THE BIOGRAPHICAL DICTIONARY
OF
MUSICIANS

THE BIOGRAPHICAL DICTIONARY
OF
MUSICIANS

ORIGINALLY COMPILED BY
RUPERT HUGHES

Completely Revised and Newly Edited by
DEEMS TAYLOR
And RUSSELL KERR

OVER 8500 ENTRIES
Together with a Pronouncing Dictionary
of Given Names and Titles and a Key
to the Pronunciation of Sixteen
Languages

BLUE RIBBON BOOKS
GARDEN CITY, NEW YORK

PRINTED AT THE *Country Life Press*, GARDEN CITY - N. Y.. U. S. A.

1940

BLUE RIBBON BOOKS, INC.

CL

COPYRIGHT, 1903
BY McCLURE, PHILLIPS & CO.
COPYRIGHT, 1913
BY DOUBLEDAY, DORAN & COMPANY, INC.
COPYRIGHT, 1939
BY GARDEN CITY PUBLISHING CO., INC.

PHONETIC MEANING
OF THE LETTERS AND SYMBOLS USED
IN THE PRONUNCIATION OF NAMES

ä as in father; *ā* as in fate; *ă* as in fat; *än* and *ăn* as in French *élan* and *fin*.

b as in bob.

c used only in *ch*, as in church. The Scotch and German guttural as in *loch* and *ich* is indicated by *kh*.

d as in deed; *dh* as *th* in these; *dj* as in adjoin.

ē as in bean; *ĕ* as in pet—at the end of words it is almost like *ŭ*.

f as in fife.

g as in gig.

h as in hate.

ī as in fight; *ĭ* as in pin.

j as in jug.

k as in kick; *kh* is used here to indicate the German or Scotch *ch* or *g*.

m as in mum.

n as in nun; *ṅ* indicates the French nasal *n* or *m*.

ō as in note; *oi* as in noise; *oo* as in moon or foot; *ô* as in wrong; *ow* as in cow; *ôṅ* as in French *bon*.

p as in pop.

r as in roar.

s as in sense.

t as in tot; *th* as in think; the sound of *th* in these is indicated by *dh*.

ū always with the sound of you; the French *u* and the German long *ü* are both indicated by *ü*.

v as in revive.

w as in will.

x as in fix.

y as in yoke.

z as in zone.

PRONOUNCING DICTIONARY OF
GIVEN NAMES, TITLES, EPITHETS, ETC.

abbate (äb'-bä-tĕ), *I.* abbé (ăbbā), *F.*
Abbot (often honorary).

l'ainé (lĕn-ā), *F.* The elder. cadet
(kă-dā), *F.* The younger. Usually
of brothers.

camerlingo (kä-mĕr-lēn'-gō), *I.* Chamberlain.

cantab(rigiensis). Of Cambridge University.

cavaliere (kä-väl-yä'-rĕ), *I.* Knight,
sir.

chevalier (shŭ-văl-yä), *F.* Knight.

cie, *F.* Company; et cie (ā sē). & Co.

comte (kôṅt), *F.*

conte (kōn'-tĕ), *I.* Count.

detto or -a (dĕt'-tō). "Called."

duc (dük), *F.* duca (doo'-kä), *I.*
Duke.

Edler von (āt'-ler fōn). Nobleman of.

fils (fēs), *F.* Son.

Frau (frow), *G.* Mrs. Fräulein (frī'-lin). Miss.

Freiherr (frī'-hăr), *G.* Baron.

Geheimrath (gĕ-hīm'-rät), *G.* Privy
counsellor.

Gesellschaft (gĕ-zĕl'-shäft), *G.* Association, society.

Graf (gräf), *G.* Count. Gräfin (grä-fĭn). Countess.

Herr (härr), *G.* Mr.

Hauptkirche (howpt-kēr'-khĕ), *G.*
Chief church.

Hofkapellmeister (mī-shtĕr). Courtconductor. Hofmusik'intendant
(moo-zek'), *G.* Supt. of court-music.

le jeune (lŭ zhŭn), *F.* The younger.

Justizrath (yoos'-tēts-rät), *G.* Counsellor of justice; often honorary.

Kammersänger (zĕngk-ĕr), *G.* Chamber-singer (to the court).

maestro (mä-ās'-tro), *I.* Master.

il maggiore (ēl mäd-jō'-rĕ), *I.* The
greater.

maistre (old French), or maître
(mĕtr), *F.* Master.

marchesa (mär-kä'-zä), *I.* Marchioness.

il minore (ēl-mē-nō'-rĕ), *I.* The lesser.

mus. bach(elor) and mus. doc(tor).
Vide the D. D.

oxon(ensis). Of Oxford University.

père (păr), *F.* Father.

Reichsfreiherr (rīkhs'-frī-hăr), *G.*
Baron of the empire.

Ritter (rĭt'-tĕr), *G.* Knight, chevalier.

sieur (s'yŭr), *F.* Sir, Mr.

und Sohn (oont zōn), *G.* & Son. und
Söhne (oont zä'-nĕ), *G.* & Sons.

van (vän), *Dutch.* von (fōn), *G.* de
(dŭ), *F.* di (dē), *I.* and *Sp.* From,
of.

vicomtesse (vē-kôn-tĕs). Viscountess.

le vieux (lŭ v'yŭ), *F.* The elder.

y (ē), *Sp.* "And," used in joining two
proper names somewhat as we use a
hyphen; the Spaniard keeping his
mother's as well as his father's name.

zu (tsoo), *G.* To.

(Others will be found in the D. D.)

NOTE.—In the Biographical Dictionary, given names are regularly abbreviated as in the following list, the same abbreviation serving for one name in its different forms in different languages.

Abramo (ä'-brä-mō), *I.*

Adam (ä'-däm), *G.*

Adalbert (ä'-däl-bĕrt), *G.*

Adelaide (ä-dä-lä-ē'-dĕ), *I.* and *G.*

(Ad.) Adolf (ä'-dôlf), *G.*

(Ad.) Adolph, *G.*

(Ad.) Adolphe (ăd-ôlf), *F.*

(Adr.) Adriano (ä-drĭ-ä'-nō), *I.*

Adrien (ăd'-rĭ-äṅ), *F.*

Agathon (ä'-gä-tōn), *G.*

(Ag.) Agostino (ä-gôs-tē'-nō), *I.*

Aimable (ĕm-äb'']), *F.*

(Alb.) Albrecht (äl'-brĕkht), *G.*

(Ales.) Alessandro (ä-lĕs-sän'-drō), *I.*

(Alex.) Alexan'der.

(Alex.) Alexandre (ăl-ĕx-äṅdr'), *F.*

Alexis (ăl-ĕx-ēs), *F.*

Aloys (ä-lois).

Aloysia (ä-loi'-zĭ-ä), *G.*

Amadeo (äm-ä-dä'-ō), *I.* -deus (dä'-oos), *G.*

Amalie (ä'-mäl-ē), *G.*

Ambroise (äṅ-bwäz), *F.*

Amédée (ăm'-ä-dä), *F.*

Amélie (ăm'-ä-lē), *F.*

Anatole (ăn-ä-tôl), *F.*

André (äṅ-drä), *F.*

(And.) Andrea (än'-drä-ä), *I.*

(Ands) Andreas (än'-drä-äs), *G.*

Ange (äṅzh), *F.*

Angelica (än-jä'-lē-kä), *I.*

(Ang.) Angelo (än'-jä-lō), *I.*

(A. or Ant.) Antoine (äṅ'-twăn), *F.*

(Ant.) Anton (än'-tōn), *G.*

3

PRONOUNCING DICTIONARY

(A. or Ant.) Anto'nio, *I.*
(Ap.) Apollon (ăp-ôl-lóń), *F.*
Aristide (är-ĭs-tēd), *F.*
Armin (är'-mēn), *G.*
Arnaud (ăr-nō), *F.*
Arrigo (är'-rē-gō), *I.*
Arsène (är-sĕn), *F.*
Arthur (är-tür), *F.*
Attilio (ät-tē'-lĭ-ō), *I.*
(Aug.) August (ow'-goost), *G.*
Auguste (ō-güst), *F.*
Augustin (ow'-goos-ten, *G.*) (ō-güs-tăń, *F.*).
(Aug.) Augusto (ä-oo-goost'-ō), *I.*

Baldassare (bäl-däs-sä'-rĕ), *I.*
(Bal.) Balthasar (băl-tă-zăr'), *F.*
(Bap.) Baptiste (bă-tēst), *F.*
(Bart.) Bartolommeo (bär-tō-lôm-mä'-ō), *I.*
(Bat.) Battista (bät-tē'-stä), *I.*
Benedikt (bā'-nĕ-dēkt), *G.*
Beniamino (bān-yĕ-mē'-nō), *I.*
(Bv.) Benvenuto (bān-vĕ-noo'-tō), *I.*
(Bdo.) Bernardo (bĕr-när'-dō), *I.*
(Bd.) Bernhard (bărn'-härt), *G.*
Bertrand (băr-träń), *F.*
Bianca (bē-än'-kä), *I.*
Blasius (blä'-zĭ-oos), *G.*
Bonaventure (bôn-äv-äń-tür'), *F.*
Bonifacio (bō-nē-fä'-chō), *I.*
Bonafazio (bōn-ē-fä'-tsĭ-ō), *I.*
Brigida (brē'-jē-dä), *I.*

Camille (kăm-ē'-yŭ), *F.*
Carlo (kär'-lō), *I.*
Casimir (kăs-ĭ-mēr), *F.*
Catherino (kät-tĕr-rē'-nō), *I.*
Caytan (kä'-ē-tän), *Sp.*
César (sā-zăr), *F.*
Cesare (chä-zä'-rĕ), *I.*
(Chas.) Charles (shärl), *F.*
Chrisostomus (krē-sôs'-tō-moos), *G.*
(Chr.) Christian (krēst'-ĭ-än), *G.*
(Chp.) Christoph (krēs-tôph), *G.*
Cinthie (săń-tē), *F.*
Claude (klōd), *F.*
Clément (klā-mäń), *F.*
Clotilde (klō-tēl'-dĕ), *G.*
Colin (kô-lăń), *F.*
Constanze (kôn-stän'-tsĕ), *G.*
Cornelius (kôr-nā'-lĭ-oos), *G.*
Costanzo (kō-stän'-tsō), *I.*

Damaso (dä-mä'-sō), *Sp.*
(D.) David (dä-vēd), *I.*
(D.) David (dä'-fēt), *G.*
Delphin (dĕl-făń), *F.*
Dietrich (dēt'-rĭkh), *G.*
Dieudonné (d'yŭ-dŭn-nä), *F.*
Diogenio (dē-ō-jä-nē'-ō), *I.*
Dioma (dē-ō'-mä), *I.*

(Dion.) Dionisio (dĕ-ō-nē'-sĭ-ō), *Sp.*
Dionys (dē'-o-nēs), *G.*
(Dom.) Domenico (dō-mä'-nĭ-kō), *I.*
(Dom.) Dominique (dôm-ĭ-nēk), *F.*
Dufrèsne (dü-frĕn), *F.*

(Edm.) Edmond (ĕd-môń), *F.*
(Edm.) Edmund (ät'-moont), *G.*
(Edw.) Edward (ād-văr), *F.*
Egidio (ā-jē'-dĭ-ō), *I.*
Eleonore (ā-lā-ō-nō'-rĕ), *G.*
Eléonore (ā-lā-ō-nôr), *F.* Also a masculine name.
Elias (ā-lē'-äs), *G.*
Eligio (ā-lē'-jō), *I.*
Eliodoro (ā-lĭ-ō-dō'-rō), *I.*
Eliseo (ā-lē'-zā-ō), *I.*
Eliza (ā-lē'-zä), *I.*
(Em.) Emanuel (ä-män-wĕl), *F.*
Emil (ä-mēl), *G.*
Emilie (ā'-mĭ-lē), *F.*
(Em.) Emilío (ā-mēl'-yō), *I.*
(Emm.) Emmanuele (ĕm-män-oo-ā'-lĕ), *I.*
(Eng.) Engelbert (ĕng'-ĕl-bĕrt), *G.*
Enrico (ĕn-rē'-kō), *I.*
Erasmo (ā-räs'-mō), *I.*
Ercole (är'-kō-lä'), *I.*
(Erh.) Erhard (är'-härt), *G.*
Ernst (ärnst), *G.*
Errico (ĕr'-rĭ-kō), *I.*
(Et.) Etienne (ät'-yĕn), *F.*
(Eug.) Eugen (oi-gān), *G.*
(Eug.) Eugène (ŭ-zhĕn'), *F.*
(Eug.) Eugenio (ā-oo-jä'-nē-ō), *I.*
Eustache (ŭs-tăsh), *F.*
Evarista (ā-vä-rē'-stä), *I.*

Fabio (fäb'-yō), *I.*
(F.) Felice (fä-lē'-chĕ).
Félicien (fä-lēs-yäń), *F.*
(F.) Félix (fä'-lĕx), *F.*
(F.) Felix (fā-lĕx), *G.*
(Fd.) Ferdinand (făr'-dĭ-nänt, *G.*) (fär-dĭ-näń, *F.*).
(Fdo.) Ferdinando (fĕr-dē-nän'-dō), *I.*
Ferencz (fĕr'-ĕns), *Hung.*
Féréol (fā-rā-ôl), *F.*
Fernandez (fĕr-nän'-dĕth), *Sp.*
Fernando (fĕr-nän'-dō), *I.*
Ferruccio (fĕr-root'-chō), *I.*
Firmin (fēr-măn), *F.*
Florence (flôr-äńs), *F.* Commonly a masculine name.
Florian (flôr-yäń, *F.*) (flôr'-ĭ-än, *G.*).
(Ft.) Fortunato (fôr-too-nä'-tō), *I.*
(Fran.) Francesco (frän-chäs'-kō), *I.*
Francesco (frän-thäs'-kō), *Sp.*
(Fran.) François (frän-swä), *F.*
Frantisek (frän'-tĭ-shĕk), *Bohemian.*

(Fz.) **Franz** (fränts), *G.*
(Fr.) **Frédéric** (frä-dā-rēk), *F.*
Fridolin (frē'-dō-lēn), *G.*
(Fr.) **Friedrich** (frēt'-rĭkh), *G.*

Gabriele (gä-brĭ-ä'-lĕ), *G.*
(Gaet.) **Gaetano** (gä-ā-tä'-nō), *I.*
(Gasp.) **Gasparo** (gäs-pä'-rō), *I.*
Gellio (jĕl'-lĭ-ō), *I.*
Geminiano (jĕm-ēn-ĭ-ä'-nō), *I.*
Gennaro (gĕn-nä'-rō), *I.*
(G.) **Georg** (gä-ôrkh'), *G.*
(G.) **George,** *E.*
(G.) **Georges** (zhôrzh), *F.*
(Ger.) **Gerolamo** (jĕ-rō'-lä-mō), *I.*
(Geron.) **Geronimo** (jĕ-rō'-nĭ-mō), *I.*
Gervais (zhĕr-vĕ'), *F.*
Gesu (hä'-zoo), *Sp.*
Ghislein (ges-lăn), *F.*
Giacinto (jä-chēn'-tō), *I.*
Giacomo (jäk'-ō-mō), *I.*
Gialdino (jäl-dē'-nō), *I.*
Gioacchino (jō-ä-kē'-nō), *I.*
Giordano (jôr-dä-nō), *I.*
Gioseffo (jō-sĕf'-fō), *I.*
(Giov.) **Giovanne** (jō-vän'-nĕ), *I.*
Giuditta (joo-dĭt'-tä), *I.*
Giulia (jool'-yä), *I.*
Giulio (jool'-yō), *I.*
(Gius.) **Giuseppe** (joo-sĕp'-pĕ), *I.*
Gjula (gū'-lä), *Hung.*
Gotifredo (gō-tē-frä'-dō), *I.*
(Gf.) **Gottfried** (gôt'-frēt), *G.*
Gotthard (gôt'-härt), *G.*
(Gh.) **Gotthilf** (gôt'-hĭlf), *G.*
(Gl.) **Gottlieb** (gôt'-lēp), *G.*
Gottlob (gôt'-lōp), *G.*
Gregorio (grä-gō'-rĭ-ō), *I.*
Guido (goo-ē'-dō), *I.*
(Guil.) **Guillaume** (gē-yōm), *F.*
(Gv.) **Gustav** (goos'-täf), *G.*
(Gve.) **Gustave** (güs-tăv), *F.*

Hamish (hä'-mēsh), *Gaelic.*
Hans (häns), *G.*
(H.) **Heinrich** (hīn'-rĭkh).
(H.) **Henri** (äṅ-rē), *F.*
(H.) **Hen'ry.**
(Hn.) **Hermann** (hăr'-män), *G.*
Hieronymus (hē-ĕr-ōn'-ē-moos), *G.*
(Hip.) **Hippolyte** (ēp-ō-lēt), *F.*
Hugo (hoo'-gō, *G.*) (ü-gō, *F.*).

(Ign.) **Ignace** (ēn-yăs), *F.*
(Ign.) **Ignazio** (ēn-yät'-sĭ-ō), *I.*
(I.) **Igraz** (ēkh'-räts), *G.*
Ilitch (ē'-lĭtsh), *Rus.*
Ilja (ēl'-jä), *Rus.*
Ingeborg (ĭng'-ĕ-bôrkh), *G.*
(Ipp.) **Ippolito** (ēp-pō-lē'-tō), *I.*
Isidore (ē-zē-dôr), *F.*
Italo (ēt'-ä-lō), *I.*

Jacob (yäk'-ōp), *G.*
Jacopo (yäk'-ō-pō), *I.*
(Jac.) **Jacques** (zhăk), *F.*
Jan (yän), *Dutch.*
Jan (yän), *Polish.*
Javier (häv-yăr), *Sp.*
(J.) **Jean** (zhäṅ), *F.*
Jefte (yĕf'-tĕ), *I.*
Jérome (zhā-rôm), *F.*
(Joa.) **Joachim** (yō'-ä-khēm), *G.*
Joaquin (wä'-kēn), *Sp.*
(Jn.) **Johann** (yō'-hän), *G.*
(Jns.) **Johannes** (yō-hän'-nĕs), *G.*
(J.) **John.**
José (hō-zā'), *Sp.*
(Jos.) **Josef,** or **Joseph** (yō'-zĕf, *G.*) (zhō-zĕf, *F.*).
Josquin (zhôs-kăṅ), *F.*
Juan (hoo-än'), *Sp.*
Jules (zhül), *F.*
Julie (zhü-lē), *F.*
Julien (zhül-yăṅ), *F.*
Juliette (zhül-yĕt), *F.*
Julius (yoo'-lĭ-oos), *G.*
Juste (zhüst), *F.*
Justin (zhüs-tăṅ), *F.*

Karl (kärl), *G.*
Karoline (kä-rō-lē'-nĕ), *G.*
Kasper (käs'-pĕr), *G.*
(Kd.) **Konrad** (kôn'-rät), *G.*
(Konst.) **Konstantin** (kōn-stän-tēn), *G.*

Ladislaw (lăd'-ĭs-läf), *Pol.*
Laure (lōr), *F.*
Laurent (lō-räṅ), *F.*
Leberecht (lā'-bĕ-rĕkht), *G.*
Léon (lā'-ôṅ), *F.*
Léonard (lā-ō-nǎr), *F.*
Léonce (lā-ôṅs), *F.*
Leone (lā-ō'-nĕ), *I.*
(Ld.) **Léopold** (lā-ŭ-pôld), *F.*
(Ld.) **Leopold** (lā-ō-pōlt), *G.*
Lopez (lō'-pĕth), *Sp.*
(Lor.) **Lorenz** (lō'-rĕnts), *G.*
(L.) **Louis** (loo-ē), *F.*
Louise (loo-ēz), *F.*
Luca (loo'-kä), *I.*
Lucien (lüs-yăṅ), *F.*
Lucrezia (loo-krä'-tsē-ä), *I.*
(Lud.) **Ludovico** (loo-dō-vē'-kō), *I.*
(L.) **Ludwig** (loot'-vĭkh), *G.*
(L.) **Luigi** (loo-ē'-jē), *I.*
Luigia (loo-ē'-jä), *I.*
Luise (loo-ē'-zĕ), *I.*

Manfredo (män-frä'-dō), *I.*
Manuel (män'-oo-ĕl), *G.*
Marcello (mär-chĕl'-lō), *I.*
Marco (mär'-kō), *I.*
Marguerite (măr-gŭ-rēt), *F.*
(M.) **Maria** (mä-rē'-ä), *G., I.* and *Sp.*
Commonly a masculine name.

Marie (mă-rē), *F.* Commonly a masculine name.
Mathias (mä-tē′-ăs), *F.* and *G.*
Mathieu (măt-yŭ), *F.*
(Mat.) Matteo (mät-tä′-ō), *I.*
Matthäus (mät-tä′-oos), *G.*
Mattia (mät-tē′-ä), *I.*
Maturin (măt-ŭ-răn), *F.*
Maurice (mō-rēs), *F.*
Max (măx), *G.*
Maximilian (mäx-ĭ-mēl′-ĭ-än), *G.*
Melchior (mĕl-shĭ-ôr), *F.*
Melchiore (mĕl-kĭ-ō′-rĕ), *I.*
Michael (mē′-kä-ĕl), *I.*
Michel (mē-shĕl), *F.*
Michele (mē-kä′-lĕ), *I.*
Miroslaw (mē′-rō-släf), *Russian.*
Modeste (mō-dĕst), *F.*
Moritz (mō′-rēts), *G.*
Muzio (moo′-tsĭ-ō), *I.*

Napoléon (nă-pō′-lä-ôṅ), *F.*
Natale (nä-tä′-lĕ), *I.*
Nepomuk (nä′-pō-mook), *G.*
Niccola (nĕk′-kō-lä), *I.*
(N.) Nich′olas, *E.*
(N.) Nicolas (nē-kō-lăs), *F.*
(N.) Nicolò (nē-kō-lō′), *I.*
Nikolai (nē′-kō-lä′), *G.*
(N.) Nikolaus (ne′-kō-lows), *G.*

Octave (ôk-tăv), *F.*
Orazio (ō-rä′-tsĭ′-ō), *I.*
Otto (ôt′-tō), *G.*
Ottokar (ôt′-tō-kär), *Pol.*

Pantaléon (pän-tä-lä-ôṅ), *F.*
Paolo (pä′-ō-lō), *I.*
Pascal (păs-kăl), *F.*
Pasquale (päs-kwä′-lĕ), *I.*
Paul (pōl), *F.*
Pedro (pā′-dhrō), *Sp.*
Peregrino (pä-rä-grē-̇nō), *I.*
(P.) Peter.
(P.) Peter (pā′-tĕr), *G.*
Philibert (fē-lĭ-băr), *F.*
(Ph.) Philipp (fē′-lĭp), *G.*
(Ph.) Philippe (fē-lēp), *F.*
Pierluigi (pē-är-loo-ē′-jē), *I.*
(P.) Pierre (pĭ-ăr′), *F.*
(P.) Pietro (pĭ-ā′-trō), *I.*
Polibio (pō-lē′-bē-ō), *I.*
Pompeo (pôm-pā′-ō), *I.*
Primo (prē′-mō), *I.*
Prosper (prôs′-pār), *F.*
Prudent (prü-däṅ), *F.*

Rafael (rä′-fä-ĕl), *I.* and *Sp.*
Regnault (rĕn-yō), *F.*
Reichardt (rīkh′-ärt), *G.*
Reinhold (rīn′-hōlt), *G.*

Réné (rā-nä), *F.*
(R.) Rob′ert, *E.* (in *F.* rō′-băr, in *G.* rō′-bărt).
Roberte (rō-bărt), *F.*
(R.) Rober′to, *I.*
Romano, *I.*
Romualdo (rōm-oo-äl′-dō), *I.*
Rose (rôz), *F.*
(Rud.) Rudolf (roo′-dôlf), *G.*
Ruggiero (rood-jä′-rō), *I.*
Ruprecht (roo′-prĕkht), *G.*

Sabine (zä-bē′-nĕ), *G.*
(S.) Salvatore (säl-vä-tō′-rĕ), *I.*
(Sml.) Samuel (zäm′-oo-ĕl), *G.*
Scipione (shē-pĭ-ō′-nĕ), *I.*
Sebald (zä′-bält), *G.*
(Séb.) Sébastian (sä-băst-yäṅ), *F.*
(Seb.) Sebastiano (sä-bäs-tĭ′-ä′-nō), *I.* and *Sp.*
Siegfried (zēkh′-frēt), *G.*
Siegmund (zēkh′-moont), *G.*
Simon (zē′-mōn), *G.*
(Sim.) Simone (sē′-mō-nĕ), *I.*
Spiro (spē′-rō).
Steffano (stĕf-fä′-nō), *I.*
Sylvain (sĕl-văṅ), *F.*

Teodulo (tä-ō-doo′-lo), *I.*
Teresa (tä-rā′-sä), *I.*
Theobald (tä′-ō-bält), *G.*
Theodor (tä′-ō-dôr), *G.*
(The.) Théodore (tä-ŭ-dôr), *F.*
(T.) Thomas.
Thueskon (too-ĕs′-kōn), *G.*
(Tim.) Timothée (tē-mô-tä′), *F.*
(T.) Tommasso (tôm-mäs′-sō), *I*
Traugott (trow′-gôt), *G.*
Turlogh (toor′-lôkh), *G.*

(Val.) Valentin (văl-äṅ-täṅ), *F.*
Venanzio (vä-nän′-tsĭ-ō), *I.*
(V.) Vincent (văṅ-säṅ), *F.*
(V.) Vincent (fēn′-tsĕnt), *G.*
(V.) Vincenzo (vēn-chän′-tsō), *I.*
Vincesleo (vēn-chĕs-lä′-ō), *I.*
Violante (vē-ō-län′-tĕ), *I.*

Wendela (vĕn′-dĕ-lä), *G.*
Wenzel (vĕn′-tsĕl), *G.*
Werner (vär′-nĕr), *G.*
(Wm.) Wilhelm (vēl′-hĕlm), *G.*
Wilhelmine (vēl-hĕl-mē′-nĕ), *G.*
Wilibald (vē′-lĭ-bält), *G.*
Willem (wĭl′-lĕm), *Dutch.*
(Wm.) William, *E.*
Woldemar (vōl′-dĕ-mär), *G.*
(Wg.) Wolfgang (vôlf-gäng), *G.*
Wulf (voolf), *G.*

(X.) Xavier (ksăv-yä), *F.*
(X.) Xavier (zä-fēr′), *G.*

A LIST OF ABBREVIATIONS, TITLES, DIGNITIES, INSTITUTIONS, ETC.

Acad., Academy.
a capp. (*I.*, *a cappella*), unaccompanied.
acc., according(ly).
accomp., accompaniment.
allg., allgem. (*G.*, *allgemein*), universal, general.
app., appointed.
apt., appointment.
Arab., Arabian.
Archbp., Archbishop.
arr., arranged, arrangement.
asst., assistant.

b., born.
bandm., bandmaster.
bar., barytone.

biog., biography, biographical.

c., composed.
ca, circa (*L.*), about.
cath., cathedral.
Cav. (*I.*, *Cavaliere*), Chevalier.
cent., century, as *18th cent.*
cf. (*L.*, *confer*), compare.
ch., church, chorus, choir.
chapelle (*F.*), chapel, choir.
Chev., Chevalier.
choirm., choirmaster.
clar., clarinet.
coll., collected, collection, collector, college.
collab., collaborated, collaboration.
comp(s)., composition(s).
cond., conducted, conductor (this abbreviation is here used for the equivalents in various languages, *Kapellmeister*, *maestro di cappella*, *maître de chapelle*, etc.).
Cons., Conservatory (Conservatoire, Conservatorio, Conservatorium).
cpt., counterpoint.
cptist., contrapuntist (used of an early composer of highly contrapuntal works).
ct., court; **ct.-cond.**, court-conductor; **ct.-Th.**, court-theatre; **ct.-opera**, court-opera.

d., died.

dict., dictionary.

dir., director.
do., ditto.
dram., dramatic.
Dr. jur. (*L.*, *doctor juris*), Doctor of Law(s).
Dr. phil. (*L.*, *doctor philosophiæ*), Doctor of Philosophy. *h. c.* (*L. honoris causa*, i.e., honorarily.)

eccl., ecclesiastical.
ed., edited, editor, edition.
e. g. (*L.*, *exempli gratia*), for example.
eng., engaged.
Engl., England, English.
est., establ., established.
et seq. (*L.*, *et sequentes, sequentia*) and the following.

F., Fr., French.
Fest., Festival.
fl., flute.
fragm., fragmentary; fragment(s).
F. (R.) C. O., Fellow of the (Royal) College of Organists, London.
Frl. (*G.*, *Fräulein*), Miss.

G., Ger., German.
gen., general.
Govt., Government.
Gr., Greek.
gr., grand.
grossherzöglich (grôs-hăr-tsäkh-lĭkl., *G.*), Granducal.
Gym., Gymnasium.

harm., harmony.
harps., harpsichord.
h. c. (*L.*, *honoris causa*), used of honorary titles.
Heb., Hebrew.
herzöglich (*G.*), Ducal.
H. M.'s Th., Her Majesty's Theatre, London.
Hochschule (hôkh'-shoo-lĕ, *G.*), "High School," college, university.
Hof (hôf, *G.*), court; a frequent prefix, as in *Hof-kapelle*, court-chapel, or court-orchestra; *Hof Kapellmeister*, court-conductor; *Hofmusikintendant*, superintendent of the court-music, etc.
hon., honorary.
Hun., Hungarian.

I., It., Ital., Italian.
ib., ibid. (*L., ibidem*), in the same place.
id. (*L., idem*), the same.
i. e. (*L., id est*), that is.
Imp., Imperial.
Incid. music, incidental music (to a drama).
incl., including.
inst., institute, institution.
instr(s)., instrument(s), instrumental.
introd., introduction, introduced.
inv., invented, inventor.

Jap., Japanese.

L., Latin.
libr., librarian.
lit., literally.
lyr., lyric.

m., married.
M(aestro) (*I.*), teacher, conductor; *m. al cembalo,* the conductor, who formerly sat at the harpsichord; *m. dei putti,* Master of the choir-boys.
m. de chap. (*F., maître de chappelle*), conductor.
m. di capp. (*I., maestro di cappella*) conductor.
M. E., Methodist Episcopal.
melodr., melodrama.
Met. Op., Metropolitan Opera House, New York.
mfr., manufacturer.
mgr., manager.
mid., middle.
min., minor.
mod., moderately.
m.-sopr., mezzo-soprano.
M. T. (N.) A., Music Teachers' (National) Association.
mus., music, musical, musician.
Mus. Antiq. Soc., Musical Antiquarian Society, London.
Mus. Bac. (Doc.), Bachelor (Doctor) of Music. Vide D. D.

n., near.
Nat. Cons., National Conservatory, New York.
N. E. Cons., New England Conservatory, Boston.
n. s., new style (referring to the use of our calendar in place of the Russian or old style).
N. Y., New York, U. S. A.

O., Ohio, U. S. A.
Obbl., obbligato.
obs., obsolete.

op., opus, opera.
Op. com., opéra-comique; or the Opéra Comique at Paris.
Oper (*G.*), opera.
Opéra, used of the Grand Opéra at Paris.
orch., orchl., orchestra, orchestral.
org., organ, organist.
o. s., old style, see **n. s.** above.
Oxon. (*L., Oxoniae*), of Oxford.

p., part.
pcs., pieces.
P. E., Protestant Episcopal.
perf., performed.
pf., pianoforte.
Philh., Philharm., Philharmonic.
Pol., Polish.
pop., popular.
Port., Portuguese.
pres., president.
Presb., Presbyterian.
prod., produced.
Prof., Professor (a special title of great distinction in Germany).
pseud., pseudonym.
pt., pianist.
pub., published, publisher.

R., Royal.
R. A. M., Royal Academy of Music, London.
R. C., Roman Catholic.
R. C. M., Royal College of Music, London.
Regius musicus, Royal musician.
ret., retired, retiring, returned.
rev., revised.
Rev., Reverend.
Rus., Russian.

sch., school.
sec., secretary.
soc., society.
sopr., soprano.
Sp., Spanish.
st., studied, studying, student.
succ., successfully, success.
supt., superintendent.
symph., symphonic, symphony.

t., teacher, taught.
th., theatre.
th., theorist (writer of treatises).
th.-cond., conductor of theatre-orchestra.
transcr., transcribed, transcription.
transl., translated, translation, translator.
Tur., Turkish.

Unit., Unitarian.
U. S., United States.
U., Univ., university.

l., 1. (*L., vide*) see;

2. very, as *v. succ.,* very successful-
(ly).

var.(s), variation(s).
vla., viola.
vln., violin.
vt., violinist.

w., with.
Wis., Wisconsin, U. S. A.

Ztg. (*G., Zeitung*), Gazette.

A TABLE OF
PRONUNCIATIONS

Giving the Code of Symbols used in this Book;
and also a Guide to the Pronunciations of sixteen
Languages, arranged in a novel Tabular Form
by Letters

This top row gives the phonetic meaning of the letters and symbols AS USED IN THIS BOOK.	**A** as used in this book : ä as in father ; ā as in fate ; ă as in fat ; ăṅ and ăṅ, see Note 1.	**B** as in bob.	**C** see *ch*, at end of the alphabet.
ARABIAN : very difficult even for sojourners among the people.	as in fat ; before *r* as in far.	as in bob.	as in English ; *ch* like German, *ch*, see Note 3.
BOHEMIAN : See Note 4. In diphthongs the vowels are pronounced separately, as in Italian.	as *u* in fun ; *á* as in father.	as in bob.	*c* like *ts*, or German *z* ; *č* like *ch* in child.
DANISH : doubled vowels are simply prolonged.	as in father ; *aa* as *a* in fall.	as in bob.	like Swedish *c*.
DUTCH : *e* in be and ge ; *i* before *k*, *g* and *ng* ; and *ij* in the suffix lijk are silent.	when short as in half ; also before *ch* ; when open as in father : *aa*, *aai* (see *ai*), prolonged as in father.	beginning a syllable, as in bet ; ending, as *p* in trap.	only in foreign words ; like *s* before *e*, *i* and *y* ; like *k*, otherwise.
FLEMISH : dead as a literary language, but of great historic importance.	*a* or *â*, as in father or mica ; *aa* or *ae*, the same prolonged.	as in bob.	like *k* ; *ch* like German *ch*.
FRENCH : a silent final consonant is usually sounded with the following word when that begins with a vowel. This is called liaison. French syllables have duration rather than accent ; the tendency is, to give a slight stress to the final syllable. In this book accent is rarely marked.	as in făt ; *â* as in father ; see *ai*, *au*, and Note 1.	as in bob.	as *s* before *e*, *i* and *y* ; as *k* otherwise, except that *ç* is always *s*. See *ch*.
GERMAN : long words usually accent the first syllable most strongly, and give a lesser accent to one or more of the others.	as in father ; *ä*, see Note 2 ; *ä* is sometimes spelled *ae* ; *ai* = *i* in bite ; for *äu* and *aeu*, see *au*.	beginning a syllable, as in bet ; ending a syllable, as *p* in trap.	like *ts* in hats before *e*, *i* and *ä* ; like *k* before *a*, and *u* ; *ch*. See Note 3.
HUNGARIAN : long and short vowels are so rather in duration than in sound. There are no silent letters and no accents.	as in what ; *á* is prolonged, as in father.	as in bob.	*cs* = *ch* in church ; *cz* = *ts*, as in hats.
ITALIAN : doubled consonants are distinctly pronounced, as fred-do. Doubled vowels are also separately pronounced.	as in father and mica ; *á* as in far.	as in bob.	before *e* and *i* as *ch* in chime ; *cc* before *e* and *i* = *tch*, as wretched ; *ch* = *k*.
NORWEGIAN :	*a* as in father ; *aa* as *o* in no ; *au* as *o* in no.	as in bob.	only in foreign words ; as *s* before *e*, *i* and *y* ; as *k* otherwise.
POLISH : consonants strongly sounded are accented thus : *b*, 1 7 7 7 7 1 7 1 *e*, *f*, *m*, *n*, *p*, *s*, *w*, *z*.	as in father ; *g* as in ball.	as in bob.	*c* = *ts*, as in hats ; *ch* = German *ch* ; *cz* = *ch* in church.
PORTUGUESE : a very difficult language ; placed usually just back of the teeth. The nasal vowels are also unique. Note 5.	as in father ; when two as occur in a word the first is more like *a* in fat ; *ā*, see Note 5.	nearly as in bob ; but softer.	like *s* before *e*, *i* and *y* ; *k* otherwise ; *ç* always like *s* ; in *cc* the first *c* is like *k*, the second is determined by the following letter.
RUSSIAN : has 36 letters, including 12 vowels. It is usually written phonetically and in German pronunciation as follows :	when accented, as in father ; unaccented, as in bat ; at the beginning, as *ya* in yacht ; if unaccented, as in yank.	this letter resembling our *f* is pronounced *v*, as in vane, or *f*, as in foe ; the equivalent of our *b* sounds as *b* or *p* in bet or trap.	as in cent or zone ; *ch* = German *ch* at the end ; at the beginning, as in chest.
SPANISH : a language of ideal regularity and precision ; all vowels are separately pronounced.	as in father or in hat ; *â* as in father.	like *v* in very.	before *e* or *i*, as *th* in think, otherwise as *k* ; *ch* as in church ; *cu* as *qu* in quart.
SWEDISH :	as in father or in mica ; *â* as *o* in go, when long ; when short, as *a* in what ; *ä* as in hare.	as in bob.	before *e*, *i* or *y*, as in cent ; otherwise as in cash ; *ch* = *k*, except in foreign words.
WELSH : all vowel combinations are separately pronounced ; the letter w = oo in moon.	as in fat ; *â* as in dare.	as in bob.	always like *k* ; *ch* = German *ch*, see Note 3.

12

D	E	F	G
as in deed ; *dh* as *th* in these : *dj* as in adjoin.	*ē* as in bean ; *ĕ* as in pet—at the end of words almost like *ŭ*.	as in fife.	as in gig.
soft like Italian *d*.	as in prey ; *ĕ* as in pet.	as in fife.	as in gig.
as in deed. For *d'*, *dĕ* and *di*, see Note 4.	as in pet ; *ê* as in ere ; *ĕ* = *ya*, as in beatitude. See also Note 4.	as in fife.	as in gig.
beginning a syllable as in date ; ending as *th* in bathe ; after *l*, *n*, and *r*, silent ; *ds* = *ss* in hiss.	as in prey and there ; *ej* like *i* in bite.	as in fife.	as in gig ; after *e* or *ö* likely in yoke ; between vowels often mute.
at the beginning of syllables as in date ; at the end as *t* in hot.	when short as in met ; when open as in prey ; *ee* simply prolongs the sound ; see also *eu*.	as in fife ; *fl* as in flow ; *fr* as in fresh.	like German *g* ; *ng* as in looking.
like German *d* and *dt*.	*e* or *ê* as in pet ; *eu* like French *eu*; *e* after a vowel usually simply prolongs it ; *ee* = *a* in fate or as in seen ; see *eu*.	as in fife.	as German *g*, very guttural.
at the beginning or in the middle as *d* in deadlock ; usually silent at the end of the word ; in liaison it becomes *t*.	as *e* in father or *u* in cut ; as a final syllable generally silent ; *ê* as in prey when it has stress, otherwise as in pet ; *ê* as *ai* in fair ; *ê* as in pet ; see *ei*, *d*, *s*, *t*, *z*, *r*.	as in fife, not silent at the ends of words, except in clef ; in liaison it becomes *v*.	as in gate except before *e*, *i* and *y*, then as *s* in pleasure (marked here as *zh*) ; silent when final, becoming *k* in liaison ; *gn* as *ni* in minion.
beginning a syllable as in date ; ending a syllable as *t* in hat ; *dt* = *t* in hat.	when long as in prey ; when short as in pet ; *ei* = *i* in right ; see *eu*.	as in fife.	at the beginning of a syllable as in gate, but softer ; at the end, see Note 3 ; *ng* when final vanishes in a faint *k* sound as sang = zangk.
as in deed ; *dj* same as *'gy* ; *djs* = *j* in judge.	before *m* or a sharp consonant as in fat ; otherwise as *e* in ten ; *ê* as in prey.	as in fife.	as in gig ; *gy* = *d* in due (not doo) ; *ggy* = gygy or *d'* *d'*.
as in deed, but softer and more palatal.	as in prey when long ; when short as in pet ; *ê* as in pet.	as in fife.	before *e* and *i* as in gem ; *gg* as *dj* in adjoin ; *gli* = *ly'* like *ll* in million, *gn* = *ny'* or *ni* in pinion : *gu* = *gw* ; *gui* = *wē*.
as in deed.	as in prey ; but when final as *e* in father.	as in fife.	as in gig, but before *j* and *y* as *y* in yoke.
as in deed ; *dz* as in adze ; *dż* as *dge* in judge.	*e* as in met ; *ę* = French in, see Note 1 ; *ē* = *a* as in pate.	as in fife.	as in gig.
as in deed.	*e* and *é* usually as in prey ; *ê* has a curious closed sound.	as in fife.	as in gate ; but before *e*, *i* and *y* as in gem.
as in deed.	at the beginning of words = yo in yolk if accented ; if unaccented as *ye* in yesterday ; otherwise as *e* in pet.	usually represented by the German *v* or *w*.	at the beginning usually as in go ; sometimes at the beginning, always at the end as German *ch* ; see Note 2.
much like *th* in those (marked in this book by *dh*) ; when two *d*s occur in a word, only the second has this sound, the first as in date.	as in prey when long ; when short as in pet ; *ê* as in prey or pet.	as in fife.	as in gate ; but before *e* and *i*, as a very harsh *h* in hate ; *gue* = *ga* as in gate ; *gui* = *ge* as in gear ; *gn* as in ignite ; *gl* as in glow.
as in deed, but silent in *ndn* and *nds* and before *j* or *t*.	as in film when long ; when short as in pet ; *er* as *ar* in bare.	as in fit at the beginning of syllables or after a short vowel ; at end of syllable like *v* in slave ; before *v* silent.	as in gig ; before *ă*, *e*, *i*, *ö*, *y* and after *l* and *r*, like *y* in yoke ; silent before *j* ; *gn* = *ng* in sing.
as in date ; *dd* as *th* in these.	as in pet ; *ê* as in bean.	like *v* in revive ; *ff* like *f* in off.	as in gate ; *ng* as in wrong

Phonetic meaning of the letters and symbols AS USED IN THIS BOOK.	**H** as in hate.	**I** *ī* as in fight ; *ĭ* as in pin.	**J** as in jug.	**K** as in kick ; *kh* = German *ch* or *g* ; see Note 3.
ARABIAN :	strongly aspirated at end or beginning of a word.	as in pin ; *i* as in bird.	as in jug.	strongly guttural.
BOHEMIAN :	as in hate.	as in pin ; *ĭ* as in machine.	like *y* in yes ; after vowels it prolongs their sounds somewhat as *y* in day, whey, etc.	as in kick.
DANISH :	as in hate but silent before *j* and *v*.	as in machine ; after *a, e, o, ö*, and *u* like *y* in yoke.	even with vowels *aj, ej,* like *y* in yoke.	as in kick.
DUTCH :	as in hate.	when short as in pin ; when open as *e* in rely ; *ie* prolongs the open sound only before *r*, otherwise as *e* in rely ; *ij* same as *ei*.	as *y* in yoke.	as in kick ; *ks* = *x* in fix ; *kw* = *qu* in quart.
FLEMISH :	as in hate.	*i* or *ĭ* as in pin ; *ŭ* or *ie* the same prolonged ; *ieu* sounds like *ē-ŭ*.	as *y* in yoke.	as in kick ; *ks* = *x* in fix.
FRENCH :	always silent.	as in pin, see *ei, oi* ; *ĭ* as *i* in machine, but see *ai*.	as *s* in measure (marked in this book as *zh*).	as in kick.
GERMAN :	as in hate.	as in machine ; *ie* as in believe.	as *y* in yoke.	as in kick.
HUNGARIAN :	as in hate.	as the quick *e* in rely ; *ĭ* as in machine.	as *y* in yoke ; *jj* as *y* in paying.	as in kick.
ITALIAN :	silent ; after *c* or *g* it has simply a hardening effect.	as in machine, but when short as in pin ; at the beginning of words like *y* in yoke.	same as *i* ; at the beginning of words like *y* in yoke ; as a vowel like *i* in machine.	....
NORWEGIAN :	as in hate.	as in machine ; at the beginning as *y* in yoke.	as in yoke.	as in kick ; before *i* and *y* like *h* ; *kv* = *qu* in quarter.
POLISH :	as in hate ; see *c, l* and *n*.	*i* as in machine ; after a consonant it has the effect of the imaginary *y* in due (not doo) ; *iu* = *u* in gun.	as *y* in yoke.	as in kick.
PORTUGUESE :	silent.	as in machine.	as in jug.	only in foreign words, as in kick.
RUSSIAN :	used only in a few native words, and in foreign derivations.	as in machine, but well back in the throat ; after labials (*b, f, m, p* and *v*) as *i* in pin.	as *y* in yet.	as in kick ; before *k, t* and *ch* softly as in German *ch*.
SPANISH :	usually silent or very slight ; see *c*.	as in machine when long ; when short as in pin ; *ĭ* as in machine.	as a very harsh *h* in hate ; almost like German *ch*.	....
SWEDISH :	as in hate ; silent before *j* or *v*.	as in machine.	as *y* in yoke.	as in kick but before *ä, e, i, ö* and *y* in the same syllable like *ch*.
WELSH :	as in hate.	as in machine.	....	as in kick.

14

L	M	N	O	P
as in lull.	as in mum.	as in nun ; ǹ, see Note 1.	ō as in note ; oi as in noise ; oo as in moon or foot ; ŏ as in wrong ; ow as in cow ; ŏǹ, see Note 1.	as in pop.
as in lull.	as in mum.	as in nun.	as in note ; ŏ = German ö, see Note 2.	as in pop.
as in lull.	as in mum.	as in nun ; ñ as in cañon.	as in note ; ŏ as in wrong.	as in pop.
as in lull.	as in mum.	as in nun.	when open as in bother ; when closed as in move ; Φ = French eu closed as in peu ; ŏ = the same open as in coeur ; see Note 2.	as in pop.
as in lull, but when followed by another consonant a short e is interpolated, as if elk were spelt elek.	as in mum.	as in nun.	as in bother when short, when long as in over ; oo = o in over ; ooi = o in over followed by i in pin ; see oe.	as in pop; ph = f.
as in lull.	as in mum.	as in nun.	o as in note or not ; oo or oe usually the same prolonged, sometimes like wa in was, oei or oey as ō-ē.	as in pop.
as in lily, t sometimes l (called "l mouillé") is liquid, as y in yoke or paying.	at the beginning, as in mate. See Note 1.	at the beginning, as in name. See Note 1.	as in not ; often almost as ŭ in nut ; ŏ as in note ; see oi.	at the beginning and middle, as in paper ; pui = almost pwe ; ph = f ; silent when final.
as in lull.	as in mum.	as in nun.	as in wrong ; ŏ see Note 2 ; ŏ is sometimes spelled oe.	as in pop.
as in late ; ll or ly = y in paying.	as in mum.	as in nun ; ny = n as in new (not noo) ; nny = nyny, or n' n'.	o as in note ; ŏ is prolonged as in slow ; ŏ = French eu ; ŏ or ö = German long ō.	as in pop.
as in lull; see g.	as in mum.	as in nun ; see g.	as in note ; ∂ as in wrong.	as in pop.
as in lull.	as in mum.	as in nun.	as u in full, but often as o in note or not ; oe = a in sale ; ŏ like French eu long or short.	as in pop.
as in lull ; t is sounded by closing the teeth on the tip of the tongue as l is pronounced.	as in mum.	as in nun.	o as in note ; ŏ is between note and move.	as in pop.
as in lull; lh like lli in million.	as in meet, but at end of syllables or after e, like French nasal n. See Note 1.	as in note ; but at end of syllables or after e, like French nasal n, see Note 1 ; nh = ni in minion.	as in note or in not ; ō see Note 5.	as in pop ; ph = f.
as in lull ; before a or o, as ll in collar.	as in mum.	as in nun.	as in not.	as in pop.
as in look : ll like lli in billiards.	as in mum.	as in nun ; ñ divides into ny as ni in minion, thus cañon = canyon.	when long as in note ; when short o as in not ; ŏ as in note.	as in pop ; silent before s, n and t.
as in lull: but usually silent before j.	as in mum.	as in nun ; gn = ng in sing.	as in move or not, according to complex rules ; ŏ = German ö.	as in pop.
as in look ; ll has a curious mingling of th and l	as in mum.	as in nun.	as in gone : ∂ as in bone ; the sound oo is represented by w.	as in pop ; ph = f.

15

Phonetic meaning of the letters and symbols AS USED IN THIS BOOK.	Q	R as in roar.	S as in sense.	T as in tot ; *th* as in think.
ARABIAN :	....	as in roar.	as in sis ; *ss* strongly hissed ; *sh* as in show.	strongly palatal.
BOHEMIAN :	as *qu* in quart.	as in roar ; *ř* = *rzh* or *rsh* as in "for sure," thus Dvořák is dvŏr-zhäk.	*s* as in sis ; *š* as *sh* in show.	as in tot ; see also Note 4.
DANISH :	*qv* = *qu* in quart.	as in roar.	as in sense ; *ski* or *sky* as in skim.	as in tot.
DUTCH :	*qu* as in quart.	as in hurry.	sharply as in sense ; *sj* = *sh* in show ; see *sch.*	after a hard vowel it is soft as in note, otherwise as in hot-
FLEMISH :	*qu* as in quart.	as in roar.	as in suppose.	as in tot ; *dt* as *t* in hat.
FRENCH :	*qu* always as *k* in kick ; *cq* as *k.*	commonly rolled on the back of the tongue ; in Paris almost like *w* in bower ; as a final letter it is sounded except after *e* ; *er* = *a* in sale.	as in suppose ; when final it is silent except in proper names ; in liaison it becomes *z.*	as *t* in tub ; like *s* in such suffixes as -tion ; almost always silent when final ; *et* = *a* in sale.
GERMAN :	*qu* as *kv* ; thus q u a r t = k'värt.	usually rolled and always strongly sounded.	beginning a syllable before a vowel usually as *z* in zone ; as the end of a syllable as in this ; *sp* and *st* = *shp* and *sht* ; *sch* = *sh.*	as in tot ; *th* = *t* in hat.
HUNGARIAN :	....	always trilled.	as *sh* in show ; *sz* = *sh.*	as in tot ; *ty* strongly as *t* in tube ; *tty* = *ty'* *ty'* or *t'* *t'* ; *ts* = *ch.*
ITALIAN :	*qu* as in quart.	usually trilled.	as in suppose ; *sce* = *shā* ; *sci* = *shē* ; *sch* = *sk.*	as in tot ; *ti* usually = *tsi.*
NORWEGIAN :	*qu* as in quart.	as in hurry.	as in sis ; *ski* = *sh* in show.	as in tot.
POLISH :	....	as in roar ; *rz* = French *j* or *s* in measure.	as in sense ; *sz* = *sh* in show.	as in tot.
PORTUGUESE :	*qua* as in quart ; before *e* or *i*, *qu* is like *k.*	as in roar and hurry.	as in suppose ; having the *z* sound between vowels.	as in tot.
RUSSIAN :	....	with a burr as *rr* in worry.	as in sense ; *sh* as in show ; *ski* = *shk* ; *sz* = *sh.*	as in tot ; *ts* beginning or ending as in hats ; *tsch* as *shtch* in wa*sht-ch*urn.
SPANISH :	*qu* as *k* in kick.	as in roar.	as in sense.	as in tot.
SWEDISH :	*qv* = *k* in kin.	as in hurry.	as in sense ; *sk*, *sj*, and *stj* all = *sh* in show.	as in tot ; *tj* = *ch* in church ; but if followed by *a* or *e* = *ts* in hats ; *th* = *t* in tot.
WELSH :	....	as in roar.	as in sense.	as in tot ; *th* as in think.

U	V	W	X	Y
ū always with the sound of you ; ŭ, see Note 2.	as in revive.	as in will.	as in fix.	as in yoke.
as in full.	as in revive.	as in will.	....	as in why.
as in full ; ū or ŭ, as in rule.	as in revive.	as in will ; w is silent before z and another consonant, as wzd.	as in fix.	as t in pin ; ŷ as t in machine.
as in rule or full.	as in revive ; silent after l and r.	only in foreign words.	as in xebec.	like u in fur.
when short, as in cut ; when long, as in rule ; uu as oo in moon.	at the beginning, as in vote ; at the end, as f in off.	as in will.	as in fix.	as in why.
like a short German ü, see Note 2 ; uu or ue, the same prolonged ; see ui.	as in revive.	as in will.	as in fix.	like i in machine ; sometimes nasal like French in, see Note 1 ; see ai.
see Note 2.	as in revive.	in foreign words only, and sounded like v in vote ; wh sounded as w in was.	as in fix or exile ; silent when final ; becoming z in liaison.	when alone or when a consonant precedes or follows it, as e in bean. When it lies between two vowels it may be said to be divided into two sounds. After an a or e it is sounded like ĕ in pet followed by y in yoke (thus rayon becomes ré-yôǹ) ; with an o it sounds like wă in was followed by y, as in yoke (thus joyeux becomes zhwä-yŭ) ; with u it becomes ē — y' (thus appuyant becomes ăp-pwē-yăǹ).
as oo in moon or foot ; ū (sometimes spelled ue), see Note 2.	like f in fife.	like v in revive, but with a soft trace also of the w in was.	as in fix, even at the beginning of a syllable.	as e in bean, sometimes like ŭ ; see Note 2.
u as in pull ; ū as in rule ; ū = French u ; ŭ or ü the same prolonged.	as in revive.	....	....	see g, l, n and t.
as in rule ; ū as in full.	as in revive.	....	....	....
as in rule.	as in revive ; kv = qu in quart.	....	as in fix.	like French u.
as in rule ; preceded by i it is the French u.	....	as v in revive.	as in fix.	yj = e in bean.
as in rule ; ŭ, see Note 5.	as in revive.	....	after e, as in vex ; otherwise as sh in show.	as i in machine.
as in due, or as oo in moon ; except in words of French or German origin, then as French u.	as f in far or off.	as f in far or off.	....	same as Russian i.
as in rule, when long ; when short, as in full ; ŭ as in rule or full ; ue = wa in wait.	as in revive.	....	as in fix ; even at the beginning ; in some proper names as h in hate.	as i in machine.
as in rule ; or in full.	as in revive.	like v in revive.	....	like French u ; see Note 2.
a little broader than i in this ; ū = ee in seen.	....	sounded like oo in moon.	....	as u in turn ; at the end of a syllable as in pretty.

Phonetic meaning of the letters and symbols AS USED IN THIS BOOK.	Z as in zone and buzz.	Æ	AI	AU	EUA
ARABIAN :	as in zone.	....	....	....	....
BOHEMIAN :	as in zone ; ž as in azure.	....	....	....	....
DANISH :	only in foreign words, then like s in sis.	like *ai* both in sail and in said.	like *i* in bite.	as *ow* in cow.	....
DUTCH :	as in zone.	....	*aai* combines *a* in father with a quick *e* in meet, almost like *y* in why.	combines *a* in fat with *oo* in moon ; sharper than *ow* in cow.	....
FLEMISH :	as in zone ; often used interchangeable with s.	same as *aa* = *a* prolonged ; *aei* or *aey* = *ai* prolonged.	*ai* and *ay* as *ai* in said ; *aei* or *aey* the same prolonged.	....	....
FRENCH :	as in zone.	....	*ai*, *at*, *ay* as *e* in pet.	as *o* in zone.	as *o* in zone.
GERMAN :	like *ts* in hats, even at the beginning of a syllable.	only another spelling of *ä*. See Note 2.	like *i* in bite.	as *ow* in cow ; *äu* almost like *i* in bite (actually *ah—ē*).	....
HUNGARIAN :	as in zone ; *zs*, see *d*.	....	....	....	....
ITALIAN :	*z* as *ts* in hats ; *zz* as *ds* in Windsor.	in vowel combinations the vowels are always separately pronounced in Italian.	....	....	....
NORWEGIAN :	like *ts* in hats.	....	....	like *o* in note.	....
POLISH :	as in zone ; *ż* as *s* in measure ; *zg* = *g* preceded by a buzz.	....	....	....	....
PORTUGUESE :	as in zone ; but at the end of syllables like *s* in this.	....	....	....	....
RUSSIAN :	as German *z* = *ts ;* or as French *z* = *g* in menagerie.	same	as	German	diphthongs.
SPANISH :	as *th* in think.	....	....	....	....
SWEDISH :	like *s* in sis.	....	....	....	....
WELSH :	....	....	....	....	....

EI	EU	IE	OE	OI as in noise.	OU
. . . .	. . . .	. . . .	. . . .	. . . .	. . . .
. . . .	. . . .	. . . .	. . . .	. . . .	. . . .
. . . .	. . . .	. . . .	. . . .	. . . .	. . . .
combines *e* in met with *i* in pin; in the suffix heid = *a* in fate.	same as German short *ŏ*, see Note 2; *eeu* = *a* in fate, with a whispered *v* after it.	see *i* ; *ieu* = *a* in fate, with a soft *w* after it.	same as *oo* in moon; *oei* = *oo* followed by a short *ĭ*.	. . . .	combines *o* in not with *u* in rule; softer than, but often confused with, *au*.
. . . .	same as French *eu* ; *eeu* the same prolonged.	. . . .	as *oo* in moon; sometimes a simple prolonged *ō* ; or like *wa* in was; *oei* or *oey* = *we*.	. . . .	. . . .
as *ĕ* in pet.	like *e* in father when short ; when long, the same sound prolonged ; it lies between *e* in pet and *u* in cut, and resembles German *ŏ*. See Note 2.	. . . .	*oe* = *wa* in was ; *oeu* like *eu*.	*oi* or *oy* = *wa* in was ; *oin* = *w* followed by the nasal in. See Note 1.	*ou* = *oo* in boot ; *ouin* = *oin* ; see *oi* and Note 1.
like *i* in bite.	almost like *i* in bite with a hint of *oi* in noise.	as in believe.	only another spelling of *ŏ*. See Note 2.	. . . .	. . . .
. . . .	. . . .	. . . .	. . . .	. . . .	. . . .
. . . .	. . . .	. . . .	. . . .	. . . .	. . . .
. . . .	. . . .	. . . .	like *a* in sale.	. . . .	. . . .
. . . .	. . . .	. . . .	. . . .	. . . .	. . . .
. . . .	. . . .	. . . .	. . . .	. . . .	almost as *ɔ* in note.
same	as	the	German	diph-	thongs.
. . . .	. . . .	. . . .	. . . .	. . . .	. . . .
. . . .	. . . .	. . . .	. . . .	. . . .	. . . .

Phonetic meaning of the letters and symbols AS USED IN THIS BOOK.	UE	UI	CH as in church ; German _ch_ is represented by _kh_, see Note 3.	SCH	SP
ARABIAN :	....	....	like German _ch_.	....	....
BOHEMIAN :	....	....	....	....	....
DANISH :	....	....	as _k_, except in foreign words.	....	....
DUTCH :	....	almost _y_ in why; but verging on the French _eu_.	like German _ch_, but more palatal at the beginning of foreign words ; as _sh_ in show.	beginning a syllable, as _stch_ ; at the end, as simple _s_ in this.	as in span.
FLEMISH :	same as a prolonged _u_.	_ui_ and _uy_ like German _eu_.	like German _ch_. See Note 3.	....	....
FRENCH :	_uei_ like _eu_.	....	as _sh_ before a vowel ; before a consonant as _k_.	....	....
GERMAN :	only another spelling of _ü_. See Note 2.	....	see Note 3.	like _sh_ in show.	like _shp_ in dishpan.
HUNGARIAN :	....	....	....	....	....
ITALIAN :	....	....	as _k_ in kin.	as _sk_ in skip.	as in span.
NORWEGIAN :	....	....	....	....	....
POLISH :	....	....	like German _ch_, see Note 3.	....	....
PORTUGUESE:	....	....	....	....	....
RUSSIAN :	....	....	....	....	....
SPANISH :	....	....	as in church.	....	....
SWEDISH :	....	....	....	....	....
WELSH :	....	....	like German _ch_, see Note 3.	....	....

ST	TH as in thing ; the *th* in those is represented by *dh*.
....	....
....	....
....	....
as in stone.	....
....	....
....	....
like *sht* in washtub.	like *t* in tot.
....	....
as in stone.	....
....	....
....	....
....	....
....	....
....	....
....	like *t* in tot.
....	....

NOTES

No. 1.—The French nasal sounds are easily obtained :

(1) Though spelled with an *m* or *n* (and indicated in this book by an *ṅ*) they have really no *n* sound in them, much less the *ng* sound that some foreigners give them. Though variously spelled they are reducible to four vowel sounds pronounced, as we say, "through the nose," though actually with closed nasal passages. If one will pronounce or rather snort the word "wrong" without producing the final *g* at all, one will have exactly the French *on* (1) ; the word "thank" similarly sounded without the *k* will give the French *in* (2) ; the word "trunk" without the *k* gives the French *un* (3) ; the word "donkey" (not pronounced like monkey) contains the French *en* (4). These four are indicated in this book by (1) *ôṅ ;* (2) *ăṅ ;* (3) *ŭṅ ;* (4) *än.*

The French nasals may be grouped as follows : Those pronounced like (1) are *om*, *on*, and *eon* after *g ;* like (2) *ĭm*, *in*, *aim*, *ain*, *ein* and also *en* as an ending ; like (3) *ŭn*, *un* and *evn ;* like (4) *am*, *an*, *ean*, *aen*, *aon* and *en* at the beginning of words.

These letters *m* and *n*, however, lose their nasal quality when doubled or when preceding a vowel ; *onne* is pronounced as *one* in done, *ome* or *omme* as in come, *eme* as in *em* in them, etc.

No. 2.—French *u* (which is the same as the German *ü* when long) is easily pronounced if one will pucker his lips to say *oo*, as in moon ; and keeping them strongly puckered, say *e* as in bean. Those who have eaten green persimmons, or had their lips distended with peach fuzz, have the correct position for this *e* sound. There is really no *oo* sound in the French *u* at all, and if one cannot say the *u* correctly he will come much nearer the truth if he uses a plain English long *e*, as in bean, rather than the sound of *u*, as the spelling might suggest.

The German *ü* when short is formed by keeping the lips puckered and saying *i* as in fit, instead of *e* in serene.

The other German modified (or umlauted) vowels are (2) *ä*, pronounced, when long, almost like *a* in sale, but verging on *a* in care (it is marked here simply as *ā*) ; when short much like *e* in pet ; (3) *ö* when long can be secured by puckering the lips for a round, full *o*, as in note and then saying *a* as in sale (it is marked in this book simply as *ā* to avoid the danger of saying a plain *o*) ; when it is short the lips should be puckered for the round *o*, and a short *e* as in pet then pronounced. The caution must be emphasised that in the experiments the lips must be firmly kept in the first, or puckered position, in spite of the temptation to alter it.

No. 3.—German *ch* is not difficult, once caught. Our sound *th* as in think will be found if prolonged to be produced by the simple device of holding the tip of the tongue lightly between the teeth and then breathing. The German *ch* results from pressing the two sides of the tongue firmly against the bicuspid teeth (the two upper teeth on each side back of the canine or eye teeth) and leaving the tip of the tongue free, then breathing the necessary vowel as in *ach*, *ich*, etc. German *g* is much the same but even softer. Both are indicated in this book by *kh*.

No. 4.—Certain Bohemian letters and combinations insert the sound *y* closely allied to a consonant, as in the French *diable* and *tien*, or the English "How *d' ye* do?" or "I've caugh*tye*." Bohemian *d*, *n* and *t* are given this *d'y* and *t'y* sound when followed by *ě* or *i* or by an apostrophe as *d'*, *ň* or *t'*.

Many Bohemian combinations of consonants seem unspeakable because they are spelt with no vowels between. They are no harder to say, however, than such words of ours as "twelfths." Among such consonant chains are *drn*, *kb*, *kd*, *krl*, *prst*, *skrz*, *sr*, *wl* and *zr*. They must be run together as smoothly as possible.

No. 5.—Portuguese diphthongs are of three sorts ; the first two cannot be distinguished here, they are simply combinations of vowels (sometimes of three vowels or triphthongs) in which each vowel is sounded independently ; in the first class the first vowel takes the accent, in the second class the second vowel is accented. The third class contains a nasal vowel marked *ã*, *õ* or *ũ*, and pronounced with a strong nasal twang.

No. 6.—In vowel combinations other than those specially mentioned here, the vowels are pronounced separately, each in its own way

No. 7.—Combinations of consonants other than those mentioned here will be found under their first letter.

No. 8.—As Greek and Latin pronunciations are matters of controversy and personal taste, no system is attempted here. Chinese, Japanese, Hebrew, Hindu, and various other languages are usually spelled phonetically, but on such different national or personal standards that they can hardly be generalised.

BIOGRAPHICAL DICTIONARY
OF MUSICIANS

N.B. The German modified vowels ä, ö, ü, are often spelled ae, oe, ue. For convenience they will here be arranged alphabetically as if a, o, u. For the system on which given names are abbreviated, and for their pronunciation, see the pages devoted to them. The word "Gerbert," or "Coussemaker" in a parenthesis means that some of the composer's works are in the great collections of Gerbert or Coussemaker (q. v.). Where not otherwise stated the man is a composer.

A

Aaron (ä'-rōn), (1) d. Cologne, 1052; abbot and theorist. (2) (or **Aron**), **Pietro**, Florence, 1480 or '90—bet. 1545–62; theorist.

Abaco (dĕl ä'-bä-kō), **E. Fel. dall'**, Verona, July 12, 1675—Munich, July 12, 1742; court-conductor and composer.

Abbà-Cornaglia (äb-ba' kôr-näl'-yä), Alessandria, Piedmont, 1851—1894; composed operas and church-music.

Abbadia (äb-bä-dē'-ä), (1) **Natale,** Genoa, 1792—Milan, ca. 1875; dram. and ch. composer. (2) **Luigia,** daughter of above, b. Genoa, 1821; mezzo-soprano.

Abbatini (äb-bä-tē'-nē), **A. M.,** Castello, ca. 1595—1677; composer.

Abbé (ăb-bā), (1) **Philippe P. de St. Sevin,** lived 18th cent.; 'cellist. (2) **Pierre de St. Sevin,** bro. of above; 'cellist.

Ab'bey, (1) **J.,** Northamptonshire, 1785—Versailles, 1859; organ-builder. (2) **Henry Eugene,** Akron, O., 1846—New York, 1896; impresario; manager of Met. Op., N. Y., 1883–4, 1891–2, and 1894–6.

Ab'bott, (1) **Emma,** Chicago, 1850—Salt Lake City, 1891; operatic soprano; toured America with great popular success. (2) **Bessie** (Ab'ott), Riverdale, N. Y., 1878—New York, 1919; soprano; pupil of Mrs. Ashford, N. Y., and of Koenig, Paris; début 1902 at the Opéra there, after singing in ballad concerts in England; 1906, U. S.

Abeille (ä-bī'-lĕ), **Jn. Chr. L.,** Bayreuth, 1761—Stuttgart, 1838; composer and court-conductor.

Abel (ä'-bĕl), (1) **Clamor H.,** b. Westphalia 17th cent.; court-mus. (2) **Chr. Fd.,** gambist at Köthen, 1720–37. (3) **Ld. Aug.,** b. Köthen, 1717, son of above; court-violinist. (4) **K. Fr.,** Köthen, 1725—London, 1787; bro. of above and the last virtuoso on the gamba. (5) **L.,** Eckartsberga, Thuringia, Jan. 14, 1834—Neu-Pasing, Aug. 13, 1895; violinist.

Abell', **J.,** London, ca. 1660—Cambridge (?) ca. 1724; alto (musico) and lutenist; collector and composer.

Abendroth (ä'-bĕnd-rōt), **Hermann,** b. Frankfort, Jan. 19, 1883; conductor; pupil of Thuille; cond. in Munich, 1903–4; Lübeck, 1905–11; Essen, 1911; after 1915, civic music dir. and head of Cons. at Cologne; in 1922–3 also led concerts of Berlin State Op. and as guest in London and other European cities; cond. Gewandhaus Orch., Leipzig, after 1934.

Abenheim (ä'-bĕn-hīm), **Jos.,** Worms, 1804—Stuttgart, 1891; conductor and violinist.

Abert (ä'-bĕrt), (1) **Jn. Jos.,** Kochowitz, Bohemia, Sept. 21, 1832—Stuttgart, April 1, 1915; double-bass virtuoso and important composer for the instr.; also composed operas, etc. (2) **Hermann,** Stuttgart, March 25, 1871—Aug. 13, 1927; son of (1); noted musical historian; Ph. D., Tübingen Univ.; 1902, docent in mus. science, Halle Univ.; 1909, prof.; 1919, do., Heidelberg Univ.; 1920, Leipzig Univ. (vice Riemann); 1923, Berlin Univ.; author of biog. of Schumann and large number of important historical and scientific works on music; after 1914 ed. the "Gluck-Jahrbuch."

Aborn (ä'-bōrn), (1) **Milton,** Marysville, Cal., May 18, 1864—New York, Nov. 13, 1933; impresario; early in life an actor; after 1902 managed Aborn Op. Co., in productions in English; 1913–15, seasons at Century

Theat., N. Y.; later Gilbert and Sullivan productions. (2) **Sargent,** b. Boston, 1866; brother of Milton, assoc. in his work as impresario and in Aborn Op. Sch., N. Y.

Abos (ä'bōs) (or **Avos, Avos'sa**), **Gir.,** Malta, ca. 1708—Naples, 1786 (?); composer of operas, etc.

A'braham, (1) **Jonn.** Vide BRAHAM. (2) (Dr.) **Max.** Vide PETERS, C. F.

Abrányi, (1) **Kornel,** d. Budapest, Dec. 20, 1903; nobleman; editor and composer. His son (2) **Emil,** b. Budapest, Sept. 22, 1882; c. operas *Monna Vanna* (Budapest, 1907), *Paolo and Francesca* (do. 1912), etc.

Abt (äpt), **Franz,** Eilenburg, Dec. 22, 1819—Wiesbaden, March 31, 1885; court-conductor at Bernburg, Zurich and Brunswick; visited America, 1872; immensely popular as a writer in the folk-song spirit, of such simple and pure songs as *"When the Swallows Homeward Fly,"* etc.; c. 500 works comprising over 3,000 numbers (the largest are 7 secular cantatas) and numerous choruses and other cantatas.

Ab'yngdon, Henry, d. Wells, England, 1497; composer.

Achenbach. Vide ALVARY.

Achron (äkh'-rŏn), **Joseph,** b. Losd-seye, Russia, May 1, 1886; composer; studied Petrograd Cons., violin with Auer (grad. gold medal), harmony with Liadoff, orchestration with Steinberg. Toured Russia at age of 11; head of vln. and chamber music, Kharkov Cons., 1913–16; later toured widely, Russia, Palestine and Europe. Since 1925, res. in New York. C. chamber music and vln. works.

Achscharumov (äsh-tshä'-roo-mŏf), **Demetrius Vladimirovitsch,** b. Odessa, Sept. 20, 1864; violinist and c.; pupil of Auer.

Ack'ermann, A. J., Rotterdam, April 2, 1836—The Hague, April 22, 1914; composer.

Ackté (äk'-tä), **Aïno,** b. Helsingfors, Finland, April 23, 1876; soprano; sang at Paris Opéra; 1904–5, Met. Op., New York.

Ac'ton, J. B., b. Manchester (?), 1863; singing-teacher and composer.

Adalid y Gurréa (ä-dhä'-lēd h-ē-goo-rä'-ä), **Marcel del.,** Coruna, Aug. 26, 1826—Longara, Dec. 16, 1881; pianist; pupil of Moscheles and Chopin; c. opera, etc.

Adam (ăd-äṅ), (1) **Louis,** Muttersholtz, Alsatia, 1758—Paris, 1848; teacher and composer. (2) **Adolphe Charles,** Paris, July 24, 1803—May 3, 1856; son of above; c. many successful operas; *Pierre et Catherine* (1829), *Le Châlet* (1834), *Postillon de Longjumeau* (1836), *Le Fidèle Berger,* *Le Brasseur de Preston* (1838), *Le Roi d' Yvetot* (1842), *La Poupée de Nuremberg, Cagliostro,* and *Richard en Palestine* (1844), the ballets *Giselle, Le Corsaire, Faust,* etc.; in 1847 he founded the Théâtre National, but was made bankrupt by the revolution of 1848, and entered the Conservatoire as prof. of composition to succeed his father.

Adam (ät'-äm) **K. F.,** Constappel, Saxony, Dec. 22, 1806—Leisnig, 1867; cantor and composer.

Adam de la Hale (or **Halle**) (ăd-äṅ dŭ lä äl), Arras, ca. 1240—Naples, 1287; called "Le bossu d'Arras" (Hunchback of Arras); a picturesque trouvère of great historical importance; c. chansons, jeux (operettas) and motets; his works were pub. 1872.

Adamberger (ät'-äm-bĕrkh-ĕr), **Valentin** (not **Joseph**), Munich, 1743—Vienna, 1804; dram. tenor; assumed name "Adamonti"; Mozart wrote the rôle of Belmonte, etc., for him.

Adami da Bolsena (or **da Volterra**) (ä'-dä-mē dä bŏl-sä'-nä), **And.,** Bologna, 1663—Rome, 1742; theorist.

Adamon'ti. Vide ADAMBERGER.

Adamowski (äd-ä-mŏf'-shkĭ), (1) **Timothée,** b. Warsaw, March 24, 1858; violinist and composer; pupil of Kontchi, Warsaw Cons. and Massart, Paris Cons.; 1879 travelled to America as soloist with Clara Louise Kellogg, and later with a company of his own 1885–86; teacher, New Engl. Cons., Boston; organised the Adamowski String-quartet (1888). (2) **Joseph,** Warsaw, 1862—Boston, May 8, 1930; bro. of above; 'cellist; member of the same quartet; married Szumowska; 1903, New Engl. Cons. teacher.

Ad'ams, (1) **Th.,** London, 1785—1858; organist. (2) **Charles R.,** Charleston, Mass., ca. 1834—July 3, 1900; tenor (3) **Suzanne,** b. Cambridge, Mass., 1873; soprano; studied with Bouhy in Paris; sang at the Op. there, 1894–7; then in Nice; from 1898 to 1906 at Covent Garden; 1898,

Chicago; 1899 at Met. Op. House; m. Leo Stern, 'cellist; lived in England after 1903.

Ad'cock, Jas., Eton, England, 1778—Cambridge, 1860; choir-master and composer.

Ad'dison, J., London, ca. 1766—1844; double-bass player, dram. composer.

Adelburg (fōn ä'-dĕl-boorkh), **Aug.**, Ritter von, Constantinople, 1830—(insane) Vienna, 1873; violinist.

Adler (ät'-lĕr), **Guido**, Eibenschütz, Moravia, Nov. 1, 1855—Vienna, February, 1941; pupil at Academic Gym. in Vienna, and Vienna Cons.; ('78) Dr. jur., and ('80) Ph. D.; 1885 prof. of mus. science Prague Univ.; ('95) prof. of mus. history, Univ. of Vienna (vice Hanslick); from 1894, ed.-in-chief, "*Denkmäler d. Tonkunst in Oesterreich*"; after 1913, ed. "*Studien zur Musikwissenschaft*"; author of many valuable essays on music.

Ad'lgasser (ät'-'l-gäs-sĕr), **Anton Cajotan**, Innzell, Bavaria, 1728—1777; organist.

Adlung (ät'-loongk), or **A'delung, Jakob**, Bindersleben, near Erfurt, 1699—1762; organist, teacher and writer.

Adolfati (ä-dōl-fä'-tē), **And.**, Venice, 1711—Genoa (?) 1760; composer.

Adriano di Bologna. Vide BANCHIERI.

Ad'riansen (or **Hadrianus**), **Emanuel**; lived Antwerp 16th cent.; lutenist and collector.

Adrien (ăd-rĭ-ăn) or **Andrien. Martin Joseph** (called la Neuville, or l'Ainé), Liége, 1767—Paris, 1824; bass and composer.

Ægid'ius de Muri'no, 15th cent.; theorist. (Coussemaker.)

Ælsters (ĕl'-stĕrs), **Georges Jacques**, Ghent, 1770—1849.

Ærts (ĕrts), **Egide**, Boom, Antwerp, 1822—Brussels, 1853.

Afanassiev (ä-fä-näs'-sĭ-ĕv), **Nikolai Jakovlevich**, Tobolsk, 1821—St. Petersburg, June 3, 1898; violinist and c.

Affer'ni, Ugo, b. Florence, Jan. 1, 1871; pianist and cond.; studied at Frankfort and Leipzig; m. the violinist Mary Brammer, 1872; c. operas, etc.

Affilard (lăf'-fē-lär'), **Michel l'**, 1683—1708; singer to Louis XIV.

Afranio (ä-frä'-nĭ-ō), b. Pavia, end of 15th cent.; canon at Ferrara; inv. the bassoon.

Afzelius (äf-tsä'-lĭ-oos), **Arvid A.**, Enköping, Sweden, 1785—1871; collector.

Agazza'ri (ä-gäd-zä'-rē), **Ag.**, Siena, 1578—1640; church-conductor.

Agnelli (än-yĕl'-lē), **Salv.**, Palermo, 1817—1874; pupil of Naples Cons.; lived Marseilles and c. operas, cantata "*Apothéose de Napoléon I.*," etc.

Agnesi (dän-yā'-sē), (1) **M. Theresia d'**, Milan, 1724—1780; pianist and dram. composer. (2) **Luigi** (rightly **F. L. Agniez**), Erpent, Namur, 1833—London, 1875; bass.

Agniez (än-yĕz). Vide AGNESI (2).

Agostini (äg-ōs-tē'-nē), (1) **Paolo**, Vallerano, 1593—Rome, 1629; wonderful contrapuntist, some of his works being in 48 parts. (2) **P. Simone**, b. Rome, ca. 1650. c. an opera, etc.

Agrel (ä'-grĕl), **J.**, Loth, Sweden, 1701—Nürnberg, 1765; court-violinist and conductor.

Agric'ola, (1) **Alex.**, Germany (?) ca. 1446—Valladolid, Spain, 1506; court-singer and church-composer. (2) **Martin**, Sorau, Saxony, 1486—Magdeburg, June 10, 1556; eminent writer and theorist. (3) **Jn.**, b. Nürnberg ca. 1570; prof. and composer. (4) **Wolfgang Chp.**, German composer (1651); (5) **G. L.**, Grossfurra, 1643—Gotha, 1676; conductor. (6) **Jn. Fr.**, Dobitschen, 1720—Berlin, 1774; court-cond.

Agthe (äkh'-tĕ), **K. Ch.**, (1) Hettstadt, 1762—Ballenstedt, 1797; composer. (2) **W. Jos. Albrecht**, Ballenstedt, 1790—Berlin, 1873; son of above; teacher. (3) **Fr. W.**, Sangershausen, 1796—(insane) Sonnenstein, ca. 1830; cantor.

Aguado (ä-gwä'-dhō), **Dionisio**, Madrid, 1784—1849; performer and composer for guitar.

Aguiari, Lucrezia. Vide AGUJARI.

Aguilar (ä'-gē-lär), (1) **Emanuel Abraham**, London, Aug. 23, 1824—London, Feb. 18, 1904; pianist of Spanish origin; c. 2 operas, 3 symph. (2) **Elisa**, (3) **Ezequiel**, (4) **Francisco**, (5) **José**, lute players, comprising Aguilar Lute Quartet; toured widely in Europe and America, New York début 1929-30.

Aguilera de Heredia (ä-gwĭ-lā'-rä dä ä-rä'-dhē-ä), **Seb.**, b. Sargossa, 17th cent.; monk and composer.

Agujari (ä-goo-hä'-rē), **Lucrezia** (called La Bastardina, or Bastardella, being the natural daughter of a nobleman), Ferrara, 1743—Parma, May 18, 1783; a phenomenal singer; Mozart remarked her "lovely voice, flexible throat, and incredibly high range,"¹ which reached from middle C three octaves up; she could shake on f''' (vide CHART OF PITCH); she m. Colla, 1780, and retired from the stage.

Ahle (ä'-lĕ), (1) **Jn. Rud.**, Mülhausen, 1625—1673; theorist and church-composer. (2) **Jn. G.**, Mülhausen, 1651—1706; son of above; organist, poet and theorist.

Ahlström (äl'-shträm), (1) Olof, Stockholm, Aug. 14, 1756—Aug. 11, 1835; organist. (2) **Jakob Niklas**, Wisby, Sweden, June 5, 1805—Stockholm, May 14, 1859; son of above; dram. composer.

Ahna. Vide DE AHNA.

Aibl (ī'-bl), **Jos.**, founded publishing firm, Munich, 1824; later heads were Eduard Spitzweg (1836) and his sons, Eugen and Otto.

Aiblinger (ī'-blĭng-ĕr), **Jn. Kasper**, Wasserburg, Bavaria, 1779—Munich, 1867; court-conductor, collector and composer.

Aichinger (ī'-khĭng-ĕr), **Gregor**, Regensburg ca. 1564—Augsburg, 1628; canon and composer.

Aigner (īkh'-nĕr), **Engelbert**, Vienna, 1798—1851; dram. composer.

Aimo (ä'-ē-mō). Vide HAYM, N. F.

Aimon (ĕm-ôṅ), **Pamphile Ld. Fran.**, b. L'Isle, near Avignon, 1779; 'cellist, conductor, theorist.

Ajolla. Vide LAYOLLE.

À Kem'pis, Nicholas, organist and c., at Brussels, ca. 1628.

Akimen'ko, Theodore, composer; b. Kharkov, Russia, Feb. 8, 1876; studied St. Petersburg Cons., 1895—1900, harmony with Rimsky-Korsakoff and Liadoff, piano with Balakireff. C. two symphonies, orchestral poems, chamber music works, opera *"Rudy."* Resident in France.

Ala (ä'-lä), **Giov. Bat.**, Monza, 1580—1612 (?); organist and composer.

Alabieff (ä-lä-bĭ-ĕf), **Alex.**, Moscow, Aug. 16, 1787—March 6, 1851; composer.

Alaleona (äl-äl-ā'-ō-nä) **Domenico**, composer, musicologist; Montegiorgio, Italy, Nov. 16, 1881—Dec. 29, 1928; grad. St. Cecilia Acad., Rome, 1906; studied piano with Bustini, composition with De Sanctis and

Renzi; cond., Augusteo concerts, Rome, and prof., Rome Conservatory, after 1910. C. opera, *"Mirra,"* choral works, chamber music, songs; author articles on Cavalieri and other early Italian composers.

Alard (äl-är), **J. Delphin**, Bayonne, March 8, 1815—Paris, Feb. 22, 1888; violinist, teacher and composer.

Al'ayrac. Vide DALAYRAC.

Albanesi (äl-bä'-nä'-zē), **Luigi**, Rome, March 3, 1821—Naples, Dec. 4, 1897; pianist and composer.

Albani (äl-bä'-nĭ) (stage name of **Marie Louise Cecilia Emma La Jeunesse**), Chambly, near Montreal, Nov. 1, 1852—London, April 3, 1930; operatic soprano; sang in Cathedral, Albany, N. Y., whence her name was mistakenly supposed to have been taken; pupil of Duprez, and of Lamperti; début at Messina in 1870; sang much in England, at Covent Garden and a favourite in concert; 1878, m. Ernest Gye, impresario; retired from stage, 1906; author *"Forty Years of Song"* (1911).

Albani, Mathias, Bozen, 1621—1673; famous father of more famous son of same name and trade, violin-making; the younger A.'s violins (1702-9) rival Amati's.

Albeniz (äl-bā'-nēth), (1) **Pedro**, Logroño, 1795—Madrid, 1855; court-organist. (2) **Pedro**, b. Biscay, San Sebastian, 1755; monk, church-cond. and composer. (3) **Isaac**, Camprodon (Gerona), Spain, May 29, 1860—Cambo-les-Bains, June 16, 1909; eminent composer; a leading representative of the "New Spanish" school of nationalistic composers. He was markedly precocious as a child and appeared as a pianist at the age of 4 in Madrid. At 6 he was taken to Paris, where he studied with Marmontel, and from 11 to 15 appeared as a concert player in North and South America. He attended the Leipzig Cons. for a short time, and later the Brussels Cons. with the aid of funds provided by Alfonso XII. He studied at various times with Brassin and Jadassohn, and also with Liszt at Weimar and Rome. His life was one of continuous uncertainties. As a composer he was prolific, his compositions falling into two separate groups, the first extending from 1883 to about 1890, during which time he composed over 200 piano works including concertos and sonatas and many smaller pieces; after 1890 he undertook the study of composition in Paris with d'Indy and composed the operas "*Pepita Jiminez*," "*Henry Clifford*," a trilogy "*King Arthur*," and the orch. suite "*Catalonia*." Among other compositions are "*Iberia*" suite for piano (several numbers orch. by Arbos), an oratorio "*Cristo*," and many songs. His piano music carries on the traditions of Chopin and Liszt, but is endowed with quite individual folk-colour and intensity of feeling, and also has many impressionistic influences. His trilogy "*King Arthur*" was left unfinished at his death. In 1923 his "*Pepita Jiminez*" was restored with success at the Paris Op.-Comique.

Albergati (däl-bĕr-gä'-tē), (1) **Pirro Capacelli**, Conte **d'**. Lived in Bologna, 17th cent.; composer. (2) **Aldobrandini**, lived in Bologna, 17th cent.; dram. composer.

Al'bert, Prinz von **Sachsen-Coburg Gotha**, Schloss Rosenau, 1819—1861; consort of Queen Victoria, patron of music and composer of an opera, "*Jean le Fol*" (Bagnières de Bigorre, 1865), an operetta, masses, etc.

Albert (äl'-bĕrt), (1) **H.**, Lobenstein, Saxony, 1604—Königsberg, 1651; poet, organist and composer, called the father of the German *Lied*, and, as he alludes to a "Comödien-musik" (1644), he must have been, with Schültz, one of the founders of German opera. (2) **Charles L. N. d'**, Nienstetten, near Hamburg, 1809—London, 1886; dancing master and composer. (3) **Eugen d'**, rightly **Eugène (Francis Charles)** (dăl-băr, or däl'-bĕrt), Glasgow, April 10, 1864—Riga, March 3, 1932; son and pupil of above; pianist; Newcastle scholar in the London Nat. Training School, 1876; pupil of Pauer (pf.) and Stainer, Prout and Sullivan (harm. and comp.); 1881, Mendelssohn scholar and pupil of Richter and Liszt, who called him "the young Tausig"; 1881, he played the Schumann concerto at the Crystal Palace, London; Oct. 24, a concerto of his own, at a Richter concert; he performed 5 Beethoven sonatas (op. 31, 53, 90, 109, 110) at a Gewandhaus recital, 1893; he married the pianist Carreño in 1892 (divorced 1895); first

conductor at Weimar, vice Lassen, but soon resigned; composed a symphony, 2 overtures ("*Hyperion*" and "*Esther*"), 2 pf.-concertos, libretto and music of the operas "*Der Rubin*" (Carlsruhe, Oct. 12, 1893), "*Ghismonda*" (Dresden, 1895), "*Gernot*" (Mannheim, 1897), 1-act mus. comedy "*Die Abreise*" (Frankfort, 1898); operas "*Kain*" and "*Der Improvisator*" (both Berlin, 1900), "*Tiefland*" (Prague, 1903), "*Flauto solo*" (Prague, 1905), "*Tragaldabas*" (Hamburg, 1907), "*Die Verschenkte Frau*" or "*The Bartered Wife*" (1912, Munich). His opera "*Tiefland*" (based on Guimera's play, "*Marta of the Lowlands*") has had immense success; in Berlin alone (prod. 1907) it reached its 400th performance in Feb., 1912; it was sung at the Met. Op., 1908, and throughout Europe; also c. the operas "*Liebesketten*," "*Izeil*," "*Die Toten Augen*" (1917); perf. also in N. Y. by German Op. Co., 1924); "*Der Stier von Oliveira*" (Leipzig, 1918); "*Revolutionshochzeit*" (do, 1919); "*Scirocco*" (Darmstadt, 1921); "*Mareike von Nymwegen*" (1923); "*Der Golem*"; "*Die Schwarze Orchidee*" (musical detective drama, using jazz effects); and a posth. work, "*Mr. Wu*," (prod. 1932); string quartets, violin con certo; pf. pieces, etc. His later marriages were to Hermine Finck, singer (1895–1910); Ida Theumann (1910–12); he is esp. remembered for his piano transcriptions of Bach organ works; his revision of the "*Well-Tempered Clavichord*"; his editions of various Liszt works and of the sonatas of Beethoven.

Albertazzi (äl-bĕr-täd'-zē), **Emma** (née **Howson**), London, 1814—1847; operatic contralto.

Alberti (äl-bĕr'-tē), (1) **Jn. Fr.**, Tonning, 1642—Merseburg, 1710; organist. (2) **Giusi Matteo**, Bologna, 1685—1746; violinist and composer. (3) **Domenico**, Venice, ca. 1717—Formio, 1740; singer then pianist; in his piano music he made use of the since-called "Alberti bass" (vide D. D.).

Alberti'ni (äl-bĕr-tē'-nē), (1) **Gioacchino**, b. 1751—Warsaw, April, 1812; conductor and dram. composer.

Albicas'tro, Henrico (rightly, **Weissenburg**), b. Switzerland, 17th cent.; court-violinist.

Albino'ni, Tommaso, Venice, 1674—1745; violinist.

Albo'ni, Marietta, ·Cesena, Romagna, March 10, 1823—Ville d'Avray, near Paris, June 23, 1894; eminent dram. contralto, compass g–g'' (vide PITCH, D. D.); pupil of Rossini; début La Scala, Milan, 1843; m. Count Pepoli, 1854.

Albrechtsberger (äl-brĕkhts-bĕrkh-ĕr), **Jn. G.,** Klosternenburg, near Vienna, Feb. 3, 1736—Vienna, March 7, 1809; eminent composer, court-organist, theorist and teacher (Beethoven was his unappreciated pupil).

Albri'ci (äl-brē'-chē), **V.,** Rome, 1631—Prague, 1696; court-conductor.

Alcarrot'ti, Giov. Fran., lived in Italy 16th cent.; organist, 1740–91.

Al'cock, (1) **John,** London, 1715—Lichfield, 1806, organist. (2) **J.,** son of above; organist.

Alda, Frances (rightly **Davis**), b. Christchurch, New Zealand, May 31, 1883; soprano; studied with Mathilde Marchesi; début as Manon (Massenet), Paris Op.-Comique, 1905; sang in Brussels, London, Warsaw, Milan, and Buenos Aires; début with Met. Op. Co., New York, 1908, as Gilda; sang more than 30 rôles with this company. Retired from opera, 1929; also active in concert and radio; m. Giulio Gatti-Casazza, 1910; divorced 1929.

Aldovrandini (äl-dō-vrän-dē'-nē), **Gius. A. V.,** b. Bologna, 1665; court-conductor and dram. composer.

Al'drich, (1) **H.,** Westminster, 1647—Oxford, 1710, theorist and composer. (2) **Richard,** Providence, R. I., July 31, 1863—Rome, June 2, 1937; graduated Harvard, 1885, won scholarships and honours; studied music under J. K. Paine; 1885 he went on the staff of the *Providence Journal*, soon reaching an editorial position, and being put in charge of the musical and other critical departments of the paper; 1888 he spent in study abroad, chiefly of music; 1889 to 1891, private secretary to U. S. Senator N. F. Dixon; 1891—1902 joined the staff of the *New York Tribune* as associate musical critic with H. E. Krehbiel, and as collaborator in their "*History of the Philharmonic Society*"; 1902–24, music critic, *N. Y. Times*; author of various magazine articles, and editor of a series of musical biographies; also guides to

Wagner music-dramas, etc. (3) **Mariska,** b. Boston, 1881; soprano; pupil of Giraudet and Henschel; début, New York, 1908; sang with Met. Op. Co., 1909–13; Brünnhilde at Bayreuth, 1914. (4) **Perley Dunn,** Blackstone, Mass., 1863—New York, Nov. 21, 1933; singer and teacher; pupil of Shakespeare, Trabadello and Sbriglia; taught at Univ. of Kansas, 1885–7; Utica Cons., 1889–91; after 1903 in Philadelphia.

Alembert (däl-än̈-bǎr), **J. Le Rond d',** Paris, 1717—1783; theorist.

Alessan'dri, (1) **Giulio,** c. an oratorio (ca. 1690). (2) **Felice,** Rome, 1747—Casalbino, 1798; pianist and conductor.

Alessan'dro Merlo (or **Alless. Romano**), called **Della Viola,** b. Rome (?) ca. 1530; monk, singer and composer.

Alfano (äl-fä'-nō), **Franco,** composer; b. Naples, March 8, 1877; studied at Naples and Leipzig Cons.; succeeded Busoni as dir. Bologna Liceo, 1917; later, at Liceo Verdi, Turin. Toured as pianist. C. (operas), "*Miranda,*" Leipzig, 1897; "*La Fonte d'Enshir,*" Breslau, 1898; "*Risurrezione*" (based on Tolstoy's work), Turin, 1904, Chicago, 1925, with Mary Garden as Katiusha; "*Il Principe Zilah,*" Genoa, 1909; "*L'Ombra di Don Giovanni,*" 1913; "*La Leggenda di Sakuntala,*" 1921; "*Madonna Imperia,*" 1925 (Met. Op., New York, 1927–8); "*Il Piccolo Lord,*" comic opera (based on "*Little Lord Fauntleroy*"); "*Cyrano de Bergerac*" (based on Rostand drama), 1935–6. Chosen to complete final act of Puccini's posth. opera, "*Turandot.*" Also c. symphony, suites, ballet and piano works.

Alfarâbi (äl-fä-rä'-bē), or **Alphara'bius,** properly **El Farâbi** (abbr. **Farâbi**) Farâb (now Othrax), 900 (?)—Damascus, 950; Arabian theorist who vainly advocated Greek theories.

Alfieri (äl-fē-ā'-rē), **Abbate Pietro,** Rome, 1801—1863; Camadulian monk; teacher and theorist.

Alfvén (älf'-vĕn), **Hugo,** b. Stockholm, May 1, 1872; violinist; studied at the Cons. and with César Thomson; 1900 received Jenny Lind scholarship for 3 years foreign study; from 1904 prof. of comp. Stockholm University: from 1910 mus. dir. Upsala Univ., in 1912 conducting a concert of Upsala students in Berlin; c. 3 symphonies; symph. poem "*Aus der Schären*": cantata "*The Bells,*" "*The Lord's Prayer,*" for chorus; scene with orch., male choruses, etc.

Algarot'ti, Count **Fran.,** Venice, 1712—Pisa, 1764; writer.

Alipran'di, (1) **Bdo.,** b. Tuscany, Bavaria, ca. 1730; his son (2) **Bdo.,** 'cellist at Munich, 1780.

Alkan (ăl-kän), (1) **Chas. H. Val.** (*l'ainê*), Paris, Nov. 30, 1813—March 29, 1888; pianist, teacher, and brilliant composer for piano.

Allacci (äl-lät'chē), **Leone** (or **Leo Allatius**), Chios, 1586—Rome, 1669; writer.

All'chin; conductor Oxford Music Society, 1869–81.

Allegran'ti, Maddalena; dram. soprano; début, Venice, 1771.

Allegri (äl-lā'-grē), (1) **Gregorio,** Rome, 1584—Feb. 18, 1652; pupil of Nanini; composed a celebrated Miserere in 9 parts, sung during Holy Week at the Sistine Chapel; its publication was forbidden on pain of excommunication; but Mozart after twice hearing it, wrote it out, and it has since been frequently published. (2) **Dom.;** lived 1610–29 at Rome; one of the first to write instrumental accompaniments not in mere unison with the voices.

Al'len, (1) **H. R.,** Cork, 1809—London, 1876; bass. (2) **G. B.,** London, 1822—Brisbane, Queensland, 1897; singer, organist, conductor, manager, and composer. (3) **Nathan H.,** Marion, Mass., 1848—1925; pupil of Haupt, Berlin; organist, teacher in Hartford, Conn.; composer of cantatas, etc. (4) **Sir Hugh Percy,** b. Reading, Dec. 23, 1869; organist at 11, 1887—1892 org. Chichester Cathedral; 1901 at Oxford, where he was made Mus. Doc. 1898, and University Choregus 1909; 1908, mus. dir. Reading University College; 1909, mus. dir., Oxford; 1918–38, dir. R. C. M., London.

Allihn (äl-lēn'), **H. Max.,** b. Halle-on-Saale, Aug. 31, 1851—Nov. 15, 1910; writer on organ-building.

Al'lison, (1) **Richard,** teacher at London, 1592. (2) **Robt.,** member of Chapel Royal till 1609. (3) **Horton Claridge,** b. London, July 25, 1846; pianist; pupil R. A. M. and Leipzig Cons.; Mus. Doc. (Dublin), c. piano and organ music and songs.

Almeida (däl-mä'-ē-dhä), **Fernando d',** Lisbon, ca. 1618—1660; monk and church-composer.

Almenräder (äl'-mĕn-rä-dĕr), **Karl,** Ronsdorf, 1786—Nassau, 1843; virtuoso and manufacturer of the bassoon.

Alois (ä'-lō-ês), **Ladislaus,** Prague, 1860—Russia, 1917; 'cellist; pupil Paris Cons.; soloist Royal orch., St. Petersburg; c. concertos, etc.

Al'paerts, Flor, b. Antwerp, Sept. 12, 1876; composer; pupil of Cons. in native city, and after 1902 its dir.; also active as orch. cond.; c. operas, orch., chamber and choral works, piano pieces.

Al'sager, Thos. Massa, Cheshire, 1779—1846; English amateur and patron.

Al'sen, Elsa, b. Germany; early sang as contralto, later dram. soprano; début as Fidelio, sang rôle in several German op. houses, also Isolde; came to U. S. 1923 with German Op. Co., singing leading Wagner rôles with succ.; Chicago Op., 1926–8; also widely in concert.

Alsleben (äls'-lä-bĕn), **Julius,** Berlin, 1832—1894; editor and writer.

Alsted(t) (äl'-shtät), **Jn. H.,** Herborn, Nassau, 1588—Weissenburg, 1638; writer.

Altenburg (äl'-tĕn-boorkh), (1) **Michael,** Alach, near Erfurt, 1584—Erfurt, 1640; pastor and composer. (2) **Jn. Ernst,** Weissenfels, 1736—Bitterfield, 1801; trumpet-virtuoso; son of (3) **Jn. Kasper,** do.

Altès (äl-tĕs), (1) **Jos. H.,** Rouen, 1826—Paris, 1895; flutist. (2) **Ernest-Eugène,** Paris, March 28, 1830—St. Dye, July 8, 1899; bro. of above; pupil Paris Cons.; violinist and conductor; 1871 deputy conductor of the Opéra; 1879–87, conductor.

Alt'house, Paul, tenor; b. Reading, Pa., Dec. 2, 1889; grad. Bucknell University; début, Met. Op. Co., 1913, as Dmitri in "*Boris Godounoff*"; sang Berlin State Op., Stockholm Royal Op., Landestheatre, Stuttgart; Philadelphia Civic Op., Chicago Civic Op. (1930–31), returned to Met. Op. Co., as singer of Wagner rôles, 1934. Also heard widely in concert, oratorio, festivals.

Alt'mann, Wilhelm, b. Adelnau, Germany, April 4, 1862; editor and musical historian; from 1900, chief librarian of Berlin Royal Library; after 1914, chief of mus. section,

Prussian State Library; 1906, dir. of Deutsche Musiksammlung; 1904, critic, "*National-Zeitung*"; a prolific and scholarly writer on a great number of musical subjects; ed. letters of Wagner and Brahms, etc.

Altnikol (ält′-nē-kôl), **Jn. Chp., d.** Naumberg, 1759; son-in-law and pupil of J. S. Bach; organist and composer.

Altschuler (ält′-shŏŏl-ĕr), **Modeste,** conductor; b. Mohilev, Russia, Feb. 15, 1873; studied Moscow Cons., 'cello, orch., with Arensky, Safonoff, Taneieff; European tour with Moscow Trio; came to America as 'cellist and teacher, 1900; founded Russian Symph. Orch., New York, 1903; cond. many first perf. of Russian works with this group, now disbanded. Res. Los Angeles.

Alvarez (ăl-vä′-rĕth), (1) **Fermin Maria,** b. Saragossa; d. Barcelona, 1898; c. popular songs, etc. (2) (ăl-vä-rĕz), stage name of **Albert Raymond Gourron;** Bordeaux, 1861 —Nice, Feb. 1, 1933; tenor; pupil of A. de Martini; début at Ghent, later at Paris Opéra as leading tenor for many years; 1898 Met. Op. House, New York.

Alvary (ăl-vä′-rē), **Max** (rightly **Achenbach**), Düsseldorf, 1856—Datenberg, Thuringia, Nov. 8, 1898; eminent Wagnerian tenor; début at Weimar.

Alvsleben, Melitta. Vide OTTO-ALVS-LEBEN.

Amadé (ăm-ä-dä), (1) **Ladislaw,** Baron von, Kaschau, Hungary, 1703— Felbar, 1764; poet and composer. (2) **Thaddäus,** Graf von Pressburg, 1782—Vienna, 1845; pianist.

Amadei (ăm-ä-dä′-ē), **R.,** Loreto, Italy, Nov. 29, 1840—Dec. 13, 1913; succeeded his father as organist and conductor.

Amati (ä-mä′-tē), a family of famous violin-makers at Cremona, Italy. (1) **Andrea,** 1530 (?)—1611 (?), evolved the violin from the viol; his younger bro., (2) **Niccolò,** made fine bass-viols 1568–86. A.'s 2 sons, (3) **Antonio,** 1555—1638, and (4) **Geronimo,** d. 1630, produced violins of the same style. The most famous was Geronimo's son, (5) **Niccolò,** Sept. 3, 1596—Aug. 12, 1684, who built the "Grand Amatis," large violins of powerful tone; his label is "Nicolaus Amati Cremonens. Hieronimi filius Antonii nepos. Fecit anno 16—";

he trained Andrea Guarneri and Antonio Stradivari. (6) His son **Giralomo,** the last of the family, was inferior. (7) **Giuseppe A.,** b. 17th cent., Bologna, a violin-maker, may have been of the same family. (8) **V.** (called **Amatus**), Cimmina, Sicily. 1629—Palermo, 1670, conductor and composer. (9) **Antonio** and (10) **Angelo,** brothers, and organ-builders at Pavia, ca. 1830.

Amato (ä-mä′-to), **Pasquale,** b. Naples, March 21, 1878; barytone; début Naples, 1900; sang at Milan, then at Trieste, etc.; 1909, Manhattan Opera; from 1911 Met. Op., singing leading rôles in variety of operas for a decade; heard widely in concerts and opera in U. S. and Europe; res. in Louisiana, opera dir. at University.

Ambrogetti (äm-brō-jĕt′-tē), **G.,** sang 1807—1838, basso-buffo.

Ambros (äm′-brôs), **Aug. W.,** Mauth, near Prague, Nov. 17, 1816—Vienna, June 28, 1876, eminent historian and critic.

Ambrose (**Ambro′sius**), Trèves A. D. 333—Milan April 4, 397; Bishop of Milan, regulated (384) and developed Western church-music by introducing ritual as practised in the Eastern Church; the adoption of the four authentic church-modes was probably due to him; he has been called "The Father of Christian Hymnology," though his authorship of the so-called Ambrosian Hymn is discredited further than the translation of the text into the "*Te Deum*"; it is improbable that he was acquainted with the use of letters for notation.

Am(m)erbach (äm′-ĕr-bäkh), **Elias Nikolaus,** ca. 1530—Leipzig, 1597; organist, theorist and composer.

Amfitheâtrov, Daniele, b. Russia, 1901; assoc. cond. Minneapolis Symph. 1937.

Amiot (äm-yō), **Father,** b. Toulon, 1718; Jesuit missionary and writer on Chinese music.

Am(m)on (äm-mōn), (1) **Blasius,** b. in the Tyrol—d. Vienna, June, 1590, court-sopranist, later Franciscan friar, composer. (2) **Jn. Ands.,** Bamberg, 1763—Ottingen, 1825; virtuoso on the Waldhorn.

Am′ner, (1) **John,** b. late 16th cent.— d. 1641; organist. (2) His son **Ralph,** bass at Windsor, 1623—1663.

Amorevoli (ä-mō-rä′-vō-lē), **Angelo,** Venice, 1716—Dresden, 1798; singer.

Anacker (ä′-näk-ĕr), **Aug. Fd.,** Freiberg, Saxony, 1790—1854; cantor and composer.

Ancot (äṅ-kō), a family of pianists and composers at Bruges. (1) **Jean** (*père*), 1779—1848. His two sons, (2) **Jean** (*fils*), 1799—Boulogne, 1829, (3) **Louis,** 1803—Bruges, 1836.

Ander (än′-dĕr), **Aloys,** Liebititz, Bohemia, 1824—Bad Wartenberg, 1864; tenor.

An′ders, Gf. Eng., Bonn, 1795—Paris, 1866; writer.

Andersen (1) **Joachim,** Copenhagen, April 29, 1847—May 7, 1909. Soloist at 13. Toured widely; court musician, Copenhagen, Petersburg and Berlin; for 8 years solo flutist and assistant conductor of Berlin Phil. Orch., of which he was one of the founders; 1895—1909, the ruling musical force in Copenhagen, as conductor of the Palace concerts, the Tivoli Orchestra, the Municipal Summer concerts, his orchestral school, and Inspector (with rank of Captain) of all the military music of Denmark. Made Knight of Dannebrog Order by King Charles IX; received the "Palms" of the Acad. from the Pres. of France, and was made "Prof." by King Frederik of Denmark. (2) **Vigo,** Copenhagen, April 21, 1852—Chicago, Jan. 29, 1895; solo flutist with Thomas orch.; brother of (1).

An′derson, (1) **Lucy,** née **Philpot,** Bath, 1790—London, 1878; pianist. (2) **Geo. Fr.,** King's bandmaster in England, 1848. (3) **Thomas,** Birmingham, England, April 15, 1836—Sept. 18, 1903; critic, organist and c. (4) **Marian,** b. Philadelphia; eminent Negro contralto; studied with Giuseppe Boghetti; first gained prominence as soloist with Philadelphia Phil. Symph., and in New York recital début; winner of contest to appear with N. Y. Phil. at Stadium concerts, 1925; European appearances, 1930–5, incl. Berlin, Vienna, Paris, where she gained remarkable triumphs and returned to U. S. in latter year, giving several N. Y. recitals with outstanding succ. Chosen to sing in Brahms' alto rhapsody with Vienna Phil. under Bruno Walter during festival there in 1936.

Ándrade (dän-drä-dhĕ) **Fran. d',** Lisbon, 1859—Berlin, Feb. 8, 1921; barytone; studied with Miraglia and Ronconi; sang leading rôles in many European cities.

André (äṅ-drä), a musical family of Offenbach. (1) **Jn.,** 1741—1799, publisher and pianist; he originated in 1783 the *durchkomponirte Ballade* (vide D. D.). (2) **Jn. Ant.,** 1775—1842; third son of above; pianist, publisher, theorist. (3) **Karl Aug.,** 1806—Frankfort, 1887; publisher and writer. (4) **Julius,** 1808—Frankfort, 1880; organist. (5) **Jn. Aug.,** 1817—1887; publisher; his 2 sons, (6) **Karl** (b. 1853) and (7) **Adolf** (b. 1885), were later the proprietors. (8) **Jean Baptiste** (de St. Gilles), 1823—Frankfort, 1882; pianist and composer.

An′dreae, Volkmar, b. Berne, July 5, 1879; conductor and composer; studied Cologne Cons.; led choruses in Winterthur and Zurich; after 1906, led symph. concerts of the Tonhalle Soc.; 1914, dir. of Zurich Cons.; president of the Swiss Composers' Soc. after 1920; has appeared as guest cond. in other European cities; c. (operas) "*Ratcliff*" and "*Abenteuer des Casanova*"; also orch. and chamber music.

Andreoli (än-drä-ō′-lē), (1) **Evangalista,** 1810—1875; organist at Mirandola; his two sons, (2) **Guglielmo** (Modena, 1835—Nice, 1860) and (3) **Carlo** (Mirandola, 1840—Regio Emilia, 1910 ?), were pianists, the latter also organist and composer. (4) **Giuseppe,** Milan, 1757—1832; double-bassist and harpist.

Andreozzi (än-drä-ŏd′-zē), **Gaetano,** Naples, 1763—Paris, 1826; dram. composer.

Andrésen (än-drä′-zĕn), **Ivar,** b. 1895; bass; sang Dresden Op., 1925–33; Bayreuth, 1927; Met. Op., 1930; Berlin Op., 1931.

Andreva (än-drä′-vä), **Stella,** b. London, of Scotch-German ancestry; coloratura soprano; studied singing at R. A. M.; sang in operettas, then engaged for three years at Stockholm R. Op.; 1934–5, Covent Garden; Met. Op., N. Y., 1936–37.

Andrevi (än-drä′-vē), **Fran.,** Sanabuya, near Lerida, 1786—Barcelona, 1853; critic and writer.

Andrien. Vide ADRIEN.

An′dries, Jean, Ghent, 1798—1872; teacher and writer.

Andriessen. Vide STAHMER.

Androt (än-drō), **Albert Auguste,** Paris, 1781—Aug. 9, 1804; c. opera, requiem, etc.

Anerio (ä-nä'-rē-ō), (1) **Felice,** Rome, 1560—Sept. 26, 1614; successor to Palestrina. (2) **Giovanni Fran.,** Rome, ca. 1567—1621 (?), bro. of above; conductor and church-composer.

Anfos'si, Pasquale, Taggia, near Naples, 1727—Rome, 1797; pupil and rival of Piccinni; composed 54 operas, etc.

Angelet (äṅ'-zhŭ-lä), **Chas. Fran.,** Ghent, 1797—Brussels, 1832.

Angeli (dän-jä'-lē), **Andrea d',** b. Padua, Nov. 9, 1868; historian; c. opera "L'Innocente" (Bologna), etc.

Angelini (än-jä-lē'-nǐ), **Bontempi Giov. And.,** Perugia, ca. 1624—1705; court-singer and dram. composer.

Angeloni (än-jä-lō'-nǐ), **Luigi,** Frosinone, Papal States, 1758—London, 1842; writer.

An'gerer, Gottfried, Waldsee, Feb. 3, 1851—Zurich, Aug. 19, 1909; c. male choruses.

Anglebert (dän-glŭ-bär), **J. Bapt. H. d',** 1628 (?)—Paris, 1691; court-clavicembalist to Louis XIV.

Animuccia (än-ē-moot'-chä), (1) **Giov.,** Florence, ca. 1500—Rome, March, 1571; wrote the first *Laudi spirituali* for the lectures of Neri in the oratory of S. Philippo, has hence been called "Father of Oratorio"; he was Palestrina's predecessor as conductor at the Vatican. (2) **Paolo,** d. Rome, 1563, bro. of above.

Ankerts, D'. Vide DANKERS, GHISELIN.

Anna Amalia. Vide AMALIA.

Annibale (än-nǐ-bä'-lĕ), (1) (called **Il Padova'no,** or **Patavi'nus,** from Padua, where he was born 1527) d. Groz 1575; organist and composer. (2) **Domenico,** Italian sopranist in London, 1756.

An'rooy, Peter van, b. Zalt-Bommel, Holland, Oct. 13, 1879; conductor; composer; pupil of Joh. Wagenaar and Taneiev; cond. orchestras in Amsterdam, Groningen, Arnhem, and after 1917 of the Residentie Orch. in The Hague; hon. doctorate from Univ. of Gronigen; c. chamber, orch., and choral works.

Ansani (än-sä'-nē) **Giovanni,** b. Rome, 18th cent.; dram. tenor.

Anschütz (än'-shüts), **K.,** Coblenz,

1815—New York, 1870; cond. and composer.

Ansermet (än-sĕr-mä'), **Ernest,** b. Vevey, Switzerland, Nov. 11, 1883; conductor; studied with Denéreaz, Gédalge, Barblan, Bloch; after 1912, cond. of concerts at Montreux Kursaal; cond. Geneva subscription concerts, 1915-18; founder, Orchestre de la Suisse-Romande, Geneva, 1918; conductor after 1915 with Diaghileff Ballet Russe, in Paris, London, Italy, Spain, America. Made guest tours of other countries, also America. C. symphonic poem "*Feuilles au printemps*" and other works.

Ansorge (än-sôr'-gĕ), (1) **Max,** b. Striegau, Silesia, Oct. 1, 1862; organist; son of a cantor; studied at Berlin; c. songs, motets, etc. (2) **Konrad (Eduard Reinhold),** Buchwald, Silesia, Oct. 15, 1862—Berlin, Feb. 13, 1930; pianist; pupil Leipzig Cons. and of Liszt; toured America; c for orchestra, and piano.

Ant'cliffe, Herbert, b. Sheffield, Engl., July 30, 1875; writer on music; author of studies of Schubert, Brahms, etc.

Antegnati (än-tän-yä'-tǐ), **Costanzo,** Brescia, 1557—ca. 1620; organbuilder, etc.

Antheil (än'-tīl), **George,** b. Trenton, N. J., July 8, 1900; composer; studied Sternberg Cons., Philadelphia; res. in Europe for some years; c. (opera) "*Transatlantic*", based on modern American "jazz age" theme (Frankfort State Op., 1930); Symphony in F (Paris, 1926); Piano Concerto in A (Paris, 1927); music to Sophocles' "*Oedipus*" (Berlin State Theat., 1929); (ballet) "*Fighting the Waves*" (text by W. B. Yeats), Abbey Theatre, Dublin; (opera) "*Helen Retires*" (book by Erskine), N. Y., 1934; two string quartets, orchestral, chamber music. Earlier manner radical to extent of introducing noise-making non-musical instruments in orchestra; later chamber works more conservative in manner than that of his "*Ballet mécanique*", a curiosity which created sensation at its Paris première.

An'tipov, Constantin, b. Russia, Jan. 18, 1859; c. symph. allegro for orch., and piano pieces.

Apel (ä'pĕl), **Jn. Aug.,** Leipzig, 1771—1816; writer.

Apell (ä-pĕl'), **Jn. D. von,** Cassel, 1754—1833; conductor and dram. composer.

Apol'lo, Greek sun-god, and god of music.

Appel (äp'-pĕl), **K.,** Dessau, 1812—Dec. 9, 1895; violinist, court-leader, composed opera *"Die Rauberbraut"* (Dessau, 1840), and humorous male quartets.

Appun (äp-poon'), **G. A. I.,** Hanau, 1816—1885; versatile performer on nearly every instr.; writer on and experimenter in acoustics; made an harmonium of 53 degrees to the octave.

Aprile (ä-prē'-lĕ), **Gius,** Bisceglia, 1738—Martina, 1814; celebrated contralto musico and vocal teacher; writer and composer.

Ap'thorp, W. Foster, Boston, Mass., Oct. 24, 1848—Vevey, Feb. 19, 1913; Harvard, '69, studied piano, harmony, cpt. with J. K. Paine and B. J. Lang; teacher of theory, and for many years distinguished critic and writer on music; author of *"Hector Berlioz"*; *"Musicians and Music-Lovers, and other Essays"*; *"By the Way, About Music and Musicians"*; *"Opera and Opera Singers"*, etc.

Aptom'mas, (1) **John,** (2) **Thomas,** brothers; b. Bridgend, England, 1826, and 1829; harp-players and teachers.

Ar'a, Ugo, Venice, 1876—Lausanne, 1936; pupil of Tirindelli, Thomson and Fuchs; 1903-17, viola player in Flonzaley Quartet.

Araja (ä-rä'-yä), **Fran.,** Naples, 1700—Bologna, ca. 1767; dram. composer; composed the first opera written in Russian.

Arauxo (ä-rä-ooks'-ō) (or **Araujo** (ä-rä-oo'-hō)), **Francisco Correa de,** ca. 1581—Segovia, 1663; bishop, theorist.

Arbeau, Thoinot (twä-nō ăr-bō). Vide TABOUROT.

Arbós (är'-vōs), **E. Fernandez,** b. Madrid, 1863—San Sebastian, 1939; violinist; grandfather & father were bandmasters in army; pupil Madrid Cons.; took prizes at 12; then studied with Vieuxtemps, Gevaërt and Joachim; cond. Berlin Phil. Society; taught at Hamburg, Madrid, and Royal College, London; c. comic opera, *"El Cientro de la Tierra,"* Madrid, 1895; also for violin and orch.; after 1908, cond. Madrid Orquesta Sinfonica; guest cond. in Europe and U. S.

Ar'cadelt, Jacob (or **Jachet Arkadelt, Archadet, Arcadet, Harcadelt),** ca. 1514—after 1557; distinguished Flemish composer and teacher; 1540, singer in Paris; 1557, *Regius musicus;* composed masses, etc.

Archadet (är-chä-dā'). Vide ARCADELT.

Archambeau (är'-shän-bō), **Iwan d',** b. Liége, 1879; 'cellist; pupil of his father, Massau and Jacobs; after 1903 mem. of Flonzaley Quartet.

Archangel'ski, Alexander A., Pensa, Russia, Oct. 23, 1846—Prague, 1924; organist and cond.; c. masses, a requiem, much church music.

Ar'cher, Fredk., Oxford, England, June 16, 1838—Pittsburgh, Pa., Oct. 22, 1901; pupil of his father; studied in London and Leipzig; organist and opera-director in London; 1881, organist of Plymouth Church, Brooklyn, later in New York; 1887, conductor of Boston Oratorio Soc.; 1895-98, Pittsburgh (Pa.) Orchestra; composed cantata, organ-pieces, etc.

Arditi (är-dē'-tē), (1) **Michele,** Marchese, Naples, 1745—1838; composer. (2) **Luigi,** Crescentino, Piedmont, July 16, 1822—Hove, England, May 1, 1903; pupil of Milan Cons.; violinist, then director of opera, 1843, Milan, Turin, and Havana. He visited New York with the Havana opera company, 1847, and at intervals thereafter until 1856. Composed 3 operas, vocal waltzes, *"Il Bacio,"* etc.; wrote *"My Reminiscences"* (London, 1896).

Arens (ä'-rĕns), **Fz. Xaver,** Neef, Germany, Oct. 28, 1856—Los Angeles, Jan. 28, 1932; came to America early in youth; pupil of his father, and of Rheinberger, etc.; conductor, organist; composer of symphonic fantasia, etc.

Arensky (ä-rĕn'-shkǐ), **Anton Stepanovitch,** Novgorod, Russia, July 31, 1861—Tarioki, Finland, Feb. 25, 1906; composer and pianist; pupil of Johanssen and Rimsky-Korsakov; Prof. Imp. Cons. Moscow, and conductor Imperial Court Choir; composed a symphony, 4 suites for orch., 1-act opera *"Rafaello,"* string quartets, concerto for piano, etc., including *"Essais sur des rythmes oubliés,"* f. pf. 4 hands.

Aretino. Vide GUIDO D'AREZZO.

Argentina (ärkh-ĕn-tē'-nä), **La** (stage name of **Antonia Mercè**) Buenos Aires—Bayonne, France, July 18, 1936; noted dancer, esp. famed for her perf. of Spanish dances and remarkable skill in playing on castanets; her parents were members of the R. Op. ballet, Madrid, of which she became *prima ballerina* at 19; later made world tours with great succ., incl. United States

Aria (ä'-rĭ-ä), **Cesare**, Bologna, 1820—1894; singing-teacher.

Aribo (ä-rē'-bō), **Scholas'ticus**, d. ca. 1078; probably from the Netherlands; writer. (Gerbert.)

Arien'zo (där-ĭ-ĕn'-tsō), **Nicolà d'**, Naples, Dec. 24, 1842—April 25, 1915; composed 5 operas in Neapolitan dialect, "*Monzu Gnazio*" (Naples, 1860), and "*I Due Mariti*" (Naples, 1866), the most successful, realistic and original; also an oratorio, a "*Pensiero Sinfonico*," overtures, etc.; wrote a treatise advocating pure intonation instead of temperament, and a third mode (the Minor Second), besides the usual major and minor.

A'rion, partly traditional Greek singer and lyrist (7th cent., B. C.), hence, the name of a vocal society.

Arios'ti, **Attilio**, Bologna, 1660—ca. 1740; composed 15 operas; 1716 a rival of Buononcini, and of Händel; in London in 1720, the three composed the opera "*Muzio Scaevola*."

Aristi'des Quintilia'nus, Greek teacher and writer on music, ca. 160.

Ar'istotle, (1) Stagyra, 384 B.C.—322 B. C.; Greek philosopher, whose works include valuable information concerning Greek music. (2) Pseudonym of a writer on mensurable music, 12th—13th cent.

Aristox'enos, b. Tarentum, ca. 354 B.C.; one of the first Greek writers on music.

Arl'berg, **Georg Ephraim**, **F.**, Leksand, Sweden, 1830—Christiania, Feb. 21, 1896; barytone.

Armbrust (ärm'-broost), **K. F.**, Hamburg, 1849—Hanover, 1896; teacher and critic.

Armbruster (ärm'-broo-stĕr), **K.**, Andernach-on-Rhine, July 13, 1846—London, June 10, 1917; pupil of Hompesch; pianist and lecturer: Hans Richter's assistant conductor at the Wagner concerts, 1882–84;

later conducted at various London theatres.

Armes, **Philip**, b. Norwich, England, 1836; Mus. Doc. Oxon, 1864; organ composer; d. Durham, Feb. 10, 1908.

Armingaud (är-măn-gō), **Jules**, Bayonne, May 3, 1820—Paris, Feb. 27, 1900; was refused admission to the Paris Cons. at 19 since he was "too far advanced"; leader of a string quartet enlarged to the *Société Classique;* said to have introduced Beethoven's quartets into Paris.

Arms'heimer, **Ivan Ivanovitch**, b. St. Petersburg, March 19, 1860; pupil at the cons.; c. 1-act opera "*Sous la feuillée*" (French text); 2-act opera "*Der Oberförstfer*" (German text); 3-act opera "*Jaegerliv*" (Danish text); cantatas, songs, etc.

Arnaud (är-nō), (1) Abbé **Fran.**, Aubignan, 1721—Paris, 1784; writer. (2) **J. Et. Guil.**, Marseilles, 1807—Jan., 1863; composer.

Arne (ärn), (1) Dr. **Thomas Augustine**, London, March 12, 1710—March 5, 1778; by secret nightly practice he learned the spinet and violin, his father wishing him to study law; 1736, m. Cecilia Young, a favourite singer of Händel's; 1738, he was composer to the Drury Lane Th. and set Dalton's adaptation of Milton's "*Comus*"; in his masque "*Alfred*" (1740) is "Rule Britannia"; in Dublin (1742–44) he produced two operas, "*Britannia*" and "*Eliza*", and a musical farce "*Thomas and Sally*"; 1745, composer to Vauxhall Gardens, London; set to music the songs in "*As You Like It*," "*Where the Bee Sucks*," in "*The Tempest*," etc.; Mus. Doc. Oxon, 1759; he was the first to use female voices in oratorio-choruses ("*Judith*"); composed 2 oratorios, many masques, orch. overtures, vln.-sonatas, organ-music, harpsichord-sonatas, glees, catches, canons, etc. (2) **Michael**, London, 1741—Jan. 14, 1786 (not 1806); natural son of above; conductor and dram. composer.

Arneiro (där-nā'-ē-rō), **Jose Aug. Ferreira Veiga**, Viscount **d'**, Macao, China, Nov. 22, 1838—San Remo, July, 1903; of Portuguese parents; composed 2 operas.

Arnold (är'-nôlt), (1) **G.**, b. Weldsberg, Tyrol, 17th cent.; organist. (2) **Samuel**, London, 1740–1802; organist Westminster Abbey. (3) **Jn. Gottf.**, near Oehringen, 1773—Frankfort, 1806; 'cellist, etc. (4) **Ignaz Ernst Fd.**, Erfurt, 1774—1812; writer. (5) **K.**, near Mergentheim, Würtemberg, 1794—Christiania, 1873; son of (3) **J. G.**; pianist and composer. (6) **K.**, b. St. Petersburg, 1820; son of (5); 'cellist in Royal Orch.; studied Stockholm. (7) **Fr. W.**, near Heilbronn, 1810—Elberfeld, 1864; collector and composer. (8) **Yourij von**, St. Petersburg, 1811—Simferopol, Crimea, 1898; singing-teacher and dram. composer. (9) **Richard**, Eilenburg, Jan. 10, 1845—New York, June 21, 1918; at 8 taken to U. S.; pupil of Fd. David, 1869–76; 1st violinist of Theo. Thomas' orch., 1878; leader New York Philh. Club, 1891; 1897, organised a sextet. (10) **Maurice** (real name Strothotte), b. St. Louis, Jan. 19, 1865—New York, 1937; pupil of the Cincinnati Coll., 1883; Vierling and Urban, Berlin; Cologne Cons. and Max Bruch, Breslau; lived St. Louis, then New York as teacher in the Nat. Cons. and pupil of Dvořák; composed notable *"Plantation Dances,"* a *"Dramatic Overture,"* 2 comic operas, etc. Wrote *"Some Points on Modern Orchestration."*

Ar'noldson, (1) **Oscar**, Stockholm, 1839—Carlsbad, 1881; tenor. (2) **Sigrid**, b. Stockholm, 1864; daughter of above; operatic soprano; pupil of Maurice Strakosch and Desirée Artot; début, Moscow, 1886; has sung in Europe and America (1894) with success; m. Alfred Fischof.

Arnould (är-noo), **Madeleine Sophie**, Paris, 1744—1802; soprano, created Gluck's *"Iphigénie."*

Ar'rau, **Claudio**, b. Chillan (Chile) Feb. 6, 1903; pianist; pupil of Paoli, Martin Krause; made first appearances as piano prodigy, winning international prize; later toured Europe and U. S., developing into mature artist of strong powers.

Arres'ti, **Giulio Cesare**, ca. 1630—ca 1695; organist and c. at Bologna.

Arriaga y Balzola (där-rĭ-ä'-gä e bäl'-thō-lä), **Juan C. J. A. d'**. Bilboa, 1806—1826.

Arrieta (är-rĭ-ā'-tä), **J. Emilio**, Puenta la Reina, 1823—Madrid, 1894; dram. composer.

Arrigoni (är-rē-gō'-nĕ), **Carlo**, Florence, ca. 1705—Tuscany (?) ca. 1743; lutenist and composer, rival in London to Händel.

Arronge (lär-rôn̄zh), **Adolf l'**, Hamburg, March 8, 1838—Berlin, 1908; pupil of Genée, and at Leipzig Cons.; 1874, theatre-manager, Breslau; composed comic operas, *"Singspiele,"* etc.

Artaria (är-tä-rē'-ä), music publishing house in Vienna, founded by Carlo A., 1780.

Arteaga (är-tä-äg'-ä), **Stefano**, Madrid, 1730—Paris, 1799; Span.sh Jesuit; theorist.

Artot (är-tō), (1) **Maurice Montagney** (ancestor of a line of musicians named Montagney), Gray (Haute-Saône), 1772—Brussels, 1829; bandmaster. (2) **J. Désiré M.**, Paris, 1803—St. Josse ten Noode, 1887; son of above; horn-player and teacher. (3) **Alex. Jos.**, son of Maurice, Brussels, 1815—Ville-d'Avray, 1845; notable violinist and composer. (4) **Marguerite Josephine Désirée**, Paris, July 21, 1835; Vienna, April 3, 1907; daughter of (2) Jean-Désiré; dram.-soprano, pupil of Viardot-Garcia (1855–57); début Brussels, 1857; sang Grand Opera, Paris, 1858, etc., m. the Spanish barytone, Padilla, in 1869. (5) **Lola (A. de Padilla)**, Sèvres, 1885 —Berlin, 1933; daughter of the preceding, also a noted operatic soprano.

Artusi (är-too'-zē), **Giov. M.**, Bologna ca. 1545—1613; canon and theorist.

Asantchevski (Asantschewski, Asantchevski) (ä-sänt-shĕf'-shkĭ), **Michael Pavlovitch**, Moscow, 1838—1881; composer.

Aschenbren'ner (ä'-shĕn-) **Chr. H.**, Altstettin, 1654—Jena, 1732; violinist and court-conductor.

Ash'ley, (1) **John**, d. 1805; bassoonist and manager; his three sons were (2) **General**, d. 1818, violinist. (3) **Chas. Jane**, 1773—1843, 'cellist and manager. (4) **J. Jas.**, 1771—1815, organist and singing teacher. (5) **J.**, "Ashley of Bath," 1780—1830, bassoonist. (6) **Richard**, 1775—1837, London viola-player.

Ash'ton, Algernon Bennet Langton, b Durham, Dec. 9, 1859—London, April 11, 1937; pupil Leipzig Cons., pf. teacher, R. C. M., London: after 1913 at London and Trinity Colleges; composer.

Ash'well, Thos., 16th cent., organist and composer in England.

Asioli (äs-ē-ō'-lē), **Bonifacio**, Correggio,

1769—1832; at the age of 8 he had composed 3 masses, 20 other sacred works, a harpsichord-concerto, a vln. concerto, with orch., and 2 harp-sonatas for 4 hands; pupil of Morigi; successful cembalist, improviser; his first opera buffa, *"La Volubile"* (1785), was successful; his opera *"Cinna,"* favourably received in 1793; prof. of cpt. at Milan Cons.

Asola (or) **Asula** (ä'-sō-lä), **Giov. Mat.,** Verona ca. 1560—Venice, 1609; church-composer.

Aspa (äs'-pä), **Mario,** Messina, 1799—1868; composed 42 operas.

Assantsheffsky. Vide ASANTCHEVSKI.

Assmayer (äs'-mī-ĕr), **Ignaz,** Salzburg, 1790—Vienna, 1862; conductor.

Astarit'ta, Gennaro, Naples, ca. 1749—1803; composed 20 operas.

As'ton, Hugh, English organist and composer in reign of Henry VIII.

Astorga (däs-tôr'gä), **Emmanuele,** Baron d', Sicily, 1680—Madrid (?), 1736; church-composer.

Ath'erton, Percy Lee, b. Roxbury, Mass., Sept. 25, 1871; composer; graduated Harvard, 1893, studying music under Paine; studied two years in Munich with Rheinberger and Thuille, then a year in Berlin with O. B. Boise; 1900 studied with Sgambati and Widor; c. symph., tone poem for orch., *" Noon in the Forest,"* opera-comique *"The Maharaja,"* comic opera, and many songs.

At'kins, Sir Ivor Algernon, b. Cardiff, Nov. 29, 1889; organist and cond.; son and pupil of an organist; later pupil and assistant of C. L. Williams; since 1897, org. Worcester Cath.; cond. of three Choirs Festivals in that city, Mus. D., Oxford; knighted 1921.

Attaignant (ăt-tīn'-yäň), **Pierre** (also **Attaingnant, Atteignant**), 16th cent. music-printer.

Attenhofer (ät'-tĕn-hôf-ĕr), **K.,** Wettingen, Switzerland, May 5, 1837—Zurich, May 22, 1914; pupil of Leipzig Cons.; cond., organist, and teacher; notable composer of male choruses.

At'terberg, Kurt; b. Gothenburg, Sweden, Dec. 12, 1887; composer, conductor; studied to be electrical engineer; also 'cello and composition; début with Gothenburg Symph. Orch., 1912; pres., Swedish Soc. of Composers; c. six symphonies, 2 operas, 2 ballets, violin and 'cello

concertos, chamber music works; winner, Intern. Prize, Schubert Centennial Contest, 1928.

Attrup (ät'-troop), **K.,** Copenhagen, March 4, 1848—Oct. 5, 1892; pupil of Gade, whom he succeeded as organ-teacher Copenhagen Cons.; composed studies for organ and songs.

Att'wood, Thos., London, Nov. 23, 1765—Chelsea, March 24, 1838; important English composer; chorister and court-organist; pupil of Mozart; 1796 organist St. Paul's Cathedral; composed 19 operas, anthems, sonatas for piano, etc.

Auber (ō-bār), **Daniel François Esprit,** Caen, Normandy, Jan. 29, 1782—Paris, May 12 (13?), 1871; notable opera-composer; his father an art-dealer in Paris, sent him to London to learn the trade; but in 1804 he returned to Paris; composed opera *"Julie,"* produced by amateurs in 1812 with an orch. of six stringed instrs.; Cherubini heard of it, recognised A.'s talent and taught him; 1842 dir. the Cons. of Music, Paris, as Cherubini's successor; 1857 imperial conductor to Napoleon III. A.'s first public productions were 2 unsuccessful operas; *" La Bergère Chatelaine"* (1820) was a success; before 1869, he composed over forty operas; his one serious opera, *"Masaniello ou la Muette de Portici"* (1828), with Meyerbeer's *"Robert le Diable"* and Rossini's *"Guillaume Tell,"* established French grand opera; its vivid portrayal of popular fury caused riots in Brussels; his comic operas (to Scribe's librettos) are the best of France; his last opera, *"Rèves d'Amour,"* was produced when he was 87 years old. Other operas are: *"La Marquise de Brinvilliers"* (1831 with eight other composers), *"Le Domino Noir"* (1837), *"Zanetta"* (1840), *"Les Diamants de la Couronne"* (1841), *"La Sirène"* (1844), *"Haydée"* (1847), *"L'Enfant Prodigue"* (1850), *"Zerline,"* *"Manon Lescaut"* (1856).

Aubert (ō-bār), (1) **Jac.** ("le vieux"), b. 1678—Belleville, 1753; violinist. (2) **Louis,** 1720—after 1779; son of above; violinist, etc. (3) **T. Fran. Olivier,** b. Amiens, 1763; 'cellist and composer. (4) **Louis,** b. Paramé, France, Feb. 19, 1877; studied Paris Cons., mem. jury, Paris Cons., music critic; Chevalier, Legion of Honour; c. (opera) *"La Forêt Bleue"*, (Boston, 1913); (symphonic poem) *"Habanera"* (Paris, 1919); (ballet) *"La Nuit Ensorcelée"* (1922); chamber music works, songs, choruses, piano pieces.

Aubery du Boulley (ō-bā-rē' dŭ bool-lĕ'), **Prudent-L.**, Verneuil, Eure, 1796—1870; teacher and composer.

Aubry (ō-brē), **Pierre**, Paris, Feb. 14, 1874—Dieppe, Aug. 31, 1910; historian of liturgical music.

Audran (ō-dräṅ), (1) **Marius-P.**, Aix, Provence, 1816—Marseilles, 1887; 1st tenor at the Paris Opéra-Comique. (2) **Edmond**, Lyons, April 11, 1842—Tierceville, n. Gisors, Aug. 17, 1901; son of above; pupil of École Niedermeyer, Paris; Marseilles, 1862, his first opera; produced 36 others, chiefly of a light character. Among his most pop. works are, *"Olivette,"* *"La Mascotte"* (1880), given over 1700 times; *"Miss Helyett,"* *"La Poupée,"* etc.

Auer (ow'-ĕr), (1) **Ld.**, Veszprem, Hungary, June 7, 1845—near Dresden July 16, 1930 (of pneumonia); vln.-virtuoso; pupil of Khonetol at Pesth, of Dont, Vienna, then of Joachim; soloist to the Czar, who conferred on him the order of St. Vladimir, carrying hereditary nobility; from 1868 violin-Prof. at the St. Petersburg Cons.; 1887–92, dir. Imp. Mus. Soc.; teacher of many eminent violinists; after 1918 he lived principally in New York, author book on vln.-playing (1921).

Au'gener & Co., London firm of music pub., founded by G. A., 1853.

Aulin (ow'-lēn), **Tor**, Stockholm, Sept. 10, 1866—March 1, 1914; violinist; pupil of Sauret and Ph. Scharwenka; from 1889 Konzertmeister Stockholm, court-opera; 1887 organised the Aulin Quartet.

Auric (ō'-rēk), **Georges**, b. Lodève, France, Feb. 15, 1899; composer; pupil of Paris Cons., and of d'Indy; c. ballets, orchestral and chamber music works, piano pieces, songs; member of former Group of Six: his ballets *"Les Facheux"* and *"Les Matelots"* had particular succ. when given by Diaghileff.

Aus der Ohe (ows'-dĕr ō'-ĕ), **Adèle**, Hanover, Germany, Dec. 11, 1864—Berlin, Dec. 8, 1937; noted pianist; pupil of Kullak and Liszt; composed

2 piano suites, concert étude, etc.; toured widely with great success.

Aus'tin, (1) **Frederic**, b. London, Mar. 30, 1872; barytone; organist at Liverpool for some years; then teacher at the College of Music, there till 1906; then studied voice with Lunn; début, 1902, favourite in oratorio and in Wagner operas; c. overture *"Richard II"* (Liverpool, 1900); rhapsody *"Spring"* (Queens Hall, 1907), symph. poem *"Isabella,"* also arr. music of *"Beggar's Opera"* by Gay and Pepusch, which had 1463 consecutive perfs. in London, 1920–3. His brother (2) **Ernest**, b. London, Dec. 31, 1874; on the Board of Trade till 33 years old, then studied comp. with J. Davenport; c. symph., idyll, march; *"Love Songs from Don Quixote,"* for voices and orch.; piano sonata, etc.

Aus'tral, **Florence** (rightly **Wilson**); b. Richmond near Melbourne, Australia, April 26, 1894; studied Melbourne Cons. and London; début in opera as Brünnhilde, London, 1922; toured with British Nat'l. Op. Co., and heard as soloist with orchestras and in oratorio, London; début, Covent Garden Op., 1929; concert tours, England, Australia, New Zealand, South Africa, and America. M. John Amadio, flutist.

Auteri-Manzocchi (ä-oo-tā'-rĭ mäntsŏk'-kē), **Salv.**, Palermo, Dec. 25, 1845—Parma, Feb. 21, 1924; pupil of Platania at Palermo, and Mabellini at Florence; composed successful operas, among them *"Graziella"* (Milan, 1894).

Auvergne (dō-vĕrn), **A. d'**, Clermont-Ferrand, Oct. 4, 1713—Lyons, Feb. 12, 1797; violinist and dram. composer.

A'verkamp, **Anton**, Willige Langerak, Holland, Feb. 18, 1861—Bussum, Holland, June 1, 1934; composer and conductor; pupil of Daniel de Lange, Kiel, Rheinberger, Messchaert; dir. of a singing school in Amsterdam and (1890–1914) of a famous *a cappella* choir with which he perf. old church music; c. orch., chamber music, choral works, songs, etc.

A'very, **J.**, d. England, 1808; organ-builder.

Av'ison, **Chas.**, Newcastle-on-Tyne, 1710—May 9, 1770; organist, writer and composer; vide Robert Browning's "PARLEYINGS."

Aylward (āl'-wärd), **Th.**, ca. 1730—1801; teacher and composer.

Ayrton (ăr'-tŭn), (1) **Edm.**, Ripon, Yorks, 1734—Westminster, 1808; composer. (2) **W.**, London, 1777—1858; son of above; writer and editor.

Azzopardi (äd-zō-pär'-dē), **Francesco**, conductor and theorist at Malta, 1786.

Azevedo (äth-ā-vā'-dhō), **Alexis Jacob**, Bordeaux, 1813—Paris, 1875; writer.

B

Babbi (bäb'-bē), **Christoph** (or **Cristoforo**), Cesena, 1748—Dresden, 1814; violinist and composer.

Babbini (bä-bē'-nē), **Mat.**, Bologna, 1754—1816; tenor, début, 1780.

Ba'bell, **Wm.**, ca. 1690—Canonbury, England, 1723; organist, teacher and composer; son of a bassoon-player.

Baccusi (bäk-koo'-sē), **Ippolito**, monk; composer and cathedral cond., Verona, 1590.

Bac'fark (or **Bacfarre**), **Valentin** (rightly **Graew** (gräv), Kronstadt, 1507—Padua, 1576; lutenist and writer.

Bach (bäkh), the name of a Thuringian family prominent in music and furnishing so many organists, Kapellmeisters and cantors that town musicians were called "the Bachs," after them. Outstanding were: (1) **Bach, Jn. Sebastian**, Eisenach, March 21, 1685—Leipzig, July 28, 1750; youngest son of **Jn. Ambrosius B.** and Elizabeth (née Lammerhit), of Erfurt; early left an orphan; both parents died when he was 10, his father having begun teaching him the violin. He went to the home of his brother Jn. Christoph, who taught him the clavichord, but forbade him inspection of a MS. vol. of works by Frohberger, Buxtehude, etc., obtaining it secretly **B.** copied it by moonlight for 6 months, though near-sighted, with results fatal to his eyes in later life. This desire to study other men's work characterised his whole career. At 15 his fine soprano voice secured him free tuition at St. Michael's Ch. in Lüneberg (he having already attended the Ohrdruff Lyceum). He went on foot on holidays to Hamburg to hear the great Dutch organist Reinken, and at Celle he heard the French instr. music used in the Royal Chapel. He studied also the work of Böhm, organist at Lüneberg, and practised violin, clavichord and org. often all night; 1703, in the Weimar ct.-orch.; 1704, organist at Arnstadt; 1705, walked 50 miles to Lübeck to hear Buxtehude, and stayed till a peremptory recall from the Church at Arnstadt; 1707, organist at Mühlhausen. On Oct. 17, he m. Maria Barbara Bach, his cousin, who bore him 7 children, of whom 4 died, leaving a daughter, Wm.-Friedemann, and K. P. E. (See below.) 1708, he played before the Duke at Weimar, and was made ct.-organist; 1714 Konzertmeister. In his vacations he made clavichord and org. tours. 1714, he furnished the organ-music for a service conducted in the Thomaskirche, Leipzig, and produced a cantata. Dresden, 1717, he challenged Marchand, a French organist of high reputation, who was afraid to compete. 1717 Kapellmeister to Prince Leopold of Anhalt, at Köthen, and composed much orch.- and chamber-music. In 1719 he revisited Halle, to meet Händel, but he had just gone to England. 1720, his wife died. He applied for the organ of the Jacobskirche, Hamburg. **B.** was now famous, but a young rival offered to pay 4,000 marks for the place and got it. In 1721 he m. Anna Magdalene Wülken, daughter of the ct.-trumpeter at Weissenfels. She bore him 13 children, 9 of them sons, of whom only 2 survived him: Jn., Christoph, Fr., and Jn. Christian. His second wife had a fine voice and musical taste, and wrote out the parts of many of his cantatas; for her he prepared 2 books of music. In May, 1723, cantor at the Thomasschule, Leipzig, vice Jn. Kuhnau; also organist and dir. of mus. at the Thomaskirche and the Nicolaikirche, continuing as "Kapellmeister vom Haus aus." to Prince Leopold. He was made, 1736, hon. cond. to the Duke of Weissenfels, and court-composer to the King of Poland, and Elector of Saxony. He kept his place at Leipzig for twenty-seven years, and there wrote most of his sacred music. He often visited Dresden, where he could hear the Italian opera, cond. by Hasse. Frederick the Great having asked to hear him, on May 7, 1747, with his son Wilhelm Friedemann,

B. arrived at Potsdam. He improvised upon the various Silbermann pianos in the palace, followed from room to room by the king and his musicians. The next day he tried the principal organs in Potsdam, improvising a 6-part fugue on a theme proposed by the king. He afterward wrote a 3-part fugue on this theme, a Ricercare in 6 parts, several canons inscribed "Thematis regii elaborationes canonicae," and a trio for flute, violin, and bass, dedicating the "*Musikalisches Opfer*" to the king. 1749, two operations to restore his sight, weakened by copying his own and other men's works and engraving his "*Art of Fugue*," left him totally blind and ruined his previous vigour. His sight was suddenly restored, July 10, 1750; but 10 days later he died of apoplexy. He dictated the choral "*Vor deinen Thron tret' ich hiemit*," shortly before his death.

Among his distinguished pupils were Krebs, Homilius, Agricola, Kirnberger, Goldberg, Marpurg; J. Kasper Vogler; Altnikol, his son-in-law, and his sons for whom he wrote the "*Klavierbüchlein*," and the "*Kunst der Fuge*." He engraved on copper; invented the "viola pomposa" and the "Lauten-Clavicembalum"; he advocated equal temperament (vide D. D.), tuning his own pianos and writing "*Das Wohltemperirte Klavier*," to further the cause. This work (known in English as "*The well-tempered Clavichord*," or "*The 48-Fugues*") is a set of 48 preludes and fugues, two of each to each key, major and minor. The works are very chromatic and use the keys enharmonically. Some of his improvements in fingering still survive. Bach was little known as a composer during his life, and few of his works were published then. He was not indeed established on his present pinnacle till Mendelssohn took up his cause, in 1829; Franz was also an important agent in preparing his scores for general use. In 1850, a hundred years after his death, the BACH-GESELLSCHAFT began to publish his complete works. Many other Bach societies now exist. **B's.** enormous list of works includes: VOCAL, 5 sets of church Cantatas for Sundays and feast-days, "*Gottes Zeit ist die*

beste Zeit," etc., various secular cantatas, 2 comic cantatas, the "*Bauern Cantate*" and "*Coffee-Cantate*," a protest against the excessive use of the beverage, and *Trauerode*, on the death of the Electress of Saxony; 5 Passions, incl. the *St. Matthew*, the *St. John*, and the *St. Luke* (doubtful); a *Christmas Oratorio*, in 5 parts; 4 small masses and the Grand Mass in B min.; motets; 2 Magnificats; 5 Sanctus. INSTRUMENTAL, numerous pieces for clavichord: inventions in 2 and 3 parts; 6 "small" French suites; 6 "large" English suites; Preludes and Fugues, incl. "*Das Wohltemperirte Klavier*"; the remarkable "*Goldberg Variations*"; pf.-sonatas with instrs., incl. 6 famous sonatas for pf. and vln.; solo sonatas for vln. and 'cello; solos, trios, etc., for various combinations of instrs., concertos for 1 to 4 pfs. vln. and other instrs., concertos with orch.; 6 notable "*Brandenburg*" concertos; overtures and suites, and fantasias, toccatas, preludes, fugues, and chorale-arrangements for organ. The modern-minded musicians of the twentieth century have found new formal and harmonic interest in **B's.** works, and an entire school has used as its slogan, "Back to Bach," in an effort to throw off the influence of Romantic styles of thought and feeling. Such a work as his monumental "*Art of the Fugue*" has gained wide popularity in the concert-room, the latter arr. for orch. by W. Graeser, heard in Europe and U. S. often after 1926. The best biography of **B.** is by Spitta (Leipzig, 1873–80, 2 vols.; Eng. transl., London, 1884–85). Other memoirs by Forkel, Schweitzer, Parry, Pirro, C. S. Terry, Boughton, Buhrman and C. F. A. Williams. The Bach "*Jahrbücher*," pub. by Breitkopf & Härtel, also hold much material of value. Books on **B's.** music have been issued in great numbers, incl. works by Fuller-Maitland, Grace, Iliffe, Prout, Riemann, Schweitzer, Whittaker and C. S. Terry.

(2) **Karl Philipp Emanuel** ("the Berlin" or "Hamburg Bach"), Weimar, March (8?) 14, 1714—Hamburg (Sept. ?) Dec. 14, 1788. Son of above (Johann Sebastian Bach). Studied philosophy and law at Leip-

zig and Frankfort; cond. a singing society at Frankfort, for which he composed. 1737 (38?) in Berlin. Chamber-mus. and clavecinist to Frederick the Great, 1746–57 [or 1740–67?]. 1757 Hamburg as Ch. mus.-dir.; 1767 as Musik-director of the principal church there, vice Telemann, a position held till death. He was one of the chief virtuosos of the day. He was the founder of the modern school of piano-playing, and a pioneer of greatest importance in the sonata and symphony-forms and orchestration, his works having a graceful modernity not possessed even by most of his father's. He wrote *"Versuch über die wahre Art das Clavier zu spielen"* (2 parts, 1753–62), an important work containing detailed explanations concerning ornaments. His very numerous comps. include 210 solo pieces; 52 concertos with orch.; quartets, trios, duets, sonatas, sonatinas, minuets, polonaises, solfeggi, fugues, marches, etc., for clavier; 18 symphonies; 34 miscellaneous pieces for wind-instrs., trios; flute-, 'cello-, and oboe-concertos; soli for flute, viola di gamba, oboe, 'cello, and harp, etc., and 2 oratorios (*"Die Israeliten in der Wüste,"* and *"Die Auferstehung und Himmelfahrt Jesu"*), 22 Passions; cantatas, etc.
(3) **Johann Chr.** ("the London Bach"), Leipzig, Sept. 7 (?), 1735—London, Jan. 1, 1782; youngest son of J. S. Bach; pupil of his brother Emanuel and Martini in Bologna; 1760–2, org. Milan Cathedral; after 1762 lived in London as music master. C. over 15 operas, choral works, many symphonies or overtures, clavier concertos and sonatas. (4) **Wilhelm Friedemann,** Weimar, 1710—Berlin, 1784; eldest son of J. S. Bach; gifted but dissolute; 1733, org. in Dresden; 1747–64, Halle; c. 25 cantatas, many concertos, etc.
Bache (bäch), (1) **Francis Edw.,** Birmingham, 1833—1858; violinist. (2) **Walter,** Birmingham, 1842—London, 1888, bro. of above; pianist and teacher. (3) **Constance,** Edgbaston, March 11, 1846—Montreux, June 28, 1903; sister and pupil of above; pupil of Klindworth and Hartvigson; teacher, translator, and composer in London.

Bachelet (bäsh-lā'), **Alfred,** b. Paris, Feb. 26, 1864; composer; studied at Cons. in Paris; won Prix de Rome; from 1919 dir. of Nancy Cons.; after almost a quarter century of obscurity, he prod. several lyric dramas that placed him in front rank of contemporary French composers, esp. *"Quand la Cloche Sonnera"* (Paris Op.-Comique, 1922) and *"Scemo"* (Paris Op., 1914, later revived).
Bachmann (bäkh'-män), (1) **Anton,** 1716—1800; court-musician at Berlin, instr.-maker; inv. the machinehead. His son and successor, (2) **Karl L.,** 1743—1800, court-violinist, player, married the pianist and singer (3) **Charlotte Karoline Wilhelmine Stowe,** Berlin, 1757—1817. (4) Pater **Sixtus,** Kettershausen, Bavaria, July 18, 1754—Marchthal, near Vienna, 1818; organist and pianist of unusual precocity, and memory; said to have played by heart over 200 pieces at 9; at 12 equalled Mozart, then 10 years old, in organ-competition, at Biberach; became a Premonstrant monk, composed Masses, etc. (5) **G. Chr.,** Paderborn, 1804—Brussels, 1842; clarinet-maker, soloist and teacher. (6) **Georges,** ca. 1848—Paris, 1894. (7) **Gottlob,** Bornitz, Saxony, 1763—Zeitz, 1840, organist. (8) **Alberto** (rightly **Abraham**), b. Geneva, Switzerland, March 20, 1875; violin virtuoso; pupil of Thomson, Hubay and Petri; lived in Paris as teacher; made many tours of Europe and after 1916 in U. S.; ed. *"Encyclopedia of the Violin"* (1925).
Bachofen (bäkh'-ôf-ĕn), **Jn. Kaspar,** Zurich, 1697—1755; organist.
Bachrich (bäkh'-rĭkh), **Sigismund,** Zsambokreth, Hungary, Jan. 23, 1841—Vienna, July 16, 1913; violinist, pupil and then teacher at Vienna Cons.; composed 4 comic operas incl. *"Der Fuchs-Major"* (Prague, 1889), etc.
Ba(c)ker-Gröndahl (bäk'-ĕr grön'-däl), **Agathe,** Holmestrand, Norway, Dec. 1, 1847—Christiania, June 6, 1907; pianist and composer; pupil of Kjerulf, Bülow and Liszt; she married 1875, Gröndahl, singing-teacher in Christiania.
Back'ers, Americus. Vide BROADWOOD.
Bac(k)haus (bäk'-hows), **Wilhelm,** b. Leipzig, March 26, 1884; eminent pianist; pupil of Reckendorf and at the Cons., later of d'Albert; from

2900 toured; 1905, piano teacher R. C. M., Manchester, but won the Rubinstein prize and toured again; 1911 the U. S.; 1907 taught master-courses at Sondershausen Cons.

Back'ofen, Jn. G. H., Durlach, Baden, 1768—Darmstadt, 1839; virtuoso and manufacturer of wind-instrs. at Darmstadt; writer and composer.

Ba'con, (1) **Richard Mackenzie,** Norwich, Engl. 1776—1844; teacher and writer. (2 **Katherine,** b. Chesterfield, Engl., June 2, 1896; pupil of Arthur Newstead, whom she married 1916; toured United States and Canada, including series of Beethoven and Schubert sonatas, New York; member, faculty, Juilliard School of Music, New York.

Bader (bä'-dĕr), K. Adam, Bamberg, 1789—Berlin, 1870; cathedral-organist, Bamberg (1807); later first tenor Berlin court opera (1820–45).

Badia (bä-dē'-ä), (1) **Carlo Ag.,** Venice, 1672—Vienna, 1738; court-composer at Vienna. (2) **Luigi,** Tirano, Naples, 1819—Milan, 1899; composed 4 operas.

Badiali (bä-dĭ-ä'-lē), **Cesare,** Imola, 1810—Nov. 17, 1865; basso; début, Trieste, 1827; sang throughout Italy; 1859 in London.

Bagge (bäg'-gĕ), **Selmar,** Coburg, 1823 —Basel, 1896; editor and composer.

Bahn, Martin. Vide TRAUTWEIN.

Bai (or **Baj**) (bä'-ē'), **Tommaso,** Crevalcuore, near Bologna, ca. 1650—Rome, Dec. 22, 1714; tenor at the Vatican; conductor, 1713; composed a "*Miserere*," sung in the Papal Chapel, during Holy Week, alternately with those by Allegri and Baini.

Baif (bīf), **Jn. A. de,** Venice, 1532—Paris, 1589; composer.

Bai'ley Apfelbeck, Marie Louise, b. Nashville, Tenn., Oct. 24, 1876; Leipzig, Cons. Pupil of C. Reinecke, winning a scholarship, and with Leschetizky; début, 1893, Gewandhaus, Leipzig; former chamber-virtuoso to King Albert of Saxony; after 1900 toured Europe and U. S.

Bailly (bī'-yē), **Louis,** b. Valenciennes, France; violist; pupil of Paris Cons., first prize for viola; played with Capet, Geloso, Flonzaley, Elman and Curtis Quartets; soloist with leading Amer. orchestras; head of dept. of viola and chamber music, Curtis Inst., Philadelphia; cond. at

Pittsfield Fest., 1918, and also of chamber ensemble of Curtis school.

Baillot (bī'yō), (1) **P. M. Fran. de Sales,** Passy, Oct. 1, 1771—Paris, Sept. 15, 1842; eminent violinist, pupil of Polidori, Sainte, Marie, and Pollani; later prof. of vln. at the Paris Cons.; toured Europe; 1821, leader at the Grand Opera; 1825, solo violinist, Royal Orch.; wrote famous "*L'Art du Violon*" (1834) and "*Méthode du Violon*"; composed 10 vln. concertos, 3 string-quartets, 24 preludes in all keys, etc. (2) **Réné Paul,** Paris, 1813—1889; son of above, Prof. at Paris Cons.

Baini (bä-ē'-nē), **Abbate, Gins.,** Rome, 1775—1844; composer and conductor at St. Peter's; wrote famous life of Palestrina.

Bain'ton, Edgar Leslie, b. London, Feb. 14, 1880; composer; studied R. Coll. of Music, under Davies, Stanford and Wood, winning several state prizes; after 1912, dir. of Cons. at Newcastle-on-Tyne, and led Phil. Orch. there, retiring in 1918; appeared as guest cond. with Amsterdam Concertgebouw; c. symph., choral, piano works, etc.

Baj (bä'-ē). Vide BAI.

Bajetti (bä-yĕt'-tē), **Giov.,** Brescia, ca. 1815—Milan, 1876; violinist, conductor and dram. composer.

Ba'ker, (1) **G.,** Exeter, England, 1773 —Rugeley, 1847; organist, violinist, and composer. (2) **Benj. Franklin,** Wenham, Mass., July 10, 1811—Boston, 1889; singer, teacher, and editor. (3) **Theodore,** New York, June 3, 1851—Leipzig, Oct. 13, 1934; editor and author; Ph.D., Leipzig Univ., 1882, with thesis on music of North American Indians; also studied with Oscar Paul there; after 1892, literary ed. for publishing house of G. Schirmer, N. Y.; ed. Baker's '*Dictionary of Musical Terms*' and "*Biographical Dictionary of Musicians*"; tr. many technical works on music.

Baklanoff (bäk-län'-ŏf), **Georges,** b. St. Petersburg, 1882—Basle, 1938; barytone; LL. B., Petersburg Univ., 1904; studied singing with Vittorio Vanzo; début in Rubinstein's "*Demon*," 1905; sang Covent Garden Op., Berlin Royal Op., Vienna Imp. Op., Moscow, Petrograd, Monte Carlo, Budapest, Stockholm, Munich; first visited U. S., 1909; member

Boston Op. Co., and after 1917 of Chicago Op. Co.

Balakirew (bä-lä-kē'-rĕf), **Mily Alexejevitch,** Nijni-Novgorod, Jan. 2, 1837 —St. Petersburg, May 28, 1910; eminent composer; member Group of Five; studied at Kasan Univ., as a musician, self-taught; début as pianist in St. Petersburg, 1855; founded the "Free Music School," 1862; 1866, opera-conductor Prague; 1867-70, conductor Imp. Music Society, St. Petersburg, retired 1872; composed symph. poems "*Russia*" and "*Tamara*"; music to "*King Lear*"; 4 overtures; an Oriental fantasia, "*Islamey*," for pf., also symphonies in C and in D minor; piano concerto, many smaller works for the instrument and two collections of songs. His letters to and from Tschaikowsky were ed. by Liapunov (1912).

Balart (bä-lärt'), **Gabriel,** Barcelona, 1824—1893; studied in Paris; conductor, later director, Barcelona Cons.; composed zarzuelas

Balat'ka, Hans, Hoffnungsthal, Moravia, 1827—Chicago, 1899; studied at Vienna; 1849, America; 1851, founded the Milwaukee Musikverein; 1860, conductor of Chicago Philh. Soc.; composed cantatas, etc.

Balbâtre or **Balbastre** (băl-bätr'), **Claude Louis,** Dijon, 1729—Paris, 1799; pupil and friend of Rameau; organist and composer.

Balbi (băl'-bē), (1) **Ludovico,** composer and conductor at S. Antonio, Padua; d. 1604, Franciscan monastery, Venice. (2) (Cav.) **Melchiore,** Venice, 1796—Padua, 1879; churchconductor, theorist and composer.

Baldewin (băl-dĕ-vēn). Vide BAULDEWIJN.

Bald'win, (1) **Ralph Lyman,** Easthampton, Mass., March 27, 1872; educator and composer; active as organist, choir director and music supervisor in Northampton, Mass., and Hartford, Conn; after 1900 faculty member of Inst. of Music Pedagogy at former city. (2) **Samuel Atkinson,** b. Lake City, Minn., Jan. 22, 1862; organist; studied at Dresden Cons.; active as org. in Chicago, St. Paul, Minneapolis, and after 1895 in New York, where he taught at City College and gave a memorable series of recitals during many years.

Balfe (bălf), **Michael Wm.,** Dublin, May 15, 1808—Rowney Abbey, Hertfordshire, Oct. 20, 1870; operatic composer; pupil of O'Rourke, Ireland, and C. F. Horn, London; 1824, violinist Drury Lane; also sang in London; went to Italy with his patron Count Mazzara, and studied comp. with Frederici at Rome, and singing with F. Galli at Milan; his ballet "*La Pérouse*," prod. there (1826); pupil of Bordogni, and first barytone at the Ital. Opera, Paris (1828), and elsewhere till 1835; composed several Italian operas; m. the Hungarian singer **Lina Rosen** (1808 —London, 1888); he ret. to England 1835, and prod. "*The Siege of Rochelle*" (Drury Lane); failed as manager; went to Paris, returned 1843, and prod. "*The Bohemian Girl*," very successful everywhere; prod. Paris, 1850, in 5-act version as "*La Bohémienne*." In 1857, his daughter **Victorie** made her début in Italian opera; 1864, he retired to his countryseat, Rowney Abbey; he composed 31 operas in all, including "*The Rose of Castile*" (1857); "*Satanella*" (1858); "*Il Talismano*" (1874); biog. by C. L. Kenny (London, 1878), and W. A. Barrett (do. 1882).

Bal'lantine, Edward, b. Oberlin, O., Aug. 8, 1886; pianist and composer; pupil of Schnabel and Ganz (piano); Spalding and Converse (comp.); after 1912 taught theory at Harvard; c. orch. works incl. "*The Eve of Saint Agnes*" (Boston Symph., 1917); chorus, piano, violin pieces, etc.

Ballard (băl-lär'), a family of French music-printers; founded 1552 by **Robert B.,** with a patent, from Henri II., as "Seul imprimeur de la musique de la chambre, chapelle et menus plaisirs du roy." The patent expired 1776.

Bal'ling, Michael, Heidingsfeld, Bavaria, Aug. 28, 1866—Darmstadt, Sept. 1, 1925; noted conductor; pupil of Würzburg Mus. Sch.; at 18 played 'cello in Mainz City Orch.; and later in Schwerin and Bayreuth orchs.; founded mus. sch. in Nelson, Australia; later a viola virtuoso in England; 1896, assistant cond. at Bayreuth; choral dir. at Hamburg Op.; 1898, first cond. at Lübeck; after 1906, regularly cond. at Bayreuth; 1911-14, succeeded Richter as cond. in Manchester, Engl.; after 1919, gen. mus. dir. in Darmstadt; one of the leading Wagner conductors of his day and ed. that composer's works for the Breitkopf and Härtel complete edition.

Baltzell, Winton J., Shiremanstown, Penn., Dec. 18, 1864—New York, Jan. 10, 1928; graduated Lebanon Valley College; at 24 took up music, studied with Emery and Thayer; later in London with Bridge and Parker, later with H. A. Clarke, Philadelphia, as editor; taught musical history and theory at Ohio Wesleyan University one year, then returned to Philadelphia; edited a *"Dictionary of Musicians"* (1911).

Bamp'ton, Rose, b. Cleveland, O., 1910; soprano; studied at Curtis Inst. of Music, Philadelphia, with Horatio Connell and Queena Mario; sang with Chautauqua, N. Y., Op. Ass'n., 1929; with Philadelphia Grand Op. Co. for three seasons; with Philadelphia Orch., in Schönberg's *"Gurrelieder"*; and after 1933 with Met. Op. Co.; toured Europe with succ., 1937.

Banchieri (bän-kĭ-ā'-rē), Adr., Bologna, 1565 (?)—1634; theorist and organist.

Banck (bänk), K., Magdeburg, 1809—Dresden, 1889; critic and vocal teacher.

Banderali (bän-dä-rä'-lē), Davidde, Lodi, 1780—Paris, 1849, buffo tenor, then teacher at Paris Cons.

Bandini (bän-dē'-nē) (1) Primo, Parma, Nov. 29, 1857—Piacenza, May 3, 1928, where he was dir. of Cons. after 1886; pupil R. School of Music there; composed successful operas *"Eufemio di Messina"* (Parma, 1878), *"Fausta"* (Milan, 1886), *"Janko"* (Turin, 1897). (2) Uberto Rieti, Umbria, March 28, 1860—near Naples, Nov. 20, 1919; pupil of Giustiniani, Boldoni, Rossi Tergiani, and Sgambati; composed prize overture *"Eleonora,"* symphony, etc.

Bandrowski (bän-drôf'-shkĭ), Alex. Ritter von, Lubackzow, Galicia, April 22, 1860—Cracow, May 28, 1913; operatic tenor, studied Cracow University, then with Sangiovanni, Milan, and Salvi, Vienna; début Berlin, for some years leading tenor Cologne opera, also in Russia, and oratorio in England; sang Paderewski's *"Manru"* at Warsaw and in New York, 1902.

Ban'ester, Gilbert, 16th cent.; English composer of Flemish influences.

Bang, Maia, b. Norway, April 1877; N. Y. Oct. 1940; violinist, pedagogue; pupil of Leipzig Cons., Marteau and Auer; début in Oslo, 1900, where she founded a music school; 1919 taught in Auer's Academy in New York; has toured and lectured extensively and is author of methods for violin.

Ban'ister, (1) J., London, 1630—1676 (79?); court-violinist and composer. (2) J. (Jr.), d. 1735, son of above; court-violinist. (3) Chas. Wm., 1768—1831; composer. (4) Hy. Joshua, London, 1803—1847. (5) Hy. Chas., London, 1831—1897, son of (3); pianist, teacher, and writer, pub. *"Lectures on Musical Analysis,"* etc.

Banti-Giorgi (bän'-tē-jôr'-jē), Brigida, Crema, Lombardy, 1759—Bologna, Feb. 18, 1806; dram. soprano; first a *chanteuse* in a Paris café, later engaged at the Grand Opera; toured Europe with great success; her voice was remarkable in compass and evenness, but she was musically illiterate; m. the dancer Zaccaria Banti.

Ban'tock, Sir Granville, b. London, Aug. 7, 1868; studied R. A. M., took 1st. Macfarren Prize for comp.; his first work, dram. cantata *"The Fire-Worshippers,"* successfully prod., 1889; successful 1-act romantic opera *"Caedmar"* (London, 1892), conductor of Gaiety Theatre Troupe; 1898 he founded the New Brighton Choral Society; 1900 Principal Birmingham and Midland Inst. School of Music and cond. various societies; 1908 succeeded Elgar in Peyton Chair of Music at Birmingham Univ.; 1898 he married Helena von Schweitzer. He c. *"Omar Khayyam"* for voices and orch. Part I (Birmingham Fest., 1906), Part II (Cardiff Fest., 1907), Part III (Birmingham Fest., 1909); comedy overture, *"The Pierrot of the Minute,"* overture to *"Oedipos at Kolonos"* (Worcester Fest., 1911); mass for male voices; chamber music; choral symphs., *"Atalanta in Calydon"* and *"Vanity of Vanities"*; festival symph., *"Christus"*; choral suite, *"Pageant of Human Life"*; tonepoems, *"Thalabra," "Dante," "Hudibras," "Witch of Atlas," "Lalla Rookh," "Great God Pan," "Dante and Beatrice," "Fifine at the Fair," "Hebridean"* Symph.; overtures *"Saul," "Cain," "Belshazzar," "Eugene Aram," "To a Greek Tragedy"*; suites, *"Russian Scenes," "English*

Scenes," "*Dances and Scenes from Scottish Highlands*," "*Pagan*"? Symph.; ballets, songs, etc.; symph. overture "*Saul*"; dram. symphony in 24 parts, "*The Curse of Kehama*," etc.

Bap′tie, David, Edinburgh, Nov. 30, 1822—Glasgow, March 26, 1906; composed anthems, etc.; compiled hymn-books.

Barbaco′la. Vide BARBIREAU.

Barbaja (bär-bä′-yä), **Domenico,** Milan, 1778—Posilippo, 1841; impresario.

Barbarieu. Vide BARBIREAU.

Barbedette (bărb-dĕt) **H.,** Poitiers, 1827—Paris, 1901; writer and composer.

Barbel′la, Emanuele, d. Naples, 1773; violinist and composer.

Bar′ber, Samuel, b. West Chester, Pa., 1910; composer; nephew of Mme. Louise Homer; grad. Curtis Institute of Music; awarded fellowship at American Academy in Rome and Pulitzer Prize, 1935; c. (orch.) "*Music for a Scene from Shelley*" (N. Y. Phil., 1935); 'cello and piano sonata; "*Dover Beach*" for voice and string quartet; songs and piano works, etc.

Bar′bi, Alice, b. Brodena, 1862; mezzosopr.; pupil of Zamboni, Busi, and Vannucceni; début, Milan, 1882; toured Europe in concert; also a violinist and poet; (1) m. Baron Wolff-Stomersee; (2) Marchese della Torretta, Italian ambassador to London, 1920.

Barbier (bărb-yā), (1) **Fr. Ét.,** Metz, 1829—Paris, 1889; teacher and leader; composed over 30 operas. (2) **Jules Paul,** Paris, 1825—Jan., 1901. collaborator with Carré, in the libretti of many operas including "*Les Noces de Jeannette*" (Massé); "*Le Pardon de Ploërmel*" (Meyerbeer); "*Faust*" (Gounod); "*Philemon et Baucis*" (Gounod); "*Roméo et Juliette*" (Gounod); "*Hamlet*" (Ambr. Thomas).

Barbieri (bär-bĭ-ā′-rē), (1) **Carlo Emm. di,** b. Genoa, 1822—Pesth, 1867; conductor and dram. composer. (2) **Francisco Asenjo,** Madrid, 1823 —1894, very pop. composer of "*Zarzuelas*" (Vide D. D.).

Barbireau (bär-bĭ-rō) (or **Barbiriau, Barbarieu, Barbyria′nus, Barberau, Barbingaut** (bär-băn-gō), or **Bar-**

baco′la), d. Aug. 8, 1491; from 1448 choirmaster of Nôtre-Dame; notable cptist., composed masses, etc.

Barbirolli (bär-bē-rôl′-ē), **John,** b. London, 1899; 'cellist and conductor; of Italian-French parentage; studied at R. Acad. of Music; début as 'cellist, Queen's Hall, 1911; member of Intern. String Quartet, with which toured Europe; founded Barbirolli Chamber Orch., 1925; cond. Brit. Nat'l. Op. Co., 1926; later appeared with London Symph. and Royal Phil.; cond. Scottish Orch. and Leeds Symph.; guest appearances in Russia; 1936-7, cond. N. Y. Phil. for 3 season term; m. Marjorie Parry, soprano.

Barbot (bär-bō), **Jos. Th. Désiré,** Toulouse, 1824—Paris, 1897; tenor; created "*Faust*," 1859; 1875, prof. Paris Cons.

Barcewicz (bär′-tsĕ-vĭts), **Stanislaus,** Warsaw, April 16, 1858—Sept. 2, 1929; violinist; pupil of Moscow Cons.; opera cond. at Warsaw; from 1885 violin prof. at the Cons.; c. violin pieces.

Bardi (bär′-dē), **Giov., conte del Vernio,** Florentine nobleman and patron of the 16th cent., under whose influence the attempted revival of the Greek lyric drama led to modern opera. At his house "*Dafne*" was performed.

Barge (bär′-gĕ), **Jn. H. Wm.,** Wulfsahl, Hanover, Nov. 23, 1836—Hanover, July 16, 1925; self-taught flutist; 1867-95 first flute, Leipzig Gewandhaus Orch., retired on pension; teacher Leipzig Cons.; wrote "Method for Flute"; composed 4 orchestral flute-studies, etc.

Bargheer (bär′-khăr), (1) **K. Louis,** Bückeburg, Dec. 31, 1831—Hamburg, May 19, 1902; violinist; pupil of Spohr, David, and Joachim; 1863, court-conductor at Detmold; made concert-tours; 1879-89, leader Hamburg Phil. Soc., teacher in the Cons.; later leader in Bülow orch. (2) **A.,** Bückeburg, Oct. 21, 1840—Basel, March 10, 1901; brother of above, pupil of Spohr; court-violinist Detmold; 1866, Prof. Basel Sch. of Music.

Bargiel (bär′-gēl), **Woldemar,** Berlin, Oct. 3, 1828—Feb. 23, 1897; composer; pupil, Leipzig Cons.; later Prof. in Cologne Cons.; 1865, dir. and cond. of the Mus. Sch., Amsterdam; 1874 Prof. R. Hochschule, Berlin; 1882, Pres. "Meisterschule für musikalische Komposition"; composed 3 overtures *"Zu einem Trauerspiel (Romeo and Juliet)"*: *"Prometheus," "Medea"*; a symphony; 2 psalms for chorus and orchestra; pf.-pcs. etc.

Bar'ker, Chas. Spackmann, b. Bath, 1806—Maidstone, 1879; organ-builder; invented the pneumatic lever.

Bar'low, Howard, b. Plain City, Ohio, May 1, 1892; conductor; grad. Reed College, Portland, Ore.; studied music with Lucien Becker, also with Frank E. Ward and Cornelius Rybner (at Columbia Univ., N. Y.); cond. Reed Coll. choral soc.; after 1915, Riverdale Choral Soc., N. Y.; then at Neighborhood Playhouse, N. Y., and in recent years active as a leading cond. of radio programmes.

Bärman (bär'-män), (1) **H. Jos.,** Potsdam, 1784—Munich, 1847; clarinet-virtuoso and composer. His brother (2) **K.,** 1782—1842, was a bassoonist; (3) **K. (Sr.),** (1811–1885), son of H. J. B., was a clarinettist; his son (4) **K. (Jr.),** Munich, July 9, 1839—Newton, Mass., Jan. 17, 1913; pupil of Liszt and Lachner; teacher at Munich Cons.; later lived in Boston, Mass., as pianist and teacher; composed piano pieces.

Bar'nard, Mrs. Chas. (née **Alington**), 1830—Dover, 1869; composed popular songs, etc., under name **"Claribel."**

Barn'by, (1) **Rob.,** York, England, 1821—London, 1875; alto-singer, Chapel Royal. (2) **Sir Jos.,** York, Engl., Aug. 12, 1838—London, Jan. 28, 1896; choirboy at 7; at 10 taught other boys; at 12 organist; at 15 music-master; 1854 entered the R. A. M., London; then organist various churches and cond.; 1875, precentor and dir. at Eton; 1892 Principal of Guildhall Sch. of Mus.; knighted, July, 1892; composed, *"Rebekah,"* a sacred idyll; Psalm 97; Service in E, etc.

Bar'nekov, Christian, St. Sauveur, France, July 28, 1837—Copenhagen, March 20, 1913; musician; of Danish parentage; pianist and organist; pupil of Helfstedt, Copenhagen; c. women's choruses with orch.; chamber music and songs.

Barnes, Robt., (1) violin-maker, London, 1760—1800. (2) **Edward Shippen,** b. Seabright, N. J., Sept. 14, 1887; organist, composer; studied Yale Univ., with Parker and Jepson; ass't. org. there; later pupil of Paris Schola Cantorum with d'Indy, Vierne and Decaux; org. at various N. Y. churches; c. organ and choral works, songs.

Barnett, (1) **J.,** Bedford, England, July 1, 1802—Cheltenham, April 17, 1890, "The father of English opera"; pupil of C. E. Horn, Price, and Ries; brought out his first opera *"Before Breakfast,"* 1825; *"The Mountain Sylph"* (1834); the very succ. *"Fair Rosamond"* (1837), and *"Farinelli"* (London, 1838); 1841, singing teacher at Cheltenham; left 2 unfinished oratorios, a symphony, etc. (2) **Jos. Alfred,** London, 1810 (?), 1898; bro. of above; composer. (3) **J. Francis,** London, 1837—1916; nephew of above; studied with Dr. Wylde; and at R. A. M., and Leipzig Cons.; début as pianist, 1853; 1883, prof. at R. Coll. of Mus.; composed oratorio *"The Raising of Lazarus,"* symphony in A min., *"Ouverture symphonique,"* overture to *"Winter's Tale,"* cantatas, etc.

Barome'o, Chase, b. Augusta, Ga., Aug. 19, 1893; bass; grad. school of music, Univ. of Michigan; studied singing in Italy; sang at La Scala, in Buenos Aires; with Chicago Op., and after 1935 with Met. Op. Co., N. Y.

Baron (bä'-rōn), **Ernst Gl.,** Breslau, 1696—Berlin, 1760; court-lutenist and theorist; writer and composer.

Barré (or Barra) (bär-rä or bär'-rä), (1) **Léonard,** b. Limoges; singer in Papal Chapel (1537) and special musical envoy to the Council of Trent (1545); composed madrigals and motets. (2) **A.,** printer, etc., Rome, 1555-70, later Milan.

Barrère (bär-âr'), **Georges,** b. Bordeaux, France, Oct. 31, 1876; flutist, conductor; studied Paris Cons., 1st prize, 1895; member orchestra, Paris Op., Colonne Orch.; teacher, Schola Cantorum, Paris; founder, Modern Society of Wind Instruments, Paris, 1895; member N. Y. Symph. Orch., 1905-1928; taught Inst. of Musical Art, New York, after 1910; founded Barrère Little Symphony Orchestra, 1914; member trio with Carlos Salzedo. harp, and Horace Britt, 'cello; c. chamber music works.

Barret (bär-rä), **A. M. Rose,** Paris, 1808 —London, 1879; oboist.

Bar′rett, (1) **J.,** 1674—London, 1735 (8 ?); organist. (2) **Thos.,** violin-maker, London, 1710–30. (3) **Wm. Alex.,** Hackney, Middlesex, 1836—London, 1891; editor and writer; co-editor with Sir John Stainer of a "Dict. of Music. Terms."

Barrien′tos, Maria, b. Barcelona, March 4, 1885; coloratura soprano; sang with success in Rome at 11 years; took two medals for violin-playing; later heard in Madrid and various Italian theatres as a singer; at Met. Op., N. Y., for several seasons after 1916; also in South America.

Bar′rington, Daines, London, 1727—1800; lawyer and musical essayist.

Bar′ry, Chas. Ainslie, London, June 10, 1830—March 21, 1915, pupil of Cologne Cons. and Leipzig Cons.; editor and organist; composed a symphony, 2 overtures, etc.

Barsanti (bär-sän′-tē), **Fran.,** Lucca, ca. 1690—1760; flutist, oboist, and composer; 1750, viola-player at London.

Barsot′ti, Tommaso G. F., Florence, 1786—Marseilles, 1868; teacher and composer.

Bartay (bär′-tä-ē), (1) **Andreas,** Szé-plak, Hungary, 1798—Mayence, 1856; 1838 dir. Nat. Th., Pesth; composed Hungarian operas, etc. (2) **Ede,** Oct. 6, 1825—Sept., 1901, son of above; pupil Nat. Mus. Academy, Pesth; founded pension-fund for musicians; composed overture, "Pericles," etc.

Bartei (bär-tä′-ē), **Girolamo,** general of Augustinan monks at Rome; publisher and composer (1607–18).

Barth (bärt), (1) **Chr. Samuel,** Glaucheau, Saxony, 1735—Copenhagen, 1809; oboist. (2) **F. Phil. K. Ant.,** b. Cassel, ca 1775; son of above; composer. (3) **Jos. Jn. Aug.,** b. Grosslippen, Bohemia, 1781; 1810–30, tenor, Vienna. (4) **Gustav,** Vienna, 1800—Frankfort, 1897; son of (3); pianist and conductor. (5) **K. H.,** Pillau, Prussia, July 12, 1847—Berlin, Dec. 23, 1923; pianist, pupil of Von Bülow, Bronsart, and Tausig; 1871, teacher at R. Hoch-schüle für Musik, conductor of the Philh. concerts at Hamburg (vice von Bülow). (6) **Richard,** Gros-swanzleben, Saxony, June 5, 1850—Hamburg, 1923; left-handed violin-

virtuoso; Univ. Mus. Dir. Marburg, till 1894; then Dir. of Hamburg Philh. Concerts; 1908, dir. Cons. there; sonatas, string quartet, etc.

Barthe, Grat-Norbert (grä-nòr-bĕr-bärt), Bayonne, 1828—Asniéres, Aug. 1898; pupil Paris Cons., 1854; won the Grand Prix de Rome; wrote cantata "Francesca da Rimini"; composed operas "Don Carlos" and "La Fiancée d'Abydos" (1865); oratorio, "Judith," etc.

Barthel (bär′-tĕl), **Jn. Chr.,** Plauen, Saxony, 1776—Altenburg, 1831; court-organist.

Barthélemon (bär-tä-lŭ-môṅ) (in English **Bar′tleman**), **Fran. Hip.,** Bordeaux, 1741—London, 1808; violinist and composer.

Barthol′omew, Wm., London, 1793—1867; translator.

Bart′lett, (1) **J.,** 17th century English composer. (2) **Homer Newton,** Olive, N. Y., Dec. 28, 1846—Hoboken, N. J., April 3, 1920; pupil of S. B. Mills, Max Braun, Jacobson, etc. From 14 organist New York churches, including Madison Av. Bapt. Ch.; published a sextet, a cantata "The Last Chieftain," many songs, etc.; opera, "La Vallière," oratorio, "Samuel," etc.

Bart′muss, Richard, Bitterfeld, Dec. 23, 1859—Dessau, Dec. 25, 1910; organist; pupil of Grell, Haupt, Löschhorn; 1896 royal music director; 1902, professor; c. oratorio "Der Tag des Pfingsten," 4 organ sonatas and much sacred music.

Bartók, Béla (bä′-lä bär-tŏk′), b. Nagy Szent Miklos, Hungary, March 25, 1881; composer, pianist, noted for his researches in folk-music and for compositions in original modern idiom; studied with Kersch and Erkel, and at Budapest Acad.; prof. at latter school after 1906; his music employs various ancient scales and harmonies, abandoning traditional diatonic and chromatic system, and treating twelve tones of chromatic scale as separate entities; the influence of archaic folk music was noted in B's. turning, about 1907, to this new style, which then sounded extremely formidable to listeners and roused considerable opposition; for a time he retired from active composition, visiting Biskra to collect Arabian folk music; his first major recognition came in 1917 when the dance-play "*Der Holzgeschnitzte Prinz*" was prod. at Budapest Op.; since that time his works have aroused keen interest among modern-minded musicians, his greatest succ. probably coming with the perf. of his "*Dance Suite*" for orch., based on folk airs, at Prague in 1925; **B.** has visited the U. S. as lecturer on music and for concerts of his chamber music; c. (opera) "*Ritter Blaubarts Burg*" (1918); (pantomime) "*Der wunderbare Mandarin*" (1924); orchestral and chamber music works, among which several string quartets have had international hearings; two violin sonatas, and many piano works; made valuable collections of Hungarian, Rumanian and Slovak folk-songs (including some 7,000 specimens).

Bartoli (bär-tō'-lē), Padre **Erasmo,** Gaeta, 1606—Naples, 1656; church-composer under the name "Padre Raimo."

Barzin (bär-zăň'), **Léon,** b. Brussels; conductor and violist; brought to U. S. at age of two; had early lessons from his father, who was first violist in Met. Op. orchestra; later a pupil of Henrotte, Deru, Megerlin and Ysaye; harmony and counterpoint with Lilienthal; was mem. of Nat'l. Symph. Orch., N. Y., 1919; the next year, second violinist, N. Y. Phil. Orch.; first violist in same, and member of Phil. Quartet, 1925; after 1929 cond. American Orch. Soc., N. Y., which was reformed as the Nat'l. Orch. Ass'n., 1930.

Baselt (bä'zĕlt), **Fritz (Fr. Gv. O.),** Oels, Silesia, May 26, 1863—Nov. 12, 1931; pupil of Köhler and Bussler; music-dealer, teacher, and conductor Breslau, Essen and Nürnberg; 1894, director of Philh. Verein, and "Sängervereinigung" (ca. 1,200 voices), Frankfort-on-Main; composed 9 operettas, nearly 100 male choruses, etc.

Basevi (bä-sä'-vē), **Abramo,** Leghorn, 1818—Florence, 1885; journalist and composer.

Ba'sil (Saint), **The Great,** Caesarea, 329—Cappadocia, 379; bishop; reputed introducer of congregational (antiphonal) singing into the Eastern Ch., preceding St. Ambrose in the Western.

Basili (bä-zē'-lē), (1) **Dom. Andrea,** 1720—Loreto, 1775; conductor and

composer; his son (2) **Fran.,** Loreto, 1767—Rome, 1850; prod. 11 operas, and several dram. oratorios in Rome; 1837, conductor at St. Peter's, Rome; composed also symphonies, etc.

Basiron (bä'-sĭ-rōn), **Giovanni,** developed the motet, ca. 1430—1480.

Bassani (bäs-sä'-nē), (1) **Giov.,** ca. 1600; conductor at St. Mark's, Venice. (2) (or **Bassiani**), **Giov. Bat.,** Padua, ca. 1657—Ferrara, 1716; violinist, conductor, and composer. (3) **Geron.,** b. Padua, 17th cent.; singer, teacher, and composer.

Bassevi (bäs-sä'-vē), **Giacomo.** Vide CERVETTO.

Bass'ford, Wm. Kipp, New York, April 23, 1839—Dec. 22, 1902; pupil of Samuel Jackson; toured the U. S. as pianist; later organist at East Orange, N. J.; also composer.

Bassi (bäs'-sē), **Luigi,** Pesaro, 1766—Dresden, 1825; barytone and director; Mozart wrote the rôle of "Don Giovanni" for him.

Bassiron (bäs-sĭ-rōň), **Ph.,** 15th cent.; Netherland contrapuntist; composed masses.

Bastardella. Vide AGUJARI.

Bastiaans (bäs'-tē-äns), (1) **J. G.,** Wilp, 1812—Haarlem, 1875; organist and teacher at Amsterdam and at St. Bavo's; his son and successor (2) **Jn.,** 1854—1885; teacher and composer.

Baston (bäs-tŏň), **Josquin,** lived, 1556, Netherlands; contrapuntist.

Bates, (1) **Joah,** Halifax, 1741—London, 1799; conductor; promoter and conductor of the famous "Händel Commemoration" festivals in London (1784–91). (2) His wife was a singer. (3) **Wm.,** 1720—1790 (?); English opera composer.

Ba'teson, T., England, ca. 1575—after 1611; organist and composer of madrigals.

Bath, Hubert, b. Barnstaple, England, Nov. 6, 1883; 1901 pupil of Beringer and Corder at R. A. M., London; 1904, won Goring Thomas scholarship; c. 1-act opera, "*The Spanish Student*"; symph. poems; cantata "*The Wedding of Shon Maclean*"; variations for orch., and many songs.

Bathe (bāth), **Wm.,** Dublin, 1564—Madrid, 1614; writer.

Batiste (bä-tēst), **A. Éd.,** Paris, 1820–1876; organist, teacher, and composer.

Batistin (bä-tēs-tăň). Vide STRUCK, J. B.

Bat'ka, Richard, Prague, Dec. 14, 1868
—Vienna, April 24, 1922; critic, historian, and librettist.

Batta (bät'-tä), (1) **Pierre,** Maastricht,
Holland, 1795—Brussels, 1876;
'cellist and teacher. His sons were
(2) **Alex.,** Maastricht, July 9, 1816
—Versailles, Oct. 8, 1902; 'cellist and
composer. (3) **J. Laurent,** Maastricht, 1817—Nancy, 1880; pianist
and teacher.

Battaille (băt-tī'-yŭ), **Chas. Aimable,**
Nantes, 1822—Paris, 1872; dram.
bass.

Battanchon (băt-tän-shôn), **F.,** Paris,
1814—1893; 'cellist; inv. (1846) a
small 'cello, the "barytone."

Bat'ten, Adrian, ca. 1585—ca. 1637;
English organist.

Bat'tishill, Jonathan, London, 1738—
Islington, 1801; conductor and dram.
composer.

Battista (bät-tēs'-tä), **V.,** Naples, 1823
—1873; dram. composer.

Battistini (bät-tēs-tē'-nē), **Mattia,**
Rome, Feb. 27, 1857—Rieti, Nov. 7,
1928; dram. barytone; début, Rome,
1878; sang at Buenos Aires and
principal theatres in Europe; one of
most accomplished "*bel canto*" singers of his period; was often reported
to be contemplating tour of U. S.,
for which he received tempting offers,
but his terror of seasickness is said
to have caused him to refuse them;
he knew about eighty rôles, principally Italian; a notable "Don Giovanni," etc.

Batton (băt-tôn), **Désiré Alex.,** Paris,
1797—Versailles, 1855; teacher and
dram. composer.

Battu (băt-tü), **Pantaléon,** Paris, 1799
—1870; violinist and composer.

Baudiot (bōd-yō), **Chas. N.,** Nancy,
1773—Paris, 1849; 'cellist.

Baudoin (or **Baudouyn**) (bō-dwăn).
Vide BAULDEWIJN.

Bauer (bow'-ĕr), (1) **Harold,** b. London,
April 28, 1873, of English mother and
German father; eminent pianist;
played violin in public at 9; studied
with Gorski, Paris; then the piano,
in 1892, under Paderewski; début as
pianist, Paris, 1893; has toured Europe and, since 1900, America, with
great success; res. in New York for
many years; he has long been ranked
as one of leading solo and ensemble
players; pres., Beethoven Ass'n. of
New York; also active as master
teacher and as ed. of musical works.

(2) **Marion,** b. Walla Walla, Wash.,
Aug. 15, 1887; composer; incid. music
for "*Prometheus Bound*," string quartet, songs, etc.; asst. prof. of music,
N. Y. Univ., 1926; mem. bd. of dirs.,
League of Comps.

Bauldewijn (bōd-wăn) (or **Baulduin,
Baldewin, Balduin, Baudoin, Baudouyn**), **Noël** (**Natalis**), Antwerp,
1513 (or 1518?)—1529; conductor at
Nôtre Dame; and composer.

Baumfelder (bowm'-fĕlt-ĕr), **Fr.,** Dresden, May 28, 1836—Aug. 8, 1916;
pianist; pupil of J. Otto, and Leipzig
Cons.

Baumgarten (bowm'-gärt-ĕn), **K. Fr.,**
Germany, 1740 (?)—London, 1824;
violinist and dram. composer.

Baumgärtner (bowm'-gĕrt-nĕr), (1)
Aug., Munich, 1814—1862; writer on
"musical shorthand," etc. (2) **Wm.**
(**Guillaume**), 1820—Zurich, 1867;
composer and mus. dir. at St. Gallen.

Bäumker (bīm'-kĕr), **Wm.,** Elberfeld,
Oct. 25, 1842—Rurich, 1905; chaplain and school-inspector, Niederkrüchten; wrote biogs. of Palestrina,
Lassus, etc.

Bausch (bowsh), (1) **L. Chr. Aug.,**
Naumburg, 1805—Leipzig, 1871;
maker of violins and bows. His 2
sons were also vln.-makers: (2)
Ludwig (1829—Leipzig, 1871), lived
New York, then in Leipzig; and (3)
Otto, 1841—1874.

Bausznern (bows'-nĕrn), **Waldemar
von,** Berlin, Nov. 29, 1866—Potsdam, Aug. 20, 1931; studied at
Kronstadt, Budapest, Vienna, and
with Bargiel and Fr. Kiel at the
Berlin Hochschule; 1894 in Dresden,
as dir. Singakademie and Liedertafel; 1903, docent at Cologne Cons.
and dir. of Soc. of Musicians there;
1908, dir. of Weimar School of
Music; 1916, dir. of Hoch Cons.,
Frankfort; c. 4 symphonies; operas,
"*Dürer in Venedig*," "*Herbort und
Hilda*," "*Der Bundschuh*," "*Satyros*"; choral works, chamber music,
song cycles, etc.

Bax (băks), **Sir Arnold,** b. London,
Nov. 8, 1883; composer; pupil R. A. of
Music, studying piano with Matthay
and comp. with Frederick Corder;
one of leading contemporary British
creative figures, with Celtic, neo-Romantic spirit and clarity of form
among his salient characteristics,
individual type of chromaticism and
reticence of expression; c. (orch.) five

symphonies; Festival Overture; Four Pieces; Symphonic Variations for piano and orch.; *"Tintagel," "Summer Music," "Mediterranean," "The Happy Forest," "The Garden of Fand," "Overture to a Picaresque Comedy," "The Tale the Pine Trees Knew," "In the Faery Hills"; "Enchanted Summer"* for two sopranos, chorus and orch.; *"Christmas Eve in the Mountains," "Spring Fire," "In Memoriam," "November Woods," "Moy Mell,"* (chamber music) trio; sonata for violin and piano; quintet; string quartet; quintet for strings and harp; quartet for piano and strings; quintet for oboe and strings; sonata for violin and piano; 'cello sonata; sonata for two pianos; sonata for viola and harp; (ballet scores) *"Between Dusk and Dawn," "The Frog-skin," "The Truth about the Russian Dancers,"* also piano music and songs. Knighted, 1937.

Bayer (bī'-ĕr), **Josef**, Vienna, Mar. 6, 1852—March 12, 1913; composer of ballets and operettas; studied at Vienna Cons.; cond. at Court Opera.

Bazin (bä-zăṅ), **Fran. Em. Jos.**, Marseilles, 1816—Paris, 1878; dram. composer.

Bazzini (bäd-zē'-nē), **A.**, Brescia, March 11, 1818—Milan, Feb. 10, 1897; violinist; pupil of Camisani; at 17 conductor Church of S. Filippo, where he prod. masses and vespers, and 6 oratorios with full orch., and gave successful concert-tours through Europe. 1873, prof. of comp., 1882, dir. of Milan Cons. In his compositions his native melodiousness gained unusual value from a German solidity of harmony.

Bé, Le. Vide LE BÉ.

Beach, Mrs. **H. H. A.** (née **Amy Marcy Cheney**), b. Henniker, N. H., Sept. 5, 1867; pianist and composer; pupil of E. Perabo and K. Baermann (pf.), and Junius W. Hill (harmony); self-taught in cpt., comp. and orchestration, having transl. Berlioz and Gevaert for her own use; Pres. Board of Councillors, N. E. Cons., Boston; composed *"Gaelic"* symphony, Mass with orch., piano quintet, piano concerto, choral works, a number of attractive songs, etc.

Beale, (1) **Wm.**, Landrake, Cornwall, 1784—London, 1854; famous glee-composer. (2) **J.**, London, ca. 1796; pianist.

Beard, J., England, ca. 1717—Hampton, 1791; eminent tenor for whom Händel wrote the tenor rôles in his chief oratorios.

Beauchamps (bō-shäṅ), **P. Fran. Godard de**, Paris, ca. 1689—1761; writer.

Beaulieu (rightly **Martin**) (bōl-yŭ', or mär-tăṅ), **M. Désiré**, Paris, 1791—Niort, 1863; patron, writer, and composer.

Beauquier (bōk-yā), **Chas.**, 1833— ?; writer of "Philosophie de musique" (1865), and librettist.

Beauvarlet - Charpentier (bō-văr-lä-shär-päṅt-yā), (1) **Jean Jacques**, Abbeyville, 1730—Paris, 1794; organist and comp. (2) **Jacques Marie**, Lyons, July 3, 1776—Paris, Nov. 1834; organist and comp., son of (1).

Becher (bĕkh'-ĕr), (1) **Alfred Julius**, Manchester, 1803—Vienna, 1848; editor. (2) **Jos.**, Neukirchen, Bavaria, Aug. 1, 1821—Sept. 23, 1888; composed over 60 masses, etc.

Bechstein (bĕkh'-shtīn), **Fr. Wm. K.**, Gotha, June 1, 1826—Berlin, March 6, 1900; 1856, worked in German factories, later established the well-known piano factory in Berlin.

Beck, (1) **David**, Germany, ca. 1590; organ-builder. (2) **Reichardt K.**, lived in Strassburg, ca. 1650; composer. (3) **Jn. Philip**, 1677; editor. (4) **Michael**, b. Ulm, 1653; writer. (5) **Gf. Jos.**, Podiebrad, Bohemia, 1723—Prague, 1787; Dominican (later Provincial) friar, organist. (6) **Chr. Fr.**, b. Kirchheim, ca. 1755; composer. (7) **Fz.**, Mannheim, 1730—Bordeaux, 1809; court-violinist. (8) **Fr. Ad.**, pub. at Berlin, *"Dr. M. Luther's Gedanken über die Musik,"* 1825. (9) **K.**, 1814—Vienna, 1879; tenor; created *"Lohengrin."* (10) **Jn. Nepomuk**, Pesth, 1827—Pressburg, 1904; dram. barytone. (11) **Jos.**, Mainz, June 11, 1850—Pressburg, Feb. 15, 1903; son of above, barytone, sang in Austria, Berlin (1876), and Frankfort (1880). (12) **Johann Heinrich**, Cleveland, Sept. 12, 1856—May 26, 1924; violinist; pupil Leipzig Cons.; founded the Cleveland "Schubert Quartet"; composed overtures to Byron's *"Lara,"* to *"Romeo and Juliet"*; cantata *"Deukalion"* (Bayard Taylor), etc. (13) **Conrad**, b. Schaffhausen, Switzerland, June 16, 1901; composer; studied with Andreae and at Zurich Cons.; res. in Berlin, later Paris, where studied with Honegger; c. in neo-classic manner, but modern harmonisation, cantata *"Death of Oedipus"*; four symphonies, concertino for piano and orch., concerto for string quartet and orch.; three string quartets, choral works, etc.

Beck'er, (1) **Dietrich** (1668), composer at Hamburg, 1668. (2) **Jn.,** Helsa, near Cassel, 1726—1803; court-organist. (3) **K. Fd.,** Leipzig, 1804 —1877; organist and writer. (4) **Konstantin Julius,** Freiberg, Saxony, 1811—Oberlössnitz, 1859; editor. (5) **Val. Ed.,** Würzburg, 1814— Vienna, 1890; dram. composer. (6) **Georg,** Frankenthal, Palatinate, June 24, 1834—Geneva, July 18, 1928; pianist and writer; lived in Geneva; pub. *"La Musique en Suisse,"* etc. (7) **Albert Ernst Ant.,** Quedlinburg, June 13, 1834—Berlin, Jan. 10, 1899, pupil of Bonicke and Dehn; 1881, teacher of comp. at Scharwenka's Cons.; also conductor Berlin cathedral choir; composed a noteworthy symphony, a Grand Mass in B♭ min. (1878), and oratorio *"Selig aus Gnade,"* etc. (8) **Jean,** Mannheim, May 11, 1833—Oct. 10, 1884; violinist, leader Mannheim orch.; after concert-tours, lived in Florence and founded the famous "Florentine Quartet"; toured with his children. (9) His daughter **Jeanne,** Mannheim, June 9, 1859— April 6, 1893; pianist, pupil of Reinecke and Bargiel. (10) **Hans.,** Strassburg, May 12, 1860—May 1, 1917; viola-player, pupil of Singer. (11) **Hugo,** b. Strassburg, Feb. 13, 1864; 'cellist; son of **Jean B.;** pupil of his father, Grützmacher, Piatti, etc.; 'cellist at the Opera Frankfort, 1884–86 and 1890–1906; 1896, Royal Prof.; succeeded Piatti as 'cellist at London Monday concerts; 1909–29, taught Berlin Hochschule; later lived in Switzerland; made many concert tours, including U. S., 1900. (12) **Rheinhold,** Adorf, Saxony, 1842— Dresden, Dec. 4, 1924; violinist; lived in Dresden; composed succ. operas *"Frauenlob"* (Dresden, 1892), and *"Ratbold"* (Mayence, 1896), 1-act; symph. poem *"Der Prinz von Homburg,"* etc. (13) **K.,** Kirrweiler, near Trier, June 5, 1853—Berlin, Aug. 31, 1928; teacher at Neuwied; pub. songbooks. (14) **Jakob,** founder (1841) of large Russian pf.-factory.

Beck'mann, Jn. Fr. Gl., 1737—Celle, 1792; organist, harpsichord-virtuoso, and dram. composer.

Beck'with, J. Christmas, Norwich, England, 1750–1809; organist and writer.

Becquié (bĕk-yā), (1) **A.** (?), Toulouse, ca. 1800—Paris, 1825; flutist. His brother (2) **("De Peyre Ville"), Jean Marie,** Toulouse, 1797—Paris, 1876; violinist.

Bečvafovsky (bĕch'-var-shóf'-shkǐ), **Ant. F.,** Jungbunzlau. Bohemia, 1754—Berlin, 1823; organist and composer.

Bed'ford, Herbert, b. London, Jan. 23, 1867; composer; lectured on un-accompanied vocal music and published an essay on this subject; c. (opera) *"Kit Marlowe,"* symph., chamber and vocal music; m. Liza Lehmann, composer.

Bedos de Celles (bŭ-dō du -sĕl), Caux, near Bézières, 1706—St. Maur, 1779; Benedictine monk and writer.

Beech'am, (1) Sir **Thomas,** b. near Liverpool, Engl., April 29, 1879; eminent conductor; son of Sir Joseph Beecham; educated at Rossall Sch.; studied comp. with Dr. Sweeting, later with Varley Roberts at Oxford Univ.; from 1899 founder and leader of amateur orch. soc. at Huyton; also substituted for Richter in a concert given by his father; 1902, cond. of Kelson 'Truman's touring op. co.; studied comp. for a year and prod. three operas; 1905, led his first orch. concert in London; 1906–8 founded New Symph. Orch. there and in latter year formed Beecham Symph. Orch.; 1910 organised season of opera at Covent Garden, following this with others until 1915, in which a number of first perfs. in England were given, esp. Strauss operas, Wagner and works in English; later cond. of Royal Op. Syndicate and after 1915 of London Phil. Soc.; knighted 1916; in recent years artistic dir. of Covent Garden Op.; has appeared widely as guest cond. in other countries, incl. N. Y. Phil. Orch. and Philadelphia Orch. in U. S. (2) **Adrian,** b. London, Sept. 4, 1904; son of (1); composer of music to *"The Merchant of Venice,"* songs, etc.

Beecke (bā'-kĕ), **Ignaz von,** 1733 —Wallerstein, 1803; captain of dragoons, then "Musikintendant" to

Prince of Ottingen-Wallerstein; harpsichordist; composer of 7 operas, etc.

Beellaerts (bāl-lärts), **Jean.** Vide BELLERE.

Beer (bār), (1) **Jacob Liebmann.** Vide MEYERBEER. (2) **Josef,** Grünwald, Bohemia, 1744—Potsdam, 1811; player of the clarinet, for which he invented the fifth key. (3) **Max Josef,** Vienna, Aug. 25, 1851—Nov. 25, 1908; pianist; pupil of Dessoff; lived in Vienna; composed 4 operas, incl. the succ. "*Der Strick der Schmiede*" (Augsburg, 1897), etc.

Beer-Walbrunn, Anton, Kohlberg, June 29, 1864—Munich, March 22, 1929; studied with Rheinberger, leader in Regensburg orch., later lived in Munich; taught piano and theory at Akad. there after 1901; prof., 1908; c. operas, many orch., chamber, piano works, etc.

Beethoven (bāt'-hō-fĕn, not bā-tō'-vĕn), **Ludwig van,** b. Bonn-on-Rhine, Dec. 16 (baptised, Dec. 17, 1770) (Beethoven said Dec. 16, 1772); d. Vienna, March 26, 1827; grandson of **Ludwig van B.** (a native of Maestricht, bass singer, opera composer, and conductor to the Elector Clemens August, at Bonn), 2d child of **Jn. van B.** (a tenor singer in the Electoral choir), who had m. a widow, Magdelena Laym (née Keverich), a daughter of the chief cook at Ehrenbreitstein. **B.** studied at the public schools at Bonn till 14. From his fourth year, his father taught him music with great severity till 1779. He played the vln. well at 8; at 11 he knew Bach's "*Wohltemperirte Clavier.*" Became pupil of Pfeiffer, a music-dir. and oboist; and Van der Eeden, court-organist, who predicted that he would be "a second Mozart"; 1785, studied vln. with Franz Ries; 1787, took a few lessons of Mozart; 1792, Haydn, passing through Bonn, praised a cantata of his (now lost). The Elector sent **B.** to Vienna, where he studied cpt. with Haydn, who seemed to neglect him, so that he secretly studied with Schenck; later he went to Albrechtsberger, who said "he has learnt nothing, and will never do anything in decent style"; he studied the vln. with Schuppanzigh and consulted Salieri and Aloys Förster; 1781, he is believed to have written a Funeral Cantata in memory of the English *chargé d'affaires* at Bonn, who had advanced money to the family; 1781 (1782 ?), his first publication, 3 pf.-sonatas, 1782; deputy organist, 1783; cembalist for rehearsals of the opera-orch., without compensation 1784–92; asst. organist at an annual salary of 150 florins (about $63); from 1788 also 2d viola of the theatre orch. Visited Vienna, 1787, and made a sensation by extemporising, Mozart exclaiming "He will make a noise in the world some day." In July his tender-hearted mother died of consumption; his father lost his voice and became a sot. **B.'s** only home was in the family of the widow von Breuning, to whose daughter and son he gave lessons. Here he acquired his passion for English literature. He now made acquaintance of young Count Waldstein, who became his life-long patron, and in 1792 sent him to Vienna, where he henceforward lived. The decade 1782–92 does not show much fertility in composition, half a dozen songs, a rondo, a minuet, and 3 preludes for pf., 3 pf.-quartets, a pf.-trio, a string-trio, op. 3; 4 sets of pf. variations; a rondino for wind; the "*Ritter Ballet*" with orch. (pub. 1872); "*The Bagatelles,*" op. 33; 2 vln.-rondos, op. 51; the "*Serenade Trio*" op. 8; the lost cantata, a lost trio for pf., flute, and bassoon, and an Allegro and Minuet for 2 flutes. 1792, he was sent to Vienna by the Elector, who paid him his salary for 2 years; he had growing royalties from his comps., also 600 florins annually from Prince Lichnowsky, his warmest admirer. March 29, 1795, he played his C major pf.-concerto in the Burgtheater, his first public appearance; 1796, he played before King Fr. Wm. II.; 1798, at Prague, he gave 2 sensational concerts and met two piano virtuosi: Steibelt who challenged **B.** to extemporise and was sadly worsted, and Wölffl, who became his friend. 1800 ends what is called (after von Lenz's book "*B. et ses trois styles*") his "first period" of composition; the "second period," extending to 1815; the "third" to 1827. This first period includes op. 1–18, pf. and string-trios, string-quartets, 9 pf.-sonatas, 7 variations on "*God Save the Queen,*" and 5 on "*Rule Britan-*

nia," the aria *"Ah perfido,*" etc.
Now a severe and early venereal
trouble affected his liver, and began
to ruin his hearing, which by 1822
was entirely gone. Though he had
always been brusque (especially with
the aristocracy, among whom he had
an extraordinarily long list of friend-
ships and love-affairs), his former
generosity and geniality speedily developed into atrocious suspiciousness
and violence toward his best friends.
The wild life of a nephew whom he
supported brought him great bitter-
ness. Until the beginning of the
"third period," however, he had large
stores of joy in life, open-air Nature,
and the details of his compositions
which were worked up with utmost
care from "sketch-books," always
carried with him, and still extant as
a unique example of genius at work.
In the arbitrary but somewhat con-
venient von Lenz classification the
2d period includes the symphonies
III—VIII; the opera *"Fidelio"*; the
music to *"Egmont"*; the ballet
"Prometheus"; the Mass in C, op. 86,
the oratorio *"Christus am Oelberg"*
(1803); the *"Coriolanus"* overture;
2 pf.-concertos, 1 vln.-concerto; 3
quartets; 4 pf.-trios and 14 pf.-
sonatas (among them op. 27, op. 28,
31, No. 2, 53, 57, and 81); the
"Liederkreis," etc. The "third period" incl. the five pf.-sonatas, op. 101,
111, the *"Missa solennis,"* the Ninth
Symphony, the overture *"Ruins of
Athens,"* the overtures op. 115, 124;
the grand fugue for string-quartet,
and the string-quartets op. 127, 130,
131, 132, 135 (F).
"Fidelio," first named *"Leonore,"*
was prod. Nov. 20, 1805, just a week
after the French army entered Vienna. It was withdrawn after three
consecutive performances; revised
and prod. March 29, 1806, but withdrawn by B. after two performances.
Once more revised, it was revived in
1814, very successfully; the present
overture is the result of various versions known as the *Leonore* overtures
1, 2, and 3. The *"Eroica"* symphony (No. 3) was called *"Sinfonia
grande Napoleon Bonaparte"* in honour of his advocacy of "liberty,
equality, and fraternity." When
Napoleon proclaimed himself emperor, B. tore up the title-page in
wrath and changed the name to

*"Sinfonia eroica composta per fes-
teggiare il sovvenire d'un gran uomo."*
(Heroic symphony, composed to
celebrate the memory of a great
man.) In the Ninth Symphony, a
choral Finale is used as the final
addition to the orchestral climax of
ecstasy (the words from Schiller's
"Hymn to Joy"). In 1809 Jerome
Bonaparte invited **B.** to become conductor at Cassel with a salary of 600
ducats (about $1,500); but his Vien-
nese patrons Archduke Rudolf and
the Princes Lobkowitz and Kinsky,
settled on him an annuity of 4,000
florins ($2,000). Dec., 1826, a vio-
lent cold resulted in pneumonia;
dropsy followed, **B.** saying to the
doctors who tapped him three times
and drew out the water, "Better from
my belly than from my pen." After
an illness of 3 months he took the
Roman Catholic sacraments, a two-
days' agony of semi-consciousness
followed and he died, just after shak-
ing his clenched fist in the air, during
a terrific thunderstorm, the evening
of March 26, 1827. 20,000 persons
attended his funeral.
His complete works comprise 138
opus-numbers and about 70 unnumbered comp. The following are
those published. INSTRUMENTAL.—
9 Symphonies—No. 1, op. 21, in C;
2, op. 36, in D; 3, op. 55, in E♭ (the
"Eroica"); 4, op. 60, in B♭; 5, op.
67, in C min.; 6, op. 68, in F (*"Pastoral"*); 7, op. 92, in A; 8, op. 93, in
F; 9, op. 125, in D min. (*"Choral"*).
"The Battle of Vittoria" (op. 91);
music to the ballet *"Prometheus"*
(op. 43), and to Goethe's *"Egmont"*
(op. 84), both with overtures, besides, nine overtures—*"Coriolanus"*;
"Leonore" (Nos. 1, 2, and 3); *"Fidelio"*; *"King Stephen"*; *"Ruins of
Athens"*; *"Namensfeier,"* op. 115;
"Weihe des Hauses" (op. 124). Also
for orch.; Allegretto in E♭; March
from *"Tarpeia,"* in C; *"Military
March,"* in D; *"Ritter-Ballet"*; 12,
Minuets; 12, "deutsche Tänze"; 12,
Contretänze; violin-concerto, op. 61.
Five pf.-concertos, the last op. 73, in
E (*"Emperor"*); also a pf.-concerto
arranged from the violin-concerto.
A triple-concerto, op. 56, for pf.,
vln., 'cello and orch.; a *"Choral
Fantasia"* for pf., chorus and orch.;
a Rondo in B, for pf. and orch.;
cadences to the pf.-concertos.

Two Octets for wind, both in E♭. Septet for strings and wind. Sextet for strings and 2 horns. One sextet for wind, E♭. Two quintets for strings; fugue for string-quintet; also quintet arr. from pf.-trio in C min. Sixteen string-quartets; Op. 18, Nos. 1-6 in F, G, D, C min., A and B♭ (first period); op. 59, Nos. 1-3; op. 74, in E♭ (the "*Harfenquartett*"); op. 95 (second period); op. 127; op. 130; op. 131; op. 132; op. 135. A grand fugue for string-quartet, op. 133, in B♭ (third period). One pf.-quartet (arr. from the pf.-quintet); 3 juvenile pf.-quartets; five string-trios; eight pf.-trios, that in E♭ being juvenile; an arr. of the "*Eroica*" symphony. Grand trios for pf., clar. and 'cello op. 11; in B♭ and in E♭ (arr. from septet, op. 20); trio for 2 oboes and *cor anglais*, in C op. 87. Ten sonatas for pf. and violin, incl. op. 47 ("*Kreutzer*"); rondo for pf. and vln.; 12 variations for do. Five sonatas and 31 variations for pf. and 'cello. Sonata for pf. and horn. Sonata for pf., 4 hands. 38 Sonatas for piano, incl. op. 27. Nos. 1 and 2 ("*Quasi Fantasia*"), op. 28 ("*Pastorale*") in D; op. 53 ("*Waldstein*") in C; op. 57 ("*Appassionata*") in F min.; op. 81 ("*Caractéristique*"—"*Les adieux, l'absence, le retour*") in E♭. Also 6 easy sonatas, 3 of them composed at age of 10; 21 sets of variations for pf.; 3 sets of bagatelles; 4 rondos; fantasia in G min.; 3 preludes; polonaise; andante in F ("*Favori*"); 7 minuets; 13 Ländler, for 4 hands; 3 marches; 14 variations.

VOCAL.—Opera "*Fidelio*," in 2 acts, op. 72. 2 Masses, in C and D ("*Solennis*"). Oratorio "*Christus am Oelberg*," op. 85. Cantata "*Der glorreiche Augenblick*," op. 136 (1814); also arr. as *Preis der Tonkunst. Meeresstille und Glückliche Fahrt*, op. 112 (poem by Goethe). Scena and aria for soprano, "*Ah Perfido*," with orch., op. 65. Trio for soprano, tenor, and bass, "*Tremate, Empi, Tremate*," op. 116. "*Opferlied*" for soprano solo, chorus, and orch. "*Bundeslied*" for 2 solo voices. 3-part chorus and wind. "*Elegischer Gesang*" for 4 voice-parts and strings; 66 songs with pf.-accomp.; one duet, "*Gesang der Mönche*"; 3 voice-parts *a capp.* 18

vocal canons. 7 books of English, Scotch, Irish, Welsh, and Italian songs, with pf., vln, and 'cello. A symphony supposed to be a youthful work of his was discovered 1911 in the library of the University of Jena, by Prof. Fritz Stein, was performed there Jan. 17, 1910, and published 1911; performed in Leipzig, Nov., 1911, and by Boston Symph., 1912. It is not generally accepted as Beethoven's but is found weak and uninteresting, of Haydnlike simplicity, with echoes of Mozart. The best biography is Alex. W. Thayer's. Partial collections of Beethoven's letters are pub. and his sketch-books are discussed in Ignaz von Seyfried's "*Ludwig van Beethoven's Studien im Generalbass, Kontrapunkt und in der Kompositionslehre.*" Selections from these have been published; a complete edition projected (1935) in Germany. Biogs. also by Schindler, Nohl, Crowest, etc. Wagner wrote an estimate. The vast Beethoven literature includes studies of the composer by Bekker, Grace, Grove, Kalischer, Kerst, Herriot, Kullak, Mason, d'Indy, Mies, Newman, Rolland, Marion Scott, Sonneck, Specht, J. W. N. Sullivan, Ernest Walker, etc. Studies of his sonatas by Behrend, Elterlein, Harding, Marx, McEwen, Milne, Shedlock and Tovey; of the symphonies, by Berlioz, Edwin Evans, Sr., Grove, Tovey, and Weingartner; the string quartets by J. de Marliave (1928). A thematic index of his works was made by Nottebohm.

Beffara (bĕf'-fä-rä), **Louis François**, Nonancourt, Eure, 1751—Paris, 1838; 1792-1816, commissaire de police, at Paris; musical historian.

Begnis (bān'-yēs), (1) **Gius or Wm. de**, Lugo, Papal States, 1793—Bath(?), England, 1849; buffo singer; in 1816, he m. (2) Signora **Ronzi**, Paris, 1800 (?)—Italy, 1853; comic soprano.

Behaim (bĕ-hīm'), **Michel**, Sulzbach, 1416—murdered there, 1474; soldier and minnesinger.

Behm (bām), **Eduard**, b. Stettin, April 8, 1862; studied with Paul, Weidenbach, Reinecke, Härtel, Raif and Kiel; pianist and teacher in various cities, then at Berlin as dir. (until 1901) Schwantzer Cons.; composed an opera, "*Schelm von Bergen*" (Dresden, 1899), a symphony, pf.-concerto, etc.

Behnke (bān'-kē), **Emil**, Stettin, 1836 —Ostend, 1892; teacher and writer.

Behr (bār), (1) **Fz.**, Lubtheen, Mecklenburg, July 22, 1837—Dresden, Feb. 15, 1898; composed pf.-pieces, under pseud. of "William Cooper," "Charles Morley," or "Francesco d'Orso." (2) **Therese**, b. Stuttgart, Sept. 14, 1876; alto; pupil of J. Stakhausen, of Schulz-Dornberg and of Etelka Gerster; m. Artur Schnabel, pianist.

Beier (bī'-ĕr), **Fz.**, Berlin, April 18, 1857—Cassel, June 25, 1914; son of a military band-master; pupil Stern and Kullak Cons.; cond. at the Royal Theatre; composed succ. opera "*Der Posaunist von Scherkingen*" (Cassel, 1889), a parody on Nessler's well-known "*Der Trompeter von Säkkingen*"; succ. comic operetta "*der Gaunerkönig*" (Cassel, 1890), etc.

Bek'ker, Paul, Berlin, Sept. 11, 1882— New York, Feb., 1937; writer; originally a violinist; pupil of Rehfeld, Sormann, and Horwitz; became critic of Berlin Neueste Nachrichten, 1906; Allgemeine Zeitung, 1909; Frankfurter Zeitung, 1911–23; intendant of Cassel Stadttheat., 1925–7; and of Wiesbaden Op., 1927–32; after 1934 critic of Staats-Zeitung, New York; author of many books on music, incl. "*Beethoven*" (1911); "*Das Deutsche Musikleben*" (1916); "*Die Symphonien Gustav Mahlers*" (1921); "*Richard Wagner*" (1925); "*Die Oper*," etc.

Belaiev, (1) **Mitrofan**, St. Petersburg, Feb. 10, 1836—Jan. 10, 1904; noted music patron and eccentric millionaire, who sponsored the work of the Russian Nationalist group of composers, also establishing in 1885 the important pub. house in Leipzig for works by his countrymen. (2) **Victor Michailovitch**, b. Uralsk, Russia, Feb. 5, 1888; eminent musicologist and writer on music.

Belce. Vide REUSS-BELCE.

Belcke (bĕl'-kĕ), (1) **Fr. Aug.**, Lucka, Altenburg, 1795—1874; the first trombone virtuoso. (2) **Chr. Gl.**, Lucka, 1796—1875; bro. of above; flutist.

Beldoman'dis (or **Beldeman'dis, Beldeman'do**), **Prosdo'cimus de**, b. Padua, 15th cent.; prof. of philosophy, ca. 1422; theorist.

Beliczay (bā'-lĭ-chä-ĕ), **Julius von**, Komorn, Hungary, 1835—Pesth, 1893; violinist.

Belin (or **Bellin**) (bŭ-lăn), (1) **Guil.**, ca. 1547; tenor Chapelle Royale, Paris. (2) **Julien**, b. Le Mans, ca. 1530; lutenist.

Bell, William Henry, b. St. Albans, Aug. 20, 1873; pupil at the R. A. M.; won Goss scholarship, 1889; 1903, prof. of harmony there; c. symphonies "*Walt Whitman*" and "*The Open Road*," 3 symph. poems to the "*Canterbury Tales*"; symph. poems, "*Love Among the Ruins*"; "*The Shepherd*," etc. 1912, dir. of Cape Town Cons.

Bellaigue (bĕl-lĕg), **Camille**, Paris, May 24, 1858—Oct. 4, 1930; critic and essayist; pupil of Paladilhe and Marmontel.

Bellasio (bĕl-lä'-sĭ-ō), **Paolo**, 1579–95; pub. madrigals, etc., at Venice.

Bel'lasis, Edw., b. Jan. 28, 1852; English writer and composer; wrote biog. of Cherubini (1912).

Bell'avere (or **Bell'haver**) (bĕl-ä-vä'-rĕ), **V.**, Venice, 1530 (?)—1588 (?); organist and composer.

Bellazzi (bĕl-läd'-zē), **Fran. C.**, at Venice, 1618–28.

Bellère (bĕl-lăr') (or **Belle'rus**, rightly **Beellaerts**) (bāl-lärts'), (1) **Jean**, d. Antwerp, ca. 1595; publisher. His son and successor was (2) **Balthasar**.

Bel'lermann, (1) **Konstantin**, Erfurt, 1696—Münden, 1758; rector and composer. (2) **Jn. Fr.**, Erfurt, 1795 —Berlin, 1874; writer on Greek music. His son (3), **Jn. Gf. H.**, Berlin, March 10, 1832—Potsdam, April 10, 1903; pupil R. Inst. for ch.-music, 1866; prof. of mus. Berlin U. (vice Marx.); theorist and composer.

Bellet'ti, Giov. Bat., Sarzana, Feb. 17, 1813—Dec. 27, 1890; barytone; pupil of Pilotti at Bologna; début, 1838, Stockholm; sang with Jenny Lind on tour; retired, 1862.

Bellezza, Vincenzo (vĭn-chĕn'-tsō bĕl-lĕts'-ä), b. Bitonto, Italy, Feb. 17, 1888; operatic conductor; studied Naples Cons.; has conducted at Met. Op. House, N. Y.; Covent Garden Op., London; Teatro Colon, Buenos Aires; also in various opera houses of Italy, Spain, Portugal, and South America.

Bell'haver, V. Vide BELL'AVERE.

Belli (bĕl'-lē), (1) **Gir.**, pub., 1586–94;

madrigals, etc. (2) **Giulio,** b. Longiano, ca. 1560; ch.-composer and cond. (3) **Dom.,** 1616; court-musician at Parma.

Bellin, G. Vide BELIN.

Bellincioni (bĕl-lĭn-chō'-nē), **Gemma,** b. Monza, Aug. 17, 1864; notable Italian soprano; toured U. S. in opera, 1899; after 1911 taught in Berlin; and later at Academy of Sta. Cecilia, Rome; pub. a vocal method; she created Santuzza in "*Cavalleria Rusticana.*"

Bellini (bĕl-lē'-nē), (1) **Vincenzo,** Catania, Sicily, Nov. 3, 1801—Puteaux, near Paris, Sept. 23, 1835; opera composer; son and pupil of an organist; a nobleman sent him (1819) to the Cons. at Naples; studied under Furno, Tritto, and Zingarelli, until 1827; privately studied with Haydn and Mozart, and chiefly Pergolesi; as a student composed a symphony, 2 masses, several psalms, a cantata, etc.; his first opera, "*Adelson e Salvini,*" was performed by Cons. pupils, 1825, whereupon the manager of La Scala, Milan, commissioned him to write an opera; 1826, "*Bianca e Fernando*" was prod. with succ.; 1827, "*Il Pirata*"; 1829, "*La Straniera.*" The librettist of the latter 2 was Felice Romani, who wrote the books of all B.'s operas, except "*I Puritani.*" "*Zaira*" (1829) was a failure; "*I Capuleti e Montecchi,*" written in forty days (1830), was a great succ.; "*La Sonnambula,*" and "*Norma*" (1831), with Malibran in the title-rôle, established his fame; "*Beatrice di Tenda*" (Venice, 1833) failed; "*I Puritani*" (libretto by Count Pepoli), written to order 1834, for the Théâtre Italien, Paris, was a great success, and his last finished work. B.'s work abounds in delightful, spontaneous melodies, though the lack of variety in his rhythmic scheme and orchestral accompaniments makes his scores today sound rather pale; Norma remains a great rôle for sopranos of a heroic vocal equipment. He died youngest of all prominent composers—at the age of 33, from dysentery due to overwork. Biog. by Scherillo (Milan, 1885), Pougin (Paris, 1868), etc. Other studies by Cicconetti, Amore, Voss, Lloyd and Parodi; collections of B.'s letters ed. by Scherillo and Salvioli. (2) **Carmelo,** Catania, 1802—1884;

brother of above; composed church-music.

Belloc (bĕl-lôk'), **Teresa** (G. **Trombet'ta-Belloc**), San Begnino, Canavese, 1784—S. Giorgio, 1855; mezzosoprano; repertoire of 80 operas.

Belloli (bĕl-lō'-lē), (1) **Luigi,** Castelfranco, Bologna, 1770—Milan, 1817; horn-player and composer. (2) **Ag.,** b. Bologna; first horn (1819–29) at La Scala, Milan, and dram. composer.

Bemberg (bän-bĕrg), **Henri,** b. Paris, March 29, 1861; pupil of Dubois, Franck and Massenet, Paris Cons.; 1887 took Rossini prize; composed 1-act opera "*Le Baiser de Suzon*" (Paris, Op.-com., 1888), mod. succ.; opera "*Elaine*" (London, 1892: New York, 1894), cantata, "*Mort de Jeanne d'Arc,*" and songs.

Bemetzrieder (bā'-mĕts-rē-dĕr), **A.,** b. Alsatia, 1743; Benedictine monk; composer and writer.

Ben'da, (1) **Franz,** Alt-Benátek, Bohemia, Nov. 25, 1709—Potsdam, March 7, 1786; court-violinist to Frederick II., whom he accompanied for 40 years in flute-concertos; composed symphonies, etc. His 3 brothers (2) **Jn.,** Alt-Benátek, 1713—Potsdam, 1752; violinist. (3) **G.,** Jungbunzlau, Bohemia, 1722—Koestritz, Nov. 6, 1795; court-cond., 1748 (Gotha); 1764–66, Italy; prod. at Gotha 10 operas in which he originated the idea of spoken words with orchestral accompaniment, literal "melodrama." (4) **Jos.,** 1724—Berlin, 1804; violinist. His sister, (5) **Anna Frangiska,** 1726—Gotha, 1780; singer. (6) **Fr. Wm. H.,** Potsdam, 1745—1814; son and pupil of (1); composed operas, etc. (7) **Fr. L.,** Gotha, 1746—Königsberg, 1793; son of (3); cond. and composer. (8) **K. Hermann H.,** Potsdam, 1748—1836; son of rich father; court-violinist and composer.

Ben'del, Fz., Schönlinde, northern Bohemia, March 23, 1832—Berlin, July 3, 1874; pianist; composed symphonies, 4 masses, songs, and piano pieces.

Ben'deler, Jn. Ph., Riethnordhausen, near Erfurt, ca. 1660—Quedlinburg, ca. 1712; clavecinist, organist, and writer.

Ben'der, Paul, b. Driedorf, Germany, July 28, 1875; operatic bass; first studied medicine; singing with Luise

Ress and Baptist Hoffmann; member Breslau Op., after 1900; Munich Op. after 1903; sang at Bayreuth Festivals, beginning 1902; was member of Metropolitan Op., N. Y., in 1922–6.

Ben'dix, (1) **Victor E.,** Copenhagen, May 7, 1851—Jan. 5, 1926; pianist, pupil and protégé of Gade; lived in Copenh. as pf.-teacher and cond.; composed 4 symphonies, incl. *"Zur Höhe,"* in C (also named *"Felsensteigung"*); and *"Sommerklänge aus Südrussland"* in D. (2) **Max,** b. Detroit, Mich., March 28, 1866; violinist; early played in orchestras; studied with Jacobsohn; 1886, concertm. at Met. Op. House; also of Thomas Orch., of which ass't. cond.; founded Bendix Quartet; cond. at Manhattan Op. House, 1906; at Met. Op., 1909–10; 1915, San Francisco Exp.; later teacher in New York.

Ben'dl (běnt'-'l), **K.,** Prague, April 16, 1838—Sept. 20, 1897; important Czech composer; pupil of Blažok and Pitsch, at Prague; chorus-master, Amsterdam (1864); 1866, cond. Prague choral society, *"Hlahol"*; composed Czech operas incl. *"Díte Tábora"* (Child of the Camp), 1892 (3 acts); given at Prague; 3 masses, cantatas, an overture, a *"Dithyramb,"* *"Slavonic Rhapsody,"* for orch., etc.

Ben'edict, Sir **Julius,** Stuttgart, Nov. 27, 1804—London, June 5, 1885; son of a Jewish banker; pupil of Abeille, Hummel, and Weber, 1825 at Naples, where his first opera was prod. 1829, without success; his next (Stuttgart, 1830) was not a success; settled in London as pf.-teacher and concertgiver; 1836, cond. opera buffa; 1837 at Drury Lane, there his first English opera, *"The Gypsy's Warning,"* was prod. (1838); he accompanied Jenny Lind to America, then cond. at Her Majesty's Th., and Drury Lane; 1859 at Covent Garden, and "Monday Popular Concerts"; cond. also Norwich festivals, and (1876–80) the Liverpool Philharmonic; knighted in 1871; composed 11 operas; 2 oratorios, *"St. Cecilia"* (1866), and *"St. Peter"* (1870); 2 symphonies, 2 pf.-concertos, etc.; wrote a biog. of Weber.

Benedic'tus Appenzelders (äp'-pěn-tsělt-ěrs) (B. of **Appenzell**), b. Appenzell, Switzerland; choir-master in Brussels (1539–55) and composer;

often confused with Benedictus Ducis.

Benel'li, (1) **Alemanno.** Vide BOTTRIGARI. (2) **A. Peregrino,** Forli, Romagna, 1771—Bornichau, Saxony, 1830; tenor.

Benevoli (bā-nā'-vō-lē), **Orazio,** Rome, 1602—1672; natural son of Duke Albert of Lorraine, but lived in poverty; cond. at the Vatican (1646); remarkable contrapuntist; in writing chorals with instrs. he was a pioneer; his Salzburg mass being written on 54 staves.

Beninco'ri, Ang. M., Brescia, 1779—Paris, 1821; dram. composer.

Ben'net, (1) **J.,** English composer (1599). (2) **Saunders,** d. 1809; English organist and composer. (3) **Theodore.** Vide TH. RITTER.

Ben'nett, (1) **Wm.,** b. Teignmouth, ca. 1767; organist. (2) **Thos.,** ca. 1774–1848; organist. (3) **Alfred,** 1805—1830; English organist. (4) Sir **Wm. Sterndale,** Sheffield, April 13, 1816—London, Feb. 1, 1875; son of an organist (who died 1819); at 8 entered the choir of King's College Chapel; at 10 pupil of R. A. M.; at 17 played there an original pf.-concerto, later pub. by the Academy, sent 1837 by the Broadwoods to Leipzig for one year; friend of Schumann and Mendelssohn; 1844 m. Mary Anne Wood, founded the Bach Society, 1849; cond. Philh. Society, 1856–66; 1856, Mus. Doc. Cambridge and prof. of mus. there; 1866, Principal there; 1871, knighted; buried in Westminster Abbey; composed 1 symphony, an oratorio *"The Woman of Samaria,"* music to Sophokles' *"Ajax"*; 5 overtures, *"Parisina,"* *"The Naiads,"* *"The Wood-nymph,"* *"Paradise and the Peri,"* *"Merry Wives of Windsor,"* sonatas, etc. (5) **Jos.,** Berkeley, Gloucestershire, Nov. 29, 1831—June 12, 1911; organist of Westminster Chapel; then music critic for various London newspapers; finally *The Telegraph;* wrote various libretti; pub. *"Letters from Bayreuth"* (1877); *"The Musical Year"* (1883), etc. (6) **Robert Russell,** b. Kansas City, Mo., 1894; composer; early pupil of Carl Busch; res. in New York after 1916, where active as orchestrator and arranger; won Guggenheim Fellowship; studied with Nadia Boulanger, Paris; c. (opera) *"Maria Malibran,"* text by

Robert A. Simon, prod. by Juilliard School, N. Y., 1935; (ballet) *"Endymion"* (orch.) symphony; *"Charleston Rhapsody,"* *"Sights and Sounds"* (won RCA-Victor Co. prize); *"Abraham Lincoln"*; concerto grosso; March for two pianos and orch.; Six Variations on a Theme of Jerome Kern; chamber music, incl. "Toy" Symphony and string quartet.

Bennewitz (bĕn'-nĕ-vēts), (1) **Wm.**, Berlin, 1832–1871; dram. composer. (2) **Anton**, Privat, Bohemia, March 26, 1833—Hirschberg near Leipzig, May 30, 1926; violinist; 1882–1901, dir. of Prague Cons.

Benoist (bŭn-wä), **François**, Nantes, 1794—Paris, 1878; organ-prof. Paris Cons.; composed operas, etc.

Benoît (bŭn-wä), (1) **Pierre Léonard Ld.**, Harlebecke, Belgium, Aug. 17, 1834—Antwerp, Mar. 4, 1901; Flemish composer and writer; pupil Brussels Cons., 1851–55; at same time prod. a small opera and wrote music for Flemish melodramas; 1856, cond. Park Th.; 1857, won the Prix de Rome, with the cantata *"Le Meurtre d'Abel"*; studied at Leipzig, Dresden, Munich, and Berlin, and wrote a thesis for the Brussels Academy *"L'école de musique flamande et son avenir."* In 1861 his opera *"Le Roi des Aulnes,"* was accepted by Théâtre Lyrique, Paris, but not given; cond. at the Bouffes-Parisiennes; from 1867, dir. Antwerp Cons.; 1882, member of the R. A., Berlin; composed *"Messe solennelle"* (1862); *"TeDeum"* (1863); *"Requiem"* (1863); 2 oratorios, *"Lucifer"* and *"De Schelde"*; 2 operas, *"Het Dorp int Gebergte"* and *"Isa"*; *"Drama Christi,"* a sacred drama in Flemish; a cantata *"De Oorlog War"*; *"Children's Oratorio"*; a choral symphony, *"De Maaiers"* (The Reapers); music to *"Charlotte Corday,"* and to *"Willem de Zwijger"* (1876); the "Rubens cantata" *"Flanderens kunstroem"*; *"Antwerpen,"* for triple male chorus (1877); vocal works with orch. incl. *"Joncfrou Kathelijne,"* scena for alto (1879); *"Muse der Geschiednis"* (1880); and "Hucbald," *"Triomfmarsch"* (1880); grand cantata *"De Rhyn"* (1889); a mass, etc. Wrote *"De vlaamsche Musiek-school van Antwerpen"* (1873), *"Verhandelung over de nationale Toonkunde"* (2 vols., 1877–79), etc. (2) **Camille**, Roanne,

Nov. 7, 1851—Paris, July 1, 1923; pupil of César Franck; 1888–1895, assistant conservator at the Louvre; 1895, conservator; c. overture, 1880; text and music of opera *"Cléopatre,"* etc.; author of *"Souvenirs,"* 1884, and *"Musiciens, poetes et philosophes,"* 1887; also translator.

Bentonel'li, **Joseph** (rightly **Benton**), b. Oklahoma; tenor; grad. Okla. State Univ.; studied with Jean de Reszke in France, coached operatic rôles in Italy for three years, and made début at Bologna as Alfredo; sang in Italian theatres, also in Austria, France, Belgium, and Holland; mem. Chicago Op. Co., 1934–5, singing with this company in latter year leading tenor rôle in Am. prem. of Respighi's *"La Fiamma,"* also with Philadelphia Orch. in its stage prod. of Gluck's *"Iphigénie en Aulide"*; concert tour in U. S.; audition with Met. Op. Co. was followed by sudden call two days later to take place of indisposed tenor as Des Grieux in *"Manon,"* 1936, which he sang with succ. and was engaged as regular mem. of company.

Benvenuti (bĕn-vā-noo'-tē), **Tommaso**, Venice, 1838—Rome, 1906; dram. composer.

Berardi (bā-rär'-dē), **Ang.**, b. Bologna, 1681; conductor and theorist.

Ber'ber, **Felix**, Jena, March 11, 1871—Nov. 2, 1930; violinist; pupil of Dresden Cons. and Leipzig Cons.; concertmaster in various cities; 1904–1907 prof. Royal Acad., London; 1907 at Frankfort-on-Main; 1908 at Geneva Cons.; toured widely; 1910, America; after 1912 in Munich; 1920, teaching at Cons. there.

Berbiguier (bĕr-bĭg-yä), **Benoît Tranquille**, Caderousse, Vaucluse, 1782—near Blois, 1838; flute-virtuoso and composer.

Berchem (or **Berghem**) (bĕrkh'-ĕm), **Jachet de** (also **Jaquet, Jacquet,** and **Giachetto di Mantova**), Berchem (?) near Antwerp, ca. 1500–1580; contrapuntist and conductor.

Berens (bā'-rĕns), (1) **Hermann**, Hamburg, 1826—Stockholm, 1880; son and pupil of (2) **K. B.** (1801–1857); court-conductor and composer.

Beret'ta, **Giov. Batt**, Verona, 1819—Milan, 1876; theorist, editor, and composer.

Berezowsky (bĕr-ē-sŏf'-skē), **Nicolai**, b. St. Petersburg, May 17, 1900;

violinist, composer; at 8 entered Imp. Capella and grad. with honours; 1918, concertm. Saratov Nat'l. Op.; 1921, dir. Sch. of Mod. Art, Moscow; after 1922 in U. S.; studied with Josef Borisoff, then at Juilliard Sch. of Mus. with R. Goldmark and Kochanski; played in N. Y. Phil.; c. sextet for strings, piano, and clarinet (heard Washington Chamber Mus. Fest., 1926); four string quartets; quartet for soprano and strings; piano trio; quintet for wind instruments; (orch.) two symphonies (the first played by Boston Symph., as well as his 'cello concerto); "*Hebrew*" *Suite* (N. Y. Phil.); Sinfonietta; violin concerto (played by Flesch with Dresden Phil. under composer's baton); (opera) "*Prince Batrak.*"

Berg (bĕrkh), (1) **Adam,** 1540—1599; music-printer, Munich. (2) **Jn. von,** 1550; music-printer, Ghent, Nürnberg. (3) **G.,** German composer in England, 1763–71. (4) **Kon. Mat.,** Colmar, Alsatia, 1785—Strassburg, 1852; violinist, pianist, and writer. (5) **Alban,** Vienna, Feb. 7, 1885—Dec. 24, 1935; eminent composer; studied with Schönberg, 1904–08, whose radical doctrines in harmony and tonality he combined in his work with an original capacity of expression that makes him the outstanding member of that composer's school; served as director of concerts given by Private Performing Society organized by Schönberg in Vienna; c. piano sonata (1908); string quartet (1910); songs with piano and orchestra (1908–09); four pieces for clarinet and orchestra (1913); three orchestral pieces (1914); chamber concerto for piano, violin, and 13 wind instruments (1924); the expressionistic music-drama "*Wozzeck*" (based on play by Georg Büchner, nineteenth-century German poet), which is written in novel style, partly atonal, and utilizing antique forms such as suite, passacaglia, etc., in its operatic texture (première after many rehearsals evoked sensational impression at Berlin State Op., Dec. 14, 1925); Lyric Suite for string quartet (1926); concert aria, "*Le Vin,*" for soprano and orchestra (1929); partially completed music drama, "*Lulu*" (based on Wedekind dramas, "*Erdgeist*" and "*Pandora's Box*"), which after his death aroused wide interest when premiered, Zurich, 1937; also posth. violin concerto (Barcelona, 1936, Intern. Society for Contemp. Music Festival). One of the most original figures in early twentieth-century music, **B.** in his "*Wozzeck,*" relates the heart-rending tragedy of an ignorant soldier who, oppressed by his superiors, murders his sweetheart and drowns himself; this work made a definite contribution to post-Wagnerian music drama. The opera was given its American première by the Philadelphia Orch. and Grand Opera Co., under Stokowski, both in Phila. and N. Y., with impressive effect in 1931. **B.** also served as editor of the Vienna publication "*Musikblätter des Anbruch,*" for a period after 1920.

Berger (bĕr'-gĕr), (1) **L.,** Berlin, 1777—1839; from 1815 pf.-teacher and composer. (2) **Francesco,** London, June 10, 1834—April 25, 1933; pupil of Ricci and Lickl (pf.), Hauptmann and Plaidy; from 1855 pf.-prof. R. A. M., and Guildhall Sch. of Mus.; for years dir., and 1884–1911, sec., Philh.; composed an opera, a mass (prod. in Italy), etc.; wrote "*First Steps at the Pianoforte.*" (3) **Wm.,** Boston, Mass., Aug. 8, 1861—Jena, Germany, Jan. 16, 1911; taken by parents to Bremen; pupil of Kiel, etc.; lived Berlin as teacher and composer; 1898 won a prize of 2,000 marks, with a setting of Goethe's "*Meine Göttin*" (op. 72); composed "*Gesang der Geister über den Wassern,*" mixed choir and orch. in overture form, a dram. fantasy, etc. (4) **Siegfried.** Vide CHELIUS. (5) **Otto,** Machau, Bohemia, 1873 (?)—1897; 'cellist.

Berggreen (bĕrkh'-grän), **Andreas P.,** Copenhagen, 1801—1880; teacher.

Berghem. Vide BERCHEM.

Bergmann (bĕrkh'-män), **K.,** Ebersbach, Saxony, 1821—New York, Aug. 16, 1876; in America, 1850, with "Germania" Orch., later its cond. till 1854; cond. "Händel and Haydn" Soc., Boston, 1852–54; in 1855 alternate cond. Philh. Soc., New York; 1862–76, sole cond.; also cond. "Arion" Society; active in introducing Wagner, Liszt, etc., to America.

Bergner (bĕrkh'-nĕr), **Wm.,** Riga, Nov. 4, 1837—June 9, 1907; organist; founded a Bach Society and a cathedral choir.

Bergonzi (bĕr-gŏn'-tsē), (1) **Carlo,** d. 1747; vln.-maker at Cremona; best pupil of Stradivari. His son (2) **Michelangelo,** and his 2 nephews, (3) **Niccolo** and (4) **Carlo,** were less important. (5) **Benedetto,** Cremona, 1790—1840; horn-player and inventor.

Bergson (bĕrkh'-zōn), **Michael,** Warsaw, May 20, 1820—London, March 9, 1898; pianist and composer; pupil of Schneider, Rungenhagen, and Taubert, Paris (1840); Italy, 1846, where hir opera "*Louisa di Montfort*" was succ. (Florence, 1847); Paris, 1859, prod. a 1-act operetta; 1863, 1st pf.-teacher and for a time dir. Geneva Cons.; later in London as teacher.

Bergt (bĕrkht), **Chr. Gl. Aug.,** b. Oderan, Saxony, 1772—Bautzen, 1837; organist, violinist, and conductor.

Beringer (bā'-rĭng-ĕr), **Oscar,** Furtwangen, July 14, 1844—London, Feb. 21, 1922; pupil of Plaidy, Moscheles, Leipzig Cons., 1864–66; later of Tausig, Ehrlich, and Weitzmann, Berlin; teacher there, 1869; London, 1873–97; after 1885, pf.-prof. in R. A. M.; composed Technical Exercises, etc.

Bériot (dŭ bār-yō), (1) **Chas. Auguste de,** Louvain, Feb. 20, 1802—Brussels, April 8, 1870; vln.-virtuoso; pupil of Viotti and Baillot, but chiefly of his guardian, Tiby; at 9 he played a concerto; 1821, made a brilliant début, Paris; chamber-violinist to the King of France, solo-violinist to the King of the Netherlands (1826–30); 1830–35 toured Europe with Mme. Garcia-Malibran, whom he m. in 1836; from 1843–52, prof. at Brussels Cons.; became blind and paralysed in left arm; pub. method and 7 concertos, etc., for vln. (2) **Chas. Vilfride de,** Paris, Feb. 12, 1833—near Paris, 1914; son of above; pupil of Thalberg; prof. of pf., Paris Cons.; composed symphonies, etc.; wrote with his father a "*Methode d'accompagnement.*"

Berlijn (or **Berlyn**) (bär'-lēn), **Anton** (or **Aron Wolf?**), Amsterdam, 1817—1870; conductor.

Berlin', Irving (rightly **Baline**), b. Russia, May 11, 1888; composer of popular music; was largely responsible for start of "ragtime" craze with his "*Alexander's Ragtime Band*"

several years before the war; has since c. more elaborate scores for musical comedies and the radio; pres. of his own publishing firm, Irving Berlin Inc., New York; m. Ellin Mackay, daughter of Clarence H. Mackay.

Berlioz (bār-lĭ-ōs not bār-lĭ-ō), **Hector (Louis),** Côte-Saint-André, near Grenoble, France, Dec. 11, 1803—Paris, March 9, 1869; "Father of modern orchestration"; conductor, critic, writer of verse and electric prose; sent to Paris to study medicine, he accepted disinheritance and took up music, though he could never play any instr. save the guitar and flageolet; while pupil at the Cons., he earned a bare living; joined the chorus of the Gymnase Dramatique; left the Cons. in disgust with Reicha's formalism, and plunged with characteristic energy—or rather fury—into the cause of romanticism; 1825, an orchestral mass given at St. Roch brought the ridicule he usually had in France where he was little thought of as a composer though admired as a writer; 1828 saw the production of two overtures, "*Waverley*" and "*Les Frances-Juges,*" and a Symphonie fantastique, "*Épisode de la vie d'un artiste*"; 1829, his "*Concerts des Sylphes,*" publicly produced at 26, show him an ardent believer in programme-music (vide D. D.) and a marvellous virtuoso in instrumentation. He reëntered the Cons. under Lesueur, in spite of Cherubini, who fought his admission; 1830, he took the Prix de Rome with a cantata, "*Sardanapale*"; after 18 months in Italy he returned to Paris and took up journalism with marked success. His symphony "*Harold en Italie*" (1834), the "*Messe des Morts*" (1837), the dram. symphony "*Roméo et Juliette,*" with vocal soli and chorus (1839), and the overture "*Carneval romain,*" were well received, but the 2-act opera semi-seria "*Benvenuto Cellini*" failed both in Paris and in London, 1838. In 1839 he was made Conservator of the Cons.; librarian, 1852, but was never made professor as he desired. Concert tours through Germany and Russia, 1843–47, were very successful and are described in his book "*Voyage musical.*" London (1852) he cond. the "New Philh. Concerts"; prod. comic opera "*Béat-*

rice et Bénédict (1862, Baden-Baden); 1865, member of the Académie, and decorated with cross of Legion of Honour. He m. Henrietta Smithson, an Irish actress who made a sensation in Paris in Shakespearian rôles, but later was hissed off, and became a peevish invalid. His opera, "*Les Troyens à Carthage*," (1863) was a failure. His son Louis died 1867. "*Les Troyens*," in two parts; "*La Prise de Troie*," 3 acts, and "*Les Troyens à Carthage*," in 5 acts was given complete for the first time, at Carlsruhe, 1897. His most succ. work was his "oratorio," "*La Damnation de Faust*" (1846). His "*Traité d'instrumentation*" is a classic in orchestration, though its then sensational modernity is lost. B. strangely despised Wagner, who, however, confessed his large indebtedness to B. Other books are "*Soirées d'orchestre*" (1853), "*Grotesques de la musique*" (1859), "*A travers chants*" (1862), and an autobiography, "*Mémoires*," from 1803-65. In original verse are the text to the sacred trilogy "*L'Enfance du Christ*" (*Part I.*, *Le songe d'Hérode; II.*, *La fuite en Égypte; III.*, *L'Arrivée à Sais*); and his operas "*Les Troyens*" and "*Béatrice et Bénédict*." He composed also a "*Te Deum*" for 3 choirs, orch. and org.; a "*Grand symphonie funèbre et triomphale*" for full military band, with strings and chorus ad lib.; overture to "*Le Corsaire*"; "*Le Cinq Mai*," for chorus and orch. (on the anniversary of Napoleon's death), etc. Recent studies of B. have been published in English by W. J. Turner (1934) and Tom S. Wotton (1935); coinciding with a resurgence of interest in this composer on the part of a modern-minded coterie of musicians in Britain. Revivals of Berlioz operas have also taken place, notably of "*Les Troyens*," and "*Béatrice and Bénédict*," at Glasgow.

Berlyn, Anton. Vide BERLIJN.

Bermudo (bĕr-moo'-dhō), **Juan,** Astorga, ca. 1510; writer.

Bernabei (bĕr-nä-bā'-ē), (1) **Gius, Ercole,** Caprarola, ca. 1620—Munich, 1687; 1672 cond. at the Vatican; 1674 cond. at Munich; composed three operas (prod. in Munich), etc. (2) **Gius. A.,** Rome, 1649—Munich,

1732; son of above and his successor at Munich.

Bernacchi (bĕr-näk'-kē), **A.,** Bologna, 1685—1756; soprano-musico, engaged by Händel for London, 1729, as the greatest living dram. singer; 1736 founded a singing-school at Bologna.

Bernard (bĕr-năr, in *F.*), **Émile,** Marseilles, Nov. 28, 1843—Paris, Sept. 11, 1902; until 1895 organist of Nôtre-Dame-des-Champs, Paris; composer of vln.-concerto; concertstück for pf. with orch.; overture "*Beatrice*"; cantatas; much chamber-music, etc.

Bernardel. Vide LUPOT.

Bernar'di, (1) **Steffano,** ca. 1634; canon at Salzburg; theorist and composer. (2) **Francesco.** Vide SENESINO. (3) **Enrico,** Milan, 1838—1900; conductor and dram. composer.

Bernardini (bĕr-när-dē'-nē), **Marcello** ("**Marcello di Capua**"), b. Capua, ca. 1762; dram. composer.

Bernasco'ni, (1) **Andrea,** Marseilles, 1706—Munich, 1784; court-conductor. (2) **P.,** d. Varese, May 27, 1895; organ-builder.

Bern'eker, Constanz, Darkehmen, E. Prussia, Oct. 31, 1844—Königsberg, June 9, 1906; conductor and comp.

Ber'ner, Fr. Wm., Breslau, 1780—1827; organist.

Ber'ners, Lord (Gerald Tyrwhitt), b. Bridgnorth, Engl., Sept. 18, 1883; composer; studied in Dresden and London; chiefly self-taught in music, but orchestration with Stravinsky, some of whose modern musical devices are reflected in his work; entered diplomatic service, 1909; after 1912 connected with British Embassy in Rome; succeeded to British peerage, 1918; c. (opera in one act) "*Le Carrosse de Saint-Sacrement*"; (orchestra) "*Fantaisie Espagnole*" (1919); "*Funeral Marches for a Statesman, a Canary, and a Rich Aunt*" (for two pianos); "*Valse Bourgeoise*" (Salzburg Festival, 1923); Fugue for Orchestra (danced by Diaghileff Ballet, London, 1925); also an amusing nautical ballet, "*The Triumph of Neptune*," suggested by Rowlandson prints, from which a succ. orch. suite has been drawn.

Bernhard (bĕrn'-härt), (1) **der Deutsche** (dĕr doit'-shĕ); organist, Venice, 1445-59; known as "Bernardo di Steffanino Murer"; perhaps inv., certainly introduced, into Italy, the organ-pedal. (2) **Chr.**, Danzig, 1627 —Dresden, 1692; court-conductor and notable contrapuntist.

Ber'no, Augien'sis, d. Riechenau, 1048; abbot and theorist.

Bernoulli (băr-noo'-yē), (1) **Jn.**, Basel, 1667—1747. His son (2) **Daniel**, Groningen, 1700—Basel, 1781, also was prof. and writer on acoustics.

Berns'dorf, Eduard, Dessau, March 25, 1825—Leipzig, June 27, 1901; Leipzig critic and composer.

Bernuth (băr'-noot), **Julius von,** Rees, Rhine Province, Aug. 8, 1830—Hamburg, Dec. 24, 1902; studied law and music at Berlin, 1854; studied at Leipzig Cons. till 1857; founded the "Aufschwung Society," and 1859 "Dilettante's Orchestral Society"; also cond. 3 other societies; later cond. at Hamburg; 1873, dir. of a cons. there; 1878, "Royal Prussian Professor."

Berr (bĕr), **Fr.**, Mannheim, 1794—Paris, 1838; bandmaster; 1831, prof. of clar., Paris Cons.; 1836, dir. School of Military Music; writer and composer.

Bertali (bĕr-tä'-lē), **Ant.**, Verona, 1605 —Vienna, 1669; court-conductor and dram. composer.

Ber'telmann, Jan. G., Amsterdam, 1782—1854; prof. and composer.

Ber'telsmann, K. Aug., Gütersloh, Westphalia, 1811—Amsterdam, 1861; director and composer.

Berthaume (bĕr-tōm), **Isidore,** Paris, 1752—St. Petersburg, 1802; violinist and conductor.

Berthold (bĕr'-tŏlt), **K. Fr. Theodor,** Dresden, 1815—1882; court-organist.

Bertin (bĕr'-tăṅ), **Louise Angélique,** Roches, near Paris, 1805—Paris, 1877; singer, pianist, and dram. composer.

Bertini (bĕr-tē'-nē), (1) **Abbate Gius.**, Palermo, 1756—1849 (?); court-cond. and lexicographer. (2) **Benoît Auguste,** b. Lyons, 1780; writer. (3) **H. Jérome,** London, 1798—Meylau, near Grenoble, 1876; bro. and pupil of above; pianist and composer; at 12, toured the Netherlands and Germany; retired, 1859; wrote technical studies. (4) **Dom.**, Lucca, 1829—Florence, 1890; teacher, critic, theorist, and director.

Bertinot'ti, Teresa, Piedmont, 1776—Bologna, 1854; operatic soprano; m.

Felix Radicati, a violinist and composer.

Bertolli (tōl'-lĭ), **Fran.**, Italian contralto in Händel's operas, London, 1729-37.

Berton (bĕr-tôṅ), (1) **P. Montan,** Paris, 1727—1780; conductor grand opera and dram. composer. (2) **H. Montan,** Paris, 1767—1844; son of above; composer. (3) **François,** Paris, 1784 —1832; natural son of (2); pupil, later prof. of singing, at Cons.; composed operas and songs.

Berto'ni, Fdo Giu., Venice, 1725—Desenzano, 1813; organist and dram. composer.

Bertrand (bĕr-träṅ), **J. Gv.**, Vaugirard, near Paris, 1834—Paris, 1880; writer and critic.

Berwald (bĕr'-vält), (1) **Jn. Fr.**, Stockholm, 1787—1861; precocious violinist, etc.; pupil of Abbé Vogler; composed a symphony at 9. (2) **Fz.**, Stockholm, 1796—1868; nephew of above; dram. composer.

Besekirsky (bā-zĕ-kēr'-shkĭ), (1) **Vasily Vasilevitch,** Moscow, 1835—St. Petersburg, 1910; concert violinist and composer. (2) **Vasily,** b. Moscow, 1879; son of (1); violinist; pupil of his father; 1910-13, prof. Odessa Cons.; after 1914 toured and taught in U. S.

Besler (bās'-lĕr), (1) **Samuel,** Brieg, Silesia, 1574—Breslau, 1625; rector and composer. (2) **Simon,** cantor at Breslau, and composer, 1615-28.

Besozzi (bā-sôd'-zē), the name of 4 brothers, all oboists except (3). (1) **Ales.**, Parma, 1700—Turin, 1775. (2) **Antonio,** Parma, 1707—Turin, 1781; (3) **Girolamo,** Parma, 1713 —1786, bassoonist. (4) **Gaetano,** b. Parma, 1727. (5) **Carlo,** b. Dresden, 1745; oboist, son of (2). (6) **Hieronimo,** d. 1785; son of (3); oboist. His son (7) **Henri** was a flutist, and father of (8) **Louis Désiré,** Versailles, 1814—Paris, 1879; teacher and composer.

Bessems (bĕs'-säms), **A.**, Antwerp, 1809—1868; violinist and composer.

Besson (bŭs-sôṅ), **Gv. Aug.**, Paris, 1820—1875; improver of valves in wind-instruments.

Best, Wm. T., Carlisle, Engl., Aug. 13, 1826—Liverpool, May 10, 1897; org.-virtuoso; pupil of Young; organist at various ch., and the Philh. Society; in 1880, declined knighthood, but accepted Civil-List pen-

sion of £100 per annum; 1894,
retired; 1890 went to Sydney, Australia, to inaugurate the organ in the
new Town Hall; composed overtures,
sonatas, preludes, etc., for organ,
also 2 overtures and march for orch.;
and pf.-pcs.; wrote *"The Art of
Organ-playing,"* etc.

Beständig (bĕ-stĕn'-dĭkh), **Otto,** Striegau, Silesia, Feb. 21, 1835—Wands-
beck, Feb., 1917; cond. and comp.;
pupil of Mettner, etc., in Breslau;
founded a conservatory in Hamburg;
c. oratorio *"Der Tod Baldurs"*[1] and
"Victoria Crucis," etc.

Bet'ti, Adolfo, b. Bagni di Lucca, Italy,
March 21, 1875; violinist; studied
with César Thomson, Liége Cons.,
1st prize, harmony and chamber
music, 1895; gold medal in violin,
1896; début Vienna, 1897; toured in
solo recitals in various European
countries; assist. prof., Brussels
Cons., 1900–03; first violinist, of
Flonzaley Quartet, 1903–29, touring
widely in Europe and U. S.; now
makes home in America, where he is
active as violin teacher; has edited
and arranged early Italian music for
orchestra, including works of Geminiani.

Betz (bĕts), **Fz.,** Mayence, March 19,
1835—Berlin, Aug. 12, 1900; barytone; created "Wotan,"[2] and "Hans
Sachs."

Bev'an, Fr. Chas., b. London, July 3,
1856—Adelaide, 1939; pupil of Willing and Hoyte; organist; then
studied singing with Schira, Deacon,
and Walker; 1877 Gentleman of the
Chapel Royal; composed pop. songs.

Bevignani (bā-vēn-yä'-nē), Cavaliere
Enrico, Naples, Sept. 29, 1841—
Aug. 29, 1903; pupil of Albanese,
Lillo, etc., 1st opera, *"Caterina
Bloom,"*[2] succ.; Czar made him
Knight of the Order of St. Stanislas,
and conferred a life-pension; noted
as cond. in London, Moscow, and
New York; after 1894 at Met. Op.,
N. Y.

Bev'in, Elway, Wales, 1560 (-70 ?)—
1640 (?); Gentleman of the Chapel
Royal; organist, writer, and composer.

Bex'field, Wm. Rd., Norwich, 1824
—London, 1853; organist and composer.

Biaggi (bē-äd'-jē), **Gir. Ales.,** Milan,
1819—Florence, 1897; prof., dram.
composer, writer under pseudonym
"Ippolito d'Albano."

Bianchi (bē-än'-kē), (1) **Fran.,** Cremona, 1752—London, 1810; organ-
ist; composed 47 operas. (2) **Valentine,** Wilna, 1839—Candau, Kurland,
1884; dram. soprano; début, 1855.
(3) **Bianca** (rightly **Schwarz**), b.
Heidelberg, Jan. 28, 1855; dram.-
soprano; pupil of Wilczek and
Viardot-Garcia; Pollini (whom she
m., 1894) paid her tuition and then
engaged her for 10 years; début
Carlsruhe, 1873; taught Munich
Akad., 1902–25; later at Salzburg
Mozarteum. (4) **Eliodoro,** 1773—
1848, a tenor singer who composed
operas; *"Gara d'Amore"* (Bari, 1873);
"Sarah"; *"Almanzor."*[2] (5) **Renzo,**
b. Maggianico, Italy, July 29, 1887;
composer; grad. of Milan Cons.; c.
(operas) *"Fausta"*[2] (Florence), *"Ghismonda"* (La Scala, 1918), *"Ghi-
bellina"*[2] (Costanzi Theat., Rome,
1924), also orch. works.

Biber (bē'-bĕr), (1) **H. Jn. Fz. von,**
Wartenberg, Bohemia, 1644—Salz-
burg, May 3, 1704; violinist, and
one of the founders of the German
school of vln.-playing; Leopold I.
ennobled him. (2) **Aloys,** Ellingen,
1804—Munich, 1858; piano-maker.

Bibl (bēb-'l), (1) **Andreas,** Vienna,
1797—1878 organist and composer.
His son and pupil (2) **Rudolf,**
Vienna, Jan. 6, 1832—Aug. 2, 1902;
pupil of Lechter; organist and composer of organ sonata, etc.

Bie (bē), **Oskar,** b. Breslau, Feb. 9,
1864; critic; pupil of Ph. Scharwenka;
1886, Dr. Phil.; 1890, Privat Docent
at Technical High School, Berlin;
author of books; also comp.

Biehr (bēr), **Oskar,** Dresden, 1851—
Munich, March 7, 1922; violinist;
pupil of David; for twenty-five years
member of Munich court orchestra.

Bierey (bēr'-ī), **Gl. Benedikt,** Dresden,
1772—Breslau, 1840; conductor and
dram. composer.

Biernacki (bē-ĕr-nät'-skē), **Michael
Marian,** b. Lublin, Sept. 9, 1855;
comp.; pupil of Warsaw Cons.; later
director there; comp. 2 masses,
Prologue for orch., etc.

Bignami (bēn-yä'-mē), (1) **Carlo,** Cremona, Dec. 6, 1808—Voghera, Aug.
2, 1848; cond., violinist and dir.,
Cremona; Paganini called him "the
first violinist of Italy."[2] (2) **Enrico,**
1836—Genoa, 1894; violinist, dram.
composer.

Bigot (bē-gō), **M.** (née **Kiene**), Colmar,

Upper Alsatia, 1786—Paris, 1820; pianist.

Bilhon (or **Billon**) (bē-yòṅ), **J. de**, 16th cent.; composer and singer in the Papal Chapel.

Bil'lings, Wm., Boston, Mass., Oct. 7, 1746—Sept. 29, 1800; composed hymns; introduced the pitch-pipe and the 'cello into American church-choirs, and is said to have given the first concert in New England.

Bil'lington, (1) **Th.**, pianist, harpist, and composer, latter part of 18th cent. (2) **Elizabeth** (née **Weichsel**), London, ca. 1768—near Venice, Aug. 23, 1818; pupil of her father, a clarinet-tist; then of J. Chr. Bach; handsome operatic soprano, had a compass of 3 octaves, *a-a'''* 1784, Dublin; 1786, Covent Garden; retired, 1818.

Billrot(h) (bēl'-rōt), (1) **Jn. Gv. Fr.,** Halle, near Lübeck, 1808—Halle, 1836; composer and writer. (2) **Theodor**, Bergen, Isle of Rügen, 1829 —Abbazia, 1894; surgeon and writer.

Bilse (bēl'-sě), **Benj.**, Liegnitz, Aug. 17, 1816—Berlin, July 13, 1902, where 1868-84 he cond. notable popular series of orch. concerts; originally "Stadtmusikus" at Lieg-nitz, and trained a remarkable or-chestra; retired 1894 as "Hofmusi-kus."

Binchois (**Gilles de Binche**, called **Binchois**) (băṅsh-wä), Binche, in Belgian Hainault, ca. 1400—Lille, 1460; one of the early Netherland composers; 3-part chanson, ron-deaux, etc., of his are extant.

Binder (bĭnt'-ĕr), (1) **K. Wm. Fd.,** b. Dresden, 1764; harp-maker at Weimar, ca. 1797. (2) **K.**, Vienna, 1816—1860; conductor and dram. composer.

Bini (bē'nē), **Pasqualino**, b. Pesaro, ca. 1720; violinist.

Bioni (bē-ō'-nē), **A.**, b. Venice, 1698; composed 26 operas.

Birch'all, Robt., d. 1819; music-pub-lisher, London.

Birckenstock (bĕr'-kĕn-shtôk), **Johann Adam**, Alsfeld, 1687—Eisenach, 1733; conductor.

Bird, (1) **Wm.** Vide BYRD. (2) **Arthur**, Cambridge, Mass., July 23, 1856—Berlin, Dec. 22, 1923; pupil of Haupt, Löschhorn, and Rohde, Ber-lin, 1875-77; organist and teacher at Halifax, N. S.; founded the first male chorus in N. S., 1881; studied comp.

and orchestration with Urban, Ber-lin; 1885-86 with Liszt at Weimar; 1886, gave a successful concert, and lived, later, in Berlin-Grünewald; composed symphony and 3 suites for orch.; various pieces for piano; comic opera "*Daphne*" (New York, 1897); and a ballet, "*Rübezahl.*" (3) **Henry Richard**, Walthamstow, Nov. 14, 1842—London, 1915; organist; son of **George B.**, an organist; at 9, be-came org.; pupil of Turle; since 1872 org. at St. Mary Abbots, London; conducted concerts, and won promi-nence as accompanist.

Birnbach (bērn'-bäkh), (1) **K. Jos.**, Köpernick, Silesia, 1751—Warsaw, 1805; conductor. (2) **Jos. Benj. H.**, Breslau, 1795—Berlin, 1879, pianist and composer; son and pupil of above.

Bischoff (bēsh'-ôf), (1) **G. Fr.**, Ellrich, Harz Mts., 1780—Hildesheim, 1841; conductor; founded the German mus. festivals. (2) **L. Fr. Ch.**, Dessau, 1794—Cologne, 1867; translator; son of (3) **K. B.**, court-mus., Dresden. (4) **Kasper Jakob**, Ansbach, 1823—Munich, 1893; teacher and composer. (5) **Hans**, Berlin, 1852—Nieder-schönhausen, near Berlin, 1889; pf.-teacher, conductor, and editor.

Bish'op, (1) Sir **H. Rowley**, London, Nov. 18, 1786—April 30, 1855; noted Engl. composer; pupil of Bianca; his first opera, "*The Circassian Bride*," was prod. Drury Lane, when he was 20; 1810-11 comp. and cond. at Co-vent Garden; 1813 alternate cond. Philh. Soc.; 1825 cond. at Drury Lane; 1830 musical dir. at Vauxhall; 1841-43, prof. music, Edinburgh; knighted, 1842; 1848 prof. of music at Oxford; 1853, Mus. Doc. (Oxon); prod. over 80 operas, farces, ballets, an oratorio, cantata, etc. (2) **J.**, b. Cheltenham, 1814; organist, editor, and composer. (3) **Ann**, or **Anna**, London, 1814—New York, March 18, 1884; soprano; daughter of Jules Rivière; married Sir Henry Bishop, 1831, deserted him for the harpist Bochsa, with whom she toured the world in concert; after his death, in 1856, she married a Mr. Schulz.

Bispham (bĭsp'-hăm), **David**, Philadel-phia, Jan. 5, 1857—New York, Oct. 2, 1921; dram. barytone; sang in church and oratorio; 1885-87 pupil of Vannuccini and Wm. Shakespeare; from 1891 in opera at Covent Garden, and America, with much success and versatility; and also in recitals, in both of which fields his high dramatic intelligence played an unusual part; brilliant in comic or tragic rôles; he had a huge repertoire, including 50 operatic rôles, more than 100 oratorio parts, and some 1500 recital numbers. After 1909 he withdrew from opera and sang in concerts. A brilliant teacher.

Bitt'ner, Julius, b. April, 1874, Vienna, d. there Jan. 9, 1939; composer and jurist; active for many years as a judge in Vienna, he was a pupil in music of Josef Labor and also for a time of Bruno Walter. He is best known for a series of popular operas many of which are written to his own texts, including "*Der Musikant*" (Vienna, 1910), "*Der Bergsee*" (Vienna, 1911), "*Der Abenteurer*" (Cologne, 1912), "*Das Höllisch Gold*" (Dresden, 1916), usually considered his most successful work; "*Die Kohlhaimerin*" (Vienna, 1921); and "*Das Rosengärtlein*" (Mannheim, 1923); also dance plays, piano works, songs, etc.

Bizet (bē-zā), **G. (Alex. César Léopold),** Paris, Oct. 25, 1838—Bougival, June 3, 1875; distinguished composer. At 9, pupil at Paris Cons. of Marmontel (pf.), Benoist (org.), Zimmerman (harm.), and Halévy (whose opera "*Noë*" he finished, and whose daughter Geneviéve he m.); 1857, too, Offenbach 1st prize for an opera buffa, "*Le Docteur Miracle*," prod. at Bouffes Parisiens, 1863; also won the Grand Prix de Rome. In place of the Mass prescribed he sent from Rome a 2-act Ital. opera buffa "*Don Procopio*"; 2 movements of a symphony, "*La Chasse D'Ossian*," an overture; and "*La Guzla de l'Emir*," a comic opera, 1836, his grand opera, "*Les Pêcheurs de Perles*," was prod. Paris (Th. Lyrique); it failed, as did "*La Jolie Fille de Perth*" (1867), and the 1-act "*Djamileh*" (1872). In all his music B. revealed a strong leaning toward Wagner, then so unpopular in France; but 1872 his overture "*Patrie*," the 2 symphonic movements, and incidental music to Daudet's "*L'Arlésienne*," brought him success; and "*Carmen*" (Opéra-Com., March 3, 1875) brought him a fame, which he hardly knew, as he

died three months later of heart disease; he composed also 2 operas, "*Numa*" (1871) and "*Ivan le Terrible*"; 150 pf.-pcs., songs, etc.; collaborated with Délibes, Jonah and Legouix in opera "*Malbrough, s'en va-t-en-guerre*." Biog. by Pigot, 1886, and D. C. Parker, 1926.

Björling, Jussi (Yōō'-sĭ byär'-ling), b. Dalarna, Sweden, February 2, 1910; eminent tenor; son of operatic singer; one of three brothers, all singers, who with father formed quartet and made American concert tour when B. was eight years old, singing in churches, etc.; on return to Sweden B. began vocal study with Julia Svedelius; in 1929 admitted to Royal Op. Sch., Stockholm, where in one year of intensive study under John Forsell, Opera director, he prepared for his début as Don Ottavio (Don Giovanni); won permanent contract there and sang some fifty rôles in less than decade; 1935, made guest appearances in Vienna, Prague and Dresden with sensational success; engaged for America; début N. Y. as soloist on General Motors Radio Hour, with symphony orchestra, 1937-8; same season sang in "*La Bohème*" and "*Rigoletto*" with Chicago Op. Co., and gave concerts; engaged for Met. Op., 1938-9.

Black, Frank, b. Philadelphia; conductor; studied to be chemical engineer, but after graduation decided on musical career; studied piano with Joseffy; active in radio programmes, esp. as cond.; appointed mus. dir. of Nat'l. Broadcasting Co., 1930, in which post has taken leading part in direction of musical programmes; he has appeared as guest cond. with other Amer. orchs.; hon. Mus. D., and Officer with Palms of the French Académie.

Blahag (blä'häkh) (or **Blahak**), **Josef,** Raggendorf, Hungary, 1779—Vienna, 1846; tenor, conductor, and composer.

Blahet'ka (or **Piahet'ka**), **Marie-Léopoldine,** Gumtramsdorf, near Vienna, 1811—Boulogne, 1887; pianist and dram. composer.

Blainville (blăṅ-vē'-yŭ), **Chas. H.,** near Tours, 1711—Paris, 1769; 'cellist, writer, and composer.

Blanchet (blän-shä'), **Emile,** b. Lausanne, Switzerland, July 17, 1877;

pianist and composer; studied at Cologne Cons. and with Busoni; was for three years dir. of Cons. in native city and taught there afterward; c. piano works rich in colour and of refined harmonic style.

Blanckenburgh (blänk'-ĕn-boorkh), **Gerbrandt van**, organist at Gouda, 17th century.

Bland (blänt), (1) **Maria Theresa** (née Romanzini), 1769—1838; pop. Italian singer in England; married an actor, Bland, and had two sons. (2) **Chas.**, tenor. (3) **James**, 1798—1861, bass.

Blangini (blän-jē'-nē), **Giu. Marco, M. Felice**, Turin, 1781—Paris, 1841; organist.

Blankenburg (blänk-ĕn-boorkh), (1) **Quirin van**, Gouda, Holland, 1654—The Hague, ca. 1740; probably son of GERBRANDT VAN BLANCKENBURGH (q. v.); organist and writer. (2) **Chr. Fr. von**, Kolberg, Pomerania, 1744—Leipzig, 1796; Prussian officer and composer.

Blaramberg (blä'-räm-bĕrkh), **Paul I.**, Orenburg, Russia, Sept. 26, 1841—Nice, Feb. 28, 1907; pupil of Balakirew; lawyer, then editor; composed succ. operas, "*Maria Tudor*," (St. Petersburg, 1882); "*The First Russian Comedian*,"; "*Tuschinsky*," (Moscow, 1895).

Blaser'na, Pietro, Fiumicello, Feb. 29, 1836—Rome, 1917; teacher and theorist.

Blasius (bläz'-yüs), **Mathieu Fr.**, Lauterburg, Alsatia, 1758—Versailles, 1829; cond. Op. Comique, Paris; composer.

Blassmann (bläs'-män), **Ad. Jos. M.**, Dresden, 1823—Bautzen, 1891; pianist, court-conductor, and writer.

Blauvelt (blou'-fĕlt), **Lillian**, b. Brooklyn, N. Y., March 16, 1873; soprano; studied Nat. Cons., N. Y., and in Paris; after years of success at home, toured Europe, 1900; decorated in Italy with the order of St. Cecilia; she made her début in opera in "*Faust*," at Covent Garden, 1903, with success; until 1914 sang much in Europe.

Blauwart (blow'-värt), **Emil**, St. Nicholas, Belgium, 1845—Brussels, 1891; barytone.

Blavet (blä-vä), **Michel**, Besançon, Mar. 13, 1700—Paris, Dec. 28, 1768; composer of comic operas, etc.

Blaze (bläz), (1) (Called **Castil-Blaze**), **Fran. H. Jos.**, Cavaillon Vaucluse,

1784—Paris, 1857; "The father of modern French musical criticism"; son and pupil of Henri Sebastian B.; wrote scathing "*L'Opéra en France*," (1820); was made critic on "*Journal des Débats*," where his articles were signed "*XXX*"; transl. libretti of German and Italian operas; composed 3 operas, several "pastiches," etc. (2) **H.**, Baron de Bury, Avignon, 1813—Paris, 1888; son of above; writer.

Blech (bläkh), **Leo**, b. Aachen, April 22, 1871; conductor; pupil of Berlin Hochschule; 1893—1896, cond. at Municipal Theatre, Aachen, and pupil of Humperdinck; 1899—1906, cond. German Landestheatre at Prague; 1906, Royal Opera, Berlin; 1908, cond. first East-Prussian Festival at Königsberg; c. 3 symph. poems, successful 1-act opera, "*Das War Ich*," (Dresden, 1902); 3-act opera "*Aschenbrödel*," (Prague, 1905); "*Versiegelt*," (Hamburg, 1908; New York, 1912); operetta "*Die Strohwitwe*,"; orch. works, etc.; 1925, cond. in Stockholm; after 1926 again at Berlin Op.

Bleichmann (blīkh'-män), **Julius Ivanovitch**, St. Petersburg, Dec. 5, 1868—Jan. 10, 1909; conductor; pupil at the Cons., and of Reinecke and Jadassohn; cond. various orchs. at St. Petersburg; c. 2 operas, chamber music, etc.

Bleuer (bloi'-ĕr), **L.**, Budapest, 1863—Berlin, 1897; violinist; 1883-93, leader of Philh. orch., Berlin; 1894, of Philh. Club, Detroit (Michigan).

Blew'itt, (1) **Jonathan**, London, 1782—1853; organist and director; son and pupil of (2) **Jonas**, organist and writer.

Bleyle (blī'-lĕ), **Karl**, b. Feldkirch, May 7, 1880; pupil of Wehrle and de Lange; later at Stuttgart Cons. and of Thuille; gave up violin on account of nervous affliction of the arm; lived in Munich; c. symph., "*An den Mistral*," (from Nietzsche), for mixed chorus and orch., "*Lernt lachen*," (from Nietzsche's "*Zarathustra*"), do.; symph. poem "*Flagellantenzug*," etc.

Bliss, Arthur, b. London, Aug. 2, 1891; composer; educated Pembroke Coll., Cambridge, and R. Coll. of Mus.; pupil of Stanford, Charles Wood and Vaughan Williams; his early string quartet in A and piano quartet in

A minor were perf. during his period of war service, but though pub., were later withdrawn by him; incid. mus. to *"As You Like It"* heard at Stratford, 1919; his rhapsody for soprano and tenor, flute, *"cor anglais,"* string quartet, and bass (winning Carnegie Pub. Fund award and heard at Salzburg Fest., 1922) and his *"Rout"* (for soprano and chamber orch.) both date from 1920; also c. *"Colour Symphony"* (the movements portraying different colours), heard Three Choirs Fest., 1922; *"Melée Fantasque"* and *"Madame Noy,"* Pastorale, string quartet; concerto for two pianos and orch.; (orch.) *"Two Studies,"* *"Battle Variations,"* *"Hymn to Apollo"*; Introduction and Allegro: Serenade (for barytone and orch.); songs, piano pieces, etc.; his earliest works marked by lively and sometimes ironic touch, freshness and audacity of invention and pronounced modern tendencies; later productions showed a more serious spirit; notably his *"Morning Heroes"* for chorus, orator and orch. (1930); arranged suite of music by Purcell; visited U. S., 1923–25.

Blitzstein (blĭts'-stīn), **Marc**, b. Philadelphia, March 2, 1905; composer; studied piano with Siloti; comp. with Scalero at Curtis Inst. of Mus.; Nadia Boulanger and Schönberg; composer of modern tendencies; c. (orch.) *"Romantic Piece"*; piano concerto; music for film *"Surf and Seaweed"*; (chamber works) *"Gods"* for mezzo-soprano and chamber orch.; *"Serenade"*; string quartet; (opera-farce) *"Triple-Sec"*; (short operas) *"Parabola and Circula"*; *"Harpies"*; *"The Condemned"* (latter written for four choruses); (ballet) *"Cain"*; (song cycle) *"Is Five"*; *"Percussion Music"* and other pieces for piano; mus. play, *"The Cradle Will Rock."*

Bloch (blôkh) (1) **G.**, Breslau, Nov. 2, 1847—Berlin, Feb. 11, 1910; pupil of Hainsch, J. Schubert, Taubert, and F. Geyer; teacher in Breslau's Cons., Berlin; founded Opera Society, 1879; composer. (2) **Ernest**, b. Geneva, Switzerland, July 24, 1880; now American citizen; studied violin with Ysaye; composition with Dalcroze, Rasse, and Knorr; acted as lecturer at Geneva Cons.; conducted symphony concerts, Lausanne

and Neuchatel; made first American tour as conductor for Maud Allan, dancer, 1916; has led owr works with various American orchestras; director of Cleveland Institute of Music, 1920–25; also of San Francisco Cons., 1925–30; received fund with annual income of $5,000 for ten years, beginning 1930, from family of late Jacob and Rosa Stern, San Francisco, on agreement that he devote himself to creative work entirely; c. symphony in C sharp minor (1902); (Symphonic poems) *"Winter-Spring"* (1905); (opera) *"Macbeth"* (Paris Op. Comique, 1910); Prelude and Two Psalms, for sopr. or ten. and orch. (1914); *"Psalm 22"* for bar. or alt. and orch. (1916); *"Israel"* Symphony with 5 solo voices (1915); *"Schelomo,"* Hebrew rhapsody for 'cello and orch. (1916); *"Trois Poèmes Juïfs,"* for orchestra; Suite for viola and piano or orch. (Coolidge Prize, 1919); *"Baal Shem,"* for violin and piano (1923); Concerto Grosso for strings and piano (1925); *"America,"* epic rhapsody for orchestra (won Musical America $3,000 prize, 1927–28); string quartets, piano quintet, violin and piano works; also sacred service for barytone, mixed chorus and orchestra, a setting of Jewish liturgy (1935). B. combines a strong sense of modern orchestral colour, formal ingenuity, and emotional fervour. Racial colouring predominates in many of his works.

Blockx (blôx), **Jan.**, Antwerp, Jan. 25, 1851—May 22, 1912; pianist and composer; pupil, Flemish Mus. School; from 1886, teacher of harm. there; 1901 succeeded Bénoît, at Antwerp Cons.; composed succ. operas, incl. *"Maître Martin,"* etc.

Blodek (blôd-ĕk), (1) **P. Aug. L.**, Paris, 1784—1856; viola-player and dram. composer. (2) **Wm.**, Prague, 1834—1874; prof. and dram. composer.

Blon (blôn), **Franz von**, b. Berlin, July 16, 1861; cond.; pupil of Stern's Cons.; 1898, c. operettas *"Sub rosa"* (Lübeck, 1887); *"Die Amazone"* (Magdeburg, 1903), etc.

Blondeau (blôn-dō), **Pierre Auguste Louis**, Paris, Aug. 15, 1784—1865; viola-player at the Opéra; pupil of the Cons., taking the Prix de Rome, 1808; c. opera, ballet, etc.

Bloom'field-Zeisler (tsīs'-lĕr), **Fanny,**

Bielitz, Austrian Silesia, July 16, 1863—Chicago, Aug. 21, 1927; pianist; at 2 was brought to Chicago, where she lived; played in public at 10; was pupil of Ziehn and Karl Wolfsohn, and 1876-81 of Leschetizky; from 1883 toured America with distinction; from 1893, Germany, Austria, England, and France with great success.

Blow, John (Mus. Doc. Oxon.), Collingham, Nottinghamshire, 1649—Westminster (London), Oct. 1, 1708; organist Westminster Abbey, 1680; was superseded by Purcell, whom he in turn succeeded; he is buried in the Abbey; 1674, organist and (1699) composer to the Chapel Royal; beginning to compose as a boy, he achieved a vast amount of church-music.

Blum (bloom), **K. L.**, Berlin, 1786—July 2, 1844; actor, singer, poet, organist, 'cellist, cond., and composer; chamber-musician to the Prussian Ct., 1822; stage mgr.; prod. nearly 30 operas, ballets, songs, etc.; also vaudevilles, which he introduced to the German stage.

Blumenfeld (bloo'-mĕn-fĕlt), **Felix M.**, Kovalevska, Russia, April 19, 1863 —Moscow, Jan. 23, 1931; pianist; pupil of Th. Stein; took gold medal at St. Petersburg Cons.; composed "Allegro de Concert," with orchestra, etc.; many pf. works; 1898-1912 cond. Imperial Opera, St. Petersburg; also after 1885 prof. at Cons. there. His brothers (2), **Stanislaus**, Kiev, 1850-97, pianist and teacher; (3) **Sigismund**, Odessa, Dec. 27, 1852—St. Petersburg, 1920; song-composer.

Blumenthal (bloo'-mĕn-täl), (1) **Jos. von**, Brussels, 1782—Vienna, 1850, violinist and dram. composer. (2) **Jacob** (Jacques), Hamburg, Oct. 4, 1829—Chelsea, May 17, 1908; pupil of Grund, Bocklet, and Sechter (Vienna), and 1846 of Herz and Halévy; after 1848 in London; pianist to the Queen, and composer. (3) **Paul**, Steinau-on-Oder, Silesia, Aug. 13, 1843—Frankfort-on-Oder, May 9, 1930; pupil of R. A., Berlin, 1870; organist, Frankfort-on-Oder; from 1870, "R. mus. dir."; composed masses, motets, etc.

Blumner (bloom'-nĕr), **Martin**, Fürstenberg, Mecklenburg, Nov. 21, 1827—Berlin, Nov. 6, 1901; pupil

of S. W. Dehn; 1876, cond. of Berlin Singakademie; titles "R. Musik-dir.," and "Prof."; composed 2 oratorios, "Abraham" and "Der Fall Jerusalems"; cantata "Columbus"; "Te Deum," etc.

Blüthner (blüt'-nĕr), **Julius Fd.**, Falkenhain, near Merseburg, March 11, 1824—Leipzig, April 13, 1910; piano-maker, Leipzig, from 1853.

Boccabadati (bôk-kä-bä-dä'-tē), **Luigia**, Parma—Turin, 1850; soprano.

Boccherini (bôk-kĕ-rē'-nē), **Luigi**, Lucca, Italy, Feb. 19, 1743—Madrid, May 28, 1805; 'cellist; toured with success; 1797, made chamber-composer to Friedrich Wilhelm II., of Prussia, in return for a dedication; after the king's death B.'s fortune left him, and he died in dire poverty. His prolific and often fascinatingly graceful compositions include 20 symphonies, an opera, an orchestral suite, a 'cello-concerto, 2 octets, 16 sextets, 125 string-quintets, 12 pf.-quintets, 18 quintets for strings and flute (or oboe), 91 string-quartets, 54 string-trios, 42 trios, sonatas and duets for vln., etc.; biog. by Picquot (Paris, 1851), and Schletternd (Leipzig).

Bochsa (bôkh'-sä), (1) **K.**, Bohemia—Paris, 1821; oboist; music-seller. (2) **Rob. Nic. Chas.**, Montmedy, Meuse, Aug. 9, 1789—Sydney, Australia, Jan. 6, 1856; son and pupil of above; composed a symphony at 9, an opera at 16; pupil of Fr. Beck; harpist to Napoleon and to Louis XVIII.; he eloped with Sir Henry Bishop's wife, made tours in Europe and America, and finally to Australia; composed 9 French operas, prod. in Lyons (1804), and in Paris (1813-16); 4 ballets; an oratorio, etc.; wrote a standard method for harp.

Bock'elmann, Rudolf, b. Bodenteich, Germany, April 2, 1892; barytone; studied at Leipzig Univ.; voice with Oscar Lassner in that city; sang at Neues Theat. there, 1921-26; after latter year heroic rôles at Hamburg Stadtheat.; also guest engagements at Covent Garden, with Chicago Op., etc.; esp. noted for his Wotan and other Wagnerian portrayals.

Bockshorn (bôks'-hôrn) ("Capricornus"), **Samuel**, Germany, 1629—Stuttgart, 1665; composer and conductor.

Bodanzky (bō-däntz'-shkĭ), **Artur,** b. Vienna, Dec. 1877—N. Y., Nov. 23, 1939; grad. Vienna Cons., 1896; début, Budweiss, Bohemia, 1900; from 1896 violinist at the Vienna Op.; in 1901, took up baton activities in native city; in 1903 assistant to Mahler at the Opéra; 1904, cond. Theater an der Wien, Vienna; 1905, at Lortzing Theatre, Berlin; 1906-09, orchestra and theatre cond., Prague; 1909-15, Grand Ducal Theatre, Mannheim, also appearing widely as guest conductor; 1912, Mahler Fest., in Mannheim; 1914, London première of *"Parsifal"*; engaged Met. Op., N. Y., in 1915, where he has since served as principal conductor and leader of German opera performances; in 1919 conducted National Symphony Orchestra (since merged with N. Y. Philharmonic); cond. New York Friends of Music Society in programmes of rare music by older composers, Bruckner, Mahler, etc.

Bodenschatz (bō'-d'n-shäts), **Erhard,** Lichtenberg, Saxony, 1576—Gross-Osterhausen, near Querfurt, 1636; publisher.

Boedecker (bā'-děk-ĕr), **Louis,** Hamburg, 1845—1899; teacher, critic, and composer.

Boehm, Boehme. Vide BÖHM (E).

Boekelman (bā'-kĕl-män), **Bernardus,** Utrecht, Holland, 1838—New York, Aug. 2, 1930; pupil and son of A. J. B.; director, studied with Moscheles, Richter and Hauptmann, at Leipzig Cons.; von Bülow, Kiel, and Weitzmann, at Berlin; from 1866, lived in New York; founded and cond. (till 1888) the N. Y. Trio Club; 1883-97, mus. dir. Miss Porter's School, Farmington, Conn.; later pianist and teacher in New York; composed orch.-pcs., etc.; ed. an analytical edition of Bach's *"Well-tempered Clavichord,"* in colours, etc.

Boëllmann (bwĕl'-män), **Léon,** Ensisheim, Alsatia, 1862—Paris, 1897; composer and teacher.

Boëly (bwĕl'-ē), **Alex. P. Fran.,** Versailles, 1785—Paris, 1858; pianist and composer.

Boers (boors), **Jos. Karel,** Nymwegen, Holland, 1812—Delft, 1896; cond. and writer.

Boesset (bwôs-sā), (1) **A.,** Sieur de Villedieu, ca. 1585—1643; intendant of music to Louis XIII. (2) **J. B.,**

1612—1685; son and successor of above; and in turn succeeded by his son. (3) **C. J. B.,** b. ca. 1636.

Boe'tius (or **Boethius**), **Ani'cius Man'lius Torqua'tus Severi'nus,** Rome ca. 475—executed 524 (?); eminent poet and writer on music.

Bohlmann (bōl'-man), **Th. H. Fr.,** Osterwieck am Harz, Germany, June 23, 1865—Memphis, Tenn., Feb., 1926; pianist; pupil of Dr. Stade, Barth, Klindworth, Tiersch, d'Albert, and Moszkowski; début Berlin, 1890; toured Germany 1890, pf.-prof. Cincinnati Cons.; later head of his own school in Memphis.

Bohm (bōm), **K.,** Berlin, Sept. 11, 1844 —April 4, 1920; pupil of Löschhorn, Reissmann, and Geyer; pianist and composer in Berlin.

Böhm (bām), (1) **G.,** Goldbach, Thuringia, 1661—Lüneburg, 1733; organist and clavichordist; composed important organ preludes and suites. (2) **Elizabeth Riga,** 1756—1797; soprano, m. the actor B. (3) **Theobald,** Munich, April 9, 1793 —Nov. 15, 1881; inv. the "Böhm flute" (vide D. D.); flutist and composer for flute; "Hofmusikus," and player in royal orch. (4) **Jos.,** Pesth, 1795—Vienna, 1876; son and pupil of above; violinist and prof. (5) **Heinrich,** Blatu, Bohemia, 1836— (?); composed 35 operas in Bohemian. (6) **Jos.,** Kühnitz, Moravia, 1841— Vienna, 1893; organist, cond., and director. (7) **Karl,** b. Graz, Aug. 28, 1894; cond. Munich, 1921; 1927, Darmstadt; 1933, dir. Dresden Op.

Böhme (bā'-mĕ), (1) **Jn. Aug.,** 1794; founder of pub. house at Hamburg. His son, (2) **Justus Eduard,** succeeded him in 1839; and his grandson, (3) **August Eduard,** in 1885. (4) **Aug. Julius Fd.,** Ganderheim, Brunswick, 1815—1883; conductor. (5) **Fz. Magnus,** Wellerstedt, near Weimar, 1827—Dresden, 1898; teacher, Dresden, later prof.; composer, writer, and collector.

Böhmer (bā'-mĕr), **K. (Hermann Ehrfried),** The Hague, 1799—Berlin, 1884; dram. composer.

Bohn (bōn), **Emil,** Bielau, near Neisse, Jan. 14, 1839—Breslau, July 5, 1909; organist, 1884, founded the Bohn Choral Society, giving historical concerts; lecturer, writer, critic, and composer; R. Prof. of Music.

Bohnen, Michael (mē'-kĕl bō'-nĕn),

b. Keulen, Germany, Jan. 23, 1888; opera bass; studied Cologne Cons., début in *"Der Freischütz,"* Düsseldorf; has sung in opera at Berlin, Bayreuth, London, Vienna, Barcelona, Stockholm, and New York (member of Met. Op. Co. for a number of years after 1923); also has appeared in motion pictures in Germany; m. Mary Lewis, soprano; divorced.

Böhner (bā'-nĕr), **Jn. L.,** Tôttelstedt, Gotha, 1787—near Gotha, 1860; composer; led a roving life of drunkenness and talent; said to be the original of Hofmann's *"Kreisler"* (vide SCHUMANN); composed opera, etc.

Bohrer (bō'-rer), (1) **Anton,** Munich, 1783—Hanover, 1852; violinist; composer for vln.; a co-member of the Bavarian Court-orch. and concertgiver with his brother, (2) **Max,** Mannheim, 1785—Stuttgart, 1867; 'cellist.

Boïeldieu (bō-ĕld-yŭ), (1) **Fran. Adrien,** Rouen, Dec. 16 (not 15), 1775—Jarcy, near Grosbois, Oct. 8, 1834; son of secretary of Archp. Larochefoucauld and a milliner; apprenticed to the intemperate, brutal cathedral organist Broche, he ran away, at 12, and walked to Paris, but was brought back. He is not known to have had other teaching. At 18, he prod. succ. *"La fille coupable"* (Rouen, 1793); 1795, *"Rosalie et Myrza,"* text of both by his father. Discouraged in a planned Cons. at Rouen, he again walked to Paris, and subsisted as teacher and piano-tuner to Erard. The tenor Garat sang his still pop. songs, in public, and won him a publisher. 1796, *"La Dot de Suzette,"* in one act, was prod. with succ. (Opéra-Com.); 1797, *"La famille Suisse"* (ran 30 nights at the Th. Feydeau); 1798, he pub. sonatas, and a pf.-concerto, etc.; 1800, prof. of piano, Paris Cons. *"Zoraime et Zulnare"* (1798), *"Beniowski,"* and *"Le Calife de Bagdad"* (1800) were succ. and ended his first period, one of light gracefulness. He now studied cpt. seriously, probably with Cherubini, who had criticised him. After 3 years' silence, he reappeared with enlarged powers, succ. in *"Ma Tante Aurore"* (Th. Feydeau, 1803). In 1802 he m. Clotilde Mafleuroy, a ballet-dancer; 1803, he went to St. Petersburg, partially perhaps (but not surely) because of domestic unhappiness, and became cond. of the Imperial Opera, writing by contract 3 operas annually and a number of marches. He returned to Paris, 1811; had immense succ., particularly with *"Jean de Paris,"* 1812; 1817 prof. of comp. at the Cons. and member of Institut; 1821, Chévalier of the Legion of Honour; 1818, *"Le Petit Chaperon rouge"* was succ., followed, after 7 years' silence, by *"La Dame Blanche,"* his masterpiece. His last opera, *"Les Deux Nuits"* (1829), failed. His wife d. 1825, and 1827 he m. Mlle. Phillis, a singer, who was a devoted wife. The poverty of their last years was relieved by Thiers, minister of Louis Philippe, who made him an annuity of 6,000 francs. He died at his country-home, of pulmonary trouble. B.'s work has great vivacity and vitality combined with musical sweetness, and rhythm without jingle. His large gifts in the construction of ensembles are seen in the septet and chorus at the end of the 2d act of *"La Dame Blanche,"* which up to 1875 had been performed 1340 times at the same theatre; its libretto is a combination of 2 of Scott's novels "The Monastery" and "Guy Mannering." He collaborated with Cherubini in *"La Prisonnière"* (1799); with Méhul, Kreutzer, and others, in *"Le Baiser et la Quittance"* (1802); with Cherubini, Catel, and Niccòlo Isouard, in *"Bayard à Mézières,"* with Kreutzer in *"Henri IV. en Voyage"* (1814); with Mme. Gail, in *"Angela"* (1814); with Hérold in *"Charles de France"*; with Cherubini, Berton, and others, in *"La Cour des Fées"* (1821) and *"Pharamond"*; with Auber, in *"Les Trois Genres"*; with Berton, and others, in *"La Marquise de Brinvilliers."* Biog. by A. Pougin, 1875. (2) **Adrien L. V.,** b. Paris, 1816—near Paris, 1883; son and pupil of above; dram. composer.

Boisdeffre (bwä-dĕfr), **Chas. H. Réné de,** Vesoul (Haute-Savoie), 1838—Vézelise, Dec., 1906; Chev. of Legion of Honour; composer of religious and chamber music, the latter taking Chartier prize, 1883.

Boise (bois), **Otis Bardwell,** Oberlin, Ohio, Aug. 13, 1844—Baltimore,

Md., Dec. 16, 1912; organist; 1861 pupil of Hauptmann, Richter, Moscheles, etc., Leipzig; 1864, of Kullak, at Berlin; 1864-70, organist and teacher in Cleveland; 1870-76, in New York; 1876-78, spent in Europe; for some years prominent in Berlin as a teacher; 1901, settled in Baltimore; composed symphonies, overtures, pf.-concertos, etc., wrote *"Music and Its Masters"* (1902), etc.

Boismortier (bwä-môrt-yä), **Josef Bodin De**, Perpignan, ca. 1691—Paris, ca. 1765; c. ballet operas, cantatas, etc.

Boisselot (bwäs-lō), (1) **J. Louis**, Montpellier, 1785—Marseilles, 1847; piano-maker at Marseilles; his eldest son (2) **Louis** (1809—1850) was the manager. His grandson, (3) **François**, was later the proprietor. (4) **Xavier**, Montpellier, 1811—Marseilles, 1893; second son of above; composer.

Boïto (bō-ē'-tō), **Arrigo**, Padua, Feb. 24, 1842—Milan, June 10, 1918; poet, soldier, novelist, editor, essayist, librettist, and composer; son of an Italian painter and a Polish woman. Pupil, 1853-62, of Milan Cons., almost dismissed for mus. incompetence (cf. VERDI); composed 2 cantatas, *"Il 4 di Giugno"* (1860), and *"Le Sorelle d'Italia"* (1862), in collab. with Faccio; they met with such great succ. that the Govt. gave F. and B. funds for 2 years in Paris and Germany. B. had already taken up Goethe's *"Faust,"* long before Gounod, at the suggestion of his bro. Camillo, an eminent architect. B. brought back from Germany a passion for Beethoven, then little heeded in Italy. 1867 at Paris, as journalist; then Poland, where he sketched out text and music of *"Mefistofele,"* which was prod. at Milan, 1868 (La Scala), after 52 rehearsals, and with great hopes; but it was then in a rather shapeless state, and Gounod's *"Faust"* having meanwhile been prod. at Milan with succ., B.'s work was hissed by some, and having provoked riots and duels was withdrawn by order of the police. It was remodelled with more attention to stage requirements and prod. with great succ. at Bologna, Oct. 4, 1875. An earlier opera, *"Ero e Leandro,"* was never prod., B. lending his own libretto to Botte-

sini, and later to Mancinelli. Other libretti of his are, Ponchielli's *"Gioconda,"* Verdi's *"Otello"* and *"Falstaff,"* Faccio's *"Amleto"* and Coronaro's *"Un Tramonto."* His opera, *"Nerone,"* on which he worked for many years and which was repeatedly announced for production, finally saw the stage posthumously when Toscanini cond. the work at La Scala, with great scenic splendour of production, May 1, 1924, before a distinguished international audience. Its succ. proved not to be lasting. B. translated 2 of Wagner's libretti into Italian, and wrote often under the pseud. "Tobia Gorrio." The King made him "Cavaliere" and "Commendatore"; 1892, Inspector-Gen. of Technical Instruction in the Italian Cons. and Lyceums; 1895 Chevalier of the Legion of Honour.

Bok, Mary Louise Curtis (Mrs. Edward Bok), b. Boston, Aug. 6, 1876; music patron; d. of Cyrus H. K. Curtis and Louisa (Knapp); founder (1923) and pres. Curtis Institute of Music, Philadelphia, est. in memory of her father, the prominent publisher; also active in many other musical and civic philanthropies.

Bolck (bôlk), **Oskar**, Hohenstein, 1839—Bremen, 1888; dram. composer.

Bolm, Adolph, b. St. Petersburg, Russia, Sept. 25, 1884; dancer and ballet director; educated Imp. Ballet School; début, Maryinsky Theatre, St. Petersburg, 1904; soloist, Diaghileff Ballet Russe, 1909-17; org. his own ballet company, 1917; has also directed ballets and appeared as soloist at Met. Op. House, N. Y.

Bölsche (bĕl'-shĕ), **Franz**, b. Wegenstedt, Aug. 20, 1869—Bad Oeynhausen, 1935; theorist; pupil Berlin Royal Hochschule; 1896, teacher Cologne Cons.; c. overture *Judith*, etc.

Bomtempo (bōm-täm'-pō), **João Domingos**, Lisbon, 1775—1842; pianist, director, and writer.

Bona (bō'-nä), **Giov.**, Mondovi, 1609—Rome, 1674; cardinal and composer.

Bonawitz (bō'-nä-vēts) (or **Bonewitz**), **Jn. H.**, Dürkheim-on-Rhine, Dec. 4, 1839—London, Aug. 15, 1917; pupil Liége Cons. till 1852, then brought to America; 1872-73 cond. "Popular Symphony Concerts," New York; 1873, toured U. S.; prod. 2 operas in Philadelphia; 1876, ret. to Europe; lived in Vienna and London.

Bonci (bôn'chē), **Alessandro**, b. Cesena, Feb. 10, 1870—Milan, Aug. 10, 1940; lyric tenor; at 7 sang in choir, studied singing with Coen at Pesaro Lyceum for 5 years; then member of choir at Loreto; operatic début in *"Falstaff"*; sang with great success at Covent Garden, 1900, and in 1908 at Metropolitan Opera House; toured U. S., 1911-12; 1912-13, Chicago Op. Co.

Bond, Carrie Jacobs, b. Janesville, Wis.; composer; studied with Bischoff; c. many songs of ballad variety, usually with sentimental texts, among which wide popularity has been won by *"A Perfect Day," "Just A-Wearyin' For You,"* and *"I Love You Truly"*; also composed scores for motion pictures.

Bonel'li, Richa'rd, b. Port Byron, N. Y.; barytone; educated Syracuse Univ.; studied voice with Arthur Alexander and William Vilonat; début as Valentine, Brooklyn, N. Y., 1915; member San Carlo Opera, in America; later sang with Monte Carlo Op., La Scala Op., Milan and in Germany; member Chicago Civic Op., 1925-31; since 1933 with Met. Op. Co.; m. Pauline Cornelys, soprano.

Bönicke (bä'-nĭ-kě), **Hermann**, Endorf, 1821—Hermannstadt, Transylvania, 1879; conductor, composer, and writer.

Bo'niforti, Carlo, Arona, Sept. 25, 1818—Trezzo d'Adda, Dec. 10, 1879; organist and comp.

Bonini (bō-nē'-nē), **Severo**, b. Florence, 17th century; Benedictine monk, one of the first writers in monodic style; c. madrigals, etc., 1607-13.

Boniventi (bō-nĭ-věn'-tē) (or **Boneventi**), **Gius**, b. Venice, ca. 1660; conductor and dram. composer.

Bonnet (bŭn-nā), (1) **Jacques**, Paris, 1644—1724; writer. (2) **J. Bap.**, b. Montauban, 1763; organist and composer. (3) **Joseph**, b. Bordeaux, France, March 17, 1884; organist; studied with Tournemire, Gédalge, and Guilmant; 1st prize, organ playing and improvisation, Paris Cons., 1906; won competition in 1906 as organist at St. Eustache, Paris; organist Société des Concerts du Conservatoire, 1911-20; soloist with various European and American orchestras; has made many tours of Canada and U. S.

Bonno (bôn'-nō) (or **Bono**), **Jos.**, Vi-

enna, 1710—1788; court-cond. and dram. composer.

Bononcini (bō-nôn-chē'-nē), (1) **Giov. M.**, Modena, 1640—Nov. 19, 1678; conductor, composer, and writer of Bologna. (2) Who usually wrote it **Buononcini** (boo-ō-nôn-chē'-nē), **Giov. Bat.**, Modena, 1660 (?)—Venice (?), 1750 (?); son and pupil of above; studied with Colonna and Buoni ('cello), at Bologna; 1685-91, pub. 7 vols. masses and instr. mus.; in 1690, court 'cellist of Vienna; 1694, Rome, prod. 2 operas, *"Tullo Ostilio"* and *"Serse"*; 1699-1701 prod. 2 operas at Vienna; 1703-05, at Berlin as court-composer; prod. *"Polifemo"* (1703); ret. to Vienna, where 6 new operas were prod. In 1716, invited to London as cond. and composer for the new King's Theatre, and to rival Händel; this provoked a famous and bitter war with some success for **B.**, who prod. 8 operas, 1702-27; but in 1731 he was caught in a plagiarism from A. Lotti (a crime of which Händel was by no means guiltless himself); 1733 an alchemist swindled him from affluence to bankruptcy. Later he appeared in Paris and prod. a motet for the "Chapelle royale," playing the 'cello-accomp. before the King; 1737 his opera *"Alessandro in Sidone,"* and an oratorio, *"Ezechia,"* were prod. in Vienna; 1748, he was called to Vienna to write peace-festival music and later went to Venice as theatre-composer, a post retained at least till he was 90. (3) **Marc An.**, Modena, 1675 (?)—1726; bro. of above; court-cond. there; prod. 11 operas highly rated by Padre Martini; also composed an oratorio.

Bonporti (bôn-pôr'-tē), **F. A.**, Trent, ca. 1660; Imperial Counsellor and composer.

Bontempi (bôn-těm'-pē) (surnamed **Angelini**), **Giov. Andrea**, Perugia, ca. 1624—Bruso, near Perugia, 1705, dram. composer and writer.

Bonvin (bôn-văn), **L.**, b. Siders, Feb. 17, 1850—Buffalo, Feb. 18, 1939; self-taught; studied medicine, Vienna; entered Jesuit novitiate in Holland; became organist and choir-master; from 1887, mus. dir. Canisius College, Buffalo, N. Y.; pub. masses, etc.

Boom (bōm), (1) **Jan. E. G. van** (Senior), b. Rotterdam, April 17,

1783; flutist and composer for flute. (2) **Jan.** (Jns.) **van,** Utrecht, 1807—Stockholm, 1872; son of above; pianist, professor, and dram. composer. (3) **Hermann M. van,** Utrecht, 1809—1883; son and pupil of (1); flutist.

Boo′sey, Thos. (1825), founded the London pub. house of Boosey & Co.

Boott, Francis, Boston, Mass., June 21, 1813—Cambridge, Mass., March 2, 1904; pupil of L. Picchianti, in Florence; lived in Cambridge, Mass.; composed under pseud. **"Telford."**

Bopp, Wilhelm, Mannheim, Nov. 4, 1863—Bühler Höhe, June 11, 1931; pupil of Leipzig Cons., and of Emil Paur; 1884, dir. in Freiburg; 1886, assistant to Mottl at Bayreuth; 1889, teacher at Mannheim Cons.; 1900, opened a High School of Music; 1907–19, dir. Royal Cons., Vienna; cond. His wife, born **Glaser,** a court opera singer at Stuttgart.

Bordes (bôrd), **Charles,** Vouvray-sur-Loire, May 12, 1863—Toulon, Nov. 8, 1909; composer; important figure in the revival of French church music; pupil of César Franck; 1887, church-conductor at Nogent-sur-Marne; 1889 commissioned by the govt. to collect Basque folk music; from 1890 chapel-master at St. Gervais, Paris; founder of the *"Association of the Singers of St. Gervais"* and of the *"Schola Cantorum de St. G.,"* 1898 with d'Indy and Guilmant; 1905 retired to Montpellier and founded a *Schola* there; 1909 went to Nice to give a concert and died on his way home. He resuscitated many forgotten master works, and wrote many articles on them; c. *"Phantasie"* and *"Rapsodie Basque"* for orch.; opera *"Les trois Vagues,"* religious music, choruses, and songs and piano pieces.

Bordese (bôr-dā′-zĕ), **Luigi,** Naples, 1815—Paris, 1886; singing teacher and dram. composer.

Bordier (bôrd-yä), (1) **L. Chas.,** Paris, 1700—1764; abbé, conductor, composer, and writer. (2) **Jules,** 1846 (?) —Paris, 1896; dram. composer.

Bordogni (bôr-dōn′-yē), **Giulio Marco,** Gazzaniga, Bergamo, 1788—Paris, July 31, 1856; distinguished tenor and singing teacher; prof. Paris Cons.; pub. standard *"Vocalises."*

Bordo′ni, Faustina. Vide HASSE, FAUSTINA.

Borghi (bôr′-gē), **Luigi,** Italian violinist, came to London, ca. 1774; pub. symphonies, excellent music for vln., etc.

Borghi-Mamo (mä′-mō), (1) **Adelaide,** Bologna, 1826—1901; mezzo-soprano; début, 1846, at Urbino, where she was engaged; then in Vienna and Paris; later lived in Florence; her daughter (2) **Erminia,** soprano; début 1874, Bologna; sang in Italy and Paris.

Borgioli (bôr-jō′-lē), **Dino,** b. Florence, Italy; operatic tenor; became member of Dal Verme Op., Milan, 1918, following war service; has sung at Costanzi, Rome; San Carlo, Naples; Covent Garden, London; Monte Carlo, Lisbon, Madrid, and La Scala Op., Milan, also as assisting artist to Dame Nellie Melba in tour of Australia, 1924; came to America, 1928, making début in California; New York début, Dec., 1930, and sang with Met. Op. Co., N. Y., 1934.

Bori (bō′-rē), **Lucrezia** (rightly **Borgia**), b. Valencia, Spain, Dec. 24, 1888; noted soprano; pupil of Vidal; made début at Rome, in *"Carmen,"* 1908, singing rôle of Micaela; appeared in other leading opera theatres with succ., incl. Naples, Milan, Buenos Aires, and at Paris in 1910 when the Met. Op. Co. made a guest appearance there; 1912–13, made début with that company in *"Manon"* in the autumn at New York; quickly became one of most popular members of forces; owing to vocal indisposition, retired for brief period in 1915, but returned to New York several seasons later and resumed place as an important singer, esp. in lyric rôles; member of Met. Op. until 1935–36, portraying large variety of French, Italian, Spanish, and English parts; a distinguished actress and an exemplary vocalist; she took active part in assisting company to raise fund to cover deficit in 1933–34, and was elected a member of the Met. Op. board of directors.

Borodin (bō′-rō-dēn), **Alex. Porphyrjevitch,** St. Petersburg, Nov. 12, 1834—Feb. 29, 1887; composer of the neo-Russian school; Prof. at the St. P. Medico-surg. Institute; Counsellor of State; Knight; pres. Mus. Soc. of Amateurs; at Balakirev's suggestion studied music; composed opera, *"Prince Igor"* (finished after his death by Rimsky-Korsakov, and prod. succ. 1891); 3 symphonies, A flat, B minor, and A minor (last left incomplete, ed. by Glazounov), symphonic poem, "*On the Steppes of Central Asia*"; scherzo for orch., 2 string-quartets, piano quintet; string trio; pf. pcs., etc.; biog. by A. Habets, in English, London, 1895. Memoirs by Stassov and Gerald Abraham also published.

Boroni (bō-rō'-nē) (or **Buroni**), **A.,** Rome, 1738—1792; court-conductor.

Borovsky (bōr-ŏf'-skē), **Alexandre,** b. Libau, Russia, March 19, 1889; pianist; studied at Petersburg Cons. with Essipov.; studied to be lawyer; won gold medal and Rubinstein prize as pianist, 1912; taught at Moscow Cons. after 1915; following 1920 he made tours of France, England, Germany, and U. S.

Borowski (bōr-ŏf'-skē), **Felix,** b. Burton, Engl., March 10, 1872; studied Cologne Cons. and London; taught composition and history, Chicago Musical College, 1897; pres. of this school, 1916–24; music ed., Chic. *Eve. Post*, 1908, and Chic. *Herald*, 1909–17; ed. programme book, Chic. Symph. Orch.; c. orchestral and chamber music works, organ, piano, and other pieces; (ballet) "*Boudour*" (Chic. Op., 1919).

Bortnianski (bōrt-nyän'-shkĭ) (or **Bartñansky**) **Dimitry Stepanovitch,** Gluchov, Ukraine, 1751—St. Petersburg, Sept. 28 (Oct. 9), 1825; choir dir. and dram. composer, called "the Russian Palestrina"; pupil of Galuppi, under patronage of Empress Catherine, 1779–96 dir. of her choir; then of her orchestra.

Bor'wick, Leonard, Walthamstow, Essex, Engl., 1868—Le Mans, France, Sept. 17, 1925; pianist; pupil H. R. Bird, and Clara Schumann, B. Scholtz, and Ivan Knorr at Frankfort Cons.; début, at London Philh. Concert, 1890; toured Europe, 1895–96; 1914, U. S.

Bos (bōs), **Coenraad V.,** b. Leiden, Dec. 7, 1875; pianist; studied Amsterdam Cons.; played in Berlin, a member of the "Dutch Trio" with J. M. van Veen and J. van Lier; after 1908 toured U. S. as accompanist to noted singers; also active as vocal coach.

Boschetti (bŏs-kĕt'-tē), **Viktor,** Frankfort-on-Main, Aug. 13, 1871—April

12, 1933; pupil of Prague Cons.; organist at Vienna (1896–1921, St. Stephen's Cath.); and Dir. Court Opera, 1900–03; c. 5 operas, church music, etc.

Bösendorfer (bā'-zĕn-dôrf-ĕr), firm of Vienna pf.-makers founded by (1) **Ignaz B.,** Vienna, 1796—1859, later managed by his son (2) **Ludwig,** b. Vienna, 1835.

Bosio (bō'-zĭ-ō), **Angiolina,** Turin, 1830—St. Petersburg, 1859; mezzo-soprano.

Bos'si, (bôs'-sē), (1) **Pietro B.,** Morbegno, 1834—1896; organist. (2) **Marco Enrico,** Salè, Brescia, Italy, April 25, 1861—Feb. 21, 1925, while returning from America; son and pupil of above, 1881–91, conductor and organist at Como Cath.; then till 1895, prof. of org. and harm. Naples; 1896, dir. and prof. Liceo Benedetto Marcello, Venice; 1902–12, dir. Bologna Liceo; after 1916, dir. Liceo of Santa Cecilia, Rome; member of the permanent govt. commission for musical art, Chevalier of the Italian Crown and of the Spanish order of Isabella la Catolica; composed 2 1-act operas, "*Paquita*" and "*Il Veggente*"; 4-act melodrama "*L'Angelo Della Notte*" (Como); symph. poem "*Il Cieco*" (1897), with tenor solo, and chorus; "*Westminster Abbey*," *Inno di Gloria*, for chorus and organ, Requiem Masses, etc.; wrote important "*Metodo di Studio per l'Organo moderno*," with G. Tebaldini (Milan, 1893). (3) **Renzo,** b. Como, Italy, April 9, 1883; composer, pianist; son of (2); active as conductor in Italy, Germany, and Austria; later prof. of organ and comp. at Parma Cons.; and then of comp. at Milan Cons.; appeared widely with the Polo and Bolognese Quartets; c. orch., chamber and vocal works, also stage music, incl. "*Volpino*," which won a national lyric prize and was given at the Carcano Theat., Milan, 1924.

Bote und Bock (bō'-tŭ̌ oont bôk), firm of mus. pubs., Berlin, est. 1838 by Eduard Bote and Gustav Bock.

Bott (bôt), **Jean Jos.,** Cassel, March 9, 1826—New York, April 30, 1895; violinist; son and pupil of a court-musician; 1852, court-conductor; 1878 pensioned; 1885 came to New York; composed 2 operas, etc.

Bot'ta, Luca, Italy, 1882—New York,

1917; tenor; sang with Pacific Coast Op. Co., 1912; after 1914 until his death, mem. of Met. Op. Co., also appearing in South America with success.

Bottée, de Toulmon (dŭ toomôṅ bôt-tā), Aug., Paris, 1797—1850; 'cellist and writer.

Bottesini (bôt-tĕ-sē'-nē), **Giov.**, Crema, Lombardy, 1821—Parma, 1889; double-bass virtuoso; conductor and dram. composer.

Bottrigari (bôt-trē-gä'-rē), **Ercole**, Bologna, Aug. 1531—S. Alberto, Sept. 30, 1612; wrote 3 learned theoretical treatises, each called by the name of a friend (a) Patrizio, (b) Desiderio, and (c) Melone.

Boucher (boo-shā), **Alex J.**, Paris, April 11, 1778—Dec. 29, 1861; vln.-virtuoso; a charlatan but amazing in technic; played before the court at 6; composed vln.-concertos; his wife was a clever harpist, also eccentric, playing duets with one hand on harp and one on a piano.

Boughton (bow'-tŏn), **Rutland**, b. Aylesbury, England, Jan. 23, 1878; composer; educated, Royal College of Music, London; studied with Stanford and Walford Davies; teacher at Birmingham School of Music; founder, Glastonbury Festival, 1914, aim of which was to produce music dramas based on Arthurian legend; c. (operas) "*The Immortal Hour*" (London, 1922) which had a long run and subsequent revivals, also having brief New York production without pronounced success; "*Bethlehem*" (London, 1923); "*Alkestis*" (Covent Garden Op., 1924); also choral works "*The Birth of Arthur*," "*The Skeleton in Armor*," "*The Invincible Armada*"; in 1921–22 **B.** founded the Bristol Fest. School; he has also c. chamber music.

Bouhy (boo'-ē), **Jacques**, Pepinster, Belgium, 1848—Paris, 1929; barytone; pupil at Liège Cons., then Paris Cons.; 1871 the Opéra Paris; after 1872 at Opéra Comique creating the Toreador rôle in "*Carmen*," etc.; 1885–89, director of New York Conservatory; returned to Paris Opéra; later a famous teacher; c. songs.

Bouichère (bwē-shăr), **Émile**, 1860 (?)—Paris, Sept. 4, 1895; pupil of G. Lefèvre's Acad.; est. a vocal acad. 1892; composed valuable sacred and chamber music.

Boulanger (boc-läṅ-zhā), (1) **Marie Julie** (née **Halliger**), 1786—1850; dram. singer. (2) **Henri Alex, André Ernest**, Paris, Dec. 16, 1815—April 14, 1900. Son of above. Pupil of Lesueur and Halévy at the Cons., taking Grand Prix de Rome, 1835; prof. there 1871. Composed many operettas for Opéra Comique. Legion of Honour, 1868. (3) **Nadia**, b. Paris, Sept. 16, 1887; studied Paris Cons., 1st prizes in harmony, organ and accompanying, fugue and counterpoint; third Rome Prix; teachers incl. Chapuis, Guilmant, Vierne, Vidal, Fauré and Widor; prof. of harmony, counterpoint, history of music, at École Normale, Paris; prof. history of music and harmony, American Cons., Fontainebleau; has had among her pupils many of the younger American composers. (4) **Lili**, Paris, Aug. 21, 1893—March 15, 1918; composer; sister of (3); trained at Paris Cons.; won Prix de Rome, 1913; composed various orch., chamber music, and vocal works of considerable promise and left incomplete at her early death the opera "*La Princesse Maleine*."

Boult (bōlt), **Sir Adrian**, b. Chester, Engl., April 8, 1889; ed. Westminster School, Christ Church, Oxford; studied Leipzig Cons.; Mus. D., Oxford; début as conductor, Covent Garden Op., 1914; led Birmingham Orch., 1923–36; London Bach Choir, after 1928; guest cond., Royal Philharmonic Soc., London Symphony and Queens Hall Orch.; prof. conducting at Royal College of Music since 1919; cond., Patron's Fund Concerts and of British Broadcasting Corp. Orch.; visited America as guest cond. of Boston Symph. Orch., 1935. Knighted, 1937.

Bouman (boo'-man), **Martin G.**, Herzogenbusch, Holland, Dec. 29, 1858—Gouda, May 11, 1901; pupil of Brée and Holl; city director at Gouda; c. operas, masses, etc.

Bourgault-Ducoudray (boor-gō-dü-koo-drĕ), **Louis-Albert**, Nantes, Feb. 2, 1840—Vernouillet, July 4, 1910; pupil of Thomas at Paris Cons., taking Grand Prix de Rome, 1862; prof. of mus. hist. at the Cons. 1878; wounded as volunteer at siege of Paris; later visited Greece and wrote on Oriental. music.

Bourgeois (boor'-zhwä), (1) **Loys**

(**Louis**), Paris, ca. 1510—(?); disciple of Calvin; 1545–57, Geneva; one of the first to harmonise the French melodies; wrote "*Le droict chemin de musique*," proposing the naming the tones after solmisation-syllables, a system since prevalent in France. (2) **Louis Thomas**, Fontaine l'Évêque, 1676—Paris, 1750; tenor and composer; d. in poverty.

Bourges (boorzh), (1) **Clémentine de**, d. 1561; notable woman-composer. (2) **J. Maurice**, Bordeaux, 1812—Paris, 1881; critic and dram. composer.

Bousquet (boos-kā), **G.**, Perpignan, 1818—St. Cloud, 1854; conductor at the Paris Opéra (1847); critic and dram. composer.

Bovéry (bō-vā-rē), **Jules** (rightly **Bovy** (bō'-vē), **A. Nic. Jos.**), Liége, 1808—Paris, 1868; self-taught violinist, conductor and dram. composer.

Bovy (bō'-vē), (1) **Chas. Sml.** (known under pseud. **Lysberg**), Lysberg, near Geneva, 1821—Geneva, 1873; composer. (2) **Vina**, b. Ghent; soprano; début Met. Op., 1936.

Bo'wen, York, b. London, Feb. 22, 1884; composer and pianist; 1898—1905, pupil of the R. A. M.; then piano teacher there; c. 3 pf.-concertos; symph. fantasia for orch., concerto and sonatas for the viola; Phantasy Trio; string quartet, pf.-pieces, etc.

Bow'man, Ed. Morris, Barnard, Vt., July 18, 1848—Brooklyn, N. Y., Aug. 27, 1913; pupil Wm. Mason, and J. P. Morgan, at New York, 1866; 1867–70, organist St. Louis, Mo.; studied in Berlin and Paris, 1873; 1874, St. Louis; 1881 studied under Bridge, Macfarren, Turpin, and Guilmant; was the first American to pass the examination of the London R. Coll. for Organists; 1884, one of the founders of Amer. Coll. of Musicians; organist, Brooklyn, N. Y.; 1891–95, prof. of music Vassar Coll.; 1895 founded the "Temple Choir," Brooklyn (200 voices); cond. also the Newark Harmonic Soc. and the Cecilian Choir.

Boyce (bois), **Wm.**, London, 1710—Kensington, 1779; organist and composer.

Boyd, Chas. N., Pleasant Unity, Pa., Dec. 2, 1875—Pittsburgh, April 24, 1937; pupil of Fred K. Hodge, Leo Oehmler, and von Kunits; grad. Univ. of Pittsburgh: Mus. D.. 1926;

beginning 1894 active in that city as conductor and organist; after 1903, instructor in church music, Western Theol. Sem.; 1915 appointed dir. Pittsburgh Mus. Inst.; after 1924, treasurer, Nat'l Ass'n. of Schools of Music; ass't. ed. Amer. vol., *Grove's Dictionary*; author of articles on music.

Boyle, Geo. Frdk, b. Sydney, Australia, June 29, 1886; pianist, composer and teacher; 1910, at Peabody Cons., Baltimore; later at Curtis Inst. of Music; then at Inst. of Musical Art, Juilliard School, N. Y.; c. piano concerto, which he cond. with success Feb. 1912 at New York Phil. concert; also chamber works, cantatas, etc.

Brade (brä'-dĕ), **Wm.**, b. England, lived and died at Frankfort, 1630; player of the viol, etc.

Brad'ford, Jacob, London, June 3, 1842—April 19, 1897; organist; pupil of Goss and Steggal; Mus. Doc. Oxford, 1878; 1892 organist at St. Mary's, Newington; c. oratorio "*Judith*"; "*Sinfonia Ecclesiastica*" with double chorus; overtures, etc.

Bradsky (brät'-shkē), **Wenzel Th.**, Rakovnik, Bohemia, 1833—1881; dram. composer.

Braga (brä'-gä), **Gaetano**, Giulianova, Abruzzi, June 9, 1829—Milan, Nov. 21, 1907; 'cellist, pupil of C. Gaetano (1841–52); lived at Florence, Vienna, Paris, and London and toured Europe; dram. composer; also wrote "*Metodo di Violoncello*."

Braham (rightly **Abraham**), **J.**, London, 1774—Feb. 17, 1856; noted tenor; compass 3 octaves; composed pop. ballads.

Brahms (bräms), **Johannes**, Hamburg, May 7, 1833—Vienna, April 3, 1897; son and pupil of a double-bass player in the Hamburg City Theatre, later studied with Marxsen of Altona; début Hamburg, at 14, playing his own variations on a folk-song; 1853, toured with Remenyi. Joachim heard him and sent him to Schumann, at Düsseldorf. Schumann, with characteristic openness of mind) and enthusiasm, pub. an article in the *Neue Zeitschrift für Musik*, greeting B. as the new Messiah of music, a welcome that was a mixture of blessing and bane, embarrassing the young **Brahms** with a mission that was a white elephant on his hands; for he forsook the romanticism which Schumann, and later Liszt expected of him, and took up a determined classicism in the matter of form, in which, however, he made many modifications to suit his enormous intellectuality and technical resource. This early welcome also gave him over to be bandied between believers like Hanslick who were frantic to find an opponent to the progress of Wagner, and sceptics who would not have him praised for any quality. Schumann's advocacy did not save B.'s publication and concert performance of his 3 pf.-sonatas and 3 books of songs from failure. After serving for a time as cond. to the Prince of Lippe-Detmold, he retired for study to Hamburg, 1858–62. 1862 Vienna; 1863–64 cond. of the *Singakademie* there; 1864–69 Hamburg, Zurich, Baden-Baden, etc., and made tours with Stockhausen; 1869, Vienna, which was afterward his headquarters. In 1871–74, cond. "Gesellschaft der Musikfreunde." In 1877 Cambridge University offered him the degree of Mus. Doc., which offer he ignored, accepting, 1881, Dr. Phil. from Breslau and writing in acknowledgment the "*Akademische Festouvertüre*"; 1886, a knight of the Prussian Ordre pour le Mérite, with voting privilege, and a member of the Berlin Acad. of Arts. 1889 presented with the freedom of Hamburg. His "*German Requiem*," op. 45 (the first 3 choruses given in Vienna, 1867), was given complete in the Bremen cathedral, April, 1868, and established him on a peak where he has since remained while the storms of debate rage below him. He wrote in almost every form but opera (he had considered that at one time) but admitted he "knew nothing about the theatre." He valued Wagner's scores, and owned several Wagner autographs; Wagner, however, said "Brahms is a composer whose importance lies in not wishing to create any striking effect." His first symphony, on which he had spent 10 years, made a sensation when prod. 1876. His vln.-concerto when first shown to Joachim was so impossible to the vln. that J. laughed at it till tears poured down his cheeks; he is said to have materially assisted in its

revision. **Brahms** was a brilliant pianist in his youth; in his 20th year, at a concert with Remenyi, the piano was discovered to be a semitone below concert-pitch; B., playing without notes, transposed the accompaniment to Beethoven's "*Kreutzer Sonata*," a semitone higher throughout. (Beethoven similarly transposed his own concerto in C to C♯ at a rehearsal.)

COMPOSITIONS (exclusive of Songs for one voice with pf.). For orch. Symphonies, Op. 68, in C minor, Op. 73, D, op. 90, F, op. 98, E minor; overtures, op. 80, "*Akademische Festovertüre*"; op. 81, "*Pragische Ouvertüre*"; op. 11–16, serenades; op. 56, variations on a theme of Haydn's. CHAMBER MUSIC. Op. 8, trio for pf., vln., 'cello; 18, 36, sextet for strings; 40, trios, pf., vln., horn; 114, pf., clar. and 'cello; 51, two string-quartets; 67, string-quartet; 88, 111, string-quintet; 115, quintet for clar. and strings.

For piano, op. 1, 2 and 5, sonatas, 4, scherzo; variations on a theme by Schumann; 10, four ballads; 15, 83, concertos; 21, 35, variations; 24, variations and fugue on theme by Händel; op. 76, 8 pcs.; 79, 2 Rhapsodies; 116, Fantasien; 117, 3 Intermezzi; 118, 6 Clavierstücke (3 Intermezzi, Ballades, Romanze); 119, 4 Clavierstücke (3 Intermezzi, Rhapsodie;—unnumbered—Gluck's gavotte, and 2 studies). For piano, 4 hands, op. 23, variations on a theme by Schumann; 34, sonata arr. from op. 34; 39, 16 waltzes; op. 25, 26, 60, pf.-quartets; 34, pf.-quintet; 87, 101, pf.-trios. For piano and 'cello, op. 38, and 99; sonatas; for vln., 77, concerto; 78, 100—108, sonatas pf. and vln.; for vln. and 'cello, op. 102, concerto; for clarinet (or viola) and pf., op. 120, 2 sonatas; for organ, Prelude and fugue, and fugue (unnumbered). For voices, op. 50, "*Rinaldo*" cantata (Goethe); 63, Rhapsodie (from Goethe's "*Harzreise*"), for alto solo, male chor. and orch.; 54, "*Schicksalslied*" (Song of Destiny), for chor. and orch.; 55, "*Triumphlied*" (Revelations, chap. XIX.), for 8-part chor. and orch.; 82, "*Nänie*" (Schiller), for chor. and orch.; 89, "*Gesang der parzer*" (Goethe), for 6-part chor. and orch.; op. 12, "*Ave Maria*," female chor.

with orch. (or org.); 13, funeral hymn, 109. Deutsche Fest-und Gedenkspruche, for double chorus, also numerous works for choruses of all sorts accompanied or a cappella. Brahms' songs are generally admired even by those opposed to him; they are very numerous and are pub. in sets, op. 121 being his last published work, except for several posth. songs for Ophelia in Shakespeare's "*Hamlet*," which were pub. in 1936 by Schirmer.

Memoirs and studies of the composer's music have been written by Deiters, Köhler, Mesnard, Reimann, Dietrich, Widmann, Kalbeck (most imp. biography, in 8 vols.), Erb, Antcliffe, Jenner, Imbert, Henschel, Pauli, Leyen, Von Perger, Colles, Fuller-Maitland, Thomas-San Galli, Evans, Lee, Niemann, Friedländer, May, Murdoch, Parker, Pulver, Specht, and Eugenie Schumann. His letters pub. in part by the German B.—Gesellschaft; thematic catalogue of his works, by Simrock.

Brailowsky (brä-ē-lŏf'skē), **Alexander**, b. Kiev, Russia; pianist; studied with his father and after 1911 with Leschetizky, Vienna; res. in Switzerland 1914–18; thereafter in Paris, where made his début with striking succ.; toured Europe, South America, Australia, and after 1926 in U. S.; one of most brilliant younger virtuosi.

Brambach (bräm'-bäkh), (1) **Kaspar Jos.**, Bonn, July 14, 1833—June 19, 1902; pupil in comp. of A. zur Nieden, then of Cologne Cons.; won Mozart scholarship, and studied under Fd. Hiller, Frankfort; 1858–61, teacher Cologne Cons.; 1861–69, dir. at Bonn, where he composed important secular cantatas; also an opera "*Ariadne*"; concert-overture "*Tasso*"; pf.-concerto, etc. (2) **Wm.**, Bonn, Dec. 17, 1841—Carlsruhe, Feb. 26, 1932; where from 1872, librarian; writer.

Brambilla (bräm-bēl'-lä), (1) **Paolo**, Milan, 1786—1838; dram. composer. (2) **Marietta**, Cassano D'Adda, 1807—Milan, 1875; singer, teacher, and composer; contralto and eldest of five singers. (3) **Teresa**, Cassano d'Adda, 1813—Milan, 1895; sister of above, soprano; she created "Gilda" in "*Rigoletto*," 1851.

Branca (brän'-kä), **Guglielmo**, b. Bo-logna, April 13, 1849; pupil of A. Busi, Bologna Cons., where he taught after 1890; composed succ. operas "*La Catalana*" (Florence, 1876); "*Hermosa*" (Florence, 1883); and "*La Figlia di Jorio*" (Cremona, 1897).

Brancaccio (brän-kät'-chō), **A.**, Naples, 1813—1846; dram. composer.

Brandeis (brän'-dīs), **Fr.**, Vienna, 1835 —New York, 1899; toured the U. S., then lived in N. Y., later Brooklyn, as organist and prolific composer.

Brandenburg (brän'-děn-boorkh), **Fd.**, b. Erfurt—d. Rudolstadt, 1850; violinist and dram. composer.

Brandl (bränt'-'l), (1) **Jn.**, Kloster Rohr, near Ratisbon, 1760—Carlsruhe, 1837; dir. and dram. composer. (2) **Johann**, Kirchenbirk, Bohemia, Aug. 30, 1835—Vienna, June 10, 1913; c. operettas.

Brandstetter. Vide GARBRECHT.

Brandt (bränt), **Marianne** (rightly **Marie Bischof**), Vienna, Sept. 12, 1842—July 9, 1921; dram. contralto; pupil Frau Marschner and of Viardot-Garcia; 1868–86 at Berlin Ct. Opera; created "Kundry" in "*Parsifal*" at Bayreuth, 1882; 1886–90, sang in New York, at Met. Op.; later active as teacher in Vienna.

Brandts-Buys (bränt-bois), (1) **Cornelius Alex.**, Zalt-Bommel, April 3, 1812—Dordrecht, Nov. 18, 1890; from 1840 lived in Deventer as organist and cond. His sons are (2) **Marius Adrianus** (b. 1840); (3) **L. F.** (1847—1917) organist and conductor at Rotterdam; (4) **H.** (1851—1905), conductor at Amsterdam and dram. composer. (5) **Jan** (1868—1933), son of (2); composer of operas, songs, etc.; pupil of Frankfort Cons.; lived in Vienna and after 1910 at Bozen.

Bran'dukov, **Anatol Andrejevitch**, Moscow, Jan. 6, 1859—Oct., 1930; 'cellist; pupil Moscow Cons.; spent many years in Paris; founded a quartet there with Marsick; 1890 returned to Moscow; c. for 'cello and orch., etc.

Brant (bränt), **Jobst** (or **Jodocus**) **vom**, Junior, 16th cent. captain and gov. of Liebenstein; cptist.

Branzell, **Karin** (kär'-ĭn bränt-sĕl), b. Stockholm, Sept. 24, 1891; mezzo-soprano; studied with Thekla Hofer and Louis Bachner (Berlin); début Stockholm; member Berlin State

Op., after 1919; Met. Op. Co., N. Y. after 1924; has also sung at Buenos Aires, and in various European cities; repertoire includes principal Wagner contralto rôles.

Braslau (bräs'-lä), **Sophie**, New York, Aug. 16, 1892—Dec. 22, 1935; contralto; studied piano with Alexander Lambert and voice with A. Buzzi-Peccia, Gabriele Sibella, and Dr. M. Marafioti; début Met. Op. Co., 1913, as Feodor in *"Boris Godounoff"*; member of company for seven years, singing title rôle in Cadman's opera *"Shanewis,"* 1918; sang in concerts and with leading orchestras; toured Scandinavia, Netherlands, and England, 1931.

Brassart, Johannes, priest, composer, and singer; in Papal Choir in 1431; probably same as **Johannes de Ludo;** c. sacred music.

Brassin (bräs-säṅ), (1) **Louis,** Aix-la-Chapelle, 1840—St. Petersburg, 1884; pianist. (2) **Ld.,** Strassburg, 1843—Constantinople, 1890; bro. and pupil of above; pianist. (3) **Gerhard,** Aix-la-Chapelle, June 10, 1844—Constantinople (?); leader; teacher at Stern Cons., Berlin; 1875–80, cond. of *Tonkünstlerverein* in Breslau; then, St. Petersburg and Constantinople.

Brauer (brow'ĕr , **Max,** Mannheim, May 9, 1855—Carlsruhe, Jan. 2, 1918; pupil of V. Lachner, Hiller, Jensen, and De Lange; 1880–88, dir. Kaiserslautern; 1888, dir. courtchurch at Carlsruhe; prod. *"Der Lotse,"* succ. 1-act opera, Carlsruhe, 1885.

Braun, (1) **Anton,** Cassel, Feb. 6, 1729—1785; violinist and c.; perhaps the son of (2) **Braun,** whose flute compositions were pub. in Paris, 1729–40. His brother (3) **Johann,** Cassel, 1753—Berlin, 1795, violinist and comp. (4) **Johann Fr.,** Cassel, 1759—Ludwigslust, 1824; oboist and comp.; father of (5) **Karl A. P.,** b. Ludwigslust, 1788; oboist; and of (6) **Wilhelm,** b. Ludwigslust, 1791; oboist, whose wife was his cousin (7) **Kathinka B.,** a singer.

Braunfels (brän'-fĕls, **Walter,** b. Frankfort, Dec. 19, 1882; composer of neo-Romantic tendency, with satiric elements and modern outlook; grad. Hoch Cons. in native city; also pupil of Kwast, Leschetizky, Navratil and Thuille; res. in Munich after

1903, but several years in war service; c. (operas) *"Prinzessin Brambilla"* (1919), *"Ulenspiegel"* (1913), *"Die Vögel"* (1920, a work portraying denizens of birdland and enjoying popularity when prod. in Munich), *"Don Gil von den grünen Hosen"* (1924), *"Galatea"*; (orch.) Variations on an Old Nursery Song; *"Ariel's Song"*; Serenade; Fantastic Variations on a Theme by Berlioz; *"Don Juan"* (variations on the champagne song from Mozart's opera); Praeludium and Fugue; Symphonic Suite; 'cello concerto; *"Funk"* (Radio) Music; (choral) *"Te Deum"*; Mass; *"Revelation of St. John"* (tenor solo and orch.); *"Neues Federspiel"* for voices and orch.; *"Die Ammen-Uhr"* for boys' chorus and orch.; orch. songs; music to *"As You Like It"* and *"Macbeth"*; *"Witches' Sabbath"* for piano and orch.; piano concerto and many pieces for this instrum.; songs, etc.; after 1925 dir. (with H. Abendroth) of Cologne Cons.

Brebos, Gilles. Vide GILLES.

Bree (brā) (**Jn. Bernardus**), **J. Bernard van,** Amsterdam, 1801—1857; violinist; 1840, founded the "Cecilia."

Breil (brīl), **Jos. Carl,** Pittsburgh, 1870—Los Angeles, Cal., Jan. 23, 1926; composer and tenor; studied in Leipzig and Milan; sang in Juch Op. Co., later at Pittsburgh; after 1897 theat. cond.; c. comic operas, also a one-act grand opera, *"The Legend,"* given by Met. Op. Co., 1919.

Breithaupt (brīt-howpt), **Rudolf Maria,** b. Braunschweig, Aug. 11, 1873; critic and teacher; pupil Leipzig Cons., 1897; after 1918 taught at Stern Cons., Berlin; author of influential works on piano technique, espousing a system of "weight"; c. songs.

Breitkopf und Härtel (brīt'-kŏpf oont hĕrt"-l), mus.-publishers, founded (as a printing-office) 1719 by **B. C. Breitkopf;** Klausthal, Harz, 1695—1777. His son, **J. G. Immanuel Breitkopf** (1719—1794), succeeded and revived Petrucci's invention of movable types and took up music printing. 1795, **Gottfr. Chr. Härtel** (Schneeberg, 1763—1857) added a piano-factory, founded the "Allg. musikalische Zeitung" (1798); later heads were **Florenz Härtel** (1827–35), **Dr. Hermann Härtel** (d. 1875), and his bro. **Reimund** (d. 1888); two

nephews, Wm. Volkmann (1837–
1896 ?) and Dr. Oskar von Hase
(b. 1846).

Brema (brā'-mä), **Marie**, London, Feb.
28, 1856—March 22, 1925; notable
dramatic soprano; début in opera,
Shaftesbury Theatre, 1891; sang in
New York, 1895–96; 1897 at Bayreuth; long a favourite in oratorio
perfs. in England; later prof., Manchester Coll. of Music.

Brem'mer, **Robt.**, Scotland, 1720—
Kensington, 1789; teacher.

Brendel (brĕnt'-'l), **K. Fz.**, Stolberg,
1811—Leipzig, 1868; critic, prof., and
writer.

Brenet (brŭ-nā), **Michel**, Luneville,
France, April 11, 1858—Paris, Nov.
4, 1918; wrote "*Histoire de la symphonie à orchestre depuis ses origines*"
(prize-essay), etc.

Brenner (brĕn'-nĕr), **L.**, **Ritter von**,
Leipzig, 1833—1902; pupil of the
Cons.; toured the Continent; 15
years member of the Imp. orch.;
1872–76, cond. Berlin Symphony
Orch.; 1897, cond. Meyder's Concert
Orch., Breslau; composed 4 grand
masses; symphonic poems.

Brent, Charlotte, d. 1802, Engl.; soprano; m. Pinto, a violinist, 1766.

Brescianello (brĕ'-shä-nĕl'-lō), **Giuseppe Antonio**, Mus. Director at
Stuttgart, 1717–57; published violin concertos, etc.

Breslaur (brās'-lowr), **Emil**, Kottbus,
May 20, 1836—Berlin, July 26, 1899;
pupil Stern Cons., Berlin; 1868–79,
teacher Kullak's Acad.; 1883 choirm.,
Reformed Synagogue; founder and
dir. Piano-Teachers' Seminary; ed.
"*Klavierlehrer*"; wrote technical
works, etc.

Bress'ler-Gianoli (jä-nō'-lē), **Clotilde**,
b. Geneva, 1875; d. there after opera-
tion for appendicitis, May 12, 1912.
Operatic mezzo-sopr.; studied Paris
Cons., début Geneva, at 19; 1900,
Paris Op. Com.; 1903 with New
Orleans Op. Co.; from 1907 sang
with success at Manhattan Opera,
N. Y.; 1910 with Metropolitan
Opera, N. Y.; her "Carmen" was
famous.

Brethol. Vide PIERSON-BRETHOL.

Breton y Hernàndez (brā-tôn ē ĕr-nän'-
dĕth), **Tomas**, Salamanca, Dec. 23,
1850—Madrid, Dec. 10, 1923; leading Spanish composer of zarzuelas,
an oratorio "*Apocalypsia*"; for orch.

"*Andalusian Scenes*"; funeral march
for Alfonso XII., etc.

Breuer (broi'-ĕr), **Hans**, b. Cologne,
1869; tenor; studied at the Cons.
at Stolzenberg. Sang "Mime" and
"David" at Bayreuth; d. Vienna,
1929.

Breuning (broi'-nĭng), **Fd.**, Brotterode,
Thuringia, 1830 — Aix-la-Chapelle,
1883; pf. prof., Cologne Cons.;
1865, director.

Bréval (brā-vǎl), (1) **J. Bap.**, Dept. of
l'Aisne, France, 1756—Chamouille,
1825; 'cellist and teacher. (2) **Lu-
cienne**, Berlin, Nov. 4, 1869—Paris,
Aug. 15, 1935; pupil of Warot at
Paris Cons.; notable dramatic soprano at Grand Opéra, Paris, for
years; début there in "*L'Africaine*,"
1892; created "*Brünnhilde*" in
French; sang at Covent Garden, and
1900 in New York.

Bréville (brā-vēl), **Pierre Onfroy de**,
b. Bar-le-Duc, France, Feb. 21, 1861;
composer and critic, diplomatic
career; then studied at Paris Cons.
and with César Franck; teacher at
the Schola Cantorum; c. masses,
sacred chorus with orch., "*Sainte Rose
de Lima*"; symph. poem, "*Nuit de
décembre*"; overture, "*Princesse Maleine*," music for "*Les sept Princesses*,"
and "*Sakuntala*," etc., orch. fantasie
"*Portraits des Musiciens*"; songs, etc.

Brew'er, (1) **Thos.**, 1609—1676; viol.-
player, "father of the glee." (2) **J.
Hyatt**, Brooklyn, N. Y., 1856—
Nov. 30, 1931; for 7 years boy-
soprano; studied with Dudley Buck
and others; 1871 organist various
churches, 1881 at the Lafayette Av.
Presby. Ch.; cond. various vocal
societies; composed cantatas, etc.

Briccialdi (brĕt-chäl'-dē), **Giulio**, Terni,
Papal States, 1818—Florence, 1881;
flutist.

Bridge, (1) **Sir J. Fr.**, Oldbury, Worcestershire, Engl., Dec. 5, 1844—
London, March 16, 1924; son and
pupil of J. Bridge, lay-clerk; pupil
later of J. Hopkins and Sir J. Goss;
organist 1869 Manchester cathedral;
1882 of Westminster Abbey; 1868
Mus. Bac. (Oxford), with the oratorio "*Mount Moriah*"; prof. of harm.
and cpt. R. A. M.; cond. Western
and the Madrigal Societies; 1897,
knighted; composed cantatas, overtures, etc. 1902, made member of
the Victorian Order; 1903, King
Edward Prof. of Music, London

University and R. C. M. (2) **Frank,**
b. Brighton, 1879—London, Jan. 11,
1941; Viola pupil, R. A. M., gaining
a scholarship in composition; c.
prize quartet in E. Minor (Bologna
competition); string quartet "*Three
Idylls*"; rhapsody for orch. and
symp. poem, "*Isabella*"; "*Sea*" *Suite*;
"*Dance Rhapsody*"; "*Dance Poem*";
piano trio and many chamber works;
member of various quartets; cond.
Covent Garden, 1913.

Bridge'tower, G. A. P., Poland, 1779—
ca. 1845; son of an African father
and European mother; brilliant violinist.

Briegel (brē'gĕl), **Wg. K.,** Germany,
1626—Darmstadt, 1712; conductor
and composer.

Brighenti (or **Brighetti**) (brē-gĕt'-tē),
Maria (née **Giorgi**), b. Bologna, 1792;
soprano; created "Rosina" in "*Barbiere di Siviglia.*"

Bright, Dora Estella, b. Sheffield,
Aug. 16, 1863; pianist; pupil R. A.
M., London; 1892 married Capt.
Knatchbull; c. 2 piano concertos;
variations with orch., etc.

Brink, Jules Ten (tän brēnk), Amsterdam, 1838—Paris, 1889; director and
dram. composer.

Brins'mead, (1) **J.,** North Devon,
Oct. 13, 1814—London, Feb. 17,
1908; 1835, founded piano-factory,
London; inv. "Perfect Check Re-
peater Action"; in 1863 his sons
(2) **Thomas** and (3) **Edgar** were
taken in partnership.

Bris'tow, (1) **W. R.,** England, 1803
—N. Y., 1867; cond. in New York.
(2) **G. Fr.,** Brooklyn, N. Y., Dec. 19,
1825—New York, Dec. 13, 1898;
son of above; violinist N. Y. Philh.
Soc.; cond. of the Harmonic Soc.,
later of the Mendelssohn Union; organist various churches; composed
operas, oratorios, etc.

Britt, Horace, b. Antwerp; 'cellist;
studied Paris Cons. with Delsart and
Lavignac, 1st prize at 14; soloist
with Paris orchestras; U. S. recital
tours and appearances with leading
orchestras; cond., Sunday concerts,
Boston Op. Co.; member Chamber
Mus. Soc. of San Francisco, also at
various times of Letz Quartet,
Mischa Elman Quartet; more recently of trio with Barrère, flute, and
Salzedo, harp.

Brit'ton, Thos., 1651—1714; called
"Musical Small-coal Man," because

he earned his living by hawking coal;
gave concerts in a room over his shop,
which were patronised by the aristo-
racy; Händel and Pepusch were performers at these concerts.

Brixi (brĕx'-ē), **Fz. Xaver,** Prague,
1732—1771; conductor and com-
poser.

Broad'wood & Sons, firm of London
pf.-makers; est. 1730 by the Swiss
harpsichord-maker **Burkhard Tschudi** (or **Shudi**), succeeded by his son-
in-law **J. Broadwood** (1732—1812),
later by **James** and **Thos. Shudi;**
then by **H. Fowler Broadwood** (d.
London, 1893).

Brock'way, Howard A., b. Brooklyn,
N. Y., Nov. 22, 1870; studied pf.
with Kortheuer; 1890–95, Berlin,
pupil of Barth (pf.) and O. B. Boise
(comp.); since 1895, has lived in
N. Y. teaching and touring; his
symphony in D succ., prod. Berlin;
composed also cantata, Ballade and
Scherzo for orch., etc.

Brod (brō), **H.,** Paris, 1801—1839;
oboist and conductor.

Brode (brō'-dĕ), **Max,** Berlin, Feb. 25,
1850—Königsberg, Dec. 30, 1917;
studied with Paul Mendelssohn and
at Stern Cons., Leipzig Cons., and
Berlin Hochschule; début Frankfort-
on-Main; prof. and teacher at
Königsberg, violinist, conductor.

Brodsky (brôd'-shkĭ), **Adolf,** Taganrog,
Russia, March 21, 1851—Manches-
ter, Jan. 22, 1929; violinist; pupil of
J. Hellmesberger and Vienna Cons.;
member Hellmesberger Quartet;
1868–70 Imp. Opera orch.; pupil of
Laub, Moscow, later prof. at the
Cons.; 1879, cond. symphony concerts at Kiev; toured, 1881; 1883,
vln.-prof. at Leipzig Cons.; 1891–94,
N. Y.; 1894 in Berlin; 1895, prof. of
vln., later dir. R. C. M., Manchester,
England.

Bron'ner, Georg, Holstein, 1666—
Hamburg, 1724; organist; c. for the
Hamburg Opera "*Echo and Nar-
cissus,*" "*Venus,*" etc.

Bronsart (brôn'-zärt), (1) von **Schel-
lendorf, Hans** (**Hans von Bronsart**),
Berlin, Feb. 11, 1830—Munich,
Nov. 3, 1913; pupil, Dehn, Kullak,
Liszt; concerts in Paris; 1867, intendant R. Th. at Hanover; 1887–95,
"Hofmusikintendant," Weimar; composed opera, cantata, symphony "*In
den Alpen,*" etc. (2) **Ingeborg, von**
(née **Starck**), St. Petersburg, Aug. 24,

1840—Munich, June 17, 1913; wife (since 1862) of above; pupil of Liszt; composed 3 operas, etc.

Bro'sa, Antonio, violinist; founder, 1925, in London of noted Brosa Quartet, with himself as 1st vln., David Wise, 2nd vln., Leonard Rubens, viola, and Livio Mannucci, 'cello; début, 1926, London; next year heard at Siena Fest. of I. S. C. M.; toured England, Germany, France, Holland, Italy; 1930, Amer. début at Coolidge Fest., Washington, D. C.

Brosig (brō'-zĭkh), **Moritz,** Fuchs-winkel, Upper Silesia, 1815—Breslau, 1887; organist and theorist.

Brossard (dŭ brôs-săr), **Sébastien de,** 1654—Meux, France, 1730; conductor, lexicographer, and composer.

Brounoff (broo'-nôf), **Platon,** Eliza-bethgrad, Russia, 1869—New York, July 11, 1924; composer; pupil of Rubinstein and Rimsky-Korsakov, St. Petersburg Cons.; cantata *"The Angel,"* prod. at court; lived in New York as cond. of Russian choral society, etc.; c. operas, piano suites, and songs.

Broustet (broo-stä), **Ed.,** Toulouse, April 29, 1836—Louchon, Dec., 1901; pupil of Stamaty, Litolff, and Ravina; pianist and composer; toured Russia, etc.; lived in Toulouse; composer.

Brown, (1) Dr. **J.,** Northumberland, 1715—1766; writer. (2) **Eddy,** b. Chicago, July 15, 1895; violinist; studied with Hubay and Auer; début with London Philh. Orch., 1909; toured widely in Europe and America; active also in chamber music groups, particularly in radio programmes.

Brown'lee, John, b. Geelong, Australia, 1901; operatic barytone; studied with Gilly; discovered by Melba and came to England, sang at her Covent Garden Op. farewell, 1926; début Paris Op. 1927, of which he has been a member since; has also sung at Monte Carlo and Covent Garden, principally in Italian and French rôles; engaged for Met. Op. Co., 1936-37.

Bruch (brookh), **Max,** Cologne, Jan. 6, 1838—near Berlin, Oct. 2, 1920; noted pianist and composer; at first, pupil of his mother (née Almenra-der), a singer; later with Breiden-stein, Bonn; 1853 he gained the four-year scholarship of the Mozart Foundation at Frankfort, and stud-

ied with Hiller, Reinecke, and Breuning; at 14, prod. a symphony, Cologne; 1858, his first dram. work, Goethe's *Singspiel*, *"Scherz, List und Rache"* (op. 1); 1864, prod. opera *"Loreley,"* etc.; male chorus *"Frith-jof"*; 1865-67, at Coblenz, composed his first pop. vln.-concerto (G minor); 1867-70, court-cond. at Son-dershausen; in 1878 cond. Stern Choral Union, Berlin; in 1880, cond. Liverpool Philh. Soc.; 1883, dir. Breslau Orchestral Soc.; 1881, m. Frl. Tuczek, of Berlin, a singer; lived in Breslau till 1890; 1892-1910, at K. Hochschule in Berlin; he received in 1908 the Prussian order for merit in art and learning, and many honours from England, France, etc.; prod. 1872, *"Hermione,"* based on *"Win-ter's Tale"*; 1873-78, prod. the chorals *"Arminius"* and *"Lied von der Glocke,"* and the 2d vln.-concerto; 1883, came to U. S. and prod. his *"Arminius,"* Boston. The epic can-tata is his special field; among his works of this sort are *"Odysseus," "Arminius," "Lied von der Glocke,"* and *"Achilleus"*; for male chorus, *"Frithjof," "Salamis," "Normannen-zug"* and *"Leonidas"* (op. 66). He arranged the old Hebrew melody *Kol Nidre,* and composed a cantata *"Das Feuerkreuz"* (op. 52, 1888); three symphonies; oratorio, *"Moses"* (1895); 3 vln.-concertos, which have won great popularity; secular orato-rio, *"Gustav Adolf"*; *"Nal und Dama-jant"*; *"Die Macht des Gesanges,"* for barytone, mixed chor. and orch., etc.

Brückler (brük'-lĕr), **Hugo,** Dresden, 1845—1871; composer.

Bruckner (brook'-nĕr), **Anton,** Aus-felden, Upper Austria, Sept. 4, 1824 —Vienna, Oct. 11, 1896; eminent composer; mainly self-taught as or-ganist; 1867, court-organist at Vien-na; prof. of org., harm. and cpt. at Vienna Cons.; 1875, "Lektor" of music at Vienna Univ.; 1891, Dr. hon. causa; noted organ-virtuoso and a disciple of Wagner; he composed nine symphonies: 1, C minor (1868); 2, C minor (1873); 3, D minor (1877); 4, E flat, known as the *"Romantic"* (1881); 5, B flat (1894); 6, A (1899); 7, E (1884); 8, C minor (1892); 9, left incomplete but often played with his *"Te Deum"* as concluding choral movement.

In 1936 the publication of the

original version of Bruckner's symphonies by the Musikwissentschaftliche Verlag, Vienna, led to a controversy as to whether the previously known copies had been indefensibly altered and ed. by his pupils Ferdinand Loewe and the brothers Franz and Josef Schalk. But evidence was adduced to show that B. approved these changes.

His choral works include three Grand Masses, a *"Te Deum,"* a Requiem, motets, psalms, and various church music, pcs. for male chorus. C. also a string quintet. The fame of B. has grown to great proportions since his death, not only in Germany and Austria, where he is considered a classic in the great line of Romantic composers, but also in other countries. An International Bruckner Soc. devotes itself to furthering perfs. of his music. The best passages in his works are undoubtedly of noble fervour and breadth, some even approaching sublimity, but other pages are clumsy, repetitious, and lacking in contrast. The influence of Wagner is evident in his scores.

Biog. by Fz. Brunner (Linz-on-Danube, 1895). Other memoirs by Louis, Funtek, Gräflinger, Morold, Halm, Krug, Grunsky and Göllerich.

Brückner (brük'-nĕr), **Oscar,** Erfurt, Jan. 2, 1857—Wiesbaden, June 8, 1930; 'cellist; pupil of Grützmacher and Draeseke; toured Germany, Russia, etc.; Ducal chamber-virtuoso at Strelitz; 1889 teacher in the Wiesbaden Cons., and composer.

Brugnoli (broōn-yō'-lē), **Attilio,** b. Rome, Sept. 7, 1880—Bolzano, July 10, 1937; won 1st prize in international Rubinstein contest, Paris, 1905; appointed prof. of piano at Parma Cons. in competition same year; 1907, Naples Cons.; 1916, at Rome Cons. and after 1921, Florence Cons.; has c. music for orch., piano, violin, also ed. complete works of Chopin.

Bruhns (broons), **Nikolaus,** Schwabstadt, Schleswig, 1665 — Husum, 1697; organist and violinist.

Brüll (brȳl), **Ignaz,** Moravia, Nov. 7, 1846—Vienna, Sept. 17, 1907; pianist; pupil of Epstein, Rufinatscha and Dessoff; 1872–78, pf.-prof. Horak Institute, Vienna; his first opera

"Die Bettler von Sammarkand" (1864) was not succ., but *"Das Goldene Kreuz"* (Berlin) (1875) was very pop.; followed by 6 other operas and the succ. comic opera *"Der Husar"* (Vienna, March 2, 1898); composed also hunting overture *"Im Walde,"* etc.

Brumel (broo'-mĕl), **Anton,** ca. 1480—ca. 1520; Flemish cptist.

Bruneau (brü-nō) (**Louis Chas. Bonaventure**), **Alfred,** Paris, March 3, 1857—June 15, 1934; pupil of Franchomme at the Cons.; took first 'cello prize, 1876; studied with Savart and Massenet; 1881, took first prize with cantata *"Sainte Geneviève";* composed operas *"Kerim"* (Opéra-Populaire, 1887), *"Le Rêve"* (Paris, 1892), and the very succ. drame lyrique *"L'Attaque du Moulin"* (Opéra-Comique, Paris, 1893); unsucc. drame lyrique *"Messidor"* (Paris, Gr. Opera, Feb. 19, 1897); the last three are on texts from Zola, as are *"L'Ouragan"* (Op. Com., 1901); lyric comedy in 3 acts, *"L'Enfant Roi"* (Op. Com., 1905); 1-act lyric drama *"Lazare"* (1905); incid. music to *"La Faute de l'Abbé Mouret"* (Odéon, 1907); lyric drama *"Naïs Nicoulin"* (Monte Carlo, 1907); *"Le Roi Candaule"* (1920); *"Le Jardin du Paradis"* (1921); ballets, orch. and choral works; songs set to Catulle Mendès' *"Lieds en prose";* 1893–95, critic of *"Gil Blas,"* 1895 of *"Le Figaro,"* officier of Legion of Honour.

Brunelli (broo-nĕl'-lē), **A.,** 17th cent.; conductor to Duke of Florence; writer and composer.

Brunetti (broo-nĕt'-tē), **Gaetano,** Pisa, 1740?—Madrid, 1808; composer.

Bruni (broo'-nē), **A. Bart.,** Coni, Piedmont, 1759—1823; violinist, cond. and dram. composer.

Brun'skill, Muriel, b. Kendall, England, Dec. 18, 1899; contralto; début, London, in recital, 1920; member British Nat'l. Op. Co., 1922–27; has sung with leading British orchs. and at festivals; also appeared in United States.

Bruyck (broik), **K. Debrois van,** Brünn, March 14, 1828—Waidhofen, Aug. 1, 1902; studied law, Vienna, 1850; and theory with Rufinatscha; writer on Bach, etc.

Bryen'nius, Manuel, lived ca. 1320; last Greek theorist.

Buchholz (bookh'-hŏlts), (1) **Jn. Simeon**, Schlosswippach, 1758—Berlin, 1825; founded firm of organ-builders; succeeded by his son (2) **K. Aug.** (1796—1884), whose son (3) **K. Fr.**, d. Feb. 17, 1885.

Buchner (bookh'-nĕr), **Philipp Fr.**, Wertheim, 1614—Würzburg, 1669; cond. and comp.

Büchner (bükh'-nĕr), **Emil**, Osterfield, near Naumburg, Dec. 25, 1826—Erfurt, June 9, 1908; pupil of Leipzig Cons.; 1865, court-conductor; composed 2 operas, etc.

Buck, (1) **Zechariah**, Norwich, England, 1798—Newport, Essex, 1879; organist Norwich Cathedral; teacher and composer. (2) **Dudley**, Hartford, Conn., March 10, 1839—Orange, N. J., Oct. 6, 1909; pupil W. J. Babcock (pf.), then of Plaidy and Moscheles (pf.); Hauptmann (comp.) and J. Reitz (instrumentation), Leipzig Cons.; later Dresden, under Reitz and Johann Schneider (organ); and 1861–62 in Paris; 1862, organist of the Park Ch., Hartford, U. S. A.; St. James, Chicago, 1872, St. Paul's and of the Music Hall Association, Boston; 1875, organist Cincinnati May Festival; then, asst. cond. to Th. Thomas, New York; organist of Holy Trinity Ch., Brooklyn; director Apollo Club; composed comic opera *"Deseret"* (prod. 1880); symphonic overture *"Marmion"* (1880), many cantatas; the 46th Psalm; *"The Christian Year,"* a series of 5 cantatas; wrote 2 books of Pedal-phrasing Studies, and *"Illustrations on Choir-accompaniment, with Hints on Registration"*; pub. *"The Organist's Repertoire"* (with A. P. Warren); *"The Influence of the Organ in History"* (1882); and a *"Dictionary of Musical Terms."* (3) **Percy Carter**, b. West Ham., March 25, 1871; pupil at R. A. M., London; won scholarship 1891-4, organist at Oxford; 1893, Mus. Doc.; 1896-9, organist Wells Cathedral, 1899–1901, Bristol Cathedral; 1910, prof. of music Dublin University, vice-pres.; 1927, prof. of music, Univ. of Sheffield; c. overture *"Coeur de Lion"*; chamber music, etc.

Buhl (bül), **Joseph David**, b. Amboise, 1781; famous trumpet-player at Paris; author of trumpet-method.

Bühler (bü'-lĕr), **Fz. P. Gregorius**, Schneidheim, 1760—Augsburg, 1824;

Benedictine monk, 1794; conductor at Botzen; dram. composer and theorist.

Buh'lig, Richard, b. Chicago, Dec. 21, 1880; pianist; studied in native city and with Leschetizky in Vienna; after 1901 taught in Berlin, and toured in Europe and U. S. as recitalist; Amer. début, 1907, with Phila. Orch.; 1918–20, taught at Inst. of Mus. Art, N. Y.; now lives on Pacific Coast.

Bull, John, Dr., Somersetshire, England, 1563—Antwerp, March 12, 1628; 1582, organist; 1592, Mus. Doc. Oxon.; 1596, prof. of music at Gresham Coll. on Queen Elizabeth's recommendation; resigned on his marriage, 1607; 1617, organist Nôtre Dame, Antwerp; an early English composer whom Oscar Bie credits with remarkable originality in the midst of over-ornamentation.

Bull (bool), **Ole** (**Bornemann**), Bergen, Norway, Feb. 5, 1810—Lysoen, Aug. 17, 1880; enormously popular and brilliant violin-virtuoso, a whit charlatanic; pupil of Paulsen; then self-taught, using a bridge almost level and a flat fingerboard; studied theology, but failed in examinations; 1828, dir. Philh. and Dram. Soc., Bergen; 1829, studied with Spohr briefly; 1832, début, Paris, after living there a year observing Paganini's methods; toured Europe frequently, and North America 5 times (1843–79); he died at his country-seat. He played his own comps. almost altogether; wrote 2 concertos, and characteristic solos; biog. by Sara C. Bull, his second wife, Boston, 1883, and by Vlik (Bergen, 1890).

Bul'lard, Fred. F., Boston, Mass., Sept. 21, 1864—June 24, 1904; 1888-92, studied comp. under Rheinberger, Munich; teacher of comp., critic and composer, Boston; pub. many successful ballads and four-part songs for male voices, also sacred music.

Bülow (fōn bü'-lō), **Hans Guido von**, Dresden, Jan. 8, 1830—Cairo, Egypt, Feb. 12, 1894; versatile and influential musician; pianist and conductor of remarkable accuracy and memory, popularising the custom of conducting without score; often called the best interpreter of Beethoven, but rather cold as a pianist; at 9, studied pf. with Fr. Wieck; harmony with

Ebewein; 1848, entered Leipzig Univ. as law-student, but studied cpt. with Hauptmann; 1849, Wagner's *"Die Kunst und die Revolution"*[2] stirred him deeply, and having heard *"Lohengrin"*[2] at Weimar under Liszt's direction, he joined Wagner, then exiled at Zurich, 1850–51; studied conducting with him, and acted as cond. in theatres at Zurich and St. Gallen, and later with Liszt; 1853 and 1855 toured Germany and Austria, with success; 1855–64, first pf.-teacher Stern Cons., Berlin. 1857, m. Cosima, Liszt's natural daughter, whom he later surrendered to his friend Wagner (q. v.); 1858, court-pianist; 1863, Dr. Phil. *hon. causa*, Univ. of Jena; 1864, court-pianist, Munich; 1867–69, court-conductor and dir. School of Music; 1869–72, teacher and pianist in Florence; 1875–76, gave 139 concerts in America; 1878–80, court-conductor at Hanover; then till 1885, Hofmusik-intendant, Saxe-Meiningen; 1882, m. Marie Schanzer; 1885–88, teacher Raff Cons., Frankfort, Klindworth Cons., Berlin, and dir. Berlin Philh. Concerts; in 1888, founded the succ. "Subscription Concerts."[2] Composed music to *"Julius Cæsar"* (op. 10); a Ballade for orch., *"Des Sängers Fluch"*[2] (op. 16); *"Nirwana,"*[2] a symphonic Stimmungsbild (op. 20); 4 Charakterstücke for orch. (op. 23); a few pf.-pcs. and songs; also many piano arrangements. His critical ed. of Beethoven's sonatas, and Cramer's études, are standard; biog. by his 2d wife (Leipzig, 1895).

Bulss (bools), **Paul**, Birkholz Manor, Priegnitz, Dec. 19, 1847—Temesvar, Hungary, March 20, 1902; pupil of G. Engel; barytone at Dresden (1876–89), later at Berlin court opera.

Bulthaupt (boolt'-howpt), **H.**, Bremen, Oct. 26, 1849—Aug. 21, 1905; wrote a valuable *"Dramaturgie der Oper"*[2] (Leipzig, 1887).

Bungert (boong'-ěrt), **August**, Mühl-heim-on-Ruhr, March 14, 1846—Leutesdorf-on-Rhine, Oct. 26, 1915; pupil of Kufferath (pf.), later at Cologne Cons.; for 4 years at Paris Cons.; then (1869) with Mathias; lived (1873–81) at Berlin, and studied cpt. with Kiel; lived near Genoa. C. *"Das Homerische Welt,"*[2] in 2 Homeric opera-cycles, occupying 6

"evenings"[2] (*Abende*), each with a "Vorspiel"[2]; The Iliad (*"Die Ilias"*[2]) is unfinished: (a) *Achilles;* (b) *Klytemnestra.* The Odyssey (*"Die Odyssee"*[2]) consists of *Circe; Nausikaa; Odysseus'* *Heimkehr* (Berlin, March 31, 1898; succ.), and *Odysseus'* *Tod* (Dresden, 1902). Other comp. are (comic opera) *"Die Studenten von Salamanca"*[2] (Leipzig, 1884); symph. poem, *"Auf der Wartburg"*[2]; *"Hohes Lied der Liebe,"*[2] with orch.; overture, *"Tasso,"*[2] pf. quartet, op. 18; Florentine quartet (prize, 1878); *"Italienishe Reisebilder,"*[2] etc., for pf.; songs to Carmen Sylva's *"Lieder einer Königin,"*[2] etc.

Bun'nett, Edw., near Norwich, England, 1834—1923; articled to Dr. Buck, 1849; organist various churches, Mus. Doc. Oxon, 1869; 1871–92, cond. Norwich Mus. Union; 1872 organist of the Norwich Festivals; composed cantata, etc.

Bun'ning, Herbert, b. London, May 2, 1863—Thundersley, 1937; pupil of V. Ferroni; c. Italian scena, *"Ludovico il Moro"*[2] (prod. with succ., 1892), also 2 symphonic poems, opera *"The Last Days of Pompeii"*[2] (M.S.)

Bun'ting, Edw., Armagh, Feb., 1773—Belfast, 1843; historian and collector of Irish music.

Buonamente (boo-ō-nä-měn'-tě), **Giov. Bat.**, cond. Franciscan monastery at Assisi; early and important composer for violin, also cornetti (1623–36); confused by Fétis with Bonometti.

Buonamici (boo-ō-nä-mē'-chē), (1) **Giu.**, Florence, Feb. 12, 1846—March 18, 1914; pianist; pupil of his uncle Ceccherini, and of Bülow and Rheinberger at Munich; 1873, cond. Florentine Choral Society "Cherubini"; founded the Flor. "Trio Society"; pub. études, etc. (2) **Carlo**, Florence, June 20, 1875—Boston (?), 1920; pianist; son and pupil of Giuseppe (q. v.), later studied at Würzburg Royal Musicsch., with Van Zeyl, taking first prize; after year in the army, settled in Boston, 1896, as teacher and pianist with Boston Symph. Orch., etc.; 1908 toured Europe.

Buongiorno (boo-ōn-jôr'-nō), **Crescenzo**, Bonito, 1864—Dresden, Nov. 7, 1903; c. operas.

Buononcini. Vide BONONCINI.

Burbure de Wesembeck (bür-bür dŭ vä-zäň-běk), **Léon Ph. M.**, Chevalier

de, Termonde, 1812—Antwerp, 1889; Flemish nobleman; writer and composer.

Bürde-Ney (bür'-dĕ-nī'), **Jenny,** Graz, 1826—Dresden, 1886; soprano; 1855, m. the actor E. Bürde.

Burette (bü-rĕt), **P. J.,** Paris, 1665—1747; Prof. of Medicine, Paris Univ.; writer on Greek music.

Burgk (boorkh'), **Joachim Moller** (or **Müller**), called **Joachim A. Burgk** (or **Burg,** or **Burck**), Burg, near Magdeburg; ca. 1541—Mülhausen, Thuringia, May 24, 1610; organist and eminent composer of Protestant music.

Burgmein, J., pen-name of "Giulio Ricordi."

Burgmüller (boorkh'-mül-lĕr), **Norbert,** Düsseldorf, 1810—Aix-la-Chapelle, 1836; pianist and composer.

Burgstaller (boorkh'-shtäl-lĕr), **Alois,** b. Holzkirchen, Sept. 27, 1871; tenor; studied with Bellurth and Kniese; sang small rôles at Bayreuth from 1894, "Siegfried" (1897); "Siegmund" (1899); sang Met. Op., from 1903.

Bur'leigh, (1) **Cecil,** b. Wyoming, N. Y., April 17, 1885; violinist; studied in Berlin with Grünberg and Witek (vln.), Leichtentritt (comp.) and in Chicago with Sauret, Hugo Heermann and Felix Borowski; made concert tours, and taught after 1909 in Denver, Sioux City and Missoula; res. in N. Y., 1919-21; thereafter taught at Univ. of Wis. (vln.); c. violin works and songs. (2) **Harry Thacker,** b. Erie, Pa., Dec. 2, 1866; Negro barytone and composer; studied Nat'l. Cons. in N. Y., where he has lived since 1892; active as concert singer in U. S. and Europe; has c. or arr. more than 100 songs, esp. Negro spirituals.

Burmeister (boor'-mī-shtĕr), (1) **Richard,** b. Hamburg, Dec. 7, 1860; pianist; pupil of Liszt, accompanying him as he travelled; teacher Hamburg Cons.; for 12 years head of pf. dept., Peabody Inst., Baltimore; 1898, dir. N. Y. Scharwenka Cons.; 1903-06, Dresden Cons.; 1906-25, lived in Berlin; 1925-33 in Merano; c. pf.-concerto (op. 1), "*The Chase after Fortune*" ("*Die Jagd nach dem Glück*"), a symphonic fantasy in 3 movements; rescored Chopin's F minor concerto, and wrote orch. accomp. for Liszt's "*Pathetic*" concerto. (2) **Dory** (née **Peterson**), b.

Oldenburg, 1860; pianist; **wife of** above.

Burmester (boor'-mä-shtĕr), **Willy,** Hamburg, March 16, 1869—Jan. 16, 1933; violin-virtuoso; studied with his father and Joachim; toured with his sister, a concert-pianist. Von Bülow aided him and brought public attention to his abilities; toured Europe, and 1899, America. Long a leading virtuoso, but in later years also a serious interpreter; revisited America a few years before his death.

Bur'ney, Chas., Shrewsbury, England, 1726—Chelsea, 1814; toured Europe; Mus. Doc. Oxon, 1769; pub. very interesting and gossipy "*The Present State of Music in France and Italy*," etc. (1771); "do. *in Germany, the Netherlands*," etc. (1773); "*General History of Music*" (4 vols., 1776-89), etc.

Bur'rian, Carl (rightly **Karel Burian**), Rausinow near Rakonitz, Jan. 12, 1870—Senomat, Sept. 25, 1924; opera tenor; pupil of Pivoda in Prague; début, 1891, in Brünn; sang in Reval, Cologne, Hanover, Hamburg; 1898-1911 at the Dresden Op.; then several years in Vienna and Budapest; at Met. Op., N. Y., and at Bayreuth.

Bur'rowes, J. Freckleton, London, 1787—1852; organist, pianist and writer.

Bur'tius (or **Burci** (boor'-chē)) or **Burzio** (boor'-tsī-ō), **Nicolaus,** Parma, 1450—1518; wrote the earliest specimen of printed mensural music.

Bur'ton, Frederick R., Jonesville, Mich., 1861—Lake Hopatcong, N. J., 1909; graduated at Harvard; l. Yonkers, N. Y.; founded there, 1896, a choral society; c. pop. cantata "*Hiawatha*," etc.

Bus'by, Thos., Westminster, England, 1755—London, 1838; Mus. Doc.; composer and writer.

Busch, (1) **Adolf,** b. Siegen, Germany, Aug. 8, 1891; violinist, composer; studied at Cologne Cons.; first vln., Vienna Orch., 1912-18; toured as solo performer in European cities, 1918-22; in sonata recitals with Rudolf Serkin, pianist, and in trio with Serkin and H. Busch; succeeded Marteau as teacher at Berlin Hochsch., 1919, where formed string quartet; has toured in U. S., as soloist with leading orchs.; c. orchestral and chamber works, songs. (2) **Carl,**

b. Bjerre, Denmark, March 29, 1862; studied Copenhagen and Brussels Cons., with Gade, Svendsen, Godard and others; res. in Kansas City, Mo., since 1887; org. and cond. Symph. Orch. there for some years, beginning 1912; knighted by Danish Gov't. same year; c. cantatas, orchestral and chamber music works, anthems and part-songs. (3) **Fritz**, b. Siegen, Germany, March 13, 1890; conductor; bro. of Adolf (q. v.); studied Cologne Cons., conductor Riga Op., 1909; summer concerts, Bad Pyrmont, 1910–12; choral director, Gotha Musikverein, 1911–12; court music director, Stuttgart, and cond. Opera there, 1918; conductor Dresden Op. and Symph. Concerts, 1922 until 1933, during which time he made guest tours to other countries including U. S., where led N. Y. Symph. Orch. as guest in 1925–26; has conducted opera and concerts in Buenos Aires, 1933 and subsequent years; also led Mozart opera festivals at Glyndebourne, Sussex, beginning 1934; lives in Zurich.

Busi (boo'-zē), (1) **Giu.**, Bologna, 1808 —1871; Prof. (2) **Alessandro**, Bologna, 1833—1895; son of above; 'cellist and conductor.

Busnois (bün-wä), **A.** (rightly **de Busne** (dŭ bün)), d. 1481; Netherland contrapuntist.

Busoni (boo-sō'-nē), **Ferruccio Benvenuto**, Empoli, near Florence, April 1, 1866—Berlin, July 27, 1924; noted comp. and pianist; pupil of his father (**Fdo.**), clarinettist, and his mother (*née* **Weiss**), a pianist; at 8, début at Vienna; then studied with W. A. Remy; 1881, toured Italy; at 15, elected a member of the Reale Accademia Filarmonica, Bologna; 1886, Leipzig, where he c. a fantastic opera, a string-quartet (D min.), symphonic suite, etc.; 1888–89, Prof. Helsingfors Cons.; 1890, won Rubinstein prizes for comp. and pf.-playing, with a *Concertstück* for pf. and orch., op. 31a; sonata for pf. and vln.; pf. arr. of Bach's Eb *Organ Prelude*, and *Fugue;* and other pf. pcs. incl. 2 Cadenzas to Beethoven's *Concerto in G;* 1890, Prof. in the Moscow Imp. Cons.; 1891–93 at New England Cons., Boston; in 1907 he succeeded Sauer as teacher of the master class at Vienna Cons.; 1911 toured America; 1913–15, dir. Bologna

Liceo; 1915, took up residence in Zurich; after 1920, taught master class in comp. at Berlin Acad. of Arts. He made notable transcriptions of Bach organ works for piano, which have held a place in the repertoire; also Liszt piano pieces; mem. Legion of Honour, 1913. Wrote treatise on notation (1910); edited Bach's *"Well-tempered Clavichord"* with études; other comps., *"Lustspiel Ouvertüre";* 4 choruses with orch.; 2 suites for orch.; a *"Symphonisches Tongedicht"* for orch., symph. tone-poem *"Pojohla's Tochter,"* festival overture, 1897; music to *"Berceuse élégiaque,"* for orch.; wrote *"Entwurf einer neuen Aesthetik der Tonkunst."* His opera, *"Der Brautwahl,"* was prod. Hamburg, April 13, 1912, based on Hoffman's *"Serapeons' Brüder."* His operas *"Turandot"* and *"Arlecchino"* were planned on old Italian *"Commedia dell' Arte"* (latter, Zurich, 1918). He left unfinished an opera, *"Doktor Faust,"* on which he had worked for many years; completed by Jarnach, it was prod. with succ. (Dresden, 1925). Wrote memoirs.

Büsser (büs-sä), **Henri**, b. Toulouse, Jan. 16, 1872; pupil of Guiraud and Gounod; took first Grand Prix de Rome, with cantata *"Antigone";* 1892, organist at St. Cloud; after 1902, cond. at Op.-Comique; c. succ. 1-act pastorale *"Daphnis et Chloe"* (Paris, Op. Com.), 1897; cantata *"Amadis de Gaule,"* 1892 (taking 2d Grand Prix de Rome); ballets *"Colomba"* and *"Les Noces Corinthiennes";* *"Sommeil de l'Enfant Jesus"* for vln. and orch.; also overtures, suites, organ works, harp and orch. comp. Member, Institut de France.

Bussler (boos'-lĕr), **L.**, Berlin, Nov. 26, 1838—Jan. 18, 1901; theorist; son of the painter-author, Robert Bussler; pupil of von Hertzberg, Dehn, Grell, and Wieprecht; 1865, teacher of theory, Ganz School of Music; from 1879, at the Stern Cons., Berlin; critic and writer of various treatises.

Bussmeyer (boos'-mī-ĕr), (1) **Hugo**, Brunswick, 1842—Rio de Janeiro, ?; pianist; pupil of K. Richter, Litolff (pf.), and Methfessel (comp.); 1860, toured in South America; 1860, N. Y.; settled in Rio de Janeiro; composer and writer. (2) **Hans**, Bruns-

wick, 1853—Poecking, Sept. 21, 1930;
bro. of above; pianist; pupil of Royal
School of Music at Munich, and
teacher there, 1874; also studied with
Liszt; toured S. America, 1872–74;
1879, founded Munich Choral Society.

Bustini (boos-tē'-nē), **Aless.; b.** Rome,
Dec. 24, 1876; Italian composer,
prod. succ. opera "*Maria Dulcis*,"
Rome, 1902; libretto by Luigi Ilica.

Buths (boots), **Julius,** Wiesbaden,
May 7, 1851—Düsseldorf, March 12,
1920; pianist; pupil of his father (an
oboist), also of Gernsheim, Hiller and
Kiel; 1871–72, cond. the "Cecilia,"
at Wiesbaden; 1873, won Meyerbeer
Scholarship, and lived in Milan and
Paris; 1875–79, cond. in Breslau; in
Elberfeld, 1879–90; cond. Mus. Soc.
at Elberfeld; 1890–1908, civic mus.
dir., Düsseldorf and, 1902, head of
Cons. there; c. concerto, etc., for pf.

Butt, Clara, Southwick, Sussex, Feb. 1,
1873—near Oxford, Jan. 23, 1936;
eminent English contralto; won
scholarship at London R. C. M.;
pupil of Bouhy and Mme. Gerster;
début, London, 1892; toured America several times after 1899; long a
favourite soloist at festivals in Great
Britain, and one of the most popular
concert singers of her day; made
world tour in 1913–14 with her husband, R. Kennerly Rumford, barytone; works esp. written for her included Elgar's "*Sea Pictures*"; Dame
Commander of the British Empire.

But'terworth, George, London, July 12,
1885—died in battle, at Pozières,
Aug. 5, 1916; composer; grad. of
Oxford Univ., studied music privately; a short time at R. College of
Music; c. orch. works incl. "*A Shropshire Lad*," chamber music and songs.

Buttstedt (boot'-shtĕt), **Jn. H.,** Bindersleben, 1666—Erfurt, 1727; writer
of a famous defence of sol-mi-sa-tion;
also organist and composer.

Buus (boos), **Jachet (Jacques) de,**
Bruges (?), 1510—Vienna, 1565;
Flemish cptist; 1541, asst. organist,
San Marco.

Buxtehude (boox'-tĕ-hoo-dĕ), **Dietrich,**
Helsingör (Elsinore), Denmark, 1637
—Lübeck, 1707; organist; 1673, he
established the "Abendmusiken,"
which J. S. Bach walked 50 miles to
hear; great composer of fugues and
suites.

Byrd (Byrde, Bird, or Byred), Wm.;
according to his will, discovered in
1897, he was born London, 1542, or
1543 (not 1538 or 1546, as stated); d.
July 4, 1623; organist and notable
English composer, in whose work
there is much modernity; 1554, organist; 1563, choirmaster and organist Lincoln Cathedral; 1575, procured
with Tallis, his former teacher, an
exclusive patent for the privilege of
printing music and selling music-
paper; has been called "English
Palestrina" for his supreme church
choral music; also celebrated for
his harpsichord comps.

C

Caballero (kä-bä-yä'-rō), **Manuel Fer-
nandez,** Murcia, March 14, 1835—
Madrid, Feb. 20, 1906; pupil of
Fuertes (harm.) and Eslava (comp.),
Madrid Cons.; c. pop. *Zarzuelas*
(v. D. D.) and church-music.

Cabel (kä-bĕl), rightly **Cabu,** (1) **Ed.,**
singer Op. Com., Paris. (2) **Marie
Josephe** (née **Dreulette**), Liége,
1827—1885; sister-in-law, or perhaps
mother, of above; soprano.

Cabezon (kä'-bä-thōn), (1) **(Felix),
Antonio De,** Santander, March 30,
1510—May 26, 1566; composer;
cembalist and organist to Philip II;
called "The Spanish Bach"; blind
from birth; c. harp and lute pieces,
published in 1578 by his son (2)
Hernando, who succeeded him.

Cabo (kä'-bō), **Francisco Javier,** Na-
guera, near Valencia, 1768—Valen-
cia, 1832; organist, conductor and
composer.

Caccini (kät-chē'-nē), **Giulio** (called
Romano), Rome, ca. 1546—Florence,
1618; a revolutionary composer
well called "The father of a new style
of music"; studied singing and flute-
playing with Scipione della Palla.
Wrote and sang "*Musica in Stile
Rappresentativo*," and c. "*Il Rapti-
mento di Cefalo*" (Oct. 9, 1600), the
first opera ever publicly prod.; he
had also set to music other works by
Bardi (q. v.), and collaborated with
Peri (q. v.) in "*Dafne*," the first
opera ever composed. He c. also
a novel set of madrigals justly called
"*Le nuove musiche*," and other works
of notable originality and importance
to progress.

Cad'man, Charles Wakefield, b. Johns-
town, Pa., Dec. 24, 1881; at 13 began

piano studies, at 19 composed a comic opera, prod. at Pittsburgh, but did not study composition till 20; pupil of W. K. Steiner (organ), Luigi von Kunits (orchestration), with critical advice from Emil Paur; took up Indian music, 1906 published *"Four Indian Songs"*; 1909 spent summer among the Omaha Indians, taking phonograph records and transcribing them; gives lecture-recitals on Indian music. C. *"Three Moods"* for symph. orch.; chamber music; cantata for male voices *"The Vision of Sir Launfal,"* Japanese romance for two voices, *"Sayonara"*; three *"Songs to Odysseus"*; Indian songs, operas, *"Shanewis"* (Met. Op., 1918); *"Witch of Salem"* (Chicago Op., 1926); *"Sunset Trail"* (Denver, Col., 1922); *"Garden of Mystery"* (N. Y., 1925); song cycle, *"White Enchantment"*; also *"Dark Dancers of the Mardi Gras"* for piano and orch., in which the comp. has played as soloist with many orchs.

Cafaro (kä-fä'-rō), **Pasq.** (called **Cafariel'lo**), San Pietro, Glatina, Italy, 1706—Naples, 1787; noted composer; c. operas, oratorios, a notable *"Stabat mater,"* etc.

Caffarelli (rightly **Gaetano Majorano**) (käf-fä-rĕl'-lĭ), Bari, April 16, 1703—Santo-Dorato, near Naples, Nov. 30, 1783; famous male soprano; discovered as a peasant boy, by Caffaro, a musician, he took the name Caffarelli out of gratitude; he studied 5 years with Porpora; was a skilful sight-reader and harpsichordist, a marvellous singer of florid music, and also gifted with pathos; had most successful début, Rome, 1724, in a female rôle, and sang with enormous success everywhere except London; made money enough to buy a dukedom.

Caffi (käf'-fē), **Fran.**, Venice, 1780—Padua, 1874; writer.

Cagnoni (kän-yō'-nĭ), **A.**, Godiasco, 1828—Bergamo, 1896; conductor and dram. composer.

Cahen (kä-än), (1) **Ernest**, Paris, 1828—1893; pianist and dram. composer. (2) **Albert**, Paris, Jan. 8, 1846—Cap d'Ail, March, 1903; pianist; pupil of Mme. Szarvady and César Franck; c. *"Jean le Précurseur,"* biblical poem (1874); com. opera *"Le Bois"* (1880, Op. Com.); fairy opera *"La Belle au Bois Dormant"* (Geneva, 1886); 4-

act opera *"Le Vénitien"* (Rouen, 1890); unsucc. opera *"La Femme de Claude"* (Paris, Op. Com., 1896), etc.

Cahier (kä-yā), **Mme. Charles** (née **Walker**), b. Nashville, Tenn., Jan. 6, 1875; contralto; sang in concert as Mrs. Morris Black, then studied with Jean de Reszke; début in opera as "Orfeo" (Nice, 1904); sang in other cities and from 1909 at Vienna Royal Opera. 1912 at Met. Op., N. Y.; also widely in concert; a noted teacher.

Caimo (kä'-ē-mö), **Joseffo**, b. Milan, ca. 1540; composer.

Caland (kä'-länt), **Elizabeth**, Rotterdam, Jan. 30, 1862—Berlin, Jan. 26, 1929; teacher and author of piano methods.

Caldara (käl-dä'-rä), **A.**, Venice, 1670—Vienna, Dec. 28, 1736; court-conductor and noted composer, Vienna; c. operas, 70 sacred dramas, etc.

Cal'dicott, Alfred Jas., Worcester, England, 1842 — near Gloucester, Oct. 24, 1897; organist of St. Stephen's Church, Worcester, and Corporation organist; 1883, prof. at R. C. M., London; from 1885, cond. at the Albert Palace; c. cantatas, 13 operettas, etc.

Calegari (käl-ā-gä'-rē), (1) (or **Callegari**) **Fran. A.**, d. Padua, 1740?; a Franciscan monk, 1702–24; conductor and writer at Venice, then Padua. (2) **A.**, Padua, 1757–1828; dram. composer and writer.

Cal'kin, J. Bapt., London, March 16, 1827—May 15, 1905; pianist, organist and composer; prof. Guildhall School of Mus.; pub. services, etc.

Callaerts (käl'-lärts), **Jos.**, Antwerp, Aug. 22, 1838—March 3, 1901; pupil of Lemmens at Brussels Cons.; organist at Antwerp Cathedral, and teacher at the Music School from 1867; c. a prize symphony and pf. trio, comic opera; *"Le Retour Imprévu"* (Antwerp, 1889), etc.

Call'cott, (1) **J. Wall**, Kensington, Nov. 20, 1766—May 15, 1821; mainly self-taught; organist; 1789 he won all the prizes offered by the "Catch Club"; 1790, pupil of Haydn; 1800, Mus. Doc. (Oxon); 1806, lectured at the Royal Institute; projected unfinished musical dictionary; mental disorder overtook him before it was concluded; his *"Grammar of Music"* (1806) is standard.

(2) **Wm. Hutchins,** Kensington, 1807 —London, 1882; son of above; organist and pianist.

Calliope (kăl-lĭ'-ō-pĕ or kăl-lē'-ō-pă), the Greek muse of heroic verse.

Calo'ri, Angiola, Milan, 1732—1790; soprano.

Calsabigi (kăl-sä-bē'-jē), **Raniero da,** Livorno, 1715 — Naples, 1795; Gluck's librettist and aide in opera-reformation.

Calvé (kăl-vä), **Emma (de Roquer),** b. Décazeville, France, 1863 (1866?); eminent operatic actress and soprano; pupil of Marchesi and Pugets; 1882, début in Massenet's "*Hérodiade,*" Th. de la Monnaie, Brussels; 1884, Paris Th. Italien; 1885, Op. Com.; also in London; after 1893 sang in New York, making great furore with her inimitable and rakish "Carmen"; also feted for her "Santuzza," "Juliette," etc., at Met. Op.; a concert singer of note; she is an Officier d'Académie, and lives in Paris.

Calvis'ius, Sethus (rightly **Seth Kallwitz** (kăl'-vēts)), Feb. 21, 1556—Leipzig, Nov. 24, 1615; son of a peasant; singer for alms, then as a teacher obtained funds to study; (1581) mus. dir.; writer of important treatises and composer.

Calvocores'si, Michel D., b. Marseilles (of Greek parents), Oct. 2, 1877; critic and musicologist; studied Paris Cons.; writer and lecturer on French and especially Russian music; wrote biogs. of Liszt, Moussorgsky, Glinka, Schumann, and author of "*La Musique Russe*"; has contributed to many periodicals, and translated into French Rimsky-Korsakoff's treatise on orchestration, as well as mus. texts into various languages; lives in London.

Calvör (kăl'-fär), **Kaspar,** Hildesheim, 1650—Clausthal, 1725; theorist.

Camar'go, (1) **Felix Antonio,** b. Guadalajara, 16th cent.; cathedral cond. at Valladolid; c. remarkable hymn to St. Iago, etc. (2) see CUPIS.

Cambert (kăn-băr), **Rob.,** Paris, ca. 1628—London, 1677; first composer of French operas; organist at St. Honoré; 1659, "*La Pastorale*" was succ. prod. at the Château d'Issy; and followed by others on the texts of Perrin, who received letters patent for establishing the "Académie royale de musique" (now the **Gr.**

Opéra); with Perrin he also wrote the first genuine opera, "*Pomone,*" prod. 1671, before Lully, who later took the patent for himself; he went to England where he died as Master of the Music to Charles II.

Cambini (käm-bē'-nē), **Giov. Giu.,** Leghorn, 1746—Bicêtre, 1825 (?); cond. at Paris, and prolific but cheap composer of over 60 symphonies, 144 string-quartets, several operas, etc.; he died in the almshouse.

Cam'eron, Basil, b. Reading, England, 1885; conductor; sang as choir boy; began vln. study at 8 with Otto Milani, harmony and comp. from Tertius Noble; 1902, studied with Joachim in Berlin, conducting with Hausmann; played in Queen's Hall Orch. as violinist, also studying with Auer; 1913 cond. Munic. Orch., Torquay, where gave a Wagner Fest.; after war in charge of music at Harrogate and Hastings; guest cond. R. Phil. Soc., London; 1930, cond. San Francisco Symph. with Dobrowen, re-engaged for 2nd season; after 1932, cond. Seattle Symph. with pronounced succ.

Camet'ti, Alberto, b. Rome, May 5, 1871—1935; pupil at Academy of St. Cecilia; organist of the French church of St. Louis at Rome; historian of music and comp.

Cam'idge, (1) **J.,** ca. 1735—York, Engl., 1803; organist York cath., 47 years; composer. (2) **Mat.,** York, 1764—1844; son and successor of above. (3) **J.,** York, 1790—1859; son and successor of (2).

Campagnoli (käm-pän-yō'-lē), **Bart.,** Cento, 1751—Neustrelitz, 1827; violinist and court-conductor.

Campana (käm-pä'-nä), **Fabio,** Leghorn, 1819—London, 1882; singing-teacher and dram. composer.

Campanari (käm-pä-nä'-rē), (1) **Leandro,** b. Rovigo, Italy, Oct. 20, 1857; pupil at Milan Cons.; toured Europe 2 years; America, 1879; lived in Boston; organised "C. String-quartet"; 1883 1st prof. of vln. in N. E. Cons.; 1890, 1st. prof. of vln. and head of orch. dept. Cincinnati Cons.; 1897-1905, conductor at Milan; 1906, at Manhattan Op. House, N. Y.; after 1907, taught in San Francisco; where d. April 23, 1939. (2) **Giuseppe,** Venice, Nov. 17, 1858— Milan, May 31, 1927; eminent dram. barytone; at first a 'cellist at La

Scala; engaged to play in Boston Symph.; also in Adamowski Quartet; 1893, after vocal study, sang with Hinrichs Op. Co.; also with Juch and Grau companies; 1895–08, Met. Op.; later in Europe.

Campanini (käm-pä-nē'-nē), (1) **Italo**, Parma, 1846—Vigatto, near Parma, Nov. 22, 1896; operatic tenor, a blacksmith when discovered; début, 1869, at Odessa, without much success; then studied with Lamperti, and reappeared, Florence, 1871, as "Lohengrin," with great succ.; toured Europe and U. S. with Nilsson, Patti, etc. (2) **Cleofonte**, Parma, Sept. 1, 1860—Chicago, Dec. 19, 1919; conductor; pupil Milan Cons., later teacher there; cond. at La Scala, Covent Garden, and 1906–09, at Manhattan Opera House, New York; married Eva Tetrazzini, operatic soprano (sister and teacher of Luisa); from 1910 he was cond. and after 1913 artistic dir. of the Chicago Op. Co. He was instrumental in founding the Edith Rockefeller McCormick Prize for opera composers at the Milan Cons.

Campbell-Tipton, Louis, Chicago, Nov. 21, 1877—Paris, May 1, 1921; studied in Chicago, Boston and Leipzig; lived in Paris; his important compositions played abroad, notably his "*Heroic*" sonata for piano, piano suites, "*The Four Seasons*," "*Suite Pastorale*," for piano and violin; also c. striking songs.

Cam'pion, (1) **Thos.**, d. London, Feb., 1620; English physician, poet, dramatist and noteworthy writer and composer; pub. two books of Ayres, etc. (1610); 2 more (1612). (2) **Fran.**, 1703–19, theorbist, Paris Gr. Opéra.

Campio'ni, Carlo A., Leghorn, ca. 1720 —Florence, 1793; court-conductor.

Camporese (käm-pō-rä'-zĕ), **Violante**, b. Rome, 1785; operatic sopr. of Napoleon's private music; début, London, 1817; retired, 1829.

Campos (käm'pōs), **João Ribeiro de Almeida de**, b. Vizen, Portugal, ca. 1770; cond. and professor.

Campra (kän-prä), (1) **André**, Dec. 4, 1660—Versailles, July 29, 1744; cond. at Nôtre Dame; prod. 2 succ. operas under his bro.'s name and gave up church-mus.; cond. Royal Orch. and c. 18 operas. (2) **Jos.**, bro. of above; double-bass player.

Camps y Soler (kämps ē sō'-lär), **Oscar**, Alexandria, Nov. 21, 1837—Madrid, ?; Spanish pianist; pupil of Döhler and Mercadante; played in public at 13; lived in Madrid; writer and theorist.

Canal (kä'-näl), **Abbate Pietro**, Crespano, April 13, 1807—Dec. 15, 1883; historian and comp.

Canale (or **Canali**) (kä-nä'-lē), **Floriano**, organist at Brescia, 1585–1603; c. church-music.

Candeille (kän-dĕ'-yŭ), (1) **P. Jos.**, Estaires, 1744 — Chantilly, 1827; dram. composer. (2) (**Simons-Candeille**) **Amélie Julie**, Paris, 1767 —1834; operatic sopr., actress, and composer; daughter of above; lived in Paris as teacher; she wrote libretto and music of the succ. operetta "*La Belle Fermière*" (1792); she played the leading rôle and sang to her own accomp. on piano and harp.

Cange (dü känzh), **Chas.-Dufrèsne**, sieur du, Amiens, 1610—Paris, 1688; lawyer and lexicographer.

Cannabich (kän'-nä-bĭkh), (1) **Chr.**, Mannheim, 1731—Frankfort, 1798; noteworthy violinist and conductor, a pioneer in orchestral diminuendo; son of (2) **Mathias**, a flutist in the Electoral Orch. at Mannheim of which **Chr. C.** became leader in 1765, and cond. 1775. (3) **K.**, Mannheim, 1764—Munich, 1806; son of (1); court-conductor. (4) **Rose**, b. about 1762 according to Mozart, whose pupil she was; daughter of (1); notable pianist.

Canniciari (kän-nē-chä'-rĕ), **Don Pompeo**, d. Rome, 1744; conductor and composer.

Capet (kä-pā'), **Lucien**, Paris, Jan. 8, 1873—Dec. 19, 1928; violinist and chamber music performer; pupil of Paris Cons., where won 1st prize; taught at Bordeaux; after 1907 led chamber music classes at Paris Cons., and after 1924 artistic dir. of Paris Inst. de Violon; founded noted Capet Quartet in 1903, with which he appeared with succ. in many European cities.

Caplet (käp-lä), **André**, Havre, Nov. 25, 1878—Paris, April 24, 1925; eminent composer; pupil of Wollett; violinist at Havre Theatre, 1896; pupil of Leroux at Paris Cons., winning first harmony prize, 1898, and Prix de Rome, 1901; lived in Rome, then in Germany; acted as assistant to Colonne, 1898; 1900, was the first to cond. Debussy's *"Martyre de San Sebastien"*; 1911–12 cond. at Boston Op.; also at Covent Garden, London; c. piano quintet; *"Legend"* for harp and orch. after Poe's *"Masque of the Red Death"*; *"Suite Persane"* for wood-winds; Septet for three women's voices and strings; Mass for three-part women's chorus; Sonata for voice, 'cello and piano; *"Le Miroir de Jésus,"* 15 pieces for soloists, chorus and orch., which has been perf. frequently in France; a number of songs and choruses.

Capocci (kä-pòt'-chē), (1) **Gaetano,** Rome, Oct. 16, 1811—Jan. 11, 1898; notable teacher; pub. much sacred music. (2) **Filippo,** Rome, May 11, 1840—July 25, 1911; son of above; Italian organist; 1875 organist of San Giovanni at the Lateran; c. works for organ.

Capoul (kä-pool) (Jos. **Amédée**), **Victor,** Toulouse, Feb. 27, 1839—Pujandran-du-Gers, Feb. 18, 1924; tenor; pupil of Révial and Mocker, Paris Cons.; 1861–72 at the Op. Com.; 1892 prof. of operatic singing in Nat. Cons., New York; 1897, stage manager, Paris Opéra.

Capuzzi (kä-pood'-zē), **Giuseppe Antonio,** Brescia, 1753–1818; c. 5 operas, etc.

Caraccioli (kä-rät-chō-'lē), **Luigi,** Andria (Bari), 1849—London, 1887; dram. composer.

Carado'ri-Allan, Maria C. R. (née de **Munck**), Milan, 1800 — London, 1865; soprano.

Carafa de Colobrano (kä-rä'-fä dä kō-lō-brä'-nō), **Michele Enrico,** Naples, Nov. 17, 1787—Paris, July 26, 1872; son of Prince Colobrano; while very young c. an opera, 2 cantatas, etc., with much success; 1837, member of the Academy; 1840, prof. of comp. at Cons.; c. also ballets, cantatas, and good church-music.

Cardon (kär-dôṅ), (1) **Louis,** Paris, 1747—Russia, 1805; harpist. (2) **P.,** b. Paris, 1751; 'cellist and singer.

Cardo'so, Manuel, Fronteira, 1569; Spanish priest and composer.

Caresana (kär-ä-sä'-nä), **Cristoforo,** b. Tarentum, 1655; lived in Naples as composer.

Carestini (kä-räs-tē'-nē), **Giov.** (stage name **Cusanino**), Mente Filatrano (Ancona), ca. 1705—1760; male soprano (musico).

Ca'rey, (1) **Henry,** 1685 (?)—London, Oct. 4, 1743; a reputed natural son of Marquis of Halifax, and disputed composer of *"God Save the King"*; c. the song *"Sally in Our Alley"*; ballad operas, etc. (2) **Bruce,** b. Hamilton, Ontario, 1877; conductor; studied at R. Coll. of Music, London, also in Florence and Munich; founded and cond. Hamilton Elgar Choir for 17 years; later Phila. Mendelssohn Club and music dir. at Girard Coll. there; succeeded the late Dr. J. Fred Wolle as cond. of Bethlehem Bach Choir, 1933–8.

Carissimi (kä-rïs'-sē-mē), **Giacomo,** Marino, near Rome, ca. 1604—Rome, Jan. 12, 1674; ca. 1624, church-conductor at Rome; important ch.-composer and writer; many of his MSS. are lost; 5 oratorios and other pieces remain.

Carl, Wm. Crane, Bloomfield, N. J., March 2, 1865—New York, Dec. 8, 1936; pupil of S. P. Warren, Mad. Schiller (pf.) and Guilmant, Paris; after 1892, orgauist First Presby. Ch., N. Y.; made tours as concertorganist; 1899, founded Guilmant Organ School, New York; had pub. collections of organ music; active as lecturer.

Car'michael, Mary Grant, Birkenhead, Engl., 1851—London, March 17, 1935; pupil of O. Beringer, W. Bache, and F. Hartvigson (pf.) and E. Prout (comp.); accompanist; c. operetta, *"The Snow Queen"*; a pf.-suite; and many pop. songs.

Carnicer (kär'-nē-thär), **Ramon,** Taregga, Catalonia, Oct. 24, 1789—Madrid, March 17, 1855; cond. Royal Opera, Madrid, 1830–54, prof. of comp. Madrid Cons.; one of the creators of the *Zarzuela* (v. D. D.).

Caro (kä'rō), **Paul,** b. Breslau, Dec. 25, 1859; pupil of Schäffer and Scholz, and Vienna Cons.; c. 2 operas, 5 symph., 30 string-quartets, etc.

Caron (kä-rôṅ), (1) **Philippe,** 15th cent., cptist. (of Netherlands ?). (2) **Rose Lucile** (née **Meuniez**), Monerville, France, Nov. 17, 1857—Paris, April 9, 1930; soprano; after her marriage entered Paris Cons., 1880, as pupil of Tharset, later of Marie Sasse; début Brussels, 1883; 1885–88, Opéra Paris; 1888–90, Brussels; from 1890, Opéra Paris; also at the Op. Com., from 1902 prof. at the Cons. She created many of the chief rôles in modern

French Opera and in French versions of Wagner. She sang "Salammbô" at the Opéra, 1908.

Carpani (kär-pä'-nē), **Giu. A.,** b. Vilalbese (Como), 1752—Vienna, 1825; writer.

Car'penter, John Alden, b. Park Ridge, Ill., Feb. 28, 1876; composer; grad., Harvard Univ.; studied with Bernard Ziehn and Seeboeck; a prominent business executive in Chicago, he has made much more than an avocation of music, taking his place among the most accomplished American comps.; his musical idiom is modern and his output fairly large. C. (ballets) "*The Birthday of the Infanta*" (Chicago Op., 1919–20); "*Krazy Kat*"; "*Skyscrapers*" (Met. Op., 1926); the orch. works, "*Adventures in a Perambulator*"; symphony (Norfolk Fest., 1917); concertino with piano; "*Sea Drift*" (N. Y. Philh., 1935); also a string quartet (Coolidge Fest., Washington); violin sonata; "*Water Colors*" for mezzo-soprano and chamber orch.; "*Improving Songs for Anxious Children*"; and many songs incl. the cycle "*Gitanjali*."

Carpentras (Il Carpentras'so). Vide ELEAZER GENET.

Carré (kär-rä), (1) **Louis,** Clofontaine Brie, 1663—Paris, 1711; writer. (2) **Albert,** b. Strassburg, June 22, 1852; 1898–1912, dir. Op. Com., Paris; librettist; d. Paris, Dec. 12, 1938.

Carreño (kär-rän'-yō), **Teresa,** Caracas, Venezuela, Dec. 22, 1853—New York, June 13, 1917; pupil of L. M. Gottschalk, and G. Mathias; notable pianist; played in public at 12; at 22 toured the U. S.; 1889–90 toured Germany with much success; for some years wife of E. Sauret; then of Giov. Tagliapietra; 1892–95, wife of Eugen d'Albert; 1902, m. Arturo Tagliapietra, bro. of Giov. T.; c. a string-quartet and pf. salon pieces. Her daughter **Teresita Tagliapietra,** also a pianist.

Carreras (kä-rä'-räs), **Maria,** b. Italy; pianist; at six awarded 1st prize at Acad. of Santa Cecilia, Rome, by Liszt, then hon. pres. of this school; studied with Sgambati, under whose baton at 15 she played his concerto with Rome Philh. with much succ.; immediately engaged for concerts in Russia with Imp. Music. Soc. under Safonoff; toured widely in Europe and South America; later in U. S., where she has been res. for some years and has given master classes.

Carrillo (kär-ē'-yō), **Julian,** b. Mexico, 1875; composer who has embodied novel harmonic system in his orch., chamber music and choral works; also author of "*Synthetic Treatise of Harmony*."

Carro'dus, J. Tiplady, Keighley (Yorkshire), 1836—London, 1895; violinist.

Car'ron, Arthur (rightly **Cox**), b. England; tenor; pupil of Florence Easton; sang with Old Vic. Op. Co., London; début, Met. Op. Co., summer popular season, 1936, as Canio; engaged for regular roster of company following unusual succ. in this rôle.

Carse, Adam, b. Newcastle-on-Tyne, May 19, 1878; pupil R. A. M., with the Macfarren scholarship; made an associate there in 1902; c. symph. in C minor; symph. in G minor, symph. poem, "*In a Balcony*"; concert overture, etc.; writer on music.

Car'ter, (1) **Thos.,** Ireland, ca. 1735—London, 1804; composer. (2) **Ernest Trow,** b. Orange, N. J., 1866; organist, conductor, composer; studied New York and Berlin; org. of Amer. Ch. in latter city, and 1899–1901 at Princeton Univ.; c. comic op., "*The Blonde Donna*"; opera, "*The White Bird*" (Chicago, 1924; Osnabrück, Germany, 1927); pantomime, "*Namba*," etc.

Cartier (kärt-yä), **J. Bap.,** Avignon, 1765—Paris, 1841; violinist and dram. composer.

Carulli (kä-rool'-lē), (1) **Fdo.,** Naples, 1770—Paris, 1841; self-taught guitar-virtuoso and teacher; c. 400 concertos. (2) **Gustavo,** Leghorn, 1801—Bologna, 1876; son of above; teacher and dram. composer.

Caruso (kä-roo'-zō), **Luigi,** Naples, 1754—Perugia, 1821; conductor, c. 69 operas. (2) **Enrico,** Naples, Feb. 25, 1873—Aug. 2, 1921; famous Italian tenor; pupil of Vergine; début, 1895, winning gradual success in Italy (Naples, 1898; 1899 La Scala), and creating the tenor rôles in Giordano's "*Fedora*," Cilea's "*Lécouvreur*," and Franchetti's "*Germania*"; 1899–1903 sang in St. Petersburg, and Buenos Aires; 1902, appeared with Melba at Monte Carlo, began his tremendous vogue;

1902 at Covent Garden; 1903–21, Met. Op. House, N. Y.; 1908, his voice was threatened, but an operation restored it. He created the tenor rôle in Puccini's *"Girl of the Golden West,"* in addition to a large number of first Amer. perfs. His repertoire incl. more than 50 rôles, chiefly in Italian and French works, both old and modern. In his later years the voice which was unique among singers of his period for robustness of timbre and fine cultivation, changed slightly from its earlier lyric quality to a darker dram. colour. His powers of characterisation developed also and he made a deep and poignant impression as Eleazar in *"La Juive,"* the rôle he last sang at the Met. Op., Christmas Eve, 1920, when stricken with a hemorrhage of the throat. An emergency operation later performed to relieve an abscessed condition of one lung resulted in a partial convalescence and he sailed for Naples, but passed away suddenly there during the summer. He was for long the most fêted vocalist throughout the world and sang for the highest fees in European capitals, but from 1903 made N. Y. his headquarters. A clever cartoonist, he pub. a book of his drawings and also c. several popular songs.

Carvalho (kär-väl'-ō) (rightly **Carvaille**), (1) **Léon,** in a French colony, 1825–Paris, 1897; from 1875 dir. Op. Com. (2) **Carvalho-Miolan** (mē-ō-läṅ), **Caroline M.-Félix,** Marseilles, 1827–Puys, near Dieppe, 1895; soprano; wife of above; début 1849.

Ca'ry, Annie Louise, Wayne, Kennebec County, Me., Oct. 22, 1842—Norwalk, Conn., April 13, 1921; noted operatic and concert contralto; studied in Boston and Milan, and with Viardot-Garcia, etc.; début 1868, at Hamburg; later Stockholm, Copenhagen, Brussels, London, New York (1870), St. Petersburg (1875); 1882, m. C. M. Raymond, Cincinnati.

Casadesus (cäs-ä-dĕs-üs'), (1) **Francis,** b. Paris, Dec. 2, 1870; conductor, composer; studied Paris Cons., with Lavignac and Franck (harmony prize); Tremont Prize, French Inst.; cond. symph. concerts, Trocadero, Paris, 1918–24; dir. American Cons., Fontainebleau, 1921–23; has cond. radio concerts and been active as

music critic; among his dram. works, *"Un Beau Jardin de France"* was given at Paris Op. Comique, 1918; also c. orchestral works and songs. (2) **Henri,** b. Paris, Sept. 30, 1879; violist; dir. Société des Instruments Anciens, which he founded in collaboration with Saint-Saëns, 1901; of which members are Henri, viole d'amour; Marius C., quinton; Maurice Devilliers, basse de viole; Lucette C., viole de gambe, and Regina C.-Patorni, clavecin; this group has toured widely in Europe, also visiting U. S., and presenting programmes of rare interest from historical standpoint; C. has also been an assiduous collector of old music and instruments; he is a Chevalier of the Legion of Honor. (3) **Marius,** b. Paris, Oct. 24, 1892; composer, violinist; studied Paris Cons., 1st prize, 1914; c. works for vln., orch., voice, 'cello, also chamber music; has appeared as vln. soloist with Boston Symph. Orch. (4) **Robert,** b. Paris, April 7, 1899; pianist; received early training from Mme. Marie Simon, an aunt; at 13 entered Paris Cons., winning 1st prize in piano; has appeared widely in concerts in France, Belgium, Holland, etc., after 1935–36 in U. S., where made début as soloist with N. Y. Philh.; dir. piano dept., Amer. Cons., Fontainebleau.

Casali (kä-sä'-lē), **Giov. Bat.,** d. 1792; conductor and dram. composer.

Casals', Pablo, b. Vendrell, Spain, Dec. 30, 1876; eminent 'cellist; pupil of Jose Garcia, Rodereda and Breton; 1897, prof. at Barcelona Cons.; toured widely; c. *"La Vision de Fray Martin,"* for chorus and orch.; 'cello pieces, etc.; after 1919 cond. of Orquesta Pau Casals, Barcelona, and made few concert appearances as 'cellist; member of noted trio including Cortot and Thibaud; m. Guilhermina Suggia, 'cellist, 1906; divorced, 1912; (2) Susan Metcalfe, singer.

Casamorata (kä-sä-mō-rä'-tä), **Luigi Fdo.,** Würzburg, 1807–Florence, 1881; editor, writer, and composer.

Casati (kä-sä'-tē), **Gasparo,** d. Novara, 1643; cond. at Novara Cathedral; c. church music.

Casa'vola, Franco, b. Bari, Italy, July 13, 1892; composer; pupil of La Rotella, Mapelli and Respighi; his music has been called "futuristic" and includes various ballets and a comic opera, "*Il Gobbo del Califfo*," which won 1st prize in a nat'l. contest and was given at the Rome R. Op., 1929.

Case, Anna, b. Clinton, N. J., Oct. 29, 1889; soprano; studied with Augusta Ohrstrom-Renard; mem. Met. Op. Co., 1909–16; has also sung in concerts and at festivals; m. Clarence H. Mackay, chm. board of directors, N. Y. Philh. Soc.

Casel'la, P., (1) Pieve (Umbria), 1769 —Naples, 1843; dram. composer. (2) **Alfredo,** b. Turin, Italy, July 25, 1883; composer, pianist, conductor; studied with Diémer, Leroux and Fauré, Paris Cons., 1st piano prize, 1899; début, Paris, 1911; cond. popular concerts, Trocadero, Paris, 1912; prof. advanced pf., Paris Cons., 1912–15; also at Liceo Musicale di S. Cecilia, Rome, 1915; has served as guest cond. of many orchs. in various Eur. and Amer. cities; leading spring concert series with Boston Symph. Orch., 1927–29; is best known as a versatile, somewhat eclectic but highly accomplished composer of works in modern idiom, incl. "*Italia*," rhapsody for orch.; the ballet, "*La Giara*" (Met. Op. House production, 1926–27); 2 symphonies; "*Prologue pour une Tragedie*," "*Notte di Maggio*" (with chorus), string-quartet, 'cello sonata, and other chamber music, songs, piano pieces; Serenata for small chamber ensemble, etc. C. in 1917 founded a Societa di Musica Moderna in Rome; he has lectured in America and also appeared here with the Trio Italiano; winner in 1928 of 1st prize of Philadelphia Musical Fund Soc. for composition. Has also c. an opera, "*La Donna Serpente*" after a fairy tale by Gozzi (1932); symph. suite, "*Le Couvent sur l'Eau*" from a ballet of the same name; "*Elegia Eroica*" and "*Pagine di Guerra*" for orch.; "*Pupazzetti*," 5 pieces for marionettes; "*Concerto Romano*" for organ and orch.; "*Siciliana e Burlesca*" for vln., 'cello and pf.; "*Cinque Pezzi*" for string-quartet, etc. His earlier style was markedly dissonantal as shown in his "*A Notte Alta*"; later comps. show a reversion to a simpler manner based on pre-classic models. Author, "*The Evolution of Music*," "*Stravinsky*," etc.

Caser'ta, Philippe de, Neapolitan theorist, 15th century.

Casimiro (kǎ-sē-mē'-rō), **da Silva Joaquim,** Lisbon, May 30, 1808— Dec. 28, 1862; Portuguese comp. of church music.

Casini (kä-sē'-nē), **G. M.,** b. 1670 (?); Florentine priest; he tried to revive Greek modes.

Cassado (cä-sä'-dō), **Gaspar,** b. Barcelona, 1898; 'cellist; pupil of Casals; has toured widely as outstanding virtuoso, incl. Spain, France, Germany, Austria, and in 1936 for first time in U. S.; also active as composer; his Rapsodia Catalana played by N. Y. Philh. under Mengelberg, 1928; c. 3 string quartets, trio for piano, vln. and 'cello; ed. works of Mozart, Weber and Schubert.

Castagna (käs-tän'-yä), **Bruna;** Ital. mezzo-soph.; sang Met. Op. after 1935.

Castel (käs-tĕl), **Louis Bertrand,** Montpellier, 1688—Paris, 1757; a Jesuit writer who attempted without success to construct a "Clavecin oculaire," to prod. colour harmonies.

Castellan (käs-tel-läṅ), **Jeanne A.,** b. Beaujeu, Oct. 26, 1819; retired, 1859; singer.

Castel'li, (1) **Ignaz Fz.,** Vienna, 1781 —1862; editor.

Castelmary (käs-tĕl-mä-rē) (stage name of Comte **Armand de Castan**), Toulouse, Aug. 16, 1834—New York, Feb. 9, 1897; barytone; died on the stage of the Met. Op., N. Y., just after the first act of "*Martha*."

Castelnuovo-Tedesco (cäs-tĕl-nōō-ō'-vō tĕ-dĕs'-kō), **Mario,** b. Florence, April 3, 1895; composer; studied Cherubini Cons., Florence; composition with Pizzetti; c. opera "*La Mandragola*," which won national lyric prize in 1925 and had première at Venice, 1926; "Italian" Concerto for vln. and orch., concerto for piano and orch. (1926); Symphonic Variations for vln. and orch. (N. Y. Philh., under Toscanini, 1930); also many madrigals, part-songs, songs and piano works; in the last category are some 30 "*Poemetti*" and 3 "*Poemi Campestri*"; he is known for his "*Three Chorales on Hebrew Melodies*" for voice and piano; also about 100 settings of lyrics in various languages, incl. original series of "*Shakespeare Songs*"; a trio, a quartet; "*Cipressi*," an orch. sonata: "*Tre Fioretti di*

Santo Francesco" for voice and orch.; and "*Bacco in Toscana,*" a "dithyramb in one act" for soloists, chorus, orch. and dancers, to a poem by Redi; has written extensively on music.

Castil-Blaze. Vide BLAZE, F. H. J.

Castillon (kăs-tē-yôn̄), **Alexis de, Vicomte de Saint Victor,** Chartres, Dec. 13, 1838—Paris, March 5, 1873; composer; pupil of Massé and César Franck; c. symphony; overture, *Torquato Tasso, Psalm 84* with orch.; piano concerto and important chamber music.

Cas'tro, (1) **Jean de,** played Lyons, 1570; composer and lutenist. (2) **Juan Jose,** b. Buenos Aires, March 7, 1895; composer; pupil of d'Indy at Paris Schola Cantorum; cond. of orch. at Colon Theatre, in native city, introd. many modern scores; c. of orch. works, incl. "*Biblical*" *Symphony.*

Castrucci (käs-troot'-chē), (1) **P.,** Rome, 1679—Dublin, 1752; violinist; leader of Händel's opera-orch.; inv. and played the *violetta marina.* His bro. (2) **Prospero** (d. London, 1769); violinist and composer.

Catalani (kät-ä-lä'-nē), (1) **Angelica,** Sinigaglia, Oct., 1780—Paris, June 12, 1849; famous operatic soprano of great beauty; her voice was notably flexible and reached to g''' ; in 1806, at London, she earned over £16,000 ($80,000) in one year; 1814–17, she took up management of the Th. Italien, Paris, without succ. After final appearance, York festival, in 1828, she retired to her country-seat, near Florence. (2) **Alfredo,** Lucca, June 19, 1854—Milan, Aug. 6, 1893; pupil of his father, an organist; at 14, c. a mass sung at the cathedral; pupil of Magi, and of Paris Cons. and Milan Cons.; c. operas "*La Falce*" (Milan, 1875); "*Elda*" (Turin, 1880; revised as "*Loreley,*" 1890); "*Dejanice*" (1883); "*Ero e Leandro* (1885), "*Edmea*" (1886), "*La Wally*" (La Scala, 1892); symph. poem "*Ero e Leandro,*" etc.

Catel (kă-tĕl), **Chas. Simon,** L'Aigle, Orne, 1773—Paris, 1830; dram. composer and writer.

Catelani (kät-ä-lä'-nē), **Angelo,** Guastalla, 1811—S. Martino di Mugnano, 1866; dram. composer and writer.

Catoire (kăt-wăr), **Georg L.,** Moscow, April 27, 1861—May, 1926; pupil

of Klindworth, Willborg, and Liadov; c. symphony; symph. poem, "*Mzyri*"; cantata, "*Russalka,*" piano concerto, quintet, quartet and trio for strings, "*Poème*" for vln., choruses, songs, etc.

Catrufo (kä-troo'-fō), **Giu.,** Naples, 1771—London, 1851; dram. composer.

Caurroy (kôr-wä), **Fran. Eustache du,** sieur de St.-Fremin, Gerberoy 1549—Paris, 1609; singer and conductor.

Cavaccio (kä-vät'-chō), **Giovanni,** Bergamo, ca. 1556—Rome, 1626; conductor.

Cavaillé-Coll. (kä-vī'-yä-kôl'), **Aristide,** Montpellier, 1811—Paris, 1899; famous organ-builder; son of **Hyacinthe Cavaillé,** c. 1771—1862, org.-builder and inv. of separate windchests with different pressures, etc.

Cavalieri (dĕl kä-väl-yä'-rē), (1) **Emilio del,** Rome, ca. 1550—March 11, 1602; appointed "Inspector-Gen. of Art and Artists" to the Tuscan court; advocated non-polyphonic music; his "*Rappresentazione di Anima e di Corpo*" (Rome, 1600) is the first oratorio. (2) **Katherina,** Vienna, 1761 —1801; singer, whom Mozart wrote for and praised. (3) **Lina,** b. Rome, Dec. 24, 1874; soprano; won notoriety as beauty and singer in cafés chantants; then studied with Mme. Mariani-Maesi; succ. début in "*Pagliacci,*" Lisbon, 1900; sang Naples, Warsaw, and 1902, at Dal Verme Th., Milan; 1906, Met. Op.; 1908–9, Manhattan Op.; 1915–16, Chicago Op.; m. Lucien Muratore, tenor; divorced.

Caval'li, **Fran.,** Crema, Feb. 14, 1602—Venice, Jan. 14, 1676 (rightly Pier Francesco, **Caletti-Bruni**), son of **Giambatt. Caletti,** called **Bruni,** Maestro at Crema. A Venetian nobleman, Federigo Cavalli, had him taught and he took his name. He sang at S. Marco, 1665; first organist there; 1668, conductor; he was a pupil of Monteverde and developed M.'s principles, composing 41 operas, the most succ. being "*Giasone*" (Venice, 1649); "*Serse*" (1654); "*Ercole Amante*" (Paris, 1662); he c. also a notable requiem, and other church-music.

Cavallini (lē'-nē), **Ernesto,** Milan, 1807 —1874; clarinettist and composer.

Cavos (kä'-vōs), **Catterino,** Venice,

1776—St. Petersburg, 1840; 1799, court-conductor; c. 13 Russian operas; also others.

Cazzati (käd-zä'-tē), **Maurizio**, Mantua, ca. 1620—1677; composer and conductor.

Cecil'ia (Saint), d. Rome, A.D. 230, in Christian martyrdom; her feast-day is Nov. 22d; legendary inventor of the organ, and patron saint of Christian music.

Celler, Ludovic. Vide LECLERQ.

Cellier (sĕl'-yĕr), **Alfred**, Hackney, London, Dec. 1, 1844—Dec. 28, 1891; conductor in London, etc.; c. 15 operettas, incl. the very succ. "*Dorothy*" (1886); "*The Mountebanks*" (London, 1892), etc.

Cerone (chā-rō'-nĕ), **Dom. P.**, b. Bergamo, ca. 1566; theorist.

Cerreto (chĕr-rā'-tō), **Scipione**, Naples, 1551—ca. 1632; lutist and theorist.

Certon (sĕr-tôṅ), **P.**, 16th cent., contrapuntist; choirm. Sainte Chapelle, Paris.

Cerù (chā-roo'), **Dom. Ag.**, b. Lucca, Aug. 28, 1817; engineer and writer.

Červeny (chär'-vā-nĕ), **V. F. (Wenzel Fz.)**, Dubec, Bohemia, 1819—Königgrätz, Jan. 19, 1896; maker and improver of brass instrs. and inv. of the important "roller" cylinder mechanism, also of the contrabass (1845), metal contrafagotto ('56), althorn obbligato ('59), primhorn ('73), and the complete waldhorn quartet (primhorn, E♭ alto, waldhorn in F, tenor in B♭, basso, 11 in D♭), subcontrabass and subcontrafagotto; improved the family of cornets, the euphonion, the screwdrum, and the church-kettledrum, etc.

Cervetti. Vide GELINEK.

Cervetto (chĕr-vĕt'-tō), (1) **Giacomo** (rightly **Bassevi**), Italy, ca. 1682—London, Jan. 14, 1783; 'cellist. (2) **Giacomo**, London, 1749 (?)—Feb. 5, 1837; son of above; 'cellist and composer.

Cesi (chā'-zē), **Beniamino**, Naples, Nov. 6, 1845—Jan. 19, 1907; pupil of Naples Cons. under Mercadante and Pappalardo, pf.-pupil of Thalberg; 1866, prof. Naples Cons.; c. an opera, "*Vittor Pisani*" (not prod.), etc.

Cesti (chās'-tē), **Marc A.**, Arezzo, 1618—Venice, 1669; Franciscan monk; conductor and tenor singer; first opera, "*Orontea*," succ. at Venice, 1649; wrote 10 other operas

mainly succ.; all lost now except "*La Dori*" (Venice, 1663); his cantatas are better preserved; he wrote them for the stage.

Chabran (shă-bräṅ), or **Ciabrano** (cha-brä'-nō), **Francesco**, b. Piedmont, 1723; violinist and comp.; 1751, toured Europe with success.

Chabrier (shăb-rĭ-ā), **Alexis Emm.**, Auvergne, Jan. 18, 1841—Paris, Sept. 13, 1894; studied law in Paris, then music; 1881, choirm., under Lamoureux; c. operettas, rhapsodie "*España*" for orch., etc. After his death in 1894 his unfinished opera, "*Briséis*," was given at the Opéra Paris, 1899; his opera "*Gwendoline*" (text by Catulle Mendès), at the Op. Com., 1911. C. also opera "*Le Roi malgré lui*" (1887); scena, "*La Sulamite*"; choral, orch. and piano works. Memoirs pub. by Séré and Servières.

Chad'wick, George Whitefield, Lowell, Mass., Nov. 13, 1854—Boston, April 7, 1931; studied organ, etc., under Eugene Thayer at Boston; 1876 head of mus. dept. of Olivet Coll., Mich.; 1877-78 studied Leipzig Cons. (Reinecke, Jadassohn), his graduation piece being an overture to "*Rip Van Winkle*"; studied at Munich with Rheinberger; 1880, organist Boston and teacher of harm., comp. and instrumentation at the N. E. Cons.; 1897-1931, dir.; cond. the Worcester Mus. Festivals, resigned, 1902; c. 3 symphonies; overtures, "*Rip Van Winkle*" ('79) "*Thalia*" ('83), "*Melpomene*" ('87), "*The Miller's Daughter*" ('88); 3 symphonic sketches for orch.; comic opera "*Tabasco*" (New York, '94); many choral works; "*The Columbian Ode*" (Chicago, '93); overtures "*Adonais*" (1900); "*Euterpe*" (1904); "*Cleopatra*" (1906); symphonic sketches (1908); theme, variations and fugue for organ and orch. (1909); "*Sinfonietta*" (1910); "*Suite Symphonique*" for orch. winning $700 prize of Nat. Federation of Clubs (1910); c. also "*Noel*" (1909); "*Lochinvar*," ballad for barytone and orch., 1909. "*Judith*" lyric drama, Worcester Fest., 1900; incid. music to "*Everywoman*" (1911); symph. poem "*Aphrodite*" (Norfolk, 1912); "*Tam O'Shanter*" (1917); opera "*Love's Sacrifice*" (1915), 5 string quartets, trio, piano quintet, church music, songs, etc.; wrote a text-book on "Harmony" (Boston, 1898).

Chaliapine (shäl-yä′-pēn), **Fedor Ivanovich**, Kazan, Feb. 11, 1873—Paris, April 12, 1938. Eminent Russian bass; pupil of Oussatov, in Tiflis; sang in various cities, finally at Moscow, and with immense success in European capitals; 1908, New York, at Met. Op. in Italian rôles, but on his return in 1921 to U. S. he established his full artistic stature as a powerfully eloquent protagonist in *"Boris Godounoff,"* and as Mephistopheles, King Philip in *"Don Carlos,"* etc.; also a highly individual concert singer, mostly of Russian songs.

Challier (shäl′-lĭ-ĕr), **Ernst**, Berlin, July 9, 1843—Giessen, Sept. 19, 1914; music-publisher, Berlin.

Cham′berlain, Houston Stewart, Portsmouth, England, Sept. 9, 1855—Bayreuth, Jan. 9, 1927; son-in-law of Richard Wagner, whose daughter, Eva, he m. 1908; renounced British citizenship and became German subject; son of a British Admiral, took doctor's degree in Germany, and lived at Vienna because of his health; pub. famous book "Richard Wagner" (Leipzig, 1892), followed by others.

Chambonnières (shän-bŭn-yăr), **Jacques Champion** (called "Champion de Chamb."), d. ca. 1670; first chamber cembalist to Louis XIV.

Chaminade (shăm′-ĭ-năd′), **Cécile (Louise Stéphanie),** b. Paris, Aug. 8, 1861; pianist and composer of spirit and originality; pupil of Lecouppey, Savard, Marsick and Godard; c. the succ. "ballet-symphonie" *"Callirhoë"* (Marseilles, 1888); the "symphonie lyrique" *"Les Amazones"* (Anvers, 1888); 2 suites for orch.; "Concert-stück" for pf. with orch. and many pop. songs and pf.-pieces; opéra comique, *"La Sevillane,"* etc.

Cham′lee (chăm′-lē), **Mario,** b. Los Angeles, 1892; tenor; Mus. M., Univ. of Calif., 1924; studied with Achille Alberti and Riccardo Dellera; début Met. Op. Co., 1920, as Cavaradossi in *"Tosca";* also sang with Scotti and Ravinia Op. Cos., and has made appearances in concerts and radio programmes; m. Ruth Miller, soprano.

Champein (shän-păn), **Stanislas,** Marseilles, 1753—Paris, 1830; dram. composer.

Champion (shänp-yôn), **Jacques.** Vide CHAMBONNIÈRES.

Chanot (shä-nō), **Fran.,** Mirecourt, 1787—Brest, 1823; retired as a naval engineer; designed a violin which the Academy pronounced equal to Stradivari's; his bro., a Paris luthier, manufactured it, but found it impracticable.

Chapi (y Lorente) (chä-pē′ ē lō rĕn′-tĕ), **Ruperto,** Villena, March 27, 1851—Madrid, March 25, 1909; pupil Madrid Cons.; c. operas and 78 zarzuelas; also a symph.; oratorio, etc.

Chap′man, William Rogers, Hanover, Mass., Aug. 4, 1855—Palm Beach, Fla., March 27, 1935; composer, choral conductor; founded and led Apollo Club of New York; after 1897, the Maine Festivals in Bangor and Portland; and the Rubinstein Club, a N. Y. women's chorus, which had a continuous existence under his baton from 1887.

Chap′pell & Co., music-publishers, London; founded 1812 by (1) **Samuel C.,** the pianist, Cramer, and F. T. Latour (1809—1888). (2) **Wm. C.** became the head of the firm; in 1840 he founded the "Antiquarian Society," and pub. colls. of old Engl. music. His brothers, (3) **Thomas,** founded, and (4) **Arthur,** conducted, the Monday and Saturday Pop. Concerts.

Chap′ple, Samuel, Crediton (Devon), 1775—Ashburton, 1833; organist and pianist, blind from infancy; composer.

Chapuis (shäp-wē), **Aug. Paul J. Bap.,** Dampierre-sur-Saône, France, April 20, 1862—Paris, Dec., 1933; pupil of Dubois, Massenet, and César Franck, Paris Cons., took first prize in harm., 1st prize for org., and the Rossini prize; organist at Saint Roch.; from 1894, prof. of harm. at the Cons.; 1895, inspector-gen. of music instruction in Paris schools; c. unsucc. lyric drama *"Enguerrande"* (Op. Com., 1892); lyric drama *"Tancred"* (Op. Com., 1898 ?); an oratorio; a pf.-suite "on the oriental scale," etc.; pub. a treatise on harm.

Char (khär), **Fr. Ernst ("Fritz"),** Cleves-on-Rhein, May 5, 1865—Velden, Sept. 21, 1932; pupil of C. Kistler, Wüllner and Neitzel; cond. opera at Zwickau, Stettin, and

St. Gallen; later at Ulm; wrote book and music of succ. opera *"Der Schelm von Bergen"* (Zwickau, 1895); c. cantata *"Spielmann,"* etc.

Chard, G. W., ca. 1765—May 23, 1849; English organist and composer.

Charpentier (shär-pänt-yā), (1) **Marc A.,** Paris, 1634—March, 1704; conductor to the Dauphin; c. 16 operas for the stage and many "tragédies spirituelles" for the Jesuits, masses, etc. (2) **Gustave,** b. Dieuze, Lorraine, June 25, 1860; pupil of Massart, Pessard, and Massenet, Paris Cons.; 1887, took grand prix de Rome; c. orch. suite *"Impressions d'Italie"*; scène lyrique *"Didon"*; symphonic drama (or concert opera) *"La Vie du Poète"* (Grand Opera, 1892), and *"Italien"* (Hamburg, 1902); symph. poem *"Napoli"* (1891); book and music of succ. opera *"Louise,"* impressionistic study of poet life in Montmartre, première Op.-Comique, 1900, and heard at Manhattan Op., N. Y., 1907, with Mary Garden, and with Farrar at Met. Op., 1921; he wrote a sequel, *"Julien,"* Op.-Com., 1913, also at Met. Op., with Farrar and Caruso, but not succ.; also c. *"Marie," "Orphée,"* and *"Tête Rouge,"* unprod.; and songs, *"Les Fleurs du Mal," "Quinze poèmes,"* some of them with chorus and orchestra. He founded Cercle Mimi Pinson and Cons. of same name for working girls.

Chasins (chās'-ins), **Abram,** b. New York, Aug. 17, 1903; pianist, composer; studied piano with Hutcheson, Hofmann and others; composition with Rubin Goldmark; début as soloist with Phila. Orch., 1929, playing his own concerto; member of piano faculty, Curtis Inst., Phila.; has composed numerous piano pieces, some of which he has arranged for orch.; his *"Parade"* and *"In a Chinese Garden"* played by N. Y. Philh.

Chat'terton, J. B., Norwich, 1805—London, 1871; court-harpist and composer.

Chaumet (shō-mā), **J. B. Wm.,** Bordeaux, April 26, 1842—Gajac, Gironde, Oct. 28, 1903; won the Prix Cressent, with the comic opera *"Bathyle"* (prod. 1877), also the Prix Rossini; c. comic operas; lyric drama *"Mauprat"* (MS.), etc.

Chausson (shōs-sôṅ), **Ernest, Paris,** June 21, 1855—(killed in bicycle accident), Limay n. Mantes, June 10, 1899; pupil of Massenet and César Franck; c. symph.; symph. poems *"Viviane"* and *"Les caprices de Marianne"*; operas *"Helene," "Le roi Arthus"* (Brussels, 1903; text by the composer); songs and piano pieces; *"Poème de l'Amour et de la Mer,"* and *"Chanson Perpetuelle,"* dram. scenas; lyric scene, *"Jeanne d'Arc"; "Un Soir de Fête"* and *"Solitude dans le Bois"* for orch.; piano and vln. concertos; string quartet; piano quartet; string trio; and popular *"Poème"* for vln. and orch. A highly individual genius. Memoir by Séré.

Chauvet (shō-vā), **Chas. Alexis,** Marnies. June 7, 1837—Argentan, Jan. 28, 1871; organist; c. noteworthy org.-music.

Chavanne (shä-vän'-nĕ), **Irène von,** b. Gratz, 1868; contralto; pupil, Vienna Cons., 1882–85; 1885 at the Dresden Court-opera.

Chavez (chä'-vĕth), **Carlos,** b. Mexico City, June 13, 1899; composer, conductor; studied with Manuel Ponce and Pedro Ogazon, also in Europe; founded and led Symph. Orch. of Mexico after 1928; same year appointed dir. of Nat'l. Cons. of Mexico, resigned 1934; guest cond. of Boston and Phila. Orchs., 1936; N. Y. Philh., 1937; c. modern style works of originality, incl. (ballet) *"H. P."* ("Horsepower"), staged by Stokowski in Phila., 1932; (orch.) *"Sinfonia de Antigona,"* sonatinas for various chamber combinations; piano sonata, etc.

Cheath'am, Kitty, b. Nashville, Tenn., mezzo-soprano; esp. known for her concerts of folk music and children's songs; ed. two collections of these works; res. in New York for some years.

Chelard (shŭ-lăr), **Hippolyte André J. Bap.,** Paris, Feb. 1, 1789—Weimar, Feb. 12, 1861; 1815, prod. his first opera, *"La Casa a Vendere,"* Naples; entered the Paris Operatic orch. as violinist; in 1827 his opera *"Macbeth"* (text by Rouget de Lisle) was prod., but failed; he went to Munich, and 1828 prod. a revised version of *"Macbeth"* with such succ. that he was made court-conductor; he returned to Paris,

1829, and failed with 3 other operas; conducted the German Opera in London, which failed; returned to Munich, and prod. his best work, *"Die Hermannsschlacht,"* 1835; 1836, court-conductor at Weimar, where he prod. 2 comic operas.

Chelleri (kĕl'-lĕ-rē), **Fortunato** (rightly **Keller**), Parma, 1686—Cassel, 1757; court-conductor and dram. composer.

Chemin-Petit (shŭ-măṅ-pŭ-tē'), **Hans,** d. Potsdam, 1917; c. operas, including *"Der Liebe Augustin"* (Brandenburg, 1906).

Chéri (shā-rē), **Victor** (rightly **Cizos**), Auxerre, 1830—suicide, Paris, 1882; cond. and dram. composer.

Cherkass'ky, Shura, b. Odessa, Oct. 7, 1911; pianist; studied with Josef Hofmann; début as youthful pianist prodigy; developed into excellent performer of mature ability; has appeared with leading orchs. and as recitalist, in many Eur. and Amer. cities, also extensive tours of Russia and Far East.

Cherniav'sky, (1) **Jan,** b. Odessa, June 25, 1892; pianist; pupil of Leschetizky, Vienna; founded Cherniavsky Trio with his brothers, (2) **Leo** (b. Odessa, Aug. 30, 1890), violinist, who was pupil of Wilhelmj; and (3) **Michel** (b. Odessa, Nov. 2, 1893), 'cellist, pupil of Popper. Tours in U. S. and other countries.

Cherubini (kā-roo-bē'-nē) (**M.**) **Luigi (Carlo Zenobio Salvatore),** Florence, Sept. 14, 1760—Paris, March 15, 1842; one of the greatest masters of counterpoint; pupil of his father, (cembalist, at the Pergola Th.), then of B. and A. Felici, Bizarri and Castrucci; 1779 sent (under patronage of the future Emperor Leopold III.) to Milan, to study cpt. with Sarti; at 13, had c. a mass and an intermezzo for a society theatre; at 15, another intermezzo; 1780, *"Quinto Fabio"* was prod. without succ. though with better results in a revised version (1783); he had succ. with 6 other operas, and was in 1784 invited to London, where he prod. an opera buffa, with some success, and another with none; he was court composer for one year; 1788 he prod. *"Ifigenia in Aulide"* at Turin; and then lived in Paris, where his French opera *"Démophon"* (Grand Opéra, 1788) failed; he then cond. at a small opera house, until 1792. His opera *"Lodoiska,"* 1791, showed a new style of emotional strength, powerful ensemble, and novel orchestral colour that founded a school of imitators. 7 other operas and a ballet followed, incl. his masterpiece (1800), *"Les deux journées"* (in Germany called *"Der Wasserträger";* in England, "The Water-carrier"). 1795 he had been made one of the inspectors of the new Cons., Paris, but was not liked by Napoleon, whose musical opinion he had not flattered. On invitation he wrote for Vienna *"Faniska,"* a great succ. (1806); an invitation to write a mass for the Prince of Chimay resulted in the famous 3-part mass in F. He wrote 4 more operas, but found church-music more satisfactory. 1815, visited London; wrote a symphony, an overture, and a *Hymn to Spring*, for the Philh. Soc. After many vicissitudes he became in 1816 prof. of comp. at the Cons., Paris, and 1821–41 dir. His enormous list of works includes 15 Italian and 14 French operas, 17 cantatas, 11 solemn masses, 2 requiems, 1 oratorio; 1 symphony, 1 overture; 6 string quartets; 6 pf.-sonatas, and a mass of smaller works, mus. for pf., etc. The best biog. is by Bellasis (London, 1874).

Chessin (chĕs'-sēn), **Alexander Borissovich,** b. St. Petersburg Oct. 19, 1869; conductor; pupil of the Cons., and of Nikisch at Leipzig; 1901, cond. at St. Petersburg and 1903 of Philharmonic concerts at Moscow; c. cantata, etc.

Chevé (shŭ-vā), **Emile Jos. Maurice,** Douarnenez, Finistere, 1804—1864; a physician; wrote pamphlets attacking the methods at the Paris Cons. His wife (née **Manine,** Paris) collaborated with him.

Chevillard (shŭ-vē-yăr), **Camille,** Paris, Oct. 14, 1859—May 30, 1923; pupil of G. Mathias; took 2d pf. prize at Cons.; till 1886, asst.-cond. of the Lamoureux Concerts; 1897, cond.; after 1907, prof. at Paris Cons.; 1913 also concert master at the Opéra; 1903, won Prix Chartier for chamber music; pres., Chamber Mus. Soc.; Officier of Public Instruction and mem. of the Legion of Honour; c. a symph. ballade, *"Le chêne et le roseau"*; a symph. poem, a symph.

fantàsie; incid. mus. to *"La Rous-salka* (1903); allegro for horn and piano, 1905; piano pieces and songs; 2 string quartets, trio, piano quintet, sonatas for vln. and for 'cello, etc.

Chiaromonte (kē-är-ō-mŏn'-tĕ), **Fran.** Castrogofovanni, 1809—Brussels, 1886; tenor; prof. of singing and dram. composer.

Chick'ering & Sons, American firm of pf.-makers, est. 1823, by (1) **Jonas Chickering** (New Ipswich, N. H., 1798—Boston, 1853); and his sons (2) **Col. Thos. E. C.** (Boston, 1824—1871), (3) **Geo. H.** (1830–96), and (4) **C. Frank** (1827–91). Last was named Chev. of the Legion of Honour, and took first pf.-prize at the Paris Exposition, 1867. In 1908 the firm was merged with the Amer. Piano Co.

Child, Wm., Bristol, 1606—Windsor, 1697; organist.

Chilesotti (kē-lā-sŏt'-tē), **Oscare,** Bassano, Italy, July 12, 1848—June 20, 1916; law graduate Padua Univ.; flutist and 'cellist; self-taught in harm.; lived in Milan; wrote important historical works.

Chipp, Edm. Thos. (Mus. Doc.), London, 1823—Nice, 1886; organist.

Chladni (khlät'-nē), **Ernst Florens Fr.,** Wittenberg, Nov. 30, 1756—Breslau, April 3, 1827; prof. of law and investigator in physics and acoustics; discovered the sound-figures which sand assumes on a vibrating plate, and which bear his name; inv. the euphonium and clavicylinder

Chollet (shôl-lä), **J. B. M.,** b. Paris, May, 1798; violinist and singer in opera.

Chop (khôp), **Max,** Greuszen, Thuringia, May 17, 1862—Berlin, Dec. 20, 1929; mus. writer, critic in Berlin, under the name "Monsieur Charles"; c. piano concerto, etc. Was ed. of the *"Signale,"* Berlin mus. publication. M. Celeste Groenvelt,

Chopin (shô-pǎn) **(François) Frédéric,** Zelazowa Wola (Jeliasovaya Volia), near Warsaw, Feb. 22, 1810—Paris, Oct. 17, 1849; eminent composer for the piano; son of Nicholas C. (a native of Nancy, France, who was at first bookkeeper in a cigar factory, then teacher in the Warsaw Gymnasium), and a Polish woman (née Justine Kryzanowska). **C.** studied

at his father's private school, among young Polish noblemen; Albert Zwyny taught him pf. and Joseph Elsner, harm., etc. At 9 he played in public a pf.-concerto and improvisations; c. polonaises, mazurkas, and waltzes; in 1825, pub. as op. 1 a rondo; op. 2 a fantasie with orch. He played in German cities and had at 19 an individual style of comp., having written his 2 pf.-concertos, mazurkas, nocturnes, rondos, etc. He started for London, and played in Vienna, 1829, with such success that a critic called him "one of the most remarkable meteors blazing on the musical horizon": and at Paris he had such succ. in his first concert, 1831, that he settled there for life as a teacher of the pf. and occasional giver of concerts. His pupils were of the most aristocratic, and his friends included Liszt, Berlioz, Meyerbeer, Bellini, Balzac, and Heine. Schumann with typical spontaneity (cf. BRAHMS) was moved in 1831 by Chopin's op. 2 to say, "Hats off, gentlemen:—a genius"; and in 1839, in reviewing certain of his preludes, mazurkas, and valses, to say "He is and remains the keenest and staunchest poet-soul of the time." C.'s liaison with Mme. Dudevant ("George Sand"), begun in 1836 and ended in 1844, has caused endless controversy. In 1838 an attack of bronchitis drove him to Majorca, where she seems to have been a devoted nurse, but the peevishness and weakness due to his developing consumption caused bitter quarrels, and she is believed to have caricatured him as Prince Karol in her novel *"Lucrezia Floriani."* Concert tours and social life in England and Scotland in 1841–49 destroyed his strength.

His comps. include beside those mentioned (74, with opus-number 12 lacking): *"Don Giovanni,"* fantasia, op. 2; *"Krakoviak,"* rondo, op. 14; E♭ *Polonaise,* op. 22; and a fantasia on Polish airs for pf. with orch; duo concertant on themes from *"Robert le Diable"*; an introd. et Polonaise, op. 3, and a sonata, op. 65 for pf. and 'cello; pf. trio, op. 8; and a rondo for 2pfs. op. 73. FOR PF. SOLO: *Allegro de concert;* 4 ballades; barcarolle, op. 60; berceuse, op. 57; bolero, op. 19; 3 écossaises, op. 72; 12 grandes études, op. 10; 12 études, op. 25; 3 études; 4 fantasies; 3 impromptus; marche funèbre, op. 72; 52 mazurkas. "*Morceau de concert sur la Marche des Puritains de Bellini*"; 19 nocturnes, 11 polonaises; 24 préludes, op. 28; prélude, op. 45; 3 rondos; 4 scherzos; 3 sonatas; tarantelle, op. 43; 13 valses; variations on "*Je vends des scapulaires*," op. 12; "*Variation dans l' Hexaméron*"; 16 Polish songs op. 74. A collection of his letters was pub. (Dresden, 1877). A collection by Opienski was tr. into English by Voynich and pub. 1931. His many biographers include Liszt, M. Karasowski (Dresden, 1877), M. A. Audley, Fr. Niecks (Leipzig, 1889). Other studies by Huneker, Finck, Bidou, Dry, J. P. Dunn, Hadden, Jachimecki, Kelley, Kleczynski, Maine, Murdoch, Pourtalès, Tarnowski, Niggli, Schucht, Willeby, Hoesick (3 vols.), Leichtentritt, Opienski, Poirée, Redenbacher, Weissmann, Ganche, Scharlitt, etc.

Chor'ley, H. Fothergill, Blackley Hurst, Lancashire, 1808—London, 1872; critic and widely travelled writer.

Choron (shô-rôn), **Alex. Ét.,** Caen, Oct. 21, 1772—Paris, June 29, 1834; an ardent student of musical theory and practice, historian and benefactor who devoted his fortune to the advance of the art.

Chotzinoff (khôt'-zē-nôf), **Samuel,** pianist, critic; toured as accompanist with Heifetz and Zimbalist; former mus. critic., N. Y. "*World*"; critic, N. Y. "*Post*" after 1934; author "*Eroica*," novel based on life of Beethoven.

Choudens (shoo-däns), **A.,** Paris, 1849 —1902; son of a music publisher; c. 2 operas, "*Graziella*" (Paris, 1877), and "*La Jeunesse de Don Juan*," etc.

Chouquet (shoo-kä), **Ad. Gv.,** Havre, 1819—Paris, 1886; teacher and writer of historical works.

Chris'tiansen, F. Melius, b. Eidsvold, Norway, April 1, 1871; choral conductor and composer; pupil of Oscar Hansen, in organ and conducting, at Larvik; came to America, 1888; later studied at Northwestern Cons. and at Leipzig Cons.; after 1903 dir. of mus. at St. Olaf Coll., Northfield, Minn., where he has led the notable

St. Olaf Choir; c. and arr. choral music; wrote books on theory.

Chris'tie, Winifred, Scottish pianist; studied R. Coll. of Music, London, winning Liszt scholarship; also studied in Leipzig; and with Harold Bauer; toured in Eur. countries; res. in America 1915–19; later returned here for tours; plays double-keyboard piano invented by Emanuel Moór (1863—1931), whom she married.

Christ'mann, Jn. Fr., Ludwigsburg, Würtemberg, 1752—Heutingsheim, 1817; composer and writer.

Chrysander (krē'-zänt-ĕr), **Fr.,** Lübtheen, Mecklenburg, July 8, 1826— Bergedorf, Sept. 3, 1901; editor and writer of the standard biography of Händel, and with Gervinus of the monumental H.-Gesellchaft edition of that master's works.

Chrysan'thos of Madyton; writer 19th century; teacher of church singing, Constantinople, later Archbishop of Durazzo in Albania.

Chva'la (shvä'-lä), **Emanuel,** Prague Jan. 1, 1851—Oct. 31, 1924; pupil of Förster and Fibich; historian and c. of chamber music, etc.

Chwatal (khwä'-täl), **Fz. Xaver,** Rumburg, Bohemia, 1808—Elmen (Soolbad), 1879; teacher and composer.

Chybinski (khe-bēn'-yĕ-shkĭ), **Adolf,** b. Cracow, March 29, 1880; historian of Polish music; after 1912 taught at Lemberg Univ.

Ciaja (chä'-yä), **Azzolino Bdo. della,** b. Siena, 1671; organist, amateur org.-builder, and composer.

Ciampi (chäm'-pē), **Legrenzio V.,** b. Piacenza, 1719; dram. composer.

Cianchettini (chän-kĕt-tē'-nē), (1) **Veronica,** (née **Dussek**), Czaslau, Bohemia, 1779; composer and teacher. (2) **Pio,** London, 1799—1840; son of above; composer and pianist; first appearance at 5 years; at 10 performed an original concerto in public.

Cibber (sĭb'-bĕr), **Susanna M.** (née **Arne**), 1714—1766; great English actress and notable singer, sister of Dr. Arne.

Ciconia (chĭ-kōn'-yä), **Johannes,** canon at Padua about 1400; theorist and comp.

Cifra (chē'-frä), **A.,** Rome, 1584— Loreto, 1629; important composer of the Roman School; pupil of Palestrina and B. Nanini; courtconductor.

Cigna (chēn'-yä), **Gina;** dramatic soprano, of French-Italian ancestry; early studied piano, composition and theory at Paris Cons.; awarded gold medal; later instruction in singing; after 1928 active as vocalist; from 1930 mem. of La Scala; has also sung at Paris Op., Rome Teatro Reale and Augusteo, Budapest Op., Teatro Colon (Buenos Aires), Teatro Municipal (Rio de Janeiro), and in many Italian cities; created title role in Respighi's *"La Fiamma"* at Milan; sang Norma at centenary festival of Bellini in Catania; and Gioconda at La Scala on Ponchielli centenary; engaged for Met. Op., N. Y., 1936-37.

Cilèa (chē'-lĕ-ä), **Francesco,** b. Palmi, July 29, 1866; leading Italian opera comp.; at 9 had c. a notturno and a mazurka; at 15 entered the Naples Cons.; while yet a student he had success with a suite for orch., and a 3-act opera *"Gina"* (1889); 1896-1904, professor at Royal Institute, Florence; 1913-16, dir. Palermo Cons.; from 1917 of Naples Cons.; c. operas *"La Tilda"* (1892); *"L'Arlesiana"* (Milan, 1896); *"Adrianna Lécouvreur"* (Milan, 1902, Covent Garden, 1904); *"Gloria,"* (La Scala, Milan, 1907); also *"Poema Sinfonica"*; orch. suite, piano trio, 'cello sonata, etc.

Cimarosa (chē-mä-rō'-sä), **Domenico,** Aversa, near Naples, Dec. 17, 1749—Venice, Jan. 11, 1801; the orphan of a poor mason; studied at Minorite charity-school, his first teacher being Polcano, monastery organist; when 12 years old was given a scholarship in the Cons. di S. Maria di Loreto, where he studied singing with Manna and Sacchini, cpt. with Fenaroli, and comp. with Piccinni. 1770 his oratorio *"Giuditta"* was prod. in Rome; 1772, his first opera, *"Le Stravaganze del Conte,"* at Naples, without succ., which was won, however, next year by *"La Finta Parigina."* Of phenomenal facility, he c. 76 operas in 29 years. He lived alternately in Rome and Naples. 1781, he prod. two operas in Naples, one in Rome, and two in Turin; invited 1789 to be court-composer at St. Petersburg (vice Paesiello), he spent 5 months of triumphal progress thither, being lionised at various courts; he stayed there 3 years, prod. 3 operas and wrote 500 pieces of

music for the court; but he could not tolerate the climate, and was reluctantly released, being engaged as cond. to Emperor Leopold at Vienna, with a salary of 12,000 florins. He prod. 3 operas incl. his masterpiece *"Il Matrimonio Segreto"* (1787), which won an all-effacing success. 1793, he returned to Naples. 1799, he took part in the Neapolitan revolutionary demonstration on the entrance of the French army, and was condemned to death by King Ferdinand, but banished instead; he died suddenly at Venice. It being everywhere claimed that he had been poisoned by order of Queen Caroline of Naples, the Pope's physician made an examination, and swore that he died of a gangrenous abdominal tumour. Particularly in comic, but at times also in serious opera, C. almost challenges comparison with Mozart for fluency of melody and orchestral richness. His best operas are *"La Finta"* (Naples, 1773), *"L'Italiana in Londra"* (Rome, 1774), *"Il Fanatico per gli Antichi Romani"* (Naples, 1777), in which were introduced dramatically vocal-trios and quartets, *"La Ballerina Amante"* (Naples, 1782), *"Le Trame Deluse"* (Naples, 1786), *"L'Impresario in Angustie"* (Naples, 1786), *"Giannina e Bernadone"* (Naples, 1788), *"La Vergine del Sole"* (St. Petersburg, 1791), *"Il Matrimonio Segreto"* (Vienna, 1792), *"Le Astuzie Femminile"* (Naples, 1794). He also prod. 2 oratorios, 7 symphonies, several cantatas; masses, etc.

Cimini (chǐ'-mǐ-nē), **Pietro,** b. Carpi (Modena), Italy, 1876; conductor; studied at the Bologna Liceo with Sarti, Dall'Olio, and Martucci; early active as violinist; cond. opera in Italy, Warsaw (1910-14), also in Russia, at Madrid Reale, Chicago Auditorium, Manhattan Op. House, New York; later for some years on the Pacific Coast.

Cipollini (chē-pôl-lē'-nē), **Gaetano,** Tropea, Italy, Feb. 8, 1857—Milan, Oct. 2, 1935; pupil of Francesco Coppa; lived at Milan as dram. composer.

Cirri (chēr'-rē), (1) **Ignazio,** organist and comp.; his son (2) **Giovanni Baptista,** b. Forli, ca. 1740; 'cellist; spent many years in London, then returned to Italy; c. important 'cello music.

Cisneros (sĭs-nā'-rŏs), **Eleanora de** (née **Broadfoot**), New York, Nov. 1, 1880—Feb. 3, 1934; soprano; studied with Mme. Murio-Celli, and made début as Rossweise in "*Die Walküre*" at Met. Op. House, 1900; later studied with Jean de Reszke, Maurel, Trabadello and Lombardi; after 1902, sang widely in Europe, South and Central America, and Australia; 1906–08, Manhattan Op. House, N. Y.; sang "Clytemnestra" in "*Elektra*" at Milan; after 1910 with Chicago Op.

Claassen (kläs'-sĕn), **Arthur**, Stargard, Prussia, Feb. 19, 1859—San Francisco, March 16, 1920; graduated from Danzig Gym.; 1875, studied under Müller-Hartung, Gottschalk and Sulze, Weimar Music School; 1880–84, cond. Göttingen and Magdeburg; 1884, cond. "Arion" and other societies of Brooklyn, N. Y.; est. the "Claassen Mus. Inst."; after 1910 active as choral and orch. cond., San Antonio, Tex.; c. choruses, incl. "*Der Kamerad*" (prize), and symph. poem "*Hohenfriedberg*," etc.

Clag'get, Chas., London, 1755—1820; violinist and inventor.

Clapisson (klä-pĭs-sôń), **Antoine L.**, Naples, 1808—Paris, 1866; violinist, professor and dram. composer.

Clapp, Philip Greeley, b. Boston, Aug. 4, 1888; composer, educator; grad. Harvard Univ., *magna cum laude*; cond. Pierian Sodality there; studied in Europe as Sheldon Fellow of that Univ.; Ph.D.; dir. of music, Dartmouth Coll., 1915–19; after la ter year prof. of mus., Univ. of Iowa; for a time associated with Juilliard Foundation, N. Y.; c. symph., choral works, etc., two of former played by Boston Symph.

Clari (klä'-rē), **Giov. M.**, Pisa, 1669—Pistoia, ca. 1754; conductor and composer.

Clar'ibel. Vide MRS. CHAS. BARNARD.

Clark(e), (1) **Jeremiah**, London, 1670 —(?), ca. 1707; organist and dram. composer; a suicide for love. (2) **Richard**, Datchet (Bucks), 1780—London, 1856; composer and writer. (3) Vide SCOTSON CLARK.

Clarke, (1) **Jas. Peyton**, Scotland, 1808—Toronto, Canada, 1877; organist and professor. (2) **Hugh**

Archibald, Toronto, Aug. 15, 1839— Philadelphia, Dec. 16, 1927; son of above; organist in Philadelphia churches; 1875, prof. of music in the Univ. of Pennsylv.; made Mus. Doc. (1886) by the Univ. when his music to Aristophanes' "*Acharnians*" was prod.; also c. an oratorio, "*Jerusalem*" (Phila., 1891), etc. (3) **J.** (Whitfield-Clarke), Gloucester, England, 1770—Holmer, 1836; organist, professor and editor. (4) **James Hamilton Smee**, Birmingham, England, Jan. 25, 1840—Banstead, July 9, 1912; at 12 organist; 1866 at Queen's College, Oxford; Mus. Bac., 1867; cond. various theatres; 1893, cond. Carl Rosa Opera Co.; c. operettas, 2 symphonies, etc. **Wm. Horatio**, Newton, Mass., March 8, 1840—Reading, Mass., 1913; 1878–87, organist at Tremont Temple, Boston, then retired to Reading, Mass., where he had an estate and a chapel of music, Clarigold Hall, containing a large 4-manual organ with 100 stops; wrote 15 instructive works "*Outline of the Structure of the Pipe-Organ*" (1877), etc. (6) **Maria Victoria** (Cowden-Clarke). Vide NOVELLO. (7) **Rebecca**, b. Harrow, England, Aug. 27, 1886; composer and 'cellist; studied with Stanford at R. Coll. of Music; after 1916 she visited New York as performer; c. chamber music, her piano trio being awarded a Coolidge Prize.

Clarus (klä'-roos), **Max.**, Mühlberg-on-Elbe, March 31, 1852—Brunswick, Dec. 12, 1916; pupil of his father, the municipal mus. dir. there, and of Haupt, Schneider, and Löschorn, Berlin; cond. in various German, Austrian and Hungarian theatres; 1890, mus. dir. Brunswick court; from 1884 cond. the "Orpheus," and from 1890 the "Chorgesangverein"; c. "Patriotic spectacular" opera, "*Des Grossen Königs Rekrut*" (Brunswick, 1889); succ. romantic opera "*Ilse*" (Brunswick, 1895); "*Der wunschpeter*" (1910), "*Hans Däumling*" (1911), "*Der Zwerg Nase*" (1912), choral works, ballets, etc.

Clasing (klä'-zĭng), **Jn. H.**, Hamburg, 1779—1829; teacher and dram. composer.

Claudin (klō-dăń), (1). Vide SERMISY. (2) **Le Jeune.** Vide LEJEUNE.

Claus'sen, Julia, (née **Ohlson**), b.

Stockholm, 1879–1941; contralto; studied R. Acad. in native city; début there at R. Op., 1903; mem. Chicago Op., 1912–17; after 1917 sang for some years with Met. Op. Co., N. Y., esp. in Wagnerian rôles.

Clausz-Szarvady (klows'-shär-vä'-dē), **Wilhelmine**, Prague, 1834—Paris, 1907; pianist.

Clavé (klä-vä'), **José Anselmo**, Barcelona, April 21, 1824—Feb., 1874; founder of male choral societies in Spain; c. very popular songs and choruses.

Clavijo Del Castillo (klä-vē'-hō dĕl käs-tĕl'-yō), **Bernardo**, d. Madrid, Feb. 1626; Spanish organist and comp.

Clay, Fr. (of English parents), Paris, 1840—Great Marlow, near London, 1889; dram. composer.

Clegg, J., Ireland (probably), 1714—Nisane, 1742; remarkable violinist and composer.

Clem'ens, Jacob (called **"Cl. Non Papa"**) (i.e., "not the Pope" Clement VII.); d. ca. 1557 (?); played several instrs. and composed.

Clem'ens, Charles Edwin, b. Devenport, England, March 12, 1858—Cleveland, O., Dec. 27, 1933; organist; 1889—1895, organist of the English church, and to Empress Frederick in Berlin, and teacher at Scharwenka Cons.; then moved to Cleveland, Ohio; prof. Western Reserve Univ.; author of organ-methods.

Clement (klä'-mĕnt), **Fz.,** Vienna, 1780—1842; violinist and dram. composer.

Clément (klä-mäṅ), (1) **Félix,** Paris, 1822—1885; organist. (2) **Edmond,** France, 1867—Nice, Feb. 23, 1928; eminent lyric tenor; early made succ. at Paris Op.-Comique; 1909–10, sang at Met. Op. House; 1911–13, with Boston Op. Co.; after the war returned to U. S. for concert tour.

Clementi (klä-mĕn'-tē), **Muzio,** Rome, 1752—near Evesham, England, March 10, 1832; son of a goldsmith and musical amateur who had him taught by A. Buroni, then by the organist Condicelli. At 9 he was chosen as an organist in competition with older players; until 14, studied under G. Carpani (comp.) and Sartartelli (voice); 1766, an Englishman named Beckford secured permission to educate him in England, and till

1770 he lived and studied in Dorsetshire; then made a sensation as pianist in London. 1773, pub. pf.-sonatas dedicated to Haydn, and highly praised by Emmanuel Bach; 1777–80, cembalist at the Italian Opera; 1781 toured the continent, meeting Mozart in "friendly" rivalry, without victory for either; lived in London, 1782–1802; he amassed a fortune as a teacher, pianist and composer in spite of losses from the failure of Longman and Broderip, instr.-makers; he estab. a succ. piano-factory and pub. house (now Collard's). 1802, he made a brilliant tour with his pupil Field; he taught other famous pupils, incl. Moscheles, Kalkbrenner, Meyerbeer. His comps. incl. symphonies and overtures; 106 pf.-sonatas (46, with vln., ?cello, or flute); fugues, preludes, and exercises in canon form, toccatas, etc. His book of études, the *"Gradus ad Parnassum,"* 1817, is a standard; biog. by Giov. Frojo (Milan, 1878); O. Chilesotti (Milan, 1882), and Clement (Paris, 1878).

Clérambault (klā-räṅ-bō), **Louis Nicolas,** Paris, 1676—1749; organist and comp.

Clérice (klä-rēs), **Justin,** Buenos Aires, Oct. 16, 1863—Toulouse, Sept, 1908; 1882, pupil of Délibes and Pessard, Paris Cons.; lived in Paris; prod. comic operas, etc.

Cleve (klĕv), (1) **Johannes De, Cleve** (?) 1529—Augsburg, 1582; court tenor at Vienna and Prague; c. church music; (2) **Halfdan,** b. Kongsberg, Norway, Oct. 5, 1879; pianist; pupil of his father and of Raif and the two Scharwenkas at Berlin; c. piano-concertos, etc.

Clicquot (klē-kō), **Fran. H.,** Paris, 1728—1791; organ-builder.

Cliffe (klĭf), **Frederick,** Lowmoor, May 2, 1857—Dec., 1931; organist; pupil of Sullivan, Stainer, and at R. C. M.; toured Europe with success; after 1901, taught R. A. M.; c. 2 symph.; symph poem *"Clouds and Sunshine"*; alto solo with orch., *"The Triumph of Alcestis,"* etc.

Clif'ford, Rev. **Jas.,** Oxford, 1622—London, 1698; composer.

Clif'ton, Chalmers, b. Jackson, Miss., April 30, 1889; conductor, composer; grad. Cincinnati Cons. and Harvard Univ.; studied with d'Indy and Gédalge; cond. Cecilia Soc., Boston-

1915-17; Amer. Orch. Soc., N. Y., 1922-30; also guest cond. with orch. in Boston, New York, Cincinnati, Baltimore and Conservatoire Orch., Paris; c. orch., piano works and songs; orchestrated MacDowell piano works.

Clive, Catherine (née **Raftor**) (called "Kitty Clive"), London, 1711—Dec. 6, 1785; famous actress, also singer.

Clough-Leiter (klŭf-lī'-tĕr) **Henry,** b. Washington, D. C., May 13, 1874; composer and musical editor; pupil of his mother, Edw. Kimball, H. Xande, and Dr. J. H. Anger; org. at Washington and various churches at Providence, R. I. c. "*Lasca*" for tenor and orch.; 4 cantatas, "*A Day of Beauty*," for string quintet; 200 songs.

Clu'er, J., d. London, 1729, English publisher, reputed inventor of engraving on tin plates.

Coates, (1) **John,** b. Girlington, June 29, 1865—Northwood, Aug. 16, 1941; tenor; sang choir at 5; pupil of Burton and Bridge, later of Shakespeare; sang in light opera, London and America, as barytone, 1893-1899; decided he was a tenor; studied and made début, 1900, at Covent Garden; favourite festival tenor; also in opera in Germany and 1910 chief tenor at Beecham's season. (2) **Albert,** b. St. Petersburg, Russia, April 23, 1882; of English parents; versatile conductor and composer; studied piano with Carreño, conducting with Nikisch; after baton experience in opera at Elberfeld, Dresden, Mannheim and Covent Garden (1914), he became dir. of the St. Petersburg Op., 1914-17, and continued in this post under the Soviets until 1918, subsequently returning to Russia for many engagements; has also appeared with Beecham and British Nat'l. Op. Cos., with Covent Garden Op. Syndicate, Royal Philh. and London Symph. Orchs.; in Paris, Berlin, Vienna, in Spain, Italy and Scandinavia; in U. S. with N. Y. Symph. (1921), Rochester Philh. (1921-22), N. Y. Stadium and Hollywood Bowl (1928-30); c. (operas) "*Sardanapolus*" (St. Petersburg, 1916), "*Samuel Pepys*" (Munich, 1930); "*Pickwick*"; also a "*Launcelot*" Symphony (N. Y. Philh. Stadium Concerts, 1930). (3) **Eric,** b. Hucknall, England, Aug. 27, 1886;

composer; studied at R. Coll. of Mus., viola with Tertis. comp. with Corder; played with Hamburg String Quartet and in Queen's Hall Orch.; after 1918 devoted himself increasingly to composition, esp. orch. music and songs.

Cobb, Gerard Francis, Nettlestead, Kent, Oct. 15, 1838—Cambridge, March 31, 1904; Fellow Trinity Coll., Cambridge, 1863; studied music, Dresden; 1877-92, chairman Board of Music Studies, Cambridge; c. Psalm 62, with orch., etc.

Cob'bett, Walter Willson, Blackheath, July 11, 1847—London, Jan. 22, 1937; music patron, violinist, author; organised first Cobbett Competition, 1905; had given many prizes, particularly for chamber music works; also annual prizes for chamber music performances at R. Coll. and Acad. of Mus.; particularly known as editor of monumental "*International Encyclopedia of Chamber Music*" (1929).

Cocchi (kôk'-kē), **Gioacchino,** Padua, 1715?—Venice, 1804; dram. composer.

Coccia (kôt'-chä), **Carlo,** Naples, 1782—Novara, 1873; cond. and dram. composer.

Coccon (kôk-kōn), **Nicolò,** Venice, Aug. 10, 1826—Aug. 4, 1903; pupil of E. Fabio; 1856 organist, 1873 conductor at San Marco; c. over 450 numbers, an oratorio, "*Saul*," 8 requiem masses, 30 "messe da gloria," 2 operas, etc.

Cochläus (kôkh'-lĕ-oos), **Jns.** (rightly **Jns. Dobnek,** pseud. "**Wendelstein**"), 1479—Breslau, 1552; writer; opponent of Luther.

Cocks, Robt., & Co., firm of London mus. publishers, founded, 1827, by (1) **Robt. C.,** succeeded by his sons, (2) **Arthur Lincoln C.,** and (3) **Stroud Lincoln C.,** d. 1868; (4) **Robt. Macfarlane C.** in charge until 1908; on his retirement it was bought by Augener & Co.

Coclico (kō'-klē-ko) (**Co'clicus**), **Adrian Petit,** b. in the Hennegau (Hainaut), ca. 1500; singer and composer.

Coenen (koo'-nĕn), (1) **Jns. Meinardus,** The Hague, Jan. 28, 1824—Amsterdam, Jan. 9, 1899; bassoonist, pupil of Lübeck Cons. 1864, cond. at Amsterdam; later municipal mus. dir.; c. ballet-mus., 2 symphonies, cantatas, etc. (2) **Fz.,** Rotterdam,

Dec. 26, 1826—Leyden, Jan. 24, 1904; violinist; pupil of Vieuxtemps and Molique; lived in Amsterdam, 1895, dir. of the Cons. and prof. of vln. and comp.; solo violinist to the Queen; leader of a quartet; and composer of a notable symphony, cantatas, etc. (3) **Willem**, Rotterdam, Nov. 17, 1837—Lugano, March 18, 1918; bro. of above; pianist, toured S. America, and W. Indies; 1862, concert-giver in London; c. oratorio, *"Lazarus"* (1878), etc. (4) **Cornelius**, The Hague, 1838—Arnhem, March, 1913; violinist; 1859, cond. at Amsterdam; 1860 bandm. Garde Nationale, Utrecht; c. overtures, etc.

Coerne (kĕr′-nĕ), **Louis Adolphe**, Newark, N. J., 1870—New London, Conn., Sept. 11, 1922; 1876–80 studied at Stuttgart and Paris, then entered Harvard College and studied with Paine and Kneisel, Boston, U. S. A.; 1890 studied with Rheinberger and Hieber, Munich; 1893 organist at Boston, also at the Columbian Exposition; 1893–96 dir. Liedertafel, Buffalo; 1897, in Columbus, O.; 1902–03, taught Harvard; 1903–04, Smith Coll.; 1907–09, dir. of mus., Troy, N. Y.; 1909–10, dir. Olivet Coll.; 1910, prof. at Univ. of Wis.; 1915, Conn. Coll.; his opera, *"Zenobia"* was prod. at Bremen, 1905; author of *"The Evolution of Modern Orchestration"*; c. great variety of chamber, orch., vocal music; an opera *"The Maid of Marblehead,"* symph. poem *"Hiawatha,"* etc.

Co′gan, Phillip, b. Cork, 1750; organist, teacher and composer.

Cohen (kow′-ĕn or kō′-ĕn), (1) **H.,** Amsterdam, 1808—Brie-sur-Marne, 1880; writer. (2) **Jules Émile David**, Marseilles, Nov. 2, 1830—Paris, Jan. 14, 1901; pupil of Zimmerman, Marmontel, Benoist, and Halévy, Paris Cons.; won first prize for pf., organ, cpt. and fugue; 1870, teacher of ensemble singing at the Cons.; since 1877 *Chef de Chant,* and chorusmaster Gr. Opéra; prod. 4 operas; c. 3 cantatas, several symphonies, masses, oratorios, etc. (3) **K. Hubert,** b. Laurenzkirg (near Aix), Oct. 18, 1851; a priest, studied at Aix and Raliston, 1879–87 cond. Bamberg; 1887–1910 at Cologne Cath.; c. masses, etc. (4) **Harriet,** b. London, England; pianist; her

father a composer, mother a pianist; studied with them and with Matthay; won Ada Lewis Scholarship, R. Acad. of Mus.; début, London, at 13; has appeared widely in Bach programs and works of modern school, incl. Salzburg Fest.; soloist with orch., London, Vienna, Barcelona, Warsaw, New York; also in sonata recitals with Joseph Szigeti, Beatrice Harrison, Lionel Tertis; Amer. début, 1930. Dame Commander.

Colasse (kȯ-lǎs), **Pascal,** Rheims, Jan. 22, 1649—Versailles, 1709; cond. and dram. composer.

Col′bran, (1) **Gianni,** court-musician to King of Spain, 18th century. (2) **Isabella A.,** Madrid, 1785—Bologne, 1845, daughter of above; singer and composer.

Cole, Rossetter G., b. near Clyde, Mich., Feb. 5, 1866; composer; 1888, graduated from Michigan Univ., taking musical courses also; at his graduation the Univ. Mus. Soc. performed his cantata with orch. *"The Passing of Summer"*; 1888–90, he taught English and Latin in high schools; 1890–92 in Berlin, winning competitive scholarship at Royal Master-school, and studying with Max Bruch; 1892–94, prof. of music Ripon College; 1894–1901, Iowa College; from 1902 in Chicago as teacher, and from 1908 also in charge of summer music classes of Columbia Univ., N. Y. c. *"King Robert of Sicily"* and *"Hiawatha's Wooing,"* as musical backgrounds for recitation, ballade for 'cello and orch.; sonata for violin, songs, etc.

Co′leridge-Taylor, Samuel, London, Aug. 15, 1875—Thornton Heath, Sept. 1, 1912 (of African descent; his father a native of Sierra Leone, his mother, English); composer; pupil (vln.) of the R. A. M., 1890; won composition-scholarship in 1893; until 1896 pupil of V. Stanford; 1892 pub. an anthem; c. a nonet for pf., strings, and wind (1894); a symphony (1896); a quintet for clar. and strings (1897), a string-quartet, and a Morning and Evening Service; pub. a ballade for viola and orch., operetta *"Dream Lovers,"* 4 waltzes for orch.; he was made cond. Handel Society, 1904; his *"Hiawatha"* was developed as a trilogy, *"Hiawatha's Wedding Feast."* (R. C. M., London, 1898).

"The Death of Minnehaha" (North Staffordshire Fest., 1899); *"Hiawatha's Departure"* (London, 1900), the overture the same year; c. also for voices and orch., *"The Blind Girl of Castel-Cuillé"* (Leeds Fest., 1901), *"Meg Blane"* (Sheffield Fest., 1902), *"The Atonement"* (Hereford Fest., 1903), *"Kubla Khan"* (Handel Society, 1906); incid. music to Stephen Phillips's plays, *"Herod,"* *"Ulysses,"* *"Nero,"* and *"Faust"* (1908); concert march, *"Ethiopia Saluting the Colours"*; 5 ballads by Longfellow, with orch. (Norwich Fest., 1905); *"A Tale of Old Japan,"* voices and orch. (London, 1912), etc.

Colin (kô-lăṅ), **P. Gilbert (Colinus, Colinaus, Chamault),** singer and notable composer, Paris, 1532.

Col'la, Giuseppe, cond. at Parma, 1780, m. Agujari.

Collard (kôl-lăr'), a London family of pf.-makers. (1) **Fr. W. Collard** (1772—1860), in partnership with Clementi, bought out Longman & Broderip, 1798, then C. bought out Clementi; he inv. various devices; the firm name now Collard & Collard, (2) **Chas. Lukey C.** being the head until his death, 1891; then (3) **J. C. (Collard)** was dir.

Colles (côl'-lĕs), **Henry Cope,** b. London, April 20, 1879; critic, editor; educated R. Coll. of Mus., Worcester Coll., Oxford; M. A. Oxon.; asst. music critic, *"London Times,"* after 1906, and critic since 1911; prof., R. Coll. of Mus.; ed. new edition Grove's Dictionary, 1928; served as guest critic, New York *"Times,"* 1923; author, *"Brahms,"* *"The Growth of Music."*

Colombani (kō-lôm-bä'-nē), **Orazio,** monk, conductor, and cptist. at Verona, 1576–92.

Colonna (kō-lôn'-nä), **Giov. Paolo,** Bologna (or Brescia), 1637—Bologna, 1693; organist, conductor, and dram. composer.

Colonne (kô-lŭn'), **Edouard** (rightly **Judas),** Bordeaux, July 23, 1838—Paris, March 28, 1910; pupil of Girard and Sauzay (vln.), Elwart, and A. Thomas (comp.), Paris Cons.; 1874, founded the famous "Concerts du Chatelet"; 1878, cond. official Exposition concerts; 1892 cond. at the Gr. Opéra; cond. often in London, and 1902, Vienna and 1905, New York.

Colyns (kō-lăns), **Jean Baptiste,** Brussels, Nov. 25, 1834—Oct. 31, 1902; violinist and comp.

Combs, Gilbert Raynolds, Philadelphia, Jan. 5, 1863—Mt. Airy, Pa., June 14, 1934; son and pupil of a pianist, organist and composer; organist and conductor in Philadelphia; 1885 founded the Broad St. Cons. of Mus., of which he was for many years the enterprising dir.

Comes (kō'-mäs), **Juan Baptista,** Valencia, ca. 1560; conductor and composer.

Comettant (kôm-ĕt-täṅ), **(J. P.) Oscar,** Bordeaux, Gironde, 1819—Montvilliers, 1898; writer and composer.

Commer (kôm'-mĕr), **Fz.,** Cologne, 1813—Berlin, 1887; editor and composer.

Compère (kôṅ-păr), **Louis** (diminutive, **Loyset),** Flanders, 15th cent.—St. Quentin, Aug. 16, 1518; famous contrapuntist.

Concone (kôn-kō'-nĕ), **Giu.,** Turin, 1810—June, 1861; organist, famous singing-teacher in Paris, 1832–48, later court-organist Turin; c. 2 operas and famous vocal exercises.

Co'ninck, Jacques Félix de, Antwerp, 1791—Schaerbeck-les-Bruxelles, 1866; conductor at Berlin, and composer.

Conradi (kōn-rä'-dē), (1) **Jn. G.,** 17th cent.; conductor; one of the first composers of German opera, his works prod. at Hamburg. (2) **Johan G.,** Tönsberg, Norway, 1820—Christiania, 1896; composer. (3) **Aug.,** Berlin, 1821—1873; organist and dram. composer.

Conried (kän'-rēd), **He'nrich,** Bielitz, Silesia, Sept. 13, 1855—Meran, April 27, 1909; impresario; came to New York 1878; 1901, succeeded Grau as manager of the Metropolitan Opera House, where in 1903 he made the first production outside Bayreuth of *"Parsifal"*; 1905, Franz Leopold decorated him and gave him the privilege of the prefix "von"; ill health forced his retirement in 1908.

Con'solo, (1) **Frederigo,** Ancona, 1841—Florence, Dec. 14, 1906; violinist and comp. (2) **Ernesto,** London, Sept. 15, 1864—Florence, March 21, 1931; noted pianist; pupil of Sgambati and Reinecke; toured widely; 1906–09, taught Chicago Mus. Coll.; later at Geneva and Florence Cons.; ed. Beethoven sonatas for pf.

Constantin (kŏṅ-stäṅ-tăṅ), **Titus Chas.**, Marseilles, Jan. 7, 1835—Pau, Oct., 1891; pupil of Thomas, Paris Cons., 1860; cond. of the "Fantasies Parisiennes"; 1875, Op. Com.; c. a comic-opera, *"Dans la Forêt"* (1872), etc.

Conti (kŏn'-tē), (1) **Fran. Bart.**, Florence, 1682—1732; court-theorbist and dram. composer. (2) ("Contini") **Ignazio**, Florence, 1699—Vienna, 1759; son and successor of above; composer. (3) **Gioacchino** (named **Gizziello**, after his teacher Dom. Gizzi), Arpino, Naples, 1714—Rome, 1761; famous male soprano; 1739, in London with Händel; retired to Arpino in 1753. (4) **Carlo**, Arpino, Naples, 1796—Naples, 1868; prof. and dram. composer.

Contino (kŏn-tē'-no), **Giov.**, d. Mantua, 1565; conductor and contrapuntist.

Co'nus (or Conius or Konius), (1) **George Edwardovich**, composer; Moscow, Oct. 1, 1862—Aug., 1933; theorist; pupil of the Cons.; 1891–99 teacher of theory there; 1902 prof. at the Opera School; c. symph. poem *"From the Realm of Illusions,"* orch. suite, *"Child-Life,"* cantata, etc. His brother, (2) **Julius**, b. Moscow, 1869; gold medallist at the Cons. and later teacher of violin there; c. violin concerto, etc. (3) **Leo**, pianist; pupil at the Cons.; later founded a school of his own.

Converse, Frederick Shepherd, b. Newton, Mass., Jan. 1, 1871—Westwood, Mass., June 8, 1940; grad. Harvard and studied music with Bährmann and G. W. Chadwick; 1896–98 with Rheinberger, then taught theory and comp. at the New England Cons.; 1901–07, Harvard Univ.; c. operas *"The Pipe of Desire"* (in concert form, Boston, 1906, as an opera, Met. Op., N. Y., 1910, Boston Op., 1911); symph. (1907); overtures, *"Youth"* and *"Euphrosyne"*; orch. romance, *"The Festival of Pan"*; orch. fantasie, *"The Mystic Trumpeter"*; symph. poem *"Ormazd,"* (Boston Symph. Orch., 1912); violin concerto and sonata, 2 string quartets, etc.

Conver'si, Girolamo, b. Correggio, 16th cent.; c. madrigals, etc.

Cooke, (1) **H.**, d. July 13, 1672; buried Westminster Abbey; court-composer and teacher. (2) **Nathaniel**, b. Bosham, 1773; organist. (3) **Benj.**, London, 1734—1793; conductor and composer. (4) **Thos. Simpson**, Dublin, 1782—London, 1848; conductor, later tenor, then prof. at the R. A. M.; prod. nearly 20 operas at Drury Lane. (5) **H. Angelo Michael** (called **Grattan**), son of above; oboist and bandmaster. (6) **James Francis**, b. Bay City, Mich., Nov. 14, 1875; pianist, composer, editor, teacher; studied in New York with W. H. Hall, Woodman, Eberhard and Medorn; also at Würzburg R. Cons. with Meyer-Olbersleben and Hermann Ritter; for some years active as piano teacher in New York, also org. and vocal teacher; beginning 1907 ed. *"The Etude"*; pres. Presser Foundation, Phila., after 1917; Mus. D., Ohio Northwestern Univ., 1919; c. piano pieces and songs; author; *"Great Pianists upon Piano Playing"*; *"Standard History of Music"*; *"Mastering the Scales and Arpeggios"*; *"Musical Playlets"*; *"Music-Masters Old and New,"* etc.

Coolidge, Elizabeth Sprague (Mrs. Frederick Shurtleff Coolidge), noted music patron, composer, pianist; founder and sponsor for many years of the Pittsfield, Mass., Music Fests., on her estate, where invited audiences attended these events; in recent years transferred to auditorium in Library of Congress, Washington, which she donated and endowed by means of trust fund; commissioned works from many leading contemporary composers; has established a Coolidge Chamber Music Prize for such awards, and has sponsored festivals in Chicago (1930) and in many European cities, in which eminent solo artists and chamber music groups have participated; c. chamber music, incl. trio, quartet, etc.

Coombs, Chas. Whitney, b. Bucksport, Me., Dec. 25, 1859—Montclair, N.J., Jan. 24, 1940; pupil of Speidel (pf.) and Max Seifriz, Draeseke (comp.), Hermann John, P. Janssen, and Lamperti; 1887–91, organist Amer. Ch., in Dresden; 1892, as organist Church of the Holy Communion, New York, 1908, St. Luke's; pub. *"The Vision of St. John,"* cantata with orch. and org., songs, etc.

Coo'per, (1) **G.**, Lambeth, London, 1820—London, 1876; organist and composer. (2) **Emil**, Russian conductor; pupil of Taneyeff; cond. at Moscow Imp. Op. and Imp. Mus.

Soc. of Cons. in that city before the world war; led 50th anniversary concerts of latter organization, presenting works of Scriabin, Taneyeff and Rachmaninoff in presence of composers; 1909–14, led seasons of Russian opera in London and Paris; after 1917 lived in Paris, cond. of opera in Champs-Elysées Theat.; also guest appearances in other European countries; cond. of Chicago Op. Co., 1929–31, presenting American premières of Moret's *"Lorenzaccio"* and Hamilton Forrest's *"Camille."*

Coperario (kō-pĕr-ä'-rĭ-ō) (rightly J. Cooper), famous English lutenist and viola-da-gambist, 17th century.

Copland (cōp'-lănd), **Aaron,** b. Brooklyn, N. Y., Nov. 14, 1900; composer; studied with Rubin Goldmark, also with Nadia Boulanger, Fontainebleau; piano with Victor Wittgenstein and Clarence Adler; lecturer on modern music, New School for Social Research, N. Y.; organized and promoted Copland-Sessions Concerts of Contemporary Music, N. Y. (with Roger Sessions); mem. board of directors, League of Composers; c. (ballet) *"Grotto,"* (1925); symphony (1924); *"Music for the Theatre"* (1915); concerto for piano and orch. (1926); Symphonic Ode (1929); variations for piano, etc.

Coppet (kŏ-pā), **Edward J. de,** New York, May 28, 1855—April 30, 1916; of Swiss descent; music patron; founded series of chamber music programmes at his home, 1886, more than a thousand being given before his death; in 1902, the Flonzaley Quartet (Adolfo Betti, Alfred Pochon, Ugo Ara and Iwan d'Archambeau) was organised to play at these events, being named after his summer home in Switzerland; this group became one of world's leading ensembles and made many Amer. and Eur. tours, first under his patronage and later as a public concert-giving enterprise: after 1917 Ara being succeeded as violist by Louis Bailly.

Cop'pola, (1) **Giu.,** singer in London, 1777. (2) **P. A. (Pierantonio),** Castrogiovanni, Sicily, 1793—Catania, 1877; dram. composer and conductor. (3) **Piero,** b. Milan, Oct. 11, 1888; conductor and composer; grad. Cons. Verdi, in native city; has appeared as cond. in Turin, Milan (La Scala), Modena, Florence, Bo-

logna, Brussels (La Monnaie), London, Oslo, Gothenberg, Copenhagen, Palermo, etc.; after 1923 res. in Paris as artistic dir. of French Gramophone Co. and as cond. of concerts; c. of stage and orch. music.

Coquard (kô-kăr), **Arthur,** Paris, May 26, 1846—Noirmoutier, Aug. 20, 1910; pupil of César Franck; mus. prof. Nat. Inst. of the Young Blind; critic for *"Le Monde"*; c. operas *"L' Epée du Roi"* (Angers, 1884); *"Le Mari d'un Jour"* (Paris, 1886); lyric dramas, *"L'oiseau bleu"* (Paris, 1894); *"La Jacquerie"* (Monte Carlo and Paris, 1895), *"Jahel"* (Lyons, 1900), *"La troupe Jolicoeur"* (1902), etc. Won prize from French Acad. for his study, *"De la Musique en France depuis Rameau"* (1892).

Cor'bett, Wm., 1669 (?)—London (?), 1748; Engl. violinist and composer.

Cordans (kôr-däns), **Bart.,** Venice, 1700 —Udine, 1757; Franciscan monk, then conductor and dram. composer.

Cordel'la, Giacomo, Naples, 1783—1847; dram. composer.

Cor'der, Fr., Hackney, London, Jan. 26, 1852—Sept. 21, 1932; pupil of R. A. M.; 1875, won the Mendelssohn Scholarship; 1875–78, pupil of Ferd. Hiller; 1880, cond. of Aquarium Concerts at Brighton where he lived as a transl. and critic, and composer of operas, cantatas, etc.; after 1886 prof. at R. A. M., London; 1889, curator there; wrote *"The Orchestra and How to Write for It,"* etc., ed. a musical encyclopedia (1915).

Corel'li, Arcangelo, Fusignano, near Imola, Italy, Feb. 17, 1653—Rome, Jan. 8, 1713; pupil of Bessani and Simonelli; toured Germany, then lived under patronage of Cardinal Ollobone; one of the founders of vln.-style, systematiser of bowing and shifting, introducer of chord-playing; a composer for the vln. whose works still hold favour. On invitation from the King of Naples he gave a succ. court-concert, but at a second made various blunders and returned to Rome, in chagrin, increased with fatal results on finding or imagining himself supplanted there by a poor violinist named Valentini. His masterpieces *"Concerti grossi,"* were pub. just before his death. Many spurious comps. were issued under his name.

Corfe, (1) **Jos.,** Salisbury, 1740—1820; organist and composer. (2) **Arthur T.,** Salisbury, 1773—1863; son of above; pianist, organist and writer. (3) **Chas. W.,** son of above; organist Christ Church, Oxford.

Cornelius (kôr-nā'-lǐ-oos), **Peter,** Mayence, Dec. 24, 1824—Oct. 26, 1874, unsucc. actor; then studied cpt. with Dehn at Berlin, and joined the Wagnerian coterie at Weimar. His opera *"Der Barbier von Bagdad"* was a failure through organised opposition which led Liszt to leave the town, but in 1886-87 it succeeded. C. wrote his own libretti and transl. others. 1886-87, at Dresden, and other cities; 1859, with Wagner at Vienna, and Munich, where he became reader to King Ludwig, and prof.; prod. the opera *"Der Cid,"* Weimar, 1865; he left *"Gunlöd"* unfinished; Lassen completed it, and it was prod., Strassburg, 1892; he pub. many songs. Biog. by Sandberger (Leipzig, 1887).

Cornell', J. H., New York, 1828—1894; organist, composer and writer.

Cornet (kôr'-nāt), (1) **Julius,** S. Candido, Tyrol, 1793—Berlin, 1860; tenor and dir. His wife, (2) **Franziska** (1806—1870), was also a singer.

Coronaro (kō-rō-nä'-rō), (1) **Gaetano,** Vicenza, Italy, Dec. 18, 1852— Milan, April 5, 1908; violinist; till 1873, pupil, Milan Cons., then in Germany; prod. the succ. opera *"Un Tramonto"* (Milan Cons. Th., 1873); 3-act *"La Creola"* (Bologna, 1878); *"Il Malacarne"* (Brescia, 1894); for several years prof. of harm., and 1894, prof. of comp., Milan Cons. (2) **Antonio,** Vicenza, 1851—March 24, 1933; brother of **Gaetano** C., and comp. of operas; his son was (3) **Arrigo,** Vicenza, 1880—October, 1906; c. opera *"Turiddu"* (Turin, 1905). (4) **Gellio Bv.,** Vicenza, Nov. 30, 1863—Milan, July 26, 1916; pianist (protégé of Sonzogno); début at 8; at 9, organist in Vicenza; at 13, th. cond., Marosteca; at 15, chorusm.; at 16, pupil Bologna Cons., graduating with first prizes; c. a symphony; opera, *"Jolanda"* (1889 ?); unsucc. *"Claudia"* (Milan, 1895).

Corri (kôr'-rē), **Dom.,** Rome, 1744— London, 1825; dram. composer and writer.

Cor'si, Jacopo, ca. 1560—1604; Florentine nobleman, in whose house and in Bardi's, Peri, Caccini, Emilio de' Cavaliere, Galilei, Rinuccini, and others met and inaugurated modern opera (v. PERI); C. was a skilful gravicembalist.

Corteccia (kôr-tĕt'-chä), **Fran. Bdo. di,** Arezzo, 16th cent., Florence, 1571; organist, conductor and composer.

Cortellini (kôr-tĕl-lē'-nē), **Camillo,** called "Il violino" from his skill; at Bologna, 1583, as municipal musician and comp.

Cortesi (kôr-tā'-zē), **Francesco,** Florence, 1826—Jan. 3, 1904; conductor, composer of operas, and teacher of voice.

Cortot (côr-tō'), **Alfred,** b. Nyon, Switzerland, Sept. 26, 1877; pianist; studied at Paris Cons., with Decombes and Diémer; début, Colonne Concerts, Paris, 1896; served as *répétiteur* at Bayreuth; founder and leader of Assoc. des Concerts Cortot in Paris (1902–04) and led performances of Wagnerian operas; prof., Paris Cons., 1907; after 1904 toured as pianist in many Eur. cities and in America with great succ.; also has been associated with Thibaud and Casals in trio of exemplary merit, and with these musicians has been leading factor in the École Normale de Musique, Paris; mem. of the Legion of Honor.

Coss'mann, B., Dessau, May 17, 1822 —Frankfort, May 7, 1910; 'cellist; pupil of Espenhahn, Drechsler, Theo. Müller and Kummer; 1840, member of Gr. Opéra Orch., Paris; 1847–48, solo 'cellist at Gewandhaus, Leipzig; then studied comp. under Hauptmann; 1850, at Weimar, with Liszt; 1866, prof. Moscow Cons.; 1870–78 at Baden-Baden; then prof. of 'cello, Frankfort Cons.; composer.

Cossoul (kôs'-sool), **Guilherme Antonio,** Lisbon, April 22, 1828— May 26, 1880; 'cellist and comp.

Cos'ta, (1) Sir **Michael** (rightly **Michele**), Naples, Feb. 4, 1808— Brighton, England, April 29, 1884; son and pupil of (2) **Pasquale C.** (composer ch.-mus.); pupil also of Tritto, Zingarelli (comp.), and Crescentini (singing) at the Naples Cons.; prod. 4 succ. operas at Naples, was sent to Birmingham, England, to cond. a psalm of Zingarelli's, but through a misunderstanding, had to sing the tenor part; he thereafter lived in England as dir. and cond.

of King's Th., London, where he prod. three ballets; 1846, cond. of the Philh. and the new Ital. Opera; 1848, Sacred Harmonic Society; from 1849, cond. Birmingham festivals; from 1857, the Handel festivals; knighted in 1869; 1871 dir. of the music and cond. at H. M.'s Opera; c. 3 oratorios, 6 operas, 3 symphonies, etc. (3) **Andrea,** b. Brescia, settled London, 1825; composer and teacher. (4) **Carlo,** Naples, 1826 — 1888; teacher Naples Cons. (5) **P. Mario,** Tarento, July 26, 1858—San Remo, Sept. 27, 1933; nephew of above; c. chamber-music and pop. songs in Neapolitan dialect; also 2 panto-mimes, "*Le Modèle Rêve,*" and the succ. "*L'Histoire d'un Pierrot*" (Paris, 1894 ?).

Costantini (tē'-nē), **Fabio,** b. Rome ca. 1570; composer and teacher.

Costanzi (kō-stän'-tsĭ), **Juan** (or **Gioannino**), Rome, 1754—1778; conductor.

Cotes (kō'-tĕs), **Ambrosio de,** d. Seville, Sept. 9, 1603; Spanish composer and cond.

Cott'low, Augusta, b. Shelbyville, Ill., April 2, 1878; pianist; pupil in Chicago of Wolfsohn and Gleason; orch. début there, 1889; N. Y., under Seidl, 1891; later studied in Berlin with Busoni and Boise; toured Eur. countries and after 1900 in U. S.

Cot'to (Cotto'nius), **Jns.,** 11th to 12th cent.; writer.

Cottrau (kŏt-trō, or kŏt-trä'-oo), (1) **Guillaume** (Guglielmo), Paris, 1797 —Naples, 1847; composer. His sons (2) **Teodoro** (pen-name **Eutalindo Martelli**) (Naples, 1827—1879) and (3) **Giulio** (Jules), (Naples, 1831— Rome, 1916) also song-composers; the latter c. operas.

Coucy (dŭ koo-sē), **Regnault,** Chatelain, de, d. Palestine, 1192; troubadour to Richard Cœur de Lion; his songs are in MSS. in the Paris Library, and have been re-published.

Couperin (koo-pŭ-răṅ), a family of French musicians, famous for two centuries. The first known were three brothers: (1) **Louis,** 1626— 1661; organist of St. Gervais and composer. (2) **Fran.** (Sieur de Crouilly), 1631—1698; organist and composer. (3) **Chas.,** 1638—1669; organist; his son, (4) **Fran.** (called **Le Grand**), Paris, 1668—1733; the first great composer to write exclusively for the harpsichord (or clavecin); pupil of Thomelin, and successor of his uncle François, at St. G., 1698; 1701, clavecinist and organist to the King; c. brilliant and fascinating music pub. at Paris, and wrote "*L'Art de toucher du Clavecin*" (1711). (5) His son **Nicholas,** Paris, 1680—1748, was organist. (6) **Armand Louis,** Paris, 1725—1789, son of (5), a remarkable org.-virtuoso. His wife (7) **Élisabeth Antoinette** (née **Blanchet**), b. 1721, was an organist and clavecinist, and played in public at 81. They had 2 sons (8) **P. Louis** (d. 1789), his father's asst. organist, and (9) **Gervais Fran.,** his father's successor.

Courboin (kōōr'-bwän), **Charles-Marie,** b. Antwerp, April 2, 1886; organist; pupil of Blockx at Cons. in native city; also at Brussels Cons. of Mailly, Gilson, Huberti and Tinel; won prizes in several fields, also internat'l. competition; after 1902, org. Antwerp Cathedral; appeared widely as recitalist; after 1904 in U. S., at Syracuse, Springfield, Mass., etc.; c. choral and organ music.

Courtois (koor-twä), **Jean,** 16th cent., French contrapuntist; conductor and composer.

Courvoisier (koor-vwäs-yā, or koor'-foi-sēr), (1) **K.,** Basel, Nov. 12, 1864 —1908; violinist; pupil of David, Röntgen and Joachim; 1871, a member of the Thalia Th., orch., Frankfort; then, till 1875, cond. of singing with Gustav Barth; '76, cond. Düsseldorf Th., orch., and choral societies; 1885, singing-teacher at Liverpool; c. a symphony, 2 concert-overtures, a vln.-concerto (MS.), etc.; wrote "*Die Violintechnik*" (transl. by H. E. Krehbiel; N. Y., 1896); an "*École de la velocité*" and a "*Méthode*" (London, 1892). (2) **Walter,** near Basel, Feb. 7, 1875 —Locarno, Dec. 27, 1931; pupil of Bagge and Thuille; after 1910, prof. of theory, Munich Akad.

Coussemaker (koos-mă-kăr'), **Chas. Ed. H.,** Bailleul, Nord, April 19, 1805— Boubourg, Jan. 10, 1876; a remarkable sight-reader, studied cpt. with V. Lefèbvre; while serving as a judge he made musical research his avocation, and pub. important works on Hucbald and mediæval instruments, theory and composers, incl. his

"*Scriptores de musica medii evi, nova series*" (1864–76, 4 vols.), a great collection intended as supplement to Gerbert.

Cousser. Vide KUSSER.

Cow'ard, (1) **Jas.,** London, 1824–1880; organist, conductor, composer. (2) Sir **Henry,** b. Liverpool, Nov. 26, 1849; grad. Tonic-sol-fa Coll. 1889 Mus. Bac.; 1894 Mus. Doc. Oxon; Univ.-teacher and cond. at Sheffield; after 1904, docent in music; c. choruses pf.-pcs.; knighted 1926; pub. his memoirs, 1919.

Cow'ell, Henry, b. Menlo Park, Cal., March 11, 1897; composer, pianist; studied Univ. of Calif. and in Europe; début, Munich, 1923; toured in Europe and America; his compositions early attracted attention because of use of "tone-clusters," groups of notes which might be performed on the piano keyboard with forearm or fist; in recent years has also c. orchestral and chamber music; carried on research under Guggenheim Fellowship in European folk music; dir. New Mus. Soc. of Calif., which issued contemporary Amer. music in quarterly form and recordings.

Cow'en, Sir **Frederic Hymen,** Kingston, Jamaica, Jan. 29, 1852—London, Oct. 6, 1935; at 4 brought to London to study, pupil of Benedict and Goss, then of Hauptmann, Moscheles, Reinecke, Richter, and Plaidy, Leipzig; and Kiel, Berlin; 1882, dir. Edinburgh Acad. of Music; 1887, cond. London Philh.; 1888–89, mus.-dir. Melbourne Centennial Exhibition; 1896–1914, cond. Liverpool Phil., and the Manchester Concerts; 1900, of Scottish Orch.; knighted 1911; prod. four operas; two oratorios, "*The Deluge*" (1878), and "*Ruth*" (1887); 7 cantatas; 6 symphonies (No. 3 "*Scandinavian*" (1880), 4 "*Welsh*," 6 "*Idyllic*"); four orchestral suites, "*The Language of Flowers*," "*In the Olden Time*," "*In Fairyland*," "*Suite de Ballet*," Sinfonietta in A for orch.; 2 overtures; pf.-concerto; pf.-trio; pf.-quartet; pf.-pcs.; over 250 songs.

Crabbé (kräb-ā), **Armand,** b. Brussels, 1884; barytone; pupil of Cons. in native city; 1904–08, sang at La Monnaie, Brussels; 1908–10, Manhattan Op. House, New York; after 1910 for several seasons with Chicago

Op. Co., also at Covent Garden, Berlin, etc.

Craft, Marcella, b. Indianapolis, Aug. 11, 1880; soprano; studied with Charles Adams, also 1901 in Milan with Guagni and Mottino; op. début, Morbegno, 1902; sang in Italy, at Mainz, Kiel, and at Munich Op., 1909–14; in America, 1917–18; after 1923 lived in Germany as singer and teacher.

Cramer (krä'-mĕr or krā'-mĕr), (1) **Wm.,** Mannheim, 1745 (1743?)—London, 1799 (1800?); violinist and conductor. (2) **K. Fr.,** Quedlinburg, 1752—Paris, Dec. 1807; professor. (3) **Jn. Bap.,** Mannheim, Feb. 24, 1771—London, April 16, 1858; eldest son and pupil of (1). Brought to London when a year old; pupil of Benser, Schroeter, then of Clementi; in comp., chiefly self-taught; toured as concert-pianist at 17; in 1828 est. a mus.-pub. firm (now Cramer & Co.) in partnership with Addison; managed it till 1842; 1832–45, lived in Paris, pub. "a Method for pf. ("*Grosse praktische Pfte.-Schule*"), in 5 parts," the last containing the celebrated "*84 Studies*" (op. 50), still a standard; c. 7 concertos, 105 sonatas, quartet, quintet, and many pf.-pcs.

Cranz (kränts), **August,** Hamburg, mus.-pub. firm, founded 1813 by **A. H. Cranz** (1789–1870). His son **Alwin** (b. 1834) succeeded him, and in 1896 his grandson **Oscar** became head.

Craywinckel (krī'-vĭnk-ĕl), **Fd. Manuel Martin Louis Barthélemy de,** Madrid, Aug. 24, 1820—?; pupil of Bellon; cond. St. Bruno, at Bordeaux, where he lived from 1825; c. excellent masses and other church-mus.

Cre(c)quillon (krĕk-wē-yôṅ), **Thos.,** n. Ghent (?)—Béthune, 1557; ca. 1544–47 conductor and composer.

Crescentini (krā-shĕn-tē'-nē), **Girolamo,** Urbania, near Urbino, Feb. 2, 1766—Naples, April 24, 1846; famous male soprano and composer.

Cre'ser, William, York, Sept. 9, 1844—1933; organist, composer; pupil of Macfarren; 1880, Mus. Doc. Oxford; 1881, 1891–1902, org. Chapel Royal; St. James, and comp. to Chapel Royal; married Amelia Clarke mezzo-soprano; c. oratorio, "*Micaiah*"; cantatas "*Eudora*"

(Leeds, 1882); *"The Sacrifice of Freia"* (Leeds, 1889), etc.

Cressent (krěs-säň), **Anatole**, Argenteuil, 1824—Paris, 1870; lawyer and founder of the triennial prize "prix Cressent," endowed with 120,000 francs, to be equally divided between the librettist, and the composer of the best opera; first awarded to Chaumet, 1875.

Creyghton (krā'-tŭn), Rev. **Robt.**, b. ca. 1639; English composer.

Crist, Bainbridge, b. Lawrenceburg, Ind., 1883; composer; pupil of Juon, Emerich and Shakespeare; after 1914 was active as teacher in Boston; c. dance-drama, *"Le Pied de la Momie,"* orch. and chamber music, and songs.

Cristofo'ri, Bart. (wrongly **Cristofali** and **Cristofani**), Padua, May 4, 1655 —Florence, Jan. 27, 1731; inv. the first practical hammer-action to which he gave the name "pianoforte" (v. D. D.); in 1711 he substituted for the plucking quills "a row of little hammers striking the strings from below," the principle adopted by Broadwood, and called the "English action."

Crivel'li, (1) **Arcangelo**, Bergamo, 1546 —1617; tenor and composer. (2) **Giov. Bat.**, Scandiano, Modena (?)— Modena, 1682; organist and conductor. (3) **Gaetano**, Bergamo, 1774 —Brescia, 1836; famous tenor. (4) **Dom.**, b. Brescia, 1793; son of above, dram. composer.

Croce (krō'-chě), **Giov. della** (called "Il Chiozzotto"), Chioggia, ca. 1557 —Venice, 1609; conductor and composer.

Croes (kroos), **H. Jas. de**, Antwerp, 1705—Brussels, 1786; violinist and conductor.

Croft(s), Wm., Nether-Eatington, Warwickshire, Engl., 1678—Bath, 1727 (buried Westm. Abbey); 1704, joint organist, 1707, sole organist Westm. Abbey; pub. *"Musica sacra"* (the first English church-music engraved in score on plates).

Crooks, Richard, b. Trenton, N. J.; tenor; sang as boy soprano in church choir at 8; pupil of Sydney H. Bourne; concert appearances at 12; following war service, was soloist at First Presbyterian Church, N. Y.; first came into prominence as soloist with N. Y. Symph., 1922; made U. S. concert tours, also of England,

Scandinavia and Central Europe, 1927; as Cavaradossi, Hamburg Op., same year; also at Berlin Op.; soloist with leading Amer. orchs.; mem. Met. Op. Co., after 1933, singing leading French and Italian rôles.

Cros'dill, J., London, 1751—Escrick, Yorkshire, 1825; 'cellist.

Cross, Michael Hurley, Philadelphia, 1833—1897; composer and director.

Cross'ley, Ada, near Bairnsdale, Australia, March 3, 1874—London, Oct. 17, 1929; noted mezzo-soprano; début, Melbourne as a girl; after 1894 lived in London; studied with Santley and later with Marchesi; sang at many English festivals; 1904 toured Australia; later also U. S.; m. F. E. Muecke.

Crotch, Wm., Norwich, Engl., July 5, 1775—Taunton, Dec. 29, 1847; at the age of 2½ he played on a small organ, built by his father, a mastercarpenter; at 10 played in public at London; at the age of 11 asst. organist of Trinity and King's Colleges Cambridge; at 14 c. on oratorio, *"The Captivity of Judah"* (perf. 1789), became organist of Christ Ch., Oxford; 1797, prof. of mus. Oxford; 1799, Mus. Doc. there; 1822 principal of the new R. A. M., c. 2 oratorios.

Crouch, (1) Mrs. **Anna M.** (née **Philips**), 1763—Brighton, 1805; Engl. operatic singer. (2) **Fr. Nicholls**, London, July 31, 1808—Portland, Me., Aug. 18, 1896; basso, 'cellist and singing-teacher; c. 2 operas, and songs, incl. *"Kathleen Mavourneen."*

Cro'west, Fr. J., London, Nov. 30, 1850 —Birmingham, June 14, 1927; eminent organist, writer and composer.

Crüger (krü'-gěr), **Jns.**, Gross-Breese, near Guben, 1598—Berlin, 1662; organist.

Crusell (kroos'-sěl), **Bernhard**, Finland, 1775—Stockholm, 1838; composer.

Cruvel'li (rightly **Crüwell**) (krü'-věl), (1) **Friederike M.**, Bielefeld, Westphalia, 1824—1868; noted contralto in London, but lost her voice. (2) **Jne. Sophie Charlotte**, Bielefeld, Mar. 12, 1826—Nice, Nov. 6, 1907; sister of above; also contralto, illtrained, but had enormous success at Paris Gr. Opéra, 1854, at a salary of 100,000 francs; in 1856 m. Comte Vigier, and left the stage.

Cui (kwē), **César Antonovitch**, Vilna,

Russia, Jan. 18, 1835—d. at Vilna, September 14, 1918; one of the most important of Russian composers; pupil of Moniuszko and Balakirev; a military engineer; Prof. of fortification at the St. Petersburg Engineering Acad.; from 1864–68, critic of the St. P. *"Gazette"*; 1878–79, pub. articles in Paris, on *"La musique en Russie"*; c. operas, *"William Ratcliffe"* (St. P., 1869); *"The Prisoner in the Caucasus"* (1873); *"Angelo"* (1876); *"The Mandarin's Son"* (1878); lyric comedy, *"Le Filibustier"* (Paris, 1894); the very succ. *"The Saracen"* (1899); *"A Feast in Time of Plague"* (1901); *"Mam'zelle Fifi"* (1903); *"Matteo Falcone"* (1908); *"The Captain's Daughter"*; some thirty mixed choruses; string quartet, many vln. works, 2 scherzos and a tarantella for orch.; suite for pf. and vln.; pf.-pcs.; some 200 songs. *"Esquisse critique"* on Cui and his works by the Comtesse de Mercy-Argenteau; also studies by Koptiaev, Weimarn, etc.

Cul'bertson, Sasha, b. Russia, Dec. 29, 1893; violinist; pupil of Suchorukoff; at 9 entered Cons. at Rostoff; in 1905 pupil of Sevcik, Prague; début, Vienna 1908; toured Europe and America.

Culp (koolp), **Julia,** b. Groningen, Oct. 1, 1881; mezzo-soprano; well-known Liedersinger; pupil of Amsterdam Cons. and of Etelka Gerster; has toured Europe with great success; after 1912, America.

Culwick (kŭl'-lĭk), **James C.,** West Bromwich, April 28, 1845—Dublin, Oct. 5, 1907; organist, theorist and comp. Prof. Alexandria College, Dublin; cond. Dublin Philharmonic Soc., etc. 1903, Mus. Doc. Univ. of Dublin.

Cum'mings, Wm. Hayman, Sudbury, Devon, Eng., Aug. 22, 1831—London, August, 1915; organist Waltham Abbey; prof. of singing R. Coll. for the Blind, Norwood; 1896, principal of Guildhall Sch. of Mus.; founded the Purcell Society, ed. its pubs.; wrote biog. of Purcell (London, 1882); had also pub. a music *"Primer,"* 1877; and a *"Biog. Dictionary of Musicians"* (1892); c. a cantata, *"The Fairy Ring,"* etc.

Curci (koor'-chē), **Giu.,** Barletta, 1808 —1877; singing teacher and dram. composer.

Cur'ry, Arthur Mansfield, b. Chelsea, Mass., Jan. 27, 1866; violin pupil of Franz Kneisel, and of MacDonald in harmony; teacher and cond. in Boston; c. overture *"Blomidon"* (Worcester, Mass., Fest. 1902); symph. poem *"Atala"* (Boston Symph., 1911); *"The Winning of Amarac"*; Keltic legend for a reader, chorus and orch., etc.

Curschmann (koorsh'-män), **K. Fr.,** Berlin, 1805—Langfuhr, near Danzig, 1841; singer, dram. composer and pop. song-writer.

Curti (koor'-tē), **Fz.** (or **Francesco**), Cassel, 1854—Dresden, 1898; dram. composer.

Curtis, (1) **H. Holbrook,** New York, Dec. 15, 1856—1920; grad. Yale, 1877; 1880, M.D.; vice-pres. Am. Social Science Assn., prominent throat specialist and writer on the voice, pub. *"Voice Building and Tone Placing."* (2) **Natalie,** New York—Paris, Oct. 23, 1921; writer on Indian and Negro music; studied with Friedheim, Busoni, Giraudet, Wolff and Kniese; early active as pianist; made collection of 200 songs of Am. Indians, also Negro folk-songs; m. Paul Burlin, painter.

Cur'wen, (1) Rev. **J.,** Heckmondwike, Yorkshire, Engl., 1816—near Manchester, 1880; 1862, resigned his pastorate, and founded a college, also a pub.-house, to exploit Tonic-sol-fa. (2) **J. Spencer,** Plaistow, 1847—London, 1916; son and pupil of above; pupil also of G. Oakey and R.A.M.; writer, and 1880 pres. Tonic-sol-fa Coll.

Cusani'no. Vide CARESTINI.

Cusins (kŭz'-ĭns), Sir **Wm. G.,** London, 1833 — Remonchamps (Ardennes), 1893; pf.-prof. R.A.M.; knighted 1892; conductor and composer.

Cuzzoni (kood-zō'-nē), **Fran.,** Parma, 1700—Bologna, 1770; début 1719; m. the pianist Sandoni; very successful contralto till her latter days, when it is said she earned a pittance by covering silk buttons.

Czernohorsky (chĕr-nō-hôr'-shkĭ), **Bohuslav,** Nimburg, Bohemia, Feb. 26, 1684—Graz, July 2, 1740. Franciscan monk, organist and comp.

Czerny (Cerny) (chär'-nē), **Karl,** Vienna, Feb. 20, 1791—July 15, 1857; pupil of his father **Wenzel C.,** later of Beethoven; and had advice from

Clementi and Hummel; made an early reputation as pianist and was an eminent teacher from his 16th year; Liszt, Döhler, and Thalberg were among his pupils; pub. over 1,000 works, his pf.-studies, still standard, incl. many such works as *"Die Schule der Geläufigkeit"* (School of Velocity) (op. 299); c. also masses, symphonies, overtures, etc.

Czersky (chär'-shkĭ). Vide TSCHIRCH.

Czerwonky (chĕr'-vŏn-kē), **Richard**, b. Birnbaum, Germany, May 23, 1886; violinist, conductor; studied at Klindworth-Scharwenka Cons. and Hochsch., Berlin; pupil of Zajic, Moser and Joachim; début with Berlin Philh., 1906; later concertm. of Boston and Minneapolis Symphs.; head of Bush Cons., Chicago, vln. dept., after 1919.

Czibulka (chē-bool'-kä), **Alphons**, Szepes-Várallya, Hungary, May 14, 1842—Vienna, Oct. 27, 1894; pianist and conductor; c. 5 operettas, incl. *"Der Bajazzo"* (Vienna, 1892), waltzes, etc.

D

Dachs (däkhs), **Jos.**, Ratisbon, 1825— Vienna, 1896; teacher and pianist.

Daff'ner, Hugo, b. Munich, May 2, 1882; author and comp.; pupil of Thuille, Schmid-Lindner and Max Reger; 1904, Ph.D.; c. symph., sonatas, etc.

Dalayrac (or **D'Alayrac**) (däl-ĕ-răk), **Nicolas**, Muret, Haute-Garonne, June 13, 1753—Paris, Nov. 27, 1809; prod. about 60 operas.

Dalberg (däl'-bărkh), **Jn. Fr. Hugo**, Reichsfreiherr von, Herrnsheim, 1760 —1812; writer and composer.

D'Albert, Eugen. Vide ALBERT, d'.

Dalcroze (däl-krôz), **Emile Jaques**, b. Vienna, July 6, 1865, of Swiss parentage; composer and founder of notable system of rhythmic exercises known as "Eurhythmics"; 1910-15, founded school at Hellerau, near Dresden; pupil of Fuchs, Bruchner and Délibes; teacher, lecturer and critic at Geneva Cons.; c. lyric comedies *"Janie"* (Geneva, 1893), and *"Sancho Panza"* (1897); *"Poème Alpestre"* for voices and orch. (1896, London, 1897); a violin concerto played by Marteau on his tours, and Swiss songs of popularity and national feeling; his theories of bodily movement have had deep influence on the internat'l. world of music and dance; author of many works on the subject.

Dale, Benjamin James, b. Crouch Hill, London, July 17, 1885; organist; prof. of R. A. M.; c. symph., 2 overtures, successful piano sonata in D Minor, etc.

Dal'lam, Engl. family of organ-builders 17th cent. (also spelled **Dallans, Dallum, Dalham**).

Dalmores (dăl-mō'-rĕs), **Charles**, b. Nancy, France, Dec. 31, 1871; tenor; pupil Paris and Lyons Cons.; sang in France; 1896, at Manhattan Opera, N. Y.; 1910, Chicago Op.; also widely in Europe, incl. Bayreuth; later res. in Los Angeles as vocal teacher.

D'Alvarez (däl-vär'-ĕth), **Marguerite**, b. England; contralto; of Peruvian and French ancestry; daughter of nobleman and diplomat; studied at Brussels Cons., winning 1st prizes in singing and declamation, also Prix de la Reine; appointed Court Singer to King of Belgians; studied opera in Milan; début at Rouen; also with succ. at La Scala; Amer. début with Manhattan Op. Co., 1909; with Boston Op. Co., 1913; later at Covent Garden; 1920, Chicago Op.; has sung widely in recitals.

Dalvimare (däl-vē-mä'-rĕ) or **d'Alvimare** (dăl-vĭ-măr), **Martin P.**, Dreux, Eure-et-Loire, 1772—Paris, 1839; composer.

Dambois (däm-bwä'), **Maurice**, b. Liége, Belgium, 1889; 'cellist; pupil of Cons. in native city; 1st public appearance at 12; later toured extensively; dir. Liége Académie, 1910-14; first visited the U. S. in 1917 in company with Ysaye, where he later lived; c. orch., chamber music, songs, etc.

Damcke (däm'-kĕ), **Berthold**, Hanover, 1812—Paris, 1875; conductor.

Damoreau (däm-ō-rō), **Laure-Cinthie** (née **Montalant**, first known as "Mlle. Cinti"), Paris, 1801—Chantilly, 1863; soprano, later prof. of singing, Paris Cons.; wrote *"Méthode de chant."*

Da Mot'ta, José Vianna, b. Isle St. Thomas, Africa, April 22, 1868; Portuguese pianist; studied at Lisbon; début there 1881, then studied Scharwenka Cons., with Liszt and Von Bülow; toured widely; lived in

Berlin for some years; 1915–17, taught at Geneva Cons.; later in Lisbon as dir. of Cons. and cond. of symph. orch.; c. symph. *"An das Vaterland,"* 5 Portuguese rhapsodies on native melodies, etc.; also critic and author.

Damrosch (däm'-rôsh), (1) **Dr. Leopold**, Posen, Prussia, Oct. 22, 1832 —New York, Feb. 15, 1885; 1854, M.D.; took up music as solo-violinist; then as cond. at minor theatres; 1855, solo violinist Grand Ducal Orch., at Weimar; here he m. Helene von Heimburg, a singer; 1859–60 cond. Breslau Phil. Soc., etc.; 1871, invited to New York to conduct the Arion Society, made his first appearance as conductor and composer and violinist; 1873, founded the Oratorio Society, 1878 the Symphony Society; 1880 Mus. Doc. Columbia Coll.; 1884, cond. German opera at Met. Op.; c. 7 cantatas; symphony; music to Schiller's *"Joan of Arc,"* etc. (2) **Frank**, Breslau, June 22, 1859— New York, Oct. 21, 1937; son and pupil of above; pupil of Pruckner, Jean Vogt, and von Inten (pf.), Moszkowski (comp.); 1882–85, cond. Denver (Col.) Chorus Club; 1884–85 supervisor of music in public schools, also organist in various churches; 1885–91, chorusm. Met. Op.; till 1887 cond. the Newark Harmonic Society; 1892 organized the People's Singing Classes; 1897, supervisor of music, N. Y. City public schools; cond. 1898–1912, Oratorio Society, and 1893–1920, Mus. Art Soc. (N. Y.), Oratorio Soc., Bridgeport (Conn.), *"Orpheus"* and *"Eurydice"* Phila., etc.; for nearly 30 years from 1905 he was the first and sole dir. of the Inst. of Music. Art, noted New York school, which was later merged with the Juilliard School of Music but still functions; he wrote treatises; Mus. D., Yale Univ., 1904; pub. songs and choruses, and a method of sight-singing. (3) **Walter** (**Johannes**), b. Breslau, Silesia, Jan. 30, 1862; son and pupil of (1); pupil of Rischbieter and Draeseke (harm.), von Inten, Boekelman, and Max Pinner, (pf.), von Bülow (conducting); 1885–99 cond. N. Y. Oratorio and Symphony Societies; 1892 founded the N. Y. Symphony Orch.; 1894, organized and cond. the Damrosch Opera Co.; 1899, cond. at

Philadelphia; 1902, cond. **N. Y.** Philh. (vice Paur); he toured Europe with the N. Y. Symphony, 1920, and remained its permanent cond. for more than 40 years; during this time he developed esp. popularity as a cond. and lecturer at children's orch. concerts; he resigned this post in 1926 to become musical counsel of the Nat'l. Broadcasting Co., and annually led a notable series of "music appreciation" concerts for the school children of the country over this radio chain. He is the recipient of many honours, incl. the Legion of Honour and a half-dozen doctorates from American univs. Pub. his memoirs, *"My Musical Life"* (1930); prod. opera, *"The Scarlet Letter"* (Boston, 1896), text by Geo. Parsons Lathrop; c. also *"The Dove of Peace"* (1912), *"Cyrano de Bergerac"* (text by W. J. Henderson after Rostand play, Met. Op. 1913); *"The Man Without a Country"* (libretto by Arthur Guiterman), Met. Op. 1937; choruses, songs, etc.

Da'na, **Chas. Henshaw**, West Newton, Mass., 1846—Worcester, 1883; pianist, organist and composer.

Danbé (däň-bā), **Jules**, Caen, France, Nov. 15, 1840—Vichy, Nov. 10, 1905; violinist; pupil of Paris Cons.; till 1892 2nd dir. of the Cons. Concerts; 1895, cond. Op. Com., Paris; composer.

Dan'by, **J.**, 1757—London, May 16, 1798; English organist and composer.

Dancla (däň-klä), (1) **J. Bap. Chas.**, Bagnères-de-Bigorre, Dec. 19, 1818— Tunis, Nov. 9, 1907; 1828 pupil of Baillot, Halévy, and Berton, Paris Cons.; 1834, 2nd solo vln. Op.-Com.; 1857, prof. of vln. at the Cons., giving famous quartet soirées; c. four symphonies, over 130 works for vln., etc.; wrote 5 technical books, *"Les compositeurs chefs d'orchestre,"* etc. (2) **Arnaud**, Bagnères-de-Bigorre, 1820—1862, bro. of above; 'cellist and writer. (3) **Léopold**, Bagnères-de-Bigorre, 1823 — Paris, 1895, bro. of above; composer.

Dan'do, **Jos. H. B.**, b. Somers Town, London, 1806; violinist.

d'Andrieu or **Dandrieu**, vide ANDRIEU.

Danhauser (dän-how'-zĕr or däň-ō-zā), **Ad. Ld.**, Paris, 1835—1896; prof. of solfeggio at Cons. and dram. composer.

Danican. V. PHILIDOR.

Daniel, Salvador, b. Bourges, 1830 (?); for a few days dir. Paris Cons., under the Commune; killed in battle, May 23, 1871; writer.

Danise (dä-nē'-zä), **Giuseppe,** b. Naples, Jan. 11, 1883; opera barytone; 1st studied law, then singing with Colonnese and Petillo; début, Naples, 1906; has sung in leading Italian theatres, also Russia, South and Central America and U. S.; Met. Op. Co., N. Y., for some years after 1920; also in America with Ravinia Op. Co.

Danjou (dän'-zhoo), **J. L. F.,** Paris, 1812—Montpellier, 1866; 1840, organist and erudite historian.

Dan'kers (or **Danckerts**), **Ghiselin,** b. Tholen, Zealand; chorister in Papal chapel, 1538-65; composer and writer.

Dann, Hollis, b. Canton, Pa., May 1, 1861—N. Y., Jan. 3, 1939; Mus. D., Alfred Univ., 1906; dir. public school music, Ithaca, N. Y., 1887-1903; 1906-21, headed dept. of music, Cornell Univ., leading Glee Club and Music Fest.; began work in training music supervisors which he continued at Penna. State Coll., 1921-25; head dept. of music education, N. Y. Univ., 1925-35; author of works on school music; ed. collections of school songs, hymns, etc.

Dannreuther (dän'-roi-tĕr), **(1) Edward,** Strassburg, Nov. 4, 1844—Pimlico, London, Feb. 12, 1905; at 5 taken to Cincinnati, where he studied with F. L. Ritter; later, pupil of Richter, Moscheles, Hauptmann, Leipzig Cons.; 1863, London, as pianist; 1872 founded and cond. London Wagner Society; wrote *"Richard Wagner, His Tendencies and Theories"* (London, 1873); also composer. (2) **Gustav,** Cincinnati, July 21, 1853—New York, Dec. 19, 1923; pupil of de Ahna and Joachim (vln.) and Heitel (theory), Berlin; lived in London till 1877; joined Mendelssohn Quintet Club of Boston, where in 1880 he settled as a member of the newly formed Symphony Orch.; 1882-84 dir. Philh. Soc., Buffalo, N. Y.; founded the "Beethoven String-Quartet" of N. Y. (called "Dannr. Q." from 1894); for 3 years leader Symphony and Oratorio Societies, N. Y.; 1907, taught Vassar Coll.; wrote musical treatises.

Danzi (dän'-tsē), (1) **Fz.,** Mannheim,

May 15, 1763—Carlsruhe, April 13, 1826; dram. composer.

Da Ponte (dä pôn'-tĕ), **Lorenzo,** Ceneda, near Venice, March 10, 1749—New York, Aug. 17, 1838; of Jewish race; poet-laureate to Joseph II. at Vienna, until 1792; wrote text of Mozart's *"Don Giovanni"* and *"Cosi Fan Tutte"*; London, 1803, teacher of Italian and poet to the Italian Opera; made a failure of different pursuits in the U. S. A., and was finally teacher of Italian at Columbia College, N. Y.; pub. *"Memorie"* (Memoirs). There is a sketch of his life in Krehbiel's *"Music and Manners"* (N. Y., 1899).

Daquin (dä-kăn'), **L. Claude,** Paris, 1694—1772; notable organist, clavecinist and composer.

D'Aranyi, Yelly (yĕl'-ē dä-rän'-yē), b. Budapest, May 30, 1895 (grandniece of Joachim); violinist; studied piano at 6; later vln. with Hubay; made début at 13; has toured Germany, Austria, France, Italy, England, U. S.; appeared in sonata recitals with Myra Hess; res. in London since 1913; among composers who have created works for her are Bartok, Ravel and Vaughan Williams.

Dargomyžsky (där-gō-mēsh'-shkē), **Alex. Sergievitch,** Toula, Feb. 14, 1813—St. Petersburg, Jan. 17, 1869; pianist and composer; pupil of Schoberlechner; his opera *"Esmeralda"* (c. 1839) was prod. 1847 with succ.; his best opera *"Russalka"* followed in 1856; in 1867, at Moscow, an opera-ballet, *"The Triumph of Bacchus"* (written 1847) was instrumented; left an unfinished opera, *"Kammennoi Gost"* ("The Marble Guest") (finished by Rimsky-Korsakov). *"Rogdana,"* a fantasy-opera, was only sketched; c. also pop. orch. works.

Da(s)ser (dä'-sĕr), **(Dasserus) Ludwig,** until 1562 conductor and composer at Munich, predecessor of Lassus.

Daube (dow'-bĕ), **Fr.,** Cassel (Augsburg ?), 1730—Augsburg, 1797; composer and writer.

Dau'ney, Wm., Aberdeen, 1800—Demerara, 1843; writer.

Dauprat (dō-prä), **L. Fr.,** Paris, 1781—July 16, 1868; notable horn-player and composer.

Daussoigne-Méhul (dōs'-swän-mā'-ül), **L. Jos.,** Givet, Ardennes, 1790—Liége, 1875; dram. composer.

Dauvergne (dō-věrn), **Ant. C.**, Ferrand, 1713—Lyons, 1797; violinist and dram. composer.

Davaux (dǎ-vō), **Jean Baptiste**, Côte-St-André, 1737—Paris, Feb. 22, 1822; c. many symphonies, chamber music, etc.

Davenport, Francis W., Wilderslowe, near Derby, England, 1847—London, Nov., 1925; pupil of Macfarren, whose daughter he m.; 1879, prof. R. A. M., and 1882 Guildhall Sch. of Music; c. two symphonies (the 1st winning 1st prize at Alexandra Palace, 1876), and other comps.; wrote text-books.

Davico (dä-vē'-kō), **Vincenzo**, b. Monaco, Jan. 14, 1889; pupil of Reger; c. operas, orch., chamber music, songs, etc.

David (dä'-fēt), **Fd.**, Hamburg, June 19, 1810—near Klosters, Switzerland, July 19, 1873; pupil of Spohr and Hauptmann; at 15 played in the Gewandhaus, Leipzig; 1827, in Königstadt Th. orch., Berlin; at 19, 1st vln. in the private quartet of the wealthy Baron von Liphardt, at Dorpat, whose daughter he m.; gave concerts till 1835 in Russia; at 26 leader of the Gewandhaus Orch. at Mendelssohn's invitation; his rigorous precision of drill is still a terrifying tradition. In the composition of Mendelssohn's vln.-concerto he was almost a collaborator (cf. Joachim and Brahms). The Cons. was estab. in 1843, and **D.**'s unsurpassed gifts as a teacher had a large influence in making its reputation, among his pupils being Wilhelmj and Joachim; as a leader he had a wonderful faculty of inspiring the players with his own enthusiasm. His student editions of classical works embrace nearly all compositions of standard vln. literature; edited many classics, including the "*Hohe Schule des Violinspiels.*" His comp. include an opera, "*Hans Wacht*" (Leipzig, 1852); 2 symphonies; 5 vln.-concertos, etc.; wrote a standard meth. for vln.

David (dä-vēd), (1) **Félicien César**, Cadenet, Vaucluse, April 13, 1810—St. Germain-en-Laye, Aug. 29, 1876; at 7 a pupil and chorister in the maîtrise of Saint-Sauveur at Aix; c. hymns, motets, etc.; 1825–28 studied in the Jesuit college, but ran away to continue his music, and became asst.-cond. in the theatre at Aix, and at

19 cond. at Saint-Sauveur; 1830 Paris Cons., under Bénoist (org.), Reber and Millot (harm.), Fétis (cpt. and fugue). 1831, his rich uncle withdrew his allowance of 50 francs a month, and he took up Saint-Simonism, composing hymns for this socialistic sect, which coming under ban of the law in 1833, he went with other members on a tour through Turkey, Egypt, etc.; he returned in 1835 with a fund of Oriental musical impressions, resulting in an unsucc. volume of "*Mélodies Orientales.*" He retired to the country home of a friend and c. 2 symphonies, 24 string-quintets, etc. 1838 his first symphony was prod.; and 1844, his ode-symphonie "*Le Désert*" had a "delirious succ."; the oratorio, "*Moïse au Sinaï,*" 1846; a second symphonic-ode "*Christophe Colombe*" and "*L'Eden,*" a "mystery" in 2 parts (Grand Opéra, 1848) had no succ.; his opera "*La Perle du Brésil*" (Th. Lyrique, 1851) is still popular; the opera "*La Fin du Monde*" was rejected by the Gr. Opéra, and put in rehearsal, but not produced, by the Th. Lyrique, and in 1859 produced at the Gr. Opéra as "*Herculaneum,*" the great state prize of 20,000 francs being awarded it in 1867; "*Lalla Rookh*" (1862) was a decided succ., but "*Le Saphir,*" (1865) also at the Op. Com., failed, and he now abandoned dram. comp., withdrawing "*La Captive.*" 1869, Academician and librarian of the Cons. Biog. by Azevedo (Paris, 1863). (2) **Samuel**, Paris, 1836—1895; professor, director and dram. composer. (3) **Ad. Isaac**, Nantes, 1842—Paris, 1897; dram. composer. (4) **Ernst**, Nancy, 1824—Paris, 1886; writer.

Davide (dä-vē'-dĕ), (1) **Giacomo** (called le père), Presezzo, near Bergamo, 1750—Bergamo, 1830; famous tenor. (2) **Giovanni**, 1789, St. Petersburg, ca. 1851; son of above; tenor of remarkable range B♭–b''.

Davidov (dä'-vĭ-dôf), **Karl**, Goldingen, Kurland, 1838—Moscow, 1889; solo 'cellist to the Czar; 1876–87, dir. St. Petersburg Cons.; c. symph. poem, "*The Gifts of Perek,*" etc.

Davies (dā'-vĭs), (1) **Ben**, Pontardaroe, near Swansea, Wales, Jan. 6, 1858—1923 (?); opera and concert tenor; 1880–83 pupil of Randegger at R. A.

M.; won bronze, silver, and gold medals, and the Evill prize for declamatory Engl. singing; 3 years with Carl Rosa Opera-troupe; most prominent in oratorio; after 1893 often sang in U. S. (2) **David Ffrangcon,** Bethesda, Carnarvonshire, Dec. 11, 1860—Hampstead, April 5, 1918; barytone; M. A. Oxford; pupil of Shakespeare; début Manchester, 1890; sang with Carl Rosa Opera Co., then oratorio; toured U. S. (3) **Fanny,** Guernsey, July 27, 1861—London, Sept. 1, 1934; eminent pianist; pupil of Reinecke, Paul and Jadassohn, Leipzig Cons.; later of Frau Schumann and Dr. Scholz; début Crystal Palace, London, 1885; toured in England, Germany and Italy. (4) Sir **Henry Walford,** b. Oswestry, 1869—Wrington, March 11, 1941; pupil of Sir Walter Parratt; 1898, organist of the Temple Church; 1898, Mus. Doc., Cantab.; 1895, prof. of cpt. R. C. M.; knighted 1922; 1923, national mus. dir. for Wales; 1934 made Master of King's Music (vice Elgar). C. 2 symphonies, many notable oratorios and other choral works; 2 string quartets, 3 violin sonatas, part-songs, etc.

Da′vis, John David, Edgbaston, Oct. 22, 1869—June 21, 1926; pupil Raff and Brussels Cons.; 1889, teacher at Birmingham; c. opera *"The Cossacks"* (Antwerp, 1903), also symph. variations (London, 1905), symph. ballade *"The Cenci"*; symph. poem *"The Maid of Astolat"*; chamber music; prize *"Coronation March"* (1902), etc.

Da′vison, (1) **Arabella.** Vide GODDARD. (2) **J. W.,** London, 1813—Margate, 1885; pianist, critic and composer.

Da′vy, (1) **Richard,** Engl., comp. 16th century. (2) **John,** Upton-Helion, Exeter, 1763—London, 1824; violinist.

Day, Charles Russell, Horstead, Norfolk, 1860—killed Feb. 18, 1900, in the battle of Paardeberg; major in British army and writer of books on musical instruments.

Dayas (dī′-äs), **W. Humphries,** b. New York, Sept. 12, 1863—Manchester, May 3, 1903; pupil of S. Jackson, Warren, S. B. Mills and Joseffy; organist of various churches; then studied with Kullak, Haupt, Erlich, Urban, and Liszt; made concert-tour 1888; 1890 pf.-teacher Helsingfors

Cons.; in Düsseldorf (1894), Wiesbaden Cons., and Cologne Cons.; c. organ and piano sonatas, etc.

De Ahna (dā-ä′-nä), (1) **H. K. Hermann,** Vienna, 1835—Berlin, 1892; violinist, teacher and composer. His sister (2) **Eleonore,** Vienna, 1838—Berlin, 1865; mezzo-soprano.

De Angelis (dā än′-jä-lēs), **Girolamo,** Civita Vecchia, Jan. 1, 1858—Calolzio, Feb. 9, 1935; pupil of Bazzini, Milan Cons.; 1881, prof. there of vln. and vla.; 1879–97, solo violinist at La Scala; 1897 teacher Royal Irish Acad. of Music, Dublin; c. (text and music) *"L'Innocente"* (Novi Ligure, 1896).

Debain (dŭ-băṅ), **Alex. Fran.,** Paris, 1809—Dec. 3, 1877; 1834 made pianos and organs in Paris; inv. the harmonium 1840, also "antiphonel"[1] and "harmonichorde"; improved the accordion.

Debefve (dŭ-bŭv′), **Jules,** b. Liége, Jan. 16, 1863; pianist; pupil and later teacher at the Cons.; c. opera, rhapsody for orch., etc.; d. Paris, 1932.

Debillemont (dŭ-bē′-yŭ-môṅ), **J. Jacques,** Dijon, 1824—Paris, 1879; dram. composer.

De Boeck (dĕ-book), **Auguste,** Merchtem, Belgium, May 9, 1865—Merchtem, Belgium, Oct. 9, 1937; organist, son of an organist; pupil of Brussels Cons., later a teacher there; c. symph., *Rhapsodie Dahomienne* for orch., organ music, etc.

Debussy (dŭ-bü′-sē), **Claude Achille,** St. Germain-en-Laye, Aug. 22, 1862—Paris, March 26, 1918; one of the most important composers of recent times, and the instigator of the entire "modern" movement in music; already acknowledged to be a classic, **D.** has had a profound influence on creative musicians of every country. He came from a family of tradespeople with no musical background. At 11 he entered the Paris Cons. where he won several prizes for piano and studied with Massenet, winning the Prix de Rome with his cantata, *"L'Enfant Prodigue."* During his sojourn in Italy, his originality began to assert itself, so much so that his orch. suite, *"Printemps,"* shocked the conservatives by its harmonic audacities; he also c. a work for two women soloists and female chorus, *"La Demoiselle Élué,"* at this time. Returning to Paris, he was attracted by the school of the poetic Symbolists and frequented their circle, composing meanwhile his *"Arabesques"* for piano, *"Suite Bergamasque"* (do.), *"Ariettes Oubliées,"* etc.

His early works were influenced by the French school of Massenet, Chabrier, Lalo, Fauré, and by Wagner, but he soon developed an original style which came to be known as "impressionism" and consisted in painting with brilliant but rare and elusive tonal colours, applied in little, independent units, as the painters of the *"pointillist"* school were doing. His Prelude to *"L'Après-midi d'un Faune,"* based on Mallarmé's cryptic nature poem, was completed 1894 and created a deep impression, entirely revising the possibilities contained in orchestral tone-colour. **D's.** use of distantly related overtones widened harmonic boundaries, and his use of chords not as a part of a continuous structure, but as individual entities introduced a new principle into modern music.

He carried on this revolutionary work with a string quartet (1893), *"Proses Lyriques"* for voice to his own text, the *"Chansons de Bilitis,"* and the 3 *"Nocturnes"* for orch. (*"Clouds," "Festivals"* and *"Sirens,"* the last employing a wordless women's chorus.)

D's. masterpiece is commonly acknowledged to be his music drama, *"Pelléas et Mélisande,"* a setting of Maeterlinck's symbolic play, which had its première at the Paris Op.-Comique in 1902 before a somewhat irreverent audience. Here, as in most of his works, **D.** creates an atmosphere of half-lights, mystery and poetry by the use of an original harmonic system in which dissonance takes the place of consonance; old church modes are used or suggested; as are the whole-tone scale and other exotic progressions. The voices employ a form of recitative; all climaxes are rigidly restrained. The popular following developed by this singular but highly artistic work came a few years later.

The most important productions of **D's.** final period include music for D'Annunzio's "mystery," *"The Martyrdom of St. Sebastian,"* the ballet *"Jeux,"* written for Diaghileff's company; and the notable orch. works,

"La Mer," "Rondes de Printemps" and *"Iberia,"* in which his original art of novel form, orchestration and objectivity of impression reach their climax. His final period saw the production of many works for chamber combinations, piano, etc., but with a slight growth of austerity in his manner.

His compositions include also: (voice and orch.) *"Le Jet d'Eau"*; (vocal quartet) *"Trois Chansons"*; (orch.) *"Images"*; (Harp and orch.) *"Danse Sacrée et Danse Profane"*; (voice) *"Cinq Poèmes"*; *"Mandoline"*; *"Fêtes Galantes"*; *"Trois Chansons de France"*; *"Trois Ballades de François Villon"*; *"Le Promenoir des Deux Amants"*; *"Trois Poèmes"*; *"Noël des Enfants qui n'ont plus de Maison"*; (piano) *"L'Isle Joyeuse"*; *"Estampes"*; *"Masques"*; *"Images"* (2 series); *"Children's Corner"*; *"La Plus que Lente"*; 2 series of 12 preludes each; *"La Boîte à Joujoux"*; *"Berceuse Héroïque"*; 12 etudes; (piano, four hands) *"Marche Écossaise"*; *"Petite Suite"*; 6 *"Épigraphes Antiques"*; (2 pianos, 4 hands) *"En Blanc et noir."* Many of his piano works have been orchestrated.

The Debussy literature is a large one, with the composer's own critical writings appearing under the title *"M. Croche, Anti-Dilettante"* (1923). **D.**-studies have been pub. by Daly Liebig, Laurencie, Laloy, Sartoli-quido, Caillard and De Bérys, Setaccioli, Rivière, Séré, Rolland, Chennevière, Paglia, Jean-Aubry, Cortot, Boucher, Dumesnil, Gilman, Shera, etc. Léon Vallas has issued a thematic catalogue, and countless magazine articles exist on his music.

Dechert (děkh'-ĕrt), **Hugo**, Potschappel near Dresden, Sept. 16, 1860—Nov. 28, 1923; 'cellist; studied with his father, then with H. Tiets, and at the Berlin Hochschule; toured; 1894 soloist court-chapel, Berlin; mem. of Halir and Hess Quartets.

Deck'er, Konst., Fürstenau, Brandenburg, 1810—Stolp, Pomerania, 1878; pianist and dram. composer.

Dedekind (dā'-dĕ-kĭnt), (1) **Henning**, ca. 1590 cantor, theorist and composer at Langensalza, Thuringia. (2) **Konst. Chr.**, Reinsdorf, Anhalt-Köthen, 1628—ca. 1697, comp.

Dedler (dāt'-lĕr), **Rochus**, Oberammergau, Jan. 15, 1779—Munich, Oct. 15, 1822; c. music still used in the Passion-Play.

De(e)r'ing, Richard, b. Kent, d. London (?), 1630; studied in Italy; court-organist; pub. the oldest extant comp. with basso continuo, etc.

De Falla, Manuel (män'-ōō-ĕl dä fä'-yä), b. Cadiz, Spain, Nov. 23, 1877; composer; pupil of Trago, Pedrell, Dukas and Debussy; passed student years in Paris but retired to Granada, 1914, where he has made his home regularly since; one of most original and characteristic modern Spanish comps., esp. noted for his ballets and orchestral works in impressionistic style; c. (opera) "*La Vida Breva*" (Paris Op.-Comique, 1914, has also been given at Met. Op. House, N. Y.); (ballets) "*El Amor Brujo*" and "*Sombrero de Tres Picos*"; (puppet opera) "*El Retablo de Maese Pedro*"; 3 symphonic nocturnes, "*Noches en los Jardines de España*" (with piano), "*En el Generalife*" and "*Danza Lejana*" (the first esp. popular); concerto for harpsichord and small ensemble; "*Don Quixote*," fantasy for 3 voices and orch., and numerous songs and piano works; one of the outstanding modern comps., with folk-music ingredients especially prominent in his works; a master of orchestration, and influenced by the music of Debussy and atonalists such as Schönberg; a vivid imagination, colorful and passionate romantic subjects and an ingredient of mysticism are features of his work. He was reported in 1935 to be at work on "*L'Atlantide*," a choral trilogy of large scope depicting the coming of Columbus to the New World.

Defesch (dä-fĕsh'), **Wm.,** d. ca. 1758; Flemish organist and violinist.

Deffès (dŭf-fĕs), **L. P.,** Toulouse, July 25, 1819—June 10, 1900; pupil of Halévy and Barbereau, Paris Cons., took Grand prix de Rome for cantata "*L'Ange et Tobie*"; his 1-act com.-op. "*l'Anneau d'argent*" was prod. Paris, 1855; 14 others since, the last very succ., "*Jessica*" (Toulouse, 1898); dir. of the Toulouse branch of the Cons.; c. also masses, etc.

Degele (dä'-gĕ-lĕ), **Eugen,** Munich, 1834—Dresden, 1886; barytone and composer.

De Gogorza, Emilio (ā-mē'-yō dä gō-gōr'-thä), b. Brooklyn, N. Y., May 29, 1874; barytone; studied with Moderate and Agramonte, N. Y.; boy soloist in English churches; res. as youth in Spain and France; concert début with Sembrich, 1897; toured widely in concert incl. appearances with Emma Eames, whom he married in 1911; member of faculty, Curtis Inst., Phila., during later years.

De Greef, Arthur, b. Löwen, Belgium, Oct. 10, 1862; composer and pianist; studied with Brassin at Brussels Cons. and with Liszt; taught piano at Brussels Cons., 1885; toured throughout Europe as virtuoso; has also cond., and c. chamber and piano works.

Degtarev (dĕkh'-tä-rĕv), **Stepoan Ankiewitsch,** 1766-1813; Russian director in St. Petersburg and Italy; c. 60 concertos, and church choral music.

De Haan, Willem, Rotterdam, Sept. 24, 1849—Berlin, Sept. 26, 1930; pupil of Nicolai, de Lange, and Bargiel, also at Leipzig Cons.; 1873 dir. at Bingen; cond. "Mozartverein" at Darmstadt, 1876; 1895 court-conductor there; c. 2 operas "*Die Kaiserstochter*" and the succ. "*Die Inkasöhne*" (Darmstadt, 1895); 3 cantatas.

Dehn (dān), **Siegfried Wm.,** Altona, Feb. 25, 1799—Berlin, April 12, 1858; noteworthy theorist and teacher; among his pupils Rubinstein, Kullak, Glinka, Kiel, Hofmann, etc.

Deiters (dī'-tĕrs), **Hermann,** Bonn, June 27, 1833—Coblentz, May 11, 1907; 1858, Dr. jur., and Dr. Phil., at Bonn; dir. of gymnasia at Bonn, 1858, and other cities; 1885 of the "Provincial Schulrath" at Coblentz; writer and translator.

De Ko'ven, (Henry Louis) Reginald, Middletown, Conn., April 3, 1859—Chicago, Jan. 16, 1920; composer; educated in Europe, took degree at Oxford, Engl., 1879; pupil of W. Speidel (pf.) at Stuttgart, Lebert (pf.), and Pruckner (harm.), Dr. Hauff (comp.), Vanuccini (singing), Genée (operatic comp.); after 1889, critic in Chicago and 1891, New York, incl. period on the "*World*"; 1902–05, organised and cond. Philharmonic Orch. at Washington, D. C.; c. about a score of succ. comic operas, incl. "*Robin Hood*" (Chicago, 1890); "*The Fencing Master*" (Boston, 1892); "*The Highwayman*" (New Haven, 1897); "*Maid Marian*" (1901); and two grand operas, "*The Canterbury Pilgrims*" (Met. Op., 1917) and "*Rip Van Winkle*" (Chicago Op., 1920), neither a succ.; also many songs; an orch. suite, a pf.-sonata, etc.

Delaborde (dŭ-lä-bôrd), (1) **J. Benj.,** Paris, 1734—guillotined, 1794; dram. composer and writer. (2) **Élie Miriam,** Chaillot, France, Feb. 8, 1839 —Paris, Dec., 1913); pupil of Alkan, Liszt, and Moscheles; pf.-prof. at Paris Cons. and dram. composer.

DeLamar'ter, Eric, b. Lansing, Mich., Feb. 18, 1880; conductor, composer, organist; studied with Middelschulte, Widor and Guilmant; org. in various Chicago churches; asst. cond., Chicago Symph., 1918-1936; taught at Olivet Coll., Mich., and Chicago Mus. Coll.; critic.

De Lara. Vide LARA.

De Lange. Vide LANGE.

Delâtre (dŭ-lắt'r), (1) **Olivier,** Belgian music-pub. Antwerp, (1539-55). (2) **Claude Petit Jan.,** conductor and composer at Liége, 1555.

Deldevez (dŭl-dŭ-věs), **Ed. Ernest,** Paris, 1817—1897; 1859, asst.-cond. Gr. Opéra and Paris Cons., dram. composer and writer.

Delezenne (dŭ-lŭ-zěn), **Chas. Ed. Jos.,** Lille, 1776—1866; writer.

Delhasse (děl-ăs), **Félix,** Spaa, Jan. 5, 1809—Brussels, 1898; founder and ed. of "*Guide Musicale*"; writer.

Delibes (dŭ-lēb'), **Clément Philibert Léo,** St. Germain-du-Val, Sarthe, Feb. 21, 1836—Paris, Jan. 16, 1891; composer of graceful and polished operatic and ballet scores; entered the Paris Cons. in 1848, Le Couppey, Bazin, Adam, and Bénoist being his chief teachers, 1853 organist at the Ch. of St.-Jean et St.-François; his first operetta, "*Deux Sacs de Charbon*," was followed by nearly a score more; 1865, 2nd chorus-master Gr. Opéra; his first ballet "*La Source*" was prod. here 1866 with striking succ., later in Vienna as "*Naila*"; the second, "*Coppelia*" (Gr. Opéra, 1870), is still popular, as is "*Sylvia*" (1876); 1881, prof. of comp. at the Cons.; c. also the succ. opera "*Lakmé*"

"*Le Roi l'a dit*" (1873); "*Jean de Nivelle*" (1880) and an unfinished stage work, "*Kassya*," which was completed by Massenet and prod. 1893; also songs, etc.

Delioux (De Savignac) (dŭl-yoo dŭ säv-ēn-yăk), **Chas.,** Lorient, Morbihan, April, 1830—Paris, ca. 1880; self-taught as pianist; studied harmony with Barbereau, and comp. with Halévy; 1846 took Grand Prix for cpt.; prod. 1-act comic opera "*Yvonne et Loie*" (Gymnase, 1854); c. pf.-pcs. and wrote technical works.

Delius (dā'-lē-ōōs), **Frederick,** Bradford, England, Jan. 29, 1863— Grez-sur-Loing, France, June 10, 1934; highly original and important composer; son of a naturalised German, a wool merchant; 1876-79 educated in Bradford schools and at Internat'l. Coll., Spring Grove; refusing to enter the family business, he was sent by his father to an orange plantation in Florida, where he had lessons in music from an Amer. musician, Thomas F. Ward; 1885, he taught music in Danville, Virginia, and the following year persuaded his parents to send him to Leipzig, where he made little progress at the Cons. but learned much from Grieg, who lived there; in 1888 he moved to Paris, where he worked as a solitary comp.; his first public perf. was in 1899, when a concert of his music was given in London at St. James's Hall; after an interval of 8 years his works began to have hearings in Germany; his "*Appalachia*" for orch. with choral finale given at the Lower Rhenish Fest., 1905; his "*Sea-Drift*" for orch., barytone and chorus at the fest. of the Allgemeine Deutscher Musikverein in 1906; in England his recognition was slower, but owing to the championship of Beecham, who gave many of works, and organised a fest. of 6 programmes in 1929, D. came into his own as one of the most important comps. of the day. After 1890 he lived on a small estate at Grez-sur-Loing; he m. Jelka Rosen, painter, in 1897; his latter years were clouded by the affliction of blindness and paralysis, but he continued his work in composition by dictating his music. His style is original, partaking somewhat of French impressionism, and also showing the influence of Scandinavian comps. His work is marked by an almost complete absence of polyphony, but achieved a markedly personal force and beauty through his sensitiveness to moods of Nature. His chief works include: fantasy overture, *"Over the Hills"* (Elberfeld, 1897); *"Norwegian Suite"* for orch.; piano concerto in C minor; the music dramas, *"Koanga"* (Elberfeld, 1904); *"Romeo und Julia auf dem Dorfe"* (Berlin, 1907); *"Margot la Rouge"*; *"Fennimore und Gerda"* (Frankfort, 1919); music for Flecker's *"Hassan"* (Darmstadt, 1923); *"Paris,"* a Night Piece for orch.; *"Dance of Life"* for orch.; *"Legende"* for vln. and orch.; *"A Mass of Life"* for soloists, chorus and orch.; orch. rhapsody, *"Brigg Fair,"* *"Songs of Sunset"* for soloists, chorus and orch.; *"Song of the High Hills"* for orch. with concluding chorus; the orch. works, *"In a Summer Garden,"* *"Dance Rhapsody,"* *"On Hearing the First Cuckoo in Spring,"* *"North Country Sketches,"* *"Eventyr,"* *"Summer Night on the River"*; vln. concerto, 'cello concerto; double concerto for vln. and 'cello; songs and choral pieces. Studies of his music were pub. by Chop and Heseltine.

Della Maria (dĕl'-lä mä-rē'-ä), **Doménique**, Marseilles, 1769—Paris, March 9, 1800; son of an Italian mandolinist; played mandolin and 'cello; at 18 prod. a grand opera; studied comp. in Italy, and c. 7 operas, incl. the very succ. *"Le Prisonnier"* (1798).

Delle Sedie (dĕl-lĕ sād'-yĕ), **Enrico**, Leghorn, June 17, 1826—Paris, Nov. 28, 1907; pupil of Galeffi, Persanola, and Domeniconi; 1848, imprisoned as a Revolutionist; then studied singing; début, Florence, 1851; later prof. of singing Paris Cons.; lived in Paris as singing teacher.

Dellinger (dĕl'-lǐng-ĕr), **Rudolf**, Graslitz, Bohemia, July 8, 1857—Dresden, Sept. 24, 1910; 1883, conductor at Hamburg; 1893, Dresden Ct. Opera; c. operettas, incl. succ. *"Capitän Fracasse"* (Hamburg, 1889), *"Don Cesar,"* etc.

Dell' Orefice (dĕl ō-rä-fē'-chĕ), **Giu.**, Fara, Abruzzio, Chietino, 1848—Naples, 1889; cond. and dram. composer.

Delmas (dĕl-mäs), **Jean Fr.**, Lyons, France, April 14, 1861—Paris, Sept. 29, 1933; bass; pupil Paris Cons.; 1886, joined the Opéra where he created many rôles with great success. (2) **Marc**, St. Quentin, March 28, 1885—Paris, Nov. 30, 1931; composer of operas, orch. and chamber music.

Delmotte (dĕl-môt), **Henri Florent**, Mons, Belgium, 1799—1836; writer.

Delprat (dŭl-prä'), **Chas.**, 1803—Pau, Pyrenees, 1888; singing-teacher and writer there.

Delsarte (dŭl-särt), **Fran. Alex. Nicholas Chéri**, Solesmes, Nord, 1811—Paris, 1871; tenor; teacher of a well-known physical culture; 1855 inv. the Guide-Accord, or Sonotype, to facilitate piano-tuning.

De Lu'ca, Giuseppe, b. Rome, Dec. 25, 1876; barytone; grad. St. Cecilia Acad., Rome; début as Valentin at Piacenza, 1897; sang as regular mem. of La Scala, Milan, for 8 years, prior to engagement for Met. Op., N. Y., 1915; sang with latter company until 1935, in great variety of Italian and French barytone rôles; also prominent in concert; commander, Order of the Crown of Italy.

Delune (dŭ-lün), **Louis**, b. Charleroi, March 15, 1876—Jan. 1940; Belgian cond. and pupil at Brussels Cons., winning prize, 1900, and Prix de Rome, 1903; c. sonatas and songs.

Del Valle de Paz (dĕl väl'-lä dä pätz), **Edgardo**, Alexandria, Egypt, Oct. 18, 1861—Florence, April 5, 1920; pf.-pupil at Naples Cons., of Cesi (pf.), and Serrao (comp.); at 16 toured in Italy and Egypt, 1890, prof. in Florence Cons.; pub. pf.-method, etc.; c. orchestral suites, etc.; dir. of *"La Nuova Musica,"* 1896–1914.

Demantius (dä-män'-tsĭ-oos), **Chr.**, Reichenberg, 1567—Freiburg, Saxony, 1643; prolific composer of church-music and songs; wrote a vocal method.

Demeur (dŭ-mŭr'), (1) **Anne Arsène** (née **Charton**), Sanjon, Charente, 1827—Paris, 1892; soprano; m. (2) **J. A. Demeur**, flutist and composer.

Demol (dŭ-môl), (1) **Pierre**, Brussels, 1825—Alost, Belgium, 1899; dir. and composer. (2) **Fran. M.**, Brussels, 1844—Ostend, 1883; nephew of above; cond., prof., and dram. composer.

Demunck', (1) **François,** Brussels, 1815
—1854; 'cellist and prof. (2) **Ernest,** Brussels, Dec. 21, 1840—London, Feb. 6, 1915; son and pupil of
above; pupil of Servais; 1870, 'cellist
Weimar Court orch.; 1879 m. Carlotta Patti; 1893, prof. R. A. M.,
London.

Denefve (dŭ-nŭf), **Jules,** Chimay,
1814—Mons, 1877; 'cellist and dram.
composer.

Dengremont (däṅ-grŭ-môṅ), **Maurice,**
b. of French parents, Rio de Janeiro,
1866—Buenos Aires, 1893; violinist;
at 11 played with succ. in Europe.

Dennée (dĕn-nā), **Chas.,** b. Oswego,
N. Y., Sept. 1, 1863; studied with
Emery, Boston; teacher and com-
poser of comic operas, etc.

Den'ner, Jn. Chp., Leipzig, 1655—
Nürnberg, 1707; maker of wind-
insts.; inv. 1690 or 1700 the clarinet,
perhaps also the Stockfagott and the
Rackettenfagott.

Dent, Edward Joseph, b. Ribston,
England, July, 18, 1876; educator
and writer on music; pupil of Wood
and Stanford at Cambridge Univ.,
fellow of King's Coll.; an ed. of
Encyclopedia Britannica; ed. second
edition of Grove's Musical Dictionary; pres. of Internat'l. Soc. for
Contemp. Music; after 1926 prof.
of musical science, Cambridge Univ.;
author of life of A. Scarlatti; "*A
Jesuit at the Opera in 1680*"; "*Italian
Chamber Cantatas*," "*Mozart's
Operas*," "*Foundations of English
Opera*," "*Busoni*," etc.; has also tr.
librettos of Mozart operas into
English.

Denza (dĕn'-tsä), **Luigi,** Castellam-
mare di Stabia, Feb. 24, 1846—
London, Feb. 13, 1922; pupil of
Naples Cons.; c. opera "*Wallenstein*"
(Naples, 1876), many pop. songs
(some in Neapolitan dialect), incl.
"*Funiculi-Funicula*"; after 1898,
prof. R. A. M., London.

Deppe (dĕp'-pĕ), **Ludwig,** Alverdissen,
Lippe, 1828—Pyrmont, Sept. 5-6,
1890; notable pf.-teacher and conductor.

Deprès (or Després) (dŭ-prĕ' or dä-
prä), **Josse** (known as **Josquin**),
Condé (?) in Hainault, Burgundy,
ca. 1450—Condé, Aug. 27, 1521.
[His epitaph reads "**Josse Despres**";
other spellings are Després, De(s)prez,
Depret, De(s)pret(s), Dupré, and by
the Italians, Del Prato, Latinised as

a Prato, a Pratis, Pratensis, etc.;
Josquin appears as Jossé, Jossien,
Jusquin, Giosquin, Josquinus, Jaco-
bo, Jodocus, Jodoculus, etc.] One
of the most eminent of musicians and
the chief contrapuntist of his day;
pupil of Okeghem; 1471–84 a singer
in the Sistine Chapel, and about
1488 in Ferrara; he was already now
accepted as "princeps musicorum,"
and had international vogue. He was
received with honour by various
princes, and was court-musician to
Louis XII., many amusing anecdotes
of his musical humour being told. He
finally returned to Condé as Provost
of the Cathedral Chapter. Burney
called him "the father of modern
harmony." The florid and restless
cpt. of his church-works and the secular *cantus firmus* (v. D. D.) that was
the basis of most of them, brought
his school into disfavour and disuse
when the revolutionary Palestrina appeared. But he was at least the cul-
mination of his style, and his erudition
was moulded into suave and emotional effects, so that Ambros says
that he was the "first musician who
impresses us as being a genius." His
period coinciding with the use of
movable types for music, his works
are preserved in large quantities in
volumes and in the collections of Petrucci and Peutinger. His French
chansons were pub. by T. Susato,
1545, P. Attaignant, 1549, and Du
Chemin, 1553; excerpts in modern
notation are in the "*Bibliothek für
Kirchenmusik*," 1844; in Commer's
"*Collectio*," Rochlitz' "*Sammlung
vorzüglicher Gesangstücke*," 1838,
Choron's "*Collection*," and in the
histories of Ambros, Burney, Haw-
kins, etc.

De Reszké (dŭ rĕsh'-kā), (1) **Jean,**
Warsaw, Jan. 14, 1850—Nice, April
3, 1925; perhaps the chief tenor of
his generation, great in opera of all
schools; pupil of Ciaffei, Cotogni,
etc.; 1874, début as barytone at
Venice, as Alfonso in "*La Favorita*,"
under the name "De Reschi"; after
singing in Italy and Paris and studying with Sbriglia, he made his début
as tenor in "*Robert le Diable*"
(Madrid, 1879); 1884, Th. des
Nations; 1885 at the Gr. Opéra,
Paris, creating Massenet's "*Le Cid*";
from 1887 he sang constantly in London, and 1891–1901 at the Met.

Op., N. Y., where he was an unforgettable "Tristan," etc.; retired from stage 1902 and taught singing in Paris. (2) **Édouard**, Warsaw, Dec. 23, 1855—near Piotrkow, May 25, 1917; bro. of above; pupil of his brother, of Ciaffei, Steller, and Coletti; début, Paris, April 22, 1876, as the King in "*Aïda*" (Th. des Italiens), sang there two seasons, then at Turin and Milan; 1880–84 at the Italian Opera, London; then in Paris, London, America; a magnificent basso of enormous repertory and astonishing versatility as an actor; a master in tragic, comic, or buffa opera. His sister, (3) **Josephine**, was a soprano of greatest promise, but left the stage on her marriage.

Dering, v. DEERING.

De Sabata (dā sä-bä'-tä), **Victor**, b. Trieste, 1892; composer, conductor; studied Milan Cons. (gold medal) with Orefice and Saladino; has led symph. concerts at La Scala, Augusteo (Rome), Turin, Bologna, Palermo, Trieste; guest cond., Cincinnati Symph., 1927–28; and with much succ. at Berlin and Vienna both as op. and symph. cond.; c. (opera) "*Il Macigno*" (La Scala, 1917); (orch.) "*Juventus*," Andante and Scherzo; Orch. Suite; "*La Notte di Platon*," "*Getsemane*" (N. Y. Philh. under Toscanini, 1926); chamber music, etc.

De Sanctis (dā sänk'-tēs), **Cesare**, b. Rome, 1830—ca. 1900; 1876, prof. of harm. in the Liceo; c. overture, Requiem Mass, "100 fugues," a cappella in strict style; pub. treatises.

Désaugiers (dā-sō-zhā), **Marc Ant.**, Fréjus, 1742—Paris, 1793; prod. numerous succ. short operas.

Deshayes (dŭz-ĕz), **Prosper Didier**, prod., 1780, oratorio "*Les Machabées*"; c. operettas and ballets, etc.

Deslandres (dē-län'-drŭ), **Adolphe Eduard Marie**, Paris, Jan. 22, 1840—July 30, 1911; pupil Paris Cons.; organist at St. Marie at Batignolles, where his father was director; c. operettas and church music.

Desmarets (dā-mă-rā), **H.**, Paris, 1662—Luneville, 1741; dram. composer.

Dessau (dĕs'-sow), **Bd.**, Hamburg, March 1, 1861—Berlin, 1923; pupil of Schradieck, Joachim, and Wieniawski; leader at various theatres;

1898 Konzertmeister at the court-opera, Berlin, and teacher Stern Cons.

Dessauer (dĕs'-sow-ĕr), **Jos.**, Prague, May 28, 1798—Mödling, near Vienna, July 8, 1876; c. 5 operas and many pop. songs.

Dessoff (dĕs'-sôf), (1) **Felix Otto**, Leipzig, 1835—Frankfort, 1892; courtcond. at Carlsruhe. (2) **Margarete**, b. Vienna, June 11, 1874; conductor; daughter of (1); studied at Hoch Cons. in Frankfort; founded women's chorus which made début at Wiesbaden Brahms Fest. in 1912; later a madrigal chorus; was choral cond. at Hoch Cons., 1912–17; of Bach Soc., in Frankfort, 1917–20; after 1920 res. for fifteen years in N. Y., where she led the Adesdi Chorus and A Cappella Singers in programmes incl. rare old and modern music; gave Amer. première of Vecchi's "*L'Amfiparnaso*."

Destinn (dā'-shtĭn), **Emmy**, Prague, Feb. 26, 1878—Budweis, Bohemia, Jan. 28, 1930; soprano; studied with Loewe-Destinn; her real name was Kittl—she chose "Destinn" in honour of her teacher; she sang at Bayreuth, 1891; from 1908 she had great success at the Met. Op., N. Y., also at Covent Garden and Berlin Royal Op.; she created the rôle of "*Minnie*" in Puccini's "*Fanciulla del West*"; during the war she was interned in her estate in Bohemia on the ground of enemy sympathies; and after 1918 toured again in the U. S., and sang for one season at the Met. Op.; her voice was of rare purity; her repertoire embraced 80 rôles; also a poet and writer.

Destouches (dā-toosh), (1) **André Cardinal**, Paris, 1672—1749; dram. composer. (2) **Franz Seraph von**, Munich, 1772—1844; dram. composer.

Desvignes (dā-vēn'-yŭ), **Fran.**, Trier, 1805—Metz, 1853; violinist; founded conservatory at Metz; dram. composer.

Deswert (dā-vār), (1) **J. Caspar Isidore**, Louvain, 1830—Schaerbeck, near Brussels, 1896; 'cellist; prof. Brussels Cons. (2) **Jules**, Louvain, 1843—Ostend, 1891, brother of above; conductor and dram. composer.

Dé'thier (dā'-tē-ā), (1) **Gaston Marie**, b. Liége, April 19, 1875; organist and teacher; pupil of Liége Cons., grad. at 17 with gold medals in piano, organ and 1st prize for fugue; early active as concert org.; after 1894 at St. Xavier's Ch., N. Y.; beginning 1907 excl. in concert work and as teacher at Inst. of Mus. Art. (2) **Edouard,** b. Liége, 1885; violinist; pupil of Liége and Brussels Cons.; taught at latter; début in concert, 1903; after 1906 taught at Inst. of Mus. Art, N. Y., and toured as soloist; with his bro. Gaston gave series of sonata recitals in N. Y.

Dett, Robert Nathaniel, b. Drummondsville, Quebec, Oct. 11, 1882; Negro composer; studied at Oberlin, Ohio and Columbia Univs.; taught at Lane Coll., Lincoln Inst., and after 1913 at the Hampton (Va.) Inst., where he led a choral group; won Bowdoin prize, Harvard Univ., for essay on *"The Emancipation of Negro Music"*; c. choral works, motets, piano music, songs, many of them based on Negro folk themes.

Dett'mer, Wm., Breinum, near Hildesheim, 1808—Frankfort, 1876; operatic bass; 1842 engaged for leading rôles Dresden; retired 1874.

Deutz (doits). Vide MAGNUS.

Devienne (dŭv-yĕn), **Fran.,** Joinville, Haute-Marne, Jan. 31, 1759—(insane), Charenton, Sept. 5, 1803; flutist and bassoonist; important in improving wind instr.; prof., composer and writer.

Devries (dü-vrēz'), **Herman,** b. New York, Dec. 25, 1858; sang Paris Op. and Op.-Comique; Met. Op., Covent Garden, etc.; after 1900 in Chicago as teacher and critic of the *"American"*; Chev., Legion of Honour.

Diabelli (dē-ä-bĕl'-lē), **Antonio,** Mattsee, near Salzburg, Sept. 6, 1781 —Vienna, April 7, 1858; pf.-and guitar-teacher; partner of Cappi, the music-publisher; c. opera and pop. sonatinas, etc.

Diaghileff (dē-ä'-gē-lyĕf), **Serge,** govt. of Novgorod, Russia, March 19, 1872—Venice, Aug. 19, 1929; ballet director; studied law in St. Petersburg, also music theory with Cotogni, Sokoloff and Liadoff; served as critic of the newspaper *"Les Nouvelles"*; in 1899 founded periodical and promoted art exhibitions; after 1907, arranged concerts of Russian music in Paris; prod. *"Boris Godounoff"* at the Op. there with Chaliapin

and chorus of Petersburg **Imp. Op.,** in 1908; in 1909 the first season of the Russian ballets was organized by him in Paris, incl. Nijinsky, Pavlowa, Karsavina, Fokine, etc.; this group established world-wide fame, and toured in Europe and America with brilliant succ. (N. Y., 1916); **D.** gave the impetus to a notable renaissance of ballet art, and was responsible for the development of many composers who later became famous, incl. Stravinsky; the Diaghileff Ballet Russe commissioned and prod. new scores of more advanced creators than any other organisation of its period.

Diamandy. Vide NUOVINA.

Diaz (de la Peña) (dē'-äth dŭ-lä-pän'-yä), **Eugène Émile,** Paris, Feb. 27, 1837—Sept. 12, 1901; son of the painter; pupil of Paris Cons. (Halévy, Réber); prod. the com. opera *"Le Roi Candaule"* (1865, Th. Lyrique); 1867 won the prize for opera, *"La Coupe du Roi de Thule"* (Grand Opéra); 1890 prod. lyric drama *"Benvenuto"* (Op.-Com.); pub. many songs.

Dib'din, (1) **Chas.,** Dibdin, near Southampton, 1745—London, 1814; composer, singer, accompanist, actor, manager and writer. (2) **Henry Edward,** Sadlers Wells, 1813—1866; harpist, organist, violinist and composer; youngest son of above.

Dick'inson, Clarence, b. Lafayette, Ind., May 7, 1873; organist and composer; studied with Singer, Reimann, Guilmant, Moszkowski, and Vierne; founded Mus. Art Ass'n., Chicago; res. in New York since 1909, where he is organist at Brick Presbyterian Church, teacher of church music at Gen'l. Theological Seminary; also active as composer and writer on music.

Didur (dē'-dōōr), **Adamo,** b. Sanok, Galicia, Dec. 24, 1874; bass; studied with Wysocki in Lemberg and Emerich in Milan; début, Rio de Janeiro, 1894; sang at La Scala, 1899-1903; also in England, Russia, Spain, South America, and for a number of years at the Met. Op. House, N. Y.

Did'ymus, b. Alexandria, Egypt, 63 B. C.; wrote 4,000 works in all, incl. a treatise on harmony.

Diémer (d'yä-mä), **Louis,** Paris, Feb.

14, 1843—Dec. 21, 1919; pianist; pupil at Cons. of Marmontel; took 1st pf.-prize at 13, later 1st harm., 2nd org. and 1st cpt.-prizes; pupil Ambr. Thomas and Bazin; after 1887 pf.-prof. at the Cons. (vice Marmontel); besides brilliant concerts of modern music, he presented programmes of old keyboard works played on ancient instrs.; c. pf.-concerto, chamber-music, etc., ed. collections.

Diener (dē'-nĕr), **Fz.**, Dessau, 1849—1879; tenor.

Diepenbrock (dē'-pĕn-brŏk), **A. J. M.**, Amsterdam, Sept. 2, 1862—April 5, 1921; teacher and comp. of church music.

Dierich (dē'-rĭkh), **Carl**, b. Heinrichau, March 31, 1852; tenor in concert, opera and oratorio; studied with Graben-Hoffman.

Diës (dē'-ĕs), **Albert K.**, Hanover, 1755—Vienna, 1822; writer.

Diet (dē-ā), **Edmond M.**, Paris, Sept. 25, 1854—Oct., 1924; pupil of César Franck, and Guiraud; officier of the Academy; prod. 3 comic operas, incl. *"Stratonice"* (1887), many ballets and pantomimes, etc.

Diet(t)er (dē'-tĕr), **Chr. L.**, Ludwigsburg, 1757—Stuttgart, 1822; dram. composer.

Dietrich (dē'-trĭkh) (or **Dieterich**), (1) **Sixtus**, Augsburg (?) 1490 (95)—St. Gallen, Switzerland, 1548; composer. (2) **Albert Hn.**, Golk, near Meissen, Aug. 28, 1829—Berlin, Nov. 20, 1908; composer; pupil of J. Otto, Moscheles, Reitz and Schumann; 1855–61, concert-cond., 1859, principal mus.-dir. at Bonn; 1861, court-cond. at Oldenburg; 1894 Leipzig; c. succ. opera *"Robin Hood"* (Frankfort, 1879); a symphony; overture, *"Normannenfahrt"*; cantatas with orch., 'cello- and vln.-concertos, etc.

Dietsch (dētsh), **Pierre L. Ph.**, Dijon, 1808—1865; composer and conductor.

Dieupart (d'yŭ-pär), **Chas.**, 18th cent., violinist and harpsichordist.

Dil'liger, **Jn.**, Eisfeld, 1593—Coburg, 1647, cantor and composer.

Dippel (dĭp'-pĕl), **Andreas**, Cassel, Nov. 30, 1866—Hollywood, Cal., May 12, 1932; notable tenor; studied with Hey, Leoni and Rau; 1887–92, Bremen opera, then in New York for several seasons, also in Breslau, Vienna; 1889 at Bayreuth, from 1897 at Covent Garden; associated with Gatti-Casazza in management of Met. Op. House, N. Y., 1908; then directed opera seasons in Chicago and Philadelphia, 1910–13; later organised his own Wagnerian op. company, with financial fiasco; taught singing on Pacific Coast in latter years.

Diruta (dē-roo'-tä), (1) **Gir.**, b. Perugia, ca. 1560; organist; pub. technical books on org., cpt., etc. (2) **Ag.**, b. Perugia, 1622; Augustine monk; composer.

Dit'son, (1) **Oliver**, 1811—1888; founder of the music-pub. firm O. Ditson Co., at Boston, Mass.; 1867, his eldest son, (2) **Chas.**, took charge of N. Y. branch (C. H. Ditson & Co.). After 1875 (3) **J. Edward Ditson** cond. Philadelphia branch (J. E. D. & Co.), but this was discontinued in 1910. A branch for the importation of instrs., etc., was est. at Boston in 1860 as John C. Haynes & Co.; and 1864 a Chicago branch, Lyon & Healy. In 1932 the publishing activities were taken over by the Theodore Presser Co.

Ditters (dĭt'-tĕrs) (**von Dittersdorf**), **Karl**, Vienna, Nov. 2, 1739—Neuhof, Bohemia, Oct. 24, 1799; noteworthy as forerunner of Mozart, and early writer of programme-music (v. D. D.); pupil of König and Ziegler, of Trani (vln.), and Bono (comp.); he played in the orch. of his patron Prince Joseph of Hildburghausen, 1759, and then in the ct.-Th. at Vienna (1761); toured Italy with Gluck, and made great succ. as violinist; 1764–69 conductor to the Bishop of Gross-Wardein, Hungary. Prod. his first opera, *"Amore in Musica,"* 1767; followed by various oratorios, and much orchestral and chamber-music. Later conductor to the Prince-Bishop of Breslau; built a small theatre and prod. several pieces. 1770 the Pope bestowed on him the Order of the Golden Spur; 1773 the Emperor ennobled him as "von Dittersdorf." Prod. 28 operas; *"Doktor und Apotheker"* (Vienna, 1786), still pop.; several oratorios and cantatas, 12 symphonies on Ovid's *"Metamorphoses"* (Vienna, 1785) (noteworthy as early attempts at programme-music); 41 other symphonies; a "Concerto grosso" for 11 concerted instrs. with orch.; 12

vln.-concertos, etc. Autobiography (Leipzig, 1801). Studies by Arnold, Krebs, Klob and Riedinger. Krebs also issued a thematic catalogue, with additions later by Istel.

Divitis (dē'-vĭ-tēs), **Antonius** (rightly **Antoine Le Riche**), French contrapuntist and singer, 16th century.

Dizi (dē-zē), **Fran. J.**, Namur, France, Jan. 14, 1780—Paris, Nov., 1847; composer and harpist.

Dlabacz (dlä'-bäch), **Gottf. J.**, Böhmisch-Brod, Bohemia, 1758—Prague, 1820; pub. a biog. dict., etc.

Dobrowen (dō-brō-věn'), **Issay, b.** Nishni-Novgorod, Russia, Feb. 27, 1893; conductor, composer; pupil of Moscow Cons., where won gold medal, 1911; also studied piano with Godowsky in Vienna; prof. at Moscow Philharmonie, 1917–21, and after 1919 cond. at the Great Theatre there; beginning 1923 he was cond. and scenic director at the Dresden Op.; 1924–25, Berlin Volksoper; 1931–32, Museum Concerts, Frankfort; until 1931 he was the regular cond. of the Oslo Philh. Orch., and the San Francisco Symph. Orch, 1931–33; c. chamber and orch. music and piano works.

Dobrzynski (dō-brŭ-tsēn'-shkĭ), **Ignacy Félix**, Romanoff, Volhynia, Feb. 25, 1807—Oct. 9, 1867; pupil of Elsner; pianist and dram. composer.

Doebber (děp'-běr), **Js.**, Berlin, March 28, 1866—Jan. 26, 1921; pupil of Radecke, Bussler and Agghazy, Stern Cons.; taught the 1st pf.-class in Kullak's Cons.; then conductor at Kroll's Th.; at Darmstadt ct.-Th.; 1895, cond. at the ct.-Th. in Coburg-Gotha, and tutor to Princess Beatrice; later in Hanover, and after 1908 in Berlin as critic and voice teacher; c. succ. operas, *"Die Strassensängerin"* (Gotha, 1890); *"Der Schmied von Gretna-Green"* (Berlin, 1893); burlesque-opera *"Dolcetta"* (Brandenburg, 1894); *"Die Rose von Genzanô"* (Gotha, 1895); *"Die Grille"* (Leipzig, 1897), a symphony, songs, etc.

Döhler (dä'-lěr), **Th.**, Naples, 1814—Florence, 1856; pianist and dram. composer.

Dohnanyi (dōkh-nän'-yē), **Ernst von, b.** Pressburg, Hungary, July 27, 1877; notable pianist and composer; first lessons from his father, an amateur ꞌcellist; later studied with Foerster,

Koessler, Thoman, and **Eugen** D'Albert; début, Vienna; 1898, won prize there with his pf.-concerto. 1900 and 1901 toured in America with great succ.; after 1907 taught at Berlin Hochsch.; 1919, dir. Budapest Acad. of Mus.; he cond. State Symph. in New York 1925–6 season; c. operas *"Tante Simona,"* *"The Tenor,"* *"The Voyevode's Tower"*; also pantomimes; 2 symphonies, 2 pf.-concertos, 4 rhapsodies, string sextet, piano quintet, 2 string quartets, 3 ꞌcello sonatas, 2 piano sonatas, songs, etc.

Doles (dō'-lěs), **J. Fr.**, Steinbach, Saxe-Meiningen, 1715—Leipzig, 1797; director and composer.

Dol'metsch, Arnold, b. Le Mans, France, Feb. 24, 1858—London, Feb. 29, 1940; of mixed French and Swiss parentage; studied with Vieuxtemps in Brussels and at R. Coll. of Mus., London; taught at Dulwich Coll., in latter city; began collecting and playing ancient instruments; was active in Chickering's workshop, Boston, 1902–09; and in that of Gaveau, Paris, 1910–14; in latter year settled at Haslemere, Surrey, where he in 1925 began a series of notable annual chamber music fests., in which he has restored rare old music and dances, his entire family participating in programmes; also has constructed his own instruments for these events.

Domanievski (dō-män-yĕf'-shkĭ), **Boleslaus, b.** Gronówek, Poland, 1857—1925; Polish piano teacher; pupil of Jos. Wieniawski and Rubinstein; 1890–1900, prof. at Cracow Cons., 1902, director Warsaw Music School; author of piano methods; from 1906, dir. of Warsaw Musikgesellschaft.

Dominiceti (dō-mē-nē-chä'-tē), **Cesare**, Desenzano, Lago di Garda, 1821—Sesto di Monza, 1888; prof. of comp. at Milan Cons., and dram. composer.

Dom'mer, Arrey von, Danzig, Feb. 9, 1828—Treysa, Feb. 18, 1905; pupil of Richter and Lobe (comp.), and Schallenburg (org.); 1863 Hamburg as a lecturer, critic, and (1873–79) sec. to the Town Library; 1892, Dr. phil. hon. causa (Marburg Univ.); writer and composer.

Domnich (dôm'-nĭkh), **Heinrich**, Würzburg, May 13, 1767—Paris, June 19, 1844; horn virtuoso; first teacher of the horn at Paris Cons., 1795; author of methods.

Donal'da, Pauline (rightly **Lightstone**), b. Montreal, March 5, 1884; soprano; studied at Victoria Cons., and with Duvernoy at Paris Cons.; début at Manon, Nice, 1904; sang at La Monnaie, Brussels, Covent Garden, Manhattan Op. House, N. Y. (1905); at Paris Op., 1907, etc.

Donati (dō-nä'-tē), (1) **Ignazio**, Casalmaggiore, near Cremona, 16th cent., composer and conductor. (2) **Baldassaro**, d. Venice, 1603; cond. and composer.

Donaudy (dō-nä'-oo-dē), **Stefano**, Palermo, Feb. 21, 1879—Naples, May 30, 1925; c. operas *"Folchetto"* (Palermo, 1892); *"Theodor Körner"* (Hamburg, 1902), and *"Sperduti nel Buio"* (Palermo, 1907), songs, etc.

Done (dōn), **Wm.**, Worcester, 1815—1895; Engl. organist and conductor.

Doni (dō'-nē), (1) **A. Fran.**, Florence, 1519—Monselice, near Padua, 1574; pub. a *"Dialogue on Music."* (2) **Giov. Bat.**, 1594—1647; Florentine nobleman of great learning and research in ancient music; inv. the Lyra Barberina or Amphichord.

Donizetti (dō-nē-tsĕt'-tē), (1) **Gaetano**, Bergamo, Nov. 25, 1797—April 8, 1848; son of a weaver; pupil of Salari (voice), Gonzales (pf. and accomp.), and Mayr (harm.); Pilotti and Padre Mattei (cpt.); his father opposing his making mus. a profession, he entered the army, was posted at Venice, where he c. and prod. with succ. *"Enrico di Borgogna"* (1819); *"Il Falegname di Livonia"* (Venice, 1820), first given as *"Pietro il Grande,"* also succeeded; *"Le Nozze in Villa"* (Mantua, 1820) failed; *"Zoraide di Granata"* (1822) succeeded and he left the army; 1823 he m. Virginie Vasselli (d. 1837); 1822–29 he c. 23 operas, none of them of great originality or importance. With *"Anna Bolena"* (Milan, 1830), he began a better period, incl. the great successes *"L'Elisir d'Amore"* (Milan, 1832), *"Lucrezia Borgia"* (La Scala, Milan, 1833), *"Lucia di Lammermoor"* (Naples, 1835). 1835 at Paris he prod. *"Marino Faliero."* 1837 dir. Naples Cons. The censor forbade his *"Poliuto"* (it was prod. at Naples after his death, 1848), and in wrath he left for Paris, where he prod. with much succ. *"La Fille du Régiment"* (Op.-Com., 1840), *"Les Martyrs"* (a new version of *"Poliuto"*) (Opéra, 1840?) and *"La Favorita"* (Opéra, 1840). Returned to Italy, and succ. prod. *"Adelasia"* (Rome, 1841), and *"Maria Padilla"* (Milan, 1841). At Vienna, 1842, c. and prod. with great succ. *"Linda di Chamounix."* The Emperor made him Court Composer and Master of the Imperial Chapel; c. a Miserere and an Ave Maria in strict style. *"Don Pasquale"* was prod. in Paris, 1843. Violent headaches and mental depression now assailed him, but he continued to write and prod. *"Caterino Cornaro"* (Naples, 1844), his last work; he was found stricken with paralysis, never recovered, and died in 1848 at Bergamo. Besides 67 operas, all of them produced, he c. 6 masses, a requiem; cantatas; 12 string-quartets; pf.-pcs. and songs. Biog. by Cicconetti (Rome, 1864). (2) **Alfredo** (rightly **Ciummei**), b. Smyrna, Sept. 2, 1867—Rosario de Santa Fe, Argentina; Feb. 4, 1921; pupil of Ponchielli and Dominiceti, Milan Cons., graduating with a noteworthy "Stabat Mater" with orch.; lived at Milan as cond. and teacher of cpt.; c. 1-act operas *"Nana"* (Milan, 1889), and *"Dopo l'Ave Maria"* (Milan, 1897), *"La Locandiera,"* etc.

Dont (dônt), (1) **Jos. Val.**, Georgenthal, Bohemia, 1776—Vienna, 1833; 'cellist. (2) **Jakob**, Vienna, 1815—1888; son of above; violinist and composer.

Donzelli (dôn-jĕl'-lē), **Dom.**, Bergamo, 1790—Bologna, 1873; tenor.

Door (dōr), **Anton**, Vienna, June 20, 1833—Nov. 7, 1919; pupil of Czerny and Sechter; court pianist at Stockholm; 1859 teacher at the Imp. Inst., Moscow; 1864 prof. at the Cons.; 1869 1st prof. Vienna Cons., resigned 1901; edited classical and pedagogic works.

Dopp'ler, (1) **Albert Fr.**, Lemberg, 1821—Baden, near Vienna, 1883; flutist, conductor, professor, and dram. composer. (2) **Karl**, Lemberg, 1825—Stuttgart, March 10, 1900; bro. of above; flutist, and conductor; c. operas, incl. *"Erzebeth"* in collab. with his bro. and Erkel. (3) **Arpad**, Pesth, June 5, 1857—Stuttgart, Aug. 13, 1927; son and pupil of (2); pupil of Stuttgart Cons., later pf.-teacher; 1880–83 New York;

returned to Stuttgart Cons., 1889 chorusm. at the ct.-Th.; c. opera *"Viel Lärm um Nichts"* (Leipzig, 1896); suite, *Festouvertüre*, etc.

Doret (dō-rā), **Gustave,** b. Aigle, Switzerland, Sept. 20, 1866; studied violin with Joachim and Marsick, and composition at Paris Cons.; lived at Paris as cond.; c. operas *"Les Armailles"* (Op. Com., 1906), and *"Le nain de Hassli"* (Geneva, 1908), oratorio, etc.

Dörffel (dĕrf'-fĕl), **Alfred,** Waldenburg, Saxony, Jan. 24, 1821—Leipzig, Jan. 22, 1905; pupil at Leipzig of Fink, Muller, Mendelssohn, etc.; mus.-libr. Leipzig City Library; critic and editor; 1885 Dr. phil. h. c., Leipzig U.

Do'ria, Clara, v. MRS. C. K. ROGERS.

Döring (dā'-rĭng), (1) **G.,** Pomerendorf, near Elbing, 1801—1869; cantor; pub. choral books and historical essays. (2) **Karl,** Dresden, July 4, 1834—March 26, 1916; pupil Leipzig Cons.; 1858, Dresden Cons.; 1875, prof.; c. suites for string-orch., Grand Mass., etc.

Dorn, (1) **H. (L. Edm.),** Königsberg, Nov. 14, 1804—Berlin, Jan. 10, 1892; pupil of Berger, Zelter, and Klein, Berlin; ct.-cond. at Königsberg; cond. Cologne; founded the "Rheinische Musikschule," which, 1850, became the Cologne Cons.; cond. Royal Opera, Berlin; teacher and critic; notable composer of 12 operas, symphonies, etc. (2) **Julius Paul,** Riga, June 8, 1833—Berlin, Nov. 27, 1901; son and pupil of above; pianist; teacher in Poland, Cairo, and Alexandria; 1865-68 cond. the Crefeld "Liedertafel"; then pf.-teacher at the R. Hochschule, Berlin, with title "Royal Prof."; c. over 400 works, incl. 3 masses with orch. (3) **Otto,** Cologne, Sept. 7, 1848—Wiesbaden, Nov. 8, 1931; son and pupil of (1); studied at Stern Cons., took the Meyerbeer scholarship (1st prize), 1873; lived in Wiesbaden; c. succ. opera *"Afraja"* (Gotha, 1891); symphony, *"Prometheus"*; overtures, *"Hermannsschlacht,"* and *"Sappho,"* etc. (4) **Edward,** Pen-name of **J. L. Röckel.**

Dorus-Gras (dō-rü-gräs), **Julie Aimée Josèphe** (rightly **Van Steenkiste**) (Dorus, stage-name); Valenciennes, 1805—Paris, 1896; operatic soprano; created important rôles.

Doss (dôs), **Adolf von,** Pfarrkirchen, Lower Bavaria, 1825—Rome, 1886; Jesuit priest and dram. composer.

Dotzauer (dôt'-tsow-ĕr), (1) **Justus J. Fr.,** Hasselrieth, near Hildburghausen, 1783—Dresden, 1860; 'cellist, and dram. composer. (2) **Justus B. Fr.,** Leipzig, 1808—Hamburg, 1874; son of above; teacher. (3) **K. L.** ("Louis"), Dresden, Dec. 7, 1811—1897; son and pupil of (1); 'cellist.

Dourlen (door-lăn), **Victor Chas. Paul,** Dunkirk, 1780—Batignolles, near Paris, 1864; prof. and dram. composer.

Dow'land, (1) **John,** Westminster, London, 1562—London, April, 1626; famed for polyphonic vocal music; lutenist and composer to Christian IV. of Denmark. (2) **Robert,** 1641; son of above; lutenist and editor.

Downes, Olin, b. Evanston, Ill., Jan. 27, 1886; music critic, pianist; studied piano with Carl Baermann, harmony with Homer Norris and Clifford Heilman, mus. hist. and analysis with Dr. Louis Kelterborn and John P. Marshall; mus. critic, Boston *"Post,"* 1906-24; music critic, New York *"Times,"* after 1924; has appeared widely as a lecturer on music and has written works on symphonic analysis; also has participated as pianist in chamber music programmes.

Draeseke (drā'-zĕ-kĕ), **Felix Aug. Bhd.,** Coburg, Oct. 7, 1835—Dresden, Feb. 26, 1913; important composer; pupil of Rietz, Leipzig Cons., and of Liszt at Weimar; 1864-74 Lausanne Cons., except 1868-69, in the R. M. S. at Munich; 1875 Geneva, then Dresden as teacher; 1884 prof. of comp. at the Cons.; c. 4 operas; *"Sigura,"* *"Gudrun"* (Hanover, 1884), *"Bertrana de Born"* (book and music), and the succ. *"Herrat"* (Dresden, 1892); 3 symphonies (op. 40 *"Tragica,"* in C); Grand Mass with orch.; *"Akademische Festouvertüre"*; symphonic preludes to Calderon's *"Life a Dream,"* Kleist's *"Penthesilea"* (both MS.), etc.; wrote treatises and a *"Harmony"* in verse.

Draghi (drä'-gē), (1) **Antonio,** Rimini, 1635—Vienna, 1700; c. 87 operas, 87 festival plays, etc. (2) **Gio. Bat.,** 1667—1706, harpsichordist, organist and composer, London.

Dragonet'ti, Dom., Venice, April 7,

1763—London, April 16, 1846; called "the Paganini of the contra-basso"; composed, played and taught.

Drago'ni, Giovanni Andrea, Mendola, ca. 1540—Rome, 1598; composer; pupil of Palestrina; cond. at the Lateran.

Draud (drowt) **(Drau'dius), Georg,** Davernheim, Hesse, 1573—Butzbach, ca. 1636; pub. *"Bibliotheca Classica,"* and other musical works of great informational value.

Drdla, Franz, Saar, Moravia, Nov. 28, 1868; violinist and composer; pupil of Prague and Vienna Cons.; c. over 200 smaller instrumental works, among which his *"Souvenir"* had world-wide popularity; also two stage works; 1923-25, lived in New York.

Drechsler (drĕkhs'-lĕr), (1) **Jos.,** Wallisch-Birken (Vlachovo Brezi), Bohemia, 1782—Vienna, 1852; organist, conductor and dram. composer. (2) **Karl,** Kamenz, 1800—Dresden, 1873; 'cellist teacher.

Dregert (drā'-gĕrt), **Alfred,** Frankfort-on-Oder, 1836—Elberfeld, 1893; conductor, dir. and composer.

Drese (drā'-zĕ), **Adam,** Thüringen, Dec., 1620—Arnstadt, Feb. 15, 1701; director and comp.

Dresel (drā'-zĕl), **Otto,** Andernach, 1826—Beverly, Mass., 1890; composer.

Dreszer (drĕsh'-ĕr), **Anastasius W.,** Kalisch, Poland, April 28, 1845—Halle, June 2, 1907; a brilliant pianist at 12; studied with Döring, Krebs, and Früh, Dresden Cons.; lived in Leipzig; 1868, Halle; founded a music-school of which he was dir.; c. 2 symphonies, opera *"Valmoda,"* etc.

Dreyschock (drī'-shôk), (1) **Alex.,** Zack, Bohemia, Oct. 15, 1818—Venice, April 1, 1869; one of the most dextrous of pf.-virtuosi; c. an opera, etc. (2) **Raimund,** Zack, 1824—Leipzig, 1869, br. of above; leader. His wife (3) **Elisabeth** (née **Nose),** Cologne, 1832, a contralto. (4) **Felix,** Leipzig, Dec. 27, 1860—Berlin, Aug. 1, 1906; son of (1); pianist; student under Grabau, Ehrlich, Taubert, and Kiel at the Berlin Royal Hochschule; prof. Stern Cons., Berlin; c. a vln.-sonata (op. 16), etc.

Drieberg (drē'-bĕrkh), **Fr. J. von,** Charlottenburg, 1780—1856; writer on Greek music; dram. composer.

Drigo (drē'-gō), **Riccardo,** Padua, 1846—Oct. 1, 1930; composer; active as conductor at St. Petersburg Imp. Op. and piano teacher there for many years; after 1919 again lived in Padua; c. operas, and ballets; among the latter *"Il Flauto Magico"* and *"Les Millions d'Arlequin"* have had wide popularity; also salon works for piano.

Drobisch (drō'-bĭsh), (1) **Moritz W.,** Leipzig, Aug. 16, 1802—Sept. 30, 1896; from 1842 prof. of phil., Leipzig Univ.; pub. important treatises on the mathematical determination of relative pitches. (2) **Karl L.,** Leipzig, 1803—Augsburg, 1854; bro. of above; c. 3 oratorios.

Drouet (droo-ā), **L. Franç. Ph.,** Amsterdam, 1792—Bern, Sept. 30, 1873; flutist and composer.

Duben'sky, Arcady, b. Russia, 1890; composer, violinist; pupil of Moscow Cons.; played vln. in Phila. Orch.; guest cond. of his works in America; c. (opera) *"Romance with Double Bass"* (Moscow Imp. Op., 1916); *"The Raven,"* a melo-declamation to text by Poe; orch. works, incl. symphony, *"Russian Bells"* (N. Y. Symph., 1927); Fugue for 18 violins, etc.

Dubois (dü-bwä) (1) **(Clément Fran.) Th.,** Rosnay, Marne, Aug. 24, 1837—Paris, June 11, 1924; studied at Rheims, then under Marmontel, Bénoist, Bazin, and Thomas (fugue and cpt.) at Paris Cons.; took Grand prix de Rome with the cantata *"Atala";* also first prizes in all departments; sent from Rome a Solemn Mass (perf. at the Madeleine in 1870), a dram. work, *"La Prova d'un Opera Seria,"* and 2 overtures; returned to Paris as a teacher; cond. at Saint-Clotilde; organist at the Madeleine; 1871 prof. of harm. at the Cons.; 1891 prof. of comp.; 1894, elected to Acad.; 1896, dir. of the Cons., and officier of the Legion of Honour; c. operas; oratorios: *"Les Septs Paroles du Christ"* (1867), *"Le Paradis Perdu"* (1878) (city of Paris prize), and *"Nôtre Dame de la Mer"* (1897); cantatas; masses, etc.; 3 overtures, incl. *"Frithioff."* (2) **Léon,** Brussels, Jan. 9, 1859—1935; pupil of Cons., took Grand prix de Rome; 1890 second cond., Th. de la Monnaie, Brussels, 1912-25, dir. of Brussels Cons. (vice Tinel); c.

operas, ballet, symphonic poem, *"Atala,"* etc.

Duburg, Matthew, London, 1703—1767; violinist and conductor.

Ducange. Vide CANGE, DU.

Ducasse (dü-kăs), **Roger,** b. Bordeaux, April 18, 1873; pupil Paris Cons., with Gabriel Fauré, winning Prix de Rome, 1902; from 1909 inspector in elementary schools; c. *suite française* for orch. (Colonne concerts, 1909, twice. Boston Symph., 1910); *"Variations plaisantes sur un thème grave"* for harp and orch. (Colonne concerts, 1909), *"Sarabande"* with solo voices, etc.

Ducis (dü-sē), **Benoît** (**Benedictus Ducis**), b. Bruges, 1480; important composer; not to be confused with Benedictus of Appenzell.

Dufay (dü-fĕ), **Guill.,** ca. 1400—Cambrai, Nov. 27, 1474; a canon; said to have inv. white (open) notes.

Dufranne (dü-frän'), **Hector,** b. Belgium; tenor; sang at Brussels Op., 1896; then in London and after 1899 at Paris Op.-Comique; 1908, Manhattan Op. House, N. Y.; 1910–13 with Chicago Op.; sang in the premières of *"Griselidis," "Monna Vanna"* and *"Pelléas et Mélisande."*

Dugazon (dü-gă-zôn), **Louise-Rosalie** (née Lefèvre), Berlin, 1753—Paris, 1821; untrained singer in light opera, so charming in both young and old rôles as to give rise to the descriptive terms "Jeunes Dugazon," and "Mères Dugazon."

Dug'gan, Jos. Francis, Dublin, July 10, 1817—London, 1900(?); opera-conductor and teacher in various cities in America, also Paris and London; c. succ. operas, *"Pierre,"* and *"Léonie,"* and 3 not produced; 2 symphonies, etc.

Duiffopruggar (rightly **Tieffenbrücker**) (dwĕf'-fō-proog'-gär or tĕf'-fĕn-brük-ĕr), (1) **Gaspar,** Freising, Bavaria, 1514—Lyons, 1571; long considered the first vln.-maker; went to Lyons in 1553, naturalised in 1559, and made violas da gamba and lutes. Other instr.-makers of the same surname were (2) **Wendelin,** (3) **Leonhard,** (4) **Leopold,** (5) **Ulrich,** and (6) **Magnus.** The latest made lutes at Venice, 1607.

Dukas (dü-kăs), **Paul,** Paris, Oct. 1, 1865—May 17, 1935; one of the most original of French composers; pupil at the Cons. of Dubois, Mathias and Guiraud; won prize in counterpoint, 1888, second Prix de Rome with cantata *"Velleda"*; spent a year in Rome, then a year of military service; his overture *"Polyeucte"* was played by Lamoureux in 1892; his symphony, 1896, and elsewhere; 1897 *"L'Apprenti-Sorcier"*; 1900, piano sonata; 1906, *Villanelle* for horn and piano; 1907, his opera *"Ariane et Barbe Bleue"* made a great stir and was played in Vienna, 1908, Met. Op., N. Y., 1911, etc.; had edited texts of Rameau, and c. for piano *"Variations, Interlude et Final,"* on a theme of Rameau's 1902; *Prélude élégiaque* on the name of Haydn, 1909; also a ballet *"La Péri,"* dance-poem in one act (Paris, 1911), etc.; after 1909 he was prof. at the Paris Cons. Studies by Séré and Samazeuilh.

Dukelsky (dōō-kĕl'-skē), **Vladimir,** b. Parifianova near Polotzk, Russia, Sept. 27, 1903; composer; studied in Moscow and Kiev; came into prominence through prod. of his ballet, *"Zephyr et Flore"* by Diaghileff at Monte Carlo, 1925; he has c. a large amount of chamber music, orch. works, etc.; also popular stage revues and ballads under the pseudonym of **"Vernon Duke";** res. in America for a time, but usually in Paris.

Dulcken (dool'-kĕn), (1) **Louise** (née **David**), Hamburg, 1811—London, 1850, a sister of Fd. David; pianist. (2) **Fd. Quentin,** London, June 1, 1837—Astoria, N. Y., 1902; son of above; pupil of Mendelssohn, Moscheles, Gade, Hauptmann, Becker and F. Hiller; prof. Warsaw Cons.; toured in Europe; lived for years in New York; c. an opera, *"Wieslav"*; a mass, etc.

Dulichius (dō-lĭkh'-ĭ-oos) also (**Deulich** or **Deilich**) **Philip,** Chemnitz (christened Dec. 19), 1562—March 25, 1631; teacher and comp.

Dülon (doo'-lōn), **Fr. L.,** Oranienburg, near Potsdam, 1769—Würzburg, 1826; a blind flutist and composer.

Dumont (dü-môn), **Henri,** Villers, near Liége, 1610—Paris, May 8, 1684; organist and comp.

Dunc'an, William Edmondstoune, Sale, Cheshire, 1866—June 26, 1920; organist; at 16 an associate of the Royal College of Organists: 1883, obtained scholarship at R. C. M., pupil of Parry, Stanford and Macfarren; critic for some years, then prof. at Oldham College; c. successful odes with orch., notably "*Ye Mariners of England*" (1890), etc.

Dun'ham, Henry Morton, Brockton, Mass., July 27, 1853—1929; grad. New England Cons., as pupil of G. E. Whiting (organ), J. C. D. Parker (piano), Emery and Paine (theory); held various church positions till 1911, and gave organ recitals on the Great Organ at Boston, at St. Louis Exposition; long prof. of organ at N. E. Cons.; author of an organ method; c. symph., poem "*Easter Morning*," a book of organ studies, Meditation for organ, harp and violin; 3 organ sonatas, etc.

Dun'hill, Thomas Frederick, b. Hampstead, London, Feb. 1, 1877; composer; studied at R. Coll. of Mus., after 1905 prof. there; also taught at Eton Coll., and toured colonies as examiner; 1907, founded concerts of British chamber music that have been influential in introducing new works and composers; c. large variety of orch. and esp. chamber works of tasteful quality and traditional form; opera, "*The Ice Queen*," etc.

Duni (doo'-nē), **Egidio Romualdo,** Matera, near Otranto, Feb. 9, 1709 —Paris, June 11, 1775; pupil of Durante; his first opera, "*Nerone*," prod. Rome, 1735, with great succ., triumphing over Pergolesi's last opera "*Olimpiado*," which the generous Duni said was too good for the public, declaring himself "frenetico contre il pubblico Romano"; he c. French operettas with such succ. that he settled in Paris, where he is considered the founder of French opera-bouffe; c. 13 Italian operas and 20 French.

Dunk'ley, Fd. (Louis), b. London, England, July 16, 1869; pupil of G. A. Higgs, Bainbridge, J. Higgs (cpt.), and E. H. Turpin (comp.); and at R. A. M. (Scholarship), under Parry, Bridge, Martin, Gladstone, Sharpe and Barnet; 1893, dir. at St. Agnes' School, Albany, N. Y.; also organist 1897 at Trinity M. E. Ch.; pub. "*The Wreck of the Hesperus*," ballade for soli, chor., and orch., etc.; 1889 took prize of 50 guineas

with orch. suite; lived in various cities; after 1920 in Birmingham, Ala.

Dunoyer (dün-wä-yā'). Vide GAUCQUIER.

Dun'stable (Dunstaple), John, Dunstable, Bedfordshire, England, 1370 (?)—Walbrook, Dec. 24, 1453; called by Tinctor one of the "fathers" of counterpoint.

Duparc (dü-păr) **(Fouques Duparc), Henri,** Paris, Jan. 21, 1848—Mont de Marsan, Feb. 12, 1933; pupil of César Franck; soldier in war of 1870–71; ill health led to a life of seclusion to César Franck's great regret; c. symph. poem "*Lenore*," orch nocturne, "*Aux Étoiles*"; 6 pf.-pieces; vocal duet, "*La Fuite*"; other works destroyed by the comp., and some songs of the highest importance.

Dupont (dü-pôn), (1) **Pierre,** Rochetaillée, near Lyons, April 23, 1821—Saint-Étienne, July 25, 1870; c. the words and tunes of popular and political songs which Reyer wrote out; provoked such riots that Napoleon banished him, 1851. (2) **Joseph** (ainé), Liége, 1821—1861; violinist; prof. and dram. composer. (3) **J. Fran.,** Rotterdam, 1822—Nürnberg, 1875; violinist and dram. composer. (4) **Aug.,** Ensival, near Liége, 1827—Brussels, 1890; composer. (5) **Alex.,** Liége, 1833—1888; bro. of above; pub. a "*Répertoire dramatique Belge.*" (6) **Jos.** (le jeune), Ensival, near Liége, Jan. 3, 1838—Brussels, Dec. 21, 1899; bro. of (3), pupil at Liége and Brussels Cons., took Grand prix de Rome at Brussels; 1867 cond. at Warsaw; 1871, in Moscow; 1872, prof. of harm., Brussels Cons.; cond. Th. de la Monnaie, the Society of Musicians, and the Popular Concerts. (7) **Jos. D.,** d. The Hague, June 26, 1867; bro. of above; dir. German Op. at Amsterdam. (8) **Gabriel,** Caen, March 1, 1878—Vésinet, Aug. 3, 1914; composer, esp. known for his operas "*La Cabrera*" which won the Sonzogno prize, 1904; "*La Glu*" (1910); "*La Farce du Cuvier*" (1912) and "*Antar*" (prod. 1921), also orch. works, chamber music, etc.

Duport (dü-pôr), (1) **J. P.,** Paris, 1741—Berlin, 1818; 'cellist. (2) **J. L.,** Paris, 1749—1819; more famous bro. of above; also 'cellist; composer and writer.

Duprato (dü-prä'-tō), **Jules Laurent,** Nîmes, 1827—Paris, 1892; prof. of harm. and dram. composer.

Dupré (dü-prä'), **Marcel,** b. Rouen, May 3, 1886; organist; pupil of his father, Albert, Rouen organist, then of Guilmant, Diémer, and Widor; won many 1st prizes at Cons. in Paris; succeeded Widor as org. at St.-Sulpice and played at Notre Dame; toured as recitalist in Europe and U. S.; noted for his ability at improvisation; c. org. and choral works.

Duprez (dü-prä'), **Gilbert L.,** Paris, 1806—1896; tenor and composer.

Dupuis (dü-pwē), (1) **Thomas Sanders,** London, Nov. 5, 1733—July 17, 1796; comp. and organist of Chapel Royal London; of French parentage, but lived in London, and is buried in Westminster Abbey. (2) **José** (**Joseph Lambert**), Liége, 1833—Nogent-sur-Marne, 1900; opera-bouffe singer. (3) **Sylvain,** Liége, Nov. 9, 1856—Bruges, Sept. 28, 1931; pupil Liége Cons., 1881 Prix de Rome; teacher of cpt. and cond. of a singing-society; 1900-11, cond. at La Monnaie, Brussels; and of Concerts Populaires; c. operas, incl. the succ. com. opera "*L'Idylle*," 3 cantatas, symphonic poem, "*Macbeth*," etc. (4) **Albert,** b. Verviers, France, March 1, 1877; prod. opera "*L'Idylle*" (Verviers, 1896); "*Bilitis*" (Verviers, 1899); won Prix de Rome at Brussels with opera "*Hans Michel*," 1903; c. cantata, etc.

Dupuy (dü-pwē). Vide PUTEANUS.

Durand (rightly **Duranowski**) (dü-räṅ or doo-rän-ôf'-shkĭ), (1) **Auguste Frédéric,** b. Warsaw, 1770; violinist and cond., son of a court-mus. (2) **Émile,** St.-Brieue, Côtes du Nord, Feb. 16, 1830—Neuilly, May 6, 1903; while still a pupil at the Paris Cons. he was appointed teacher of an elementary singing-class; 1871 prof. of harm.; dram. composer and writer. (3) **Marie Auguste,** Paris, July 18, 1830—May 31, 1909; pupil of Benoist; 1849-74 organist at various churches; 1870 est. mus.-pub. business of "Durand et Schöne-werk," later "Durand et Fils"; a critic and composer.

Durante (doo-rän'-tĕ), **Fran.,** Fratta Maggiore, Naples, March 15, 1684—Naples, Aug. 13, 1755; director and conductor; an important teacher and composer of the "Neapolitan School"; c. 13 masses, etc.

Durey (dü'-rē), **Louis,** b. France, May 27, 1888; composer; mem. of former Group of Six; studied with Léon Saint-Requier; after 1914 c. various orch., chamber music and other works; also wrote critical study of Ravel's music and magazine articles.

Durutte (dü-rüt), **Fran. Camille Ant.,** Ypres, East Flanders, 1803—Paris, 1881; wrote a new but erroneous system of harm.; c. operas, etc.

Du(s)sek (**Dušek, Duschek**) (doos'-sĕk or better doo'-shĕk), (1) **Fz.,** Chotiborz, Bohemia, 1736—Prague, 1799; composer, pianist and teacher. (2) **Joséphine,** b. Prague, 1756; pianist, composer, singer. (3) **J. Ladislaus,** Caslav (Tschaslau), Bohemia, Feb. 12, 1760—Saint-Germain-en-Laye, March 20, 1812; a boy-soprano at Iglau, pupil of Father Spenar at the Jesuit College; organist Jesuit Church, Kuttenburg, for 2 years; studied theology at Prague Univ., also music; became organist of Saint-Rimbaut's, Mechlin; lived Bergenop-Zoom; Amsterdam; The Hague, 1783; studied with C. P. E. Bach, Hamburg; became famous pianist and performer on Hessel's "Harmonica," Berlin and St. Petersburg; lived in Lithuania a year at Prince Radziwill's Court; lived Italy, Paris, London; 1792 m. (4) **Sofia Corri** (b. Edinburgh, 1775; a singer, harpist and composer). He entered a mus.-business with his father-in-law, 1800, failed and fled to Hamburg to escape creditors. He was in the service of various princes, and (1808) of Prince Talleyrand in Paris. A pioneer among Bohemian and Polish virtuosi and composers he disputed with Clementi the invention of the "singing-touch." Prod. 2 English operas in London with success, and pub. a Mass (comp. at the age of 13), oratorios and church-music; pub. nearly 100 works for pf., incl. 12 concertos, 80 sonatas with vln.; 53 sonatas for pf.-solo, etc.; pub. a "*Method.*"

Dushkin (dōōsh'-kēn), **Samuel,** b. Suwalki, Russian Poland, Dec. 13, 1898; violinist; studied with Auer, Kreisler, Remy; European début, 1918; 1st Amer. tour in 1924; has appeared widely in Europe, Egypt,

Palestine, and U. S., esp. in joint programmes with Igor Stravinsky.

Dustmann (doost'-män), **Marie Luise** (née **Meyer**), Aix-la-Chapelle, 1831—1899; soprano.

Duvernoy (or **Duvernois**) (dü-věrnwä), (1) **Fr.**, Montbéliard, 1765—Paris, 1838; prof. at the Cons.; composer. (2) **Charles**, Montbéliard, 1766—Paris, 1845; bro. of above; clarinettist; prof. and composer. (3) **Chas. Fran.**, Paris, 1796—1872; singer. (4) **H. L. Chas.**, Paris, Nov. 16, 1820—Jan., 1906; son of (3); pupil of Halévy and Zimmermann, Paris Cons.; 1839, assist.-prof.; 1848, prof. there of solfeggio; composer. (5) **Victor Alphonse**, Paris, Aug. 30, 1842—March 7, 1907; pupil of Bazin and Marmontel Paris Cons.; took first pf. prize; teacher of piano at the Cons.; a Chev. of the Legion of Honour, and officier of public instruction; 1892 prod. the succ. opera "*Sardanapale*" (Lyons), also opera "*Helle*" (Gr. Opéra, 1896); his symph. poem, "*La Tempête*," won the City of Paris prize.

Dux (dōoks), **Claire**, b. Witkowicz, Poland, Aug. 2, 1885; soprano; studied voice with Teresa Arkel, also in Milan; début, Cologne, 1906; sang with Berlin Op., 1911–18; Stockholm Op., 1918–21; Chicago Op., 1921–23; also at Covent Garden, and widely as concert performer in Europe and U. S.; m. Charles H. Swift; res. in Chicago since 1926, with occasional appearances.

Dvořák (dvôr'-shäk), **Antonin**, Mühlhausen, Bohemia, Sept. 8, 1841—Prague, May 1, 1904; one of the most eminent Bohemian composers; son of an inn-keeper, who wished him to be a butcher, but he learned the vln. from the schoolmaster, and at 16 entered the Prague Org.-Sch. under Pitzsch, earning a livelihood as violinist in a small orchestra; graduated in 1862, became vla.-player at the Nat. Theatre. He was 33 before an important comp. was prod., a hymn for male chorus and orch., which attracted such attention that 1875 he received a government stipend and devoted himself to composition. 1891 Mus. Doc. Cambridge Univ.; 1892–95 dir. Nat. Cons., New York; later lived at Prague; 1901, director of the Prague Cons; 1902, prod.

opera "*Armida*," Pilsen Nat. Th. He was a disciple of nationalism in music, and provoked much controversy by advising American composers to found their school on the harmonic and melodic elements of plantation-music. In his highly popular 5th symphony, op. 95, "*From the New World*," he made some use of such a manner. His other comp. are: Bohemian operas "*The King and the Charcoal-Burner*" (Prague, 1874); "*Wanda*" (1876); "*Selma Sedlák*" (1878); "*Turde Palice*" (1881); "*Dimitrije*" (1882); "*The Jacobins*" (1889); "*Rusalka, the Water Nixie*" (Nat. Th. Prague, 1901); "*Armida*" (1904); oratorio "*St. Ludmila*" (Leeds Mus. Fest., 1886); Requiem Mass, op. 89, with orch. (Birmingham Fest., 1891); cantatas "*The Spectre's Bride*," op. 69, with orch. (Birmingham Fest., 1885), and "*The American Flag*" (N. Y., 1895); Hymn of the Bohemian Peasants, for mixed ch.; hymn for mixed ch. and orch.; "*Stabat Mater*" with orch. (London, 1883); Psalm 149 with orch.; 5 symphonies; 3 orchestral ballades, "*Der Wassermann*," "*Die Mittagshexe*," and "*Das goldene Spinnrad*"; 2 sets of symphonic variations for orch.; overtures, "*Mein Heim*," "*Husitska*," "*In der Natur*," "*Othello*," "*Carneval*"; concertos for 'cello, pf., vln.; "*Slavische Tänze*" and "*Slavische Rhapsodien*"; scherzo cappriccioso for orch.; string-sextet; 2 string-quintets; pf.-quintet; 6 string-quartets; 2 pf.-quartets; a string-trio; 2 pf.-trios; mazurek for vln. with orch., serenade for wind with 'cello and double-bass; notturno for string-orch.; pf. music, "*Legenden*," "*Dumka*" (Elegy), "*Furiante*" (Boh. natl. dances); "*Klänge aus Mahren*," and "*Silhouetten*" for pf. 4-hands; violin-sonata, op. 57; songs, etc.

Dwight, **J. Sullivan**, Boston, Mass., 1813—1893; editor and critic; one of the founders of the Harvard Musical Association; was a member of the Brook Farm Community; 1852–81, edited "*Dwight's Journal of Music*."

Dykema (dī'-kĕ-mä), **Peter W.**, b. Grand Rapids, Mich., Nov. 25, 1873; educator; studied N. Y. and Berlin, with Arens, Frank Shephard and at Inst. of Music. Art; dir. of music,

Ethical Culture School, N. Y., 1901-13; prof. of music, Univ. of Wis., 1913-24; thereafter, prof. of music. education, Teachers College, Columbia Univ., author of *"School Music Handbook"* (with Cundiff), and ed. song series.

Dykes (Rev.), **J. Bacchus,** Kingston-upon-Hull, Eng., 1823—St. Leonard's, 1876; conductor.

Dy'son, Sir George, b. Halifax, England, May 28, 1883; composer and educator; pupil of R. Coll. of Mus., where won Mendelssohn Stipend; dir. of music at R. Naval Coll., Marlborough Coll., and Wellington Coll.; 1918, Mus. D., Oxford; has c. orch. and choral music; author of *"The New Music."* Dir., R. C. M., 1938; knighted, 1940.

E

Eames (āmz), **Emma,** b. (of American parents) at Shanghai, Aug. 13, 1865; noted soprano; at 5 went with her mother, her first teacher, to Bath, Maine; pupil of Miss Munger at Boston; 1886-88 at Paris, of Madame Marchesi (voice), and Pluque (acting, etc.); 1888, engaged at the Op.-Com., but made début with succ. at the Gr. Opéra, March 13, 1889, as "Juliette" in Gounod's *"Roméo et Juliette,"* a rôle previously sacred to Patti; sang at the Opera for 2 years, creating "Colombe" in St.-Saens' *"Ascanio"* and as "Zäire" in De La Nux's opera; 1891, Covent Garden in *"Faust"*; m. the painter Julian Story the same year, and in Oct. appeared in New York at Met. Op.; from then until 1909, when she retired from the stage, she sang regularly in N. Y. and London, except 1892-93, at Madrid, and 1895-96, during ill-health; "Sieglinde" was perhaps her best rôle. In 1911 she m. Emilio de Gogorza, barytone, and toured in concert with him. In later years she has lived in Paris.

Ear'hart, Will, b. Franklin, O., April 1, 1871; educator; after 1913 mus. dir. of School of Education, Univ. of Pittsburgh; author of works on school music; pres. Music Supervisors' Nat'l. Conference, 1915-16; Mus. D., Univ. of Pittsburgh, 1920.

East'man, George, Waterville, N. Y., July 12, 1854—Rochester, N. Y., March 14, 1932 (suicide); music

patron; in 1919 made gift of $3,500,-000 to found Eastman School of Music, as part of the Univ. of Rochester, and the next year added another million, the permanent endowment fund being about three millions; Rochester as a result has become an active centre of music, with the Eastman Theatre, Philh. Orch., and other enterprises incl. annual fests. of American music deriving their impetus from his generosity.

East'on, Florence, b. Middlesbrough, England, Oct. 25, 1884; soprano; studied R. Coll. of Mus., London, and with Elliott Haslam, Paris; made appearance as pianist at 8; opera début as Madame Butterfly with Moody-Manners Op. Co., London, 1903; toured U. S. with Savage Op. Co., 1904-05 and 1906-07; sang with Berlin Op., 1907-13; Covent Garden in *"Elektra,"* 1910; Hamburg Op., 1913-15; Met. Op., where she sang German and other rôles with marked versatility, 1917-28, and again in 1936; has also sung widely in concert, and as orchestral and festival soloist; a gifted lieder singer; m. Francis Maclennan, tenor; divorced.

Eaton, Louis H., b. Taunton, Mass., May 9, 1861; organist; pupil of Guilmant; 1901, org. at San Francisco.

Eb'don, Thos., Durham, 1738—1811; organist and composer.

Ebeling (ā'-bĕ-lĭng), (1) **J. G.,** Lüneburg, 1637—Stettin, 1676; prof. and composer. (2) **Chp. Daniel,** Garmissen, near Hildesheim, 1741—Hamburg, 1817; prof. and writer.

Ebell (ā'-bĕl), **H. K.,** Neuruppin, 1775—Oppeln, 1824; conductor and dram. composer.

Eberhard (1) **von Freisingen** (ā'-bĕr-härt fōn frī'-zĭng-ĕn), **Eberhar'dus Frisengen'sis,** Benedictine monk, 11th cent.; wrote on the scale of pipes and bell-founding. (2) **J. Aug.,** Halberstadt, 1739—Halle, 1809; professor.

Eberl (ā'-bĕrl), **Anton,** Vienna, June 13, 1766—March 11, 1807; famous pianist, conductor and dram. composer.

Eberlin (ā'-bĕr-lēn), (1) **Daniel,** Nürnberg, ca. 1630—Cassel, 1692; contrapuntist and violinist; famous as a composer in his day. (2) (or **Eberle**) **J. Ernst,** Jettenbach, Swabia, 1702

—Salzburg, 1762; conductor and composer.

Ebers (ā'-bĕrs), **K. Fr.**, Cassel, 1770 —Berlin, 1836; conductor and dram. composer.

Ebert (ā'-bĕrt), **Ludwig**, Kladrau, Bohemia, April 13, 1834—Coblenz, 1908; 'cellist; pupil Prague Cons.; 1854–74, first 'cellist at Oldenburg; 1875–88, teacher at Cologne Cons.; 1889, founded Cons. at Coblenz; c. 'cello pieces.

Eberwein (ā'-bĕr-vīn), (1) **Traugott Maximilian**, Weimar, 1775—Rudolstadt, 1831; dram. composer. (2) **Karl**, Weimar, 1786—1868, bro. of above; dram. composer.

Ebner (āp'-nĕr), **Wolfgang**, Augsburg, ca. 1610—Vienna, Feb., 1665; organist and comp.

Eccard (ĕk'-kärt), **J.**, Mühlhausen, Thuringia, 1553—Berlin, 1611; important composer of church-music.

Eccles (ĕk'-kĕls), (1) **John**, London (?), 1668—Kingston, Surrey, 1735; son and pupil of the violinist, (2) **Solomon E. C.** His brother (3) **Henry**, was violinist and composer. (4) **Solomon Thomas**, bro. of above, also violinist.

Eck (ĕk), (1) **J. Fr.**, Mannheim, 1766— Bamberg (?), 1809 (1810 ?); violinist and composer. (2) **Fz.**, Mannheim, 1774—insane, Strassburg, 1804; bro. and pupil of above; violinist.

Eckelt (ĕk'-ĕlt), **J. Val.**, Werningshausen, near Erfurt, 1673—Sondershausen, 1732; writer.

Eckert (ĕk'-ĕrt), **K. Ant. Florian**, Potsdam, 1820—Berlin, 1879; at 10 c. an opera, at 13 an oratorio; court-conductor and dram. composer.

Ed'dy, (1) **Clarence H.**, Greenfield, Mass., June 23, 1851—Chicago, Jan. 10, 1937; organist; pupil of J. G. Wilson and Dudley Buck; 1871 of Haupt and Löschhorn (pf.); toured in Germany, Austria, Switzerland, and Holland; 1874, organist, Chicago; 1876, dir. Hershey School of Musical Art; toured America and Europe, 1879 gave 100 recitals at Chicago without repeating a number; for some years cond. Chicago Philh. Vocal Soc.; after 1910 in San Francisco; c. organ and church music, etc.; pub. "*The Church and Concert Organist*," "*The Organ in Church*" and transl. Haupt's "*Cpt. and Fugue.*" (2) **Nelson**, b. Providence, R. I., June 29, 1901; barytone;

sang as boy soprano in choir of Grace Church, New York; pupil of David Bispham and William Vilonat; début, in benefit perf., Phila., 1922; sang with Savoy Op. Co. and Phila. Civic Op., making New York début in "*Wozzeck*," 1931; sang leading male rôle in Respighi's "*Maria Egiziaca*" with N. Y. Philh. under baton of composer; later won outstanding reputation as concert singer, in radio programmes and as featured performer in musical films.

Edelmann (ā'-dĕl-män), **Joh. Fr.**, Strassburg, May 6, 1749—Paris, July 17, 1794; c. opera, ballets, etc.

Ed'son, **Lewis**, Bridgewater, Mass., 1748—Woodstock, N. Y., 1820; pub. a coll. of hymns, etc.

Edwards, (1) **Henry Sutherland**, b. London, Sept. 5, 1829—Jan. 21, 1906; writer; historian and critic for many years of the *St. James Gazette*. (2) **Henry John**, b. Barnstaple, Feb. 24, 1854—April 8, 1933; of an organist, then pupil of Bennett, Macfarren; 1885, Mus. Doc. Oxford; c. oratorios, etc. (3) **Julian** (rightly **D. H. Barnard**), Manchester, England, Dec. 11, 1855—Yonkers, N. Y., Sept. 5, 1910; pupil Sir H. Oakley, Edinburgh, then of Macfarren, London; 1875, pianist to Carl Rosa Opera Co.; 1877, cond. Royal Eng. Opera Co. and prod. "*Victorian*" Covent Garden. 1880, prod. "*Corinne*" at St. James's Hall, London; cond. Engl. Opera at Covent Garden, and prod. 2 operas, "*Corinne*" and "*Victorian*," at Sheffield, 1883; came to the U. S., 1889, and prod. with success various comic operas, incl. "*Madeleine or the Magic Kiss*" (Boston, 1894), and "*Brian Boru*" (N. Y., 1896); "*The Wedding Day*," "*The Jolly Musketeer*," "*Princess Chic*" (1899), "*Dolly Varden*" (N. Y., 1902), and "*When Johnny Comes Marching Home*"; prod. also romantic opera "*King Rêné's Daughter*"; c. gr. opera "*Elfinella*" (MS.), symphonies, overtures, etc.

Eeden (ā'-dĕn), **Jean Baptiste van den**, Ghent, Dec. 26, 1842—Mons, April 4, 1917; pupil of Ghent and Brussels Cons.; 1st prize for comp. (1869) with the cantata "*Faust's Laaste Nacht*"; 1878 dir. of Cons. at Mons; c. opera "*Numance*" (Antwerp, 1897), oratorios and the trilogy "*Judith*," cantatas with orch., a symph. poem, "*La Lutte au XVI. Siècle*," etc.

Egenolff (or **Egenolph**) (ā'-gĕn-ôlf), 1502—55; a slovenly and piratical German mus.-printer.

Egidi (ā'-khē-dē), **Arthur**, b. Berlin, Aug. 9, 1859; organist; pupil of Kiel and Taubert; 1885–92, teacher at the Hoch Cons., Frankfort-on-Main; then org. at Berlin, and Royal Prof.; c. overture, etc.

Egk, Werner, b. Auchsesheim, Bavaria, May 17, 1901; composer; studied in Germany and Italy; after 1929 lived in Munich; c. an opera, "*Zaubergeige*" (première, Frankfort, 1935) based on nursery tale and with South German peasant songs utilised, which had succ. on several German stages; also popular orch. work, "*Georgica*," etc.

Egli (āl'-yē or ā'-glē), **Johann Heinrich**, Seegräben, canton Zurich, 1742—1810; c. "*Oden*," etc.

Ehlert (ā'-lĕrt), **Louis**, Königsberg, 1825—Wiesbaden, 1884; teacher and critic; conductor and composer.

Ehnn-Sand (ān'-zänt), **Bertha**, Budapest, Nov. 30, 1847—Aschberg, March 2, 1932; dramatic soprano, pupil of Frau Andriessen.

Ehrlich (ār'-lĭkh), (1) **Fr. Chr.**, Magdeburg, 1807—1887; conductor, singing-teacher, and dram. composer. (2) **Alfred H.**, Vienna, Oct. 5, 1822—Berlin, Dec. 30, 1899; pupil of Henselt, Bocklet, Thalberg (pf.), and Sechter (comp.); court-pianist to King George V.; 1864–72 pf.-teacher Stern Cons., and 1866–98 critic in Berlin; composer and editor.

Eibenschütz (ī'-bĕn-shüts), (1) **Albert**, Berlin, April 15, 1857—Vienna, Nov. 15, 1930; pianist; pupil of Reinecke and Paul, Leipzig Cons., won the Diploma of Honour. 1876–80, prof. in Charkoff (Russia); 1880–84 at Leipzig Cons., then Cologne Cons.; 1893, dir. Cologne Liederkranz; 1896, 1st pf.-prof. Stern Cons., Berlin; c. pf.-sonatas, etc. (2) **Ilona**, Budapest, May 18, 1872; cousin of above; pianist; at 5 she played in a concert with Liszt; 1878–85, pupil of Hans Schmitt; 1885–89, studied with Frau Schumann; lived in Vienna and made tours.

Eichberg (īkh'-bĕrkh or īch'-bŭrg), (1) **Julius**, b. Düsseldorf, June 13, 1824—Boston, Mass., Jan. 18, 1893; violinist and notable teacher; c. 4

operettas, etc. (2) **Oskar**, **Berlin**, 1845—1898; singing-teacher, conductor, critic, editor, and composer.

Eichborn (īkh'-bôrn), **H. L.**, Breslau, Oct. 30, 1847—near Bozen, April 15, 1918; studied pf., flute, trumpet, horn, etc., at an early age; at 14 pupil of the trumpeter Ad. Scholz; studied theory with Dr. E. Bohn; became a Waldhorn virtuoso; 1882 inv. the Oktav (or soprano) Waldhorn; wrote musical essays, etc.; cond. at Gries, near Bozen; editor, writer and composer.

Eichheim (īkh'-hīm), **Henry**, b. Chicago, Jan. 3, 1870; composer, violinist; grad. Chicago Music. Coll. with vln. prize; studied with Carl Becker, Jacobsohn and Lichtenberg; played 1st vln. in Boston Symph., 1890–1912; has toured as soloist in modern programmes, and cond. own works as guest in Eur. and Amer. cities; c. orch. works based on native folk material of the Orient, also chamber music, piano pieces and songs.

Eichner (īkh'-nĕr), **Ernst**, Mannheim, 1740—Potsdam, 1777; c. important symphonies, concertos, etc.

Eijken (ī'-kĕn) (or **Eyken**), **van** (1) **Jan Albert**, Amersfoort, Holland, April 25, 1822—Elberfeld, Sept. 24, 1868; organist and comp.; his son. (2) **Heinrich**, Elberfeld, July 19, 1861—Berlin, Aug. 28, 1908; composer; pupil of Leipzig Cons.; teacher of theory; c. songs with orch.

Ein'stein, Alfred, b. Munich, Dec. 30, 1880; critic and writer on music; studied with Sandberger and Beer-Walbrunn; after 1917, critic of Munich "*Post*"; later of Berlin "*Tageblatt*"; now res. in U. S. A.; after 1919 he ed. 9th edition of Riemann's Music Lexicon; ed. "*Neue Musik-Lexicon*" (1926), a revision of Eaglefield Hull's "*Dictionary of Modern Music and Musicians*"; until 1933 he was the ed. of the "*Zeitschrift für Musikwissenschaft*."

Eisfeld (īs'-fĕlt), **Th.**, Wolfenbüttel, April 11, 1816—Wiesbaden, Sept. 2, 1882; cond., N. Y. Philh. (with Bergmann), 1849–64; previously conductor at Wiesbaden; then of "Concerts Viviennes," Paris.

Eis'ler, Hanns, b. Leipzig, July 6, 1898; composer; pupil of Schönberg and Anton Webern; after 1925 taught at Klindworth-Scharwenka Cons., Berlin; visited America, 1935; esp. noted for his works written to revolutionary song texts, also chamber music.

Eitner (īt'-nĕr), **Rob.**, Breslau, Oct. 22, 1832—Templin, Jan. 22, 1905; pupil of Brosig; 1853, teacher at Berlin; est. a pf.-sch., 1863; from 1865 he was engaged in musicological work of the highest value, incl. the compilation of a *"Source Lexicon of Musicians and Musical Scientists"* (10 vols.), which has not been surpassed in its particular field; important for work in musical literature, and research in 16th and 17th centuries, Dutch music, etc.; c. "Biblical opera," *"Judith"*; overture to *"Der Cid"*; etc.

El'dering, Bram, b. Groningen, Holland, July 8, 1865; violinist; studied with Poortmann, Hubay, and Joachim; Konzertmeister Berlin Philh.; then do. in Meiningen ct.-chapel; and 1899 in Gürzenich Orch.; after 1903 taught at Cologne Cons.

Elers (ā'-lĕrs) (called **El'erus**), **Fz.**, Uelzen, ca. 1500—1590, Hamburg; teacher, director, and composer.

Elewyck (vän ā'-lŭ-vēk), **Xavier Victor** (Chevalier) **van**, Ixelles les Bruxelles, Belgium, 1825—in an insane asylum, Zickemont, 1888; writer.

El'gar, Sir Edward, Broadheath, Worcester, Engl., June 2, 1857—London, Feb. 23, 1934; important English composer; violinist, and organist; cond. Worcester Instrumental Soc., 1882–89; 1885–89, organist at St. George's; as part of his early training he was bandmaster 1879–1884 at the County Asylum with attendants as musicians; he retired to Malvern in 1891 discouraged with his prospects in London; lived as teacher and occasionally cond. His *"King Olaf"* (1896) brought his first real success, which his orch. variations (1899) increased and the *"Dream of Gerontius"* (1900) established; Cambridge made him Mus. Doc. that year; Strauss cond. *"Gerontius"* in Germany, 1902; 1904 an Elgar Festival was given for 3 days at Covent Garden, and the same year he was knighted. He c. Imperial March, 2 military marches, called *"Pomp and Circumstance"*; *"Sea Pictures,"* contralto and orch.; Coronation Ode (1902), *"The Apostles"* (Birmingham Fest., 1903); Symphony No. 1 in A flat (1908); Symphony No. 2 in E flat *"To the*

Memory of Edward VII" (London Mus. Fest., 1911, and the same year by Cincinnati Symph., N. Y. Phil., Boston Symph., etc.).

In 1906 he visited the U. S. and conducted his music at the Cincinnati Fest.; he served as prof. of music in Birmingham Univ., 1905–08; in 1924 he was created Master of the King's Musick. He lived at Hereford (after 1904), but in later years, though he maintained an estate there, he passed much of his time in London. Honorary degrees of Mus. D. were conferred upon him by Durham, Oxford and Yale Univs.; LL. D., by Leeds, Aberdeen and Pittsburgh Univs. His large output of compositions includes also a symph. study, *"Falstaff"* (1913), symph. poem; *"Polonia"* (1915), a much played vln. concerto in B minor (1910); Introduction and Allegro for strings (1905); incidental music for *"Grania and Diarmid,"* the notable *"Enigma"* Variations for orch. (1899) in which the identity of various of his friends is concealed; *"The Kingdom,"* oratorio (1906, Birmingham Fest.); *"The Music-Makers"* (1912) for chorus; *"The Crown of India"* (1912); *"The Spirit of England"* (1916), do.; 2 string quartets, oratorio, *"The Light of Life"* (1896); cantata, *"Caractacus"*; overtures, *"Froissart," "In the South," "Cockaigne"* (1901); 6 Scenes from the Bavarian Highlands, for chorus and orch. (1896); Spanish serenade for ch. and orch.; romance for vln. and orch.; church-music; pcs. for vln. and pf.; organ-sonata; songs, etc.

Elias (ā'-lĭ-äs), **Salomonis**, monk at Saint-Astère, Perigord, wrote in 1274 the oldest extant book of rules for improvised counterpoint.

El'kus, Albert, b. Sacramento, Cal., April 30, 1884; composer; studied with Oscar Weil, Robert Fuchs, Karl Prohaska, Georg Schumann, Harold Bauer and Lhevinne; c. orch., chamber music and choral works.

El'ler, Louis, Graz, 1820—Pau, 1862; vln.-virtuoso; c. *"Valse Diabolique,"* a *"Rhapsodie Hongroise,"* etc., for vln.

El'lerton, J. Lodge, Chester, 1807—London, 1873; dram. composer.

El'man, Mischa, b. Talnoe, Russia, Jan. 21, 1891; violinist; played at 5 in public; studied 16 months at

Odessa with Fidelmann, 1903 invited by Auer to become his pupil; début at St. Petersburg, 1904, and greeted as a great artist though only 12; toured widely; 1908, America; he has long ranked as one of the most eminent performers in his field. He has made his home in N. Y. for some years.

Elmblad (ĕlm'-blät), **Jns.**, b. Stockholm, Aug. 22, 1853; bass; studied with Stockhausen and Garcia; 1876, Wagner chose him for "Donner" (Rheingold), but his father, a prof. of theology, objected; 1880, he went into opera and sang in various cities, as well as in London and America; 1896, sang "Fafner" at Bayreuth; 1897 at ct.-Th., Stockholm; d. 1911.

El'mendorff, Karl, b. Düsseldorf, Germany, Jan. 25, 1891; conductor; pupil of Steinbach and Abendroth at Cologne Cons.; active as cond. at native city, Mainz, Hagen, Aachen; 1925–32, first cond. of Munich State Op.; after 1932 in Wiesbaden; appeared at Bayreuth, beginning 1927.

Elsenheimer (ĕl'-zĕn-hī-mĕr), **Nicholas J.,** Wiesbaden, 1866—Limburg, Germany, July 12, 1935; pupil of his father and of Jakobsthal, Strassburg, LL.D., Heidelberg; 1890, America; 1891, prof. at Coll. of Music, Cincinnati; c. cantata *"Valerian,"* with orch. *"Belshazzar,"* etc.

Elsner (ĕls'-nĕr), **Jos. Xavier,** Grottkau, Silesia, 1769—Warsaw, 1854; writer and composer of 19 operas.

El'son, (1) **Louis Chas.,** Boston, April 17, 1848—Feb. 14, 1920; writer and teacher; pupil of Kreissmann (singing), Boston, and Gloggner-Castelli (theory), Leipzig; edited the *"Vox Humana"*; then on the *"Music Herald"*; for years critic of the *"Boston Courier,"* then of the *"Advertiser"*; 1881 prof. of theory and lecturer on the orch. and musical history at N. E. Cons.; lectured on much with success; pub. *"Curiosities of Music,"* *"The History of German Song,"* *"The Theory of Music,"* *"The Realm of Music,"* *"German Songs and Songwriters,"* *"European Reminiscences,"* *"Syllabus of Musical History,"* and *"Great Composers and Their Work"* (1899), *"The National Music of America"* (1900), *"Home and School Songs"*; c. operettas, songs, and instr.-works; transl. and arranged over 2,000 songs, operas, etc. (2)

Arthur B., b. Boston, Nov. 18, 1873; d. N. Y., Feb. 24, 1940; son and pupil of (1); grad. Harvard Univ.; and Mass. Inst. of Technology; author of books on music.

El'terlein, Ernst von. Vide GOTTSCHALD.

El'vey, (1) **Stephen,** Canterbury, 1805 —Oxford, 1860; organist. (2) Sir **George** (Job), Canterbury, 1816— Windlesham, Surrey, 1893; bro. of above; c. oratorios.

Elwart (ĕl'-värt), **Antoine Aimable Elie,** Paris, 1808—1877; violinist and dram. composer.

El'wes, Gervase Cary, Northampton, England, Nov. 15, 1866—Boston, Mass., 1921 (killed by locomotive while on American tour); tenor; studied Vienna, Paris, etc.; at first in diplomatic life; professional début, 1903; sang in Europe and America; excelled in Brahms songs.

Em'ery, Stephen Albert, Paris, Maine, Oct. 4, 1841—Boston, April 15, 1891; prof. of harm. and cpt.; asst.-ed. *"Musical Herald"*; graceful composer and pop. theorist.

Emman'uel, Maurice, b. Bar-sur-Aube, May 2, 1862—Paris, Dec. 14, 1938; writer on music; pupil of Paris Cons., and Gevaert in Brussels; also at Sorbonne, Paris; won Kastner-Boursault prize from French Acad. for his *"Histoire de la Langue Musicale"*; has also written treatises on Greek music and modal accompaniment to the psalms; 1909, appointed prof. of music. hist. at Paris Cons.; c. orch., chamber and choral music, org. pieces and songs.

Emmerich (ĕm'-mĕr-īkh), **Robt.,** Hanau, 1836—Baden-Baden, 1891; composer.

Enckhausen (ĕnk'-how-zĕn), **H. Fr.,** Celle, 1799—Hanover, 1885; court-organist, pianist and director.

Enesco (ā-nĕs'-koo), **Georges,** b. Cordaremi, Roumania, Aug. 7, 1882; violinist, conductor, composer; at 4 played and composed, at 7 was admitted to Vienna Cons., by Hellmesberger, in whose family he lived; at 11, took first prizes for violin and harmony; 1896, studied in Paris Cons. with Marsick and Fauré; in 1897, he took second accessit for counterpoint and fugue, and a concert of his works was given in Paris, including a violin sonata, a piano suite, quintet, 'cello pieces and songs;

1898, Colonne prod. his *"Poème Roumain"* for orch.; 1899, he took first violin prize at the Cons.; toured and became court violinist to the Roumanian queen; c. symph. (Colonne orch., 1906; N. Y. Phil., 1911) and symph. in E flat, op. 13 (Berlin, 1912) Pastoral fantasie for orch. (Colonne orch., 1899); Dixtuor, or symphony for wind instrs., do. for 'cello and orch. (Lamoureux orch., 1909); suite for orch. (Boston Symph., 1911); 3 Rhapsodies Roumaines, (1911), etc. He has appeared in the U. S. both as violinist and conductor, and was engaged for guest appearances in latter capacity with N. Y. Philh. Orch., 1936–37; his music drama *"Oedipe,"* on which he had worked for many years, was prod. at the Paris Op., 1936, creating a marked impression by its nobility and original form of expression.

Engel (ĕng'-ĕl), (1) **Jn. Jakob**, Parchim, Mecklenburg, 1741–1802; dir. and composer. (2) **David Hn.**, Neuruppin, 1816—Merseburg, 1877; organist, writer and dram. composer. (3) **K.**, Thiedewiese, near Hanover, 1818—suicide, London, 1882; organist and writer. (4) **Gv. Ed.**, Königsberg, 1823—Berlin, 1895; singing-teacher, composer and theorist. (5) **Carl**, b. Paris, July 21, 1883; editor, musicologist; educated at Strasbourg and Munich Univ., studied composition with Thuille; res. U. S. since 1905, became Amer. citizen, 1917; chief of music division, Library of Congress, Washington, 1921–29; pres. publishing firm of G. Schirmer, Inc., N. Y., and ed. of *"Musical Quarterly"*; has written extensively on musical subjects.

En'na, Aug., Nakskov, Denmark, May 13, 1860—Copenhagen, Aug. 3, 1939; grandson of an Italian soldier in Napoleon's army; son of a shoemaker; self-taught in pf. and instrumentation, and had almost no teaching in vln. or theory; went with a small orch. to Finland (1880); played various insts., even a drum before a circus-tent; returned to Copenhagen; prod. the operetta *"A Village Tale"* (1880) in provincial theatres; played at dancing-lessons, and gave pf.-lessons at 12 cents an hour; 1883, cond. for a small provincial troupe, for which he wrote act-tunes, and 10 overtures; pub. songs,

pf.-pcs., an orchl. suite, and a symphony; this gained him, through Gade's interest, the Ancker scholarship, enabling him to study in Germany (1888–89). After producing an operetta *"Areta,"* he prod. with unequalled succ. for a Dane, the opera *"The Witch,"* 1892, at the R. Opera House, Copenhagen. The opera *"Cleopatra"* (Copenhagen, 1894) failed, but 1895, with new cast, was succ. as also *"Aucassin and Nicolette"* (Copenhagen, 1896; Hamburg, 1897). Opera *"Aglaia,"* in MS. Pub. a vln.-concerto, etc.

E'noch & Co., London music-pub. firm, est. 1869.

Épine (dĕ-lā-pē'-nĕ), **Francesca Margerita de l'**, extremely popular Italian singer and harpsichordist in London, from ca. 1698—1718, when she m. Dr. Pepusch; her sister sang in London from 1703–1748 as Maria Gallia.

Epstein (ĕp'-shtīn), (1) **Julius**, Agram, Aug. 7, 1832—Vienna, March 1, 1926; pupil of Lichtenegger, Halm (pf.), and Rufinatscha (comp.); 1867–1902, prof. of pf. Vienna Cons. Among his pupils were Mahler, Ignace Brüll, Ugo Reinhold, August Sturn, etc., and he is said to have discovered the voice of Marcella Sembrich, when she studied piano with him. His two daughters, (2) **Rudolfine** ('cellist), and (3) **Eugénie** (violinist), toured Austria and Germany, 1876–77. (4) **Richard** (1869–1919), his son, pianist; toured Europe, and 1914 in U. S.

Érard (ā'-răr), (1) **Sébastien**, Strassburg, April 5, 1752—near Paris, Aug. 5, 1831; notable piano-maker and inventor; inv. a "Clavecin Mécanique"; the "Piano organisé," finally the double-action mechanism, which made a new instr. of the harp (v. D. D.); perfected in 1811 his greatest achievement, the repetition action of the piano (v. D. D.). His successor as a piano-maker was his nephew, (2) **Pierre** (1796—1855), succeeded by Pierre Schaffer (d. 1878); he was succeeded by Count de Franqueville.

Erb (ĕrp), (1) **M. Jos.**, b. Strassburg, Oct. 23, 1860; pupil of St.-Saëns, Gigout, and Loret, Paris; lived in Strassburg as teacher and organist at the Johanniskirche and the Synagogue; c. a symphony; a symphonic suite; sonatas and "dram.

episode" "*Der letzte Ruf*" (Strassburg, 1895), with some succ., etc. (2) **Karl**, b. Ravensburg, July 13, 1877; tenor; sang as choir boy; later entered chorus of Stuttgart Op. when it was on guest tour in his native town; 5 months later made début at Stuttgart without formal vocal study; 1913-25, member of Munich Op.; also active as recital and oratorio singer. (3) **John Lawrence**, b. Reading, Pa., 1877; organist; studied Metropolitan Coll., N. Y., and Virgil School; headed mus. dept. of Wooster Univ., later dir. school of music, Univ. of Illinois; after 1922 dir. at Conn. Coll., New London; wrote life of Brahms; c. organ, piano and vocal music.

Er'ba, Don Dionigi, nobleman and composer at Milan, 1694; Händel appropriated some of his best works.

Erbach (ĕr'-bäkh), **Chr.**, Algesheim, Palatinate, 1570—Augsburg, 1635; composer and organist.

Er'ben, Robert, Troppau, March 9, 1862—Berlin, Oct. 17, 1925; 1894, conductor at Frankfort-on-M.; 1896, at Mannheim; prod. the succ. 1-act opera "*Enoch Arden*" (Frankfort-on-M., 1895), and a "fairy comedy," "*Die Heinzelmännchen*" (Mayence, 1896).

Erdmannsdörffer (ĕrt'-mäns-dĕrf-fĕr), (1) **Max**, Nürnberg, June 14, 1848—Munich, Feb. 14, 1905; pupil Leipzig Cons., and in Dresden of Rietz; 1871-80, ct.-cond., Sondershausen; 1882, dir. Imp. Mus. Soc. at Moscow, and prof. at the Cons.; 1885, founded a students' orch. society; returned to Germany, cond. the Bremen Philh. Concerts till 1895; 1896, cond. Symphony Concerts St. Petersburg; 1896, cond. at the ct.-Th., Munich; c. "*Prinzessin Ilse*," "a forest-legend"; and other works for soli, chor. and orch.; overture to Brachvogel's "*Narciss*," etc.; 1874 he m. (2) **Pauline Fichtner Oprawill**, b. Vienna, June 28, 1847—Munich, Sept. 24, 1916; pupil of Pirkhert and Liszt; court-pianist.

Erk (ĕrk), (1) **Adam Wm.**, Herpf, Saxe-Meiningen, 1779—Darmstadt, 1820; organist and composer. (2) **Ludwig (Chr.),** Wetzlar, 1807—Berlin, 1883; son of above; conductor. (3) **Fr. Albrecht,** Wetzlar, 1809—Düsseldorf, 1879; bro. of above; pub. the "*Lehrer Commersbuch*," etc.

Erkel (ĕr'-kĕl), (1) **Franz (or Ferencz)**, Gyula, Hungary, Nov. 7, 1810—Pesth, June 15, 1893; the father of Hungarian opera; conductor and prof., composer of operas incl. "*Hunyády László*" and "*Bank Ban*." (2) **Alexander (or Alexius)**, Pesth, 1846—1900, son of above; dir. of Philh. Conc., Pesth, 1875-93; 1896, dir. Royal Opera, Pesth; prod. opera "*Tempeföi*" (Pesth, 1883). (3) **Julius**, d. Budapest, March 22, 1909; son of (1); prof. at Acad. of Mus., Pesth; conductor for many years at R. Opera.

Erlanger (ĕr-län-zhā), (1) **Camille**, Paris, May 25, 1863—April 24, 1919; pupil of Délibes, Paris Cons.; 1888 took Grand prix de Rome with cantata "*Velleda*"; c. symphonic piece, "*La Chasse Fantastique*"; dram. legend, "*Saint Julien L'Hospitalier*" (Paris, 1896); the succ. lyric drama "*Kermaria*" (Paris, Op.-Com., 1897), "*Aphrodite*," (1906) etc. (2) Baron **Frédéric d'** (pen-names **Fr. Regnal** or **Federico Ringel**), b. Paris, May 29, 1868; son of a banker; prod. succ. opera "*Jehan de Saintre*," Hamburg (1894), and mod. succ. opera "*Inez Mendo*" (London, 1897), "*Tess*," "*Noel*," etc.

Erlebach (ĕr'-lĕ-bäkh), **Ph. H.**, Essen, July 25, 1657—Rudolstadt, April 17, 1714; court-cond.; c. overtures, etc.

Er'ler, Hermann, Radeberg, near Dresden, June 3, 1844—Berlin, Dec. 13, 1918; 1873 est. a mus.-pub. business (now Ries and Erler); editor and critic.

Ernst, Heinrich Wilhelm, Brünn, Moravia, May 6, 1814—Nice, Oct. 8, 1865; violinist; pupil Vienna Cons. and with Bohm and Mayseder; followed Paganini about to learn his methods; 1832-38 lived at Paris; 1838-44 toured Europe with greatest success; c. violin-concerto, etc.

Errani (ĕr-rä'-nē), **Achille**, Italy, 1823—New York, 1897; operatic tenor and notable singing-teacher in N. Y.

Er'skine, John, b. New York, Oct. 5, 1879; educator, novelist and musician; pres. Juilliard School of Music, N. Y., until 1937; heard as lecturer, and as piano soloist with leading Amer. orchestras; prof. of English lit., Columbia University; among many academic degrees, hon. D. Litt., Bordeaux Univ.; Chevalier of the Legion of Honour; author of librettos to operas, *"Jack and the Beanstalk"* (Gruenberg) and *"Helen Retires"* (Antheil).

Er'tel, Jean Paul, Posen, Jan. 22, 1865 —Berlin, Feb. 11, 1933; critic and composer; pupil of Tauwitz, Brassin and Liszt; self-taught in instrumentation; teacher at Brandenburg Cons.; 1897–1905, edited the *"Deutsche Musiker Zeitung"*; c. symphony *"Harald"*; symph. poems *"Maria Stuart," "Der Mensch," "Belsazar," "Hero und Leander"* (1909); a double fugue for orchestra and organ, etc.

Ert'mann, Baroness, ca. 1778—Vienna, 1848; pianist; intimate friend of Beethoven.

Eschmann (ĕsh'-män), **Jn. K.,** Winterthur, Switzerland, 1826—Zurich, 1882; pianist, teacher and composer at Leipzig.

Escudier (ĕs-küd-yā), two brothers, of Castelnaudary, Aude, (1) **Marie,** 1819—1880, and (2) **Léon,** 1821—Paris, 1881; journalists.

Eslava (ĕs-lä'-vä), **Don Miguel Hilario,** Burlada, Navarra, 1807—Madrid, 1878; court-conductor, editor and theorist.

Espagne (ĕs-päkh'-nĕ), **Fz.,** Münster, Westphalia, 1828—Berlin, 1878; director and editor.

Esplá, Oscar, b. Alicante, Aug. 5, 1886; Spanish composer; one of the leading composers of his country, his works based on folk music of eastern Spain; utilises original musical scale drawn from folk music; forswears impressionism and romanticism for classical method; c. orch., chamber and other music of marked originality.

Espo'sito, Michele, Castellammare, near Naples, Sept. 29, 1855—Dublin, Nov. 19, 1929; pianist; pupil of Naples Cons., under Cesi; 1878–82, at Paris; from 1882, piano-prof., Royal Irish Acad. of Music, Dublin; 1899 organised and cond. an orchestra in Dublin; c. cantata *"Deirdre"* winning Feis Ceoil prize (1897); operetta, *"The Postbag," "Irish"* symph. (Feis Ceoil prize, 1902), etc.

Es'ser, H., Mannheim, 1818—Salzburg, 1872; court-conductor.

Es'sipoff (or **Essipova**) (ĕs-sĭ-pôf'-ä), **Annette,** St. Petersburg, Feb. 1, 1851 —Aug. 18, 1914; pianist; pupil of Wielhorski; of Leschetizky, whom

she m. 1880; début, 1874, St. Petersburg; toured Europe with great succ.; toured America (1876); 1885, pianist to the Russian Court; 1893–1908, pf.-prof. St. Petersburg Cons.

Este (or **Est, East, Easte**), (1) **Thomas,** London music-printer, ca. 1550—ca. 1609. (2) **Michael,** son of above; 17th cent. composer.

Esterházy (esh'-tĕr-hä-zē), Count Nicholas, 1839—Castle Totis, Hungary, 1897; generous patron of music.

Ett (ĕt), **Kaspar,** Erringen, Bavaria, 1788—Munich, 1847; court-organist and composer.

Ett'inger, Max, b. Lemberg, Dec. 27, 1874; comp. of operas, *"Clavigo," "Judith,"* etc.

Eulenburg (tsoo oi'-lĕn-boorkh), (1) **Ph.,** Graf zu, Königsberg, Feb. 12, 1847 —Liebenberg, Sept. 17, 1921; Royal Prussian Ambassador, Stuttgart; c. songs (words and music). (2) **Ernst,** Berlin, 1847—Leipzig, 1926; founder of Leipzig publishing house.

Ev'ans, (1) **Edwin,** 1844—London, Dec. 21, 1923; organist; writer; author, *"Beethoven's Nine Symphonies," "Record of Instrumentation,"* etc.; his son (2) **Edwin;** b. London, Sept. 1, 1874; music critic; educated at Lille, Echtemach, Luxembourg; self-taught in music; critic, *"Pall Mall Gazette,"* 1914–23; contributor to many periodicals; one of the founders of the Internat'l Soc. for Contemporary Music; wrote work on Tschaikowsky.

Evers (ā'-vĕrs), **K.,** Hamburg, 1819—Vienna, 1875; pianist and composer.

Ew'er & Co., London mus.-publishers; founded 1820 by J. J. Ewer, succeeded by E. Buxton; 1860, W. Witt; 1867, became Novello, Ewer & Co.

Eximeno (ĕx-ĭ-mā'-nō), **Ant.,** Valencia, 1729—Rome, 1808; Jesuit priest; had historical controversy with Padre Martini.

Expert (ĕx-pĕr), **Henri,** b. Bordeaux, May 12, 1863; pupil of César Franck and Gigout; authority on 15–16th century music and editor of many important texts; from 1909 librarian Paris Cons., succeeding Weckerlin.

Eybler (ī'-blĕr), **Jos.** (later, in 1834, Edler von Eybler), Schwechat, near Vienna, 1765—Schönbrunn, 1846; conductor and composer.

Eyken (ī'-kĕn), (1) **Simon van** (or

Eycken; du Chesne). Vide QUERCU.
(2) (Eijken), Jan Albert van, Amersfoort, Holland, 1822—Elberfeld, 1868;
organist and composer; c. valuable
chorals, etc.

Eymieu (ĕm'-yŭ), Henri, b. Saillans
Drôme, France, May 7, 1860; a lawyer, but studied with E. Gazier
(theory) and Widor (comp.); writer
and critic for "Le Ménestrel," etc.;
c. a stage-piece, "Un Mariage sous
Néron" (Paris, 1898), and an oratorio, "Marthe et Marie" (Asnières,
1898), etc.

Eysler (īs'-lĕr), or Eisler, Edmund, b.
Vienna, Mar. 12, 1874; c. operettas
"The Feast of Lucullus" (Vienna,
1901), and "Brother Straubinger"
(1903), "Vera Violetta," 1907, etc.

F

Faber (fä'-bĕr), (1) Nikolaus (Nicol),
priest at Halberstadt, 1359–61, built
there what is considered the first
organ made in Germany. (2) Nikolaus (II.), a native of Bozen, Tyrol;
pub. "Rudimenta musicae," Augsburg, 1516. (3) Heinrich, "Magister," b. Lichtenfels, d. Oelsnitz, Saxony, 1552; rector of a school, whence
he was expelled for satirical songs
against the Pope; then rector of
Brunswick; pub. a pop. book of rudiments. (4) Benedikt, Hildburghausen, 1602—Coburg, 1631; composer.

Fabio. Vide URSILLO.

Fabri (fä'-brē), (1) Stefano (il maggiore), b. Rome, ca. 1550; 1599—
1601, conductor. (2) Stefano (il
minore), Rome, 1606—1658; conductor and composer. (3) Annibale Pio
(called Balino), Bologna, 1697—Lisbon, 1760; tenor, etc.

Fabricius (fä-brē'-tsĭ-oos), (1) Werner,
Itzehoe, 1633—Leipzig, 1679; composer. (2) J. Albert, Leipzig, 1668—
Hamburg, 1736, son of above; professor.

Faccio (fät'-chō), Franco, Verona,
March 8, 1840—Monza, July 21,
1891; an important composer; criticised as Wagnerite; notable cond.;
prof. at Milan Cons. (harmony, later
cpt.). Vide BOITO.

Faelten (fĕl'-tĕn), (1) K., Ilmenau,
Thuringia, Dec. 21, 1846—Read-
field, Me., Jan. 5, 1928; studied as a
school-boy with Montag; for 6
years orchestra-violinist; 1867 stud-

ied with J. Schoch, Frankfort, and
was for 10 years friend of Raff; 1868–
82, Frankfort; 1878, Hoch Cons.;
1882–85, Peabody Institute, Baltimore, U. S. A.; 1885–97, N. E. Cons.,
Boston; dir. 1890–97; 1897, founded
the Faelten Pf.-School (Teachers'
Seminary), at Boston; pub. text-
books. (2) Reinhold, b. Ilmenau,
Jan. 17, 1856; brother of (1); pupil
of Klughardt and Gottschalg in
Weimar; also for many years in the
U. S., active in Baltimore and Boston as teacher, writer.

Fago (fä'-gō), Nicola (called "Il Taren-
tino"), Tarento, 1674—1745 (?); c.
oratorio, masses; prod. several very
succ. operas.

Fahrbach (fär'-bäkh), (1) Jos., Vienna,
1804—1883; flutist, conductor, and
composer. (2) Ph. (Sr.), Vienna,
1815—1885; conductor and dram.
composer. (3) Wm., Vienna, 1838
—1866; conductor and composer.
(4) Ph. (Jr.), Vienna, 1840—1894;
son of (2); conductor.

Fährmann (fär'-män) Ernst Hans, b.
Beicha, Dec. 17, 1860; organist; 1892,
teacher at Dresden Cons.; c. organ
sonatas, etc.

Faignient (fīn-yäṅ), Noë, b. Antwerp,
ca. 1570, Flemish contrapuntist.

Fair'child, Blair, Belmont, Mass., June
23, 1877—Paris, April 23, 1933;
composer; studied at Harvard Univ.,
with Paine and W. Spalding, also in
Florence with Buonamici; entered
diplomatic service in Constantinople
and Persia; Oriental impressions
notable in his music; after 1903 lived
in Paris, studied with Widor and
Ganaye; c. (pantomime) "Dame
Libellule" (Paris Op.-Comique, 1921);
also many orch., chamber music,
vocal and piano works.

Faiszt (fīst), Immanuel G. Fr., Essligen,
Würtemberg, 1823—Stuttgart, 1894;
organist.

Falcke (fälk), Henri, Paris, 1866—
May, 1901; pupil of Saint-Saëns,
Massenet, Dubois, and Mathias,
Paris Cons.; won 1st prizes in pf. and
harm.; studied in Germany; pub. a
useful text-book on arpeggios.

Falcon (fäl-kôṅ), M. Cornélie, Paris,
1812—1897; soprano singer.

Falk Mehlig (fälk mā'-lĭkh), Anna,
Stuttgart, July 11, 1846—Berlin,
July 16, 1928; studied at the Cons.,
also with Liszt; toured as concert
pianist throughout Germany, Eng-

land, and America; court-pianist to the king of Würtemberg.

Fall, Leo, Olmütz, Feb. 2, 1873—Vienna, Sept. 15, 1925; composer of light operas; *"Irrlicht"* (Mannheim, 1905), *"Der Rebell"* (Vienna, 1905), *"Der fidele Bauer"* (Mannheim, 1907), *"Die Dollar Prinzessin,"* (Vienna, 1907, London and America as *"The Dollar Princess"*), etc.

Falla, De. Vide DE FALLA.

Faltin (fäl'-tēn), **R. Fr.,** Danzig, Jan. 5, 1835—Helsingfors, June 1, 1918; pupil of Markull, Schneider, and Leipzig Cons. Since 1869 lived at Helsingfors, Finland, as cond.; pub. *"Finnish Folk-Songs"* and a *"Finnish Song-Book."*

Faminzin (fä-mēn'-tsēn), **Alex. Sergievitch,** Kaluga, Russia, 1841—Ligovo, near St. Petersburg, 1896; critic and dram. composer.

Fanel'li, Ernest, Paris, 1860—1917; studied Paris Cons.; violinist; played in cafés, dance halls, acted as music copyist; in 1912 his symphony *"Tableaux Symphoniques,"* written in 1883, prod. by the Colonne orch., received with greatest approval. His works, in modern style of much originality, are prophetic of Debussy.

Fan'ing, Eaton, Helston, Cornwall, May 20, 1850—Brighton, Oct. 28, 1927; pupil of the R. A. M., took Mendelssohn Scholarship in 1873 and the Lucas Medal in 1876; 1894 Mus. Bac., Cantab.; 1885 dir. music at Harrow School; c. 3 operettas, cantata for female voices, symphony in C minor, overture, *"The Holiday,"* etc.

Farabi. Vide ALFARABI.

Farina (fä-rē'-nä), **Carlo,** b. Mantua; one of the earliest of violin virtuosos; 1625 court chamber musician at Vienna; c. violin pieces.

Farinel'li, (1) **Carlo Broschi** (brôs'-kē), Naples, June 24, 1705—Bologna, July 15, 1782; famous male soprano; début 1722 at Rome; he sang with the utmost brilliancy and success, being only once overcome by a rival (Bernacchi) from whom he immediately took lessons; he joined the opposition to Händel in London, and Händel went into bankruptcy and took to oratorio. He amassed great wealth and became the chief adviser of Philip V. of Spain; biog. by Sacchi (Venice, 1784). (2) **Giu.,** Este, 1769—Trieste, 1836; org.; c. 60 operas.

Far'jeon, Harry, b. Hohokus, N. J., May 6, 1878; composer; of English parentage, and taken to England in infancy; pupil of Landon Ronald, Storer, and 1895–1901, R. A. M.; prod. operetta *"Floretta,"* 1899; from 1903, prof. of theory at the R. A. M.; c. piano concerto, orch. suite *"Hans Andersen"*; symph. poems, *"Mowgli,"* and *"Summer Vision"*; chamber music, songs, etc.

Farkas (fär'-käsh), **Edmund** (Hung., Ödön), Puszta-Monostor (Heves), Hungary, 1852—Klausenburg, Sept. 1, 1912; important figure in national Hungarian music; of noble family, intended to be a civil engineer; but studied 3 years at the R. Mus. Acad., Pesth; next year became dir. at the Cons. at Klausenburg, Transylvania; was for a time op. cond. and wrote mus. articles; 1876, while still studying engineering, he prod. a 1-act opera *"Bayadér"* (Pesth); won the Haynald prize of 300 florins with a mass; c. also mixed choruses, and the orch. works *"Dawn"* (Virradat), *"Evensong"* (Estidal), *"Twilight"* (Alkony), and *"Dies iræ"*; a pop. symphony and 5 string-quartets; a prize *"Festouvertüre"*; and the operas *"Fairy fountain"* (Tünderhorrás), 1-act (Klausenburg, 1892); *"The Penitent"* (Veseklök) (Pesth, 1893); *"Balassa Balint,"* comic (Pesth, 1896); and *"The Blood-ordeal"* (Tetemre Hivás) (not prod.).

Far'mer, (1) **John,** important English composer of madrigals; author of a treatise pub. 1591, and madrigals, 1599–1602. (2) **Thomas,** d. 1694 (?); composer; graduated at Cambridge, 1684; published songs, stage music, etc., 1675–1695; Purcell wrote an elegy to Nahum Tate's words, on his death. (3) **H.,** Nottingham, England, 1819–1891; violinist and organist. (4) **J.,** Nottingham, Aug. 16, 1836—July, 1901; nephew of above; pupil of Leipzig Cons. and of Spath; teacher in Zurich for some years; 1862–85 mus.-master at Harrow School, then organist at Balliol Coll., Oxford, where he founded a mus. society; edited song-books, etc.; c. an oratorio; a fairy opera; comic cantata; a requiem, etc.

Far'naby, Giles, English composer, ca. 1565—1600 (?).

Far'rant, (1) **John,** English organist, ca. 1600. (2) **John,** English or-

ganist, Salisbury cath., ca. 1600.
(3) **Richard,** d. Nov. 30, 1580;
English organist and notable composer of church-music.

Farrar', Geraldine, b. Melrose, Mass.,
Feb. 28, 1882; soprano; at 12, pupil
of J. H. Long, Boston; later of
Trabadello and Lilli Lehmann; 1901,
début at Berlin Royal Opera; also at
the Op. Com., Paris, and 1906–22,
at the Met. Op. House in N. Y.,
creating the rôle of the Goosegirl
in Humperdinck's "*Königskinder*"
(1910). Her striking dram. and
music. gifts, coupled with charm of
personality, placed her in the front
rank of Amer. singers, and she was
heard widely as a concert and fest.
soloist. She made several successful
silent motion pictures, and also
toured with her own company in a
version of "*Carmen,*" a rôle in which
she had enjoyed favour at the Metropolitan. After retiring from the
stage and later the concert field, she
sang in radio programmes and also
acted as commentator for the Met.
Op. broadcast performances, 1935.

Farrenc (fär-ränk), (1) **Jacq. Hipp, Aristide,** Marseilles, 1794—Paris, 1865;
teacher and composer. (2) **Jeanne
Louise** (née **Dumont**), Paris, 1804–
1875; wife of above, pf.-professor.

Far'well, Arthur, b. St. Paul, Minn.,
April 23, 1872; American composer;
pupil of H. A. Norris, Boston, and of
Humperdinck; founded at Newton
Center, Mass., 1901, the "Wawan
Press" for the artistic pub. of comps.
by Americans, particularly music
based on Indian themes. In 1905 he
established the Amer. Music Soc.
From 1909–15 he was a member of
the staff of "*Musical America*" and
in 1910–13, dir. of municipal concerts
in New York; 1915–18, dir. of Music
School Settlement there; 1918–19,
acting prof., Univ. of Calif. His
comps. include for orch. "*Dawn,*"
"*The Domain of Hurakan,*" "*Navajo War-Dance*" (all on Indian
themes). "*Cornell*" overture, and
"*Love Song*"; for piano many pieces
of Indian theme, and numerous fine
songs.

Fasch (fäsh), (1) **Jn. Fr.,** Buttlestadt,
near Weimar, 1688—Zerbst, 1758;
court-conductor, composer. (2) **K.
Fr. Chr.,** Zerbst, 1736—Berlin, 1800;
cembalist; son of above; conductor.

Faugues, Vincent (or **Fauques, Fa'gus,**

La Fage) (fōg, fōk, lä fäzh), 15th
cent. contrapuntist.

Faure (fōr), **J. Bapt.,** Moulins, Allier,
Jan. 15, 1830—Paris, Nov. 9, 1914;
1841, Paris Cons.; choir-boy at the
Madeleine, and studied with Trevaux; took 1st prize for comic opera;
1852–76, at the Op. Com. as leading
barytone with great succ.; 1857,
teacher in the Cons.; after 1876 sang
in concert; pub. "*L'Art du Chant*";
c. songs, etc.

Fauré (fō-rā), **Gabriel Urbain,** Pamiers,
Ariège, May 13, 1845—Paris, Nov. 4,
1924; eminent French composer;
pupil of Niedermayer, Dietsch, and
Saint-Saëns; 1866, organist at Rennes,
then at St.-Sulpice and St.-Honoré;
1885 took Prix Chartier for chamber
music; 1896 organist at the Madeleine, and prof. of comp., cpt., and
fugue at the Cons. (vice Massenet);
1905–20, he became director; c.
music to "*Prométhée*" (Béziers, 1900),
"*Julius Cæsar*" (1905), "*Pelléas et
Mélisande,*" 1898; arranged as an
orch. suite, 1901; also much chamber
music, and religious choruses, piano
pieces and many highly important
songs; 1-act opera "*L'Organiste*"
(1887); "*La Naissance de Venus,*"
for soli, chorus, and orch.; "*Chœur
de Djinns*"; requiem; symphony;
vln.-concerto; orchestral suite; 2 pf.-
quartets; *Élégie,* for 'cello; *Berceuse
and Romance,* for vln. and orch., a
vln.-sonata, etc.; 1909, elected to
French Académie; 1910, commander,
Legion of Honour. Memoirs pub.
by Séré and Vuillemin.

Fayolle (fī-yôl), **Fran. Jos. M.,** Paris,
1774—1852; mus. biographer and
lexicographer.

Fayr'fax, Robt., Mus. Doc., Cantab.
and Oxon, 1504–11; organist and
composer.

Fechner (fĕkh'-nĕr), **Gv. Th.,** Gross-
Sarchen, Niederlausitz, 1801—Leipzig, 1887; writer.

Fedele (fā-dā'-lĕ). Vide TREU.

Federici (fā-dā-rē'-chē), **V.,** Pesaro,
1764—Milan, 1826; went to London,
where he became cembalist; returned
to Italy in 1803 and prod. many succ.
operas.

Federlein (fā'-dĕr-līn), **Gottfried,** b.
New York, 1883; organist; pupil of
his father, Goetschius and Saar;
active as church organist and recitalist; former Warden, A. G. O.

Fein'berg, Samuel Eugenievitch, b.

Odessa, May 26, 1890; composer; pupil of Jensen and Goldenweiser; grad. of Moscow Cons., as pianist; representative of the more advanced modern Russian school of composition; c. piano works and songs.

Felix (fā-lĕks), Dr. **Hugo,** Vienna, Nov. 19, 1866—Los Angeles, Aug. 24, 1934; c. operettas *"Husarenblut,"* Vienna, 1894; *"Rhodope,"* Berlin, 1900; *"Mme. Sherry"* (Berlin, 1902, with great success in America, 1910).

Fel'lowes, Edmund Horace, b. London, Nov. 11, 1870; author, lecturer, editor; specialist in Elizabethan madrigal; grad. Winchester Coll. and Oriel Coll., Oxford; hon. Mus. D., Trinity Coll., Dublin; dir. Choir of St. George's Chapel, Windsor Castle, 1923–27; has toured Canada as cond. of Westminster Abbey singers, and U. S. as lecturer on Tudor music.

Felstein (fĕl'-shtīn) (called **Felstinen'-sis**), **Sebastian von,** ca. 1530; church-conductor and composer, Cracow.

Fenaroli (fā-nä-rō'-lĕ), **Fedele,** Lanciano, Abruzzi, 1730—Naples, 1818; teacher and composer.

Feo (fā'-ō), **Francesco,** b. Naples, ca. 1685; composer and teacher.

Fer(r)abosco (fĕr-rä-bôs'-kō), (1) **Alfonso,** Italy, 1543—1588; c. madrigals. (2) **Dom. M.,** Rome, 16th cent., member Papal Choir; composer. (3) **Costantino,** court-musician and composer at Vienna, 1591. (4) **Alfonso,** Greenwich, England, ca. 1575—1628; probably son of (1); composer. (5) **John,** d. 1682, **son of** (4); organist Ely Cathedral.

Ferrari, (1) **Benedetto** (called **della Tiorba** "the theorbist") (fĕr-rä'-rĕ dĕl-la tĕ-ôr'-bä), Reggio d'Emilia, 1597 — Modena, 1681; court-conductor and composer and dram. composer. (2) **Domenico,** Piacenza, (?)—Paris, 1780; violinist, conductor and composer. (3) **Carlo,** Piacenza, ca. 1730 —Parma, 1789, bro. of above; 2cellist. (4) **Giacomo Gotifredo,** Roveredo, Tyrol, 1759—London, 1842; cembalist, writer, teacher, and composer. (5) **Francisca,** Christiania, ca. 1800—Gross-Salzbrunn, Silesia, 1828; harpist. (6) **Serafino Amadeo de',** Genoa, 1824—1885; pianist and dram. composer. (7) **Carlotta,** Lodi, Italy, Jan. 27, 1837—Bologna, 1907; pupil of Strepponi and Panzini (1844–50) of Mazzucato at Milan Cons.; wrote text and music of succ.

operas *"Ugo"* (Milan, 1857); *"Sofia"* (Lodi, 1866); *"Eleanora d'Arborea"* (Cagliari, 1871); also masses; a *Requiem for Turin,* 1868, etc. (8) **Gabrielle,** Paris, March 14, 1860 —July 4, 1921; pupil of Ketten, Duprato, later of Gounod and Leborne; at 12 début as pianist, Naples; c. opera *"Le Colzar,"* given at Monte Carlo in one act, enlarged to two (Paris Opéra, 1912); also orch. suites and many popular songs.

Ferrari-Fontan'a, Edoardo, Rome, July 8, 1878—Toronto, Can., July 4, 1936; tenor; early in life entered medical career, later diplomatic service at Italian consulate in Montevideo and Rio de Janeiro; opera début, Turin, 1910, as "Kurwenal" in *"Tristan und Isolde";* sang later in leading Italian theatres, South America, Paris, Boston and New York, with Met. Op. Co. after 1914; m. Margarete Matzenauer, contralto; divorced.

Ferreira (fĕr-rä'-ĕ-rä), **Da Costa, Rodrigo,** 1776—1825; Portuguese writer.

Fer(r)et'ti, Giov., b. Venice, ca. 1540; composer.

Ferri (fĕr'-rē), (1) **Baldassare,** Perugia, 1610—Sept. 8, 1680; one of the most gifted and successful of singers; through a boyhood accident became a male soprano; possessed extraordinary endurance of breath, flexibility of voice, and depth of emotion; at 65 returned to Perugia; on his death left 600,000 crowns for a pious foundation. (2) **Nicolà,** Mola di Bari, Italy, 1831—London, 1886; Naples, singing teacher and dram. composer.

Ferro'ni, V. Emidio Carmine, Tramutola, Italy, Feb. 17, 1858—Milan, Jan. 11, 1934; pupil Paris Cons.; 1st prize in harm. and comp., 1880–83; 1881, asst.-prof. of harm. at the Cons.; 1888 prof. of comp. at Milan Cons., and mus. dir. of the "Famiglia Artistica." 1897, Chevalier of the Ital. Crown; c. operas *"Rudello"* (Milan, 1892); and (text and mus. of) *"Ettore Fieramosca"* (Como, 1896).

Ferroud (fā-rōōd'), **Pierre-Octave,** Chesselay, France, 1900—near Debrecen, Hungary, Aug. 17, 1936 (motor accident); composer; had shown sensitive impressionistic manner in his works; studied with Florent Schmitt; served as critic on various periodicals; c. (orch.) *"Foules,"* perf. with succ. by various

Amer. orchestras; *"Au Parc Monceau"*; Serenade; also a comic opera *"Chirurgie,"* given at Monte Carlo, 1928; ballet, *"Jeunesse,"* etc.

Fes'ca, (1) **Fr. Ernst,** Magdeburg, 1789 —Carlsruhe, 1826; violinist and composer. (2) **Alex. Ernst,** Carlsruhe, May 22, 1820—Brunswick, Feb. 22, 1849; son of above; brilliant pianist and dram. composer.

Fes'ta, (1) **Costanzo,** Rome, ca. 1490 —April 10, 1545; singer and contrapuntist. (2) **Giu. M.,** Trani, 1771— Naples, 1839; violinist, conductor and composer. (3) **Francesca,** Naples, 1778—St. Petersburg, 1836; operatic singer; m. Maffei.

Fest'ing, Michael Christian, London, ca. 1700—1752; son of a flutist, of same name; conductor, violinist, and composer.

Fétis (fā-tēs), (1) **François Joseph,** Mons, Belgium, March 25, 1784— Brussels, March 26, 1871; indefatigable scholar and historian; he worked 16-18 hours a day; his father, organist and conductor at the Cathedral, was his first teacher; he learned the vln., and c. at 9 a concerto for vln. and orch.; the same year became organist to the Noble Chapter of Saint Waudra; 1800-03 in the Paris Cons.; 1803, Vienna, for study of fugue, and master-work of German music; here began an investigation of Guido d'Arezzo's system and the history of notation. 1804 he started a short-lived mus. periodical. 1806 he began the 30 years' task (still unpub.) of revising the plain-song and entire ritual of the Roman Church. He m. a wealthy woman, and was enabled to pursue his studies comfortably till 1811, when her fortune was lost. He returned to the Ardennes and made researches into harmony, which led to his formulating the modern theory of tonality. 1813, organist and teacher at Douai; wrote *"La Science de l'Organist,"* and *"Méthode élémentaire d'harmonie et d'accompagnement."* 1818, Paris, where he prod. various operas with succ. 1821, prof. of comp. at the Cons., later librarian. 1827-35 founded and edited *"La Revue Musicale."* In 1832 began historical lectures and concerts. 1833, cond. to King Leopold I., Brussels, and for 39 years dir. of the Cons. there, and 1845 member of the Belgian

Academy. On his wedding-jubilee a Mass of his was sung, and his bust was unveiled. In 1806, he began collecting and preparing for his great *"Biographie universelle des musiciens et bibliographie générale de la musique"* in 8 volumes (1837-1844). This invaluable monument is, like everything else of its kind, bristling inevitably with error, bias, and excess; yet is a standard of highest repute. Pub. many treatises and c. 6 operas (1820-32); 2 symphonies, an overture for orch.; masses, a requiem, motets, etc. Biog. in his Dictionary by L. Alvin (Brussels, 1874); and Gollmick (Leipzig, 1852). (2) **Ed. L. Fran.,** Bouvignes, near Dinant, May 16, 1812—Brussels, Jan. 31, 1909; son of above; editor; for years libr. Brussels Library; pub. *"Les musiciens Belges"* (1848). (3) **Adolphe L. Eugène,** Paris, 1820— 1873; son and pupil of (1); pianist, teacher and dram. composer.

Feuermann (foi'-ĕr-män), **Emanuel,** b. Kolomea, Poland, Nov. 22, 1902; 'cellist; pupil of Anton Walter and Julius Klengel; concert début at age of 11; at 17 appointed teacher at Cologne Cons., where he was active until 1923; solo 'cellist with Gürzenich Orch. and mem. Gürzenich Quartet; later res. in Vienna; taught Berlin Hochsch.; solo 'cellist in Philh. Orch. in that city; has made world tours with succ., incl. U. S., where made début in recital and as soloist with N. Y. Philh., 1935-36.

Feurich (foi'-rĭkh), **Julius,** Leipzig, 1821—1900; founded pf. factory, 1851.

Fevin (fū-văṅ), **Ant. (Antonius) de,** ca. 1473—1515 (?); Netherlandish (?) contrapuntist; contemporary with Josquin Deprès, and rated second only to him. (2) **Robert (Robertus),** Cambrai, 15th cent.; c. masses.

Février (fāv'-rē-ā), (1) **Henri Louis,** Abbeville—Paris, ca. 1780; composer of clavecin music, of which he pub. 2 collections in 1734 and 1755. (2) **Henry,** b. Paris, 1875; composer; pupil of H. Woollett and the Paris Cons., studying with Pugno, Leroux and Massenet; also privately with Messager; his first compositions were chamber music, incl. a piano trio and sonata for vln. and piano; he has also written pieces for the latter instrument, choruses and songs, but is chiefly known for his operas, among which are "*Le Roi aveugle*" (Paris, 1906), "*Monna Vanna*" after Maeterlinck (Paris, 1909), "*Gismonda*," taken from Sardou drama (Chicago, 1919), and a number of operettas.

Fiala (fē'-ä-lä), **Jos.**, Lobkowitz, Bohemia, 1749—Donauchingen, 1816; oboist, 'cellist, composer, and conductor.

Fibich (fē'bǐkh), **Zdenko**, Seborschitz, Bohemia, Dec. 21, 1850—Prague, Oct. 15, 1900; pupil at Prague, Leipzig Cons. (1865), and of Lachner; 1876 asst. cond. at the National Th., Prague; 1878, dir. Russian Church Choir; notable Czech dram. composer. Prod. at Prague 6 operas incl. "*Sarka*" (1898); c. the symphonic poems "*Othello*," "*Zaboj and Slavoj*," "*Toman and the Nymph*," and "*Vesna*"; "*Lustspiel Ouvertüre*," etc. "*A Night on Kaarlstein*," and other overtures.

Fiby (fē'-bē), **Heinrich**, Vienna, May 15, 1834—Znaim, Oct. 23, 1917; pupil of the Cons.; from 1857 city mus. dir., Znaim; founded a music-school and a society; c. 3 operettas; pop. male choruses, etc.

Fiebach (fē'-bäkh), **Otto**, b. Ohlau, Silesia, Feb. 9, 1851—Königsberg, 1937; mus. dir., Königsberg University; royal conductor; c. operas, and an oratorio; author of "*Die Physiologie der Tonkunst*" (1891).

Fiedler (fēt'-lĕr), (1) **August Max**, b. Zittau, Dec. 31, 1859; piano pupil of his father, and studied organ and theory with G. Albrecht; 1877–80 Leipzig Cons.; won the Holstein Scholarship; 1882 teacher, Hamburg Cons.; in 1903, became director of the Hamburg Cons.; 1904 cond. the Philharmonic concerts; 1908–12, cond. Boston Symphony Orchestra with great success during the leave of absence of Karl Muck (q. v.), c. 'cello sonata (Boston, 1909), chamber music, etc.; 1916–33, he was dir. of music in Essen. (2) **Arthur**, b. Boston, Dec. 17, 1894; studied Berlin R. Acad. of Mus.; after 1930, cond. Boston "Pop" Concerts; teacher Boston Univ.

Field (1) **John**, Dublin, July 26, 1782—Moscow, Jan. 11, 1837; a great though gentle revolutionist of music, to whom much of Chopin's glory belongs, for Field developed the more lyric manner of pf.-playing and carried it into his composition, in which he gave the piano-song or poem its first escape from the old stiff forms. He created the Nocturne, and many of his comps. in this form have practically every quality and mannerism characteristic of those of Chopin, who excelled him in passion, resource, and harmonic breadth. He was the son of a violinist, and grandson and pupil of an organist, who compelled him to practise so hard that he ran away, but was brought back and later was apprenticed to Clementi as a salesman. He also had lessons from C., and went with him to Paris in 1802, making a great stir with his interpretation of Bach's and Händel's fugues; he was kept at his salesman's tasks till 1804, when he settled at St. Petersburg as a teacher and pianist of great vogue. After touring Russia, in London, 1832, he played a concerto of his own at the Philh.; then to Paris; 1833 Belgium, Switzerland, Italy, where he was not a succ. Intemperance and fistula kept him nine months in a Naples hospital; whence he was rescued by a Russian family Raemanow and taken to Moscow, playing in Vienna with greatest succ.; but his health was lost and he died a few years later and was buried in Moscow. Besides 20 nocturnes (of which only 12 were so named by Field) he c. 7 concertos (No. 4 in E flat the most popular); 4 sonatas; "*Air russe*"; "*Air russe varié*" (4 hands); "*Chanson russe varié*," in D min.; polonaise, "*Reviens, reviens*." Romanza and Cavatina in E; 4 romances; 7 rondeaux; rondeau with 2 vlns., viola, and bass; variation in C; 2 divertissements with 2 vlns., viola and bass; 2 fantasias; and pf.-exercises in all keys. (2) **Henry**, "Field of Bath," Dec. 6, 1797—May 19, 1848; pianist and teacher.

Fielitz (fōn fē'-lǐts), **Alexander von**, Leipzig, Dec. 28, 1860—Bad Salzungen, July 29, 1930; pupil in Dresden of J. Schulhoff (pf.) and Kretschmer (comp.); he became opera-cond. in Zürich, Lübeck, and Leipzig (City Th.); a nervous disorder compelled his retirement; lived in Italy as a composer of choruses, orch. pcs., songs, which attained popularity. 1906–08, cond. and teacher, Chicago;

taught Stern Cons., Berlin (dir. 1915).

Filippi (fē-lǐp′-pǐ) (1) **Giu. de**, Milan, 1825—Neuilly, near Paris, 1887; writer. (2) **Filippo**, Vicenza, 1830 —Milan, 1887; critic, writer, and composer.

Fil′ke, Max, Staubendorf-Leobschütz, Silesia, Oct. 5, 1855—Breslau, Oct. 8, 1911; organist and singing teacher; pupil of Brosig and Leipzig Cons.; 1891, cathedral cond. at Breslau, teacher 1893 at the Royal Inst. for Church music; 1899, Royal Music director; c. several masses with orch.; choruses, etc.

Fill′more, J. Comfort, Franklin, Conn., 1843—1898; studied at Oberlin (O.) Coll., and Leipzig Cons.; 1884–95 founder and dir. of Sch. of Mus. in Milwaukee; then mus. dir. Pomona Coll., Claremont, Cal.; pub. "*A Study of Omaha Indian Music*" (with Miss Fletcher and F. La Flesche; Peabody Museum, 1893); and other treatises; tr. Riemann's works.

Finck (fǐnk), (1) **Heinrich**, 1482, conductor to John Albert I., Cracow; eminent contrapuntist. (2) **Hermann**, Pirna, Saxony, 1527—Wittenburg, 1558, grand-nephew of above; composer and writer. (3) **Henry Theophilus**, Bethel, Missouri, Sept. 22, 1854—Rumford Falls, Minn., Sept. 29, 1926; prominent American critic and essayist; influential advocate of Wagner; lived in Oregon, then (1876) graduate of Harvard, having studied theory and hist. of mus. with J. K. Paine; 1876, attended the first Bayreuth festival, and studied at Munich; pub. the valuable "*Wagner and His Works*" (N. Y., 1893, 2 vols., Germ. transl., Breslau, 1897); 1877–78, studied anthropology at Harvard; received a Fellowship and spent 3 years at Berlin, Heidelberg, and Vienna, studying comparative psychology and sending mus. letters to N. Y. "*Nation*"; and for some 40 years was mus.-ed. of the N. Y. "*Evening Post*"; pub. "*Chopin, and other Mus. Essays*," "*Paderewski and His Art*," "*Songs and Song-Writers*" (1901); "*The Pictorial Wagner*," "*Anton Seidl*," "*Grieg and His Music*," "*Success in Music*," "*Massenet and His Operas*," "*Richard Strauss*"; also four collections of songs; 3 books of

travel: "*Pacific Coast Scenic Tour*," "*Lotos-time in Japan*," "*Spain and Morocco*"; "*Romantic Love and Personal Beauty*," "*Primitive Love and Love Stories*" (1900), etc.

Findeisen (fǐnt′-ī-zĕn), **Otto**, b. Brünn, Dec. 23, 1862; theat. conductor in Magdeburg and Leipzig, prod. succ. operetta "*Der Alte Dessauer*" (Magdeburg, 1890); and the succ. folk-opera "*Henings von Treffenfeld*" (ib. 1891).

Finger (fǐng′-ĕr), **Gf.**, b. Olmütz, Bavaria; in England, 1685–1701; then chamber-mus. to queen of Prussia, till 1717.

Fink, (1) **Gf. Wm.**, Sulza, Thuringia, 1783—Halle, 1846; editor, writer, and composer. (2) **Chr.**, Dettingen, Würtemberg, Aug. 9, 1831—Esslingen, Sept. 5, 1911; pupil Esslingen Seminary; Leipzig Cons., and Schneider, Dresden; till 1860 lived as organist and teacher, Leipzig; then teacher and organist, Esslingen, and prof. in 1862; composer.

Fink′enstein (shtīn), **Jettka**, b. Seni, Russia, March 22, 1865; alto; studied at Berlin Hochschule, and with Viardot Garcia; 1st. alto at Darmstadt ct.-theatre till 1891, then toured; lived in Breslau.

Fioravanti (fē-ôr-ä-vän′-tē), (1) **Valentino**, Rome, 1764—Capua, June 16, 1837; opera-cond. and composer. (2) **Vincenzo**, Rome, 1799—Naples, 1877, son of above; conductor and dram. composer.

Fiore (fǐ-ō′-rě), **Andrea Stefano**, Milan, 1675—Turin, 1739; composer of operas.

Fiorillo (fē-ô-rǐl′-lō), (1) **Ignazio**, Naples, 1715—Fritzlar, near Cassel, 1787; court-conductor and composer. (2) **Federigo**, b. Brunswick, 1753 (?): son and pupil of above; viola player and composer.

Fiqué (fē-kā), **Karl**, Bremen, 1861— Brooklyn, N. Y., Dec., 1930; pupil of Leipzig Cons.; lived in Brooklyn, N. Y.; pianist and composer.

Fischer (fǐsh′-ĕr), (1) **Johann Kaspar Ferdinand**, ca. 1650—1746; important composer for organ and clavier; cond. to Markgraf Ludwig in Bohemia, 1688. (2) **Jn. Chr.**, Freiburg, Baden, 1733—London, 1800; oboist and composer. (3) **K. Aug.**, Ebersdorf, Saxony, 1828— Dresden, 1892; organist. (4) **Emil**, Brunswick, Germany, 1838—Hamburg, 1914; notable German basso in Wagnerian rôles; début 1849; sang at Met. Op., N. Y., 1885-98; 1899 m. Camille Seygard; divorced 1902. (5) **Edwin,** b. Basel, Oct. 6, 1886; pianist; pupil of Basel Cons., and Stern. Cons., Berlin, where he taught from 1905 to 1914; since then has toured as concert pianist, having esp. rank as performer of Bach and Beethoven; also has conducted and c. songs and piano works; ed. Bach's piano works.

Fischhof (fĭsh'-ôf), **Jos.,** Butschowitz, Moravia, 1804—Vienna, 1857; prof., composer and writer.

Fish'er, (1) **John A.,** b. Dunstable, 1774, pf.- and organ-virtuoso; violinist and composer. (2) **Wm. Arms,** b. San Francisco, April 27, 1861; pupil of J. P. Morgan (org. and pf.), H. W. Parker, and Dvořák, New York; also studied singing in London; from 1897, ed. and mgr. Oliver Ditson Co., Boston; composer. (3) **Susanne,** b. West Virginia; soprano; grad. Cincinnati Cons.; studied at Juilliard Grad. School, N. Y.; heard with Little Theatre Op. Co. in New York; sang at Berlin State Op., début as "Butterfly"; later at Paris Op.-Comique; début, Met. Op. Co., N. Y., 1935.

Fissot (fĭs-sō) **Alexis Henri,** Airaines (Somme), 1843—Paris, 1896; pf.- and organ-virtuoso and composer.

Fitelberg (fē'-tĕl-bĕrkh), (1) **Georg,** b. Dünaburg, Oct. 18, 1879; important Polish composer; pupil Warsaw Cons., taking Paderewski prize with a violin sonata, 1896, and 1901 the Zamoyski prize with a piano trio; concertmaster, and 1908 conductor Warsaw Philharmonic; 1912, engaged for 6 years to cond. Vienna Royal Opera; later cond. in England and Russia; c. 2 symphonies, orch.; chamber music, songs, etc. (2) **Jerzy,** b. Warsaw, May 20, 1903; composer; pupil of Schreker; won Coolidge Prize, 1936, for 4th str. qt.

Flagstad (fläg'-shtät), **Kirsten,** b. Oslo, Norway; dramatic soprano; her father an orchestral conductor, her mother a well-known pianist and coach; received her training from the latter; early designed for medical career, but at 15 began voice study; made début at Oslo when 18; engaged for Gothenburg Op. Co.; for a time retired from singing on marriage to Henry Johansen, industrial-

ist; consented to sing at Oslo as substitute for indisposed artist, and her succ. led to permanent engagement at the Op. there; had sung entirely in Scandinavian countries before engagement at Bayreuth, 1933-34; was offered Berlin contract but declined it; engaged for Met. Op. Co. and made début in 1934-35 season as "Sieglinde" with sensational effect, and at once became celebrated in New York for her "Isolde," "Brünnhilde," "Elsa," etc.; next season also sang in "Fidelio"; Covent Garden début, spring of 1936, as "Isolde," the three Brünnhildes; also a high-ranking concert singer.

Flecha (flĕ'-chä), (1) **Juan,** music teacher; Catalonia, 1483-1553; Carmelite monk and teacher; his nephew (2) **Fray Matheo,** 1520—Feb. 20, 1604, was an abbot and cond. to Charles V. at Prague; both were composers.

Flégier (flā-zhä), **Ange,** Marseilles, Feb. 25, 1846—Oct. 8, 1927; pupil of Marseilles Cons. and Paris Cons. 1870; returned to Marseilles; c. 1-act comic opera, "Fatima" (Mars. 1875), "Ossian" and "Françoise de Rimini," cantata, with orch., etc.

Fleischer (flī'-shĕr), (1) **Reinhold,** Dabsau, Silesia, April 12, 1842— Görlitz, Feb. 1, 1904; pupil of the R. Inst. for Church-music, and R. Akademie, at Berlin; 1870, organist at Görlitz and dir. Singakademie; 1885, Royal Mus. Dir.; c. a cantata, "Holda," etc. (2) **Oskar,** Zörbig, Nov. 1, 1856—Berlin, Feb. 8, 1923; studied in Italy on govt. stipend; pupil and, since 1896, successor of Spitta as Prof. Extraordinary, at the Berlin Univ., also custodian of the Royal Coll. of Mus. Instrs., and teacher of history at the Hochschule für Musik; pub. a study of neumes, 1895, etc. (3) **Fleischer-Edel** (ā'-dĕl), **Katharina,** Mülheim, Sept. 27, 1873—Dresden, July 17, 1928; soprano; studied with Iffert; sang at court-opera, Dresden.

Flem'ming, Fr. Fd., Neuhausen, Saxony, 1778—Berlin, 1813; c. pop. "Integer vitæ," etc.

Flesch, Carl, b. Moson, Hungary, Oct. 9, 1873; eminent violinist; pupil of Grün at Vienna, and Marsick at Paris Cons.; in 1897-1902 prof. at Bucharest Cons.; and chamber musician to the Roumanian queen; 1903-8, teacher at Amsterdam Cons.;

1925 at Curtis Inst., Phila.; later taught in Baden-Baden, London, etc.; author of vln. method.

Fleta (flä'-tä), **Miguel**, Albalete, 1897—Corunna, 1938; Spanish tenor; studied Barcelona Cons.; sang Met. Op. 1923-4, also widely in Europe.

Floridia (flō-rēd'-yä), (**Baron Napolino**), Modica, Sicily, March 5, 1860—New York, Aug. 16, 1932; pianist, pupil of S. Pietro a Majello, Naples; while there he pub. succ. pf.-pcs.; prod. succ. comic opera *"Carlotta Clepier"* (Naples, 1882), retired for 3 years to Sicily; toured 1885–86; 1888-90, prof. of pf. Palermo Cons.; 1889, his symphony won 1st prize of the Soc. del Quartetto, Milan; w. text and music of succ. opera *"Maruzza"* (Venice, 1894). He came to America in 1904, was for a year piano-prof. at Cincinnati Cons., and was commissioned to write the opera *"Paoletta,"* for the Exposition of 1910; after 1913 he lived in N. Y. where he cond. Italian Symph.; c. (with Luigi Illica) *"La Colonia Libera," "Festouvertüre,"* opera *"The Scarlet Letter," "Madrigal"* for barytone and orch., songs, etc.

Florimo (flō'-rĭ-mō), **Fran.**, San Giorgio Morgeto, Calabria, 1800—Naples, 1888; writer, teacher, and composer.

Flo'rio, Caryl, pen-name of **Wm. Jas. Robjohn.**

Flotow (flō'-tō), **Friedrich**, Freiherr von, Teutendorf, Mecklenburg, April 27, 1812—Darmstadt, Jan. 24, 1883; composer of 2 extremely popular and melodious, also extremely light, operas; son of a landed nobleman; studied composition with Reicha, Paris; he fled from the July Revolution to Mecklenburg, where he c. 2 operettas; returning to Paris, he prod. *"Séraphine,"* 1836, *"Rob Roy,"* and the succ. *"Le Naufrage de la Méduse,"* 1839 (given Hamburg, 1845, as *"Die Matrosen"*), in which he collaborated with Paloti and Grisan; 3 later works failed, incl. the ballet *"Lady Harriet"* (Opéra, 1843); afterwards rewritten with great succ. as *"Martha"* (Vienna, 1847). *"Alessandro Stradella"* (Hamburg, 1844; rewritten from a "pièce lyrique," *"Stradella,"* Paris, 1837), made his name in Germany. He fled from the March Revolution (1848), and prod. *"Die Gross-fürstin"* (Berlin, 1853), and *"Indra"* (Berlin Opera,

1850); 3 later works failed. 1856–63, he was intendant of court-music, Schwerin, and c. a "Torch-Dance" and excellent music to Shakespeare's *"Winter's Tale"*; 1863–68, he prod. 2 operettas, 2 operas, and 2 ballets, without succ.; 1868, he retired to one of his estates, near Vienna, made visits to Vienna, Paris, Italy; 1870, *"L'Ombre"* (Paris, Op. Com., 1870; prod. in London, 1878, as the *"Phantom"*) was very succ.; *" Naïda"* (Milan, 1873) and *"Il Fior d'Harlem"* (Turin, 1876) were revisions, and he rewrote *"Indra"* as *"l'Enchanteresse"* (Paris and London, 1878); Italy, *"Alma l'Incantatrice"*; Germany *"Die Hexe"*; after his death *"Rosellana,"* *"Der Graf Saint-Mégrin"* (Cologne, 1884), and *"Die Musikanten"* (Hanover, 1887) were produced.

Flügel (flü'-gĕl), (1) **Gustav**, Nienburg-on-Saale, July 2, 1812—Stettin, 1900; cantor, organist, writer, and composer. (2) **Ernest Paul**, Stettin, Aug. 31, 1844—Breslau, Oct. 20, 1912; son and pupil of above; studied at the R. Inst. for Church-music, and the Akademie, Berlin; private pupil of von Bülow; 1867, organist and teacher at the Prenzlau Gymnasium; in 1879, cantor, Breslau, and founded a singing soc.; 1901, gained title of professor; writer and composer.

Fo'dor, (1) **Jos.**, Venloo, 1752—1828, violinist and composer. (2) **Josephine**, b. Paris, 1793; soprano; retired, 1833; daughter of above; m. the actor Mainvielle.

Foerster (fĕr'-shtĕr), **Ad. Martin**, Pittsburgh, Pa., Feb. 2, 1854—Aug. 10, 1927; American composer; pupil of his mother and of Leipzig Cons.; 1875–76, teacher at Ft. Wayne (Ind.), Cons., then Pittsburgh as a teacher of singing and pf.; c. orch., chamber music, choruses, songs, etc.

Fogg, Eric, b. Feb. 21, 1903 at Manchester—London, Sept. 4, 1941; studied with his father (a well-known organist) and Bantock; c. orch., chamber, piano music, songs, etc.

Foggia (fôd'-jä), **Fran.**, Rome, 1605-1688, composer and conductor.

Fogliani (fōl-yä'-nē), (1) **Ludovico**, Modena, ca. 1490—ca. 1559, theorist and composer. (2) **Giacomo**, Modena, 1473—April 4, 1548; brother of **Ludovico F.**, organist and comp.

Földesy (fŭl'-dě-shē), **Arnold**, b. Budapest, Dec. 20, 1882; 'cellist, succ. in London, 1902; son of a military bandman at Budapest; pupil of Popper.

Fo'ley ("Signor Foli"), **Allan Jas.,** Cahir, Tipperary, Ireland, 1835—Southport, England, Oct. 20, 1899; concert and operatic bass.

Folville (fôl-vē'-yŭ), (**Eugénie Émilie**) **Juliette**, b. Liége, Jan. 5, 1870; brilliant pianist, violinist, teacher, conductor and composer; pupil of her father, a distinguished lawyer; studied vln. with Malherbes, Musin, and César Thomson; in 1879, début at Liége as concert-violinist; frequently directed her own orchestral works; annually conducted at Liége Cons. a concert of ancient music, and gave clavecin-recitals; prod. 1893, succ. opera *"Atala",* (Lille, 1892; Rouen, 1893); 1898, pf. prof. at Liége Cons.; c. orchestral suites: *"Scènes champêtres, de la mer, d'hiver,"* etc.

Fontana (fôn-tä'-nä), **Giov. Bat.,** d. Brescia, 1630; composer.

Foote, Arthur Wm., Salem, Mass., March 5, 1853—Boston, April 9, 1937; composer; pupil of B. J. Lang (pf.), S. A. Emery, and J. K. Paine (comp.) 1875, A. M. Harvard (for mus.); 1878–1910, organist of the first Unitarian Ch., Boston; pub. overture, *"In the Mountains,"* symphonic prologue, *"Francesca da Rimini,"* 'cello concerto; orch. suite and choral works, *"Farewell of Hiawatha,"* *"The Wreck of the Hesperus,"* and *"The Skeleton in Armour"*; pf.-quintet, quartet in C; pf.-trio in C min.; sonata for pf., and vln.; 2 string-quartets; pcs. for vln. and 'cello; orch. suite in D minor (played in Boston, London, N. Y., etc.) Suite for strings (do.); 4 character pieces for orch. (Thomas Orch., Boston Symph., 1912, etc.) "Bedouin Song," male chorus sung very widely; organ suite in D (played by Guilmant on American tour); two piano suites, 5 poems from Omar Khayyám for piano, songs, etc.

Forchhammer (fôrkh'-häm-měr), **Th.,** Schiers, Gray Cantons, July 29, 1847—Magdeburg, Aug. 1, 1923; pupil of Stuttgart Cons.; 1885, organist at Magdeburg Cath.; 1888 Royal Mus. Dir.; writer and composer.

Ford, Thos., England, ca. 1580—1648; composer and writer.

For'kel, Jn. Nikolaus, Meeder, near Coburg, 1749—Göttingen, 1818; historian, organist, harpist, and teacher. Wrote biography of Bach, 1803.

For'mes, (1) **K. Jos.,** Mülheim-on-Rhine, 1816—San Francisco, 1889; operabass. (2) **Theodor,** Mülheim, 1826—Endenich, near Bonn, 1874; tenor, bro. of above.

Formschneider (fôrm'-shnī'-děr). Vide GRAPHÄUS.

Fornari (fôr-nä'-rē), **V.,** Naples, May 11, 1848—Aug., 1900; pupil of Sira (pf.) and Battista (comp.); c. operas, *"Maria di Torre"* (Naples, 1872), *"Salammbo,"* *"Zuma"* (Naples, 1881), and 1-act opera-seria *"U Dramma in Vendemmia"* (Florence, 1896), succ.

Fornia, Rita (P. Newman), San Francisco, July 17, 1879—Paris, Oct. 27, 1922; soprano; pupil of Jean de Reszké and Frau Kempner; début, 1901, Hamburg Stadttheater; sang at Covent Garden and Met. Op., N. Y.

Forsell', John, b. Stockholm, Nov. 6, 1868—Sept. 4, 1941; barytone; studied at Cons. in native city with Günther; mem. R. Op. there, also guest appearances in Paris, Berlin, and (1909–10) at Met. Op., N. Y., a notable exponent of Mozart rôles; also known as concert singer; after 1913 he was dir. of the Stockholm Op.

Forster (fôr'-shtĕr), **G.,** (1) Amberg (?)—Nürnberg, 1568; editor and coll. (2) **G. (II),** d. Dresden, 1587; double-bass; conductor. (3) **Nikolaus** (called **Fortius**), 1499—1535; contrapuntist. (4) (or **Förster**) **Kaspar,** Danzig, 1617—1673; composer, theorist and conductor. (5) **Wm.** (Sr.), Brampton, Cumberland, 1739—London, 1808; vln.-maker; his son and successor was (6), **Wm.,** London, 1764—1824.

För'ster (fĕr'-shtĕr), (1) v. FORSTER (4). (2) **Chr.,** Bebra, Thuringia, 1693—Rudolstadt, 1745; organist, conductor and composer. (3) **Emanuel Aloys,** Neurath, Austrian Silesia, 1748—Vienna, 1823; theorist and composer. (4) **Jos.,** Osojnitz, Bohemia, Feb. 22, 1833—Prague, Jan. 3, 1907; noted organist in various churches; since 1887, Prague Cath.; prof. of theory, Prague Cons.; c. masses and requiems, org.-pcs;

wrote a treatise on harmony. (5) Vide FOERSTER. (6) **Alban**, Reichenbach, Saxony, Oct. 23, 1849—Neustrelitz, Jan. 18, 1916; violinist; pupil R. Blume, later of Dresden Cons.; leader at Carlsbad, Breslau, Stettin; 1871, court mus., and cond. Neustrelitz, 1881, teacher in Dresden. (7) **Josef B.**, b. Prague, Sept. 30, 1859; son of (4); pupil of Prague Cons.; c. 5 operas, 2 symphonies, chamber music, etc.; critic, teacher.

Fortlage (fôrt′-lä-gĕ), **K.**, Osnabruck, 1806—Jena, 1881; writer.

Förtsch (fĕrtsh), **Jn. Ph.**, Wertheim, Franconia, 1652—Eutin, 1732; conductor, singer, and dram. composer.

Fos′ter, (1) **Stephen Collins**, Lawrenceville (Pittsburgh), Pa., July 4, 1826—New York, Jan. 13, 1864; chiefly self-taught as flageolet-player and composer; a writer of words and music of genuine American folk-song; he enjoyed enormous vogue, receiving $500 for the privilege of singing "Old Folks at Home" (or "Suwanee River"); died poor in the Bowery; c. 160 songs, incl. "My Old Kentucky Home," "Nellie Was a Lady," and many war-songs; his melody, though simple, was rarely banal and has elements of immortality. (2) **(Myles) Birket**, London, Nov. 29, 1851—Dec. 18, 1922; organist and composer; pupil of Hamilton Clarke, and at R. A. M. of Sullivan, Prout, and Westlake; 1873–74, organist at Haweis′ Church; 1880–92, at the Foundling Hospital; then mus.-ed. for Boosey & Co.; c. 2 Evening Services; symphony, "Isle of Arran"; overtures, etc. (3) **Muriel**, Sunderland, Nov. 22, 1877—London, Dec. 23, 1937; contralto of remarkable range, g to b′′ flat; pupil of Anna Williams at the R. A. M., winning a scholarship, 1897; début 1896 in oratorio; sang with her sister **Hilda** in 1899; and at festivals; also in Germany, Russia and America.

Foulds, John, b. Manchester, Nov. 2, 1880—Calcutta, April, 1939; conductor; early played in Hallé Orch.; after 1921, dir. of Univ. of London Mus. Soc.; c. stage music, orch. and piano works.

Fourdrain (fōōr′-drăn), **Félix**, Paris, Feb. 3, 1880—Oct. 23, 1923; composer; studied with Widor at Cons., organist in several Paris churches; made esp. succ. with his lighter operatic works; c. (stage works) "La Grippe"; "Echo" (1906); "La Légende de Point d'Argentan" (1907); also heard in America at Ravinia Op.; "La Glaneuse" (1909); "Vercingétorix" (1912); "Madame Roland" (1913); "Les Contes de Perrault" (1913); well known for his art-songs.

Fournier (foorn-yā), (1) **P. Simon**, Paris, 1712—1768; introducer of round-headed notes, and writer on history of music-types. (2) **Émile Eugène Alex.**, Paris, 1864—Joinville-le-Pont, 1897; pupil of Délibes and Dubois at Cons.; 1891 took 2d Grand prix de Rome, and 1892 Prix Cressent, for 1-act opera "Stratonice" (Gr. Opéra, Paris, 1892); c. opera "Carloman," etc.

Fox, Félix, b. Breslau, Germany, May 25, 1876; pianist, pedagogue; brought to Boston as a child; studied there, in N. Y., and after 1892 at Leipzig with Reinecke and Jadassohn, also with Philipp in Paris; début, Leipzig, 1896; Paris in 1897; same year returned to U. S., giving concerts; and in 1898 (with Carlo Buonamici) founded school of piano in Boston that continued under his own name for more than three decades; officier of French Académie.

Fox-Strang'ways, Arthur Henry, Norwich, England, Sept. 14, 1859; noted critic, writer on music; studied Wellington Coll., and Balliol, Oxford, also at Berlin Hochsch.; dir. of music, Wellington Coll., 1893-1901; visited India and wrote "The Music of Hindustan"; in 1920 he founded the quarterly periodical, "Music and Letters"; was critic of London "Times" after 1911 and co-editor of the London "Mercury."

Fragerolle (frä-zhĕ-rŭl), **Georges Auguste**, Paris, March 11, 1855—Feb. 21, 1920; pupil of Guiraud; c. patriotic songs, operettas, pantomimes, etc.

Framery (frăm-rē), **Nicolas Ét.**, 1745—Paris, 1810; writer.

Fran'çaix, Jean, b. Mans, May 23, 1912; composer.

Franchetti (frän-kĕt'-tē), (1) **Alberto** (Baron); b. Turin, Sept. 18, 1850; pupil of N. Coccon and F. Magi; then of Draeseke, and at the Munich Cons.; 1926, dir. of Cherubini Cons., Florence; prod. "dram. legend" "Asraële" (Brescia, 1888); opera,

"Cristoforo Colombo" (Genoa, 1892), *"Fior d'Alpe"* (Milan, 1894), *"Il Signor di Pourceaugnac"* (Milan, 1897), all succ.; his opera *"Germania"* (prod. Milan, 1902) has been performed widely, at Covent Garden 1907 and 1911 at the Metropolitan Opera House, N. Y.; also *"La Figlia di Jorio"* (1906), *" Notte di Leggenda"* (1914); (with Giordano) *"Giove a Pompei"* (1921); *"Glauco"* (1922), etc.

Franchinus (frän-kē'-noos). Vide GAFORIO.

Franchi-Verney (frän'-kē-věr'-nä), Giu. Ip., Conte della Valetta; Turin, Feb. 17, 1848—Rome, May 15, 1911; 1874 gave up law for music; 1875-77 under the pen-name "Ippolito Valetta" contributed to various papers; 1889, m. Teresina Tua; c. succ. lyric sketch *"Il Valdese"* (Turin, 1885), and succ. ballet, *"Il Mulatto"* (Naples, 1896).

Franchomme (frän-shŭm), **Auguste,** Lille, April 10, 1808—Paris, Jan. 21, 1884; 'cellist; teacher at the Cons. and composer.

Franck (fränk), (1) **Melchior,** Zittau, ca. 1573—Coburg, June 1, 1639; from 1603 court-cond. at Coburg; a prolific and important c. of secular and church-music, a pioneer in improving instrumental accompaniment; two of his chorales *"Jerusalem, das hochgebaute Stadt,"* and *"Wenn ich Todesnöthen bin,"* are still sung; he is said to have written the text for many hymns. (2) **Jn. W.,** Hamburg, 1641—London, ca. 1696; opera-cond.; c. 14 operas. (3) (frän) **César Auguste,** Liége, Dec. 10, 1822 —Paris, Nov. 8, 1890; important and influential Belgian composer; pupil Liége Cons., then of Paris Cons., where he took 1st prize for piano, and 2d for comp., also succeeding his organ-teacher, Benoist, as prof. there in 1872, and as organist at Ste. Clothilde; c. a notable symph. poem with chorus *"Les béatitudes,"* symph. poems *"Le chasseur maudit,"* *"Psyché"* and *"Les Eolides"*; a universally popular symphony in D minor, a succ. com. opera *"Hulda"* (Monte Carlo, 1894), 2 oratorios, an unfinished opera *"Ghisella,"* a sonata for pf. and vln.; quintet for piano and strings; pf.-pcs.; organ-music, songs, etc.; biog. by Derepas (Paris, '97), Destranges, the superb volume of Vincent d'Indy, one of the best estimates; and other studies by Coquard, Meyer, Garnier, Baldensperger, Canudo, Van den Borren, Séré, de Rudder, etc.

A peculiarly lovable figure in music, F. has gained a great discipleship since his death both among musicians and the general public. His modesty and nobility of soul were allied with a highly original musical equipment, in which the sensuous and mystical elements are balanced by a strong sense of form. He entirely revolutionised the pattern of French instrumental music by reviving the polyphony which had long ceased to be a prominent factor in it; his harmonic modulations were also much freer than those previously in vogue in France. Through his disciple, d'Indy, he set in motion a whole school of "Franckists," who were opposed in aim to the extreme modernists who took their start from Debussy. These two tendencies are still warring in French music. (See article, page 496.) (4) **Eduard,** Breslau, 1817—Berlin, 1893; professor and composer. (5) **Jos.,** Liége, 1820 —Paris, 1891; bro. of (3); organist and teacher, Paris; pub. *"Ode to St. Cecilia"* (with orch.); cantatas, etc.

Franck'enstein, Clemens, Freiherr von, b. Wiesentheid, Lower Franconia, July 14, 1875; composer and impresario; pupil of Thuille, also of Knorr at Hoch Cons.; visited America; cond. in London, 1902-07; then in Wiesbaden and Berlin; 1912-18 and 1924-34, general intendant at Munich Op.; c. (operas) *"Griseldis,"* *"Rahab,"* *"Fortunatus,"* *"Li-Tai-Pe"* (the last with succ. in Hamburg and Munich); also orch., chamber music, songs.

Fran'co, a name honoured in mensural music and probably belonging to two, perhaps three, men: (1) **F. of Paris** (the *elder*), cond. at Nôtre-Dame, Paris, ca. 1100 (?) A.D.; and (2) **F. of Cologne,** Dortmund and prior of the Benedictine Abbey at Cologne in 1190, author of 2 treatises.

Francœur (frän-kŭr), (1) **François,** Paris, 1698—1787; violinist and dram. composer. (2) **Louis Jos.,** Paris, 1738—1804; nephew of above; violinist, conductor and dram. composer.

Frank (1) **Melchior.** Vide FRANCK.
(2) **Ernst,** Munich, 1847—(insane),
Oberdöbling, near Vienna, 1889;
court-organist and dram. composer.
Frankenberger (fränk'-ĕn-bĕrkh-ĕr),
H., Wümbach, Schwarzburg-Sondershausen, 1824—Sondershausen, 1885;
conductor, violinist, and dram. composer.
Frank'lin, Benj., Boston, Mass.,
1706—Philadelphia, 1790; the eminent philosopher; inv. the harmonica
(v. D. D.), and wrote wittily on
Scotch and contemporary music, etc.
Frank'o, (1) **Sam,** New Orleans, Jan.
20, 1857—New York, May 6, 1937;
violinist; pupil of Wilhelmj, Joachim
and Vieuxtemps; toured with Patti;
cond. concerts of ancient music in
New York; 1912, Berlin; arr. music
for orch., etc. (2) **Nahan,** New
Orleans, July 23, 1861—Amityville,
L. I., June 7, 1930; violinist and
cond.; at 8, toured the world with
Patti; later studied with Rappoldi,
De Ahna, Wilhelmj, and Joachim;
member of Met. Op. orchestra,
N. Y.; from 1883 concertmaster;
1905–07 conductor; later cond. his
own orchestra.
Franz (fränts), (1) **K.,** Langenbielau,
Silesia, 1738—Munich, 1802; virtuoso on the waldhorn, and the bary-
ton. (2) **J. H.,** pen-name of Count
B. von Hochberg. (3) **Robt.,** Halle,
June 28, 1815—Oct. 24, 1892; 1847,
changed his family-name **Knauth,**
by royal permission; long opposed
by his parents, he finished his musical studies 1835–37, under Fr.
Schneider, Dessau; returned to Halle,
and spent six years studying Bach,
etc.; 1843, his first album of 12
songs appeared, and was cordially
rec'd. by Liszt and Mendelssohn
and by Schumann, who wrote about
him in his periodical. He became
organist at the Ulrichskirche, and
later cond. of the Singakademie, and
mus. dir. at Halle Univ., which made
him Mus. Doc., 1861. In 1868,
deafness attacked him, and nervous
disorders prevented his writing further. His distress was relieved by
the receipt of $25,000, from a series
of concerts organised 1872, in Germany, by Helene Magnus, Joachim,
Liszt, and in America, by Dresel,
Schlesinger, and B. J. Lang. His
wife (4) **Marie** (née **Hinrichs,**
1828–91) pub. many excellent songs.

His supplementing of the old musical
shorthand of Bach and Händel, by
full scores with modern instrumentation has been of invaluable service.
He also pub. essays and "open
letters" to Hanslick on Bach and
Händel. He pub. 257 songs; the
117th Psalm, for double chorus *a
cappella;* Kyrie for soli and 4-part
chorus, *a cappella,* a liturgy for
6 chorals, 6 part-songs for mixed
chorus, and 6 do. for male chorus.
Biog. sketches, by Ambros, Liszt,
Dr. W. Waldmann (Leipzig, 1895),
Schuster, La Mara, Prochazka, Gol-
ther, Bethge, etc.
Fränzl (frĕnts'l), (1) **Ignaz,** Mannheim,
1736—1811; violinist, conductor and
composer. (2) **Fd.,** Schwetzingen,
Palatinate, 1770—Mannheim, 1833;
son and pupil of above; conductor
and dram. composer.
Fraschini (fräs-kē'-nē), **Gaetano,**
Pavia, 1815—Naples, May 24, 1887;
tenor in Italy and England.
Frauenlob (frow'-ĕn-lōp). Vide VON
MEISSEN.
Frederick II. (the Great), of Prussia;
Berlin, 1712—Potsdam, 1786; flute-
player and composer of remarkable
skill—for a king.
Frédérix (frā-dā-rĕx), **Gv.,** Liége, 1834
—Brussels, 1894; critic.
Freer, Eleanor Everest, b. Philadel-
phia, May 14, 1864; composer;
pupil of Marchesi and Godard;
theory with Ziehn; c. operas, incl.
"The Court Jester" and *"The Legend
of the Piper"* (Amer. Op. Co.,
1928–29).
Frege (frā'-gĕ), **Livia** (née **Gerhard**),
Gera, June 13, 1818—Leipzig, Aug.
22, 1891; singer; pupil of Pohlenz;
début at 15 with Clara Wieck, who
was then 13, at the Gewandhaus,
Leipzig.
Freiberg (frī'-bĕrkh), **Otto,** Naumburg, April 26, 1846—Göttingen,
Nov. 2, 1926; studied, Leipzig Cons.;
from 1865, violinist in court-orch.,
Carlsruhe; studied with V. Lachner;
became mus. dir. Marburg Univ.;
1887, mus. dir. and prof. Göttingen.
Fremstad (frĕm'-shtät), **Olive (Anna
Olivia),** b. Stockholm, 1872; dramatic soprano; at 9, a pianist;
brought to America by her parents,
at 12; 1890, soloist at St. Patrick's
Cathedral, N. Y.; 1893–94, pupil of
Lilli Lehmann at Berlin; 1895,
début; 1896 sang at Bayreuth;

1897-1900, Vienna Royal Opera; later at Munich, Covent Garden and 1903-14 at Met. Op. House, N. Y.; officer of the French Academy, and 1907 of Public Instruction. One of the most notable Isoldes of her generation, and a fine dram. artist, whose powers were superbly schooled. She toured as a concert singer, but for some years has lived in retirement; 1906, m. Edson Sutphen; 1916, Harry L. Brainard.

Frère (frăr), **Marguerite Jeanne** (called **Hatto**), b. Lyons, Jan. 30, 1879; soprano; pupil of the Cons., took 2 opera prizes, 1899; début Opéra, 1899; created "Floria" in Saint-Saëns' "*Les Barbares*"; sang at Monte Carlo, etc.

Freschi (frĕs'-kē), **Giov. Dom.**, Vicenza, 1640—1690; conductor and dram. composer.

Frescobaldi (frĕs-kō-bäl'-dē), **Girolamo**, Ferrara, 1583—(buried) Rome, March 2, 1644; the greatest organist of his time, a revolutionist in harmony and important developer of fugue and notation; he was so famous that 30,000 people attended his first performance as organist of St. Peter's, Rome (1610, or –14); pupil of Luzzacchi; organist at Mechlin probably 1607; c. org.-pcs., fugues, double-choir church-music, etc.; biog. by Haberl.

Freudenberg (froi'-dĕn-bĕrkh), **Wm.**, Raubacher Hütte, Prussia, March 11, 1838—Schweidnitz, May 22, 1928; studied in Leipzig; th.-cond. in various places; 1865, cond. of the Cecilia Singing Society, and the Synagogenverein, Wiesbaden; 1870, founded a Cons., and till 1886, cond. the Singakademie; later opera-cond. at Augsburg and (1889) Ratisbon; 1895, choir dir. at Gedächtniskirche, Berlin; c. many operas, chiefly comic; symph. poem, etc.

Frezzolini (frĕd-zō-lē'-nē), **Erminia**, Orvieto, 1818—Paris, 1884; soprano; début, 1838.

Friberth (frī'bĕrt), **K.**, Wullersdorf, Lower Austria, 1736—Vienna, 1816; tenor; conductor.

Frick (or **Frike**) (frĭk, or frē'-kĕ), **Ph. Jos.**, near Würzburg, 1740—London, 1798; organist and composer.

Frick'er, **Herbert Austin**, b. Canterbury, England, Feb. 12, 1868; conductor and organist; studied at Canterbury Cath. School, and lived in Leeds, 1898-1917, serving as civic org. and choral dir. at the fests. there; founded Leeds Orch. and led choral groups at Bradford, Halifax and Morley; after 1917, org. at Metropolitan Church and cond. of noted Mendelssohn Choir in Toronto, Can.

Friderici (or **Friederich**), **Daniel**, Eisleben (?) before 1600—after 1654; cantor at Rostock; c. madrigals, etc.

Fried (frēt), **Oskar**, b. Berlin, Aug. 10, 1871; pupil of Humperdinck; since 1904 director Stern Gesangverein and the Gesellschaft der Musikfreunde; later guest cond. in England, Russia and of N. Y. Symph., 1926; c. choral works with orch., double fugue for strings; a work for 13 wind instruments and 2 harps, etc.

Friedberg (frēd'-bĕrkh), **Carl**, b. Bingen-on-Rhine, Germany, Sept. 18, 1872; pianist; pupil of Clara Schumann and James Kwast; début with Vienna Philh. Orch., 1892; has appeared widely with leading orchestras in Europe and America, and as recitalist; has taught at Juilliard School of Music, N. Y., and as head of piano dept., Inst. of Music. Art.

Friedenthal (frē'-dĕn-täl), **Albert**, Bromberg, Sept. 25, 1862—Batavia, Jan. 17, 1921; pianist; pupil of Fr. and W. Steinbrunn, and of Kullak; toured the world.

Friedheim (frēt'-hīm), **Arthur**, St. Petersburg, Oct. 26, 1859—New York, Oct. 19, 1932; pianist and conductor; pupil of Rubinstein one year, and of Liszt, 8 years; spent many years in America as teacher and pianist; prof. at R. C. M., Manchester, England, till 1904; c. opera "*Die Tänzerin*" (Cologne, 1905); also pf. pieces and arrangements.

Friedländer (frēt'-lĕnt-ĕr), **Max.**, Brieg, Silesia, Oct. 12, 1852—Berlin, May 2, 1934; concert-bass and editor; pupil of Manuel Garcia and Stockhausen; début, 1880, London; 1881-83, Frankfort; since in Berlin; 1882, Dr. Phil. h. c. (Breslau); after 1894, prof., Berlin Univ.; lectured at Harvard, 1911; LL.D., Univ. of Wis.; wrote works on Schubert, and discovered more than 100 of that composer's songs which were previously unknown; with Bolte and

Meier made valuable collection of German folk-songs.

Friedman (frēt'-män), **Ignaz,** b. Podgorze, near Cracow, Feb. 14, 1882, pianist; pupil of his father and of Leschetizky; toured with success; c. piano pieces and songs. One of most notable piano virtuosi, esp. in Chopin performances.

Frike. Vide FRICK.

Friml, Rudolf, b. Prague, Dec. 2, 1879; composer; studied Prague Cons.; in 1901–06 toured with Kubelik; since latter year has lived in N. Y.; best known for a number of tuneful and musicianly light operas, among which are *"The Firefly," "High Jinks," "Katinka," "Rose Marie," "The Vagabond King"* and others, some of which have had internat'l. popularity; also piano concerto, and pieces for orch., piano, vln., 'cello, songs.

Frimmel (frĭm'-mĕl), **Th.,** Amstetten, Lower Austria, Dec. 15, 1853— Vienna, Dec. 27, 1928; M. D. (Vienna) writer.

Fris'kin, James, b. Glasgow, Mar. 3, 1886; pianist; pupil of London R. C. M., winning scholarship in 1900 and composition scholarship 1905; member of faculty Inst. of Musical Art, New York; active as recitalist; c. piano quintet in C minor, 'cello sonata, etc.

Fritzsch (frĭtsh), **Ernst Wm.,** Lützen, Aug. 24, 1840—Leipzig, Aug. 14, 1902; pupil Leipzig Cons.; acquired the music-pub. business of Bomnitz in Leipzig; 1870, ed. the radical *"Musikalisches Wochenblatt,"* and 1875 started the *"Musikalische Hausblätter";* a member of the Gewandhaus Orch.; pub. the works of Wagner, Grieg, etc.

Froberger (frō'-bĕrkh-ĕr), **Jn. Jakob,** 1605 (?)—Héricourt, France, May 7, 1667; chief German organist of the 17th cent.; son of a cantor at Halle; studied in Rome with Frescobaldi; court organist at Vienna; travelled, and in England, being robbed, became a bellows-treader; he overblew during Chas. II's marriage and was beaten by the organist Gibbons; he fell to improvising shortly after, and was recognised by a pupil who presented him to the king.

Frö(h)lich (frā-lĭkh), (1) **Jos.,** Würzburg, 1780—1862; musical director; writer and dram. composer. (2) The name of three sisters b. Vienna,

(a) **Nanette (Anna),** 1793—1880; pianist, teacher, and singer. (b) **Barbara,** 1797—1879; contralto and painter, m. F. Bogner. (c) **Josephine,** 1803—1878, notable singer and teacher.

Fromm (frôm), **Emil,** Spremberg, Niederlausitz, Jan. 29, 1835—Flensburg, Dec. 12, 1916; pupil of R. Inst. for Church-music, Berlin; 1866, Royal Mus. Dir.; 1869, organist and conductor at Flensburg; c. 2 Passion cantatas, an oratorio, etc.

Frontini (frôn-tē'-nē), **F. Paolo,** b. Catania, Aug. 6, 1860; pupil of P. Platania, and Lauro Rossi; dir. Catania Mus. Inst.; c. succ. opera *"Malia"* (Bologna, 1893); oratorio *"Sansone"* (1882), etc.

Frost, (1) **Chas. Jos.,** Westbury-on-Tyne, Engl., June 20, 1848—London, 1918; son and pupil of an organist at Tewkesbury, also pupil of Cooper, Goss, and Steggall; organist various churches; 1882, Mus. Doc. Cantab.; 1880 prof. of organ Guildhall Sch. of Mus.; c. oratorio, *"Nathan's Parable"* (1878); a symphony, etc. (2) **H. Fr.,** London, March 15, 1848—June, 1901; studied organ with Seb. Hart; 1865–91, organist of the Chapel Royal, Savoy; 1880–88, pf.-prof. Guildhall Sch. of Mus.; from 1877 critic of *"The Academy,"* later of *"The Athenæum,"* and *"The Standard";* pub. biog. of Schubert, and the *"Savoy Hymn-tunes and Chants."*

Frugatta (froo-gät'-tä), **Giu.,** Bergamo, May 26, 1860—Milan, May 30, 1933; pianist; pupil of Bazzini (comp.) and Andreoli (pf.) at Milan Cons.; prof. there; also at the "Collegio reale delle Fanciulle"; composer.

Fruytiers (froi'-tĕrs), **Jan.,** Flemish composer at Antwerp 16th century.

Fry, Wm. H., Philadelphia, 1813—Santa Cruz, 1864; dram. composer; critic N. Y. *Tribune.*

Fuchs (fookhs), (1) **G. Fr.,** Mayence, 1752—Paris, 1821; clarinettist and bandm. (2) **Aloys,** Raase, Austrian Silesia, 1799—Vienna, 1853; collector and writer. (3) **K. Dorius Jn.,** Potsdam, Oct. 22, 1838—Danzig, Aug. 24, 1922; pupil of his father and v. Bülow, Weitzmann and Kiel; Dr. phil., Greifswald; 1871–75, concert pianist, teacher and critic, Berlin; 1875–79, Hirschberg; 1879, Danzig; '86, organist at the Petrikirche, there. Pub. numerous valuable musical treatises. (4) **Jn. Nepomuk**, Frauenthal, Styria, May 5, 1842—Vienna, Oct. 5, 1899; from 1893, dir. of Vienna Cons.; dir. and dram. composer. (5) **Robt.**, Frauenthal, Feb. 15, 1847—Vienna, Feb. 19, 1927; bro. of above; 1875—1912, prof. theory at Vienna Cons.; pub. 3 symphonies, serenades, etc.; prod. succ. "Spieloper" "*Die Teufelsglocke*" (Leipzig, 1893) and the succ. com. opera "*Die Königsbraut*" (Vienna, 1889). (6) **Albert**, Basel, Aug. 6, 1858—Dresden, Feb. 15, 1910; pupil of Leipzig Cons.; 1880, mus. dir. at Trier; 1889, owner and manager Wiesbaden Cons.; comp.

Füchs (füks), **Fd. K.**, Vienna, 1811—1848; dram. composer.

Fuenllana (fwĕn-lĭ-än'-nä), **Miguel de**, flourished 1554 in Spain; lute-virtuoso and court composer; blind from birth.

Fuentes (foo-än'-tĕs), **Don Pasquale**, b. Albayda, Valencia, d. there 1768; conductor and composer.

Fuertes, M. S. Vide SORIANO.

Fugère (fü-zhăr), **Lucien**, Paris, March 3, 1848—July 15, 1935; barytone; pupil of Raguenau; début, 1870; sang for many years with notable succ. at Paris Op. and Op.-Comique; occasionally made operatic appearances when over 80.

Führer (fü'-rĕr), **Robt.**, Prague, 1807—Vienna, Nov., 1861; organ-composer.

Fuhrmann (foor'-män), (1) **G. Ld.**, wrote work on the lute, Nürnberg, 1615. (2) **Martin H.**, 1669—after 1740; theorist and writer.

Fuller-Maitland. Vide MAITLAND.

Fumagalli (foo-mä-gäl'-lē), name of four bros. b. at Inzago, Italy: (1) **Disma**, 1826—Milan, 1893; professor and composer. (2) **Adolfo**, 1828—Florence, May 3, 1856; pianist. (3) **Polibio**, Nov. 2, 1830—Milan, June 21, 1901; pianist and composer. (4) **Luca**, Inzago, May 29, 1837—Milan, June 5, 1908; pupil Milan Cons.; concert-pianist; prod. opera "*Luigi XI*" (Florence, 1875).

Fumi (foo'-mē), **Vinceslao**, Montepulciano, Tuscany, 1823—Florence, 1880; conductor, violinist, dram. composer and collector.

Furlanetto (foor-lä-nĕt'-tō), **Bonaventura** (called **Musin**), Venice, 1738—1817; singing-teacher, conductor and composer.

Furno (foor'-nō), **Giov.**, Capua, 1748

—Naples, 1837; professor and dram. composer.

Fursch-Madi (foorsh'-mä-dē), **Emmy**, Bayonne, France, 1847—Warrenville, N. J., Sept. 20, 1894; pupil of Paris Cons., début, Paris; came to America, 1874, with the New Orleans French Opera Company; 1879–81, Covent Garden, London; her final appearance was as "Ortrud," N. Y., 1894.

Fürstenau (fürsht'-ĕ-now), (1) **Kaspar**, Münster, Westphalia, 1772—Oldenburg, 1819; flute-virtuoso; composer. (2) **Anton B.**, Münster, 1792—Dresden, 1852; son and pupil of above; flutist and composer. (3) **Moritz**, Dresden, 1824—1889; son and pupil of (2); flutist and writer.

Fürstner (fürsht'-nĕr), **Ad.**, Berlin, 1833—Bad Nauheim, 1908; founded (1868) notable mus.-pub. house, Berlin.

Furtwängler (foort'-väng-lĕr), **Wilhelm**, b. Berlin, Jan. 25, 1886; conductor; pupil of Beer-Walbrunn, Rheinberger and Schillings; following early engagements as cond. in Zurich, Strasbourg, Lübeck, etc., succeeded Bodanzky at Mannheim Op., 1915; Vienna Tonkünstler Orch., 1919; Berlin Op. and symph. concerts, after 1920; cond. Museum Concerts, Frankfort; Leipzig Gewandhaus, after 1922; N. Y. Philh. Orch., 1925–26; Berlin Philh. Orch., incl. tours to other countries with this organisation; Berlin State Op., also several seasons at Bayreuth; guest cond. at Vienna Op. and with Philh. Orch.; nominated to succeed Toscanini as cond. N. Y. Philh., 1936, but cancelled engagement owing to controversy among subscribers of this orch. as to his political and racial sympathies; has at times enjoyed the highest honours from the Nat'l. Socialist regime in Germany, incl. vice-presidency of Reich Music Chamber, as well as virtual dictator of music in Berlin, at other times has either resigned or been relieved of his posts; one of these instances occurred in 1934 following a stand which he took in championing the music of Paul Hindemith, outlawed by German Ministry of Culture and Propaganda as showing traits of "cultural Bolshevism"; later restored to his orchestral and operatic baton posts, but in 1936–37 again granted year's leave of absence.

Fux (foox), **Jn. Jos.,** Hirtenfeld, Upper Styria, 1660—Vienna, Feb. 14, 1741; eminent theorist, organist, and court-conductor and writer; c. 405 works (few pub.), incl. 18 operas, 10 oratorios, 50 masses, incl. *missa canonica.* He wrote the famous treatise on cpt. *"Gradus ad Parnassum".* in dialogue form; it is based on the church-modes. Biogr. by Köchel (Vienna, 1872).

G

Gabler (gäp'-lĕr), **Jn.,** d. ca. 1784; organ builder at Ulm.

Gabriel (1) (gā'-brĭ-ĕl), **Mary Ann Virginia,** Banstead, Surrey, Engl., 1825—London, 1877; c. cantatas, operas, etc. (2) (gä'-brĭ-ĕl), **Max,** b. Elbing, 1861; 1890, cond. Residenz Th., Hanover; later in America, then at Rembrandt Theatre, Amsterdam; prod. succ. operettas.

Gabrieli (gä-brĭ-ā'-lē), (1) **Andrea,** Venice, ca. 1510—1586; eminent organist and teacher and composer of the first "real" fugues (v. D. D.). (2) **Giov.,** Venice, 1558—Aug. 12, 1613 (acc. to his monument); nephew and pupil of above, and equally famous; an extraordinary contrapuntist, his "symphoniæ sacræ" employing 3 simultaneous choirs independently handled; he has been called "the father of the chromatic style". because of his bold modulations. (3) **Dom.** (called "Menghino del violoncello"), Bologna, ca. 1640—ca. 1690; 'cellist, conductor, and composer.

Gabrielli (gä-brĭ-ĕl'-lē), (1) **Catterina,** Rome, Nov. 12, 1730—April, 1796; daughter of Prince G.'s cook (and hence called **"La Cochetta,"** or **"Cochettina"**); one of the most beautiful and brilliant of singers; her extraordinarily flexible voice had a "thrilling quality" (Burney); her caprices and her high-handed treatment of the nobility and royalty enamoured of her make her a most picturesque figure; she sang with greatest succ. all over Europe and retired wealthy. Her sister (2) **Francesca** (called **"La Gabriellina,"** or **"La Ferrarese"**), Ferrara, 1755—Venice, 1795, was a celebrated prima donna buffa. (3) Conte **Nicolo,** Naples, 1814—1891; prod. 22 operas and 60 ballets.

Gabriels'ki, (1) **Jn. Wm.,** Berlin, 1791 —1846; flutist and composer. (2) **Julius,** Berlin, 1806—1878; bro. and pupil of above; flutist.

Gabrilowitsch (gä-brē-lō'-vĭtsh), **Ossip,** St. Petersburg, Jan. 26, 1878—Detroit, Mich., Sept. 14, 1936; eminent pianist and conductor; studied at the Cons. with Glazounoff, Liadoff and Rubinstein; at 16 took the Rubinstein prize; studied with Leschetizky at Vienna, 1894–96; 1896 began touring with success; 1900, America. He was resident in Munich for the most part between 1904 and 1914, and cond. the Konzertverein concerts there, 1910–14. From 1907 he also led orch. programmes in N. Y. Between 1912 and 1916 he gave a series of historical piano recitals in Eur. cities and U. S., illustrating growth of the concerto. He was appointed cond. of the Detroit Symph. Orch. in 1918, a post which he filled with distinction until 1935. He also served as one of the leaders of the Phila. Orch. for several seasons and appeared as guest with other orchs. in this country. A notable ensemble perf. as well as one of the most brilliant and scholarly soloists. He m. Clara Clemens, daughter of "Mark Twain," a mezzo-soprano. C. *"Overture-Rhapsody"* for orch.; *"Elegy".* for 'cello; piano pieces, songs, etc.

Gabussi (gä-bōos'-sē), **V.,** Bologna, 1800—London, 1846; teacher and composer.

Gade (gä'-dĕ), **Niels Wm.,** Copenhagen, Feb. 22, 1817—Dec. 21, 1890; son of an instr.-maker; at 15 refused to learn his father's trade, and became pupil of Wexschall (vln.) Berggreen (theory); at 16 a concert-violinist. His overture, *"Nachklänge von Ossian,"* took first prize at the Copenhagen Mus. Soc. competition (1841) and won for him a royal stipend. In 1842 the C min. symphony, and 1846 the cantata *"Comala,"* were prod. by Mendelssohn at the Gewandhaus. He travelled in Italy; then, 1844, lived in Leipzig as sub-cond. to Mendelssohn, and regular cond. at his death (1847); 1848, he returned to Copenhagen as cond. of the Mus. Soc. and as organist; 1861, court-cond., made Prof. by the King, and Dr. Phil. *h. c.* by the Univ.; 1886, Commander in the

Order of Danebrog; 1876 the govt. voted him a life-pension. Autobiog. *"Aufzeichnungen und Briefe"* (Basel, 1893). Pub. 7 symphonies (D minor, No. 5 with pf.); 4 overtures, *"Nachklänge von Ossian," "Im Hochlande," "Hamlet," "Michelangelo,"* octet, sextet, and quartet for strings; 7 cantatas, *"Elverskind"* (Erl-King's Daughter),*"Frühlingsbotschaft," "Die Heilige Nacht," "Zion," "Kalanus," "Die Kreuzfahrer," "Psyche,"* etc.; 2 vln.-concertos; pf. sonata and pcs., songs, etc.

Gads'by, H. Robt., Hackney, London, Dec. 15, 1842—Putney, Nov. 11, 1907; pupil of Wm. Bayley, but mainly self-taught; organist at St. Peter's, Brockley; 1884, prof. of harm. Queen's Coll., London; also at Guildhall Sch. of Mus.; c. *"Festival Service"*; 3 symphonies; 3 overtures, *"Andromeda," "The Golden Legend,"* and *"The Witches' Frolic,"* etc.

Gad'ski, Johanna, Anclam, Prussia, June 15, 1871—Berlin, Feb. 23, 1932 (in automobile accident); notable soprano, educated at Stettin; 1892, m. H. Tauscher; sang in U. S. A. for many years, 1899 Covent Garden and as "Eva" (*Meistersinger*) at Bayreuth. She was a leading member of the Met. Op. Co., in Wagnerian rôles, from 1898 to 1917, also appearing widely in concerts. During the war she was accused of anti-American activities and retired to Berlin. She was again heard in the United States as leading singer with the Wagnerian Op. Co. in two tours, 1930 and 1931. A large and freely produced voice of striking dram. timbre and much dignity of stage deportment marked her interpretations of a great variety of rôles, including "Senta" and "Brünnhilde."

Gaforio (gä-fō'-rĭ-ō) (or **Gafori, Gafuri, Gaffurio**), **Franchino** (Latinised "Franchinus Gafurius," or "Franchinus"), Lodi, Jan. 14, 1451—Milan, June 24, 1522; priest, eminent theorist, choirmaster and singer.

Gagliano (gäl-yä'-nō), (1) **Marco di Zanobi da,** b. Florence; d. there, Feb. 24, 1642; conductor and composer. (2) A family of Naples vln.-makers, (a) **Alessandro,** pupil of Stradivari, worked ca. 1695—1725. His sons, (b) **Nicolò** (1700–40), and (c) **Gennaro** (1710–50), and his grandson, (d) **Ferdinando** (1736–81)

succeeded him; later descendants est. factory of strings, still famous.

Gährich (gā'-rĭkh), **Wenzel,** Zerchowitz, Bohemia, 1794—Berlin, 1864; violinist, ballet-master, and dram. composer.

Gaïl (gä-ēl), **Edmée Sophia** (née **Garre**), Paris, Aug. 28, 1775—July 24, 1819; singer and dram. composer.

Gailhard (gī'-yăr), **Pierre,** Toulouse, Aug. 1, 1848—Paris, Oct. 12, 1918; bass; pupil Paris Cons.; début, 1867, Op. Com., Paris; later at the Opéra, of which he was director 1899–1907.

Gál, Hans, b. Brünn, Austria, Aug. 5, 1890; composer; Ph.D., Univ. of Vienna; pupil of Mandyczewski and Robert; c. (operas) *"Der Arzt der Sobeide"* (Breslau, 1919); *"Die Heilige Ente"* (Düsseldorf, 1923); *"Das Lied der Nacht"* (Breslau, 1926); also orchestral and chamber music, choruses; won Austrian State Prize, 1915, for his 1st symphony; after 1918 lecturer in counterpoint, harmony and musical form at Univ. of Vienna.

Galeazzi (gä-lä-äd'-zē), **Fran.,** Turin, 1758—Rome, 1819; violinist.

Galeffi (gä-lä'-fē), **Carlo,** b. Rome; barytone; début in *"Aïda"* at Rome, 1907; created rôle of Gianni Schicchi in Puccini's opera at Costanzi Theat.; has also sung in other Eur. countries, and North and South America.

Gal'eotti, Cesare, b. Pietrasanta, June 5, 1872; c. operas *"Anton"* (La Scala, Milan, 1900) and *"La Dorise"* (1910), etc.; d. Paris, Feb. 19, 1929.

Galilei (gä-lǐ-lā'-ē), **V.,** Florence, ca. 1533—1591; lutenist, violinist and theorist; father of the astronomer.

Galin (gä-lăň), **P.,** Samatan Gers, France, 1786—Bordeaux, 1821; wrote pop. method *"Meloplaste"* (v. D. D.).

Galitzin (gä-lē'-tshĕn), (1) **Nicolas Borissovitch,** 1794—1866; a Russian prince, to whom Beethoven dedicated an overture, and 3 quartets; he advanced Beethoven liberal sums for his dedications; a skilful 'cellist. (2) **G.** (Prince), St. Petersburg, 1825—1872; son of above; composer and cond.; maintained in Moscow (1842) a choir of 70 boys; later an orchestra.

Gal'kin, Nikolai Vladimirovich, St. Petersburg, Dec. 6, 1856—May 21, 1906; violinist and composer for violin; pupil of Kaminsky, Auer, Joachim, Sauret and Wieniawski;

toured Europe and after 1877 was cond. in St. Petersburg and from 1880 teacher at the Cons.; from 1892, prof.

Gall, (1) **Jan,** Warsaw, Aug. 18, 1856 —Lemberg, Oct. 30, 1912; pupil of Krenn and Rheinberger 1886, teacher of song at Cracow Cons. then pupil of Mme. Lamperti, director of the Lemberg "*Echo*" society; composer of some 400 vocal numbers. (2) **Yvonne,** b. Paris, March 6, 1885; soprano; studied Paris Cons., début as "Marguerite," Paris Op.; has also sung with Op.-Comique, and widely in various Eur. countries and America; several seasons with Ravinia Op. Co., after 1927; also as recitalist in U. S.

Gallay (găl-lĕ), (1) **Jacques Fran.,** Perpignan, 1795—Paris, 1864; horn-virtuoso and composer. (2) **Jules,** Saint-Quentin, 1822—Paris, 1897; amateur 'cellist of wealth; made researches and pub. valuable treatises.

Gallenberg (gäl'-lĕn-bĕrkh), **Wenzel Robt.,** Graf von, Vienna, 1783—Rome, 1839; c. ballets.

Gallet'ti-Gianoli (jä-nō'-lē), **Isabella,** Bologna, Nov. 11, 1835—Milan, Aug. 31, 1901; operatic soprano; later contralto.

Gal'li, Filippo, Rome, 1783—Paris, June 3, 1853; first most successful as a tenor; illness changed his voice, and he achieved great success as a bass.

Galli-Curci, Amelita (äm-ā-lē'-tä gäl-lĭ-kōōrt'-chē), b. Milan, Nov. 18, 1889; coloratura soprano; studied piano, Milan Cons., in voice largely self-taught; début as "Gilda," "Costanzi," Rome, 1910; sang in various Eur. theatres and in South America; American début with Chicago Op., with sensational success, as "Gilda," 1916; member of this company until 1924; Met. Op., N. Y., 1921–30; many concert tours in U. S., Great Britain, Australia and Orient; m. Homer Samuels, pianist-composer.

Gal'lia. Vide ÉPINE.

Galliard (gäl'-lĭ-ärt), Jn. **Ernst,** Celle, Hanover, 1687—London, 1749; oboist and organist.

Gal'lico, Paolo, b. Trieste, May 13, 1868; at 15 gave a pf.-recital at Trieste; then studied Vienna Cons. with Julius Epstein; at 18 graduating with first prize and "Gesellschafts" medal; toured Europe; 1892

pianist and teacher, New York; his oratorio, "*The Apocalypse*," won Nat'l. Fed. of Mus. Clubs prize, 1921; c. operettas, pf.-pieces, songs, etc.

Gallic'ulus, Jns., contrapuntist at Leipzig, 1520–48.

Galli-Marié (gäl-lĭ mä̆r-yä), **Celéstine** (née Marie de l'Isle), Paris, Nov., 1840—Nice, 1905; mezzo-soprano; daughter of an opera-singer; début Strassburg, 1859; sang Toulouse, 1860, Lisbon, 1861, Rouen, 1862; 1862–78, and 1883–85, Paris Opéra Comique; she created "Mignon" (1866), "Carmen" (1875), etc.

Gal'lus, (1) **Jacobus** (rightly **Jacob Händl, Handl** or **Hähnel**); Carniola, ca. 1550—Prague, 1591; composer and conductor. (2) **Jns.** (**Jean le Cocq, Maître Jean,** or **Mestre Jhan**), d. before 1543; a Dutch contrapuntist, conductor and composer. (3) Vide MEDERITSCH, JN.

Gal'ston, Gottfried, b. Vienna, Aug. 31, 1879; pianist and pedagogue; studied Vienna Cons., piano with Leschetizky, theory with Jadassohn and Reinecke, Leipzig; toured Australia and (1913–14) U. S. as pianist; taught Stern Cons., Berlin, 1903–07, and again after 1921; also appeared in series of historical recitals and as orch. soloist in leading capitals, incl. Russia; later active as pedagogue in America; author of "*Studienbuch*."

Galuppi (gä-loop'-pĭ), **Baldassare** (called **Il Buranel'lo**), Island of Burano, near Venice, Oct. 18, 1706—Venice, Jan. 3, 1785; harpsichord virtuoso; organist 1765–68; conductor; c. 54 comic operas.

Gambale (gäm-bä'-lĕ), **Emm.,** music-teacher, Milan; pub. "*La riforma musicale*" (1840), etc., advocating a scale of 12 semitones.

Gambini (gäm-bē'-nē), **Carlo Andrea,** Genoa, 1819—1865; c. operas, etc.

Gamucci (gä-moot'-chē), **Baldassare,** Florence, 1822—1892; pianist and writer.

Ganassi (gä-näs'-sē), **Silvestro,** b. Fontego, near Venice, ca. 1500 (called "del Fontego"); editor and writer on graces.

Gand (gäṅ), **Ch. Nicolas Eugène,** ca. 1826—Boulogne-sur-Seine, 1892; vln.-maker. V. LUPOT.

Gandini (gän-dē'-nē), (1) **A.,** Modena, 1786—Formigine, 1842; conductor and dram. composer. (2) **Alessan-**

dro, Modena, ca. 1807—1871; son, pupil (1842) and successor of above; dram. composer and writer.

Ganne (găn), **L. Gaston,** Buxières-les-Mines, Allier, April 5, 1862—Paris, July 14, 1923; pupil of Dubois and Franck, Paris Cons.; cond. at Monte Carlo; c. comic opera *"Rabelais"* (1892), vaudeville, operetta, ballets, etc.

Gänsbacher (gĕns'-bäkh-ĕr), **Jn.,** Sterzing, Tyrol, 1778—Vienna, 1844; conductor and composer.

Ganz (gänts), (1) **Ad.,** Mayence, 1796 —London, 1870; violinist and cond.; his 2 brothers were, (2) **Moritz,** Mayence, 1806—Berlin, 1868; 'cellist; (3) **Ld.,** Mayence, 1810—Berlin, 1869; violinist and composer; Adolf's 2 sons were, (4) **Eduard,** Mayence, 1827—1869; pianist. (5) **Wilhelm,** Mayence, Nov. 6, 1833—London, Sept. 12, 1914; pianist, professor, conductor. (6) **Rudolph,** b. Zürich, Feb. 24, 1877; début at 10 as 'cellist, at 12 as pianist; then pupil of his uncle, Eschmann-Dumur, and later of Busoni; début as pianist and composer Berlin, 1899; 1901–05 succeeded Friedheim in Chicago; has toured widely; cond. St. Louis Symph., 1921–27; also guest cond. in New York Stadium series, Hollywood Bowl, in Los Angeles, San Francisco, Denver, etc.; after 1929, dir. of Chicago Mus. Coll. and of modern music soc. in that city; c. orch., piano music, songs; mem. Legion of Honour.

Garat (gä-rä), **P. J.,** Ustaritz, Basses-Pyrénées, April 25, 1764—Paris, March 1, 1823; most remarkable French singer of his time, a barytone of great compass and amazing memory and mimicry; professor and composer.

Garaudé (gär-ō-dä), **Alexis de,** Nancy, 1779—Paris, 1852; professor, composer and writer.

Garbou'sova, Raya, b. Tiflis, 1909; 'cellist; grad. State Cons. of Tiflis; pupil of Hugo Becker; début Moscow, 1923; has toured in European cities and America as orch. soloist and in recitals.

Garbrecht (gär'-brĕkht), **Fr. F. W.** (d. 1874), founded at Leipzig (1862) a music engraving establishment, owned since 1880 by Os. Brandstetter.

Garcia (gär-thē'-ä), a notable family of Spanish vocal teachers. (1) **Don Fran. Saverio** (Padre Garcia, called "lo Spagnoletto"), Nalda, Spain, 1731—Saragossa, 1809; conductor and composer. (2) **Manuel del Popolo Vicente,** Sevilla, Jan. 22, 1775 —Paris, June 2, 1832; eminent as tenor, teacher, and progenitor of singers; successful as manager, cond. and composer; took his family, his wife, son (3), and daughter (5) and others to America for a v. succ. opera season, 1825–26. Produced 43 operas and c. others. (3) **Manuel,** Madrid, March 17, 1805—London, July 1, 1906; son of above; bass (in Paris); he was a scientific investigator, and inv. the laryngoscope, receiving Dr. Phil. *h. c.* Königsberg Univ.; 1847, prof. at the Cons., 1850, London, R. A. M. Jenny Lind was one of his pupils; pub. *"Traité complet de l'art du chant,"* 1847. (4) **Eugènie** (née **Mayer**), Paris, 1818 —1880; wife and pupil of (3); soprano and teacher. (5) **M. Félicité,** v. MALIBRAN. (6) **Pauline,** v. VIARDOT GARCIA.

Garcin (gär-săn), **Jules Aug. Salomon,** Bourges, 1830—Paris, 1896; violinist, conductor and professor.

Gardano (gär-dä'-nō), (1) **A.** (till 1557 called himself **Gardane**), ca. 1500— Venice, 1571 (?); early Italian mus.-printer, succeeded by sons, (2) **Alessandro** and (3) **Angelo.**

Gar'den, Mary, b. Aberdeen, Feb. 20, 1877; notable soprano; as a child brought to America; pupil of Mrs. Duff; (1896) Paris with Trabadello and Fugère; début, 1900, Paris Op. Com.; has created various rôles there, including "Mélisande" in Debussy's *"Pelléas et Mélisande,"* 1902; sang at Covent Garden, 1902; leading singer with Manhattan Op. Co., N. Y., after 1907, in French rôles; 1910–30, one of the guiding artistic personalities in the Chicago Op. Co., of which she was also artistic dir., 1921–22. Sang in Amer. premières of many operas; an outstanding concert singer; in later years has taught, lectured.

Gar'diner, H. Balfour, b. London, Nov. 7, 1877; pupil of Knorr at Frankfort; also studied with Uzielli, and 1895 at New Coll. Oxford; he was for a short time a singing teacher in Winchester, then for the most part devoting himself to composition; dir. of concert series in London, 1912–13, of modern English orch. and choral music; c. popular "*Shepherd Fennel's Dance*"; overture; Suite and Fantasy for orch.; Humoresque for small orch.; string quintet and quartet; piano pieces, songs, choral works, etc.

Gard'ner, Samuel, b. Elizabethgrad, Russia, 1892; violinist, composer; studied vln. with Winternitz and Kneisel, composition with Goetschius; début, N. Y., 1912; res. in U. S.; has appeared as soloist and guest cond. in his works with leading Amer. orchestras.

Gardo'ni, Italo, b. Parma, 1821; retired, 1874; operatic singer; d. 1882.

Garlan'dia, Johannes de, ca. 1210–32; French theorist.

Garnier (gärn-yā), **Fran. Jos.,** Lauris, Vaucluse, 1759—ca. 1825; oboist and composer.

Gar'rett, Geo. Mursell, Winchester, England, 1834—Cambridge, 1897; pianist, conductor, composer and lecturer.

Gar'rison, Mabel, b. Baltimore, Md.; coloratura soprano; studied Peabody Cons.; début as "Filina" in "*Mignon*," Boston, 1912; sang with Met. Op. Co., N. Y., for 6 years after 1914; also as concert artist in U. S.; toured Orient; m. George Siemonn, conductor.

Gas'par van Weerbeke (vär'-bĕ-kĕ), b. Oudenarde, Flanders, ca. 1440; eminent contrapuntist and teacher.

Gaspari (gäs-pä'-rē), **Gaetano,** Bologna, 1807—1881; librarian, professor and composer.

Gasparini (or **Guasparini**) (gäs-pä-rē'-nē), (1) **Fran.,** Camaiore, near Lucca, 1668—Rome, 1727; director, conductor and theorist. (2) **Michelangelo,** Lucca, 1685—Venice, 1732; male contralto and dram. composer. (3) **Don Quirino,** 'cellist at Turin; 1749–70; conductor and composer.

Gasparo da Salo (gäs-pä'-rō dä sä'-lō) (family name **Bertolot'ti**), Salo, Brescia, Italy, ca. 1542—Brescia (?), 1609; famous maker of viols.

Gassier (gäs-yā), **L. Éd.,** France, 1822—Havana, 1871; barytone.

Gassmann (gäs'-män), **Florian L.,** Brux, Bohemia, 1723—Vienna, 1774; court-conductor and dram. composer.

Gass'ner, F. Simon, Vienna, 1798—Carlsruhe, 1851; violinist, teacher, editor and composer.

Gast, Peter. Vide KÖSELITZ.

Gastaldon (gäs-täl'-dōn), **Stanislas,** b. Turin, 1861—Florence, March, 1939; pub. nocturnes, *ballabili*, songs, etc., some of them v. pop.; c. succ. 1-act opera-seria, "*Il Pater*" (Milan, 1894).

Gastinel (gäs-tĭ-nĕl), **Léon G. Cyprien,** Villers, near Auxonne, Aug. 15, 1823—Paris, Nov., 1906; pupil of Halévy, Paris Cons.; took first Gr. prix de Rome with cantata "*Velasquez*"; prod. comic operas; ballet "*Le Rêve*" (Gr. Opera, 1890), etc.

Gastoldi (gäs-tōl'-dē), **Giov. Giacomo,** Caravaggio, ca. 1556—Milan (?), 1622; conductor, contrapuntist and composer.

Gastoué (gäs-too'ā), **Amadée,** b. Paris, March 13, 1873; writer; prof. of church music.

Gatayes (gä-tĕz'), (1) **Guill. P. A.,** Paris, 1774—1846; guitar-player and composer. (2) **Jos. Léon,** Paris, 1805—1877; son of above; harpist, critic and composer. (3) **Félix,** b. Paris, 1809; bro. of above; pianist, chiefly self-taught; for 20 years toured Europe, America, Australia.

Gathy (gä-tē), **Aug.,** Liége, 1800—Paris, 1858; editor, teacher and composer.

Gat'ti, Guido M., b. Chieti, May 30, 1893; writer on music; ed. monthly pub., "*Il Pianoforte*" (Turin) which he founded 1920; also organized modern chamber music and orch. concerts in that city; author of many articles on music.

Gatti-Casazza (gät'-tĭ kä-sät'-sä), **Giulio,** Udine, Feb. 5, 1869—Ferrara, Sept. 2, 1940; operatic impresario. Naval engineer; 1894–08 dir. Municipal Theatre at Ferrara; 1898–1909, dir. La Scala, Milan; 1909 co-director with A. Dippel of the Metropolitan Opera House, N. Y.; 1910–35, in full charge; he gave a number of native American operas, and the first prods. anywhere of Humperdinck's "*Königskinder*,"[2] and Puccini's "*Girl of the Golden West*."[2]

Gat'ty, (1) **Sir Alfred Scott,** Ecclesfield, Yorks., April 25, 1847—London, 1919; 1880 Poursuivant of Arms, Heralds' Coll. London; c. operettas, many pop. songs, particularly in imitation of American Plantation songs, pf.-pieces. (2) **Nicholas Comyn,** b. Bradfield, Sept. 13, 1874; composer; critic, organist and comp., pupil R. C. M., where he produced orch.-variations on *"Old King Cole"*; 1907-14, critic on *"Pall Mall Gazette"*; assistant at Covent Garden; c. 1-act operas *"Greysteel"* (Sheffield, 1906), and *"Duke or Devil"* (Manchester, 1909); Milton's *"Ode on Time,"* for chorus w. orch., (Sheffield Festival, 1905); operas *"Prince Ferelon"* (Old Vic, London, 1921); *"The Tempest"* (1920); *"Macbeth,"* etc.

Gaubert (gō-bār'), **Philippe,** b. Cahors, 1879; Paris, 1941; pupil at Paris Cons. of Taffanel; won 2 Rome prizes, 1905; 1919, chosen to succeed Messager as cond. of Société des Concerts du Conservatoire; after 1920, 1st cond. at Opéra; c. opera, ballets, chamber and orch. music.

Gaucquier (gōk-yā), **Alard** (rightly **Dunoyer** Latinized **Nuceus**), called **du Gaucquier** and **Insulanus** from Lille-l'isle, court-bandm. to Maximilian II.; famous 16th cent. contrapuntist.

Gaul (gôl), (1) **Alfred Robt.,** Norwich, England, April 30, 1837—Birmingham, Sept. 13, 1913; at 9 a cath. chorister articled to Dr. Buck; 1863, Mus. Bac. Contab.; 1887, cond. Walsall Philh.; later teacher and cond. at the Birmingham and Midland Inst., etc.; c. oratorio *"Hezekiah"*; cantatas, incl. *"Ruth"* and *"The Holy City,"* etc. (2) **Harvey Bartlett,** b. New York, April 11, 1881; organist and composer; pupil of LeJeune; later in Paris with Decaux and d'Indy at Schola Cantorum, with Widor and Guilmant; res. in Pittsburgh after 1910 as church org.; mem. faculty, Pittsburgh Inst.; critic on several newspapers of that city; c. choral, org. works, songs.

Gau(l)tier (gōt-yā), (1) **Jacques** (G. *d'Angleterre*, or *l'ancien*), Lyons, ca. 1600—Paris, ca. 1670; lutenist. (2) **Denis** (*le jeune*, or *l'illustré*), Marseilles, ca. 1610—Paris, 1672; cousin of above, and his partner in a lutenist school; famous lutenist and collector of lute-music.

Gaunt'lett, H. J., Wellington, Shropshire, 1805—London, 1876; organist and composer.

Gauthier (gōt-yā), (1) **Gabriel,** b. in Saône-et-Loire, France, 1808; became blind when 11 months old; was pupil and (1827-40) teacher Paris Inst. for the Blind, then organist of St. Étienne-du-Mont, Paris; pub. treatises. (2) **Eva,** b. Ottawa, Can.,

Sept. 20, 1886; soprano; studied with Bouhy, Shakespeare, Carigiani and Oxilla; début in Carmen, Pavia, Italy; sang rôle of "Yniold" in London première of *"Pelléas"*; best known as soloist and recitalist in programmes of modern music; active in U. S. for some years; made researches in Javanese and Malay folk-songs.

Gautier (gōt-yā), (1) v. GAULTIER. (2) **J. Fran. Eug.,** Vaugirard n. Paris, 1822—Paris, 1878; conductor and dram. composer.

Gaveaux (gă-vō), **P.,** Béziers, Hérault, Aug., 1761—insane, Paris, 1825; tenor; c. operas, incl. *"Leonore"* (1788), the same subject afterwards used in Beethoven's *"Fidelio."*

Gaviniès (gă-vēn-yĕs), **P.,** Bordeaux, 1726—Paris, 1800; violinist, professor and dram. composer.

Gavron'ski, Woitech, b. Seimony near Wilna, June 27, 1868; pupil Warsaw Mus. Inst.; toured Russia, taught in Orel and Warsaw; c. symph.; 2 operas and a string quartet (Paderewski prize, Leipzig, 1898); d. 1913.

Gay (gī), **Maria,** b. Barcelona, Spain, June 13, 1879; contralto; studied violin, and originally self-taught in voice; sang at some of Pugno's concerts, and while in Brussels was heard by director of La Monnaie, where she made her début as "Carmen" in 1902 on five days' notice; studied with Madame Adiny in Paris; toured Europe; sang Covent Garden as "Carmen," 1906; Met. Op. Co. 1908-09; Boston Op. Co. 1910-12; 1913, Chicago Op. and later again Boston; m. Giovanni Zenatello, tenor.

Gayarré (gě-yăr-rā'), **Julian,** Roncal, Jan. 9, 1844—Madrid, Jan. 2, 1890; operatic tenor, son of a blacksmith.

Gaztambide (gäth-täm-bē'-dhĕ), **Joaquin,** Tudela, Navarra, 1822—Madrid, 1870; composer, teacher and conductor.

Gazzaniga (gäd-zän-ē'-ga), **Giu.,** Verona, 1743—Crema, 1818; conductor and dram. composer.

Gear (gēr), **Geo. Fr.,** b. London, May 21, 1857; pianist; pupil of Dr. Wylde and J. F. Barnett; 1872 scholarship London Acad. of Mus., later prof. there; 1876-92 mus.-dir. German-Reed Company; composed scena for sopr. solo and orch., etc.

Gebauer (zhŭ-bō-ā), (1) **Michel Jos.,** La Fère, Aisne, 1763—1812, on the retreat from Moscow; oboist, violinĭst and viol-player; also extraordinary virtuoso on the Jew's harp. He had 3 brothers, (2) **François Réné,** Versailles, 1773—Paris, 1844; bassoonist, prof., writer, and composer. (3) **P. Paul,** b. Versailles, 1775; died young; pub. 20 horn-duets. (4) **Et. Fran.,** Versailles, 1777 —Paris, 1823, flutist and composer. (5) (gĕ-bow'-ĕr), **Fz. X.,** Eckersdorf, near Glatz, 1784—Vienna, 1822; ²cellist, conductor, teacher and composer.

Gebel (gā'-bĕl), (1) **Georg** (Sr.), Breslau, 1685—1750; organist; inv. clavichord with quarter tones and clavicymbalum with pedal-keyboard; composer; he had 2 sons, (2) **Georg** (Jr.), Brieg, Silesia, 1709—Rudolstadt, 1753; son of above; conductor, organist and composer. (3) **Georg Sigismund,** d. 1775; organist and composer. (4) **Fz. X.,** Fürstenau, near Breslau, 1787—Moscow, 1843; conductor, pf.-teacher, and composer.

Gebhard (gĕp'-härt), **Heinrich,** b. Sobernheim, near Bingen, July 25, 1878; pianist; taken to America at 10; pupil of Clayton Johns, début, 1896, Boston, playing his violin and piano sonata, then studied with Leschetizky and Heuberger; 1899 reappeared Boston with symph. orch. 1900–04, pianist of Longy Club; c. quartet, piano pieces, etc.

Gebhar'di, **Ludwig Ernst,** Nottleben, Thuringia, 1787—Erfurt, 1862; organist, composer and teacher.

Gédalge (zhā-dälzh), **André,** Paris, Dec. 27, 1856—Feb. 26, 1926; pupil of Guiraud at the Cons.; took 2nd Grand prix de Rome, 1885; prof. of theory at Paris Cons. for many years, his pupils including Ravel, Milhaud, Honegger, Florent Schmitt and many others who attained eminence; wrote notable treatise on fugue; lyric drama "*Hélène*"; pantomime "*Le Petit Savoyard*" (Paris, 1891); a succ. 1-act opera-bouffe "*Pris au Piège*" (Paris, 1895); 2 symphonies, etc.

Gehring (gā'-rĭng), **F.,** 1838—Penzing, near Vienna, 1884; writer.

Gehr'kens, **Karl Wilson;** b. Kelleys Island, O., April 19, 1882; educator; A. M., Oberlin Coll. and Cons., prof. at this inst., author of many works on music; has served as pres. of Music Supervisors Nat'l. Conference and Music Teachers Nat'l. Ass'n.,

ed. of School Music, periodical of latter organization.

Gehrmann (gār'-män), **Hermann,** Wernigerode, Dec. 22, 1861—Cassel, July 8, 1916; historian and theorist; pupil Stern Cons., Berlin; 1908, Royal Prof.; c. string-quartet and songs.

Geijer (gī'-ĕr), **Erik Gustaf,** Ransätter, Wermeland, 1783—Upsala, 1847; coll. of Swedish folk-songs; prof.

Geisler (gīs'-lĕr), (1) **Jn. G.,** d. Zittau, 1827; writer. (2) **Paul,** Stolp, Pomerania, Aug. 10, 1856—Posen, April 3, 1919; grandson and pupil of a mus.-dir. at Mecklenburg; studied also with K. Decker; 1881–82 chorusm. Leipzig City Th., then with Neumann's Wagner Co.; 1883–85 at Bremen (under Seidl); then lived in Leipzig; prod. 5 operas; c. 12 symphonic poems, incl. "*Der Rattenfänger von Hameln*," "*Till Eulenspiegel*," etc.

Geistinger (gīs'-tĭng-ĕr), **Maria ("Marie")** **Charlotte Cäcilia,** Graz, Styria, July 26, 1836—Rastenfield, Sept. 29, 1903; soprano; sang at Vienna Op., 1865–75; in U. S., 1897–99.

Gelinek (gā'-lĭ-nĕk), (1) **Hn. Anton** (called **Cervetti**), Horzeniowecs, Bohemia, 1709—Milan, 1779; ex-priest, violinist and composer. (2) **Joseph,** Abbé; Selcz, Bohemia, 1758—Vienna, 1825; teacher and composer.

Geminiani (jĕm-ē-nĭ-ä'-nē), **Fran.,** Lucca, 1687—Dublin, Dec. 17, 1762; brilliant and original violinist of great importance in English progress, author of the first vln. method pub. (1740), c. concerti, sonatas, etc.

Gemünder (gĕ-münt'-ĕr), **Aug. Martin,** Würtemberg, March 22, 1814—New York, Sept. 7, 1895; a maker whose vlns. were of the very highest perfection; his sons succeeded him.

Genast (gĕ-näst'), **Ed.,** Weimar, 1797 —Wiesbaden, 1866; barytone and composer.

Genée (zhŭ-nā), **Franz Friedrich Richard,** Danzig, Feb. 7, 1823—Baden, near Vienna, June 15, 1895; pupil of Stalleknacht, Berlin; theatre conductor various cities; a student, then conductor and operatic composer; 1868–78 at Th. an der Wien, Vienna; wrote libretti for many of his own works and for Strauss and others; c. light operas with succ., incl. "*Der Geiger aus Tirol*," "*Nanon*," etc.

Generali (jā-nĕ-rä'-lē), **Pietro** (rightly

Mercandet'ti), Masserano, Piedmont, 1783—Novara, 1832; conductor and dram. composer.

Genet (zhŭ-nä), **Eleazar** (called **il Carpentras'so**, or **Carpentras** (kăr-päñträs)), Carpentras Vaucluse, ca. 1470 —Avignon, June 14, 1548; singer, then cond., then bishop; his admired masses, etc., were the first printed in round notes without ligature.

Genss (gĕns), **Hermann**, b. Tilsit, Jan. 6, 1856; pianist; pupil of the Royal Hochsch. für Mus., Berlin; teacher in various cities; 1893, co-dir. Scharwenka-Klindworth Cons., Berlin; after 1899 teacher in and 1905 dir. of Irving Inst., San Francisco, Cal.; c. orch. works, etc.

Georges (zhôrzh), **Alex.**, Arras, France, Feb. 25, 1850—Paris, Jan. 19, 1938; pupil, later prof. of harm., Niedermeyer Sch., Paris; c. operas "*Le Printemps*" (1888) and "*Poèmes d'Amour*" (1892); "*Charlotte Corday*" (1901); 2 oratorios, a mystery "*La Passion*" (1902); symph. poem, songs, etc.

Gérard (zhä-răr), **H. P.**, Liége, 1763— Versailles, 1848; teacher and writer.

Gérardy (zhä-răr-dē), **Jean**, Spa, Belgium, Dec. 7, 1877—July 4, 1929; notable 'cellist; studied with Bellmann; a pupil of Grützmacher; played as a child in England; at 13 in Dresden; 1899, etc., toured America.

Ger'ber, (1) **H. Nikolaus**, Wenigen-Ehrich, near Sondershausen, 1702— Sondershausen, 1775; organist and composer. (2) **Ernst L.**, Sondershausen, 1746—1819; son, pupil and successor (1775) of above; 'cellist, organist, lexicographer and composer.

Gerbert (gĕr'-bĕrt), **(von Hornau) Martin**, Harb-on-Neckar, Aug. 12, 1720—St. Blaise, May 13, 1793; collector of the invaluable "*Scriptores ecclesiastici de musica sacra potissimum*," noteworthy treatises of the Middle Ages, reproduced exactly (the compilation was continued by Coussemaker). The work is briefly referred to in this book as "Gerbert."² He became in 1736 cond. at St. Blaise; when he died, the peasants erecting a statue to him; pub. also other very important works, and c. offertories, etc.

Ger'hardt, (1) **Paul**, b. Leipzig, Nov. 10, 1867; organ-virtuoso; pupil at the Cons.; since 1898 org. at Zwickau; c. organ works, etc. (2) **Elena**, b. Leipzig, Nov. 11, 1883; soprano, esp. noted as a Lieder singer; pupil of cons. in native city, with Madame Hedmondt; after 1903 appeared in many recitals with Nikisch; sang at Leipzig Op., but gave up stage career for concert activity; has toured widely in Europe, England, and in America after 1912.

Gericke (gä'-rĭ-kĕ), **Wilhelm**, Graz, Styria, April 18, 1845—Vienna, Oct. 27, 1925; pupil of Dessoff, Vienna, Cons., then cond. at Linz; 1874, 2d. cond. Vienna ct.-opera (with Hans Richter); 1880, cond. of the "Gesellschaftsconcerte" (vice Brahms); also cond. the Singerverein; 1884-89, cond. Boston (Mass.) Symphony Orch., resuming the post 1898-1908, (vice Emil Paur) after being dir. "Gesellschaftsconcerte" at Vienna until 1895; pub. several choruses, pf.-pcs. and songs; also c. operetta "*Schön Hännchen*" (Linz, 1865); a Requiem; a concert-overture, etc.

Gerlach (gĕr'-läkh), (1) **Dietrich**, d. Nürnberg, 1574; music-printer, 1566-1571. (2) **Theodor**, b. Dresden, June 25, 1861; pupil of Wüllner; at 22 prod. a notable cantata, "*Luther's Lob der Musica*," 1884; Italy, 1885; cond. Sondershausen Th., then of German Opera in Posen; his "*Epic Symphony*" caused his appointment as ct.-cond. in Coburg, 1891; 1894, cond. at Cassel; then living in Dresden and Berlin; after 1904 dir. of a mus. school at Carlsruhe; c. succ. opera (book and music) "*Matteo Falcone*" (Hanover, '98, Berlin, 1902); orch. pieces, etc.

Gerle (gĕr'-lĕ), (1) **Konrad**, d. Nürnberg, 1521; lute-maker. (2) **Hans,** d. Nürnberg, 1570; probably son of above; violinist and vln.-maker.

Ger'man, Sir Edward (rightly **Jones**), Whitechurch, Feb. 17, 1862—London, Nov. 11, 1936; violin pupil of R. A. M.; 1889, dir. Globe Th., London; 1901 completed Arthur Sullivan's unfinished opera "*The Emerald Isle*," prod. with succ. London, 1901; c. operas, 2 symphonies; various suites, including the "Gipsy" suite, chamber-music, songs, etc. His incidental music to Shakespeare's plays is especially notable, and much popularity has been won by his suites for "*Nell Gwynne*" and "*Henry VIII.*" Knighted, 1928.

Germer (gĕr'-mĕr), **H.**, Sommersdorf, Province of Saxony, Dec. 30, 1837 —Dresden, Jan. 4, 1913; pupil Berlin Akademie; teacher, pianist and writer.

Gernsheim (gĕrns'-hīm), **Fr.**, Worms, July 17, 1839—Berlin, Sept. 11, 1916; of Hebrew parents; pupil of Rosenhain and Hauff, Frankfort, and Leipzig Cons.; 1865, teacher of comp. and pf. Cologne Cons.; 1872, Prof.; 1874, dir. of the Cons. at Rotterdam and cond. "Winter Concerts"; 1890 at Stern Cons., Berlin; c. 4 symphonies, overtures, etc.

Gero (gä'-rō), **Jhan (Johann)** (called **Maister Jan** or **Jehan**, or **Joannes Gallus**), conductor and composer at Orvieto Cath., 16th cent.

Gersh'win, George, Brooklyn, N. Y., Sept. 26, 1898—Hollywood, July 12, 1937; one of the most talented pioneers in the creation of music with jazz idiom as basis, incl. orchestral works on symph. scale; studied piano with Hambitzer, composition with Kilenyi and Rubin Goldmark; c. many pop. operettas and musical revues; came into internat'l. prominence with his "*Rhapsody in Blue*," first heard at a Paul Whiteman concert in N. Y., a work written for piano and orchestra, exploiting jazz idiom treated in elaborate form; this work heard widely in U. S. and in Europe; also c. "*An American in Paris*," symph. poem; piano concerto in F (latter commissioned by Walter Damrosch for N. Y. Symph. Orch.), and a Negro folk opera, "*Porgy and Bess*," presented by N. Y. Theatre Guild, 1935.

Gerster (gĕr -shtĕr), **Etelka**, Kaschau, Hungary, June 16, 1857—near Bologna, Aug. 20, 1920; one of the most remarkable coloratura-sopranos of her time; 1874-75, a pupil of Marchesi, Vienna Cons.; v. succ. début Venice, Jan. 8, 1876; in her impresario Dr. Carlo Gardini and toured Europe and America after 1878 until her retirement in 1890; lost her voice suddenly and opened (1896) a singing-school in Berlin.

Gervasoni (jĕr-vä-sō'-nē), **Carlo**, Milan, 1762–1819; writer and theorist.

Gerville-Réache (jĕr'-vēl-rä-äsh'), **Jeanne**, Orthez, France, 1882—New York, 1915; contralto; studied with Laborde, Madame Viardot-Garcia and Criticos; after 1900 sang at Paris Op.-Comique; 1902, Brussels; 1907-10, Manhattan Op. Co., New York; 1911-12, Chicago Op.; 1913-14, Gr. Op. of Canada.

Gervinus (gĕr-vē'-noos), **Georg Gf.**, Darmstadt, 1805—Heidelberg, 1871; professor and writer.

Geselschap (gĕ-zĕl'-shäp), **Marie, b.** Batavia, Java, Dec. 15, 1874; pianist; pupil of X. Scharwenka, Berlin; played in America, etc.; 1895 in London.

Gesius (rightly **Göss**) (gä'-sĭ-oos; gĕs), **Bartholomäus**, Müncheberg, ca. 1555 —Frankfort-on-Oder, 1613; cantor and composer.

Gesualdo (jä-zoo-äl'-dō), **Don Carlo**, Prince of Venosa, d. 1614; one of the most intellectual and progressive mus. of his time; wishing to revive the chromatic and enharmonic genera of the Greeks, he strayed out of the old church-modes and, becoming one of the "chromaticista," wrote almost in modern style.

Gevaërt (zhŭ-värt'), **François Auguste**, Huysse, near Oudenarde, July 31, 1828—Brussels, Dec. 24, 1908; pupil of Sommère (pf.) and Mengal (comp.) at Ghent Cons., taking Gr. prix de Rome for comp.; 1843, organist at the Jesuit church; he prod. 2 operas; lived in Paris (1849-50); then went to Spain and c. "*Fantasia sobre motivos espanoles*," still pop. there, for which he was given the order of Isabella la Catolica; he sent back reports on Spanish music (pub. by the Academy, 1851); he returned to Ghent 1852, prod. 9 operas, 2 of them, "*Georgette*" and "*Le billet de Marguerite*," with much success; in 1857 his festival cantata "*De Nationale Verjaerdag*" brought him the Order of Leopold; 1867-70 *chef de chant* Gr. Opéra, Paris; 1871, dir. Brussels Cons. (vice Fétis); created a baron by Belgian Government, 1908; pub. colls. of Italian music, also the valuable fruits of much research in old plain-song. His "*Traité d'instrumentation*" (1863) revised as "*Nouveau traité*," etc. (1885); he prod. also cantatas, "*Missa pro Defunctis*" and "*Super Flumina Babylonis*" for male chorus and orch.; overture "*Flandre au Lion*," etc.

Geyer (gī-ĕr), Flodoard, Berlin, 1811 —1872; prof., critic, theorist and dram. composer.

Gheyn (gĕn), Matthias van den, Tirlemont, Brabant, 1721 — Louvain, 1785; one of a Flemish family of bell founders; organist. Of his 17 children his son Jossé Thos. (b. 1752) was his successor as organist.

Ghione (gē-ō'-nä), Franco, Italian cond., appointed to lead Detroit Symph. Orch., 1937.

Ghiselin(g) (gē-zĕ-lŭng) (or **Ghiselinus**), Jean, Netherlandish; contrapuntist 15–16th cent.

Ghislanzoni (gēs-län-tsō'-nē), A., Lecca, 1824 — Caprino-Bergamasco, 1893; barytone and writer; wrote more than 60 opera librettos, incl. that of "Aïda."

Ghizeghem. Vide HEYNE.

Ghizzolo (gēd'-zō-lō), Gio., b. Brescia. 1560 (?); monk and composer.

Ghys (gēs), Joseph, Ghent, 1801—St. Petersburg, 1848; violinist, teacher and composer.

Giacomelli (jäk-ō-mĕl'lē), Geminiano, Parma, 1686—Naples, 1743; dram composer.

Gianelli (jä-nĕl'-lē), Pietro, (Abbate) Friuli, Italy, ca. 1770—Venice, 1822 (?); lexicographer.

Gianettini (jä-nĕt-tē'-nē) (or **Zanettini**), A., Venice, 1649—Modena. 1721; dram. composer.

Giannini, (1) Dusolina (dōōs-ō-lē'-nä jä-nē'-nē), b. Philadelphia, Dec. 19, 1902; soprano; studied with Marcella Sembrich; début, New York, in concert, 1923; has appeared widely in opera in Europe, including Hamburg, Berlin, Paris, Budapest, also at Covent Garden; Met. Op. Co., N. Y., début as "Aïda," 1935-36; has made concert tours of U. S., Europe, Australia, New Zealand; also sang in opera at Salzburg Fest. (2) **Vittorio,** bro. of Dusolina; b. 1903, Philadelphia; composer; studied composition with Rubin Goldmark; also trained as violinist; c. (operas) "Lucedia" (Munich, 1934), "The Scarlet Letter"; "Symphony in Memoriam T. Roosevelt"; Requiem; songs; awarded fellowship at Amer. Acad. in Rome.

Gianotti (jä-nôt'-tē), P., Lucca—Paris, 1765; double-bassist, composer and writer.

Giarda (jär'-dä), Luigi Stefano, b.

Castelnuovo, Pavia, March 19, 1868; 'cellist; pupil Milan Cons.; teacher at Padua, 1893-07; 1897-1920, at Royal Cons., Naples; then at Santiago Cons., vice-dir.; c. opera "Reietto" (Naples, 1898), 'cello-music and method.

Giardini (jär-dē'-nē), Felice de, Turin, 1716—Moscow, 1796; violinist and dram. composer.

Gib'bons, (1) Orlando, Cambridge, England, 1583—Canterbury, June 5, 1625; esteemed as one of the foremost of Engl. organists and composers; Mus. Doc. Oxon; 1604, organist Chapel Royal; 1623, organist Westminster Abbey. (2) **Christopher,** London, 1615—Oct. 20, 1676; son of (1), organist and composer.

Gibbs, Cecil Armstrong, b. Great Baddow, Engl., Aug. 10, 1889; composer; studied at Winchester and Trinity Coll., Cambridge, with Dent and Wood; also with Vaughan Williams and Boult; teacher of composition and theory at R. Coll. of Mus.; c. many orch., chamber music and other works, in conservative style, well constructed and imaginative.

Gibert (zhē-bâr), Paul César, Versailles, 1717—Paris, 1787; dram. composer.

Gibert (hē-bĕrt) (or **Gisbert, Gispert**), Francisco Xavier, Granadella, Spain —Madrid, 1848; priest, cond. and composer.

Gide (zhēd), Casimir, Paris, 1804— 1868; composer.

Gieseking (gē'-sĕ-kĕng), Walter, b. Lyons, France, Nov. 5, 1895; German pianist; trained at Hanover Cons., study with Karl Leimer; début, 1920; has made many tours of Germany, Switzerland and other Eur. countries; Amer. début 1926; a brilliant virtuoso, with reputation as interpreter of modern music, particularly Debussy; c. quintet for piano and wind instruments, piano pieces, songs.

Gigli, Beniamino (bĕn-yä-mēn'-ō jēl'-yē), b. Recanati, Italy, March 20, 1890; operatic tenor; studied at Rome Liceo di Santa Cecilia with Cotogni and Enrico Rosati; début as "Enzo," Rovigo, 1914; sang widely in Italian opera houses, incl. Rome, Naples, Milan, also in South America; Met. Op. Co., N. Y., début in

"Mefistofele," 1920; sang leading rôles with this co. until 1934; has also sung in London, Berlin and elsewhere, enjoying internat'l. reputation; concert tours in U. S. and Europe; Grand Ufficiale, Order of the Crown of Italy.

Gigout (zhē-goo)₊ **Eugene,** Nancy, France, March 23, 1844—Paris, Dec. 9, 1925; organ-virtuoso, critic, etc.; pupil in the *maitrise* of Nancy cath.; at 13 entered Niedermeyer Sch., Paris, and was later teacher there for over 20 years; studied also with Saint-Saëns; 1863, organist at the Ch. of St. Augustin; succ. concert organist throughout Europe; 1885, founded an organ-sch. subsidized by the govt.; commander of the order of Isabella la Catolica; 1885, officier of pub. instruction; 1895, Chev. of the Legion of Honour; pub. over 300 Gregorian and plain-song compositions.

Gil'bert (1) **Alfred,** Salisbury, Oct. 21, 1828—London, Feb. 6, 1902; organist and composer; his brother, (2) **Ernest Thos. Bennett,** Salisbury, Oct. 22, 1833—London, May 11, 1885; organist, teacher and composer. (3) **Walter Bond,** Exeter, April 21, 1829—Oxford, 1910; organist; pupil of Wesley and Bishop; 1886, Mus. Doc. Oxford; 1889, came to New York; c. oratorios, etc. (4) **Henry Franklin Belknap,** Somerville, Mass., Sept. 26, 1868—Cambridge, Mass., May 19, 1928; violin pupil of Mollenhauer; studied harmony with G. H. Howard and for 3 years with MacDowell; 1892–1901 in business, then took up composition. His work is full of originality and character; c. Comedy Overture on Negro Themes (Boston Symph., 1911); *Americanesque, Two Episodes, I, Legend; II, Negro Episode,* Boston (1896, and often elsewhere); *"Salammbo's Invocation to Tanith"* for soprano and orch. (1906); *"American Dances in Rag-Time"* for orch.; symph. poem, *"The Dance in Place Congo"*; for piano *"Indian Scenes,"* *"Negro Episode,"* etc., many beautiful songs, including the well-known *"Pirate Song"*; also *"Negro Rhapsody"* (1913), and symph. prologue *"Riders to the Sea"* (1915). He lectured at Harvard and Columbia Univs.; his *"Place Congo"* was given as a ballet at Met. Op., 1918.

Gil'christ, W. Wallace, Jersey City₊ N. J., Jan. 8, 1846—Easton, Pa., Dec. 20, 1916; pupil of H. A. Clarke at the U. of Penn.; from 1877 organist and choirm. Christ Ch., Germantown; from 1882 teacher Phila. Mus. Acad.; cond. of orch. and choral societies; c. prize *Psalm xlvi.* for soli, chorus, orch. and org. (Cincinnati Festival, 1882), *"Song of Thanksgiving"* for chorus and orch.; a cantata *"The Rose,"* etc.

Giles (jīlz), **Nathaniel,** near Worcester, Engl., ca. 1550—Windsor, Jan. 24, 1633; organist; Mus. Doc. Oxon; writer and composer.

Gilibert (zhēl-ē-bār'), **Chas.,** Paris, 1866—New York, 1910; barytone; pupil of Paris Cons.; after about 1888 sang at Brussels; 1900–03, Met. Op. Co.; 1906–10, Manhattan Op. Co.; was to have returned to Met. but died suddenly; an excellent song interpreter.

Gille (gĭl'-lĕ), **Karl,** Eldagsen, Hanover, Sept. 30, 1861—Hanover, June 14, 1917; pupil of J. Fischer, Bott and Metadorf; theatre-cond. in various cities; 1891–97 court cond., Schwerin; 1897 succeeded Mahler at Hamburg Stadttheater; 1906, first cond. Vienna Volksoper; after 1910 in Hanover.

Gilly (zhē'-lĕ), **Dinh,** Algeria—London, May 19, 1940; barytone; Met. Op. 1909–14.

Gil'man, Lawrence, b. Flushing, N. Y., July 5, 1878—Franconia, N. H., Sept. 8, 1939; ed. Collins St. Classical School, Hartford, Conn.; self-trained in music; 1901–13, music critic for Harper's *Weekly*; after 1913, music and dram. critic, *The North American Review*; beginning 1923, music critic of N. Y. *Tribune* (later *Herald-Tribune*), succeeding the late H. E. Krehbiel; for some seasons he has written the annotations for the N. Y. Philh. Orch. programmes, in which he has shown distinguished literary and musical taste; author, *"Phases of Modern Music," "Edward MacDowell," "The Music of Tomorrow," "Guide to Strauss' Salome," "Stories of Symphonic Music," "Guide to Debussy's Pelléas et Mélisande"; "Aspects of Modern Music," "Life of Edward MacDowell," "Nature in Music,"* etc.; c. *"A Dream of Youth,"* etc.

Gil'more, Patrick Sarsfield, near Dublin, Dec. 25, 1829—St. Louis, Mo.,

Sept. 24, 1892; an immensely popular conductor, some of whose influence went to the popularising of good music; on occasions he cond. an orch. of 1,000 and a chorus of 10,000, also an orch. of 2,000 and a chorus of 20,000, reinforced with cannon fired by electricity, an organ, anvils, chimes, etc. (cf. Sarti); he c. pop. military and dance music.

Gilson (zhĕl-sōṅ), **Paul,** b. Brussels, June 15, 1865; self-taught; his cantata *"Sinai"* won the Grand prix de Rome, 1892; 1896 prod. opera *"Alvar,"* Brussels; completed Ragghianti's opera *"Jean-Marie"*; 1904, teacher of harmony Antwerp Cons., and critic of the *"Soir"*; composed operas, *"Gens de mer,"* (based on Victor Hugo's novel, Brussels, 1902; Antwerp, 1904) and *"Prinses Zonnenschijn"* (Antwerp, 1903); ballet, *"La Captive,"* Brussels, 1902; symph. *"La Mer,"* 1892; orch. fantasy on Canadian folk-songs, symph. poems, etc.

Giner (hē-nār'), **Salvador,** Valencia, Jan. 17, 1832—Nov. 3, 1911; pupil of Gascons; dir. Valencia Cons.; c. a symph. *"The Four Seasons,"* operas, etc.

Ginguené (zhăṅ-gŭ-nā), **P. L.,** Rennes, 1748—Paris, 1816; writer.

Giordani (jôr-dä'-nē), name of a family, father, 3 sisters and 2 brothers, all singers in comic opera at Naples, till 1762 when they came to London (except Giuseppe); one of the brothers wrote the still pop. song *"Caro mio ben."* (1) **Tommaso** (rightly **Carmine**), Naples, ca. 1740—Dublin after 1816; dram. composer. (2) **Giuseppe** (called **Giordanel'lo**), Naples, 1744—Fermo, 1798; bro. of above; conductor; c. 30 operas.

Giordano (jôr-dä'-nō), **Umberto,** b. Foggia, Aug. 27, 1867; studied with Paolo Serrao at the Naples Cons.; c. operas; very succ. *"Andrea Chénier"* (La Scala, Milan, 1896; in Berlin, 1898, and U. S.); also *"Miranda,"* unsucc., *"Regina Diaz"* (Naples, 1894); and succ. 3-act melodrama *"Mala Vita"* (Rome, 1892, prod. as *"Il Voto,"* Milan, 1897); *"Fédora"* (Milan, 1898), *"Siberia,"* (do, 1903, Leipzig, 1907), and *"Marcella"* (Milan, 1907); *"Mme. Sans Gene"* (Met. Op., 1915); mus. comedy, *"Giove a Pompei"* (Rome, 1921); *"La Cena delle Beffe"* (La Scala,

1924, at Met. Op., 1926) and *"Il Re"* (1928).

Giorgetti (jôr-jĕt-té), **Ferdinando,** Florence, 1796–1867; violinist, teacher and comp.

Giorgi (jôr'-jē). Vide BANTI.

Giorni (jōr'-nē), **Aurelio,** Perugia, Italy, Sept. 15, 1895, Pittsfield, Mass., Sept. 23, 1938; composer, pianist; studied St. Cecilia Acad., Rome, piano with Sgambati, composition with Humperdinck, piano with Busoni, Gabrilowitsch, Lhevinne and Da Motta; début as orch. soloist, Rome, 1912; appeared also in Berlin, London and U. S. (after 1914); mem. of Elshuco Trio; taught formerly at Inst. of Music. Art, N. Y., later at Phila. Cons.; composed orchestral, chamber music, choral and piano works.

Giornovichi. Vide JARNOVIC.

Giorza (jôr'-tsä), **Paolo,** Milan, Nov. 11, 1838—Seattle, Wash., May 4, 1914; son and pupil of an organist and dram. singer; studied cpt. with La Croix; lived New York some years, later London; prod. unsucc. opera *"Corrado"* (Milan, 1869), and many succ. ballets.

Giosa, Nicola de. Vide DE GIOSA.

Giovanelli (jō-vä-nĕl'-lē), **Ruggiero,** Velletri, ca. 1560—Rome, 1625; 1599 successor of Palestrina as conductor at St. Peter's, Rome; an important composer.

Giraldoni (zhē-räl-dō'-nē), **Leone,** Paris, 1824—Moscow, 1897; barytone.

Girard (zhē-rär), **Narcisse,** Nantes, France, 1797—Paris, 1860; conductor and violin professor.

Girardeau (zhē-rär-dō), **Isabella,** called **la Isabella,** Italian singer in London, ca. 1700.

Gizziello (gĭd-zĭ-ĕl'-lō), **Gioacchino.** Vide CONTI.

Glad'stone, Francis Edw., Summertown, near Oxford, May 2, 1845—Hereford, Sept. 5, 1928; pupil of S. Wesley; organist various churches; 1879 Mus. Doc., Contab; 1881, prof. of cpt. Trinity Coll., London; prof. of harm. and cpt. R. C. M.; c. an overture, chamber-music, etc.

Glarea'nus, Henricus (rightly **Heinrich Lo'ris,** Latinized, **Lori'tus**), Glarus, 1488 — Freiburg, Baden, March 28, 1563; poet and important theorist.

Glasenapp (glä'-zĕ-näp), **Karl Fr.,**

Riga, October 3, 1847—April 14; 1915; studied philosophy at Dorpat, since 1875 head-master at Riga; wrote on Wagner, a biography in 3 vols., a lexicon, and a Wagner Encyclopædia, etc.

Gläser (glä'-zĕr), (1) **K. G.**, Weissenfels, 1784—Barmen, 1829; mus. dir. and later dealer, composer and writer. (2) **Fz.**, Obergeorgenthal, Bohemia, 1798—Copenhagen, 1861; conductor, violinist, and dram. composer.

Glaz(o)unow (glä'-tsoo-nôf), **Alex.**, St. Petersburg, Aug. 10, 1865—Paris, March 21, 1936; eminent Russian composer; studied till 1883 at Polytechnic Inst., then took up music; studied with Rimsky-Korsakov; 1881 his first symphony was produced, repeated under Liszt in 1884 at Weimar; he cond. his second symphony in Paris, 1889; his fourth symphony, London Phil.; 1896-97, with Rimsky-Korsakov and Liadov, cond. Russian Symphony Concerts at St. P.; from 1899 he was prof. of instrumentation, St. Petersburg Cons.; 1909-12 director; honoured by Soviets but lived Paris after 1930. He c. 8 symphs. 5 suites, ballets, 4 overtures, a symph. poem, "*Stenka Rasin*," a symphonic fantasy, "*Through Night to Light*," and a great number of other orch. works, chamber music in large quantity and high quality, cantatas, the "*Memorial*" (Leeds, Fest., 1901), ballets, violin concerto (1904), etc.

Gleason (glē'-sŭn), **Fr. Grant**, Middletown, Conn., Dec. 17, 1848—Chicago, June 12, 1903; pupil of Dudley Buck and at Leipzig Cons.; later at Berlin, of Loeschorn, Weitzmann and Haupt; later with Beringer (pf.) in London; 1875 organist Hartford; 1877, teacher Hershey Sch. of Music, Chicago; critic for years of Chicago *Tribune*; c. (text and music) grand operas "*Otho Visconti*" and "*Montezuma*"; cantata "*The Culprit Fay*," with orch.; "Praise-song to Harmony," symphonic cantata; "Auditorium Festival Ode," symph. cantata with orch.; op. 21, "*Edris*," symphonic poem (after the prologue to "*Ardath*" by Marie Corelli), etc.

Gleich (glīkh), **Fd.**, Erfurt, 1816—Langebrück, near Dresden, 1898; critic and writer; c. symphonies.

Gleissner (glīs'-nĕr), **Fz.**, Neustadt-on-the-Waldnab, 1760—Munich, after 1815; printed songs of his own by lithographic process, the first music so printed.

Gleitz (glīts), **K.**, Hetzerode, near Cassel, Sept. 13, 1862—Torgau, June, 1920; studied Leipzig Cons. and Munich Music School, and in Berlin; c. symph.-poem "*Fata Morgana*" (played by Nikisch at the Berlin Philh. concerts, 1898); "*Ahasuerus*," "*Venus and Bellona*," etc., for orch.; "*Hafbur and Signild*," for chorus; "*Inlichter*," a pf.-fantasy with orch.; vln.-sonata, etc.

Glière (glē-âr), **Reinhold Moritzovich**, composer; b. Kiev, Dec. 30, 1874 (O. S.), or Jan. 11, 1875, (N. S.); pupil of Moscow Cons., winning gold medal; in 1913, prof. Kiev Cons.; 1914, dir. of same; after 1920, prof. of comp., Moscow Cons. He has enjoyed honours under the Soviet regime, and has striven to embody revolutionary and proletarian ideals in his later productions. His ballet, "*The Red Poppy*," became for a time most popular on the stages of the U. S. S. R., and a lively "*Sailor's Dance*" from this work has been perf. widely in other countries, incl. U. S. His principal works include 2 symphonies, "*Les Sirènes*," "*Ilya Mourometz*"; and "*Triana*" for orch.; 3 string quartets, 3 string sextets, octet for strings; the ballet "*Chrysis*," etc.

Glinka (glĭnk'-ä), **Michail Ivanovitch**, Novospasköi, near Smolensk, Russia, June 1 (new style), 1804—Berlin, Feb. 15, 1857; piano-virtuoso and composer, father of the new nationalistic Russian Musical School; of noble birth; pupil of Bohm (vln.), Mayer (theory and pf.), John Field (pf.). Of very weak health, he studied vocal composition in Italy; 1834 with Dehn in Berlin; prod. at St. Petersburg, 1836, the first Russian national opera "*A Life for the Czar*" (*Zarskaja Skisu* or *Ivan Sussanina*), with succ. still lasting; the next opera "*Russlan and Ludmilla*" (St. P., 1842) was also succ. (book by Pushkin); 1844 in Paris he gave orch. concerts strongly praised by Berlioz; 1845-47, Madrid and Seville, where he c. "*Jota Aragonese*," a "*Capriccio brillante*" for orch., and "*Souvenir d'une nuit d'été à Madrid*," for orch.; 1851, Paris; 1854–55, near St. Petersburg writing his autobiography, planning a never-attempted opera; he visited Dehn at Berlin in 1856, and died there suddenly; Glinka's other comp. incl. 2 unfinished symphonies; 2 polonaises for orch.; a fantasia, *"La Kamarinskaja"*; a septet; 2 string-quartets; trio for pf., clar. and oboe; dramatic scenes; vocal-quartets, songs and pf.-pcs.

Glöggl (glĕg'-gl), (1) **Fz. X.,** Linz-on-Danube, 1764—July 16, 1839; conductor, mus. dir.; writer. (2) **Fz.,** Linz, 1797—Vienna, 1872; son of above; est. music business, 1843; writer and mus. director.

Glover (glŭv'-ĕr), (1) **Sarah Ann,** Norwich, Engl., 1785—Malvern, 1867; inv. the Tonic Sol-fa system of notation and wrote about it. (2) **Chas. W.,** Feb., 1806—London, 1863; violinist, etc. (3) **Stephen,** London, 1812—Dec. 7, 1870; teacher and composer. (4) **W. Howard,** London, 1819—New York, 1875; violinist and critic; sang in opera. (5) **John Wm.,** Dublin, June 19, 1815—Jan. 15, 1900; violinist and choirmaster at the Cathedral from 1860; c. opera *"The Deserted Village"* (London, 1880), etc.

Gluck (glook), (1) **Christoph Wilibald** (Ritter **von**), Weidenwang, near Neumarkt, Upper Palatinate, July 2, 1714—Vienna, Nov. 15, 1787; son of head-gamekeeper to Prince Lobkowitz; at twelve went to the Jesuit Coll. at Komotau (1726–32), where he learnt the violin, clavecin, and organ, and was chorister in the Ch. of St. Ignaz; at eighteen he went to Prague, earning a living by playing at rural dances, giving concerts and singing and playing in various churches; under the tuition of Father Czernohorsky he mastered singing and the 'cello, his favourite instr.; 1736 entered the service of Prince Melzi, Vienna, who took him to Milan and had him study harm. and cpt. with Sammartini. After four years' study he prod. *"Artaserse"* (La Scala, 1741) with great succ. and was commissioned to c. for other theatres; prod. 8 operas 1742–45. On invitation he went to London 1745 as composer for the Haymarket, in opposition to Händel. *"La Caduca dei Giganti"* was given on the defeat of the Pretender, 1746,

"Artamene," followed by *"Piramo e Tisbe,"* a pasticcio of his best arias, had no succ. and led Händel to say that the music was detestable, and that Gluck knew no more counterpoint than his cook. The operas **G.** had written up to this time were thoroughly Italian. The influence of Händel and Rameau's works heard at Paris awakened him, and led him to that gradual reform which made him immortal, though it brought on him the most ferocious opposition. *"La Semiramide Riconosciuta"* (Vienna, 1748) began the change to more serious power. 1750–62 he prod. *"Telemaco"* (Rome, 1750), *"La Clemenza di Tito"* (Naples, 1751), and 4 others. 1754–64 he was dir. court-opera Vienna and prod. 6 more works. He made great succ. in spite of opposition with *"Orfeo ed Euridice"* (1762), *"Alceste"* (1767), *"Paride ed Elena"* (1769), libretti by Calzabigi. 2 other inferior works were performed by members of the royal family (1765). In the dedicatory prefaces to *"Alceste"* and *"Paride ed Elena,"* **G.** expressed his protest against the Italian school, and declared for dramatic consistency unhampered by rigid formulæ for arias, duets, etc., and interpolated cadenzas. He had such harsh criticism at home and such encouragement from du Rollet of the French Embassy at Vienna in 1772 that he went to Paris. But here also he met such opposition that all his diplomacy and all the power of his former pupil, Queen Marie Antoinette, hardly availed to bring about the presentation of *"Iphigénie en Aulide"* (1774); its great succ. was repeated in *"Orphée"* (Aug., 1774), *"Alceste"* (1776), and *"Armide"* (1777). Piccinni was brought to Paris as a rival, and prod. *"Roland"* while Gluck was preparing the same subject. Gluck burned his score and published a letter which precipitated an unimaginably fierce war of pamphlets. Both men now set to composing *"Iphigénie en Tauride"*; here Gluck forestalled his rival by two years (1779), and Piccinni's work on appearing was not a succ., while Gluck's succeeded enormously. His last opera, *"Echo et Narcisse,"* was not succ. (Sept. 21, 1779); 1780, he retired to Vienna and lived on his

well-earned wealth, till apoplexy carried him off. He wrote a De profundis for chorus and orch., 6 overtures and an incomplete cantata, *"Das Jüngste Gericht,"* finished by Salieri, and 7 odes for solo voice and pf. Biog. by A. Schmidt (1854); Marx (1863); Desnoiresterres (1872); also studies of his operas by Berlioz and Newman. (2) **Alma** (née **Reba Fierson**), Bucharest, Roumania, May 11, 1866—New York, Oct. 26, 1938; pupil of Buzzi-Peccia; début New Theatre, N. Y., 1909; the same year at the Met. Op.; of which mem. until 1912; sang widely in concert; m. Efrem Zimbalist, violinist.

Gluth (gloot), **Victor,** Pilsen, May 6, 1852—Munich, Jan. 17, 1917; taught Akademie der Tonkunst, Munich; c. operas *"Zlatorog"* and *"Horand und Hilde."*

Gmeiner (g'mī'nĕr), **Lula, Mysz-,** b. Kronstadt, Aug. 16, 1876; alto; studied vln. with Olga Grigorourcz; then studied voice with Gr. Walter and Emilie Herzog; noted Lieder singer.

Gnecchi (nyĕ'-kē), **Vittorio,** b. Milan, July 17, 1876; composer; private pupil of Saladino, Coronaro, Serafin and Gatti; c. (operas) *"Virtu d'Amore"* (1895); *"Cassandra"* (Bologna, 1905, also heard in Phila., 1914); *"La Rosiera"* (prod. in Germany); *"Judith"*; orch. works, songs; his *"Cassandra"* is asserted by Giovanni Tebaldini to have suggested certain details of Strauss's *"Elektra."*

Gnecco (n'yĕk'-kō), **Francesco,** Genoa, 1769—Milan, 1810; dram. composer.

Gniessin (gnyĕs'-ĕn), **Michael,** b. Rostoff, Russia, Jan. 23, 1883; composer; studied at Moscow and Petrograd Cons.; since 1923 teacher at the State Cons. in Moscow; his music utilises Jewish folk themes and shows an impressionistic manner; c. (opera) *"The Youth of Abraham,"* symphonic, choral and chamber music, songs.

Gobbaerts (gŭb'-bărts), **Jean Louis,** Antwerp, 1835—Saint Gilles, near Brussels, 1886; pianist and composer.

Göbel (gä'-bĕl), **K. H.,** Berlin, 1815—Bromberg, 1879; pianist, conductor, and dram. composer.

Gockel (gŏk'ĕl), **Aug.,** Willibadessen, Westphalia, 1831—1861; pianist and composer.

Godard (gō-dăr), **Benjamin (Louis Paul),** Paris, Aug. 18, 1849—Cannes, Jan. 11, 1895; studied vln. with Hammer and played in public at 9; then studied with Reber (comp.) and Vieuxtemps (vln.), Paris Cons.; 1865 pub. a vln.-sonata, later other chamber-compositions; rec'd the Prix Chartier from the Institut de France for merit in the department of chamber-music; prod. 5 operas, incl. *"Jocelyn"* (Brussels, 1888), and the very succ. posthumous *"La Vivandière"* (Paris Op.-Com., 1895), the last 2 acts orchestrated by Paul Vidal; 2 operas not prod.; he c. also incid. mus. and 6 symphonies; *"Le Tasse"* (Tasso), dram. symphony with soli and chorus took the city of Paris prize in 1878; concerto for vln.; a pf.-concerto, songs and pf.-pcs.

God'dard (Davison), **Arabella,** St. Servan, near Saint Malo, Brittany, Jan. 12, 1836—Boulogne, April 6, 1922; pianist; at 4 played in public, at 6 studied with Kalkbrenner at Paris, at 8 played to Queen Victoria; pub. 6 waltzes and studied with Mrs. Anderson and Thalberg; at 12 played at the Grand National Concerts; 1850-53 pupil of J. W. Davison, whom she m. (1860); toured Germany and at 17 played at Leipzig Gewandhaus etc.; 1873-76 toured the world; retired 1880 and lived in Tunbridge Wells.

Godebrye. Vide JACOTIN.

Godefroid (gôd-fwä), (1) **Jules Joseph,** Namur, Belgium, 1811—Paris, 1840; harpist and dram. composer. (2) **Dieudonné Jos. Guil. Félix,** Namur, 1818—Villers-sur-mer, 1897; bro. of above; harpist and dram. composer.

God'frey, (1) **Chas.,** Kingston, Surrey, 1790—1863; bassoonist and conductor. (2) **Daniel,** Westminster, Engl., Sept. 4, 1831—Beeston, near Nottingham, June 30, 1903; conductor; son of above; pupil R. A. M., later Fellow and Prof. of Military Mus.; 1856 bandm. of the Grenadier Guards; 1872 and 1898 toured the U. S. with his band, composer. (3) **Sir Daniel Eyers,** b. London, 1868; son of (2); noted conductor; after 1894 led symph. concerts at Bournemouth for more than 40 years, presenting series of eminent soloists and also organising fests. there; retired 1934; d. Bournemouth, July 20, 1939.

Godowsky (gō-dôf'-skē), **Leopold,** b. Wilna (Vilno), Russian Poland, Feb. 13, 1870—N. Y., Nov. 21, 1938; pianist; pupil of Rudorff; 1881–84 R. Hochschule, Berlin; 1887–90 studied with Saint-Saëns; 1890–91 toured America 'again; 1894 dir. pf.-dept., Broad St. Cons., Phila.; 1895–99 head of pf.-dept., Chicago Cons.; then toured Europe; 1902 lived in Berlin; succeeded Busoni in 1910, as head of the Master-School of the Vienna Imperial Academy; 1904, married Frieda Saxe; after 1912 made home in U. S.; c. symphonic Dance-pictures from Strauss "Fledermaus"[2]; sonata E minor, for piano;. left-hand transcriptions of Chopin Études, 50 études on Chopin's Études, and many brilliant piano works, incl. "Java"[2] suite, etc.

Goedicke (gĕd'-č-kē), **Alex. Fedoro-vitch,** b. Moscow, March 3, 1877; composer, pianist and organist; pupil of Pabst and Safonoff at the Cons. in his native city; won Vienna Rubin-stein prize in 1900 for his piano concerto; after 1907 taught at Mos-cow Cons.; c. orch., chamber and piano works of classical trend.

Goepfart (gĕp'-färt), (1) **Chr. H.,** Wei-mar, 1835—Baltimore, Md., 1890; organist and composer. (2) **Karl Eduard,** b. Weimar, March 8, 1859; son of above; 1891, cond. Baden-Baden Mus. Union; 1909–27, active in Potsdam; after 1928 in Weimar; c. "Sarastro,"[2] a sequel to Mozart's "Magic Flute,"[2] etc. (3) **Otto Ernst,** Weimar, July 31, 1864—Jan. 13, 1911; bro. of above; since 1888 Weimar town cantor and composer.

Goepp (gĕp), **Philip Henry,** New York, June 23, 1864—Philadelphia, Aug. 25, 1936; composer, writer; grad., Harvard Univ., studied comp. with Paine; 1892, founded Manuscript Soc.; after 1900 wrote programme notes for Phila. Orch.; prof. of theory, Temple Univ.; c. orch., chamber music, choral works, songs; author, "Symphonies and Their Meaning."[2]

Goes (gō'-ĕs), **Damião de,** Alemquer, Portugal, 1501—Lisbon, 1572; am-bassador, theorist and composer.

Goethe (gä'-tĕ), **Walther Wg. von,** Weimar, 1818—Leipzig, 1885; grand-son of the poet; c. 3 operettas, etc.

Goetschius (gĕt'-shī-oos), **Percy,** b. Paterson, N. J., Aug. 30, 1853; pupil Stuttgart Cons.; 1876, teacher there;

1885, Royal Prof.; critic for various German music papers; 1890–92, prof. Syracuse (N. Y.) Univ. and Mus. Doc.; 1892–96, taught comp. and lectured on mus., hist., etc., N. E. Cons., Boston; 1896, private teacher Boston, and essayist; 1897, organist First Parish Ch., Brookline; 1905–25, prof. at Inst. of Music. Art, N. Y.; pub. important and original treatises; ed. piano works of Mendelssohn; c. piano pieces and songs.

Goetz (gĕts), **Hn.,** Königsberg, Prussia, 1840—Hottingen, near Zurich, 1876; 1863, organist and conductor; c. operas, notably "Taming of the Shrew"; orch., chamber music, cho-ruses, songs, etc.

Göhler (gä'-lĕr), **Karl Georg,** b. Zwickau, June 29, 1874; author and comp.; pupil of Vollhardt and Leip-zig Cons.; 1896, Ph.D.; from 1898 director of the Riedelverein, also from 1903 court cond. at Altenburg; 1907–09 at Carlsruhe; 1909–13, Leipzig; 1913–14, Hamburg Op.; 1915–18, cond. Philh. Chorus and Orch., Lübeck; 1922–33, cond. Halle Philh. Orch.; c. 2 symphs.; orch. suite "Indian Songs."[2]

Goldbeck (gōlt'-bĕk), **Robert,** Pots-dam, April 19, 1839—St. Louis, May 16, 1908; pupil of Kohler and H. Litolff; gave succ. concerts in London and prod. operetta; 1857–67 in New York as teacher; 1868 founded a Cons. at Chicago; dir. till 1873; cond. the Harmonic Society, and co-dir. Beethoven Cons., St. Louis; New York, 1885; c. 3 operas; cantata, Burger's "Leonore,"[2] etc.

Goldberg (gōlt'-bĕrkh), (1) **Jn. G. (Theophilus),** Königsberg, ca. 1730 —Dresden (?), 1760 (?); organ and clavichord player. (2) **Jos. Pas-quale,** Vienna, 1825—1890; vln.-pupil of Mayseder and Seyfried, then operatic bass and teacher. His 2 sisters, (3) **Fanny G.-Marini** and (4) **Catherine G.-Strossi,** were singers.

Goldmark (gōlt'-märk), (1) **Karl,** Kesz-thely, Hungary, May 18, 1830— Vienna, Jan. 2, 1915; noted com-poser; violinist and pianist, pupil of Jansa (vln.), later of Bohm (theory) at the Vienna Cons., then mainly self-taught; début 1858 Vienna, with his own pf.-concerto; the popular overture "Sakuntala"[2] (op. 13); and a Scherzo, Andante, and Finale for Orch. (op. 19) won him success strengthened by his opera *"Die Königin von Saba"* (Vienna, 1875); c. also operas *"Merlin"* (Vienna, 1886) v. succ.; *"Das Heimchen am Herd"* based on Dickens' "Cricket on the Hearth" (Vienna, 1896); *"Die Kriegsgefangene"* (Vienna Ct.-opera, 1899); *"Der Fremdling"* (not prod.) and *"Götz von Berlichingen"*; c. also 2 symphonies, incl. *"Landliche Hochzeit"*; overtures, *"Im Frühling," "Prometheus Bound,"* and *"Sappho,"* also a pop. vln. concerto, suite for vln. and piano, choruses, songs, piano works; author, *"Reminiscences of My Life."* (2) Rubin, New York City, Aug. 15, 1872—March 6, 1936; composer; nephew of above; at 7 began to study with A. M. Livonius, with whom he went to Vienna, 1889; studied there also with Door and Fuchs; later in New York with Joseffy and Dvořák; 1892–1901, in Colorado Springs, Colorado; founder and dir. of a Coll. of Mus. there, *"Theme and Variations"* for orch. (performed by Seidl, 1895); c. a pf.-trio, cantata with orch. *"Pilgrimage to Kevlaar,"* overture *"Hiawatha"* (played by Boston Symph. Orch.), vln.-sonata, etc.; after 1902 lived again in N. Y. as teacher and comp.; 1924 until his death, head of comp. dept., Juilliard Grad. School; c. *"Gettysburg Requiem"* (N. Y. Philh., 1917); *"Negro Rhapsody"* (1922, played by many orchs.); founder and long pres., N. Y. Bohemians' Club.

Goldner (gŏlt′-nĕr), **Wm.,** Hamburg, June 30, 1839—Paris, Feb. 8, 1907; pupil Leipzig Cons.; lived in Paris as a pianist and composer.

Goldschmidt (gŏlt-shmĭt), (1) **Sigismund,** Prague, 1815—Vienna, 1877, pianist and composer. (2) **Otto,** Hamburg, Aug. 21, 1829—London, Feb. 24, 1907; pianist; pupil of Jakob Schmitt and F. W. Grund, Mendelssohn, and Chopin; 1849 London with Jenny Lind, whom he accompanied on her American tour and m. (Boston, 1852); 1852–55 Dresden; 1858–87 London; 1863 vice-principal of the R. A. M., 1875 founded Bach Choir, also cond. mus. festivals at Düsseldorf (1863) and Hamburg (1866); c. oratorio *"Ruth"* (Hereford, 1867); pf.-concerto and trio, etc. (3) **Adalbert von,** Vienna, May 5, 1848—Dec. 21, 1906; pupil

Vienna Cons.; amateur composer; prod. with great succ. cantata *"Die Sieben Todsünden"* (Berlin, 1875), and succ. opera *"Helianthus"* (Leipzig, 1884); prod. trilogy *"Gaea"* 1889. (4) **Hugo,** Breslau, Sept. 19, 1859—Wiesbaden, Dec. 26, 1920; 1884 Dr. jur.; studied singing with Stockhausen (1887–90); 1893–1905, co-dir. Scharwenka-Klindworth Cons., Berlin; writer.

Gold′win, John, d. Nov., 1719; Engl. organist and composer.

Golinel′li, Stefano, Bologna, Oct. 26, 1818—July 3, 1891; pianist; pupil of B. Donelli and N. Vaccai; pf.-prof. Liceo Musicale till 1870; c. 5 pf.-sonatas, etc.

Gollmick (gŏl′-mĭk), (1) **Fr. K.,** Berlin, 1774—Frankfort-on-Main, 1852; tenor. (2) **Karl,** Dessau, 1796—Frankfort-on-Main, 1866; son of above; theorist and writer. (3) **Adolf,** Frankfort-on-M., 1825—London, 1883; pianist; son and pupil of (2); studied also with Riefstahl, 1844; c. comic operas, etc.

Golsch′mann, Vladimir, b. Paris, Dec. 16, 1893; conductor; studied vln. with Möller, Berthelier, piano with de Saunieres and Braud, comp. with Dumas, and Caussade; founded Golschmann Orch., Paris, 1919, and led this series until 1923; guest cond. in other European cities; came to America as musical dir. of Swedish Ballet, invited to lead N. Y. Symph. as guest by Damrosch; cond. St. Louis Symph. Orch. after 1934.

Goltermann (gŏl′-tĕr-män), (1) **G. Ed.,** Hanover, 1824 — Frankfort-on-M., 1898; 'cellist and composer. (2) **Jn. Aug. Julius,** Hamburg, 1825—Stuttgart, 1876; 'cellist. (3) **Aug.,** 1826—Schwerin, 1890; court pianist.

Gombert (gôm′-bĕrt), **Nicolas,** Bruges, ca. 1495—after 1570; a most important 16th cent. composer, one of the first to take up secular music seriously; a lover of Nature and a writer of descriptive and pastoral songs of much beauty; his motet *"Pater Noster"* was prod. at Paris by Fétis with impressive effect.

Gomes (or Gomez) (gō′-mäs), **Antonio Carlos,** Campinas, Brazil, July 11, 1839—Para, Sept. 16, 1896; pupil of Rossi, Milan Cons.; Dir. of Para Cons.; c. succ. operas *"Il Guarany," "Salvator Rosa," "Lo Schiavo," "Maria Tudor,"* etc.

Gomiz (gō'-mĕth) **Jose Melchior,** Valencia, Jan. 6, 1791—Paris, July 26, 1836; military bandmaster and singing teacher at Paris; c. operas and patriotic songs.

Gom'pertz, Richard, Cologne, April 27, 1859—Dresden, 1921; violinist; pupil at the Cons., and of Joachim; toured, then invited to teach at Cambridge University; from 1883, teacher at R. C. M., 1895, prof.; from 1899 at Dresden; c. violin sonatas, etc.

Good'rich, (1) **Alfred John,** Chile, Ohio, May 8, 1847—Paris, April 25, 1920; eminent theorist; except for a year's instruction from his father, wholly self-taught; teacher theory Grand Cons., N. Y., 1876; voice, pf. and theory Fort Wayne Cons., Ind.; dir. vocal-dept. Beethoven Cons., St. Louis; 2 years at Martha Washington Coll., Va.; lived in Chicago, New York as teacher; pub. theoretical essays and books of radical and scholarly nature, the important products of research and individuality, incl. *"Complete Musical Analysis"* (1889), *"Analytical Harmony"* (1894), *"Theory of Interpretation"* (1898), *"Counterpoint."* (2) **(John) Wallace,** b. Newton, Mass., May 27, 1871; educator, organist and conductor; studied in Boston and Munich, and with Widor, Paris; taught New England Cons.; dean after 1907; became dir., succeeding Chadwick, 1931; 1897–1909, org. for Boston Symph., also in various churches in that city; 1902–08, cond. and founder, Boston Choral Art. Soc.; until 1907, dir. of choral work, Worcester Fest.; 1907–10, cond. Cecilia Soc.; in latter year also of orch. concerts; cond. with Boston Op. Co., 1907–12, when it disbanded; c. choral music; also author and translator of works on organ, etc.

Good'son, Katharine, b. Watford, England, June 18, 1872; pianist; at 12 pupil at the R. A. M., till 1892, then four years with Leschetizky—début, 1896, London Pop. Concerts; has toured widely; 1903, married Arthur Hinton (q.v.).

Goos'sens, (1) **Eugene,** b. London, May 26, 1893; conductor, composer; studied Bruges Cons. and Liverpool Coll. of Mus., later grad. R. Coll. of Mus., London; 1911–15, played in Queen's Hall Orch. and Philh. String Quartet; 1916, cond. Stanford's opera, *"The Critic"*; 1915–20, cond. in association with enterprises of Beecham; 1921, founded own orch. in London for a season; later with Brit. Nat'l. Op. Co. and Carl Rosa Co., the Russian Ballet, and London Symph.; 1923–31, cond. Rochester Symph. Orch. in U. S.; founded chamber music concerts in London; after 1931 cond. Cincinnati Symph. with which he has also given operas and ballets; c. (operas) *"Judith,"* to libretto by Arnold Bennett, (Covent Garden, 1929); *"Don Juan de Mañara"*; (orch.) *"Tam o' Shanter"*; *"Four Conceits"*; *"The Eternal Rhythm"*; *"Kaleidoscope"*; *"Rhythmic Dance"*; Sinfonietta; Fantasy for 9 wind instruments; 3 Greek Dances; Concertino for double string orch.; Poem for viola and orch.; Rhapsody for 'cello and orch.; *"By the Tarn"* for strings and clarinet; *"Silence"* for chorus and orch.; (chamber music) Fantasy Quartet; Sextet (commissioned for Berkshire Fest., 1923); Spanish Serenade; String Quartet in C; sonata for piano and vln.; piano sonatas, songs, piano pieces; *"Five Impressions of a Holiday"* for piano, flute (or vln.) and 'cello; (ballet) *"L'École en Crinoline."* (2) **Léon,** bro. of **Eugene;** oboist; pupil of R. Coll. of Mus.; mem. Philh. Trio; soloist in Covent Garden, Philh. and Queen's Hall orchs.; later active as solo performer; gave N. Y. recital, 1927.

Goovaerts (gō'-värts), **Alphonse, J. M. André,** Antwerp, May 25, 1847—Brussels, Dec. 25, 1922; 1866, assist. librarian, Antwerp; founded an amateur cathedral choir to cultivate Palestrina and the Netherland cptists; 1887 royal archivist, Brussels; writer and composer.

Göpfert (gĕp'-fĕrt), (1) **K. And.,** Rimpar, near Würzburg, 1768—Meiningen, 1818; clarinetist and dram. composer. (2) **K. G.,** Weesenstein, near Dresden, 1733—Weimar, 1798; vln. virtuoso; conductor and composer.

Gordigiani (gôr-dēd-jä'-nē), (1) **Giov. Bat.,** Mantua, 1795—Prague, 1871; son of a musician; dram. composer. (2) **Antonio,** a singer. (3) **Luigi,** Modena, 1806—Florence, 1860; bro. of (1); dram. composer.

Goria (gō-rē'-ä), **Alex. Éd.,** Paris, 1823 —1860; teacher and composer.

Go'ritz, Otto, Berlin, June 8, 1872—

Hamburg, April 11, 1929; barytone; studied with his mother; début, Neustrelitz, 1895; thereafter at Breslau and Hamburg Ops.; Met. Op. Co., N. Y., 1903–17; noted for Wagnerian character rôles.

Görner (gĕr'-nĕr), (1) Jno. **Gottlieb**, Penig, 1697—Leipzig, 1778; organist; his brother, (2) **J. N. Valentin**, b. Penig, 1702, cond. at Hamburg Cathedral; c. songs.

Gorno (gôr'-nō), **Albino**, b. Cassalmorano (Cremona), Italy, March 10, 1859; pupil Milan Cons., graduating with 3 gold medals; pianist and accompanist to Adelina Patti on Amer. tour 1881–1882; then pf.-prof. Cincinnati Coll. of Music; c. opera, cantata "*Garibaldi*," etc.

Göroldt (gā'-rôlt), **Jn. H.**, Stempeda near Stolberg (Harz), 1773—after 1835; mus. dir., writer and composer.

Gorria, Tobio. Vide BOITO, ARRIGO.

Gorter (gôr'-tĕr), **Albert**, Nürnberg, Nov. 23, 1862—March 14, 1936; studied medicine; then music at R. Mus. Sch., Munich; took 3 prizes for composition; studied a year in Italy; assist. cond. Bayreuth Festivals; cond. Breslau, etc.; 1894–99 assist. cond. Carlsruhe Ct.-Th., then cond. Leipzig City Th.; 1903, Strasbourg, 1910–25, munic. cond. in Mainz; c. (text and mus.) opera "*Harold*" and comic opera "*Der Schatz des Rhampsinnit*" (Mannheim, 1894); 2 symphonic poems, etc.

Goss, (1) John **Jeremiah**, Salisbury, 1770—1817; alto. (2) Sir **John**, Fareham, Hants, England; 1800—London, 1880; organist; knighted, 1872; composer and writer.

Gossec (gôs'sĕk) (rightly Gossé, Gosset or Gossez) (gôs-sā), **François Joseph**, Vergniers, Belgium, Jan. 17, 1734—Passy, near Paris, Feb. 16, 1829; 1741–49 chorister Antwerp cath.; for 2 years he then studied vln. and comp.; 1751 Paris, cond. private orch. of La Pouplinière; then *fermier-général*; 1754 he pub. his first symphonies (5 years before Haydn's); 1759 his first string-quartets which became pop.; 1769 his "*Messe des Morts*" made a sensation (the "*Tuba mirum*" being written for 2 orch., one for wind. instrs., concealed, a new effect he repeated in his first oratorio); 1762 cond. of Prince Conti's orch. at Chantilly; from 1764 prod. 3-act operas "*Le Faux Lord*,"

etc., incl. succ. "*Les Pêcheurs*" (Comédie It., 1766); 1770 founded Concerts des Amateurs; 1773 reorganised and cond. the Concerts Spirituels till 1777; 1780–82 assist. cond. Académie de Musique (later Gr. Opera); 1784 founded and dir. École Royale de Chant, the beginning of the Cons. of which (1795) he was an inspector and prof. of comp.; c. 26 symphonies, 3 symphonies for wind, "*Symphonie concertante*" for 11 insts., overtures, 3 oratorios, etc.; masses with orch.; string-quartets, etc.

Gottschalg (gôt'-shälkh), **Alex. W.**, Mechelrode, near Weimar, Feb. 14, 1827—Weimar, May 31, 1908; pupil Teachers' Seminary, Weimar; succeeding Göpfer there later; court organist, teacher, editor and writer.

Gottschalk (gôts'-chôlk), (1) Louis **Moreau**, New Orleans, La., May 8, 1829—Rio de Janeiro, Dec. 18, 1869; brilliant and original pianist and composer; studied in Paris; began c. at 10; c. operas, etc., and 90 pf.-pcs. of distinct and tropical charm. (2) **Gaston**, bro. of above, singer and for years teacher in Chicago.

Götze (gĕt'-zĕ), (1) **Jn. Nik. K.**, Weimar, 1791—1861; violinist and dram. composer. (2) **Fz.**, Neustadt-on-Orla, 1814—Leipzig, 1888; tenor, teacher and composer. (3) **Karl**, Weimar, 1836—Magdeburg, 1887; pianist and dram. composer. (4) **H.**, Wartha, Silesia, April 7, 1836—Breslau, Dec. 14, 1906; studied singing with (2); lost his voice; teacher in Russia and Breslau; 1885 Ziegenhals, Silesia; 1889 Royal Mus. Dir.; wrote 2 technical books; c. a mass with orch., etc. (5) **Auguste**, Weimar, Feb. 24, 1840—Leipzig, April 29, 1908; daughter of (2); teacher Cons., Dresden; founded a school there; 1891 taught at Leipzig Cons.; wrote under name "**Auguste Weimar.**" (6) **Emil**, Leipzig, July 19, 1856—Charlottenburg, Berlin, Sept. 28, 1901; pupil of Scharfe, Dresden; 1878–81, tenor Dresden Ct.-Th., then at Cologne Th., then toured as "star," 1900 lived in Berlin as court-singer. (7) **Otto**, 1886, conductor at Essen-on-Ruhr; prod. succ. opera "*Riscatto*" (Sondershausen, 1896). (8) **Fz.**, 1892, prod. Volksoper "*Utopia*" (Stettin, 1892) and 1-act opera "*Die Rose von Thiessow*"

(Glogau, 1895). (9) **Marie**, Berlin, Nov. 2, 1865—Feb. 18, 1922; alto, studied Stern Cons. and with Jenny Meyer and Levysohn; sang Berlin opera, then at Hamburg City Th.; 2 years in America; 1892 Berlin ct.-opera.

Goudimel (goo-dĭ-mĕl), **Claude**, Vaison, near Avignon, ca. 1505—killed in St. Bartholomew massacre, Lyons, Aug. 24, 1572; pupil perhaps of Josquin Desprès; est. a school and formed Palestrina and other pupils, winning name "Father of the Roman School"; a music printer for a time; his important comp. incl. *"The Psalms of David,"* complete.

Gould, Nathaniel Duren, Chelmsford, Mass., 1781—Boston, 1864; conductor and writer.

Gounod (goo-nō), **Charles François,** Paris, June 17, 1818—Oct. 17, 1893; son of a talented painter and engraver; his mother taught him the pf. and he entered the Lycée Saint-Louis; 1836 studied at the Paris Cons. with Reicha (harm.), Halévy (cpt. and fugue), Lesueur and Paer (comp.); took 2nd Prix de Rome with cantata *"Marie Stuart et Rizzio"* in 1837; his cantata *"Fernanda"* won the Grand Prix de Rome in 1839, and he studied church music at Rome; 1841 his orch. mass was performed; in 1842 he cond. his *Requiem* at Vienna with great succ.; returned to Paris as precentor and organist of the Missions Étrangères; studied theology 2 years, intended to take orders and was called l'Abbé Gounod by a publisher in 1846; after 5 years of seclusion, parts of his *Messe Solennelle* were played with profound succ. in London; he prod. a symphony, but his opera *"Sappho"* failed (Gr. Opéra, 1851); revised 1884, it failed again; a gr. opera, *"La Nonne Sanglante"* (1854), and a comic opera, *"Le Médecin Malgré Lui"* (played in London as "The Mock Doctor") (1858), both failed; 1852-50 cond. the *"Orphéon,"* Paris, and c. choruses and 2 masses. The opera *"Faust"* (Th. Lyrique, 1859) was and still is a great succ. *"Philémon et Baucis"* (1860); *"La Reine de Sabā"* (in London as "Irene") (1862); *"Mireille"* (1864), *"La Colombe"* (1866), were not great works, but *"Romeo et Juliette"* (1867) still holds the stage; 1866 member of the Institut de France and commander of the Legion of Honour. In 1870, during the war he lived in London; founded Gounod's Choir. In 1871 he prod. *"Gallia,"* a cantata based on "Lamentations"; 1875 returned to Paris, prod. *"Cinq Mars"* (Opéra Comique, 1877), *"Polyeucte"* (Gr. Opéra, 1878), and *"Le Tribut de Zamora"* (1881), none succ. The sacred trilogy *"La Rédemption"* (Birmingham, 1882) (music and French words), and *"Mors et Vita"* (Birmingham, 1885) (Latin text arranged by Gounod) are standard. He also c. *"Messe Solennelle à Ste. Cecile"*; masses; *"Angeli custo des"* (1882); *"Jeanne d'Arc"* (1887); a Stabat Mater with orch.; the oratorios *"Tobie," "Les Sept Paroles de Jésus," "Jésus sur le Lac de Tibériade"*; the cantatas *"A la Frontière"* (1870, Gr. Opéra), *"Le Vin des Gaulois,"* and *"La Danse de l'Épée,"* the French and English songs, etc. He left 2 operas, *"Maître Pierre"* (incomplete) and *"Georges Dandin"* (said to be the first comic opera set to prose text, cf. Bruneau). He wrote *"Méthode de cor a pistons,"* essays, etc. Biog. by Jules Clarétie (Paris, 1875); Mme. Weldon (London, 1875); Paul Voss (Leipzig, 1895); *"Mémoires"* (Paris, 1895).

Gouvy (goo-vē), **Louis Théodore,** Goffontaine, Rhenish Prussia, 1819—Leipzig, 1898; pianist and composer.

Gow, (1) **Niel,** Strathband, 1727—Inver, Scotland, 1807; violinist and composer. (2) **Nathaniel,** 1763—1831; son of above, also violinist and composer. (3) **Donald,** brother of (1), was a 'cellist. And (4) **Niel, Jr.,** 1795-1823, son of (2), was violinist and composer. (5) **George Coleman,** b. Ayer Junction, Mass., Nov. 27, 1860—Jan. 12, 1938; pupil of Blodgett, Pittsfield and Story (Worcester); graduate Brown Univ., 1884, and Newton Theol. Seminary, 1889; then teacher of harm. and pf. Smith College; studied with Büssler in Berlin; 1895 prof. of music Vassar Coll.; composer and writer.

Graben-Hoffmann (grä'-bĕn hôf'-män), **Gustav** (rightly **Gustav Hoffmann**), Bnin, near Posen, March 7, 1820—Potsdam, May 21, 1900; singing teacher, writer and composer.

Grädener (grä'-dĕ-nĕr), (1) **K. G. P.,** Rostock, 1812—Hamburg, 1883; dir., conductor, writer, and dram. composer. (2) **Hermann (Th. Otto),** Kiel, May 8, 1844—Vienna, Sept. 18, 1929; son and pupil of above; later studied Vienna Cons.; 1873 teacher harmony Horak's Pf. Sch., later Vienna Cons.; from 1890 lecturer on harm. and cpt. Vienna Univ.; cond. Singakademie; c. Capriccietta and Sinfonietta for orch. (op. 14), etc.

Graen'er, Paul, b. Berlin, Jan. 11, 1872; composer; studied Berlin Music. Acad.; mus. dir., Haymarket Theat. and teacher at Royal Acad., London, 1896-1904; principal, Mozarteum, Salzburg, 1910-14; taught master class in comp., Leipzig Cons., 1920-24; dir. of Stern Cons., Berlin, 1930-33; until 1935 mem. of the presiding council of the German Music Chamber; associate of the Berlin Acad. of Arts; c. (operas) "*Don Juans Letztes Abenteuer*," "*Schirin und Gertraude*," "*Friedemann Bach*," "*Hanneles Himmelfahrt*" (after Hauptmann drama), "*Der Prinz von Homburg*"; also symphonic works, piano and 'cello concertos, chamber music, and many songs.

Graew (grāv). Vide BACFART.

Graf (gräf), (1) Fr. Hartman, Rudolfstadt, 1727—Augsburg, 1795; flutist and comp. (2) **Max,** b. Vienna, Oct. 1, 1873; music critic; grad. Vienna Univ.; critic of *Wiener Allgemeine Zeitung,* and prof. of mus. hist. and aesthetics, State Acad. of Mus.; author of books on Wagner, etc. His son (3) **Herbert,** b. Vienna, April 10, 1903; noted stage director; studied at State Acad. of Mus. and Vienna Univ., Ph.D.; filled early posts as operatic *régisseur* at Münster, Breslau and Frankfort-am-Main; 1933, stage manager, Munic. Theat., Basel; then with German Theat., Prague; staged opera perfs. of Phila. Orch., 1934-35; at Florentine Musical May Fest., 1935; Salzburg Fest., 1936; engaged for Met. Op., N. Y., 1936-37.

Graffigna (gräf-fēn'-yä), Achille, San Martino dell' Argine, Italy, 1816—Padua, 1896; conductor, teacher, and dram. composer.

Gra'ham, Geo. F., Edinburgh, 1789—1867; composer and writer.

Grahl (gräl), Heinrich, Stralsund, Nov. 30, 1860—Berlin, March 14, 1923; concert tenor in Berlin; pupil of Felix Schmidt.

Grainger (grān-jĕr), Percy, b. Brighton, Australia, July 8, 1882; composer and pianist; pupil of Louis Pabst, Melbourne, and James Kwast, Frankfort; after 1900, appeared in London and other centres with succ.; 1907, chosen by Grieg to play his piano concerto at Leeds Fest.; 1909, made tour of Scandinavia and other parts of Europe; after 1915 made his home for the most part in the U. S., becoming an Amer. citizen in 1917; he was for a time dir. of the mus. dept., N. Y. Univ., but resigned in 1934 to engage in a world tour; his compositions include many arrangements of folk-song material; c. (orch.) "*Molly on the Shore*"; "*Shepherd's Hey*"; "*Colonial Song*"; "*Mock Morris*"; "*Irish Tune from County Derry*" for strings; "*Handel in the Strand*" for piano and orch.; (chorus) "*The Bride's Tragedy*," "*Father and Daughter*," "*Sir Eglamore*," "*Two Welsh War Songs*"; "*The Hunter in His Career*"; "*Marching Song of Democracy*," "*Brigg Fair*," "*The Warriors*," "*Hill-Songs*" Nos. 1 and 2; "*To a Nordic Princess*"; and many settings of British folk music; m. Ella Viola Strom, sculptress, 1928, the marriage ceremony taking place after a concert at the Hollywood Bowl in view of the audience.

Grammann (gräm'-män), Karl, Lübeck, 1844—Dresden, 1897; dram. composer and writer.

Granados y Campina (grä-nä'-dhōs ē käm-pē'-nä), Enrique, Lerida, July 27, 1867—March 24, 1916, perished on torpedoed ship, Sussex, when returning from a visit to the U. S.; Spanish composer of strong nationalistic leanings and marked individuality; son of a military officer, he had his first musical instruction from the army conductor Junceda; later studied piano with Jurnet and Pujol in Barcelona, also comp. with Felipe Pedrell, and had further piano work with de Beriot in Paris. He founded and dir. (after 1900) the Sociedad de Conciertos Clasicos; toured Spain and France as an excellent pianist. His opera, "*Goyescas*," was composed in his latter years, using material from some of his pop. piano works, and was premièred at the Met. Op., N. Y., in the presence of the composer, 1915-16. His output included also the operas "*Petrarca*," "*Foilet*,"

"Maria del Carmen" as well as numerous *zarzuelas;* (orch.) *"Dante"; "Elisenda"* Suite; *"La Nit del Mort"; "Serenata"; Suites Gallega and Arabe; "Marcha de los Vencidos"; "Tres Danzas Espagnoles";* piano trio; works for 'cello and piano, piano and orch., songs with piano acc.; but his princ. legacy remains his large collection of keyboard music, which has won a wide popularity with performers.

Grandi (grän'-dē), **Ales. de**, Venice (?) —Bergamo, 1630; singer and composer.

Grandval (gräñ-văl), Mme. **Marie Félicie Clémence de Reiset, Vicomtesse de,** Saint-Rémy-des-Monts (Sarthe), France, Jan. 20, 1830— Paris, Jan., 1907; pupil of Flotow and Saint-Saëns (comp.); prod. the operas *"Piccolini"* (Op.-Com., 1868), *"Les Fiances des Rosa"* (Th.-Lyr., 1863), *"Atala"* (Paris, 1888), *"Mazeppa"* (Bordeaux, 1892) and others; won the Prix Rossini with oratorio *"La Fille de Jaïre,"* "drame sacré," *"Sainte-Agnès"* in MS.; had prod. symph. works and songs; sometimes wrote under pen names **"Tesier, Valgrand, Jasper, Banger,"** etc.

Gras (dorü-gräs), Mme. **Julia Aimée Dorus,** Valenciennes, 1807—retired, 1850; operatic singer Paris and London.

Grasse (gräs), **Edwin,** b. New York City, Aug. 13, 1884; blind violinist, pianist and composer; pupil of Carl Hauser, N. Y.; at 13, of César Thomson, Brussels, then at the Cons., taking 1st prize; 1901 took "Prix de Capacité"; début Berlin, Feb. 22, 1902, with succ. N. Y., 1903; has given many concerts in U. S., incl. his own works for piano, vln., org., etc.

Grasset (gräs-sä), **J. Jacques,** Paris, ca. 1767—1839; violinist, conductor, professor, etc.

Grassini (gräs-sē'-nē), **Josephina,** Varese, Lombardy, 1773—Milan, 1850; Italian soprano of remarkable talent and beauty.

Gratiani. Vide GRAZIANI.

Grau (grow), **Maurice,** Brünn, Austria, 1849—Paris, March 13, 1907; impresario of Met. Op., 1883, 1891–1903.

Graumann (grow'-män), **Mathilde.** Vide MARCHESI.

Graun (grown), (1) **Aug. Fr.,** 1727–71,

tenor, cantor. (2) **Jn. Gl.,** 1698— Berlin, 1771; bro. of above; violinist; pupil of Pisendel and Tartini; in service of Fredk. the Great and cond. of Royal band; c. 40 symphonies, etc. (3) **K. H.,** Wahrenbrück, Prussian Saxony, May 7, 1701—Berlin, Aug. 8, 1759; bro. of above; organist, singer, court-conductor, and composer.

Graupner (growp'-nĕr), **Chp.,** Kirchberg, Saxony, 1687 — Darmstadt, 1760; dram. composer.

Graveure (gräv-ĕr'), **Louis,** American tenor; originally sang as barytone; N. Y. début, 1915; has appeared widely as Lieder singer; formerly faculty member, Mich. State Inst. of Mus. and Allied Arts; held private classes in several Amer. cities; now res. in Europe; m. Eleanor Painter, soprano; divorced.

Gray, Alan, York, Dec. 23, 1855— Cambridge, England, Sept. 27, 1935; organist; studied law, then music under Dr. E. G. Monk; 1883–92, musical dir. Wellington College; then org. Trinity College, Cambridge, and cond. of the University Musical Society; c. cantatas *"Arethusa"* (Leeds Festival, 1892) and *"A Song of Redemption"* (do., 1898), 4 organ sonatas, string quartet, piano quartet, violin sonata, part-songs, etc.

Graziani (grä-tsē-ä'-nē), (1) (Padre) **Tommaso,** b. Bagnacavallo, Papal States; conductor and composer of 16th cent. (2) (or **Gratiani**) **Boniface,** Marino, Papal States, ca. 1606 —Rome, 1664; cond. and composer. (3) **Ludovico,** Fermo, Italy, 1823— 1885; tenor. (4) **Francesco,** Fermo, April 16, 1829—Fermo, June 30, 1901, bro. of above; barytone, sang in Italy, Paris, New York.

Grazzini (gräd-zē'-nē), **Reginaldo,** Florence, Oct. 15, 1848—Oct. 6, 1906; studied R. Cons. with T. Mabellini; op.-cond. in Florence, later prof. of mus. theory and artistic dir. Liceo Benedetto Marcello, Venice; c. symphonies; a mass with orch., etc.

Great'orex, Thos., North Wingfield, Derby, Engl., 1758—Hampton, near London, 1831; organist, teacher, and composer (1789–93); then conductor.

Green, Samuel, London, 1740—Isleworth, 1796; organ-builder.

Greene, (1) **Maurice,** London, 1696 (1695 ?)—1755; teacher and composer. (2) (**Harry**) **Plunket,** Old

Connaught House, Co. Wicklow, Ireland, June 24, 1865—London, Aug. 19, 1936; basso; studied with Hromada and Goetschius, Stuttgart, 1883–86, and 6 months with Vannuccini of Florence; later with J. B. Welch and Alf. Blume, London; début, Jan. 21, 1888, in "*Messiah*"; début in opera at Covent Garden, 1890; heard widely in recitals; sang frequently in America.

Grefinger (or **Gräfinger**) (grä'-fǐng-ěr), **Jn. W.**, Vienna, 16th cent. composer.

Gregh (grěg), **Louis,** Paris, 1843—Dourdan, 1915; Paris music-publisher; 1894 prod. pantomime; vaudeville operettas, etc.

Gregoir (grüg-wăr), (1) **Jacques Mathieu Joseph,** Antwerp, 1817—Brussels, 1876; teacher and dram. composer. (2) **Ed.,** Turnhout, near Antwerp, Nov. 7, 1822—Wyneghem, June 28, 1890; bro. and pupil of above; pianist, dram. composer and writer.

Gregoro'vitch, Charles, St. Petersburg, Oct. 25, 1867—(suicide) 1926 (?); violinist; pupil of Wieniawski, Dont and Joachim; 1896–97 toured Europe and America.

Greg'ory I. ("The Great"), Rome, 540–604; Pope from 590; reformer and reviser of Roman Catholic ritual.

Greith (grīt), **Karl,** Aarau, Feb. 21, 1828—Munich, Nov. 17, 1887; org. and comp. of church music.

Grell, Ed. Aug., Berlin, 1800—Steglitz, near Berlin, 1886; organist, conductor, prof. and composer.

Grenié (grün-yā), **Gabriel Jos.,** Bordeaux, 1756—Paris, 1837; inv. of the *orgue expressif*

Gren'ville, Lillian, b. New York, Nov. 20, 1888; soprano; studied with Algier, Aramis, Rossi and Sebastiani; début as "Juliette," Nice, 1906; sang also in Milan, Brussels, Naples, Genoa and Lisbon; mem. Chicago Op., 1910–11; d. Paris, 1928.

Gresnich (grěn-ǐsh), **Ant. Frédéric,** Liége, 1755—Paris, 1799; conductor and dram. composer.

Gretchaninoff (grä-chä'-nē-nôf), **Alex. Tikhonovich,** b. Moscow, Oct. 26, 1864; composer; pupil of Safonoff at the Cons.; later at St. Petersburg Cons., under Rachmaninoff; prof. of comp. Moscow Cons. until 1928;

visited U. S. 1930, and now resides in N. Y.; appeared in concerts of his works; c. succ. opera "*Dobringa Nikitich*" (Moscow, 1903); incidental music to Tolstoi's "*Feodor*," and "*Ivan*," and to Ostroski's "*Snow-Maiden*"; 2 symphonies; 3 string quartets; (opera) "*Sœur Beatrice*" after Maeterlinck play (prod. Moscow, 1912, but later withdrawn because appearance of the Virgin on stage considered sacrilegious); also sacred choruses and liturgies; "*At the Cross-roads*" for bass and orch.; vln. works, songs, chamber comps., etc.

Grétry (grä-trwē), (1) **André Ernest Modeste,** Liége, Feb. 9, 1741—Montmorency, near Paris, Sept. 24, 1813; dram. composer; son of a violinist. Chorister at 6, but dismissed for incapacity at 11, then pupil of Leclerc and Renekin. R. failing to keep him to the strict course of cpt. Moreau later tried with equal failure; 1758 he prod. 6 symphonies at Liége; 1759 a mass for which the Canon du Harlez sent him to study in Rome, to which he walked; he studied cpt. and comp. with Casali and Martini for 5 years, but was again dismissed as impossible; a dramatic intermezzo, "*Le Vendemmiatrice*," was succ. 1765, but reading Monsigny's "*Rose et Colas*," he decided that his restless dramatic longings were best adapted for French opéra comique. He was a long time finding a fit librettist (Voltaire declining his invitation). He reached Paris slowly *via* Geneva, where he taught singing a year and prod. the succ. 1-act "*Isabelle et Gertrude.*" In Paris after 2 years' hardships his "*Les Mariages Samnites*" was rehearsed, and though not prod., won him a patron in Count Creutz, the Swedish Minister, who secured him as libretto Marmontel's comedy "*Le Huron.*" This was prod. (Op.-com., 1768) with a great succ., enjoyed also in extraordinary degree by an astounding series of works, mostly comic and mostly successful, the best of which are "*Lucile*," "*Le Tableau Parlant*" (1769), "*Les Deux Avares*," "*Zémire et Azor*" (1771), "*Le Magnifique*" (1773); "*La Rosière de Salency*" (1774); "*La Fausse Magie*" (1775), "*Le Jugement de Midas*" (in which he satirised the old French music and its rendition at the Académie), and "*L'Amant Jaloux*" (1778); the grand opera "*Andromaque*" (1780) (in which the chief rôle is accompanied by 3 flutes throughout); "*La Double Épreuve*" (or "*Colinette à la cour*") (1782); "*Théodore et Pauline*" (or "*L'Épreuve villageoise*"); and "*Richard Cœur de Lion*" (his best work, still played in Paris); the gr. opera "*La Caravane du Caïre*" (1785) performed 506 times; (libretto by the Comte de Provence, later Louis XVIII.); "*La Rosière Républicaine*" (1793); "*La Fête de la Raison*" (prod. 1794 during the Revolution); "*Lisbeth*"; "*Anacreon chez Polycrate*" (1797); c. 50 operas in all, remarkable for spontaneity, grace and fervour of melody, dramatic effect and general charm, but open to serious criticism as works of formal art. He was called "the Molière of music." Mozart and Beethoven wrote Variations on themes of his. Once launched, his progress was a triumph of honour of all kinds; in 1802 Napoleon made him Chevalier of the Legion of Honour with a pension of 4,000 francs. He bought Rousseau's former residence at Montmorency and retired there; wrote *Memoirs*, etc. He had several children, including the gifted Lucille (v. *infra*), all of whom he outlived. He left 6 unprod. operas and c. also 6 symphonies; 6 pf.-sonatas, 6 string-quartets, church-mus., etc. Biog. by his nephew, A. J. G. (1815); Grégoir (1883); Brunet (1884), etc. (2) **Lucille**, Paris, 1773–93; daughter of above, who instrumented her opera "*Le Mariage d'Antonio*," written and prod. at the Op.-Com., with succ. when she was only 13; the next year her opera "*Toinette et Louis*" was not a success; she married unhappily and died at 20.

Greulich (groi'-lĭkh), (1) **K. W.**, Kunzendorf, Silesia, 1796—1837; teacher and composer. (2) **Ad.**, Posen, 1819—Moscow, 1868; teacher and composer. (3) **Ad.**, Schmiedeberg, Silesia, 1836—Breslau, 1890; conductor, bass., organist and composer.

Grey, Madeleine, b. Villaines, France, June 11, 1897; soprano; studied piano with Cortot, voice with Hettlich; début, Paris, 1921; appearances in recital and with orch. in many Eur. countries, South America,

Egypt, U. S.; specialist in modern French and Spanish music and folksongs.

Grieg (grēg), **Edvard Hagerup**, Bergen, June 15, 1843—Sept. 4, 1907; pupil of his mother, a pianist; at 15 entered Leipzig Cons.; pupil of Hauptmann and Richter (harm. and cpt.); Rietz and Reinecke (comp.); Wenzel and Moscheles (pf.); then with Gade, Copenhagen. With the young Norwegian composer Rikard Nordraak, he conspired, as he said, "Against the effeminate Mendelssohnian-Gade Scandinavianism, turning with enthusiasm into the new, well-defined path along which the Northern School is now travelling." 1867 Grieg founded a Musical Union in Christiania and was cond. till 1880; 1865 visited Italy, again in 1870, meeting Liszt in Rome. 1879 he performed his pf.-concerto at the Gewandhaus, Leipzig. After 1880 lived chiefly in Bergen; cond. the Christiania Phil.; 1888 played his concerto and cond. his 2 melodies for string-orch. at London Phil. 1894 Mus. Doc. Cantab. C. concert-overture "*In Autumn*"; op. 20, "*Vor der Klosterpforte*," for solo, female voices and orch.; "*Landerkennung*" for male chorus with orch.; "*Der Einsame*" for barytone, string orch. and 2 horns; op. 35, "*Norwegische Tänze*," for orch.; op. 40, "*Aus Holzberg's Zeit*," suite for string orch.; "*Bergliot*," melodrama with orch.; "*Peer Gynt*," suites 1 and 2 for orch.; op. 50, "*Olav Trygvason*," for solo, chorus, and orch.; "*Sigurd Jorsalfar*" for orch., etc.; op. 22, 2 songs for male voices and orch.; various pcs. for string orch., string-quartet in G min.; pf.-concerto; pf.-sonatas, 3 vln.-sonatas, a 'cello-sonata, also for pf.-"*Poetische Tonbilder*," Romanzen and Balladen; several sets of "*Lyrische Stücke*," "*Symphonische Stücke*" (4 hands), "*Norwegische Volkslieder und Tänze*," "*Bilder aus dem Volksleben*," *Peer Gynt* suite No. 1 (4 hands), and many songs, incl. song-cycle to Garborg's "*Haugtussa*." Biog. by Ernest Closson, Mason, Schelderup, Finck, Lee, La Mara.

Griepenkerl (grē'-pĕnk-ĕrl), (1) **F. K.**, Peine, Brunswick, 1782—Brunswick, 1849; Prof. (2) **W. Rob.**,

Holwyl, 1810—Brunswick, 1868; son of above; teacher and writer.

Griesbach (grēs'-bäkh), (1) **John Hy.,** Windsor, 1798—London, 1875; son of the 'cellist. (2) **J. C. G.,** pianist, 'cellist, dir. and writer.

Griesbacher (grēs'-bäkh-ĕr) **Peter,** Egglham, March 25, 1864—Regensburg, Jan. 29, 1933; priest and teacher at Regensburg; c. 40 masses, and other church music, also cantatas, etc.

Griesinger (grē'-zĭng-ĕr), **G. Aug.,** d. Leipzig, 1828; writer.

Griffes (grĭf'-ĕs), **Charles Tomlinson,** Elmira, N. Y., Sept. 7, 1884—New York, April 8, 1920; composer; one of the most gifted and individual creators of Amer. impressionistic music, particularly for orch. and piano; studied with Jedliczka, Galston, Klatte, Loewengard and Humperdinck; taught in Berlin, later at Tarrytown, N. Y., and N. Y.; c. *"The Pleasure Dome of Kubla Khan"* for orch.; Poem for flute and orch.; (dance-drama) *"The Kairn of Koridwen"* for wind, harp, celesta and piano; Japanese mime-play, *"Schojo"*; 2 pieces for string quartet; piano sonata, and many shorter works for this instrument, incl. *"Four Roman Sketches"* (among which *"The White Peacock"* is particularly pop. in its orchestrated version); and a quantity of original songs, incl. Japanese poems set in pentatonic scale; his early death was a deep loss to Amer. music.

Grif'fin, (1) **Thos.,** English organ builder 18th cent. (2) **George Eugene,** 1781—London, 1863; Engl. pianist and composer.

Griffith, **Frederick,** Swansea, Nov. 12, 1867—London, May, 1917; at 14 won prize at a Welsh national Eisteddfod; pupil at R. A. M.; 1889–91 with Svendsen, later with Jaffanel, Paris; toured widely; flutist at Covent Garden, and prof. at R. A. M.

Grigny (grēn'-yē), **Nicolas de,** Reims, 1671—1703; organist and comp.

Grillet (grē-yā), **Laurent,** Sancoins, Cher, France, May 22, 1851—Paris, Nov. 5, 1901; pupil of A. Martin ('cello), E. Mangin (harm.), and Ratez (cpt. and fugue); cond. various theatres; 1886 Nouveau-Cirque, Paris; writer; c. comic opera *"Graciosa"* (Paris, 1892), ballets, etc.

Grill'parzer, **Fz.,** Vienna, Jan. 15, 1791—Jan. 21, 1871; friend of Beethoven and Schubert. Comp.

Grimm, (1) **Fr. Melchior,** Baron **von,** Ratisbon, 1723—Gotha, 1807; one of the advocates and controversialists for the Ital. *opera buffa.* (2) **Karl,** Hildburghausen, 1819—Freiburg, Silesia, 1888; 'cellist and composer. (3) **K. Konst.,** lived in Berlin, 1820—1882; harpist. (4) **Julius Otto,** Pernau, Livonia, March 6, 1827—Münster, Dec. 7, 1903; pianist; pupil of Leipzig Cons.; founded vocal society at Göttingen, then R. Mus. Dir. Münster Academy and cond.; c. a symphony, 2 suites in canon-form, etc.

Grim'mer, **Chr. Fr.,** Mulda, Saxony, 1798—1850; composer.

Grisar (grē-zär), **Albert,** Antwerp, Dec. 26, 1808—Asnières, near Paris, June 15, 1869; prolific dram. composer; biog. by Pougin, Paris.

Grisart (grē-zär), **Chas. J. Bapt.,** prod. light operas in minor theatres, the last *"Le Petit Bois"* (1893) and *"Voilà le Roi"* (1894).

Grisi (grē'-zē), (1) **Giuditta,** Milan, July 28, 1805—near Cremona, May 1, 1840; famous mezzo-soprano; pupil of Milan Cons.; m. Count Barni, 1834. (2) **Giulia,** Milan, July 28, 1811—Berlin, Nov. 29, 1869; sister and pupil of above; famous dramatic soprano; pupil of Giacomelli, Pasta and Marliani; m. Count Melcy, later m. Mario.

Griswold, **Putnam,** Minneapolis, Dec. 23, 1875—New York, Feb. 26, 1914; bass; pupil of Randegger, Bouhy, Stockhausen and Emerich; début, Covent Garden, 1901; sang in Berlin and with Savage Op. Co. in *"Parsifal"*; Berlin R. Op., 1906–11; Met. Op. Co., after latter year, winning succ. in Wagnerian rôles.

Grofé (grō'-fā), **Ferde** (rightly **Ferdinand Rudolph von Grofe**), b. New York, 1892; conductor and composer; studied harmony and theory with his mother, Elsa von Grofe, a grad. of Leipzig Cons.; at 16 pub. first composition; following year mem. of Los Angeles Symph.; won increasing reputation as cond. of modern syncopated music; known as comp. particularly of picturesque descriptive suites, in which he has employed novel jazz scoring devices.

Groningen (grō'-nĭng-ĕn), **Stefan van,**

Deventer, Holland, June 23, 1851—Laren, March 25, 1926; pupil of Raif and Kiel, Berlin; pianist; teacher in Zwolle, The Hague, Leyden; composer.

Grosheim (grōs'-hīm), **G. Chr.**, Cassel, 1764—1847; dram. composer.

Grosjean (grō-zhäṅ), **J. Romary,** Rochesson, Vosges, France, 1815—St. Dié, 1888; org. composer and writer.

Gross (grôs), **Jn. Benj.**, Elbing, West Prussia, 1809—St. Petersburg, 1848; 'cellist and composer.

Grosz, Wilhelm, b. Vienna, Aug. 11, 1894—N. Y., 1939; pupil of Schreker and Guido Adler; Ph. D.; c. (opera) "*Sganarell*"; chamber and vocal music in modern, satiric style.

Gross'man, Ludwig, Kalisz, Poland, 1835—Warsaw, July 15, 1915; c. overtures "*Lear*" and "*Marie*," and succ. operas "*Fisherman of Palermo*" (Warsaw, 1866) and "*Woyewoda's Ghost*" (1872).

Grove, Sir George, Clapham, Surrey, Aug. 13, 1820—London, May 28, 1900; civil engineer; Sec. to the Society of Arts; 1852, Sec., and 1873 a member of the Board of Directors, Crystal Palace; edited *Macmillan's Magazine;* later dir. of the Royal Coll. of Mus.; 1883, knighted; 1875 D.C.L. Univ. of Durham; 1885 LL.D., Glasgow; wrote important book "*Beethoven and His Nine Symphonies*" (1896), etc., and was the editor-in-chief 1879–89 of the musical dictionary known by his name.

Grovlez (grôv'-lāz), **Gabriel,** b. Lille, April 4, 1879; composer, conductor, pianist; educated Paris Cons., 1st prize in piano; studied with Diémer, Lavignac, Fauré; cond. at Paris Op.-Comique, Chicago Op.; c. incidental music for plays, orchestral and piano works, songs, also a ballet, "*La Fête à Robinson*," given by Chicago Op., 1921.

Grua (groo'-ä), (1) **C. L. P.,** court-conductor at Mannheim and composer, 1700—1755. (2) **Paul,** Mannheim, 1754—Munich, 1833; son of above; conductor and dram. composer.

Gruber (groo'-bĕr), **Jn. Sigismund,** Nürnberg, 1759—1805; lawyer and writer.

Gruen'berg, Louis, b. Russia, Aug. 3, 1883; composer, pianist; taken to America at age of 2; studied Vienna Cons. and with Busoni and Friedrich Koch; c. (orch.) "*The Hill of Dreams*" (N. Y. Symph. Orch. prize, 1919); "*The Enchanted Isle*" (Worcester Fest.); "*The Valley of Voices,*" "*The Blue Castle,*" "*Vagabondia*" (Prague Philh., under comp.); "*Jazz Suite*" (Boston Symph.); symph. "*Music to an Imaginary Ballet*"; "*Daniel Jazz*" for tenor and 8 instruments (Internat'l. Soc. for Contemporary Music Fest.); "*The Creation*" for barytone and 8 instruments (N. Y. League of Comp.); 2 suites for vln. and piano, 2 vln. sonatas; "*Indiscretions*" and "*Diversations*" for string quartet; (operas) "*Jack and the Beanstalk*" (Juilliard Op. School, N. Y., and Chicago Op., 1936–37); "*Emperor Jones*" (after O'Neill drama), Met. Op. Co., 1932, one of the most graphic and stageworthy of Amer. operas, in impressionistic modern idiom; his music in general has many colourful elements, strikingly orchestrated and dissonantal in harmony; mem., board of directors, N. Y. League of Comp.; has taught at Chicago Musical College.

Grün (grün), **Friederike,** Mannheim, June 14, 1836—Jan., 1917; soprano, at first in the opera-chorus, then sang solo parts at Frankfort, later (1863) at Cassel and 1866–69 Berlin; 1869 m. Russian Baron von Sadler; studied with Lamperti at Milan and continued to sing with success.

Grünberger (grün'-bĕrkh-ĕr), **Ludwig,** Prague, 1839—1896; pianist and composer.

Grund (groont), **Fr. Wm.,** Hamburg, 1791—1874; conductor and dram. composer.

Grünfeld (grün'-fĕlt), (1) **Alfred,** Prague, July 4, 1852—Vienna, Jan. 5, 1924; pianist and composer; pupil of Hoger and Krejci, later at Kullak's Academy, Berlin; 1873, chamber-virtuoso, Vienna; toured Europe and the U. S. (2) **Heinrich,** Prague, April 21, 1855—Berlin, Aug. 26, 1931; bro. of above; 'cellist; pupil of Prague Cons.; 1876, teacher in Kullak's Academy; 1886 'cellist to the Emperor; wrote memoirs, "*In Dur und Moll*" (1924).

Grützmacher (grüts'-mäkh-ĕr), (1) **Fr. Wm. L.,** Dessau, March 1, 1832—Dresden, Feb. 23, 1903; eminent 'cellist; son and pupil of a chamber-musician at Dessau; later studied with Drechsler ('cello) and Schneider (theory); at 16 joined a small Leipzig orch.; was "discovered" by David, and at 17 made 1st 'cello, Gewandhaus orch. and teacher at the Cons.; 1869 Dresden, later Cologne; 1902 Philadelphia; c. concerto for 'cello, orch.-and chamber-music, pf.-pcs., songs, etc. (2) **Ld.**, Dessau, Sept. 4, 1835—Weimar, Feb. 27, 1900; bro. and pupil of above; studied with Drechsler ('cello) and Schneider (theory); played in the Gewandhaus orch., Leipzig; then 1st 'cello Schwerin court-orch.; 1876 chamber virtuoso at Weimar. (3) **Friedrich**, Meiningen, July 20, 1866—Cologne, July 25, 1919; son and pupil of (2); 1st 'cello Sondershausen court-orch., then Pesth (1890); 1892-94 prof. at the Cons., Pesth; 1894 in the Gürzenich Orch. and teacher at the Cons., Cologne.

Guadagni (goo-ä-dän'-yē), **Gaetano**, Lodi, 1725 (?)—1785 (97?); male contralto (later a soprano) of 18th cent.; Gluck wrote "*Telemaco*" for him.

Guadagnini (goo-ä-dän-yē'-nē), family of vln.-makers of the Cremona school. (1) **Lorenzo** and (2) **John Baptiste**, worked 1690-1740. (3) **J. B.**, the younger (son of Lorenzo), also made excellent violins.

Guarducci (goo-är-doot'-chē), Montefiascone, ca. 1720 (?); Italian singer in London, 1766-71.

Guarneri (goo-är-nä'-rē) (Latinized **Guarne'rius**), family of famous vln.-makers at Cremona. (1) **Pietro Andrea**, b. ca. 1626; worked 1650-95; pupil of N. Amati; his label *Andreas Guarnerius Cremonæ sub titolo Santæ Theresiæ* 16—. (2) **Giuseppe**, b. 1666; son of above; worked 1690-1730; his label *Joseph Guarnerius filius Andreas fecit Cremonæ sub titolo St. Theresiæ* 16—. (3) **P.**, b. ca. 1670; son of (1); worked 1690-1700. (4) **P.**, son of (2); worked 1725-40. (5) **Giuseppe Antonio** (known as Guarneri del Gesù, i.e., "the Jesus," from the "I H S" on his labels), Oct. 16, 1687—ca. 1745; the best of the family, nephew of (1); his label, *Joseph Guarnerius Andreæ Nepos Cremonæ* 17—, I H S.

Gudehus (goo'-dĕ-hoos), **H.**, Altenhagen, Hanover, March 30, 1845—Dresden, Oct. 9, 1909; tenor, son of a village schoolmaster; pupil of Frau Schnorr von Karolsfeld at Brunswick; 1870-73 engaged for the court opera, Berlin; 1872, studied with Louise Ress, Dresden; reappeared 1875; 1880-90 at Dresden ct.-opera, creating "*Parsifal*" at Bayreuth, 1882; in New York 1890-91, later at Berlin ct.-opera.

Guénin (gā-năṅ), **Marie Alex.**, Maubeuge (Nord), France, 1744—Paris, 1819; violinist and composer.

Guercia (goo-är-chē'-ä), **Alphonso**, b. Naples, Nov. 13, 1831—June, 1890; pupil of Mercadante; dram. barytone for a time; after 1859 vocal teacher, Naples; c. succ. opera "*Rita*" (Naples, 1875), etc.

Guérin (gā-răṅ), **Emmanuel**, b. Versailles, 1779; 'cellist.

Guerrero (gĕr-rä'-rō), **Francisco**, Sevilla, Spain, 1528—1599; conductor, singer and composer.

Gueymard (gĕ'-măr), **Louis**, Chapponay (Isère), France, 1822—Corbeil, near Paris, 1880; tenor, 1848-68 at the Gr. Opéra.

Guglielmi (gool-yĕl'-mē), (1) **Pietro** cond. to Duke of Modena. His son (2) **P.**, Massa di Carrara, Italy, Dec. 9, 1728—Rome, Nov. 19, 1804; conductor, teacher and composer of over 200 operas. (Perhaps the (3) **Signora G.** who sang in London 1770-72 was the wife he treated so shamefully.) Rival of Paisiello and Cimarosa; 1793 cond. at the Vatican, composed only church-music. (4) **Pietro Carlo** (called **Guglielmini**), Naples, ca. 1763—Massa di Carrara, 1827; son of above; dram. composer, teacher and conductor.

Gui (goo-ē'), **Vittorio**, b. Rome, Sept. 14, 1885; conductor, composer; pupil of Santa Cecilia Liceo, Rome, with Setaccioli and Falchi; début at Teatro Adriano in that city, 1907; later cond. in Parma, Turin, at Naples San Carlo Op., Bergamo, La Scala, at Augusteo (Rome), and at Lisbon; c. (lyric fable) "*Fata Malerba*," also orch. music, cantatas, song cycles.

Guicciardi (goo-ēt-chär'-dē), **Giulietta** (or *Julie*), Countess (or Gräfin), Nov. 24, 1784—March 22, 1855; pianist; pupil of Beethoven and his enamoured *inamorata*; a Viennese woman, m. Count Gallenberg, 1803.

Gui de Châlis (gē dŭ shäl-ēs) (**Guido**), end of the 12th cent.; writer.

Guidetti (goo-ē-dĕt'-tē), **Giov.**, Bologna, 1530—Rome, 1592; pupil and assistant of Palestrina; conductor and composer.

Guido d'Arezzo (goo-ē'-dō där-rĕd'-zō) (Latinized Areti'nus), (?) ca. 995—Avellano (?), May 17 (?), 1050 (?); eminent revolutionist in music; a Benedictine monk at Pomposo, near Ferrara, later perhaps at Arezzo; some investigators identify him with a Benedictine monk in the Monastery of St. Maur des Fosses, a Frenchman who went to Italy, not an Italian; his abilities as a singing-teacher and musician led Pope John XIX. to summon him to Rome; he was later probably a Prior at Avellano; though he is being stripped of many of his early honours, it seems true that he introd. the 4-line staff, and ledger-lines and Solmisation

Guido de Châlis. Vide GUI DE CHÂLIS.

Guignon (gēn-yôṅ), **J. P.**, Turin, 1702 —Versailles, 1774; violinist and composer.

Guilbert, Yvette (gēl-bār, ē-vĕt') b. Paris, Jan. 20, 1867; diseuse and singer; début as actress, 1885, as singer, 1890; especially noted for her dram. gifts and as singer of *chansons;* appeared in leading Eur. capitals, also in America at various times after 1906; estab. school for dram. artists with branch in N. Y.

Guillemain (gē'-yŭ-măṅ), **Gabriel,** Paris, Nov. 15, 1705—(suicide) Oct. 1, 1770; c. violin pieces.

Guilmant (gēl-mäṅ), (1) **Félix Alex.,** Boulogne, March 12, 1837—Meudon near Paris, March 29, 1911; son and pupil of the org. (2) **Jean Baptiste G.** (Boulogne, 1793—1800); later pupil of Lemmens and G. Carulli (harm.); at 12 substitute for his father at the church of St. Nicolas; at 16 organist at St. Joseph; at 18 prod. a solemn mass; at 20 choirm. at St. Nicholas, teacher in Boulogne Cons. and cond. of a mus. soc.; 1871 organist of Ste. Trinité; 1893 chev. of Legion of Honour; 1896 org.-prof., Paris Cons.; 1893, 1897-98, toured Europe and U. S. with much succ.; 1901 resigned from Ste. Trinité; made concert tours of England, Italy, Russia; one of the founders of the Schola Cantorum; after 1906 prof. of org., Paris Cons.; c. "lyric

scene" *"Belsazar"* for soli, chorus and orch.; *"Christus Vincit,"* hymn for chorus, orch., harps and org.; org. sonatas, symphonies for organ and orch., etc., wrote treatise on instrumentation; ed. collection of Gregorian music.

Guiraud (gē-rō), (1) **Ernest,** New Orleans, June 23, 1837—Paris, May 6, 1892; son of (2) **Jean Baptiste G.** (Prix de Rome, Paris Cons., 1827), at 12 in Paris; at 15 prod. opera *"Le roi David"* at New Orleans; studied Paris Cons., and took Grand Prix de Rome; later prof. of Paris Cons. and dram. composer.

Gulbranson (gool'-brän-zōn), **Ellen,** b. Stockholm, March 3, 1863; notable soprano; studied with Marchesi, sang in concert; 1889 entered opera, singing "Brünnhilde," 1899 "Kundry" at Bayreuth and other rôles in other cities; lives on her estate near Christiania.

Gumbert (goom'-bĕrt), **Fd.,** Berlin, 1818—1896; tenor and barytone; also critic and dram. composer.

Gumpeltzhaimer (goom'-pĕlts-hī-mĕr), **Adam,** Trostberg, Bavaria, 1559—Augsburg, 1625; composer and theorist.

Gumpert (goom'-pĕrt), **Fr. Ad.,** Lichtenau, Thuringia, April 27, 1841—Leipzig, Dec. 31, 1906; pupil of Hammann; from 1864 1st horn Gewandhaus Orch., Leipzig; writer and composer.

Gumprecht (goom'-prĕkht), **Otto,** b. Erfurt, April 4, 1823—Merano, 1900; Dr. jur.; 1849 critic and writer.

Gungl (or **Gung'l**) (goong'-l), (1) **Joseph,** Zsámbék, Hungary, Dec. 1, 1810—Weimar, Jan. 31, 1889; oboist, bandmaster and composer of pop. dance-music. (2) **Virginia,** daughter of above; opera-singer; début ct.-opera, Berlin, 1871; later at Frankfort. (3) **Jn.,** Zsámbék, 1828—Pecs, Hungary, 1883; nephew of (1); composer.

Gunn, (1) **Barnaby,** 1730-53, organist. (2) **John,** Edinburgh (?), 1765 (?)—ca. 1824; Chelsea Hospital, 1730-53; 'cello-teacher and writer. (3) **Glenn Dillard,** b. Topeka, Kans., Oct. 2, 1874; pianist, educator; studied in Leipzig with Reinecke, Teichmüller, Schreck; début as pianist, 1896; toured Germany; taught Amer. Cons., Chicago, 1900-01; Chicago Mus. Coll. from latter year to 1906;

founded his own school of music, 1906; mus. ed., Chicago *Herald Examiner;* has appeared as soloist with leading orchs.

Günther (gün'-tĕr), (1) **Hermann**, Leipzig, 1834–71; a physician; c. opera under name "F. Hesther." (2) **Otto**, Leipzig, 1822—1897; bro. of above; dir. (3) **Günther-Bachmann, Karoline**, Düsseldorf, 1816—Leipzig, 1874; singer.

Gunz (goonts), **G.**, Gaunersdorf, Lower Austria, 1831—Frankfort, 1894; tenor.

Gura (goo'-rä), (1) **Eugen**, Pressern, n. Saatz, Bohemia, Nov. 8, 1842—Aufkirchen, Aug. 26, 1906; barytone; pupil of Polytechnic and the Akademie, Vienna; then Munich Cons., début 1865, Munich; 1867–70 Breslau; 1870–76 Leipzig with great succ.; 1876–83 Hamburg, Munich, 1883–95. His son (2) **Hermann** (b. Breslau, April 5, 1870) barytone, operatic stage director and after 1927 a singing teacher in Berlin.

Gurlitt (goor'-lĭt), **Cornelius**, Altona, near Hamburg, Feb. 10, 1820—Berlin, 1901; pupil of the elder Reinecke and Weyse; army mus. dir. in the Schleswig-Holstein campaign; prof. Hamburg Cons.; 1874 Royal Mus. Dir.; c. 3 operas, incl. "*Die römische Mauer*" (Altona, 1860), etc.

Gürrlich (gür'-lĭkh), **Jos. Augustin**, Munsterberg, Silesia, 1761—Berlin, 1817; organist, bass, court-conductor and dram. composer.

Gusikow (goo'-zĭ-kôf), **Michael Jos.**, Sklow, in Poland, Sept. 1806—Aix-la-Chapelle, Oct., 1837; remarkable virtuoso on the xylophone.

Gutheil-Schoder (goot'-hĭl-shō'-dĕr), **Marie**, Weimar, Feb. 10, 1874—Ilmenau, Oct. 4, 1935; mezzo-soprano; pupil of Virginia Gungl, and Weimar Music School; 1891–1900 at Weimar court opera; later at Vienna opera; m. Gustav Gutheil, conductor at Vienna Volksoper.

Gyrowetz (gĕ'-rō-vĕts), **Adalbert**, Budweis, Bohemia, Feb. 19, 1763—Vienna, March 19, 1850; son and pupil of a choirm.; c. symphonies, operettas, etc.; court-conductor.

H

Haack (häk), **Karl**, Potsdam, Feb. 18, 1751—Sept. 28, 1819; violinist and teacher; court cond. to Fr.

Wilhelm II. at Potsdam; c. violin pieces.

Haas (häz), **Jos.**, b. Maihingen, Bavaria, Mar. 19, 1879; composer; pupil of Reger; 1911, taught Stuttgart Cons.; 1921, Manich Akad.; c. oratorios, orch. and chamber works, songs, based on German folk-style.

Ha'ba (ä'-bä), (1) **Alois**, b. Wisowitz, Moravia, June 21, 1893; comp. esp. known for his researches and works in style of quarter-tone music; pupil of Vienna and Prague Cons., won Mendelssohn Prize, 1921; taught at Berlin Hochsch., 1921–23; c. of much chamber music in which he has used a quarter-tone scale, and in later works a sixth-tone system; has given concerts on specially constructed quarter-tone piano; author of "*The Theory of Quarter-tones*", "*Treatise on the Foundations of Tonal Differentiation.*" (2) **Karel**, his bro., has also c. music in the same style.

Habeneck (äb'-ĕ-nĕk), **François Ant.**, Mézières (Ardennes), France, June 1 (Jan. 25 ?), 1781—Paris, Feb. 8, 1849; son and pupil of a German musician; studied Paris Cons.; later cond. of its concerts and vln.-prof.; introd. Beethoven's symphonies to the French public; composer.

Haberbier (hä'-bĕr-bēr), **Ernst**, Königsberg, Oct. 5, 1813—Bergen, Norway, March 12, 1869; son and pupil of an organist; court-pianist at St. Petersburg; later toured with great success; composer.

Haberl (hä'-bĕrl), **Fz. X.**, Oberellenbach, Lower Bavaria, April 12, 1840—Ratisbon, Sept. 7, 1910; took orders 1862; 1862–67 cath. cond. and mus. dir. Passau Seminary; 1867–70 organist, Rome; 1871–82 cath.-cond. at Ratisbon; 1875 founded famous sch. for church-music; edited Palestrina's works, etc.; 1889, Dr. Theol. *h. c.*, Univ. of Würzburg.

Habermann (hä'-bĕr-män), **Fz. Jn.**, Königswarth, Bohemia, 1706—Eger, 1783; conductor, teacher and composer.

Habert (hä'-bĕrt), **Jns. Evangelista**, Oberplan, Bohemia, 1833—Gmunden, 1896; editor and collector.

Hack'ett, (1) **Charles**, b. Worcester, Mass., 1889; tenor; studied with Arthur Hubbard and Lombardi; opera début in Mignon, Genoa, 1916; sang at Milan, Rome, London, Paris,

Madrid, and in South America; début Met. Op. as "Almaviva," 1919, sang with co. for 3 years, and again after 1935; was regular mem. of Chicago Op. from 1923 for more than a decade; also heard with Ravinia and Los Angeles Op. and in concert. (2) **Arthur,** b. Portland, Me., tenor; bro. of **Charles H.;** studied vln. in youth, also voice with Hubbard; appeared at Paris Op., recital tours in U. S. and Great Britain, well known as oratorio soloist; prof. of voice, Univ. of Mich. (3) **Karleton,** Brookline, Mass., Oct. 8, 1867—Chicago, Oct. 7, 1935; mus. critic, teacher of singing; grad. Harvard Univ., 1891; vice-pres. and head of vocal dept., Amer. Cons., Chicago; was critic of the Chicago *Evening Post* for a number of years; for a brief time before his death he had been pres. of the Chicago City Op. Co.

Hackh (häk), **Otto (Chp.),** Stuttgart, Sept. 30, 1852—Brooklyn, N. Y., 1917; pupil of Stuttgart Cons. and of A. de Kontski (pf.), at New York; 1872-75 teacher at the Cons.; 1877-78 toured; 1878 teacher in London; in 1880-89 Ger. Cons., New York; later private teacher and composer.

Hadley, Henry Kimball, b. Somerville, Mass., Dec. 20, 1871—New York, Sept. 6, 1937; showed early musical precocity; studied with Heindl, Emery and Chadwick; in 1893 toured with the Mapleson Opera Co. as violinist in its orch.; the next year went to Vienna for study under Mandyczewski; returned to U. S. and taught music (1896) at St. Paul's Episcopal School for Boys, Garden City, L. I.; made début as cond. in concert at Waldorf-Astoria, N. Y., 1900; again toured Europe, 1904-10, having further study with Thuille in Munich and acting as guest cond. of orchs. in Warsaw and Mainz; in the latter city his opera "*Safie*" was prod., 1909 (he had already had a symph., "*Youth and Life,*" perf. by Seidl in 1897). On his return from Europe, he became cond. of the Seattle Symph. Orch., 1909-11; and of the San Francisco Symph. Orch., 1911-15. He also appeared as guest leader in Europe, America and Japan. In later years he had been assoc. cond. of the N. Y. Philh. Orch., beginning 1920; cond.

Manhattan Symph. in N. Y., 1931-32; and of the Berkshire Fest., 1934-35. Among the very large number of his comps., the following are outstanding: (operas) "*Azora*" (Chicago, 1917); "*Bianca*" (one-act work winning award of Amer. Soc. of Singers, 1918, and perf. N. Y.); "*Cleopatra's Night*" (Met. Op. Co., 1920); also 4 symph., the 2nd of which, subtitled "*The Four Seasons,*" took two prizes simultaneously in 1901, the Paderewski and the New England Cons. His fourth symph. "*North, East, South and West*" he cond. himself with the London Philh., Boston Symph., and other orch.; c. overtures "*Hector and Andromache*" (Boston, 1901); "*In Bohemia*" (1903), "*Herod,*" symph. fantasie "*Salome*" (Boston Symph., 1907, Monte Carlo, 1907; Warsaw, 1908, Cassel, 1908); lyric drama "*Merlin and Vivien,*" piano quintet, (1907), etc. poetic rhapsody, "*The Culprit Fay*" (N. Y., 1912); a music drama, "*The Atonement of Pan*" (San Francisco, 1912); cantatas, "*In Music's Praise*" (winning Ditson Prize, 1899); "*A Legend of Granada,*" "*The Nightingale and the Rose,*" "*The Fate of Princess Kiyo,*" "*The Golden Prince*" for women's voices; "*Mirtil in Arcadia,*" large-scale choral work; also the lyric drama, "*Ode to Music,*" for soloists, chorus and orch., a setting of a poem by Henry Van Dyke (Worcester, Mass., Fest., 1917); 7 Ballads for chorus and orch.; tone-poem, "*Lucifer*" (Norfolk Fest., 1915); Concertino for piano and orch.; 3 ballet suites for orch.; the descriptive suite, "*Streets of Pekin*"; and a quantity of chamber music, incl. string quartet; vln. sonatas, and more than 150 songs; m. Inez Barbour, soprano.

Had'ow, Sir **William Henry,** b. Ehrington (Gloucester), England, Dec. 27, 1859—London, April 9, 1937; writer; grad. Oxford Univ., in 1885, a fellow, and 1888-1909, dean of Worcester Coll. at that Univ.; after 1909 principal of Armstrong Coll., Newcastle-on-Tyne; he was knighted in 1918; 1919-30, vice-Chancellor of Sheffield Univ.; Mus. D., Oxford and Durham Univs.; author of "*William Byrd,*" "*Studies in Modern Music,*" 2 series; "*Sonata Form*"; "*A Croatian Composer,*" a study of

Haydn; *"The Viennese Period"*, comprising Vol. V of the Oxford Hist. of Music, of which he was the ed. (1901–05); also ed. *"Songs of the British Isles."*

Hadria'nus. Vide ADRIANSEN.

Häffner (hĕf'-nĕr), Jn. Chr. Fr., Oberschönau, near Suhl, 1759—Upsala, Sweden, 1833; organist, court-conductor, dram. composer and collector.

Hageman (hä'-gĕ-män), (1) **Maurits Leonard**, Zutphen, Sept. 23, 1829—Dutch East Indies, 1900; violinist and pianist; pupil of Brussels Cons.; 1865–75 dir. Cons., Batavia; 1875 founder and dir. of a Cons., Leeuwarden; c. oratorio *"Daniel,"* etc. (2) **Richard,** b. Leeuwarden, Holland; composer, conductor; son of (1); studied with his father, and at Brussels under De Greef and Gevaert; asst. cond. Amsterdam Op., at 16; came to U. S. in 1906 as accompanist for Yvette Guilbert; asst. cond. Met. Op., N. Y., 1908–21; has also cond. at Chicago Op., Ravinia and Los Angeles Op.; and has appeared with Amer. orch.; c. opera *"Caponsacchi"* (based on Browning's *"Ring and the Book,"* libretto by Arthur Goodrich), première, Freiburg, Germany, 1931; later at Vienna, and was prod. by Met. Op. Co., in English, 1936–37; he again cond. with latter co. in 1936; known also as composer of many songs.

Hagen (hä'-gĕn), (1) **Fr. H. von der,** Schmiedeberg, Ukraine, 1780—Berlin, 1856; prof. and writer. (2) **Jn. Bapt.,** Mayence, 1818—Wiesbaden, 1870; conductor and composer. (3) **Ad.,** Bremen, Sept. 4, 1851—Dresden, June 6, 1926; son of above; violinist; 1879–82 cond. Hamburg Th.; 1883, court cond. Dresden, and 1884 manager of the Cons.; c. comic opera *"Zwei Komponisten,"* Hamburg, 1882, etc. (4) **Theodor,** Hamburg, 1823—New York, 1871; teacher, critic and composer.

Hahn (hän), (1) **Albert,** Thorn, West Prussia, 1828—Lindenau, near Leipzig, 1880; teacher. (2) **Reynaldo,** b. Caracas, Venezuela, Aug. 9, 1874; pupil of Massenet, Paris Cons.; lives in Paris; c. 3-act "idylle polynésienne" *"L'Ile du Rêve"* (Paris, Op.-com., 1898); opera, *"La Carme-*

lite," was prod. at the Opéra Comique, Paris, 1902; incidental music to C. Mendés' *"Scarron,"* Racine's *"Esther,"* and V. Hugo's *"Angelo"* (all in 1905); 2-act ballet *"La fête chez Thérèse"* (Opéra, 1910); *"Le Dieu Bleu"* (1912); *"Le Bois Sacré"* (1912); *"Nausicaa"* (Monte Carlo, 1919; Paris Op., 1923); music for Guitry's comedy *"Mozart"* (1925); also symph. poems, *"Nuit d'Amour,"* *"Bergamasque,"* *"Promethée Triomphant,"* etc.; songs of remarkable beauty and originality, etc.

Hähnel (hä'-nĕl). Vide GALLUS, J.

Haines, **Napoleon J.,** London, 1824—New York, 1900; founder of Haines Bros. Piano Mfrs., N. Y.

Hainl (ăňl), **Georges François,** Issoire, Puy-de-Dôme, 1807—Paris, 1873; 'cellist; conductor, writer and composer.

Haizinger (hī'-tsĭng-ĕr), **Anton,** Wilfersdorf, Lichtenstein, 1796—Vienna, 1869; tenor.

Hale (1), **Philip,** Norwich, Vt., March 5, 1854—Boston, Nov. 30, 1934; notable American critic and essayist; as a boy, organist Unit. Ch., Northampton, Mass.; 1876 grad. Yale Univ.; 1880 admitted to the Albany bar; pupil of D. Buck, 1876; 1882–87 studied organ and comp. with Haupt, Faiszt, Rheinberger and Guilmant, Urban, Bargiel, Raif and Scholz; 1879–82 organist St. Peter's, Albany; 1887–89 St. John's, Troy; 1889 of First Religious Soc., Roxbury, Mass.; 1887–89 also cond. of Schubert Club at Albany; 1889–91 critic successively of the Boston *Home Journal,* *Post;* 1891, *Journal;* 1897–1901 edited *Mus. Record;* 1901, ed. *Musical World;* lecturer on mus. subjects; critic, Boston *Herald,* 1903–34; wrote series of notable programme annotations for Boston Symph. (after 1901), extending over 3 decades; Mus. D., Dartmouth Coll.

Hale (or Halle). Vide ADAM DE LA HALE.

Halévy (ă-lā-vē), **Jac. Franç. Fromental Élie,** Paris, May 27, 1799—of consumption, Nice, March 17, 1862; of Jewish parentage; pupil of Cazot, Lambert (pf.), and Berton (harm.), Cherubini (cpt.); Paris Cons. winning 2nd harmony prize; 1816 and 1817, 2nd Prix de Rome; 1819 won Prix de Rome; 1827 prof.

of harmony and accomp. at the Cons.; 1833 prof. of cpt. and fugue; 1829 prod. 2 succ. operas; 1830 succ. ballet *"Manon Lescaut"*; 1830–46 *chef de chant* at the Opera; 1832 he completed Herold's *"Ludovic"* with succ.; 1835 he wrote and prod. 2 great successes, his masterpiece *"La Juive"* (Gr. Opéra) and a comic opera *"L'Eclair"*; Chevalier of the Legion of Honour; 1836 member of the Académie; 1854, secretary for life. In 1836 Meyerbeer appeared, and in efforts to rival his prestige H. wrote too much with inferior librettos, among his works being (1841) *"La Reine de Chypre."* He collaborated with Adam, Auber and Carafe in 4 operas; he left 2 unfinished operas, *"Vanina d'Ornano"* (completed by Bizet) and *"Le Déluge."* Biog. by his brother Léon (1862), etc.

Halff'ter, Ernesto, b. Madrid, Jan. 16, 1905; composer; studied with Esplá, Salazar and de Falla; cond. chamber orch. in Seville, 1924; c. Sinfonietta, *"Deux Esquisses"* and other works for orch., string quartets, piano music; won National State Prize, 1924–25; one of the most promising younger Spanish comps., whose style shows influences of Ravel and Stravinsky.

Halir (hä'-lēr), (1) **Karl,** Hohenelbe, Bohemia, Feb. 1, 1859—Berlin, Dec. 21, 1909; violinist; pupil of Bennewitz, Prague Cons. and Joachim in Berlin; 1884 leader of the ct.-orch., Weimar; 1896 toured the U. S.

Hall, (1) **Henry,** Windsor, ca. 1655–1707; organist and composer. (2) **Henry, Jr.,** d. 1763; son of above; organist and composer. (3) **Wm.,** 17th cent. violinist and composer. (4) **Marie** (Mary Paulina), b. Newcastle-on-Tyne, April 8, 1884; violinist; as a child played in Bristol streets; pupil of her father and Hildegarde Werner; later of J. Kruse; at 15 won an exhibition at the R. A. M.; from 1901, pupil of Sevcik; toured widely. (5) **Walter Henry,** London, April 25, 1862—New York, Dec. 11, 1935; choral cond.; pupil of R. Coll. of Mus.; came to America, 1883; org. in various churches; 1893, founded Brooklyn Oratorio Soc., after 1901 taught at Columbia Univ., and, beginning 1913, was prof. of

church music and leader of Univ. Chorus there.

Halle (äl). Vide ADAM DE LA H.

Hallé (äl-lā), Sir **Charles** (rightly **Karl Halle**), Hagen, Westphalia, April 11, 1819—Manchester, Oct. 25, 1895; pianist and conductor, Paris, 1836–48; later pop. cond. at Manchester and dir. of "Gentlemen's Concerts" there; also closely connected with London Popular Concerts; 1888 m. Mme. Neruda (q.v.); after his death appeared his autobiography, *"Life and Letters"* (1896).

Hallen (häl'-lĕn), **Anders,** Gotenburg, Dec. 22, 1846—Stockholm, March 11, 1925; pupil of Reinecke, Rheinberger, and Rietz; cond. of the Mus. Union, Gotenburg; 1892–97, cond. Royal Opera, Stockholm; 1902–07, cond. in Malmö; after 1907, taught comp., Stockholm Cons.; c. 3 operas, *"Herald der Viking"* (Leipzig, 1881; Stockholm, 1883); v. succ. *"Hexfallen"* (*"Der Hexenfang"*) (Stockholm, 1896); *"Waldemar"* (Stockholm, 1899); 2 Swedish Rhapsodies; ballad cycles with orch.; symphonic poem *"Ein Sommermärchen"*; romance for vln. with orch.; German and Swedish songs, etc.

Haller (häl'-lēr), **Michael,** Neusaat (Upper Palatinate), Jan. 13, 1840—Regensburg, Jan. 4, 1915; 1864 took orders; studied with Schrems; 1866 cond. *"Realinstitut"*; teacher of vocal comp. and cpt. at the Sch. of Church-music; writer and composer; completed the lost 3rd-choir parts of six 12-part comps. of Palestrina's.

Hallström (häl'-strām), **Ivar,** Stockholm, June 5, 1826—April 10, 1901; dram. composer; librarian to the Crown Prince, later King of Sweden; 1861 dir. of Sch. of Music. His first opera failed—having 20 numbers in minor keys; his 2d also; but others were succ., incl. *"Nyaga"* (1885; book by "Carmen Sylva").

Halm (hälm), **Anton,** Altenmarkt, Styria, 1789—Vienna, 1872; pianist and composer.

Halvor'sen, Johan, Drammen, Norway, March 15, 1864—Oslo, Dec. 4, 1935; composer, conductor; pupil of Stockholm Cons. also of Brodsky in Leipzig; toured as vln. virtuoso; taught Helsingfors Cons.; studied with Albert Becker and César Thomson; after 1899 cond. at the Nat'l. Theat., Christiania, where he also led symph. concerts; c. 2 symphs., and much other orch., chamber and vln. music, incidental scores for plays, etc.; best known for his *"March of the Boyars"* and his arr. of a Handel Passacaglia.

Hambourg (häm′-boorg), (1) **Mark,** b. Gogutschar-Woronesch, Russia, May 31, 1879; notable piano-virtuoso; studied with his father (a teacher in London), and with Leschetizky; toured widely with brilliant success; 1900, America; lived in London. (2) **Boris,** b. Woronesch, S. Russia, Dec. 27, 1884; 'cellist; studied with Walenn, Hugo Becker and at Hoch Cons., Frankfort; début in Pyrmont, 1903; toured Australia, Belgium, Great Britain, U. S. (lived in Pittsburgh, 1910); with father and bro. opened a school in Toronto, 1911. (3) **Jan,** bro. of **Mark** and **Boris,** b. at Woronesch, Aug. 27, 1882; violinist; studied with Wilhelmj, Sauret, Heermann, Sevcik and Ysaye; début, 1905, in Berlin; toured widely in concerts.

Ham′boys. Vide HANBOYS.

Hamel (ä-mĕl), **M. P.,** Auneuil (Oise), France, 1786—Beauvais, after 1870; amateur expert in organ-building; writer.

Ham′erik, Asger, Copenhagen, April 8, 1843—July 13, 1923; pupil of Gade, Matthison-Hansen and Haberbier; 1862 of von Bülow; c. two operas; 1870 at Milan prod. an Ital. opera *"La Vendetta"*; 1871-98, dir. of the Cons. of the Peabody Institute and of the Peabody symphony concerts, Baltimore, Md.; 1890 knighted by the King of Denmark; c. 1866 a festival cantata to commemorate the new Swedish constitution, *"Der Wanderer"* (1872); 1883 *"Oper ohne Worte"*; a choral work *"Christliche Trilogie"* (a pendant to a *"Trilogie judaique"* brought out in Paris); 7 symphonies, etc.

Ham′ilton, (1) **Jas. Alex.,** London, 1785 —1845; writer. (2) **Clarence Grant,** b. Providence, R. I., June 9, 1865; pianist, educator; grad. Brown Univ.; pupil of Dannreuther and Matthay; after 1904 prof. at Wellesley Coll.; author and ed. of books on mus. hist. and pedagogy.

Ham′lin, (1) **George John,** Elgin, Ill., 1868—New York, 1923; tenor; sang in concert after 1895, and from 1911 a mem. of Chicago Op. with notable succ. as recitalist and as soloist at fests. (2) **Anna,** b. Chicago, Sept. 10, 1902; daughter of preceding; soprano; début, Albenga, Italy, 1926; sang with Chicago Op., also in concerts.

Ham′merich, Angul, Copenhagen, Nov. 25, 1848—April 26, 1931; 'cellist; pupil of Rüdinger and Neruda; 1896 prof. of musical science Copenhagen University; brother of Asger Hamerik (q.v.)

Hammerschmidt (häm′-mĕr-shmĭt), **Ands.,** Brüx, Bohemia, 1611—Zittau, Oct. 29, 1675; organist, 1639, at Zittau; c. important and original concertos, motets, madrigals, etc.

Ham′merstein, (1) **Oscar,** Berlin, 1847 —New York, Aug. 1, 1919, impresario; came to America at 16; made a fortune by the invention of a cigar-making machine; wrote a comic opera in 24 hours on a wager, and produced it at his own theatre; built five theatres in N. Y. and the Manhattan Opera House; where he gave opposition to the Metropolitan, 1906-08; built also an opera house in Philadelphia; sold out his interests to the Metropolitan Co., and built opera house in London; opened, 1911, but it was a complete fiasco and closed after one season; he then built the Lexington Op. House in N. Y. and planned to open opera season there, but the Met. prevented it by legal measures; he died while in the midst of other plans. His son (2) **Arthur,** a leading producer of operettas and musical shows in N. Y.

Hammond, (1) **Richard,** b. Kent, England, Aug. 26, 1896; composer; grad. Yale Univ. where studied music, also with Mortimer Wilson and Nadia Boulanger; mem. board of dir., League of Comps., N. Y.; c. (ballet) *"Fiesta,"* also chamber and orch. works, piano pieces, songs. (2) **John Hays, Jr.,** his bro., invented novel contrivance known as "sustaining pedal" for piano, which makes tones on that instrument capable of being held or released at the player's will; this was demonstrated in concerts under the sponsorship of Stokowski and Phila. Orch. and promised to make possible technical innovations in comp. (3) **William Churchill,** b. Rockville, Conn., Nov. 25, 1860; organist, pupil of Allen and S. P. Warren; gave notable series of more than 1,000 recitals at Holyoke, Mass.; 1890, teacher of org., Smith Coll., Northampton, Mass.; after 1900 head of mus. dept., Mount Holyoke Coll.

Han'boys (or **Hamboys**), **John**, English theorist ca. 1470.

Hand (hänt), **F. G.**, b. Plauen, Saxony, 1786—Jena, 1851; writer.

Handel (or **Händel, Handl**). (1) Vide GALLUS. (2) Vide HÄNDEL.

Händel (hĕnt'-l) (**Hendel, Hendeler, Handeler** or **Hendtler**), **Georg Friedrich** (at first spelt **Hendel** in England; later he anglicised it to **George Frederic Handel** (hăn'-dĕl, the form now used in England), Halle, Feb. 23, 1685—London, April 14, 1759; son of a barber (afterwards surgeon and valet to the Prince of Saxe-Magdeburg) and his second wife Dorothea Taust. Intended for a lawyer; in spite of bitter opposition he secretly learned to play a dumb spinet. At 7 on a visit to his elder step-brother, valet at the court of Saxe-Weissenfels, Händel while playing the chapel-organ was heard by the Duke, who persuaded the father to give the boy lessons. Zachau, organist of Halle, taught him cpt., canon and fugue, and he practised the oboe, spinet, harpsichord and organ; he soon c. sonatas for 2 oboes and bass, became assist. organist, and for 3 years wrote a motet for every Sunday. In 1696 his skill on organ and harpsichord won him at Berlin the friendship of Ariosti and the jealousy of Bononcini. The Elector offered to send him to Italy; but his father took him back to Halle; the next year his father died, and he went to Halle Univ. (1702–03) to study law, at the same time serving as organist at the cathedral at a salary of $50 a year. 1703 he went to Hamburg as *violino di ripieno*. He fought a duel with Mattheson, later his friend and biographer, and was saved by a button. When Keiser the dir. fled from debt, **H.** was engaged as clavecinist. He c. a "Passion" and prod. 2 operas, "*Almira*" (succ.) and "*Nero*" (1705); he was also commissioned to write "*Florindo und Daphne*" (1708), an opera filling two evenings. In 1706, with 200 ducats earned by teaching, he went to Italy and made success and powerful acquaintances,

incl. the Scarlattis. In Florence (1707) he prod. with succ. "*Rodrigo*" (Venice, 1708), and "*Agrippina*" with great succ. In Rome he prod. 2 oratorios, and in Naples a serenata, "*Aci, Galatea e Polifemo*," in which is a bass solo with a compass of 2 octaves and a fifth. 1709, in Germany as cond. to the Elector of Hanover; 1710 visited England on leave of absence. In 2 weeks he c. the opera "*Rinaldo*," a pasticcio of his older songs. It was prod. at the Haymarket Th. with great succ.; 1712 he returned to London on leave; but stayed. His first two operas were not succ.; but an ode for the Queen's birthday, and a Te Deum and Jubilate in celebration of the Peace of Utrecht won him royal favour and an annuity of £200; 1714 his Hanover patron became George I. of England, and he was for a time out of that monarch's good graces, but had already been restored when, at the request of Baron Kilmanseck, he produced the delightful 25 pieces called the "*Water-Music*," at a royal aquatic fête. 1716–18 he went to Hanover with the King. He there c. his only German oratorio, the "*Passion*"; 1718 cond. to the Duke of Chandos and c. the English oratorio "*Esther*," the secular oratorio "*Acis and Galatea*," and the Chandos Te Deums and Anthems. He taught the Prince of Wales' daughters, and c. for Princess Anne "*Suites de Pièces*" for harpsichord (*The Lessons*) including "*The Harmonious Blacksmith*."

He was dir. of new R. A. of M. 1720 prod. the succ. opera "*Radamisto*" (prod. 1721 in Hamburg as "*Zenobia*"). Now Bononcini and Ariosti appeared as rivals and a famous and lasting feud arose around the three after they had prod. one opera, "*Muzio Scaevola*," in which each wrote an act. B. had rather the better of it, when he was caught in a plagiarism (a crime not unknown in Händel's works (v. LOTTI). B. left England without reply (1731). Up to this time **H.** had prod. 12 operas.

1726 he was naturalised. 1729–31 he was in partnership with Heidegger, proprietor of the King's Th., where he prod. "*Lotario*," followed by 4 more operas. 1732 he prod. his two oratorios revised; 1733 the oratorios "*Deborah*" and "*Athaliah*" at Oxford, when he was made Mus.Doc. *h.c.* 1733 he began a stormy management of opera, quarrelled with the popular singer Senesino, and drove many of his subscribers to forming a rival troupe "The Opera of the Nobility," with Porpora and afterwards Hasse as composer and conductor; 1737 the companies failed, **H.** having prod. 5 operas; the ode "*Alexander's Feast*" (Dryden), and the revised "*Trionfo del Tempo e della Verita.*" Overexertion brought on a stroke of paralysis in one of his hands and he went to Aix-la-Chapelle, returning to London with improved health. He now prod., under Heidegger, 5 operas, incl. "*Faramondo*," "*Serse*" (1738), and "*Deidamia*" (1741). Now he abandoned the stage and turned to oratorio, producing "*Saul*," and "*Israel in Egypt*" (1739); the "*Ode for St. Cecilia's Day*," and in 1740 "*L'Allegro and Il Penseroso*" (Milton), and a supplement "*Il Moderato*," written by Chas. Jennens, who also wrote the text of the Messiah. 1741 he visited Dublin and prod. there his masterpiece the "*Messiah*," April 13, 1742. This re-established him in English favour and raised him from bankruptcy. It was followed by "*Samson*," the "*Dettingen Te Deum*," "*Semele*," "*Joseph*" (1743), "*Belshazzar*," and "*Heracles*" (1744). His rivals worked against him still, and in 1745 he was again bankrupt, writing little for a year and a half, when he prod. with renewed success and fortune his "*Occasional Oratorio*," and "*Judas Maccabaeus*" (1746); "*Joshua*" (1747), "*Solomon*" (1748); "*Susannah*" (1748); "*Theodora*" (1749); "*The Choice of Hercules*" (1750); and "*Jephthah*" (1752), his last. During the comp. of "*Jephthah*" he underwent three unsuccessful operations for cataract. He was practically blind the rest of his life, but continued to play org.-concertos and accompany his oratorios on the organ up to 1759. He was buried in Westminster Abbey. His other comp. incl. the "*Forest Musick*" (Dublin, 1742), etc., for harps.; the "*Fireworks Musick*" (1749) for strings; 6 organ-concertos; concertos for trumpets and horns; and for horns and side drums (MS.);

sonatas for vln., viola and oboe, etc. A complete edition of his works in 100 vols. was undertaken in 1856 for the German Händel Soc. by Dr. Chrysander as editor. Biog. by Mattheson (1740); Mainwaring (1760); Forstemann (1844); Schölcher (1857); Rockstro (1883); Chrysander (unfinished at his death), Leichtentritt and Müller-Blattau (in German). Various aspects of Händel's life and art are considered in studies in English by Benson, Davey, Flower, Marshall, Romain Rolland, Streatfeild, C. F. A. Williams.

Händel as an opera composer has been rediscovered by the 20th cent., after the long dominance of his oratorios. Esp. in Germany there occurred a remarkable "**H.** Renaissance" from about the year 1920, centring in the Univ. of Göttingen, where German adaptations of such works as "*Rodelinda*," "*Ottone*," "*Giulio Cesare*," etc., were staged in annual fests. Productions also took place in Berlin, and in America at Smith Coll., Northampton, Mass.

Hand'lo, Robert de, Engl. theorist of 14th century.

Hand'rock, Julius, Naumburg, 1830 —Halle, 1894; teacher and composer.

Hänel von Cronenthal (hä'-něl fōn krō'-něn-täl), **Julia,** Graz, 1839— Paris, March 9, 1896; wife of the Marquis d'Héricourt de Valincourt; studied in Paris; c. 4 symphonies. 22 pf.-sonatas, etc.

Hanff, J. Nicolaus, Wechmar, 1630— Schleswig, 1706; cathedral organist at Schleswig and important predecessor of Bach in choral-writing.

Hanfstängel (hänf'-shtěng-ěl), **Marie** (née **Schröder**), Breslau, April 30, 1848—Munich, 1917; soprano; pupil of Viardot-Garcia; début, 1867, Paris; studied 1878 with Vannucini; 1882–97 Stadt-theatre, Frankfort.

Hanisch (hä'-nǐsh) **Jos.,** Ratisbon, 1812—1892; organist, teacher and composer.

Hanke (hänk'-ě), **K.,** Rosswalde, Schleswig, 1754—Hamburg, 1835; conductor and composer.

Hansen (hän'-sěn), **Cecilia,** b. Stanitza Kamenska, Russia, Feb. 17, 1898; violinist; studied with Auer; has appeared as orchestral soloist and recitalist in many Eur. centres, also in U. S. 1923–24; m. Boris Sacharoff, pianist.

Hanslick (häns'-lĭk), **Eduard**, Prague, Sept. 11, 1825—Baden near Vienna, Aug. 6, 1904; eminent critic and writer; Dr. Jur., 1849; studied piano under Tomaschek at Prague 1848–49; critic for the *Wiener Zeitung;* among his many books his first is most famous, *"Vom Musikalisch-Schönen"* (Leipzig, 1854); a somewhat biassed, yet impressive plea for absolute music as opposed to programme (v. D. D.) or fallaciously sentimental music; a bitter opponent of all Wagnerianism and an ardent Brahmsite; 1855–64 mus. editor *Presse;* then, of the *Neue freie Presse;* lecturer on mus. hist. and æsthetics Vienna Univ.; 1861 prof. extraordinary, 1870 full prof.; 1895 retired.

Hanson, Howard, b. Wahoo, Nebr., Oct. 28, 1896; composer, conductor, educator; grad. Luther Coll., Inst. of Music. Art, N. Y., hon. Mus.D., Northwestern Univ.; first to be awarded music fellowship at Amer. Acad. in Rome, 1921–24; dir. Eastman School of Music at Univ. of Rochester, N. Y., after latter year; has been active in nat'l. educational organisations in music field, and has carried on a unique series of several annual American Comps. Concerts at Rochester as well as fests. of native music there; has served as guest cond. of his works with many Amer. orchs.; c. (opera) *"Merry Mount"* (libretto by Richard Stokes), Met. Op. Co. (commissioned), 1933; two symphonies (*"Nordic"* and *"Romantic"*), also for orch. *"Before the Dawn," "Exaltation," "North and West," "Lux Aeterna," "Pan and the Priest,"* Symphonic Legend; (chorus and orch.) *"The Lament for Beowulf," "Heroic Elegy," "Drum Taps"* (after Walt Whitman); concerto for org. and orch., 2 quintets for piano and strings, string quartet.

Hanssens (häns'-sĕns), (1) **Chas. L. Jos.** (ainé), Ghent, 1777—Brussels, 1852; conductor and composer. (2) **Chas. L.** (cadet), Ghent, 1802—Brussels, 1871; conductor, professor, 'cellist and composer.

Harcourt (dǎr-koor), **Eugene d',** Paris, 1855—March 8, 1918; composer; pupil Paris Cons., and of Schulze and Bargiel, in Berlin; 1890 gave concerts in his own Salle Harcourt; 1900 gave oratorios at St.

Eustache; c. mass (Brussels, 1876); opera *"Tasso"* (Monte Carlo, 1903); 3 symph., etc.

d'Hardelot (gē-dǎrd'-lō), **Guy (Mrs. Rhodes**), near Boulogne, France—London, Jan. 7, 1936; c. operetta *"Elle et Lui"* and many pop. songs.

Hark'nes. Vide SENKRAH.

Harling, W. Franke, b. London, Jan. 18, 1887; composer; studied Grace Church Choir School, N. Y., Acad. of Mus., London, and with Théophile Ysaye, Brussels; active as org. in Brussels and at West Point Mil. Acad.; c. (opera) *"A Light from St. Agnes"* (Chicago Op., 1925); (lyric drama) *"Deep River"* (N. Y., 1926); Jazz Concerto; *"Venetian Fantasy,"* cantatas and songs; also scores for motion pictures.

Harma'ti, Sandor, Budapest, July 9, 1892—Flemington, N. J., Apr. 4, 1936; composer, violinist, conductor; grad. Budapest Acad. of Mus.; concertm. State Orch., Budapest, 1912–14; People's Op. there, 1912–14; coming to America, led Lenox String Quartet; cond. N. Y. Women's String Orch., Omaha Symph. Orch., 1924–28; Westchester, N. Y. Fest. also led orchs. as guest in Paris, Berlin, Frankfort, St. Louis; c. symph. poem winning Pulitzer Prize, 1923; string quartet (Phila. Chamber Music Ass'n. Prize, 1925), other orch. works and songs.

Harp'er, (1) **Thos.,** Worcester, 1787—London, 1853; trumpet virtuoso. His 3 sons were (2) **Thomas,** his successor. (3) **Charles,** horn-player. (4) **Edward,** pianist.

Har'raden, Samuel, Cambridge, Engl., 1821 (?)—Hampstead, London, 1897; org.-professor.

Harriers-Wippern (här'-rĭ-ĕrs vĭp'-pĕrn), **Louise** (née **Wippern**), Hildesheim, 1837—Grobersdorf, Silesia, 1878; soprano.

Har'ris, (1) **Jos. M.,** London, 1799—Manchester, 1869; organist and composer. (2) **Augustus** (Sir), Paris, 1852—Folkestone, Engl., June 22, 1896; an actor, début as "Macbeth" in Manchester, 1873; then stage manager; 1879 leased Drury Lane Th. for spectacle; 1887 he took up opera and controlled successively H. M.'s Th., the Olympia, etc., finally Covent Garden. (3) **(Wm.) Victor,** b. New York, April 27, 1869; pupil of Charles Blum (pf.), Wm. Court-ney (voice), Fredk. Schilling (harm. and comp.), Anton Seidl (cond.); 1889–95 org. various churches; 1892–95 *répétiteur* and coach at Met. Op.; 1893–94 cond. Utica Choral Union; 1895–96 asst.-cond. to Seidl, Brighton Beach Concerts; vocal teacher and accompanist, N. Y.; long cond. of Cecilia Chorus; c. a pf.-suite, a cantata, an operetta *"Mlle. Mai et M. de Septembre,"* songs, etc. (4) **Roy,** b. Lincoln Co., Okla., Feb. 12, 1898; composer; educated Univ. of Calif.; studied with Fanny Dillon, Arthur Farwell, Modeste Altschuler, Arthur Bliss, Rosario Scalero and Nadia Boulanger; awarded Guggenheim Fellowship for study in Europe, 1927–28; Intercollegiate Fellowship for Comp., California; has lectured extensively and taught at Westminster Choir School, Princeton, N. J., where he organised fest. of modern Amer. music, 1936; c. symph.; andante for orch.; sextet for clarinet, strings and piano; suite for string quartet; symphonic poem, trio and chorus; suite for women's chorus and 2 pianos; *"A Song for Occupations"* for mixed chorus to Whitman's words; symph. for voices, etc.

Har'rison, (1) **Wm.,** London, 1813—London, 1868; tenor. (2) **Beatrice,** b. Roorkee, India, 1892; 'cellist; senior medal of Assoc. Board, London; exhibitor R. Coll. of Music at 11; won Mendelssohn Prize, Berlin Hochsch.; studied with Whitehouse and Hugo Becker; début, Berlin, 1910; has appeared in chief Eur. centres, also in U. S. after 1913. (3) **May,** b. Roorkee, India, 1890; sister of **Beatrice H.;** violinist; studied in London, also with Fernandez Arbos and Auer; has toured as soloist since 1907 and in joint recitals with her sister. (4) **Julius,** b. Stourport, England, March 26, 1885; composer and conductor; studied on stipend with Bantock; cond. of Beecham Op. Co., later the Scottish Orch., and the British Nat'l. Op. Co.; c. orch., chamber music, choral works; also an opera, *"The Canterbury Pilgrims."*

Har'rold, Orville, Muncie, Ind., 1878—Darien, Conn., Oct. 23, 1933; operatic tenor; reputed to have been discovered singing in vaudeville, by Oscar Hammerstein, N. Y.,

taught by Oscar Saenger, 1909–10; début Manhattan Op., N. Y., 1910; sang with Mme. Trentini in comic opera; 1911 at Hammerstein's London Opera; Met. Op. Co. after 1919.

Harsan'yi, Tibor, b. Ober-Kanizsa, Hungary, June 27, 1898; composer; pupil of the Budapest Acad. of Mus.; lives in Paris; c. 2 orch. suites; *"Les Invités,"* setting of text by Jean-Victor Pellerin; sonatina for piano and vln.; sonata for vln. and piano; piano trio; string quartet; duo for vln. and 'cello; nonette for wind quintet and string quartet; piano sonata and other pieces for this instrument.

Hart, (1) **James,** d. 1718; Engl. bass and composer. (2) **Philip,** d. ca. 1749; Gentleman of Chapel Royal; son of above (?); organist and composer; wrote music for *"The Morning Hymn"* from Book V. of Milton's *"Paradise Lost."* (3) **J. Thos.,** 1805—London, 1874; vln. maker. (4) **George,** London, 1839—1891; son of above; writer.

Härtel (hěr'-těl), (1) Vide BREITKOPF UND HÄRTEL. (2) **G. Ad.,** Leipzig, 1836—Homburg, 1876; violinist, conductor and dram. composer. (3) **Benno,** Jauer, Silesia, May 1, 1846—Berlin, Aug. 4, 1909; pupil of Hoppe (pf.), Jappsen (vln.), Kiel (comp.); 1870 teacher of theory, Berlin Royal High Sch. for Music; c. an opera, over 300 canons, etc. (4) **Luise** (née **Hauffe**), Düben, 1837—Leipzig, 1882; pianist; wife of (5) **Hermann H.** Vide BREITKOPF.

Hart'mann, (1) **Johan Peder Emilius,** Copenhagen, May 14, 1805—Copenhagen, March 10, 1900; organist and dram. composer; grandson of a German court-cond. (d. 1763); son of an organist at Copenhagen. (2) **Emil** (Jr.) Copenhagen, 1836—1898; son and pupil of above, and court-organist; composer. (3) **Ludwig,** Neuss-on-Rhine, 1836—Dresden, Feb. 14, 1910; pianist, composer and critic (son and pupil of (4) **Friedrich,** song-composer, b. 1805); also studied at Leipzig Cons. and with Liszt; lived in Dresden; prominent Wagnerian champion; c. an opera, etc. (5) **Arthur,** b. Maté Szalka, Hungary, July 23, 1881; taken to Philadelphia at the age of two months; violinist; all his schooling in America; has toured Europe and America with great success. 1911, soloist with Colonne orch., Paris; c. orch. works, violin pieces, etc.

Har'tog, (1) Edouard de, Amsterdam, Aug. 15, 1829—The Hague, Nov. 8, 1909; pupil of Hoch, Bartelmann, Litolff, etc.; 1852 in Paris as teacher of pf., comp. and harm.; decorated with the orders of Leopold and the Oaken Crown; c. operas, the 43rd psalm with orch., etc. (2) **Jacques,** Zalt-Bommel, Holland, Oct. 24, 1837—Amsterdam, Oct. 3, 1917; pupil of Wilhelm and Fd. Hiller; prof. Amsterdam Sch. of Music.

Hartvigson (härt'-vĭkh-zōn), (1) **Frits,** Grenaa, Jutland, May 31, 1841—Copenhagen, 1919; pianist; pupil of Gade, Gebauer, Ree, and von Bülow; 1864, London; 1873 pianist to the Princess of Wales; 1875 prof. at the Norwood Coll. for the Blind; 1887 pf.-prof. Crystal Palace. (2) **Anton,** Aarhus, Oct. 16, 1845—Copenhagen, Dec. 29, 1911; bro. of above; pianist; pupil of Tausig and Neupert; lived in London.

Har'ty, Sir Hamilton, b. Hillsborough, Co. Down, Ireland, Dec. 4, 1879; d. Brighton, England, Feb. 19, 1941; pupil of his father, an organist; later studied in Dublin; début, London, as an accompanist; after 1920, cond. Hallé Orch. Soc., Manchester; guest cond., London and U. S.; c. setting of Keats's "*Ode to a Nightingale,*" for soprano and orch.; "*Irish Symphony*"; vln. Concerto in D minor; "*Wild Geese,*" symph. poem; "*Comedy Overture*"; Piano Quartet in F major; also 'cello pieces, chamber music and songs; m. Mme. Agnes Nicholls, singer.

Har'wood, Basil, b. Woodhouse, Gloucestershire, April 11, 1859; pianist, composer; pupil of Roeckel, Risley, Corfe, and at Leipzig Cons.; 1880, Mus. Bac., Oxford; 1896, Mus. Doc.; organist various churches; from 1892 at Christ Church, Oxford; retired in 1909 from his posts there as organist and *choragus;* c. church music; "*Capriccio,*" "*Three Cathedral Preludes,*" and Sonata No. 2, in F-sharp minor, for org.; Concerto in D for organ and orchestra; cantata, "*Song on May Morning,*" psalm, "*Inclina, Domine,*" voices and orch. (Gloucester Fest., 1898); ed. Oxford Hymn Book.

Häsche (hĕsh'-ĕ), **William Edwin,** b.

New Haven, April 11, 1867; pupil of Listemann, Perabo, and Parker; dir. New Haven Symph. Orch.; 1903 teacher of instrumentation at Yale; cond. N. H. Choral Union (250 voices); c. symph., symph. poems "*Waldidylle,*" "*Fridjof and Ingeborg*"; cantata "*The Haunted Oak,*" etc.; d. Roanoke, Va., Jan. 26, 1929.

Hase (Dr.), **Oskar von.** Vide BREITKOPF UND HÄRTEL.

Häser (hä'zĕr), (1) **Aug. Fd.,** Leipzig, 1799—Weimar, 1844; theorist, conductor, writer and composer. (2) **Charlotte Henriette,** Leipzig, 1784—1871; sister of above; singer; m. a lawyer Vera.

Has(s)ler (häs'-lĕr), (1) **Hans Leo von,** Nürnberg, 1564—Frankfort, June 5, 1612; the eldest of 3 sons of ((2) **Isaac H.,** town-mus., Nürnberg); pupil of his father; organist and composer. (3) **Jakob,** Nürnberg, 1566—Hechingen (?), 1601; bro. of (1), conductor, organ virtuoso and composer. (4) **Kaspar,** Nürnberg, 1570—1618; bro. of above; organist.

Haslinger (häs'-lĭng-ĕr), (1) **Tobias,** Zell, Upper Austria, 1787—Vienna, 1842; conductor and publisher. (2) **Karl,** Vienna, 1816—1868; son and successor of above; pianist; c. opera "*Wanda,*" etc.

Hasse (häs'-sĕ), (1) **Nikolaus,** ca. 1650; organist and writer at Rostock. (2) **Jn. Ad.,** Bergedorf, near Hamburg, March 25, 1699—Venice, Dec. 16, 1783; famous tenor and v. succ. operatic cond.; rival of Porpora; c. over 100 operas, etc. (3) **Faustina** (née Bordoni), Venice, 1693 (1700?)—1781; of noble birth; one of the most cultivated mezzo-sopr.; m. the above 1730, a happy union, she collaborating in his success. (4) **Gustav,** Peitz, Brandenburg, Sept. 4, 1834—Berlin, Dec. 31, 1889; studied Leipzig Cons., afterward with Kiel and F. Kroll; settled in Berlin as teacher and composer.

Has'selbeck, Rosa. Vide SUCHER.

Has'selmans, (1) **Louis,** b. Paris, July 25, 1878; conductor; studied at Paris Cons. with Delsart, Lavignac, Godard and Massenet; 1st prize in 'cello; mem. Caplet Quartet; début as cond. at Lamoureux Concerts, Paris, 1905; founded and led Hasselmans Orch., after 1907; cond. at Op.-Comique, 1909-11; Montreal Op., 1911-13;

Marseilles Concerts Classiques, 1913–14; Chicago Op., 1918–20; also at Ravinia Op., and at Met. Op. House, N. Y., 1921–36; m. Minnie Egener, soprano. (2) **Alph. J.,** Liége, 1845—Paris, 1912; harpist.

Hasselt-Barth (häs'-sĕlt-bärt), **Anna Maria Wilhelmine** (née van Hasselt), Amsterdam, July 15, 1813—Mannheim, Jan. 4, 1881; soprano; début Trieste (1831).

Hässler (hess'-lĕr), (1) **Jn. Wm.,** Erfurt, March 29, 1747—Moscow, March 29, 1822; organist and famous teacher; toured widely; 1792–94 royal cond. St. Petersburg; then teacher at Moscow; c. important piano and organ pieces; his wife, (2) **Sophie,** was a singer who travelled with him.

Hast'ings, Thos., Washington, Conn., 1787—New York, 1872; editor and composer.

Hastreiter (häst'rī-tĕr), **Helene,** b. Louisville, Ky., Nov. 14, 1858; operatic contralto, popular in Italy; pupil of Lamperti, Milan; m. Dr. Burgunzio.

Hatto. Vide FRÈRE.

Hat'ton, J. Liptrott, Liverpool, Oct. 20, 1809—Margate, Sept. 20, 1886; cond. and dram. composer.

Hattstädt (hät'-shtĕt), **J. J.,** Monroe, Mich., Dec. 29, 1851—Chicago, Dec., 1931; studied in Germany; pf.-teacher and writer in Detroit, St. Louis, and for 11 years, Chicago Coll. of Mus.; 1886, dir. Amer. Cons., Chicago.

Haubiel (hō'-bĕl), **Charles,** b. Delta, Ohio, Jan. 31, 1894; composer, educator; studied with Ganz, Lhevinne (piano) and Scalero (comp.); toured with Kocian; taught at Oklahoma City Mus. Art Inst., later at N. Y. Univ.; has toured as pianist and lecturer; c. "*Karma,*" symph. variations which won prize in Schubert Centenary contest; also other orch., chamber music and piano works, incid. music to plays, etc.

Hau(c)k (howk), **Minnie,** New York, Nov. 14, 1852—Villa Triebschen, Lucerne, Feb. 6, 1929; notable soprano; pupil of Errani and Moritz Strakosch; début 1866, N. Y., as "Norma"; 1868–72 Vienna ct.-opera; 1875, Berlin; sang with great succ. in Europe and America. She was court-singer in Prussia, Officier d'Académie, Paris, and member of the Roman Mus. Academy.

Hauer (how'-ĕr), **K. H. Ernst,** Halberstadt, 1828—Berlin, 1892; organist and composer.

Hauff (howf), **Jn. Chr.,** Frankfort, 1811—1891; founder and prof., Frankfort School of Music; writer and composer.

Hauffe (howf'-fĕ), **Luise.** Vide HÄRTEL, LUISE.

Haupt (howpt), **K. Aug.,** b. Kunern, Silesia, Aug. 25, 1810—Berlin, July 4, 1891; pupil of A. W. Bach, Klein, and Dehn; famous as organist and teacher at Berlin; composer.

Hauptmann (howpt'-män), **Moritz,** Dresden, Oct. 13, 1792—Leipzig, Jan. 3, 1868; violinist; pupil of Spohr; famous as theorist and teacher; from 1842 prof. of cpt. and comp. Leipzig Cons., and dir. Thomasschule. His canon was "unity of idea and perfection of form," exemplified in his comps., enforced upon his many eminent pupils and exploited in many essays and standard works, incl. "*Die Natur der Harmonik und Metrik*" (1833); the posthumous, "*Die Lehre von der Harmonik,*" 1868, etc.; c. opera, "*Mathilde*" (Cassel, 1826); quartets, masses, etc.

Hauptner (howpt'-nĕr), **Thuiskon,** Berlin, 1821—1889; conductor and composer.

Hauschka (howsh'-kä), **Vincenz,** Mies, Bohemia, 1766—Vienna, 1840; 'cellist and barytone player; composer.

Hause (how'-zĕ), **Wenzel,** b. Bohemia, ca. 1780; prof. of double-bass, Prague Cons.; writer.

Hausegger (hows'-ĕg-gĕr), (1) **Fr. von,** Vienna, April 26, 1837—Graz, Feb. 23, 1899; pupil of Salzmann and Dessoff; barrister at Graz; 1872 teacher of history and theory, Univ. of Graz; writer. (2) **Siegmund von,** b. Graz, Aug. 16, 1872; pupil of his father, of Degners and Pohlig; 1896 cond. at Graz; 1899 of the Kaim concerts at Munich; 1903–06 the Museum Concerts at Frankfort-on-Main; 1910, dir. of Hamburg Philh.; 1920–34, dir. Acad. der Tonkunst, Munich, and leader of orch. concerts there; c. mass, an opera "*Helfrid*" (Graz, 1893); "*Zinnober*" (Munich, 1898); "*Dionysian Fantasie*" for orch., symph. poems, "*Barbarossa,*" "*Wieland der Schmied,*" choruses, etc.

Hauser (how'-zĕr), (1) **Fz.,** b. Crasowitz, near Prague, 1794—Freiburg,

Baden, 1870; bass-barytone; teacher.
(2) **Miska** (**Michael**), Pressburg, Hungary, 1822—Vienna, 1887; vln.-virtuoso; composer.

Häuser (hī-zĕr), **Jn. Ernst**, b. Dittchenroda, near Quedlinburg, 1803; teacher, Q. Gymnasium; writer.

Haussmann (hows'-män), **Valentin**, the name of five generations, (1) **V. I.**, b. Nürnberg, 1484; a friend of Luther; composer and conductor. His son (2) **V. II.**, organist and composer. His son (3) **V. III.**, organist at Löbejün, expert in org.-building. His son (4) **V. IV.**, organist and court-conductor at Köthen; writer. His son (5) **V. V.** Vide BARTHOLOMAUS; Löbejün, 1678—Lauchstadt, after 1740; cath. organist and theorist. (6) **Robt.**, Rottleberode, Harz Mts., Aug. 13, 1852—Vienna, Jan. 19, 1909, while on a concert tour; 'cellist; pupil of Th. Müller, and Piatti in London; teacher, Berlin Royal "Hochschule"; 1879, member Joachim Quartet.

Hav'ergal, Rev. **Wm. H.**, Buckinghamshire, 1793—1870; composer.

Haweis (hôz), Rev. **H. R.**, Egham, Surrey, 1838—London, Jan. 30, 1901; amateur violinist and popular writer on music.

Hawes (hôz), **Wm.**, Engl., London, 1785—1846; conductor and composer.

Haw'kins (Sir), **J.**, London, March 30, 1719—Spa, May 14, 1789; an attorney; eminent historian of music; knighted, 1772.

Haydn (hīd'-'n), (1) (**Fz.**) **Josef**, Rohrau-on-Leitha, Lower Austria, March 31, 1732—Vienna, May 31, 1809; second son of a wheelwright who was the sexton and organist of the village church, and a fine tenor, and whose wife, Maria Koler, had served as cook for Count Harrach. She sang in the choir. At 5, H. was taken to the home of a paternal cousin, Frankh, who taught him Latin, singing, the vln. and other instrs. He was engaged as a chorister for St. Stephen's, and taught by Reutter the cond., who gave him no encouragement and dismissed him in 1748. At 8, he went to Vienna, and studied singing, vln. and clavier, with Finsterbusch and Gegenbauer. He studied harmony chiefly from Fux' *"Gradus ad Parnassum"* and Mattheson's *"Volkommener Kappell-*

meister." At 13 he c. a mass. He obtained a few pupils, and a Viennese tradesman lent him 150 florins, with which he rented an attic-room and an old harpsichord. He practised C. P. E. Bach's first 6 sonatas and the vln.; Metastasio taught him Italian, and recommended him to a Spanish family as teacher for their daughter, who was studying with Porpora. From Porpora, in return for menial attentions, H. received some instruction in comp. and a recommendation to the Venetian ambassador for a stipend of 50 francs a month. At 20, he had c. 6 trios, sonatas, his first mass, and a comic opera *"Der neue krumme Teufel"* (Stadttheater, 1752), a satire on the lame baron Affligi the ct.-opera dir.; this work was suppressed but revived afterwards, and he received 24 ducats for it. He began to make powerful friends, and became Musikdirektor and Kammercompositeur to Count Fd. Maximilian Morzin. 1759 Prince Paul Anton Esterházy heard his 1st symph. and 1760 took him into his service as 2d (later 1st) conductor; the same year H. m. Maria Anna, the elder sister of the girl whom he loved and who had entered a convent. This marriage was as unhappy as one would expect. Prince Nikolaus Esterházy, who succeeded his bro. in 1762, retained H. as conductor and in his service H. c. 30 symphonies, 40 quartets, a concerto for French horn, 12 minuets, most of his operas, etc. He was soon very pop. through Europe, and royalty sent him gifts. 1785 commissioned to write a mass, *"The Seven Words on the Cross,"* for the Cath. of Cadiz; in 1790 Prince Nikolaus was succeeded by his son Anton, who kept H. as cond. and increased his stipend of 1,000 florins to 1,400. In 1791 on a pressing invitation brought by Salomon, he went to England and was for 18 months the lion of the season. Oxford made him Mus. Doc.; and he c. the so-called *"Salomon Symphonies,"* for his concerts. On his way home, he visited his native place to witness the unveiling of a monument erected in his honour by Count Harrach. In this year Beethoven became his pupil. 1794, he revisited London, with renewed triumph, the King urging him to stay, but, at the invitation of a new Prince Esterházy, he returned. 1797, he c. the Austrian national anthem. At 65, he prod. his great oratorio *"The Creation"* *("Die Schöpfung")*; in 1801 *"The Seasons"* *("Die Jahreszeiten")*. His health failing he went into retirement, appearing in public only once in 1808, when he was carried in a chair to hear a special performance of the *"Creation."* His agitation was so great that he had to be taken away after the first half; the throng giving him a sad farewell, and Beethoven bending to kiss his hands and forehead. In 1809, his death was hastened by the shock of the bombardment of Vienna by the French. His astounding list of works includes besides those mentioned, 125 symphonies and overtures, incl. the *"Farewell"* *("Abschiedssymphonie,"* 1772), the *"Fire S."* *("Fuersymph.,* 1774), the *"Toy S."* *("Kindersymph.),* *"La Chasse"* (1870), the *"Oxford"* (1788), the *"Surprise"* *("S. mit dem Paukenschlag,"* 1791); *"S. with the drumroll"* *("S. mit dem Paukenwirbel,"* 1795); 51 concertos for harpsichord, vln., 'cello, lyre, barytone, doublebass, flute and horn; 77 stringquartets; 175 numbers for barytone; 4 vln.-sonatas; 38 pf.-trios; 53 sonatas and divertimenti; an oratorio *"Il Ritorno di Tobia"*; 14 masses; 4 operas; 4 Italian comedies; 14 Ital. opere buffe, and 5 marionette-operas; music to plays; 22 arias; cantatas, incl. *"Ariana a Naxos,"* *"Deutschlands Klage auf den Tod Friedrichs des Grossen,"* *"The* 10 *Commandments"* in canon-form; 36 German songs; collections of Scotch and Welsh folk-songs, etc. Biog. by S. Mayr, 1809; K. F. Pohl (Leipzig, 1875, 1882; completed by E. von Mandyczewski). Haydn's diary is quoted from extensively in Krehbiel's *"Music and Manners"* (New York, 1898). Studies of Haydn have been published by Brenet, Hadden, Hadow and Runciman. (2) **Jn. Michael,** Rohrau, Sept. 14, 1737—Salzburg, Aug. 10, 1806; bro. of above; soprano chorister, with compass of 3 octaves, at St. Stephen's, Vienna, replacing his brother Josef. Studied vln. and organ, and became asst.-organist; 1757, cond. at Grosswardein; 1762, dir. to Archbishop Sigismund, Salz-

burg; 1777, organist of the Cath. and St. Paul's Ch. He m. Maria Magdalena Lipp, an excellent soprano; 1880 he lost his property, by the French occupation, but was aided by his bro. and 2 others, and the Empress Maria Theresa rewarded him for a mass c. at her command, in which she sang the soprano solos. He founded a school of composition, and had many pupils, incl. Reicha and Weber. Prince Esterházy twice offered to make him vice-cond.; but **H.** refused, hoping to reorganise the Salzburg Chapel. His best works were sacred music, which his brother esteemed above his own. He declined publication, however; c. 360 church-comps., incl. oratorios, masses, etc., 30 symphonies; operas, etc. Biog. by Schinn and Otter (Salzburg, 1808).

Hayes (hāz), (1) **Wm.,** Hanbury, Worcestershire, Dec., 1706—Oxford, July 27, 1777; organist, conductor and writer. (2) **Philip,** Oxford, April, 1738—London, March 19, 1797; son and pupil of above, and his successor as Univ. Prof. of Mus. at Oxford; also organist there; c. oratorio; a masque; 6 concertos, etc. (3) **Roland,** b. Chattanooga, Tenn., June 3, 1887; Negro tenor; has made recital tours of Europe and U. S., with succ.; specialist in Lieder, classic and modern songs, spirituals.

Haym (hīm), (1) (or **Hennius**), **Gilles,** Belgian composer 16th cent. (2) Italian composer, **Aimo** (ä'-ē-mō), (3) **Niccolo Franc.,** Rome, ca. 1679—London, 1729; 'cellist and librettist.

Heap, Chas. Swinnerton, Birmingham, Engl., April 10, 1847—June 11, 1900; won the Mendelssohn scholarship and studied at Leipzig Cons.; also organ with Best; Mus. Doc. Cambridge, 1872; cond. Birmingham Phil. (1870–86) and other societies; c. an oratorio *"The Captivity"*; cantatas, etc.

Hebenstreit (hāb'-'n-shtrīt), **Pantaleon,** Eisleben, 1660 (9?)—Dresden, 1750; conductor; improved the dulcimer as the "Pantalon" (v. D. D.).

Hecht (hěkht), **Ed.,** Dürkheim, Rhine Palatinate, 1832—Didsbury, near Manchester, 1887; pianist; prof. and composer.

Heckel (hěk'-ĕl), **Wolf,** lutenist at Strassburg, 16th cent.

Heckmann (hĕk'-män), (1) **G. Julius Robt.**, Mannheim, 1848—Glasgow, 1891; violinist. His wife (2) **Marie** (née **Hartwig**), Greiz, 1843—Cologne, 1890; pianist.

Hédouin (ād-wăṅ), **P.**, Boulogne, 1789 —Paris, 1868; lawyer, writer, librettist and composer.

Heermann (här'-män), **Hugo**, Heilbronn, March 3, 1844—Merano, Switz., Nov. 6, 1935; violinist; studied with J. Meerts, Brussels Cons. 1878, also with Joachim; in Frankfort as soloist and teacher at the Hoch Cons.; 1906–09, taught Chicago Mus. Coll.; 1910, Stern Cons., Berlin; 1911, Geneva Cons.; ed. de Bériot vln. method.

Heeringen (hā'-rĭng-ĕn), **Ernst von**, Grossmehlza, near Sondershausen, 1810—Washington, U. S. A., 1855; unsuccessful innovator in notation and scoring.

Hegar (hā'-gär), (1) **Fr.**, Basel, Oct. 11, 1841—Zurich, June 2, 1927; studied Leipzig Cons., 1861; from 1863 cond. Subscription Concerts, and of the Choral Soc., Zürich; 1875 founded Cons. at Zürich; c. vln.-concerto in D; succ. dram. poem, *"Manasse,"* for soli, chorus and orch.; *"Festouvertüre,"* etc. (2) **Emil**, Basel, Jan. 3, 1843—June 13, 1921; bro. of above; pupil, later 'cello-teacher at Leipzig Cons., and 1st 'cello Gewandhaus Orch.; then studied singing; vocal-teacher Basel Sch. of Mus. (3) **Julius**, bro. of above; 'cellist at Zurich.

Hegedüs (hĕg-ĕ-düsh), **Ferencz**, b. Fünfkirchen, Feb. 26, 1881; violinist; succ. début, London, 1901; lives in Zurich.

Heger (hā'-gĕr), **Robert**, b. Strasbourg, Aug. 19, 1886; German conductor and composer; studied with Stockhausen in Strasbourg Cons., later in Zurich and with Schillings at Munich; cond. at Strasbourg, Ulm, Barmen, Nuremberg, Munich and after 1925 at Vienna State Op., also guest cond. at Covent Garden; c. operas, orch. works, chamber music, choruses.

Hegner (hăkh'-nĕr), (1) **Anton**, b. Copenhagen, March 2, 1861—N. Y., Dec. 4, 1915; 'cellist; studied Copenh. Cons.; début at 14; later a teacher N. Y.; c. 4 quartets; 2 concertos for 'cello, etc. (2) **Otto**, Basel, Nov. 18, 1875—Hamburg, Feb. 22, 1907;

pianist; pupil of Fricker, Huber, and Glaus; made début very early at Basel (1888), England and America, at the Gewandhaus, Leipzig, 1890; c. pf.-pcs.

Hegyesi (hĕg'-yā-zē), **Louis**, Arpad, Hungary, 1853—Cologne, Feb., 1894; 'cellist.

Heide, von der. Vide VON DER H.

Heidingsfeld (hī'-dĭngs-fĕlt), **L.**, Jauer, Prussia, March 24, 1854—Danzig, Sept. 14, 1920; pupil, later teacher Stern Cons., Berlin; composer.

Heifetz, Jascha (hī'-fĕtz yä'-shä), b. Vilna, Russia, Feb. 2, 1901; violinist; grad. Vilna School of Music at 8; studied with Auer at St. Petersburg Cons.; 1st appearance at 5; début, Berlin Philh. under Nikisch, 1912; toured Europe; Amer. début, N. Y., Oct. 27, 1917, in recital, with sensational succ.; at 15 estab. as one of foremost technicians of vln., a reputation he has subsequently enhanced with ripening of stylistic and interpretative powers; has made appearances around world, incl. Orient; became U. S. citizen, 1925; soloist with leading orchs. in the princ. cities of Europe and America; has arranged many comps. for vln.; m. Florence Vidor, film actress.

Hein (hīn), **Carl**, b. Rendsburg, 1864; 'cellist; pupil Hamburg Cons.; 1885– 90 'cellist Hamburg Philharmonic Orch.; 1890 teacher in New York at German Cons.; 1903, joined with a fellow-pupil from the Hamburg Cons., August Fraemcke, in its direction; school later known as N. Y. Coll. of Mus.

Heinemeyer (hī'-nĕ-mī-ĕr), (1) **Chr. H.**, 1796—1872; flutist at Hanover; composer. (2) **Ernst Wm.**, Hanover, 1827—Vienna, 1869; son of above; flutist and composer.

Heinichen (hī'-nĭkh-ĕn), **Jn. D.**, Krössuln, near Weissenfels, 1683—Dresden, 1729; dram. composer and writer.

Heinrich (hīn'-rĭkh), (1) **Jn. G.**, Steinsdorf (Silesia), 1807—Sorau, 1882; organist, writer and composer. (2) **Heinrich XXIV.**, Prince Reuss j. L., Dec. 8, 1855—Einstbrunn, Oct. 2, 1910; pianist; c. a symphony, a pf.-sonata, etc.

Heinroth (hīn'-rōt), (1) **Chp. Gl.**, for 62 years organist at Nordhausen. (2) **Jn. Aug. Günther**, Nordhausen, 1780—Göttingen, 1846; son of above;

director and composer. (3) **Charles,** b. New York, Jan. 2, 1874; organist; studied piano with Friedheim and Spicker, org. with John White and comp. with Herbert; also in Munich with Hieber and Rheinberger; after 1893, org. in various N. Y. and Brooklyn churches and taught at Nat'l. Cons.; after 1907, org. and dir. of music at Carnegie Inst., Pittsburgh, Pa., where he has given notable series of weekly recitals; also heard in other cities.

Heintz (hīnts), **Albert,** Eberswalde, Prussia, March 21, 1882—Berlin, June 14, 1911; organist "Petrikirche," Berlin; writer on Wagner; composer.

Heinze (hīnts'-ĕ), (1) **Wm. H. H.,** b. 1790; clarinettist in the Gewandhaus Orch. (2) **Gv. Ad.,** Leipzig, Oct. 1, 1820—near Amsterdam, Feb. 2, 1904; son and pupil of above; at 15 clarinettist in the Gewandhaus; 1844, 2d cond. Breslau Th., and prod. 2 operas (of which his wife wrote the libretti); 1850, Amsterdam as cond.; c. 5 oratorios, 3 masses, 3 overtures, etc. (3) **Sarah** (née **Magnus**), Stockholm, 1836—Dresden, Jan. 27, 1901; pianist; pupil of Kullak, Al. Dreyschock, and Liszt; lived in Dresden.

Heise (hī'-zĕ), **Peder Arnold,** Copenhagen, 1830—1879; teacher and dram. composer.

Heiser (hī'-zĕr), **Wm.,** Berlin, 1816—Friedenau, 1897; singer, bandmaster, and composer.

Hek'king, Anton, b. The Hague, Sept. 7, 1855—Nov. 18, 1935; noted 'cellist; teacher at the Stern Cons.; toured widely.

Hel'ler, Stephen, Pesth, May 15, 1813 —Paris, Jan. 14, 1888; notable composer who, like Chopin, confined his abilities to the pf. Lacking the breath, passion and colour of Chopin's, his music has a candour and vivacity and a fascinating quaintness that give it peculiar charm; his études, simpler than Chopin's, are as well imbued with art and personality. Studied piano with F. Bräuer; at 9 played in pub. with succ.; then studied with Czerny and Halm; at 12, gave concerts in Vienna, and toured; at Pesth studied a little harmony with Czibulka; at Augsburg, fell ill, and was adopted by a wealthy family, who aided his

studies; 1838, Paris. Schumann praised his first comp. highly. 1849, London, he played with succ. though infrequently because of nervousness; thereafter lived in Paris. C. several hundred pf.-pcs., incl. 4 sonatas and the famous Études. Biogr. by H. Barbadette (1876).

Hel'linck, Joannes Lupus (often called Lupus or Lupi), d. 1541; Flemish choir master at Cambrai and Bruges; c. many masses, influencing Palestrina; important motets, hymns and songs.

Hellmesberger (hĕl'-mĕs-bĕrkh-ĕr), (1) **G.** (Sr.), Vienna, 1800—Neuwaldegg, 1873; violinist, conductor and composer. (2) **G.** (Jr.), Vienna, 1830—Hanover, 1852; son and pupil of above; violinist and dram. composer. (3) **Rosa,** daughter of (2), was a singer, début 1883, ct.-opera, Vienna. (4) **Jos.** (Sr.), Vienna, 1828—1893; son of (1); conductor, violinist and professor. (5) **Jos.** (Jr.), Vienna, April 9, 1855—April 26, 1907; son of (4); violinist and composer of operettas, ballets, etc. 1902, cond. Vienna Philh. Orch. (6) **Fd.,** b. Vienna, Jan. 24, 1863; bro. of above; 'cellist in ct.-orch. from 1879; from 1883 with his father's quartet; 1885 teacher at the Cons.; 1886, solo 'cellist, ct.-opera; 1905-06, cond. at same; 1908-11, cond. in Abbazia.

Hellwig (hĕl'-vĭkh), **K. Fr. L.,** Künersdorf, 1773—Berlin, 1838; conductor and dram. composer.

Helm, Theodor, Vienna, April 9, 1843 —Dec. 23, 1920; studied law, entered govt. service; 1867 critic for various journals, and writer; 1874, teacher of mus. hist. and æsthetics, Horak's School of Music; author, studies of music of Beethoven and Mozart.

Helmholtz (hĕlm'-hôlts), **Hermann L. Fd.,** Potsdam, Aug. 31, 1821—Charlottenburg, Sept. 8, 1894; eminent scientist; pub. famous treatises such as *"Sensations of Tone as a Physiological Basis for the Theory of Music"* (*Lehre von den Tonempfindungen als physiologische Grundlage für die Theorie der Musik*) (Brunswick, 1863; English trans. by Ellis, 1875); this work, the result of much experiment, is the very foundation of modern acoustics, though Riemann, who was in some opposition to **H.,** says his conclusions are not infallible.

H. inv. also a double harmonium with 24 vibrators to the octave; this lacks the dissonant 3rds and 6ths of equal temperament (v. D. D.) and permits the same modulation into all keys.

Hem'pel, Frieda, b. Leipzig, June 26, 1885; soprano; studied the piano at Leipzig Cons., 1903–05; then voice with Frau Lempner; début in Stettin; 1906, at Bayreuth; 1907 Covent Garden; has sung in Paris Opéra, Brussels, Vienna, etc.; from 1908 Berlin Royal Opera; engaged for Met. Op., N. Y., 1912; and sang with that co. for nearly a decade with distinction in wide variety of German and Italian rôles; thereafter prominent as a concert singer.

Henderson, William James, b. Newark N. J., Dec. 4, 1855—New York, June 5, 1937; noted critic; grad. Princeton Univ., 1876; Litt. D., 1922; from 1887–1902 critic, New York *Times*; 1902–1937, critic New York *Sun*; lectured, N. Y. Coll. of Music and Inst. of Music. Art; wrote librettos for Damrosch's operas *"The Scarlet Letter"* and *"Cyrano de Bergerac"*; author of *"The Story of Music," "Preludes and Studies," "What Is Good Music?", "How Music Developed," "The Orchestra and Orchestral Music," "Wagner, His Life and Dramas," "Modern Music Drift," "The Art of the Singer," "Some Forerunners of Italian Opera," "The Early History of Singing," "The Soul of a Tenor"* (novel), *"Pipes and Timbrels,"* poems. He long upheld a high standard of musical commentary, combined with a vast knowledge of musical hist. and an experience of actual concert and opera-going covering a half-cent.; his style, urbane, pithy and often marked by gentle satire, retaining its pungency, while he also saluted with an open mind some of the more advanced musical manifestations of latter days.

Henkel (hěnk'-ĕl), (1) **Michael,** Fulda, 1780—1851; composer. (2) **G. Andreas,** Fulda, 1805—1871; organist and composer. (3) **H.,** Fulda, Feb. 16, 1822—Frankfort-on-Main, April 10, 1899; son and pupil of (1), also studied with Aloys Schmitt, and theory with Kessler and Anton Andre; 1849, teacher, etc.,

Frankfort. (4) **K.,** Brünn, May 28, 1867—near Vienna, Dec. 2, 1924; son of (3); studied in Berlin Hochschule; lived in London, as violinist.

Henneberg (hěn'-ně-běrkh), **Jn. Bapt.,** Vienna, 1768—1822; organist, conductor and composer.

Hennig (hěn'-nǐkh), (1) **K.,** Berlin, 1819—1873; organist, dir. and composer. (2) **K. Rafael,** Berlin, Jan. 4, 1845—Posen, Feb. 6, 1914; son of above; pupil of Richter and Kiel; 1869–75, organist Posen; 1873, founder of "Hennig" Vocal Soc.; 1883, Royal Mus. Dir.; 1892, R. Prof.; composer and writer.

Hen'nius. Vide HAYM, GILLES.

Henrion (än-rǐ-ôn), **Paul,** Paris, July 20, 1819—Oct. 24, 1901; c. operettas and over a thousand popular songs.

Henriques (hěn-rē'-kěs), **Fini Baldemar,** b. Copenhagen, Dec. 20, 1867; violinist; pupil of Tofte, Svendsen, and Joachim; member of court orch. at Copenhagen; c. incidental mus. to *"Wieland der Schmied"* (1898), piano pieces, etc.

Henschel (hěn'-shěl), (1) **Sir George,** Breslau, Feb. 18, 1850—Aletna-Criche, Scotland, Sept. 10, 1934; prominent barytone, pianist, and teacher; pupil of Wandelt and Schaeffer, Breslau; of Leipzig Cons. also Kiel and Ad. Schulze (singing); Berlin; 1877–80, lived in London; 1881–84, cond. Boston (U. S. A.) Symph. Orch.; 1885, London; founded the *"London Symphony Concerts"*; 1886–88, prof. of singing R. C. Mus.; c. operas, *"Friedrich der Schöne"* and *"Nubia"*; operetta, *"A Sea Change, or Love's Castaway"*; an oratorio, etc. (2) **Lillian** (née **Bailey**), Columbus, Ohio, Jan., 1860 —London, Nov. 4, 1901; pupil and (1881) wife of above; also studied with C. Hayden and Viardot-Garcia; concert-soprano; she and her husband gave recitals with great art and success. (3) **Helen,** daughter of above, soprano; sang N. Y. 1902.

Hensel (hěn'-zěl), (1) **Fanny Cäcilia** (née **Mendelssohn**), Hamburg, Nov. 14, 1805—Berlin, May 14, 1847; eldest sister of FELIX M., whose devoted companion she was, and who died six months after her sudden death. He said she was a better pianist than he, and six of her songs are pub. under his name: viz., his op. 8 (Nos. 2, 3, 12), and op. 9 (7, 10,

12); she pub. under her own name "*Gartenlieder*," part-songs and songs; c. also pf.-trios and pcs. (2) **Octavia.** Vide FONDA.

Henselt (hĕn'-zĕlt), **Ad. von,** Schwabach, Bavaria, May 12, 1814—Warmbrunn, Silesia, Oct. 10, 1889; eminent pianist who played with remarkable sonority and emotion; to obtain his remarkable reach he c. and practised incessantly very difficult studies; he c. a famous pf.-concerto, études, etc.

Hentschel (hĕnt'-shĕl), **Theodor,** Schirgiswalde, Upper Lusatia, 1830—Hamburg, 1892; conductor, pianist and dram. composer.

Herbart (hĕr'-bärt), **Jn. Fr.,** Oldenburg, 1776—Göttingen, 1841; writer.

Herbeck (hĕr'-bĕk), **Jn. Fz. von,** Vienna, Dec. 25, 1831—Oct. 28, 1877; important cond., mainly self-taught; dir. 1866, ct.-cond. at Vienna and prof. at the Cons.

Her'bert, Victor, Dublin, Ireland, Feb. 1, 1859—New York, May 26, 1924; a grandson of Samuel Lover, the novelist; at 7, sent to Germany to study music; 1st 'cello ct.-orch. Stuttgart, and elsewhere; 1886 solo 'cellist, Metropolitan Orch., New York; later Theodore Thomas' and Seidl's orchs. (also associate-cond.); 1894, bandm. 22d Regt., vice Gilmore; 1898—1904 cond. of Pittsburgh (Pa.) Orch. (70 performers); then founded and cond. the Victor Herbert Orch., with which he toured widely; c. pcs. for orch. and 'cello; 'cello-concerto; an oratorio, "*The Captive*" (Worcester Festival); and numerous comic operas, incl. "*Prince Ananias*," a failure, "*The Wizard of the Nile*," "*The Serenade*," "*The dol's Eye*," "*The Fortune Teller*," "*The Singing Girl*," "*Babes in Toyland*," "*The Red Mill*," "*Naughty Marietta*," "*The Enchantress*," "*Mlle. Modiste*," "*The Lady of the Slipper*," "*The Madcap Duchess*," "*Sweethearts*," "*The Debutante*," "*The Only Girl*," "*Princess Pat*," "*Eileen*," "*Her Regiment*," etc. He c. also the grand opera "*Natoma*," libretto by Jos. D. Redding, which was prod. by the Philadelphia Opera Co., 1911, in Philadelphia and at the Met. Op., N. Y., the same year; and a one-act lyric opera, "*Madeleine*" (book by Grant Stewart), Met. Op., Jan. 24, 1914.

Heritte - Viardot (ŭr-ēt-v'yär-dō), **Louise Pauline Marie,** Paris, Dec. 14, 1841—Heidelberg, Jan. 17, 1918; daughter of Viardot-Garcia; vocal teacher St. Petersburg Cons.; later at Frankfort, and Berlin; m. Consul-General Heritte; c. opera "*Lindora*" (Weimar, 1879), and cantatas.

Hermann (hĕr'-män), (1) **Matthias,** called **Verrecoiensis,** or **Verrecorensis,** from his supposed birthplace, Warkenz or Warkoing, Holland; Netherland cptist. 16th cent. (2) **Jn. D.,** Germany, ca. 1760—Paris, 1846; pianist and composer. (3) **Jn. Gf. Jakob,** Leipzig, 1772—1848; writer. (4) **Fr.,** Frankfort, 1828—Leipzig, 1907; pupil Leipzig Cons.; 1846–75, viola-player, Gewandhaus and theatre orchs.; 1848, vln.-teacher at the Cons.; 1883 Royal Saxon Prof.; c. symphony, etc.; editor and collector. (5) **Rheinhold L.,** Prenzlau, Brandenburg, Sept. 21, 1849—1919; pupil of Stern Cons., Berlin; 1878–81 dir. of it; 1871–78 singing-teacher and cond. New York; 1884, cond. N. Y. "Liederkranz"; 1887, prof. of sacred history at the Theol. Seminary; 1898, cond. Handel and Haydn Soc., Boston; 1900 returned to Berlin; c. 4 operas incl. "*Vineta*" (Breslau, 1895), and "*Wulfrin*" (Cologne, 1896); 5 cantatas, overtures, etc. (6) **Robt.,** Bern, Switzerland, April 29, 1869—Ambach, Oct. 10, 1912; studied Frankfort Cons; previously self-taught in zither, pf., comp. and had c. works of much originality in which Grieg encouraged him; 1893, studied with Humperdinck, then went to Leipzig and Berlin, where (1895) his symphony and a concert-overture were prod. at the Philh., provoking much critical controversy; lived in Leipzig; c. also "*Petites variations pour rire*," for pf. and vln.; etc. (7) **Hans,** Leipzig, Aug. 17, 1870—Berlin, May 18, 1931; contrabassist and composer; studied with Rust, Kretschmer and von Herzogenberg; c. string-quartets, pf.-pcs., etc., and many songs. (8) **J. Z.** Vide ZENNER. (9) Vide HERRMANN.

Herman'nus (called **Contrac'tus** or **"der Lahme,"** for his lameness), Graf von Vehrhgen, Saulgau, Swabia, July 18, 1013—Alshausen, near Biberach, Sept. 24, 1054; important writer and theorist.

Hermesdorff (hĕr'-mĕs-dôrf), **Michael,** Trier (Trèves), 1833—1885; organist, composer and editor.

Hermstedt (hĕrm'-shtĕt), **Jn. Simon,** Langensalza, near Dresden, 1778—Sondershausen, 1846; composer.

Hernandez (ĕr-nän'-dĕth), **Pablo,** b. Saragossa, Jan. 25, 1834—187–; pupil Madrid Cons.; organist and (1863) auxiliary prof. there; c. *zarzuelas;* a mass, symphony, etc.

Hernando (ĕr-nän'-dō), **Rafael José M.,** Madrid, May 31, 1822—after 1867; pupil of R. Carnicer, Madrid Cons.; 1848–53, he prod. several succ. *zarzuelas,* some in collab.; later dir and composer to Th. des Variétés; 1852, secretary, later prof. of harm., Madrid Cons.; founded a Mutual Aid Mus. Soc.

Hérold (ā-rôl), (1) **Louis Jos. Fd.,** Paris, Jan. 28, 1791—(of consumption) Thernes, near Paris, Jan. 19, 1833; son of (2) **Fran. Jos. H.** (d. 1802; pf.-teacher and composer, pupil of P. E. Bach), who opposed his studying music, though Fétis taught him solfège and L. Adam, pf. After his father's death (1802), he studied piano with Louis Adam, Paris Cons. (first prize, 1810); harmony with Catel and (from 1811) comp. with Méhul; 1812 won the Prix de Rome, with cantata "*Mlle. de la Vallière*"; studied at Rome and Naples, where he was pianist to Queen Caroline, and prod. opera "*La Gioventù di Enrico Quinto*" (1815); Paris, 1815, finished Boieldieu's "*Charles de France*" (prod. with succ. 1816, Op. Com.); "*Les Rosières*" and "*La Clochette*" followed 1817, both v. succ.; others followed; the last (1820) failing, he imitated Rossini in several operas, but recovered himself in the succ. "*Marie*" (1826); 1824, pianist, later chorusm. at the Ital. Opera, but soon relinquished. 1827 Chef du Chant at the Gr. Opéra, for which he wrote several succ. ballets, incl. "*La Somnambule,*" which gave a suggestion to Bellini; 1828, Legion of Honour. "*Zampa*" (1831) gave him European rank and is considered his best work by all except the French, who prefer his last work "*Le Pre aux Clercs*" (1832); he prod. also "*L'Auberge d'Airey*" (1830) (with Carafa), "*La Marquise de Brinvilliers*" (1831), with Auber, Boïeldieu,

Cherubini, and 5 others; and "*La Médicine sans Médecin*" (1832); he left "*Ludovic*" unfinished, to be completed by Halévy with succ.; c. also much pf.-mus. Biogr. by Jouvin (Paris, 1868).

Herrmann (hĕr'-män), (1) **Gf.,** Sondershausen, 1808—Lübeck, 1878; violinist, pianist, organist and dram. composer. (2) **K.,** d. Stuttgart, 1894; 'cellist.

Herschel (hĕr-shĕl), **Fr. Wm.** (Anglicised, Sir William Herschel, K.C. H., D.C.L.), Hanover, 1738—Slough, near Windsor, 1822; oboist; organist at Bath; astronomy, in which he won such fame, was till 1781 only his diversion.

Hertel (hĕr'-t'l), (1) **Jn. Chr.,** Oettingen, Swabia, 1699—Strelitz, 1754; singer, viola da gambist, violinist and composer. (2) **Jn. Wm.,** Eisenach, 1727—Schwerin, 1789; son and pupil of above; violinist, conductor and composer. (3) **K.,** 1784–1868; violinist. (4) **Peter L.,** Berlin, 1817—1899; son of above; composer.

Hertz (hĕrtz), **Alfred,** b. Frankfort-on-Main, July 15, 1872; studied Raff Cons.; from 1895 2d-cond. various cities; 1899 cond. city theatre Breslau; 1899, London; 1909-15, Met. Op., N. Y., 1915-30, cond. San Francisco Symph. Orch.; lives on Pacific Coast.

Hertzberg (hĕrts'-bĕrkh), **Rudolph von,** Berlin, 1818—1893; conductor and editor.

Hervé rightly **Florimond Ronger** (ĕr-vā or rôn-zhā), (1) Houdain, near Arras, June 30, 1825—Paris, Nov. 4, 1892; singer, then organist, conductor; in Paris acting as librettist, composer and actor, and producing flippant but ingenious little works in which French operetta finds a real origin; c. over 50 operettas, also heroic symphony "*The Ashantee War,*" and ballets. (2) **Gardel,** son of above, prod. 1871 operetta "*Ni, ni, c'est fini.*"

Hervey (här'-vĭ), **Arthur,** of Irish parents, Paris, Jan. 26, 1855—London, March 10, 1922; pupil of B. Tours (harm.) and Ed. Marlois (instr.); intended for the diplomatic service, till 1880; critic of "*Vanity Fair*"; from 1892, London "*Post*"; c. a 1-act opera, a dram. overture "*Love and Fate,*" etc.; author of biog. and other works.

Herz (hĕrts or ĕrs), (1) Jacques Simon, Frankfort, Dec. 31, 1794—Nice, Jan. 27, 1880; of Jewish parentage; studied at Paris Cons. with Pradher; pianist and teacher in Paris; then London; 1857, acting-prof. Paris Cons.; c. vln.-sonatas, etc. (2) **Henri**, Vienna, Jan. 6, 1806—Paris, Jan. 5, 1888; 1st prize pf.-pupil Paris Cons.; very popular as touring pianist; succ. as mfr. of pianos; obtained extravagant prices for his comps.; prof. at the Cons.; writer.

Herzog (hĕr'-tsōkh), (1) **Jn. G.**, Schmolz, Bavaria, Sept. 6, 1822—Munich, Feb. 4, 1909; pupil of Bodenschatz, and at Altdorf Seminary; 1842, organist at Munich; 1848, cantor; 1850, organ-prof. at the Cons.; 1854, mus. dir. Erlangen Univ.; 1866, Dr. Phil.; later prof.; retired 1888; composer. (2) **Emilie**, Ermatingen, Switzerland, 1859—Aarburg, Sept. 16, 1923; soubrette coloratura-singer; pupil Zurich Sch. of Mus., then of Gloggner, and Ad. Schimon, Munich; début, Munich (1879); 1889–1916, Berlin ct.-opera; 1922 taught Zurich Cons.

Herzogenberg (hĕr'-tsōkh-ĕn-bĕrkh), (1) **H. von**, Graz, Styria, June 10, 1843—Wiesbaden, 1900; prof. at Berlin, etc.; director, professor and composer. (2) **Elizabeth** (née von Stockhausen) (?) 1848—San Remo, 1892; pianist, wife of above.

Hes'eltine, (1) **Jas.**, d. 1763; English organist and composer. (2) **Philip**, London, Oct. 30, 1894—Dec. 17, 1930; composer and author, known under pseudonym of "*Peter Warlock*"; studied at Eton, and with Colin Taylor, Delius and van Dieren; founded and ed. periodical, "*The Sackbut*," 1920–21; wrote books on Delius, Gesualdo; also "*The English Ayre*"; c. chamber and orch. music, many songs.

Hess, (1) **Joachim**, organist, writer and carillonneur, Gouda, Holland, from 1766—1810. (2) **Willy**, b. Mannheim, July 14, 1859—Berlin, Feb. 17, 1939; pupil of Joachim; at 19 Konzertmeister at Frankfort, 1886 at Rotterdam, then England; 1895 1st vln.-prof. Cologne Cons., and 1st vln. Gürzenich Quartet. He was made Royal Prof., 1900; 1903–4 he was violin prof. R. A. M., London; resigned and became concertmaster Boston Symph. Orch., and leader of the Quartet; 1908 co-founded the Hess-Schroeder Quartet; 1910–28, taught Berlin Hochsch. (3) **Ludwig**, b. Marburg, March 23, 1877; pupil Berlin Royal Hochsch. and Vidal in Milan; toured as concert singer; from 1907 succeeded Felix Mottl as dir. Munich Konzertgesellschaft; c. symphony "*Hans Memling*," an epic "*Ariadne*," and other works for voices and orch.; songs, etc.; 1912 engaged to tour America; 1925–34, prof. Berlin Acad. for Church and School Music. (4) **Myra**, b. London, Feb. 25, 1890; pianist; studied R. Coll. of Mus. with Tobias Matthay; has toured France, Holland, Belgium, Canada, also U. S. annually after about 1920; one of pre-eminent pianists of her generation; has made arr. of Bach chorales for piano: created Dame Commander of British Empire, 1936.

Hesse (hĕs'-sĕ), (1) **Ernst Chr.**, Grossen-Gottern, Thuringia, 1676—Darmstadt, 1762; viola-da-gambist, conductor. (2) **Ad.** (Fr.), Breslau, 1809—1863; org.-virtuoso and composer. (3) **Julius**, Hamburg, 1823—Berlin, 1881; introduced the present measurement for pf.-keys; and pub. a method. (4) **Max**, Sondershausen, Feb. 18, 1858—Leipzig, Nov. 24, 1907; 1880 founded mus. pub. house in Leipzig; in 1883, founded H. und Becker.

Hetsch (hĕtsh), **K. Fr. L.**, Stuttgart, 1806—Mannheim, 1872; pianist, violinist and dram. composer.

Heuberger (hoi'-bĕrkh-ĕr), **Richard Fz. Jos.**, Graz, Styria, June 18, 1850—Vienna, Oct. 28, 1914; a civil engineer; in 1876 took up music, which he had previously studied; chorusm., Vienna academical Gesangverein; 1878 cond. Singakademie; c. operas "*Abenteuer einer Neujahrsnacht*" (Leipzig, 1886); "*Manuel Venegas*" (do., 1889), remodelled as "*Mirjam*" (Vienna, '94); 2 operettas; critic, and teacher at Vienna Cons.

Heubner (hoip'-nĕr), **Konrad**, Dresden, 1860—Coblenz, June 6, 1905; pupil of the "Kreuzschule"; 1878–79, at Leipzig Cons. and writer; with Riemann, later Nottebohm, Vienna; Wüllner, Nicodé and Blassmann, Dresden; 1882, cond. Leipzig Singakademie; 1884, asst. cond. Berlin Singakademie; 1890, dir. Coblenz

Cons. and Mus. Soc.; c. a symphony, overtures, etc.

Heugel (ŭ-zhĕl), **Jacques Ld.**, La Rochelle, 1815—Paris, 1883; editor and publisher.

Hey (hī), **Julius**, Irmelshausen, Lower Franconia, April 29, 1832—Munich, April 22, 1909; studied with Lachner (harm. and cpt.), and F. Schmitt (singing); later with von Bülow at the Munich Sch. of Mus. (estab. by King Ludwig II. on Wagner's plans); attempted a reform in the cultivation of singing, but resigned at Wagner's death (1883), and pub. important vocal method, *"Deutscher Gesangsunterricht"* (4 parts, 1886), exploiting Wagner's views. Wagner called him "the chief of all singing-teachers." 1887, Berlin; later Munich; composer.

Heyden (hī'-d'n), (1) **Sebald**, Nürnberg, 1498 (1494?)—1561; cantor, writer. (2) **Hans**, Nürnberg, 1540—1613; son of above; organist; inv. the "Geigenclavicimbal."

Heydrich (hī'-drĭkh), **Bruno**, b. Leuben, Feb. 23, 1863—Halle, August, 1938; pupil of Dresden Cons.; 1879-82, took prizes as double-bass player, pianist and composer; for a year in von Bülow's Weimar orch.; 4 years Dresden ct.-orch.; also studied singing with Scharfe, Hey and v. Milde; succ. début as tenor at Sondershausen theatre; prod. 1-act opera-drama, with pantomimic prologue, *"Amen,"* Cologne, 1895; c. songs; after 1909, dir. of a mus. school in Halle.

Hey'man, Katherine Ruth, b. Sacramento, Cal.; pianist; studied in America and Europe; début, Boston, 1899, also heard in Europe; known particularly as an interpreter of Scriabin, for which she has won internat'l. reputation.

Heymann (hī'-män), (1) **Karl**, pianist, Filehna, Posen, Oct. 6, 1854—Haarlem, Nov., 1922. Son of (2) **Isaac H.** (cantor); pupil of Hiller, Gernsheim, Breunung and Cologne Cons. and of Kiel; ill-health ended his promising career as virtuoso; 1874, mus. dir. at Bingen; court-pianist to the Landgrave of Hesse; 1879-80, Hoch Cons., Frankfort; c. concerto *"Elfenspiel,"* *"Mummenschanz,"* *"Phantasiestücke,"* etc., for piano.

Heymann-Rheineck (hī'-män-rī'-nĕk) (**K. Aug. Heymann**), b. Burg-

Rheineck on Rhine, Nov. 24, 1852; pianist; pupil Cologne Cons., and R. Hochschule, Berlin; 1875-1920, teacher there; composer.

Heyne Van Ghizeghem (also **Hayne**, or **Ayne**, "**Henry**"), Netherland contrapuntist and court-singer, ca. 1468.

Hiebsch (hēpsh), **Josef**, Tyssa, Bohemia, 1854—Carlsbad, 1897; teacher and writer in Vienna.

Hientzsch (hēntsh), **Jn. Gf.**, Mokrehna, near Torgau, 1787—Berlin, 1856; teacher, composer and writer.

Hig'ginson, Henry Lee, New York, Nov. 18, 1834—Boston, Nov. 15, 1919; music patron; banker; had studied music in Vienna; founded Boston Symph., 1881, with a million-dollar endowment; directed its policies until 1918, when gave control to a board of directors; also a trustee of N. E. Cons.

Hignard (ēn-yăr) (**J. L.**), **Aristide**, Nantes, 1822—Vernon, 1898; the preface to his *"Hamlet"* written 1868, not prod. till Nantes, 1888, shows him to have attempted a new and serious manner, but he found production only for comic operas which were usually succ.

Hildach (hĭl'-däkh), (1) **Eugen**, Wittenberg-on-the-Elbe, Nov. 20, 1849—Berlin-Zehlendorf, July 28, 1924; barytone; pupil of Frau Prof. El. Dreyschock. (2) **Anna** (née **Schubert**), Königsberg, 1852—Nov. 18, 1935; wife of above; mezzo-soprano; teacher Dresden Cons., 1880-86.

Hildebrand (hēl'-dĕ-bränt), **Camillo**, b. Prague, 1879; conductor 1912-19, Berlin Philh.; 1921-24, Berlin Symph.; composer.

Hiles (hīlz), (1) **J.**, Shrewsbury, 1810—London, 1882; organist, writer and composer. (2) **H.**, Shrewsbury, Dec. 31, 1826—Worthing near London, Oct. 20, 1904; bro. and pupil of above; organist various churches; 1867, Mus. Doc. Oxon; 1876, lecturer; later, prof. R. Manchester Coll. of Music; 1885, editor and writer; c. 2 oratorios, 3 cantatas, an historic opera, etc.

Hilf (hēlf), (1) **Arno**, Bad Elster, Saxony, March 14, 1858—Aug. 2, 1909; vln.-virtuoso; son and pupil of (2) **Wm. Chr. H.**; from 1872 he also studied with David, Röntgen, and Schradieck, Leipzig Cons.; second concertm., 1878, and teacher at Moscow Cons., (1888) Sondershausen; 1889–91, concertm. Gewand-haus orch., Leipzig; after 1892, 1st vln. prof. at the Conservatorium.

Hill, (1) **Wm.,** London, 1800—1870; org.-builder. (2) **Wm. Ebsworth,** London, 1817—Hanley, 1895; vln.-maker. (3) **Thos. H. Weist,** London, 1828—1891; violinist, conductor and composer. (4) **Ureli C.,** New York, 1802 (?)—1875; violinist. (5) **Wm.,** Fulda, March 28, 1838—Homburg, June 6, 1902; pianist; pupil of H. Henkel and Hauff; lived in Frankfort; c. prize-opera *"Alona";* vln.-sonatas, etc. (6) **Edward Burlingame,** b. Cambridge, Mass., Sept. 9, 1872; composer; grad. Harvard, 1894, with highest honours in mus.; pupil of Lang and Whiting, piano; Widor, comp.; Bullard, theory; Chadwick, instrumentation; 1887–1902, taught piano and harmony in Boston; instructor of mus., Harvard Univ., after 1908; in recent years, head of the mus. dept. there; a prolific comp.; among his works: fantastic pantomime for orch. *"Jack Frost in Midsummer"?* (Chicago Orch. 1907, N. Y. Symph. 1908); women's chorus with orch. *"Nuns of the Perpetual Adoration"?* (Musical Art Soc., 1907, Birmingham Orch., etc.); Stevensonia Suite Nos. 1 and 2, symphonies, *"Sinfonietta,"?* *"Lilacs";* Concertino, for orch.; chamber music, 3 piano sonatas, songs.

Hille (hĭl′-lĕ), (1) **Ed.,** Wahlhausen, Hanover, 1822—Göttingen, 1891; cond. and teacher. (2) **Gv.,** b. Jerichow-on-Elbe, near Berlin, May, 31, 1850; violinist; pupil of R. Wüerst (theory), Kullak's Acad., 1869–74 w. Joachim (vln.); lived in Berlin, as a solo-player; 1879, invited to the Mendelssohn Quintet Club, Boston, Mass.; toured; then teacher at Mus. Acad., Phila.; co.-dir. of Leefson-Hille Cons. there; 1910, returned to Germany; c. 5 vln.-concertos with orch., etc.

Hillemacher (hĭl′-lĕ-mäkh-er, or ēl-mă-shä), two brothers. (1) **Paul Jos. Wm.,** Paris, Nov. 25, 1852—Versailles, Aug. 13, 1933. (2) **Lucien Jos. Ed.,** Paris, June 10, 1860—June 2, 1909; both studied at the Cons., and took the first Grand Prix de Rome, (1) in 1876; (2) in 1880. For some years they wrote all their scores in collaboration. C. symph. legend *"Lorely"* (1882, City of Paris

prize); succ. opera *"St. Megrin"?* (Brussels, 1886), etc.; *"Orsola"* (Gr. Opéra, Paris, 1902).

Hiller (Hüller) (hĭl′-lĕr), (1) **Jn. Adam,** Wendisch-Ossig, near Görlitz, Dec. 25, 1728—Leipzig, June 16, 1804; pupil of Homilius (Kreuzschule) and U. of Leipzig; flutist in concerts, and teacher; 1754 tutor to the son of Count Brühl; 1758, accompanied him to Leipzig, where he lived thereafter; 1763, revived, at his own expense, the subscription concerts, which developed into the famous "Gewandhaus"? concerts, of which he was cond.; 1771, founded a singing-school; 1789–1801, cantor and dir. Thomasschule. He founded the *"Singspiel,"* from which German "comedy-opera" developed, contemporaneously with *opera buffa* and *opéra comique.* In his dram. works the aristocratic personages sing arias, while the peasants, etc., sing simple ballads, etc. His *Singspiele,* all prod. at Leipzig, had immense vogue, some of the songs being still sung; 1766–70, he wrote, edited collections, etc.; c. also a Passion cantata, funeral music (in honour of Hasse), symphonies and partitas, the 100th Psalm, etc. Biog. by Carl Peiser (Leipzig, 1895). (2) **Fr. Adam,** Leipzig, 1768—Königsberg, Nov. 23, 1812; violinist and tenor; son and pupil of above; mus. dir. of Schwerin Th.; 1803, cond. of Königsberg Th.; c. 4 operettas, etc. (3) **Fd. von,** Frankfort, Oct. 24, 1811—Cologne, May 12, 1885; of wealthy Jewish parentage; a pupil of Hofmann (vln.), Aloys Schmitt (pf.) and Vollweiler (harm. and cpt.); at 10 played a Mozart concerto in public, at 12 began comp.; from 1825 pupil of Hummel; at 16 his string-quartet was pub. Vienna; at 15, he saw Beethoven on his death-bed; 1828–35, taught Choron's School, Paris; then independently giving occasional concerts; 1836, he returned to Frankfort, and cond. the Cäcilien-Verein; 1839, prod. succ. opera *"Romilda,"?* at Milan; oratorio, *"Die Zerstörung Jerusalems"* (Gewandhaus, 1840); 1841, studied church-music with Baini, Rome; 1843–44 he cond. the Gewandhaus; prod. at Dresden, 2 operas; 1847, municipal cond. at Düsseldorf; 1850 at Cologne, where he organised the Cons.; cond. Gürzenich Concerts, and the Lower Rhine Festivals; 1852–53, cond. Opera Italien, Paris; 1868, Dr. Phil. *h. c.* Bonn Univ.; 1884 he retired. He was a classicist in ideal of the Mendelssohn type and his comp. are of precise form and great clarity. He was also a lecturer and writer on music. He c. 3 other operas, 2 oratorios, 6 cantatas, 3 overtures, 3 symphonies, a ballad "*Richard Löwenherz,*"[2] with orch. (1883), etc. (4) **Paul,** Seifersdorf, near Liegnitz, Nov. 16, 1850—Breslau, Dec. 27, 1924; 1870, asst.-organist, and 1881 organist St. Maria-Magdalena, and dir. of a music school, Breslau; composer.

Hil'pert, W. Kasimir Fr., Nürnberg, 1841—Munich, 1896; 'cellist.

Hils'berg, (1) **Ignace,** b. Warsaw, July 8, 1894; pianist; pupil of St. Petersburg Cons., with Essipov and Sauer; soloist with orchs. in Europe and U. S., also Far East; mem. of faculty, Inst. of Musical Art, Juilliard School, N. Y. (2) **Alexander,** his bro.; b. Warsaw; violinist; mem. of faculty, Curtis Inst. of Mus., Phila.; also heard in concerts here and in Europe.

Hilton, (1) **John,** d. before 1612; organist at Cambridge, 1594; perhaps the father of (2) **John,** 1599—1656-7; organist at Westminster; c. anthems, madrigals, etc.

Him'mel, Fr. H., Treuenbrietzen, Brandenburg, 1765—Berlin, 1814; court-cond. and dram. composer.

Hinck'ley, Allen Carter, b. Boston Oct. 11, 1877; bass; pupil of Carl Schachner and Oscar Saenger; début with Bostonian Light Op. Co., 1901; op. début, Hamburg as "King Henry" in "*Lohengrin,*" 1903; sang at Covent Garden and Bayreuth; Met. Op. Co., 1908–11; later with Chicago Op. Co., also in other cities of Europe and U. S. and in concerts.

Hindemith (hǐn'-dĕ-mǐt), (1) **Paul,** b. Hanau, Germany, Nov. 16, 1895; composer, viola player; one of the most prolific, scholarly and original comps. among the younger German school, combining remarkable command of cpt. with original harmonic style, including use of atonality; there are both romantic and parodistic elements in his work; studied comp. with Arnold Mendelssohn and Sekles; played in Frankfort Op.

orch., 1915–23; after which he was active mainly as composer and as a member of the Amar String Quartet; taught at Berlin Hochsch., 1927–34; in latter year his music fell under ban in Germany as opposed to cultural policies then enforced by the state regime, although he had in his opera "*Mathis der Maler*" (1934) shown a return to orthodox tonality and romantic subject matter; c. (operas) "*Mörder, Hoffnung der Frauen,*"[2] "*Das Nusch-Nuschi*"[2] and "*Sankta Johanna,*" 3 one-act works (1921); "*Cardillac*" (1926), in which there was a return to set forms and contrapuntal writing for voices; "*Neues vom Tage*"[2] (1929), a work introducing the more banal features of contemporary life as recorded in newspapers of sensational sort; "*Hin und Zurück,*" short opera using, then reversing, a film; dance-pantomime "*Der Dämon,*" an oratorio "*Das Unaufhörliche,*" (cantata) "*Die Serenaden*"; (vocal works) "*Marienleben,*" "*Junge Nonne,*" and a large amount of ingenious chamber music, incl. 4 string quartets, sonatas for piano and vln., viola and 'cello, piano suite "*1912,*"[2] orchestral, piano, vln., 'cello, viola and viola d'amour concertos, various forms of writing known as "Kammermusik"[2] with pieces for piano and 'cello, songs; Prof. of music, Yale Univ., 1941. (2) **Rudolf,** bro. of **Paul,** b. Jan. 9, 1900, in Hanau; 'cellist; pupil of Hoch Cons.; was solo 'cellist at Munich and Vienna State Op.; mem. of Amar Quartet and of Munich Trio; after 1927 taught at Carlsruhe Cons.

Hinrichs (hǐn'-rǐkhs), (1) **Fz.,** Halle-on-the-Saale, ca. 1820—Berlin, 1892; composer and writer on music. His sister (2) **Maria.** Vide FRANZ. (3) **Gustav,** b. Ludwigslust, Mecklenburg, 1850; conductor; studied with his father, Marxsen and Reisland; early active as a violinist, after 1870 in San Francisco; cond. of Amer. Op. Co., assisting Theodore Thomas, 1885–86; 1886–96, manager of his own opera company; 1899–1906, dir. of music at Columbia Univ.; 1903-08, cond. at Met. Op.; c. operas, orch. works, choral pieces, songs, etc.

Hin'shaw, William Wade, b. Union, Iowa, Nov. 3, 1867; bass and impresario; studied with R. A. Heritage, L. G. Gottschalk and L. A. Phelps; early active as voice teacher and choir dir.; début at St. Louis with Savage Op. Co., 1899, as "Mephistopheles"; organised school of opera, Chicago, 1903; 1909 founded Internat'l. Gr. Op. Co.; sang at Met. Op. House, 1910–13; after 1917, manager of Soc. of Amer. Singers, N. Y., and later of his own touring opera company which gave Mozart and other works in chamber form.

Hin'ton, Arthur, b. Beckenham, Nov. 20, 1869; violinist; pupil R. A. M., later with Rheinberger at Munich Cons., where his first symph. was played; his second symph. was played in London, 1903; c. also opera "Tamara"; operettas for children, and piano pieces played by his wife, Katharine Goodson, whom he married in 1903.

Hip'kins, Alfred Jas., Westminster, June 17, 1826—London, June 3, 1903; writer; an authority on ancient instrs., etc.; was for a time in business with Broadwood; wrote many articles for the "Encyclopædia Britannica," and "Grove's Dictionary of Music," also books on old instr. and pitch.

Hirn (hērn), Gv. Ad., Logelbach, near Colmar (Alsatia), 1815—Colmar, 1890; writer.

Hirsch (hērsh), (1) Dr., Rudolf, Napagedl, Moravia, 1816—Vienna, 1872; critic, poet and composer. (2) Karl, Wemding, Bavaria, March 17, 1858—Faulenbach, Nov. 3, 1918; studied in Munich; 1885–87, church mus.-dir., Munich; 1887–92, Mannheim; then Cologne; after 1893 lived in other cities as dir. various societies, etc.; c. numerous pop. a cappella choruses.

Hirschbach (hērsh'-bäkh), H., Berlin, 1812—Gohlis, 1888; editor and composer.

Hirschfeld (hērsh'-fĕlt), Robt., Moravia, Sept. 17, 1857—Salzburg, April 2, 1914, where he was dir. of Mozarteum; studied Vienna Cons.; later lecturer there; 1884 teacher of musical æsthetics; took Dr. Phil. with dissertation on "Johannes de Muris"; he wrote a pamphlet against Hanslick in defence of ancient a cappella music, and founded the "Renaissance-Abende" to cultivate it.

Hirsch'mann, Henri, b. St. Maudé, 1872; composer, under pen-name of V. H. Herblay, of operas, "L'Amour à la Bastille" (Paris, 1897), "Lovelace" (do., 1898), "Hermani" (do., 1909); operettas "Das Schwalbennest" (Berlin, 1904, in Paris, 1907, as Les hirondelles); "La petite Bohême" (Paris, 1905; in Berlin 1905, as "Musette"), etc.

Hobrecht (hō'-brĕkht) (or Obrecht, Obreht, Ober'tus, Hober'tus), Jakob, Utrecht, ca. 1430—Antwerp, 1505; church composer of great historical importance.

Hochberg (hōkh'-bĕrkh), Bolko, Graf von (pseud. J. H. Franz), Fürstenstein Castle, Silesia, Jan. 23, 1843—Bad Salzbrunn, Dec. 1, 1926; maintained the H. quartet at Dresden; 1876 founded the Silesian music festivals; 1886–1903, general intendant Prussian Ct. Th.; prod. 2 operas; c. symphonies, etc.

Hoffmann (hôf'-män), (1) Eucharius, b. Heldburg, Franconia, cantor at Stralsund; writer and composer, 1577–84. (2) Ernst Th. (Amadeus) Wm. (he added Amadeus from love of Mozart), Königsberg, 1776—Berlin, 1822; gifted poet, caricaturist, and dram. composer. (3) H. Aug. (called H. von Fallersleben), Fallersleben, Hanover, 1798—Castle Korvei, 1874; writer. (4) Richard, Manchester, Engl., May 24, 1831—Mt. Kisco, N. Y., Aug. 17, 1909; pianist and teacher; pupil of his father, and de Meyer, Pleyel, Moscheles, Rubinstein, Döhler, Thalberg, and Liszt; 1847, New York; solo pianist with Jenny Lind on tours, etc.; also with von Bülow, in N. Y. (1875); c. anthems, pf.-pcs., etc. (5) Karl, Prague, Dec. 12, 1872—1936; violinist; studied Prague Cons.; founder and 1st vln. the famous "Bohemian String-quartet"; after 1922 taught master class at Prague Cons.

Hoffmeister (hôf'-mī-shtĕr), Fz. Anton, Rotenburg-on-Neckar, 1754—Vienna, 1812; conductor and dram. composer, etc.

Hofhaimer (hôf'-hī-mĕr) (Hoffheimer, Hoffhaimer, Hoffhaymer), Paulus von, Radstadt, Salzburg, 1459—Salzburg, 1537; eminent organist; lutenist, composer and teacher.

Hofmann (hôf'-män), (1) Chr., ca. 1668; cantor at Krossen; writer.

(2) **H. (K. Jn.)**, Berlin, Jan. 13, 1842 —July 19, 1902; pupil of Würst, Kullak's Academy; famous pf.-virtuoso and teacher; prod. succ. operas "*Cartouche*" (Berlin, 1869) and "*Donna Diana*," and 4 others; and succ. orch. works, "*Hungarian Suite*" (1873) and "*Frithjof*" symph. (1874); was a Prof., and a member of the Berlin R. Acad. of Arts; c. 6 other operas, "secular oratorio" "*Prometheus*" (1896); cantatas; "*Schauspiel*" overture; "*Trauermarsch*," etc., for orch.; a vln.-sonata, etc. (3) **Richard**, Delitzsch, Prussian Saxony, April 30, 1844—Leipzig, Nov. 11, 1918; son of municipal mus.-dir.; pupil of Dreyschock and Jadassohn; lived in Leipzig as teacher; pub. a valuable "*Praktische Instrumentationsschule*" (Leipzig, 1893), a catechism of instrs., etc. (4) **Casimir** (rightly **Wyszkowski**) (wĕsh-kôf'-shkĭ), Cracow, 1842—Berlin, 1911; pianist; prof. of harm. and comp. at Cons., and cond. of opera, Warsaw. (5) **Josef**, b. Cracow, Jan. 20, 1876. Son and (till 1892) pupil of (4); at 6 played in public; at 9 toured Europe; at 10 gave 52 concerts in America; then studied 2 years with Rubinstein and made new début in Dresden, 1894, and has toured Europe since and (beginning 1899) America; from being a sensational prodigy, he developed into a brilliant pianist of great power, virtuosity and charm; his technique is probably unsurpassed in his generation; after 1924 dir. of Curtis Inst. of Mus., Phila.; c. symph. work, "*The Haunted Castle*"; pf.-concerto, and numerous other pieces; author, "*Piano Playing*," etc.

Hofmeister (hôf'-mī-shtĕr), (1) **Fr.**, 1782—1864; publisher; his son and successor (2) **Ad. H.**, ca. 1818—Leipzig, 1870; was succeeded by **Albert Rothing**, 1845—1907.

Ho'garth, G., Carfrae Mill, near Oxton, Berwickshire, 1783—London, 1870; 'cellist and composer; his daughter m. Charles Dickens.

Hohlfeld (hōl'-fĕlt), **Otto**, Zeulenroda, Voigtland, 1854—Darmstadt, 1895; vln.-virtuoso and composer.

Hohnstock (hōn'-shtôk), **Carl**, Brunswick, 1828—1889; teacher, violinist, pianist and composer.

Hol, Richard, Amsterdam, July 23, 1825—Utrecht, May 14, 1904; pupil

Martens (org.) and of Bertelman (harm. and cpt.); teacher at Amsterdam; 1862, city mus.-dir., Utrecht; 1869, cath.-organist; 1875, dir. Sch. of Mus.; also cond. "Diligentia" Concerts at The Hague, Classical Concerts at Amsterdam; 1878, officer of the French Academy; c. oratorio "*David*" (op. 81); 2 operas; 2 symphonies, etc.

Hol'borne, Antony and **Wm.**, English composers, 1597.

Hol'brooke, Josef, b. Croyden, July 6, 1878; English composer; pupil of the R. A. M., till 1898; c. symph. poems "*The Raven*" (Crystal Palace, 1900); "*Ode to Victory*," "*The Skeleton in Armour*," "*Ulalume*" (London Symph., 1904), "*Queen Mab*" (Leeds Fest., 1904), "*The Masque of the Red Death*," overture, "*The New Renaissance*," etc. His opera "*The Children of Don*" (libretto by Lord Howard de Walden) was prod. at the London Op., June 15, 1912, with Nikisch conducting. Other works include: (operas) "*Pierrot and Pierrette*," "*Dylan*," "*Bronwen, Daughter of Llyr*," "*The Wizard*," "*The Stranger*"; chamber music, ballets, suites for orch., vln. concerto. Author, "*Contemporary British Composers*" (1931).

Hol'der, Rev. Wm., Nottinghamshire, 1616—Amen Corner, 1697; writer, editor and composer.

Holländer (hôl'-lĕnt-ĕr), (1) **Alexis**, Ratibor, Silesia, Feb. 25, 1840— Berlin, Feb. 5, 1924; pianist; pupil of Schnabel and Hesse at Breslau; cond. of the Gymnasium Singing Society; 1858-61, studied with Grell and A. W. Bach, and K. Bohmer, Berlin, R. Akad.; 1861, teacher at Kullak's Acad.; 1864, cond.; 1870-1902, cond. the "Cäcilienverein"; 1888, professor; c. 6 pf. Intermezzi for left hand, etc. (2) **Gv.**, Leobschütz, Upper Silesia, Feb. 15, 1855 —Berlin, Dec. 4, 1915; played in public early; pupil of David, of Joachim (vln.), and Kiel (theory); 1874, principal teacher Kullak's Acad. and royal chamber-mus.; toured Austria with Carlotta Patti; 1881, teacher at the Cons., Cologne; 1884, leader at the Stadttheater; 1894, dir. Stern Cons., Berlin; c. vln. and pf.-pcs. (3) **Victor**, b. Leobschütz, April 20, 1866; pupil of Kullak; c. succ. comic operas and stage music, also for films; after 1934 comp. in Hollywood.

Hollander (hŏl'-lĕn-dĕr), **Benno,** b. Amsterdam, June 8, 1853; violinist; played as child, then studied with Massart and Saint-Saëns at Paris Cons., winning first violin prize, 1873; after 1876 toured, then settled in London as viola player; 1882, cond. German Opera season; 1887 violin prof. at the Guildhall; cond. London Symph. Concerts; 1903, organised the Benno H. Orchestral Society; c. symph. *"Roland"*; violin concertos, pastoral fantasia played by Ysaye, 1900, etc.

Hollangue. Vide MOUTON.

Hol'lins, Alfred, b. Hull, Sept. 11, 1865; pianist, and org.; blind from birth; pupil of Hartvigson; played Beethoven concerto as a boy; at 16 played for the Queen; pupil of Bülow, later at Raff Cons.; played for crowned heads, and toured America; 1884, org. at Redhill; 1888 at People's Palace; 1897 at Edinburgh, Free St. George's Church; c. 2. overtures, organ music, etc.

Hollmann (hŏl'-män), **Josef,** Maestricht, Holland, Oct. 16, 1852— Paris, Jan. 1, 1927; notable 'cellist; studied with Gervais; toured Europe, England and America; court-mus., Holland, and many decorations.

Holmes (hōmz), (1) **Edw.,** near London, 1797—U. S., 1859; pf.-teacher, editor and critic. (2) **Wm. H.,** Sudbury, Derbyshire, 1812—London, 1885; pianist and professor. (3) **Alfred,** London, 1837—Paris, 1876; son of above; dram. composer. (4) **Hy.,** London, Nov. 7, 1839—San Francisco, Cal., Dec. 9, 1905; bro. of above; after 1866 was long vln.-prof. R. C. M.; c. 4 symphonies, etc.

Holmès (ŏl'-mĕs) (rightly **Holmes**), **Augusta Mary Anne,** (of Irish parents) Paris, Dec. 16, 1847—Jan. 28, 1903; at first a pianist; studied comp. with Lambert, Klosé and César Franck; 1873, prod. a psalm, *"In Exitu"*; 1874, a 1-act stage work *"Héro et Leandre"* (Chatelet); the symphonies *"Lutece"* and *"Les Argonautes,"* 1883; symph. *"Irlande,"* 1885; unsucc. drama *"La Montagne Noire"* (Gr. Opera), 1895; symphonic poems, *"Roland," "Pologne,"* *"Au Pays Bleu"*; 2 operas, etc.; she sometimes uses pseud. *"Hermann Zenta."*

Holst, Gustav, Cheltenham, England, Sept. 21, 1874—London, May 25, 1934; studied R. Coll. of Mus. with Stanford; fellow and prof. of comp., R. Coll. of Mus.; formerly dir. of music, Morley Coll.; lectured on music, Harvard Univ., one of the most accomplished of modern English comps., though of Teutonic ancestry; introduced British folk-song elements into some of his works, also arranged many traditional pieces in choral transcriptions; showed interest in and influence of Oriental themes; modern French school and Stravinsky among others contributed to his style; c. (operas) *"Savitri,"* one-act work with chamber ensemble (London, 1916); *"The Perfect Fool"* (a ballet-opera, said to satirise Wagner's *"Parsifal"*), Covent Garden, 1923; *"At the Boar's Head,"* based on Shakespeare's *"Henry IV"* and using actual folk melodies (British Nat'l. Op. Co., 1927); also *"Ave Maria"* for 8 women's voices; (masque) *"The Vision of Dame Christian"* (1909); *"The Mystic Trumpeter,"* scena for soprano and orch. (1905); Cotswolds Symphony (1900); *"The Planets"* (1915) and *"Beni-Mora"* suite (1910); *"Phantasies"* (1912), *"Indra"* (1903), *"Japanese"* suite (1916); *"A Somerset Rhapsody"* for orch. (1907); (choral works) *"King Estmere"* (1903), *"Choral Hymns from the Rig-Veda"* (1912), *"The Cloud-Messenger"* (1910), *"Hymn of Jesus"* and *"Ode to Death"* (Leeds Fest., 1921), Choral Symphony (do., 1924); Fugal Concerto, St. Paul's Suite, *"Songs without Words," "Songs of the West,"* and numerous choruses and part-songs, besides 2 wind quintets and other chamber works.

Holstein (hŏl'-shtīn), **Fz. (Fr.) von,** Brunswick, 1826 — Leipzig, 1878; dram. composer.

Holten (hŏl'-tĕn), **K. von,** Hamburg, July 26, 1836—Altona, Jan. 12, 1912; pianist; pupil of J. Schmitt, Ave-Lallemant and Grädener, and at Leipzig Cons.; after 1874, teacher Hamburg Cons.; c. a *Kindersymphonie,* etc.

Holy (ō'-lē), **Alfred,** b. Oporto, Aug. 5, 1866; harp-virtuoso; son and pupil of a cond. and teacher from Prague; studied at Prague Cons., and lived there till 1896, when he went to the

Berlin ct.-opera; after 1913, solo harpist, Boston Symph.

Holzbauer (hôlts'-bow-ĕr), **Ignaz**, Vienna, 1711—Mannheim, 1783; court-conductor and dram. composer; highly praised by Mozart.

Hölzl (hĕl'-ts'l), **Fz. Severin**, Malaczka, Hungary, 1808—Fünfkirchen, 1884; conductor and composer.

Ho'mer, (1) **Sidney**, b. Boston, Mass., Dec. 9, 1864; prominent American song-composer; pupil of G. W. Chadwick, then of Rheinberger, O. Hieter and Abel in Germany; 1888–96 teacher of theory in Boston; c. many important songs. In 1895 he married (2) **Louise (Dilworth Beatty)**, b. Pittsburgh, Pa.; famous operatic contralto, pupil of Miss Whinnery and Miss Goff, W. L. Whitney, and of her husband in theory; then studied in Paris with Fidèle Koenig; début, 1898, at Vichy; 1899 at Covent Garden, also at La Monnaie, Brussels; 1900–19 sang regularly at Met. Op. House as a leading member of co. in Italian, German, French rôles; created title rôle in Parker's *"Mona,"* etc.; guest appearances with co. after the latter year; also an eminent concert singer. (3) **Louise (Homer-Stires)**, their daughter, also active as a concert singer (soprano) in joint programmes with her mother.

Homeyer (hō'-mī-ĕr), name of a musical family. The most prom. of them is **Paul Joseph M.**, Osterode, Harz, Oct. 26, 1853—Leipzig, July 27, 1908; famous organist at the Gewandhaus, and teacher Leipzig Cons.

Homilius (hō-mē'-lĭ-oos), **Gf. Aug.**, Rosenthal, Saxony, 1714—Dresden, 1785; eminent organist and composer.

Honegger (ŏn'-ĕg-ĕr), **Arthur**, b. Le Havre, France, March 10, 1892, of Swiss ancestry; composer; studied with Martin, Gédalge, Widor and Capet; an exponent of Polytonality, but classic in form; one of most gifted members of former "Group of Six"; since 1913 active in Paris; c. (operas) *"Morte de Ste. Almeenne"*; *"Antigone," "Judith,"* produced by Chicago Op. with Mary Garden; (cantata with narrator) *"Le Roi David"* to text by Morax, widely performed (N. Y., 1925); music to Méral's *"Dit des Jeux du Monde"*; (ballet) *"Verité Mensonge?"*, Concertino for piano

and orch., and (orch.) *"Horace Victorieux," "Pastorale d'Été," "Pacific 231"* (literal depiction in sound of the journey of a locomotive), prelude to *"The Tempest,"* prelude to Act II of d'Annunzio's *"Phaedre," "Skating Rink," "Rugby"* (descriptive of a football game), Hymne for 10 stringed instruments; Rhapsodie for piano, flutes and clarinet, sonatas for 2 violins, for viola and for 'cello, etc.

Hood, Helen, b. Chelsea, Mass., June 28, 1863; pupil of B. J. Lang (pf.) and Chadwick (comp.), Boston; and Moszkowski (pf.); composer.

Hook, Jas., Norwich, 1746—Boulogne, 1827; organist and composer.

Hope'kirk, Helen, b. near Edinburgh, Scotland, May 20, 1856; studied with Lichtenstein and A. C. Mackenzie; for 2 years at Leipzig, later with Leschetizky; début as pianist at Gewandhaus, Leipzig, 1878; gave concerts in Great Britain and (1883–84) U. S.; 1897–1901, teacher N. E. Cons.; later private teacher, Boston, Mass.; c. Concertstück for pf. and orch.; 1894, orch. pcs.; a pf.-concerto; sonata for pf. and vln., and songs.

Hopffer (hôp'-fĕr), **L. Bd.,** Berlin, 1840 —Niederwald, near Rüdesheim, 1877; dram. composer.

Hop'kins, (1) **Edw. J.,** Westminster, June 30, 1818—London, Feb. 4, 1901; self-taught organist at various churches; 1843–1898, to the Temple Ch., London; wrote *"The Organ; Its History and Construction"* (Rimbault); contributed to *"Grove's Dict. of Mus."*; c. 3 prize anthems, hymntunes, chants and church-services. (2) **Edw. Jerome,** Burlington, Vt., 1836—Athenia, N. J., 1898; self-taught in harmony; began composing at 9; organist, editor and lecturer; (3) **Harry Patterson,** b. Baltimore, 1873; graduated Peabody Inst., 1896; studied with Dvořák in Bohemia; after 1899 active as organist and teacher, Baltimore; c. a symphony, songs, etc.

Hop'kinson, Francis, composer; 1737–91; one of the earliest American composers; inventor of the *"Bellarmonica."*

Hoplit. Vide POHL, R.

Horák (hō'-räk), (1) **Wenzel (Václav) Emanuel,** Mscheno-Lobes, Bohemia, 1800—Prague, 1871; organist, teacher and composer. (2) **Ed.,** Holitz,

Bohemia, 1839—Riva, Lake of Garda, 1892; teacher and writer. (3) **Ad.**, Jankovic, Bohemia, Feb. 15, 1850—Vienna (?); pianist; bro. of above and co-founder, "Horák" Pf.-School, Vienna; writer.

Horn, (1) **K. Fr.**, Nordhausen, Saxony, 1762—Windsor, Engl., 1830; organist, writer and theorist. (2) **Chas. Edw.**, London, 1786—Boston, Mass., 1849; son of above; singer, teacher, cond., and composer. (3) **Aug.**, Freiberg, Saxony, 1825—Leipzig, 1893; dram. composer.

Horneman (hôr'-nĕ-män), (1) **Johan Ole Emil**, Copenhagen, 1809—1870; composer. (2) **Emil Chr.**, Copenhagen, Dec. 17, 1841—June 9, 1906; son and pupil of above; studied at Leipzig Cons.; dir. of sch. of mus. in Copenhagen; c. overtures "*Aladdin*" and "*Heldenleben*," etc.

Hornstein (hôrn'-shtīn), **Robt. von**, Donaueschingen, 1833 — Munich, 1890; dram. composer.

Horowitz (hŏr'-ō-vētz), **Vladimir**, b. Kiev, Russia, Oct. 1, 1904; pianist; grad. Kiev Cons. at 17; studied with Blumenfeld; début, Kharkov; since 1924 has made appearances in leading Eur. capitals with pronounced succ.; a brilliant virtuoso, he has appeared with the princ. orchs. in Germany, France, England, Italy and U. S. (Amer. début with N. Y. Philh., 1928); m. Wanda, daughter of Arturo Toscanini.

Hors'ley, (1) **Wm.**, London, 1774—1858; organist, theorist and composer. (2) **Chas. Edw.**, London, 1822—New York, 1876; son and pupil of above; organist, writer and composer.

Horszowski (hôr-shŏf'-skē) **Miecio**, b. Lemberg, Poland, 1892; pianist; pupil of Leschetizky, Cyrill Kistler and Heuberger; after early successes went into retirement for several years, then reappeared in concerts 1913; toured widely in Europe, South America and also visited U. S.; lives in Paris.

Hor'vath, (1) **Cecile de** (née Ayres), b. Boston, 1889; pianist; studied with her father, Eugene Ayres, and with Safonoff and Gabrilowitsch; after 1910 active as concert artist in Europe and U. S., later taught in Chicago. (2) **Zoltan**, her husband, b. Chicago, 1886; also a pianist and teacher, was long active in Phila.

Horwitz (hôr'-vĭts), **Benno**, Berlin, March 17, 1855—Berlin, June 3, 1904; violinist and composer; pupil of the Rl. Hochschule, and of Kiel and Albert Becker; c. symph. poem "*Dionysos*," etc.

Hostinsky (hô-shtēn'-shkĭ), **Ottokar**, Martinoves, Bohemia, Jan. 2, 1847 —Prague, Jan. 19, 1910; Dr. Phil., Prague; writer.

Hoth'by (or **Hothobus, Otteby, Fra Ottobi**), **John** (or **Johannes**), d. London, Nov., 1487; English Carmelite monk; famous for science.

Hotteterre (ôt'-tăr), (1) **Henri**, d. 1683; instr.-maker, musette player, ct.-musician. (2) **Louis** (called "*Le Romain*," having lived in Rome); son of above; notable flutist and writer. (3) **Nicolas**, d. 1695; noted bassoonist and oboist; bro. of (2).

Ho'ven, J., pen-name of **V. von Puttlingen.**

How'ard, (1) **Samuel**, 1710—1782; English organist and composer. (2) **Kathleen**, b. Clifton, Canada; contralto; pupil of Saenger and Jean de Reszke; début, Metz, 1906; 1909–12, Darmstadt Op., Century Op. Co., N. Y., 1913–15; Met. Op. Co., 1916–28; also toured in Europe; author "*Confessions of an Opera Singer.*" (3) **John Tasker**, b. Brooklyn, N. Y., Nov. 30, 1890; composer and writer; educated Williams Coll.; studied comp. with Howard Brockway and Mortimer Wilson; c. orch., piano and vocal works; author, "*Studies of Contemporary American Composers*," "*Our American Music*," "*Stephen Foster*," etc.

How'ell, Jas., b. Plymouth, England, d. 1879; singer and double-bass player.

How'ells, Herbert, b. Lydney, Australia, 1892; composer; pupil of Brewer and of R. Coll. of Mus., London, where has been prof. since 1920; c. piano concerto, orch. and chamber music, choral works, org. pieces and songs.

Hrimaly (h'rĭm'-ŭ-lē), **Adalbert**, Pilsen, Bohemia, July 30, 1842—Vienna, June 17, 1908; violinist; pupil of Mildner, Prague Cons., 1861; cond. Gothenburg orch., 1868; National Th., Prague; at the German Th., there in 1873, and at Czernowitz, Bukowina, in 1875; his succ. opera "*Der Verzauberte Prinz*" (1871) played at Prague.

Hubay (hoo'-bä-ē) (or **Huber**), (1) **K.**, Varjas, Hungary, 1828—Pesth, 1885; vln.-prof., Pesth Cons.; conductor and dram. composer. (2) **Jeno**, Budapest, Sept. 15, 1858—Vienna, March 12, 1937; son and pupil of above, and 1886 his successor as prof.; also studied with Joachim; gave succ. concerts in Hungary and at Paris; 1882 principal vln.-prof., Brussels Cons.; 1886, prof. and 1919–34, dir. Budapest Cons.; 1894, m. Countess Rosa Cebrian; c. succ. opera "*Der Geigenmacher von Cremona*" (Pesth, 1893); opera "*Alienor*" (Pesth, 1892); succ. Hungarian opera "*A Falu Rossza*" (The Townloafer) (Budapest, 1896); opera, "*Anna Karenina*"; 3 symphonies, many notable vln. works, incl. 4 concertos.

Huber (hoo'-bĕr), (1) **F.**, d. Berne, Feb. 23, 1810; poet and song-composer. (2) **Fd.**, 1791—St. Gallen, 1863; Swiss song-writer. (3) **K.** Vide HUBAY. (4) **Jos.**, Sigmaringen, 1837—Stuttgart, 1886; violinist and dram. composer. (5) **Hans**, Schönewerd, Switzerland, June 28, 1852—Locarno, Dec. 25, 1921; pupil Leipzig Cons.; teacher at Wesserling for 2 years, then at Thann (Alsatia), later Basel Music School; 1892, Dr. Phil. *h. c.*, Basel Univ.; 1896, dir. of the Mus. Sch.; c. succ. operas "*Weltfrühling*" (Basel, 1894); and "*Gudrun*" (Basel, 1896); cantatas, sonatas, concertos, overtures "*Lustspiel*," symph. "*Tell*," etc. (6) **Eugen.** Vide HUBAY, JENO.

Huberdeau (ü'-bĕr-dō), **Gustave**, b. Paris, 1878 (?); notable operatic bass; studied at Paris Cons.; début, 1898; sang at Op.-Comique; 1908, Manhattan Op. Co., N. Y.; after 1910 with Chicago Op. Co. in French and Italian rôles.

Hu'berman, **Bronislaw**, b. Czenstochova near Warsaw, Dec. 19, 1882; Polish violinist; succ. début as prodigy; retired for five years' study; reappeared, Bucharest, 1902; has since won world-wide reputation as a leading virtuoso, and has toured continuously in Europe and at intervals in the U. S. (first Amer. tour, 1896–97); founded Palestine Orch., 1935.

Hubert (hoo'-bĕrt), **Nikolai Albertovitch**, 1840—1888; prof. and writer at Moscow.

Huberti (ü-bĕr'-tē), **Gve. Léon**, Brussels, April 14, 1843—July 23, 1910;

pupil Brussels Cons.; 1865, won Prix de Rome; 1874–78, dir. of Mons. Cons.; 1880–89, Antwerp; then prof. at Brussels Cons., and dir. of the Mus.-School of St. Josse-ten-Noode-Schaerbeek; 1891, member of the Belgian Academy; 1893, Chevalier of the Legion of Honour. C. oratorios, the dram. poem "*Verlichting*" ("*Fiat lux*"), with orch.; symphonic poem "*Kinderlust en Leed*," chorus and orch., etc.; symphonie funèbre, festival marches, etc.

Hucbald (hook'-bält, or ük-bäl) (**Hugbal'dus, Ubal'dus, Uchubal'dus**) **de S. Amand(o)**, ca. 840—St. Amand, near Tournay, June 25 (or Oct. 21), 930 (or June 20, 932). He is perhaps credited with some works belonging to a monk of the same name living a century later; pupil of his uncle, Milo, a mus.-dir., whose jealousy drove him to Nevers, where he taught singing; 872 he succeeded his uncle; ca. 893, the Archbishop of Rheims invited him to reform the music of the diocese. His works (Gerbert) contain the first known notation showing difference of pitch on lines.

Hué (ü), **Georges Ad.**, b. Versailles, May 6, 1858; pupil of Paris Cons., took 1st Grand prix de Rome; later Prix Cressent; 1922 elected mem. of French Acad. to take place of late Camille Saint-Saëns; c. op. com. "*Les Pantins*" (Op.-Com., 1881); "*Rübezahl*," symphonic legend in 3 parts ("Concerts Colonne," 1886); succ. "Féerie dramatique" "*La Belle au Bois Dormant*" (Paris, 1894); "épisode sacré" "*Resurrection*"; a symphony, a symphonic overture; the operas "*Le roi de Paris*," 1901; "*Titania*," 1903; "*Le Miracle*," 1910; "*Dans l'Ombre de la Cathédrale*" (Op.-Comique, 1921), ballet "*Siang-Sin*" (Opéra, 1922), etc.

Hueffer (hüf'-fĕr), **Francis**, Münster, 1843—London, Jan. 19, 1889; 1869, lived in London; from 1878, critic of *The Times;* librettist and writer.

Hughes, (1) **Edwin**, b. Washington, D. C., Aug. 15, 1884; pianist, pedagogue; pupil of S. M. Fabian, Joseffy, and Leschetizky; appeared in concerts in Europe and U. S., active in Munich, 1912; taught at Inst. of Mus. Art, N. Y., 1916–22; later cond. many master classes in Amer. cities; ed. piano works. (2) **Herbert**, b. Belfast, March 16,

1882—Brighton, Engl., May 2, 1937; pupil of R. Coll. of Mus.; founder of Irish Folk-Song Soc. (1904); after 1911, music ed. on London *Daily Telegraph*; visited America in 1922; ed. Modern Festival Series; Irish Country Songs, Historical Songs and Ballads of Ireland; c. chamber music and songs. (3) **Rupert**, b. Lancaster, Mo., Jan. 21, 1872; Amer. writer on music; novelist, dramatist; grad. Adelbert Coll. (Western Reserve Univ.); A. M., Yale Univ.; studied comp. with Wilson Smith, Edgar Stillman Kelley, and C. W. Pearce; music critic and mem. of editorial board of various Amer. periodicals, incl. *Current Literature, The Criterion*; mem. of the N. Y. editorial board of the Encyclopedia Britannica; author "*Contemporary Amer. Composers*," "*Love Affairs of Great Musicians*," "*Music Lovers' Cyclopedia*"; ed. "*Songs by Thirty Americans*."

Huguenet (üg-nā). Vide GIRARD.

Huhn, Bruno (Siegfried), b. London, 1871; org. and pianist; pupil of Sophie Taunton, later in New York of S. B. Mills and L. Alberti; has toured Europe as pianist; prominent composer, choral conductor and accompanist in New York; c. "*Te Deum*" with orch., and many songs.

Hull, Arthur Eaglefield, Market Harborough, England, March 10, 1876—Huddersfield, Nov. 4, 1928; organist, teacher, composer, writer; pupil of Wood, Matthay and Pearce; Mus. D., Oxford; ed. "*The Music Lover's Library*"; c. oratorios, org. and piano pieces; ed. org. works of Bach and Mendelssohn; wrote books on Bach, Scriabin, Cyril Scott, also "*Modern Harmony*" and ed. "*Dictionary of Modern Music and Musicians*."

Hul'lah, John Pyke, Worcester, June 27, 1812—London, Feb. 21, 1884; professor, conductor, writer and dram. composer.

Hüller, J. A. Vide HILLER.

Hüllmandel (hĭl'-mänt-'l), **Nicholas Jos.**, Strassburg, 1751 — London, 1823; pianist and harmonica-player; c. 12 piano trios, 14 vln. sonatas, 6 piano sonatas, etc.

Hüllweck (hĭl'-vĕk), **Fd.**, Dessau, 1824 —Blasewitz, 1887; concert-violinist and composer.

Hulsteyn (hŭl'-shĭn), **Joai'n C. Van**, b. Amsterdam, 1869; violinist; pupil at Liége Cons. of César Thomson; won

first prize; played in Lamoureux orch., Paris; prof. at Peabody Inst., Baltimore.

Humbert (ŭn-bär), **Georges**, b. St. Croix, Switzerland, Aug. 10, 1870; organist; pupil Leipzig and Brussels Cons., and of Bargiel; teacher of mus. history at Geneva Cons. and org. at Nôtre Dame; from 1893 at Lausanne; after 1918 dir. of a mus. school at Neuchâtel, where he d. Jan. 1, 1936.

Hum'frey (Humphrey, Humphrys), Pelham, London, 1647—Windsor, July 14, 1674; English composer. Charles II. sent him to Paris to study with Lully; 1672 master Chapel Royal children and with Purcell ct.-composer.

Hu'miston, William Henry, Marietta, O., April 27, 1869—New York, Dec. 5, 1923; pianist, conductor, writer; grad. Lake Forest Coll., studied piano with Mathews and org. with Eddy; also later comp. with MacDowell; active as teacher, lecturer, and cond. with opera companies on tour; after 1912 ed. programme notes of N. Y. Philh.; and following 1916 was asst. cond. of this orch.; 1914 led MacDowell Club perf. of Mozart's "*Bastien et Bastienne*" and Bach programmes in 1916 and 1918; c. orch. works and songs.

Hummel (hoom'-mĕl), (1) **Jos.**, music-master Wartberg Military Acad.; 1786, conductor at Vienna. (2) **Jn. Nepomuk**, Pressburg, Nov. 14, 1778 —Weimar, Oct. 17, 1837; son of above; a famous pianist and improviser, and a composer of once popular pieces in which ornament outweighs matter; and form, interest; protégé of Mozart; début 1787; toured Europe frequently; 1793 studied with Albrechtsberger; asst.-cond. to Haydn, 1804–11; 1830 and 1833 cond. German opera in London; c. operas, cantatas, ballets, 3 masses, sonatas; he pub. a notable pf.-method; c. dram. pcs., concertos, sonatas, septet in D minor, etc. (3) **Elisabeth** (née Röckl), 1783—Weimar, 1883; wife of above; opera-singer. (4) **Jos. Fr.**, Innsbruck, Aug. 14, 1841—Salzburg, Aug. 29, 1919; pupil Munich Cons., 1861–80; th.-cond. Vienna, 1880–1907, dir. Mozarteum at Salzburg, and cond. *Liedertafel*. (5) **Fd.**, Berlin, Sept. 6, 1855—April 24, 1928; son and pupil of a musician; at 7 a harp virtuoso;

1864–67 toured Europe, and received a royal grant for study at Kullak's Akademie, Berlin; 1871–75, studied R. High Sch. of Mus., then at Akademie; for years active as cond. and comp. for the Berlin ct.-theatres. c. succ. operas, *"Mara"* (Berlin, 1893); *"Ein Treuer Schelm"* (Prague, 1894); *"Assarpai"* (Gotha, 1898); a symphony, sonatas, etc.

Humperdinck (hoom'-pĕr-dĭnk), **Engelbert,** Siegburg, near Bonn, Sept. 1, 1854—Neustrelitz, Sept. 27, 1921; studied architecture, Cologne, then mus. at the Cons.; won Mozart scholarship at Frankfort; studied 2 years with Franz Lachner, Munich, also with Rheinberger and Barmann at the Cons.; pub. Humoreske for orch. and *"Die Wallfahrt nach Kevelaar"* for chorus; 1878 won the Mendelssohn prize (3,000 marks), 1880 the Meyerbeer prize (7,600 marks); 1885–86, prof. Barcelona Cons.; 1881–82, a special protégé of R. Wagner in Bayreuth; made pf.-scores, and aided in the preparation of *"Parsifal."* Returned to Cologne, 1887, went to Mayence in the employ of Schott & Co.; 1890 teacher Hoch Cons., Frankfort, critic on the Frankfort *Zeitung;* later lived at Boppard-on-Rhine. In 1900–20, he was dir. of Master-School of the Berlin Royal Acad. of Arts. His first international succ. was the graceful 2-act fairy-opera *"Hänsel und Gretel,"* Munich, 1893 (prod. at Milan, 1897, as *"Nino e Rita"*), which has taken its place in the repertoire as an enduring little masterpiece. **H.** never again quite equalled this work, though he made an approach to it in *"Die Königskinder,"* originally conceived as incid. music to the spoken play but re-written as opera; prod. at Met. Op., N. Y., 1910; with success, later in Europe. *"Dornröschen"* was prod. Frankfort-on-Main (1902); com. op. *"Die Heirat wider Willen"* (Berlin, 1905); he also c. incid. music to Aristophanes' *"Lysistrata"* (do., 1908); Shakespeare's *"Winter's Tale"* and *"Tempest"* (do. 1906); to the pantomime, *"The Miracle"* by Vollmoeller (staged in U. S. by Max Reinhardt). His last 2 operas, *"Die Marketenderin"* (1914) and *"Gaudeamus,"* (1919) were not successful.

Huneker (hū'-nĕk-ĕr), **James Gibbons,** Philadelphia, Jan. 31, 1860—New York, Feb. 9, 1921; eminent critic and writer; pupil of Michael Cross, L. Damrosch and Joseffy, and for 10 years asst. to Joseffy at the Nat'l. Cons. in N. Y.; music and dram. critic of the *Commercial Advertiser* and *The Recorder,* transferring in 1901 to the New York *Sun;* after 1918 to the New York *Times;* and for a short period before his death, to the New York *World;* wrote for Philadelphia *Press,* and for many years for the *Musical Courier;* champion of Brahms and some moderns, an outstanding stylist; author of *"Mezzotints in Modern Music," "Chopin, the Man and His Music," "Melomaniacs," "Franz Liszt," "Overtones (in) Music and Literature," "Iconoclasts," "Visionaries," "Egoists," "Promenades of an Impressionist," "The Pathos of Distance," "Old Fogy," "New Cosmopolis," "Ivory Apes and Peacocks," "Unicorns," "The N. Y. Philharmonic Soc.," "Charles Baudelaire," "Steeplejack," "Bedouins," "Mary Garden,"* etc.

Hunke (hoon'-kē), **Jos.,** Josephstadt, Bohemia, 1801—St. Petersburg, 1883; choirm. Russian ct.-chapel; composer.

Hünten (hĭn'-tĕn), **Fz.,** Coblenz, 1793—1878; c. pop. pf.-pcs., etc.

Huré (ü-rā'), **Jean,** Gien, Loiret, Sept. 17, 1877—Paris, Jan. 27, 1930; studied in monastery at Angers; lived in Paris after 1895; active as pianist and comp.; founded Paris Normal School for pianists, organists; c. operas, symphonies, chamber and choral works; author, *"La Technique du Piano," "La Technique de l'Orgue";* pub. periodical, *L'Orgue et les Organistes.*

Hurel de Lamare (ü'-rĕl-dŭ-lä-mär), **Jacques Michel,** Paris, 1772—Caen, 1823; 'cellist and composer; his friend Auber pub. some comp. under **H.'s** name.

Hurlstone, Wm. Yeates, London, Jan. 7, 1876—May 30, 1906; composer; at 9 pub. 5 waltzes; at 18 held scholarship at R. A. M.; later prof. there of harmony and counterpoint; c. piano concerto, etc.

Huss (hoos), **Henry Holden,** b. Newark, N. J., June 21, 1862; concert-pianist and teacner; studied with O. B. Boise (cpt. and comp.), also at

Munich Cons.; lives in N. Y. as teacher of pf., comp. and instr. He and his wife, the soprano, **Hildegard Hoffman,** have given joint recitals throughout America, and 1910 in London. His piano concerto in B major was played with the composer as soloist by the N. Y. Philh., Boston Symph., Pittsburgh and Cincinnati Symph. orch's. and by the Monte Carlo Symph., with Pugno as soloist; his violin sonata by Kneisel, Spiering, etc.; also c. *"Recessional"* for mixed chorus, organ, and orch. (Worcester, Mass., Festival, 1911); string quartet in E minor (Kneisel Quartet); 'cello sonata; songs, etc.

Hutch'eson, Ernest, b. Melbourne, July 20, 1871; pianist; pupil of Leipzig Cons., 1886–1892, winning Mozart prize with a trio; toured Australia; studied with Stavenhagen; 1898 married Baroness von Pilsach; from 1900 teacher Peabody Cons., Baltimore; c. symph. poem *"Merlin and Vivien"* (Berlin, 1899); orch. suite (do.), piano concerto (1899); symphony; two-piano concerto; vln. concerto, etc.; 1912–14, toured Europe; after latter year in N. Y.; after 1911 taught Chautauqua Inst.; and has been dean of Juilliard Grad. School of Music, N. Y., since 1926; author, *"Guide to Strauss' Elektra."*

Hutschenruijter (hoot'-shěn-roi-těr), (1) **Wouter,** Rotterdam, 1796—1878; horn- and trumpet-virtuoso; professor, conductor, director and dram. composer. (2) **Wouter,** b. Rotterdam, Aug. 15, 1859; noted conductor; after 1890 asst. cond. of Concertgebouw, Amsterdam; then of Utrecht Orch.; 1917–25, dir. Rotterdam Munic. School of Music.

Hüttenbrenner (hǐt'-těn-brěn-něr), **Anselm,** Graz, Styria, 1794—Ober-Andritz, 1868; pianist, conductor and dram. composer.

Huygens (hī'-gěns), (1) **Constantin,** The Hague, Sept. 4, 1596—March 28, 1687; poet and military secretary to William II. and William III.; also skilful performer; c. over 700 airs for lute, theorbo, etc.; his son (2) **Christian,** The Hague, April 14, 1629—June 8, 1695; mathematician and musician.

Hyllested (hŭl'-lě-städh), **Aug.,** b. (of Danish parents) Stockholm, June 17, 1858; violinist; at 5 played in public;

studied with Holger Dahl till 1869, and then made succ. tour through Scandinavia; entered the Royal Cons. at Copenhagen; 1876, organist of the Cath. and dir. of a mus. soc.; 1879, studied with Kullak, Kiel, and later Liszt; 1885, toured U. S.; 1886–91, asst.-dir. Chicago Mus. Coll.; 1891–94, Gottschalk Lyric Sch.; 1894–97, toured Europe; prod. in London symph. poem *"Elizabeth,"* with double chorus; 1897, Chicago; c. romantic play *"Die Rheinnixe,"* orch. "suite romantique," etc.

I

Ibach (ē'-bäkh), (1) **Jns. Ad.,** 1766—1848; pf. and organ-builder. His son (2) **C. Rudolf** (d. 1862), and (3) **Richard,** joined the firm; a third son (4) **Gustav J.** founded another business 1869. (5) **Rudolf** (d. Herrenalb, Black Forest, July, 1892) son of (2), continued the pf.-factory, and **Richard,** the organ-factory.

Ibert (ē-bār'), **Jacques,** b. Paris, Aug. 15, 1890; composer; studied Paris Cons., Prix de Rome, 1919; an accomplished modern-style comp., especially known for his colourful orchestral compositions in which one finds the influence of Franck, Ravel and Debussy; *"Escales,"* a suite depicting marine ports, has had internat'l. hearings; also c. a light opera, *"Angélique,"* given with succ. in Paris; (opera) *"Le Roi d' Yvetot"*; the symph. poems, *"Noël en Picardie,"* *"The Ballad of Reading Gaol"* (after Wilde); *"Persée et Andromède,"* orchestral phantasy; lyric scene, *"La Poète et la Fée"*; wind quartet, vln. sonata, 'cello concerto, concerto for saxophone and orch.; org. and piano pieces; his ballet, *"Gold Standard,"* was prod. by Chicago Op. in 1934.

If'fert, August, Braunschweig, May 31, 1859—near Dresden, Aug. 13, 1930; singer and teacher in various cities; author of a vocal method.

Igumnoff (ē-goom'-noff), **Konstantin Nikolajavich,** b. Lebedjana, Tambouv, May 1, 1873; Russian pianist; pupil of Svereff, Siloti and Pabst; 1898, teacher in Tiflis; 1900 prof. at Moscow Cons.

Iliffe (ī'-lǐf), **Fr.,** Smeeton-Westerby, Leicester, Engl., Feb. 21, 1847—Oxford, Feb. 2, 1928; 1883, organist and choirm. St. John's Coll., Oxford; cond. of Queen's Coll. Mus. Soc., 1873, Mus. Bac. Oxon.; wrote *"Critical Analysis of Bach's Clavichord"* (London, 1896; 4 parts); c. oratorio, *"The Visions of St. John the Divine"*; cantata with orch. *"Lara,"* etc.

Ilinski (ē-lĭn'-shkĭ), Count **Jan Stanislaw,** b. Castle Romanov, 1795; composer.

Iljinski (ĕl-yēn'-shkĭ), **Alexander Alexandrovich,** Tsarkoe Selo, Jan. 24, 1859—Moscow, 1919?; composer; pupil of Kullak and Bargiel; 1885 prof. of theory at the Philharmonic Music School in Moscow; c. opera *"The Fountain of Bastchi-Sarai"*; symph.; symphonic scherzo; pf.-pcs., songs, etc.

Imbert (ĕn-bār), **Hugues,** Moulins-Engilbert 1842—Paris, 1905; noted writer of biogs., etc.

Inc'ledon, Chas., Bery St. Kevern, Cornwall, 1763—1826; tenor, called "The Wandering Melodiste."

Indy (dăn-dē), (**Paul M. Th.**) **Vincent d',** Paris, March 27, 1851—Dec. 3, 1931; pupil of César Franck (comp.) and at the Cons., 1875, chorusm. with Colonne; played drum-parts for 3 years to learn instrumentation; pres. of various concert-societies; mus.-inspector of Paris schools; Chev. of the Legion of Honour; 1896 he became prof. of composition at Paris Cons.; 1896 with Bordes and Guilmant founded the *Schola Cantorum,* and became director; c. a 3-part symph. poem *"Wallenstein"* (Part II., *"I Piccolomini,"* prod. 1874 by Pasdeloup); symphonies (1) *"On a French mountaineer-song,"* and (2) *"Jean Hunyadi,"* symphonic legend *"La forêt enchantée"*; overture to *"Antony and Cleopatra"*; *"La Chevauchée du Cid,"* for orch.; symphonic pf.-concerto; prod. 1-act comic opera, *"Attendez-moi sous l'Orme"* (Op.-com., 1882); c. text and mus.; succ. mus. drama, *"Fervaal"* (Brussels, 1897); *"L'Étranger"* (do. 1903); *"Le chant de la cloche,"* dramatic legend in seven pictures, with his own text, for soli, double chorus and orch. Festival cantata *"Pour l'inauguration d'une Statue"* for barytone, chorus and orch., *"Ode à Valence,"* do. symph. in B flat, 1902; *"Jour d'été à la montagne,"* 1905; *"Souvenirs"* for orch. 1906;

songs, piano pieces and choruses, author of a *"Cours de Composition Musicale,"* 1902, and a life of César Franck, 1906.

Infante (ēn-fän'-tā), **Manuel,** b. Osuna near Seville; composer; has c. many piano works of graceful sort and attractive folk colouring, first made pop. by the pianist Iturbi; res. in Paris.

Ingegneri (ēn-gän-yā'-rē), **Marco A.,** Verona, ca. 1545—Cremona, July 1, 1592; conductor, composer and publisher.

Inghelbrecht (ēn'-gĕl-brĕkht), **Desiré Emile,** b. Paris, Sept. 17, 1880; composer; pupil of Cons.; a friend of Debussy in the composer's latter days, whose works he excels in conducting; after 1908 active at various Paris theatres and following 1925 music. dir. at the Op.-Comique; c. ballet, *"Le Diable dans le beffroi"* (after Poe), and numerous orch., chamber music, and vocal works; arr. works of Couperin and Albeniz for orch.

In'gram, Frances, b. Liverpool, England, 1888; contralto; studied with Maurel; after 1911 sang for several years with Chicago Op. Co.; 1913, Montreal Op. Co., and also in concerts.

Insanguine (ēn-sän-gwē'-nā), **Giacomo** (called **Monopoli**), Monopili, ca. 1740 —Naples, 1795; teacher and dram. composer.

Ippolitov-Ivanov (ēp-pō'-lē-tŏf-ē'-vänŏf), **Mikhail Mikhailovitch,** Gatchina, Nov. 19, 1859—Moscow, Jan. 26, 1935; added his mother's name to Ivanoff, to distinguish him from Ivanoff (2); pupil of Rimsky-Korsakov; at St. Petersburg Cons.; 1882 dir. of the Music School and cond. in Tiflis; 1884 cond. at the Imperial Theatre; from 1893 prof. of theory Moscow Cons.; dir., 1906–22; from 1899 cond. the Private Opera; c. operas *"Ruth"* (Tiflis, 1887), *"Asja"* (Moscow, 1900); and *"Sabava Putjatischna"* (St. Petersburg, 1901); overtures *"Jar Chmel,"* *"Spring,"* and *"Medea"*; orch. suite, *"Caucasian Sketches"*; violin-sonata (rearranged as a Sinfonietta); character-pictures for chorus and orch.; cantatas *"In Memory of Pushkin,"* of *"Gogol"* and *"Shukovski,"* and *"Legend of the White Swan of Novgorod,"* etc.; author of a book on Georgian folk-songs.

Ire'land, John, b. Bowdon, England, Aug. 13, 1879; composer; pupil of Stanford; one of the more able and original modern British creators; he destroyed his earlier comps. and 1st became known for his Phantasy Trio in A Minor (1908) and *"Songs of a Wayfarer"* (1910); his reputation grew after the prod. of his 2nd sonata for vln. and piano; c. many orch. and chamber works fairly simple in structure and of traditional form, among which are: the rhapsodies *"Mai-Dun"* and *"The Forgotten Rite"*; overtures *"Pelléas et Mélisande"* and *"Midsummer"*; symph. poem in A Minor; sextet for strings, clarinet and horn; 2 string quartets; 3 piano trios; 4 vln. sonatas; piano sonata; many piano works, incl. *"Decorations,"* *"London Pieces"* and *"Preludes,"* Mass in Dorian Mode; choral and org. pieces and songs.

Irgang (ēr'-gäng), **Fr. Wm.,** Hirschberg, Schleswig, Feb. 23, 1836—Carlsruhe, 1918 ?; teacher in Proksch's Sch., Prague; 1863, founded sch. at Görlitz; also organ composer. (2) **Irr'-gang, H. Bd.,** Krotoschin, 1869—Berlin, 1916; noted organist, teacher.

Isaak (ē'-zäk), **H.** (or **Isaac, Izak, Yzac, Ysack;** in Italy **Arrigo Tedesco,** Henry the German; Low; Lat. **Arrighus**), ca. 1450—ca. 1517; famous contrapuntist doubtless of Netherlandish birth; conductor and organist.

Iserlies (ĭs'-ĕr-lĕz), **Julius,** b. Kishinev, Russia, Nov. 8, 1888; noted pianist; 1907-9, toured U. S.; after 1913 taught Moscow Philh. Cons.

Isouard (ē-zoo-ăr), **Niccolò** (called **Niccolo de Malte**), Malta, 1775—Paris, March 23, 1818; pupil of Amendola, Sala, and Guglelmi; organist, conductor and prolific dram. composer.

Israel (ēs'-rä-ĕl), **K.,** Heiligenrode, Electoral Hesse, 1841—Frankfort-on-M., 1881; critic and bibliographer.

Is'tel, Edgar, b. Mainz, Germany, Feb. 23, 1880; composer and writer on music; pupil of Thuille and Sandberger; Ph. D., Munich Univ., 1900; lecturer on music; c. operas, choral music and songs; author of many books on music.

Iturbi (ē-tōōr'-vē), (1) **José,** b. Valencia, Spain, Nov. 28, 1895; pianist and conductor; studied Valencia Cons., 1st prize in piano at 13; grad. Paris Cons. with highest honours at 17; pupil of Joaquin Malats, Barcelona; was head of piano faculty, Geneva Cons., 1919-23; began tours of chief Eur. countries and South America, establishing reputation as one of the pre-eminent piano virtuosi of the day; Amer. début, 1928; won marked popularity, esp. for his performance of Mozart and Beethoven works, to which he brings polished readings; began conducting activities in Mexico City, 1933, and estab. permanent orch. there to give summer series under his baton; has since led N. Y. Philh. Orch. (summer series at Lewisohn Stadium), Phila. Orch., Los Angeles Philh. at Hollywood Bowl, sometimes playing concertos and conducting from the piano; appointed permanent cond. Rochester, N. Y., Philh. Orch., 1936. (2) **Amparo,** his sister, also a skilled pianist.

I'vanov, (1) **Nicholas Kusmich,** Poltava, Oct. 22, 1810—Bologna, July 7, 1887; tenor; popular in London, 1834-37; accumulated a fortune in Italy and Paris and retired in 1845; (2) **Michael Mikhailovich,** Moscow, Sept. 23, 1849—Rome, Oct. 20, 1927; pupil of Tchaikovsky and Dubuque at the Cons.; critic and comp.; 1870-76 at Rome; then critic for the *Novoe Vremya; c.* symph. *"A Night in May"*; symph. prologue *"Savonarola"*; four operas including *"Potemkin's Feast"* (1888), and *"Sabava Putjatischna"* (Moscow, 1899); incidental music to *"Medea,"* etc. His opera *"Treachery"* (Moscow, Feb. 1911) made great success.

Ives, Charles Edward, b. Danbury, Conn., Oct. 20, 1874; composer; studied with Dudley Buck, H. R. Shelley and Parker; an original figure among Amer. comps., working in seclusion and with music as an avocation, Ives' scores when prod. by modernist organizations in N. Y. and elsewhere have created considerable interest; one of his theories being that several musical units of an ensemble may proceed independently of each other; also employs much freedom in tonality, rhythm and harmony; among his productions, the work of many years, are 4 symphonies, 3 orch. suites, 2 cantatas, 4 vln. sonatas, 2 piano sonatas, 2 overtures, works for chorus and orch., chamber music incl. a string quartet and quarter-tone pieces, and especially a collection of about 200 highly original songs; some of his subjects are drawn from New England.

Ivogün, (1) **Maria** (ēf'-ō-gün mä-rē'-ä) (rightly **Inge von Günther**), b. Budapest, Nov. 11, 1891; coloratura soprano; studied Vienna Acad.; regular mem. Munich Op., 1913–25; Berlin Städtische Op., 1925–32; also sang in America with Chicago Op., and in concert; m. Karl Erb, tenor, 1921, (2) **Michael Raucheisen,** pianist, 1933.

Ivry (dēv-rē), **Paul Xavier Désiré, Marquis Richard d',** Beaune, Côte D'Or, Feb. 4, 1829—Hyères, Dec. 18, 1903; pupil of A. Hignard and Leborne; c. operas, "*Fatma,*" "*Quentin Metzys*" (1854), "*La Maison du Docteur*" (Dijon, 1855), "*Omphale et Pénélopé,*" "*Les Amants de Vérone*" (1867), under the pen-name "**Richard Irvid**"; revised as "*Roméo et Juliette,*" 1878; "*Persévérance D'Amour*" (MS.); concert-overture, songs, etc.

Izac. Vide ISAAK.

J

Jacchia, Agide (yä-kē'-ä ä-jē'-dä), Lugo, Jan. 5, 1875—Siena, Nov. 29, 1932; conductor; studied at Parma and Pesaro Cons., pupil of Mascagni; after 1898 cond. at Brescia, Ferrara and La Fenice Op., Venice; 1902, visited America with Mascagni; 1903–06, at Milan, Leghorn and Siena; 1907–09, led Milan Op. Co. tour of Canada and U. S.; 1909–10, cond. op. season at Acad. of Mus., N. Y.; 1910–14, dir. Montreal and Nat'l. Op. Cos., Canada; 1914–15, chief cond., Century Op. Co., N. Y.; 1915–16, Boston Nat'l. Op. Co.; led "Pop" Concerts, Boston Symph., 1916–23; dir. music school in Boston after 1919; c. cantata and choral works.

Jachet. Vide BERCHEM.

Jachmann-Wagner (yäkh'-män). Vide WAGNER, JOHANNA.

Jack'son, (1) **Wm.,** Exeter, 1730—1803; organist, writer, and dram. composer. (2) **Wm.,** Masham, Yorks, Engl., 1815—Bradford, 1866; organist, conductor, writer and composer. (3) **Samuel P.,** Manchester,

Engl., 1818—Brooklyn, N. Y., 1885; composer; son of (4) **James J.,** organ-builder.

Ja'cob, (1) **Benj.,** London, 1778—1829; organist, conductor and composer. (2) **F. A. L.** Vide JAKOB.

Jaco'bi, Frederick, b. San Francisco, May 4, 1891; composer; studied with Rubin Goldmark, Gallico, Joseffy, Juon and Ernest Bloch; asst. cond., Met. Op. Co., 1913–17; one of founders, Amer. Mus. Guild; mem. executive board, League of Comps., N. Y.; from 1936 teacher of comp., Juilliard School of Music; c. string quartet based on Amer. Indian themes (Zurich Fest., Internat'l. Soc. for Contemp. Music, 1926); (orch.) "*The Pied Piper,*" "*California Suite,*" "*The Eve of Saint Agnes,*" "*Indian Dances*"; "*Two Assyrian Prayers*" for voice and orch., "*The Poet in the Desert,*" for barytone, chorus and orch.; piano concerto; 'cello concerto; "*Sacred Service*" for synagogue; vln. and piano works; m. Irene Schwarz, pianist.

Jacobs (zhä-kō), **Édouard,** b. Hal, Belgium, 1851; pupil of Servais, Brussels Cons.; 'cellist Weimar ct. orch. for some years; 1885 prof. Brussels Cons.

Ja'cobsen, Sascha, b. Finland (Russian parents); violinist; studied piano at 5, violin at 8; pupil of Kneisel, also of St. Petersburg Cons.; N. Y. début, 1915; has toured England, Germany, France, Spain and U. S.

Jacobsohn (yäk'-ôp-zōn), **Simon E.,** Mitau, Kurland, Dec. 24, 1839—Chicago, 1902; violinist; pupil Leipzig Cons.; 1860 leader Bremen orch.; 1872, of Theodore Thomas's orch., N. Y.; teacher Cincinnati Cons., then Chicago.

Jacobsthal (yäk'-ôps-täl), **Gv.,** Pyritz, Pomerania, March 14, 1845—Berlin, Nov. 9, 1912; 1872, lecturer on music Strassburg Univ.; 1875 professor extraordinary; writer.

Jacotin (rightly **Jacques Godebrye**), (zhäk-ô-tăn) (or gôd-brē), ca. 1445—March 24, 1529; famous Flemish cptist.; singer and composer at Antwerp.

Jacquard (zhäk-kär), **Léon J.,** Paris, 1826—1886; 'cellist; composer.

Jadassohn (yä'-däs-zōn), **Salomon,** Breslau, Aug. 13, 1831—Leipzig, Feb. 1, 1902; eminent theorist; pupil of Hesse (pf.) Lüstner (vln.) and Bro-sig (harm.); later Leipzig Cons., then with Liszt and Hauptmann (comp.); from 1852 lived in Leipzig; 1866 cond. "Balterion" choral soc.; 1867–69 cond. "Euterpe"; from 1871, prof. of pf., harm., cpt., comp. and instrumentation at the Cons. 1877, Dr. Phil., *h. c.;* 1893 Royal Prof. He m. a singing-teacher. Wrote occasionally under name "Lübenau" (lü'-bĕ-now). Pub. very succ. text-books all trans. in English. *"Harmonielehre"* (Leipzig, 1883); *"Kontrapunkt"* (1884); *"Kanon und Fuge"* (1884); *"Die Formen in den Werken der Tonkunst"* (1889); *"Lehrbuch der Instrumentation"* (1889); *"Allgemeine Musiklehre"* (1895). His comps. are notable for form, particularly his many works in canon incl. serenade for orch. (op. 35), and ballet-mus.; which have won him the name "Musical Krupp"; c. also 4 symphonies; 2 overtures; a pf.-concerto; The 100th Psalm, for double chorus with orchestration, etc.

Jadin (zhă-dăň), (1) **Louis Emmanuel,** Versailles, 1768—Paris, 1853; prof., conductor and dram. composer. Son and pupil of (2) **Jean J.,** violinist. (3) **Hyacinthe,** Versailles, 1769—Paris, 1800; prof. and composer; bro. and teacher of (1).

Jaell (yāl), (1) **Alfred,** Trieste, March 5, 1832—Paris, Feb. 27, 1882; noted touring pianist and composer, son of (2) **Eduard J.** (d. Vienna, 1849). (3) **Jaell-Trautmann, Marie,** Steinseltz, Alsatia, 1846—Paris, Feb. 7, 1925; wife of (1); pianist, composer and writer.

Jaffé (yäf'-fā), **Moritz,** Posen, Jan. 3, 1835—Berlin, May 7, 1925; violinist; pupil of Ries Bohmer (harm.), of Maurin and Massard, Laub, Wuerst and Bussler; c. operas, etc.

Ja'gel, Frederick, b. Brooklyn, N. Y., 1897; tenor; studied with Portanova and Castaldi; début in *"La Bohème,"* Livorno, Italy; sang in that country 4 years, heard in Calif. opera seasons; début, Met. Op. Co., as "Radames," 1927; has sung leading rôles with that co., also in concert.

Jahn (yän), (1) **Otto,** Kiel, June 16, 1813—Göttingen, Sept. 9, 1869; prof. of archæology, Bonn Univ.; wrote a model biog. of Mozart (1856–59, 4 vols.), etc., also composed.

(2) **Wm.,** Hof, Moravia, Nov. 24, 1835—Vienna, April 14, 1900; 1854 conductor; dir. ct.-opera, Vienna, etc.

Jähns (yäns), **Fr. Wm.,** Berlin, 1809—1888; singer, composer and writer.

James, Philip, b. Jersey City, N. J., May 17, 1890; composer, conductor; studied comp. with Norris and Schenck, also at City College, N. Y.; cond. New Jersey Orch., Brooklyn Orch. Soc. and later the Bamberger Little Symph. in weekly radio programmes; taught at N. Y. Univ. music dept., c. orch. music, including prize-winning work, RCA-Victor contest; also vln. sonata; appeared as guest cond. of several major Amer. orchestras.

Jan (yän), (1) **Maistre.** Vide GALLUS, J. (2) **K. von,** Schweinfurt, 1836—Adelboden, Sept. 4, 1899; Dr. Phil., Berlin, 1859; writer.

Jan'aček (yän-ä'-chĕk), **Leos,** Hukvaldy, July 3, 1854—Möhr.-Ostrau, Aug. 12, 1928; composer of original style, studied at Prague Organ School, Leipzig and Vienna Cons., but largely self-taught; evolved manner of expression based on natural accents and declamation of human voice, also unconventional in harmonic method; influenced by folklore; late in life he was accepted by the internat'l. music world as in some measure a pioneer; founded org. school in Brünn, 1881, where he passed most of his life; after 1919, taught comp. at the Cons. there; c. (operas) *"Jenufa,"* story of Moravian peasant life, 1901, not prod. until 1916 in Prague, but thereafter pop. in German version in Austria and Germany, heard also at Met. Op. House, 1924; *"Katja Kabanova"* (1922); *"Das Schlaue Füchslein,"* an animal fable (1925); *"Die Sache Makropoulos"* (1925) and a posth. work, *"Aus einem Totenhaus"* (after Dostoievsky novel), with libretto by composer (Brünn, 1930); also Fest. Mass, Sinfonietta for orch., string quartet, piano sonata, songs; orch. rhapsodie *"Taras Bulba,"* etc.

Janiewiecz (yän'-ē-vĕch), **Felix,** Wilna, 1762—Edinburgh, 1848; violinist and composer.

Jankó (yäng'-kō), **Paul von,** Totis, Hungary, June 2, 1856—Constantinople, March 17, 1919; pupil Polytechnic, Vienna, and at the Cons. with Hans Schmitt, Krenn, and Bruckner; 1881–82, mathematics at Berlin Univ., pf. with Ehrlich; inv. in 1882 the admirable keyboard known by his name (v. D. D.); taught in Leipzig Cons., etc.

Jan(n)aconi (yän-nä-kō'-nē), **Gius.**, Rome, 1741—March 16, 1816; eminent church-composer; conductor at St. Peter's; pupil of Rinaldini and Carpani.

Jannequin (or **Janequin, Jennekin**) (zhăn-kăn), **Clément**, a French (or Belgian) contrapuntist of the 16th cent.; nothing is known of him except that he lived to be old and poor; c. genuine "programme" music.

Janotha (yä-nō'-tä), **Nathalie**, Warsaw, June 8, 1856—The Hague, June 9, 1932; pupil of Joachim and Rudorff, Clara Schumann, Brahms, and Princess Czartoryska, F. Weber (harm.) and Bargiel; début at the Gewandhaus, Leipzig, 1874; 1885, ct.-pianist to the German Emperor, and decorated with many orders; pub. a trans. with additions of Kleczynski's "Chopin"; c. "*Ave Maria*" (dedicated to Pope Leo), "*Mountain Scenes*" (to Frau Schumann), gavottes, etc., for piano.

Janowka (yä-nôf'-kä), **Thos. Balthasar**, b. Kuttenberg, Bohemia; organist and writer at Prague ca. 1660.

Jansa (yän'-sä), **Ld.**, Wildenschwert, Bohemia, 1795—Vienna, 1875; violinist, teacher and composer.

Jansen (yän'-zĕn), **F. Gv.**, Jever, Hanover, Dec. 15, 1831—Hanover, May 3, 1910; pupil of Coccius and Riccius; teacher at Göttingen; 1855–1900, organist Verden Cath.; 1861, Royal Mus. Dir.; composer and writer.

Janssen (yäns'-zĕn), (1) **N. A.**, Carthusian monk; organist and writer at Louvain, 1845. (2) **Julius**, Venlo, Holland, June 4, 1852—Dortmund, Sept. 24, 1921; studied Cologne Cons.; 1876, cond. Mus. Soc., Minden; later cond. at Dortmund; 1890, city mus. dir.; cond. the 1st and 2d Westphalian Mus. Festivals; pub. songs. (3) **Werner**, b. New York, June 1, 1899; composer, conductor; grad. Dartmouth Coll.; studied with Converse, Stone, Friedheim and Chadwick; Mus. D., Univ. of Calif., 1923; began career as comp. of musical comedies and pop. songs;

won fellowship, Amer. Acad. in Rome, 1930; guest cond. of various Eur. and Amer. orchs., incl. Sibelius programmes in Helsingfors; engaged as one of conductors for N. Y. Philh. Orch., 1934; c. symphony, symph. poem "*New Year's Eve in New York*," given dance prod. by Neighborhood Playhouse, N. Y., "*Obsequies of a Saxophone*" for chamber ensemble (Washington Fest., 1929). Cond. Baltimore Symph. after 1937–8.

Janssens (yäns'-zĕns), **Jean Fran. Jos.**, Antwerp, 1801—insane, 1835; dram. composer.

Januschowsky (yän-oo-shôf'-shkĭ), (Frau) **Georgine von**, b. Austria, ca. 1859—New York, 1914; 1875, soprano in operetta at Sigmaringen; 1877, soubrette, Th. an der Wien, Vienna; 1879–80, Leipzig; 1880, Germania Th., New York; 1892, at Mannheim and Wiesbaden; 1893–95, prima donna, Imp. Opera, Vienna; sang Wagner, etc.; comic operas and operettas; m. Ad. Neuendorff.

Japha (yä'-fä), (1) **G. Jos.**, Königsberg, 1835—Cologne, 1892; violinist. (2) **Louise**, Hamburg, Feb. 2, 1826—Wiesbaden, Oct. 13, 1910; pianist and composer; pupil of Warendorf (pf.), Gross and Grund (comp.) and Robt. and Clara Schumann; 1858, she m. W. Langhans, with whom she gave v. succ. concerts; after 1874, Wiesbaden; c. an opera, etc.

Jaques-Dalcroze. Vide DALCROZE.

Jarecki (yä-rēts'-kē),(1) **Henri**, Warsaw, Dec. 6, 1846—Lemberg, Dec. 18, 1918; dir. at Lemberg; c. operas, incl. "*Wanda*," etc. (2) **Tadeusz**, his son, b. Lemberg, 1889; composer; in New York, 1920.

Jarnach (yär'-näkh), **Philipp**, b. Noisy, France, July 26, 1892; composer (of Catalonian ancestry); largely self-trained but studied with Lavignac and Risler; taught at Zurich Cons., 1918–21; lived in Berlin 1921–27; prof. at Cologne Hochsch. after 1927; c. 2 symphonies, overtures, string quintet, piano works, songs, string quartet, sonata for vln. alone, vln. and piano sonata, sonatinas for flute and 'cello, exhibiting a modern style of interesting originality; completed Busoni's opera, "*Doktor Faust.*"

Järnefelt (yärn'-ĕ-fĕlt), **Armas**, b.

Wiborg, Finland, Aug. 14, 1869; composer, conductor; pupil of Helsingfors Cons., Busoni, Becker and Massenet; chorusmaster, Magdeburg Op., 1896; Düsseldorf Op., 1897; cond. Wiborg Orch., 1898–1903; won a gov't. award for study in other countries; in 1904–05, was dir. of Helsingfors Op.; in 1905–07, cond. Stockholm R. Orch.; in latter year cond. also of R. Op. in same city; dir., Helsingfors Cons., 1906–07; c. the orch. works, "*Korsholm*"; "*Heimatklang*" (latter a symph. fantasy); Serenade; 4 suites; 2 overtures; the choral comps., "*Laula vuoksella*," "*Suomen synty*," "*Ago Slott*," also many notable works for male chorus; songs, piano pieces, etc.; m. Maikki Parkarinnen, singer; divorced; (2) Liva Edström, singer.

Jarnowic (or **Giornovi(c)chi**) (yär'-nō-vĕk, or jôr-nō-vē'-kē), Giov. M., Palermo, 1745—St. Petersburg, Nov. 21, 1804; violinist and composer; pupil of Lolli, whose intolerable eccentricities and immorality, as well as virtuosity, he adopted with disastrous results; J. B. Cramer challenged him, but he would not fight.

Jar'off, Serge, b. Russia, March 20, 1896; choral conductor; studied at Moscow Synodal Acad. for Church Choral Song; in 1920 founded the celebrated Don Cossack Russian Male Chorus, composed of former soldiers in the White Russian Armies; beginning 1923 began triumphal tours with this group in Europe; 1930, U. S.

Jar'vis, (1) Stephen, 1834 ?—London, 1880; composer. (2) Chas. H., Philadelphia, 1837—1895; pianist and conductor.

Jaspar (zhăs-păr), Maurice, b. Liége, June 20, 1870; pianist; pupil and (1909–16) teacher at the Cons.; 1909, founded (with Lebefve) the Walloon Music Fests.; c. piano pieces and songs.

Jean-Aubry (zhän-ō'-brē), G., b. Le Havre, France, 1885; writer on music; ed. of "*The Chesterian*," London, since 1918; author of "*La Musique française d'aujourd'hui*," etc.

Jean le Coq, or **Jehan**. Vide GALLUS, JOHANNES.

Jedliczka (yät-lēch'-kä), Ernest, Poltawa, Russia, June 5, 1855—Berlin, Aug. 8, 1904; pianist; pupil of

Moscow Cons.; teacher there till 1888, then teacher Berlin, Stern Cons.

Jeff'ries, (1) G., organist to Chas. I., 1643. Had a son (2) Christopher, organist and composer. (3) Stephen, 1660—1712; Engl. organist and composer.

Jéhin (zhā-ăn), Léon, Spa, Belgium, July 17, 1853—Monte Carlo, Feb. 15, 1928; violinist; pupil of Leonard, Brussels Cons.; cond. at Antwerp and Vauxhall, Brussels; 1879–89, asst.-prof. of theory, Brussels Cons.; cond. at Monaco; composer.

Jéhin (Jéhin-Prume) (zhā-ăn-prüm), Fz. H., Spa, Belgium, April 18, 1839—Montreal, May 29, 1899; one of the most eminent violinists of Belgian sch.; composer.

Jelensperger (yā'-lĕn-shpĕrkh-ĕr), Daniel, near Mühlhausen, Alsatia, 1797—1831; writer.

Jelinek (yĕ'-lĭ-nĕk), Fz. X., b. Kaurins, Bohemia, 1818—Salzburg, 1880; oboist and composer.

Jenk'ins, (1) J., Maidstone, 1592—Kimberley, Norfolk, 1678; court-lutist and lyra-violist to Chas. I. and II.; composed. "*12 Sonatas for 2 Vlns. and a Base, with a Thorough Base for the Organ or Theorbo*," the first Engl. comp. of the sort; the pop. "*The Lady Katherine Audley's Bells, or The Five Bell Consort*," etc. (2) David, b. Trecastell, Brecon, Jan. 1, 1849—Aberystwith, Dec. 10, 1916; 1878, Mus. Bac. Contab.; 1885, cond. America; prof. Univ. Coll. of Wales; c. operetta, 2 oratorios, 3 cantatas, *A Psalm of Life*, etc. (3) Cyril, b. Dunvant near Swansea, South Wales, Oct. 9, 1885; comp. of symph. poems, chamber music, cantatas, some of which have won prizes at the nat'l. Eisteddfod.

Jennekin (zhĕn-kăn). Vide JANNEQUIN.

Jenner (yĕn'-nĕr), Gustav, Keitum, Island of Sylt, Dec. 3, 1865—Marburg, Aug. 29, 1920; pupil of Stange and Gänge in Kiel, of Brahms and Mandyczewski in Vienna; from 1895 director in Marburg; c. songs and quartets for women's voices.

Jensen (yĕn'-sĕn), (1) Ad., Königsberg, Jan. 12, 1837—of consumption, Baden-Baden, Jan. 23, 1879; one of the most original and poetical of composers for piano and voice; his pf. pcs. have an unexcelled lyricism, and marked melodiousness. Self-taught, but advised by L. Ehlert and

Fr. Marburg; before 20 had c. overtures, a string-quartet, sonatas and songs. 1856, teacher in Russia; then studied with Schumann; 1857, cond. Posen City Th.; 1858–60, studied with Gade; 1860, returned to Königsberg; 1866–68, teacher at Tausig's Sch. in Berlin; compelled by ill-health to retire to Dresden, 1870 to Graz, finally to Baden-Baden. C. opera "*Turandot*" (finished by Kienzl); "*Nonnengesang*,". and "*Brautlied*". for solo and chorus with 2 horns, harp and a piano, "*Jephtha's Tochter*" and "*Adonis-Feier*," "*Donald Caird ist wieder da*,". and other vocal works with orch.; concert-overture; "*Geistlicher Tonstück*"; "*Hochzeitsmusik*," "*Abendmusik*," "*Lebensbilder*," 6 "*Silhouetten*,". and "*Ländliche Festmusik*,". for pf. (4 hands); and "*Innere Stimmen*," "*Wanderbilder*,". a sonata; 6 German Suites, "*Idyllen*," "*Erotikon*". (7 pcs.), a scherzo, "*Wald-Idylle*," op. 47, "*Scenes carnavalesques*," for pf.-solo; and 160 solo songs. Biog. by Niggli. (2) **Gustav**, Königsberg, 1843—Cologne, 1895; pupil of Dehn (comp.) and Laub and Joachim (vln.); violinist Königsberg Th.; 1872–75, prof. of cpt., Cologne Cons.; c. symphony, etc.

Jentsch (yĕntsh), **Max**, Ziesar, Saxony, Aug. 5, 1855—Stendal, Nov., 1918; pianist and teacher; pupil of Stern Cons.; toured the Orient; 1884–89 in Constantinople; later in Berlin; from 1894 in Vienna; c. symphony, "*Elysium*" for chorus and orch., 2 operas, etc.

Jep'son, (1) **Harry Benjamin**, b. New Haven, Conn., Aug. 16, 1870; educator; grad. Yale Univ.; studied with Stoeckel, Parker, Widor; after 1899 ass't. prof. of theory at Yale, and 1906 prof. and Univ. org.; c. numerous org. and vocal works. (2) **Helen**, b. Akron, O.; soprano; studied with Horatio Connell at Curtis Inst. of Mus., Phila.; also with Richard Hageman; sang with Chautauqua, N. Y., Op. Ass'n.; with Phila. Gr. Op. Co.; soloist with various orchs.; after 1935 with Met. Op. Co.; 1936, also Chicago Op. Co.

Jeritza (yĕr'-ĕt-sä), **Maria**, b. Brünn, Moravia, Oct. 6, 1887; soprano; family name Jedlitzka; studied singing with Auspitzer; first sang in operetta at Stadttheatre in native town; later in Olmütz; then in comic opera at Munich and Vienna; after 1912 a regular mem. of Vienna State Op., where became known as dram. actress of pronounced powers; Amer. début, Met. Op. Co. as "Marietta" in Korngold's "*Die Tote Stadt*," 1921; sang leading rôles in Wagnerian and Italian works with this co. for more than a decade; a striking "Tosca"; "Turandot" and "Helena" in Strauss's opera (creations for America); in 1933 with Chicago Op., also appeared at Covent Garden and widely in concert; m. Baron Leopold Popper; divorced; (2) Winfield Sheehan, motion picture executive.

Jiminez (hĭ'-mĭ-nĕth), **Jeronimo**, Seville, 1854—Madrid, 1923; comp. of 50 zarzuelas.

Jimmerthal (yĭm'-mĕr-täl), **Hn.**, Lübeck, 1809—1886; organist, org.-builder and writer.

Jiránek (yē'-rä-nĕk), (1) **Anton**, ca. 1712—Dresden, Jan. 16, 1761; studied at Prague; later joined the royal chapel at Warsaw. (2) **Josef**, b. Ledec, Bohemia, March 24, 1855; pianist; pupil of Smetana, and of the organ school at Prague; studied the harp with Stanek, the violin with Hrimaly, and was a harpist at first; 1877–91 piano teacher at Charkov; 1891–1913, prof. at Prague Cons.; c. "*Ballade*". and "*Scherzo fantastique*" for orch., piano pieces; author of methods. His brother (3) **Aloys,** b. Ledec, Sept. 3, 1858; pupil of Prague Organ School, and in composition of Fibich; from 1881, piano teacher at Charkov; c. opera "*Dagmar*,". etc.

Joachim (yō'-ä-khēm), (1) **Jos.**, Kittsee, near Pressburg, June 28, 1831—Berlin, Aug. 15, 1907; eminent violinist; studied at 5 with Szervacinski, Pesth, with whom he appeared in public at 7; from 1841, at Vienna Cons. with Böhm; at 12, played in Leipzig, and soon after at the Gewandhaus, with much succ.; frequently leader of the Gewandhaus Orchestra; 1844, made his first of many appearances in London; 1849, Concertmeister of the Weimar orch.; 1854, cond. and solo violinist to the King of Hanover; 1863 m. Amalie Weiss (v. infra); 1868 head of the Hochschule, Berlin; 1877, Mus. Doc. *h. c.*, Cambridge Univ.; had many degrees from German universities, and various orders of knighthood; undisputed pre-eminence as a classicist and solo-performer; his famous J. Quartet included De Ahna, Wirth and Hausmann. He c. "Hungarian" concerto for violin, and 2 others, and variations with orch., also overture to "*Hamlet*"; 4 overtures incl. "*Dem Andenken Kleists*"; Hebrew Melodies, for vla. and pf.; Op. 14, "*Szene der Marfa*" (from Schiller's *Demetrius*), for contralto solo with orch.; three cadenzas to Beethoven's vln.-concerto, etc. (2) **Amalie** (née **Weiss**, rightly, **Schneeweiss**), Marburg, Styria, May 10, 1839—Berlin, Feb. 3, 1899; eminent concert and operatic soprano; then contralto and teacher; wife of above.

João IV. (zhown), King of Portugal, Villa-Vicosa, 1604—Lisbon, 1656; theorist and composer.

Johns, Clayton, New Castle, Del., Nov. 24, 1857—Boston, March 7, 1932; pupil of J. K. Paine, and W. H. Sherwood, Boston; later with Kiel, Grabow, Raif, and Rummel (pf.) in Berlin; in Boston, Mass., as a concert-pianist and teacher; after 1912 taught N. E. Cons.; c. a Berceuse and Scherzino for string-orch. (played by Boston Symph. orch.); many songs, etc.

John'son, (1) **Edw.,** English composer, 1594. (2) **Robert,** Engl. 16th cent. ecclesiastic and church composer. (3) **Robert,** lutenist and prominent composer, 1573—1625. (4) **John,** d. 1594—95; musician to Queen Elizabeth; c. lute-music. (5) **Edward,** b. Guelph, Ontario, tenor and impresario; studied Univ. of Toronto; singing with Lombardi in Florence; early sang in concerts and in light operas in N. Y.; opera début at Padua; heard in several Italian theatres, incl. La Scala (1st Ital. perf. of Parsifal, 1914); sang Chicago Op. Co. 1920, also Ravinia Op.; Met. Op. Co., after 1921, interpreting romantic rôles such as "Pelléas" and in Italian works with succ.; created parts in 1st Amer. hearings of operas by Puccini, Pizzetti, Montemezzi, Zandonai and Deems Taylor ("*King's Henchman*" and "*Peter Ibbetson*"); chosen as asst. general manager, Met. Op. Co., 1935, and same year succeeded

to managership on death of Herbert Witherspoon; hon. LL. D., Univ of Western Ontario; Cav. Ufficiale, Order of the Crown of Italy; Commander of the British Empire. (6) **Horace,** b. Waltham, Mass., October 5, 1893; composer; studied comp. with Bainbridge Crist, org. and pf. with John P. Marshall; c. (orch.) suite, "*Imagery*," based on Tagore; "*Streets of Florence*"; tone-poem, "*Astarte*"; "*In the American Manner*"; (string orch.) "*Joyance*"; vln. and pf. pieces, songs, etc. Managing editor, *Musical Courier.*

Jommelli (yôm-měl'-lĭ), **Niccolò,** Aversa, near Naples, Sept. 11, 1714 —Naples, Aug. 28, 1774; eminent operatic and church-composer; pupil of Canon Mozzillo, Durante, Feo, Leo, Prato and Mancini. C. ballets and songs, then dram. cantatas; at 23 prod. opera "*L'Errore Amoroso*" (Naples, 1737), under the name "**Valentino**"; its succ. relieved his anxiety and removed his anonymity and he followed it with other succ. works in various cities under various patronage. He was made Dir. of the Cons. del Ospedaletto, Venice; 1748–54 asst. *Maestro* at St. Peter's, Rome, until 1754; cond. to the Duke of Würtemberg. Lived in Germany 15 years and made great succ. He profited artistically by German influence, but when the Stuttgart opera was disbanded and he retired to Italy his style was too serious and perhaps his best works "*Armida Abbandonata*" (1770), "*Demofoönte*" (1770), and "*Ifigenia in Tauride*" (1771), were failures when prod. at Naples. The humiliation after such long triumph brought on apoplexy (1773), from which he recovered only long enough to write a cantata on the birth of a prince, and his masterpiece, a "*Miserere*." The King of Portugal commissioned him to write 2 operas and a cantata; but he did not live to finish them; he c. over 50 known operas and divertissements, and equally fine sacred mus., incl. 4 oratorios, a magnificat, with echo, etc.

Jonás (zhō-năs), (1) **Émile,** Paris, March 5, 1827—St. Germain-en-Laye, Paris, May 21, 1905; pupil of Carafa at the Cons.; from 1847 teacher there also mus.-dir. Portuguese synagogue. (2) (hō'-năs).

Alberto, b. Madrid, June 8, 1868; pf. pupil of Olave and Mendizabal; also at the Cons.; at 18 with Gevaert, Brussels Cons.; won 1st prize for pf., and later 2 first prizes in harm.; début, Brussels, 1880; 1890, studied St. Petersburg Cons. under Rubinstein's tuition; since toured Europe and America; 1894 head of the pf.-dep. Univ. of Michigan; since 1914 has taught in N. Y.; composer and writer.

Joncières (zhôn-sï-ărs), **Victorin de,** Paris, April 12, 1839—Oct. 26, 1903; studied painting, then mus. with Elwart at the Cons.; an ardent Wagnerian, he left the Cons. because of Elwart's adverse opinion; pres. "Soc. des Compositeurs de musique," Chev. of the Legion of Honour, and officer of public instruction; 1871 critic of "*La Liberté,*" etc.; prod. 4 operas, incl. "*Le Chevalier Jean*" (Op.-com., 1885), a symph. ode, "*La Mer*"; a "*Symphonie romantique*"; "*Li Tsin,*" a Chinese theme for soli and orch., etc.

Jones, (1) **Robt.,** Engl. lutenist and composer, 1601–16; one of his songs, "*Farewell deere love,*" is alluded to in "*Twelfth Night.*" (2) **Wm.** ("of Nayland"), Lowick, Northamptonshire, 1726—Nayland, Suffolk, 1800; writer and composer. (3) **J.,** 1728—London, 1796; organist and composer. (4) (Sir) **Wm.,** London, 1746—Calcutta, 1794; writer. (5) **Edw.** ("**Brady Brenin**"), Llanderfel, Merionethshire, April 18, 1752—London, April 18, 1824; Welsh harpist, writer and composer. (6) **Griffith,** British writer, pub. "*A History of the Origin and Progress of Theoretical and Practical Music,*" 1819. (7) **Sidney,** b. Leeds, 1869; theater conductor and composer of the succ. operetta "*The Gaiety Girl*" (London, 1893); "*An Artist's Model*" (Daly's Th., London, 1895); "*The Geisha*" (ibid., 1896), etc.

Jongen (zhôn'-gĕn), (1) **Joseph,** b. Liége, Dec. 14, 1873; composer; pupil of Cons. in native city, winning many prizes incl. Prix de Rome; 1903 prof. of harmony and cpt. there; after 1904 res. in Brussels; 1920 taught at Cons. there; 1925, dir.; with Lekeu and Vreuls, one of leading Belgian comps., influenced by Franck and Debussy; c. much orch. and chamber music, 'cello

concerto, cantatas, piano and org. music, and stage works. (2) **Léon,** b. Liége, March 2, 1884; bro. of **Joseph;** studied Liége Cons., won Prix de Rome; c. dram. works, incl. opera, "*Le Rêve d'une Nuit de Noël,*" string quartet, piano pieces, songs, etc.

Jor'dan, Jules, Willimantic, Conn., Nov. 10, 1850—Providence, R. I., March 5, 1927; studied singing with Osgood, Boston, Shakespeare, London, and Sbriglia, Paris; for 13 years choirm. of Grace Ch., Providence; 1880 cond. Arion Club; c. comedy-opera "*Rip Van Winkle*" (pub. 1898); cantata with orch.; songs, etc.

Jörn (yărn), **Karl,** b. Riga, Jan. 5, 1876; tenor; pupil of Lohse, Schutte, Harmsen and Elis. Jacobs, also Mme. Ress and Weiss; made début at Freiburg, 1896; sang at Zurich, Hamburg, Berlin; also in London, 1905–08, and Met. Op., 1908–11.

Joseffy (yŏ-zĕf'-fï), **Rafael,** Miskolcz, Hungary, July 3, 1853—New York, June 25, 1915; eminent pianist; pupil of Moscheles, Leipzig Cons., Liszt, Tausig; toured Europe with succ.; lived in Vienna; for many years at New York; teacher Nat. Cons.; c. pf.-pcs.

Josephson (yŏ'-zĕf-zōn), **Jacob Axel,** Stockholm, March 27, 1818—Upsala, March 29, 1880; Swedish cond. and composer.

Josquin. Vide DESPRÈS.

Josten (yōs'-tĕn), **Werner,** b. Elberfeld, Germany, June 12, 1888; composer; since 1923 prof. of music, Smith Coll., Northampton, Mass.; also dir. music fests. there, incl. perfs. of Händel operas, etc.; c. "*Jungle*" for orch.; "*Concerto Sacro*" for strings and piano; "*Hymnus to the Quene of Paradys,*" for alto solo, women's chorus, strings and org.; "*Crucifixion,*" for bass solo and mixed chorus; "*Indian Serenade,*" for tenor and orch., "*Ode for St. Cecilia's Day*" for soprano, barytone, mixed chorus, orch.; "*A Une Madone*" for tenor and orch.; string quartet; (ballet) "*Joseph and His Brethren*" (Juilliard School of Music, 1936).

Jouret (zhoo-rā), (1) **Th.,** Ath, Belgium, 1821—Kissingen, 1887; critic and dram. composer. (2) **Léon,** Ath, Oct. 17, 1828—Brussels, June 6,

1905; bro. of above; pupil Brussels Cons. and after 1874 vocal teacher there; c. 2 operas, cantatas, etc.

Journet (zhoor'-nä), **Marcel**, Grasse, 1869—Vittel, Sept. 6, 1933; bass; pupil of the Cons.; début Th. de la Monnaie, Brussels; sang often at Covent Garden; 1900 at Met. Op., N. Y.; 1914, Chicago Op. Co.

Jousse (zhoos), **J.**, Orleans, France, 1760—1837; teacher and writer.

Juch (yookh), **Emma**, Vienna, July 4, 1865—N. Y., March 6, 1939; soprano; studied in New York with Mme. Murio-Celli; concert début, 1882; in opera at Her Majesty's Theat., London, the following year in *"Mignon"*; sang under Mapleson's mgt. there for 3 seasons in leading rôles; 1886–87 with Amer. Op. Co. under Thomas; 1889 founded her own co. and sang in U. S. and Mexico; also heard in concerts and with orchs. in U. S.

Judenkunig (yoo'-den-koo-nĭkh), **Hans**, b. Schwäbisch-Gmünd; lutenist, violist and composer at Vienna, 1523.

Jue (zhü), **Edouard**, b. Paris, 1794 (?); violinist and writer.

Jul(l)ien (zhül-yäň), (1) **Marcel Bd.**, Paris, 1798—1881; writer. (2) **Jean Lucien Ad.**, Paris, June 1, 1845—1932; son of above; prominent critic and writer. (3) **Louis Ant.**, Sisteron, Basses-Alpes, April 23, 1812—insane, Paris, March 14, 1860; pop. conductor and composer of dance music, etc. (4) **Paul**, Brest, France, Feb. 12, 1841—at sea, 1866; violinist; pupil Paris Cons., took 1st prize; toured America, 1853–66.

Jumilhac (zhü-mēl-yăk), **Dom P. Benoît de**, near Limoges, 1611—St. Germain-des-Pres, 1682; writer.

Junck (yoonk), **Benedetto**, Turin, Aug. 24, 1852—Vigilio (Bergamo), Oct. 3, 1903; pupil of Bazzini and Mazzucato; lived in Milan; c. stringquartet, etc.

Jüngst (yĭnkst), **Hugo**, Dresden, Feb. 26, 1853—Feb. 6, 1923; studied at Cons. there; founded the Julius Otto Soc.; and cond. Male Choral Soc.; 1898 made prof. by King of Saxony; c. male choruses.

Junker (yoonk'-ĕr), **K. L.**, Öhringen, ca. 1740—Kirchberg, 1797; writer and composer.

Juon (zhwôñ), **Paul**, Moscow, Mar. 8, 1872—Vevey, Switz., Aug. 21, 1940;

violinist; pupil Hrimaly, Taneiev and Arensky, later of Bargiel in Berlin, where he won the Mendelssohn Scholarship; 1896 taught theory at Baku; 1897 settled in Berlin; 1906–34, teacher of composition at the High School for Music; c. 2 symph., the second prod. with much interest at Meiningen, 1903, and in London, 1904 and 1905; fantasie for orch., *"Wächterweise,"* on Danish folk-themes, orch. suite, *"Aus meinem Tagebuch"*; chamber music, *"Satyrs and Nymphs,"* and other piano pieces, 3 vln. concerti, etc.

Jupin (zhü-păň), **Chas. Fran.**, Chambéry, 1805—Paris, 1839; violinist, professor, conductor, and dram. composer.

Jürgenson (yür'-gĕn-zōnĭ, **Peter**, Reval, 1836—Moscow, Jan. 2, 1904; founded mus.-pub. house, Moscow, 1861.

K

Kaan (kän) **("Albést-Kahn")**, **H. von**, Tarnopol, Galicia, May 29, 1852—Rudna, May, 1926; pianist; pupil of Blodek and Skuhersky, Prague; since 1890, prof. at the Cons. there; director of same, 1907 to 1918; c. ballets, symphonic poem *"Sakuntala"*; etc.

Kade (kä'-dĕ), **Otto**, Dresden, 1825—Schwerin, 1900; ct.-conductor, writer and composer.

Kaempfert (kĕmp'-fĕrt), **Max**, b. Berlin, Jan. 3, 1871; studied in Paris and Munich; 1899—1923 cond. at Frankfort-on-Main; c. opera; 4 rhapsodies for orch., etc.

Kahl (käl), **H.**, Munich, 1840—Berlin, 1892; conductor.

Kahlert (kä'-lĕrt), **Aug. K. Timotheus**, Breslau, 1807—1864; writer and composer.

Kahn (kän), (1) **Robt.**, b. Mannheim, July 21, 1865; pianist; pupil of Ernst Frank and V. Lachner, Kiel, and Jos. Rheinberger (Munich, 1885); 1891 founded Ladies' Choral Union, Leipzig; 1898—1930, prof. of comp., Berlin Hochschule für Musik; c. orch., chamber and choral music, songs, etc. His bro. (2) **Otto Hermann**, Mannheim, Germany, Feb. 21, 1867—New York, March 29, 1934; patron of music; 1908–31, chairman of board of directors, Met. Op. Co., and for some years dominated its artistic policies;

possessing wide interests, he was also a generous supporter of many of the foreign musical and other productions brought to N. Y.; influential in sponsoring the Century Op. Co., Boston Op. Co., Chicago Op. Ass'n., the French-American Ass'n. for Mus. Art, and other projects; he was interested in promoting a plan for a new opera house in N. Y. and even bought up parcels of land for such a structure, but opposition in the Met. Op. directorate caused the matter to be shelved.

Kahnt (känt), **Chr. Fr.**, 1823—Leipzig, 1897; mus.-publisher.

Kaiser (kī'-zĕr), (1) **K.**, Leipa, Bohemia, 1837—Vienna, 1890; founded sch. continued by his son (2) **Rudolf.** (3) **Fr. Emil**, Coburg, Feb. 7, 1853—Munich, 1929; regimental bandm. Prague; prod. 5 operas, incl. *"Der Trompeter von Säkkingen"* (Olmütz, 1882).

Kajanus (kä-jä'-noos), **Robert,** Helsingfors, Dec. 2, 1856—July 6, 1933; Finnish composer; pupil Leipzig Cons.; returned to Helsingfors, founded an orchestra school, and developed the Phil. orch.; 1897 mus. director of the University; c. 2 Finnish rhapsodies, symph. poems *"Aino"* and *"Kullervo"*; orch. suite *"Summer Memories,"* cantata, etc.

Kal'beck, Max, Breslau, Jan. 4, 1850—Vienna, May 5, 1921; studied Munich Sch. of Mus.; 1875, writer, critic at Breslau; then on the *"Wiener Montags-Revue,"* and the *"Neues Tageblatt."*

Kalin'nikov, Vassili Sergeievich, Voina, Jan. 13, 1866—Jalta, Crimea, Jan. 11, 1901; pupil of Iljinski and Blaramberg at Moscow; 1893 assistant cond. at the Italian Opera there; compelled to retire because of pulmonary trouble and go south; c. 2 symph., the first in G minor, much played; 2 symph. poems, *"The Nymphs"* and *"Cedar and Palm"*; music to Tolstoi's *"Czar Boris,"* (Little Theatre, Moscow, 1899); *"Russalka,"* ballade with orch., cantata, *"St. John of Damascus,"* etc.

Kalisch (kä'-lǐsh), **Paul,** b. Berlin, Nov. 6, 1855; tenor; studied with Leoni; sang Berlin ct.-opera; m. Lilli Lehmann; sang at Cologne and 6 times in America.

Kalischer (kä'-lǐsh-ĕr), **Alfred,** Thorn, March 4, 1842—Berlin, Oct. 8, 1909; Dr. Phil., Leipzig U.; studied with Bürgel and Böhmer; lived in Berlin, as a writer and teacher; editor *"Neue Berliner Musikzeitung"*; pub. *"Lessing als Musikästhetiker"*; *"Musik und Moral,"* *"Beethoven und seine Zeitgenossen"*; ed. collection of Beethoven's letters.

Kalkbrenner (kälk'-brĕn-nĕr), (1) **Chr.**, Minden, Hanover, 1755—Paris, 1806; writer and dram. composer. (2) **Fr. Wm. Michael**, b. on a journey from Cassel to Berlin, 1788—d. of cholera Enghien-les-Bains, near Paris, June 10, 1849; son and pupil of above; very succ. pianist and teacher; developed modern octave-playing, lefthand technique and pedalling; wrote valuable études and other comps.; also studied Paris Cons. and with Clementi and Albrechtsberger. (3) **Arthur**, d. near Paris, 1869; son of (2); composer.

Kalliwoda (käl'-lǐ-vō-dä), (1) **Jn. Wenzel**, Prague, 1801—Carlsruhe, 1866; pianist, conductor and dram. composer. (2) **Wm.**, Donaueschingen, 1827—Carlsruhe, 1893; son and pupil of above; dir., ct.-conductor, pianist and composer.

Kallwitz, or **Kalwitz.** Vide CALVISIUS.

Kal'man, Emmerich, b. Siofok, Hungary, Oct. 24, 1882; composer of operettas, some of which have had world-wide popularity; pupil of Koessler; c. among other works *"Die Czardasfürstin,"* *"Gräfin Maritza,"* *"Die Zirkusprinzessin"*; res. in Vienna.

Kamienski (käm-ǐ-ĕn'-shkǐ), **Mathias,** Odenburg, Hungary, 1734—Warsaw, 1821; teacher and composer of the first Polish opera *"The Wretched Made Happy"* (1778), etc.

Kamin'ski, Heinrich, b. Tiengen, Baden, Germany, July 4, 1886; composer; studied at Heidelberg Univ., and with Klatte, Kaun and Juon; his works based on pre-Bach polyphonic style; c. (music drama) *"Jürg Jenatsch"* (prod. Dresden Op.), concerto grosso and suite for orch., chamber music, many choral works and motets, Magnificat, (widely sung, incl. Boston perf.); Psalms for chorus and orch.; Passion (mystery play); org. works, etc.; 1930–32, leader of master school in comp. at Berlin Akad. der Künste; also cond. of orch. concerts in Bielefeld, 1930–33.

Kam'mel, Anton, Hanna, Bohemia, 1740—London, before 1788; violinist and composer; pupil of Tartini; c. masses, violin duets, etc.

Kammerlander (käm'-mĕr-länt-ĕr), **K.,** Weissenhorn, Swabia, 1828—Augsburg, 1892; conductor and composer.

Kandler (känt'-lĕr), **Fz. Sales,** Klosterneuburg, Lower Austria, 1792—Baden, 1831; writer.

Kapp, Julius, b. Steinbach, Baden, Oct. 1, 1883; Ph. D.; editor; writer of biogs. of Wagner, Berlioz, Liszt, etc.

Kappel (kä'-pĕl), **Gertrude;** b. Halle, Germany; studied piano and singing Leipzig Cons., with Nikisch and Noe; has appeared in opera at Hanover, Vienna, Munich, London, Madrid, Amsterdam, and after 1927 with Met. Op. Co., N. Y., singing leading Wagnerian rôles, also Strauss's *"Elektra."*

Kapsberger (käps'-bĕrkh-ĕr), **Jn.** Hieronymus von, b. of noble German family, d. Rome, ca. 1650; virtuoso on theorbo, chitarrone, lute, and trumpet; notable composer.

Karajan (kä'-rä-yän), **Th. G. von,** Vienna, 1810—1873; writer.

Karasowski (kä-rä-shôf'-shkĭ), **Moritz,** Warsaw, 1823—Dresden, 1892; 'cellist, writer and composer.

Karg-Elert (kärkh-ā'-lĕrt), **Sigfrid,** Oberndorf, Nov. 21, 1879—Leipzig, April 9, 1933; pupil Leipzig Cons.; teacher and composer; after 1919, taught at Leipzig Cons.; eminent concert organist; toured U. S. shortly before his death; c. a large variety of works for org., incl. sonatas, etc.

Karl, Tom, Dublin, Jan. 19, 1846—Rochester, N. Y., 1916; tenor; studied with H. Phillips, Sangiovanni and Trivulzi; sang in Italian opera for years, went to America with Parepa-Rosa, then with "The Bostonians" in comic opera many years; retired 1896; later vocal teacher, N. Y.

Karlovicz (kärl'-yō-vĭch), **Mieczyslav,** Wisznievo, Lithuania, Dec. 11, 1876—(in an avalanche), Zakopane, Galicia, Feb. 10, 1909; composer; studied in Warsaw and Berlin; c. symph., symphonic-trilogy *"Three Ancient Songs"* (1907), *"Lithuanian Rhapsody"* (1908), also published Chopin letters and documents (Warsaw and Paris, 1905).

Karpath (kär'-pät), **Ludwig,** Budapest, 1866—Vienna, 1936; singer and critic; pupil Budapest Cons.; sang with Nat'l. Op. Co., N. Y., 1886-88; after 1894, critic *"Neues Wiener Tageblatt";* 1910-17, ed., *"Merker";* author of books on Wagner.

Kasan'li, Nicolai Ivanovich, Tiraspol, Dec. 17, 1869—St. Petersburg, 1913 (?); Russian composer; pupil Odessa Music School and St. Petersburg Cons.; had cond. Russian symph. concerts in Germany, Bohemia, etc.; c. symph., Sinfonietta, cantata *"Russalka"* (Munich, 1897), and *"Leonore"* (do.).

Kasatchen'ko, Nicolai Ivanovich, b. Russia, May 3, 1858; cond.; pupil St. Petersburg Cons.; 1883 chorus master at the Imperial Opera; cond *"Russian Concerts"* in Paris, 1898; after 1924 prof. of choral singing, Leningrad Cons.; c. symph., 2 oriental suites, 2 operas, *"Prince Serebrianni"* (St. Petersburg, 1892), and *"Pan Sotkin"* (do., 1902).

Kasch'in, Daniel Nikitich, Moscow, 1773-1844; composer of Polish folk and patriotic songs; also three operas.

Kash'perov, Vladimir Nikitich, Simbirsk, 1827—Romanzevo, July 8, 1894; Russian composer; pupil of Voigt and Henselt; and comp. an opera in 1850, then went to Berlin to study with Dehn; thence with Glinka to Italy, where he produced various operas. *"Maria Tudor"* (Milan, 1859), *"Rienzi"* (Florence, 1863), *"Consuelo"* (Venice); 1866-72 he was singing teacher at Moscow Cons., and organised public chorus-classes; c. also operas *"The Weather"* (St. Petersburg, 1867), and *"Taras Bulba"* (Moscow, 1893).

Kaskel (käs'-kĕl), Freiherr **K. von,** b. Dresden, Oct. 10, 1866; studied law at Leipzig, also mus. in the Cons. with Reinecke and Jadassohn (1886-87), and later with Wüllner and Jensen, Cologne; lived in Dresden; c. succ. 1-act opera *"Hochzeitsmorgen"* (Hamburg, 1893); v. succ. opera *"Sjula"* (Cologne, 1895), etc.

Kässmeyer (kĕs'-mī-ĕr), **Moritz,** Vienna, 1831—1884; violinist; c. 5 string-quartets, some of them humorous.

Kastal'sky, Alexander Dmitrievitch, Moscow, Nov. 28, 1856—Dec. 17, 1926; important Russian church composer; after 1887 teacher and conductor at the School of the Synodal Chorus, renamed the People's Choral Acad. in 1918 and merged with Moscow Cons. in 1923; also c. operas, etc.

Kastner (käst'-něr), (1) **Jn. G.**, Strassburg, March 9, 1810—Paris, Dec. 19, 1867; pupil of Maurer and Romer; at 10, organist; at 20, bandm.; at 25 had prod. 4 operas, and was sent ʰy the town council to Paris, to study with Berton and Reicha; 1837, pub. treatise "*On Instrumentation*" among others; also methods adopted at the Paris Cons.; lived thereafter at Paris as teacher; wrote learned essays and an "*Encyclopédie de la musique.*" C. 3 later operas incl. "*Le dernier roi de Juda,*" his masterpiece, also 3 symphonies, 5 overtures, 10 serenades for wind; "*Livrespartitions*" (symphony-cantatas, prefaced by brilliant historical essays, incl. "*Les danses des morts*"), a vol. of 310 pages; "*La harpe d'éole*" (1856); "*Les voix de Paris,*" followed by "*Les cris de Paris,*" grande symphonie humoristique voc. et instr. (1857); "*Les Sirènes,*" etc. Biog. by Jan (Leipzig, 1886). (2) **G. Fr. Eugen**, Strassburg, 1852 —Bonn, 1882; son of above; inv. the pyrophone (v. D. D.), and pub. work on it. (3) **Emmerich**, Vienna, March 29, 1847—1916; editor and writer.

Kate (kä'-tĕ), **André Ten**, Amsterdam, 1796—Haarlem, 1858; 'cellist and dram. composer.

Kauders (kow'-děrs), **Albert**, b. Prague, Jan. 20, 1854; critic in Vienna, and composer of comic operas.

Kauer (kow'-ĕr), **Fd.**, Klein-Thaya, Moravia, Jan. 8, 1751—Vienna, April 13, 1831; prolific c. of *Singspiele;* organist, conductor, 'cellist; c. 2,000 operas and operettas.

Kauffmann (kowf'-män), (1) **Ernst Fr.**, Ludwigsburg, 1803—Stuttgart, 1856; pianist and composer. (2) **Emil**, Ludwigsburg, Nov. 23, 1836—Tübingen, June 18, 1909; violinist; son of above; pupil of Stuttgart Cons.; musical dir. Tübingen Univ.; Dr. Phil., 1885. (3) **Fritz**, Berlin, June 17, 1855—Magdeburg, Sept. 29, 1934; a druggist, Leipzig and Hamburg; took up music, 1878, entered the Akademische Hochschule at Berlin, won Mendelssohn prize for comp. 1881; till 1889, lived in Berlin as a teacher and then cond. of the "Gesellschaftsconcerte" at Magdeburg; 1893, Royal Musik-Direktor;

c. comic opera, "*Die Herzkrankheit*"; symphony, etc.

Kaun (kown), **Hugo**, Berlin, March 21, 1863—April 2, 1932; pupil at Royal High School under Grabau and Fr. Schulz; also with K. and O. Raif, and Fr. Kiel; 1887 took up residence in Milwaukee, Wis., as teacher and cond.; 1900 returned to Berlin; 1912, elected to Berlin Royal Academy; c. symph. "*An Mein Vaterland,*" symph. prolog "*Marie Magdalene*"; symph. poems; festival march "*The Star Spangled Banner,*" chamber music with orch., "*Normannen Abschied*"; 1-act opera "*Der Pietist*" or "*Oliver Brown,*" and important songs and piano pieces.

Kazynski (kä-zēn'-shkĭ), **Victor**, Wilna, Lithuania, Dec. 18, 1812—St. Petersburg, 1870; pupil of Elsner, Warsaw; prod. 3 operas; 1843, cond. Imp. Th. St. Petersburg.

Ke'fer, **Paul**, Rouen, 1875—Rochester, N. Y., 1941; 'cellist; pupil Verviers Mus. School and Paris Cons.; after 1900 played in Paris orchs., and 1908–13 with N. Y. Symph., also heard as soloist.

Keiser (kī'-zĕr), **Reinhard**, Teuchern, near Weissenfels, Jan. 9, 1674—Hamburg, Sept. 12, 1739; the father of German opera, the first to employ popular subjects and to leave the Italian and French pattern; also noteworthy for his instrumentation and dramatic force; pupil of his father; c. 116 operas at Hamburg from 1694; mgr. the opera there, ct. cond. and later canon and cantor; c. also oratorios, masses, etc.

Kel'berine, **Alex**, Kiev, 1903—N. Y., Jan. 30, 1940; pupil of Busoni and Siloti; toured in Europe; N. Y. début, 1928; head of piano dept., Sternberg Cons., Phila.; has appeared as soloist with leading Amer. orchs.

Keler-Bela (rightly **Adabert von Keler**) (kä'-lĕr bā'-lä), Bartfeld, Hungary, Feb. 13, 1820—Wiesbaden, Nov. 20, 1882; violinist, conductor and composer.

Kel'ler, (1) **Gottfried** (called **Godfrey**), b. in Germany; teacher and writer in London, 1707. (2) **Max**, Trostberg, Bavaria, 1770—Altötting, 1855; organist and composer. (3) **K.**, Dessau, 1784—Schaffhausen, 1855; ct.-flutist, conductor and composer. (4) **F. A. E.**, inv., 1835, the unsucc.

"pupître-improvisateur"

Kel'lermann, (1) **Berthold,** Nürnberg, March 5, 1853—Munich, June 14, 1926; pianist; pupil of his parents and of Liszt, 1878-81 Wagner's secretary; 1882, teacher Munich R. Mus. Sch.; conductor and ct.-pianist. (2) **Chr.,** Randers, Jutland, 1815—Copenhagen, 1866; 'cellist and composer.

Kel'ley, Edgar Stillman, b. Sparta, Wis., April 14, 1857; American composer; pupil of F. W. Merriam, Clarence Eddy, and N. Ledochowski (Chicago), and 1876-80 of Seifriz (comp.), Krüger and Speidel (pf.) and Fr. Finck (org.), at Stuttgart; organist at Oakland and San Francisco, Cal.; cond. comic opera, 1890-91; teacher pf., org., and comp. in various schools, incl. N. Y. Coll. of Mus.; critic for the *"Examiner,"* San Francisco, 1893-95; and essayist for various periodicals; 1896 lecturer on music for the Univ. of New York; 1901-02 at Yale University; 1902-10, taught in Berlin; then head of comp. dept., Cincinnati Cons.; later held comp. fellowship, Western Coll., Oxford, Ohio; c. *"Gulliver,"* humorous symph.; Chinese suite, *"Aladdin,"* for orch.; comic opera, *"Puritania"* (Boston, 1892); succ. incid. music to *"Macbeth"* and to *"Ben Hur,"* both for chorus and orch.; string-quartet and quintet; *"Wedding-Ode,"* for tenor solo, male chorus and orch. (MS.); 6 songs, *"Phases of Love"*; notable songs, *"Eldorado"* and *"Israfel,"* and others.

Kell'ner, (1) **David,** dir. German ch. and Th. at Stockholm, 1732. (2) **Jn. Chp.,** Gräfenroda, 1736—Cassel, 1803; ct.-organist and dram. composer.

Kel'logg, Clara Louise, Sumterville, S. C., July, 1842—New Hartford, Conn., May 13, 1916; noted soprano; 1856-61, studied in New York; début Acad. of Mus. (1861); début, London, at H. M's. Th. (1867), as "Margherita," with great succ.; sang in many capitals.

Kel'ly, Michael, Dublin, 1764—Margate, 1826; tenor and dram. composer; friend of Mozart; wrote musical "Reminiscences."

Kelterborn, Louis, Boston, April 28, 1891—Neuchâtel, July 9, 1933; composer and conductor; of Swiss parentage; studied at Basel and Geneva Cons.; 1917-19, teacher of theory at Wolff Cons., Basel; after 1919, org. in Burgdorf; 1927, taught Neuchâtel Cons.; c. symph., choral and org. music.

Kempff, Wilhelm, b. Jüterbog, Germany, Nov. 25, 1895; composer, pianist; studied at Berlin Hochsch., winning both Mendelssohn prizes, 1917; toured as piano and org. virtuoso; 1924-29, dir. Stuttgart Cons.; c. orch., chamber and choral music.

Kemp'ter, (1) **K.;** Limbach, Bavaria, 1819—Augsburg, 1871; conductor. (2) **Lothar,** Lauingen, Bavaria, Feb. 5, 1844—Vitznau, July 14, 1918; cond., professor, and dram. composer; son and pupil of (3) **Fr. K.** (music-teacher); studied Munich Univ., then with Rheinberger; chorus-dir.; 1886 prof. of mus. theory, Zurich Mus. Sch.

Ken'nedy, Daisy, b. Burra-Burra near Adelaide, Australia, 1893; violinist; studied at Adelaide Cons. and with Sevcik, in Vienna Master School; toured Great Britain, Austria and U. S.; m. Benno Moiseiwitsch, pianist; divorced; (2) John Drinkwater, dramatist.

Ken'nedy-Fra'ser, Marjory, Perth, Scotland, Oct. 1, 1857—Edinburgh, Nov. 21, 1930; composer, alto singer and pianist; esp. known for her *"Songs of the Hebrides."*

Ker'by, Paul, b. South Africa; conductor, composer; studied at London R. Coll. of Mus. (Associate); began baton career at Capitol Theat., N. Y.; 1926, foreign adviser to Salzburg Fest.; res. in Vienna 1926-33, appearing as cond. with Philh. and Symph. in that city, also as guest in Budapest, Frankfort, Wiesbaden; mus. dir. in Vienna for Columbia Phon. Co.; 1933 led Chicago Symph. in Viennese concert as official repr. of Austrian gov't.; cond. at Chicago Op., 1933-34, own English translation of *"Le Coq d'Or"*; 1936, cond. of part of summer season N. Y. Philh. at Lewisohn Stadium.

Kerekjar'to, Duci de (rightly **Julius**), b. Budapest, 1898; violinist; studied at Acad. of Mus. there, also with Hubay; toured in Europe and after 1922 in America.

Kerle (kĕrl), **Jacques de,** b. Ypres,

Flanders, 16th cent.; conductor and composer.

Kerl(1) (Kherl, Cherl), **Jn. Caspar**, Gaimersheim, near Ingolstadt, 1627 —Munich, Feb. 13, 1693; organist, ct.-conductor, teacher, and notable composer of the "Missa nigra" (all in black notes), etc.

Kern, Jerome David, b. New York, Jan. 27, 1885; composer of operettas and musical comedies; studied with Gallico, Lambert and Pierce, also at N. Y. Coll. of Mus.; has produced since 1915 many operetta scores marked by pleasing melody and tasteful style, among which some of the outstanding were: *"Sally,"* *"Sunny,"* *"Show Boat,"* *"Music in the Air,"* *"The Cat and the Canary,"* *"Roberta,"* etc.

Ker'nochan, Marshall Rutgers, b. New York, Dec. 14, 1880; composer, editor; pupil of Wetzler, Knorr and Goetschius; musical editor of *The Outlook* for a period; later pres. of Galaxy Music Corp., N. Y. publishing firm; c. (cantata) *"The Foolish Virgins"*; *"The Sleep of Summer"* for women's chorus and orch.; and numerous songs.

Kes (käs), **Willem**, Dordrecht, Holland, Feb. 16, 1856—Munich, Feb. 21, 1934; violinist; pupil of Böhm, etc., then of David, and, under royal patronage, of Wieniawski, and Joachim; 1876, leader Park Orch. and Felix Meritis Soc., Amsterdam; then cond. "Society" concerts, Dordrecht; 1883–95 cond. at Amsterdam; 1895 Glasgow orch.; 1898 cond. Philh. and dir. Moscow Cons.; 1905–26, dir. Coblenz Musikverein.

Kess'ler, (1) **Fr.**, preacher and writer, (2) **Fd.**, Frankfort-on-Main, 1793– 1856; violinist and composer. (3) (rightly Kötzler) (kĕts'-lĕr), **Jos. Chp.**, Augsburg, 1800—Vienna, 1872; teacher, organist and composer.

Ketel'bey, Albert William, b. Birmingham, England; composer and conductor; studied Trinity Coll., London; cond. at theatres there; was music ed. and also dir. of Columbia Gramophone Co.; c. pop. orch. works, of which *"In a Monastery Garden"* has wide currency.

Ket'ten, H., Baja, Hungary, 1848— Paris, 1883; pianist and composer.

Kettenus (kĕt-tä'-noos) (or kĕt-nüs), **Aloys**, Verviers, 1823—London, 1896; violinist and dram. composer.

Ketterer (kĕt-tŭ-rā), **Eugène**, Rouen, 1831—Paris, 1870; pianist and composer.

Keurvels (kŭr'-vĕls), **Edw. H. J.**, Antwerp, 1853—Eeckeren, Jan. 19, 1916; pupil of Benoît; till 1882, chorusm. Royal Th.; cond. Nat. Flemish Th., Antwerp, c. operas, cantatas, etc.

Keussler (kois'-lĕr), **Gerhard von**, b. Schwanenburg, Livonia, July 6, 1874; pupil Leipzig Cons.; cond. 2 singing societies in Prague; 1918–31, Hamburg; after 1931 in Melbourne; c. symph. poems, etc.

Kewitsch (Kiewics) (kā'-vĭtsh or kē'-vēch), (**Karl**) **Theodor**, Posilge, W. Prussia, Feb. 3, 1834—Berlin, July 18, 1903; son and pupil of an organist; studied with Maslon; oboist, then teacher and organist in different towns; pensioned 1887; editor, etc.

Kiefer (kē'-fĕr), **Heinrich**, Nuremberg, Feb. 16, 1867—Eisenach, Aug. 15, 1922; 'cellist; pupil of Royal Cons., 1883 at Munich, 1884, Stuttgart, 1887–90, Frankfort-on-Main with Cossmann; 1896, soloist of Leipzig, Phil.; 1898 do. of Berlin Phil.; 1900, teacher at Stern Cons.; from 1902, co-founder of the Munich string quartet; toured widely.

Kiel (kēl), **Fr.**, Puderbach, near Siegen (Rh. Prussia), Oct. 7, 1821—Berlin, Sept. 13, 1885; notable teacher and composer of classic sch.; self-taught as pianist and composer; vln.-pupil of Prince Karl von Wittgenstein and later, on stipend from Fr. Wm. IV.. studied with Dehn; lived in Berlin; 1868 "Royal Prof."; c. oratorios, etc.

Kiene (kē'-nĕ). Vide BIGOT.

Kienle (kēn'-lĕ), **Ambrosius**, b. Siegmaringen, May 8, 1852; Benedictine monk and writer, d. Einsiedeln Convent, June 18, 1905.

Kienzl (kĕnts'-'l), **Wm.**, b. Waizenkirchen, Jan. 17, 1857—Vienna, Oct. 3, 1941; pupil of Buwa, Uhl, Remy, Mortier de Fontain, Jos. Krejci, and later, Liszt; 1879 Dr. Phil. at Vienna; 1880 lectured at Munich; 1881–82 toured as pianist; 1883–84 chief cond. of German Opera, Amsterdam; 1886 m. the concert-singer Lili Hoke; 1886–90 dir. Styrian Musikverein at Graz and cond.; 1890–92, 1st cond. Hamburg Opera; 1892–93, at Munich; 1899–1901 at Graz as composer. His first opera *"Urvasi"* (Dresden,

1886) was succ., as was "*Heilmar, der Narr*" (Munich, 1892), and still more so "*Der Evangelimann*"; his opera, "*Kuhreigen*" (Vienna Volksoper, Nov. 25, 1911) a succ. in Europe; c. also "*Don Quichote*," a "musical tragi-comedy"; he finished Jensen's "*Turandot*," and c. also songs, etc.; author of books on music, volumes of memoirs, etc.

Kiepura (kĕ-ä-poō'-rä), **Jan**; Polish tenor; after 1924 sang at Vienna State Op. with sensational succ., while still in his twenties; also heard as guest artist in many other Eur. cities; with Chicago Op. Co., 1930; has sung in motion pictures in England and Hollywood. Met. Op., 1937–8.

Kiesewetter (kē'-zĕ-vĕt-tĕr), **Raphael G.** (Edler von Wiesenbrunn), Holleschau, Moravia, 1773—Baden, near Vienna, 1850; important coll. of mus. MSS. and historian of many obscure periods, etc.; later ennobled.

Kiewics. Vide KEWITSCH.

Kilen'yi, Edward, b. Hungary, Jan. 25, 1884; composer; pupil of Nat'l. Mus. School, Rome, and Cologne Cons.; 1913, Mosenthal Fellow at Columbia Univ.; studied with Mason and Rybner; c. opera, overture, string quartet, vln. pieces and songs.

Kilpinen (kĭl-pē'-nĕn), **Yrö**, b. Helsingfors, Feb. 4, 1892; studied in native city, Vienna and Berlin; comp. of Lieder in romantic style, incl. more than 400 works, some to German texts.

Kind (kĭnt), **J. F.,** Leipzig, 1768— Dresden, 1843; librettist of "*Der Freischütz*," afterwards composer.

Kindermann (kĭnt'-ĕr-män), (1) **Jn. Erasmus,** b. Nürnberg, 1616—Venice, 1655; organist and composer. (2) **Aug.,** Potsdam, 1817—Munich, 1891; barytone. (3) **Hedwig,** daughter of above. Vide REICHER, K.

Kind'ler, Hans, b. Rotterdam, Jan. 8, 1893; 'cellist and conductor; studied at Rotterdam Univ. and Cons., also with Mossel, Casals and Gerardy; served as teacher of 'cello at Scharwenka Cons., Berlin, and chief 'cellist at Charlottenburg Op., has toured widely in Eur. countries; also in U. S., where he has been resident for some years; organised and cond. Nat'l. Symph. Orch., Washington, D. C., after 1930; also in Paris, Brussels, Vienna, Prague, Rome, Milan, and world première

of Stravinsky's "*Apollon Musagète*" at Washington Fest.

King, (1) **Wm.,** 1624—1680; Engl. organist and composer. (2) **Robt.,** d. after 1711; Engl. composer. (3) **Chas.,** Bury St. Edmunds, 1687— London, 1748; composer. (4) **Matthew Peter,** London, 1773—1823; theorist and dram. composer. (5) **Oliver A.,** London, 1855—Sept., 1923; pianist; pupil of W. H. Holmes, and Reinecke, Leipzig Cons.; pianist to the Princess Louise, 1879; toured Canada and New York; 1899 pf.-prof. at R. A. M.; c. cantatas, 147th Psalm, with orch. (Chester Festival, 1888), a symphony, "*Night*." (6) **Julie.** Vide RIVE-KING.

King'ston, Morgan, Nottinghamshire, 1875—England, 1936; operatic tenor; in early life a coal miner; after period of struggle secured mus. education and made début at Queen's Hall, London, with succ., 1909; Amer. début as "Radames" at Century Theat., N. Y., 1913; mem. of Met. Op. Co., for several seasons after 1916; also sang with Chicago Op. Co., and at Covent Garden, 1924–25.

Kinkeldey (kēn'-kĕl-dī), **Otto,** b. New York, Nov. 27, 1878; musicologist; M. A., N. Y. Univ. and Columbia; Ph. D., Univ. of Berlin; studied with MacDowell, Radecke, Thiel, Fleischer, Kretzschmar, Egidi, Wolf and Friedländer; was choir dir. and teacher, N. Y., 1898–1902; prof. org. and theory, Univ. of Breslau, 1909; royal Prussian prof., 1910–14; chief of mus. div., N. Y. Public Library 1915–23; prof. of mus., Cornell Univ., 1923–27; wrote and ed. scientific works on music.

Kipke (kĭp'-kĕ), **K.,** Breslau, Nov. 20, 1850—Leipzig, Nov. 14, 1923; editor.

Kip'nis, Alexander, b. Schitomir, Ukrainia, Feb. 1, 1891; bass; grad. Warsaw Cons., also studied Klindworth-Scharwenka Cons., Berlin, with Ernst Grenzebach; début, Hamburg Op., 1915; 1916–18 in Wiesbaden; after latter year sang at Deutsche Opernhaus, Berlin; toured America with Wagnerian Op. Co., 1923; sang for several years with Chicago Op., also in Munich, London, Milan, Paris, Buenos Aires; after 1932 engaged at Berlin State Op., and in 1936 at Vienna State Op., has a wide following as a concert singer.

Kip'per, Hn., Coblenz, Aug. 27, 1826—Cologne, Oct. 25, 1910; pupil of Anschütz and H. Dorn; teacher and critic at Cologne; c. operettas.

Kircher (kĕrkh'-ĕr), **Athanasius**, Geisa (Buchow ?), near Fulda, 1602—Rome, 1680; Jesuit archæologist and coll. of airs, some of them supposed to have curative effects.

Kirchhoff (kĕrkh'-hōf), **Walther**, b. Berlin, March 17, 1879; tenor; studied with Lilli Lehmann and in Milan; 1906–1920, a leading heroic tenor of the Berlin Op., thereafter appearing in Buenos Aires and for several seasons at the Met. Op. House in Wagnerian rôles.

Kirchner (kĕrkh'-nĕr), (1) **Fz.**, Potsdam, Nov. 3, 1840—Berlin, May 14, 1907; pianist; pupil Kullak's Acad., where he taught 1864–89, then in the Mädchenheim sch., Berlin; c. pf.-pcs., etc. (2) **Hn.**, Wolfis, Jan. 23, 1861—Breslau, Dec. 26, 1928; tenor, and composer at Berlin. (3) **Theodor**, Neukirchen, Saxony, Dec. 10, 1823—Hamburg, Sept. 18, 1903; pupil of J. Knorr (pf.), K. F. Becker (org.), Jn. Schneider, and at Leipzig Cons.; 1843–62, organist Winterthur; 1862–72, teacher Zurich Mus. Sch., and cond.; 1873–75, dir. Würzburg Cons., Leipzig; 1883; Dresden; 1890, Hamburg; c. pf.-pcs., etc.

Kirnberger (kĕrn'-bĕrkh-ĕr), **Jn. Ph.**, Saalfeld, Thuringia, 1721—Berlin, 1783; eminent theorist, conductor and composer.

Kist (kĕst), **Florent Corneille (Florens Cornelius)**, Arnheim, 1796—Utrecht, 1863; horn-player and flutist; editor, conductor and composer.

Kistler, Cyrill, Grossaitingen, near Augsburg, March 12, 1848—Kissingen, Jan. 1, 1907; studied with Wüllner, Rheinberger, and Fr. Lachner; 1883 teacher Sondershausen Cons.; since 1885 lived in Bad Kissingen as principal of a sch., pub. of text-books, incl. "*A Harmony, based on Wagner*," etc.; c. 2 operas; a succ. "musical comedy" "*Eulenspiegel*" (Würzburg, 1893); etc.

Kist'ner, (1) **Fr.**, Leipzig, 1797—1844; pub. His son (2) **Julius** succeeded him.

Kittel (kĭt'-tĕl), (1) **Jn. Chr.**, Erfurt, Feb. 18, 1732—May 18, 1809; J. S. Bach's last pupil; organist in Erfurt; famous but ill-paid virtuoso and teacher. (2) **Bruno**, b. Entenbruch,

Posen, May 26, 1870; conductor: studied with Sauret and others in Berlin; early played as violinist; founded chorus named after him in Berlin, 1902, which has played important rôle in that city's music; cond. at R. Theat. there, later founded and dir. Brandenburg Cons.; after 1935, dir. of Stern Cons., Berlin.

Kittl (kĭt'-'l), **Jn. Fr.**, b. Schloss, Worlik, Bohemia, 1806—Lissa, 1868; conductor and dram. composer.

Kitzler (kĭts'-lĕr), **Otto**, Dresden, March 16, 1834—Graz, Sept. 6, 1915; pupil of Schneider, Otto, and Kummer ('cello), later of Servais and Fétis, Brussels Cons.; 'cellist in opera-orchs. at Strassburg and Lyons; cond. at various theatres; 1868 dir. Brünn Mus. Soc. and Mus. Sch., also cond. of the Männergesangverein; he was Anton Bruckner's teacher; pub. orch.-mus., pf.-pcs., etc.

Kjerulf (k'yä'-roolf), **Halfdan**, Christiania, Sept. 15, 1815—Bad Grafsee, Aug. 11, 1868, composer; gave up theology for music; studied at Leipzig; settled in Christiania; c. songs and pf.-pcs.

Klafsky (Lohse-Klafsky) (kläf'-shkĭ), **Katharina**, St. Johann, Hungary, 1855—Hamburg, 1896; sopr.; pupil of Mme. Marchesi; sang in comic opera chorus, later leading Wagnerian rôles in Europe and America; m. Otto Lohse.

Klatte (klä'-tĕ), **Wilhelm**, b. Bremen, Feb. 13, 1870; author biog. of Schubert, etc.

Klauser (klow'-zĕr), (1) **K.** (of Swiss parents), St. Petersburg, Aug. 24, 1823—Farmington, Conn., Jan. 9, 1905; chiefly self-taught; 1850, New York; 1856, Mus.-Dir. Farmington Cons.; editor. (2) **Julius**, New York, July 5, 1854—Milwaukee, 1907; pupil of Wenzel, Leipzig Cons.; mus.-teacher, Milwaukee; pub. "*The Septonate and the Centralization of the Tonal System*" (1890).

Klauwell (klow'-vĕl), (1) **Ad.**, Langensalza, Thuringia, 1818 — Leipzig, 1879; teacher, writer, etc. (2) **Otto**, Langensalza, April 7, 1851—Cologne, May 12, 1917; nephew of above; pupil of Schulpforta, and at Leipzig Cons.; Dr. Phil.; 1875 prof. Cologne Cons.; 1885, dir. Teachers' Seminary; writer and dram. composer.

Klee (klā), **L.**, Schwerin, April 13, 1846

—Berlin, April 14, 1920; pupil of Th. Kullak, and until 1875, teacher Kullak's Acad., then dir. of his own sch.; "Musik-Direktor," writer and editor.

Kleeberg (klā-bĕr), **Clotilde**, Paris, June 27, 1866—Brussels, Feb. 7, 1909; pianist; pupil of Mmes. Rety and Massart at the Cons., won 1st prize; début, at 12, with Pasdeloup orch.; toured Europe with great succ.; 1894, Officier de l'Académie.

Kleefeld (klā'-fĕlt), **Wilhelm**, b. Mayence, April 2, 1868; author and comp.; pupil of Radecke, Härtel and Spitta; 1891 cond. in Mayence, etc.; 1897 Ph. D., 1898–'01 teacher at the Klindworth-Scharwenka Cons.; c. opera "*Anarella*" (Königsberg, 1896), string suite, etc.

Kleemann (klā'-män), **K.**, Rudolstadt, Sept. 9, 1842—Gera, Feb. 18, 1923; pupil of Müller, 1878, studied in Italy; then 2nd opera cond. and ct. mus.-dir. Dessau; c. 2 symphonies, etc.

Kleffel (klĕf'-fĕl), **Arno**, Possneck, Thuringia, Sept. 4, 1840—near Berlin, July 15, 1913; studied Leipzig Cons., and with Hauptmann; 1863–67, dir. Riga Mus. Soc.; then th. cond. in Cologne; later teacher of theory, Stern's Cons., Berlin; 1895, professor; c. opera, Christmas legend, overtures, etc.

Kleiber (klī'-bĕr), **Erich**, b. Vienna, Aug. 5, 1890; conductor; served in theatres at Darmstadt, 1912–19; Barmen-Elberfeld, Düsseldorf and Mannheim; general mus. director at Berlin 1923–35, incl. chief conductor-ship of one of the city's State Op. Houses and symph. concerts; also cond. as guest in Rome, Paris, Barcelona, Budapest, Prague, Buenos Aires, Copenhagen, Bucharest, Vienna, Leningrad; N. Y. Philh. Orch., 1930–31; in Feb., 1935, he resigned Berlin post as consequence of artistic differences with Nat'l. Socialist regime and took up res. in Mondsee, near Salzburg, Austria; in the autumn of that year he was invited to direct German opera at La Scala, Milan.

Klein (klīn), (1) **Jn. Jos.**, Arnstadt, 1740—Kahla, near Jena, 1823; writer. (2) **Bd.**, Cologne, 1793—Berlin, 1832; teacher and composer. (3) **Joseph,** 1801—1862, bro. of above; lived as composer in Berlin and Cologne.

(4) **Bruno Oscar,** Osnabrück, Hanover, June 6, 1856—New York, June 22, 1911; son and pupil of (5) **Carl K.** (organist Osnabrück Cath.); (4) studied at Munich Cons.; 1878, gave concerts in America; 1883, New York; 1884, chief pf.-teacher Convent of the Sacred Heart; also, 1884–94, organist St. Francis Xavier, and 1887–92, prof. of cpt. and comp. Nat. Cons.; 1894–95, gave concerts in Germany; prod. succ. gr. opera, "*Kenilworth*" (Hamburg, 1895), vln.-sonata, etc. (6) **Hermann,** Norwich, Eng., 1856—London, March 10, 1934; critic and teacher; studied law; 1874 singing with Manuel Garcia; 1881–1901, critic London *Sunday Times;* 1887, prof. of singing at Guildhall; 1896, dir. opera-class (vice Weist Hill); 1901–09, taught N. Y.; then again in London; author, "*30 Years of Musical Life in London,*" "*The Reign of Patti,*" etc.

Kleinmichel (klīn'-mĭkh-'l), (1) **Hermann;** (?) 1816—Hamburg, 1894; bandmaster. (2) **Richard,** Posen, Dec. 31, 1846—Berlin, 1901; son and pupil of above; studied also at Hamburg and at Leipzig Cons.; teacher, Hamburg; 1876, Leipzig; 1882, mus. dir. City Th.; c. 2 operas; 2 symphonies; chamber-music, valuable études, etc.; m. a dramatic soprano, (3) **Clara Monhaupt.**

Klem'perer, Otto, b. Breslau, May 15, 1885; conductor; studied Frankfort Cons., with P. Scharwenka and Pfitzner; after 1907 cond. at Prague Op., on recommendation of Mahler; Hamburg Op., 1909, also in Bremen, Strasbourg and Cologne (1917–24); general mus. director, Wiesbaden, 1924–27; similar post at State Op. on Platz der Republik, Berlin, 1927–31, and that on Unter den Linden, 1931–33, where he inst. a regime of notable enterprise in the prod. of modern works and novel scenic dress, also cond. symph. concerts; resigned Berlin posts on accession to political power of Nat'l. Socialists; after 1935, cond. Los Angeles Philh. Orch., also led part of season with N. Y. Philh. Orch., 1934 and 1935; c. opera, choral works and songs.

Kle'nau, Paul von, b. Copenhagen, Feb. 11, 1883; composer; pupil of Bruch, Thuille and Schillings; theatre cond., Freiburg, 1897–1908, and after 1920 of Copenhagen Philh.; c.

(operas) "*Sulamith*" (Munich, 1913); "*Kjartan und Gudrun*" (Mannheim, 1918); "*The School for Scandal*" (after Sheridan), prod. Frankfort; (dance-play) "*Klein Idas Blumen*" (Stuttgart, 1916); 4 symphonies, (orch.) "*Paolo and Francesca*"; "*Gespräch mit dem Tod*" for alto and orch.; "*Ebba Skammelsen*," ballade for barytone and orch.; piano quintet, string quartet, songs.

Klengel (klĕng'-ĕl), (1) **Aug. Alex.** ("Kanon-Klengel"), Dresden, 1783—1852; organist and composer of an attempt to rival Bach's "Well-tempered Clavichord," etc. (2) **Paul,** b. Leipzig, May 13, 1854—April 24, 1935; violinist; Dr. Phil., Leipzig; 1881–86, cond., Leipzig, "Euterpe" concerts; 1888–93, 2nd ct.-cond., Stuttgart; cond. "Arion," Leipzig; 1898, New York. (3) **Julius,** Leipzig, Sept. 24, 1859—Oct. 26, 1933; bro. of above; 'cellist, pupil of Emil Hegar ('cello) and Jadassohn (comp.); 1st 'cello in Gewandhaus Orch., and teacher at the Cons.; composer.

Klenov'ski, Nicholas Semenovich, b. Odessa, 1857; pupil Moscow Cons.; leader of private concerts there 1883–93; when he became cond. at the Imperial Theatre, then a teacher at Tiflis till 1902, then assistant cond. of the Imperial Chapel at St. Petersburg; c. ballets, "*Hasheesh*," Moscow, 1885; "*Salanga*" (St. Petersburg, 1900); orch. suite "*Fata Morgana,*" cantatas, etc.

Kliebert (klē'-bĕrt), **K.,** Prague, Dec. 13, 1849—Würzburg, May 23, 1907; Ph. D., Prague; pupil of Rheinberger and Wüllner, Munich; 1876, dir. R. Sch. of Mus., Würzburg.

Klindworth (klĭnt'-vôrt), **K.,** Hanover, Sept. 25, 1830—Oranienburg (Berlin), July 27, 1916; pianist, eminent teacher and editor; self-taught pianist; at 6 played in public; at 17, cond. of an opera-troupe; 1849, teacher at Hanover; 1852, a Jewish woman advanced him money to study with Liszt; 1854, music-début, London; Wagner admired him, and they became friends. 1854–68, he gave concerts and lessons, London; then pf.-prof. Imp. Cons., Moscow; while here he completed two monumental works, his pf.-scores of Wagner's "*Ring des Nibelungen*," and a rev. ed. of Chopin. 1882–92, cond. at Berlin the Wagnerverein

and (with Joachim and Wüllner) the Philharm. Concerts. Est. a "Klavierschule" (Sch. of Pf.-playing), later united with the Scharwenka Cons., 1893, when he retired to Potsdam; composed piano-pieces.

Kling, H., Paris, Feb. 14, 1842—Geneva, May 2, 1918; prof. Geneva Cons. and teacher in city schools; writer and dram. composer.

Klitzsch (klĭtsh), **K. Emanuel,** Schönhaide, Saxony, 1812—Zwickau, 1889; writer and composer.

Klose (klō'-zĕ), **Friedrich,** b. Karlsruhe, Nov. 29, 1862; composer; pupil of Lachner, Ruthardt and Bruckner; 1907–19, teacher of comp. at the Akademie der Tonkunst, Munich; c. dramatic symph. "*Ilsebill*," or "*The Fisher and His Wife*" (Karlsruhe, 1903); mass with orch.; symph. poem in three parts "*Das Leben ein Traum*" with organ and women's chorus, chamber, orch. and vocal music.

Klosé (klô-zā), **Hyacinthe Eléonore,** Isle of Corfu, 1808—Paris, 1880; clarinettist and prof., Paris Cons.; composer.

Klotz (klôts), family of Bavarian violinmakers at Mittenwald. The first (1) **Ægidius,** sen., the best; another, (2) **Matthias** (1653—1743). Matthias's sons were (3) **Sebastian** and (4) **Joseph,** and their sons (5) **Georg,** (6) **Karl,** (7) **Michael,** and (8) **Ægidius, Jr.**

Klughardt (klookh'-härt), **Aug. (Fr. Martin),** Köthen, Nov. 30, 1847—Dessau, Aug. 3, 1902; pupil of Blassmann and Reichel, Dresden; ct.-cond. at Neustrelitz and later at Dessau; prod. 4 operas, the symphonic poem, "*Leonore*"; 3 symph. (1. "*Waldweben*"), overtures "*Im Frühling*"; "*Sophonisbe*," "*Siegesouvertüre*," and "*Festouverture*," etc.

Knabe (k'nä'-bĕ), (1) **Wm.,** Kreuzburg, Prussia, 1797—Baltimore, 1864; founder of pf.-factory at Baltimore, Md.; succeeded by his sons (2) **Wm.** (1841—89) and (3) **Ernest,** and they by (4) **Ernest J.** (b. July 5, 1869) and (5) **Wm.** (b. March 23, 1872). In 1908 the business was amalgamated with the Amer. Piano Co. of N. Y.

Knap'pertsbusch, Hans, b. Elberfeld, Germany, March 12, 1888; conductor; studied Bonn Univ. and Cologne Cons.; cond. in Elberfeld,

Leipzig, Dessau, and 1920–35 succeeded Bruno Walter as general music director of Munich Op.; he resigned this post following controversy with Nat'l. Socialist authorities as to his political views, and in 1936 was active as guest cond. at Vienna State Op.

Knecht (knĕkht), **Justin H.,** Biberach, Würtemberg, Sept. 30, 1752—Dec. 1, 1817; rival of Vogler as organist, and important theorist, conductor and composer.

Kneisel (knī'-zĕl), (1) **Fz.** (of German parents), Bucharest, Jan. 26, 1865—Boston, March 27, 1926; violinist; pupil of Grün and Hellmesberger, Vienna; *Konzertmeister*, Hofburg Th.-Orch.; then of Bilse's Orch., Berlin; 1885–1903, concertm. and soloist, Boston Symphony Orch.; 1887, founded the "Kneisel Quartet," which played with greatest succ. in America and Europe until 1917; 1902, cond. Worcester (Massachusetts) Festival; after 1905, prof. of vln., Inst. of Mus. Art, N. Y. (2) **Frank,** his son, and (3) **Marianne,** his daughter, both accomplished string players.

Kniese (knē'-zĕ), **Julius,** Roda, near Jena, Dec. 21, 1848—Dresden, April 22, 1905; pianist and organist; pupil of Stade, at Altenburg, Brendel and C. Riedel, Leipzig; 1884–89, mus.-dir. at Aix; 1882, chorusm. at Bayreuth, where he lived; 1889, dir. Preparatory Sch. for Stage-Singers; c. opera, "*König Wittichis*"; symphonic poem, "*Frithjof*," etc.

Knip'per, Lyof, b. Tiflis, Dec. 16, 1898; composer; studied in Russia, also with Jarnach in Berlin; c. works in modern style, some in satirical vein, incl. (operas) "*Til Eulenspiegel*," "*Cities and Years*"; (orch.) "*Legend of a Plaster God*" (Phila. Orch., 1930); symphonies; chamber music; (ballet) "*Santanella.*"

Knoch (knŏkh), **Ernst,** b. Carlsruhe, Aug. 1, 1875; conductor; pupil of Mottl; esp. known as interpreter of Wagner works; 1914, cond. for Century Op. Co.; 1916, Ravinia Park Op.; also with many other touring organisations in U. S.

Knorr (knôr), (1) **Julius,** Leipzig, 1807—1861; pf.-teacher and deviser of standard rudimentary exercises; pub. "*Methods,*" etc. (2) **Ivan,** Mewe, West Prussia, Jan. 3, 1853—Frank-

fort-on-Main, Jan. 22, 1916; studied Leipzig Cons. with Richter, Reinecke; 1883, prof. of theory, Hoch Cons. Frankfort-on-Main; c. 2 suites, etc.

Knote, Heinrich, b. Munich, Nov. 20, 1870; tenor; studied with Kirschner in native city, where he was mem. of Op., 1892–1914; guest appearances in America, incl. Met. Op. Co., 1903; also at Charlottenburg Op., and after 1924 again in Munich; one of leading Wagner tenors of his period.

Kny'vett, (1) **Chas.,** England, 1752—London, 1822; tenor and organist. (2) **Chas.,** 1773—1852; son of above; organist and teacher. (3) **Wm.,** 1779—Ryde, 1856; bro. of above; composer and conductor.

Kobbé (kŏb-bā), **Gustav,** New York, March 4, 1857—Bay Shore, N. Y., July 27, 1918; studied pf. and comp. with Adolf Hagen, Wiesbaden; later with Jos. Mosenthal, New York; 1877, graduated Columbia Coll.; 1879, Sch. of Law; served as music critic on various N. Y. papers; wrote "*Wagner's Life and Works*" "*The Ring of the Nibelung*," etc.; teacher; pub. a few songs.

Kobelius (kō-bā'-lĭ-oos), **Jn. Augustin,** Wählitz, near Halle, 1674—Weisenfels, 1731; ct.-cond. and dram. composer.

Koch (kōkh), (1) **H. Chp.,** Rudolstadt, 1749—1816; violinist; writer and composer. (2) **Eduard Emil,** Schloss Solitude, near Stuttgart, 1809—Stuttgart, 1871; writer. (3) **Emma,** b. Mayence; pianist; pupil of Liszt, Moszkowski, etc.; 1898, teacher Stern Cons. (4) **Fr.,** Berlin, July 3, 1862—Jan. 30, 1927; pupil of the Hochschule; conductor; 'cellist and c. of operas, "*Die Halliger*" and "*Lea*" (Cologne, 1896), etc.; 1901, mem. of the Prussian Acad. of Arts; 1917, head of theory dept., Berlin Hochsch.

Kochanski (kō-hän'-skē), **Paul,** Odessa, 1887—New York, Jan. 12, 1934; violinist; studied with Mlynarski, and César Thomson, Brussels Cons., début with Musical Soc., Warsaw, 1898; toured Europe and U. S.; estab. high reputation as solo and chamber music player; was dir. of vln. dept., Juilliard School of Mus., N. Y., until his death.

Köchel (kěkh'-'l), **L. Ritter von,** Steinon-Danube, Lower Austria, 1800—Vienna, 1877; writer.

Kocher (kōkh'-ĕr), **Conrad,** Ditzingen,

near Stuttgart, 1786 — Stuttgart, 1872; mus.-dir. and dram. composer.

Kocian (kō'-tsǐ-ŭn), **Jaroslav**, b. Wildenschwert, Bohemia, Feb. 22, 1884; violinist, son and pupil of a school-teacher; studied violin at 3½ years; at 12, Prague Cons. under Sevcik (vln.), and Dvořák (comp.); début, 1901; toured Europe with much succ.; 1902, America.

Koczalski (kō-chäl'-shkǐ), **Raoul** (**Armand G.**), b. Warsaw, Jan. 3, 1885; studied pf. with his mother; then with Godowski at Warsaw; at 4 played in public with great succ.; at 7, played at Vienna, St. Petersburg, etc.; at one time ct.-pianist to the Shah of Persia; c. 1-act operas, "*Hagar*," "*Rymond*," etc.

Kodaly (kō-dä'-ē), **Zoltan**, b. Kecskemet, Hungary, Dec. 16, 1882; composer; Ph. D., Budapest Univ., 1905; studied Budapest Acad., under Koessler; made researches in folk music of his country, incl. about 3500 melodies; prof. of comp. at Budapest Acad. since 1907; his works incl. modern harmonic treatment, with some elements of atonality, and abound in colourful folk inspiration and brilliant orchestration; c. (comic folk opera) "*Hary Janos*" (Budapest, 1926); (opera) "*Szekely Spinning Room*"; a highly praised "*Psalmus Hungaricus*" for tenor solo, chorus and orch., heard widely in Europe, also in U. S.; "*Summer Evening*," tone poem; "*Dances of Marosszek*" for orch. (perf. by N. Y. Philh.); Serenade for 2 violins and viola; 2 string quartets, 'cello sonata; songs with orch., choruses, etc.

Koechlin (kěsh'-lěn), **Charles**, b. Paris, Nov. 27, 1867; studied Paris Cons., c. ballets, choral and chamber music, orch. works, suites for various instruments; choral, piano and org. pieces, songs; contrib. to Lavignac's Encyclopedia and periodicals.

Koemmenich (kěm'-mě-nǐkh), **Louis**, Elberfeld, Germany, Oct. 4, 1866— New York, 1922; pupil of Anton Krause, Barmen and at Kullak's Acad. 1890, New York, as conductor and teacher; since 1894, cond. Brooklyn Sängerbund; 1898, organised an Oratorio Soc.; 1912–17, cond. N. Y. Oratorio Soc.; 1913–19, Mendelssohn Glee Club; after 1917 New Beethoven Soc.; c. a cantata, choruses. etc.

Koenen (kā'-něn), (1) **Fr.**, Rheinbach, near Bonn, 1829—Cologne, 1887; conductor and composer. (2) (koo'-něn), **Tilly**, b. Java, Dec. 25, 1873, of Dutch parents, her father a cavalry general and Governor of the Province; pupil of the Amsterdam Cons. and with Cornelie van Zanten; 1899, sang in London, Berlin, etc.; after 1909 in the U. S.

Koessler (kěs'-lěr), **Hans**, Waldeck, Jan. 1, 1853—Ansbach, May 23, 1926; organist; pupil Munich Cons.; 1877 teacher at Dresden Cons., and cond. of the Liedertafel; 1882–1908, teacher at Budapest Landesakad.; c. Psalm for 16 voices, winning a prize at Vienna; a symph., an opera "*Der Münzenfranz*" (Strassburg, 1902), etc.; a personal friend of Brahms and an eminent teacher, numbering among his pupils a whole generation of younger Hungarian comps.; after 1908 he was pensioned and lived in Berlin and other cities, but returned to Budapest to cond. a master class in comp., 1920–25.

Kofler (kôf'-lěr), **Leo**, Brixen, Austrian Tyrol, March 13, 1837—New Orleans, 1908; from 1877, organist and choirm. of St. Paul's Chapel, New York; writer and composer.

Kogel (kō'-gěl), **Gv.**, Leipzig, Jan. 16, 1849—Frankfort-on-Main, Nov. 13, 1921; pupil of the Cons.; th.-cond. various cities; 1891–1902, cond. Museum Concerts, Frankfort; editor and composer.

Köhler (kā'-lěr), (1) **Ernst**, Langenbielau, Silesia, 1799—Breslau, 1847; organist and composer. (2) (**Chr.**) **Louis** (**H.**), Brunswick, 1820—Königsberg, 1886; pianist, teacher and dramatic composer, also notable critic.

Kohut (kō-hoot'), **Ad.**, Mindszent, Hungary, Nov. 10, 1847—Berlin, Sept. 21, 1917; writer.

Kolachev'ski, Michail Nicolaievich, b. Oct. 2, 1851; pupil Leipzig Cons.; c. "*Ukranian*" symph. and church music.

Ko'lar, Victor, b. Budapest, Feb. 12, 1888; composer, violinist, conductor; grad. Prague Cons., 1904; mem. N. Y. Symph., 1907–19; assoc. cond. Detroit Symph., after 1919; c. symphonic and chamber music.

Kolbe (kôl'-bě), **Oskar**, Berlin, 1836—1878; composer and writer.

Kol'berg, Oskar, near Radom, 1815—Warsaw, 1890; comp. of Polish dances and songs.

Ko'lisch, Rudolf, b. Klamm, Austria, June 20, 1896; violinist; pupil of Egghard, Grädener, Sevcik, Schreker and Schönberg; studied at Vienna Akad. für Musik and Univ.; after 1922 leader of the Kolisch String Quartet (with Felix Khuner, E. Lehner and B. Heifetz), which toured with succ. in Europe and after 1933 in U. S. (début Coolidge Fest., Washington, D. C.)

Kollmann (kôl'-män), **Aug. Fr. K.,** Engelbostel, Hanover, 1756—London, 1829; organist, theorist and composer.

Kömpel (kĕm'-pĕl), **Aug.,** Brückenau, 1831—Weimar, 1891; violinist.

Kom'zak, (1) **Karl,** Prague, Nov. 8, 1850 —Baden near Vienna, April 23, 1905; cond. of military bands; composer of many pop. dances, operettas, etc. His son (2) **Karl, Jr.,** d. Vienna, Sept. 5, 1924, also a comp. of dance music.

Königslöw (kä'-nĭkhs-läv), (1) **Jn. Wm. Cornelius von,** Hamburg, 1745—1833; organist and composer. (2) **Otto Fr. von,** b. Hamburg, Nov. 13, 1824—Bonn, Oct. 6, 1898; pupil of Fr. Pacius and K. Hafner, and at Leipzig Cons.; toured for 12 years; 1858–81, leader Gürzenich Orch., Cologne; vice-dir. and vln.-prof. at the Cons.; Royal Prof.; retired to Bonn.

Königsperger (kä'-nĭkhs-pĕrkh-ĕr), **Marianus,** Roding, Bavaria, Dec. 4, 1708 — Ratisbon, Oct. 9, 1769. Benedictine monk who devoted the proceeds of his very successful works to the Abbey; c. church music, also operas.

Koning (kō'-nĭng), **David,** Rotterdam, 1820—Amsterdam, 1876; pianist, conductor and composer.

Konradin (kōn'-rät-ēn), **K. Fd.,** St. Helenenthal, near Baden, 1833—Vienna, 1884; dram. composer.

Kontski (kônt'-shkē), (1) **Antoine de,** Cracow, Oct. 27, 1817—Ivanitchi, Novgorod, Russia, Dec. 2, 1899; pianist; pupil of Markendorf and Field; made v. succ. tours; teacher, London; lived in Buffalo, N. Y.; at 80 toured round the world; c. an opera, an oratorio; symph.; pop. pf.-pcs., incl. "Le Réveil du Lion," etc. (2) **Chas.,** 1815—Paris, 1867; com-

poser. (3) **Apollinaire de,** Warsaw, 1825—1879; violinist; bro. and pupil of (2). (4) **Stanislas,** Cracow, Oct. 8, 1820—?; bro. of above; vln.-teacher and composer, Paris.

Koptjajev (kôpt'-yä-yĕf), **Alexander Petrovich,** b. St. Petersburg, Oct. 12, 1868; author and composer of "Oriental Dances" and "Elégie," for orch., etc.

Kopylow (kō'-pē-lôf), **Alex.,** St. Petersburg, July 14, 1854—Feb. 20, 1911; pupil of Liadoff and Rimsky-Korsakoff; teacher of singing at the Imp. Court Chapel; c. finale for chorus and orch. to "The Bride of Messina"; also orch. and chamber music, piano works, etc.

Korestchenko (kôr-ĕsht-chĕn'-kō), **Arseni Nicholaievich,** Moscow, Dec. 18, 1870—1918; pupil Cons., winning a gold medal in 1891; later teacher there and in the School of the Synod; c. 1-act opera "Belshazzar's Feast" (Moscow, 1892), 2-act "The Angel of Death," "The Ice Palace" (Moscow 1892); two "Symphonic Pictures," "Symphonie Lyrique" (op. 23), chamber music, etc.

Kor'ganov, Gennari Ossipovich, Kwarelia, May 12, 1858—Rostov, April 12, 1890; pianist and composer; pupil of Leipzig and St. Petersburg Cons.; c. piano pieces, etc.

Kornauth (kôr'-naut), **Egon,** b. Olmütz, Austria, May 14, 1891; composer; studied at Vienna Acad. of Mus.; with Fuchs, Schreker, Schmidt, also at Univ. there with Guido Adler; Ph. D.; toured America as accompanist, 1910; solo répetiteur at Vienna Op.; teacher and lecturer; c. many works in neo-Romantic style, esp. chamber, orch. and vocal music.

Körner (kĕr'-nĕr), **Gotthilf Wm.,** Teicha, near Halle, 1809—Erfurt, 1865; publisher.

Korn'gold, Erich Wolfgang, b. Brünn, May 29, 1897; composer and pianist; son of Julius K., Viennese mus. critic; at early age showed remarkable prowess as a comp.; at a concert in Berlin, March, 1911, his trio in D Major, op. I., composed at the age of 13, was played; also portions of two piano sonatas, and a series of "Fairy Pictures"; he c. a ballet given at the Royal Opera and elsewhere; trio (Rosé Quartet, Berlin); serenade and pantomime, "The Snowman" (London, 1912); his one-act operas,

"Violanta" and *"Der Ring des Polykrates,"* were given in Munich, 1916; the former work was sung at the Met. Op., 1928, and the latter prod. by the Phila. Civic Op. 1927-28; a marked succ. was won by his *"Die tote Stadt"* (Hamburg, 1920; Met. Op. Co., 1921, with Jeritza in chief rôle), this work showing a somewhat modernistic idiom; his opera *"Das Wunder der Heliane"* (1927) was sung on a number of Central Eur. stages; **K.** was a cond. in 1919-20 at the Hamburg Stadttheat.; and for a time after 1927 taught at the Vienna Akad. für Tonkunst; he modernised a number of Johann Strauss operettas and cond. them in Berlin and elsewhere; after 1934 he was active as comp. for motion pictures in Hollywood; c. also incid. music to *"Much Ado about Nothing"*; Sinfonietta; string sextet; 2 piano sonatas; piano trio; vln. sonata, etc.

Kort'schak, Hugo, b. Graz, Austria, Feb. 24, 1884; violinist, conductor; grad. Prague Cons., studied with Sevcik; début, Prague, 1904; mem. Berlin Philh., Frankfort Museum Quartet, Chicago Symph., founded Kortschak Quartet (later reorg. as Berkshire String Quartet), which played at Berkshire Fests., also appeared as soloist; prof. vln., Yale Univ. School of Mus.

Koschat (kō'-shät), **Thos.,** Viktring, near Klagenfurt, Aug. 8, 1845—Vienna, May 19, 1914; studied science at Vienna; joined the ct.-opera chorus, soon became leader; 1874, joined cath.-choir; 1878, the Hofkapelle. 1871, he began the pub. of original poems in Carinthian dialect, which he set to music for male quartets; these had great popularity; 1875, founded the "Kärnthner Quintett"; prod. 4-act "Volksstück mit Gesang," *"Die Rosenthaler Nachtigall,"* and succ. "Singspiel" *"Der Burgermeister von St. Anna,"* etc.

Köselitz (kä'-zĕ-lĭts), **H.,** Annaberg, Saxony, 1854—1918; pupil of Richter, Leipzig Cons. and Nietzsche, Basel, lived in Italy; under the name **"Peter Gast"** prod. opera, *"Die Heimliche Ehe"* (Danzig, 1891), etc.

Kosleck (kôs'-lĕk), **Julius,** Neugard, Pomerania, Dec. 1, 1825—Berlin, Nov. 5, 1905; trumpet- and cornet-virtuoso; member of the royal band, Berlin; teacher.

Kossmaly (kôs'-mä-lē), **Karl,** 1812—Stettin, 1893; teacher, conductor and writer.

Köstlin (kĕst'-lēn), (1) **K. Rheinhold,** Urach, Würtemberg, 1819—1894; prof. and writer. (2) **H. Ad.,** b. Tübingen, Sept. 4, 1846—Kannstadt, June 4, 1907; preacher; 1875 he united the choirs of three towns, which became in 1877 the Würtemberg Evangelical "Kirchengesangverein," and which he cond.; 1891, Darmstadt; writer.

Kotchetov, Nikolai, b. Oranienbaum, 1864; composer.

Kothe (kō'-tĕ), **Bd.,** Gröbnig, Silesia, 1821—Breslau, 1897; teacher and composer.

Köttlitz (kĕt'-lĭts), (1) **Ad.,** Trier, 1820—Siberia, 1860; dir. and composer. His wife (2) **Clothilde** (née **Ellendt**), 1822-67, was an excellent singing-teacher.

Ko(t)že'luch (kŏt'-zĕ-lookh or kō'-zhĕ-lookh), (1) **Jn. A.** (rightly **Jan Antonin**), Wellwarn, Bohemia 1738—Prague, 1814; mus.-dir.; conductor and dram. composer. (2) **Ld. Anton,** Wellwarn, 1748—Vienna, 1818; pupil and cousin of above; conductor, teacher and composer.

Kotzolt (kŏt'-tsôlt), **H.,** Schnellwalde, Upper Silesia, 1814—Berlin, 1881; conductor and composer.

Kotzschmar (kôtsh'-mär), **Hn.,** Finsterwalde, Germany, July 4, 1829—Portland, Me., 1909; his father taught him various instrs.; studied also with his uncle Hayne and Jul. Otto, Dresden; in the opera-orch.; 1848, America, with Saxonia Band; from 1849 lived Portland, Me.; cond. "Haydn Assoc.," and was long active as organist there; a memorial org. in his honour was presented to the city by Cyrus H. K. Curtis.

Koussevitzky (kōō-sĕ-vēt'-skē), **Serge,** b. Vishni Volochok, Russia, June 30, 1874; conductor; grad. Moscow Cons., 1894; hon. Mus. D., Brown Univ.; 1926; after 1900 prof. at the Philh. Mus. School, Moscow; began career as double-bass virtuoso in the Imp. Theat. orch. there; in 1910 founded his own symph. orch., which he led until 1918, making 3 tours of Russia with it on chartered steamer down the Volga; his reputation as a cond. grew rapidly when he led the Koussevitzky Concerts in Paris after 1920, winning rank as one of the most brilliant leaders of the day, and making guest appearances in Germany, Italy, England and Spain; since 1924, cond. of the Boston Symph., where he has maintained an aggressive campaign for the introd. of outstanding modern compositions; founder publishing house for Russian music in Paris, 1909; French Legion of Honour, 1924; cond. Berkshire Fest., Stockbridge, Mass., after 1935.

Kovařovic (kō-vär'-zhō-vĭts), **Karl,** Prague, Dec. 9, 1862—Dec. 6, 1920; pupil of the Cons., and of Fibich; from 1899 cond. at the Bohemian Landestheater in Prague; where many of his operas given from 1884 to *"Fraquita"* (1902); c. ballet *"Hasheesh,"* piano concerto, etc.

Kowalski (kō-väl'-shkĭ), **H.,** b. Paris, 1841—Bordeaux, 1916; pianist; pupil of Marmontel (pf.) and Reber (comp.); composer.

Kozlovski (kôs-l'yôf'-ski), **Joseph Antonovich,** Warsaw, 1757—St. Petersburg, Feb. 11, 1831; teacher in the household of Prince Oginski; went to the Turkish war, attracting the notice of Prince Potemkin, who took him to St. Petersburg, where he became director of the court balls, and c. a war song which was for a long time the Russian national anthem; c. also requiem to the Polish King Stanislas, and the Czar Alexander I, etc.

Kraft (kräft), (1) **Anton,** Rokitzan, 1752—Vienna, 1820; 'cellist and composer. (2) **Nicolaus,** Esterháza, Hungary, 1778—Stuttgart, 1853; 'cellist and composer; son and pupil of above; became a member of the famous "Schuppanzigh Quartett."

Kram'er, A. Walter, b. New York, Sept. 23, 1890; composer, editor; studied with father, Maximilian Kramer, also with Carl Hauser, Richard Arnold and James Abraham; mem. editorial staff, *Musical America*, 1916–21; ed.-in-chief 1929–36; vice-pres. and exec. dir., Galaxy Mus. Corp., N. Y., publishers; c. 2 Symph. Sketches; Symph. Rhapsody for vln. and orch., *"Rococo Romance,"* choral cycle; *"Interlude for a Drama,"* for wordless solo voice, oboe, viola, 'cello and piano; *"The Hour of Prayer"* for chorus; other choruses, vln. and piano works and many songs; transc. for orchestra.

Krantz (kränts), **Eugen,** Dresden, 1844—1898; pianist and critic, teacher and composer.

Kraus (krows), (1) **Joseph Martin,** Miltenberg, 1756—Stockholm, 1792; pupil of Abt Vogler; 1778 director and cond. at Stockholm opera; c. operas, symphs., etc. (2) **Ernst,** Erlangen, 1863—April 24, 1933; tenor; pupil of Galliera and Frau Schimon-Regan; 1893 sang at Mannheim; from 1896, Berlin Royal Opera; (3) **Felix von,** b. Vienna, Oct. 3, 1870—Munich, Nov., 1937; bass; pupil of Stockhausen but largely self-taught; sang Hagen and Gurnemanz at Bayreuth; from 1908 teacher at Royal Akad. der Tonkunst, Munich. His wife (4) **Adrienne, (Osborne)** b. Buffalo, N. Y., 1873; pupil of Marie Götze, also a prominent opera singer.

Krause (krow'-zĕ), (1) **Chr. Gf.,** Winzig, 1719—Berlin, 1770; writer. (2) **Karl Chr. Fr.,** Eisenberg, Altenburg, 1781—Munich, 1832; writer. (3) **Theodor,** Halle, 1833—Berlin, 1910; rector at Berlin; cond. Seiffert Soc.; R. Mus.-Dir., 1887; composer. (4) **Anton,** Geithain, 1834—Dresden, 1907; at 6 pupil of cantor Dietrich; then of Fr. Wieck, Reissiger, and Spindler, Dresden, later Leipzig Cons., début, as pianist, Geithain, 1846; 1853–59, teacher and cond. Leipzig *Liedertafel;* 1859–97, dir. *Singverein* and the *Concertgesellschaft* (retired); 1877 Royal Mus. Dir.; prof.; c. *"Prinzessin Ilse."* "Rübezahl Legend." (5) (Prof. Dr.) **Eduard,** Swinemünde, 1837—Berlin, 1892; pianist, teacher and composer. (6) (Dr.) **Emil,** Schassburg in Transylvania, 1840 — Hamburg, 1889; barytone. (7) **Emil,** Hamburg, July 30, 1840—Sept. 5, 1916; pupil of Leipzig Cons.; since 1860, teacher of pf. and theory at Hamburg; since 1885 at the Cons.; c. an Ave Maria at 6, etc. (8) **Martin,** Lobstädt, near Leipzig, June 17, 1853—Plattling, Bavaria, Aug. 2, 1918; pianist and teacher; son and pupil of a cantor, then studied with Fuchs, Borna Teachers' Sem., and at Leipzig Cons.; toured Holland and Germany; had the friendship and advice of Liszt for years; 1885, with Siloti and others, founded the Leipzig "Lisztverein"; 1892, professor; 1901, Munich Cons; 1904, Stern Cons., Berlin.

Kraushaar (krows'-här), **Otto**, Cassel, 1812—1866; writer and composer.

Krauss (krows), (1) **Marie Gabrielle**, Vienna, March 24, 1842—Paris, Jan. 6, 1906; soprano; pupil of Vienna Cons. and Marchesi; 1860–67, Vienna ct. opera; 1867 Th. des Italiens, Paris; 1875–86, Gr. Opéra, Paris; then a teacher at Paris and officier d'Académie. (2) **Clemens**, b. Vienna, March 31, 1893; conductor; sang as boy soprano in Imp. Chapel, Vienna; grad. Cons. there, 1912; cond. German Theatre, Riga, 1913–14; Nuremberg, 1915–16; Stettin, 1916–22; Graz, 1921–22; Vienna State Op., 1922; Tonkünstler Orch., there, 1923–27; Frankfort Op. and Museum Concerts, 1924–29; dir., Vienna State Op. from 1929 to 1934, when he was appointed to similar post at Berlin State Op.; dir. Munich Op. after 1936; has also cond. as guest at Munich Fest., Salzburg Fest., at Leipzig Gewandhaus, Budapest, Barcelona, Paris, Prague, Leningrad; visited America in 1929, as guest cond. of N. Y. Philh. and Phila. Orchestra.

Krebs (kräps), (1) **Jn. L.**, Buttelstedt, Thuringia, 1713—Altenburg, 1780; organist and composer. (2) **Karl Aug.** (rightly, **Miedcke**, changed after adoption by his teacher the opera-singer **J. B. Krebs**), Nürnberg, 1804—Dresden, 1880; c. operas. (3) **Marie** (Frau **Brenning**), Dresden, Dec. 5, 1851—June 27, 1900; daughter of above; pianist and teacher. (4) **K.**, b. near Hanseberg, Würtemberg, Feb. 5, 1857; studied R. Hochschule, Berlin; lived in Berlin as critic and writer, where d. Feb. 9, 1937.

Krečman. Vide KRETSCHMANN.

Krehbiel (krā'-bēl), **H. Edw.**, Ann Arbor, Mich., March 10, 1854—New York, March 20, 1923; prominent American critic; studied law at Cincinnati, but entered journalism; 1874–78, mus.-critic Cincinnati *Gazette;* later editor New York *Mus. Review,* and, 1880 to his death, critic of the *Tribune;* pub. many succ. books, incl. *"Studies in the Wagnerian Drama,"* *"How to Listen to Music"*; *"Annotated Bibliography of Fine Art,"* with R. Sturgis; *"Music and Manners in the 18th Century,"* *"Chapters of Opera,"* *"A Book of Operas,"* *"The Pianoforte and Its Music,"* *"Afro-American Folk Songs,"* *"A*

Second Book of Operas," *"More Chapters of Opera"*; prepared English version of *"Parsifal"*; was mem. of ed. committee for *"The Music of the Modern World"* (1895–97), Amer. ed. for 2nd edition of *"Grove's Dictionary,"* and translated, revised and completed Thayer's life of Beethoven; mem. French Legion of Honour

Krehl (krāl), **Stephan**, Leipzig, July 5, 1864—April 8, 1924; studied Leipzig Cons. and Dresden Cons., 1889; teacher of pf. and theory, Carlsruhe Cons.; 1902, Leipzig Cons.; composer; wrote 5 treatises on comp.

Krein (1), **Alexander**, b. Nizhny-Novgorod, Russia, Oct. 20, 1883; composer; also active as 'cellist in Moscow; noted for the employment of ancient Jewish melodies in his works; c. *"Salome,"* symph. poem; chamber music, piano pieces; *"Kadisch,"* a requiem; incid. music to Jewish plays, songs. (2) **Grigori**, bro. of (1); b. 1879; studied with Juon and Glière; lives in Moscow; c. chamber music, piano sonata, songs.

Kreisler (krīs'-lĕr), (1) **Jns.** Vide E. T. A. HOFFMANN. (2) **Fritz**, b. Vienna, Feb. 2, 1875; violinist; pupil of Massart and Delibes; début Paris; has toured Europe and U. S. with eminent succ. for many years; he has long held a leading rank among the world's vln. artists, both for stylistic qualities and virtuosity; c. a string quartet, several operettas many pop. smaller pieces for his instrument and others, some of which are adaptations of Viennese folk music; the bulk of them he long attributed to little known composers of the past, whose works he was supposed to possess in MS.; but in 1935 he astounded the musical world by announcing that they were his own compositions.

Kreissle von Hellborn (krīs'-lĕ fŏn hĕl'-bôrn), **H.**, Vienna, 1812—1869; writer; wrote *"Biog. of Schubert."*

Krejči (krā'-chē), **Josef**, Milostin, Bohemia, 1822—Prague, 1881; organist and composer.

Krempelsetzer (krĕm'-p'l-zĕts-ĕr), **G.**, Vilsburg, Bavaria, 1827—1871; cond. and dram. composer.

Kremser (krĕm'-zĕr), **Eduard**, Vienna, April 10, 1838—Nov. 26, 1914; from 1869, chorusm. the Vienna "Männergesangverein"; c. operettas, a cantata, with orch., famous *"Altnieder-*

ländische Volkslieder," and other part-songs, etc.

Křenek (krzhěn'-ěk), **Ernst,** b. Vienna, Aug. 23, 1900 (of Czech ancestry); composer; studied with Schreker, but departed from that composer's manner in the direction of extreme modernity, his works embodying atonality; lived in Berlin 1920–24, the following year in Zurich; served as choral répétiteur at the Cassel and Wiesbaden Ops.; c. (operas) *"Die Zwingburg"* (Berlin State Op., 1924); *"Der Sprung über den Schatten"* (Frankfort, 1923); *"Orpheus und Eurydike"* (1926), *"Jonny Spielt Auf"* (Leipzig, 1927, the last making a sensational but brief effect because of its introd. of jazz motifs and story of modern "machine" age, sung on many German stages, also at Met. Op. House, in 1929); 3 one-act operas, 1928; *"Die Heimkehr des Orest"* (1929); *"Karl V,"* completed 1933, but not immediately performed, partly owing to ban upon his works by Nat'l. Socialist regime in Germany; also incid. music to Goethe's *"Triumph der Empfindsamkeit,"* ballets, symphonies, concerti grossi, piano concerto, vln. concerto, string quartet, piano sonatas, choruses and songs; m. a daughter of Mahler; prof. Vassar Coll., 1941.

Krenn (krěn), **Fz.,** Dross, Lower Austria, 1816—St. Andrä vorm Hagenthal, 1897; organist, composer and conductor; prof. harmony, Vienna Cons.

Kretschmann (or **Krečman**) (krětch'-män), **Theobald,** b. Vinos, near Prague, 1850; solo 'cellist, Vienna ct.-opera; d. Vienna, Apr. 16, 1929.

Kretschmer (krětsh'-měr), (1) **Edmund,** Ostritz, Saxony, Aug. 31, 1830—Dresden, Sept. 13, 1908; pupil of Otto and Schneider, Dresden; ct.-organist; founder and till 1897 cond. the Cäcilia Singing-Soc., etc.; teacher in the R. "Kapellknaben-Institut," where his son (2) **Fz.** succeeded him; **E. K.** c. text and music of 2 important operas, *"Die Folkunger"* (Dresden, 1874) and *"Heinrich der Löwe"* (Leipzig, 1877); operetta, *"Der Flüchtling"* (Ulm, 1881); a romantic opera *"Schön Rohtraut"* (Dresden, 1887); *"Geisterschlacht"* (prize, Dresden, 1865); 3-part mass for male chorus (Brussels Acad. prize, 1868); an orch. suite *" Hochzeitsmusik,"* etc.

Kretzschmar (krětsh'-măr) **(Aug. Fd.), Hermann,** Olbernhau, Saxony, Jan. 19, 1848—Berlin, May 11, 1924; organist and conductor; pupil of Otto at the Kreuzschule, Dresden, and at Leipzig Cons.; 1871 Dr. Phil. at Leipzig, with a thesis on notation prior to Guido d'Arezzo; then teacher of org. and harm. at the Cons. and cond. several societies; 1887, mus.-dir. of Leipzig Univ. and cond. "Paulus." 1888–97, cond. of the "Riedel-Verein," retired because of ill-health; 1890, prof., critic, lecturer and writer; 1904, prof. at Berlin Univ.; 1907–22, dir. R. Inst. for Church Music; 1909–22, of the "Hochschule für Musik.-Wissenschaft." Author, studies of Bach, Cornelius, and many pop. musical treatises; c. org.-pcs. and part-songs.

Kreubé (krŭ-bā), **Chas. Frédéric,** Luneville, 1777—at his villa, near St. Denis, 1846; cond. at Paris Op. Com.; c. 10 comic operas.

Kreu(t)zer (kroi'-tsěr), (1) **Conradin,** Messkirch, Baden, Nov. 22, 1780—Riga, Dec. 14, 1849; pupil of Riegard, Weibrauch and Albrechtsberger; toured as pianist; ct.-cond.; c. 30 operas, incl. *"Das Nachtlager von Granada"* (1834) and *"Jery und Bätely,"* still played, etc. His daughter (2) **Cäcilie** was an operatic singer. (3) (pron. in France, krŭt-zär), **Rodolphe,** Versailles, Nov. 16, 1766; —Geneva, Jan. 6, 1831; famous violinist to whom Beethoven dedicated the *" Kreutzer Sonata";* son and pupil of a German violinist and of Stawitz; prof. at the Cons.; ct.-violinist to Napoleon and to Louis XVIII., 1802–26; prod. at Paris over 40 operas, incl. *"Lodoiska,"* also collaborated with Rode and Baillot in a standard method and c. famous vln.-études, etc. (4) **Aug.,** Versailles, 1778—Paris, Aug. 31, 1832; bro. of above, and 1826, his successor as vln.-prof. at the Cons.; composer. (5) (**Chas.**) **Léon (Fran.),** Paris, 1817—Vichy, 1868. Son of (3); writer and composer. (6) **Leonid,** b. St. Petersburg, March 13, 1884; pianist and conductor; studied Petersburg Cons., with Essipov and Glazounoff; prof. at Berlin Hochschule, 1920–33; since 1935 res. in Tokyo; c. (ballet) *"Der Gott und die Bajadere"* (Mannheim, 1921); author books on piano technique; ed. works of Chopin.

Krička (krẑsh'-kä), **Jaroslav,** b. Kelč, Moravia, Aug. 27, 1882; choral dir. and after 1918 teacher at the Prague Cons., c. (opera) *"Spuk im Schloss,"* which blends jazz and folk themes in lively manner and attained succ. on several German stages; also cantatas, overtures, chamber music, choruses and song cycles.

Krieger (krē'-gĕr), (1) **Adam,** Driesen, 1634—Dresden, 1666; ct.-organist and composer. (2) (Jn.) **Phillip,** Nürnberg, 1649—Weissenfels, 1725; ct.-organist, ct.-cond., and dram. composer. (3) **Jn.,** Nürnberg, Dec. 28, 1651—Zittau, July 18, 1735; famous contrapuntist; bro. and pupil of above, and his succ. as ct.-cond.

Kriens, Christiaan, Amsterdam, April 29, 1881—West Hartford, Conn., Dec. 17, 1934; composer, conductor; studied at Hague Cons., winning gold medal; début 1895 with his father's orch. in Amsterdam, cond. own symph. and playing both vln. and piano concertos; toured France, Holland, Belgium; came to U. S. 1906 as cond. of French Op. Co., New Orleans; after 1907, active as teacher and cond. in New York, founding and leading there a Symph. Club to train young players; for 5 years before his death, **K.** was musical dir. of a radio station in Hartford, Conn.; c. orch., chamber works, etc.

Kroeger (krā'-gĕr), **Ernest R.,** St. Louis, Mo., Aug. 10, 1862—April 7, 1934; composer, organist and teacher; active as recitalist (piano), dir. of mus. at Forest Park Univ. and after 1904 head of his own music school in St. Louis; mem. French Academie and Nat'l Inst. of Arts and Letters; c. overtures, orch. suite, *"Lalla Rookh"*; various types of chamber music, a piano sonata op. 33, concert studies for the piano, violin and piano sonata; and many other piano pieces, songs, etc.

Krogulski (krō-gool'-skĭ), **Joseph,** Tarnov, 1815—Warsaw, Jan. 9, 1842; composer; pupil of Elsner; c. 10 masses, an oratorio, etc.

Krohn (krōn), **Ilmari Henrik Rheinhold,** b. Helsingfors, Nov. 8, 1867; Finnish author and comp. of sacred songs, piano sonatas, etc.

Krommer (krôm'-mĕr), **Fz.,** Kamenitz, Moravia, 1760—Vienna, 1831; violinist, organist and conductor.

Kronach. Vide KLITZSCH.

Kronke (krônk'-ĕ), **Emil,** b. Danzig, Nov. 29, 1865; pianist; pupil of Reinecke and Paul, Nicodé and Th. Kirchner, Dresden; 1886 won pf.-prize, Dresden Cons.; 1887, diploma of honour; editor of an edition of Liszt's complete works; also composer.

Kroy'er, Theodor, b. Munich, Sept. 9, 1873; author, critic and comp. studied theology, then music at the Akademie der Tonkunst; 1897, Ph. D. Munich University; 1920, taught Heidelberg Univ.; 1922, Leipzig, where developed school for musical science; after 1933 at Cologne Univ. c. 2 symphonies with chorus and soli, chamber music, etc.

Krueger (krü'-gĕr), **Karl,** b. New York, 1894; conductor; studied with Fuchs, Schalk, Weingartner and Nikisch; early active as 'cello and organ virtuoso, touring in Europe and South America; asst. cond. Vienna Op.; 1926–31, led Seattle Symph. Orch., following its reorganisation; also guest cond. Phila. Orch. and in Hollywood Bowl, Cal.; after 1933 cond. Kansas City Philh. Orch. and chamber opera perfs. in Chicago.

Krug (krookh), (1) **Fr.,** Cassel, 1812—Carlsruhe, 1892; op. barytone and dram. composer. (2) **Dietrich,** Hamburg, 1821—1880; pianist and composer. (3) **Arnold,** Hamburg, Oct. 16, 1849—Aug. 4, 1904; son and pupil of above; studied also with Gurlitt and Reinecke; won Mozart scholarship, 1869; studied with Kiel and Ed. Franck, Berlin; 1872–77, pf.-teacher, Stern Cons.; won Meyerbeer scholarship, and studied in France and Italy; 1885, ct.-cond. at the Hamburg Cons.; pub. a symph., symph. prologue *"Otello,"* and orch. suite; choral works, etc. (4) **(Wenzel) Jos.** (called **Krug-Waldsee**), Waldsee, Upper Swabia, Nov. 8, 1858—Magdeburg, Oct. 8, 1915; chiefly self-taught until 1872, then studied vln., pf., singing and comp. with Faiszt, at Stuttgart Cons.; 1882–89, cond. at Stuttgart; 1889, chorusm., mus.-dir. Municipal Th., Hamburg; 1892, th.-cond. various cities; 1889, Munich; 1900, Nürnberg; 1901, Magdeburg; c. concert-cantatas, *"Dornröschen," "Hochzeitslied," "Geiger zu Gmund"* and *"Seebilder";* succ. opera *"Astorre"* (Stuttgart, 1896); "secular oratorio" *"König Rother,"* etc.

Krüger (krü'-gĕr), **Eduard**, Lüneburg, 1807—Göttingen, 1885; prof. and writer.

Kruis (krīs), **M. H. van**, Oudewater, Holland, March 8, 1861—Lausanne, Feb. 14, 1919; pupil of Nikolai at The Hague; 1884, organist, teacher and writer, Rotterdam; 1886, founded monthly "Het Orgel"; c. an opera "*De Bloem Van Island*," 3 symph., 8 overtures, etc.

Krumpholtz (kroomp'-hŏlts), (1) **Jn. Bap.**, Zlonitz, near Prague, ca. 1745 —Paris, Feb. 19, 1790; harpist, composer; he m. his 16-year old pupil, Frl. Meyer, a brilliant harpist; they gave concerts together, until her elopement, when he drowned himself in the Seine. (2) **Wenzel**, 1750— Vienna, 1817; bro. of above; violinist and composer.

Kubelik (koo'-bĕ-lĭk), (1) **Jan**, b. Michle, July 5, 1880—Prague, Dec. 5, 1940; violinist; son and pupil of a Bohemian gardener; pupil for 6 years of Sevcik, Prague Cons.; studied later at Vienna; début there 1898; then toured Europe, played at Milan, London, 1900, and 1901 America with great success; 1902, London Philh. Society awarded him its Beethoven medal; returned to U. S., 1935, for tour after long absence; estab. res. in Calif. (2) **Rafael**, his son, pianist and conductor.

Kucharž (koo'-chärzh), **Jn. Bap.**, Chotecz, Bohemia, 1751—Prague, 1829; organist and conductor.

Kücken (kĭk'-'n), **Fr. Wm.**, Bleckede, Hanover, 1810 — Schwerin, 1882; composer of operas and pop. songs; for some time cond. at Stuttgart.

Kuczynski (koo-chĕn'-shkĭ), **Paul**, Berlin, Nov. 10, 1846—Oct. 21, 1897; Polish composer; pupil of von Bülow; c. succ. cantata "*Ariadne*."

Kudelski (koo-dĕl'-shkĭ), **K. Mat.**, Berlin, 1805—Baden-Baden, 1877; violinist, composer and conductor.

Kufferath (koof'-fĕr-ät), (1) **Jn. Hn.**, Mühlheim-on-the-Ruhr, 1797—Weisbaden, 1864; conductor. (2) **Louis**, Mühlheim, 1811 — near Brussels, 1882; pianist, teacher and composer. (3) **Maurice**, Brussels, Jan. 8, 1852— Dec. 8, 1919; studied with Servais (père and fils) 'cello; 1873–1900, editor "*Guide musicale*," later, proprietor; writer and translator; 1900, dir. Théâtre de la Monnaie, Brussels.

Küffner (kĭf'-nĕr), **Jos.**, Würzburg, 1776—1856; dram. composer.

Kugelmann (koo'-gĕl-män), **Hans**, d. Königsberg, 1542; trumpeter and composer.

Kuhe (koo'-ĕ), **Wm.**, Prague, Dec. 10, 1823—London, Oct. 9, 1912; pianist; pupil of Proksch, Tomaschek and Thalberg; 1845, London; from 1886 prof. the R. A. M.; composer.

Kuhlau (koo'-low), **Fr.**, Ülzen, Hanover, Sept. 11, 1786—Copenhagen, March 12, 1832; ct.-flutist, dram. composer, teacher and composer of important technical pf.-pcs., etc.

Kühmstedt (küm'-shtĕt), **Fr.**, Oldisleben, Saxe-Weimar, 1809—Eisenach, 1858; theorist, composer, writer and teacher.

Kuhnau (koo'-now), **Jn.**, Geysing, Saxony, April 6, 1660—Leipzig, June 5, 1722; pupil of Henry, Albrici and Edelmann; organist at the Thomaskirche, Leipzig, and 1700 cantor, before Bach; pub. the first sonata for harpsichord, of which he was a noted player; also famous Biblical sonatas; composer and writer.

Kulenkampff (koo'-l'n-kämpf), (1) **Gus.**, Bremen, Aug. 11, 1849—Berlin, Feb. 10, 1921; concert pianist and teacher; pupil of Reinthaler, Barth and Bargiel, Berlin Hochschule; organised the succ. "Kulenkampscher Frauenchor"; dir. Schwantzer Cons. at Berlin for a few years; c. succ. comic operas "*Der Page*" (Bremen, 1890) and "*Der Mohrenfürst*" (Magdeburg, 1892); "*Die Braut von Cypern*" (Schwerin, 1899); male choruses, etc. (2) **Georg**, b. Bremen, Jan. 23, 1888; noted violinist; pupil of Willy Hess; prof. at Berlin Hochschule.

Kullak (kool'-läk), (1) **Theodor**, Krotoschin, Posen, Sept. 12, 1818—Berlin, March 1, 1882; eminent teacher; Prince Radziwill had him taught by the pianist Agthe; at 11 he played at a ct.-concert; studied with Dehn, Czerny, Sechter and Nicolai; then teacher to the royal family; 1846, ct.-pianist, Berlin; 1850, founded (with Julius Stern and Bern. Marx) the Berlin (later Stern) Cons.; 1855, resigned, established his famous "Neue Akademie der Tonkunst"; 1861, royal prof.; wrote standard works, "*Sch. of Octave-playing*," "*Seven Studies in Octave-playing*," etc.; c. a concerto, sonata and other brilliant

pf.-pcs., etc., incl. "*Kinderleben*."
(2) **Ad.**, Meseritz, 1823—Berlin,
1862; bro. of above; writer and composer. (3) **Fz.**, Berlin, 1844—1913;
son and pupil of (1); studied with
Wieprecht and Liszt; 1867, pf.-
teacher and dir. orch.-class in Acad.
of his father, on whose death he became dir. in 1890; writer; c. an opera
"*Ines de Castro*" (Berlin, 1877), etc.

Kull'mann, Charles, b. New Haven,
Conn., Jan. 13, 1903; tenor; studied
Juilliard School of Music, also at
Fontainebleau, and with Francis
Rogers and Mme. Schoen-René;
toured Europe as soloist with Yale
Glee Club; op. début with Amer.
Op. Co., 1929; sang with Berlin
State Op. and at Vienna with succ.
for several years; also at Salzburg
Fest.; début, Met. Op., 1935-36.

Kummer (koom'-m'r), (1) **Kaspar,**
Erlau, 1795—Coburg, 1870; flute-
virtuoso. (2) **Fr. Aug.,** Meiningen,
Aug. 5, 1797—Dresden, Aug. 22,
1879; notable 'cellist and composer
for 'cello; wrote method.

Kümmerle (kĭm'-mĕr-lĕ), **Salomon,**
Malmsheim, near Stuttgart, 1838—
Samaden, 1896; prof. and composer.

Kun'its, Luigi von, Vienna, July 30,
1870—Toronto, Oct., 1931; violinist,
conductor; grad. Univ. of Vienna;
studied vln. with Kral, Gruen and
Sevcik, comp. with Bruckner; led
string quartet of Tonkünstlerverein
there; came to America 1893 and
taught in Chicago; 1896-1910, concertm. of Pittsburgh Orch.; taught
at Cons. there; 1910-12 in Vienna;
after latter year in Toronto, where
prof. in Canadian Acad. of Music,
and leader of Symph. Band.

Kunwald (koon'-vält), **Ernst,** b. Vienna,
April 14, 1868; studied law there,
then music at Leipzig Cons.; became
correpetitor at the city theatre; 1895,
cond. operetta at Rostock, 1901-02
at Teatro Real, Madrid, where he
gave Wagner's Ring cycle complete
and was decorated by the Queen of
Spain; 1902, cond. at opera Frankfort. 1906 cond. at Nuremberg city
theatre; conducting two concerts of
the New York Phil. as guest, Feb.
1906; 1907 director of the Berlin
Phil. orch.; 1912 engaged to conduct
the Cincinnati Symph. Orch.; held
post till 1917; interned as enemy alien;
1922-27, gen. mus. dir., Königsberg;
1928-32, cond., Berlin Symphony.

Kunz (koonts), **Konrad Max,** Schwan-
dorf, Bav. Palatinate, 1812—Munich, 1875; conductor and composer.

Kunzen (koonts'-'n), (1) **Jn. Paul,** Leisnig, Saxony, 1696—Lübeck, 1757;
organist and composer. (2) **K. Ad.,**
Wittenberg, 1720—Lübeck, 1781;
organist, pianist and composer.
(3) **Fr. L. Æmilius,** Lübeck, 1761—
Copenhagen, 1817; ct.-conductor and
composer.

Kupfer-Berger (koop'-f'r-bĕrkh-'r),
Ludmilla, Vienna, 1850—May 12,
1905; pupil of the Cons.; début Linz-
on-Danube, 1868, then at the Berlin
Ct.-opera; m. the Berlin merchant
Kupfer; later at Vienna, ct.-opera as
alternate with Materna.

Kurenko (kōōr-yĕnk'-ō) **Maria,** b.
Tomsk, Siberia; law grad. Moscow
Univ., also Cons. there, with Masetti
and Gontzoff; début in op. at Kharkov; has sung with Moscow Op.;
in N. Y., Chicago and Los Angeles;
concert appearances Europe and
America.

Kurpinski (koor-pĭn'-shkĭ), **Karl (Kasimir),** Luschwitz, Posen, 1785—
Warsaw, 1857; conductor and dram.
composer.

Kurt, Melanie, b. Vienna, 1880—
N. Y., March 11, 1941; studied at
Vienna Cons. and as pianist with
Leschetizky; toured in that capacity,
then turned to singing, working with
Lilli Lehmann; sang Lübeck and
Leipzig, after 1905 at Brunswick
Op.; 1908-12, Berlin Op.; 1915-17,
pronounced succ. in début with Met.
Op. in Wagnerian rôles.

Kus'ser (or Cous'ser), Jn. Siegmund,
Pressburg, 1660—Dublin, 1727; conductor and dram. composer.

Küster (kĭs'-tĕr), **Hn.,** Templin, Brandenburg, 1817—Herford, Westpha-
lia, 1878; ct.-organist, theorist and
composer.

Küzdö, Victor, b. Budapest, 1869;
violinist; grad. of Cons. there at 13;
tours of Europe and after 1884 in
U. S.; further study with Lotto and
Auer; after 1887, lived as concert
artist and teacher in New York.

Kuzniet'zof, Maria, b. Odessa, 1884;
operatic soprano; has appeared
widely in Russia, Spain, France,
England, U. S. (after 1915) and in
South America.

Kwast (kwäst), **Jas.,** Nijkerk, Holland,
Nov. 23, 1852—Berlin, Oct. 31, 1927;
pianist; pupil of his father and Fd.

Böhme; Reinecke and Richter, Kullak and Wuerst, Brassin and Gevaert, Brussels; 1874 teacher Cologne Cons.; 1883–1903, Hoch Cons., Frankfort; then Stern Cons.; composer.

L

Labarre (lä-bär), **Th.**, Paris, 1805–1870; harpist and dram. composer.

Labey (lä-bě'), **Marcel**, b. Dept. Besinet, France, 1875; studied law in Paris, then with d'Indy at the *Schola Cantorum*, where until 1914 taught piano and orch. classes; c. symph., fantasie for orch., sonatas, songs, etc.

Labitzky (lä-bǐt'-shkǐ), (1) **Jos.**, Schönfeld, near Eger, 1802—Carlsbad, 1881; violinist. (2) **Aug.**, Petschau, Saxony, Oct. 22, 1832—Reichenhall, Aug. 28, 1903; pupil of Prague Cons., of David and Hauptmann, Leipzig; 1853, cond. and composer at Carlsbad.

Lablache (lä-bläsh), **Luigi**, son of French father and Irish mother, Naples, Dec. 6, 1794—Jan. 23, 1858; eminent bass, with powerful and flexible voice with compass (E♭–e'); pupil of Valesi, pupil Cons. della Pietà; début Naples as buffo; later in heroic rôles throughout Europe; wrote "Méthode de chant."

Labor (lä'-bôr), **Josef**, Horowitz, Bohemia, June 29, 1842—Vienna, April 26, 1924; a blind pianist and organist; pupil of Sechter and Pirkjer, Vienna Cons.; chamber-pianist and teacher of the Princess of Hanover; after 1866 taught in Vienna, his pupils incl. Schönberg and Julius Bittner; composer.

Laborde. Vide DELABORDE.

Labro'ca, Mario, b. Rome, Nov. 22, 1896; composer and music critic; studied with Respighi and Malipiero; c. ballets, chamber symph., piano concerto, chamber music and vocal works; 1936 appointed pres. of Florence Teatro Comunale.

Lachmund (läkh'-moont), **Carl V.**, b. Booneville, Mo., 1857—Yonkers, N. Y., Feb. 20, 1928; at 13 studied in Cologne with Heller, Jensen and Seiss; then Berlin, also 4 years with Liszt at Weimar; c. trio (played by Berlin Philh. orch.), *"Japanese"* overture (perf. by Thomas and Seidl), etc.; lived in New York as teacher, conductor and composer.

Lachner (läkh'-něr), (1) **Theodor**, b. 1798; son of a poor organist at Rain, Upper Bavaria; organist at Munich. (2) **Thekla**, b. 1803; sister of above, organist at Augsburg. (3) **Christiane**, b. 1805; sister of above; organist at Rain. (4) **Fz.**, Rain, April 2, 1803—Munich, Jan. 20, 1890; half-brother of above; studied with Eisenhofer (comp.), and with Ett; 1882, organist Protestant Church. Vienna, and studied with Stadler, Sechter, and Weigl; a friend of Schubert and Beethoven; 1826, cond. Kärthnerthor Th.; 1834, Mannheim; 1836, the production of his D minor symph. at Munich won him the appointment of ct.-cond.; from 1852, was gen. mus. dir.; 1868 retired with pension in protest against the growing Wagnerianism at court; his eight orch. suites are his best work, showing his contrapuntal gifts at their best; he prod. 4 operas, 2 oratorios, 8 symphs., incl. the *"Appassionata,"* chamber-music, etc. (5) **Ignaz**, Rain, Sept. 11, 1807—Hanover, Feb. 24, 1895. Bro. of (4) and his successor as organist, 1825. 2nd cond. of court-opera, later ct.-mus.-dir., Stuttgart; 1858, ct.-cond., Stockholm; c. operas, pop. Singspiele, etc. (6) **Vincenz**, Rain, July 19, 1811—Carlsruhe, Jan. 22, 1893; bro. of above; his successor as organist and later successor of **Fz.**, as ct.-cond.; teacher and composer.

Lachnith (läk'-nǐt), **L. Wenzel**, b. Prague, 1746; horn-player, and deranger of famous works.

Lack (läk), **Théodore**, Quimper, France, Sept. 3, 1846—Paris, Nov. 25, 1921; pupil of Marmontel (pf.) and Bazin (harm.) Paris Cons.; teacher at Paris; 1881 officier of the Académie; officier of public instruction; c. much light and graceful pf.-music.

Lackowitz (läk'-ō-vǐts), **Walter**, Trebbin, near Berlin, Jan. 13, 1837—Berlin, March 11, 1916; pupil of Erk, Kullak and Dehn; editor.

Lacombe (lä-kôṅb), (1) **Louis** (Brouillon-Lacombe), Bourges, France, Nov. 26, 1818—St. Vaast-la-Hougue, Sept. 30, 1884; pianist; pupil of Paris Cons.; writer and dram. composer. (2) **Paul**, Carcassonne, Oude, France, July 11, 1837—June 5, 1927; studied with Teysseyre, but mainly self-taught; 1880 won the Prix Chartier, for chamber-mus.; c. also 3 symph., a symph. overture, etc.

Lacome (lä-kŭm), **Paul** (P. J. Jac. Lacome de L'Estaleux), Houga, Gers, France, March 4, 1838—Dec. 12, 1920; lived since 1860, Paris; essayist and composer of many light operas, incl. *"Jeanne, Jeannette et Jeanneton"*; orchestral suites; songs, incl. *"L'Estudiantina,"* etc.

La'cy, Michael Rophino, Bilbao, 1795—Pentonville, 1867; English violinist and composer.

Ladegast (lä'-dĕ-gäst), **Fr.,** b. Hochhermsdorf, near Leipzig, Aug. 30, 1818; org.-builder; d. Weissenfels, 1905.

Ladmirault (lăd-mē-rō), **Paul Émile,** b. Nantes, Dec. 8, 1877; began to study at the Cons. piano, violin, organ, and harmony at 7, and to compose at 8; at 15 his 3-act opera *"Gilles de Retz,"* was given at Nantes (1893); the next year he refused to allow its repetition; he took first harmony prize at the Nantes Cons. and 1895 entered Paris Cons. under Taudou, winning first harmony prize 1899. After a year of military service, he entered the classes of Fauré and Gédalge; failing three times to win the Prix de Rome, he left the Cons. His comps. include *"Le Chœur des âmes de la Forêt"* (1903), *"Suite Bretonne"* for orch. (1904), a *"Tantum Ergo"* (1907) crowned by the Société des Compositeurs de Musique; prélude symphonique, *"Brocéliande au Matin,"* a portion of a dramatic work *"Myrdhin";* a symphony in C major, 1910; songs, piano pieces, and pieces for military band.

Laduchin (läd'-oo-chĕn), **Nikolai Mikailovich,** b. St. Petersburg, Oct. 3, 1860; violinist and pianist; pupil of Taneiev at Moscow Cons.; c. symphonic variations; 100 children's songs, *"Liturgy of Johann Slatoust"* for chorus, etc.

Ladurner (lä-door'-nĕr), **Ignaz Ant. Fz.,** Aldein, Tyrol, 1766—Villain (Massy), 1839; pianist and composer.

Lafage (lä-făzh), **Juste Adrien Lenoir de,** Paris, 1801—Charenton Insane Asylum, 1862; singing-teacher, conductor, composer and writer.

Lafont (lä-fôṅ), **Chas. Philippe,** Paris, 1781—near Tarbes, 1839; violinist and composer.

La Forge, Frank, b. Rockford, Ill., Oct. 22, 1877; pupil of his sister-in-law, Mrs. Ruth La Forge, then of Harrison M. Wild of Chicago, 1900–04, Leschetizky, Vienna, and Josef Labor (theory); accompanist to Gadski and Sembrich on their tours; later has lived in N. Y. as voice teacher, coach of noted singers, and composer; c. piano pieces and many successful songs.

La Grange (lä gräṅzh), **Mme. Anna (Caroline) de,** b. Paris, July 24, 1825—April, 1905; colorature soprano of remarkable range and flexibility; pupil of Bordogni and Lamperti; début 1842, at Varese; m. the wealthy Russian Stankowich, lived in Paris as teacher.

La Harpe (lä-ärp), **J. Fran. de,** Paris, 1739—1803; critic.

Lahee', (1) **H.,** Chelsea, England, April 11, 1826—London, April 29, 1912; pupil of Bennett, Potter and J. Goss (comp.); concert-pianist; lived in Croydon as teacher; c. 5 cantatas, etc. His son (2) **H. Chas.,** b. London, 1856; writer; after about 1883 in U. S., and 1891–99 sec'y of N. E. Cons., Boston; author, *"Annals of Music in America,"* 1923.

Laid'law, Anna Robena (Mrs. Thomson), Bretton, Yorkshire, April 30, 1819—May, 1901; successful concert-pianist until her marriage, 1852.

Lajarte (lä-zhärt), **Th. Ed. Dufaure de,** Bordeaux, 1826—Paris, 1890; writer and dram. composer.

Lajeunesse, M. Vide ALBANI.

Lajtha (loi'-tä), **Ladislas,** b. Budapest, June 30, 1892; composer; c. chamber music, incl. four string quartets (No. 3 perf. at Coolidge Fest., Washington, 1930).

Lalande (lä-läṅd), (1) **Michel Richard de,** Paris, 1657—1726; organist, conductor and composer. (2) (**Méric-Lalande**) **Henriette Clémentine,** Dunkirk, 1798—Paris, 1867; brilliant soprano.

La Lau'rencie, Lionel de, Nantes, July 24, 1861—Paris, Nov. 21, 1934; eminent writer on music; ed. Lavignac's Encyclopedia of Music; wrote life of Rameau, etc.

Lalevicz (lä-lä'-vĭch), **Georg von,** b. St. Petersburg, Aug. 21, 1876; piano teacher; pupil of the Cons.; 1900, won the Rubinstein competition in Vienna; 1902–05 prof. in Odessa Cons., then Cracow, Vienna, Lemberg, Paris; lives Buenos Aires.

Lalo', (1) **Edouard Victor Antoine**, Lille, Jan. 27, 1823—Paris, Apr. 22, 1892; eminent French composer; studied at Paris Cons., winning the 2nd Prix de Rome in 1847; little known until 1872 when his orchestral works began to appear, and 1874 when Sarasate played his vln. concerto. C. (operas) "*Le Roi d' Ys*," "*Savonarola*" and "*La Jacquerie*" (latter 2 fragmentary, last completed by Coquard, 1895); 3 symphonies and many shorter orchestral works, a string quartet, piano trios, sonatas for vln. and for 'cello, vln. concertos; "*Symphonie Espagnole*," for vln. and orch.; choral church music and many songs. The popularity of his works, particularly the vln. concertos and the "*Symphonie Espagnole*," is owing to their genial melodic qualities. After early neglect he established his place among the more gifted French comps. of his time. "*Le Roi d' Ys*" has held the stage in France. He m. the contralto, Mlle. Bernier de Maligny. (2) **Pierre**, his son, critic in Paris.

Laloy', **Louis**, b. Graz, 1874; musicologist.

La Mara. Vide LIPSIUS, MARIE.

Lambert (län-băr), (1) **Michel**, Vivonne, Poitou, 1610—Paris, 1696; conductor and composer. (2) **Lucien**, b. Paris, Jan., 1861; pupil of Paris Cons.; 1883, took Prix Rossini w. cantata "*Promethée Enchainé*"; c. lyric dram. "*Le Spahi*" (Op.-com., 1897), "*Brocéliande*," "*Marseillaise*," etc.

Lambert (läm'-bĕrt), (1) **Jn. H.**, Mühlhausen, Alsatia, 1728—Berlin, 1777; writer. (2) **Geo.**, b. Beverley, 1795; organist there, succeeded by his son (3) **Geo. Jackson** in 1818; retired, 1874. (4) **Alex.**, Warsaw, Poland, Nov. 1, 1862—New York, Dec. 31, 1929 (killed by taxicab); pianist; son and pupil of (5) **Henry L.**; (4) studied at Vienna Cons.; graduated at 16; studied with Urban, Berlin; toured Germany and Russia; studied some months at Weimar with Liszt; 1884, America; 1888, dir. N. Y. Coll. of Mus.; long active as teacher in N. Y.; c. piano works. (6) **Constant**, b. London, 1905; composer; began piano study at early age; at 16 won gold medal award and entered R. Coll. of Music, studying with Vaughan Williams and R. O.

Morris; Adrian Boult and Malcolm Sargent (cond.); c. (ballets) "*Romeo and Juliet*" (1st work commissioned from an Englishman by Diaghileff); "*Pomona*"; also "*Music for Orch.*"; settings of 7 poems by Li Po; "*The Rio Grande*," for contralto, chorus, orch. and piano (setting of poem by Sacheverell Sitwell), with pungent use of barbaric rhythm and jazz, which had immense succ., and was given in U. S.; piano music, incl. sonata and "*Elegiac Blues*," etc.; wrote book, "*Music Ho!*" subtitled "A study of music in decline," in which post-war productions are consid. as showing falling off of originality and strength.

Lamberti (läm-bĕr'-tē), **Gius.**, Cuneo, Italy, 1820 (?)—Turin, 1894; dram. composer.

Lam'beth, **H. A.**, b. Hardway, near Gosport, 1822; organist; d. Glasgow, 1895.

Lambillotte (län-bĭ-yôt), **Père Louis**, Charleroi, Hainault, 1796—Vaugirard, 1855; organist, conductor and composer.

Lambrino (läm-brē'-nō), **Télémaque**, Odessa, Oct. 27, 1878 (of Greek parents)—Leipzig, Feb. 25, 1930; pianist; studied music at the Royal Akad. der Tonkunst, Munich, and with Teresa Carreño; from 1900 lived in Leipzig, from 1908 teacher at the Cons.

Lamond', (1) **Frederic**, b. Glasgow, Jan. 28, 1868; eminent pianist (pupil of his bro. (2) **David**); 1882 at Raff Cons., Frankfort; later with von Bülow and Liszt; début, Berlin, 1885; toured Europe; after 1902, America; c. symph., overture "*Aus dem schottischen Hochlande*," etc.

Lamont', **Forrest**, Springfield, Mass., 1880—Chicago, Dec. 17, 1937; tenor; studied in U. S. and Europe; op. début, Rome; toured Italy, West Indies and South America; after 1917 sang for several years with Chicago Op. Co., also with Cincinnati and Phila. Operas.

Lamoureux (läm-oo-rŭ'), **Chas.**, Bordeaux, Sept. 28, 1834—Paris, Dec. 21, 1899; eminent conductor; pupil of Girard, Paris Cons.; later with Tolbecque, Leborne and Chauvet; co-founder of a soc. for chamber-mus.; 1872, organist "Société de musique sacrée;" 1876, assist.-cond. Paris Opéra; 1878, first cond.;

1872–78, also assist.-cond. the Cons. Concerts; resigned from the Opéra, 1881, and est. the celebrated "Concerts Lamoureux" (Nouveaux Concerts).

Lampadius (läm-pä'-dǐ-oos), **Wm. Ad.,** 1812—Leipzig, 1892; writer.

Lamperti (läm-pěr'-tē), (1) **Fran.,** Savona, Italy, March 11, 1813—Como, May 1, 1892; eminent singing-teacher; pupil of Milan Cons. and teacher there, 1850–76; pub. treatises. (2) **Giovanni Battista,** Italy, 1839—Berlin, March 19, 1910. Famous singing master; wrote *The Technic of Bel Canto,* 1905.

Lampugnani (läm-poon-yä'-nē), **Giov. Bat.,** Milan, 1706—ca. 1780; dram. composer.

Land (länt), **Dr. Jan Pieter Nicolaas,** Delft, 1834—Arnhem, 1897; professor; pub. important results of research in Arabian and Javanese mus., etc.

Landi (län'-dē), (1) **Stefano,** Rome, ca. 1590—ca. 1655; conductor, composer and singer. (2) **Camilla,** b. Geneva 1866; mezzo-soprano, daughter and pupil of singers; début 1884 Florence; 1886–92 in Paris, then in London where her mother taught; toured widely and returned to Geneva.

Landino (län-dē'-nō), **Fran.** (called **Francesco Cieco** "the blind," or **Degli Organi**), Florence, ca. 1325—1397; notable organist and composer.

Landolfi (län-dôl'-fē) (or **Landul'-phus**), (1) **Carlo Fdo.,** l. Milan, 1750–60; maker of 'cellos, etc. (2) **Pietro,** instr.-maker at Milan ca. 1760, probably son or bro. of above.

Landormy (län-dôr-mē), **Paul Charles René,** b. Issy, near Paris, Jan. 3, 1869; studied singing with Sbriglia and Plançon; published philosophical works, biography of Brahms, etc.

Landowska (län-dôf'-skä), **Wanda,** b. Warsaw, July 5, 1877; harpsichordist and pianist; studied Warsaw Cons., and with Michalowski, Moszkowski and Urban; début at 11 in native city; teacher of piano, Schola Cantorum, Paris, 1900–13; of harpsichord (newly estab. class) at Berlin Hochsch., 1913–19; founded her own school of music at St. Leu-La-Forêt, France, 1927; has internat'l. reputation as performer of cembalo music, 17th and 18th cent. in particular; wrote "*Bach et ses Inter-*

prètes," "*La Musique Ancienne,*" "*Les Allemandes et la Musique Française au XVIII Siècle*"; toured Europe and America as recitalist and orch. soloist; Amer. début with Phila. Orch., 1923.

Lang (läng), (1) (**Lang-Köstlin**), **Josephine,** Munich, 1815—Tübingen, 1880; composer. (2) **Benj. Johnson,** Salem, Mass., Dec. 28, 1837—Boston, April 3, 1909; prominent pf.-teacher and conductor, pupil of his father and of F. G. Hill at Boston, Jaell and Satter, later in Berlin, and with Liszt; organist various churches, Boston; for over 25 years organist Handel and Haydn Soc. and cond., 1895; also cond. the Apollo Club and the Cecilia, etc.; c. an oratorio "*David*"; symphs., etc. (3) **Margaret Ruthven,** b. Boston, Nov. 27, 1867; daughter and pupil of above; studied also with Schmidt of Boston, Drechsler and Abel (vln.) and Gluth (comp.) in Munich; pub. many songs and pf.-pcs.

Langbecker (läng'-běk-ěr), **Emanuel Chr. Gl.,** Berlin, 1792—1843; writer.

Lange (läng'-ě), (1) **Otto,** Graudenz, 1815—Cassel, 1879; editor and writer. (2) **Gustav,** Schwerstedt, near Erfurt, 1830—Wernigerode, 1889; pianist and composer. (3) **Samuel de,** Rotterdam, Feb. 22, 1840—Stuttgart, July 7, 1911; son and pupil of the organist, (4) **Samuel de L.** (1811—1884); later studied with Winterberger, Vienna, and Damcke and Mikuli, Lemberg; 1863 organist and teacher Rotterdam Mus. Sch.; often touring Europe; 1876 teacher Cologne Cons., also cond.; 1885–93, cond. at The Hague, later teacher and vice-dir. Stuttgart Cons., and 1895, dir.; c. oratorio "*Moses,*" 8 organ sonatas, 3 symph., etc. (5) **Daniel de,** Rotterdam, July 11, 1841—Point Loma, Cal., Jan. 31, 1918; bro. of above; studied with Ganz and Servais ('cello), Verhulst and Damcke (comp.), at Lemberg Cons. 1860–63, then studied pf. with Mme. Dubois at Paris; chiefly self-taught as organist; 1895—1913, dir. Amsterdam Cons., and cond.; also critic; c. opera "*De Val Van Kuilenburg*"; two symphs.; overture, "*Willem van Holland,*" etc. (6) **Aloysia.** Vide WEBER. (7) **Hieronymus Gregor,** Havelberg, Brandenburg—Breslau, 1587; in 1574 cantor at Frankfort-am-Oder; comp. of Latin motets and songs. (8) **Hans,** b. Constantinople, Feb. 14, 1884; pupil of Brassin and Wondra; then of Prague Cons.; début Berlin, 1903; 1910, concertm., Frankfort Op.; also led a string quartet there; came to America and played in the N. Y. Philh. Orch., after 1924 serving as concertm. and asst. cond.; his duties in the latter capacity were extended until in 1934–36, under Toscanini's régime, he led annually a number of concerts of the organisation, showing high musicianship and presenting a number of new works; in 1936 he presented in N. Y. the 1st of a series of historical concerts by the N. Y. Philh. Chamber Orch., composed of solo players in the larger ensemble; and he has also appeared as guest cond. in several other American cities; 1936–37, assoc. cond., Chicago Symph. Orchestra.

Lange-Müller (läng'-ĕ-mĭl-lĕr), **Peter Erasmus,** Frederiksberg, Dec. 1, 1850—Feb. 25, 1926; Danish composer; pupil of Copenhagen Cons.; c. operas *"Tove"* (to his own libretto 1878); *"The Spanish Students,"* (1883); *"Frau Jeanna"* (1891) and *"Vikingeblod"* (Copenhagen and Stockholm, 1900); symph. *"Autumn"*; incid. music to *"Fulvia"* and *"Es war einmal"*; orch. suite *"Alhambra"* and songs of decidedly national feeling.

Langer (läng'-ĕr), (1) **Hn.,** Höckendorf, near Tharandt, Saxony, 1819—Dresden, 1889; organist, conductor and teacher. (2) **Fd.,** Leimen, near Heidelberg, Jan. 21, 1839—Kirneck, Aug. 25, 1905; 'cellist at Mannheim ct.-Th., and later 2nd cond.; prod. there 5 succ. operas. (3) **Victor,** Pesth, Oct. 14, 1842—March 19, 1902; pupil R. Volkmann, and Leipzig Cons.; teacher, th.-cond. and editor; pub. under the name of **"Aladar Tisza"** very pop. songs, etc.

Langert (läng'-ĕrt), (**Jn.**) **Aug.** (**Ad.**), Coburg, Nov. 26, 1836—Dec. 28, 1920; dram. composer; th.-cond. Coburg; 1872, teacher of comp. Geneva Cons.; 1873, ct.-cond., Gotha, reappointed 1893; prod. 7 operas.

Langhans (läng'-häns), (**Fr.**) **Wm.,** Hamburg, 1832—Berlin, 1892; writer.

Langlé (läṅ'-lä), **Honoré Fran. M.,**

Monaco, 1741—Villiers-le-Bel, near Paris, 1807; mus.-dir., theorist and composer.

Lanière (Lanier or Lanieri) (län-yăr, län-ēr', or län-ĭ-ā'-rē), (1) **Nicholas,** London, Sept. 10, 1588—London, Feb., 1666; son of (2) **Jos.,** and nephew of (3) **Nicholas.** (2) and (3) came to England, were mus. to Queen Elizabeth. (1) was ct.-musician to Charles I; a prolific composer and singer who introduced the recitative style into England.

Lanner (län'-nĕr), (1) **Jos.** (**Fz. K.**), Oberdöbling, near Vienna, 1801—1843; violinist, composer and conductor. (2) **Aug.** (**Jos.**), 1834—1855; son of above; violinist, conductor and dance-composer of prominence.

Lanzetti (län-tsĕt'-tē), **Salvatore,** Naples, ca. 1710—Turin, ca. 1780; one of the earliest 'cello virtuosi; c. 'cello sonatas and a method.

Lapar'ra, Raoul, b. Bordeaux, France, May 13, 1876; composer; studied Paris Cons. with Godard, Lavignac, Diémer, Gédalge, Massenet and Fauré; Prix de Rome, 1903; Chevalier, Legion of Honour, 1923; Inspector of Musical Instruction for French govt., after 1930; c. (operas) *"La Habanera"* (Paris Op.-Comique, 1908; Boston, 1910; Met. Op., 1924); *"La Jota"* (Op.-Comique, 1911); *"Le Joueur de Viole"* (do., 1925); *"Las Toreras"* (Lille, 1929); *"Amphitryon,"* *"L'Aventure Pittoresque"*; also chamber and piano works, latter incl. two series for children *"Iberian Scenes"* and *"Book of the Dawn"*; wrote *"La Musique Populaire en Espagne."*

Lapicida (lä-pĭ-chē'-dä), **Erasmus,** 16th cent. composer.

Laporte (lä-pôrt), **Jos. de,** Befort, 1713—Paris, 1779; Jesuit abbé; writer.

Lara (lä'-rä), **Isidore de** (rightly **Cohen**), London, Aug. 9, 1858—Paris, Sept. 2, 1935; of English father and Portuguese mother; studied at Milan Cons.; took 1st prize for comp. at age of 17; c. operas: *"La Luce dell' Asia,"* founded on Sir Edwin Arnold's poem (London, 1892); *"Amy Robsart"* (1893); *"Moina"* (1897); *"Messaline,"* Monte Carlo (1899), very successful; *"Le Réveil de Bouddha"* (1904), *"Sangà"* (1906), *"Solea"* (1907), *"Les Trois Masques"* (1912), etc.

Laroche (lä-rôsh), **Hermann,** St. Petersburg, May 25, 1845—Oct. 18, 1904; critic and comp; pupil of the Cons. and of Tchaikovsky, whose friend and biographer he was; prof. at Moscow, later at St. Petersburg Cons.; c. overture, etc.

La Rue (lä-rü), **Pierre de** (Latinised **Petrus Platensis;** also called **Perisone, Pierchon, Pierson, Pierzon,** or **Pierazon de la Ruellien**), eminent 16th cent. Netherland contrapuntist and composer; fellow-pupil (with Desprès) of Okeghem; ct.-singer and favourite of Margaret of Austria.

Laruette (lä-rü-ĕt), **J. L.,** Toulouse, 1731—1792; composer.

Lashan′ska, Hulda, b. New York; soprano; studied with Frieda Ashforth and Mme. Sembrich; début as soloist with N. Y. Symph.; has made concert tours and fest. appearances.

Lassale (lăs-săl), **Jean,** Lyons, France, Dec. 14, 1847—Paris, Sept. 7, 1909; studied Paris Cons.; notable barytone; début, Brussels, 1871; sang at Paris Opéra, in America, etc.; after 1903, prof. Paris Cons.

Lassen (läs′-sĕn), **Eduard,** Copenhagen, April 13, 1830—Weimar, Jan. 15, 1904; at 2 was taken to Brussels and at 12 studied in the Cons. there; won first pf.-prize, 1844; harm. prize, 1847; 2nd prize in comp. and 1851 Prix de Rome; travelled in Germany and Italy and made a long stay in Rome; 1858, ct.-mus.-dir. at Weimar; Liszt procured the prod. of his opera "*Landgraf Ludwig's Brautfahrt*" (Weimar, 1857); 1861-95, Liszt's successor as ct.-cond. at Weimar; then pensioned; c. operas "*Frauenlob*" (Weimar, 1860); "*Le Captif*" (Brussels, 1865; in German, Weimar, 1868); 11 characteristic orch.-pcs.; Bible-scenes with orch.; cantatas, 2 symphs., pop. songs, etc.

Lasserre (lăs-sắr), **Jules,** Tarbes, July 29, 1838—Feb. 19, 1906; pupil Paris Cons.; took 1st and 2nd prize as 'cellist; lived for some time in Madrid and, after 1869, in London; composer.

Lasso (läs′-sō), (1) **Orlando di** (rightly **Roland de Lattre,** Lat. **Orlan′dus Las′sus**), Mons (Hainault), 1530—Munich, June 14, 1594; most eminent of Netherland and (except Palestrina) of 16th cent. composers and conductors. Haberl claims that he was born in 1532, in spite of Vinchant's contemporary statement that 1520 was the date, and Quichelberg's that 1530 was the date. His family seems to have used the name Lassus for some time before him; he signed his own name variously. C. 2,500 compositions, still beautiful to modern ears, as his melodic suavity was not smothered by the erudition which gave him even among contemporaries the name "Prince of Music." Befriended by various noblemen and given much Italian travel, he became 1541-48 cond. at S. Giovanni in Laterano at Rome; then visited Mons and ca. 1554, England, settling in Antwerp the same year; 1557 joined on invitation the ct.-chapel of Albert V., Duke of Bavaria; from 1562 he was cond. there, full of honours. His complete works (in course of pub. by Breitkopf & Härtel) include his famous "*Psalmi Davidis poenitentiales,*" masses, psalms, and secular compositions of occasionally humorous vein. Biogr. by Dehn (1837), Bäumkehr (1878), and Sandberger. (2) **Fd. di,** d. Munich, Aug. 27, 1609, eldest son of above; ct.-cond. (3) **Rudolf di,** d. Munich, 1625; second son of (1); organist and composer (4) **Fd. di,** d. 1636; son of (2); conductor and composer.

Lászl′ó (läsh′-lō), **Alexander,** b. Budapest, Nov. 22, 1895; composer; studied at Acad., in native city; best known as inventor of a system of music synchronized with color.

Latilla (lä-tïl′-lä), **Gaetano,** Bari, Naples, 1711—Naples, 1791; conductor, teacher and composer.

La Tombelle. Vide TOMBELLE.

Latrobe, (1) Rev. **Chr. I.,** Fulnes, Leeds, 1758—Fairfield, near Liverpool, 1836; composer. (2) **J. Antes,** London, 1799—Gloucester, 1878; son of above; organist and composer.

Lattre, de. Vide LASSO.

Lattuada (lät-ōō-ä′-dä), **Felice,** b. Casella di Morimondo, Italy, Feb. 5, 1882; composer; grad. in comp. of Verdi Cons., Milan; c. (operas) "*Sandha,*" (Genoa, 1921); "*La Tempesta,*" based on Shakespeare (Dal Verme, Milan, 1922); "*Le Preziose Ridicole,*" after Molière (La Scala, 1929; Met. Op., 1930); "*Don Giovanni*" (Naples, 1929); also (orch.)

Sinfonia Romantica, and chamber music, songs; ed. *"Raccolta di canzoni popolari."*

Laub (lowp), **Fd.**, Prague, 1832—Gries, Tyrol, 1875; vln.-virtuoso; teacher and composer.

Laubenthal (lä'-bĕn-täl), **Rudolf**; b. Düsseldorf; tenor; sang with Berlin Op. at Covent Garden, and for nearly a decade until 1932 with Met. Op., N. Y., in Wagnerian rôles, etc.

Laurencie, see LA LAURENCIE.

Laurencin (low'-rĕn-sēn), **Graf Fd. P.**, Kremsier, Moravia, 1819—Vienna, 1890; writer.

Lauri-Volpi (lä-ōō-rē-vôl'-pē), **Giacomo** (rightly **Volpi**), b. Lanuvio, Italy, Dec. 12, 1892; tenor; early studied law; served in the war, winning 3 decorations; début as singer at the Costanzi, Rome, 1920, as Des Grieux; has sung in leading theatres of Europe and was mem. of Met. Op. Co. for several years after 1925.

Lauska (lä-oos'-kä), **Fz. (Seraphinus Ignatius)**, Brünn, Moravia, 1764—Berlin, 1825; teacher, composer.

Lauterbach (low'-tĕr-bäkh), **Jn. Chr.**, Culmbach, Bavaria, July 24, 1832—Dresden, March 28, 1918; pupil Würzburg Mus. Sch., and of Fétis and de Bériot at Brussels (1850), won gold medal for vln.-playing, 1851; 1853 Munich Cons.; 1860–77 ~resden Cons.; 1889, pensioned; ~~~poser.

Lavall~e~ (lä-väl-lä), **Calixa**, Verchères, Canaɑ~~a~, 1842—Boston, Mass., 1891; concert-~~pianist; toured U. S., giving frequent~~ concerts of American composers' wo.~~rks, 1886–87; c. 2 operas, an oratorio,~~ a symph., etc.

Lavigna (lä-vēn~~.'-yä), V.~; Naples, 1777 —Milan, ca. 18.37; teacher and dram. composer.

Lavignac (lä-vēn-yăk), **Albert, Paris, Jan. 21, 1846—May 28, 1916; pupil of the Cons., and from 1882 prof. there; author of many important works; ed. notable *"Encyclopédie de Musique,"* subsidized by French Gov't. (1903); new edition by Lionel de la Laurencie, 1929; pub. a *"Cours complet théorique et pratique de dictée musicale,"* 1882, which led to the general adoption in mus. schs. of courses in mus. dictation; also *"La musique et les musiciens."*

Lavigne (lä-vēn), (1) **Jacques Émile**, Pau, 1782—1855; tenor. (2) **A. Jos.,**

Besançon, France, March 23, 1816—Manchester, Aug. 1, 1886; oboist; pupil Paris Cons.; from 1841 in Drury Lane Promenade Concerts, later in Halle's Manchester orch.; he partially adapted Böhm's system to the oboe.

Lavoix (lä-vwä), **H. M. Fran.**, Paris, 1846—1897; writer and composer.

Lawes (lôz), (1) **Wm.**, Salisbury, Wiltshire, 1582—killed at the siege of Chester, 1645; composer. (2) **H.**, Dinton, near Salisbury, Dec., 1595—London, Oct. 21, 1662; bro. of above; one of the most original and important of song-writers, forestalling in his principles those of Franz, etc., in that he made his music respect the poetry he was setting; Milton, Herrick and others accordingly praised him. Pupil of Coperario. 1625, Epistler and Gentleman, Chapel Royal; on Charles I's execution he lost his places but re-found them in the Restoration in 1660; buried in Cloisters of Westminster Abbey; c. the music to Milton's *"Comus,"* etc.

Law'rence, Marjorie, b. Melbourne, Australia; dram. soprano; studied in Paris; début at Monte Carlo, 1932, as "Elisabeth"; sang heroic rôles with Paris Op., incl. "Brünnhilde", "La Juive", "Salome" and "Aïda"; début, Met. Op., N. Y., 1935–36.

Layol(l)e (or dell'**Aiole, Ajolla**) (li-yôl', or ä-yō'-lĕ), **Fran.**, Florentine composer 16th cent.

Lazar (lä'-zär), **Filip**, b. Craiova, 1894; composer of orch., piano and vocal music; played his pf.-concerto with Boston Symph., 1936.

Lázaro (lä'-thär-ö), **Hipólito**; b. in Catalonia; tenor; noted for his virile timbre of voice; sang at Teatro Real, Madrid; at Barcelona, La Scala and at Met. Op. House, N. Y.

Laz'arus, (1) **H.**, London, 1815—1895; clarinettist. (2) **Gustav**, Cologne, 1861—Berlin, 1920; pianist, composer.

Lazzari (läd-zä'-rē), (1) **Silvio,** b. Bozen, Jan. 1, 1858; studied with César Franck, Paris Cons.; composer of operas *"La Lépreuse"* (Op. Com., Paris, 1912), *"Moelenis,"* lyric drama *"Armor"* (prelude at Lamoureux concerts, 1895—prod. at opera Lyons 1903, revived 1912); *"Le Sauteriot"* (Chicago, 1917); *"La Tour de Feu"* (Paris Op., 1928,) orch., chamber music, songs, etc. (2) **Carolina,**

b. Milford, Mass., contralto; with Chicago Op., 1918; (3) **Virgilio, b.** Assisi, Italy; bass; pupil of Cotogni; sang with Chicago Op. after 1918; Met. Op., after 1934; also widely in Europe.

Le Bé (lŭ-bā), **Guil.,** 16th cent. French type-founder.

Le Beau (lŭ-bō), **Louise Adolpha,** Rastatt, Baden, April 25, 1850—Baden-Baden, July 2, 1927; concert-pianist; pupil of Kalliwoda, Frau Schumann, Sachs, Rheinberger and Fr. Lachner; c. choral works, piano works, songs, etc.; pub. memoirs.

Lebègue (lŭ-bĕg), **Nicolas A.,** Laon, 1630—Paris, 1702; ct.-organist and composer.

Lebert (lā'-bĕrt) (rightly **Levy**), **Siegmund,** Ludwigsburg, near Stuttgart, 1822—Stuttgart, 1884; teacher, writer and composer; co-founder of Stuttgart Cons. (1856–57).

Lebeuf (lŭ-bŭf), Abbé **Jean,** Auxerre, 1687—1760; writer.

Leblanc (lŭ-bläṅ), **Georgette,** b. Rouen; pupil of Bax; début Op. Com., Paris, 1893, in *"L'Attaque de Moulin."* 1895, Th. de la Monnaie, Brussels; then gave song recitals in costume with much effect.

Leborne (lŭ-bôrn), (1) **Aimé Ambroise Simon,** Brussels, 1797—Paris, 1866; teacher and writer. (2) (or **Le Borne**), **Fd.,** Charleroi, March 10, 1862—Paris, February, 1929; pupil of Massenet, Saint-Saëns, and Franck, Paris Cons.; lived in Paris as critic; c. operas; a symph. légende; symphs., etc.

Lebouc (lŭ-book), **Chas. Jos.,** Besançon, 1822—Hyères, 1893; 'cello-virtuoso.

Lebrun (lŭ-broon'), (1) **L. Aug.,** Mannheim, 1746—Berlin, 1790; greatest oboist of the 18th cent.; composer. (2) (née **Danzi**), **Franciska,** Mannheim, 1756—Berlin, 1791; wife of above; soprano. Their two daughters, (3) **Sophie** and (4) **Rosine,** were distinguished singers.

Lebrun (lŭ-brŭṅ), (1) **Jean,** Lyons, 1759—suicide, Paris, 1809; horn-virtuoso. (2) **Louis Sébastien,** Paris, 1764—1829; tenor and teacher. (3) **Paul H. Jos.,** Ghent, April 21, 1861—Louvain, Nov. 4, 1920; pupil of the Ghent Cons.; 1891 won the Prix de Rome for composition and the Belgian Academie 1st prize for a symphony; 1889, prof. of theory at

Ghent Cons., after 1913 dir. of a mus. school in Louvain.

Lechner (lĕkh'-nĕr), **Ld.,** ca. 1550, Etschthal, Switzerland (?)—Stuttgart, 1606; ct.-cond. and composer.

Léclair (lā-klăr), **J. M.,** Lyons, 1697—assassinated, Paris, 1764; violinist; c. operas, 48 notable vln.-sonatas, etc.; his wife, a singer, engraved his compositions.

Lecocq (lŭ-kôk), **(Alex.) Chas.,** Paris, June 3, 1832—Oct. 24, 1918; studied at the Cons., won 1st prize for harm., and 2d prize for fugue; his first work, *"Le Docteur Miracle,"* in conjunction with Bizet (prod., 1857), won a prize offered by Offenbach for opera buffa; smaller succ. culminated in *"Fleur de Thé"* (1868); followed by the sensational succ. *"La Fille de Mme. Angot"* (Brussels, 1872; Paris, 1873), which ran uninterruptedly over a year; its succ. was equalled by *"Giroflé-Girofla"* (1874); 1894, chev. of the Legion of Honour; prod. over 40 operas-bouffes, comic operas and operettas, written with scholarship and brilliant instrumentation; sacred and other songs, etc.

Le Couppey (lŭ koop'-pĕ'), **Félix,** Paris, April 14, 1811—July 5, 1887; prof., pf.-teacher and composer.

Ledebur (lā'-dĕ-boor), **K. Freiherr von,** Schildesche, near Bielefeld, April 20, 1806—Stolp, Oct. 25, 1872; Prussian cavalry officer and lexicographer.

Leduc (lŭ-dük), **Alphonse,** Nantes, 1804—Paris, 1868; pianist, bassoonist and composer.

Lee (lā), **Louis,** Hamburg, Oct. 19, 1819—Lübeck, Aug. 26, 1896; 'cellist; pupil of J. N. Prell; at 12 gave concerts; 'cellist in the Hamburg Th.; lived several years in Paris; organist, chamber-mus. soirées, Hamburg; until 1884, teacher in the Cons. and 1st 'cello; c. symphonies, overtures, etc.

Lefébure-Wély (lŭ-fā-bür-vā-lē), **L. Jas. Alfred,** Paris, 1817—1869; noted organist; c. opera, masses, etc.

Lefèbvre (lŭ-fĕv'-r), **Chas. Édouard,** Paris, June 19, 1843—Aix-les-Bains, Sept. 8, 1917; pupil of Ambr. Thomas, Paris Cons.; 1870, Grand prix de Rome; 1873, after touring the Orient settled in Paris; after 1895, theory prof., Paris Cons.; c. succ. opera, *"Djelma"* (1894); *"Zaïre"* (1887), etc.

Lefèvre (lŭ-fĕv′-r), **J. X.**, Lausanne, 1763—Paris, 1829; clarinettist, composer and professor.

Le Flem (lŭ flŭm′), **Paul**, b. Lèzardieux (Côtes du Nord), France, March 18, 1881; composer; pupil of d'Indy; studied at Paris Cons. and Schola Cantorum; winner Laserre Prize, 1928; Chevalier, Legion of Honour; c. (lyric fable) "*Aucassin et Nicolette*"; (orch.) 1st symphony; "*La Voix du Large*" (symph. sketch); "*Pour les Morts*," "*Danse*" and "*Invocation*," comprising symph. in form of triptych; piano quintet; vln. sonata, fantasie for piano and orch., works for piano, for chorus, and songs.

Legin′ska, **Ethel** (rightly **Liggins**), b. Hull, England, April 13, 1890; composer, pianist, conductor; studied Frankfort Cons. and with Leschetizky; toured Europe and U. S. as pianist, N. Y. début, 1913; cond. Boston Philh., Chicago Women's Symph., and similar orch. in Boston, also operatic prod. of Suppé's "*Boccaccio*"; c. orchestral and other works; also one-act opera "*Gale*," prod. by Chicago Op. 1935; m. Emerson Whithorne, composer; separated.

Legouix (lŭ-gwēx), **Isidore Éd.**, Paris, April 1, 1834—Boulogne, Sept., 1916; pupil of Reber and Thomas at the Cons.; prod. 4 operas, etc.

Legrenzi (lā-grĕn′-tsē), **Giov.**, Clusone, near Bergamo, 1626—Venice, 1690; organist, conductor and dram. composer.

Lehár (lĕ-här′), **Franz**, b. Komorn, Hungary, April 30, 1870; composer of the world sweeping operetta "*Die Lustige Witwe*" (Vienna, 1905, in New York and London as "*The Merry Widow*"); lives in Vienna; c. also operas "*Kukuska*," Leipzig, 1896, revised as "*Tatjana*," Brünn, 1905; operettas "*Wiener Frauen*" (Vienna, 1902; revised as "*Der Schlüssel zum Paradiese*," Leipzig, 1906); "*Mitislav*" (Vienna, 1907); "*Edelweiss und Rosenstock*" (1907); "*Peter and Paul reisen ins Schlaraffenland*" (Vienna, 1906); "*Der Mann mit den drei Frauen*" (1908); "*Das Fürstenkind*," "*Der Graf von Luxemburg*," "*Zigeunerliebe*," "*Die blaue Mazur*," "*Frasquita*," "*Paganini*," "*Friederike*," "*Zarevitch*," "*Das Land des Lächelns*" (revision of "*Die blaue Jacke*"), and the grand opera, "*Giuditta*" (Vienna, 1934), etc.

Lehmann (lā′-män), (1) **T. Marie**, (I.) prima donna at Cassel under Spohr; (2) **Lilli**, Würzburg, Nov. 24, 1842—Berlin, May 16, 1929; daughter and pupil of above; eminent soprano; début at Prague as "First Boy" in "*Die Zauberflöte*"; 1868, at Danzig, and Leipzig, 1870; in the same year obtained a life-engagement at the Royal Opera, Berlin, with the title (1876) of Imp. Chamber-singer; she sang "*Woglinde*," "*Helmwige*" and the "*Bird*," at their first performance, 1876; 1885, broke her contract, and sang in the U. S.; was as a result banned from German stages for several seasons but restored to favor by Emperor; sang at Met. Op. Co., N. Y., 1885–89 and 1891–92, revealing highest dram. and technical powers in such rôles as "Isolde" and even some Italian parts; she lived in Berlin after 1892, and also took active share in Salzburg Fests., devoting much of her time to teaching, but continuing to appear in opera occasionally as late as 1910; m. Paul Kalisch, tenor. (3) **Marie** (II.), Hamburg, May 15, 1851— Berlin, Dec. 9, 1931; daughter and pupil of (1); at 16 sang in Leipzig City Th.; for many years, till 1897, Vienna ct.-opera; lived in Berlin. (4) **Liza** (Mrs. Herbert Bedford), London, July 11, 1862—Sept. 19, 1918; concert-soprano; pupil of Randegger and Raunkilde at Rome (voice) and of Freudenberg (Wiesbaden), and Hamish MacCunn (comp.); début, Nov. 23, 1885, at a Monday Pop. Concert; 1887, sang at the Norwich Festival; 1894, m. and retired; c. many songs incl. the very pop. song-cycle from Omar Khayyám, "*In a Persian Garden*," also "*In Memoriam*," etc. (5) **Lotte**, b. Perleberg, Germany, July 2, 1885; soprano; studied Berlin R. Acad. of Music and with Mathilde Mallinger; début, Hamburg, 1910; won high rank as lyric-dram. soprano, being heard in Dresden, Berlin, and as a regular mem. of the Vienna State Op., where she has enjoyed much popularity for her perfs. in Wagner, Strauss and other works; created rôle of the composer in "*Ariadne auf Naxos*"; heard at Salzburg Fest.,

Covent Garden, Chicago Op., (début as "Sieglinde," 1930), and after 1934 at Met. Op., N. Y.; also holds distinguished place as Lieder singer; awarded decoration of Officer Public Instruction, France; Swedish Medal of Arts and Sciences.

Leibrock (līp'-rŏk), **Jos. Ad.**, Brunswick, 1808—Berlin, 1886; writer and composer.

Leichtentritt (līkh'-tĕn-trĭt), **Hugo,** b. Pleschen, Posen, Jan. 1, 1874; at 15 taken to America, where he studied with J. K. Paine, Boston, then at the Royal Hochschule, Berlin; 1901, Ph. D.; wrote theoretical and historical works and c. chamber music and songs; 1902–24, taught Klindworth-Scharwenka Cons., Berlin; after 1933, at Harvard Univ., dir. of the seminar in musical science.

Leider (lī'-dĕr), **Frida**, b. Berlin, April 18, 1888; soprano; studied in Berlin and Milan; sang in many opera houses of her native country, incl. Rostock, Aachen and Hamburg; after 1924 with the Berlin State Op.; beginning 1928 at Bayreuth Fest. ("Brünnhilde," "Kundry"); also at Covent Garden; Chicago Civic Op., 1930; thereafter for several seasons at Met. Op., N. Y., in Wagnerian rôles.

Leighton (lā'-tŭn), **Sir Wm.**, Engl. composer, 1641.

Leite (lī'-tĕ), Antonio da Silva, 1759—1833; cond. Oporto Cath., and composer.

Leitert (lī'-tĕrt), **Jn. G.**, Dresden, Sept. 29, 1852—1901; pianist; pupil of Kragen and Reichel (pf.) and Rischbieter (harm.); début Dresden, 1865; studied with Liszt; 1879–81 teacher Horak Mus. Sch., Vienna; composer.

Le Jeune (lŭ-zhŭn), **Claudin,** Valenciennes, 1528—1602; highly original French contrapuntist and composer.

Lekeu (lŭ-kŭ), **Guillaume,** Heusy-les-Verviers, Jan. 20, 1870—Angers, Jan. 21, 1894; composer. His death at 24 left many unfinished works, but enough were complete to assure his fame, among them 3 *études symphoniques* (1889, 1890); adagio for quatuor and orch. (1891), *epithalame*, for string quintet, organ and 3 trombones; introduction and adagio for orch. with tuba solo; *fantaisie symphonique sur deux airs populaires angévins*, 1892; (unfin.) comedy, *"Barberine"*; cantata, *"Andromède"*

(2nd Prix de Rome at Brussels, 1891); chamber music, including sonata for piano and 'cello, finished by V. d'Indy, 1910, and a quatuor finished by the same; sonata for piano and violin (ded. to and played by Ysaye), etc.

Le Maistre (lŭ-mĕtr) (or **Le Maître**), **Mattheus,** d. 1577; Netherland contrapuntist; ct.-conductor and composer.

Lemare (lĕ-măr'), **Edwin Henry,** Ventnor, Isle of Wight, Sept. 9, 1865—March 19, 1929; organist; pupil R. A. M. London, with Goss Scholarship, then made an associate, later a fellow; 1884 fellow Royal College of Organists; occupied various church positions, and gave recitals; 1902–04, organist at Carnegie Hall, Pittsburgh, Pa.; 1905, again in London; c. symph., a pastorale and much organ music.

Lemmens (lĕm'-mĕns), **Nicolas Jacques,** Zoerle-Parwys, Belgium, 1823—Castle Linterport, near Malines, 1881; organist, professor and composer.

Lemoine (lŭm-wăn), (1) **Ant. Marcel,** Paris, 1763—1817; publisher, ct.-conductor and writer. (2) **H.,** Paris, 1786—1854; son of above and his successor in business; writer. (3) **Aimé,** b. 1795 (?); pub. "Méthode du Méloplaste"; teacher.

Lemoyne (lŭm-wăn) (rightly **Moyne**) (mwăn), **J. Bap.,** Eymet, Périgord, 1751—Paris, 1796; conductor and dram. composer.

Lenaerts (lŭ-nărts), **Constant,** b. Antwerp, March 9, 1852; pupil of Benoît; at 18 dir. Flemish National Th.; teacher Antwerp Cons.; founder, 1914, Société Royale de l'harmonie; cond. of orch. concerts, etc.

Lendvai (lĕnd'-vī), **Erwin,** b. Budapest, June 4, 1882; composer; pupil of Koessler and Puccini; after 1901 lived in Germany, teaching at Dalcroze School, Hellerau, 1914; later prof. at Hoch Cons., Frankfort; 1919 at Klindworth-Scharwenka Cons., Berlin; also in Jena; 1923, choral dir. in Hamburg-Altona; 1926 at Coblentz; and since 1929 in Stockdorf and Erfurt; c. opera, "*Elga*" (1916), a symph. and other orch. works, chamber music, choral pieces, songs, etc., in modern style; a study of his work has been written by Leichtentritt.

Lenepveu (lŭ-nŭp′-vŭ), **Chas. Fd.,** Rouen, Oct. 4, 1840—Paris, Aug. 16, 1910; studied with Servais, in 1861 won 1st prize at Caen; studied with Thomas at the Cons., 1865 took Grand prix de Rome, rt. from Rome; won a prize with opera "*Le Florentin*" (Op.-com., 1874); prod. gr. opera "*Velleda*" (Covent Garden, 1882); 1891 harm.-prof. in the Cons. and 1893 prof. of comp.; 1896, Académie des Beaux-Arts; Chev. of the Legion of Honour, and officer of pub. instruction; c. lyric drama "*Jeanne d'Arc*" (Rouen Cath., 1886); "*Hymne funèbre et triomphal*" (V. Hugo) (Rouen, 1889), etc.

Léner, Jenö, b. Szabadka, Hungary, June 24, 1871; violinist; studied with Hubay, Budapest Acad. of Music; début in that city, 1913; solo player with Budapest Philh., until 1918; founded and led after 1920 the eminent string quartet named after him, with headquarters in London; N. Y. début, 1929.

Le′normand, René, Elbeuf, Aug. 5, 1846—Paris, Dec. 5, 1932; pianist, composer; c. many songs, orch. works, chamber music and stage pieces; author, study of modern harmony.

Len′ton, J., d. after 1711; band-musician and composer, London.

Lenz (lĕnts), **Wm. von,** Russia, 1808 —St. Petersburg, Feb. 12, 1883; pianist; wrote genial and enthusiastic studies of musicians, "*Beethoven et ses trois styles*" (1852), etc., being the first so to divide B.'s art.

Leo (lā′-ō), **Leonardo,** Brindisi, 1694 —Naples, 1744; eminent pioneer in the Neapolitan Sch. and noted teacher, conductor and organist; pupil of Aless. Scarlatti, Fago, and Pitoni; ct.-organist; c. 60 operas, also religious mus., incl. a noble 8-part "*Miserere*," a cappella.

Léonard (lā-ō-när), **Hubert,** Bellaire, near Liége, April 7, 1819—Paris, May 6, 1890; eminent violinist; pub. technical studies.

Leoncavallo (lā-ŏn-kä-väl′-lō), **Ruggiero,** Naples, March 8, 1858—Montecatini near Florence, Aug. 9, 1919; noted opera composer; studied Naples Cons., and at 16 made a tour as pianist; his first opera "*Tommaso Chatterton,*" failed at first but was succ. revived at Rome, 1896; a disciple whom Wagner per-

sonally encouraged, he spent 6 years in researches, resulting in an "historic" trilogy (uncompleted) "*Crepusculum*" ("Twilight"), I. *Medici,* II. *Girolamo Savonarola,* III. *Cezare Borgia;* toured as pianist through Egypt, Greece, Turkey, etc.; lived in Paris some years and had an opera "*Songe d'une Nuit d'Été,*" privately performed, and many songs published; he prod. 2-act opera seria "*I Pagliacci*" (Milan Dal Verme Th., 1892, in Germany 1893, as "*Der Bajazzo*") of which he wrote the masterfully constructed libretto as well as the strenuous music that made it a universal succ. The first part of the trilogy, the 4-act "*I Medici,*" was not succ. (La Scala, Milan, 1893); the 4-act opera "*La Bohème*" (Venice) was a succ. but was overshadowed by that of Puccini and did not hold the repertoire; other of his works were moderate successes, notably "*Zaza*" (Milan, 1900), sung in other cities and revived at Met. Op. 1919–20 as an effective vehicle for Farrar; the Kaiser commissioned "*Roland,*" but it failed (Berlin R. Op., 1904). Other later works were "*La Jeunesse de Figaro*" (sung in America, 1906); "*Maja*" (Rome, 1910); "*Malbruck*" (operetta, do.); "*La Reginetta della Rose*" (operetta, Rome, 1912); "*I Zingari*" (London and Milan, 1912); "*La Candidata*" (operetta, Rome, 1915); "*Goffredo Mameli*" (Genoa, 1916); "*Edipo Re*" (one act, Chicago Op., 1920); and a number of other works that never saw the stage. **L.** also served as librettist for Machado and Pennachio, and his song texts were set, among others, by Tosti. He also c. a symph. poem, "*Nuit de Mai,*" ballets, choral works, and an unfinished operetta, "*La Maschera Nuda,*" orchestrated by S. Allegra and given at Naples, 1925. He visited the U. S., 1906 and 1913.

Leonhard (lā′-ōn-härt), **Julius Emil,** Lauban, 1810—Dresden, 1883; professor and composer.

Leoni (lā-ō′-nē), (1) **Leone,** cond. Vicenza Cath., 1588—1623, and composer. (2) **Carlo,** Italian composer; prod. 3-act operetta "*Per un Bacio*" (Siena, 1894), and text and music of succ. comic opera "*Urbano*" (Pienza, 1896). (3) **Franco,** b.

Milan, Oct. 24, 1865; composer; pupil of Ponchielli; for 25 years res. in London; after 1914 in Milan; c. pop. realistic one-act opera "*L'Oracolo*," a melodrama of China-town, which gave striking rôle to Scotti at Met. Op.; also opera, "*Rip Van Winkle*" (London, 1897); can-tata "*Sardanapalus*," and many other stage works and pop. songs.

Leono'va, Daria Mikhailovna, in the Russian Govt. of Twer, 1825—St. Petersburg, Feb. 9, 1896; alto; début at 18 in Glinka's "*Life for the Czar*"; sang for many years at the National Opera, and toured around the world.

Leopo'lita (or **Lvovczyk**) (l'vôf'-chĕk), **Martin**, Lemberg, ca. 1540—Cracow, 1589; from 1560 Polish court com-poser; c. masses, chorales, etc.

Ler'ner, Tina, b. Odessa, 1890; pianist; toured Europe; from 1908, toured America; m. Louis Bachner; (2) Vladimir Shavitch, conductor.

Le Roi (lür-wä), **Adrien**, 16th cent.; partner of Ballard (q. v.).

Leroux (lŭ-roo), **Xavier**, Velletri, Papal States, Oct. 11, 1863—Paris, Feb. 2, 1919; pupil of Paris Cons., took Grand Prix de Rome, 1885; c. opera "*Cléopatre*" (1890), lyric drama "*Evangeline*," a dramatic overture "*Harold*," and operas "*William Ratcliff*" and "*L'Epavo*" (not prod.); "*Astarté*" (Gr. Opéra, 1901), "*La Reine Fiammette*" (1902), "*Théodora*" (Monte Carlo, 1907); "*Le Chemineau*" (Paris Op.-Comique, 1907, also with succ. at Ravinia (Chicago)); "*Le Carilloneur*" (Op.-Comique, 1913); "*La Fille de Figaro*" (Paris, 1914); "*Les Cadeaux de Noël*" (do., 1916); "18—" (do., 1918); and the posthumous "*Nausi-thoe*" (Nice, 1920); also "*L'Ingénu*" (unpub.); and partially finished work, "*La Plus For—*" orch. by Büsser and prod. Op.-Comique. He was a prof. at the Paris Cons.

Lert, (1) **Ernst**, b. Vienna, May 12, 1883; theatre and opera director; Ph. D.; stage director, Breslau Op., 1909; Leipzig Op., 1912; Basel, 1919; Frankfort Op., 1920–23; also for a season at Met. Op., N. Y.; teacher at Curtis Inst., Phila. (2) **Richard**, b. Vienna, Sept. 19, 1885; conductor; bro. of Ernst; cond. at Düsseldorf, Darmstadt, Breslau, and (1929–32) at Berlin State Op., later res. in Los Angeles as orch. and choral cond., including Hollywood Bowl appearances.

Lesage de Richée (lŭ-săzh-dŭ-rē-shä), **Philipp Fz.**, lutenist and composer.

Leschetizky (lĕ-shĕ-tĭt'-shkĭ), **Theodor**, Lancut, Austrian Poland, June 22, 1830—Dresden, Nov. 14, 1915; emi-nent pf. teacher; son and pupil of a prominent teacher in Vienna; studied with Czerny (pf.) and Sechter (comp.); at 15 began teaching; 1842 made succ. tours; 1852 teacher in the St. Petersburg Cons.; 1878 toured; 1880 m. his former pupil Annette Essipoff, and settled as a teacher in Vienna; c. succ. opera, "*Die Erste Falte*" (Prague, 1867), piano pieces, etc.

Les'lie, (1) **H. David**, London, 1822—London, 1896; 'cellist, cond. and composer. (2) **Ernest**, pen-name of **Brown, O. B.**

Les'sel, Fz., Pulaivi, Poland, 1780—Petrikow, 1838; composer.

Less'man (W. J.), **Otto**, Rüdersdorf, near Berlin, Jan. 30, 1844—Jena, April 28, 1918; critic and composer; teacher at Stern's Cons.; then at Tausig's Acad. until 1871; organised a piano-sch. of his own; 1882 pro-prietor and ed. *Allgm. Musik-Zeitung*.

Le Sueur (lŭ-sŭr) (or **Lesueur**), **J.-Fran.**, Drucat-Plessiel, near Abbe-ville, France, Feb. 15, 1760—Paris, Oct. 6, 1837; chiefly self-taught; 1786 cond. at Notre Dame, Paris, where he drew crowds and criticism by his progammatic mus.; he pub. pamphlets defending "dramatic and descriptive" church-mus.; the oppo-sition prevailed, however, and he re-tired to the country for 4 years; 1793 he prod. succ. opera "*La Caverne*," followed by others; 1804 Napoleon raised him from distress to the post of ct.-cond.

Letz, Hans, b. Ittenheim, Alsace, March 18, 1887; violinist; studied Strasbourg Cons. and Berlin Hochsch. (with Joachim); recital début, N. Y., 1909; concertm. Thomas Orch., Chicago, 1910–12; mem. Kneisel Quartet, later org. Letz Quartet; taught Juilliard School of Music and N. Y. School of Music.

Leuckart (loik'-ärt), **F. Ernst Chp.**, founded mus. business at Breslau, 1782, bought 1856 by C. Sanders.

Leva (dĕ lā'-vä), **Enrico de**, b. Naples, Jan. 18, 1867; singing teacher, pupil of Puzone and Arienzo; c. opera "*La Camargo*," (Naples, 1898); serenade "*A Capomonte*" and popular Neapolitan canzonets.

Levadé (lŭ-vă-dā′), **Charles Gaston,** b. Paris, Jan. 3, 1869; pupil of Massenet at the Cons.; c. opera "*Les Hérétiques*" (Béziers, 1905), operetta "*L'Amour d' Héliodora*" (Paris, 1903), pantomime, suites, etc.

Levasseur (lŭ-văs-sŭr), (1) **P. Fran.,** b. Abbeville, France, 1753; 'cellist, Paris Grand Opéra; composer. (2) **J. H.,** Paris, 1765—1823; 'cellist. (3) **Rosalie,** soprano, Paris Opéra, 1766–85. (4) **Nicholas Prosper,** b. in Picardy, March 9, 1791; dram.-bass and professor; d. Paris, Dec. 7, 1871.

Lev′ey, Wm. Chas., Dublin, 1837—London, 1894; dram. composer.

Levi (lā′-vē), (1) **Hermann,** Giessen, Nov. 7, 1839—Munich, May 13, 1900; eminent conductor; pupil of V. Lachner and of Leipzig Cons.; 1859–61, mus.-dir., Saarbrücken; 1861–64, cond. German Opera at Rotterdam; 1864–72, ct.-cond. at Carlsruhe; from 1872, ct.-cond. at Munich; 1894, Gen. mus. dir. Munich; 1896, pensioned. (2) **Levi** (or Levy, Lewy). Vide LEBERT.

Levitzki (lĕ-vēt′-skē), **Mischa,** b. Krementchug, Russia, May 25, 1898; d. Avon, N. J., Jan. 2, 1941; studied N. Y., and Berlin Hochsch. under Dohnanyi; grad. with artist's diploma; début, Berlin, 1914; has toured widely in Europe, America and Orient as recitalist and with orchs. following N. Y. début, 1916; a brilliant technician; has also c. piano works.

Lewalter (lĕ-väl′-tĕr), **Johann,** b. Cassel, Jan. 24, 1862; pupil Leipzig Cons.; from 1886 music teacher and essayist; c. fugues, songs, etc.

Lewinger (lā′-vǐng-ĕr), **Max,** Sulkov, near Cracow, March 17, 1870—Dresden, Aug. 31, 1908; violinist; pupil of Cracow and Lemberg Cons.; and with Grüns Scholarship, at the Vienna Cons.; from 1892 toured; teacher at Bucharest Cons.; thence to Helsingfors as concertmaster; 1897, do. at the Gewandhaus Orch., Leipzig; 1898 Royal Court concert master in Dresden.

Lewis, Mary, b. Hot Springs, Ark., Jan. 7, 1900; soprano; sang in church choir in native state, later entered musical comedy in N. Y.; op. début as "Marguerite," Vienna Volksop., 1923; sang in Monte Carlo, London and Paris, 1924–25; concert début with State Symph. Orch., N. Y.; mem. Met. Op. Co., 1926–30, début as "Mimi"; sang "Marguerite" at Berlin Op., 1927; also appeared in recitals in U. S.; m. Michael Bohnen, bass; divorced; (2) Robert Hague.

Lewy (lā′-vē), (1) **Eduard Constantin,** Saint-Avold, Moselle, 1796—Vienna, 1846; horn-virtuoso and prof. (2) Jos. **Rodolphe,** Nancy, 1804—Oberlissnitz, near Dresden, 1881; bro. and pupil of above; horn-virtuoso. (3) **Chas.,** Lausanne, 1823—Vienna, 1883; son of (1); pianist and composer. (4) **Richard Levy,** Vienna, 1827—1883; son of (1); horn-player, singing-teacher. (5) Vide LEBERT.

Leybach (lī′-bäkh), **Ignace,** Gambsheim, Alsatia, 1817—Toulouse, 1891; pianist, teacher and composer.

L'Héritier (lā-rǐt-yā), (1) **Jean,** flourished 1519–1588; French pupil of Deprès; c. masses and songs. (2) **Antoine,** court musician to Charles V. at Toledo, 1520–1531; (3) **Isaac,** probably the same as **Jean.**

Lhévinne (lā′-vēn), (1) **Josef,** b. Moscow, Dec. 3, 1874; world famous pianist; pupil of his father (first cornet soloist in Moscow Royal Orch.), and of Chrysander; début at 8; pupil of Safonoff at the Cons.; 1885, winning highest honours; 1895 won Rubinstein prize; 1902–06 teacher at the Cons., and toured Europe; 1905, the U. S.; again, 1912; resides in N. Y. and has toured widely, giving two-piano programmes with his wife, (2) **Rosina L.;** also a noted teacher.

Liadoff (or Liadow) (l'yä′-dôf), **Anatole,** St. Petersburg, May 12, 1885—Novgorod, Aug. 28, 1914; pupil Johansen (cpt. and fugue) and Rimsky-Korsakov (form and instr.) at St. P. Cons.; 1878, prof. of harmony there; also at the Imp. Chapel; 1894, cond. Mus. Soc.; in 1908 he resigned on account of the expulsion of Rimsky-Korsakov (q.v.) and was later reinstated in the Cons.; c. scherzos for orch.; the popular symphonic poems, "*The Enchanted Lake*" and "*Kikimora*"; "*Baba-Yaga*" tone-picture (1905, Boston Symph., 1910), 8 folk-songs for orch.; suite "*To Maeterlinck*" for orch., choruses with orch.; "*The Music Box*," and other piano pieces and songs.

Liapunov (or **Liapounow**) (lē-ä'-poonôf), **Serge Michailovitch**, Jarslavi, Russia, Nov. 30, 1859—Paris, Nov. 9, 1924; pupil Klindworth and Pabst (pf.) and Hubert (comp.) Moscow Cons.; sub-dir. Imp. Choir, St. Petersburg, and a member of the Imp. Geographical Soc., which 1893 commissioned him to collect the folk-songs of Vologda, Viatna and Kostroma, which he pub. 1897; 1894, mus.-master to the Grand Duke; pub. concerto, a symph., pf.-pcs., etc.

Libon (lē'-bōn), **Felipe**, Cadiz, Aug. 17, 1775—Paris, Feb. 5, 1838; violinist and comp. for violin.

Lichey (lēkh'-ī), **Rheinhold**, b. Neumark, near Breslau, March 26, 1880; organist; pupil of Baumert and Rudnick, later at the Royal High School in Berlin; from 1907 org. Königsberg; c. organ pieces, choruses, etc.

Lichtenberg (līkh'-t'n-běrkh), **Leopold**, San Francisco, Nov. 22, 1861—Brooklyn, N. Y., May 16, 1935; vln.-virtuoso; pupil of Beaujardin; at 8 played in public; at 12 pupil of Wieniawski, and his aide on a U. S. tour; studied 6 months with Lambert in Paris, then studied again with Wieniawski 3 years; won first prize of honour at the "National concourse"; toured America and Europe; member of Boston Symph. Orch.; 1899, vln. prof. Nat. Cons., New York.

Lichtenstein (līkh'-t'n-shtīn), **K. Aug., Freiherr von**, Lahm, Franconia, 1767—Berlin, 1845; c. operas.

Lichtenthal (līkh'-t'n-täl), **Peter**, Pressburg, 1780—Milan, 1853; dram. composer and writer on mus.

Lidon (lē'-thon), **José**, Bejar, Salamanca, 1752—Madrid, Feb. 11, 1827; organist; 1808, royal chapel organist and royal cond. at Madrid; c. operas, church music, etc.

Lie (lē), (1) **Erica** (Mme. **Nissen**), Kongsvinger, near Christiania, Jan. 17, 1845—Christiania, Oct. 27, 1903; pianist, pupil of Kjerulf, and of Th. Kullak; teacher at the Kullak's Acad., toured Germany, etc.; member R. Acad., Stockholm. (2) (l'yä), **Sigurd**, May 23, 1871—Sept. 29, 1904; important Norwegian conductor and composer; pupil Leipzig Cons.; 1894 cond. in Bergen, studied

again in Berlin; cond. of vocal society in Christiania; c. symph., Marche symphonique; orch. suite, "*Oriental-isk*," cantatas, chorals and songs.

Liebe (lē'-bĕ), **Ed. L.**, Magdeburg, Nov. 26, 1819—Coire, Switz., 1900; pianist, organist and dram. composer.

Liebig (lē'-bīkh), **K.**, Schwedt, 1808—Berlin, 1872; staff oboist in a Regt.; 1843, est. Berlin "Symphoniekapelle"; 1860, R. Mus. Dir.

Liebling (lēp'-līng), (1) **Emil**, Pless, Silesia, April 12, 1851—Chicago, Jan. 20, 1914; concert-pianist; pf.-pupil of Ehrlich and Th. Kullak, Berlin; Dachs, Vienna, Liszt and Dorn; since 1867, America, and since 1872, Chicago, as reviewer and concert-pianist, teacher and writer. Co-ed. in a "*Dictionary of Terms*"; pub. pf.-pcs. and songs. (2) **G.**, b. Berlin, Jan. 22, 1865; pupil of Th., and Fr. Kullak, and Liszt (pf.), H. Urban and H. Dorn (comp.); 1880–85, teacher in Kullak's Acad.; 1881–89 toured Germany and Austria, with success; 1890, ct.-pianist to Duke of Coburg; 1908–23, res. in Munich; more recently in Los Angeles. (3) **Leonard**, b. New York, Feb. 7, 1874; pianist, editor; grad. Coll. of the City of N. Y.; pupil of Kullak and Godowsky at Berlin Hochsch.; taught piano in Berlin and N. Y. for several years; after 1899, active as critic and librettist; joined staff of *Musical Courier*, 1902; and has regularly written "Variations" column in that paper; after 1911, ed.-in-chief; music critic of N. Y. *American* until 1936; wrote plays. (4) **Estelle**, b. New York, 1886; soprano and teacher; sang opera in Europe and U. S.; faculty mem., Curtis Inst.

Lienau (lē'-now), **Robt.**, Neustadt, Holstein, Dec. 28, 1838—July 22, 1920; mus.-pub., Berlin.

Lier (văn lēr), **Jacques Van**, b. The Hague, April 24, 1875; pupil of Hartog, Giese and Eberle; 1891 first 'cellist Amsterdam Palace Orch.; 1897 Berlin Phil. Orch.; teacher at Klindworth-Scharwenka Cons. until 1915; later in The Hague; 'cellist of the Dutch Trio and the Dutch String Quartet; author of methods.

Liliencron (lē'-lī-ĕn-krōn), **Rochus, Freiherr von**, Plön, Holstein, Dec. 8, 1820—Coblenz, March 5, 1912; prof.; commissioned by the Historical

Commission of Munich to collect the mediæval German folk-songs, and pub. them.

Lillo (lĭl'-lō), **Gius.**, Galatina, Lecce, Italy, 1814—Naples, 1863; teacher and dram. composer.

Lim'bert, Frank L., b. New York, Nov. 15, 1866; at 8 taken to Germany; pupil of Hoch Cons. and of Rheinberger; 1894 Ph. D. Berlin; 1901 cond. of the Düsseldorf Singing Society, and teacher at the Cons. 1906, at Hanau; c. choral works with orch., etc.

Limnan'der de Nieuwenhove (nā'-věn-hō-vě), **Armand Marie Ghislain**, Ghent, 1814—Moignanville 1892; dram. composer.

Lincke (lĭnk'-ě), (1) **Jos.**, Trachenberg, Silesia, 1783—Vienna, 1837; 'cellist. (2) **Paul**, b. Berlin, Nov. 7, 1866; comp. of pop. operettas.

Lind (lĭnt), **Jenny**, Stockholm, Oct. 6, 1820—at her villa, Wynds Point, Malvern Wells, Nov. 2, 1887; "The Swedish Nightingale," one of the most eminent and pop. of sopranos; had a remarkably sympathetic voice of great compass (d' –e''',

remarkable purity, breath, endurance and flexibility; studied with Berg and Lindblad, at the court where she made her very succ. début, 1838, in *"Der Freischütz"*; 1841, studied with Manuel Garcia, in Paris, for nine months; 1842, sang at the Opéra, but was not engaged; 1844, studied German at Berlin, and sang with greatest succ. in Germany and Sweden; 1847, made a furore in London; 1849, she left the operatic stage, and created even greater sensations in concert; 1850–52, under the management of P. T. Barnum, she toured the U. S., earning $120,000; 1852, she m. Otto Goldschmidt in Boston; lived in Dresden; 1856, London, appearing especially with the Bach Choir which her husband cond. Her last pub. appearance was in his oratorio *"Ruth,"* Düsseldorf, 1870. Her private life was unusually serene, impeccable, and generous. Her bust is in Westminster Abbey. Biogr. by A. J. Becher (1847), Rockstro and Wilkens.

Lindblad (lĭnt'-blät) **Ad. Fr.**, Löfvingsborg, near Stockholm, 1801—1878; teacher of Jenny Lind; c. excellent Swedish songs and an opera.

Lind'egren, Johan, Ullared, Sweden, Jan. 7, 1842—Stockholm, June 8, 1908; teacher of theory and contrapuntist; from 1884 cantor at the Stockholm Storkyrka; c. and edited church music.

Linden (lĭnt'-'n), **Cornelis van der**, Dordrecht, Aug. 24, 1839—Dordrecht, May 28, 1918; prominent Dutch cond.; pupil of Kwast (pf.) and F. Böhme (theory); 1860 cond. Dordrecht; later bandm. the Nat. Guard (1875); cond. Netherland Musicians' Assoc.; c. cantatas with orch., 2 operas, etc.

Linder (lĭn'-děr), **Gf.**, Ehingen, July 22, 1842—Stuttgart, Jan. 29, 1918; pupil Stuttgart Cons.; from 1868 teacher there; 1879 professor; c. 2 operas; overture *"Aus nordischer Heldenzeit,"* etc.

Lind'ley, (1) **Robert**, Rotherham, Yorkshire, 1776—London, 1855; 'cellist. (2) **Wm.**, 1802—Manchester, 1869; son of above; 'cellist.

Lindner (lĭnt'-něr), (1) **Fr.**, Liegnitz ca. 1540—Nürnberg, 1597; composer. (2) **Adolf**, Lobenstein, 1808—Leipzig, 1867; horn-player. (3) **Ernst Otto Timotheus**, Breslau, 1820—Berlin, 1867; conductor and writer.

Lindpaintner (lĭnt'-pīnt-něr), **Peter Jos. von**, Coblenz, Dec. 9, 1791—Nonnenhorn, Aug. 21, 1856; eminent conductor, ct.-conductor and dram. composer.

Lin'ley, (1) **Thos.**, Sr., Wells, 1732—London, 1795; conductor and dram. composer; owner with Sheridan of Drury Lane Th., 1776. (2) **Thos.**, Jr., Bath, 1756—drowned at Grimsthorpe, Lincolnshire, 1778; violinist and composer.

Lin'narz, Robt., b. Potsdam, Sept. 29, 1854; writer, composer.

Lipinski (lĭ-pĭn'-shkĭ), **K. Jos.**, Radzyn, Poland, Nov. 4 (Oct. 30 ?), 1790—Urlow, near Lemberg, Dec. 16, 1861; noted violinist and composer; pupil of Paganini; lived in Dresden, 1839–59.

Lipsius (lĭp'-sĭ-oos), **Marie**, Leipzig, Dec. 30, 1837—near Wurzen, Saxony, March 2, 1927; noted writer on Liszt, Beethoven; edited letters of Liszt, Berlioz, etc.; wrote under pen-name **"La Mara."**

Lischin (lēsh'-ĭn), **Grigory Andreevitch**, 1853—St. Petersburg, June 27, 1888; c. operas, incl. *"Don César de Bazan."*

Lissenko (or **Lysenko**), **Nikolai Vitalie-vich**, Grinjki, March 22, 1842—Kiev, Nov. 11, 1912; popular Little Russian comp.; pupil of Panochiny, Dimitriev and Vilczek; then of Leipzig Cons.; 1868, teacher at Kiev; c. 6 operas; children's opera, and popular songs.

Lissmann (lēs'-män), (1) **H. Fritz**, Berlin, 1847—Hamburg, 1894; barytone; m. the sopr. (2) **Anna Marie Gutzschbach.**

List, Emanuel, b. Vienna; operatic bass; sang as a boy chorister at Theater an der Wien; later toured as mem. of quartet and in solo programmes; came to U. S. from England in 1914 and studied in N. Y. with Josiah Zuro, appearing in feature radio theatre presentations; 1922, returned to Europe, studied with Édouard de Reszke and was engaged for Vienna Volksoper; later for Berlin Municipal Op. and then for State Op. on Unter den Linden, where he remained for ten years; after 1932, mem. Met. Op.; noted for his portrayal of "Baron Ochs" in *"Der Rosenkavalier"* and for Wagnerian impersonations; has sung at Covent Garden, at Bayreuth, and in other leading Eur. op. houses.

Listemann (lĭs'-tĕ-män), (1) **Fritz,** Schlotheim, Thuringia, March 25, 1839—Boston, Dec. 28, 1909; violinist; pupil of his uncle Ullrich, and of David, Leipzig Cons., 1858, chamber-virtuoso to the Prince of Rudolstadt; 1867 lived in New York; 1871, 1st vln. Thomas Orch.; from 1878, 1st vln. Philh. Orch.; 1881–85 Symph. Orch.; taught and toured with "Listemann Concert Co."; c. 2 vln.-concertos, etc. (2) **Bernhard,** Schlotheim, Aug. 28, 1841—Chicago, Feb. 11, 1917; bro. of above; pupil of Ullrich and David, Vieuxtemps and Joachim. 1859–67, 1st vln. in Rudolstadt ct.-orch.; came to America with his bro., lived in Boston; 1871–74, leader Thomas Orch.; 1874 founded the "Philharm. Club," and toured the country; 1878 founded Boston Philh.-Orch.; cond. till 1881, then 4 yrs. leader of the New "Symph.-Orch."; founded "Listemann Quartet"; 1883–93, dir. of the "Listemann Concert Co."; from 1893, prof. Chicago Coll. of Mus.; pub. a *"Method."* (3) **Paul,** b. Boston, Oct. 24, 1871; son and pupil

of (2); studied also with (1) and was a member of the Quartet and Concert Co., 1890–93; studied with Brodsky and Hilf, Leipzig, and with Joachim, at Berlin; concert m. of the Pittsburgh (Pa.) Orch.; 1896, of the "American Orch.," N. Y.; soloist of the "Redpath Concert Co." (4) **Fz.**, New York, Dec. 17, 1873—Chicago, March 11, 1930; bro. of above; 'cellist; pupil of Fries and Giese at Boston, of Julius Klengel, Leipzig; and Hausmann, Berlin; 1st 'cello Pittsburgh Orch. for a year, then lived in N. Y. as teacher and concert-performer.

Liszt (lĭst), **Franz** (originally **Ferencz**), Raiding, near Oedenburg, Hungary, Oct. 22, 1811—Bayreuth, July 31, 1886; in many ways the most brilliant of all pianists, and a composer whose poorest works are too popular, while he is not granted the credit due his more solid achievements; as great a patron of art, also, as he was creator. Son and pupil of an amateur; at nine played in public, at Oedenburg, Ries' E♭ concerto. A group of Hungarian counts subscribed a 6 years' annuity of 600 florins, and the family moved to Vienna, where L. studied with Czerny (pf.), and Salieri (theory) for 18 months. Beethoven hearing him play his trio op. 97, embraced him. At 12 he gave v. succ. concerts in Vienna and his father took him to Paris, where he was refused as a foreigner because of Cherubini's objections to "infant phenomena;" hereafter L. was his own teacher, except in comp. which he studied with Paër and Reicha. At 14, his 1-act operetta, *"Don Sancho"* had 5 performances at the Acad. royale de musique. On his father's death in 1827 he supported his mother by teaching, soon becoming the salon-idol he always remained. He was strongly influenced by Chopin, von Weber, Paganini and Berlioz. He had a brilliant series of heart-affairs, beginning with the literary Countess d'Agoult ("Daniel Stern"), with whom he lived in Geneva (1835–39). She bore him a son and three daughters; Cosima, the youngest, became the wife of von Bülow, later of Wagner. 1839, he successfully undertook to earn by concerts money enough for the completion of the

Beethoven monument at Bonn. 1849, ct.-cond. at Weimar, with royal encouragement to aid mus. progress. He made himself the greatest patron among creative artists, aiding Wagner materially by productions of his works at Weimar and by pf.-transcriptions, aiding also Raff, Schumann, and Berlioz, finally resigning before the opposition to, and failure of, an opera by Cornelius (q. v.). 1859–70, he lived chiefly at Rome, where in 1866 the Pope, Pius IX., made him an abbé. 1870 he was reconciled with the Weimar Court. 1875 pres. of the new Acad. of Mus. at Pesth; he spent his last years at Weimar, Pesth, and Rome, followed by a large retinue of disciples and pupils whom he taught free of charge. He died during a Bayreuth Festival. C. 2 SYMPHS.: "*Dante*" (after the "Divina Commedia" with female chorus); "*Eine Faustsymphonie*" ("Faust," "Gretchen," "Mephistopheles," with male chorus); SYMPH. POEMS: "*Ce qu'on entend sur la montagne*" (Victor Hugo); "*Tasso, lamento e trionfo*"; "*Les Préludes*"; "*Orpheus*"; "*Prometheus*"; "*Mazeppa*"; "*Festklänge*"; "*Héroïde funèbre*"; "*Hungaria*"; "*Hamlet*"; "*Hunnenschlacht*"; "*Die Ideale*" (Schiller); and "*Von der Wiege bis zum Grabe*" (Michael Zichy); ALSO FOR ORCH. "*Zwei Episoden aus Lenaus Faust*" (Der nächtliche Zug, 2 Mephisto-wälzer), etc. FOR PIANO: 2 concertos; "*Danse macabre*" with orch.; "*Concerto pathétique*"; 15 "*Rhapsodies hongroises*"; "*Rhapsodie espagnole*"; "*Sonata in B Min.*"; "*Fantasia and Fugue on B–A–C–H*"; variations on a theme from Bach's *B-min. mass;* 10 "*Harmonies poétiques et réligieuses*"; "*Années de pélerinage*"; 3 "*Apparitions*," 2 ballades; 6 "*Consolations*"; 2 élégies; 2 légendes ("*St. François D'Assise*" and "*St. François de Paul*"); "*Liebesträume*" (Notturnos); "*Études d'éxécution transcendante*"; "*Ab irato, étude de perfectionnement*"; concert-études, "*Waldesrauschen*" and "*Gnomenreigen*"; "*Technische Studien*" (12 books), etc., and many transcriptions of symphs., overtures, 50 songs by Schubert, etc. Vocal comps.: 4 masses, incl. *Missa solennis* (the "Graner" Festival Mass); requiem;

3 oratorios, "*Die Legende von der Heiligen Elisabeth*," "*Stanislaus*," and "*Christus*"; Psalms 13th, 18th, etc., with orch. and other church-music; 3 cantatas with orch.; male choruses, 60 songs, etc. Wrote life of Chopin, of Franz, etc. Complete ed. of his writings in 6 vols. Biogr. by L. Ramann, 1880. There is an extensive Liszt literature; among studies of his life and work are those by Göllerich, Kapp, Schrader, Raabe, Corder, Habets, Hervey, Huneker, Newman, Pourtalès, Sitwell, W. Wallace and La Mara; a complete edition of his musical works is being prepared by Breitkopf and Härtel, under the auspices of a committee headed by Raabe.

Litolff (lē'-tôlf), **H. Chas.**, London, Feb. 6, 1818—Paris, Aug. 6, 1891; prominent pianist, conductor, publisher and composer.

Litta (lĭt'-tä), Duca **Giulio,** Visconte **Arese,** Milan, 1822—Vedano, near Monza, 1891; dram. composer.

Litvinne (lēt'-vĭn), **Felia,** St. Petersburg, 1860 (?)—Paris, Oct. 12, 1936; soprano; pupil of Mme. Barth-Banderoli and Maurel; début Th. des Italiens, Paris; 1896–97, sang Wagner at Met. Op., N. Y.; then in St. Petersburg; later res. in Paris; sister-in-law of Éd. de Reszke.

Litzau (lēt'-tsow), **Jn. Barend,** Rotterdam, 1822—1893; pianist, organist and composer.

Liverati (lē-vě-rä'-tē), **Giov.,** Bologna, 1772—after 1817; noted tenor conductor and dram. composer.

Ljungberg, **Göta** (yĕt'-tä-yōōng'-bĕrkh), b. Sundsvall, Sweden, Oct. 4, 1893; soprano; studied in Stockholm; 1924, guest at Covent Garden as "Salome"; sang Met. Op., N. Y., in same rôle, also Wagner operas, and Howard Hanson's "*Merry Mount.*"

Lloyd (loid), (1) **Edw.,** London, March 7, 1845—March 31, 1927; noted concert tenor; choir-boy, Westminster Abbey, with Jas. Turle, till 1860; from 1874, first tenor, Leeds Festival; sang at Cincinnati Festival 1888, and had toured the U. S.; gave farewell concert, London, 1900. (2) **Chas. Harford,** Thornbury, Gloucestershire, Engl., Oct. 16, 1849—London, Oct. 16, 1919; 1891, Mus. Doc. Oxford· 1876,

organist Gloucester Cath.; 1892 precentor and mus.-teacher Eton Coll.; founded Oxford Univ. Mus.-Club; 1877–80, cond. Gloucester Festivals; Oxford Symph. Concerts; c. 7 cantatas, mus. to *"Alcestis"* (Oxford, 1887); full cath. service, etc.

Lobe (lō'-bĕ), **Jn. Chr.**, Weimar, May 30, 1797—Leipzig, July 27, 1881; flutist, vla.-player, and dram. composer; wrote important treatises.

Lobkowitz. Vide CARAMUEL DE L.

Lo'bo (or **Lopez**) (lō'-pĕs) (or **Lupus**), **Duarte**, Portuguese composer at Lisbon, 1600.

Locatel'li, Pietro, Bergamo, 1693—Amsterdam, 1764; vln.-virtuoso, regarded as marvellous for his double-stopping and effects procured by changed accordature (v. D. D.) in which Paganini imitated him; composer.

Locke, Matthew, Exeter, England, 1632 (33 ?)—London, 1677; composer.

Lo'der, (1) **Edw. Jas.,** Bath, 1813—London, 1865; dram. composer. (2) **Kate Fanny** (**Lady Thompson**) Bath, Aug. 21, 1825—London, Aug. 30, 1904; pianist, cousin of E. J. Loder (q. v.); pupil of the R. A. M., London, winning the King's scholarship, 1839 and 1841; from 1844 Prof. of harmony there; played with great success at Phil. concerts and elsewhere; 1851 married the surgeon Henry Thompson, afterward knighted; c. an opera, overture, violin sonata, etc.

Loeb (lāp), **Jules,** Strassburg, May 13, 1852—Paris, Nov., 1933; pupil of Chevillard, Paris Cons., won 1st prize; solo 'cellist at the Opéra, and the Cons. Concerts; member of the Marsick Quartet, and the "Société pour instrs. à vent et à cordes."

Loeffler (lĕf'-lĕr), **Chas. Martin Tornov,** Mühlhausen, Alsatia, Jan. 30, 1861—Medfield, Mass., May 20, 1935; violinist and notable composer; pupil of Massart, Leonardi, Joachim and Guiraud (comp.); played in Pasdeloup's orch.; later in Prince Dervier's orch.; resigned from the Boston Symph. Orch., 1903, to give his time entirely to composition; c. a fantastic concerto for 'cello and orch. (1894); divertimento for violin and orch. (1897); his symph. poem for 2 viole d'amore *"La Mort des*

Tintagiles" was prod. by the Boston Symph. 1897; he revised it for one viola d'amore and it was prod. 1901, with the composer as the soloist; his *"Divertissement Espagnol"* for saxophone, and orch. was prod. 1901; his 2 symph. poems, *"Avant que tu ne t'en ailles"* (after Verlaine's *"La bonne chanson,"*) and *"Villanelle du diable"* (after Rollinat) were prod. 1902; his *"Pagan Poem"* for orch., piano, 3 trumpets and Engl. horn 1907. Other works include (for orch.) *"Les Veillées de l'Ukraine"* (1891), *"Memories of My Childhood,"* both showing impressions gained in early visit to Russia; *"Poem"*; and *"Evocation"* for orch. with choral voices; (for chorus) *"Hora Mystica," "By the Rivers of Babylon," "Canticum Fratris Solis"* (setting of St. Francis' Canticle to the Sun); (chamber works) Music for 4 stringed instruments; 2 Rhapsodies for oboe, viola and piano; *"To the Memory of Victor Chapman"* for string quartet; Sextet for strings; Octet for strings, harp and two clarinets; and important songs.

Loeillet (lwä-yā'), **J. Bap.,** Ghent, 1653—London, 1728; noted virtuoso on flute and harp; composer.

Loewe. Vide LÖWE.

Loewengard (lā'vĕn-gärt), **Max Julius,** Frankfort-on-Main, Oct. 2, 1860—Hamburg, Nov. 19, 1915; writer and composer; pupil of Raff, then teacher at Wiesbaden Cons.; 1904 critic in Hamburg and 1908 teacher at the Cons.; author of text books in theory; c. comic opera *"Die 14 Nothelfer."*

Logier (lō'-jēr), **Jn. Bd.,** Cassel, 1777—Dublin, 1846; flutist, writer and composer; invented the "chiroplast."

Logroscino (lō-grō-shē'-nō), **Nicolà,** Naples, ca. 1700—1763; professor of cpt.; composer; pupil of Durante; 1747, prof. of cpt. at Palermo, then lived in Naples and prod. some 20 light operas; he was brilliantly successful, and was the first to close acts with an ensemble.

Löhlein (lā'-līn), **Georg Simon,** Neustadt, 1727—Danzig, 1782; pianist and teacher.

Lohmann (lō'-män), **Peter,** Schwelm, Westphalia, April 24, 1833—Leipzig, Jan. 10, 1907, where he had lived since 1856; 1858–61, writer for *"Neue Zeitschrift für Musik"*; wrote treatises and several dramas set to music by Huber, Goetze, etc.

Löhr (lär), (1) G. **Augustus**, Norwich, Engl., 1821—Leicester, 1897; organist and conductor. (2) **Richard H.**, Leicester, Engl., June 13, 1856— St. Leonard's-on-Sea, Jan. 16, 1927; studied R. A. M., won two medals; organist, London; 1882, concert-pianist; c. oratorios; wrote "*Primer of Music*," etc.

Lohse (lō'-zĕ), **Otto**, Dresden, Sept. 21, 1858—Baden-Baden, May 5, 1925; for years cond. Hamburg City Th., 1895-96, Damrosch Op. Co., in which the prima donna was his wife Klafsky (q. v.); cond. Covent Garden, 1901; cond. City Th., Strassburg, 1897—1904; after 1904, in Cologne; 1912-23, dir. of Leipzig Op.; c. succ. opera "*Der Prinz Wider Willen*" (Cologne, 1898).

Lolli (lōl'-lĭ), **Ant.**, Bergamo, ca. 1730 ('40 ?)—Palermo, 1802; violinist and leader; composer and writer.

Lomagne, B. de. Vide SOUBIES.

Lo'makin, Gabriel Joakimovich, St. Petersburg April 6, 1812—Gatschina, May 21, 1885; teacher in St. Petersburg, where he founded the Free School of Music, with Balakirev; c. 10 "*Cherubinische*" songs, etc.

Long'hurst, (1) **Wm. H.**, Lambeth, Engl., Oct. 6, 1819—Canterbury, 1904; chorister in Canterbury Cath.; later asst.-organist, master of the choristers and lay-clerk; 1873, organist; 1875, Mus. Doc. and mus.-lecturer; c. oratorios, cath. service, etc. (2) **J. Alex.**, 1809—1855; operatic and concert-singer; bro. of above.

Longy (lôń-zhē), (1) **Gustave Georges Léopold**, Abbéville, Aug. 29, 1868— April 14, 1930; pupil Paris Cons. taking second oboe prize 1885, first prize 1886; oboist with Lamoureux and at Op. Com.; from 1898 first oboist Boston Symph., founding 1900 the Longy Club (flute, oboe, clarinet, horn, bassoon, piano), and giving important concerts; 1890-1913, also cond. of the Orchestral Club, and from 1915 dir. of the MacDowell Orch. In 1916 he founded the notable Longy School of Music, with a faculty incl. many solo players of the Boston Symph. Orch. This institution has had a continued existence until the present day, upholding high standards and

moving its headquarters to Cambridge, Mass., after many years in Boston. (2) **Renée (Longy-Miquelle)**, his daughter, also an able musician, especially known as a teacher of *solfège;* mem. faculty, Curtis Inst. of Music, Philadelphia.

Loo'mis, Harvey Worthington, b. Brooklyn, N. Y., Feb. 5, 1865— Roxbury, Mass., Dec. 25, 1931; composer; pupil of Dvořák at the National Cons., New York, 1892, winning a 3-years' scholarship; lived in New York; c. pantomimes and music to poems; pf.-pcs. and songs.

Lopat'nikoff, Nikolai, b. Reval, March 16, 1903; composer; studied at Petrograd Cons., also with W. Rehberg, Grabner and Toch; after 1920 res. in Karlsruhe, later in Helsingfors; c. modern-style works of originality and strong formal sense, among which a symph. was performed by N. Y. Philh. Orch. under Lange; also chamber music and piano works.

Lopez. Vide LOBO.

Lorenz (lō'-rĕnts), (1) **Fz.**, Stein, Lower Austria, 1805—Vienna, 1883; writer. (2) **Karl Ad.**, Köslin, Pomerania, Aug. 13, 1837—Stettin, March 3, 1923; c. quartets, etc., as a sch.-boy; studied with Dehn, Kiel and Gehrig, Berlin, and at Berlin Univ.; 1861, Dr. Phil.; 1866, Municipal Dir., Stettin, cond. symph. concerts, etc.; teacher in two gymnasiums; founded the "Stettin Musikverein" (for oratorio); 1885, professor; c. 2 succ. operas, overtures, etc. (3) **Julius**, Hanover, Oct. 1, 1862—Glogau, Oct. 1, 1924; from 1884, cond. Singakademie, Glogau; 1895, of the "Arion," New York; c. an opera "*Die Rekruten*," and overtures. (4) **Max**, b. Düsseldorf, May 19, 1901; tenor; studied with Grenzebach; sang heroic rôles at Dresden Op., and after 1934 at Berlin State Op.; also, beginning 1933, at Bayreuth Fest. ("Parsifal," "Siegfried," "Walther"); was mem. of Met. Op. Co., N. Y., for several seasons.

Lo'ris, Lori'tus. Vide GLAREANUS.

Lortzing (lôrt'-tsǐng), (Gv.), **Albert**, Berlin, Oct. 23, 1801—Jan. 21, 1851; an actor, son of actors, and m. an actress, 1823. Had a few lessons with Rungenhagen; chiefly self-taught; 1826, actor at Detmold; prod. 2 vaudevilles with succ.; 1833-

44, tenor at Leipzig th.; prod. succ. *"Die beiden Schützen"*; 1837 and 1839, *"Czar und Zimmerman"*; 4 others followed, then *"Der Wildschütz,"* 1842; cond. at Leipzig Op., then travelled, producing 6 more operas, incl. *" Undine"* (1845); *"Der Waffenschmied"* (1846); his melodious unction keeps those works mentioned still popular, and his *"Regina"* was posthumously prod. Berlin, 1899, with succ.; he lived in poverty in spite of his succ., and a benefit was needed for his family after his death; c. also an oratorio, etc.; biogr. by Düringer (Leipzig, 1851).

Löschhorn (lĕsh'-hôrn), **Albert,** Berlin, June 27, 1819—June 4, 1905; pupil of L. Berger, Kollitschgy, Grell and A. W. Bach at the R. Inst. for Churchmusic; 1851, pf.-teacher there; 1859, professor; noted teacher; writer and composer.

Lossius, Lucas, Vacha, Hesse-Cassel, Oct. 18, 1508—Lüneburg, 1582; rector, theorist and compiler.

Lotti (lôt'-tē), **Ant.,** Venice, ca. 1667—Venice, Jan. 5, 1740; son of the ct.-cond. at Hanover; pupil of Legrenzi; at 16 prod. an opera at Venice; 1697 organist there; prod. 20 operas with general succ.; was noted as an organist, and more famed as a composer of churchmusic.

Lotze (lôt'-tsĕ), **Rudolf Hn.,** Bautzen, 1817—Berlin, 1881; professor and writer.

Louis (loo'-ēs), (1) **Fd.,** Friedrichsfelde, near Berlin, 1772—Saalfeld, 1806; Prince of Russia, nephew of Frederick II.; composer. (2) (loo'-ē), **Rudolf,** Schwetzingen, Jan. 30, 1870 —Munich, Nov. 15, 1914; pupil at Geneva and Vienna, where he was made Ph. D., studied conducting with Mottl; theatre-cond. at Landshut and Lübeck; after 1907 writer and theory teacher in Munich; c. symph. fantasie *"Proteus"* (Basel, 1903).

Lowe (lō), **Edw.,** Salisbury, Engl., 1610 (-15?)—Oxford, 1682; organist, professor and composer.

Löwe (lā'-vĕ) (**Jn.**) **Karl (Gf.),** Löbejün, near Halle, Nov. 30, 1796—Kiel, April 20, 1869; son and pupil of a cantor; studied with Türk on a royal stipend; 1821-66 town mus.-dir. at Stettin; toured Europe singing his own fine "ballades" or dramatic

solos; also c. 5 operas, 17 oratorios, etc., wrote a "Selbst-biographie (1870)." His *"Edward"* and *"Erlkönig"* famous.

Löwenstern (lā'-vĕn-shtĕrn) (or **Leuenstern** or **Leonastro**), **Matthaeus Apelles von,** Neustadt, 1594—Bernstadt, 1648; poet and composer; son of a saddler named Löwe; became a privy councillor and was ennobled by Ferdinand II., taking the name of von Loewenstern; c. words and music of *"Frühlings-Morgen"* (30 sacred songs), oratorio *"Judith"* (1646), etc.

Lualdi (loo-äl'-dē), **Adriano,** b. Larino (Campobasso), March 22, 1887; composer of stage works; editor.

Lübeck (lü'-bĕk), (1) **Vincentius,** Paddingbüttel, near Bremen, 1654—Hamburg, Feb. 9, 1740; famous organist. (2) **Jn. H.,** Alphen, Holland, 1799—The Hague, 1865; violinist and ct.-conductor. (3) **Ernst,** The Hague, 1829—Paris, 1876; son of above; pianist. (4) **Louis,** The Hague, 1838—Berlin, March 8, 1904; bro. of above; pupil of Jacquard; 1863-70, 'cello-teacher, Leipzig Cons.; then in Frankfort.

Lü'benau, L. Vide JADASSOHN, S.

Luboshutz (loo'-bō-shoots), **Lea,** b. Odessa, Feb. 22, 1889; studied at Moscow Cons., and with Hrimaly and Ysaye; violinist and soloist with orchs. in Europe and U. S.; teacher, Curtis Inst. of Music, Philadelphia.

Lubrich (loo'-brĭkh), **Fritz,** b. Bärsdorf, July 29, 1862; 1890 cantor at Peilau, Silesia; editor and composer.

Lu'cas, (1) **Chas.,** Salisbury, 1808— London, 1869; 'cellist and composer. (2) **Stanley,** after 1861 secretary to the R. Soc. of Mus.; and 1866-80 of the Philh. Soc. (3) **Clarence,** b. Canada, 1866; studied Paris Cons.; critic; conductor; comp. of operas, etc.

Lucca (look'-kä), **Pauline,** Vienna, April 25, 1841—Feb. 28, 1908; famous soprano; studied with Uschmann and Lewy; in chorus Vienna Op.; 1859 won attention as "First Bridesmaid" in *"Der Freischütz,"* engaged at Olmütz, for leading rôles; Meyerbeer chose her to create "Selika" in *"L'Africaine"* at Berlin, where she was engaged as ct.-singer for life; sang in London annually, and broke her Berlin engagement (1872) to sing in the United States for two years; 1869 m. Baron von

Rhaden (divorced, 1872); m. von Wallhofen in America; lived in Vienna.

Luck'stone, Isidore, b. Baltimore, Md., Jan. 29, 1861; pianist and teacher; pupil of P. Scharwenka; toured as accompanist for many noted artists; after 1897 in N. Y. as teacher of singing, where he headed vocal dept., N. Y. Univ., for a time.

Ludikar (lōō'-dĕ-kär), **Pavel,** b. Prague; studied law at Univ. of Prague; also music; his father a cond. of Prague Opera and prof. at Cons. there, his mother an opera singer; début as "Sarastro," Prague, 1906; sang with Boston Op. Co., 1913–14; later mem. Met. Op. Co., N. Y., for several seasons; also sang at La Scala, in Paris and at Baden-Baden Mozart festivals.

Ludwig, (1) **August,** b. Waldheim, Saxony, Jan. 15, 1865; critic and comp.; pupil of Cologne and Munich Cons.; attracted attention by the completion of Schubert's Unfinished symph., with a *"Philosophic scherzo,"* and a *"March of Fate";* c. also an overture *"Ad Astra,"* songs, etc. (2) **Friedrich,** Potsdam, May 8, 1872 —Göttingen, Oct. 3, 1930; historian of music; docent at Strassburg University; after 1920, prof. musical science, Göttingen; author works on music of 13th and 14th century.

Lugert (loo'-gĕrt), **Josef,** Frohnau, Bohemia, Oct. 30, 1841—Linz, Jan. 17, 1928; teacher; pupil of Prague Organ School, and violinist in German Landestheater there; later piano teacher at Prague Cons.; 1905 Royal Music Inspector; organised orchestra schools, and won fame as a teacher; c. symph., serenades for orch., *"In Memoriam"* for full orch. with English horn solo; also wrote technical books.

Luigini (lwē-zhē'-nē), **Alexandre (Clément L. Jos.)** Lyons, March 9, 1850 —Paris, July 29, 1906; pupil and prize-winner at the Cons.; 1869 leader in Grand Théâtre, Lyons, and founder of the Cons. concerts and prof.; 1897 cond. at Op. Comique, Paris; c. comic operas, *"Les caprices de Margot"* (Lyons, 1877), *"Faublas"* (1881), ballets, etc.

Lully (rightly Lulli) (lül-lē, or lool'-lĭ), (1) **J. Bap. de,** Florence, Nov. 29, 1632—Paris, March 22, 1687. A Franciscan monk taught him the violin and guitar. His parents were poor; the Chev. de Guise took the boy in 1646 to France to entertain Mlle. de Montpensier, but he was set to work in the scullery, where Count de Nogent heard him play the vln. and placed him in the private band. L., however, set to music a satirical poem on Mlle. de M. and she dismissed him. He studied the harps. and comp. with Métru, Roberday, and Gigault, and became a member of the King's private orchestra; 1652, he became head of the "24 violins"; he organised a second group, "les petits violons," of 16 instrs. and made it the best orchestra in France. 1653, ct.-composer and prod. masques and ballets in which Louis XIV. took part and Lully as "M. Baptiste," danced and acted. 1672, the king held him in such favour that he gave him letters patent for an "Académie royale de musique" (now the Gr. Opéra); a rival theatre was closed by the police (v. CAMPRA). With this opportunity (cf. Wagner's Bayreuth Theatre) the transplanted Italian proceeded to found French opera—idiomatic mus. to texts in the vernacular, and free of the superornamentation of the Italian Sch. He held the vogue till Gluck put him in eclipse. L. was dir., stagemanager, conductor, and even at times machinist, as well as composer. He was fortunate in his librettist, Quinault. He developed the overture, and introduced the brass into the orch. He was famous for his temper and once while cond. furiously struck his own foot with the bâton, producing a fatal abscess. His works, mainly on classical subjects, include *"Les Fêtes de l'Amour et de Bacchus";* a pastoral pasticcio (1672); *"Cadmus et Hermione";* *"Alceste";* *"Thésée";* *"Le Carnaval,"* opera-ballet; *"Atys,"* *"Isis,"* *"Psyche";* *"Bellérophon";* *"Proserpine";* *"Le Triomphe de L'Amour";* *"Persée";* *"Phaëton";* *"Amadis de Gaule";* *"Roland";* *"Armide et Renaud";* *"Acis et Galatée,"* historic pastoral (1686), etc., also symphs., a mass, etc. (2) **Louis de,** Paris, 1664—after 1713; son of above; dramatic composer.

Lum'bye, (1) **Hans Chr.,** Copenhagen, 1810—1874; conductor and composer of pop. dance-mus. His son and successor (2) **G.**, c. opera "*The Witch's Flute.*"

Lund, John Reinhold, Hamburg, Germany, Oct. 20, 1859—Buffalo, N. Y., Feb. 1, 1925; conductor, composer; studied at Leipzig Cons.; cond. of chorus, Bremen Op., 1880–83; after 1884 asst. cond. to Damrosch with German Op. Co., N. Y.; 1887–1903, cond. Buffalo Orch. and Orpheus Soc.; toured as cond. of Herbert operettas; after 1914 again in Buffalo.

Lunn, (1) **Henry Charles**, London, 1817 —Jan. 23, 1894; editor and author; pupil Royal Acad. of Music, later dir.; 1863–87, edited *The Musical Times*, London. (2) **(Louisa) Kirkby**, Manchester, Nov. 8, 1873— London, Feb. 17, 1930; mezzo-soprano; pupil of J. H. Greenwood, then of Visetti, R. A. M., London, gaining a scholarship in 1894. Appeared in a student performance of Schumann's "*Genoveva,*" 1893, with such success that she was engaged by Sir Augustus Harris; 1897–09 contralto of Carl Rosa Company; then married W. J. K. Pearsen; sang in concert; 1901 began engagements at Covent Garden; sang much at festivals; 1902 at Met. Op. House, New York and with Boston Symph. and other orchs., 1907 created "Kundry" in first English performance of "*Parsifal*" by the Henry W. Savage Company.

Luporini (loo-po-rē'-nē), **Gaetano**, b. Lucca, Italy, Dec. 12, 1865; pupil of Primo Quilici, graduating from the Pacini Mus. Inst.; c. opera "*Marcella,*" succ. lyric comedy, "*I Dispetti Amorosi*" (Turin, 1894); v. succ. opera "*La Collana di Pasqua*" (Naples, 1896), etc.; cond. at Lucca.

Lupot (lü-pō), (1) **Nicolas**, Stuttgart, 1758—Paris, 1824; chief of a French family of vln.-makers, incl. his great grandfather (2) **Jean**; his grandfather (3) **Laurent** (b. 1696); his father (4) **François**, his bro. (5) **François** (d. 1837), and his son-in-law, **Chas. Fr. Gand** of Gand & Bernardel, Paris.

Lusci'nius (Latin form of **Nachtgall** or **Nachtigall** (näkht'-(ĭ)-gäl), "Nightingale"), **Othmar**, Strassburg, 1487—ca. 1536; organist, theorist and composer.

Lussan (dŭ lüs-säṅ), **Zélie de**, b. New York, 1863; pupil of her mother; début in concert and stage, 1886; 1889 Carl Rosa Co., London; from 1894, Met. Op., N. Y., also in Spain, etc.

Lussy (loos'-sē), **Mathis**, Stans, Switz., April 8, 1828—Montreux, Jan. 21, 1910; pupil of Businger and Nägeli; pf.-teacher, Paris, and writer.

Lustig (loos'-tĭkh), **Jacob Wm.**, Hamburg, Sept. 21, 1706–1796; organist and theorist.

Lüstner (lĭst'-n'r), (1) **Ignaz P.**, Poischwitz, near Jauer, 1793—Breslau, 1873; violin teacher. His four sons were (2) **K.**, Breslau, Nov. 10, 1834—Wiesbaden, April 9, 1906; pianist and 'cellist; after 1872, teacher in Wiesbaden. (3) **Otto**, Breslau, 1839—Barmen, 1889; town mus.-dir. at Barmen. (4) **Louis**, Breslau, June 30, 1840—Wiesbaden, Jan. 24, 1918; violinist, and after 1874, cond. at Wiesbaden. (5) **G.**, 1847—1887; 'cellist; ct.-cond. at Berlin.

Luther (loo'-tĕr), **Martin**, Eisleben, Nov. 10, 1483—Feb. 18, 1546; the great reformer concerned himself also with church-mus., issuing "*Formula missae*" (1523), and a new order for the German mass. He wrote the words of at least 36 chorals, and is generally believed to have c. 13 choral-tunes (incl. the famous "*Ein feste Burg ist unser Gott,*" and "*Jesaia den Propheten das gescha*"), his method being to play them on the flute (which he played well) while his friends and assistants, the cond. Konrad Rupff and cantor Jn. Walther, wrote them out.

Lut'kin, Peter Christian, Thompsonville, Wis., March 27, 1858—Evanston, Ill., Dec. 27, 1931; teacher, conductor and composer; studied at Berlin Hochsch.; with Stepanov, Moszkowski, Leschetizky and others; after 1888 theory teacher, Amer. Cons., Chicago; and following 1891 at the school of music, Northwestern Univ., Evanston, Ill.; there after 1908 he conducted the annual Chicago North Shore Fests.; in 1911 and 1920 was pres. of the Music Teachers' Nat'l Association.

Lutz (loots), **Wm. Meyer**, Kissingen, 1822—West Kensington, Jan. 31, 1903; pianist and dram. composer; from 1848, conductor at London.

Lutzer, Jenny. Vide DINGELSTEDT.

Lux (looks), **Fr.**, Ruhla, Thuringia,

1820—Mayence, 1895; conductor, organist, pianist and dram. composer.

Luython (or **Luiton**) (lĭ-tôn), **Carl,** Antwerp (?)—Prague, 1620; important composer of madrigals, masses, fugues, etc.; 1576 court organist to Maximilian II. and to Rudolf II.

Luzzaschi (lood-zäs'-kē), **Luzzasco,** d. Ferrara, 1607; court organist; pupil of Ciprian de Rore, and teacher of Frescobaldi; c. madrigals, etc.

Luzzi (lood'-zē), **Luigi,** Olevano di Lomellina, 1828—Stradella, 1876; dram. composer.

Lvoff (or **Lwoff**) (l'vôf), **Alexis,** Reval, 1799—on his estate, Govt. of Kovno, 1871; violinist and conductor; c. the Russian national hymn and 4 operas.

Lyra (lē'-rä), **Justus W.,** Osnabrück, 1822—Gehrden, 1882; composer.

Lysberg (lēs-bĕrkh) (rightly **Bovy,** Chas. Samuel,** Lysberg, near Geneva, 1821—Geneva, 1873; pianist and dram. composer.

Lyssenko, vide LISSENKO.

M

Maas (mäs), (1) **Jos.,** Dartford, 1847—1886; tenor. (2) **Louis (Ph. O.),** Wiesbaden, 1852 — Boston, 1889; pianist, conductor and composer. (3) **Gerald Christopher,** b. Mannheim, 1888; 'cellist; pupil of Paris Cons. and of Julius Klengel; played in Munich Konzertverein orch.; 1912, Berlin Op. orch.; 1914, taught at Hoch Cons., Frankfort; played in Rebner Quartet; after 1916 in U. S., where he was a member of Letz Quartet, 1917–21.

Mabellini (mä-bĕl-lē'-nē), **Teodulo,** Pistoia, Italy, 1817—Florence, 1897; ct.-conductor and dram. composer.

Macbeth', (1) **Allan,** Greenock, Scotland, March 13, 1856—Glasgow, 1910; pupil of Leipzig Cons.; organist in Glasgow; after 1890, principal sch. of mus., Glasgow Athenæum; c. an operetta, 2 cantatas, chambermus., etc. (2) **Florence,** b. Mankato, Minn., 1891; coloratura soprano; studied with Yeatman Griffith; sang in England; op. début, Darmstadt, 1913; after 1914 sang with Chicago Op. Co., also at Ravinia Op. and in concerts.

MacCunn', **Hamish,** Greenock, Scotland, March 22, 1868—London, Aug. 2, 1916; British composer;

pupil of Parry, R. A. M., having won a scholarship for comp.; at 19, several of his orch.-pcs. were prod. by Manns; at 20 commissioned to c. a cantata for the Glasgow Choral Union; gave concerts at the studio of John Pettie, whose daughter he m., 1889; 1888–94, prof. of harm. R. A. M.; 1898, cond. Carl Rosa Op. Co.; c. operas, "*Jeanie Deans*" (Edinburgh, 1894), "*Diarmid and Ghrinè*" (Covent Garden, 1897); 5 cantatas incl. "*The Death of Parry Reed*" (male chorus and orch.), overtures "*Cior Mhor,*" "*The Land of the Mountain and the Flood*"; ballad overture, "*The Dowie Dens o' Yarrow*"; ballade, "*The Ship o' the Fiend,*" with orch.; 8th Psalm with orch., etc.

MacDow'ell, **Edward,** New York, Dec. 18, 1861—Jan. 23, 1908; eminent American composer and one of the most original and virile of creators among his countrymen; pupil of J. Buitrago, P. Desvernine and Teresa Carreño, N. Y.; 1876, Paris Cons.; 1879, with Heymann (pf.) and Raff (comp.) Frankfort; 1881–82, chief pf. teacher at Darmstadt Cons.; at 21, Raff (who was deeply interested in his progress) and Liszt procured the performance of his works at the annual festival of the "Allgemeiner deutscher Musikverein"; lived in Wiesbaden; 1888, Boston; 1896, prof. of mus. in Columbia Univ., New York; Mus. Doc. *h. c.,* Princeton Univ. and 1902, Penn. U. also; he gave frequent pf.-recitals, and played his concertos with the Boston Symph. and other orchs. In Jan. 1904, he resigned his professorship at Columbia University from dissatisfaction with the faculty's attitude toward music as a high art. He was succeeded by Cornelius Rybner (q. v.). He had cond. the Mendelssohn Glee Club for two years. In 1905 he fell a prey to cerebral trouble that ended his beautiful career. Faithfully tended by his wife, he lingered under increasing clouds, till his death, Jan. 23, 1908, at New York. So great was his hold upon the American public that a MacDowell Club with many branches was formed to carry on his ideals of art and to aid the struggling musician; a choral branch under the leadership of Kurt Schindler attained a very high standard, taking the title of "Schola Cantorum" in 1912; a biography of MacDowell was written by Lawrence Gilman, 1905. His widow has been an active force in Amer. music, having founded the MacDowell Colony on the composer's estate at Peterboro, N. H., as a creative centre for young Amer. comps., scholarships there being defrayed by M.-Clubs throughout U. S. ORCHESTRAL COMPOSITIONS: 2 poems "*Hamlet*" and "*Ophelia*"; symph. poems, "*Lancelot and Elaine*," "*Lamia*" and "*Roland*," op. 35, romance for 'cello with orch.; 3 orch. suites incl. "*In October*" and "*Indian Suite*." FOR PIANO. 4 sonatas "*Tragica*," "*Eroica*" ("*Flos regum Arthurus*"), "*Scandinavian*" and "*Celtic*"; prelude and fugue, modern suite; forest idyls, 3 poems, "*Moon-pictures*," 6 poems after Heine, 4 "*Little Poems*"; technical exercises (3 books), and 12 virtuoso-studies, etc., and many songs of great charm and individuality.

Mace, Thos., ca. 1613—1709; Engl. lutenist, inventor and writer.

Macfar'lane, W. Chas., b. London, Oct. 2, 1870; organist; brought to New York at 4; pupil of his father and of S. P. Warren; c. anthems, etc.

Macfar'ren, (1) Sir G. Alex., London, March 2, 1813—Oct. 31, 1887; notable English composer and scholar; son and pupil of the playwright G. Macfarren; also studied with Ch. Lucas and C. Potter, R. A. M.; 1834, prof. there, even after blindness overtook him; from 1875 prof. at Cambridge Univ. Mus. Doc. there 1876; from 1876, also principal of the R. A. M.; 1883, knighted; c. 13 operas, 9 of them prod.; 4 oratorios, 5 cantatas, 8 symphonies, 7 overtures, incl. "*Chevy Chase*," "*Don Carlos*," "*Hamlet*" and "*Festival*," concertos, sonatas, etc.; wrote text-books, articles; ed. old texts, etc.; biog. by Banister (London, '91). (2) **Natalia,** Lübeck, 1827—Bakewell, April 9, 1916; wife of above; contralto, translator and writer. (3) **Walter Cecil,** London, Aug. 28, 1826—Sept. 2, 1905; bro. and pupil (in comp.) of (1); studied with Turle, Holmes (pf.) and Potter (comp.); from 1846, pf.-prof. at the R. A. M., of which he was a Fellow; 1873–80,

cond. Acad. Concerts; dir. and treasurer Philharm. Soc.; pianist, lecturer, editor, and composer of a symph., 7 overtures, a cantata "*The Song of the Sunbeam*," services, etc.

Machault (or **Machau, Machaud, Machut**) (mă-shō), Guillaume (Gulielmus) de Mascandio, Machault in the Ardennes, 1300—ca. 1372; troubadour; composer.

Macken'zie, Sir Alex. Campbell, Edinburgh, Aug. 22, 1847—London, April 28, 1935; notable British composer; pupil of Ulrich (pf.) and Stein (comp.), Sondershausen Cons.; at 14 a violinist in the Ducal Orch.; 1862, won the King's scholarship, R. A. M., and studied with Sainton, Jewson, and Lucas; from 1865 teacher and cond. Edinburgh; 1888 of Cambridge; 1896 of Edinburgh U.; 1894 knighted; 1888–1924, principal R. A. M. (vice Macfarren); 1892 cond. Philh. Soc.; c. operas, "*Colomba*" (Drury Lane, 1883), "*The Troubadour*" (ibid. 1886), and "*His Majesty, or the Court of Vingotia*" (1897; comic), "*Cricket on the Hearth*" (MS.); oratorios, "*The Rose of Sharon*" (Norwich Festival, 1884), and "*Bethlehem*" (1894); cantatas, "*Jason*" (Bristol Festival, 1882), "*The Bride*," "*The Story of Sayid*" (Leeds Festival, '86), "*The New Covenant*," "*The Dream of Jubal*," "*The Cotter's Saturday Night*," and "*Veni, Creator Spiritus*"; 2 Scottish rhapsodies, a ballad, with orch., "*La belle dame sans merci*"; overtures "*Cervantes*," "*To a comedy*," "*Tempo di ballo*," "*Twelfth Night*," "*Britannia*"; a vln.-concerto, a "*Pibroch*" for vln. and orch.; "*Scottish Concertos*" for pf., etc.

Maclean', (1) **Chas. Donald,** Cambridge, March 27, 1843—London, June 23, 1916; pupil of Ferdinand Hiller; organist at Oxford, later at Eton and (after 1880) in London; for a time in India; c. oratorios, etc. (2) **Alex. Morvaren,** Eton, July 20, 1872—London, May 18, 1936; active for many years as theatre cond. and comp. of music for plays in London; also orch. and choral works. (3) **Quentin Morvaren,** b. London, May 14, 1896; son of (2); also a prolific comp. of music for the stage; a pupil of Straube, Reger and Krehl.

Maclen'nan, Francis, Bay City, Mich., 1879—Port Washington, N. Y.,

1935; tenor; studied New York, London and Berlin; sang in London, 1902; after 1904 with Savage Op. Co., in U. S.; 1907, Royal Op., Berlin; 1913, Hamburg Op.; 1915–17, Chicago Op. Co., later again in Berlin; m. Florence Easton, soprano; divorced.

MacMill'an, Sir Ernest Campbell, b. Mimico, Ontario, Aug. 18, 1893; composer, conductor, organist; studied in Toronto and Edinburgh with Niecks, Hollins and W. B. Ross; Mus. D., Oxford, 1918; Fellow of the R. Coll. of Music, London; 1926, principal, Toronto Cons., and dean of faculty of music, Univ. of Toronto; 1935, knighted by British Gov't.; c. and arr. choruses and songs, c. orch. and chamber music; cond. Toronto Symph. Orchestra.

Macmil'len, Francis, b. Marietta, Ohio, Oct. 14, 1885; violinist; pupil of Listemann, Chicago; at 10, pupil of Markees, Berlin; at 15 of César Thomson at Brussels Cons.; sharing first violin prize 1902 and taking Van Hal prize; played in Brussels, etc.; 1903 London; after 1906 toured U. S.

Macpher'son, (1) **Charles Stewart,** composer; b. Liverpool, March 29, 1865; pupil of R. A. M., London, with a scholarship; gained also the Balfe scholarship and medals; 1887 prof. there; 1892 a fellow; 1903 prof. Royal Normal College for the Blind; c. symph., 2 overtures, a fine mass with orch. (1898); *"Concerto alla fantasia"* for violin, etc.; wrote theoretical text books. (2) **Charles,** Edinburgh, May 10, 1870—May 28, 1927; 1890 pupil R. A. M., winning Lucas prize 1892; later teacher of counterpoint there; 1895, suborganist at St. Paul's, London; c. overture *"Cridhe an Ghaidhil"* (London, 1895); orch. suites, *"Highland"* and *"Hallowe'en"*; *"Psalm 187"* for choir and orch., etc.

Macque (măk), **Jean de,** Flemish choirmaster in Rome 1576–82; 1610 at Royal Chapel Naples; c. madrigals and motets.

Mad'dy, Joseph Edgar, b. Wellington, Kans., Oct. 14, 1891; conductor, educator; studied with Czerwonky, Ludwig Becker, Arthur Hartmann; hon. Mus. D., Cincinnati Cons., 1930; mem., Minneapolis Symph., 1909–14; prof. public school music,

Univ. of Mich.; organised and cond. Nat'l High School Orch. after 1926; dir. summer school and camp of this group at Interlochen, Mich.; pres. Music Educators Nat'l Conference, 1936; author of books on instr. technique and teaching.

Mader (mä'-dĕr), **Raoul (M.),** b. Pressburg, Hungary, June 25, 1856; studied Vienna Cons.; took 1st prize for pf. and comp., and the great silver medal and the Liszt prize as best pianist in the Cons.; 1882–95, 1st "coach" for solo singers, Vienna ct.-opera, also asst.-cond. From 1895 cond. Royal Opera, Budapest; 1917–19, dir. Vienna, Volksoper; 1921–25, dir. Budapest Op.; c. 2 comic operas, 4 ballets, incl. *"Die Sireneninsel,"* and *"She"* (after Rider Haggard), parody on Mascagni's *"Cavalleria Rusticana"* (Th. an der Wien, 1892), choruses, songs, etc.

Madeto'ja, Leevi, b. Oulu, Finland, Feb. 17, 1887; composer; studied at Helsingfors Univ. and at Music Institute there under Järnefelt and Sibelius; also in Paris with d'Indy and in Vienna with Fuchs; 1912–14, second cond. of Helsingfors Philh.; 1914–16, cond. Wiborg Orch.; since then teacher of comp. and mem. of directorate at Helsingfors Mus. Inst.; c. opera *"Pohjalatsia"*; 3 symphonies; *"Stabat Mater"* for women's chorus; other choral works, chamber music, piano and vocal pieces.

Maganini (mäg-ä-nē'-nē), **Quinto,** b. Fairfield, Cal., Nov. 30, 1897; composer, conductor, flutist; studied with Barrère and Nadia Boulanger; winner of Pulitzer Prize, 1927, and of Guggenheim Fellowship; played as flutist in San Francisco and N. Y. Symph. Orchs.; guest cond. with leading orchs. and also of his own Little Symph.; c. orch., chamber music and vocal works.

Mag(g)ini (mäd-jē'-nē) (or **Magino**), **Giov. Paolo,** Botticini-Marino, Italy, 1580—Brescia, ca. 1640; vln.-maker, rivaling Stradivari and Guarneri; his double-basses particularly good; label, "Gio. Paolo Maggini, Brescia."

Magnard (mĭn-yăr), **Albéric,** Paris, June 9, 1865—killed by German soldiers while defending his estate at Senlis, Sept. 3, 1914; composer; pupil of the Cons. (winning first harmony prize 1888), then of d'Indy; c. 3 symph., overture, suite in ancient style; hymns to *"Justice"* and to *"Venus,"* 1-act opera *"Yolande"* (Brussels, 1892); 3-act *"Guercœur"*; important chamber music, etc.

Mag'nus, Désiré (rightly **Magnus Deutz**), Brussels, 1828—Paris, 1884; teacher, composer and critic.

Mahillon (mä-ē-yòn), Chas. Victor, Brussels, March 10, 1841—St. Jean, Cape Ferrat, June 17, 1924; after 1877 custodian of mus. instrs., Brussels Cons.; editor and writer; manager wind-inst. factory of his father.

Mahler (mä'-lĕr), (1) **Gustav**, Kalischt, Bohemia, July 7, 1860—Vienna, May 18, 1911; highly gifted composer and conductor; pupil of the Cons. and Univ. at Prague and Vienna, with Bruckner as one of his teachers; began his career in 1880 as theatre cond. in Hall, Lubjlana and Olmütz; asst. cond., Cassel, 1883; asst. to Angelo Neumann at the Prague German Op., 1885–86; in latter year at Leipzig Op., under Nikisch; at Budapest Royal Op., 1888–91; at the Hamburg City Theatre, 1891–97, and orch. cond. as successor to Bülow. Beginning 1897 he was in Vienna, 1st as cond. at the Court Op., then from 1900 to 1907 its dir. during a most brilliant period. In 1907 he was called to the Met. Op., where he led German operas, and in 1909 was elected cond. of the N. Y. Philh. Orch. at what was then the largest salary ever paid a leader ($30,000 per annum). Partially as a result of a typhoid infection and partly of a nervous breakdown, he gave up his post and returned to Vienna in 1911, where he died the following year. He has had a strongly augmented fame as a comp. in recent years, owing to the championship of various notable conductors, such as Mengelberg, Bruno Walter, etc., and also to the organization of Mahler societies in various countries, of which there is one in the U. S. His output is highly individual, but there is a strong division of opinion as to its ultimate artistic rank. That he was a master of orchestration is generally admitted; he chose subjects of vast scope for his compositions, with programmes drawn from literature, and in several of his symphs. he employs the human voice as an adjunct; he generally uses a large musical apparatus.

His comps. include: 10 symphonies, 1, D major (1891); 2, C minor, with contralto and chorus (1895); 3, D minor, known as *"La Programmatica,"* with contralto soloist, men's and boys' choruses (1896); 4, G major, known as *"The Heavenly Life,"* with soprano soloist (1901); 5, C♯ minor (1904); 6, A minor (1906); 7, E minor (Prague, 1908); 8, E flat major, in 2 sections, known as "the symphony of a thousand" from the large choral, orch. and solo forces employed (Munich, 1910); 9, D major, posthumous, 1st heard in Vienna under Bruno Walter, 1912; and 10, left unfinished but ed. by Franz Mikorey, and prod. under the title *"Sinfonia Engadine"* in Berlin, 1913. His other principal works are: *"Das Lied von der Erde"* for tenor and alto soloists and orch., after old Chinese poems (also a posth. work, first heard 1911, and since often perf. with growing popularity); *"Das Klagende Lied,"* for soloists, chorus and orch.; 4 *"Lieder eines Fahrenden Gesellen,"* 12 songs from *"Des Knaben Wunderhorn"*; songs to poems by Rückert; 5 *"Kindertotenlieder"*; 3 *"Hefte Lieder"*; and other songs from his earlier period; fragments from a youthful opera, *"Die Argonauten"*; a fairy tale opera, *"Rübezahl"* with text by the composer; sketches for an opera based on Weber's *"Die Drei Pintos,"* early chamber music, etc. Studies of Mahler have been written by Specht, Bekker, Stefan, Guido Adler and Arthur Neisser. (2) **Alma Maria** (née Schindler), his wife, a pupil of Labor and Zemlinsky, c. songs; (3) **Fritz,** his nephew, a conductor, active in Germany and (1936) in the U. S.

Mahu (mä'-oo), **Stephan,** b. Germany, ct.-singer and composer, 1538.

Maier (mī'-ĕr), (1) **Julius Jos.,** Freiburg, Baden, 1821—Munich, 1889; teacher and writer. (2) **Guy,** b. Buffalo, N. Y., 1892; pianist; studied at New England Cons. with Proctor and Schnabel; début, Boston, 1915; has toured as solo pianist and in two-piano programmes with Lee Pattison; prof. piano, Univ. of Mich.; has given many lecture-recitals for children on lives of composers.

Maikapar (mä'-kä-pär), **Samuel,** b. Chersson, Russia, Dec. 18, 1867;

pianist; pupil of the Cons., and of Leschetizky; settled in Moscow; c. piano pieces.

Maillard (mī-yăr), **Jean,** 16th century French composer; pupil of Deprès; c. important motets and masses, from one of which Palestrina took themes for a mass of his own.

Maillart (mī-yăr), **Louis** (called **Aimé**), Montpellier, Herault, France, 1817— Moulins, Allier, 1871; dram. composer.

Mailly (mī-yē), **Alphonse J. Ernest,** Brussels, Nov. 27, 1833—Jan., 1918; pianist, and organ virtuoso; pupil of Girschner, Brussels Cons.; 1861 pf.-teacher there; 1868 organ-teacher; composer.

Mainardi (mä-ē-när'-dē), **Enrico,** b. Milan, May 19, 1897; 'cellist; studied Verdi Cons., Milan and in Berlin with Hugo Becker; début in Milan, 1909; taught at Rome Acad. after 1933; 1929-31, 1st 'cellist of Berlin State Op. orch.; has made concert appearances in Eur. countries.

Mainzer (mīn'-tsĕr), **Abbé Jos.,** Trier, 1807—Manchester, 1851; singing-teacher, writer and dram. composer.

Maison (mä-sôṅ'), **René,** b. Trameries, Belgium, Nov. 24, 1895; tenor; studied Antwerp, Brussels and Paris; mem. of Monte Carlo Op., 1922-25; later sang at Paris Op. and Op.-Comique; for several seasons with Chicago Op., and 1935 with Met. Op., N. Y., in Wagnerian and French rôles, also in "*Fidelio.*"

Maitland (māt'-lănd) **J. Alex. Fuller-,** London, April 7, 1856—Canforth, Lancashire, March 30, 1936; 1882, M. A. Trinity Coll., Cambridge; lecturer and critic for various papers; 1889-1911 London *Times;* ed. the Appendix to Grove's Dict.; pianist at the Bach choir concerts; wrote "*Masters of German Music*" and many authoritative works. Edited the "*Fitzwilliam Virginal Book*" with Barclay Squire.

Majo (mä'-yō), **Fran. di** (called **Ciccio di Majo**), Naples, ca. 1740—Rome, 1770; organist and noted composer of operas and church-mus.

Major (mä'-yôr), **Julius J.,** Kaschau, Hungary, Dec. 13, 1859—Budapest, Jan. 30, 1925; pupil of the Landes-Musik Akad. at Budapest; founded a music school and singing societies there; c. a symph., operas, "*Lisbeth*"

and "*Erysika*" (Pest, 1901), "*Szechi Maria*" (Klausenburg, 1906), etc.

Majorano. Vide CAFFARELLI.

Malash'kin, Leonid Dimitrievitch, 1842 —Moscow, Feb. 11, 1902; Russian composer of an opera, a symph., songs, etc.

Malder (mäl'-dĕr), **Pierre van,** Brussels, 1724—1768; violinist and composer.

Malherbe (măl-ărb), **Chas. Théodore,** Paris, April 21, 1853—Oct. 5, 1911; at first a lawyer, then studied with Danhauser, Wormser, and Massenet; also pub. some original comps., and transcriptions; Danhauser's sec.; 1896, asst.-archivist, Gr. Opéra; Officer of the Acad. and of Pub. Instruction; Chev. of various orders. Ed., *Le Ménestrel,* and prolific writer on Wagner, etc.; owned probably the best private coll. of mus.-autographs in the world; ed. Rameau's complete works.

Malibran (mäl-ĭ-bräṅ), (1) **M. Felicità** (née **Garcia**), Paris, March 24, 1808 —Manchester, Sept. 23, 1836 (from singing too soon after being thrown and dragged by a horse). In some respects the greatest of all women vocalists; she had a contralto voice with an additional soprano register and several well-concealed "head tones" between; she improvised frequently on the stage, and also c.; at 5 she played a child's part and one evening broke out singing the chief rôle to the amusement of the audience; at 7 studied with Pauseron; at 15 studied with her father (v. GARCIA); début, London, 1825; sang in opera in New York, 1825-27 with great succ.; she had a personality that compelled extraordinary homage. She m. Malibran; when he became bankrupt she divorced him and 1836 m. De Bériot, ct.-violinist with whom she had lived since 1830. (2) **Alex.,** Paris, 1823—1867; violinist and composer.

Malipiero (mäl-ē-pē-ä'-rō), **Gian Francesco,** b. Venice, March 18, 1882; composer; mem. of a family line of musicians for some generations; pupil of the Liceo in Bologna, studying with Enrico Bossi; after 1913 lived for a time in Paris in touch with modern musical circle incl. Casella; at this time submitted 5 scores to Italian Nat'l Contest and won 4 prizes under different names; this occasioned criticism when his earlier scores were performed in Italy, where his recognition has been slower than in other countries; after 1920 he came to be recognised as one of the leading creators of his country, a cultivated, intellectual personality, and in his music embodying romantic and poetic qualities, individual color and atmosphere, with an idiom of marked modernity; after 1921 he taught comp. at the Parma Cons.; his productions before 1911 have been disavowed by him as not representative; later works include: (operas) "*Sette Canzoni*," orig. series of short operatic sketches; "*Pantea*"; "*Three Goldoni Comedies*"; "*Filomela e l'Infatuato*"; "*Orfeo*"; "*Il Mistero di Venezia*"; "*La Favola di Figlio Cambiato*" (to Pirandello book, which had première in Brunswick, Germany, but on Rome hearing, 1934, was stormily hissed and withdrawn after one perf. owing to satire on royalty and church); "*Giulio Cesare*" (Genoa, 1935–36 with succ.); "*Antonio e Cleopatra*," Florence, 1938. (Ballets) "*La Baruffe Chiozzotte*," "*La Mascherata delle Principesse Prigionere*"; (orch.) "*Impressioni del Vero*" (2 series); "*Pause del Silenzio*"; "*Ditirambo Tragico*"; "*Oriente Immaginario*"; "*La Cimarosiana*"; Symphony; vln. concerto; (chamber music) "*Rispetti e Strambotti*" and "*Stornelli e Ballate*" for string quartet; Sonata à Tre; 'cello sonata; (choral works) "*San Francesco d'Assisi*," mystery for soloists, chorus and orch. (N. Y., 1921); "*Princess Eulalia*," for soloists, chorus and orch. (N. Y. Oratorio Soc., 1927); also piano music, songs, etc.

Mal'ling, (1) **Jörgen,** Copenhagen, 1836—July 12, 1905; Danish composer and teacher; from 1875 in Vienna. His brother (2) **Otto (Baldemar),** Copenhagen, June 1, 1848 —Oct. 5, 1915; pupil of Gade and Hartmann at the Cons., later teacher there; organist and founder of concert association; c. symph.; violin fantasie with orch., overture, chamber music, and valuable organ pieces.

Mallinger (mäl'-lĭng-ĕr), **Mathilde** (née Lichtenegger), Agram, Feb. 17, 1847 —Berlin, April 19, 1920; soprano; pupil of Giordigiani and Vogl, Prague Cons., and Lewy, Vienna; début, Munich, 1866; 1868, created "Eva" in the "*Meistersinger*"; m. Baron von Schimmelpfennig; 1890, singing-teacher, Prague Cons.

Malten (mäl'-tĕn), **Therese,** Insterburg, East Prussia, June 21, 1855— Dresden, Jan. 2, 1930; soprano; pupil of Engel (voice), and Kahle (action), Berlin; at 18 début, Dresden as "Pamina," and engaged there for life; created "Kundry" ("*Parsifal*") at Bayreuth, 1882; 1898, ct.-chamber singer.

Malvezzi (mäl-vĕd'-zē), **Christofano,** Lucca, 1547—Florence, 1597; canon in Florence; and chapel master to the Grand Dukes of Tuscany; collected and composed dramatic intermezzi, 1591, etc.

Mälzel (mĕl'-tsĕl), **Jn. Nepomuk,** Ratisbon, 1772—on a voyage, July 31, 1838; mus.-teacher; inv. "panharmonion" (a sort of orchestrion), an automaton-trumpeter, and an automatic chess-player; while experimenting with his "chronometer," a sort of metronome , he saw Winkel's invention, adopted its chief features and patented the result as Mälzel's metronome

Mana-Zuc'ca (rightly **Zuckerman**), b. New York, 1891; woman composer; studied in U. S. and Europe; toured as pianist, also sang in light opera; has c. works for orch., chamber music, and a large number of highly successful songs.

Man'chester, Arthur Livingston, b. Bass River, N. J., Feb. 9, 1862; organist, editor, educator; pupil of Zeckwer, Gilchrist, Bussmann and Tubbs; dir. of music schools; from 1904–13 at Converse Coll., Spartanburg, S. C.; 1913–18, Southwestern Univ., Georgetown, Tex., and afterward at Hardin Coll.; assoc. ed. *The Étude*, 1893–96; ed. *The Musician* (Boston), 1896–1902; pres. of M. T. N. A., 1900–02, and ed. its pub., *The Messenger*.

Mancinelli (män-chĭ-nĕl'-lĭ), **Luigi,** Orvieto, Papal States, Feb. 5, 1848— Rome, Feb. 2, 1921; intended for commerce, self-taught on the pf., but permitted to study at 14 with Sbolci (Florence, 'cello); at 15, 3rd 'cellist Pergola Th., earning his living the next 8 years; studied with Mabellini (comp.); 1870 in the orchestra of the opera at Rome; 1874, 2nd cond.; 1875, cond.; 1881, dir. Bologna Cons., which he made one of the best in Italy; 1886–88, cond. at Drury Lane, London; 1888–95, Royal Th., Madrid; till 1906 at Covent Garden, London, and, 1894–1902, at Met. Op., N. Y.; in Italy called "il Wagnerista" for his advocacy; c. opera "*Isora di Provenza*" (Bologna, 1884); succ. "*Ero e Leandro*" (Madrid, 1897, New York, 1899); an oratorio, etc.; overture and entr'actemus. to Cossa's "*Cleopatra*."

Mancini (män-chē'-nē), (1) **Fran.**, Naples, 1679—1739 cond. and dram. composer. (2) **Giambattista**, Ascoli, 1716—Vienna, 1800; writer on voice.

Manci'nus, Thomas, Schwerin, 1550—Wolfenbüttel ca. 1620; Dutch composer of "*Passions according to St. Matthew and St. John*"; cond. to Duke of Brunswick.

Mandl (mänt'-'l), **Richard,** Prossnitz, Moravia, 1859—Vienna, April 1, 1918; pianist; pupil Vienna Cons., later of Delibes, Paris, where he settled 1886; c. 1-act opera "*Rencontre Imprévue*" (Rouen, 1889); "*Chanson Provençal*" for voice and orch., orch. scherzo (Lamoureux concerts, 1894); symph. poem, with organ, mezzo-sopr. and female chorus, "*Griselidis*" (Vienna, 1906?); overture "*To a Gascon Knight drama*" (Wiesbaden, 1910), piano pieces, etc.

Mandyczewski (män-dē-chěf'-skǐ), **Eusebius,** Czernovitz, Aug. 18, 1857—Vienna, July 15, 1929; pupil of Fuchs and Nottebohm; from 1897 teacher Vienna Cons.; writer and editor of Schubert's works, for which he was made Ph. D., Leipzig. After 1914 he was comp. teacher at the Vienna Cons.; he trained the Vienna Singakademie chorus from 1887, and was librarian of the Musikfreunde, whose historic archives he kept; also chairman of the Tonkünstlerverein, and a personal friend of Brahms, whose complete works (as well as those of Haydn) he edited.

Manén (mä'-nän) **Joan,** b. Barcelona, March 14, 1883; violinist; composer; travelled as prodigy pianist, then took up violin; pupil of Alard; c. operas "*Giovanni di Napoli*" (Barcelona, 1903), "*Akté*" (do.); "*Der Fackeltanz*" (Frankfort -on - Main 1909); symph. poem "*Nuova Catalonia*," violin concertos, etc.

Manfredini (män-frĕ-dē'nē), (1) **Francesco,** b. Pistoja, 1688; violinist; 1711

cond. at Monaco; c. oratorios, concertos, etc. His son (2) **Vincenzo,** Pistoja, 1737—St. Petersburg, 1799, as court cond., c. sonatas, etc.

Mangeot (män-zhō), **Ed. Jos.,** Nantes, France, 1834—Paris, 1898; pf.-maker and editor; inv. piano "à double clavier renversé."

Mangold (män'-gôlt), (1) **G. M.,** 1776 —1835; violinist. (2) (Jn.) **Wm.,** Darmstadt, 1796—1875; conductor and dram. composer. (3) **K.** (L. Amand), Darmstadt, 1813—Oberstdorf, Algau, 1889; bro. of above; dir., conductor and composer. (4) **K. G.,** 1812—London, 1887; pianist, composer and teacher.

Mann, Arthur Henry, Norwich, Engl., May 16, 1850—Cambridge, Nov. 11, 1929; chorister at the cath. with Dr. Buck; organist various churches; since 1876, King's Coll., Cambridge; 1871, F. C. O., 1882, Mus. Doc., Oxford; Händel scholar; with Prout discovered the original wind-parts of the "*Messiah*"; ed. the *Fitzwilliam Catalogue* with Maitland, etc.; c. "*Ecce Homo,*" with orch.; "*Te Deum,*" "*Evening Service,*" for orch., etc.

Man'ners, (1) **Charles** (rightly Southcote Mansergh),** London, Dec. 27, 1857—Dublin, May 3, 1935; bass; pupil Dublin Academy and R. A. M., London, and of Shakespeare; début 1882; 1890 Covent Garden; 1893 toured America; 1896 South Africa; 1897, organised Moody-Manners Opera Co. touring the provinces with three companies, two seasons at Covent Garden. In 1890 he married (2) **Fanny Moody,** b. Redruth, Nov. 23, 1866; soprano; pupil of Mme. Sainton Dolby; début 1887 with Carl Rosa Co., from 1890 sang with her husband.

Mannes (măn'-něs), (1) **David,** b. New York, Feb. 16, 1866; violinist, conductor, educator; studied in New York, Berlin and Brussels; played in N. Y. Symph., 1898 concertm.; cond. Symph. Club after 1902; taught at Music School Settlement, N. Y., for some years; beginning 1916, founded and dir. the David Mannes Music School, with his wife (2) **Clara** (née **Damrosch**) as co-dir.; cond. of concert series at Met. Museum of Art beginning 1920; gave concerts for young people and adults in cities near N. Y.; toured in sonata recitals with his wife, an accomplished pianist; ed. *New Songs for New Voices*, with Mrs. Mannes and Louis Untermeyer, 1928. (3) **Leopold Damrosch**, b. New York, Dec. 6, 1899; son of the preceding; composer and pianist; grad. Harvard Univ.; pupil of Guy Maier, Cortot, Scalero and others; Pulitzer Prize for comp.; also Guggenheim Fellowship; teacher of comp. and lecturer at David Mannes Music School; and of theory at Inst. of Mus. Art, N. Y.; c. string quartet, variations for piano, suite for 2 pianos, suite for orch.; introd. and allegro for vln. and piano; songs; incid. music to "*The Tempest*," etc.

Man'ney, Chas. Fonteyn, b. Brooklyn, 1872; studied with Wm. Arms Fisher and J. Wallace Goodrich, Boston; composed cantatas, songs, etc.

Manns (mäns), **Sir Augustus,** Stolzenburg, near Stettin, March 12, 1825—London, March 2, 1907; noted conductor; son of a glass-blower, who with his sons formed a quintet (vlns., 'cello, horn, and flute); at 15, apprenticed to Urban of Elbing; later 1st clar. of a regimental band, Dantzig; 1848, at Posen. Wieprecht got him a place as 1st vln. in Gungl's orch. at Berlin; 1849-51, cond. Kroll's Garden; regimental bandm. Königsberg and Cologne (1854); joined Crystal Palace band, London, as asst.-cond. to Schallen, who pub. as his own **M.'s** arrangement of certain quadrilles; whereupon **M.** resigned, publicly stating the reason; 1859 he succeeded S., he later made the band a full orch., giving famous and very popular Saturday Concerts till 1900, when the public ceased to support it; he also cond. 7 Triennial Händel Festivals, concerts of the Glasgow Choral Union, 1879-92, etc. He was knighted 1904.

Mannstädt (män'-shtĕt), **Fz.,** Hagen, Westphalia, July 8, 1852—Wiesbaden, Jan. 18, 1932; pupil Stern Cons., Berlin; 1874, cond. at Mayence; 1876, Berlin Symph. Orch.; 1879, pf.-t. Stern Cons.; 1893-97, cond. Berlin Philh.; then returned to Wiesbaden, where he had been a conductor and teacher.

Mantius (män'-tsĭ-oos), **Ed.,** Schwerin, 1806—Bad Ilmenau, 1874; tenor.

Man'uel, Roland (rightly **Levy**), b. Paris, March 22, 1891; composer, critic.

Manzuoli (män-tsoo-ō'-lē), **Giov.,** b. Florence, ca. 1725; famous sopranomusico.

Ma'pleson, Col. Jas. H., London, May 4, 1828—Nov. 14, 1901; famous impresario; studied R. A. M., London; a singer, and vla.-player in an orch.; 1861, managed Italian Opera at the Lyceum; 1862-68, was at H. M.'s Th.; 1869, Drury Lane; 1877, reopened H. M.'s Th.; gave opera at Acad. of Mus., New York, with varying succ. in different seasons.

Mara (mä'-rä), **Gertrud Elisabeth** (née **Schmeling**), Cassel, Feb. 23, 1749—Reval, Jan. 20, 1833; phenomenal soprano, with compass, g-e''' (v. PITCH, D. D.), who reached a high pinnacle of art over difficulties (ranging from rickets to the Moscow fire) not surpassed in the wildest fiction; she m. in 1773, the 'cellist Mara, divorced him 1799; teacher.

Mara, La. Vide LIPSIUS, MARIE.

Marais (mǎ-rě'), (1) **Marin,** Paris, March 31, 1656—Aug. 15, 1728; the greatest viola-da-gambist of his time; c. symphonies, etc. (2) **Roland,** son of above; solo gambist; pub. pcs. for gamba.

Mar'beck, J. (or **Merbecke**), 1523—1585; Engl. organist and composer.

Marcello (mär-chĕl'-lō), **Benedetto,** Venice, July 24, 1686—Brescia, July 24, 1739; noted composer, pupil of Gasparini and Lotti; held gov't positions; pub. satires, and c. 50 psalms, madrigals, operas, oratorios, etc.

Marchand (mär-shäṅ), **Louis,** Lyons, 1669—in poverty, Paris, 1732; an org.-virtuoso whose fame wilted before his failure to meet J. S. Bach in a duel of virtuosity; c. clavecin pcs., etc.

Mar'chant, Arthur Wm., London, Oct. 18, 1850—Sterling, Nov. 23, 1922; organist in English churches; 1880-82, St. John's Cath., Denver, Col.; 1895, organist, Dumfries, Scotland; wrote text-books; c. Psalm 48, with orch.; "*A Morning Service*" and an "*Evening Service*," etc.

Marchesi (mär-kā'-zē), (1) **Luigi** ("**Marchesi'ni**"), Milan, 1755—Inzago, Dec. 14, 1829; soprano musico. (2) **Salvatore,** Cavaliere **De Castrone** (dä-käs-trō'-nĕ) (Marchese **Della Rajata**), Palermo, Jan. 15, 1822—Paris, Feb. 20, 1908; studied mus. with Raimondi, Lamperti and Fontana; exiled after the Revolution of

1848, and début as barytone, N. Y.; then studied with Garcia, London; a succ. concert-singer; 1852 m. Mathilde Graumann (v. *infra*), and they sang together in opera, later taught together at Vienna Cons., 1865-69, Cologne Cons.; 1869-81, Vienna, then in Paris; pub. a vocal method, translations, etc.; c. songs. (3) **Mathilde** (née **Graumann**), Frankfort-on-M., March 24, 1821—London, Nov. 18, 1913; famous singing-teacher; pupil of Nicolai, Vienna, and Garcia, Paris; sang in concert; wife of above (q. v.); pub. a vocal method, vocalises, and autobiog. *"Marchesi and Music,"* enlarged from *"Aus meinem Leben"* (Düsseldorf, 1887). (4) **Blanche**, Paris, 1863—London, 1940; daughter of (3) and (2); soprano; after 1896 lived in London as singing teacher; later in Paris; author, *"A Singer's Pilgrimage"*; m. Baron André Caccamisi.

Marchetti (mär-kĕt'-tĭ), **Filippo**, Bolognola, Italy, Feb. 26, 1831—Rome, Jan. 18, 1902; pupil of Lillo and Conti, Royal Cons., Naples; at 21 prod. succ. opera, *"Gentile da Varano"* (Turin), *"La Demente"* (1857); singing-teacher, Rome; went to Milan and prod. succ. *"Giulietta e Romeo"* (1865), and *"Ruy-Blas"* (La Scala, 1869). From 1881, dir. R. Accad. di Santa Cecilia, Rome; prod. 3 other operas, symphonies, and church-music.

Marchet'tus of Padua (Marchetto da Padova), lived in Cesena, ca. 1270—ca. 1320; learned theorist. (Gerbert.)

Marchisio (mär-kē'sĭ-ō), (1) **Barbara**, Turin, Dec. 12, 1834—Mira near Venice, April 19, 1919; opera singer in Paris and London; sang usually with her sister. (2) **Carlotta**, Turin, 1836—1872.

Marcoux (mär-kōō'), **Vanni**, b. Turin, 1879; barytone; of French-Italian ancestry; studied with Collino and Boyer; after 1899 appeared with succ. in Paris, London and Brussels; came to U. S. and was active with Chicago Op. for a number of seasons; refinement of character portrayal and diction distinguished his perfs. of such rôles as "Boris Godounoff" and "Don Quichotte."

Maréchal (mär-ā-shăl), (1) **Henri**, Paris, Jan. 22, 1842—May 10, 1924; pupil of Cons., 1870, won Grand Prix

de Rome; prod. 1-act op.-com. *"Les Amoureux de Cathérine"* (Op.-Com., 1876); also 3-act op.-com. *"La Traverne des Trabans"* (ibid., '81); *"Déïdamie"* (Gr. Opéra, '93); *"Calendal"* (Rouen, '94); c. sacred drama *"Le Miracle de Naïm"* ('91), etc. (2) **Maurice**, b. Dijon, France, Oct. 3, 1892; 'cellist; pupil of Paris Cons.; 1st prize in 'cello; after 1912 soloist with leading Paris orchs.; played in trio with Thibaud and Cortot; toured U. S. as recitalist.

Marenco (mä-rĕn'-kō), **Romualdo**, Novi Ligure, Italy, March 1, 1841—Milan, Oct. 10, 1907; violinist; then 2d bassoon, Doria Th., Genoa, where he prod. a ballet; studied cpt. with Fenaroli and Mattoi; 1873, dir. of ballet at La Scala, Milan; c. 4 operas, and over 20 ballets.

Marenzio (mä-rĕn'-tsĭ-ō), **Luca**, Coccaglio, near Brescia, ca. 1553—("of love disprized") Rome, Aug. 22, 1599; famous composer of madrigals, also of motets, etc.

Mareš (mä'-rĕsh), **Johann A.**, Chotebor, Bohemia, 1719—St. Petersburg, 1794; invented the Russian "hunting-horn mus.," each horn sounding one tone.

Maretzek (mä-rĕt'-shĕk), **Max**, Brünn, Moravia, June 28, 1821—Pleasant Plains, Staten Island, N. Y., May 14, 1897; well-known impresario; also dram. composer and teacher.

Mariani (mä-rĭ-ä'-nē), **Angelo**, Ravenna, Oct. 11, 1821—Genoa, June 13, 1873; famous conductor.

Marimon (mă-rē-môṅ), **Marie**, b. Liége, 1839; pupil of Duprez; début, 1857; soprano.

Marin (mä-răṅ), **M. Martin Marcelle de**, b. Bayonne, France, Sept. 8, 1769; harpist and composer.

Marini (mä-rē'-nē), (1) **Biagio**, Brescia—Padua, ca. 1660; violinist and composer. (2) **Carlo A.**, b. Bergamo; violinist and composer, 1696.

Marinuzzi (mär-ē-nōōd'-sē), **Gino**, b. Palermo, March 24, 1882; conductor and composer; dir. Bologna Liceo, 1915-18; cond. Costanzi Theatre, Rome, and 1919-21 with Chicago Op., where his *"Jacquerie"* was prod., 1921; later res. in San Remo; has also cond. in South America, in Turin, Milan and at Rome with much succ.; c. also operas, *"Il Sogno del Poeta,"* *"Barberina"*; (orch.) *"Suite Siciliano"*; a Requiem for chorus, etc.

Mario (mä'-rĭ-ō), (1) **Giuseppe, Conte**

di Candia, Cagliari, Sardinia, Oct. 17, 1810—Rome, Dec. 11, 1883; eminent tenor; pupil of Bordogni and Poncharde; début, Paris Opéra, 1838; toured Europe and America with greatest success; m. Giulia Grisi. (2) **Queena** (rightly **Tillotson**), b. Akron, Ohio, August 21, 1896; soprano; studied with Oscar Saenger and Sembrich; mem. of Met. Op. Co., author of a novel; m. Wilfred Pelletier, conductor; divorced.

Mar'iotte, Antoine, b. Avignon, Dec. 22, 1875; pupil of d'Indy; composer of operas, etc.

Markevitch (mär-kyä'-věch), **Igor,** b. Kiev, Russia, July 27, 1912; composer and pianist; studied with Nadia Boulanger in Paris, where he lived after 1926; also for a time with Vittorio Rieti; commissioned by Diaghileff to write a ballet, but that impresario died before it could be written; 1st came into prominence with perf. of his Concerto Grosso in Paris, 1929, and Piano Concerto, same year in London; his works reveal a polyharmonic style of uncompromising harshness, much rhythmic vitality and logical clarity, but an almost total lack of feeling; his music has been called highly original and significant by some, merely sensational by other critics; c. (orch.) Sinfonietta; Concerto Grosso; Piano Concerto; Partita; *"Rebus"; "Hymnes"* (an excerpt played by Boston Symph., 1934); (chamber music) Serenade for vln., clar. and bassoon; (choral works) Psalm (the last causing a bitter division of opinion between adherents and detractors when played at the I. S. C. M. Fest. in Florence); and a cantata, *"Paradise Lost"* (perf. in London and Paris, 1936).

Markull (mär-kool'), **Fr. Wm.,** Reichenbach, near Elbing, 1816—Danzig, 1887; pianist, critic and dram. composer.

Markwort (märk'-vôrt), **Jn. Chr.,** Riesling, near Brunswick, 1778— Bessungen, 1866; tenor and writer.

Marmontel (mär-môn-těl), **Ant. Fran.,** Clermont-Ferrand, Puy-de-Dôme, July 18, 1816—Paris, Jan. 15, 1898; pupil Paris Cons., 1848; pf.-teacher there, noted for famous pupils; writer of historic and didactic treatises; composer.

Marpurg (mär'-poorkh), (1) **Fr. Wm.,**

Seehausen, Altmark, Nov. 21, 1718— Berlin, May 22, 1795; important theorist; wrote treatises of great historic and theoretic value, much translated. (2) **Fr.,** Paderborn, 1825 —Wiesbaden, 1884; great-grandson of above; violinist, pianist, cond. and dram. composer.

Mar'schalk, Max, b. Berlin, April 7, 1863; composer of 2-act opera *"In Flammen"* (Gotha, 1896); musical piece *"Aucassin und Nicolette"* (Stuttgart, 1907); incid. music to *"Und Pippa tanzt"* (Berlin, 1906), and to Maeterlinck's *"Sister Beatrice"* (Berlin, 1904); critic of Berlin *"Vossische Zeitung,"* 1895-1933.

Marschner (märsh'-něr), (1) **H. (August),** Zittau, Saxony, Aug. 16, 1795 (not 1796)—Hanover, Dec. 14, 1861; eminent opera-composer of Weber's school but great modernity, and remarkable brilliance of instrumentation; studied piano from age of 6; sang as a boy, then pupil of Bergt (org.); studied law Leipzig U. 1813, then turned to mus. entirely; pupil of Schicht; the Graf von Amadée became his patron, and he went to Vienna; later taught at Pressburg; c. 3 operas, the last prod. 1820 at Dresden by C. M. von Weber; 1823, he became co.-dir. of opera there with von W. and Morlacchi; 1826, cond. Leipzig Th. and prod. *"Der Vampyr"* (1828) and *"Der Templer und die Jüdin";* both widely succ. and still heard; 1831-59, ct.-cond. Hanover, when he was pensioned; while ct.-cond. he prod. *"Hans Heiling"* (Berlin, 1833), also very succ. and still alive; he prod. 8 other operas; c. incidental music, choruses, etc. (2) **Fz.,** b. Leitmeritz, Bohemia, March 26, 1855; pupil Prague Cons., and Bruckner, Vienna; after 1886, teacher Female Teachers' Seminary, Vienna; pub. a treatise on piano-touch; d. n. Poggstall, Austria, Aug. 28, 1932.

Marshall, (1) **John Patton,** b. Rockfort, Mass., 1877—Boston, 1941; pupil B. J. Lang, MacDowell, Chadwick, and Norris; 1903 Prof. of Music, Boston University; c. songs and piano pieces. (2) **Charles;** b. Waterville, Me.; tenor; studied with William Whitney, Vannucini and Lombardi; sang in Italian opera houses after début in Florence, 1901; also in Russia, Greece and Turkey; mem. Chicago Op. for a decade after 1921, singing heroic tenor rôles in Italian and French works.

Marsick (măr-sĭk), (1) **Martin P. Jos.**, Jupille, near Liége, Belgium, March 9, 1848—Paris, Oct. 21, 1924; prominent violinist; pupil of Désiré Haynberg, Liége Cons.; at 12 organist of the cath., and a vocalist; pupil of Léonard, Brussels Cons., later of Massenet at Paris Cons. (taking 1st vln. prize); and of Joachim at Berlin; début, Paris, 1873; toured Europe and (1895–96) U. S.; 1892, vln.-prof., Paris Cons.; c. 3 vln.-concertos, etc. (2) **Armand**, b. Liége, 1878; pupil of Ropartz and d'Indy; 1900, teacher and conductor in Athens; composer.

Marteau (măr-tō), **Henri**, Rheims, March 31, 1874—Lichtenberg, Oct. 3, 1934; excellent violinist; pupil Paris Cons.; 1892, took 1st prize; toured U. S., 1893, 1898; Russia, 1899; then compelled to spend a year in the French army; founded "Marteau Prize for vln.-sonata c. by a native-born American"; 1900 toured America; from 1900 teacher at Geneva Cons.; 1908–15, successor to Joachim at the Royal Hochschule für Musik, Berlin; 1921, Prague; 1926–28, Leipzig Cons.; later Dresden; c. chamber music, vln. works, etc.

Martelli, E. Vide COTTRAU, T.

Martin (măr-tăṅ), (1) **Jn. Blaisé**, Lyons, 1768—Paris, 1837; barytone. (2) **Sir George Clement**, Lambourne, Berks, Sept. 11, 1844—London, 1916; organist various churches; teacher in R. Coll. of Mus.; c. anthems; knighted, 1889. (3) **Riccardo (Hugh Whitfield)**, b. Hopkinsville, Ky., Nov. 18, 1881; tenor; studied violin; comp. with MacDowell; singing with Escalais, Sbriglia and Lombardi; début as "Faust," Nantes, France, 1904; sang in Verona and Milan; made Amer. début with French Op. Co., New Orleans; sang with Met. Op. Co., 1907–15; Boston Op. Co., 1915–17; at Covent Garden, and after 1920 with Chicago Op., also in concerts; later res. in Europe.

Martin y Solar (măr-tēn'-ē-sō-lär'), **Vicente**, Valencia, Spain, 1754—St. Petersburg, March 3, 1806; organist at Alicante; prod. operas in Italy in succ. rivalry with Cimarosa and Paisiello and in Vienna with Mozart; his best work was "*La Cosa Rara,*"

1785; 1788–1801, dir. Italian Op. at St. Petersburg; then teacher; c. 10 operas, ballets, etc.

Martinel'li, Giovanni, b. Montagnana, Italy, Oct. 22, 1885; notable tenor; at first an instrumentalist in Milan; début 1912, Covent Garden in "*La Tosca*" with great success; mem. of Met. Op. Co., N. Y., since 1913, with outstanding rank in wide variety of Italian and French rôles; has sung in South America, in Brussels and in many Italian theatres with eminent succ.; also in concerts.

Martines (mär-tē'-něs) (or **Martinez**) (mär-tē'-něth), **Marianne di**, Vienna, 1744—1812; singer, pianist and composer.

Martini (mär-tē'-nē), (1) **Giambattista** (or **Giov. Bat.**) (known as **Padre M.**), Bologna, April 24, 1706—Oct. 4, 1784; son and pupil of a violinist ((2) **Antonio Maria M.**), he studied with Predieri and Riccieri, Zanotti and Perti; took orders 1729; cond. from 1725 at church of San Francisco, Bologna; as a composer of church-mus., a theorist and teacher he won European fame; he also pub. a history of ancient mus., and treatises. (3) (rightly **Schwarzendorf**) (shvärts'-ĕn-dôrf), **Jean Paul Egide**, Freistadt, Palatinate, 1741—Paris, 1816; dram. composer. (4) **Nino**, b. Verona, Italy, 1905; tenor; pupil of Giovanni Zenatello; op. début in Italy at 21, in "*I Puritani*"; Amer. début as the "Duke" in "*Rigoletto*" with Phila. Grand Op. Co., 1931; mem. Met. Op. Co., after 1933; also active as concert, radio and film artist.

Martin'u, Bohuslav, b. Policka, Bohemia, Dec. 8, 1890; composer; studied at Prague Cons. (violin), also comp. with Suk and Roussel; c. sacred opera, "*Mysteries of the Virgin Mary*"; many chamber music works in advanced modern manner, among which are several string quartets, quintet, concerto for string quartet and orch., harpsichord concerto; symph. music and accompaniment to films; some of his works perf. in America by Boston Symph. and at Coolidge Fest., Pittsfield, Mass.

Martucci (mär-toot'-chē), **Gius.**, Capua, Jan. 6, 1856—Naples, June 1, 1909; son and pupil of a trumpet-player; début as pianist Naples, 1867; studied at the Cons.; 1874, prof. there; cond. the orch. and concerts estab. by Prince d'Ardore, and dir. of the Società del Quartetto; from 1875, toured with succ. as pianist; 1886–1902, dir. Bologna Cons.; 1902, Naples; c. 2 symph., pf.-concerto, chamber, choral works, etc.

Marty (mär-tē), **G. Eugène,** Paris, May 16, 1860—Vichy, Oct. 11, 1908; studied at the Cons. 1882; won the Grand Prix de Rome with cantata "*Edith*"; since 1894, prof. for ensemble singing there; 1895–96, chorusm. and cond. of the Concerts de l'Opéra; 1901, dir. concerts of the Cons.; c. several suites for orch., pantomime, "*Le Duc de Ferrare*," 3-act opera (1896), etc.

Marx (märx), (1) **Ad. Bd.,** Halle, May 15, 1795—Berlin, May 17, 1866; eminent theorist; founded with Schlesinger, "*Berliner allgemeine musikalische Zeitung*"; editor, prof. and mus.-dir., 1832; c. opera; wrote v. succ. and important treatises. (2) **Joseph,** b. Graz, Austria, May 11, 1882; composer, educator; studied with Degner, also at Univ., Ph. D.; prof. Vienna Akad., after 1914; succeeded Loewe as dir., 1922–25; 1925–27, also rector of the Hochschule; known for his songs, espec. "*Italienisches Liederbuch*"; also c. orch., chamber and choral music; a symph.; "*Castella Romana*" for piano and orch., etc.

Marxsen (märx'-zĕn), **Eduard,** Nienstädten, near Altona, 1806—Altona, 1887; organist and teacher.

Marzials (mär-tsĭ-äls'), **Theodor,** Brussels, Dec. 21, 1850—Feb., 1920; pupil of M. L. Lawson, London; studied later in Paris and Milan; 1870, supt. mus.-dept. British Museum; barytone and composer of pop. songs.

Marzo (mär'-tsō), **Ed.,** Naples, 1852—June 7, 1929; pupil of Nacciarone, Miceli and Papalardo; 1867, New York, as boy pianist; became opera and concert-cond., and accompanist to Carlotta Patti, Sarasate, etc.; organist at St. Agnes' Church, N. Y.; later at All Saints; 1884, knighted by the King of Italy; 1892, member of the R. Acad. of S. Cecilia; lived in N. Y. as singing teacher; pub. 6 masses (3 with orch.), etc.

Mascagni (mäs-kän'-yē), **Pietro,** b. Leghorn, Dec. 7, 1863. Son of a baker who wished him to study law;

he secretly studied the piano, later at Soffredini's Mus.-Sch.; studied pf., harm., cpt., and comp.; his father, finding him out, locked him in the house, whence he was rescued at 14 by an uncle; upon the uncle's death he was befriended by Count Florestan, while studying with Ponchielli and Saladino, at Milan Cons. He was cond. of various small troupes, finally cond. of the mus.-soc. at Cerignola; he won the prize offered by the mus.-pub. Sonzogno, for a 1-act opera, with "*Cavalleria Rusticana*," which had a sensational succ. (Costanzi Th., Rome, 1890) and has been universally performed; while fiercely assailed by the critics it has produced a school of short operas showing a tendency to excessive realism and strenuousness, yet offering a much-needed relief from the eternal classic, mythologic or costume-play plots and bringing serious opera as close home to real life as comic opera; 1895, dir. of the Rossini Cons. at Pesaro. **M.**'s later operas have not fared so well as his "*Cavalleria Rusticana*"; they include: "*L'Amico Fritz*" (Rome and Berlin, 1891), "*I Rantzau*" (Florence, 1892), fairly succ.; "*Guglielmo Ratcliff*" (Milan, La Scala, 1895), "*Silvano*" (ibid., 1895); 1-act "bozzetto" "*Zanetto*" (Pesaro, 1896); and the fairly succ. "*Iris*" (Rome, 1898; revised La Scala, Milan, 1899); "*Le Maschere*" simultaneously prod. without succ. in 6 cities in Italy, Jan., 1901; he c. also (previously to *Cav. Rust.*) 2-act opera "*Il Filanda*," and Schiller's "*Hymn to Joy*"; also a "*Hymn in Honor of Admiral Dewey, U. S. N.*" (July, 1899), etc. 1902, toured America with his own opera-troupe; he was dir. of Pesaro Cons. until 1903; 1909, cond. at Teatro Costanzi, Rome; c. also "*Amica*" (Monte Carlo, 1905, Cologne, 1907); 1910 he c. opera "*Isabeau*" for the U. S. but not completing it on time became involved in a lawsuit. The opera was prod. at Venice and Milan simultaneously, 1912, with moderate succ. Later operas include "*Parisina*" (Milan, 1913); "*Lodoletta*" (Rome, 1917); operetta, "*Si*" (Rome, 1919); "*Il Piccolo Marat*" (Rome, 1921, with succ. of short duration); "*Nerone*" (Rome, 1935), an attempt to show Nero as an art-lover and amorist; also symph., choral and other works. M. has appeared widely in Italy as a cond. of his works, also in orch. concerts; mem. of Italian Academy.

Maschek (mä-shāk'), (1) **Vincenz,** Zwikovecz, Bohemia, 1755—Prague, 1831; pf. and harmonica-virtuoso; organist and dram. composer. (2) **Paul,** 1761—Vienna, 1826; bro. of above; pianist.

Mascheroni (mäs-kĕ-rō'-nē), **Edoardo,** Milan, 1857—March 4, 1941; cond. and composer; pupil of Boucheron; 1883 theatre cond. at Leghorn, later at Teatro Apollo, Rome; 1893 chosen to cond. Verdi's *"Falstaff"* at La Scala; c. *"Requiem"* for King Victor Emanuel, also by Royal command another *"Requiem"* for the royal chapel; c. operas *"Lorenza"* (Rome, 1901) successful throughout Europe and South America; *"La Perugina,"* etc.

Ma'son, (1) Rev. **Wm.,** Hull, Engl., 1724—Aston, 1797; writer and composer. (2) **Lowell,** Medfield, Mass., Jan. 24, 1792—Orange, N. J., Aug. 11, 1872; pioneer in American comp. and teaching; c. v. succ. and remunerative colls., principally of sacred music. (3) **Wm.,** Boston, Mass., Jan. 24, 1829—New York, July 14, 1908; prominent American teacher and technician; son of above; studied with Henry Schmidt (pf.) in Boston; at 17, début as pianist there; 1849, studied with Moscheles, Hauptmann and Richter, at Leipzig; with Dreyschock at Prague; and Liszt, at Weimar; he played in Weimar, Prague, and Frankfort, London, and 1854–55 in American cities; 1855 lived in New York as teacher; 1872, Mus. Doc. *h. c.,* Yale; pub. *"Touch and Technic, a Method for Artistic Piano playing"; "A Method for the Pf."* with E. S. Hoadley (1867); *"System for Beginners"* (1871); *"Mason's Pf.-Technics"* (1878); and *"Memoirs"* (New York, 1901); c. a serenata for 'cello and many pf.-pcs. in classical form. (4) **Luther Whiting,** Turner, Maine, 1828 — Buckfield, Maine, 1896; devised the v. succ. *"National System"* of mus.-charts and books; wrote *"Die neue Gesangschule."* (5) **Daniel Gregory,** b. Brookline, Mass., Nov. 20, 1873; pupil of Clayton Johns, E. Nevin, A. Whiting, J. K. Paine, Chadwick, d'Indy and

Goetschius; graduated Harvard, 1895; author of articles and books on musical topics; c. violin and piano sonata, piano variations, quartet in A major; pastorale for violin, clarinet and piano; elegy for piano, symphonies and other orch. works, songs, etc.; prof. of music at Columbia Univ., N. Y. Author, *"From Grieg to Brahms," "Guide to Music," "Beethoven and His Forerunners," "Great Modern Composers," "The Romantic Composers," "Appreciation of Music"* (with T. W. Surette); *"Orchestral Instruments,"* etc.; ed. *"The Art of Music."* (6) **Henry Lowell,** b. Boston, 1864; grandson of Lowell M.; mem. of firm of Mason & Hamlin, piano mfrs. after 1888; pres., 1915; author of histories of piano and reed organ, and stories of operas. (7) **Edith Barnes,** b. St. Louis, Mo., 1892; soprano; studied with Clement and Maurel; mem. Boston Op., 1913; Met. Op. Co., 1915–17, and again after 1935; appeared with Paris Op. and Op.-Comique, 1918–21; Chicago Op., 1921–30; also at La Scala, Monte Carlo, Havana, Mexico City and at Ravinia (Chicago), in lyric rôles; m. Giorgio Polacco, conductor.

Massa (mäs'-sä), **Nicolò,** Calice, Ligure, Italy, 1854—Genoa, 1894; c. operas.

Massaini (mäs-sä-ē'-nē), **Tiburzio,** b. Cremona, 16th cent.; Augustine monk; cond. and composer.

Massart (mäs-sär'), (1) **Lambert Jos.,** Liége, July 19, 1811—Paris, Feb. 13, 1892; violinist and prof. Paris Cons. (2) **Louise Aglæ** (née Masson), Paris, 1827—1887; wife of above; pianist and, 1875, teacher at the Cons. (3) **Nestor, H. J.,** Ciney, Belgium, 1849—Ostende, 1899; tenor opera singer; operatic favourite in Europe and America.

Massé (mäs-sā), **Felix M.** (called Victor), Lorient, Mar. 7, 1822—Paris, July 5, 1884; pupil Paris Cons.; won Grand prix de Rome, prof. of cpt. there 1872; c. 18 operas, 13 prod., incl. the still succ. *"Les noces de Jeannette"* (Op. Com. 1853).

Massenet (mäs-nā), **Jules** (**Émile Fr.**), Montaud, near St. Étienne, France, May 12, 1842—Paris, Aug. 13, 1912 (of cancer); eminent French opera-composer; pupil of Laurent (pf.), Reber (harm.), Savard and Ambr.

Thomas (comp.) at the Cons.; took first prizes for piano and fugue; 1863, the Grand prix de Rome with cantata "*David Rizzio*"; 1878-96 prof. of comp. at the Cons.; 1878, member of the Académie, Commander of the Legion of Honour. C. operas, almost all of them succ. and many still in the repertory of the Paris Opéra and Op. Com., 1-act comic opera "*La Grand Tanta*" (1867); the operas, "*Don César de Bazan*" (1872); "*Le Roi de Lahore*" (1877); "*Hérodiade*" (1884); "*Manon Lescaut*" (one of the greatest successes in the history of the Op.-Com.), "*Le Cid*" (1885); fairy-opera (1889) "*Esclarmonde*"; "*Le Mage*" (1891); "*Werther*" (1892); lyric comedy, "*Thaïs*" (1894); 1-act com.-op. "*Le Portrait de Manon*" (1894); lyric episode, "*La Navarraise*" (London, 1894; Paris, 1895); "*Sapho*" (Op.-Com., 1897); "*Cendrillon*" (Op.-Com., 1899); also 4-act drama "*Marie-Magdeleine*" (Odéon Th., 1873); "*Ève*," a mystery, 1875; oratorio, "*La Vièrge*," 1880; conte lyrique "*Griselidis*" (Op.-Com., 1901); "*Jongleur de Nôtre Dame*," (Monte Carlo, 1902) (sung widely; Covent Garden, 1906, New York Manhattan Opera, 1910); "*Cherubin*" (Op. Com. Paris, 1905); "*Ariane*" (1906); "*Thérèse*" (Monte Carlo, 1907); "*Don Quichotte*" (Paris, 1911); "*Roma*" (Paris, Opéra, 1912); oratorios "*La Terre Promise*" (Paris, 1900); piano concerto (1903); ballets, "*La cigale*" (Paris, 1903), "*Espada*" (Monte Carlo, 1908), "*Bacchus*" (1909), "*Panurge*" (1913), opera "*Cleopâtre*"; orch. suites; overtures incl. "*Phèdre*"; pf.-pcs., songs, etc.

Maszynski (mä-shĭn'-shkĭ), **Peter, b.** Warsaw, 1855; pianist and composer; pupil of Mikhalovski, Roguski and Noszkowski; his "*Chor zniviarzy*" won a prize at Cracow; teacher at the Musical Institute; cond.; c. violin sonata, incid. music, a cantata in honor of the jubilee of Sienkiewicz, etc.

Materna (mä-tĕr'-nä), **Amalie, St.** Georgen, Styria, July 10, 1845—Vienna, Jan. 18, 1918; noted soprano; daughter of a sch.-master; sang in church and concert at Graz; début 1865 in opera as soubrette; m. an actor, K. Friedrich, and sang with him in operetta at the Carl Th.,

Vienna; 1869-96 prima donna, Vienna ct.-opera; toured America 1884 and 1894; she created "Brünnhilde," at Bayreuth, 1876, and "Kundry" in "*Parsifal*," 1882; after 1900 taught in Vienna.

Math'ews, Wm. Smyth Babcock, New London, N. H., May 8, 1837—Denver, Col., April 8, 1912; prominent teacher and writer; studied at New London; later at Lowell and Boston; 1860-63, pf.-teacher Macon, Ga.; 1867-93, organist Chicago; 1868-72, ed. "*Musical Independent*"; 1878-86, critic of Chicago *Times*, *Morning News*, and *Tribune*; 1891, founded and ed. the magazine *Music*; pub. many books of educational value.

Mathias (mä-tē'-äs), **Georges (Amédée St. Clair)**, Paris, Oct. 14, 1826—Oct. 14, 1910; pupil of Kalkbrenner and Chopin (pf.) and of Paris Cons.; 1862, pianist and prof. there, c. symph., overtures, etc.

Mathieu (mät-yŭ), (1) **Adolphe Chas. Ghislain,** Mons, Belgium, June 22, 1840—Paris, 1883; custodian of MSS. Brussels Library; writer. (2) **Émile (Louis V.),** Lille, Oct. 16, 1844 —Sept., 1932; studied Louvain Mus. Sch. and Brussels Cons.; won 1st harm. prize, and 1st pf. prize, 1869, and 1871, won 2nd Grand prix de Rome; 1867-73, prof. pf. and harm., Louvain Mus. Sch.; 1881-98, dir. Louvain Mus.-Sch.; 1898, dir. R. Cons. at Ghent; c. 7 operas, mostly comic, a ballet, 5 cantatas and 2 children's cantatas, 3 (text and music) "*Poèmes lyriques et symphoniques*," symph. poems, etc.

Mattei (mät-tā'-ē), (1) Abbate **Stanislao,** Bologna, 1750—1825; professor, conductor and writer. (2) **Tito,** Campobasso, near Naples, May 24, 1841—London, March 30, 1914; pianist to the King of Italy; pupil at 11 and later "Professore," Accad. di Santa Cecilia, Rome; received a gold medal from Pius IX.; toured Europe; 1865-71, cond. at H. M.'s Th., London; c. 3 operas incl. "*Maria, di Gand*" (H. M.'s Th., 1880); ballet, pop. songs, etc.

Matteis (mät-tā'-ēs), (1) **Nicolà,** Italian violinist, 1672, London. (2) **Nicolà,** d. 1749, son of above; teacher.

Matthay, Tobias Augustus, b. London, Feb. 19, 1858; pianist; pupil R. A. M., teacher there; c. "*Hero and Leander*," for chorus and orch., etc. One of most eminent piano masters, with many famous pupils. An Amer. **M.** Assoc. formed among these which annually awards a scholarship in competition for study with him. Author of important treatises.

Mat(t)heson (mät'-tĕ-zōn), **Jn.,** Hamburg, Sept. 28, 1681—April 17, 1764; versatile diplomat and musician, a singer, composer and player on the org. and harps.; operatic tenor; important in the development of the church cantata afterward advanced by Bach; the first to introduce women into church-service; pub. valuable and controversial treatises; c. 88 works; 1715–28, mus. dir., Hamburg Cath.

Matthieux, Jna. Vide KINKEL.

Matthison-Hansen (mät'-tĭ-zōn-hän'-zĕn), (1) **Hans,** Flensburg, Denmark, 1807—Roeskilde, 1890; organist and composer. (2) **Godfred,** Roeskilde, Nov. 1, 1832—Copenhagen, Oct. 14, 1909; son of above; 1859, organist German Friedrichskirche, Copenhagen; 1862, won the Ancker scholarship, and studied at Leipzig; 1867, organist at St. John's and organ-teacher Copenhagen Cons.; from 1877, asst.-organist to his father; later organist of Trinity Ch.; c. vln. sonata, 'cello sonata, etc.

Matzenauer (mät'-sĕn-ow-ĕr), **Margarete,** b. Temesvar, Hungary, June 1, 1881; contralto; her father a conductor and mother an opera singer; studied with Mmes. Mielke and Neuendorf and Franz Emerich; début, Strasbourg, 1901; mem. of this co. to 1904; thereafter until 1911 with Munich. Op.; Met. Op., N. Y., 1911–30; also soloist with orchs., and in recital; has taught and appeared in films; m. Edoardo Ferrari-Fontana, tenor; divorced.

Maubourg (mō'-boorg), **Jeanne,** b. Namur, 1875; soprano; her teachers included Mmes. Labarre and Jouron-Duvernay; she sang at La Monnaie, Brussels, 1897–1907; at Covent Garden after 1900, and at Met. Op., N. Y., 1909–14; afterward teaching in New York.

Mauduit (mō-dwē), **Jacques,** Paris, Sept. 16, 1557—Aug. 21, 1627; lute player and composer of chansons and a requiem for the poet Ronsard.

Mauke (mow'-kĕ), **Wilhelm,** Hamburg, Feb. 25, 1867—Wiesbaden. Aug. 25, 1930; pupil of Löwe and Huber; then at Munich Akad. der Tonkunst; acted as critic; c. symph. poem *"Einsamkeit"* (after Stuck and Nietzsche), operas, songs, etc.

Maurel (mō-rĕl), **Victor,** Marseilles, June 17, 1848—New York, Oct. 22, 1923; eminent barytone; studied Marseilles and with Vauthrot at the Paris Cons., gaining 1st prizes in singing and opera; début, 1868 at the Gr. Opéra as "de Nevers" in *"Les Huguenots"*; 1870, sang at La Scala, Milan, then in New York, Egypt, Russia with Patti, London, etc.; 1883, co-director Th. Italien, Paris, without succ.; sang in all the capitals as the supreme dramatic artist of his operatic generation, his splendid impersonation and vocal art carrying conviction after his voice lost its youth; he created "Iago" in Verdi's *"Otello,"* 1887, and stamped "Don Giovanni" and other rôles with his own personality as a criterion; after 1909 taught in New York.

Maurer (mow'-rĕr), **L. Wm.,** Potsdam, Feb. 8, 1789—St. Petersburg, Oct. 25, 1878; distinguished violinist and dram. composer.

Maurin (mō-răn), **Jean Pierre,** Avignon, 1822—Paris, 1894; violinist and teacher.

May, (1) **Edw. Collett,** Greenwich, 1806—London, 1887; vocal teacher and writer. (2) **Florence,** pianist, London; daughter of above; wrote biography of Brahms, of whom she was a pupil.

Mayer (mī'-ĕr), (1) **Chas.,** Königsberg, 1799—Dresden, 1862; pianist and composer. (2) **Emilie,** Friedland, Mecklenburg, May 14, 1821—Berlin, April 10, 1883; pupil of Löwe, Marx and Wieprecht; lived in Berlin; c. 7 symphonies, 12 overtures, an operetta, *"Die Fischerin,"* etc. (3) **Wm.** (pseud. **W. A. Remy**), Prague, 1831—Graz, 1898; excellent teacher of cpt. and comp.; composer. (4) Vide MAYER.

Mayerhoff (mī'-ĕr-hôf), **Fz.,** b. Chemnitz, Jan. 17, 1864; pupil Leipzig Cons.; theatre-cond. various cities; from 1885, Chemnitz; 1888, cantor Petrikirche, and cond. Mus. Soc.; 1910, cond. of Lehrergesangverein; 1915, Leipzig Riedel-Verein; 1911, Royal Prof., c. sacred choruses, etc.

May'nard, Walter. Vide BEALE, TH. W.

Mayr (mīr), (1) (Jn.) **Simon,** Mendorf, Bavaria, June 14, 1763—blind, Bergamo, Dec. 2, 1845; famous teacher and dram. composer; pupil of Lenzi and Bertoni; lived in Venice as church-composer; 1794 prod. v. succ. opera "*Saffo,*" followed by 70 more; 1802, cond. Santa Maria Maggiore, Bergamo, and 1805, dir. Mus. Inst.; wrote a life of Haydn, treatises and verse; he is said to have been the first to use the orchestral crescendo in Italy; biog. by Alborghetti and Galli (Bergamo, 1875). (2) **Richard,** Salzburg, Nov. 18, 1877—Vienna, Dec. 1, 1935; bass; studied at Vienna Cons., made début as "Hagen" at Bayreuth Fest., 1902; mem. of Vienna Op., 1902–35, singing wide range of rôles, but especially renowned for his *buffo* characterizations, such as "Baron Ochs" in "*Der Rosenkavalier*"; Covent Garden, 1924; Met. Op., N. Y., 1927 (début as "Pogner" in "*Die Meistersinger*"); also heard in Wagner and Mozart rôles at Salzburg Festivals.

Mayrberger (mīr'-běrkh-ěr), **K.,** Vienna, 1828—Pressburg, 1881; conductor and dram. composer.

Mayseder (mī'-zä-děr), **Jos.,** Vienna, Oct. 26, 1789—Nov. 21, 1863; eminent violinist, teacher and composer; 2nd vln. of famous "Schuppanzigh Quartet."

Mazas (mä-zäs), **Jacques Féréol,** Béziers, France, 1782—1849; violinist, writer and dram. composer.

Mazzinghi (mäd-zēn'-gǐ), **Jos.,** of Corsican extraction, London, 1765—London, 1839; organist, teacher and dram. composer.

Mazzocchi (mäd-zôk'-kǐ), **Dom.,** Città Castellana, Rome, ca. 1590—ca. 1650; composer.

Mazzolani (mäd-zō-lä'-nē), **Antonio,** Ruina, Ferrara, Dec. 26, 1819—Ferrara, Jan. 25, 1900; composer of successful operas and choruses.

Mazzucato (mäd-zoo-kät'-tō), **Alberto,** Udine, 1813—Milan, 1877; violinist, teacher, editor and composer.

McConathy, Osbourne, b. Pitts Point, Ky., 1875; educator, conductor; studied with Luther Mason, Karl Schmidt, Percy Goetschius; dir. Louisville Fests., 1900–03; cond. in Boston, choruses, bands, etc., 1904–12; assoc. cond., Evanston, Ill.,

North Shore Fests., 1913–25; teacher of theory and methods at various Amer. univs.; has served as pres., Music Teachers Nat'l Ass'n. and Music Supervisors Nat'l Conference; author and ed. of works on school music.

McCor'mack, John, b. Athlone, 1884; tenor; pupil of Sabatini, Milan; début Covent Garden, 1907, with great success; 1910 sang with Philadelphia Opera Co.; 1911 Chicago Opera Co.; toured Australia, 1912, with the Melba Opera Co. and in concert with immense succ. in U. S. and Europe; created a Papal Count by the Vatican.

McEw'en, Sir John Blackwood, b. Hawick, April 13, 1868; Scots composer and pupil R. A. M.; from 1898 prof. there and dir., 1924; knighted, 1934; c. symph., 2 overtures, "*Hellas*" for women's voices and orch. "*The Last Chantey,*" chorus and orch. Milton's "*Nativity,*" do.; also Highland dances for strings, violin, chamber music, etc.

McKin'ley, Carl, b. Yarmouth, Me., Oct. 9, 1895; composer; grad. Knox Cons., Galesburg, Ill.; also of Harvard Univ.; studied with G. Dethier, Rothwell, R. Goldmark, and Nadia Boulanger; his symph. poem, "*The Blue Flower,*" won Flagler Prize, 1921; cond. his "*Masquerade*" at N. Y. Stadium concerts, 1926; won Guggenheim Fellowship, 1927–29; was solo répetiteur at Munich Op., later teacher of organ, theory and history of music at N. E. Cons.

McPhee', Colin, b. Canada, 1901; composer, of modern style works, incl. piano concertos with orch. and also with wind octet; sonatina for two flutes, clar., trumpet and piano; "*Sea Chanty*" suite for barytone and unison male chorus; symph. in one movement, and "*Sarabande*" for orch.; also music for films and songs.

Mederitsch (mā'-dě-rītsh), **Jn.** (called **Gallus**), b. Nimburg, Bohemia, ca. 1765—died 1835, Lemberg; pianist and composer.

Medt'ner, Nicholas, b. Moscow, Dec. 24, 1879; composer, pianist; studied with Safonoff, at Moscow Cons; won medal there and also Rubinstein prize, Vienna, 1900; prof. Moscow Cons., 1902–3; has toured in many Eur. cities, also America 1929–30 in programs of his works;

these exhibit a more or less classical approach with some descriptive qualities; c. many works for piano, incl. sonatas, *"Dithyramben," "Novellen," "Fairy-Tales," "Tragödie-Fragment"*; also vln. sonata and songs.

Meerens (mā-räṅs), **Chas.**, Bruges, Dec. 26, 1831—near Brussels, Jan. 14, 1909; 'cellist and acoustician.

Meerts (mārts), **Lambert** (**Jos.**), Brussels, 1800—1863; violinist, professor and composer.

Mees (māz), **Arthur**, Columbus, Ohio, Feb. 13, 1850—New York, April 26, 1923; pupil of Th. Kullak (pf.), Weitzmann (theory), and H. Dorn (cond.), Berlin; cond. Cincinnati May Fest. Chorus; asst.-cond. various societies in New York, Albany, etc.; 1896, asst.-cond. Thomas Orch., Chicago; 1898—1904, cond. Mendelssohn Glee Club, New York; 1887–96, wrote programme notes for N. Y. Philh. Orch., pf.-studies; pub. *"Choirs and Choral Music."*

Megerlin (mā-gĕr-lăṅ), **Alfred**, b. Antwerp, Belgium, 1880; violinist; pupil Antwerp and Brussels Cons.; after 1914 in U. S. and for a period beginning 1917, concertm. of N. Y. Philh. Orch.

Mehlig (mā'-lǐkh), **Anna**, Stuttgart, July 11, 1846—Berlin, July 16, 1928; pianist, pupil of Lebert and Liszt; m. Antwerp merchant Falk.

Mehrkens (mār'-kĕns), **Fr. Ad.**, Neuenkirchen, near Otterndorf-on-Elbe, April 22, 1840—Hamburg, May 31, 1899; pupil, Leipzig Cons.; lived in Hamburg as pianist, teacher and conductor; from 1871, cond. of the Bach-Gesellschaft; c. a symph., a Te Deum, etc.

Méhul (mā-ül), **Étienne Nicolas, (Henri)**, Givet, Ardennes, June 22, 1763—of consumption, Paris, Oct. 18, 1817; one of the great masters of French opera, a student of orch. effects, and a special master of the overture; son of a cook; pupil of an old blind organist; at 10, studied with Wm. Hauser; at 14, his asst.; 1778, taught in Paris and studied with Edelmann (pf. and comp.); Gluck's advice and assistance turned him to dram. comp., after a succ. cantata with orch. (1782). He c. 3 operas, never prod., and now lost, a 4th was accepted but not performed until after the succ. of the op.-com.

"Euphrosyne et Coradin" (Th. Italien, 1790); 15 other operas followed with general succ. incl. *"Stratonice"* (1792), *"Le Congrès des Rois"* (1793) with 11 collaborators; 1705, inspector of the new Cons., and a member of the Academie; 1797, *"Le Jeune Henri"* was hissed off as irreverent toward Henri IV., though the fine overture had been demanded three times; the opera buffa *"L'irato, ou l'emporté"* (1801) made great succ. and lightened the quality of later operas; his best work was *"Joseph"* (1807); for four years he wrote only ballets; he left 6 unprod. operas incl. *"Valentine de Milan,"* completed by Daussoigne-Méhul, and prod. 1822; he c. also inferior symphs. and pf.-sonatas, and very pop. choruses *"Chant du départ," "C. de victoire," "Chant de retour,"* etc. Biogr. by Vieillard, 1859, and A. Pougin, 1889.

Meibom (mī'-bôm) (or **Meibo'mius**), **Marcus**, Tönning, Schleswig, 1626 (?)—Utrecht, 1711; theorist and collector; his great work is a valuable historical coll. of old composers.

Meifred (mĕ-frā), **Jos. J. P. Émile**, Colmars, Basses-Alps, 1791—Paris, 1867; horn-virtuoso, professor and writer.

Meiland (mī'-länt), **Jakob**, Senftenberg, Lower Lusatia, 1542—Celle, 1577; important contrapuntist.

Meinardus (mī-nar'-doos), **L. Siegfried**, Hooksiel, Oldenburg, 1827—Bielefeld, 1896; writer and dram. composer.

Meiners (mī'-nĕrs), **Giov. Bat.**, Milan, 1826—Cortenova, Como, 1897; conductor and dram. composer.

Meisle (mīz'-lē), **Kathryn**, b. Philadelphia; contralto; studied at Phila. Cons., début as soloist with Minneapolis Symph., 1921, and won reputation as a concert singer before entering opera; début in latter field as "Erda," Chicago Op., 1923; also as guest with Cologne Op., and after 1934 with Met. Op. Co.; m. Calvin Franklin, concert manager.

Meister (mī'-shtĕr), **K. Severin**, Königstein (Taunus), 1818—Montabaur, (Westerwald), 1881; teacher and mus. director.

Mel (mĕl), **Rinaldo de**, Flemish musician, 16th cent.

Mela (mā'-lä), (1) del **M.** Vide DEL

MELA. (2) **Vincenzo**, Verona, 1821 —Cologna, Vaneta, 1897; dram. composer.

Melar'tin, Erkki, Kexholm, Finland, Feb. 7, 1875—Helsingfors, Feb. 14, 1937; pupil of Wegelius; after 1911 dir. of Helsingfors Cons.; c. orch. music, songs, etc.

Melba (měl'-bä), **Nellie** (rightly **Mitchell**), Melbourne, Australia, May 19, 1861—Feb. 23, 1931; one of the chief colorature-sopranos of her time, with a voice of great range, purity and flexibility; pupil of Mme. Marchesi; début Th. de la Monnaie, Brussels, 1887, as "Gilda" in *"Rigoletto,"* sang in Europe and America with greatest succ. in both opera and concert; after 1888 at Covent Garden; the following year in Paris as "Ophelia"; from 1893 at Met. Op., N. Y., where she was one of the notable luminaries in casts with the brothers de Reszke; 1906–07 at Manhattan Op., and in 1917, Chicago Op.; she gave a series of special perfs. in 1922–23 with the British Nat'l Op. Co. in London, then organized her own co. for a season in Australia; as a reward for her extensive work in giving benefit concerts during the war was created a Dame Commander of the British Empire; her gala "farewell" at Covent Garden, when she appeared in scenes from her favorite operas, was in 1926; founded Melba Scholarship for women singers in her native country.

Melcér (měl'-tsěr), **H. von**, Kalish, Poland, Sept. 21, 1869—killed in battle, Galicia, 1915; pianist and composer; 1895 won Rubinstein prize with Concertstück for pf. and orch.

Melchior (měl'-kǐ-ôr), (1) **Edw. A.**, b. Rotterdam, Nov. 6, 1860; teacher and lexicographer. (2) **Lauritz**, b. Copenhagen, March 20, 1890; tenor; studied at Cons. in native city, début Royal Op. there, 1913; afterward a pupil of Beigel, Grenzebach, Mme. Bahr-Mildenburg and Karl Kittel; Covent Garden, 1924, same year at Bayreuth, where his "Parsifal" roused much admiration; after 1926 mem. of Met. Op. Co., excelling in Wagnerian rôles; has also sung "Otello" at Covent Garden and with San Francisco Op. Co.

Melchiori (měl-kǐ-ō'-rē), **Ant.**, Parma 1827—Milan, 1897; violinist and composer.

Melgunow (měl'-goo-nôf), **Julius von**, Kostroma, Russia, Sept. 11, 1846— Moscow, March 31, 1893; pupil of Henselt and the Rubinsteins; also of Moscow Cons. and R. Westphal, whose system he adapted to Bach's; pub. a coll. of folk-songs.

Mel'is, Carmen, b. Cagliari, Sardinia, 1885; soprano; sang 1909 at Manhattan Op. House, N. Y.; 1911, Boston Op. Co.; after 1913 for a time with Met. Op., also appearing at the Paris Op. and widely in Italy.

Melone. Vide BOTTRIGARI.

Meltz'er, Charles Henry, London, June 7, 1853 of Russian parentage— New York, Jan. 14, 1936; critic; pupil of the Sorbonne, Paris, later journalist on various New York papers; author and translator of plays and librettos.

Meluzzi (mā-lood'-zē), **Salvatore**, Rome, July 22, 1813—April 17, 1897; eminent organist, composer and conductor.

Membrée (mäñ-brā), **Edmond**, Valenciennes, 1820—Château Damont, near Paris, 1882; dram. composer.

Mendel (měn'-děl), **Hn.**, Halle, 1834 —Berlin, 1876; writer and lexicographer.

Mendelssohn, (1) **(Jakob Ludwig) Felix** (rightly **Mendelssohn-Bartholdy**) (měn'-d'l-zōn-bär-tôl'-dē), Hamburg, Feb. 3, 1809—Leipzig, Nov. 4, 1847; eminent composer of remarkably early maturity. Great-grandson of a Jewish sch.-master, Mendel, who adopted Christianity and had his children reared in the Christian faith; grandson of the prominent philosopher Moses: son of the banker Abraham M. Pf.-pupil of his mother, Lea Salomon-Bartholdy, as was also his elder sister Fanny (v. HENSEL). The family-life of the Mendelssohns is almost unique in history for its happiness and mutual devotion. **M.** studied also with L. Berger, Zelter (theory), Hennings (vln.) and Mme. Bigot (pf.). At 10 he entered the Singakademie, as an alto; the same year his setting of the 19th Psalm was performed by the Akademie. Every Sunday a small orch. performed at his father's house, and his comps. were heard here early and often; he usually cond. these concerts even as a child. 1825 his father took him to Paris to consult Cherubini, who offered to teach him, but the father preferred to have him at home. At 12 he began the series of 44 vols., in which he kept copies of his comps. This year he c. bet. 50 and 60 pcs., incl. a cantata, a mus. comedy, a pf.-trio, 2 pf.-sonatas, a vln.-sonata, songs, etc. At 9 he had played the pf. in public; at 12 he was a notable improviser (while playing a Bach fugue at Goethe's request he extemporised the Development which he had suddenly forgotten). At 17 he c. the remarkably original, beautiful and (in advance) Wagnerian overture to "*A Midsummer Night's Dream*," and the superb octet for strings (op. 20). This same year he matriculated at Berlin Univ. with a translation of Terence, said to be the first German attempt to render Terence in his own metres. He also painted, and was proficient in gymnastics and billiards. At 18 he prod. the succ. opera "*Die Hochzeit des Camacho*," at the Berlin Opera, in which he used the leit-motif (v. D. D.). At 20 he compelled and conducted the first performance since the composer's death of the Bach "*Passion according to St. Matthew*" at the Singakademie. This was the first step in the great crusade he waged, taking Bach out of obsolescence into the pre-eminence he now keeps. 1830, **M.** declined the chair of mus. at the Berlin Univ. The year before he had made the first of nine voyages to England, where he has stood next to Händel in popularity and influence. He cond. his symph. in C minor, at the London Philh., which gave him his first official recognition as a composer. The same year he was invited (in vain) to c. a festival hymn for the anniversary of the emancipation of the natives of Ceylon, and in his letters (in which his sunny nature finds free play) he referred to himself as "Composer to the Island of Ceylon." He appeared also with brilliant succ. as pianist and organist. He now travelled in Scotland, Switzerland, and elsewhere, and returning to London, conducted the "*Hebrides*" overture, played his G min. concerto and B min. Capriccio brillant, and pub. his first 6 "Songs without Words" (c. in Ven-

ice, 1830). His race and his amazing energy and succ. made him much opposition at Berlin, and he was refused the conductorship of the Singakademie in 1833, although he had arranged a series of concerts for the benefit of the Orch. Pension Fund. 1833, he cond. the Lower Rhine Mus. Festival at Düsseldorf, and became Town Mus. Dir. of the ch.-mus., the opera, and two singing-societies, for a salary of 600 thaler (about $450). 1835, he became cond. of the Gewandhaus Orch., Leipzig, which (with Fd. David as leader) he raised to the highest efficiency; the Univ. made him, in 1836, Dr. Phil., *h. c.*; 1836, he cond. his oratorio "*Paulus*," the Lower Rhine Festival, Düsseldorf, in 1837 also at the Birmingham Festival. 1837, he m. Cécile Charlotte Sophie Jeanrenaud of Frankfort, daughter of a French Protestant clergyman. She bore him five children, Karl, Marie, Paul, Felix, and "Lili" (Elisabeth). In 1841 Friedrich Wilhelm IV. invited him to take charge of the grand orch. and choral concerts at Berlin. The hostility to him was however so general that he wished to resign, but at the King's request organised the cath. mus., later famous as the "Domchor" (cath. choir). He was made R. Gen. Mus. Dir. With Schumann, Hauptmann, David, Becker, and Pohlenz, in the faculty, he organised the since famous Conservatorium of Mus. at Leipzig (since 1876 the "R. Cons."); he again cond. the Gewandhaus Concerts. 1845 he cond. "*Elijah*" at Birmingham. He resigned the Gewandhaus conductorship to Gade, and the piano-dept. to Moscheles, whom he invited from London. Upon hearing the news of the sudden death of his idolised sister, Fanny Hensel, he fell insensible and lived only 6 months. **M.** was kept from opera by inability to find a satisfactory libretto. Besides "*Die Hochzeit des Camacho*" he left an unfinished opera "*Lorelei*," an operetta "*Son and Stranger*," and 5 small unpub. operas. He c. 3 oratorios, "*Paulus*" (St. Paul), "*Elias*" (Elijah), and "*Christus*" (unfinished), the symph. cantata "*Lobgesang*," op. 52; the ballade, with orch. "*Die erste Walpurgis-*

nacht," op. 60; 2 "*Festgesänge*," "*An die Künstler*" (for male chorus and brass), and "*Zur Säcularfeier der Buchdruckerkunst*" ("Gutenberg Cantata"), with orch.; mus. to the plays "*Antigone*" (op. 55), "*Athalie*" (op. 74), "*Œdipus in Colonos*" (op. 93), and "*A Midsummer Night's Dream*" (op. 61); c. also vocal works with orch., hymn, "*Tu es Petrus*," Psalms 114, 115, and 95, prayer "*Verleih' uns Frieden*," and sopr. concert-aria "*Infelice*" (op. 94).
4 SYMPHONIES, in C min.; A min. (or "*Scotch*"); A (or "*Italian*"); D (or "*Reformation*"). OVERTURES, "*Sommernachtstraum*" ("A Midsummer Night's Dream"), op. 21; "*Hebrides*," "*Die Fingalshöhle*" (or "Fingal's Cave"), op. 26; "*Meerstille und glückliche Fahrt*" ("Calm Sea and Prosperous Voyage"), "*Die Schöne Melusine*" ("The lovely Melusine") (op. 32), "*Ruy Blas*" (op. 95). "*Trumpet*" overture, and an overture for wind-band (op. 24); c. also andante, scherzo, capriccio, and fugue, for string-orch. (op. 81), funeral march (op. 103), and march (op. 108); 2 pf.-concertos, in G. min. and D. min.; capriccio brillant; rondo brillant, and serenade and allegro giocoso, for pf. with orch.; vln.-concerto in E min. (op. 64); a string octet, quartets, 2 quintets, a pf.-sextet, 7 string-quartets, 3 pf.-quartets, 2 pf.-trios, 2 trios for clar., basset horn, and pf.; 2 'cello-sonatas, a sonata for vln., variations concertantes (op. 17) and "*Lied ohne Worte*" (op. 109), for 'cello with pf., religious and secular choruses, 13 vocal duets, and 83 songs. FOR PIANO, 3 sonatas; capriccio; Charakterstücke; rondo capriccioso; 4 fantasias, incl. "*The Last Rose of Summer*"; "*Lieder ohne Worte*" ("Songs without Words") in 8 books; "*Sonate écossaise*," 6 preludes and fugues, "*Variations sérieuses*," etc.; 6 Kinderstücke, 3 preludes and 3 studies, op. 104; "*Albumblatt*," "*Perpetuum mobile*," etc. 4-hand variations; 4-hand allegro brillant; duo concertant (with Moscheles), for 2 pfs. on the march-theme in Weber's "*Preciosa*." FOR ORGAN, 3 preludes and fugues; 6 sonatas, op. 65; preludes in C min.
Biogr. by his eldest son Karl (1871); by Hiller (1874); S. Hensel (1879);

Eckardt (1888); an extended article by Grove (in his Dictionary), etc. Numerous editions of his letters published. Memoirs by Lampadius, Kaufman, Rockstro, Runciman and Stratton. (See article, page 504.)

(2) **Arnold**, Ratibor, Dec. 26, 1855— Darmstadt, Feb. 19, 1933; grandnephew of above; studied with Haupt, Kiel, Grell, Taubert; organist and teacher in the Univ. at Bonn; then teacher at Cologne Cons.; then at Darmstadt, professor; from 1912 taught Hoch Cons., Frankfort-on-Main; D. Theol., Giessen Univ., 1917. C. operas "*Elsi*" (Cologne City Th., 1894), "*Der Bärenhäuter*," and "*Die Minneburg*"; also many choral works of high quality; songs, etc.

Mendès (män-dĕs), **Catulle**, Bordeaux May 22, 1841—Paris, Feb. 8, 1909; poet; librettist of pop. poems and operettas.

Mengal (män-găl), **Martin Jos.,** Ghent, 1784—1851; horn-virtuoso and dram. composer.

Mengelberg (meng'-ĕl-bĕrkh), (1) **Jos. Willem,** b. Utrecht, March 28, 1871; pupil of Umland, Hol, Wurff, and Petri at Utrecht, then at Cologne Cons.; 1891, dir. at Lucerne; from 1895 to the present he has been the brilliant cond. of the Amsterdam Concertgebouw Orch., an organisation which he shaped into one of the leading ensembles in Europe; after 1898 also of the Toonkunst choral society there. Beginning 1903 he served as guest leader of many Eur. orchs., incl. the London Philh.; 1905 he visited N. Y. as one of the conductors of the Philh. Orch.; 1907 led the Frankfort Museum Concerts and, 1908, the Caecilienverein there; in 1921 he returned to N. Y. as cond. of the short-lived Nat'l Symph. Orch., and made so powerful an impression that he was engaged for the Philh. when the former orch. was merged with it. He conducted annually in N. Y. until 1930 with a pronounced musical following; he has appeared as guest cond. in the principal Eur. capitals. Also a proficient pianist, and a notable champion of the works of Mahler. (2) **Rudolf,** b. Crefeld, Germany, Feb. 1, 1892; cousin of (1); composer and writer; wrote programme notes for Amsterdam

Concertgebouw, of which after 1925 he was vice-director.

Mengés, Isolde, b. Brighton, Engl., 1894; violinist; studied with her father, who was dir. of Brighton Cons.; then with Leon Sametini and Auer; début, London, 1913; U. S., 1916.

Mengewein (mĕng'-ĕ-vīn), **K.**, Zaunroda, Thuringia, Sept. 9, 1852—near Berlin, April 7, 1908; from 1881–86, teacher at Freudenberg's Cons. Wiesbaden; co-founder of a Cons. at Berlin, 1886; c. oratorio, festival cantata, operetta, overture "*Dornröschen*," etc.

Mengozzi (mĕn-gôd'-zē), **Bdo.**, Florence, 1758—Paris, March, 1800; tenor, writer and composer of 13 operas.

Ménil (dŭ-mā-nĕl), **Félicien de**, b. Boulogne-sur-Mer, July 16, 1860; historian and comp.

Menotti, Gian-Carlo, b. Milan, 1911; composer; studied Curtis Inst., Phila.; c. one-act opera, "*Amelia Goes to the Ball*," Met. Op., N. Y., 1937–8.

Menter (mĕn'-tĕr), (1) **Jos.**, Deutenkofen, Bavaria, 1808—Munich, 1856; 'cellist. (2) (**Menter-Popper**) **Sophie**, Munich, July 29, 1846—near Munich, Feb. 23, 1918; daughter of above; eminent pianist; pupil of Schönchen, Lebert and Niest; début, 1863; in 1867, studied with Tausig; 1869, with Liszt; 1872, m. the 'cellist Popper (divorced 1886); ct.-pianist to the Emperor of Austria; 1878–87, prof. St. Petersburg Cons.; then lived at her country-seat, Castle Itter, in the Tyrol.

Menuhin (mĕn'-ōō-hĭn), (1) **Yehudi**, b. New York, Jan. 22, 1917; remarkable for his precocious genius as violinist; res. in San Francisco as child; began vln. study at 4 with Louis Persinger; at 7 début with San Francisco Orch., creating a furore as prodigy; N. Y. recital, following year, roused much interest; was then taken to Paris for study with Enesco; début at 10 in that city with Lamoureux Orch. was triumphal event, closely followed by his appearance as soloist with N. Y. Symph. in Beethoven concerto, then further Eur. conquests incl. remarkable feat of playing Bach, Beethoven and Brahms concertos in one evening with Berlin Symph. under Bruno Walter; at 15, chosen to play Brahms concerto with N. Y. Philh., showing ripened stylistic authority; has also been a pupil of Adolf Busch, and has appeared in sonata recitals with his young sister (2) **Hephzibah**, pianist, in London, Paris and New York with equal applause; following world tour, incl. Antipodes, 1935–36, he went into temporary retirement of 2 years on his ranch in Cal. for further musical study and recreation.

Merbecke, J. Vide MARBECK.

Mercadante (mĕr-kä-dän'-tĕ), **Gius. Saverio**, Altamura, Sept. 17, 1795—Naples, Dec. 17, 1870; pupil of Zingarelli and in 1840 his successor as dir. of Naples Cons.; in 1819 prod. an opera with great succ. and followed it with 60 others, incl. "*Elisa e Claudio*" (Naples, 1866), "*Il Giuramento*" (Milan, 1837); he lived in various cities; 1833 cond. at Novara Cath.; 1862 he went blind; he c. also 2 symphonies, 4 funeral symphonies, 20 masses, etc.

Méreaux (mā-rō), (1) **J. Nicolas Amédée Lefroid de**, Paris, 1745—1797; organist and dram. composer. (2) **Jos. N. L. de**, b. Paris, 1767; son of above; organist, and pianist. (3) **J. A. L. de**, Paris, 1803—Rouen, 1874; son of above; pianist, composer and writer.

Merian (mā'-rĭ-än), **Hans**, Basel, 1857—Leipzig, 1905; writer.

Méric (mā-rĭk). Vide LALANDE.

Mériel (mā-rĭ-ĕl), **Paul**, Mondoubleau, 1818—Toulouse, 1897; violinist, cond. and dram. composer; dir. Toulouse Cons.

Merikan'to, Oscar, Helsingfors, Aug. 5, 1868—Feb. 17, 1924; organist and composer; studied Helsingfors, Leipzig and Berlin; organist and cond. at Nat'l Op., Helsingfors; c. (operas) "*The Girl of Pohja*" and "*The Death of Elina*"; works for organ, piano, violin, songs; ed. collection of folksongs.

Merk (mărk), **Jos.**, Vienna, 1795—Ober-Döbling, 1852; violinist and composer.

Merkel (mär'-kĕl), (1) **Gustav (Ad.)**, Oberoderwitz, Saxony, Nov. 12, 1827—Dresden, Oct. 30, 1885; org. and composer. (2) **K. L.**, wrote treatises on throat, etc.

Merklin (mär'-klēn), **Jos.**, Oberhausen, Baden, Jan. 17, 1819—Nancy, June

10, 1905; org.-builder at Brussels; son of an org.-builder; took his brother-in-law, F. Schütze, into partnership, as "Merklin-Schütze," 1858; in 1855, est. a branch in Paris.

Mérö, Yolanda, b. Budapest, Aug. 30, 1887; pianist; studied at Cons. there, also with Liszt; début as soloist with Dresden Philh., 1907; toured in Eur. cities, also South and Central America, has lived in U. S. for a number of years, where she gave many recitals; c. "*Capriccio Ungharese*" for piano and orch.; m. Hermann Irion, mem. firm of Steinway & Sons.

Merola (mä'-rō-lä), **Gaetano,** b. Naples, Jan. 4, 1881; conductor; studied Naples Cons.; 1899, asst. cond., Met. Op.; later with Savage Op. Co., at Manhattan Op., and for some years gen'l dir. of San Francisco and Los Angeles Op. Association.

Mersenne (měr-sĕn), **Marin,** Oize (Maine), France, Sept. 8, 1588—Paris, Sept. 1, 1648; writer of mus. treatises.

Mertens (măr'-tĕns), **Jos.,** Antwerp, Feb. 17, 1834—Brussels, June 30, 1901; 1st vln. at the opera there and teacher at the Cons.; 1878–79, cond. Flemish Opera, Brussels; later, dir. at Royal Th., The Hague; prod. succ. Flemish and French operettas and operas, incl. "*De Zwarte Kapitein*" (The Hague, 1877).

Mertke (měrt'-kĕ), **Ed.,** Riga, 1833—Röga, 1895; pianist, violinist, composer and collector.

Mertz (märts), **Jos. K.,** Pressburg, Hungary, 1806—Vienna, 1856; guitar-virtuoso.

Merula (mä-roo'-lä), **Tarquinio,** b. Bergamo; violinist and composer, 1623–40.

Merulo (mä-roo'-lō) (rightly **Merlot'ti**), **Claudio** (called "Da Coreggio"), Coreggio, April 8, 1533—Parma, May 4, 1604; eminent organist, dram. composer and famous teacher; pupil of Menon and G. Donati; he was a leader of the Venetian sch. and bordered on the new tonality.

Merz (märts), **K.,** Bensheim, near Frankfort-on-Main, 1836—Wooster, Ohio, 1890; teacher and writer.

Messager (měs-să-zhä), **André (Chas. Prosper),** Montlucon, Allier, France, Dec. 30, 1853—Paris, Feb. 24, 1929; pupil of Niedermeyer School and of Saint-Saëns; 1874, organist of the choir, St. Sulpice; cond. at Brussels; organist at St.-Paul-Saint-Louis; Paris, cond. at Sainte Marie des Batignolles; 1898–1903, cond. Op. Com.; Chev. of the Legion of Honour; 1901–07, mus.-dir. Covent Garden, London; 1907–19, one of directors of the Opéra at Paris, and from 1908 cond. of the concerts of the Cons.; 1919–20, dir. Op.-Comique; completed Bernicat's unfinished score, "*François les Bas Bleus*" (Folies-Dramatiques, 1883), following it with about 20 other comic operettas, and operas, incl. the succ. "*Le Chevalier d'Harmental*" (Op.-Com., 1896); "*La Basoche*" (Op.-Com., 1890, Bremen, 1892, as "*Zwei Könige*"); "*Mirette*" (Savoy, London, 1894); "*Les P'tites Michu*" (Paris, 1894) enormous success; "*Véronique*" (1899); "*Fortunio*" (Op. Com. 1907); "*Beatrice*" (Monte Carlo, 1914); operetta, "*L'Amour Masqué*" (Paris, 1923); mus. comedy, "*Passionnément*" (do., 1926); the ballets, "*Scaramouche*," "*Les Deux Pigeons*", songs, etc.

Messchaert (mä'-shärt), **Johannes,** Hoorn, Holland, 1857—Zurich, 1922; barytone; pupil of Schneider, Stockhausen and Wüllner; teacher and cond. in Amsterdam; toured widely.

Mestrino (mäs-trē'-nō), **Niccolò,** Milan, 1748—Paris, 1789; violinist, conductor, and composer.

Metastasio (mä-täs-tä'-zĭ-ō) (rightly **Trapassi,** but changed to **M.,** a pun on **T.** to please his patron Gravina), **P. Ant. Dom. Bonaventura,** Rome, Jan. 13, 1698—Vienna, April 12, 1782; poet and dramatist; wrote librettos set to mus. by Gluck and Mozart.

Methfessel (mät'-fĕs-sĕl), **Albert Gl.,** Stadtilm, Thuringia, 1785—Heckenbeck, 1869; dram. composer.

Métra (mä-trä), **(Jules Louis) Olivier,** Rheims, 1830—Paris, 1889; violinist and double-bass player, conductor and dram. composer.

Mettenleiter (mĕt'-tĕn-lī-tĕr), (1) **Jn. G.,** St. Ulrich, near Ulm, 1812—Ratisbon, 1858; organist and composer. (2) **Dominicus,** Thannhausen, Würtemberg, 1822—Ratisbon, 1868; brother of above; writer and composer.

Metzdorff (mĕts'-dôrf), **Richard,** Danzig, June 28, 1844—Berlin, April

26, 1919; pupil of Fl. Geyer, Dehn, and Kiel, Berlin; cond. at various cities; c. opera *"Rosamunde"* (Weimar, 1875); succ. *"Hagbart und Signe"* (Weimar, 1893); c. also 3 symph. incl. *"Tragic"*; overture *"King Lear"*; *"Frau Alice,"* ballade, with orch., etc.

Meurs, de. Vide MURIS, DE.

Meursius (mŭr'-sĭ-oos), **Jns.**, Loozduinen, near The Hague, 1579— Denmark, 1639; prof. and writer.

Meyer (mī'-ĕr), (1) **Ld. von** (called "De Meyer"), Baden, near Vienna, 1816—Dresden, 1883; pianist and composer. (2) **Jenny**, Berlin, 1834 —1894; concert-singer; 1865 teacher, 1888 proprietress Stern Cons. Berlin. (3) **Waldemar**, b. Berlin, Feb. 4, 1853; violinist, pupil of Joachim; 1873-81, member of the Berlin ct. orch. (4) **Gustav**, b. Königsberg, Prussia, June 14, 1859; pupil of Leipzig Cons.; cond. various cities; 1895, Leipzig City Th. 1903, Prague; c. 4-act farce, ballet-pantomime, etc. D. Prague, ?.

Meyerbeer (mī'-ĕr-bār), **Giacomo** (rightly **Jakob Liebmann Beer**; by adding the name "Meyer" he secured a large inheritance from a wealthy relative; he then Italianised "Jacob" as "Giacomo"), Berlin, Sept. 5, 1791—Paris, May 2, 1864; son of a Jewish banker; a precocious and remarkable pianist; pupil of Lauska and Clementi; at 7 played in public; studied with Zelter, Anselm, Weber; 1810, was invited by Abbé Vogler to live in his house as a son and pupil; did so for 2 years, one of his fellow-pupils being his devoted friend C. M. von Weber. Here he c. an oratorio and 2 operas *"Jephthas Gelübde"* (Ct.-Op., Munich, 1813) and *"Alimilek"* (Munich, 1813), the first a failure, the latter accepted for Vienna, whither he went and made a great succ. as pianist though his opera was not a succ. In his discouragement Salieri told him he needed only to understand the voice, and advised an Italian journey. He went to Venice in 1815 and, carried away with Rossini's vogue, c. 6 Italian operas which had succ., especially *"Il Crociato in Egitto"* (Venice, 1824). While writing this last he went to Berlin hoping to prod. 3-act German opera, *"Das Brandenburger Thor"*; though he

found no hearing, Weber begged him not to give himself up to Italian influences. In the 6 years of silence that followed, occurred his marriage, his father's death, and the death of his two children. In 1826, he went to Paris to live, and made a profound and exhaustive study of French opera from Lully down, forming his third style, in which acc. to Mendel "he united to the flowing melody of the Italians and the solid harmony of the Germans the pathetic declamation and the varied, piquant rhythm of the French." He made a coalition with the sophisticated librettist, Scribe, and his first French opera, *"Robert le Diable"* (Gr. Opéra, 1831), was an enormous succ., financially establishing the Opéra itself, though **M.** had had to pay the manager Véron a large sum to secure its production. Less pop. succ. at first, but more critical favour attended *"Les Huguenots"* (1836); its prod. at Berlin, 1842, led King Fr. Wm. IV, to call him there as Gen. Mus.-Dir. His opera *"Das Feldlager in Schlesien"* (1843), had only mod. succ. until Jenny Lind sang it in 1844; 1847, he visited Vienna and London; returning to Berlin he prod. Wagner's new work *"Rienzi"*; later he obtained *"The Flying Dutchman"* performance, after its rejection elsewhere. The extent to which he befriended Wagner is matter of bitter controversy, some claiming that he gave only formal assistance while Wagner was obscure, and fought him with underhanded methods and a "press-bureau," when Wagner attained power. At any rate Wagner despised and publicly assailed the music of Meyerbeer. Yet, whether or no Wagner borrowed money from **M.**, he certainly borrowed numberless points of artistic construction from him. In 1849, *"Le Prophète"* (finished 1843) was prod. at the Paris Gr. Opéra (1849) followed by the successes *"L'Étoile du Nord"* (Op.-Com., 1854), some of it taken from his *"Das Feldlager in Schlesien"*; and *"Dinorah, ou le Pardon de Ploërmel"* (Op. Com., 1859). *"L'Africaine"* (worked on with constant and characteristic changes from 1838) was prod. at the Paris Gr. Opéra, 1865, a year after his death. **M.** left by will 10,000 thaler ($7,500) for the foundation of a *Meyerbeer Scholarship*, for which only Germans under 28, and pupils of the Berlin "Hochschule," the Stern Cons., and the Cologne Cons., are eligible. Competitors must submit a vocal fugue *à 8* (for double chorus), an overture for full orch., and a dram. cantata *à 3*, with orch. (text of cantata, and text and theme of fugue being given). The fund gives six months in Italy, six in Paris, and six more in Vienna, Munich and Dresden together. M. c. also incid. music to *"Struensee"* (the tragedy by his brother, Michael Beer; Berlin, 1846), choruses to Æschylus' *"Eumenides"*; festival-play *"Das Hoffest von Ferrara"*; monodrama *"Thevelindens Liebe,"* for sopr. solo, chorus with clar. obbligato (Vienna, 1813); cantatas, *"Gutenberg"* and *"Maria und ihr Genius"* (for the silver wedding of Prince and Princess Carl of Prussia); *"Der Genius der Musik am Grabe Beethoven"*; serenade *"Brautgeleite aus der Heimath"* (for the wedding of Princess Louise of Prussia); ode to Rauch (the sculptor), with orch.; 7 sacred odes *a cappella; "Festhymnus"* (for the King of Prussia's silver wedding); 3 "Fackeltänze," for wind-band, also scored for orch. (for the weddings of the King of Bavaria, and the Princesses Charlotte and Anna of Prussia); grand march for the Schiller Centenary (1859); overture in march-form (for opening of London Exhibition, 1862); coronation march for King Wilhelm I. (1863); church-music; pf.-pcs., etc. Biog. by A. de Lasalle (1864); H. Blaze de Bury (1865); Ella (1868); H. Mendel (1868), and J. Schucht, 1869. Other memoirs by Pougin, Kohut, J. Weber, Curzon, Eymieu, Dauriac, Hervey, Kapp, etc.

Meyer-Helmund (mī'-ĕr-hĕl-moont), **Erik,** St. Petersburg, April 13 (25 new style), 1861—Berlin, April 4, 1932; pupil of his father and of Kiel and Stockhausen; prod. comic operas, incl. the succ. *"Der Liebeskampf"* (Dresden, 1892); succ. ballet *"Rübezahl"* (or *"Der Berggeist"*) (Leipzig, 1893); 1-act burlesque *"Trischka"* (Riga, 1894); and pop. songs.

Meyer-Olbersleben (mī'-ĕr-ôl'-bĕrs-lā-bĕn), **Max,** Olbersleben, near Weimar, April 5, 1850—Würzburg, Dec. 31, 1927; pupil of his father, of Müller-Hartung and Liszt, on whose recommendation he was given a stipend by the Duke, and studied with Rheinberger and Wüllner; 1877, teacher of cpt., and comp. R. Cons. of Mus., Würzburg; 1907-20, dir. of same; 1879, cond. the *"Liedertafel"*; 1885, Royal Prof.; 1896, dir. *"Deutscher Sängerbund,"* and co-dir. the Fifth National *Sängerfest,* Stuttgart; c. succ. romantic opera *"Cläre Dettin"* (Würzburg, 1896), and a comic opera *"Der Hauben Krieg"* (Munich Opera); overtures, *"Feierklänge"* and *"Festouvertüre"*; fine choruses; chamber-mus., etc.

Mézeray (māz-rĕ'), **L. Chas. Lazare Costard de,** Brunswick, 1810—Asnières, near Paris, April, 1887; barytone and dram. composer.

Miaskowsky (mē-äs-kôf'-skē), **Nicolas,** b. Novogeorgievsky, near Warsaw, April 20, 1881; Russian composer; his father a general in the Russian army, and early trained to follow in the profession of military engineer; 1906, entered St. Petersburg Cons., where he studied with Glière, Liadoff, Witol and Rimsky-Korsakoff; early composed pf. sonata; after serving in Russian armies during war, came into prominence as a symph. comp. in pos-revolutionary period; composed many works in this form, several of which have been played in the U. S.; his music is neo-romantic though with some modern harmonic influence by Scriabin, Prokofieff, Debussy, etc.; but in general he carries on the tradition of Tschaikowsky in Russian music; after 1921, prof. of theory at Moscow Cons.; c. (orch.) 18 symphonies; Sinfonietta; *"The Silence"*; *"A Tale"*; *"Alastor"*; (chamber works) 3 string quartets; also piano music and songs.

Miceli (mē-chā'-lē), **Giorgio,** Reggio di Calabria, 1836—Naples, 1895; c. 6 operas, 2 biblical operas, etc.

Michael (mē'-khä-ĕl), (1) **Rogier,** d. Dresden, 1618; tenor and cond. to the Elector; c. motets. His son (2) **Tobias,** b. Dresden, 1592; church cond. Leipzig; c. church music, etc.

Michaelis (mē-khä'-ā-lēs), **Chr. Fr.,** Leipzig, 1770—1834; writer.

Micheli (mē-kā'-lē), **Romano,** Rome,

ca. 1575—ca. 1655; conductor, writer and composer of notable canons, etc.

Middelschulte (mid'-děl-shool-tě), **Wilhelm**, b. Werne, Westphalia, April 3, 1863; organist; pupil of the Berlin Inst. for church music; from 1888 organist there; in 1891 settled in Chicago; 1894–1918, org. of the Thomas orch.; c. canons and fugue on *"Our Father in Heaven"*; organ concerto on a theme of Bach's; canonic fantasie on Bach, etc.

Mielck (mēlk), **Ernst**, Wiborg, Oct. 24, 1877—Locarno, Oct. 22, 1899; Finnish composer, who, in spite of his pitifully brief life of 22 years, gained a place of national importance; pupil of Tietse, Radecke and Bruch; c. Finnish symph.; overture *"Macbeth"*; Finnish fantasie for chorus and orch.; Finnish orch. suite, etc.

Miersch (mērsh), (1) **Carl Alex. Johannes**, Dresden, 1865—Cincinnati, O., Sept. 8, 1916; violinist; pupil of the Cons. and of Massart; 1888–90 teacher in Aberdeen, then for a year with the Boston Symph. Orch.; 1894–98 artistic dir. of the Athens Cons. and court violinist; 1902, returned to the U. S.; from 1910 at Cincinnati Coll. of Music. His brother (2) **Paul Fr.**, b. Dresden, Jan. 18, 1868; 'cellist, pupil of Royal Akad., Munich; from 1892 in New York, for five years soloist N. Y. Symph. Orch., 1898, soloist Met. Opera; c. Indian rhapsody, for orch., 'cello and violin concertos, etc.

Mignard (mēn-yär), **Alexander Konstantinovich** (rightly **Scheltobrjuchov**), b. Warsaw Aug. 13, 1852; pupil of the Cons. and of Saint-Saëns at the Paris Cons.; lawyer and statesman at Warsaw; c. operas, overtures, 2 symph., etc. D. Moscow, ?.

Migot (mē'-gō), **Georges**, b. Paris, Feb. 27, 1891; composer; studied with Bouval, Ganaye and Widor; won Boulanger, Lepaulle, Halphen and Blumenthal prizes; c. chamber and orch. music; author books on aesthetics (he is also a painter).

Mihalovich (mē-hä'-lō-vĭch), **Edmund von**, Fericsancze, Slavonia, Sept. 13, 1842—Budapest, April 22, 1929; pupil of Hauptmann and von Bülow; 1887–1919, dir. R. Acad. of Mus., Budapest; c. romantic opera *"Hagbarth und Signe"* (Dresden, 1882); succ. opera *"Toldi"* (Pesth, 1893);

ballads for full orch. (*"Das Geisterschiff,"* *"Hero und Leander,"* *"La ronde du sabbat,"* *"Die Nixe"*), a symph., etc.

Mikorey, (1) **Franz**, b. Munich, June 3, 1873; conductor; son of the opera tenor, (2) **Max M.** (1850—1907); pupil of Thuille and Herzogenberg; cond. at Dessau, 1902–18; 1919 in Helsingfors; 1924–28, Braunschweig; c. operas, piano concerto, piano quintet and trio, songs, etc.; arranged Mahler's posth. *"Sinfonia Engadine."*

Miksch (mēksh), **Jn. Aloys**, Georgenthal, Bohemia, 1765—Dresden, 1845; barytone and celebrated teacher.

Mikuli (mē'-koo-lē), **Karl**, Czernowitz, Bukowina, 1821—Lemberg, 1897; pupil of Chopin and ed. of standard edition of his works, composer.

Milanollo (mī-län-ôl'-lō), (1) **Teresa**, Savigliano, near Turin, Aug. 28, 1827—Paris, Oct. 25, 1904; violinist; studied with Ferrero, Gebbaro, and Mora, at Turin, and played in public at 6; afterwards touring with great succ. till in 1857 she m. military engineer, Parmentier; lived in Toulouse. Her companion on her tours was her sister (2) **Maria**, 1832—(of consumption) Paris, 1848. Also a violinist.

Milde (mēl'-dě), (1) **Hans Feodor von**, Petronell, near Vienna, April 13, 1821—Weimar, Dec. 10, 1899; pupil of Hauser and Manuel Garcia; created "Telramund" in *"Lohengrin,"* Weimar, 1850; life-member of the Weimar ct.-opera. (2) **Rosa** (née **Agthe**), Weimar, June 25, 1827—Jan. 26, 1906; wife of above; created "Elsa," sang at Weimar till 1876. (3) **Fz. von**, Weimar, March 4, 1855—Munich, Dec. 6, 1929; son and pupil of (1) and (2); barytone, 1878 at Hanover ct.-th.

Mil'denberg, Albert, Brooklyn, Jan. 13, 1878—Raleigh, N. C., 1918; pupil of Joseffy, Bruno Oskar Klein, C. C. Müller; c. orch. suites, operas.

Mildenburg, Anna von (Bahr-), b. Vienna, Nov. 29, 1872; notable dramatic soprano; pupil of Vienna Cons.; 1895, début in Hamburg; 1897, Bayreuth; 1908–17 a leading mem. of the Vienna Ct.-Op.; esp. known for her Wagnerian interpretations; after 1919 teacher of singing at the Munich Akad.; from 1920 also dram. dir. for Wagner works at the Munich Op.; m. Hermann Bahr, poet and playwright, with whom she wrote *"Bayreuth und das Wagner-Theater"* (1912).

Milder-Hauptmann (mēl′-dĕr-howpt′-män), **Pauline Anna**, Constantinople, 1785—Berlin, 1838; soprano; Beethoven wrote the rôle of "Fidelio" for her.

Mildner (mēlt′-nĕr), **Moritz**, Türnitz, Bohemia, 1812—Prague, 1865; vln.-teacher.

Milhaud (mēl′-ō), **Darius**, b. Aix-en-Provence, France, Sept. 4, 1892; studied Paris Cons., mem. of former Group of Six, in which (with Honegger) he was most considerable figure; he was a pioneer in the use of jazz in art forms, and leading exponent of polytonal style; was at one time attached to diplomatic post at Brazil, from which he derived some folk inspiration in his pop. piano pieces *"Saudados do Brazil"* (also orch.); many of his post-war ballets and other works were flippant in manner, but he has also given modern neo-classic treatment to Greek myths; visited U. S. in 1923 and 1927, appearing as guest leader with orchs. in N. Y., Phila. and Boston and in chamber concerts of his music elsewhere; also lectured at several Amer. univ. C. (operas) *"La Brebis Égarée," "Protée," "Les Malheurs d'Orphée," "Esther de Carpentras," "Le Pauvre Matelot"*; (3 "opéras minuits" forming triptych) *"L'Enlèvement d'Europe," "L'Abandon d'Ariane"* and *"La Délivrance de Thésée"; "Maximilien," "Christophe Colombe"* (Berlin State Op., 1928); (farce) *"Le Bœuf sur le Toit"*; (ballets) *"L'Homme et son Désir"* (given by Swedish Ballet in N. Y.), *"La Création du Monde"* (in which jazz themes are artistically employed), *"Salade," "Le Train Bleu," "L'Éventail de Jeanne," "La Bien-Aimée"*; a cantata in 5 parts, *"Le Retour de l'Enfant Prodigue"* to a text by André Gide; music for the Orestes and Agamemnon; 6 symphonies, suites, serenade, hymns for orch., *"Catalogues de Fleurs"* and *"Machines Agricoles"* for voice and ensemble; *"Rag Caprices," "Actualities"*; vln. concerto; *"Cinema Fantasie"* for vln. and orch., 7 string quartets, songs, piano works. Studies of his music have been writ-

ten by Prunières, Coeuroy, Landormy; prof. Mills Coll., Cal., 1941.

Mililotti (mē-lē-lôt′-tē), (1) **Leopoldo,** Ravenna, Aug. 6, 1835—Marsiglia, Jan. 28, 1911; studied at Rome and lived there as singing-teacher; pub. songs and wrote. His brother (2) **Giuseppe,** 1833—1883, prod. 2 operettas.

Millard′, Harrison, Boston, Mass., Nov. 27, 1830—1895; studied in Italy; tenor concert-singer; toured Great Britain; lived in New York from 1856, as singer and teacher; c. an opera, grand mass, and many pop. songs.

Mil′ler, Edw., Norwich, 1731—Doncaster, 1807; organist, composer, and writer.

Millet (mēl′-yĕt), **Luis,** b. Barcelona, April 18, 1867; pupil of Vidiella and Pedrell; founded and cond. the Orféo Catalá society; c. choruses and orch. fantasies on folk-themes.

Milleville (mĭl-lĕ-vĭl′-lĕ), (1) **Fran.,** b. Ferrara, ca. 1565; conductor and composer; son and pupil of (2) **Alessandro,** organist, and composer to the Ducal Court.

Mil′lico, Giuseppe, b. Modena, ca. 1730; male soprano, and dram. composer.

Mil′ligan, Harold Vincent, b. Astoria, Ore., Oct. 31, 1888; organist, composer, writer; grad. and post-grad. courses, Guilmant Organ School, N. Y.; studied with T. Tertius Noble and Arthur E. Johnstone; toured U. S. as organ soloist; org. and choir dir. at various N. Y. churches, more recently at Riverside Church; gen'l sec'y, A. G. O.; and was pres. of Nat'l Ass'n of Org.; exec. dir., Nat'l Music League; c. operettas, songs, organ works, incid. music to plays; author, *"Stephen Foster; The First American Composer"; "Pioneer Amer. Composers,"* Vols. I and II; ed. *"Colonial Love Lyrics."*

Mil′ligen, Simon Van, Rotterdam, Dec. 14, 1849—Amsterdam, March 11, 1929; organist; pupil of Nicolai, Bargiel, etc.; for many years municipal dir. of Gouda, later in Amsterdam as critic and teacher; c. operas *"Brinio"* and *"Darthula"* (The Hague, 1898), etc.

Millöcker (mĭl′-lĕk-ĕr), **K.,** Vienna, May 29, 1842—Baden near Vienna, Dec. 31, 1899; pupil of the Cons.; 1864, th.-cond. at Graz; 1866, **Har-**

monie-Th., in Vienna; from 1869, Th. an der Wien; c. many graceful and succ. operettas, and comic operas, incl. 2 prod. at 23, *"Der todte Gast"* and *"Die beiden Binder"* (Pesth, 1865); *"Das verwünschene Schloss"* (1878), with songs in Upper Austrian dialect; the widely pop. *"Der Bettelstudent"* (Dec. 6, 1881; in Italian as *"Il Guitarrera,"* in English *"The Beggar Student"*); *"Die sieben Schwaben"* (1887, in Engl. *"The 7 Swabians"*); *"Der arme Jonathan"* (1890, in Engl. *"Poor Jonathan"*); *"Das Sonntagskind"* (1892); *"Nordlicht"* (1897); c. also pf.-pcs.

Mills, Sebastian Bach, Cirencester, England, March 13, 1838—Wiesbaden, Dec. 21, 1898; organist; pf.-teacher, New York.

Milon (mē-lôn). Vide TRIAL.

Mil'stein, Nathan, b. Odessa, Dec. 31, 1904; violinist; pupil of Auer and Ysaye; began Russian tours at 19, also appearances with Horowitz, pianist; visited various other Eur. countries and South America; U. S. début, 1929-30; has internat'l reputation as brilliant virtuoso and has appeared with leading orchs. of U. S. and Europe, also as recitalist.

Mil'ton, J., d. 1646(7?); father of the English poet; a scrivener in London, and an excellent musician and composer.

Minc'us, Ludwig, Vienna, 1827—after 1897; violinist and cond. in St. Petersburg; 1872, ballet composer at the Imperial Opera; then retired to Vienna; c. 16 ballets, including *"La Source"* in collaboration with Delibes.

Mingotti (mēn-gôt'-tĭ), **Regina** (née Valentini); b. Naples, 1721; soprano.

Minoja (mē-nō'-yä), **Ambrogio,** Ospedaletto, 1752—Milan, 1825; singing-teacher and composer.

Mirande (mē-räńd), **Hippolyte,** b. Lyons, May 4, 1862; pupil of Dubois and Guiraud, Paris Cons.; 1886-90, prof. Geneva Cons.; 1890, Sec.-Gen. Gr. Th., Lyons, and prof. of mus. history, Lyons Cons.; critic; organist at the synagogue; c. v. succ. ballet, *"Une Fête Directoire"* (Lyons, 1895); overtures, *"Rodogune," "Frithjof," "Macbeth," "Prométhée,"* and *"La mort de Roland,"* etc.

Mirecki (mē-rets'-kē), **Franz,** Cracow, April 1, 1791—May 29, 1862; pupil

of Hummel and Cherubini; after 1838 director of school of opera singing in Cracow; c. operas, ballets, etc.

Mi'rovitch, Alfred, b. St. Petersburg, 1884; pianist; studied law; grad Cons. in native city, pupil of Essipov; won gold medal and Rubinstein prize; début, Berlin, 1911; has toured Europe, Far East and U. S., also teaching in Los Angeles; c. piano works and songs.

Miry (mē'-rē), **Karel,** Ghent, 1823—1889; professor and dram. composer.

Missa (mĭs'-sä), **Edmond Jean Louis,** Rheims, June 12, 1861—Paris, Jan. 29, 1910; pupil of Massenet, Paris Cons.; won Prix Cressent; lived in Paris, as teacher; c. an op. com., *"Juge et Partie"* (Op.-Com., 1886), followed by others, also pantomimes; *"Ninon de Lenclos,"* lyric episode (1895), etc.

Mitro'poulos, Dmitri, b. Athens, 1896; composer, conductor; grad. Athens Cons., 1919; studied piano with Wassenhoven, comp. with Marsick and Busoni, organ with Desmet, Brussels; was répetiteur at Berlin Op. until 1925; later successful orch. cond., in Athens; guest leader London, Paris and Boston Symph. Orchs., 1935; 1937, appointed cond. of the Minneapolis Symph. Orch.; c. (opera) *"Sœur Béatrice"* (Athens, 1919) also orch. and chamber music.

Mit'terer, Ignaz Martin, St. Justina, Tyrol, Feb. 2, 1850—Brixen, Aug. 18, 1924, composer and director; pupil of his uncle Anton M., (a choirmaster), and of Father Huber; 1874 became a priest; studied at Regensburg under Jakob, Haberl and Haller; 1880 chaplain in Rome; 1882-85, cathedral cond. at Regensburg, later at Brixen as dir. in the cathedral; his compositions show the influence of Palestrina; c. masses with orch., offertories and a great amount of church music.

Mitterwurzer (mĭt'-tĕr-voor-tsĕr), **Anton,** Sterzing, Tyrol, 1818—Döbling, near Vienna, 1876; barytone.

Mizler (mĭts'-lĕr), **Lorenz Chp.** (ennobled as **M. von Kolof**), Heidenheim, Würtemberg, 1711—Warsaw, 1778; writer, editor and composer.

Mlynarski (m'lē-när'-skĭ), **Emil,** Kibarty, Suvalki, July 18, 1870—Warsaw, April 5, 1935; pupil St. Petersburg Cons.; 1893 cond. and teacher at Warsaw; 1894 at Odessa;

from 1899 cond. at Opera House,
Warsaw; also cond. Phil. orch.;
1904–07 director of the Cons.; 1910–
18, dir. Choral and Orch. Union,
Glasgow; 1918–24, dir. Warsaw Op.
and Cons.; after 1930 for several
seasons in Phila., U. S., as head of
orch. dept., Curtis Inst. of Music,
also guest cond. with Phila. Orch.;
he appeared as cond. in numerous
Eur. capitals, incl. London; c.
symphony, "*Polonia*," 2 vln. concertos (the 1st winning Paderewski
Prize, 1898); a comic opera "*A Summer Night*"; piano works, etc.

Mocquereau (mŏk-rō), **Dom André,**
La Tessouale, France, June 6, 1849
—Solesmes, Jan. 18, 1930; writer;
'cello pupil of Dancla; from 1875
Benedictine monk, teacher of choral
singing at the Abbey of Solesmes,
later prior; founder and editor of
the *Paléographie musicale;* in 1903
on the exile of the order, moved to
the Isle of Wight, continuing the
publication of his great work; authority on Gregorian chant, on which
he wrote "*Rhythmique Grégorienne*"
(vol. I, 1908), etc.

Modernus (mō-der'-noos), **Jacobus**
(rightly **Jacque Moderne;** called
Grand Jacques, or **J. M. de Pin-
guento,** because of his stoutness);
cond. at Notre Dame, Lyons; pub.
and composer, 1532–67.

Moe'ran, Ernest John, b. Osterley,
England, Dec. 31, 1894; composer;
of Irish extraction; in large part
self-taught; but studied at R. Coll.
of Music, London, 1913–14; made
large collection of folk-songs of
Norfolk; c. orch. rhapsody, 4 string
quartets, sonata for vln. and piano;
toccata and "*Stalham River*," variations, etc., for piano; 2 vln. sonatas,
2 piano trios, serenade-trio for
strings; "*Cushinsheean*," symph. impression for orch.; "*Lonely Waters*"
for small orch., and many songs and
piano pieces, also a symph., 1937.

Mohr (mōr), **Hn.,** Nienstedt, 1830—
Philadelphia, 1896; composer.

Möhring (mä'-rĭng), **Fd.,** Alt-Ruppin,
1816—Wiesbaden, 1887; organist,
teacher, and dram. composer.

Moir, Frank Lewis, Market Harborough, Engl., April 22, 1852—
Deal, Engl., Aug., 1902; studied
painting at S. Kensington, also mus.;
won scholarship Nat. Training Sch.
(1876); c. a comic opera, church-

services, madrigal "*When at Chloe's
Eyes I Gaze*" (Madr. Soc. prize,
1881), many pop. songs, etc.

Moiseiwitsch (mō-ĭ-sā'-ĭ-vĭch), **Benno,**
b. Odessa, Feb. 22, 1890; pianist;
studied with Klimoff at Odessa
Acad., winning Rubinstein Stipend,
also with Leschetizky, Vienna; made
début in England with succ., 1908,
followed by orchestral and recital
appearances throughout British Empire and on continent, also in U. S.;
has particular reputation for Chopin
playing, but repertoire incl. classic
and modern works.

Mojsisovics (mō-sē'-sō-vĭch), **Roderich
von,** b. Graz, May 10, 1877; pupil
of Degner, and of the Cologne Cons.,
and Munich Akad.; 1903 cond. in
various cities; 1912–30, dir. Graz
Cons.; c. symph. "*In the Alps*,"
symph. poem "*Stella*," "*Chorus
Mysticus*" from "*Faust*" for soli,
double chorus, organ and orch., etc.

Mol, de. Vide DEMOL.

Molinari (mŏl-ē-nä'-rē), **Bernardino,**
b. Rome, April 11, 1880; conductor;
studied there organ and comp.; at
St. Cecilia Liceo with Renzi and
Falchi; cond. Augusteo Orch. Rome,
beginning 1909 and after 1915 taking
this ensemble on tours of Italy, later
also to Switzerland, Germany and
Czechoslovakia; he has appeared
as guest cond. in many world
capitals, incl. Antwerp, London,
Geneva, Vienna; with New York
Philh. and St. Louis Orch., 1928; and
in subsequent years also in San
Francisco, Los Angeles, Detroit and
Phila., again in N. Y., 1930–31; he
has transcribed for orch. works by
Debussy, Monteverdi, Vivaldi and
other composers.

Molique (mŏl-ēk'), **Wm. Bd.,** Nürnberg, Oct. 7, 1802—Cannstadt, May
10, 1869; eminent violinist; son and
pupil of a town-musician; studied
with Rovelli on royal stipend; 1820,
successor of R. as leader of Munich
orch.; studied with Spohr; 1826,
"Musik-direktor" at Stuttgart; 1849-
66, London; also toured with great
succ.; c. an oratorio, 6 famous vln.-
concertos, etc.

Mollenhauer (mŏl'-lĕn-how-ĕr), three
brothers, b. at Erfurt. (1) **Fr.,** 1818
—1885; violinist and composer. (2)
H., 1825; 'cellist. (3) **Ed.,** Erfurt,
1827—Owatonna, Minn., 1914; violinist; pupil of Ernst, and of Spohr;

1853, New York, founded a vln.-sch.; one of the originators of the "Conservatory System" in America; c. 2 operas; 3 symphonies, incl. the "*Passion*," string-quartets, vln.-pcs., etc. (4) **Emil,** Brooklyn, N. Y., Aug. 4, 1855—Boston, Dec. 10, 1927; son of (1); violinist at 9, then with Boston Symph. Orch.; 1899 cond. Boston Handel and Haydn Society; 1900, Apollo Club; led Boston Symph. at various expositions.

Moller (or **Möller**) (mŏl'-lĕr, or mĕl'-ler), **Joachim.** Vide BURGK.

Molloy', Jas. Lyman, b. Cornolore, Ireland, 1837—Wooleys, Bucks, England, Feb. 4, 1909; c. operettas; pub. Irish melodies with new accompaniments and c. pop. songs.

Mol'ter, Johann Melchior, mus. director in Durlach, 1733; amazingly prolific writer; c. 169 symph., 14 overtures, etc.

Momigny (mō-mēn'-yē), **Jérome Jos. de,** Philippeville, 1762—Paris, 1838; theorist and dram. composer.

Momolet'to. Vide ALBERTINI, M.

Mompou (mŏm'-pōō), **Federico,** b. Barcelona, 1905; composer; studied with Motte Lacroix, but developed own manner of composition which he styles "primitive"; c. piano works, esp. suites.

Monasterio (mō-näs-tā'-rĭ-o), **Gesù,** Potes, Spain, April 18, 1836—Santander, Sept. 28, 1903; violinist; début at 9, then pupil of De Bériot, Brussels Cons.; made v. succ. tours; 1861 founded Quartet Soc., Madrid; ct.-violinist, prof., and (1894) dir. Madrid Cons.; c. pop. vln.-pcs.

Monath (mŏn'-ăth), **Hortense,** American pianist; studied first with her mother, then with Ernest Hutcheson in N. Y., and Schnabel in Berlin; début, Hamburg; gave recitals in Italian cities, appeared with Vienna Philh., Hamburg Philh., and at Salzburg Fest.; returned to U. S. 1934, appearing with Boston Symph. and in solo concerts.

Mendonville (mŏn-dŏn-vē'-yŭ), **J. Jos. Cassanea de** (de M. being his wife's maiden name), Narbonne, 1711—Belleville, near Paris, 1772; violinist, conductor and dram. composer.

Moniuszko (mō-nǐ-oosh'-kō), **Stanislaw,** Ubiel, Lithuania, May 5, 1819 —Warsaw, June 4, 1872; pupil of Freyer and Rungenhagen; l. Berlin, then at Wilna; c. 15 notable Polish operas incl. "*Halka*," a nat'l classic; also masses, songs, etc.; organist, director, professor. Biogr. by A. Walicki (Warsaw, 1873).

Monk, (1) **Edwin G.,** Frome, Engl., December 13, 1819—Radley, Jan. 3, 1900; pupil of G. A. Macfarren; Mus. Doc. Oxon, 1856; 1859–83, organist York Minster; ed. choral books, etc.; c. 2 odes, unison service, etc. (2) **Wm. H.,** London, 1823— Stoke Newington, London, 1889; organist, professor of vocal mus.; editor.

Monn, Georg Matthias, Lower Austria, 1717—Vienna, Oct. 3, 1750; organist and comp. of highly important instrumental works, symphonies, etc., marking a transition to the modern style.

Monod (mŭ-nō), **Edmond,** Lyons, Feb. 4, 1871; author and teacher; pupil of Roth, Stepanov and Leschetizky; 1899–1906 teacher in Berlin; 1907 prof. at Geneva Cons.; c. songs.

Monpou (mŏn-poo) (**Fran. L.**) **Hip.,** Paris, 1804—Orleans, 1841; c. of light operas and songs.

Monsigny (mŏn-sēn-yē), **P. Alex.,** Fauquembergue, near St.-Omer, Oct. 17, 1729—Paris, Jan. 14, 1817; illtrained but melodious French comic opera writer of noble birth but left poor on his father's death; became a clerk, later steward to the Duke of Orleans; he had studied the vln. as a child and now studied harm. for 5 months with Gianotti; at 30 prod. a succ. 1-act op., followed by 12 others, the last, "*Félix, ou l'enfant trouvé*" (1777), the greatest succ. of all; immediately m., ceased to write; his stewardship and his royalties had brought him riches, which the Revolution swept away; he was given a pension of 2,400 francs ($480) a year by the Op. Com.; 1800–02, inspector at the Cons.; 1813, member of the Acad.; 1816, Legion of Honour. Biogr. by Alexandre (1819), and Hédouin, 1820.

Montanari (mŏn-tä-nä'-rē), **Francesco,** Padua (?)—Rome, 1730; violinist at St. Peter's, Rome; c. 12 violin sonatas.

Monte (mŏn'-tĕ), **Filippo** (or **Philippus de**) (**Philippe de Mons**) (dŭ-môns), probably at Mons (or Malines), 1521—Prague, July 4, 1603; conductor and celebrated composer.

Montéclair (môn-tā-klăr), **Michel Pignolet de,** Chaumont, 1666—Saint-Denis, n. Paris, Sept., 1737; double-bass player; dram. composer and writer of methods.

Montefiore (môn-tĕ-fĭ-ō'-rē), **Tommaso Mosè,** composer; Livorno, 1855—Rome, March 13, 1933; pupil of Mabellini; critic under the penname of *"Puck,"* editor; c. operas *"Un bacio a portatore"* (Florence, 1884), and *"Cecilia"* (Ravenna, 1905).

Montemezzi (môn-tā-mĕd'-sē), **Italo,** b. Verona, May 31, 1875; composer; studied at Milan Cons.; c. (operas) *"Giovanni Gallurese"* (Turin, 1905, prod. at Met. Op., N. Y., with slight succ. 2 decades later); *"Hellera"* (do., 1909); *"L'Amore dei Tre Re"* (Milan, 1913) won immediate succ. for its tragic action, noble restraint and original adaptation of modern dram. and harmonic idiom to classic theme; Met. Op., following year, with equal succ. and has been periodically restored; *"La Nave"* (Chicago, 1918); *"Principezza Lontana"* (unfinished); *"La Notte di Zoraima,"* one-act opera with melodramatic story, which proved disappointing when given in Milan and at Met. Op. in 1931; also cantata, *"Il Cantico dei Cantici,"* etc.

Monteux (môn-tü'), **Pierre,** b. Paris, April 4, 1875; conductor; studied Paris Cons.; 1st prize there; after 1894 orch. and opera cond., in Paris, also as guest in London, Berlin, Vienna, Budapest; visited U. S. in 1916 with Diaghileff Ballet Russe; cond. Met. Op., 1917–19; in 1918 called to take charge of Boston Symph. for a time pending arrival of Rabaud; 1919–24 regular leader of that orch.; thereafter active also with Phila. Orch. and at Hollywood Bowl; following period as regular leader of Amsterdam Concertgebouw Orch., he returned to America for summer concerts at Los Angeles and was engaged as permanent leader of San Francisco Symph., beginning 1935; has especial rep. as interpreter of modern scores; leads series annually in spring and fall with Orchestre Symphonique in Paris, and also has a course of instruction for young conductors there.

Monteverde (môn-tā-vĕr'-dĕ) (he signed his name, **Monteverdi**), **Claudio** (**Giov. A.**), Cremona (bapt., May 15), 1567—Venice, Nov. 29, 1643; eminent composer; when young, vla.-player in the orch. of Duke Gonzaga, Mantua, and studied cpt. with Ingegneri. At 17 and at 20 pub. Canzonette à 3, and madrigals, in which appeared (among many unintentional or unbeautiful effects) the harmonic innovations for which he is famous and which led Rockstro to call him "not only the greatest musician of his own age, but the inventor of a system of harmony which has remained in uninterrupted use to the present day." His progressions include the unprepared entrance of dissonances, the dominant seventh and the ninth (v. D. D., CHORD, PROGRESSION, SUSPENSION PREPARATION, etc.). He was bitterly assailed in pamphlets, particularly by Artuso, and he replied in kind. The outcome was his complete triumph and the establishment of the new school of song and accompaniment. His victory, while salutary for art in general and dramatic song in particular, was too complete; for the bigoted defenders of polyphonic music dragged down with them in their ruin the splendid edifice of church-mus. built to perfection by Palestrina and others. 1603, **M.** became his teacher's successor as Maestro to the Duke and c. for the wedding of the Duke's son to Margherita of Savoy the opera *"Arianne,"* in which Ariadne's grief moved the audience to tears. In 1608 he prod. his opera *"Orfeo"* with the unheard-of orchestra of 36 pieces (Riemann states that *"Arianne"* was the 2d work and *"Orfeo"* the first). *"Orfeo"* was published in 1609 and in 1615, and the score shows great modernity, Rockstro comparing its preludes with one bass-note sustained throughout to the Introduction to *"Das Rheingold,"* and its continual recitative also to that of Wagner.

In 1608 appeared his mythological spectacle *"Ballo delle Ingrate."* Vespers and motets (pub. 1610) gave him such fame that he was in 1613 made Maestro di Cappella at San Marco, Venice, at the unprecedented salary of 300 ducats (the usual salary had been 200), but it was raised to 500 in 1616, and a house and travelling expenses given him. 1621, his very romantic Requiem was given with effect. In 1624, he intoduced the then startling novelty of an instrumental tremolo (which the musicians at first refused to play) into his dramatic interlude, *"Il Combattimento di Tancredi e Clorinda"*; 1627 he c. 5 dramatic episodes incl. *"Bradamante"* and *"Dido,"* for the court at Parma; 1630, opera *"Proserpina Rapita"*; in 1637 in the first opera-house opened at Venice, the Teatro di S. Cassiano, operas having hitherto been performed at the palaces of the nobility (v. PERI) M. prod. the operas *"Adone"* (Venice, 1639); *"Le Nozze di Enea con Lavinia"* (1641), *"Il Ritorno di Ulisse in Patria"* (1641), and *"L'Incoronazione di Poppea"* (1642). He earned the title of "the father of the art of instrumentation"; was the most popular and influential composer of his time.

In 1636 he joined the priesthood and is heard of no more. C. masses, psalms, hymns, magnificats, motets, madrigals, etc.

There has been a strong revival of interest in his music within recent years. D'Indy arranged *"Poppea"* and *"Orfeo"* for prod. in Paris; and the latter work was also rescored by Respighi and prod. in Rome. A biog. by Prunières was published, 1926.

Moody, Fanny, vide MANNERS (2).

Moor (mōōr), (1) **Karel,** b. Belohrad, Hungary, Nov. 26, 1873; composer; pupil of Prague Cons. and that in Vienna; played and taught violin in Prague; after 1902 active in Czech Philh. and theatres in Bohemia, Trieste and Jugoslavia; c. operas, orch. and chamber works. (2) **Emanuel,** Keskemet, Hungary, Feb. 19, 1863—Mt. Pelerin, Vevey, Switzerland, Oct. 21, 1931; pianist, composer; in 1920 invented a novel piano in which several keyboards are connected with couplers and may be played together; m. Winifred Christie, Scottish pianist, who has toured with much succ. as recitalist on this instrument in Europe and U. S.

Moore, (1) **Thos.,** Dublin, 1779—near Devizes, 1852; famous poet; pianist and singer. (2) **Douglas Stuart,** b. Cutchogue, Long Island, N. Y., 1893;

composer; studied Yale Univ. under Parker and D. S. Smith, later in Paris with d'Indy and Nadia Boulanger; formerly dir. of music, Cleveland Museum of Art; 1926, awarded Pulitzer Prize and Guggenheim Fellowship; assoc. prof. of music, Columbia Univ.; c. (orch.) *"Pageant of P. T. Barnum," "Moby Dick," "Museum Pieces," "Symphony of Autumn"*; vln. and piano sonata; author, *Listening to Music*. (3) **Grace,** b. Jellico, Tenn., Dec. 5, 1901; soprano; studied Ward-Belmont School, Nashville, and Wilson-Greene School, Washington; vocal study in Europe; began singing career in musical comedy and revues in N. Y.; later trained for opera and made début, Met. Op., 1928; also sang at Paris Op.-Comique in following year as "Louise"; after several seasons, left grand opera to star in operetta, *"The Du Barry,"* in N. Y.; then entered musical films with striking succ.; guest appearances as "Mimi" at Covent Garden, 1935, were attended with unusual manifestations of popularity.

Moraës (mō-răns), **João da Silva,** Lisbon, Dec. 27, 1689—ca. 1747; important Portuguese composer of church music; cond. at the Cathedral.

Morales (mō-răl'-ās) **Cristobal,** Seville, 1500—Malaga, 1553; entered Papal chapel ca. 1540; eminent Spanish contrapuntist and composer.

Moralt (mō'-rält), the name of four brothers famous at Munich as a quartet. (1) **Jos.,** Schwetzingen, near Mannheim, 1775—Munich, 1828, 1st violinist. (2) **Jn. Bpt.,** Mannheim, 1777—Munich, 18?5; 2d violinist; composer. (3) **Philipp,** Munich, 1780—1829; 'cellist. (4) **G.,** Munich, 1781—1818; vla.-player.

Moran-Olden (rightly F. Tappenhorn) (mō'-rän-ōl'-děn), **Fanny,** Oldenburg, Sept. 28, 1855—near Berlin, Feb. 13, 1905; pupil of Haas and Götze; début as "Fanny Olden" at the Gewandhaus, 1877; 1878, leading sopr., Frankfort; 1888–89, New York; m. in 1879 the tenor **K. Moran;** 1897, m. Bertram, ct.-singer at Munich.

Morel (mō-rěl), **Auguste Fran.,** Marseilles, 1809—Paris, 1881; dir. of the Marseilles Cons. and dram. composer.

Morelli (mō-rĕl'-lē), (1) **Giacomo,** Venice, 1745—1819; librarian, San Marco. (2) **Giov.,** Italian bass, in London, 1787.

Morelot (môr-lŏ), **Stephen,** Dijon, Jan. 12, 1820—Beaumont, Oct. 7, 1899; from 1845, co-ed, *Revue de la Musique;* 1847, sent by the Ministry of Pub. Instruction to study church-mus. in Italy; wrote a work on plain-chant, an attempt to revive ancient harmonisation, etc.

Morena (mō-rä'-nä), **Berta,** b. Mannheim, Jan. 27, 1878; pupil of Frau Röhr-Brajnin and Mme. de Sales; 1898–1923 at Munich Court Theatre; and 1908 with Met. Op., N. Y.; also in concert with Boston Symph., 1909, etc.

Mor'gan, (1) **G. Washbourne,** Gloucester, Engl., 1822—Tacoma, U. S., 1892; organist and conductor. (2) **J. Paul,** Oberlin, Ohio, 1841—Oakland, Cal., 1879; organist and composer.

Morini (mō-rē'-nē), **Erica,** b. Vienna, May 26, 1906; violinist; studied with her father, Oscar Marinka, and with Sevcik at Vienna Cons.; début in that city, 1916; 1st visited U. S., 5 years later, when she made a pronounced impression, although only 15, as a spirited and fluent technician; after several years' absence during which she appeared widely in Europe and Australia as orchestral soloist and in recital, she returned to America in 1930 and 1935 as a matured and impressive performer.

Morlacchi (môr-läk'-kē), **Fran.,** Perugia, June 14, 1784—Innsbruck, Oct. 28, 1841; pupil of Zingarelli, Padre Martini, etc., from 1810 cond. of Italian opera, Dresden; c. many succ. operas, also church-music, incl. Tuba Mirum, inspired by Michelangelo's *"Last Judgment"*; biog. by Count Rossi-Scotti (1870).

Mor'ley, (1) **Thos.,** 1557—1603; pupil of Byrd; 1588, Mus. Bac. Oxford; 1592, Gentleman of the Chapel Royal; also Epistler and Gospeller; c. the only contemporary Shakespearean song extant, *"It Was a Lover and His Lass"* from *"As You Like It,"* pub. 1600 in one of his very numerous colls.; he wrote the first English treatise on mus. (1597) still valuable, and ed. (1599) a curious treatise on ensemble playing; some of his madrigals and melodious ballets

are still heard. (2) **Wm.,** d. 1731; Mus. Bac. Oxford, 1713; 1715, Gent. of the Chapel Royal; c. one of the earliest known double-chants, songs, etc.

Mor'nington, Earl of (Garrett C. Wellesley), Dangan, Ireland, July 19, 1735—May 22, 1781; founded Academy of Music, 1757; 1764 Mus. Doc. (Dublin) and Prof.; 1760 created Viscount Wellesley and Earl of M.; c. glees and madrigals; one of his sons was the Duke of Wellington.

Morris, (1) **Robert O'Connor,** b. London, March 3, 1886; studied R. Coll. of Music, where later taught cpt.; also at Curtis Inst. of Music, Philadelphia. (2) **Harold,** b. San Antonio, Tex., 1890; composer; c. symphony, piano concerto, string quartet, piano quintet, vln. and piano sonata; *"Poem after Tagore's 'Gitanjali' "* for orch.; rhapsody for piano, vln. and 'cello; has appeared as piano soloist in his works with leading Amer. orchestras.

Morse, Chas. H., Bradford, Mass., Jan. 5, 1853—Boston, June 4, 1927; 1873, graduate New Engl. Cons.; studied with Perabo, and Baermann, 1879; 1873, teacher N. E. Cons.; 1875–84, Mus. Dir. Wellesley Coll.; from 1891, organist Plymouth Church, Brooklyn; pub. collections of organ-pieces and composed.

Mor'telmans, Lodevijk, b. Antwerp, Feb. 5, 1868; pupil of the Cons. and Brussels Cons.; c. symph. *"Germania,"* symph. poem *"Wilde Jagd,"* etc.; after 1902, prof. of comp., Antwerp Cons.

Mortier de Fontaine (môrt-yä dŭ fôṅ-tĕn), **H. Louis Stanislas,** Wisniewiec, Russia, 1816—London, 1883; pianist.

Mor'timer, Peter, Putenham, Surrey, 1750—Dresden, 1828; a Moravian brother; writer.

Mosca (môs'-kä), (1) **Giuseppe,** Naples, 1772—Messina, 1839; conductor and dram. composer. (2) **Luigi,** Naples, 1775—1824; bro. of above; prof. of singing.

Moscheles (mō'-shĕ-lĕs), **Ignaz,** Prague, May 30, 1794—Leipzig, March 10, 1870; son of a Jewish merchant; at 10 pupil of Dionys Weber, Prague Cons.; at 14 played publicly a concerto of his own; studied with Albrechtsberger and Salieri while earning his living as a pianist and teacher; at 20 was chosen to prepare the pf.-score of *"Fidelio"* under Beethoven's supervision; as a pianist a succ. rival of Hummel and Meyerbeer; he could not comprehend or play Chopin or Liszt, but had large influence on subsequent technic; after tours, he lived in London 1821–46, when Mendelssohn, who had been his pupil, persuaded him to join the newly founded Leipzig Cons., of which he became one of the pillars; c. 8 pf.-concertos, incl. *"fantastique," "pathétique"* and *"pastoral"*; *"Sonata"* and *"Sonate symphonique,"* for pf. 4 hands, and *"Sonate caracteristique," "Sonate mélancolique,"* and many standard studies; biog. (1872) by his wife Charlotte (née Embden).

Mosel (mō'-zĕl), (1) **Ignaz Fz.**, Edler von, Vienna, 1772—1844; conductor, writer and dram. composer. (2) **Giovanni Felice,** b. Florence, 1754; violinist; pupil of Nardini and his successor as court cond., 1793; c. violin music, etc.

Mosenthal (mō'-zĕn-täl), **Jos.**, Cassel, Nov. 30, 1834—New York, Jan. 6, 1896; from 1867, cond. Mendelssohn Glee Club, New York, also violinist, organist and composer.

Moser (mō'-zĕr), (1) **K.**, Berlin, 1774—1851; violinist and conductor. (2) **Andreas,** 1859—1925; pupil Joachim; noted vln. teacher in Berlin. (3) **Hans I.,** his son, b. Berlin, 1889; prof., writer.

Mosewius (mō-zä'-vĭ-oos), **Jn. Th.**, Königsberg, 1788 — Schaffhausen, 1858; opera-singer and writer.

Moson'yi (rightly **Michael Brandt**), Boldog-Aszony, Hungary, 1814—Pesth, 1870; pf.-teacher and composer.

Mos'solov, Alex., b. Kiev, Russia, Aug. 10, 1900; one of most individual and accomplished of Soviet composers; came into internat'l prominence for his descriptive works for orch. and chamber ensembles which are based on the rhythms and sounds of labor; esp. *"The Soviet Iron Foundry,"* in radical dissonantal style, which has been played by a number of Amer. orchs.; piano pieces, etc.

Moszkowski (môsh-kôf'-shkĭ), (1) **Moritz,** Breslau, Aug. 23, 1854—Paris, March 4, 1925; son of a wealthy Polish gentleman; pupil of Dresden Cons., Stern and Kullak Cons.; teacher Stern Cons. for years; later début with succ. as pianist, Berlin, 1873; until 1897 Berlin then Paris; as a composer, prod. succ. opera, *"Boabdil der Maurenkönig"* (Berlin, 1882); symph. poem *"Jeanne d'Arc"*; *"Phantastischer Zug"* for orch.; 2 orchestral suites and a vln.-concerto; c. many pop. pf.-pcs., incl. *"Aus. allen Herren Länder,"* and *"Spanische Tänze."* (2) **Alex.,** Pilica, Poland, Jan. 15, 1851—Berlin, Sept. 26, 1934; bro. of above; critic, editor and writer at Berlin.

Motta, José Da, vide **Da Motta.**

Mottl (môt'-'l), (1) **Felix,** Unter-St. Veit, near Vienna, Aug. 24, 1856—Munich, July 2, 1911; prominent conductor; as a boy-soprano, entered Löwenberg "Konvikt," then studied at the Vienna Cons., graduating with high honours; cond. the Academical Wagnerverein for some time; 1880, ct.-cond. at Carlsruhe, also, until 1892, cond. Philh. Concerts; 1893 the Grand Duke app. him Gen. Mus. Dir.; 1886, cond.-in-chief, Bayreuth; invited to be ct.-cond. but he declined; 1898 declined a similar call to Munich; led succ. concerts London and Paris; 1892, he m. (2) **Henriette Standhartner** (b. Vienna, Dec. 6, 1866, ct. opera singer at Weimar and Carlsruhe). **M.** came to N. Y., 1903–04, to conduct the first perfs. of *"Parsifal"* outside Bayreuth, but owing to protests of Wagner family did not do so; 1904 he became co-director of the Royal Academy of Music, Munich; he was cond. the United Royal Operas there, when he fell ill of arteriosclerosis and died in July, 1911. Shortly before his death he was divorced from his first wife and married Sdenka Fassbender, of the Munich Opera. He is particularly known for his orch. arrangements of ballet suites by Gluck and Rameau, but also c. succ. operas, *"Agnes Bernauer"* (Weimar, 1880), and the 1-act *"Fürst und Sänger"* (Carlsruhe, 1893); prod. also a "Festspiel," *"Eberstein,"* songs, etc.

Mount-Edg'cumbe, Richard, Earl of, 1764 — Richmond, Surrey, 1839; wrote *"Reminiscences of an Amateur"*; c. opera *"Zenobia."*

Mouret (moo-rā), **J. Jos.,** Avignon, 1682—insane asylum, Charenton, 1738; conductor and composer.

Moussorgsky (mōō-sôrg'-skĕ), **Modest Petrovich**, Karevo, Ukraine, March 28, 1839—St. Petersburg, March 28, 1881; one of the most important Russian composers, perhaps the most original of the Nationalistic school of that country and the "father" of the whole modern movement for anti-formalism, and expression by means of folk idioms. He was the son of an impoverished noble family; early learned to play the piano, 1st from his mother, then from a teacher named Herke. He was largely self-instructed in comp. and began to compose songs before he was 20. He entered the Russian army, and as a young officer was introduced by César Cui to Balakireff (with whom he had some fitful instruction in comp.). He had also come to know Dargomizhsky earlier. He lived in St. Petersburg as a minor State official, his life a constant struggle with poverty, depression and drink. One of the bright spots was a journey to South Russia as accompanist to the singer Leonowa in 1879. His death occurred at the age of 46 in the Nikolai Military Hospital at Petersburg.

Largely unappreciated by his contemporaries, but his fame has steadily increased since his death. Especially in his marvellous collection of some 60 songs, most of them grim and somewhat mordant, he has shown an outstanding gift for expression and character portrayal. He is most celebrated for his 2 principal operas, the stupendous nationalistic folk drama, "*Boris Godounoff*," conceived most originally with the people as the main protagonists and the chorus the featured performers, and the lesser but also impressive "*Khovanstchina*," both based on Russian folk and liturgical idioms. The first was originally prod. in St. Petersburg, 1874, but withdrawn after a few perfs. Fifteen years after **M.'s** death it was revised by Rimsky-Korsakoff, who added to it his brilliant orchestration, and smoothed down what he considered its "uncouth" qualities. In this form it made its way over the opera stages of the world and made a profound impression. Only in 1925 was the original version of the work published by the Soviet musical authorities and eagerly performed in Europe and the U. S. (concert hearing under Stokowski, Phila.). Other smaller operatic works are "*The Marriage*" (one-act, based on Gogol's comedy), 1868; and "*The Fair at Sorotchinsi*," partially finished and completed by Tcherepnine. As an orch. composer, **M.** is best known by the symph. poem, "*Night on the Bald Mountain*," much revised by Rimsky-Korsakoff. His famous suite of descriptive pieces for piano, "*Pictures from an Exhibition*," has been orchestrated by Ravel and has enjoyed wide popularity; also c. song cycles, "*Without Sunlight*," "*Songs and Dances of Death*," "*The Children's Room*"; (chorus) "*The Defeat of Sennacherib*," etc. The chief Moussorgsky biographies are by Calvocoressi and Riesemann; a collection of his letters has been published.

Mouton (moo-tôṅ) (**Jean de Hollingue** (ôl'-lăng) (called "Mouton")), Holling (?), near Metz—St. Quentin, Oct. 30, 1522; important contrapuntist; c. motets, masses, psalms, chansons, etc.

Mouzin (moo-zăṅ), **P. Nicolas** (called **Édouard**), Metz, July 13, 1822—Paris, 1894; studied at Metz branch of the Paris Cons.; 1842, teacher there, 1854, dir.; 1871, teacher at the Paris Cons.; writer; c. 2 operas, symphs., etc.

Mozart (mō'-tsärt) (originally **Motzert**), (1) (**Jn. G.**) Ld., Augsburg, 1719—Salzburg, 1787; father of W. A. M.; dram. composer. (2) (**Maria**) **Anna** (called "**Nannerl**"), Salzburg, 1751—1829; daughter and pupil of above; pianist; c. org. pcs. (3) **Wolfgang Amadeus** (baptised **Jns. Chrysostomus Wolfgangus Theophilus**), Salzburg, Jan. 27, 1756—Vienna, Dec. 5, 1791; son of (1), and bro. of (2); one of the major divinities of music. Of unrivalled precocity in performance, composition, and acoustic sensitiveness; at 3 his talent and his discovery of thirds (v. D. D.), led his father to teach him. He began at once to compose little minuets which his father and later he himself noted down. He and his sister made a joint début at Munich, when he was barely 6, though he had appeared as a performer 4 months before in a comedy at the Univ. at Salzburg. He appeared the same year in Vienna, fascinating the court. He now learned the vln. and org. without instruction. At 7 he was in Paris, where his first works were pub., "*II Sonates pour le clavecin.*" The next year he was in London, delighting royalty, winning the honest praise of musicians and coming victoriously out of remarkable tests of his ability as sight-reader and improviser. During his father's illness, while silence was required, he c. his first symph. Here his 6 sonatas for vln. and harps, were pub. and his first symph. performed frequently. He won the friendship of J. Chr. Bach, and was given singing lessons by Manzuoli. Before leaving England he wrote a motet to English words in commemoration of a visit to the British Museum. The family stopped at various cities on the way home, the children playing at courts with constant succ., a concert being given at Amsterdam in 1766, at which all the instrumental music was **M.'s**. At Biberach he competed as organist without result against a boy 2 years older, Sixtus Bachmann. Returning to Salzburg, in 1766, **M.** was set to studying Fux, etc. 1767 he c. an oratorio, 1768, an opera, "*La Finta Semplice*," at the Emperor's request. Its production was postponed by the now jealous musicians till 1769. Meanwhile a German opera "*Bastien und Basti-enne*" had been performed, and **M.** made his début as cond. in 1768 (aged 12), with his solemn mass. The Archbishop made him Konzert-meister, with salary, but his father wished him to enjoy study in Italy. His concerts were sensations, the Pope gave him the order of the Golden Spur (also given to Gluck), and at his father's behest he signed a few compositions by his new title Signor Cavaliere Amadeo, but soon dropped this. After tests he was elected a member of the Accademia Filarmonica of Bologna. At 14 he gave a concert at Mantua in which according to the programme he promises to play "a Symphony of his own composition; a Clavichord-concerto, which will be handed to him, and which he will immediately

play at sight; a Sonata handed him in like manner, which he will provide with variations, and afterwards re-peat in another key; an Aria, the words for which will be handed to him, and which he will immediately set to music and sing himself, accom-panying himself on the clavichord; a Sonata for clavichord on a subject given him by the leader of the violins; a Strict Fugue on a theme to be se-lected, which he will improvise on the clavichord; a trio, in which he will execute a violin-part *all' im-provviso;* and finally, the latest Symphony composed by himself." In Rome, after twice hearing Allegri's famous "*Miserere*," long kept secret, he correctly wrote out the entire score from memory. At Milan he prod. 3-act opera seria "*Mitridate, re di Ponto*" (1770), which had 20 consecutive performances under his direction. 1771, he brought out a dramatic serenade, "*Ascanio in Alba*," for the wedding of Archduke Ferdinand. 1772 his friendly pro-tector, the Archbishop of Salzburg, died; his successor, Hieronymous, Count of Colloredo, treated **M.** with the greatest inappreciation, compell-ing him to sit with the servants (though **M.** was frequently enter-tained at the houses of the nobility with great distinction); and when **M.** demanded his discharge in 1781, he had him kicked out by a servant. It was for his installation that **M.** had c. the dramatic "*Il Sogno di Scipione*" (1775), "*Lucio Silla*" (1772), and "*La Finta Giardiniera,*" prod. at Milan, under his own direc-tion, 1775; later "*Il Re Pastore*" at Salzburg during Archduke Maxi-milian's visit. 1778 he went with his mother to Paris, where he won little attention in the struggle be-tween Gluck and Piccini. At length after his mother's death he returned to Salzburg as Konzertmeister, and ct.-organist; but settled in Vienna, after prod. the opera "*Idomeneo*" (Munich, Jan., 1781). On commis-sion for the Emperor he wrote ("*Belmonte und Constance, oder*) *Die Entführung aus dem Serail,*" prod. with great succ., despite the ma-chinations of the theatrical clique, 1782; a month later he m. Constance Weber (the sister of Aloysia, whom he had loved in Mannheim). She bore him six children, four sons and two daughters. The small receipts for compositions and concerts were quickly spent on luxuries beyond their means, and as neither was a good manager of resources, many hardships followed. After two unfinished operas he prod. a mus. comedy, *"Der Schauspieldirektor"* (Schönbrunn, 1786). May 1, in Vienna, his opera buffa *"Le Nozze di Figaro"*("Marriage of Figaro") was rescued from intrigues into a very great succ. The then famous librettist Da Ponte next wrote the book for *"Don Giovanni"* ("Don Juan"), which made a very great succ. at Prague (1787), and led the Emperor to appoint **M.** "chamber composer," at 800 gulden ($400) a year (Gluck, just deceased, had 2,000 gulden). 1789 he accompanied Prince Karl Lichnowski to Berlin, playing for the Dresden court, and at the Thomaskirche, Leipzig. King Fr. Wm. II., hearing him at Potsdam, offered him the post of 1st Royal cond. with 3,000 thaler ($2,250) a year, but **M.** would not abandon his "good Kaiser"; still Fr. Wm. II. ordered three quartets, for which he paid well. Hearing this, the Emperor ordered the opera buffa *"Così fan Tutte"* (Vienna, 1790). Soon after its production the Emperor died; his successor Ld. II. cared little for **M.**, leaving him in greatest hardship. His devoted friend Jos. Haydn now went to London. **M.** made a tour, pawning his plate to pay the expenses. For the coronation of Leopold II., as King of Bohemia, at Prague, he was invited to write the festival opera *"La Clemenza di Tito,"* performed 1791. He returned to Vienna and c. *"Die Zauberflöte"* ("Magic Flute," Vienna, Sept. 30, 1791), a work in which are exploited the allegories of the Masonry of which **M.** was a member. It made a decided succ. He was, however, growing weaker and suffering from fainting fits, claiming that he had been poisoned. A mysterious stranger had commissioned him to write a requiem, and **M.** began it with a superstitious dread that the messenger had come from the other world to announce his death. It has since been learned that he was Leutgeb, the steward of

Count von Walsegg, who gave the work out as his own, not, however, destroying the MS. The work was not quite completed by Mozart, who had his pupil Süssmayer fill out the incomplete portions. Mozart died of malignant typhus. A violent rain-storm coming up in the midst of the funeral, the party turned back leaving the body to be interred in some spot, never after discovered, in the ground allotted to paupers in the St. Mary cemetery. The profits of a Mus. Festival given by the Frankfort "Liederkranz," June 25, 1838, were devoted to founding a Mozart Scholarship, the interest amounting in 1896 to 1500 marks, applied quadrennially to the aid of talented young composers of limited means. At Salzburg the *Mozarteum,* a municipal musical institute founded in his memory, consists of an orch. soc. pledged to perform his church-music in the 14 churches of the town, to give 12 concerts yearly, and to sustain a mus.-sch. in which the musicians of the orch. give instruction.

A complete ed. of **M.**'s works pub. by Breitkopf & Härtel (1876–86), contains much church-mus. inc. 15 masses, cantatas *"Davidde penitente"* (masonic), *"Maurerfreude"* and *"Kleine Freimaurercantate,"* etc.; stage-works, besides those mentioned, *"Die Schuldigkeit des ersten Gebots"* (only partially his own), *"Apollo et Hyacinthus"* (Latin comedy with mus.); *"Zaïde"* (unfinished); *"Thamos, König in Aegypten"* (choruses and entr'actes; Berlin, 1786); *"Idomeneo, re di Creta, ossia Ilia ed Idamante."* ORCH. WORKS: 41 symph.; 2 symph. movements; 31 divertimenti, serenades, and cassations; 9 marches; 25 dances, *"Masonic Funeral-Music"*; *"A Musical Jest"* for string-orch. and 2 horns; a sonata for bassoon and 'cello; phantasie for Glockenspiel; andante for barrel-organ, etc.; 6 vln.-concertos, bassoon-concerto, a concerto for flute and harp, 2 flute-concertos, horn-concertos, a clarinet-concerto, 25 pf.-concertos, a double concerto for 2 pfs., a triple concerto for 3 pfs. CHAMBER-MUSIC: 7 string-quintets; 26 string-quartets; *"Nachtmusik"* for string-quintet; 42 vln.-sonatas, etc. PF.-MUSIC: for 4 hands; 5 sonatas.

and an andante with variations; for 2 pfs., a fugue, and a sonata; 17 solo sonatas; a fantasie and fugue; 3 fantasias; 36 cadenzas to pf.-concertos; rondos, etc.; 17 organ sonatas, etc. VOCAL MUSIC: 27 arias, and 1 rondo for sopr. with orch.; German war-song; a comic duet; 34 songs; a song with chorus and org.; a 3-part chorus with org.; a comic terzet with pf.; 20 canons. His unstageworthy opera *"Idomeneo"* was provided with a new book, and extensively rescored by Richard Strauss for the Munich Fest., 1930. The best of many biographies is by Otto Jahn (1856–59, 4 volumes in English, London, 1882), etc.
His letters, ed. by Hans Mersmann, have also been published and translated in two volumes. One of his two overtures was found at the Paris Cons. 1901. Six unpublished sonatas were found in Buckingham Palace, 1902. A violin concerto (the "Adelaide"), c. at 10 yrs., was recovered in 1934.
Other memoirs have been issued by Berlioz, Dent, Holmes, Kerst, Breakspeare and Mersmann.

(4) **Wolfgang Amadeus**, Vienna, July 26, 1791—Carlsbad, July 29, 1844; son of above; pianist, teacher and composer of pf.-concertos, sonatas, etc.

Muck (mook), **Carl**, b. Darmstadt, Oct. 22, 1859—Stuttgart, March 4, 1940; pupil of Leipzig |Cons., cond. at various cities; 1892, ct.-cond. Royal Op., Berlin; 1899, cond. German Opera in London; 1903–05 alternated with Mottl as cond. of the Vienna Phil.; 1906–08 on leave of absence he cond. Boston Symph. during the winters; appearing also at Paris, Madrid, etc.; 1901, 2, 4, 6, and 8 cond. *"Parsifal"* at Bayreuth. By arrangement with the Boston Symph. he continued his contract, sending Max Fiedler to conduct in his place 1909–12; and returning 1912. He made a most brilliant impression as a musician of the highest order, and raised the orch. to hitherto unparalleled efficiency. In 1918 he was accused of anti-Amer. activity and was interned as an enemy alien during the remainder of the war and deported, 1919. He was again active in Germany, after 1922, as leader of the Hamburg Philh. **Orch.**, and conducted elsewhere, incl. Bayreuth.

Mu'die, Thos. Molleson, Chelsea, 1809 —London, 1876; teacher, organist and composer.

Muffat (moof'-fät), (1) **G.**, Schlettstadt, ca. 1645—Passau, Feb. 23, 1704; organist, conductor and composer. (2) **Aug. Gottlieb**, Passau, April, 1690—Vienna, Dec. 10, 1770; son of above; organist and composer.

Mugellini (moo-gĕl-lē'-nē), **Bruno**, Potenza, Dec. 24, 1871—Bologna, Jan. 15, 1912; pianist; pupil of Tofano, Busi and Martucci; 1898 teacher Bologna Lyceum; 1911, dir.; c. prize symph. poem *"Alle fonte del Clitumno"*; 'cello sonata, etc.; edited Bach, Czerny and Clementi.

Mugnone (moon-yō'-nā), **Leopoldo**, b. Naples, Sept. 29, 1858; noted conductor; pupil of Cons. in native city; beginning 1885 cond. at Costanzi Theatre, Rome; led première of Verdi's *"Falstaff,"* Milan, 1893; esp. known for his Wagnerian perfs.; c. operas, etc.

Mühldörfer (mül'-dĕrf-ĕr), (1) **Wm.**, 1803—Mannheim, 1897; ct.-inspector of theatres, Mannheim. (2) **Wm. K.**, Graz, Styria, March 6, 1836— Cologne, 1919; son of above; studied at Linz-on-Danube and Mannheim; actor; 1855, th.-cond., Ulm; 1867–81, 2d cond. at Cologne; c. 4 operas, incl. successful *"Iolanthe"* (Cologne, 1890), overtures, etc.

Mühlfeld (mül'-fĕlt), **Richard**, Salzungen, Feb. 28, 1856—Meiningen, June 1, 1907; clarinettist for whom Brahms c. a trio and sonata; studied with Büchner at Meiningen, where he lived after 1873; 1875–96, 1st clarinet at Bayreuth.

Mühling (mü'-lĭng), **Aug.**, Raguhn, 1786—Magdeburg, 1847; organist and composer.

Mukle (mōō'-klē), **May Henrietta**, b. London, May 14, 1880; 'cellist; appeared as child prodigy; later pupil of R. A. M., and of Hambleton; from 1900 made world tours; played in trio with Maud Powell, violinist, and her sister Anna, pianist; visited Australia, U. S., South Africa, Honolulu, etc.

Mulé (mōō-lā'), **Giuseppe**, b. Sicily, June 28, 1885; composer; studied at Palermo Cons.; early active as 'cellist; cond. opera and concerts; after 1922, dir. of Palermo Cons., and 1925 succeeded Respighi as dir. of Liceo of Santa Cecilia, Rome; c. (operas) *"La Monacella dell Fontana," "Dafni,"* etc., which have had succ. productions; also oratorio, orch. and other music.

Müller (mül'-lĕr), (1) **Chr.**, org.-builder at Amsterdam, ca. 1720-70. (2) **Wm. Chr.**, Wassungen, Meiningen, 1752—Bremen, 1831; mus. director and writer. (3) **Aug. Eberhard**, Nordheim, Hanover, 1767—Weimar, 1817; son and pupil of an organist; organist, ct.-conductor and dram. composer. (4) **Wenzel**, Tyrnau, Moravia, 1767—Baden, near Vienna, 1835; conductor and composer of 200 operas. (5) **Fr.**, Orlamünde, 1786—Rudolstadt, 1871; clarinettist, conductor and composer. (6) **Ivan (Iwan)**, Reval, 1786—Bückeburg, 1854; inv. of the clarinet with 13 keys, and altclarinet; finally ct.-mus. (7) **Peter**, Kesselstadt, Hanau, 1791—Langen, 1877; c. operas, and famous *"Jugendlieder,"* etc. (8) Two famous German quartet parties, (a) The bros. **K. Fr.** (1797—1873), **Th. H. Gus.** (1799—1855), **Aug. Th.** (1802—1875), and **Fz. Fd. G.** (1808—1855), sons of (9) **Aegidius Chp. M.** (d. 1841, Hofmus. to Duke of Brunswick), all b. Brunswick, and in the orch. there—**K.** as Konzertmeister, **Th.** 1st 'cello, **Gv.** symph.-director, and **G.** conductor. (b) The four sons of the **Karl Fr.** above, who organised 1855 a ct.-quartet. **Hugo**, 2d vln. (1832—1886); **Bd.**, 1825—1895; viola; **Wm.**, 1834—N. Y., 1897; 'cello; **Karl**, Jr., 1829—1907; 1st vln. in Stuttgart and Hamburg; m. Elvina Berghaus and took name **Müller-Berghaus**, under which he c. a symph., etc. (10) (Rightly Schmid) **Ad.** Sr., Tolna, Hungary, 1801—Vienna, 1886; singer, conductor and dram. composer. (11) **Ad.**, Jr., Vienna 1839—1901, son of above; 1875, cond. German opera at Rotterdam; prod. 4 operas and 5 operettas, incl. the succ. *"Der Blondin von Namur"* (Vienna, 1898). (12) **Jns.**, Coblenz, 1801—Berlin, 1858; writer. (13) **Fz. K. Fr.**, Weimar, 1806—1876; one of the first to recognise Wagner; pub. treatises on his work. (14) **Aug.**, 1810—1867; eminent double-bass. (15) **K.**, Weissensee, near Erfurt, 1818—Frankfort, 1894; conductor and composer.

(16) **Bd.**, Sonneberg, 1824—Meiningen, 1883; cantor. (17) **K. Chr.**, Saxe-Meiningen, July 3, 1831—New York, June 4, 1914; pupil of F. W. and H. Pfeiffer (pf. and org.), Andreas Zöllner (comp.) 1854, New York; 1879, prof. of harm. N. Y. Coll. of Mus.; translator, etc. (18) **Richard**, Leipzig, Feb. 25, 1830 —Oct. 1, 1904; pupil of Zöllner, Hauptmann and Reitz; until 1893, cond. "Arion," then the "Hellas," and the "Liedertafel"; teacher singing, Nikolai Gymnasium; c. motets, etc. (19) **Jos.**, 1839—Berlin, 1880; writer. (20) **Wm.**, Hanover, Feb. 4, 1845—July 21, 1905; tenor at the ct.-opera, Berlin. (21) **Hans**, Cologne, 1854—Berlin, 1897; prof. and writer. (22) **Gustav.** Vide BRAHMÜLLER. (23) **Maria**, b. Prague, Jan. 29, 1898; lyric soprano; début as "Elsa," Linz, 1920; sang with Linz Op., 1920—21; Prague, 1921—23; Munich State Op., 1923—24; after latter year until 1935 she was a member of Met. Op. Co., N. Y., also singing at Berlin State Op. after 1926, and at Bayreuth from 1930; her repertoire includes both Italian and German rôles.

Mül'ler-Hartung, K. (Wm.), Sulza, May 19, 1834—Charlottenburg, Berlin, June 11, 1908; pupil of Kühmstedt, Eisenach; mus.-dir. and teacher at the Seminary; 1864, prof.; 1869, opera-cond. Weimar; 1872, founder and dir. Gr. Ducal "Orchester-und-Musikschule"; wrote a system of music theory (vol. i. *"Harmonielehre"* appeared in 1879); composer.

Müller-Reuter (roi-tĕr), **Theodor**, Dresden, Sept. 1, 1858—Leipzig, Aug. 16, 1919; pupil of Fr. and Alwin Wieck (pf.); J. Otto and Meinardus (comp.); and the Hoch Cons., Frankfort; 1879—87, teacher Strassburg Cons.; 1887, cond. at Dresden; 1892, teacher in the Cons.; mus.-dir. at Crefeld, 1893—1918; c. 2 operas, Paternoster, with orch.; *"Hackelberend's Funeral"* for chorus and orchestra (1902), etc.

Munck, de. Vide DEMUNCK.

Mun'dy, (1) **William**, d. 1591(?); Gentleman of the Chapel Royal, 1563; c. anthems, etc. His son (2) **John**, d. Windsor, 1630; where he had been organist from 1585; c. madrigals and a fantasia describing the weather.

Muratore (mü'-rä-tôr), **Lucien**, b. Marseilles, 1878; tenor; grad. of Cons. there, also studied Paris Cons.; began career as actor; début at Paris Op.-Comique, 1902, in Hahn's "*La Carmelite*"; at the Opera as "Rinaldo" in "*Armide*," 1905; after 1913 he was a pop. mem. of the Chicago Op., singing romantic rôles opposite Mary Garden; he also appeared in Buenos Aires and in various Eur. capitals; m. Lina Cavalieri, soprano; divorced.

Mur'doch, **William**, b. Bendigo, Victoria, Feb. 10, 1888; pianist; début in London, 1910; thereafter toured Europe, Australia, and after 1914 gave concerts in U. S.

Muris (dŭ mü'-rēs), **Jns. de** (or **de Meurs**) (dŭ mŭrs), eminent theorist; wrote treatise "*Speculum Musicae*" (probably ca. 1325) (Coussemaker).

Mur'phy, **Lambert**, b. Springfield, Mass., April 15, 1885; tenor; grad. Harvard Univ.; studied with Thomas Cushman, Isadore Luckstone and Herbert Witherspoon; soloist in N. Y. and Boston churches; mem. Met. Op. Co., 1911–15; also active as orch. and fest. soloist and in radio programmes.

Murschhauser (moorsh'-how-zĕr), **Fz. X. Anton**, Zabern, near Strassburg, 1663—Munich, 1738; conductor and theorist.

Murska (moor'-shkä), **Ilma, di**, Croatia, 1836—Munich, Jan. 16, 1889; famous dramatic soprano, with remarkable compass of nearly 3 octaves.

Musard (mü-zăr), (1) **Philippe**, Paris, 1793—1859; c. pop. dances. (2) **Alfred**, 1828—1881; orch.-cond., and composer; son of above.

Musin (moo-zēn), **Bonaventura**. Vide FURLANETTO.

Musin (mü-zăn), **Ovide**, Nandrin, n. Liége, Sept. 22, 1854—Brooklyn, N. Y., Oct. 30, 1929; violinist; pupil of Liége Cons.; at 11 took 1st vln.-prize; studied then at Paris Cons.; at 14 won the gold medal for solo and quartet playing; taught a year at the Cons. then toured Europe with great succ.; later organised a concert-troupe and toured America, then the world; 1897, returned to Liége as vln.-teacher at the Cons.; 1898, vln.-professor; 1908–10, dir. of his own music school in N. Y.

Musiol (moo'-zĭ-ōl), **Robt. Paul Jn.**, Breslau, Jan. 14, 1846—Fraustadt, Oct. 19, 1903; from 1873–91 teacher and cantor at Röhrsdorf, Posen; pub. mus. lexicons; c. part-songs, etc.

Musorgsky, see MOUSSORGSKY.

Mustel (müs-tĕl), **Victor**, b. Havre, 1815; mfr. and improver of the harmonium.

Müthel (mē'-tĕl), **Johann Gottfried**, Mölln, 1720—Riga, after 1790; organist; c. sonatas and songs.

Muzio (moo'-tsĭ-ō), (1) **Emanuele**, Zibello, near Parma, Aug. 25, 1825—Paris, Nov. 27, 1890; pupil of Provesi and Verdi, and (for pf.) of Verdi's first wife, Margherita Barezzi; 1852, cond. It. Opera, Brussels; later, London, New York (Acad. of Mus.); 1875 noted singing teacher, Paris; c. 4 operas, etc. (2) **Claudia**, Pavia, 1892—Rome, May 24, 1936; notable soprano; daughter of Carlo Muzio, stage director at Covent Garden and at Met. Op., N. Y.; studied harp and piano; singing with Mme. Casaloni; début as "Manon" at Arezzo; sang in a number of Italian opera houses, including La Scala, also at Covent Garden; début Met. Op. as "Tosca," 1918; sang there for several seasons with notable success; after 1922 with Chicago Op. for a decade with eminent popularity; also in Rome, Paris, Buenos Aires, Monte Carlo, Naples, Genoa, Havana, and with San Francisco Op.; returned to Met. Op. for a perf. as "Violetta" in 1933 and as "Santuzza," 1934; created title rôle in Refice's opera, "*Cecilia*," in Rome and Buenos Aires.

Mysliweczek (mē-slē'-vä-chĕk), **Jos.** (called "Il Boemo," or "Venatorini"), near Prague, March 9, 1737—Rome, Feb. 4, 1781; prod. about 30 pop. operas in Italy; c. symphs.; pf.-sonatas praised by Mozart, etc.

Mysz-Gmeiner, vide GMEINER.

N

Naaff (näf), **Anton E. Aug.**, Weitentrebetitsch, Bohemia, Nov. 28, 1850—Vienna, Dec. 27, 1918; mus. editor and poet at Vienna.

Na'bokoff, **Nicholas**, b. Poland, April 7, 1903; composer; studied at St. Petersburg Imp. Lyceum; at Berlin Hochsch. with Busoni, and in Stuttgart; res. in Paris; visited U. S., 1933; c. (ballets) "*Union Pacific*," "*Aphrodite*," "*A Ballet Ode*," "*Commedie*"; (choral work) "*Job*": (orch.) Symphonie Lyrique; concerto for piano and orch.; (opera) "*Le Fiancé.*"

Nachbaur (näkh'-bowr), **Fz.**, Schloss Giessen, near Friedrichshafen, March 25, 1835—Munich, March 21, 1902; pupil of Pischek; sang at theatres in Prague and other cities; 1866–90, "Kammersänger," Munich.

Náchez (nä'-chĕs) (**Tivadar (Theodor) Naschitz** (nä'-shĭts)), Budapest, May 1, 1859—Lausanne, May 29, 1930; vln.-virtuoso; pupil of Sabatil, Joachim and Leonard; toured the continent; lived in Paris and (1889) London; c. 2 concertos for vln., 2 Hungarian Rhapsodies, requiem mass, with orch., etc.

Nadaud (nă-dō), **Gv.**, Roubaix, France, Feb. 20, 1820—Paris, 1893; celebrated poet, composer of chansons; also c. operettas.

Nadermann (nä'-dĕr-män), **François Jos.**, Paris, 1773—1835; harpist, teacher and composer.

Nagel (nä'-gĕl), **Willibald**, b. Mühlheim, Jan. 12, 1863; writer; pub. "*Geschichte der Musik in England*" (1897); d. Stuttgart, Oct. 17, 1929.

Nägeli (nä'-gĕl-ē), **Jn. Hans G.**, Wetzikon, near Zurich, 1773—1836; mus.-publisher, writer and composer.

Nagiller (nä'-gĭl-lĕr), **Matthäus**, Münster, Tyrol, 1815—Innsbrück, 1874; conductor and dram. composer.

Nanini (nä-nē'-nē) (incorrectly **Nanino**), (1) **Giov. M.**, Tivoli, Italy, 1545—Rome, March 11, 1607; noted Italian composer; pupil of Goudimel; cond. at Vallerano, 1571–75, at Santa Maria Maggiore, Rome (vice Palestrina); 1575 founded a pub. mus.-sch. in which Palestrina was one of the teachers; 1577, papal singer; 1604 cond. Sistine Chapel; his 6-part motet "*Hodie nobis cœlorum rex*" is still sung there every Christmas morning. (2) **Giov. Bernardino**, Vallerano, ca. 1560—Rome, 1623; younger bro. (Riemann says nephew) and pupil of above; conductor and notable composer.

Nantier-Didiée (nänt-yä dēd-yä), **Constance Betsy R.**, Île de la Réunion, 1831—Madrid, 1867; v. succ. mezzo-soprano.

Napo'leão, **Arthur**, Oporto, March 6, 1843—Rio de Janeiro, May 12, 1925; pianist and cond.; at 9 made a sensation at the courts of Lisbon, London (1852), and Berlin (1854), then studied with Hallé, at Manchester; toured Europe, and N. and S. America. 1868 (1871 ?) settled in Rio de Janeiro as mus.-seller, etc.

Nápravnik (Náprawnik) (nä-präf'-nēk), **Éduard**, Bejst, near Königgratz, Aug. 24, 1839—St. Petersburg, Nov. 10, 1915; pupil Prague Org.-Sch.; from 1856 teacher Maydl Inst. for Mus., Prague; 1861, cond. to Prince Yussupoff at St. Petersburg; then organist and 2nd cond. Russian Opera; from 1869 1st cond.; 1870–82, cond. the Mus. Soc.; c. 4 operas, incl. the succ. "*Dubroffsky*" (St. P., 1895); symph. poem "*The Demon*," overtures, incl. "*Vlasta*" (1861), etc.

Nardini (när-dē'-nē), **Pietro**, Fibiana, Tuscany, 1722—Florence, May 7, 1793; noted violinist; pupil of Tartini; ct.-musician at Stuttgart and Florence; composer.

Nares (närz), **Jas.**, Stanwell, Middlesex, 1715—London, Feb. 10, 1783; organist and composer.

Naret-Koning (nä'-rĕt-kō-nĭng), **Jn. Jos. D.**, Amsterdam, Feb. 25, 1838—Frankfort, March 28, 1905; violinist; pupil of David, Leipzig; from 1878 leader City Th., Frankfort; pub. songs, etc.

Nasolini (nä-sō-lē'-nē), **Sebastiano**, Piacenza, ca. 1768—(?); prod. 30 operas in Italy.

Natale (nä-tä'-lĕ), **Pompeo**, choirsinger and composer at S. Maria Maggiore, Rome, 1662.

Na'than, Isaac, Canterbury, 1792—Sydney, Australia, 1864; writer.

Natorp (nä'-tôrp), **Bd. Chr. L.**, Werden-on-Ruhr, Nov. 12, 1774—Münster, Feb. 8, 1846; reformer of church and sch.-mus.; writer.

Nau (na'-oo), **Maria Dolores Benedicta Josefina**, of Spanish parents, New York, March 18, 1818—Paris, Feb. 1891; soprano; pupil of Mme. Damoreau-Cinti, Paris Cons., taking 1st prize in 1834; début at the Opéra, 1836; sang minor rôles there 6 years, etc.; 1844–48 and 1851–53, leading rôles, singing in other cities; retired, 1856.

Naudin (nä'-oo-dēn), **Emilio**, Parma, Oct. 23, 1823—Bologna, May 5, 1890; tenor; pupil of Panizza, Milan; début, Cremona. Meyerbeer in his will requested him to create the rôle of "Vasco" in "*L'Africaine*" (1865), which he did.

Naue (now'-ĕ), **Jn. Fr.**, Halle, 1787—1858; organist and composer.

Nauenburg (now'-ĕn-boorkh), **Gv.**, Halle, May 20, 1803—after 1862; barytone and singing-teacher; writer and composer.

Naumann (now'-män), (1) **Jn. Gl.** (Italianised as **Giov. Amadeo**), Blasewitz, near Dresden, April 17, 1741—Dresden, Oct. 23, 1801; pupil of Tartini and Padre Martini; 1764, ct.-cond., Dresden; 1776, cond.; prod. 23 operas and excellent church-music. (2) **Emil**, Berlin, Sept. 8, 1827 — Dresden, June 23, 1888; grandson of above; court church mus.-dir., Berlin; c. an opera, a famous oratorio *"Christus der Friedensbote"*; pub. many valuable treatises. (3) **K. Ernst**, Freiberg, Saxony, Aug. 15, 1832—Jena, Dec. 15, 1910; grandson of (1), studied with Hauptmann, Richter, Wenzel and Langer, Leipzig (1850), Dr. Philh. at the Univ., 1858; studied with Joh. Schneider (org.) in Dresden; mus.-dir. and organist, Jena; prof., 1877; pub. many valuable revisions of classical works, for the Bach-Gesellschaft; c. the first sonata for vla., much chamber-mus., etc.

Nava (nä'-vä), (1) **Ant. Maria**, Italy, 1775—1826; teacher and composer for guitar. (2) **Gaetano**, Milan, 1802—1875; son and pupil of above; prof. at the Cons. and composer.

Navál (nä-väl'), **Fz.**, b. Laibach, Austria, Oct. 20, 1865—Vienna, (?); tenor; pupil of Gänsbacher; 1903-4, N. Y.

Navrátil (nä-vrä'-tēl), **Carl**, Prague, April 24, 1867—Dec. 23, 1936; violinist; composer; pupil of Adler and Ondříček; c. symph.; symph. poems, *"Jan Hus," "Zalco,"* etc.; opera *"Salammbô,"* lyric drama, *"Hermann"*; violin concerto, etc.; wrote biog. of Smetana.

Nawratil (nä-vrä'-tēl), **K.**, Vienna, Oct. 7, 1836—April 6, 1914; pupil of Nottebohm (cpt.); excellent teacher; pub. Psalm XXX with orch., an overture, chamber mus., etc.

Nay'lor, (1) **J.**, b. Stanningly, near Leeds, 1838—at sea, 1897; organist and composer. (2) **Sidney**, London, 1841—1893; organist. (3) **Edward Woodall**, Scarborough, Feb. 9, 1867—May 7, 1934; composer; pupil of his father, Dr. John N. (q. v.); and at the R. C. M., London; organist at various churches; 1897 made Mus. Doc. by Cambridge University, where he had taken the degrees

of B. A., M. A., and Mus. B.; organist from 1897 at Cambridge (Emanuel College); lecturer there from 1902; c. Ricordi prize opera *"The Angelus"* (Covent Garden, 1909); cantata *"Arthur the King"* (Harrogate, 1902), church music, etc.

Ned'bal, Oscar, Tabor, Bohemia, March 25, 1874—(suicide) Zagreb, Dec. 24, 1930; vla.-player in the "Bohemian" string-quartet; studied Prague Cons. (comp. with Dvořák); he was dir. Bohemian Phil., Prague 1896-1906; thereafter cond. Vienna Volksoper, also the Tonkünstler orch.; c. ballet *"Der faule Hans"* (Vienna, 1903), scherzo caprice for orch., violin sonata, etc.

Neefe (nā'-fĕ), **Chr. Gl.**, Chemnitz, 1748—Dessau, 1798; mus.-director and conductor.

Nef (näf), (Dr.) **K.**, b. St. Gall, Aug. 22, 1873—Basle, Feb. 9, 1935; Ph.D.; studied Leipzig Cons. and Univ.; after 1923, prof. of mus. science, Basle Univ.

Neitzel (nīt'-tsĕl), **Otto**, Falkenburg, Pomerania, July 6, 1852—Cologne, March 10, 1920; pupil of Kullak's Acad., Berlin; Dr. Philh., 1875, at the Univ.; toured as pianist; 1879-81, teacher Moscow Cons.; then Cologne Cons.; 1887, also critic; prod. operas: *"Angela"* (Halle, 1887), text and music of, *"Dido"* (Weimar, 1888) and *"Der Alte Dessauer"* (Wiesbaden, 1889), etc.

Nen'na, Pomponio, b. Bari, Naples; pub. madrigals, 1585—1631.

Neri (nā'-rē), **Filippo**, Florence, July 21, 1515—Rome, May 26, 1595; preacher in the oratory (It. *oratorio*) of San Girolamo. From the music c. for illustrations by Animuccia and Palestrina arose the term "oratorio."

Neruda (nä-roo'-dä), (1) **Jakob**, d. 1732; violinist. (2) **Jn. Chrysostom**, Rossiez, 1705—1763; violinist; son of above. (3) **Jn. Baptist G.**, 1707—Dresden, 1780; composer, son of Jakob. (4) (**Normann-Neruda**) (or **Lady Hallé**) **Wilma Maria Fran.**, Brünn, March 21, 1839—Berlin, April 15, 1911; noted violinist (daughter of (5) **Josef**, an organist); she studied with Jansa; at 7 played in public at Vienna with her sister (6) **Amalie** (a pianist); then toured Germany with her father, sister and bro.; 1864, in Paris, she m. L. Normann; played annually in London;

she m. Hallé (q.v.), 1888, and toured Australia with him, 1890–91; 1899, America. (7) **Franz,** Brünn, Dec. 3, 1843—Copenhagen, March 19, 1915; 'cellist, son of Josef N., and brother of **Normann-N.**, (q.v.) pupil of Royal Chapel at Copenhagen; from 1892 successor of Gade as dir. of the Copenhagen Music Society; also dir. of Stockholm Music Society; 1894, prof., c. *"Slovak"* march, orch. suite *"From the Bohemian Forest,"* 'cello pieces, etc.

Ness'ler, Victor E., Baldenheim, Alsatia, Jan. 28, 1841—Strassburg, May 28, 1890; studied with Th. Stern at Strassburg; 1864, prod. succ. opera, *"Fleurette"*; studied in Leipzig, became cond. of the "Sängerkreis" and chorusm. City Th., where he prod. with general succ. 4 operettas and 4 operas, incl. two still pop. *"Der Rattenfänger von Hameln"* (1879), *"Der Trompeter von Säkkingen"* (1884); c. also *"Der Blumen Rache,"* ballade, with orch.; pop. and comic songs, etc.

Nesvad'ba, Jos., Vyskeř, Bohemia, 1824—Darmstadt, 1876; conductor and dram. composer.

Nešvera (nĕsh-vä'-rä), **Jos.,** Proskoles, Bohemia, Oct. 24, 1842—Olmütz, April 4, 1914; cond. Olmütz Cath.; c. succ. opera *"Perdita"* (Prague, 1897); masses, De Profundis, with orch., etc.

Netzer (nĕt'-tsĕr), **Jos.,** Imst. Tyrol, 1808—Graz, 1864; teacher, conductor and dram. composer.

Neubauer (nä'-oo-bow-ĕr), **Fz. Chr.,** Horzin, Bohemia, 1760—Bückeburg, 1795; violinist, conductor and composer.

Neuendorff (noi'-ĕn-dôrf), **Ad.,** Hamburg, June 13, 1843—New York, Nov. 5, 1897; at 12 taken to America; pianist, concert-violinist, prominent conductor and composer of comic operas.

Neukomm (noi'-kôm), **Sigismund,** Ritter von, Salzburg, 1778—Paris, 1858; organist, conductor and composer.

Neumann (noi'-män), **Angelo,** Vienna, Aug. 18, 1838—Prague, Dec. 20, 1910; studied singing with Stilke-Sessi, début as lyric tenor, 1859; 1862–76, Vienna ct.-opera; 1876–82, Leipzig opera; as manager of a travelling company prod. Wagner operas; 1882–85, manager Bremen opera; then German opera, Prague.

Neumark (noi'-märk), **G.,** Langensalza. 1621—Weimar, 1681; composer.

Neupert (noi'-pĕrt), **Edmund,** Christiania, April 1, 1842—New York, June 22, 1888; pianist; pupil of Kullak's Academy and teacher at Stern Cons.; 1861 at Copenhagen cons.; 1888 at Moscow Cons.; from 1883 at New York; c. piano studies, etc.

Neusiedler (noi'-zēt-lĕr) (or **Newsidler**), (1) **Hans,** b. Pressburg—Nürnberg, 1563; lute-maker. (2) (or **Neysidler**) **Melchior,** d. Nürnberg, 1590; lutenist and composer at Augsburg; 2 books of lute mus. (Venice, 1566), etc.

Neuville (nŭ-vē'-yĕ), **Valentin,** b. Rexpoede, French Flanders, 1863; organist; pupil of Brussels Cons.; org. at Lyons and after 1894 in London; c. 2 symph., an oratorio *"Nôtre Dame de Fourvières,"* 6 operas, including *"L'Aveugle"* (1901), and *"Les Willis"* (1902).

Nevada (nĕ-vä'-dä) (rightly **Wixon**), (1) **Emma,** b. Alpha, Cal., 1862; d. Liverpool, June 20, 1940; soprano; pupil of Marchesi in Vienna; début London, 1880; sang in various Italian cities; 1883 and 1898 Paris, Op.-Com.; 1885 sang Opera Festival, Chicago, and again in 1889; 1898, Op.-Com., Paris, 1885 m. Dr. Raymond Palmer; 1900 America. (2) **Mignon,** b. ca. 1887; her daughter; soprano, heard in Europe in opera.

Nevin (nĕv'-ĭn), (1) **Ethelbert** (Woodbridge), Edgeworth, Penn., Nov. 25, 1862—New Haven, Conn., Feb. 17, 1901; prominent American composer; pupil of von der Heide and E. Günther (pf.) at Pittsburgh; of von Böhme (voice), at Dresden, 1877–78; of Pearce (N. Y.), B. J. Lang and Stephen A. Emery (Boston); von Bülow, Klindworth, and K. Bial, Berlin; lived in Florence, Venice, Paris, and New York as teacher and composer; after 1900 at Sewickley, near Pittsburgh, Pa.; c. a pf.-suite; song-cycles *"In Arcady,"* and a posthumous *"The Quest of Heart's Desire"*; highly artistic piano pieces and many song albums of well-deserved popularity. His songs are genuinely lyrical, with an exuberance of musical passion, and accompaniments full of colour, individuality and novelty. (2) **Arthur,** b. Vine Acre, Edgeworth, Pa., April 17, 1871;

bro. of above; from 1891 studied with Goetschius, Boston, then at Berlin with Humperdinck, Boise and Klindworth; spent the summers of 1903 and 1904 among the Blackfeet Indians in Montana, collecting material for his Indian opera *"Poia,"* libretto by Randolph Hartley (prod. in concert form by the Pittsburgh Orch. and as an opera at the Royal Opera, Berlin); c. also 1-act opera *"Twilight"*; orch. suites *"Lorna Doone"* (prod. by Karl Muck in Berlin), and *"Love Dreams"* (Pittsburgh Orch.); also songs; 1915–20, taught Univ. of Kansas; later res. in Memphis, Tenn.

New′comb, Ethel, b. Whitney Point, N. Y., 1879; pianist; pupil and later asst. to Leschetizky in Vienna, where she made début 1903; after 1908 toured U. S., England, Germany.

New′man, Ernest, b. Liverpool, Nov. 30, 1868; prominent critic and writer on music; studied at the univ. there; intended for civil service in India, but withdrew because of ill health and entered business in native city; beginning 1903 he took music as his life work, teaching at Midland Inst., Birmingham. In 1905 he lived in Manchester as music critic of the *Guardian;* 1906, Birmingham *Daily Post;* 1919–20, of the London *Observer;* after 1920 of the London *Sunday Times* of which his weekly column is a much-read feature; 1923 also on the ed. staff of the weekly *Glasgow Herald;* in 1924–25, he was guest critic of the New York *Evening Post.* He has been an aggressive upholder of high ideals in interpretation and as a biographer has been no less unsparing in his moral and artistic judgments, esp. in his works on Wagner and Liszt. Author of *"Gluck and the Opera," "A Study of Wagner," "Wagner," "Musical Studies," "Elgar," "Richard Strauss," "Wagner As Man and Artist," "A Musical Motley," "The Piano-Player and Its Music," "A Music Critic's Holiday," "Hugo Wolf," "Stories of the Great Operas," "The Unconscious Beethoven," "Facts and Fiction about Wagner," "The Man Liszt,"* etc. He translated Weingartner's work on conducting, Schweitzer's biography of Bach, and Wagner's music dramas for the Breitkopf and Härtel edition; dir. the collection of the series *"The New Library of Music,"*

and 1912–14 ed. *The Piano-Player Review.*

New′march, Rosa, b. Leamington Spa, Eng., 1857—Worthing, April 9, 1940; writer of music of mod. Russia; translated Deiters' *"Brahms,"* Habet's *"Borodin and Liszt,"* Modeste Tschaikowsky's biography of his brother and d'Indy's *"César Franck"* into Eng.; author, *" Henry J. Wood," "The Russian Opera," "Songs to a Singer," "Jean Sibelius," "The Russian Arts," "Life of Tschaikowsky,"* etc.

Newsidler, Neysidler. Vide NEUSIEDLER.

Ney (nī), Elly, b. Düsseldorf, Sept. 27, 1882; pianist; pupil of Cologne Cons., of Leschetizky and Sauer; won Mendelssohn-Ibach Prize; taught at Cologne Cons.; toured Europe and U. S. as recitalist and orch. soloist; a performer of strong temperament, esp. known as interpreter of Brahms; m. Willem van Hoogstraten, conductor; divorced.

Niccolò de Malta. Vide ISOUARD.

Nichelmann (nĭkh′-ĕl-män), Chp., Treuenbrietzen, Brandenburg, 1717—Berlin, 1762; cembalist and writer.

Nicholl (nĭk′-ôl), Horace Wadham, Tipton, near Birmingham, Engl., March 17, 1848—New York, March 10, 1922; son and pupil of a musician, John N.; studied with Samuel Prince; 1867–70 organist at Dudley; 1871 organist at Pittsburgh, Pa., 1878, editor, New York. 1888–95 prof. at Farmington, Conn.; contributed to various periodicals; pub. a book on harmony; c. 12 symphonic preludes and fugues for organ, suite for full orch. (op. 3); a cycle of 4 oratorios with orch.; symph. poem *"Tartarus"*; 2 symphonies; a psychic sketch *"Hamlet,"* etc.

Nich′olls, Agnes, b. Cheltenham, July 14, 1877; soprano; pupil of Visetti at the R. C. M., London, with a scholarship; début 1895 in a revival of Purcell's *"Dido and Aeneas"*; studied also with John Acton; 1901, and 1904–06 sang at Covent Garden; has sung much in concert and oratorios, and at the Cincinnati Festival, 1904; in which year she married Hamilton Harty (q.v.).

Nick′lass-Kempt′ner, Selma, Breslau, April 2, 1849—Berlin, Dec. 22, 1928; noted coloratura soprano and teacher; studied at Stern Cons.; début, 1867;

sang in Rotterdam 10 years; then teacher Vienna Cons.; 1893, Berlin.

Nicodé (nē'-kō-dā), **Jean Louis,** Jerczik, near Posen, Aug. 12, 1853—near Dresden, Oct. 5, 1919; pupil of his father and the organist Hartkäs, and at Kullak's Acad.; lived in Berlin as a pianist and teacher; 1878–85 pf.-teacher Dresden Cons.; 1897, cond. Leipzig "Riedel Verein"; c. symph. poem *"Maria Stuart"*; *"Faschingsbilder," "Sinfonische Variationen,"* op. 27; *"Das Meer,"* symph. ode, for full orch.; "Erbarmen," hymn for alto with orch., etc.

Nicolai (nē'-kō-lī), (1) **Otto,** Königsberg, June 9, 1810—of apoplexy, Berlin, May 11, 1849; son and pupil of a singing-teacher; studied with Zelter and Klein, later with Baini at Rome, where he was organist at the embassy chapel; 1837–38 theatre-cond. at Vienna; again in Rome; 1841–47 ct.-cond. at Vienna and founded the Phil., 1842; 1847 cond. of the opera and cath.-choir, Berlin; prod. 5 v. succ. operas, incl. *"Il Templario"* (Turin, 1840; known in Germany as *"Der Templer,"* based on Scott's *"Ivanhoe"*); and the unctuous and still popular opera *"Die lustigen Weiber von Windsor,"* based on and known in English as *"The Merry Wives of Windsor"* (Berlin, 1849); he c. also a symph., etc.; biog. by Mendel (Berlin, 1868); his diary ("Tagebücher") was pub. Leipizg, 1893. (2) **Wm. Fr. Gerard,** Leyden, Nov. 20, 1829—The Hague, April 25, 1896; professor; notable conductor and composer.

Nicolau (nē'-kō-lä-oo), **Antonio,** Barcelona, June 8, 1858—Feb. 26, 1933; pupil of Pujol and Balart; cond. of Catalonian Concert Society in Paris, then dir. municipal music school at Barcelona; c. opera, choral works, etc.

Nicolini (nē-kō-lē'-nē), (1) **Nicolino Grimaldi** detto, Naples, ca. 1673—Venice, (?) after 1726; tenor, whom Addison called "perhaps the greatest performer in dramatic music that ever appeared upon a stage"; he was a contralto in Italy as early as 1694 and was decorated with the Order of St. Mark; from 1708–1716 in England rousing a furore; created "Rinaldo" in Handel's opera, 1711; returned to sing in Italy. (2) **Giuseppe,** Pincenza, Jan. 29, 1762—

Dec. 18, 1842; conductor and operatic composer. (3) **Ernest [Nicholas],** Tours, France, Feb. 23, 1834—Pau, Jan. 19, 1898; tenor; 1886, m. Adelina Patti.

Nic'olson, Richard, d. 1639; Engl. organist.

Niecks (nēks), **Frederick (Friedrich),** Düsseldorf, Feb. 3, 1845—Edinburgh, June 29, 1924; lecturer, critic, etc.; pupil of Langhans, Grünewald, and Auer (vln.); début at 12; 1868, organist, Dumfries, Scotland, and viola-player in a quartet with A. C. Mackenzie; studied in Leipzig Univ. (1877), and travelled Italy; critic, London; 1891, Ried Prof. of Mus., Edinburgh Univ.; pub. notable biog. of *"Frederic Chopin as a Man and a Musician"* (1888); a *"Dict. of Mus. Terms,"* etc.

Niedermeyer (nē'-děr-mī-ĕr), **Louis,** Nyon, Switzerland, 1802 — Paris, 1861; dramatic composer and theorist.

Niedt (nēt), **Fr. Erhardt,** d. Copenhagen, 1717; writer.

Nielsen (nēl'-sĕn), (1) **Carl,** Nörre-Lyndelse, Fünen Island, June 9, 1864—Copenhagen, Oct. 2, 1931; important Danish composer; pupil of Gade, member of the Copenhagen court orch., and from 1904 assistant cond. succeeding Svendsen; after 1915 assoc. dir., Copenhagen R. Cons.; c. 6 symph., No. 2 *"The Four Seasons,"* overture, *"Helios,"* opera *"Saul and David"* (Copenhagen, 1902); chorus with orch., *"Hymnus amoris"*; chamber music, etc. (2) **Ludolf,** b. Nörre-Tolde, Zealand, Jan. 29, 1876; pupil Copenhagen and Leipzig Cons.; viola player in Andersen's orch.; c. opera *"Mascarade"* (Copenhagen 1906), etc. (3) **Alice,** b. Nashville, Tenn., 1876; soprano; sang with Bostonians Light Op. Co.; later in London; op. début at Naples, 1903 as "Marguerite"; also sang at Covent Garden; with Met. Op. Co., 1910, and with touring companies.

Niemann (nē'-män), (1) **Albert,** Erxleben, near Magdeburg, Jan. 15, 1831—Berlin, Jan. 13, 1917; 1849, without study sang in minor rôles at Dessau; then studied with F. Schneider, and the bar. Nusch; sang at Hanover, then studied with Duprez, Paris; 1860–66, dram. tenor, Hanover, later at the ct.-opera, Berlin; Wagner chose him to create "Tann-

häuser" (Paris, 1861), and "Siegmund" (Bayreuth, 1876); he sang at
Met. Op., 1886–88, making deep impression as dram. artist; retired 1889.
(2) **Rudolf (Fr.)**, Wesselburen, Holstein, 1838—Wiesbaden, 1898; pianist and composer. (3) **Walter**, b.
Hamburg, Oct. 10, 1876; son of
(2), writer, composer.

Nietzsche (nēt'-shĕ), **Fr.**, Röcken, near
Lützen, Oct. 15, 1844—(insane)
Aug., 1900; prof. at Basel Univ.;
notable, if eccentric, philosopher; as
a partisan of Wagner he pub. *"Die
Geburt der Tragödie aus dem Geiste
der Musik," "Richard Wagner in
Bayreuth"*; while *"Der Fall Wagner,"*
and *"Nietzsche contra Wagner"* attack Wagner as violently as he once
praised him; his philosophical work
"Also sprach Zarathustra" provides
the title of R. Strauss's symph. poem.

Nieviadomski (n'yäv-yä-dŏm'shkĭ),
Stanislav, b. Soposzyn, Galicia, Nov.
4, 1859; pupil of Mikuli, Krenn, and
Jadassohn; teacher at Lemberg Cons.,
where he d. 1936; comp.

Niggli (nĭg'-glē), **Arnold**, Aarburg,
Switzerland, Dec. 20, 1843—Zurich,
May 30, 1927; writer.

Nikisch (nĭk'-ĭsh), (1) **Arthur**, Szent
Miklos, Hungary, Oct. 12, 1855—
Leipzig, Jan. 23, 1922; eminent conductor; son of the head-bookkeeper
to Prince Lichtenstein; pupil of
Dessoff (comp.) and Hellmesberger
(vln.), Vienna Cons., graduating at
19 with prizes for vln., and for a
string-sextet; violinist in the ct.-
orch.; then 2nd cond. Leipzig Th.;
1882–89, 1st. cond.; 1889–93, cond.
Boston Symph. Orch., 1893–95, dir.
Royal Opera, Budapest, and cond.
Philh. Concerts; 1895, cond. Gewandhaus Concerts, Leipzig (vice
Reinecke), also Phil. concerts, Berlin;
1902–07, dir. Leipzig Cons.; 1905–06
dir. the Stadttheater; toured widely
with the Berlin Phil., and acted as
guest cond. in many capitals; April,
1912, toured the U. S. as cond. of the
London Phil. with immense success.
He c. a symph., a cantata *"Christ-
nacht,"* orch. fantasie *"Der Trompeter"*; etc. His wife (2) **Amélie**
(née Heuser), b. in Brussels; sang in
Cassel and Leipzig operas, and composed music. (3) **Mitja**, b. Leipzig,
May 21, 1899; son of (1); pianist;
toured U. S.; d. Venice, Aug. 5, 1936.

Nilsson (nēls'-sōn), **Christine**, near
Wexio, Sweden, Aug. 20, 1843—
Stockholm, Nov. 22, 1921; eminent
soprano, compass 2½ octaves (g–d'');
pupil of Baroness Leuhausen and
F. Berwald, Stockholm; later, in
Paris, of Wartel; début, 1864, Th.-
Lyrique, Paris, engaged for 3 years
there; 1868–70, Opéra; toured America (1870–74 and 1884) and Europe;
1872, she m. Auguste Rouzaud (d.
1882); 1887, m. Count Casa di
Miranda.

Nin, Joaquin, b. Havana, Sept. 29,
1859; pianist, composer; studied
piano with Moszkowski and comp.
at Schola Cantorum, Paris, where he
taught, 1906–08; toured as pianist;
he is known esp. as composer and
arranger of Spanish pop. folk music;
mem. of the French Legion of Honour
and the Spanish Academy.

Nini (nē'-nē), **Ales.**, Fano, Romagna,
1805—Bergamo, 1880; cond. and
dram. composer.

Nisard (nē-zär), **Théodore** (pen-name
of Abbé **Théodule Eleazar X. Norman**), Quaregnon, near Mons, Jan.
27, 1812—Paris, 1887; chorister at
Cambrai; studied in Douay; 1839,
dir. Enghien Gymnasium, and 1842,
2d *chef de chant* and organist St.-
Germain, Paris; then confined himself to writing valuable treatises on
plain-chant, etc.

Nissen (nĭs'-sĕn), (1) **G. Nicolaus von**,
Hadersleben, Denmark, 1765—Salz-
burg, March 24, 1826; councillor of
State; m. the widow of Mozart,
1809, and aided her in preparing his
biog. (1828). (2) (**Nissen-Saloman**)
Henriette, Gothenburg, Sweden,
March 12, 1819—Harzburg, Aug. 27,
1879; great singer and teacher; pupil
of Chopin and Manuel Garcia; début
Paris, 1843; 1850, m. Siegfried Saloman, from 1859 teacher St. Petersburg Cons. (3) **Erica**. Vide LIE.

Nivers (nē-vārs), **Guillaume Gabriel**,
Melun, 1617—after 1701; organist,
singer and composer.

Nix'on, (1) **H. G.**, Winchester, 1796—
1849; organist and composer. (2)
Jas. Cassana, 1823—1842; violinist;
son of above. (3) **H. Cotter**, London, 1842—Bromley, 1907; organist
and composer.

No'ack, Sylvain, b. Rotterdam, Aug.
21, 1881; at first a pianist, then violin
pupil of André Spoor, Amsterdam;
at 17 entered the Cons., as a pupil of
Elderling, winning first prize, 1903,

and becoming a teacher there; 1905 settled in Rotterdam, and toured widely; 1906 concertm. at Aix-la-Chapelle; from 1908 second concertmaster Boston Symph.; after 1919, concertm., Los Angeles Philh.

No'ble, Thomas Tertius, b. Bath, May 5, 1867; composer; pupil of the R. C. M., London, winning a scholarship, and later teaching there; org. at Cambridge, Ely Cathedral, and from 1898 at York Minster, founding the York Symphony Orch.; c. church music with orch., cantata *"Gloria Domini,"* music to Aristophanes' *"Wasps,"* etc.; since 1913 in N. Y. as org. and dir. of music, St. Thomas' P. E. Church.

Nohl (nōl), **(K. Fr.) L.,** Iserlohn, 1831—Heidelberg, 1885; 1880, professor and writer; wrote biogs. of Beethoven, Mozart, etc., and published many colls. of the letters of composers.

Nohr (nōr), **Chr. Fr.,** Langensalza, Thuringia, 1800—Meiningen, 1875; violinist and dram. composer.

Norblin (nôr-blăn), (1) **Louis Pierre Martin,** Warsaw, 1781—Chateau Conantre, Marne, 1854; 'cellist and professor. (2) **Émile,** 1821—1880; son of above; 'cellist.

Nor'dica, Lillian (stage-name of **Lillian Norton**), Farmington, Me., 1859—Batavia, Java, May 10, 1914, while on world tour; pupil of John O'Neill and of N. E. Cons.; Boston; concert-début, Boston, 1876; 1878, toured Europe with Gilmore's Band; studied opera with San Giovanni, Milan; début at Brescia, 1880; 1881, Gr. Opéra, Paris; 1882, m. Frederick A. Gower; 1885, he made a balloon ascension and never returned; she retired till 1887; sang Covent Garden, London same year; 1888, began appearances at Met. Op., N. Y. as striking and brilliant artist of notable powers; afterward appeared regularly in U. S., England, etc.; 1894 chosen to sing "Elsa" at Bayreuth; In 1910-11 she was with the Boston Op. Co. Throughout her career she was a prominent concert and festival singer. In early years she sang many Italian rôles but later almost wholly Wagner operas; 1896, m. Zoltan F. Doeme, Hungarian singer (divorced 1904) and in 1909, Geo. W. Young, N. Y. financier.

Nordqvist (nôrt'-kwĭst), **Johan Conrad,** Venersborg, April 11, 1840—Stockholm, April 16, 1920; Swedish composer; pupil Stockholm Musikakademie; 1864 military bandmaster, then with state funds studied in Dresden and Paris; from 1875 organist and teacher at Stockholm; 1881 teacher of harmony at the Musikakad.; 1885 court cond.; c. orch. works, etc.

Nor'draak (nôr'-dräk), **Rikard,** Christiania, June 12, 1842—Berlin, March 20, 1866; composer whose early death ended a promising career; pupil of Kiel and Kullak; c. incid. music to Björnson's *"Maria Stuart"* and *"Sigurd Slembe,"* piano pieces, etc.

No'ren, Heinrich Gottlieb, Graz, Jan. 6, 1861—Rottach, June 6, 1928; violinist; pupil of Massart; concertmaster in various countries; from 1896-1902 in Crefeld, where he founded a Cons.; teacher at Stern Cons., in Berlin; later in Dresden; c. orch. variations *"Kaleidoskop"* (Dresden, 1907), serenade for orch., etc.

Norê'na, Eidé, (née **Kaja Hansen**) b. Oslo, Norway; soprano; studied and made début in Scandinavia; sang at La Scala with succ.; at Covent Garden, 1924-25, and at Paris Op.; Amer. début in N. Y. concert, 1926; heard in opera at Baden-Baden Fest. same year; a mem. of Chicago Op., 1926-27, and after 1933 of Met. Op., N. Y.

Norman. Vide NISARD.

Nor'man(n), L., Stockholm, 1831—1885; conductor, professor and composer. Vide NERUDA.

Nor'ris, (1) **Wm.,** d. ca. 1710; English composer. (2) **Thos.,** 1741-1790; English male soprano, organist and composer. (3) **Homer A.,** Wayne, Maine, Oct. 4, 1860—New York, 1920; notable theorist; studied with Marston, Hale, Chadwick and Emery, Boston; lived there as teacher; also studied 4 years in Paris with Dubois, Godard, Gígout and Guilmant; c. overture *"Zoroaster,"* cantata *"Nain"* and songs; pub. "Harmony" and "Counterpoint" on French basis.

Noszkowski (nôsh-kôf'-shkǐ), **Sigismund** (Zygismunt von), Warsaw, May 2, 1846—July 24, 1909; pupil of Warsaw Mus. Inst.; inv. a mus.-notation for the blind, and was sent by the Mus. Soc. to study with Kiel and Raif, Berlin; 1876 cond.; 1881,

dir. of the Mus. Soc., Warsaw, and
(1888) prof. at the Cons.; prod. succ.
opéra "*Livia*" (Lemberg, 1898); c.
symph., overture "*Das Meerauge*,"
etc.

Noszler (nôsh'-lĕr), **K. Eduard,** b.
Reichenbach, Saxony, March 26,
1863; pupil of Leipzig Cons.; 1888—
93, organist Frauenkirche, Bremen;
1887, cond. Male Choral Union;
1893, organist Bremen Cath., and
1896, cond. Neue Singakademie; c.
symph., "Lustspiel-Ouvertüre," etc.

Notker (nôt'-kĕr) (called **Balbulus,**
"the stammerer"), 830–912, monk
at St. Gallen; important writer and
composer of sequences. (V. D. D.)

Nottebohm (nôt'-tĕ-bōm), **Martin Gv.,**
Lüdenscheid, Westphalia, 1817—
Graz, 1882; teacher and writer chiefly
of valuable Beethoven works and
discoveries; also composer.

Nouguès (noo-gĕs), **Jean,** Bordeaux,
1876—Auteuil, Aug. 29, 1932; composer of operas " *Yannha*" (Barcelona, 1897); "*Thamyris*" (Bordeaux,
1904); "*Quo Vadis*" (Paris Gaité,
1910, Berlin Royal Op., 1912);
"*Chiquito*," "*L'Éclaircie*," "*La Dan-
seuse de Pompeii*" (Rouen).

Nourrit (noor-rē), (1) **Louis,** Montpellier, 1780—Brunoy, 1831; leading
tenor Gr. Opéra, Paris. (2) **Ad.,**
Paris, 1802—suicide, Naples, 1839;
eminent tenor; son and successor
(1825) of above; pupil of Garcia and
teacher at the Cons.; also composer.

Nováček (nō'-vä-chĕk), **Ottokar,** Fe-
hértemplom, Hungary, May 13, 1866
—New York, Feb. 3, 1900; violinist;
pupil of his father, of Dont, and at
Leipzig Cons., where he won the
Mendelssohn prize, 1889; 1891 member Boston Symph. Orch.; 1892–03
Damrosch Orch., N. Y.; heart-
trouble forced his retirement; c.
chamber music, Bulgarian dances
and other violin pieces.

Novaes (nō-vä'-äs), **Guiomar,** b. São
Paulo, Brazil, Feb. 28, 1895; pianist;
began to study piano at 5 with
Chiafarelli; grad. Paris Cons., pupil
of Philipp, won 1st prize; made début
in Paris, 1907, followed by appearances in Germany, Italy, Switzerland
and Brazil; her début in the U. S.
took place at N. Y., 1915; her playing
won warm applause for its refinement, brilliance and expressiveness;
after a few years' retirement, returned to North America in 1934,

deepening the impression by matured
interpretative powers; m. Octavio
Pinto, composer.

No'vák, Vítězslav, b. Kamenitz, Bohemia, Dec. 5, 1870; important Bohemian composer; pupil of Prague Cons.
under Dvořák, later teacher at
Prague; from 1909 teacher of composition at the Cons.; 1919–22, its
dir.; c. overture "*Maryscha*," symph
poems "*On the High Tatra*,"
and "*Eternal Longing*"; "*Slovak*"
suite, four Moravian ballads with
orch., chamber music, piano sonata
"*Eroica*," etc.

Novello (nō-vĕl'-lō), (1) **Vincent,** London, Sept. 6, 1781—Nice, Aug. 9,
1861; son of Italian father and English mother; founded, 1811, the pub.
firm Novello & Co. (later Novello,
Ewer & Co., London); notable organist, pianist and composer. (2)
Clara Anastasia, London, Jan. 10,
1818—Rome, March 12, 1908; 4th
daughter of (1); pupil Paris Cons.,
succ. operatic début Padua, 1841,
but made her best succ. in oratorio;
1843, m. Count Gigliucci; retired
1860.

Noverre (nō-vär), **J. G.,** Paris, April 29,
1727—St. Germain, Nov. 19, 1810;
solo-dancer at Berlin; ballet-master
at the Op.-Com., Paris; inv. the
dramatic ballet.

Nowakowski (nō-vä-kôf'-shkĭ), **Jozef,**
Mniszck, 1800—Warsaw, 1865; pf.-
teacher, professor and composer.

Nowowiejski (nō-vō-vē'-shkĭ), **Felix,**
b. Wartenburg, East Prussia, Feb. 7,
1877; pupil of Stern Cons., and
Regensburg Church Mus. Sch.;
1902, won Berlin Meyerbeer prize
with oratorio "*Die Rückkehr des
verlorenen Sohnes*"; c. 2 symph.;
opera "*Quo Vadis*" (1907); oratorio
"*Die Auffindung des Kreuzes*" (Lemberg, 1906). "*Quo Vadis*" was given
as an oratorio New York, 1912.

O

Oakeley (ōk'-lĭ), Sir **Herbert Stanley,**
Ealing, Middlesex, July 22, 1830—
Eastbourne, Oct. 26, 1903; while at
Oxford, studied with Elvey (harm.),
later at Leipzig Cons., with Schnei-
der, Dresden, and Breidenstein,
Bonn.; 1865–91, Ried Prof. of Mus.,
Edinburgh Univ., developing the
annual Ried Concerts into a 3-days'
Festival; his org.-recitals had a large

influence; knighted 1876; Mus. Doc., Cantab., 1871; Oxon., Dublin, 1887; 1892, Emeritus Professor; composer to the Queen in Scotland, and 1887, Pres., Cheltenham Mus. Festival; pub. a cantata *"Jubilee Lyric,"* *"Suite in the Olden Style,"* *"Pastorale,"* Festival March, and a Funeral March (op. 23) for orch.; pf.-sonata, etc.

O'ber, Margarete, b. Berlin, 1885; contralto; studied with Stolzenberg, then with Arthur Arndt (whom she married); sang at Stettin, and at Berlin Op.; 1913–17, Met. Op., N. Y.; later again active in Berlin.

O'berhoffer, (1) **Heinrich,** Pfalzel, Dec. 9, 1824—Luxembourg, May 30, 1885; organist at Luxembourg, c. church music. (2) **Emil,** Munich, Aug. 10, 1867—San Diego, Cal., May 22, 1933; pupil of Kistler, and I. Philipp; settled in Minneapolis, Minn.; cond. Phil. Club. and 1905–22, Minn. Symph. Orch., with which he toured the U. S., 1912; c. church music, songs, etc.

Oberthür (ō'-bĕr-tür), **K.,** Munich, 1819—London, 1895; harpist, teacher and dramatic composer.

Obrecht, vide HOBRECHT.

O'brist, Aloys., San Remo, March 30, 1867—(suicide) Stuttgart, June 29, 1910; pupil of Müller Hartung at Weimar; cond. in various cities; from 1900 at Weimar; mus. director and coll. of mus. instruments.

O'Car'olan, Turlough, Newton, Meath, 1670—Roscommon, 1738; Irish harpist.

Ochs (ôkhs), (1) **Traugott,** Altenfeld, Oct. 19, 1854—Berlin, Aug. 27, 1919, where he was dir. of his own school after 1911; pupil of Stade, Erdmannsdörfer, Kiel, and the R. Inst. for Church-mus.; 1899, artistic dir. Mus.-Union and the Mus.-Sch., Brünn; then civic. dir., Bielefeld, and ct.-dir., Sondershausen; c. *"Deutsches Aufgebot"* for male chorus and orch.; requiem, etc. (2) **Siegfried,** Frankfort-on-Main, April 19, 1858—Berlin, Feb. 6, 1929; studied R. Hochschule für Musik, Berlin, later with Kiel and Urban, and von Bülow, who brought into publicity a small choral union, the "Philharmonischer Chor.," of which he was cond., and which is now the largest singing-society in Berlin; also a singing-teacher and writer, 1901, Munich; c. succ. comic

opera (text and music) *"Im Namen des Gesetzes"* (Hamburg, 1888); 2 operettas; many choruses, duets, songs, etc.; ed. some of Bach's cantatas.

Ochsenkuhn (ôkh'-zān-koon), **Sebastian,** d. Heidelberg, Aug. 20, 1574; lutenist and composer.

O'dington, Walter de ("Monk of Evesham"), b. Odington, Gloucestershire; d. ca. 1330; important theorist. (Coussemaker.)

O'do de Clugny (dŭ klün'-yē) (Saint), became in 927 abbot of Clugny, where he d. 942; writer. (Gerbert.)

Oeglin (ākh'-lēn), **Erhard,** 16th cent. German printer of Augsburg, the first to print figured mus. with types.

Oelschlegel (āl'-shlā-gĕl), **Alfred,** Anscha, Bohemia, Feb. 25, 1847—Leipzig, June 19, 1916; Prague Org.-Sch.; th.-cond. at Hamburg, etc., and Karltheater, Vienna; later bandm. Klagenfurt; c. operettas *"Prinz una Maurer"* (Klagenfurt, 1884); succ. *"Die Raubritter"* (Vienna, 1888); succ. *"Der Landstreicher"* (Magdeburg, 1893).

Oelsner (ĕls'-nĕr), (**Fr.**) **Bruno,** b. Neudorf, near Annaberg, Saxony, July 29, 1861; pupil of Leipzig Cons.; solo-vla., ct.-orch. Darmstadt; studied with de Haan (comp.); 1882, vln.-teacher Darmstadt Cons., with title Grand Ducal Chamber-mus.; prod. at Darmstadt 1-act operas, incl. succ. *"Der Brautgang"* (1894); also a cantata with orch., etc.

Oesten (ā'-shtĕn), **Theodor,** Berlin, 1813—1870; pianist and composer.

Oesterlein (ā'-shtĕr-līn), **Nikolaus,** 1842—Vienna, 1898; maker of the coll. known as the *"Wagner Museum."*

Oettingen, Arthur Joachim, 1836—1920; imp. writer and physicist.

Offenbach (ôf'-fĕn-bäkh), **Jacques,** Cologne, June 21, 1819—Paris, Oct. 5, 1880; eminent writer of light opera; studied 'cello at the Cons., then joined Op.-Com. orch., Paris; c. chansonnettes (parodying La Fontaine), played the 'cello in concerts, and c. 'cello-pcs.; 1849, cond. Th.-Français, prod. unsucc. 1-act operetta *"Pepito"* (Op.-Com., 1853); others followed till 1855–66 he had a theatre for his own work; 1872–76, manager Th. de la Gaîté; 1877, toured America; his 102 stage-works include the ballet-pantomime *"Le Papillon"* and the v. succ. operas.

"Orphée aux Enfers," 1858; *"La Belle Hélène,"* 1864; *"Barbe-Bleu"* and *"La Vie Parisienne,"* 1866; *"La Grande Duchesse de Gérolstein,"* 1867; *"Madame Favart,"* 1879. The grand opera, *"The Tales of Hoffmann,"* his masterpiece was prod. posthumously 1881.

Oginski (ō-gēn'-shkǐ), (1) Prince **Michael Cléophas**, Guron, near Warsaw, 1765—Florence, 1833; composer. (2) **Michael Casimir**, Warsaw, 1731—1803; uncle of above; said to have inv. the pedals of the harp.

O'keghem (or **Okekem, Okenghem, Ockegheim, Ock'enheim**), **Jean de** (or **Joannes**), probably Termonde, East Flanders, ca. 1430—Tours, 1495; an eminent contrapuntist; the founder of the Second (or New) Netherland Sch. Chorister, Antwerp cathedral; studied with Dufay; 1454, ct.-cond. and composer to Charles VII. at Paris; 1467, royal cond. to Louis XI.; toured Spain and Flanders on stipend; c. masses, motets, canons, etc.

Oldberg, Arne, b. Youngstown, Ohio, July 12, 1874; began piano studies with his father at 5; at 6 was playing Haydn symphonies in duet form; pupil of Aug. Hyllested, Chicago; 1893–95 of Leschetizky, Vienna; from 1895 in Chicago with Middelschulte (counterpoint); Ad. Koelling (instrumentation) and F. G. Gleason; 1898 with J. Rheinberger, Munich; from 1899 teacher at Northwestern Univ., Ill.; c. 2 symphs. (F minor, winning National Federation prize 1911); overture *"Paola and Francesca"* (played 3 times by Thomas Orch.); Festival Overture, 12 orch. variations, horn concerto, chamber music, piano sonata, etc.

Olib'rio, Flavio Anicio. Vide J. F. AGRICOLA.

Ol'iphant, Thos., Condie, Perthshire, 1799—London, 1873; theorist and collector.

Ollone (dôl-lŭn), **Max d',** b. Besançon, June 13, 1875; pupil Paris Cons., taking the Prix de Rome, 1897; for a time after 1923, dir., Amer. Cons., Fontainebleau; c. cantata *"Frédégonde,"* lyric scene *"Jeanne d'Arc à Domrémy,"* etc.

Olsen (ōl'-zĕn), **Ole,** b. Hammerfest, Norway, July 4, 1851—Christiania, Nov. 9, 1927; composer.

Olszewska (ŏl-shĕv'-skä), **Maria,** b. Augsburg, Aug. 8, 1892; contralto; début, Crefeld, Germany; later sang at Hamburg State Theatre, Vienna State Op., Berlin Städtische Op., at Munich Fest., Covent Garden; Amer. début with Chicago Op., 1930–31; after 1932 sang for several seasons with Met. Op. Co., also in various Eur. theatres and in South America; m. Dr. Emil Schipper, basso.

Ondricek (ŏn'-drǐ-chĕk), **Fz.,** Prague, April 29, 1859—Milan, April 13, 1922; violinist; pupil of his father, and at 14 member of his small orch. for dance mus.; then studied Prague Cons. and with Massart, Paris Cons., took first prize for vln.-playing; toured Europe and America; after 1907 in Vienna, where prof. at Cons.

Onegin (ŏn-yā'-gǐn), **Sigrid** (née **Hoffmann**), b. Stockholm, June 1, 1891; German contralto; pupil of Ress in Frankfort, also of Eugen Rob, and di Ranieri in Milan; after 1912 active as concert singer; studied for opera on advice of Schillings; début at Stuttgart; after 1919 at Munich Op.; Amer. début as soloist with Phila. Orch., 1922; sang at Met. Op. House same season, "Amneris," "Brangäne" and other Wagnerian rôles; one of leading contemporary singers, with great flexibility and range, incl. both soprano and coloratura contralto; has appeared widely in opera and concerts in Europe and America, also at Salzburg Festival.

O'Neill, (1) **Norman,** Kensington, March 14, 1875—London, March 3, 1934; cond., pupil of Somervell and Hoch Cons. at Frankfort; c. incid. music to *"Hamlet"* (1904), *"King Lear"* (1908), *"The Blue Bird"* (1909); overture *"In Autumn,"* *"In Springtime";* fantasy for voices and orch. *"Woldemar";* Scotch rhapsody; ballade with orch. *"La belle dame sans merci"* (London, 1910), etc.; 1899, he married (2) **Adine Rückert,** pianist; pupil of Clara Schumann and Mme. Clause-Szavardy. He taught R. A. M. after 1924.

Ons'low, G., Clermont-Ferrand, France, 1784—1852; grandson of the first Lord Onslow; amateur 'cellist and pianist; prod. 4 succ. comic operas; 34 string-quintets; 36 quartets; and other chamber-music.

Opienski (ŏp-yĕn'-shkǐ), **Heinrich,** b. Cracow, June 13, 1870; pupil of

Zelénski there, of d'Indy and Urban; critic in Warsaw, then pupil of Riemann in history, and of Nikisch in conducting; from 1907 teacher of history at the Warsaw Music School, and from 1908 cond. of the Opera; 1919, dir. of a music school in Posen; from 1926, lived in Geneva; c. prize cantata in honour of Mickiewicz; opera *"Maria,"* symph. poem *"Lilla Weneda"* (1908), etc.

Ordenstein (ôr'-děn-shtīn), **H.,** Worms, Jan. 7, 1856—Carlsruhe, March 22, 1921; pianist; pupil of Leipzig Cons., also in Paris; 1879–81, teacher at Carlsruhe; 1881–82, at Kullak's Acad., Berlin; 1884, founded Carlsruhe Cons.; made prof. by Grand Duke of Baden.

Orefice, dell'. Vide DELL' OREFICE.

Orgeni (ôr-gä'-nē) (Orgenyi) (ôr-gän'-yē), **Anna Maria Aglaia,** Tismenice, Galicia, Dec. 17, 1843—Vienna, March 15, 1926; colorature soprano; pupil of Mme. Viardot-Garcia; début, 1865, Berlin Opera; 1886, teacher Dresden Cons.

Orlan'di, Fernando, Parma, 1777—Jan. 5, 1848; 1809–28 singing teacher at Milan Cons.; then at Munich Music School; c. 26 operas.

Orlandini (ôr-län-dē'-nē), **Giuseppe Maria,** Bologna, 1688—Florence, ca. 1750; opera composer, c. 44 operas, 3 oratorios, etc.

Orlando, or **Orlandus.** Vide LASSO.

Or'loff, Nikolai, b. Jeletz, Russia, Feb. 26, 1892; pianist; pupil of Moscow Cons., gold medal; also studied comp. with Taneiev; 1913–15, prof. at Moscow Philharmonie, 1917 at Cons.; after 1921 made concert tours of Europe and U. S., winning prominent position as virtuoso.

Or'mandy, Eugene, b. Budapest, Nov. 18, 1899; studied R. Acad. of Music there, winning diploma in vln., 1914, and professor's dip., 3 years later; pupil of Hubay; toured as violinist; prof. Hungarian State Cons., 1919; came to America and played as concertm. in Capitol Theater, N. Y., 1921; guest cond. with N. Y. Philh. and Phila. Orch. in summer seasons, 1930; succeeded Verbrugghen as cond. Minneapolis Symph., also appeared as guest with other Amer. orchs., Budapest Philh., etc., and in 1936 was appointed as regular cond. Phila. Orch., sharing bâton with Stokowski.

Orn'stein, Leo, b. Krementchug, Russia, Dec. 11, 1895; composer, pianist; studied St. Petersburg Cons., with Glazounoff and Inst. of Musical Art, N. Y.; début, in latter city, 1911; played as soloist with orchs. in N. Y., Los Angeles, Phila., Boston, St. Louis, Chicago; early attracted prominence for radical style of comp., but later works more conservative; c. piano concerto, vln. sonata, 'cello sonata, piano quintet, string quartet, choral music, songs, and piano music.

Orologio (ôr-ō-lō'-jī-ō), (1) and (2), **Alessandro,** two contemporary madrigal composers of the same name, one of them in 1603 became vice-chapelmaster to Emperor Rudolph at Prague; the other vice-chapelmaster to the Electoral Court at Dresden the same year.

Ortigue (ôr-tēg), **Jos. Louis de,** Cavallon, Vaucluse, 1802—Paris, 1866; writer.

Ortiz (ôr-tĕth), **Diego,** b. Toledo, ca. 1530; from 1558 chapelmaster to Duke of Alva; c. important book of sacred music (pub. Venice, 1565).

Ort'mann, Otto, b. Baltimore, Md., Jan. 25, 1889; pianist, educator; grad. Baltimore City Coll.; also Peabody Cons.; studied piano with Coulson, Boyle, Breitner, Landow; comp. with Blackhead, Boise, Siemann, Strube; after 1913 taught at Peabody Inst., and succeeded the late Harold Randolph as dir.; noted for research in the psychology of music; author, *"The Physical Basis of Piano Touch and Tone," "The Physiological Basis of Touch and Tone,"* etc.

Orto (ôr'-tō), **Giov. de** (Italian form of **Jean Dujardin**) (dü-zhär'-dăň); Latinised as **de Hor'to** (called **"Marbriano"**); contrapuntist and composer 15th and 16th centuries.

Os'borne, G. Alex., Limerick, Ireland, 1806—London, 1893; composer.

Osiander (ō'-zē-änt-ĕr), **Lucas,** Nürnberg, 1534—Stuttgart, 1604; writer and composer.

Ostrčil (ôstr'-chĭl), **Otakar,** Smichov, Feb. 25, 1879—Prague, 1935; composer and conductor; pupil in comp. of Fibich; also of Prague Univ.; 1901, prof. at Prague Acad.; 1909–22, cond. notable orch. of amateur players in that city; 1914, chief cond. at Weinberge Stadttheater, Prague; after 1920 chief cond. at Prague Nat'l Theater; a notable propagandist for the younger generation of Czech composers; c. operas, "*Vlastas Ende*," "*Kunalas Augen*," "*Poupé*," "*Legende von Erin*," also orch., chamber music and choral works, songs, etc.

O'Sul'livan, Denis, San Francisco, April 25, 1868—Columbus, Ohio, Feb. 1, 1908; barytone of Irish descent; pupil of Talbo and Formes; later of Vannucini, Santley and Shakespeare; début 1895 in concert; also in opera with Carl Rosa Co.; 1896 created the title rôle in Stanford's "*Shamus O'Brien*" and sang it in England and America.

Othegraven (ō'-tĕ-grä-vĕn), **August von**, b. Cologne, June 2, 1864; pupil of the Cons. and from 1889 teacher there; c. fairy play "*The Sleeping Beauty*" (Cologne, 1907), songs, etc.

Othmayr (ōt'-mī-ĕr), **Kaspar**, Amberg, 1515—Nürnberg, 1553; composer.

Otho. Vide ODO.

Ott(o) (or **Ottl**), **Hans**, ca. 1533—1550; pub. in Nürnberg.

Ottani (ŏt-tä'-nē), Abbate **Bernardino**, Bologna, 1736—Turin, 1827; dram. composer.

Otterstroem (ŏt'-tĕr-strŭm), **Thorvald**, b. Copenhagen, July 17, 1868; composer; piano pupil of Sophie Menter, St. Petersburg; from 1892 in Chicago; c. 24 preludes and fugues for piano, chamber music, etc.

Otto (ŏt'-tō), (1) Vide OTT. (2) (Ernst) **Julius**, Königstein, Saxony, Sept. 1, 1804—Dresden, March 5, 1877; notable composer of cycles for male chorus, songs, operas, etc. (3) **Valerius**, organist at Prague, 1607; c. church music. (4) **Stephan**, b. Freiburg, Saxony, ca. 1594; cantor there and at Schandau; c. church music.

Otto-Alvsleben (ŏt'-tō-älf'-slä-bĕn), **Melitta** (née **Alvsleben**), Dresden, 1842—1893; soprano; married, 1866.

Oudin (oo-dăṅ), **Eugène** (Espérance), New York, 1858—London, 1894; barytone, pianist and composer.

Oudrid y Segura (oo-drēdh' ē sä-goo'-rä), **Cristobal**, Badajoz, 1829—Madrid, March 15, 1877; conductor and dram. composer.

Oulibichef. Vide ULIBISHEV.

Oury. Vide BELLEVILLE-OURY.

Ouse'ley, Sir **Fr. Arthur Gore**, London, Aug. 12, 1825—Hereford, April 6, 1889; notable theorist and composer; pianist and organist remarkable for fugal improvisation; wrote important

treatises, etc.; c. an opera at 8; M. A. Oxford, 1840, Mus. Doc. there, 1854; also from Durham and Cambridge, 1862; from 1855 Prof. of Music at Oxford, vice Sir H. R. Bishop; c. 2 oratorios incl. "*Hagar*."

P

Pabst (päpst), (1) **Aug.**, Elberfeld, May 30, 1811—Riga, July 21, 1885; director and composer of operas. (2) **Louis**, Königsberg, July 18, 1846 —?; son of above; pianist and composer. From 1899, head pf.-teacher Moscow Philh. Sch. (3) **Paul**, Königsberg, 1854—Moscow, 1897; son of (1); pf.-prof.; director.

Pacchiarotti (päk-kĭ-ä-rŏt'-tē), **Gasparo**, Fabriano, Ancona, 1744—Padua, Oct. 28, 1821; one of the greatest and most succ. of 18th cent. singers; soprano-musico.

Pacchioni (päk-kĭ-ō'-nē), **Antonio Maria**, Modena, 1654–1738, priest, court chaplain; c. oratorios, etc.

Pacelli (pä-chĕl'-lē), **Asprilio**, Varciano, ca. 1570—Warsaw, May 3, 1623; Italian choirmaster; 1604, called to Warsaw as chapelmaster to the King; c. motets, etc.

Pache (päkh'-ĕ), (1) **Johannes**, b. Bischofswerda, Dec. 9, 1857—Limbach, Dec. 21, 1897; organist and composer of male choruses, etc. (2) **Joseph**, Friedland, Silesia, June 1, 1861—Baltimore, Dec. 7, 1926; pupil Royal Akad., Munich, and of Scharwenka Cons., and Max Bruch; settled in New York and founded 1903 an oratorio society; from 1904 dir. oratorio society in Baltimore.

Pachelbel (päkh'-ĕl-bĕl), (1) **J.**, Nürnberg, Sept. 1, 1653—March 3, 1706; org.-virtuoso and composer. (2) **Wm. Hieronymus**, b. Erfurt, 1685; son of above; organist and composer.

Pachler-Koschak (päkh'-lĕr-kō'-shäk), **Marie Leopoldine**, Graz, Oct. 2, 1792 —April 10, 1855; pianist and composer; friend of Beethoven.

Pachmann (päkh-män), **Vladimir de**, Odessa, July 27, 1848—Rome, Jan. 8, 1933; notable pianist especially devoted to Chopin's mus.; son and pupil of a prof. at Vienna Univ.; studied also with Dachs, Vienna Cons.; 1869 toured Russia with great succ. that followed him throughout Europe and America; in Denmark he received the Order of the Danebrog from the King; 1916, Beethoven medal of London Philh.; returned to U. S. 1923 after a decade's absence; in final years his playing was marked by many eccentricities. He was more noted for refinement of effects in his playing than for sustained strength of interpretation. Ed. works of Chopin.

Pachulski (pä-khool'-shkĭ), **Henry**, b. Poland, Oct. 4, 1859; pupil Warsaw Cons., 1886–1917, prof. Moscow Cons.; c. pf.-pcs., etc.

Pac(c)ini (pä-chē'-nē), (1) **Andrea**, b. Italy, ca. 1700; male contralto. (2) **A. Fran. Gaetano Saverio**, Naples, 1778—Paris, 1866; singing-teacher, conductor and composer of comic operas. (3) **Giov.**, Catania, Feb. 17, 1796—Pescia, Dec. 6, 1867; son of a tenor; pupil of Marchesi, Padre Mattei and Furlanetto; 1813–35, prod. 40 operas, the last failing, he established a sch. at Viareggio, later Lucca, wrote treatises, etc.; 1840, the succ. of "*Saffo*" set him to work again, and he turned out 40 more operas, also oratorios, a symph. "*Dante*," etc. (4) **Emilio**, 1810—Neuilly, near Paris, Dec. 2, 1898; bro. of above; librettist of "*Il Trovatore*," etc.

Pacius (pä'-tsĭ-oos), **Fr.**, Hamburg, March 19, 1809—Helsingfors, Jan. 9, 1891; violinist; c. the Finnish National Hymn, operas, etc.

Paderewski (päd-ĕ-rĕf'-shkĭ), **Ignace Jan**, b. Kurilovka, Poland, Nov. 18, 1860—N. Y., June 29, 1941; famous pianist; pupil of Raguski (harm. and cpt.) Warsaw Cons., of Urban and Wuerst, Berlin; of Leschetizky, Vienna. 1878–83, pf.-teacher, Warsaw Cons.; has toured Europe and America with unprecedented success. His first wife, who died young, bore him a son. 1899, m. Mme. Gorski. He settled at Morges, Switzerland, continuing to tour the world; 1912, in South Africa; 1909 director Warsaw Cons. During the World War, **P.** gave many concerts to raise funds for his native country. He abandoned music to work for the cause of Polish nat'l independence and was elected Premier of the new Republic in 1919, having taken part in the Peace Conference at Versailles. The following year he retired from polit. life, renewing his interest in the piano, but did not resume public perf. until 1922. His return to the U. S. in a tour of remarkable interest and succ. in that year was followed by others of like import. In 1935–36 he was again announced to tour America after several years' absence, but this visit was cancelled owing to the pianist's illness. 1896 he set aside $10,000 as the Paderewski fund, the interest to be devoted to triennial prizes "to composers of American birth without distinction as to age or religion;" 1. $500 for best orchestral work in symph. form; 2. $300 for best comp. for solo instr. with orch.; 3. $200 for best chamber-music work. C. succ. opera "*Manru*" (Ct.-Th. Dresden, 1901 also at Met. Op.); opera "*Sakuntala*" (text by C. Mendès), a symphony in memory of the revolution of 1864, (1908; Boston Symph., 1909; Richter, London, 1909); a second symph., an hour and twenty minutes long (1912); piano sonata, variations, and fugue for piano (1907), etc. Polish fantasia for pf. with orch. op. 19, "*Légende No. 2*," for pf. op. 20, and many original and brilliant pf.-pcs. incl. "*Chants du voyageur*," a vln. sonata; vars. and fugue on original theme; op. 14, "*Humoresques de concert for pf.*" (*Book 1; Menuet, Sarabande, Caprice; Book 2, Burlesque, Intermezzo polacco, Cracovienne fantastique*); "*Dans le désert, toccata*".

Padilla y Ramos (pä-dēl'-yä ĕ rä'-mŏs), Murcia, Spain, 1842 — Auteuil, France, Nov. 21, 1906; pupil of Mabellini, Florence; barytone at Messina, Turin, etc., St. Petersburg, Vienna and Berlin; 1869, m. Désirée Artot. (q.v.)

Paër (pä'-ăr), **Ferdinando**, Parma, June 1, 1771—Paris, May 3, 1839. 1807, ct.-cond. to Napoleon and cond. Op.-Com.; 1812, cond. Th.-Italien (vice Spontini); violinist and c. 43 operas, of which "*Il Maestro di Capella*" is still sung.

Paesiello. Vide PAISIELLO.

Paganini (päg-ä-nē'-nē), **Niccolò**, Genoa, Oct. 27, 1782—Nice, May 27, 1840; pre-eminent violin-virtuoso. Studied with G. Servetto and G. Dosta; at 8 he c. a vln.-sonata; at 9 he played in public with greatest succ.; from 1795 he studied with Ghiretti and Aless. Rolla (though **P.**

denied this), at Parma. 1798, he ran away from his severe father after a concert at Lucca, and played at Pisa and other places. At 15 he was a passionate gambler, and very dissipated. Fits of gambling alternated with periods when he practised 10 hours a day, the result being a ruined constitution. He pawned his violin to pay a gambling debt, but a M. Levron presented him with a Joseph Guarnerius, which P. willed to Genoa. In 1804 he went home, and practised till 1805, when he had extraordinary succ. making a sensation by brilliant performances on the G string alone; soon ct.-soloist at Lucca; then to 1827 he toured Italy, crushing all rivalry with an extraordinary technic; 1827, Pope Leo XII. conferred on him the Order of the Golden Spur; he played at Vienna, receiving from the municipality the great gold medal of St. Salvator; from the Emperor the honorary title of ct.-virtuoso. 1829, Berlin; 1831, Paris; 1831, London. 1833–34, Paris; then retired to his villa at Parma. He lost 50,000 francs on a scheme to establish a gambling house with concert-annex at Paris, the gambling-license being refused. Though his earnings were enormous, he was not generous except spasmodically; he gave Berlioz $4,000 as a compliment for his *"Symphonie Fantastique"* (B. had written *" Harold in Italy"* for **P.'s** Stradivari viola). He m. the singer Antonia Bianchi, and he left his son Achille $400,000 (£80,000). He died of phthisis of the larynx. His technic was never equalled, and it provoked superstitious dread among his auditors, his ghoulish appearance aiding the impression. He was sometimes the charlatan and some of his effects were due to special tunings (scordatures), but his virtuosity has never been rivalled. C. 24 caprices for violin-solo; of which pf.-transcriptions were made by Schumann and Liszt; 12 sonatas for violin and guitar (op. 2); do. (op. 3); 3 gran quartetti; concerto in E♭ (solo part in D, for a vln. tuned a semitone high); concerto in B min.; *"La Campanella,"* with Rondo à la clochette (op. 7); variations on many themes, *"Le Streghe," "God save the King," "The Carnival of Venice,"*

etc.; concert Allegro *"Moto perpetuo"* (op. 12); a sonata with accomp. of vln., 'cello or pf., and studies, etc. Biog. by Fétis (Paris, 1851; London, 1852); A. Niggli (1882); O. Bruni (Florence, 1873). Other studies by Stratton (1907), Prod'homme (1907), Bonaventura (1911), Kapp (1913), Day (1929), and Codignola (1936).

Page, (1) **J.,** England, ca. 1750—London, 1812; tenor. (2) **Nathaniel Clifford,** b. San Francisco, Oct. 26, 1866; pupil of E. S. Kelley; after 1895 res. in N. Y. as mus. editor; c. an opera *"The First Lieutenant"* (1889); incid. mus. for *"Moonlight Blossom"* (London, 1898), using Japanese themes; orch. suites, piano pieces, songs, etc.

Paine (pān), **J. Knowles,** Portland, Me., Jan. 9, 1839—Cambridge, Mass., April 25, 1906; American composer of importance; pupil of Kotzschmar, at Portland, Haupt (cpt.), Fischer (singing), and Wieprecht (instr.), Berlin; gave org.-concerts in Berlin and American cities, then lived in Boston as organist West Church; 1862, teacher of mus. Harvard Univ., and organist at Appleton Chapel, Cambridge; from 1876, prof. of mus. and organist at Harvard; c. an opera (text and mus.) *"Azara";* oratorio *"St. Peter," "Centennial Hymn,"* with orch. (to open the Philadelphia Exposition, 1876); *"Columbus March and Hymn"* (to open the Columbian Exposition, Chicago, 1893); mus. to Sophokles' *"Œdipus Tyrannus"* for male voices and orch. (prod. at Harvard, 1881); 3 cantatas with orch. *"The Realm of Fancy," "The Nativity," "Song of Promise,"* 2 symphs. op. 23, in C min., and op. 34 in A (*"Spring symph."*); 2 symph. poems, *"The Tempest"* and *"An Island Fantasy";* overture to *"As You Like It";* Domine Salvum with orch.; mass, with orch.; chamber-mus., vln.-sonata, etc.

Paisiello (pä-ē-sĭ-ĕl′-lō) (or **Paesiello**) (pä-ā-sĭ-ĕl′-lō), Taranto, Italy, May 9, 1740—Naples, June 5, 1816. At 5 studied at Jesuit sch. in Taranto with a priest Resta; later studied with Durante, Cotumacci and Abos, Cons. di S. Onofrio, at Naples; teacher there, 1759–61. He c. masses, etc., till a comic intermezzo

(Cons. Theatre, 1763) won him a commission to c. an opera for the Marsigli Th., at Bologna, where his comic opera "*La Pupilla, ossio il Mondo alla Rovescia,*" was prod. 1764. (Grove calls this work 2 operas.) In 12 years he prod. 50 operas mainly succ., though in rivalry with Piccinni and Cimarosa; these include "*Il Marchese di Tulipano*" (Rome, 1766); "*L'Idolo Cinese*" (Naples, 1767) and "*La Serva Padrona*" (Naples, 1769). He was notable also for his jealousy and devotion to intrigue. 1776–84, St. Petersburg, with a splendid salary and on invitation from Empress Catherine. Here he prod. 1776 "*Il Barbiere di Siviglia,*" gaining such succ. that the later and better opera by Rossini was received as a sacrilege with great hostility at first; on his return from Russia he prod. at Vienna one of his best works, "*Il Re Teodoro,*" and 12 symph. for Joseph II. 1784–99, cond. to Ferdinand IV. of Naples; and prod. various works incl. "*L'Olimpiade*" (1786) and "*Nina, o la Pazza per Amore*" (1789), "*La Molinara*" and "*I Zingari in Fiera.*" During the revolution 1799–1801, he won the favour of the Republican govt., also regained the favour of royalty at the Restoration, till Napoleon who had always admired him called him to Paris, 1802–03, as cond. Here P. lived in magnificence, lording it over Cherubini and Méhul. 1803–15, he was in Naples again as ct.-cond. In 1815, on the return of Ferdinand IV., he was reduced to a small salary; soon his wife died, and he shortly after. A composer of great prolificity, melodic grace and simplicity, his works are rarely heard now. He c. 100 operas, a Passion oratorio (Warsaw, 1784); 3 solemn masses, Te Deum for double chorus and 2 orch.; requiem with orch. (performed at his own funeral); 30 masses with orch., 40 motets, 12 symphs., and other things in proportion. Biog. by Le Seuer (1816), Quatremere de Quincy (1817), Schizzi (Milan, 1833), Villarosa (Naples, 1840); other memoirs by Palma (1891), Pupino (1908), Panareo (1910), and Abert (1919).

Paix (pä'-ēx), **Jacob,** Augsburg, 1550 —after 1590; organist and composer.

Paladilhe (păl-ä-dĕl), **Émile,** Montpellier, June 3, 1844—Paris, Jan. 8, 1926; studied with Marmontel (pf.), Benoit (org.) and Halévy (cpt.), Paris Cons.; won 1st prize for pf. and org., 1857; 1860, Grand prix de Rome, with the cantata "*Le Czar Ivan IV.*" (Opéra, 1860); from Rome, he sent an Italian opera buffa, an overture and a symph.; 1872, prod. the 1-act comic opera "*Le Passant*" (Op.-Com.) followed by 5 operas incl. the still pop. "*Patrie*" (Opéra, 1886; 1889, Hamburg, as "*Vaterland*"; 1895, Milan, as "*Patria*"); and c. also 2 masses, a symph., chamber music, piano pieces, songs, etc.

Palestrina (pä-lĕs-trē'-nä) (rightly **Giovanni Pierluigi Sante,** called **da Palestrina,** from his birthplace), Palestrina, near Rome, probably Dec. 27, 1525 (though date has long been controversial)—Rome, Feb. 2, 1594. One of the most revered names in liturgical music and the foremost composer of the Roman Catholic Church; he was b. of poor parents, little is known of his early life; he is said to have earned his living first as a church-singer; probably studied in Goudimel's sch., 1540, and was, 1544–51, organist at Palestrina, then *magister puerorum* (master of the boys), in the Cappella Giula, with title "maestro della capella della Basilica Vaticana." He dedicated a book of masses to Pope Julius III., who, Jan., 1554, admitted him to the Pontifical Chapel as a singer, against the rules, P. having a wife and no voice. July 30, 1555, Paul IV. dismissed him with a pension of 6 scudi per month. This blow affected him so deeply (he had 4 children to support) that he suffered nervous prostration. On Oct. 1, however, the Pope appointed him cond. at the Lateran. 1560, he prod. his famous "*Improperia*" for Holy Week, with such succ., that the Pope secured them for the Sistine Chapel, where they have been performed on every Good Friday since. 1561, he took the better-salaried post of cond. at Santa Maria Maggiore. The Pope was determined to rid church-mus. of its astonishing secular qualities: first, the use of street-ballads, even when indecent, as *canti fermi*, many of the choir actually singing the words; and second, the riotous counterpoint with which the sacred texts and the secular tunes were overrun. The Council of Trent and a committee of 8 cardinals, considering the matter seriously, decided not to revolutionise church-music entirely, and in 1564 commissioned Palestrina, by this time famous, to write a mass which should reform, without uprooting, ecclesiastical polyphony. He wrote three, all noble, the third, the "*Missa papæ Marcelli,*" winning the most profound praise. He was called "the saviour of music," and appointed composer to the Pontifical Chapel. 1571, he became and remained till death maestro of St. Peter's. He also composed for the "Congregazione del Oratorio" (v. NERI); taught in Nanini's sch., and was from 1581 maestro concertatore to Prince Buoncompagni. Pope Sixtus V. wished to appoint him maestro of the Sistine Chapel, but the singers refused to serve under a layman. He was, however, commissioned to revise the Roman Gradual and Antiphonal, by Pope Gregory XIII.; he pub. the "Directorium chori" (1582), the offices of Holy Week (1587), and the *Præfationes* (1588), but on the death of his pupil and assist. Giudetti, he was compelled to leave the work unfinished. A complete ed. of his works is pub. by Breitkopf and Härtel: Vols. i.–vii. contain 262 motets; Vol. viii., 45 hymns; Vol. ix., 68 offertories; Vols. x.–xxiv., 92 Masses; Vol. xxv., 9 Lamentations each in various arrangements in 3, 4, 5, 6, or 8 parts; Vol. xxvi., 17 Litanies, Motets and Psalms in 3–12 parts; Vol. xxvii., 35 Magnificats; Vol. xxviii., about 90 Italian (secular) Madrigals; Vol. xxix., 56 Church-Madrigals (Latin); Vol. xxx. (from colls. of 16th-17th cent.), 12 Cantiones sacræ, 12 Cant. profanæ, and 14 Cant. sacræ; Vol. xxxi. (from archives of the Pontifical Chapel, etc.), 56 miscellaneous numbers, many doubtful, incl. 11, "Esercizi sopra la scala"; Vol. xxxii., 60 miscellaneous comp. incl. 8 Ricercari, Responses, Antiphones, etc.; Vol. xxxiii., Documents, Index, Bibliography, etc. Among his best masses are "*Æterna Christi numera,*" "*Dies*

sanctificatus," "O sacrum convivium," in 8 parts; "Assumpta est Maria in coelum," "Dilexi quoniam," "Ecce ego Joannes," "Papæ Marcelli" in 6 parts; "Tu es Petrus" in 6 parts; these, the Motet "Exaudi Domine," 3 Lamentations, also selected Madrigals, Canzonets, etc., are pub. separately. Biog. by Baini (Rome, 1828); A. Bartolini (Rome, 1870); Bäumker (1877); Cametti (Milan, 1895). Also further studies by Brenet (1905); Raf. Casimiri (1918); Zoe Kendrick Pyne (1922); P. Wagner, etc.

Pallavicini (päl-lä-vē-chē'-nē), (1) (or **Pallavicino**) **Benedetto**, Cremona —Mantua (?), after 1616; conductor and composer. (2) **Carlo**, Brescia, 1630—Dresden, 1688; conductor and dram. composer.

Palme (päl'-mĕ), **Rudolph**, Barby-on-Elbe, Oct. 23, 1834—Magdeburg, Jan. 8, 1909; pupil of A. G. Ritter; organist; R. Mus. Dir. and organist at Magdeburg; c. concert-fantasias with male chorus, sonatas, etc., for org.

Palm'er, **Horatio Richmond**, Sherburne, N. Y., April 26, 1834—Yonkers, N. Y., 1907; pupil of his father and sister, and studied in New York, Berlin and Florence; at 18, began composing; at 20 choruscond.; 1857, teacher at Rushford Acad.; after the Civil War, Chicago; ed. *Concordia;* cond. various societies from 1873, cond. New Church Choral Union, giving concerts, sometimes with 4,000 singers; 1877, Dean of the Chautauqua Sch. of Mus.; Mus. Doc. (Chicago Univ. and Alfred Univ.); pub. colls. and treatises.

Palm'gren, **Selim**, b. Björneborg, Finland, Feb. 16, 1878; composer; studied at Helsingfors Cons., and with Berger, Klathe and Busoni; toured Scandinavia as pianist, 1900; cond. Helsingfors choral society and later the orch. in Abo; c. operas, piano concertos, symphonic poems, piano pieces, choruses and songs, some of these having internat'l hearings; 1923, teacher of comp. at Eastman School of Music, Rochester, N. Y.; m. Maikki Järnefelt, singer.

Païoschi (pä-lòs'-kē), **Giov.**, 1824—1892, member of the Milan firm of Ricordi.

Palot'ta, **Matteo**, Palermo, 1680—Vienna, 1758; ct.-composer and writer.

Paminger (pä'-mǐng-ěr) (or **Pammigerus, Panni'gerus**), **Leonhardt,** Aschau, Upper Alsatia, 1495—Passau, 1567; composer.

Pancera (pän-chä'-rä), **Ella,** Vienna, Aug. 15, 1875 (of Italian parents) —Bad Ischl, May 10, 1932; pianist; pupil of Epstein and Vockner; début at 13; toured widely.

Panizza (pä-nǐd'-zä), **Ettore, b.** Buenos Aires, Aug. 12, 1875; conductor; pupil of Milan Cons.; after 1899 active as cond. in various Italian theatres; 1907-13, Covent Garden; 1916, La Scala; also in Paris, Buenos Aires; Chicago Op., and after 1934 as chief cond. of Italian works at Met. Op., succeeding Serafin; c. opera "*Il fidanzeto del mare*" (Buenos Aires, 1897); "*Medioevo latino*" (Geneva, 1900); "*Aurora*" (Buenos Aires, 1908); translated Berlioz's treatise on instrumentation (1913).

Pan'ny, Jos., Kolmitzberg. Lower Austria, 1794—Mayence, 1838; violinist, teacher and composer.

Panof'ka, H., Breslau, 1807—Florence, 1887; violinist, writer and composer.

Panseron (pän-sŭ-rôṅ), **Aug. Mathieu,** Paris, 1796—1859; writer of vocal methods, études, etc.; composer.

Panzner (pänts'-něr), **K.,** Teplitz, Bohemia, March 2, 1866—Düsseldorf, Dec. 7, 1923; pupil of Nicodé and Dräeseke; cond. at Sondershausen th.; 2 years later at Elberfeld; 1893, 1st cond. Leipzig city th.; 1899, cond. Philh. concerts, Bremen; after 1909, munic. dir. of music, Düsseldorf.

Paolucci (pä-ō-loo'-chē), **Giuseppe,** Siena, May 25, 1726—Assisi, April 26, 1776; Franciscan monk; c. church music.

Pape (pä'-pě), **Jn. H.,** Sarstedt, near Hanover, July 1, 1789—Paris, Feb. 2, 1875; distinguished maker and improver of the piano; he inv. a transposing piano, introd. padded hammers, etc.

Papier (pä-pēr'), (1) **Louis,** Leipzig, 1829—1878; organist, singing-teacher and composer. (2) **Rosa,** Baden, near Vienna, 1858—Vienna, Feb. 9, 1932; mezzo-soprano; Imp. Op., Vienna; 1881, m. Dr. Hans Paumgartner.

Papini (pä-pē'-ně), **Guido,** Camagiore, near Florence, Aug. 1, 1847—London, Oct. 20, 1912; violinist; pupil of Giorgetti; début at 13; toured Europe; composer.

Papperitz (pap'-pē-rēts), **Benj. Robt.,** Pirna, Saxony, Dec. 4, 1826—Leipzig, Sept. 29, 1903; pupil of Hauptmann, Richter and Moscheles, Leipzig Cons., 1851; teacher of harm. and cpt. there; from 1868-69, also organist of Nikolaikirche there; 1882, R. Prof.; composer.

Paque (păk), **Guil.,** Brussels, 1825—London, 1876; 'cello-virtuoso and teacher.

Paradies (or **Paradisi**) (pä-rä-dē'-ěs, or dē'-sē), **P. Dom.,** Naples, 1710—Venice, 1792; pupil of Porpora; harps.-player and teacher, also dram. composer.

Paradis (pä-rä-dēs'), **Maria Theresia von,** Vienna, May 15, 1759—Feb. 1, 1824; a skilful blind organist and pianist for whom Mozart wrote a concerto; daughter of an Imperial Councillor; teacher of pf. and voice; c. an opera.

Paray (pär-ä'-ē), **Paul, b.** Tréport, France, May 24, 1886; conductor; pupil of Paris Cons., Prix de Rome winner; after 1921 cond. Lamoureux Concerts, Paris, succeeding Chevillard in 1923 as leader of this orch.; also a pianist and composer.

Parent (pă-räṅ), **Charlotte Frances Hortense,** London, March 22, 1837—Paris, Jan. 12, 1929; pianist; pupil of Mme. Farreṅc, Paris Cons.; founded "École préparatoire au professorat," Paris; wrote a pf.-method, etc. (2) **Armand,** Liége, Feb. 5, 1863—Paris, Jan. 19, 1934; noted violinist.

Parepa-Rosa (pä-rä'-pä-rō'-zä) (née **Parepa de Boyescu**), **Euphrosyne,** Edinburgh, May 7, 1836—London, Jan. 21, 1874; daughter and pupil of Elizabeth Seguin, a singer; eminent soprano in opera and oratorio; her strong and sympathetic voice had a compass of 2½ octaves reaching to d'''   ; début at 16, Malta; 1865 m. Carl Rosa; toured Europe and America.

Par'ish-Al'vars, Elias, Teignmouth, Engl., Feb. 28, 1808—Vienna, Jan. 25, 1849; of Jewish descent; noted harp-virtuoso and composer.

Parisini (pä-rǐ-sē'-nē), **Federico,** Bologna, 1825—Jan. 4, 1891; theorist and dram. composer.

Parke, (1) **J.,** 1745—1829; Engl. oboist and composer. (2) **Wm. Thos.,**

London, 1762—1847; bro. of above; oboist, composer and writer.

Park′er, (1) **Jas. Cutler Dunn,** Boston, Mass., June 2, 1828—1916; studied Leipzig Cons.; lived in Boston and Brookline; 1862, organist "Parker Club," vocal soc.; 1864–91, organist Trinity Ch., and for years organist Händel and Haydn Soc.; prof. Boston Univ. Coll. of Mus., and Examiner N. E. Cons.; writer and transl.; c. "*Redemption Hymn*" (1877); cantata "*The Blind King*" (1886); "*St. John*," with orch.; oratorio, "*The Life of Man*"; church-services, etc. (2) **H.,** b. London, Aug. 4, 1845; pupil of Leipzig Cons., and of Lefort, Paris; singing-teacher and vocal composer. London; wrote treatise "*The Voice*"; c. comic opera "*Mignonette*" (London, 1889); "*Jerusalem*," for bass-solo and chorus (Albert Hall, 1884); gavottes, etc., for orch.; pf.-pcs. (3) **Horatio Wm.,** Auburndale, Mass., Sept. 15, 1863—Cedarhurst, N. Y., Dec. 18, 1919; prominent American composer; pupil of his mother, later of Emery (theory), J. Orth (pf.), and Chadwick (comp.), Boston; organist Dedham and Boston; studied 1882–85 with Rheinberger (org. and comp.) and L. Abel (cond.), Munich; organist and prof. of mus. St. Paul's Sch., Garden City, New York; 1886, organist St. Andrew's, Harlem; 1888, Ch. of the Holy Trinity, N. Y.; 1894, prof. of mus., Yale Univ.; 1899, cond. his notable oratorio "*Hora Novissima*" at Worcester (Engl.) Festival with great succ. (first given at Worcester [U. S. A.] Festival, 1893). Pub. coll. of org.-pcs. In May, 1911, his opera "*Mona*," libretto by Brian Hooker (b. N. Y. Nov. 2, 1880, a graduate of Yale, 1902, and instructor there 1905–10), won the $10,000 prize offered by the Met. Op. Co. for the best grand opera in English by an American. It was prod. with succ., 1912; his opera "*Fairyland*" (text by Hooker) won prize offered by Nat'l. Fed. of Women's Clubs and was perf. at the fest. of this body at Los Angeles, 1915; Mus. D., Cambridge Univ., 1902; c. oratorios, "*Hora Novissima*" (1893), and "*St. Christopher*" (1896); cantatas "*King Trojan*" (Munich, 1885), "*The Holy Child*," "*The Kobold*" and "*Harold Harfager*," prize-cantata, "*Dream King*" (1893);

symph. in C.; concert-overture; heroic-overture "*Regulus*"; overture to "*Count Robert of Paris*," "*Cohal Mahr*," for bar.-solo and orch. (1893); "*Commencement Ode*," Yale Univ. (1895); McCagg prize chorus *a cappella* (1898); "*A Northern Ballad*" for orch. (1899); also many other choruses; string quintet; string quartet; suite for piano trio; violin suite, songs, etc. (4) **Henry Taylor,** Boston, 1867—March 30, 1934; music and dramatic critic; after 1905 until his death, the distinguished critic of the Boston *Transcript*, noted for a highly analytic if somewhat involved literary style.

(Parkina) Park′inson, Elizabeth, Kansas City, Mo., 1882—Colorado Springs, Col., 1922; soprano; pupil of Mrs. Lawton, Kansas City, Miolan Carvalho, de la Nux and Mme. Marchesi; début, Paris, 1902; Covent Garden, 1904–07; also sang at English fests. and concerts; toured Australia.

Par′low, Kathleen, b. Calgary, Canada, 1890; violinist; taken to California at 5, and studied there with Conrad and Holmes; début there at 6; at 15 gave a recital in London and appeared with the London Symph. Orch.; then studied with Auer; 1907 began to tour.

Par′ratt, Sir Walter, Huddersfield, Feb. 10, 1841—Windsor, March 27, 1924; at 7 sang in church; at 10 knew Bach's "*Well-tempered Clavichord*" by heart; at 11, organist Armitage Bridge; 1872 Magdalen Coll., Oxford; 1882, St. George's Chapel, Windsor Mus. Bac. Oxon., 1873; 1883, organ-prof. R. C. M.; knighted 1892; 1893, Master of Mus. in Ordinary to the Queen and 1901 to the King; prof. of music, Oxford Univ., 1908–18; wrote articles; c. mus. to "*Agamemnon*" and "*Orestes*," "*Elegy to Patroclus*," anthems, org.-and pf.-pcs., etc.

Par′ry, (1) **J.,** Ruabon, N. Wales—Wynnstay, Oct. 7, 1782; Welsh bard, harper, and composer. (2) **J.** (called "Bardd Alaw," i.e., master of song), Denbigh, Feb. 18, 1776—London, April 8, 1851; clarinettist; cond. of the Eisteddfod for years; critic, teacher and composer in London; pub. colls., etc. (3) **J. Orlando,** London, 1810—E. Molesey, 1879; son of above; pianist, harpist, singer and composer. (4) **Jos.,** Merthyr Tydvil, Wales, May 21, 1841—Penarth, Feb. 17, 1903; the son of a labourer; at 10 worked in a puddling-furnace; 1854 emigrated to America with his family, but returned to Britain, won Eisteddfod prizes for songs; 1868 studied R. A. M. on a fund especially raised by Brinley Richards; 1871, Mus. Bac. Cambr.; prof. of music, Univ. Col., Aberystwith; 1878, Mus. Doc.; 1888, Mus. Lecturer at Cardiff; also Fellow R. A. M. C. 4 operas, cantatas *"The Prodigal Son," "Nebuchadnezzar,"* and *"Cambria";* "Druids' Chorus"; an orchestral ballade, overtures, etc. (5) Sir **Chas. Hubert Hastings,** Bournemouth, England, Feb. 27, 1848—near Littlehampton, Oct. 7, 1918; eminent English composer; from 1861, while at Eton, pupil of G. Elvy (comp.), was pianist, organist, singer, and composer at the concerts of the Musical Soc. At 18, while still at Eton, he took "Mus. Bac." at Oxford, wrote a cantata, *"O Lord, Thou hast cast us out";* 1867, Exeter Coll., Oxford; founded "Univ. Mus. Club"; 1874, M. A.; studied with Bennett and Macfarren, and Dannreuther (pf.), and Pierson, Stuttgart. At 26 prod. *"Intermezzo religioso,"* for strings (Gloucester Festival); 1883, Choragus of Oxford and Mus. Doc. Cantab.; do. Oxon, 1884, do. Dublin, 1891; 1894 dir. R. C. M.; 1898, knighted; 1902 made a baronet; active as lecturer and writer of essays and books incl. the notable *"Evolution of the Art of Music"* (1896). C. also 4 symphs.; symph vars.; overtures, *"To an Unwritten Tragedy"* and *"Guillem de Cabestanh";* oratorios *"Judith," "Job," "King Saul";* mus. to Aristophanes' *"Birds"* (1883), and *"Frogs"* (1892); and to *"Hypatia"* (1893); the following were prod. at prominent festivals: scenes from Shelley's *"Prometheus Unbound,"* with orch. (Gloucester festival, 1880); *"The Glories of Our Blood and State"; "Suite moderne," "Ode on St. Cecilia's Day," "L'Allegro ed Il Penseroso," "De profundis,"* with 3 choirs and orch.; chamber-mus.; vln.- and pf.-sonatas, songs, etc.; *"Invocation to Music";* Magnificat, in Latin. In 1908 his health forced his resignation of the Oxford Professorship; c.

also Processional Music for the coronation of Edward VII (1903); a simfonia sacra for soli, chorus and orch. (Gloucester Festival, 1904); music to Aristophanes' *"Clouds"* (Oxford, 1905); Browning's *"Pied Piper"* with orch. (Norwich Fest., 1905); symph. poem *"The Vision of Life"* (Cardiff Fest., 1907); cantata (Worcester Fest., 1908); revision of 4th symph. (Philharmonic, 1910); wrote important work on Bach; *"The Music of the 17th Century,"* for the Oxford History of Music (1902), etc.

Par'sons, (1) **Robt.,** Exeter, drowned Newark, Engl., 1569; composer. (2) **J.,** d. 1623; probably son of above; organist and composer. (3) Sir **Wm.,** 1746—1817; master of King's Band and teacher. (4) **Albert Ross,** Sandusky, O., Sept. 16, 1847—Mt. Kisco, N. Y., June 14, 1933; noteworthy American teacher; pupil of F. K. Ritter, N. Y., and at Leipzig Cons.; later of Tausig, Kullak, Weitzmann and Würst, Berlin; 1871, New York; organist 1885, Fifth Av. Presb. Ch.; same year taught at Met. Coll. of Music; 1890, pres. Music Teachers' Nat'l. Assoc.; 1893, head of Amer. Coll. of Musicians; translator, editor, and writer of various works; c. vocal quartets, songs, etc.

Pasdeloup (pä-dŭ-loo), **Jules Étienne,** Paris, Sept. 15, 1819—Fontainebleau, Aug. 13, 1887; eminent cond.; pianist; pupil Paris Cons., 1847–50; pf.-teacher, and 1855–68, teacher of ensemble there; 1851, cond. famous concerts (known from 1861 as "concerts populaires"); v. succ. till 1884, when they fell before the popularity of Colonne and Lamoureux; a benefit festival brought him 100,000 francs ($20,000).

Pasquali (päs-kwä'-lē), **Nicolò,** Italy—Edinburgh, 1757; writer and composer.

Pasqué (päs-kā'), **Ernst,** Cologne, 1821—Alsbach, 1892; barytone; director and writer.

Pasquini (päs-kwē'-nē), **Bdo.,** Massa di Valdinevole, Tuscany, Dec. 8, 1637—Rome, Nov. 22, 1710; noted organist at San Maria Maggiore; pupil of Vittori and Cesti; teacher and composer of 10 operas, 8 oratorios, cantatas, sonatas, suites, etc.

Pasta (päs'-tä) (née **Negri**), (1) **Giuditta,** Milan, April 9, 1798—villa on

Lake Como, April 1, 1865; a noted Jewish singer; pupil of Asioli; début, 1815, but had no succ.; studied with Scappa, and reappeared with greatest succ. Her powerful voice (range a-d''', v. PITCH, D. D.) had always some irregularities, but her dramatic power was great and she invented embellishments with much skill; m. the tenor (2) **Pasta**, before 1816; she created "La Sonnambula" and "Norma" and earned a fortune.

Pas'ternack, Jos. A., Czentochowa, Poland, 1881—Chicago, April 29, 1940; studied Warsaw Cons.; violist in Met. Op. orch. and asst. cond., 1909-10; cond. Century Op. Co., afterward of Phila. Philh.; Boston "Pops," 1916; mus. dir., Victor Phon. Co. and Stanley Co. of America; after 1927 cond. in radio programmes for Nat'l. Broadcasting Co.

Pa'tey, Janet Monach (née Whytock), London, 1842—Sheffield, 1894; alto.

Pa'ton, Mary Ann (Mrs. Wood), Edinburgh, 1802—Bucliffe Hall, near Wakefield, 1864; prominent soprano; m. tenor Jos. Wood, 1831.

Patti (pät'tē), (1) **Carlotta**, Florence, 1840—Paris, June 27, 1889; eminent concert colorature-soprano; pupil of her father, (2) **Salvatore P.**, a tenor, and her mother, (3) **Caterina** (née **Chiesa**), a soprano. (4) **Adelina** (**Adela Juana Maria**), Madrid, Feb. 10, 1843—Craig-y-Nos, Breconshire, Wales, Sept. 27, 1919; one of the most eminent colorature-singers in history; sister of (1), and like her a pupil of her parents; sang in public as a mere child; then studied with Max Strakosch (husband of her sister Amelia); début, at 16, New York, Nov. 24, 1859, as "Lucia" (under the stage-name "the little Florinda"); 1861, London, Covent Garden; 1862, Paris Th. Italien; 1868, m. the Marquis de Caux. Her career, covering more than 40 years, brought her phenomenal adulation in the principal music centres, although she sang only about 30 rôles and these usually in the older Italian operas. Not a great actress, she relied for her effects upon consummate vocal technique rather than emotional powers. She withdrew from the stage 1906 and, except for a brief tour in the U. S., lived at her castle Craig-y-Nos, in Wales. 1886, m. and toured with the tenor Nicolini (d.

1898); 1899 m. a Swedish nobleman, Baron Cederström. (5) **Carlo**, Madrid, 1842—St. Louis, Mo., March, 1873; bro. of above: violinist.

Pat'tison, (1) **J. Nelson**, Niagara Falls, N. Y., Oct. 22, 1845—New York, 1905; pianist; pupil of Liszt, Thalberg, Henselt and von Bülow (pf.), and Haupt (harm.); toured U. S. as pianist with Parepa Rosa, etc.; c. symph. for orch. and military band "*Niagara*"; concert overture, etc. (2) **Lee**, b. Grand Rapids, Wis., July 22, 1890; pianist and composer; grad. New England Cons. with honours; studied piano with Baermann and Schnabel; comp. with Chadwick and Juon; début, Boston, 1913; has made many tours in duo-piano recitals with Guy Maier, and in double concertos with leading Amer. orchs.; c. songs and piano works, made many transcriptions for two pianos; dir. of Met. Op. spring season, 1937.

Pauer (pow'-ĕr), (1) **Ernst**, Vienna, Dec. 21, 1826—near Darmstadt, May 9, 1905; noted pianist; son of a prominent Lutheran clergyman; pupil of Th. Dirza, W. A. Mozart, Jr. (pf.), and Sechter (comp.), later of Fr. Lachner, Munich; 1847-51, dir. mus. societies at Mayence; 1851, London; 1859, prof. at the R. A. M.; in 1861, gave historical performances of clavecin and pf.-mus.; 1866, pianist to Austrian Court; 1867, prof. at the Nat. Training Sch.; 1883, R. C. M.; 1870, lecturer; toured U. S.; ed. the classics; pub. mus. primers, colls. of old clavier-works, and many didactic works; c. a quintet, vln. arrangements of symphs., etc. (2) **Max**, b. London, Oct. 31, 1866; son and pupil of above; then studied with Lachner, Carlsruhe; 1887, pf.-prof. Cologne Cons.; 1893, chamber-virtuoso to the Grand Duke of Hesse; 1897, prof. Stuttgart Cons.; 1898, made prof. by the King of Würtemberg; he became dir. of Stuttgart Cons. 1908, succeeding De Lange; 1924, dir. Leipzig Cons.; pub. pf.-pieces.

Pauly, Rose, Hungarian sopr.; sang "*Elektra*" with striking success, Met. Op., 1937-8.

Paumann (pow'-män), **Konrad**, b. (blind) Nürnberg, ca. 1410—Munich, Jan. 25, 1473; c. the oldest extant book of org.-pcs.

Paumgartner (powm'-gärtnĕr), (1) **Dr. Hans**, 1844—Vienna, May 23, 1893; pianist; critic and composer. (2) **Bernhard**, b. Vienna, Nov. 14, 1887; after 1919 dir. Salzburg Mozarteum.

Paur (powr), (1) **Emil**, Czernowitz, Bukovina, Aug. 29, 1855—Mistek, Moravia, June 7, 1932; noted conductor; pupil of his father; at 8 he played vln. and pf. in public; studied with Dessoff (comp.) and Hellmesberger (vln.) Vienna Cons. (fellow pupil with Nikisch and Mottl); graduated with first prizes; 1870, first vln. and assist.-soloist in ct.-opera orch.; 1876, cond. at Cassel; later Königsberg; 1880, 1st ct.-cond. Mannheim; 1891, cond. Leipzig City Th.; 1893–98, cond. Boston (U. S. A.) symph. Orch. (vice Nikisch); 1898, New York Philh. Concerts (vice Seidl); 1899—1902, dir. of the Nat. Cons., N. Y. (vice Dvořák); 1900, cond. German opera of the Met. Op.; he returned to Europe, 1903; cond. concerts in Madrid; 1904–10, returned to the U. S. as cond. Pittsburgh Symph. Orch.; 1912–13, at Berlin Op.; c. symphony; piano concerto; vln. concerto, string quartet, vln. sonata, pf.-pcs., songs. (2) **Maria** (née **Burger**), Gengenbach, Black Forest, 1862—New York, 1899; wife of above; pianist; pupil Stuttgart Cons., Leschetizky and Essipoff, Vienna. (3) **Kurt**, son of (1) and (2), an accomplished pianist; res. in the U. S.

Pauwels (pow'-vĕls), **Jean Engelbert**, Brussels, 1768—1804; violinist, conductor and dram. composer.

Pavesi (pä-vä'-sē), **Stefano**, Cremona, 1779—Crema, 1850; dram. composer.

Pax'ton, **Stephen**, d. 1787; Engl. composer.

Payer (pī-ĕr), **Hieronymus**, Meidling, near Vienna, 1787—Wiedburg, near Vienna, 1845; conductor and dram. composer.

Peace, **Albert Lister**, Huddersfield, Engl., Jan. 26, 1844—Liverpool, March 14, 1912; prominent organist; pupil of Horn and Parratt; 1875, Mus. Doc. Oxon; 1873, organist Glasgow cath.; 1897, of St. George's Hall, Liverpool (vice Best); c. Psalm 138 with orch., org.-music.

Pearce, (1) **Stephen Austen**, London, Nov. 7, 1836—April 19, 1900; pupil of J. L. Hopkins; Mus. Doc. Oxford, 1864, same year U. S. and Canada; then organist 2 London churches; 1872, vocal-teacher, Columbia Coll., N. Y., and lecturer Peabody Inst. and Johns Hopkins Univ., Baltimore; 1879–85, organist Collegiate Church, N. Y.; writer and composer of a 3-act opera, a children's opera, an oratorio and a church-cantata in strict fugal style (prod. at Oxford), overture, etc. (2) **Chas. Wm.**, Salisbury, England, Dec. 5, 1856—London, Dec. 2, 1928; pupil of Ayluard, Hoyte, Read and Prout; 1881, Mus. Bac., 1884 Mus. Doc., Cambridge. From 1871 organist various London churches. 1882 Prof. of Trinity College; co-editor, organist and choir-master; wrote various text-books, and c. an oratorio.

Pear'sall, **Robt. Lucas De**, Clifton, Engl., 1795—Schloss Wartensee, Lake of Constance, 1856; writer and composer.

Pearson. Vide PIERSON.

Pedrell (pä'-dhrĕl), **Felipe**, Tortosa, Spain, Feb. 19, 1841—Barcelona, Aug. 19, 1922; composer; 1894, prof. of Mus. History and Æsthetics, Royal Cons., Madrid; editor, critic, lexicographer and writer; c. operas, including "*Quasimodo*" (Barcelona, 1875), a trilogy "*Los Pinneos*" (Barcelona, 1902), "*La Celestina*" (1904), "*La Matinada*" (1905), a Gloria mass with orch.; also wrote and edited important historical works.

Pedrotti (pä-drôt'-tē), **Carlo**, Verona, Nov. 12, 1817—suicide, Oct. 16, 1892; conductor and composer of 16 operas, etc.

Pelletan (pĕl-täṅ), **Fanny**, 1830—1876; singer and writer.

Pelletier (pĕl'-tē-ā), **Wilfred**, b. Canada; conductor; won Quebec gov't. scholarship, studied in Europe; early tours as accompanist; cond. Met. Op., N. Y., also with Ravinia, Los Angeles and San Francisco Op., and as guest with Canadian orchs.; m. Queena Mario, soprano; divorced. (2) Rose Bampton.

Pembaur (päm'-bowr), (1) **Jos.**, Innsbruck, May 23, 1848—Feb. 19, 1923; studied Vienna Cons., later at Munich R. Sch. of Mus.; 1875, dir. and headmaster, Innsbruck Mus. Sch.; prod. v. succ. opera "*Zigeunerleben*" (1898), choral works with orch.; symph. "*Im Tyrol*," etc. (2) **Jos.**, b. Innsbruck, April 20,

1875; pianist; son of (1); taught Munich Acad., 1897–1900; Leipzig Cons., 1903–21; c. piano works, songs, etc. D. Munich, Jan. 30, 1937.

Peña y Goni (pān'-yä ē gō'-nē), **Antonio,** San Sebastian, Spain, 1846–Madrid, 1896; critic and composer.

Peñalosa (pěn-yä-lō'-sä), **Francisco,** Spanish composer, 1470–1535; cond. to Ferdinand the Catholic, then singer in Papal Chapel.

Pénavaire (pā-nä-vǎr), **Jean Grégoire,** Lesparre, Sept. 15, 1840–Paris, Sept., 1906; composer; theatre-cond. at Nantes; c. overtures "*Tasso,*" "*Cervantes*"; symph. poem with chorus, "*La vision des Croisées,*" comic opera and ballets.

Pen'na, Lorenzo, Bologna, 1613–Imola, 1693; conductor and composer.

Pentenrieder (pěn'-těn-rē-děr), **Fz. X.,** Kaufbeuren, Bavaria, 1813–Munich, 1867; organist and dram. composer.

Pepusch (pā'-poosh), **John Chr. (Jn. Chp.),** Berlin, 1667–London, July 20, 1752; violinist, composer and writer; pupil of Klingenberg and Grosse; held a position at the Prussian Court, but 1697 seeing the king kill an officer without trial he went to London. 1710 founded the famous "Academy of Antient Music"; 1712 organist and composer to Duke of Chandos (succeeded by Händel), dir. Lincoln Inn's Theatre, for which he c. 4 masques, the music to the enormously pop. "*Beggar's Opera,*" etc.; 1730 m. de l'Épire, the singer.

Perabo (pā'-rä-bō), **(Jn.) Ernst,** Wiesbaden, Germany, Nov. 14, 1845–Boston, Oct. 29, 1920; at 7 brought to New York; pupil of his father; then of Moscheles and Wenzel (pf.), Papperitz, Richter, and Hauptmann (harm.), and Reinecke (comp.), Leipzig Cons., returned to America, 1865; succ. concert-pianist; lived in Boston as teacher and pianist; c. arrangements, etc.

Pereira (pā-rā'-ē-rä), **(1) Marcos Soares,** Caminha, Portugal–Lisbon, Jan. 7, 1655; c. a mass, etc. **(2) Domingos Nuñes,** Lisbon–Camarate, near Lisbon, 1729; cond. and composer.

Perepelitzin (pā-rě-pě-lēt'-shēn), **Polycarp D.,** Odessa, Dec. 26, 1818–St. Petersburg, June 14, 1887; Russian colonel; pupil of Lipinski (vln.); writer and composer.

Perez (pā'-rěth), **Davide, (1)** of Spanish parents, Naples, 1711–Lisbon, 1778; cond. at Palermo Cath.; 1752, ct.-cond., Lisbon; rival of Jomelli as c. of operas, incl. "*Demofoonte*"; c. also notable church-mus. **(2) Juan Ginez,** Orihuela, Murcia, Oct. 7, 1548–Orihuela, 1612; royal chaplain and comp. of church music.

Perfall (pěr'-fäl), **K.,** Freiherr von, Munich, Jan. 29, 1824–Jan. 14, 1907; studied mus. with Hauptmann, Leipzig; 1854–64 founded and cond. the still succ. "Oratorio Soc."; in 1864, Intendant ct.-mus.; 1867–1893, Intendant Ct.-Th.; writer and composer of operas, cantatas, etc.

Perger (pěr'-gěr), **Richard von,** Vienna, Jan. 10, 1854–Jan. 11, 1911; pupil of Brahms; 1890–95, dir. and cond. Rotterdam Cons.; 1895–99, cond. "*Gesellschafts-concerte,*" Vienna; 1899–1907, dir. of Cons. there; prod. (text and mus.) succ. comic opera "*Der Richter von Granada*" (Cologne, 1889), a vaudeville, vln.-concerto, etc.

Pergolesi (pěr-gō-lā'-sē), **Giov. Bat., Jesi,** Papal States, Jan. 4, 1710–(of consumption) Pozzuoli, near Naples, March 16, 1736; eminent composer. At 16 entered the Cons. dei Poveri di Gesù Cristo, Naples, and studied with de Matteis (vln.), Greco (cpt.), Durante, and Feo (cpt.). He speedily won attention by novel harmonies and threw off contrapuntal shackles early. His last student-work, the biblical drama "*San Guglielmo D'Aquitania*" (prod. with comic intermezzi at the convent of S. Agnello Maggiore, Naples, 1731), shows the beginnings of vivid and original fancy. He prod. at Naples in 1731 the excellent and novel opera "*Sallustia,*" and the intermezzo "*Amor Fa l' Uomo Cieco,*" which had no succ., while the opera seria "*Ricimero*" was a distinct failure. But he found a patron in the Prince of Stigliano, for whom he wrote 30 terzets for vln. with bass; he was commissioned to compose a solemn mass for Naples, which was performed after the earthquake of 1731, as a votive offering to the patron saint of the city. It brought him immediate fame. After four stage-works, prod. in 1732 the intermezzo "*La Serva Padrona*" (Naples, 1733); won him note as a dramatic composer and has served as a model of comic operas since; it has only 2 characters and the accompaniment is a string-quartet with occasional support of horns. His subsequent 6 operas were received without interest (except for the intermezzo to "*Adriano*" first given as "*Livietta e Tracollo*" and later as "*La Contadina Astuta*"), though after his death they were re-vived with immense enthusiasm, and their harmonic novelty, sweetness, delicacy and melodic charm were recognised, "*La Serva Padrona*" and "*Il Maestro di Musica*" be-coming standards in France. Of the failure of "*L'Olimpiade*," v. DUNI. Irregular habits due to regular dis-appointments undermined Pergolesi's constitution, and he died of con-sumption at the baths of Pozzuoli, finishing five days before his death his masterpiece, the celebrated "*Stabat Mater*" for soprano and alto with string orch. and org. He c. also 3 masses with orch.; Dixit for double chorus and orch.; a Kyrie cum gloria; a Miserere, and a Lau-date with orch., etc.; an oratorio, "*La Natività*," a cantata "*Orfeo*" for solo voice and orch.; a cantata, "*Giasone*"; 6 cantatas with string-accomp.; 30 trios, etc. Biog. by Blasis (1817) Villarosa (1831). Other memoirs by Boyer, Fracassetti, Schletterer, Faustina-Fasini, Radic-iotti, Barchiesi, etc.

Peri (pā'-rē), (1) **Jacopo** (called **"Il Zazzerino,"** i.e., the long-haired), Rome, Aug. 20, 1561—Florence, Aug. 12, 1633; pupil of Malvezzi; court-cond. at 3 successive courts; an enthusiast in everything classic, he haunted the salons of Count Bardi and Corsi, where he joined the attempt at revival of Greek musical recitative, with Caccini and Corsi; he set to mus. Rinuccini's text of "*Dafne*"; this was doubtless the first opera ever written; its effort at reproducing the supposed manner of Æschylos, Sophokles, etc., was called "stile rappresentativo"; the opera was given only once, and privately at Bardi's house, but it won Peri a commission to set Rinuccini's text "*Euridice*" for the wedding of Maria de' Medici and Henry IV. of France (1600); an ed. of his works was pub. 1603, incl. madrigals, etc. (2) **Achille,** Reggio d'Emilia, Italy,

1812—1880; conductor and dram. composer.

Perisine. Vide LA RUE.

Perne (părn), **Fran. L.,** Paris, 1772—May 26, 1832; pupil of Abbé d'Hau-dimont (harm. and cpt.); 1792, chorus-singer at the Opéra; 1799, double-bass player in the orch.; 1801, prod. a grand festival mass; the next year he c. a triple fugue to be sung backwards on reversing the page; 1811, prof. harm. at the Cons.; 1816, Inspector Gen.; 1819, libr., 1822, retired to an estate near Laon; he returned to Paris a few weeks before he died; he was indefatigable in re-search, and an authority on Greek notation, the troubadours, etc.; writer and composer.

Perosi (pā-rō'-sē), Don **Lorenzo,** b. Tortona, Italy, Dec. 20, 1872; a priest and organist who has com-posed a large variety of sacred mus.; it aims to use modern resources and ancient principles; pupil of Saladino, Milan Cons.; 1894, of Haberl's Domchorschule, Ratisbon; 1895, cond. at Imola; from 1897, at San Marco, Venice; his sacred trilogy "*La Passione di Cristo*" (a, "*La Cena del Signore*"; b, "*L'Orazione al Monte*"; c, "*La Morte del Reden-tore*"), Milan, 1897, at the Ital. Congress for Sacred Mus., created a sensation, and has been widely performed; 1898, Pope Leo XIII. made him honorary *maestro* of the Papal Choir; c. also 25 masses; c. also oratorios, "*La Transfigurazione del Nostro Signore Gesù Cristo*" (1898), "*La Risurrezione di Lazaro*" (Venice, July 27, 1898, in La Fenice Th., by special permission), "*Il Natale del Redentore*" (Como, 1899); "*Mosè*" (Rome, 1902); "*Leo the Great*" (1902), "*Il Giudizio Uni-versale*" (The Last Judgment), Rome, 1904; and "*In Patris Memoriam*" (1910); orch. variations (1904), can-tatas "*Anima*" (1908), and "*Dies Iste*"; requiem for Leo XIII. (1909), etc. He announced an ambitious undertaking to compose ten sym-phonies, each named after an Italian city, and had completed those de-voted to Rome, Florence, Venice and Bologna when he suffered a nervous breakdown in 1917 and was obliged to forego composition. In 1922 he was reported to be confined in a sanitarium, but the following year was able to prepare a revision of his oratorio, "*The Resurrection*," which was presented at Rome.

Peroti'nus, Magnus, Magister; 12th cent. composer; conductor at Nôtre-Dame, Paris. (Coussemaker.)

Perotti (pā-rŏt'-tē), **Giov. Ag.,** Vercelli, 1769—Venice, 1855; writer and composer.

Perrin (pĕr-răṅ), **Pierre** (called *l'abbé*, though never ordained), Lyons, ca. 1620—Paris, 1675; librettist of the first French operas.

Perron (pĕr'-rōn), **Karl,** Frankenthal, Jan. 3, 1858—Dresden, July 15, 1928; barytone; studied with Hey and Hasselbeck and Stockhausen; concert-début, 1880; 1884–91, Leipzig City th.; then at Dresden ct.-opera.

Per'ry, (1) **G.,** Norwich, 1793—London, 1862; director and composer. (2) **Edw. Baxter,** Haverhill, Mass., Feb. 17, 1855—Camden, Me., June 13, 1924; pianist; blind from an early age; pupil of J. W. Hill, Boston; later of Kullak, Clara Schumann, Pruckner and Liszt; played before the German Emperor; in 10 years he gave 1,200 concerts in America; originated the "lecture-recital"; c. fantasia "*Loreley,*" "*The Lost Island,*" etc., for piano.

Persiani (pĕr-sĭ-ä'-nē), (1) (née **Tacchinardi**) (täk-kĭ-när'-dē), **Fanny,** Rome, Oct. 4, 1812—Passy, near Paris, May 3, 1867; daughter and pupil of the tenor-singer Nicolà T.; one of the most noted and succ. colorature-sopranos of the century; lacking in appearance and possessed of a faulty voice, she compelled homage by her perfect technic; in 1830 she m. (2) **Giuseppe Persiani** (1799—1869), a composer of operas.

Per'singer, Louis, b. Rochester, Ill., Feb. 11, 1888; violinist; pupil of Becker, Ysaye and others; toured in European cities, later active as concertm. of Berlin Philh., and San Francisco Symph., led Chamber Music Soc. of latter city, 1916–28 (afterward known as Persinger Quartet); taught Cleveland Inst. of Music, 1929–30; after latter year faculty member of Juilliard School, N. Y.

Persuis (pĕr-swēs), **Louis Luc Loiseau de,** Metz, 1769—Paris, 1839; violinist, conductor, prof. and comp.

Perti (pĕr'-tē), **Jacopo A.,** Bologna,

June 6, 1661—April 10, 1756; one of the chief 17th cent. composers of operas; pupil of Padre Franceschini; at 19 prod. a mass; church-conductor and composer of oratorios, etc., also 21 operas.

Pescetti (pā-shĕt'-tē), **Giov. Bat.,** Venice, 1704—(probably) 1766; organist and dram. composer.

Peschka-Leutner (pĕsh'-kä-loit'-nĕr), **Minna,** Vienna, 1839—Wiesbaden, 1890; soprano.

Pessard (pĕs-săr), **Émile Louis Fortuné,** Montmartre, Seine, May 28, 1843—Paris, Feb. 10, 1917; pupil of Paris Cons.; won 1st harm. prize; 1866, Grand Prix de Rome, with cantata "*Dalila*" (Opéra, 1867); 1878–80, inspector of singing, Paris schools; 1881, prof. of harm. at the Cons.; dir. of mus. instruction in the Legion of Honour; after 1895, critic; prod. many comic operas and operettas, incl. "*Le Capitaine Fracasse*" (Th. Lyr., 1878); c. also masses, etc.

Peters (pā'-tĕrs), **Carl Fr.,** Leipzig pub. firm, founded 1814 by C. F. Peters; 1893, a large library was opened to the public as the "Bibliothek Peters."

Petersen (pā'-tĕr-zĕn), **Peter Nikolaus,** Bederkesa, 1761—Hamburg, 1830; player on, improver of, and composer for, the flute.

Petersilea (pā'-tĕr-sē'-lā-ä), **Carlyle,** Boston, Mass., Jan. 18, 1844—near Los Angeles, Cal., June 11, 1903; pianist and teacher; pupil of his father, and at Leipzig Cons., winning the Helbig prize for pf.-playing; toured Germany with succ.; lived in Boston; est. 1871 "The Petersilea Acad. of Mus."; 1886, teacher New Engl. Cons.; 1884 studied with Liszt at Weimar, and gave a concert at the Singakademie, Berlin; after 1894 res. in Cal.; pub. pf.-studies.

Peterson-Berger (pā'-tĕr-son-bĕrkh-ĕr), **Wilhelm,** b. Ullanger, Sweden, Feb. 27, 1867; composer; studied in Dresden and in Stockholm where he was critic and régisseur at the opera; c. dramatic work "*Ran*" (Stockholm, 1903), and other operas, orch. pieces, 2 vln. sonatas, songs, etc.

Petit, Adrien. Vide COCLICUS.

Petrejus (pā-trā'-yoos), **Jns.,** Langendorf, Franconia—Nürnberg, 1550; mus.-printer.

Petrella (pā-trĕl'-lä), **Errico,** Palermo,

Dec. 1, 1813—in poverty, Genoa, April 7, 1877; v. succ. Italian composer of operas, rivalling Verdi's popularity, "*Marco Visconti*" and "*La Contessa d'Amalfi*" most succ.; pupil of Saverio del Giudice (vln.) and Naples Conservatorium.

Petri (pā'-trē), (1) **H.**, Zeyst, near Utrecht, April 5, 1856—Dresden, April 7, 1914; violinist; pupil of David; 1882–89 leader Gewandhaus Orch. with Brodsky, then leader Dresden Ct.-orch.; composer. (2) **Egon**, b. Hanover, Germany, March 23, 1881; pianist; son of (1); studied with Carreño, Buchmayer, Busoni; also (comp.) with Draeseke; after 1921 taught at Berlin Hochsch.; one of the most intellectual of present-day pianists and an outstanding virtuoso; concert tours of U. S. and Europe.

Petrini (pā-trē'-nē), **Fz.**, Berlin, 1744—Paris, 1819; harpist and theorist.

Petrov (pā'-trôf), **Ossip Afanassjevich**, Elisavetgrad, Nov. 15, 1807—St. Petersburg, Mar. 14, 1878; famous Russian barytone-bass, with remarkable compass of nearly four octaves (B-g''); discovered on the stage of a country fair by Lebedev; created "Sussanin" in "*Life for the Czar*"; Glinka wrote "*Ruslan*" for him, and he created rôles in many of the chief Russian operas, singing up to four days before his death in his seventy-first year.

Petrucci (pā-troot'-chē), **Ottaviano dei**, Fossombrone, June 18, 1466—May 7, 1539, inv. of mus.-printing with movable types; in 1498 received from the Council of the Republic of Venice a 20 years' monopoly of mus.-printing by his method; 1511–23 at Fossombrone with a 15 years' privilege for the Papal States; his method, which required 2 impressions, one of the lines, one of the notes, was beautifully managed and specimens are valuable; he publ. many of the most important comps. of his time and of previous composers.

Pe'trus Platen'sis. Vide LA RUE.

Petsch'nikoff, Alex., b. Jeletz, Russia, Feb. 8, 1873; violinist; pupil Moscow Cons.; at 10 entered Moscow Cons. and took prize; toured Europe with great succ., 1895–96; America, 1899; 1913–21, taught Munich Conservatory, title of prof.

Petyrek (pā'-tē-rĕk), **Felix**, b. Brünn, Austria, May 14, 1892; composer, pianist; studied at Vienna Univ. and Acad., pupil of Godowsky, Sauer and Schreker; 1919–21, taught at Salzburg Mozarteum; 1921–23, at Berlin Hochsch.; c. chamber music, piano and vocal works in modern style.

Petz'et, Walter, b. Breslau, Oct. 10, 1866; pupil of Kleffel, Rheinberger and von Bülow; 1887–96 piano teacher in America, then at Helsingfors Cons., and 1898 at Karlsruhe Cons.; c. an opera, piano pieces, etc.

Petzold (pĕt'-tsôlt), **Chr.**, Königstein, 1677—Dresden, 1733; ct.-organist and composer.

Peurl (**Bäwerl, Bäurl**, or **Beurlin**), **Paul**, organist at Steyer; important composer of suites, etc. (1611–20).

Pevernage (pŭ-vĕr-näzh), **André** (or **Andreas**), Courtray, Belgium, 1543—Antwerp, 1591; choirm. Nôtre-Dame and composer.

Pezze (pĕd'-zĕ), **Ales.**, b. Milan, 1835; 'cellist; in London from 1857; pupil Merighi; d. London, June, 1914.

Pfannstiehl (pfän'-shtēl), **Bernhard**, b. Schmalkalden, Thuringia, Dec. 18, 1861; blind organist; pupil Leipzig Cons., winning the Mendelssohn prize three times; from 1903 org. at Chemnitz; 1912, Dresden Kreuzkirche.

Pfeiffer (pfīf'-fĕr), **K.**, 1833 (?)—Vienna, 1897; dram. composer. (2) (pfĕf-fā), **Georges Jean**, Versailles, Dec. 12, 1835—Paris, Feb. 14, 1908; pianist; pupil of Maleden and Damcke; 1862 début; won Prix Chartier for chamber-mus.; critic; member of the firm of Pleyel, Wolff et Cie., Paris; c. a symph., a symph. poem, "*Jeanne d'Arc*"; pf. concertos, 3 operettas, oratorio "*Hagar*," etc.

Pfeil (pfil), **H.**, Leipzig, Dec. 18, 1835—April 17, 1899; 1862, ed. "*Sängerhalle*" (the organ of the Sängerbund); c. male choruses.

Pfitzner (pfīts'-nĕr), **Hans**, b. Moscow, May 5, 1869; pupil of Hoch Cons., Frankfort; 1892–93, teacher of pf. and theory, Coblenz Cons.; 1894–95, asst.-cond. City Th., Mayence; 1897–1903, teacher in Stern Cons., Berlin; 1903–07, cond. Theater des Westens, Berlin; 1908–18, munic. music dir. and head of Cons. at Munich; 1910–16, also opera dir. in

Strassburg; 1920–26, master class, Berlin Acad. of Arts; 1929–34, prof. Munich Akad. der Tonkunst; a prolific composer in Neo-Romantic style, he produced the operas "*Der Arme Heinrich*" (1893), "*Die Rose vom Liebesgarten*" (1909), "*Palestrina*" (1917), music drama having a largely male cast; impressive but over-weighty score much sung in Germany; "*Christelflein*" (fairy-tale opera) and "*Das Herz*," based on medieval legend (1931); also incid. music to plays; cantata, "*Von Deutscher Seele*" (sung in N. Y. by Friends of Music Soc.); other choral works, piano, vln. and 'cello concertos; much chamber and orch. music, songs, etc.; he ed. and arranged E. T. A. Hoffmann's "*Undine*" and works of Marschner for modern presentation; also c. scherzo for orch.; ballad "*Herr Oluff*" for bar. and orch., pf.-trio.

Pflughaupt (pflookh'-howpt), (1) **Robt.**, Berlin, 1833—Aix-la-Chapelle, 1871; pianist and composer. (2) **Sophie** (née Stschepin), Dünaburg, Russia, 1837—Aix-la-Chapelle, 1867; pianist.

Pfohl (pfōl), **Fd.**, b. Elbogen, Bohemia, Oct. 12, 1863; critic; studied mus. at Leipzig; c. orch. music; author of books on Wagner, Nikisch. D., Hamburg (?).

Pfundt (pfoont), **Ernst Gotthold Benj.**, Dommitzsch, near Torgau, 1806—Leipzig, 1871; tympanist; inv. the "machine-head"; wrote method for kettle-drum.

Phalèse (fǎ-lĕz'), **P.** (Petrus Phale'-sius), b. Louvain, ca. 1510; 1545, est. a mus.-publishing business; 1579 removed to Antwerp, as "Pierre Phalèse et Jean Bellère."

Phelps, Ellsworth C., Middletown, Conn., Aug. 11, 1827—Brooklyn, N. Y., 1913; self-taught; at 19 organist; from 1857, Brooklyn; teacher in pub. schools for 30 years; c. 2 comic operas; symphs. "*Hiawatha*," and "*Emancipation*"; 4 symphonic poems; Psalm 145, with orch., etc.

Philidor (rightly **Danican**) (fē-lǐ-dôr or dǎ-nǐ-käṅ). A famous French family called usually **Danican-Philidor**, the name Philidor being taken from a remark of the King comparing **Jean D.** with his favourite oboist Philidor. There seem to have

been two named **Michel**, (1) the first, b. Dauphine—d. Paris, ca. 1650, the oboist whom the King praised; the other (2) **Michel**, d. 1659, ct.-mus. (3) **Jean**, d. Paris, Sept. 8, 1679, in the King's military band. (4) **André D.-P.** (l'aîné), b. Aug. 11, 1730; cromorne-player and composer. He had 16 children. (5) **Jacques** (le cadet), Paris, 1657—Versailles, 1708; bro. of (4), oboist, etc., favourite of Louis XIV.; c. military music, etc.; he had 12 children, four of whom were musicians, the best known being (6) **Pierre**, 1681—1731; flutist; c. suites, etc., for flutes. (7) **Anne**, Paris, 1681—1728; eldest son of (4); flute-player, and conductor; before he was 20, prod. operas at court. (8) **Michel**, b. Versailles, 1683, 2nd son of (4); a drummer. (9) **Fran.**, Versailles, 1689—1717(18 ?), 3rd son of (4); oboist and bass-violist; c. flute-pcs. (10) **Fran. André**, Dreux, Sept. 7, 1726—London, Aug. 31, 1795; last and greatest of the family, the youngest son of (4); remarkable chess-player of European fame; musical pupil of Campra. At 30 he suddenly began to prod. operas with great succ., his best works being the following (among 25 notable for orch. and harm. brilliance): "*Le Diable à quatre*" (Op.-Com., 1756); "*Le Maréchal*" (1761), performed over 200 times; "*Le Sorcier*" and "*Tom Jones*" (only 8 weeks apart, in 1704; the latter containing the then novelty of an unaccompanied quartet); the grand opera, his best work, "*Ernelinde*," 1767 (revised, 1769, as "*Sandomir*"). Biog. by Allen (Philadelphia, 1863). He had four sons all ct. mus.: (11) **Pierre**, Paris, 1681—1740(?); oboist, flutist and violist; c. suites and prod. a pastorale at court. (12) **Jacques**, 1686—1725, oboist. (13) **François**, 1695—1726, oboist. (14) **Nicolas**, 1699—1769; played the serpent, etc.

Phil'ipp, Isidor (**Edmond**), b. Budapest, Sept. 2, 1863; pianist; a naturalised French citizen; came to Paris as a child; at 16 pupil of Georges Mathias, at the Cons.; won 1st pf.-prize, in 1883; studied with Saint-Saëns, Stephen Heller, and Ritter; played with succ. in European cities; est. concerts (with Loeb and Berthelier), producing modern

French chamber-comps.; reorganised the "Société des instr. à vent"; cofounder and pres. of the "Soc. d'Art"; after 1903 prof. at Paris Cons.; also taught at Fontainebleau Amer. Cons.; master classes in Boston and N. Y., 1934–35; pub. a *"Suite fantastique,"* a *"Rêverie mélancolique,"*[21] a *"Sérénade humoristique,"*[22] for orch. In U. S. since 1941.

Philippe, (1) de Caserte. Vide CASERTA. (2) de Mons. Vide MONTE. (3) de Vitry. Vide VITRY.

Phil'ipps, (1) Peters (or **Petrus Philip'pus,** Pietro Filip'po), England, ca. 1560—after 1633, organist and composer. (2) **Arthur,** b. 1605, organist at Oxford, prof., and composer. (3) **Henry,** Bristol, 1801— Dalston, 1876; bass-barytone. (4) **Wm. Lovell,** Bristol, 1816—1860; 'cellist and composer. (5) **Adelaide,** Stratford-on-Avon, 1833—Carlsbad, 1882; noted contralto, taken to America as a child; pupil of Garcia; début, Milan, 1854.

Piatigorsky (pē-ăt-ē-gôr'-skē), **Gregor,** b. Ekaterinoslav, Russia, April 20, 1903; 'cellist; studied violin, later 'cello with Glehn in Moscow; 1st 'cellist of Berlin Philh., 1923; began solo appearances with leading continental orchs., also in chamber music concerts; Amer. tours after 1929; has appeared widely in recital and as a first-rank solo performer.

Piatti (pē-ät'-tē), (1) **Alfredo Carlo,** Bergamo, Jan. 8, 1822—Bergamo, July 19, 1901; 'cello-virtuoso (son of a violinist, (2) **Antonio P.,** d. Feb. 27, 1878); pupil of his granduncle, Zanetti, and of Merighi, Milan Cons.; début, Milan, 1838; at 7 had played in an orch., 1849, 1st 'cello It. opera, London; from 1859 at Monday and Saturday Pop. Concerts of chamber-mus.; pub. a method for 'cello, 2 'cello-concertos, vocal mus. with 'cello obbligato, etc.

Piccaver (pē'-kä-vĕr), **Alfred,** b. Lone Sutton, England, Feb. 5, 1897; tenor; in early youth came to America and had vocal instruction in N. Y. and Milan; 1907–12, mem. Prague Landestheatre; after 1912, sang regularly with Vienna State Op., where he enjoyed marked popularity, esp. in Italian rôles; 1923, guest appearances with Chicago Opera.

Piccinni (or **Piccini** or **Picinni**) (pĭt-chǐn'-nē), (1) **Nicolà,** Bari, Jan. 16, 1728—Passy, near Paris, May 7, 1800; operatic composer, famous as a rival of Gluck. Son of a musician who opposed his tastes. The Bishop of Bari recognising his talent and irrepressible passion for music overcame opposition, and at 14 he entered the Cons. di San Onofrio, Naples, remaining for 12 years, as favourite pupil of Leo and Durante. He entered into competition with the popular Logroscino, and prod. the v. succ. opera-buffa *"Le Donne Dispettose"* (1754), followed by (1755) *"Gelosia per Gelosia"* and *"Il Curioso del suo proprio Danno,"* which had the unprecedented run of four years; *"Alessandro nelle Indie"* (Rome, 1758), and *"Cecchina Zitella, o La Buona Figliuola"* (Rome, 1760), the most success. work of its kind in Europe, though written in 3 weeks, were hailed as masterworks. His new dramatic fervour and his extended duets and varied finales gave him such prestige that he is said to have c. 133 dramatic works, incl. *"Il Re Pastore"* (1760); *"L'Olimpiade"* (1761) previously though less succ. set by Pergolesi, Galuppi and Jomelli; revised 1771; *"Bernice"* (1764); *"La Cecchina Maretata"* (1765); *"Didone abbandonata"* (1767); *"Antigone"* (1771). 1773, the Roman public favoured his pupil Anfossi, and hissed one of P.'s operas, which prostrated him with grief; on recovering he regained favour with *"I Viaggiatori."* In response to flattering invitations in 1776 he removed with his family to Paris, spent a whole year learning the tongue and writing his first French opera, *"Roland"* (Opéra, 1778), which had a succ. said to be due largely to the necessity the anti-Gluck faction was under to find a rival. The war between the "Gluckists" and "Piccinists" was violent and incessant, though P. regretted his position and made a vain effort after Gluck's death to raise a fund for annual concerts in his memory. He had succ. with the following French operas, *"Le fat méprisé"* (1779), *"Atys"* (1780), *"Didon,"* *"Le dormeur éveillé,"* and *"Le faux Lord"* (all 3 in 1783). In 1778, as dir. It. Opéra, whose performances alternated with the French company at the Opera, he produced his best Italian works with succ. The management simultaneously commissioned both Gluck and P. to set the opera *"Iphigénie en Tauride"*; **P.** had his libretto rewritten by Ginguené, and his version was delayed till after Gluck had made a triumph and left Paris. **P.**'s opera, though usually called a failure, ran 17 nights in spite of having an intoxicated prima donna on the first night to start the joke *"Iphigénie en Champagne."* Half a dozen others failed or were never performed. A new rival, Sacchini, now appeared. When this second succ. rival died, the large-hearted Piccinni delivered a glowing funeral-eulogy over him. 1784, he was Maître de chant at the new "École royale de musique et déclamation." His last operatic attempts in French were unsucc. At the outbreak of the Revolution he lost his positions, and retired to Naples, on a pension. But his daughter m. a young French radical, and **P.**, suspected of republicanism, was kept a prisoner in his own house for four years, in extreme poverty. 1798, he returned to France, was fêted at the Cons., presented with 5,000 francs and small irregular pension. He was prostrated for some months by paralysis; a sixth inspectorship was created at the Cons. for him, but he soon fell ill and died. (2) **Luigi,** Naples, 1766—Passy, July 31, 1827; son and pupil of above; ct.-cond. at Stockholm and dr. composer. (3) **Louis Alex.,** Paris, 1779—1850; grandson and pupil of (1); conductor and dram.-composer.

Piccolomini (pĭk-kō-lō'-mē-nē), **Maria,** Siena, March 15, 1834—near Florence, Dec. 23, 1899; mezzo-soprano of "hardly one octave and a half-compass" (Chorley), but so excellent an actress, that she became a great rage; pupil of Mazzarelli and Raimondi, Florence; début there 1852, with great succ., sang in Italy, London, Paris and New York (1858); 1863, m. the Marquis Gaetani, and retired from the stage.

Pichel (or **Pichl**) (pĕsh'-'l), **Wenzel,** Bechin, Bohemia, 1741—Vienna, 1805; violinist; c. 700 works.

Picinni. Vide PICCINNI.

Pick-Mangiagalli (pĕk'-män-jĕ-ä-gäl'-ē), **Riccardo,** b. Strakonitz, Bohemia, July 10, 1882; studied Milan Cons.; c. (ballets) *"Il Salice d'Oro"* (La Scala, 1914); *"Il Carillon Magico"* (given by Met. Op. Co., N. Y.); *"Mahit"* (La Scala, 1923); *"Casanova a Venezia"* (do., 1929); (opera) *"Basi e Bote"* (Rome, 1927); also orch. works, chamber music, vln. and piano pieces, songs.

Piel (pēl), **Peter,** Kessenich, near Bonn, Aug. 12, 1835—Boppard, Aug. 21, 1904; from 1868, teacher Boppard-on-Rhine; 1887, R. Mus.-Dir.; wrote a harm.; c. 8 Magnificats (in the church-modes), etc.

Pieragon, or **Pierchon.** Vide LA RUE.

Pierné (p'yĕr-nä) (**H. Constant**) **Gabriel,** Metz, Aug. 16, 1863—Brittany, July 17, 1937; pupil Marmontel, Franck Massenet; 1st prize (1879), do. for cpt. and fugue (1881), do. for organ (1882) and Grand Prix de Rome (1882); 1890, organist Ste. Clothilde (vice César Franck); 1893, prod. spectacle *"Bouton d'or"*; opera, *"Izéïl"* (1894); succ. *"Vendée"* (Lyons, 1897); a hymn to the Russian visitors, *"La Fraternelle,"* 1893; from 1910 he cond. the Colonne concerts Paris; he c. very successful choral work, *"Croisade des Enfants"* (1905), *"La coupe enchantée"* (Paris, 1895; Stuttgart, 1907); opera *"La fille de Tabarin"* (Op. Com., 1901), oratorio *"Les enfants de Bethlehem"* (1907); *"Les Fioretti de St. Francis d'Assise"* (Paris, 1912), etc. P. had shown a wide versatility in writing incid. music for dramas. His ballet, *"Cydalise et le Chèvre-Pied,"* in which his musical style kept abreast of the more recent harmonic innovations, had a pronounced succ. when presented in Paris, 1919. Excerpts from this score have proved pop. on orch. programmes in the U. S. His works also include the opera; *"On ne badine pas avec l'Amour"*; concerto for piano and orch.; concerto for bassoon and orch.; sonata for vln. and piano; sonata da camera; chamber trio; pieces for piano, harp and other instruments; songs, etc.

Pierre (pĭ-ăr'), **Constant,** Passy, Aug. 24, 1855—Paris, Jan., 1918; pupil of Paris Cons.; bassoon-player; assist. sec. at the Cons.; ed. *Le Monde musical;* wrote a history of the Opéra orchestra (for which the

"Soc. des compositeurs" awarded a prize, 1889), etc.

Pier'son, (1) or **Pier'zon.** Vide LA RUE. (2) (rightly **Pearson**), **Henry Hugo** (early pen-name "**Edgar Mansfeldt**"), Oxford, 1816—Leipzig, 1873; prof. of mus.; prod. in Germany 4 operas.

Piéton (pǐ-ā-tóṅ), **Loyset,** French contrapuntist, 1531.

Pijper (pī'-pĕr), **Willem,** b. Zeist (Utrecht), Holland, Sept. 8, 1894; composer; studied with Johan Wagenaar, and Mme. von Luntern (piano); active as music critic; dir. Amsterdam Cons., 1929; c. orch. chamber and choral music.

Pilati (pē-lä'-tē), **Auguste** (rightly **Pilate**), Bouchain, Sept. 29, 1810 —Paris, Aug. 1, 1877; c. operettas under name of A. P. Juliano.

Pilk'ington, Francis, Engl. lutenist and composer, 1595–1614.

Pillois (pēl'-wä), **Jacques,** Paris, 1877 —New York, Jan. 3, 1935; composer; pupil of Vierne and Widor at Paris Cons.; taught music history at Fontainebleau School after 1921; also at N. Y. Univ., 1927–30, and Smith Coll., 1929–30; won Trement, Nicolo and Rousseau Prizes; laureate of French Inst.; res. in America after 1929; c. orch., chamber music and vocal works.

Pilotti (pē-lôt'-tē), **Giuseppe,** Bologna, 1784—1838; son and succ. of an org.-builder; professor, writer and dram. composer.

Pinel'li, Ettore, Rome, Oct. 18, 1843— Sept. 17, 1915; violinist; pupil of Ramaciotti and Joachim; 1866, founded (with Sgambati) soc. for classical chamber-mus.; 1874, the "Società Orchestrale Romana," which he cond.; 1877, in the Liceo Musicale of Santa Cecilia; also cond. ct.-concerts alternately with Sgambati; c. overture "*Rapsodia italiana*," etc.

Pinel'lo de Gherardi (gä-rär'-dē), **Giov. Bat.,** Genoa, ca. 1540—Prague, 1587; court cond. and composer.

Pinsuti (pǐn-soo'-tē), **Ciro,** Sinalunga, Siena, 1829—Florence, 1888; famous vocal teacher at the R. A. M., London, from 1856; composer of operas and very popular songs.

Pinza (pĕnt'-sä), **Ezio,** b. Rome; basso; early trained as civil engineer, but gave up this profession for vocal career; début at Rome R. Op.; later

heard in Turin, Naples, for 3 years at La Scala; after 1926 sang with Met. Op. Co., also at Covent Garden and widely in concerts, incl. tour of Australia.

Pipegrop (pē'-pĕ-gróp) (called **Baryphonus**), **H.,** Wernigerode, 1581— Quedlinburg, 1655; town-cantor and theorist.

Pipelare (pē-pĕ-lä'-rĕ), **Matthæus,** 16th cent. Belgian composer.

Pirani (pē-rä'-nē), **Eugenio,** b. Bologna, 1852—Berlin, 1939; pianist, pupil of Golonelli, Bologna Liceo Musicale, and of Th. Kullak (pf.) and Kiel (comp.); 1870–80 in Kullak's Acad.; lived in Heidelberg till 1895, then Berlin; after 1901 toured U. S.; 1904 estab. music school in Brooklyn, N. Y.; wrote essays; c. symph. poem "*Heidelberg,*" etc.; later in Berlin.

Pir'ro, André, b. St. Dizier, Feb. 12, 1869; organist and historian; from 1896, teacher at the Schola cantorum, Paris; 1904 taught at "École des hautes études sociales"; 1912, director.

Pisa (pē'-zä), **Agostino,** wrote earliest known treatise on conducting, etc. (2d ed., Rome, 1611.)

Pisari (pē-sä'-rĕ), **Pasquale,** Rome, 1725—1778; bass-singer and composer, whom Padre Martini called the "Palestrina of the 18th cent."

Pisaroni (pē-sä-rō'-nē), **Benedetta Rosamonda,** Piacenza, 1793—1872; high soprano; after an illness became a contralto.

Pisendel (pē'-zĕnt-ĕl), **Jn. G.,** Karlsburg, 1687—Dresden, 1755; violinist and composer.

Pisk, Paul A., b. Vienna, May 16, 1893; composer; professor, University of Redlands, Cal., 1937.

Pistocchi (pēs-tôk'-kē), **Fran. Ant.,** Palermo, 1659—Bologna, May 13, 1726; founder of famous Sch. of Singing at Bologna; c. operas.

Pis'ton, Walter, b. Rockland, Me., Jan. 20, 1894; composer; early studied at art school, then vln. and piano privately; theory at Harvard Univ., later in Paris with Nadia Boulanger; showed radical tendencies in harmony but strongly logical sense of structure in his works; c. (orch.) Symphonic Piece (Boston Symph., 1928); Orch. Suite (Phila. Orch., 1932); Symphonic poem; (chamber music) string quartet; 3

pieces for flute, clar. and bassoon, etc.; mem. of mus. faculty, Harvard University.

Pitoni (pē-tō'-nē), **Gius. Ottavîo,** Rieti, Italy, March 18, 1657—Rome, Feb. 1, 1743; an eminent teacher and composer; pupil of Natale and Froggia; from 1677 cond. Coll. of San Marco, Rome; c. a Dixit in 16 parts for 4 choirs, etc.

Pitt, Percy, London, Jan. 4, 1870—Hampstead, Nov. 23, 1932; organist and prominent English composer; pupil of Reinecke, Jadassohn and Rheinberger; 1896 organist Queen's Hall; 1902 adviser and cond. Covent Garden; dir., 1907; 1915-18, Beecham Op. Co.; 1920-24, ass't. dir. British Nat'l. Op. Co.; 1927, mus. dir. British Broadcasting Corp.; c. Sinfonietta (Birmingham Fest., 1906); symphonic prelude "*Le sang des crépuscules,*" ballade for violin and orch.; orch. suites, etc.

Piutti (pē-oot'-tē), (1) **K.,** Elgersburg, Thuringia, April 30, 1846—Leipzig, June 17, 1902; notable organist; pupil, and from 1875, teacher Leipzig Cons.; 1880, also organist Thomaskirche; wrote a harm.; c. 6 fugal fantasias, 8 preludes, "*Wedding Sonata,*" etc., for organ. (2) **Max.,** Luisenhall, near Erfurt, 1852—Jackson, Mich., 1885; brother of above; writer, teacher and composer.

Pixis (pēx'-ēs), (1) **Fr. Wm.,** Mannheim, 1786—Prague, 1842; violinist and conductor. (2) **Jn. Peter,** Mannheim, 1788—Baden-Baden, 1874; bro. of above; pianist, teacher and dram. composer.

Pizzetti (pēd-sĕt'-ē), **Ildebrando,** b. Parma, Sept. 20, 1880; composer; studied with his father and at Parma Cons., made study of Greek and Gregorian modes, which have influenced his style of comp.; in his operas he has shown original method in which voices are treated in flexible, semi-declamatory manner; a highly sensitive writer for the chorus, which is allotted some of the most important passages in his stage works; he taught comp. at the Istituto Musicale in Florence after 1909, becoming its director in 1918; visited U. S., 1930; c. (operas) "*Fedra*" (1915); "*Debora e Jaele*" (1922); "*Lo Straniero*" (Rome, 1930); "*Fra Gherardo*" (première, La Scala, Milan, May 16, 1928, also

at Met. Op., 1929); "*Orseolo*" (Florence Fest., 1935, repeated in other cities); incid. music to "*Edipo Re*" and "*La Nave*"; "*Lamento*" for tenor and orch.; Requiem in memory of King Humbert: (orch.) "*Overture per una Farsa Tragica,*" "*Sinfonia del Fuoco,*" "*Concerto dell'Estate,*" "*Rondo Veneziano*" (N. Y. Philh. under Toscanini, 1930); 'cello sonata, vln. sonata, piano pieces and songs; has written essay on Greek music, works on contemporary composers and on Bellini; "*Intermezzi Critici,*" also many articles, some under pseudonym "*Ildebrando di Parma*"; after 1936 appointed prof. of comp. at Liceo of Santa Cecilia, Rome, to succeed the late Ottorino Respighi.

Pizzi (pĭd'-zē), **Emilio,** Verona, Feb. 2, 1862—Bergamo, 1931; pupil of Ponchielli and Bazzini, Milan Cons., graduating 1884; took 1st prize Milan, 1885, for 1-act opera "*Lina*"; 1st and 2d prize, Florence, for 2 string quartets; prize of 5,000 francs, Bologna, 1889, for succ. grand opera "*Guglielmo Ratcliff*" (Bologna, 1889); 1897, dir. of mus.-sch. at Bergamo and at church of S. Maria Maggiore; c. also 2 1-act operas "*Gabriella*" and "*Rosalba*" (written for Adelina Patti, 1893-96), etc.

Plaidy (plī'-dē), **Louis,** Hubertusburg, Saxony, Nov. 28, 1810—Grimma, March 3, 1874; eminent pf.-teacher; pupil of Agthe and Haase; at first a violinist; 1843, invited by Mendelssohn to teach at the then new Leipzig Cons., and did so till 1865; wrote text-books.

Plançon (plän-sôn), **Pol Henri,** Fumay, Ardennes, June 12, 1854—Paris, 1914; famous barytone; pupil of Duprez and Sbriglia; début, 1877, at Lyons; 1883-93, at the Paris Opéra; 1891-1904, Covent Garden annually, and 1893-1906, at Met. Op. House, N. Y.

Planquette (plän-kĕt), **(Jean) Robert,** Paris, March 31, 1848—Jan. 28, 1903; studied comp. with Duprato, Paris Cons., c. chansons and "*Saynètes*" for "cafés-concerts"; prod. succ. 1-act operetta "*Paille d'Avoine*" (1874) followed by others incl. the still pop. comic opera, "*Les Cloches de Corneville*" (Folies-Dramatiques, 1877), given over 400 times, consecutively, and widely popular elsewhere (known in Engl.

as "Chimes of Normandy"); later works incl. *"Mam'zelle Quat'sous"* (Gaité, 1897) and for London *"The Old Guard"* (1887), and *"Paul Jones"* (1889).

Plantade (plän-tăd), (1) **Chas. H.,** Pontoise, 1764—Paris, 1839; prof. of singing at Paris Cons.; ct.-conductor and dram. composer. (2) **Chas. Fran.,** Paris, 1787—1870; son of above; composer.

Planté (plän-tā), **Francis,** Orthez, Basses Pyrénées, March 2, 1839—Dax, Dec. 19, 1934; noted pianist; pupil of Marmontel at Paris Cons.; won 1st prize after 7 months' tuition; pupil of Bazin (harm.) then self-taught for 10 years, during which time he studied in seclusion in the Pyrenees; reappeared with succ.; toured widely in Europe, from 1872 until 1900, when he retired except for occasional concerts; c. transcriptions.

Platania (plä-tä'-nĭ-ä), **Pietro,** Catania, April 5, 1828—Naples, April 26, 1907; pupil of P. Raimondi, at the Cons. there; 1863, dir. Palermo Cons.; later cond. Milan, 1885–1902, dir. R. Coll. of Mus. at Naples; wrote a treatise on canon and fugue; c. 5 operas; a symph. *"L'Italia"*; funeral symphony in memory of Pacini, festival symph. with choruses to welcome King Humbert in 1878, etc.

Platel (plä-tĕl), **Nicolas Jos.,** Versailles, 1777—Brussels, 1835; 'cellist; prof. and composer.

Pla'to, eminent Greek philosopher, 429 —347 B. C.; formulated in his *"Timaeus"* a system of harm., interpreted in Th. H. Martin's *"Études sur les Timée de Platon,"* etc.

Play'ford, (1) **John,** 1623—1686; London mus.-publisher. (2) **Henry,** his son and successor, 1657—1720.

Pleyel (plī'ĕl, or plĕ'-yĕl), (1) **Ignaz Jos.,** Ruppertsthal, near Vienna, June 1, 1757—at his estate near Paris, Nov. 14, 1831; pianist, ct.-cond.; founded, 1797, at Paris a piano factory later known as Pleyel, Wolff & Co.; c. 29 symphs., sonatas, etc. (2) **Camille,** Strassburg, 1788—Paris, 1855; son, pupil and successor of above; a pianist and composer; his successor in business was August Wolff. (3) **Marie Félicité Denise,** Paris, 1811 — St.-Josse-ten-Noode, 1875; wife of (2); pianist and teacher.

Plüddemann (plüt'-dĕ-män), **Martin,**

Kolberg, 1854—Berlin, 1897; conductor and singing teacher, writer and composer.

Plutarch (Plutar'chos) (ploo'-tärk), Chaeronea, Boeotia, ca. 50 A. D.—120 (131 ?); the Greek biographer; wrote treatises *"De musica,"* containing important data.

Pochhammer (pôkh'-häm-mĕr), **Adolf,** b. Rheine, Aug. 14, 1864; pupil of Hamburg Cons.; teacher at Wiesbaden Cons.; 1902–28, dir. Cons. in Aachen; c. songs.

Pochon (pôsh'-ôṅ), **Alfred,** b. Yverdon, Switzerland, 1878; violinist, composer; 1st appeared in public at 11; pupil of César Thomson, whose ass't. teacher he was at Brussels Cons. after 1898; played in Thomson Quartet, also in orch. under Ysaye there; 1902 organised Flonzaley Quartet for the Amer. music patron, de Coppet; played 1st as leader, then as 2nd vln. in this group; c. vln. and chamber works and made transcriptions.

Poenitz (pā'-nĭtsh), **Fz.,** Bischofswerda, Aug. 17, 1850—Berlin, March 19, 1913; harpist; studied with Weitzmann, Berlin; after 1861, at the ct. opera; composer.

Poglietti (pōl-yĕt'-tē), **Alessandro,** from 1661 court organist; murdered by the Turks in the siege of Vienna, 1683; c. clavier pieces.

Pohl (pōl), (1) **K. Fd.,** Darmstadt, 1819 —Vienna, 1887; writer. (2) **Richard,** Leipzig, 1826—Baden-Baden, 1896; ed. and writer (pen-name "Hant"). (3) **Bd.** Vide POLLINI.

Pohlenz (pō'-lĕnts), **Chr. Aug.,** Saalgast, Niederlausitz, 1790—Leipzig, 1843; organist, conductor and composer.

Pohlig (pō'-lĭkh), **Karl,** Teplitz, Feb. 10, 1864—Brunswick, June 17, 1928; pupil of Liszt; cond. Graz, Hamburg, Covent Garden, etc.; 1907—1912, Phila. Orch.; 1914–24, gen'l. music dir., Brunswick, Germany; c. orch. pieces and songs.

Poirée (pwä'-rā), **Elie Émile Gabriel,** Villeneuve, St. Georges, Oct. 9, 1850 —Paris, May 26, 1925; librarian, author; c. string quartet, etc.

Poise (pwäz), **Jn. Alex. Fd.,** Nîmes, 1828—Paris, 1892; dram. composer.

Poisot (pwä-zō), **Chas. Émile,** Dijon, France, July 8, 1822—March, 1904; pianist; pupil of Paris Cons.; co-founder "Soc. des Compositeurs";

founder and dir. Dijon Cons., also from 1872 cond. Soc. for Sacred and Classical Mus.; dram. composer and writer.

Poiszl (poish'-'l), **Jn. Nepomuk,** Freiherr von, Haukenzell, Bavaria, 1783 —Munich, 1865; dram. composer.

Polac'co, Giorgio, b. Venice, April 12, 1875; pupil Milan Cons.; cond. in London, Italy, Spain, South America; 1907, Royal Op., Wiesbaden; 1908, Berlin Royal Op.; 1911–12, cond. H. W. Savage's prod. of *"Girl of the Golden West"*; 1912, engaged for Met. Op., N. Y.; 1913 also at Covent Garden; 1918–31, cond. of Chicago Op.; guest appearances in Europe; c. operas, *"Rahab"* (Budapest), and *"Fortunatus,"* etc.; m. Edith Mason; divorced.

Pölchau (pĕl'-khow), **G.,** Cremon, Livonia, 1773—Berlin, 1836; librarian and collector.

Poldini (pōl-dē'-nē), **Eduard,** b. Pest, June 13, 1869; composer of opera *"Vagabond and Princess"* (Pest, 1903), children's operas and many pop. piano pieces.

Poldowski (pōl-dŏf'-skē), pen-name of **Lady Dean Paul,** d. London, June 28, 1932; composer; daughter of H. Wieniewski; c. many modern works, chamber, pf. and vocal music.

Pole, Wm., Birmingham, Engl., April 22, 1814—London, Dec. 30, 1900; Mus. Doc. Oxon., 1864; 1876–90, examiner in Mus. London Univ.; writer; c. Psalm 100 in cantata-form, etc.

Polidoro (pō-lĭ-dō'-rō), (1) **Giuseppe,** d. Naples, 1873; singing-teacher, Naples Cons. (2) **Federigo,** Naples, Oct. 22, 1845—near Naples, Aug. 14, 1903; son and pupil of above; studied with Lillo, Conti and d'Arienzo, essayist and historian under pen-name "Acuti."

Polko (pōl'-kō) (née Vogel), **Élise,** Leipzig, Jan. 13, 1822—Munich, May 15, 1899; mezzo-soprano and writer of romantic musical essays.

Pol'lak, Egon, Prague, May 3, 1879— June 14, 1933; conductor; was from 1917 to 1931 the gen'l. music dir. of the Hamburg Op., and 1929–30, cond. with the Chicago Opera.

Pollarolo (pōl-lä-rō'-lō), (1) **Carlo Francesco,** Brescia, ca. 1653—Venice, 1722; composer; organist and assist-ant-cond. at St. Mark's; c. 3 oratorios, 68 operas, etc. His son and pupil (2) **Antonio,** Venice, 1680—

Venice, 1746; 1723, cond. at St. Mark's; c. operas.

Polledro (pōl-lä'-drō), **Giov. Bat.,** Piovà, n. Turin, 1781—1853; violinist, cond. and composer.

Polleri (pōl-lä'-rē), **Giov. Bat.,** Genoa, June 28, 1855—Oct., 1923; organist; from 1887 teacher in the U. S.; 1894, in Genoa; from 1898 dir. of the Cons.; c. organ pieces, etc.

Pollini (pōl-lē'-nē), (1) **Fran.,** Laibach, Carniola, 1763—Milan, Sept. 17, 1846; pianist and pf.-prof., 1809, Milan Cons.; perhaps the first to write pf.-music on 3 staves. (2) **Bd.** (rightly **Pohl**), Cologne, Dec. 16, 1838—Hamburg, Nov. 27, 1897; tenor, later barytone; but more famous as manager; his second wife was Bianca Bianchi. (3) **Cesare,** Cavaliere de, Padua, July 13, 1858— Jan. 26, 1912; studied with Bazzini, Milan; 1883–85 dir. of a Cons. at Padua; resigned to write and compose.

Pollitzer (pōl'-lĭts-ĕr), **Ad.,** Pesth, July 23, 1832—London, Nov. 14, 1900; violinist; pupil of Böhm (vln.) and Preyer (comp.), Vienna; toured Europe, then studied with Alard at Paris; 1851 leader H. M.'s Th., London; later New Philh. Soc.; prof. of vln., London Acad. of Mus.; 1890, director.

Ponchard (pôn-shăr), (1) **L. Ant. Éléonore,** Paris, 1787—1866; tenor and prof. at the Cons. (2) **Chas.,** Paris, 1824—1891; son of above; teacher at the Cons.

Ponchielli (pôn-kĭ-ĕl'-lē), **Amilcare,** Paderno Fasolaro, Cremona, Aug. 31, 1834—Milan, Jan. 16, 1886; opera composer; pupil Milan Cons.; organist, then bandmaster, 1881; cond. Piacenza Cath. from 1856; c. 10 operas, incl. *"La Gioconda,"* widely popular; 1902 his son discovered a MS. opera *"I Mori di Valenza"* (composed, 1878–79).

Poniatowski (pō-nĭ-ä-tôf'-shkĭ), **Jozef** (**Michal Xawery Franciszek Jan**), Prince of Monte Rotondo, Rome, 1816 — Chiselhurst, Engl., 1873; tenor and dram. composer.

Pons (pôns), (1) **Charles,** French composer; from about 1901 active as composer of many operas of lighter nature, including *"L'Epreuve," "Mourette," "La Voile de Bonheur," "Francaise";* oratorio, *"La Samaritaine";* music for various plays, a

Mass, and piano works. (2) **Lily,** b. Cannes, France, April 16, 1904; coloratura soprano, of French-Italian parentage; studied piano at Paris Cons. and singing with Alberti De Gorostiaga; in her native country she had fulfilled only minor engagements in various seaside resorts, making operatic début at Mulhouse in *"Louise,"* 1928; became protégée of Maria Gay, who discovered her unusual gifts; wholly unknown in America, she made début with Met. Op. Co., New York, as "Lucia," Jan. 3, 1931, with sensational succ., and immediately became leading mem. of that co.; has sung in opera and concert in Paris, Rome, London and elsewhere as one of leading vocalists of the day; also with wide following in radio programmes and films.

Ponselle (pŏn-sĕl'), (1) **Rosa,** b. Meriden, Conn.; dramatic soprano; of Italian parents; family name, Ponzillo; early heard as church soloist in native town, later as vaudeville singer with her sister; had vocal instruction for opera from William Thorner and Romano Romani; was brought to attention of Caruso, under whose sponsorship she made Met. Op. début as "Leonora" in *"Forza del Destino"* in 1918 with impressive success; until 1936 was a leading mem. of that co., her rôles incl. "Norma," "Donna Anna," the heroine in Spontini's *"La Vestale,"* and many other Italian dramatic works, also *"Carmen"*; in these she has shown outstanding beauty and opulence of voice; has appeared at Covent Garden, making a particular succ. as "Violetta"; also in Italy; widely as a recital and orchestral soloist, and on the radio. (2) **Carmela,** her sister, mezzo-soprano; has sung with Met. Op. and with other Amer. lyric organisations; also in concert and radio.

Ponte, Lorenzo da. Vide DA PONTE.

Pop'ov, Ivan Gegorovich, b. Ekaterinodar, 1859; pupil Moscow Phil. School, from 1900, director of society in Stavropol, Caucasus; c. symph., Armenian rhapsody; symph. poem *"Freedom,"* overture, *"Ivan the Terrible,"* etc.

Popper (pŏp'-pĕr), **David,** Prague, Dec. 9, 1843—Baden near Vienna, Aug. 7, 1913; prominent 'cellist; pupil of Goltermann, Prague Cons.; a member of Prince von Hechingen's orch., at Löwenburg; toured Europe with greatest succ.; 1868–73, 1st 'cello, Vienna ct.-orch.; 1872 m. Sophie Menter (divorced, 1886); c. excellent and pop. 'cello-pcs., a concerto, etc.

Porges (pôr'-gĕs), **H.,** Prague, Nov. 25, 1837—Munich, Nov. 17, 1900; pupil of Müller (pf.), Rummel (harm.) and Zwonar (cpt.); 1863 co.-ed. *"Neue Zeitschrift fur Musik"*; friend and champion of Wagner; lived in Vienna; 1867 was called to Munich by King Ludwig II.; pf.-teacher R. Sch. of Mus. and 1871 R. Musikdirector; writer and composer.

Por'pora, Niccolò A. (wrote his name "Niccolà," printed it as here), Naples, Aug. 19, 1686—Feb., 1766; eminent vocal teacher at London, 1729–36; ct.-conductor; as dram. composer, rival of Händel, c. about 50 operas.

Porporino (-rē'-nō). Vide UBERTI.

Porsile (pôr-sē'-lĕ), **Giuseppe,** b. Naples, 1672—Vienna, 1750; court cond.; c. 6 operas, etc.

Porta (pôr'-tä), (1) Padre **Costanzo,** Cremona, ca. 1530—Padua, 1601; writer and composer. (2) **Fran. della,** Milan, ca. 1590—1666; composer. (3) **Giov.,** Venice, ca. 1690—Munich, 1755; ct.-cond. and dram. composer.

Por'ter, (1) **Walter,** d. London, 1659; tenor and composer. (2) **Quincy,** b. New Haven, Conn., 1897; composer; grad. Yale Univ. Sch. of Mus., 1921; studied with Horatio Parker and David Stanley Smith, winning two prizes; also with d'Indy, in Paris, and Ernest Bloch; taught mus. theory, Cleveland Inst. of Mus., 1922–8; then studied three years in Paris on Guggenheim Fellowship; prof. of mus., Vassar College, 1932–8; dean of faculty, New England Cons., from 1938; c. symphony (N. Y. Philh., 1938), 4 string quartets, and other orch., chamber and vocal music; mem. bd. of dirs., League of Comps. and Internat'l Soc. for Contemp. Mus.

Portugal (Portogallo) (pôr-tŭ-gäl' or pôr-tō-gäl'-lo), i.e., "The Portuguese", **Marcos A.** (acc. to Vasconcellos, rightly "Portugal da Fonseca," not **M. A. Simão** as in Fétis), Lisbon, March 24, 1762—of apoplexy, Rio de Janeiro, Feb. 7, 1830; the most eminent of Portuguese composers; studied Italy and prod.

3 operas there; 1790 ct.-cond. Lisbon, also theatre cond. and produced 20 operas; 1810 followed the court to Rio and prod. operas; 1813 dir. of a Cons. at Vera Cruz.

Pothier (pŏt-yā), **Dom Jos.**, Bouzemount, near Saint-Dié, Dec. 7, 1835 —Dec. 8, 1923; 1866, prof. of theology, Solesmes monastery; writer and theorist.

Pott, August, Northeim, Hanover, Nov. 7, 1806—Graz, Aug. 27, 1883; violinist and composer, pupil of Spohr.

Pot'ter, Philip Cipriani Hambly, London, Oct. 2, 1792—Sept. 26, 1871; pianist, writer and composer.

Pottgiesser (pŏt'-gēs-sĕr), **Karl**, b. Dortmund, Aug. 8, 1861; pupil of H. Riemann: after 1890 lived in Munich; c. opera "*Heimkehr*" (Cologne, 1903), a Festspiel, choruses, etc.; chapter 1 of *St. Paul's First Epistle*, for voices, organ and orch.; oratorio "*Gott ist der Liebe*"; choruses, etc.

Poueigh, (poo-ā) **(Marie Octave Géraud) Jean**, b. Toulouse, Feb. 24, 1876; studied with the Jesuit fathers at Toulouse; at 19 took up harmony with Hugounant of the Cons., which he entered in 1897, receiving the second harmony prize 1898; he then studied in Paris with Caussade, Lenepveu and Fauré, receiving criticisms from d'Indy. His comps. include sonata for piano and violin (performed by Enesco and Aubert, 1906); orch. suite "*Fünn*" (1906 and 1908 at Lamoureux concerts), poem with orch. "*Sentellière de Rêve*," dramatic poem for solos, choir and orch. "*Les Lointains*"; 5-act lyric drama, "*Le Meneur de Louves*"; "*Le Soir rôde*" (song with orch.), etc.

Pougin, Fran. Aug. Arthur (Paroisse), Châteauroux, Indre, France, Aug. 6, 1834—Paris, Aug. 8, 1921; pupil Paris Cons.; 1856–59, asst.-cond. Folies-Nouvelles; till 1863, violinist at Op.-Com., then important critic, essayist and biographer; ed. the supplement to "*Fétis*" (1878).

Pouishnoff (poo-ēsh'-nôf), **Lev**, b. Russia, Oct. 11, 1891; pianist; studied at St. Petersburg Cons., with Essipov, Rimsky-Korsakoff, Liadoff, Glazounoff, Tcherepnine; 1913 taught at Tiflis Cons.; also led orch. concerts there; toured Russia, Persia and England, living in the latter

country; one of leading piano virtuosi of day.

Poulenc (poo'-lŭnk), **Francis**, b. Paris, Jan. 7, 1889; composer; mem. of former Group of Six; pupil of Viñes and Koechlin; one of most gifted composers in the little circle of insouciant Parisian modernists devoted to lighter phases of music; his works parody folk-songs, military marches, tangos, etc., and he often changes his style within a composition; c. (ballet with voice) "*Les Biches*," prod. with succ. by Diaghileff, Monte Carlo, 1925 (ballet); "*Les Mariés de la Tour Eiffel*" (given in N. Y. by Swedish Ballet); "*Le Bestiaire*" for voice and piano; "*Rhapsodie Nègre*" and other chamber music pieces; two-piano concerto; sonata for 4 hands; sonata for 2 clarinets; various song cycles with small orch., and some pop. piano pieces incl. "*Mouvements perpétuels*," "*Promenades*," etc.

Pow'ell, (1) **Walter**, Oxford, 1697—1744, counter-tenor. (2) **Maud**, Peru, Ill., Aug. 22, 1868—Uniontown, Pa., Jan. 8, 1920; notable American violinist; pupil of Lewis, later in Paris and of Schradieck, Leipzig, and of Joachim; toured widely with success Europe and America; début Berlin Phil., 1885; the same year in America with Theo. Thomas orch.; married H. Godfrey Turner. (3) **John**, b. Richmond, Va., 1882; pianist and composer; pupil of Hahr, Leschetizky and Navratil; début, Vienna, 1907, followed by tours in Germany, France, England; after 1912, heard as soloist with leading Amer. orchs. and as recitalist; c. (orch.) "*Negro Rhapsody*," "*Natchez-on-the Hill*"; piano and vln. concertos, string quartets, 2 vln. sonatas (the "*Virginiesque*" being well known); 3 piano sonatas (subtitled "*Psychologique*," "*Noble*" and "*Teutonica*"); piano suites, "*At the Fair*" and "*In the South*," etc.; active in folk-music festival movement in the South.

Pradher (rightly **Pradère**) (prăd-ā, or prä-dăr), **Louis Barthélemy**, Paris, 1781—Gray, Haute-Saône, 1843; noted teacher at the Cons. and the court; pianist, and dram. composer.

Präger (prä'-gĕr), **Fd. Chr. Wm.**, Leipzig, Jan. 22, 1815—London, Sept. 1, 1891; son of **Aloys P.**, cond.;

'cellist, later pianist and writer; c. symph. poem *"Life and Love, Battle and Victory,"* overture *"Abellino,"* etc.

Prätorius (prä-tō'-rĭ-oos) (Latinised form of Schulz(e)), (1) **Gottschalk,** Salzwedel, 1528—Wittenberg, 1573; writer. (2) **Chp.,** b. Bunzlau; pub. a funeral song on Melanchthon (1560). (3) **Hieronymus,** Hamburg, 1560—1629; son of an organist; organist; c. church-mus., etc., with his son (4) **Jakob,** d. 1651, organist; (5) **Bartholomäus,** composer, Berlin, 1616. (6) (or **Praetorius**), **Michael,** Kreuzberg, Thuringia, Feb. 15, 1571—Wolfenbüttel, Feb. 15, 1621; conductor and ct.-organist. Eminent as a composer of church- and dance-mus.; wrote valuable historical "Syntagma musicum."

Pratt, (1) **J.,** Cambridge, Engl., 1772—1855; organist and composer. (2) **Chas. E.,** Hartford, Conn., 1841—New York, 1902; pianist, cond. and composer. (3) **Silas Gamaliel,** Addison, Vt., Aug. 4, 1846—Pittsburgh, Pa., Oct. 31, 1916; prominent American composer for orch.; at 12 thrown on his own resources, became a clerk in mus.-houses; studied with Bendel, and Kullak (pf.), Wuerst and Kiel (comp.); 1871 organised Apollo Club, Chicago; 1875, returned to Berlin, and studied with H. Dorn; prod. *"Anniversary Overture"* there 1876; 1877, Chicago; gave symph. concerts, 1878, and prod. his opera *"Zenobia,"* 1882, 1885, gave concerts of his own comp. Crystal Palace, London; 1890, pf.-prof. N. Y. Metropolitan Cons.; c. lyric opera *"Lucille"* (Chicago, 1887); *"The Last Inca,"* cantata with orch. which ran for three weeks; 2 symphs. (No. 2, *"Prodigal Son"*), *"Magdalena's Lament"* (based on Murillo's picture) for orch.; an excellent symph. suite, *"The Tempest"*; a grotesque suite *"The Brownies"*; cantata *"Columbus,"* etc. (4) **Waldo Selden,** b. Philadelphia, Nov. 10, 1857; d. Hartford, July 29, 1939; Mus. D. Syracuse Univ.; prof. music and Hymnology, Hartford Theol. Sem., 1882–1917; later emeritus prof.; taught Inst. of Mus. Art, New York, 1905–20; lecturer, music history and science, Smith Coll., 1895–1908; ed. of *"New Encyclopedia of Music and Musicians"*; author, *"History of Music,"*

"Musical Ministries in the Church," "The Music of the Pilgrims," etc.

Predieri (prä-dĭ-ā'-rē), (1) **Giacomo Cesare,** d. after 1743; from 1696 cond. at Bologna Cath.; c. oratorios, motets, etc. (2) **Luca Ant.,** Bologna, 1688—1767; ct.-cond. and dram. composer.

Preindl (prīnt' 'l), **Jos.;** Marbach, Lower Austria, 1756—Vienna, 1823; conductor, writer and collector.

Preitz (prīts), **Fz.,** Zerbst, Aug. 12, 1856—July 17, 1916; concert-organist; pupil of Leipzig Cons., singing-teacher, Zerbst Gymnasium, and cantor at the ct.-church; pub. a requiem, etc.

Pren'tice, **Thos. Ridley,** Paslow Hall, Ongar, Essex, 1842—Hampstead, 1895; teacher, pianist and writer.

Pres'sel, **Gv Ad.,** Tübingen, 1827—Berlin, 1890; dram. composer.

Pressen'da, **Johannes Franciscus,** Lequio-Berria, Jan. 6, 1777—Turin, Sept. 11, 1854; violin maker.

Pres'ser, **Theodore,** Pittsburgh, Pa., July 3, 1848—Philadelphia, Oct. 27, 1925; publisher; 1883, founded and ed. *The Etude*; 1906, endowed Presser Home for Musicians, Phila.; now administered by Presser Foundation; transl. text-books; c. pf.-pcs., etc.

Prévost (prä-vō), **Eugène Prosper,** Paris, Aug. 23, 1809—New Orleans, Aug. 30, 1872, conductor and singing-teacher; prod. operas in Paris and New Orleans.

Preyer (prī'-ĕr), (1) **Gf.,** Hausbrunn, Lower Austria, March 15, 1807—Vienna, 1901; organist, pupil of Sechter; 1838, prof. of harm. and cpt. at the Cons.; 1844–48, dir.; 1844, also vice ct.-cond.; 1846, ct.-organist; 1853, con. at St. Stephen's; 1876, pensioned as "Vice-Hofkapellmeister"; prod. symphony, masses, etc. (2) **Wm. Thierry,** Manchester, Engl., July 4, 1841—Wiesbaden, July 15, 1807; studied Bonn Univ.; 1869–94 prof. of physiology, Jena; acoustician.

Pribik (prē'-bĭk), **Joseph,** b. Bohemia, 1853; pupil Prague Cons.; director of opera in various cities; from 1894 of Odessa Symph. Orch.; c. orch. suites, operas, etc.

Prihoda (prē-hō'-dä), **Vasa,** b. Vodnany, Bohemia, Aug. 24, 1900; violinist; pupil of Marak at Prague Cons.; early showed unusual musical talent; his 1st major succ. came when he played in an audition for Toscanini in Milan and made his début there in concert, 1920; since that time he has played with marked succ. in many Eur. cities, also visiting U. S.

Prill (prĭl), **K.,** Berlin, Oct. 22, 1864—Vienna, Aug. 18, 1931; son and pupil of a mus.-dir., and pupil of Helmich, Wirth, and Joachim (at the Hochschule); violinist; 1883–85 leader Bilse's orch., 1885 at Magdeburg; from 1891, of the Gewandhaus Orch., Leipzig; later at Nürnberg; 1901, at Schwerin (vice Zumpe).

Primavera (prē'-mä-vä'-rä), **Giovanni Leonardo,** b. Barletta; from 1573 concertmaster at Milan; c. madrigals, etc.

Pri'oris, Johannes, organist at St. Peter's, Rome, 1490; 1507, cond. to Louis XII of France; c. motets, etc.

Proch (prōkh), **H.,** Böhmisch-Leipa, July 22, 1809—Vienna, Dec. 18, 1878; noted vocal teacher and conductor; c. comic opera and famous vocal variations.

Procházka (prō-khäz'-kä), **Rudolf,** Freiherr **von,** Prague, Feb. 23, 1864—Mar. 23, 1936; pupil of Fibich and Grünberger; magistrate in Prague; author of biographies; c. dramatic tone story. *"Das Glück"* (Vienna, 1898); sacred melody *"Christus,"* etc.

Prod'homme, Jacques Gabriel, b. Paris, Nov. 28, 1871; writer on music; pupil of the École des Hautes Études Sociales; critic on various Paris papers; 1897–9100 in Munich; author, *"Le Cycle Berlioz," "H. Berlioz," "sa Vie et Ses Oeuvres," "Les Symphonies de Beethoven," "La Jeunesse de Beethoven," "Paganini," "Wagner et la France,""L'Opéra—1669-1925,"* etc.

Pro'fe, (or Profius) Ambrosius, Breslau, Feb. 12, 1589—Breslau, Dec. 27, 1661; organist; c. church music.

Prokofieff (prō-kŏ'-fē-ĕf), **Serge,** b. Sontzovka, Russia, April 23, 1891; composer, pianist; began study with Taneieff in Moscow at 10, later with Gliere; won Rubinstein prize at Petersburg Cons. where he studied with Liadoff, Rimsky-Korsakoff and the elder Tcherepnine; while a student c. 2 operas, 6 sonatas, many piano pieces, all unpublished; made début as comp. at 18, when Petersburg Soc. for Contemp. Music gave a concert of his works; early pub. a

Sinfonietta, several symph. poems and his 1st and 2nd piano concertos; after graduation went to London, where Diaghileff commissioned a ballet, which became his "Scythian" suite for orch.; all his works show bold harmonic clashes, many are in a somewhat satiric vein; the majority exploit an original rhythmic style and spirit of experimentation; c. (operas) *"The Gambler"* (later revised); *"The Love of the Three Oranges"* (Chicago Op., 1922); *"The Flaming Angel"*; (ballets) *"Chout," "Le Pas d'Acier," "The Prodigal Son," "Sur le Borysthene"*; (orch.) 4 symphonies, Divertimento, also a much played *"Classical"* symphony in Mozartian vein; (piano) 5 concertos, 5 sonatas, various smaller pieces; two vln. concertos, sonata for 2 violins unaccompanied, 'cello concerto, string quartet, ballade for 'cello, and many songs; has appeared as piano soloist in his works with leading Eur. and Amer. orchs.; m. Lina Llubera, soprano.

Proksch (prŏksh), (1) **Josef,** Reichenberg, Bohemia, 1794—Prague, 1864; pianist, writer and composer; founded a pf.-school; his children and successors were (2) **Theodor,** 1843—1876; and (3) **Marie,** 1836—1900.

Proske (prŏsh'-kĕ), **K.,** Gröbnig, Upper Silesia, 1794—Ratisbon, 1861: canon, conductor, publisher, editor and composer.

Proth'eroe, Daniel, Wales, Nov. 24, 1866—Chicago, Feb. 24, 1934; choral conductor; after 1894 in Milwaukee, where he led Arion Chorus beginning 1899; from 1904 in Chicago; taught Sherwood Music School; Mus. D.

Prout (prowt), (1) **Ebenezer,** Oundle, Northamptonshire, March 1, 1835—Hackney near London, Dec. 5, 1909; prominent theorist and composer. Save for a few piano lessons as a boy, and with Chas. Salaman, wholly self-taught. B.A. London Univ., 1854; 1859 took up music; 1861–73, organist Union Chapel, Islington; 1861–85, pf.-prof. at the Crystal Palace Sch. of Art; from 1876 prof. of harm. and comp. at the Nat. Training Sch.; 1879, at the R. A. M. (Vice A. Sullivan), also cond. 1876–90, the Hackney Choral Assoc.; 1874 Critic on the *Acad.* 1879, on the *Athenaeum.* Contributed 53 articles to *"Grove's Dictionary."*

1894, prof. of mus., Dublin Univ.; 1895, Mus. Doc. *h. c.* Dublin and Edinburg Univ. Pub. many valuable and original treatises, incl. *"Harmony"* (1889, 10 editions); *"Counterpoint, Strict and Free"* (1890); *"Double Counterpoint and Canon"* (1891); *"Fugue"* (1891); *"Fugal Analysis"* (1892); *"Musical Form"* (1893); *"Applied Forms"* (1895); *"The Orchestra"* (1898–1900); c. 4 symphs., 2 overtures, *"Twelfth Night"* and *"Rokeby"*; suite de ballet for orch.; suite in D; cantatas; a Magnificat, Evening Service, Psalm 126 (St. Paul's, 1891); Psalm 100 *"The Song of Judith"* (Norwich, 1867), *"Freedom"* (1885), all with orch., 2 organ-concertos, 2 prize pf.-quartets, etc. (2) **Louis Beethoven,** b. London, Sept. 14, 1864; son of above; from 1888, prof. of harm. Crystal Palace Sch. of Art; pub treatises; c. Psalm 93.

Pruckner (prook'-něr), (1) **Dionys,** Munich, May 12, 1834–Heidelberg, Dec. 1, 1896; pianist and teacher. (2) **Caroline,** Vienna, Nov. 4, 1832–June 16, 1908; succ. operatic soprano; 1855, suddenly lost her voice; 1870 opened a Sch. of Opera; pub. a vocal treatise (1872) for which she was made Prof.

Prudent (prü-däṅ) (Beunie-Prudent), **Émile,** Angoulême, 1817–Paris, 1863; pianist and composer.

Prume (prüm), (1) **Fran. Hubert,** Stavelot, near Liége, 1816–1849; ct.-prof. and composer. (2) **Fz. H.,** nephew of the above. Vide JEHIN-PRUME.

Prumier (prüm-yā), (1) **Ant.,** Paris, 1794–1868; harpist; prof. at the Cons., and composer. (2) **Ange Conrad,** 1820–Paris, 1884; son, pupil and successor of above.

Prunières (prün-yĕr), **Henry,** b. Paris, May 24, 1886; critic and writer on music; pupil of Rolland; Litt. D.; after 1919 ed. *La Revue Musicale;* organised series of modern music concerts; author of many books.

Puccini (poot-chē'-nē), (1) **Giacomo,** b. Italy, 1712; pupil of Padre Martini; organist; c. church-music. (2) **Antonio,** b. 1747; son of above; c. church-music and (acc. to Fétis) operas; m. di capp. to Republic of San Lucca; his son and successor (3) **Domenico,** 1771–1815; c. church-music and many comic operas; his son (4)

Michele, 1812–1864; pupil of Mercadante; lived at San Lucca as church and opera-composer; his son (5) **Giacomo,** Lucca, Italy, Dec. 23, 1858–Brussels, Nov. 29, 1924; noted opera composer; pupil of Angeloni at Lucca; then of A. Ponchielli, Milan Cons., graduating with a *"Capriccio sinfonico"*; 1893, prof. of comp. there; prod. 1-act opera *"Le Villi"* (Milan, 1884); extended later to 2 acts and prod. at La Scala; succ. *"Edgar"* (La Scala, Milan, 1889); succ. lyric drama *"Manon Lescaut"* (Turin, 1893); widely popular opera seria *"La Bohême"* (Turin, 1896); succ. *"La Tosca"* (London, Covent Garden, 1900); *"Madame Butterfly"* (La Scala, Milan, 1904) a dire failure and withdrawn after one performance; revised and brought out at Brescia the same year with a success that has spread all over the world, being sung throughout America in English by the Henry W. Savage Company. It was based on a play by John Luther Long and David Belasco. His next opera was also based on a play of Belasco's, *"The Girl of the Golden West"* (*"La Fanciulla del West"*), and first prod. New York Met. Op., 1910, with much success and later in Italy, England, etc. He prod. also *"La Rondine,"* a lighter work on Viennese models (Monte Carlo, 1917); his Trittico or triptych of 1-act operas, *"Il Tabarro," "Suor Angelica"* and *"Gianni Schicchi"* (Met. Op., 1918), the last of which, a sparkling comedy, has won a place in the repertoire and has been called his most musicianly work; and his last opus, *"Turandot,"* not quite complete at his death, but with a final scene by Alfano, after his sketches, prod. at La Scala, April 25, 1926. A master of fluent melody, he gave perhaps the most pop. works to the modern opera stage, despite his lack in thorough contrapuntal knowledge; this was compensated for by skilled sense of the theatre and an instinct for creating mood, pathos and atmosphere. He also c. some vocal and instrumental works not for the stage. Memoirs by Dry, Specht, etc.

Puchalski (poo-chäl'-shkǐ), **Vladimir V.,** b. Minsk, April 2, 1848; pupil at St. Petersburg Cons.; pianist; 1876–1913, director Imperial Music

School in Kiev; c. Little-Russian fantasie for orch., opera, etc.

Puchat (poo'-khät), **Max,** Breslau, 1859—in the Karwendel Mountains, Aug. 12, 1919; pianist, pupil of Kiel, at Berlin; 1884, Mendelssohn prize; c. symph. poems *"Euphorion"* and *"Tragödie eines Künstlers"*; overture; a pf.-concerto, etc.

Pucitta (poo-chĭt'-tä), **V.,** Civitavecchia, 1778—Milan, 1861; cembalist and dram. composer.

Pudor (poo'-dôr), (1) **Jn. Fr.,** Delitzsch, Saxony, 1835—Dresden, 1887; from 1859 proprietor Dresden Cons. (2) Dr. **H.,** b. Dresden, 1865; son and successor of above in the Cons., which he sold 1890 to E. Krantz; wrote many essays.

Puente (poo-ĕn'-tĕ), **Giuseppe del,** Naples, April, 1845—Philadelphia, May 25, 1900; operatic barytone and teacher.

Puget (pü-zhä), **Paul Chas. M.,** b. Nantes, June 25, 1848; pupil of Paris Cons., took Grand Prix de Rome; prod. comic opera *"Le Signal"* (Op. Com., 1886); mod. succ. opera *"Beaucoup de Bruit Pour Rien"* (*"Much Ado about Nothing"*) (ibid., 1899); incid. mus. to *"Lorenzaccio,"* etc.

Pugnani (poon-yä'-nē), **Gaetano,** Turin, Nov. 27, 1731—July 15, 1798; famous violinist, dram. composer and conductor.

Pugni (poon'-yē), **Cesare,** Genoa, 1805—St. Petersburg, 1870; dram. composer.

Pugno (pün-yō), **Raoul,** Montrouge, Seine, France, June 23, 1852—Moscow, Jan. 3, 1914 (while on concert tour); prominent pianist; pupil of Paris Cons.; 1866 took 1st pf.-prize, 1867, 1st. harm.-prize; 1869, 1st org.-prize; organist and cond., Paris; from 1896, prof. of piano at the Cons.; after 1897 toured U. S. with succ.; Officier of the Académie; prod. an oratorio, *"La Resurrection de Lazare"*; comic opera *"Ninetta"*; 2 opéras bouffes; 3 1-act vaudev.-operettas *"La Petite Poucette"* (Berlin, as *"Der Talisman"*); etc.

Pujol (poo'-hôl), **Juan Bautista,** Barcelona, 1836—Dec., 1898; pianist, author of a method; c. piano pieces.

Puliti (poo-lē'-tē), **Leto,** Florence, 1818—1875; composer.

Punto, G. Vide STICH.

Puppo (poop'-pō), **Gius.,** Lucca, June 12, 1749—in poverty, Florence, April 19, 1827; an eccentric violinist, conductor and composer.

Purcell (pŭr'-sĕl), (1) **H.,** d. London, 1664; gentleman of the Chapel Royal, and Master of the Choristers at Westminster Abbey. (2) **Henry** (called "the younger"), London, 1658—of consumption, Dean's Yard, Westminster, Nov. 21, 1695; nephew of (1); one of the most eminent of English composers. Chorister Chapel Royal, and studied with Cooke, Humfrey, and Dr. Blow; at 18 c. mus. for Dryden's tragedy, *"Aurungzebe,"* and Shadwell's comedy *"Epsom Wells"*; pub. a song; at 19 an overture, etc., to Aphra Behn's tragedy, *"Abdelazor,"* and an elegy on Matthew Locke; at 20 c. music to Shadwell's version of *"Timon of Athens"*; 1680, incid. mus., and a short opera *"Dido and Æneas"* written to order for Josias Priest for his "boarding sch. for young gentlewomen"; c. also the *"Ode or Welcome Song for His Royal Highness"* Duke of York, and *"A Song to Welcome Home His Majesty from Windsor."* From 1680 organist Westminster Abbey, where he is buried. 1682, organist Chapel Royal; 1683, composer-in-ordinary to the King. His first pub. chamber-mus. is dated the year 1683. He c. *"Odes"* to King Charles 1684, and to King James in 1685, 28 in all. He c. mus. for 35 dram. works of the time. 1695 he pub. his first real opera, *"Dioclesian."* The Purcell Society (organised, 1876) has issued many of his works in a proposed complete edition (18 vols. had appeared before 1922) and has given frequent performances of them in London. The Mus. Antiq. Soc. has pub. others; his widow pub. in 1697 *"A Collection of Ayres Composed for the Theatre and upon Other Occasions"*; also songs for 1–3 voices, from his theatrical works and odes; and the *"Orpheus Brittanicus"* in 2 parts (Part i, 1698, Part ii, 1702). W. Barclay Squire issued his original works for harpsichord (4 vols.). Playford's *"Theatre of Musick"* (1687), and other colls. contain many of his works; *"Purcell's Sacred Music"* pub. in 6 vols. (Novello). Biographical works on **P.** have been

pub. by Arundell, Cummings, H.
Dupré, Holland, Runciman, Scholes,
Westrup.
(3) **Edw.**, 1689—1740; son of above;
organist and composer. (4) **Daniel,**
London, 1660—Dec. 12, 1717; bro.
of above; 1688, organist; 1695, succ.
his bro. as dram. composer; c. incid.
mus. to ten dramas; odes, incl.
funeral ode for his brother, etc.

Putea'nus, Ericius (Latinised form of
H. Van de Putte) (poot'-tĕ) (Galli-
cised to **Dupuy**), Venloo, Holland,
1574—Louvain, 1646; professor and
writer.

Pyne (pīn), (1) **Geo.**, 1790—1877, Engl.
male alto. (2) **Jas. Kendrick,** 1852—
1938; Engl. organist. (3) **Louisa
Fanny,** England, 1832—London,
March 20, 1904; soprano, daughter
of (2); pupil of Sir G. Smart; début,
Boulogne, 1849; 1868, m. Frank
Bodda, a barytone.

Pythag'oras, Samos, Greece, ca. 582,
B. C.—Metapontum, ca. 500 B. C.;
famous philosopher and mathematician; developed an elaborate system
of musical ratios.

Q

Quadflieg (kvät'-flēkh), **Gerhard
Jakob,** Breberen, Aug. 27, 1854—
Elberfeld, Feb. 23, 1915; pupil
Church Music School, Regensburg;
from 1881, teacher; from 1898, rector
at Elberfeld; also cond. and organist;
c. 7 masses, many motets, etc.

Quadrio (kwä'-drĭ-ō), **Fran. Saverio,**
Ponte, Valtellina, 1695—Milan,
1756; theorist.

Quagliati (kwäl-yä'-tē), **Paolo,** d.
Rome, ca. 1627; cembalist; c. one
of the earliest mus. dramas (1611).

Quantz (kvänts), **Jn. Joachim,** Ober-
scheden, Hanover, 1697—Potsdam,
1773; noted flutist; inv. the second
key and sliding top for tuning the
flute; taught Frederick the Great; c.
500 flute pcs.

Quaranta (kwä-rän'-tä), **Fran.,** Naples,
1848—Milan, 1897; singing-teacher
and dram. composer.

Quarenghi (kwä-rän'-gē), **Guglielmo,**
Casalmaggiore, 1826—Milan, 1882;
'cellist, professor, conductor and
dram. composer.

Quarles, Jas. Thos., b. St. Louis,
Nov. 7, 1877; organist; pupil of
Galloway, Vieh, Ehling and Kroeger;
also with Widor in Paris; active for

many years in native city, incl.
Scottish Rite Cath.; founded Choral
Art Soc. there; after 1913 at Cornell
Univ., where asst. prof., 1916; prof.
of music, Univ. of Missouri, 1923.

Quatremère de Quincey (kăt-rŭ-măr'-
dŭ-kăṅ-sē'), **Ant. Chrysostome,** Paris,
1755—1849; writer.

Queisser (kvīs'-sĕr), **Carl T.,** Döben,
1800—Leipzig, 1846; noted trombonist.

Quercu (kvĕr'-koo), **Simon de** (Latinised from **Van Eycken** or **Du
Chesne**), b. in Brabant; theorist and
ct.-chapel-singer, Milan, ca. 1500.

Quil'ter, Roger, b. Brighton, Nov.
1, 1877; composer; pupil of Knorr,
Frankfort; c. serenade for orch.
part songs, and many attractive
songs, esp. on English texts.

Quinault (kē-nō), (1) **Philippe,** Paris,
1635—1688; Lully's librettist. (2)
J. Bap. Maurice, d. Gien, 1744;
singer, actor and composer of
ballets, etc.

Quiroga (kē-rō'-gä), **Manuel,** b. Ponta-
vedra, Spain, 1890; violinist; pupil
of R. Cons. in Madrid and Paris
Cons.; one of leading virtuosi of vln.;
has toured Spain, France, England
and (1936) U. S. A.

R

Raabe (rä'-bĕ), **Peter,** b. Frankfort-
am-Oder, Nov. 27, 1872; pupil of
Bargiel; cond. at various theatres;
1899 at the Opera, Amsterdam;
1903, dir. Kaim orch., Munich;
1907-20, court cond. Weimar; c.
song and piano pieces; after 1910,
curator of Weimar Liszt museum;
also writer on this composer and
head of a committee to publish his
complete works; 1920-34, gen. mus.
dir., Aachen; 1935, pres. of Reich
Music Chamber.

Rabaud (rä'-bō), (1) **Henri,** b. Paris,
Nov. 10, 1873; eminent composer;
pupil of Massenet and Gédalge at
Paris Cons.; awarded Prix de Rome,
1894; son of the 'cellist (2) **Hippolyte R.** (who also taught at the
Cons.); he served as cond. at the
Op.-Comique and after 1908 also
at the Opéra; 1914-18, chief cond.
at latter house; 1918-19, he succeeded Muck as cond. of Boston
Symph. Orch.; after 1920 he was
dir. of the Paris Cons. (vice Fauré);
c. many works in a witty, modern

style of considerable colourfulness and charm, including the operas "*La Fille de Roland*" (Op.-Comique, 1904); "*Le Premier Glaive*" (Béziers Arena, 1908); "*Marouf*" (Paris, 1914, also at Met. Op. and with succ. at Ravinia Op., his most effective stage composition); "*Antoine et Cléopâtre*"; "*L'Appel de la Mer*" (1-act, Op.-Comique, 1924); also the oratorio "*Job*" (1900); 4 Psalms for soloists, chorus and orch.; 2 symphonies; symph. poem, "*La Procession' Nocturne*" after Lenau's "*Faust*," a much played work; "*Poème Virgilien*" and "*Divertissement sur des Airs Russes*," both for orch.; string quartet, songs, etc.

Rachmaninoff (räkh-mä'-nē-nôf), **Sergei Vassilievitch,** b. Novgorod, Russia, April 1, 1873; pianist and composer; pupil of Siloti (pf.) and Arensky (theory), Moscow Cons.; 1891, took gold medal; c. succ. 1-act opera "*Aleko*" (Moscow, 1893); in 1899 appeared in London as conductor and pianist; from 1903 piano prof. Maryinski Inst. for Girls, Moscow; 1912, appointed chief cond. of the Opera St. Petersburg. He began a series of notable tours of Europe and (after 1905) in the U. S., where from 1917 he made his home, as his estates in Russia had been confiscated by the Soviets. He also passed summers at his villa outside Paris. His fame as a pianist has become world-wide and he has toured each season as one of the most fêted of performers, invariably playing to large audiences. His comps. include 3 symphonies; the tone poem, "*Isle of the Dead*"; 4 piano concertos; and a virtuosic work for piano and orch., "*Rhapsody on a Theme of Paganini*," in which he has toured extensively as soloist; (chamber music) "*Elegiac*" Trio; sonata for 'cello and piano; (choral works) "*The Bells*" (after the poem by Poe); six choruses for women's voices; "*Fate*"; (operas) "*Aleko*" and "*Francesca da Rimini*"; a mass and other church music; also a large number of piano works, incl. several famous Preludes, and songs which have gained a wide popularity.

Radecke (rä'-děk-ě), (1) **Rudolf,** Dittmannsdorf, Silesia, 1829—Berlin, 1893; conductor, teacher and composer. (2) (**Albert Martin**), **Robert,** Dittmannsdorf, Oct. 31, 1830—Wernigerode, June 21, 1911; bro. of above; pupil of Leipzig Cons.; 1st vln. in Gewandhaus; then pianist and organist, Berlin; later mus.-dir. ct.-th.; 1871–84, ct.-cond.; 1883–88, artistic dir. Stern Cons.; 1892, dir. R. Inst. for Church-mus., Berlin; c. 1-act "*Liederspiel*," "*Die Mönkguter*" (Berlin, 1874); a symph., 2 overtures, etc. (3) **Ernst,** Berlin, Dec. 8, 1866—Winterthur, Oct. 8, 1920; son of above; Dr. Phil. at Berlin U., 1891; 1893, town mus.-director and teacher, Winterthur, Switzerland.

Radeglia (rä-dāl'-yä), **Vittorio,** b. Constantinople, 1863; composer; c. operas "*Colomba*" (Milan, 1887), "*Amore occulto*" (Constantinople, 1904), etc. C. Turkish National Anthem.

Radicati (rä-dĭ-kä'-tē), **Felice da Maurizio di,** Turin, 1778—Vienna, April 14, 1823; violinist, court composer and 1815 cond. at Bologna; c. operas and important chamber music.

Radoux (rä-doo), (1) **Jean Théodore,** Liége, Nov. 5, 1835—March 21, 1911; pupil at the Cons.; 1856, teacher of bassoon there; 1859, won Prix de Rome with cantata "*Le Juif Errant*"; studied with Halévy, Paris; 1872, dir. Liége Cons.; pub. biog. of Vieuxtemps (1891); prod. 2 comic operas, oratorio "*Cain*," cantata "*La Fille de Jephté*" with orch., 2 symph. tone-pictures, symph. overture, Te Deum, etc. His son (2) **Charles,** b. Liége, 1877; composer: pupil of Cons. in native city; won Prix de Rome, 1907; after 1900 prof. at Liége Conservatory.

Radziwill (rät'-tsē-vĭl), Prince **Anton H.,** Wilna, 1775—Berlin, 1833; singer and composer; patron of Beethoven and Chopin.

Raff (räf), (1) Vide RAAF. (2) **Jos. Joachim,** Lachen, Lake of Zurich, May 27, 1822—Frankfort-on-Main, June 25, 1882; eminent composer, particularly in the field of programmatic romanticism. Son of an organist; too poor to attend a Univ. he became a sch.-teacher; was self-taught in comp. and vln.; 1843 he sent some comps. to Mendelssohn, who recommended them to a publisher. R. accompanied Liszt on a concert-tour as far as Cologne (1846), where he lived for a time, writing reviews; later von Bülow played his "*Concertstück*"; his opera "*König Alfred*" was accepted at the ct.-th., but forestalled by the Revolution of 1848; it was prod. in revised form at Weimar by Liszt. He pub. (1854) a pamphlet *Die Wagnerfrage*. 1854, m. the actress Doris Genast, and obtained vogue at Wiesbaden as a pf.-teacher. 1863, his first symph., "*An das Vaterland*," won the prize of the Viennese "Gesellschaft der Musikfreunde"; 1870, his comic opera "*Dame Kobold*," was prod. at Weimar. 1877, dir. Hoch Cons. at Frankfort. He was a very prolific and uneven composer. The Raff Memorial Soc. pub. at Frankfort (1886) a complete list of his works which incl. 11 symphs.: No. 1, "*An das Vaterland*"; famous No. 3, in F, "*Im Walde*" (1869); No. 5, op. 177 in E, the noted "*Lenore*"; No. 6, op. 189 in D min., "*Gelebt, gestrebt-gelitten, gestritten-gestorben, umworben*"; No. 7, op. 201 in B♭, "*In den Alpen*"; No. 8, op. 205, A, "*Frühlingsklänge*"; No. 9, op. 208, E min., "*Im Sommer*"; No. 11, op. 214, A min., "*Der Winter*" (posthumous); a Sinfonietta; 4 suites No. 2, "*In ungarischer Weise*"; No. 3, "*Italienisch*"; No. 4, "*Thüringer*"; 9 overtures, the "*Jubel-Fest-*" and "*Concert-ouvertüre*"; "*Festouverture*" for wind; "*Ein feste Burg*," "*Romeo and Juliet*," "*Othello*," "*Macbeth*," and "*The Tempest*"; festival cantata "*Deutschlands Auferstehung*"; "*De profundis*" in 8 parts, op. 141; "*Im Kahn*" and "*Der Tanz*"; for mixed chorus "*Morgenlied*" and "*Einer Entschlafenen*"; "*Die Tageszeiten*"; "*Die Jägerbraut und die Hirtin*," 2 scenes for solo voice; all with orch; the oratorio "*Weltende, Gericht, Neue Welt*" (Revelations) (Leeds, 1882); "*Die Sterne*" and "*Dornröschen*" (MS.); 4 unperformed operas, "*Die Eifersüchtigen*" (text and music); "*Die Parole*," "*Benedetto Marcello*" and "*Samson*"; mus. to Genast's "*Bernard von Weimar*" (1858); "*Ode au printemps*" for pf. and orch.; "*La fête d'Amour*" suite for vln. with orch.; 2 'cello-concertos; much chamber-mus., incl. op. 192 (3 nos., "Suite älterer Form," "Die schöne Müllerin," "Suite in canon-

form"); 5 vln. sonatas; 'cello-sonata; 2 pf.-sonatas, suites, sonatinas; "*Homage au néo-romantisme*," "*Messagers du printemps*," "*Chant d'Ondine*" (arpeggio tremolo étude), Ungarische Rhapsodie, Spanische Rhapsodie, 2 études mélodique, op. 130 ("Cavatina," and the famous "La Fileuse"), many paraphrases; many songs, incl. 2 cycles, "Maria Stuart" and "Bonded de Nesle"; 30 male quartets, etc.

Rahlwes (räl'-vās), **Alf.**, b. Wesel, Oct. 23, 1878; pupil Cologne Cons.; conductor, composer.

Raida (rī'-dä), **Karl Alex.**, Paris, Oct. 4, 1852—Berlin, Nov. 26, 1923; pupil Stuttgart and Dresden Cons.; theatre-cond. in various cities; 1878-92, in Berlin; from 1895, Munich; c. operettas, ballets, etc.

Raif (rīf), **Oscar**, The Hague, 1847—Berlin, 1899; pianist, teacher and composer.

Raimondi (rä-ē-môn'-dē), (1) **Ignazio**, Naples, 1733—1813; violinist and composer. (2) **P.**, Rome, Dec. 20, 1786—Oct. 30, 1853; extraordinary contrapuntist, rivalling the ancient masters in ingenuity; prof. of cpt., and cond. at St. Peter's; prod. 62 operatic works and 21 ballets, 4 masses w. orch. and 5 oratorios, besides the monumental trilogy "*Giuseppe*" (*Joseph*) consisting of 3 oratorios ("*Potifar*," "*Giuseppe*" "*Giacobbe*"), performed at Rome, 1852 separately, then all at once by 400 musicians, producing such frantic excitement that the composer fainted away; he c. also an opera buffa and an opera seria performable together; 4 four-voiced fugues which could be combined into one fugue à 16, etc., incl. a fugue for 64 parts in 16 choirs; he wrote essays explaining his methods.

Rains, **Leon**, b. New York, 1870; basso; pupil of Saenger and Bouhy; 1897-99, sang with Damrosch Op. Co.; at Dresden Op. in latter year; Met. Op., 1908; afterward teacher and lecturer in N. Y. and on Pacific Coast.

Raisa (rä-ē'-zä), **Rosa**, b. Bielostok, Poland; soprano; studied at Naples Cons. with Marchisio; début, Parma, 1913; was member Chicago Op. for many seasons, singing Italian dram. rôles principally, also "Elisabeth"; a voice of notable size and strong dram. talents; has also appeared at Covent Garden, La Scala (where created title rôle in Puccini's "*Turandot*"), Rome, Buenos Aires, Paris Op., Mexico City, Rio de Janeiro, Los Angeles, Ravinia and Detroit Operas, in Amer. première of Rocca's "*The Dybbuk*" (in English) with last organisation; m. Giacomo Rimini, barytone.

Ramann (rä'-män), **Lina**, Mainstockheim, near Kitzingen, June 24, 1833—Munich, March 30, 1912; pupil of Franz and Frau Brendel, Leipzig; 1858, founded a mus.-seminary for female teachers, 1865–90, a mus.-sch. at Nürnberg; pub. treatises and composed. Author of life of Liszt (3 vols.), 1880–94, a translation of his literary works, and a "*Liszt-Pädagogium*" (5 vols.), his piano works with annotations.

Rameau (rǎ-mō), (1) **J. Philippe,** Dijon, Sept. 25, 1683—of typhoid, Paris, Sept. 12, 1764; eminent as theorist, composer and organist. At 7 he could play at sight on the clavecin any music given him; from 10 to 14 he attended the Jesuit Coll. at Dijon; but taking no interest in anything but music was dismissed and left to study music by himself. He was sent to Italy, 1701, to break off a love affair, but did not care to study there, and joined a travelling French opera-troupe as violinist. Later he became organist at two churches in Paris, 1717. He studied org. with Louis Marchand, who found his pupil a rival, and in a competition favoured his competitor, Daquin, as organist of St. Paul's; **R.** went as organist to Lille, later to Clermont (where lived his brother (2) **Claude,** a clever organist, and his father (3) **Jean Fran.,** a gifted but dissipated organist and poet). After 4 years he returned to Paris, and pub. a treatise on harm. which attracted some attention. He became organist Sainte-Croix-de-la-Bretonnerie; and c. songs and dances for pieces by Piron, at the Op.-Com.; 1726, he pub. his epoch-making "*Nouveau système de musique théorique,*" based on his own studies of the monochord (v. D. D.); in this work among many things inconsistent, involved and arbitrary (and later modified or discarded) was much of remarkable even sensational novelty, such as the discovery of the law of chord-inversion. He founded his system on (1) chord-building by thirds; (2) the classification of chords and their inversions to one head each, thus reducing the consonant and dissonant combinations to a fixed number of root-chords; (3) a fundamental bass ("basse fondamentale," not our thorough-bass), an imaginary series of root-tones forming the real bases of all the chord-progressions of a composition. His theories provoked much criticism, but soon won him pupils from far and wide and the pre-eminence as theorist that he enjoyed as organist. He followed his first theoretic treatises with 5 other treatises. He now obtained the libretto "*Samson*" from Voltaire (whom he strikingly resembled in appearance) but the work was rejected on account of its biblical subject. "*Hippolyte et Aricie,*" libretto by Abbé Pelegrin, was prod. at the Opéra, 1733, with so little succ. that he was about to renounce the stage, but his friends prevailed and he prod., 1735, the succ. ballet-opera "*Les Indes Galantes,*" and at the age of 54 his masterpiece "*Castor et Pollux,*" a great succ. as were most of his later works for 23 years, "*Les Fêtes d'Hébé*" (1739), "*Dardanus*" (1739), "*La Princesse de Navarre,*" "*Les Fêtes de Polhymnie,*" and "*Le Temple de la Gloire*" (1745), "*Les Fêtes de l'Hymen et de l'Amour, ou les Dieux d'Egypte*" (1747), "*Zaïs*" (1748), "*Pygmalion*" (1748), "*Platée ou Junon jalouse,*" "*Neïs*" and "*Zoroastre*" (the "*Samson*" music with another libretto) (1749), "*Acanthe et Céphise,*" "*La Guirlande,*" and "*La Naissance d'Osiris*" (1751), "*Daphnis et Églé,*" "*Lycis et Délie*" and "*Le Retour d'Astrée*" (1753), "*Anacréon,*" "*Les Surprises de l'Amour,*" and "*Les Sybarites*" (1757), "*Les Paladins*" (1760). He c. also others not prod. His mus. is full of richness, novelty and truth, though he wrote only fairly for the voice. He said himself that were he younger he would revolutionise his style along the lines of Pergolesi. 1745 the King made him chamber-composer. His patent of nobility was registered, just before his death. He c. also many books of mus. for clavecin, etc.; of these a complete ed. is pub. by Steingräber, edited by Riemann. In 1895 a complete ed. of his works was begun by Durand, Saint-Saëns and Malherbe, including his cantatas and motets. Biog. by du Charger (1761), Nisard (1867), Griqne (1876). Other memoirs by Chabanon, Maret, Poisot, Pougin, Garraud, Brenet, Laurencie, and Laloy.

Ra'min, Günther, b. Carlsruhe, Germany, Oct. 15, 1898; organist; pupil of St. Thomas School, Leipzig, and Cons. in that city; after 1918 org. at St. Thomas' Church there; later at Dresden Kreuzkirche; also active as choral cond.; has toured widely as organ virtuoso, incl. U. S.

Randegger (rän'-dĕd-jĕr), **Alberto,** Trieste, April 13, 1832—London, Dec. 18, 1911; pupil of Lafont (pf.) and Ricci (comp.); at 20 prod. 2 ballets and an opera, "*Il Lazzarone,*" in collab. with 3 others, at Trieste; then th.-cond. at Fiume, Zara, Sinigagli, Brescia and Venice, where he prod. grand opera "*Bianca Capello*" (1854); ca. 1854, London, as a singing-teacher; 1868 prof. of singing, R. A. M.; later dir. and a member of the Committee of Management; also prof. of singing R. C. M.; 1857 cond. It. Opera, St. James's Th.; 1879–85, Carl Rosa company; and from 1881, the Norwich Triennial Festival. Wrote "*Primer on Singing.*" C. comic opera "*The Rival Beauties*" (London, 1864); the 150th Psalm with orch. and org. (Boston Jubilee, 1872); dram. cantata "*Fridolin*" (1873, Birmingham); 2 dram. scenes "*Medea*" (Leipzig, 1869) and "*Saffo*" (London, 1875); cantata, "*Werther's Shadow*" (Norwich, 1902), etc.

Randhartinger (ränt-härt'-ing-ĕr), **Benedikt,** Ruprechtshofen, Lower Austria, 1802—Vienna, 1893; at 10 soprano; conductor and composer of over 600 works.

Randolph, Harold, Richmond, Va., Oct. 31, 1861—Northeast Harbor, Me., July 6, 1927; pupil of Mrs. Auerbach and Carl Faelten. at Peabody Cons., Baltimore; from 1898 its director; pianist, played with Boston Symph., etc.

Rangström (räng'-strĕm), **Ture,** b. Stockholm, Nov. 30, 1884; composer and conductor; studied singing with Julius Hey in Berlin, 1905–07; also

for a short time comp. with Johan Lindegren in his native city and with Pfitzner in Berlin; active as music critic of the *Stockholms Dagblad* and as singing teacher for a time; 1922–25, cond. Gothenburg Musikverein symph. concerts; 1919, mem. of R. Acad. of Music, Stockholm; c. (operas) "*Die Kronbraut*" (Stuttgart, 1919), "*Middelalderig*" (Stockholm, 1918); also 3 symphonies, chamber music, choral works, more than 100 songs, etc.

Raoul de Coucy. Vide COUCY.

Rapee (rä'-pā), **Erno,** b. Budapest, June 4, 1891; conductor; grad. with honours from Cons. in native city; early appeared as pianist; came to U. S. as dir. of Hungarian Op. Co., 1913; cond. of leading N. Y. film theatres, incl. the Rialto; later musical dir. of Capitol and Roxy Theatres; for a time of the Capitol in Berlin, where he made guest appearance with Philh., also of orchs in Vienna and Budapest; later assoc. with Warner Bros. and First Nat'l. Studios, Hollywood, and more recently mus. dir. of Nat'l. Broadcasting Co. and cond. of notable series of concerts by Gen'l. Motors Symph. Orch. and outdoor stadium series in Newark, N. J., 1935–6.

Rap'pold, Marie (née **Winteroth**), b. Brooklyn, N. Y., 1880(?); soprano, sang in London at 10; studied with Oscar Saenger and sang in concert; from 1905 Met. O.

Rappoldi (räp-pôl'-dē), (1) **Eduard,** Vienna, Feb. 21, 1831—Dresden, May 16, 1903; pupil at the Cons.; 1854–61, violinist ct.-opera; leader at Rotterdam, then teacher Hochschule, Berlin; then leader opera-orch., Dresden, and 1893 head vln.-teacher at the Cons.; c. chamber-mus., etc. (2) **Laura Rappoldi-Kahrer** (kä'-rĕr), Mistelbach, near Vienna, Jan. 14, 1853—Dresden, Aug. 1, 1925; wife of above; pianist; pupil of Vienna Cons. and of Liszt.

Rase'lius, Andreas, Hahnbach, upper Palatinate, ca. 1563—Heidelberg, Jan. 6, 1602; court cond. and comp.

Rastrelli (räs-trĕl'-lē), (1) **Jos.,** Dresden, 1799—1842; ct.-conductor and dram. composer; son and pupil of (2) **Vincenzo,** 1760—1839.

Ras(o)umovski (rä-zoo-mŏf'-shkĭ) Count (from 1815 Prince) **Andreas Kyrillovitch,** Nov. 2. 1752—Sept.

23, 1836; Russian ambassador at Vienna, 1793–1809; to whom Beethoven dedicated the 3 quartets, op. 59.

Ratez (rä-těs), **Émile P.**, Besançon, Nov. 5, 1851—Lille, Aug. 25, 1905; pupil of Bazin and Massenet at Paris Cons.; vla.-player, Op.-Com.; chorusm. under Colonne; 1891, dir. the Lille branch of the Paris Cons.; prod. 2 operas "*Ruse d'Amour*" (Besançon, 1885), and succ. "*Lydéric*" (Lille, 1895); c. a symph. poem with soli and chorus, "*Scènes héroiques*," etc.

Rathaus (rät'-häs), **Karel**, b. Tarnopol, Poland (then Austria), Sept. 16, 1895; composer in radical modern style; pupil of Schreker in Vienna and Berlin; his early orch. works, an overture and "*Tanzstück*," were heard in Berlin soon after the war; his first opera, "*Der letzte Pierrot*," prod. at the Berlin State Op., 1927, showed highly original methods; succ. was gained by his opera, "*Fremde Erde*," at the same theatre in 1931, a morbid study of the fate befalling refugees in America; also c. (operas) "*Sergeant Grischa*," "*Schweik*," and "*Uriel Acosta*," (orch.) 2 symphonies, suite, etc.; (chamber music) 2 string quartets, Serenade for 4 wind instruments and piano; (choral) "*Pastorale und Tanzweise*," "*Lied ohne Worte*," prof. Queens Coll., N. Y., 1941.

Rauchenecker (row'-khě-něk-ēr), **G. Wm.**, Munich, March 8, 1844—Elberfeld, July 17, 1906; pupil of Th. Lachner, Baumgartner and Jos. Walter (vln.); dir. Avignon Cons.; 1873, mus.-dir. at Winterthur; 1874, prod. prize cantata, "*Niklaus von der Flüe*" (Zurich Music Festival); for one year cond. Berlin Philh. Concerts; 1889, mus. dir. at Elberfeld, where he prod. 3 succ. operas, "*Die letzten Tage von Thule*" (1889), "*Ingo*" (1893), and "*Sanna*" (1-act, 1893); c. also "*Le Florentin*" (1910 prod.); a symph., etc.

Rauzzini (rä-ood-zē'-nē), (1) **Venanzio**, Rome, 1747—Bath, Engl., 1810; tenor and dram. composer. (2) **Matteo**, d. 1791; bro. of above; dram. composer.

Ravel (rä-věl'), **Maurice**, Ciboure, France, March 7, 1875—Paris, Dec. 28, 1937; one of the most brilliant and resourceful of modern composers, not slavishly a follower in the tradition of Debussy, but amplifying the impressionistic formulae with an individual quality and virtuosity. His birthplace is in the Pyrenees, and childhood impressions of Spanish music are evident in some of his works. At 12 he took up res. in Paris, where he entered the Cons. in 1899, a pupil of Gédalge. In 1902 he won 2nd Prix de Rome, but in 1905, although he had already composed some of his early piano works, his brilliant string quartet and his song cycle "*Shéhérazade*," he was excluded from the competition. This summary action resulted in a controversy on the part of his admirers, and as a result the head of the Cons., Théo. Dubois, resigned. Further controversy over the merits of R. was stirred in 1907, when his "*Histoires Naturelles*" for voice and piano were premièred, this opus dividing listeners into two camps on the question whether or not he was an imitator of Debussy. His music steadily gained public following, with the publication of his brilliant "*Rhapsodie Espagnole*" for orch., the piano suite, "*Gaspard de la Nuit*," and the spirited one-act opera, "*L'Heure Espagnole*," with its element of satire (Op.-Comique, 1911). The ballet, "*Daphnis et Chloe*" (one of R.'s most inspired works) was prod. by Diaghileff in 1912 to much applause. In recent years almost everything from his pen has been greeted with enthusiasm, perhaps the two outstanding successes in his orch. production being the virtuosic "*La Valse*," an "apotheosis" of the dance, which uses all the modern wizardry of instrumentation to create a brilliant and kaleidoscopic picture; and the somewhat overrated "*Bolero*," which develops a monotonous dance theme by a process of repetition until the effect on the hearer is almost hypnotic (created to be danced by Ida Rubinstein). His piano concerto and concerto for the left hand alone (composed for Paul Wittgenstein) show cerebral manipulation of material that in some instances is trite despite its engaging flippancy. His principal works, in addition to those already named, include the charming series of richly coloured nursery pictures for orch., "*Ma Mère L'Oye*"

(French equivalent of Mother Goose); his scintillant orchestration of Moussorgsky's "*Pictures from an Exhibition*"; a nursery opera, "*L'Enfant et les Sortilèges*," in which a naughty child is punished when his toys come to life; his popular Introduction and Allegro for flute and string quartet; chamber works, incl. a trio and a septet, and a large number of much-played piano pieces, some artistic songs and vln. works. A biog. of R. has been written by Roland-Manuel.

Ra'venscroft, (1) **Thos.**, 1593—London, 1635 (?); prominent early English composer and writer. (2) **John**, d. 1740; violinist, London.

Ravera (rä-vä'-rä), **Niccolò Teresio**, b. Alessandria, Italy, Feb. 24, 1851—(?); pupil Milan Cons.; won first prizes for pf., organ and comp.; cond. Th.-Lyrique de la Galérie-Vivienne, Paris; c. 7 operas.

Ravina (rä-vē'-nä), **J. H.**, Bordeaux, May 20, 1818—Paris, Sept. 30, 1906; pianist; pupil of Zimmermann (pf.) and Laurent (theory) at Paris Cons., won first pf.-prize, 1834; 1st harm.-prize, 1836; asst.-teacher there till 1837, and also studied with Reicha and Leborne; made tours; 1861, Chev. of the Legion of Honour; c. a concerto, etc.

Raway (rä'vĭ), **Erasme**, Liége, June 2, 1850—Brussels, Oct., 1918; priest; teacher and cathedral cond. at Liége; c. church works, Hindu scenes, a dramatic dialog. "*Freya*," etc.

Raymond (rĕ'-môṅ), **G. M.**, Chambéry, 1769—1839; acoustician.

Rea (rā), **Wm.**, London, March 25, 1827—Newcastle, March 8, 1903; articled pupil of Josiah Pittmann; at 16, organist; studied with Sterndale Bennett (pf., comp. and instr.) then at Leipzig and Prague; returned to London, and gave chamber-concerts; 1856, founded the Polyhymnian Choir; organist at various churches; c. anthems, etc.

Reading (rĕd'-ĭng), (1) **John**, 1645—Winchester, Engl., 1692; organist and composer of "Dulce domum," etc. (2) **John**, 1677—London, Sept. 2, 1764; son of above; organist and composer; the "*Portuguese Hymn*," "*Adeste Fideles*," is credited to him. (3) **John**, 1674—1720; organist.

Reay (rā), **Samuel**, Hexham, Engl., March 17, 1822—Newark-on-Trent,

July 21, 1905; a pupil of Henshaw and Stimpson; 1841, organist St. Andrew's, Newcastle; song-school-master, Newark Parish Ch. and cond. Philh. Soc.; c. Psalm 102, with string-orch.; Communion Service, etc.

Rebel (rŭ-bĕl), (1) **J. Ferry**, Paris, 1661—1747; conductor and composer. (2) **Fran.**, Paris, 1701—1775; violinist and dram. composer.

Rebello (rā-bĕl'-lō), **João Lourenço** (**João Soares**), Caminha, 1609—San Amaro, Nov. 16, 1661, eminent Portuguese composer.

Reber (rŭ-bā), **Napoléon H.**, Mühlhausen, Alsatia, Oct. 21, 1807—Paris, Nov. 24, 1880; 1851, prof. of comp., Paris Cons.; pub. one of the best French harm. treatises (1862); c. comic operas, etc.

Rebicek (rā'-bĭ-tsĕk), **Josef**, Prague, Feb. 7, 1844—Berlin, March 24, 1904; violinist; pupil Prague Cons.; 1861, Weimar ct.-orch.; 1863, leader royal th., Wiesbaden; 1875, R. Mus.-Dir.; 1882, leader and op.-dir. Imp. Th. Warsaw; 1891, cond. Nat. Th., Pesth; 1893, at Wiesbaden; 1897, cond. Berlin Philh. Orch.

Rebikov (rĕb'-ĭ'-kôf), **Vladimir Ivanovich**, Krasnojarsk, Siberia, June 1 (N. S.), 1866—Yalta, Crimea, Dec. 1, 1920; pupil Moscow Cons., and in Berlin; 1897-1902 cond. in Kishinev; later in Berlin and Vienna; theorist and composer of originality, as in his piece "*Satan's Diversions*," his "*Melomimik*," lyric scenes in pantomime, 1-act fairy opera, "*Der Christbaum*," etc.

Rebling (rāp'-lĭng), (1) **Gv.**, Barby, Magdeburg, July 10, 1821—Magdeburg, Jan. 9, 1902; pupil of Fr. Schneider at Dessau; 1856, R. Mus.-Dir.; 1858, organist Johanniskirche; 1846, founded and cond. a church choral soc.; 1897, c. Psalms, "*a cappella*," 'cello-sonata, etc. (2) **Fr.**, Barby, Aug. 14, 1835—Leipzig, Oct. 15, 1900; pupil of Leipzig Cons. and of Götz (singing); 1865-78, tenor at various theatres; from 1877, singing-teacher Leipzig Cons.

Red'head, **Richard**, Harrow, Engl., 1820—May, 1901; studied at Magdalen Coll., Oxford; organist of St. Mary Magdalene's Ch., London; ed. colls.; c. masses, etc.

Ree (rā), (1) **Anton**, Aarhus, Jutland, 1820—Copenhagen, 1886; pianist, teacher and writer. (2) **Louis,** b. Edinburgh, 1861; pianist.

Reed, (1) Thos. German, Bristol, 1817—Upper East Sheen, Surrey, 1888; pianist and singer. In 1844 he m. (2) **Priscilla Horton** (1818—1895), a fine actress and contralto. Their entertainments were continued by their son (3) **Alfred German** (d. London, March 10, 1895). (4) **Robt. Hopké,** and (5) **Wm.,** bros. of (1); 'cellists.

Reeve, Wm., London, 1757—1815; c. operettas.

Reeves, (1) **(John) Sims,** Woolwich, Sept. 26, 1818 (acc. to Grove, Shooters Hill, Oct. 21, 1822)—London, Oct. 25, 1900; noted tenor; at 14 organist of North Cray Ch.; learned the vln., 'cello, oboe and bassoon; and studied with J. B. Cramer (pf.) and W. H. Callcott (harm.); début as barytone, 1839, studied with Hobbs and Cooke, and sang minor tenor parts at Drury Lane; then studied with Bordogni, Paris, and Mazzucato, Milan, sang at La Scala, 1846, Drury Lane, 1847, with great succ.; début in Italian opera, 1848, at H. M.'s Th., also in oratorio at the Worcester and Norwich Festivals, the same year; retired in 1891, but on account of reverses, reappeared in 1893; and 1898 made succ. tour of South Africa; pub. "*Life and Recollections*" (London, 1888); he m., 1850, (2) **Emma Lucombe,** opera and concert soprano. (3) **Herbert,** his son and pupil, studied at Milan; concert-début, 1880.

Refice (rä-fē'-chä), **Licinio,** b. Rome, Feb. 12, 1885; composer; a Roman Catholic priest; pupil of Boezi, Falchi and Renzi, at St. Cecilia Liceo; after 1910 taught liturgical music at Pontifical School of Sacred Music; 1911, cond. Capella Liberiana at Church of S. Ma. Maggiore; c. many motets, masses, cantatas, and a sacred opera, "*Cecilia,*" which had marked succ. in Rome and Buenos Aires.

Regan, Anna. Vide SCHIMON-REGAN.

Reger (rä'-gĕr), **Max,** Brand, Bavaria, March 19, 1873—Leipzig, May 11, 1916; pupil of Lindner and H. Riemann; important composer, especially in chamber music and sacred music; 1891–96 he was teacher at Wiesbaden Cons., then took his year of military service. After a severe illness he settled in Munich, 1901,

and married there; 1905 he taught counterpoint at the Royal Academy; 1907–08 taught composition at Munich Cons., and was University music dir.; 1908 was named Royal Prof. and Dr. Phil. by Jena; 1910 Mus. D. Berlin U.; in 1911, he became General Music Dir. at Meiningen, cond. Meiningen orch., continuing to teach one day a week at Leipzig Cons. He toured with the orch., 1912. His compositions are exceedingly numerous, and include a Sinfonietta, op. 90, symph. prologue to a tragedy, op. 108, "*Lustpiel*" overture (1911), violin concerto; a vast amount of chamber music, sonatas for piano, organ, violin, clarinet, 'cello, variations, fugues, canons in all keys, left-hand studies, and transcriptions for piano; much organ music; "*Gesang der Verklärten*" for choir and orch., "*An die Hoffnung*" for contralto and orch. (1912); three orch. pieces "*Nocturne,*" "*Elfenspuk,*" and "*Helios*" (1912); organ fantasie and fugue,B-A-C-H; violin suite op. 103, sonata op. 42, for violin alone; tone-poems for pianos, "*Aus meinem Tagebuch*"; cantatas, male and mixed choruses, and many beautiful sacred and secular songs. His music as a whole is marked by elaborate formal and contrapuntal structure, sometimes developed to the point of pedantry. R., though a strong influence upon German musicians of his time, represents a type of comp. in whom ponderous scientific knowledge and great practical ability are unleavened by a sense of proportion. In the field of organ comp. he holds an honourable place. Biog. also thematic catalogue of his works, by Fritz Stein.

Régis (rä'-zhēs), **Jns.,** Belgian cptist.; contemporary of Okeghem.

Regnal, Fr. Vide FR. D'ERLANGER.

Regnart (or **Regnard**) (rĕkh'-närt), (1) **Jacob,** Netherlands, 1540—Prague, ca. 1600; Innsbruck, cond.; popular composer. His brothers (2) **Fz.,** (3) **K.,** and (4) **Pascasius,** also c. songs.

Rehbaum (rä'-bowm), **Theobald,** Berlin, Aug. 7, 1835—Feb. 2, 1918; pupil of H. Ries (vln.) and Kiel (comp.); c. 7 operas incl. "*Turandot*" (Berlin, 1888), etc.

Rehberg (rä'-bĕrkh), (1) **Willy,** Morges, Switz., 1863—Mannheim, 1937; son and pupil of (2) **Fr. R.** (a mus.-

teacher); later studied at Zurich Mus.-Sch. and Leipzig Cons.; pf.-teacher there till 1890; 1888–90, cond. at Altenburg; 1890, head pf.-teacher Geneva Cons.; 1892, also cond. Geneva Municipal Orch.; 1907, taught Hoch Cons., Frankfort; 1917, dir. Mannheim Hochsch.; 1921–26, dir. Basel Cons.; c. vln.-sonata, pf.-sonata, etc. (3) **Walter, b.** Geneva, 1900; son of (2); pianist.

Rehfeld (rā'-fĕlt), **Fabian,** Tuchel, W. Prussia, Jan. 23, 1842—Berlin, Nov. 11, 1920; violinist; pupil of Zimmermann and Grünwald, Berlin, 1868, royal chamber-mus.; 1873, leader ct.-orch.

Reicha (rī'-khä), (1) (rightly **Rejcha,** rä'-khä), **Jos.,** Prague, 1746—Bonn, 1795; 'cellist, violinist, and cond. at Bonn. (2) **Anton** (Jos.), Prague, Feb. 25, 1770—Paris, May 28, 1836; nephew and pupil of above; flutist, vla.-player, and teacher.

Rehkemper (rā'-kĕmp-ĕr), **Heinr.,** b. Schwerte, 1894; barytone; Munich Op., after 1926.

Reichardt (rī'-khärt), (1) **Jn. Fr.,** Königsberg, Nov. 25, 1752—Giebichenstein near Halle, June 27, 1814; cond., editor and dram. composer; pupil of Richter and Veichtner; 1775, ct.-cond. to Frederick the Great, later to Fr. Wm. II. and III., then to Jerome Bonaparte; he prod. many German and Italian operas and influential Singspiele; also c. 7 symphs., a passion, etc., and notable songs. (2) **Luise,** Berlin, 1779—Hamburg, 1826; daughter of above; singing-teacher. (3) **Gv.,** Schmarsow, near Demmin, 1797—Berlin, 1884; conductor; c. pop. songs. (4) **Alex.,** Packs, Hungary, 1825—Boulogne-sur-Mer, 1885; tenor.

Reichel (rī'-khĕl), (1) **Ad. H. Jn.,** Tursznitz, W. Prussia, 1817—Berne, March 4, 1896; pupil of Dehn and L. Berger; Berlin; pf.-teacher, Paris; 1857–67, taught comp. at Dresden Cons.; 1867, municipal mus.-dir. Berne, Switz.; c. pf.-concertos, etc. (2) **Fr.,** Oberoderwitz, Lusatia, 1833 —Dresden, 1889; cantor and org.-composer.

Reicher-Kindermann (rī'-khĕr-kĭn'-dĕr-män), (1) **Hedwig,** Munich, 1853 —Trieste, 1883; soprano; daughter of the barytone, A. Kindermann; m. (2) **Reicher,** an opera singer.

Reichmann (rīkh'-män), **Th.,** Rostock, March 15, 1849—Marbach, May 22, 1903; barytone, pupil of Mantius, Elsler, Ress and Lamperti; 1882–89, ct.-opera Vienna; 1882, created "Amfortas" in "*Parsifal,*" Bayreuth; 1889–90, New York; then Vienna.

Reichwein (rīkh'-vīn), **Leopold,** director and composer; b. Breslau, May 16, 1878; cond. 1909 of the Court Opera at Carlsruhe; after 1913 in Vienna; 1921, succeeded Schalk as cond. of Musikfreunde concerts and Singverein there; c. operas "*Vasantasena*" (Breslau, 1903), "*Die Liebenden von Kandahar*" (1907), and music for "*Faust*" (Mannheim, 1909).

Reid (rēd), General **John,** Straloch, Perthshire, 1721(?)—London, 1806; a musical amateur, founded a chair of mus. Edinburgh Univ.

Reijnvaan (or **Reynwaen**) (rĕn'-vän), **Jean Verschuere,** LL.D.; Middleburg, Holland, 1743—Flushing, May 12, 1809; organist and composer.

Reimann (rī'-män), (1) **Mathieu** (**Matthias Reymannus**), Löwenberg, 1544 —1597; composer. (2) **Ignaz,** Albendorf, Silesia, 1820—Rengersdorf, 1885; composer. (3) **H.,** Rengersdorf, March 14, 1850—Berlin, May 24, 1906; son and pupil of (2); 1887 asst.-libr., R. Library, Berlin; organist to the Philh. Soc.; teacher of organ and theory, Scharwenka-Klindworth Cons., and (1895) organist at the Gnadenkirche; prominent critic and writer; c. sonatas and studies for organ.

Reinagle (rī'-nä-gĕl), (1) **Jos.,** Portsmouth, 1762—Oxford, 1836; son of a German mus., horn-player and composer, 1785. (2) **Hugh,** d. young at Lisbon; bro. of above; 'cellist. (3) **Alex.,** Portsmouth, 1756—Baltimore, Md., 1809; versatile composer, pianist, cond. and theatre manager; his works are among the earliest prod. in America that have definite value and historical interest.

Reinecke (rī'-nĕk-ĕ), (1) **Ld., K.** Dessau, 1774—Güsten, 1820; leader and dram. composer. (2) **K. (H. Carsten),** Altona, June 23, 1824—Leipzig, March 10, 1910; noteworthy pianist and teacher; son and pupil of a music-teacher; at 11, played in public; at 19 toured Denmark and Sweden; at Leipzig advised by Mendelssohn and Schumann; ct.-pianist at Copenhagen; 1851 teacher Cologne Cons.; 1854–59 mus.-dir.

Barmen; 1859–60 mus.-dir. and cond. Singakademie, Breslau; 1860–95 cond. Gewandhaus Concerts, Leipzig; also prof. of pf.-playing and free comp., Leipzig Cons.; 1897 "Studiendirektor" there; Dr. Phil. *h. c.*, Leipzig Univ.; Royal Professor; toured almost annually with great succ., c. 2 masses, 3 symphs., 5 overtures: *"Dame Kobold," "Aladin," "Friedensfeier," "Festouvertüre," "In Memoriam"* (of David), *"Zenobia,"* introd. and fugue with chorus and orch.; funeral march for Emperor William I.; concertos for vln., 'cello and harp.; prod. grand opera *" König Manfred"* (Wiesbaden, 1867); 3 comic operas; fairy opera *"Die Teufelchen auf der Himmelswiese"* (Glarus, 1899); mus. to Schiller's *"Tell"*; oratorio *"Belsazar"*; 2 cantatas *"Hakon Jarl,"* and *"Die Flucht nach Ægypten,"* with orch.; 5 fairy cantatas, 4 concertos, many sonatas; *"Aus der Jugendzeit,"* op. 106; *" Neues Notenbuch fur Kleine Leute,"* op. 107; concert-arias, 20 canons for 3 female voices, and excellent songs for children.

Reiner (rī'-nĕr), (1) **Jacob**, Altdorf, Württemberg, ca. 1560–1606; composer. (2) **Fritz**, b. Budapest, Dec. 19, 1888; conductor; studied Budapest Acad. of Music, comp. with Hans Koessler, piano with Stephen Thoman; cond. Budapest Op.-Comique, 1909; Laibach Op., 1910; Budapest Volksop., 1911–14; Dresden State Op., and symph. concerts, 1914–21; Cincinnati Symph., 1922–31; thereafter headed orch. dept., Curtis Inst. of Music, Phila.; appearances with Phila. Orch.; at Hollywood Bowl and in various other Amer. and Eur. cities; cond. German opera perfs. of Phila. Orch., 1934–35; at Covent Garden, 1936, and San Francisco Op.; 1938 cond. Pittsburgh Symph. Orch.; m. Berta Gerster-Gardini; divorced; (2) Carlotta Irwin.

Rein'hardt, Heinrich, Pressburg, April 13, 1865—Vienna, Jan. 31, 1922; c. operettas for Vienna: *"Das süsse Mädel"* (1901); *"Ein Mädchen für Alles"* (Munich, 1908). *"Die Sprudelfee"* (which had marked succ. in America as *"The Spring Maid"*), etc.; music ed., Vienna *Tageblatt*.

Reinhold (rīn'-hŏlt), **Th. Christlieb**, d. Dresden, March 24, 1755; cantor, teacher and composer.

Reinke(n) (rīn'-kĕn) (or **Reinicke**), **Jn. Adam**, Deventer, Holland, April 27, 1623—Hamburg, Nov. 24, 1722; noted organist and composer.

Reinsdorf (rīns'-dôrf), **Otto**, Köselitz, 1848—Berlin, 1890; editor.

Reinthaler (rīn'-täl-ĕr), **K. (Martin)**, Erfurt, 1822—Bremen, 1896; singing-teacher, organist, conductor and dram. composer.

Reisenauer (rī'-zĕ-now-ĕr), **Alfred**, Königsberg, Nov. 1, 1863—Liebau, Russia, Oct. 3, 1907; pianist; pupil of L. Köhler and Liszt; début, 1881, Rome, with Liszt; toured; composer; taught Leipzig Cons., 1900–06.

Reiser (rī'-zĕr), **Aug. Fr.**, Gammertingen, Württemberg, Jan. 19, 1840—Haigerloch, Oct. 22, 1904; 1880–86, ed. Cologne *Neue Musikzeitung;* c. 2 symphs., choruses, incl. *"Barbarossa,"* for double ch., etc.

Reiset. Vide DE GRANDVAL.

Reiss (rīs), (1) **K. H. Ad.**, Frankfort-on-Main, April 24, 1829—April 5, 1908; pupil of Hauptmann, Leipzig; chorus-master and cond. various theatres; 1854, 1st cond. Mayence; 1856, 2d., later 1st cond. at Cassel (vice Spohr). 1881–86, ct.-th., Wiesbaden; prod. opera, *"Otto der Schütz"* (Mayence, 1856). (2) **Albert**, b. Berlin, 1870—Nice, 1940; tenor; studied law, then became an actor, discovered by Pollini; pupil of Liebau and Stolzenberg; début in opera at Königsberg, later at Posen and Wiesbaden, famous as "Mime" and "David," 1901–17, at Met. Op., N. Y.

Reissiger (rīs'-sĭkh-ĕr), (1) **Chr. Gl.**, ca. 1790; comp. (2) **K. Gl.**, Belzig, near Wittenberg, Jan. 31, 1798—Dresden, Nov. 7, 1859; son of above; pupil of Schicht and Winter; singer, pianist and teacher; 1826, on invitation, organised at The Hague the still succ. Cons.; ct.-cond. Dresden (vice Weber); c. 8 operas, 10 masses. (3) **Fr. Aug.**, Belzig, 1809—Frederikshald, 1883; bro. of above; military bandm.; composer.

Reissmann (rīs'-män), **Aug.**, Frankenstein, Silesia, Nov. 14, 1825—Berlin, Dec. 1, 1903; studied there and at Breslau; 1863–80, lectured at Stern Cons., Berlin; then lived in Leipzig (Dr. Phil., 1875), Wiesbaden and Berlin; writer of important historical works, and lexicographer; c. 3 operas, 2 dram. scenes, an oratorio, etc.

Reiter (rī'-tĕr), (1) **Ernst,** Wertheim, Baden, 1814—Basel, 1875; vln.-prof. and dram. composer. (2) **Josef,** b. Braunau, Jan. 19, 1862; composer; Viennese composer of operas, including *"Der Totentanz"* (Dessau, 1908), symph., cantatas, male choruses, etc.; 1908–11, dir., Mozarteum at Salzburg.

Rellstab (rĕl'-shtäp), (1) **Jn. K. Fr.,** Berlin, 1759—1813; son and successor of owner of a printing-establishment; critic, teacher, and composer. (2) (**H. Fr.**) **L.,** Berlin, 1799—1860; the noted novelist, son of above; wrote biog., libretti and criticisms which got him twice imprisoned; c. part-songs.

Remenyi (rĕm'-ān-yē), **Eduard,** Heves, Hungary, 1830—on the stage, of apoplexy, San Francisco, Cal., May 15, 1898; noted violinist; pupil of Böhm, Vienna Cons.; banished for his part in Hungarian Revolution; toured America; 1854, solo violinist to Queen Victoria; 1860, pardoned by Austrian Emperor and made ct.-violinist; toured widely, 1866 round the world; c. a vln.-concerto, transcriptions, etc.

Rem'mert, **Martha,** b. Gross-Schwein, near Glogau, Aug. 4, 1854; pianist; pupil of Kullak, Tausig and Liszt; 1900, founder Liszt Acad. for piano in Berlin.

Rémusat (Rémuzat) (rä-mü-zä), **Jean,** Bordeaux, 1815—Shanghai, 1880; flute-virtuoso; writer and composer.

Remy, **W. A.** Vide MAYER, WM.

Rénard (rä-năr), **Marie,** b. Graz, Jan. 18, 1863; soprano; début, Graz, 1882; 1885–88, Berlin ct.-opera; 1888–1901, Vienna ct.-opera; m. Count Kinsky and retired from stage.

Renaud (rŭ-nō), (1) **Albert,** b. Paris, 1855; pupil of Franck and Délibes; organist St. François-Xavier; critic, *La Patrie;* c. 4-act "féerie," *"Aladin"* (1891); opéra comique *"À la Houzarde"* ('91); operetta *"Le Soleil de Minuit"* (1898); ballets, etc. (2) **Maurice,** Bordeaux, 1862—Paris, Oct. 16, 1933; notable bass; pupil of Paris Cons.; 1883–90, at R. Opera, Brussels; 1890–91, Op.-Com., Paris; from 1891–1902, Gr. Opéra; equally fine in comic and serious works; had a repertory of 50 operas; sang with Chicago Op. Co. and at Manhattan Op., N. Y.

Rendano (rĕn-dä'-nō), **Alfonso,** Carolei, Calabria, April 5, 1853—Rome, Sept. 10, 1931; pianist; pupil of Naples Cons., Thalberg and Leipzig Cons.; toured; c. piano-pcs.

Renié (rŭn-yā'), **Henriette,** b. Paris, Sept. 18, 1875; harpist, composer; pupil of Paris Cons.; has appeared with leading French orchs.; c. many works for harp; a noted teacher.

Ren'ner, **Josef,** Schmatzhausen, Bavaria, 1832—Ratisbon, 1895; editor.

Respighi (rĕ-spē'-gē), **Ottorino,** Bologna, July 9, 1879—Rome, April 18, 1936; composer, conductor, pianist; studied Bologna Liceo, vln. with Sarti, comp. with Martucci; also in St. Petersburg, 1902, with Rimsky-Korsakoff; later in Berlin with Bruch; prof. of comp., Bologna Liceo, 1913; after 1924, at Liceo of Santa Cecilia, Rome; appeared as guest cond. and pianist in his works in Europe and America; c. (operas) *"Re Enzo," "Semirama," "Maria Vittoria," "Belfagor"* (1923), *"La Campana Sommersa"* (after Hauptmann's drama), heard in several Italian theatres, also at Met. Op., 1928; *"La Fiamma"* (Rome, Buenos Aires and Chicago Op., 1935, with considerable succ.); (opera-oratorio) *"Maria Egiziaca,"* world première, N. Y. Philh. in staged version, 1932, composer conducting, also later in Paris; another opera, *"Lucrezia,"* completed just before his death; (puppet play) *"The Sleeping Princess";* a series of highly succ. symph. poems of colorful descriptive nature, incl. *"Fountains of Rome," "Pines of Rome," "Roman Festivals," "Church Windows," "Primavera," "Ballade of the Gnomides";* suite to the *"Birds"* of Aristophanes; piano concerto, string quartets, and many other works for vln., organ, piano, as well as orch. transcriptions of Bach and Vivaldi music, and old works for lute; ed. Monteverdi's opera *"Orfeo"* in free, modern version; m. Elsa Sangiacomo, soprano.

Reszké. Vide DE RESZKE.

Rethberg (rāt'-bĕrkh), **Elisabeth** (née **Sättler**), b. Schwarzenberg, Germany, Sept. 22, 1894; soprano; studied piano, later voice, at Dresden Cons.; début, Dresden Op., 1915, sang with this company until 1922; début with Met. Op., N. Y., in latter year as "Aïda" and took leading place as a singer of German and Italian rôles; guest appearances, Covent Garden, La Scala, Rome R. Op., Paris Op., Budapest, Vienna, at Ravinia (Chicago), Los Angeles and San Francisco. Has toured widely as recitalist and soloist with leading orchs. in Europe and U. S.; created rôle of "Helen" in Strauss's "*Aegyptische Helena*" at Dresden, 1928.

Réti (rā'-tē), **Rudolf**, b. Uzize, Serbia, Nov. 27, 1885; composer of modern-style chamber music, songs, etc.

Reubke (roip'-kě), (1) **Ad.**, Halberstadt, 1805—1875; org.-builder at Hausendorf, near Quedlinburg. (2) **Emil**, Hausneindorf, 1836—1885; son and successor of above. (3) **Julius R.**, Hausneindorf, 1834—Pillnitz, 1858; bro. of above; pianist and composer. (4) **Otto R.**, Hausneindorf, Nov. 2, 1842—Halle, May 18, 1913; bro. of above; pupil of Von Bülow and Marx; mus.-teacher and conductor, Halle; 1892, mus.-dir. at the University.

Reuling (roi'-lǐng), (**L.**) **Wm.**, Darmstadt, 1802—Munich, 1879; conductor and dram. composer.

Reuss (rois), (1) **Eduard**, New York, Sept. 16, 1851—Dresden, Feb. 18, 1911; pupil of Ed. Krüger and of Liszt; 1880, teacher at Carlsruhe; after 1896 in Wiesbaden; dir. Cons. there, 1902; later in Dresden and Berlin as teacher. His wife, (2) **Reuss-Belce** (-běl'-tsě) **Louise**, b. Vienna, 1863; soprano; pupil of Gänsbacher; début as "Elsa," Carlsruhe, 1884; later at Wiesbaden, and Bayreuth as one of the "Norns" and "Walküre" for years; 1900 sang Wagner in Spain, 1901, Met. Op., N. Y. (3) **H. XXIV.**, Prince of Reuss-Köstritz; Trebschen, Brandenburg, Dec. 8, 1855—Ernstbrunn near Vienna, Oct. 2, 1910; pupil of Herzogenberg and Rust, Leipzig; c. 2 symphs., a mass, etc.

Reuter (roi'-těr), **Florizel von,** b. Davenport, Iowa, Jan. 21, 1893; violinist; pupil of Bendix, Chicago, and of Marteau, in Europe; has toured America with popular success; c. operas, orch. and vln. works.

Reutter (roit'-těr), (1) **G.** (Senior), Vienna, 1656—Aug., 1738; theorbist, ct.-organist and conductor. (2) (**Jn. Adam**), **G.** (Junior), Vienna, 1708—1772; son and (1738) successor of above as ct.-conductor; c. opera, etc. (3) **Hn.**, b. Stuttgart, 1900; com-

poser; after 1936, dir. Hoch Cons., Frankfurt.

Rey (rě), (1) **J. Bap.**, Lauzerte, 1734—Paris, 1810; conductor, professor of harm. and dram. composer. (2) **L. Chas. Jos.**, bro. of above; for 40 years 'cellist, Gr. Opéra. (3) **J. Bap.** (II.), b. Tarascon, ca. 1760; from 1795 till 1822, 'cellist, Gr. Opéra, and theorist. (4) **V. F. S.**, b. Lyons, ca. 1762; theorist. (5) Vide REYER.

Reyer (rě-yā) (rightly **Rey**), **L. Étienne Ernest**, Marseilles, Dec. 1, 1823—near Hyères, Jan. 15, 1909; prominent French composer; studied as a child in the free municipal sch. of mus.; while in the Govt. financial bureau at Algiers, c. a solemn mass and pub. songs; the Revolution of 1848 deprived him of his position and he retired to Paris where he studied with his aunt, Mme. Farrenc; librarian at Opéra (vice Berlioz); 1876, Académie; critic *Journal des Débats;* 1862, Chev. of the Legion of Honour; 1886, Officier. Prod. a symph. ode with choruses "*Le Sélam*" (Th. Italien 1850); 1-act comedy-opera "*Maître Wolfram*" (Th.-Lyrique, 1854), a ballet-pantomime "*Sacountala*" (Opéra, 1858); comedy-opera "*La Statue*" (Th.-Lyr., 1861, revived at the Opéra 1878 without succ.); unsucc. opera "*Erostrate*" (Baden-Baden, 1862); the still pop. opera "*Sigurd*" (Brussels, 1884), and "*Salammbô*" (Brussels, 1890). C. a cantata "*Victoire*" (1859); a hymn, "*L' Union des Arts*" (1862); a dram. scene, "*La Madeleine au Desert*" (1874); male choruses; also some church-mus. Pub. a volume of essays, 1875.

Reznicek (rěz'-nǐ-chěk), **Emil Nicolaus, Freiherr von,** b. Vienna, May 4, 1861; studied Leipzig Cons.; th.-conductor various cities; 1896, 1st cond. ct.-th., Mannheim; after 1901 lived in Berlin; 1902, founded orch. concerts there; 1906, taught Scharwenka Cons.; 1907-08, dir., Warsaw Op. and Philh.; 1909-11, cond. Komische Op., Berlin; after 1920 taught at Hochsch. there; prod. at Prague operas "*Die Jungfrau von Orleans*" (1887), "*Satanella*" (1888), "*Emerich Fortunat*" (1889), comic opera (text and music), "*Donna Diana*" (1894), all very succ.; Volks-oper. "*Till Eulenspiegel*" (Berlin, 1903), "*Eros* und Psyche" (1917), "Ritter Blaubart" (1918), etc. C. also a requiem, a symph. suite, etc.

Rhaw (Rhau) (row), **G.**, Eisfeld, Franconia, 1488—Wittenberg, 1548; mus.-printer and composer.

Rheinberger (rīn'bĕrkh-ĕr), **Jos. (Gabriel)**, Vaduz, Lichtenstein, March 17, 1839—(of nerve and lung troubles) Munich, Nov. 25, 1901; eminent teacher and composer. At 5 played the piano; at 7 a good organist; studied R. Sch. of Mus., Munich; 1859, teacher of theory there; also organist at the ct.-church of St. Michael, and cond. Oratorio Soc., 1865-67, "*Repetitor*" ct.-opera; Royal Prof. and Inspector of the Sch. of Mus.; from 1877 ct.-cond. Royal Chapel-Choir; m. Franziska von Hoffnas, a poetess (1822—1892), prod. romantic opera "*Die 7 Raben*" (Munich, 1869); comic opera "*Des Thürmers Töchterlein*" (Munich, 1873); "*Christophorus*," a mass for double choir (dedicated to Leo XIII.); mass, with orch.; requiem for soldiers of the Franco-Prussian War; 2 Stabat Maters; 4 cantatas with orch.; 2 choral ballades, "*Florentine*" symph.; symph. tone-picture "*Wallenstein*"; a symphonic fantasia; 3 overtures "*Demetrius*," "*The Taming of the Shrew*," "*Triumph*"; 2 organ-concertos; pf.-concertos; chamber-music; vln.-sonatas; pf.-sonatas ("symphonique"; op. 47; "romantic," op. 184), etc., notably 18 important org.-sonatas; left unfinished mass in A minor (finished by his pupil L. A. Coerne).

Rhené-Baton (rā-nā bä'-tôṅ), (rightly **René Baton**), b. Courseulles-sur-Mer Sept. 5, 1879—Paris, Oct., 1940; conductor; also active as composer; studied piano at Paris Cons.; comp. with André Bloch and Gédalge; choral dir., Op.-Comique in early career; later cond. of Soc. des Concerts Populaires in Angers, and St. Cecilia Soc. in Bordeaux; asst. cond., Lamoureux Concerts; after 1916, cond., Pasdeloup Concerts; c. orch. works, songs, etc.

Riccati (rĭk-kä'-tē), **Count Giordano**, b. Castelfranco, 1709—Treviso, 1790; theorist.

Ricci (rĭt'-chē), (1) **Luigi**, Naples, 1805 —insane, in asylum, Prague, 1859; conductor and dram. composer; m. (2) **Lidia Stoltz**, who bore him two children, of whom (3) **Adelaide** sang at Th. des It., Paris, 1867, and died soon after. (4) **Federico**, Naples, 1809—Conegliano, 1877; bro. of (1) and collaborator in 4 of his operas; among which "*Crispino e la Comare*" still holds the stage; also himself c. others. (5) **Ruggiero**, b. California, July 24, 1920; violinist; early attracted attention as child prodigy; studied with his father, a bandmaster; 1st San Francisco recital at 8, following training by Louis Persinger; during 1931 gave concerts in Chicago and N. Y., playing Beethoven Concerto with orch. under baton of his teacher in latter city to sensational ovation; also toured Europe.

Riccitelli (rē-chē-tāl'-lē), **Primo**, b. Cognoli, 1880—Giulianova, 1941; pupil of Mascagni at Pesaro; c. several stage works incl. 1-act opera, "*I Compagnacci*," prod. at Rome and Met. Op. House.

Riccius (rēk'-tsĭ-oos), (1) **Aug. Fd.**, Bernstadt, Saxony, 1819—Carlsbad, 1886; conductor, critic, singing-teacher and composer. (2) **K. Aug.**, Bernstadt, July 26, 1830—Dresden, July 8, 1893; nephew of above; conductor, violinist and composer of comic operas, etc.

Rice, **Fenelon B.**, Green, Ohio, Jan. 2, 1841—Oberlin, Ohio, Oct. 26, 1901; studied Boston, Mass., later Leipzig; for 3 years organist, Boston; from 1871, dir. Oberlin (Ohio) Cons. of Mus.; Mus. Doc. Hillsdale (Mich.) Coll.

Richafort (rēsh-ä-fôr), **Jean**, important Flemish composer of masses, motets and songs; pupil of Deprès; 1543, choirmaster in Bruges.

Rich'ards, **(H.) Brinley**, Carmarthen, Wales, Nov. 13, 1817—London, May 1, 1885; pop. composer and pianist.

Richault (rē-shō), (1) **Chas. Simon**, Chartres, 1780—Paris, 1866; mus.-publisher, succeeded by his sons (2) **Guillaume Simon** (1806—1877) and (3) **Léon** (1839—1895).

Riche, **A. Le.** Vide DIVITIS.

Richter (rĭkh'-tĕr), (1) **Fz. X.**, Holeschau, Moravia, 1709—1789; cond., writer and composer. (2) **Jn. Chr. Chp.**, Neustadt-am-Kulm, 1727—Schwarzenbach - on - Saale, 1779; Father of Jean Paul R.; organist. (3) **Ernst H. Ld.**, Thiergarten, Prussian Silesia. 1805—Steinau-on-Oder, 1876; notable teacher; c. an opera, etc. **(4) Ernst Fr. (Eduard)**, Gross Schönau, Saxony, Oct. 24, 1808 —Leipzig, April 9, 1879; eminent theorist; pupil of Weinlig, and self-taught; 1843 teacher at Leipzig Cons. newly founded; 1843–47, conductor Singakademie; organist various churches, 1863 mus.-dir. Nikolaikirche, 1868 mus.-dir. and cantor Thomaskirche; Prof.; wrote a standard *"Lehrbuch der Harmonie"* (1853), and *"Lehrbuch der Fuge"*; c. an oratorio, masses, etc. **(5) Alfred**, Leipzig, April 1, 1846 — Berlin, March 1, 1919; son of above; teacher at the Cons., 1872–83; then lived in London; 1897, Leipzig; pub. supplement to his father's *"Harmonie,"* and *"Kontrapunkt"*; also *"Das Klavierspiel für Musikstudierende"* (Leipzig, 1898). **(6) Hans**, b. Raab, Hungary, April 4, 1843—Bayreuth, Dec. 5, 1916; eminent conductor; son of the cond. of the local cath.; his mother was a prominent sopr. and later a distinguished teacher; choirboy in the ct.-chapel, Vienna; studied with Sechter (piano-playing), and Kleinecke (the French horn), at the Cons.; horn-player in Kärtnertor Th. orch.; then with Wagner, 1866–67 in Lucerne, making a fair copy of the *"Meistersinger"* score. On W.'s recommendation, 1867, chorusm., Munich Opera. 1868–69 ct.-cond. under von Bülow. Cond. first performance of *"Lohengrin"* (Brussels, 1870); again at Lucerne with Wagner, making fair copy of the score of the *"Nibelungen Ring"*; 1871–75, cond., Pesth National Th.; then cond. of the Imp. Opera, Vienna, 1893, 1st cond., after 1875 also cond. *"Gesellschaft der Musikfreunde"* excepting 1882–83. Selected by Wagner to cond. the *"Ring des Niebelungen"* (Bayreuth, 1876), and alternate cond. with Wagner at the Wagner Concerts, Albert Hall, London, 1877; chief-cond. Bayreuth Festivals, and 1879–97, annually cond. Philh. concerts at London. Cond. several Lower Rhenish Festivals and 1885–1912 the Birmingham Festivals. In 1885, Mus. Doc. *h. c.*, Oxford Univ. In 1898 the freedom of the city of Vienna was given him.

Ricieri (rē-chä′-rĕ), **Giov. A.**, Venice, 1679—Bologna, 1746; male soprano and composer.

Ricordi (rē-kŏr′-dē), **(1) Giov.**, Milan, 1785—1853; founder of the mus.-publishing firm in Milan; violinist and conductor; succeeded by his son **(2) Tito** (1811—1888); then by **(3) Giulio** (Milan, Dec. 19, 1840—June 6, 1912; also ed. of the *Gazetta Musicale*. **(4) Tito** (1865—1933), a grandson, was a librettist. After 1912 the firm was dir. by Dr. Carlo Clausetti (with Renzo Balcarenghi, beginning 1919).

Rider-Kelsey, Corinne, b. Le Roy, N. Y., Feb. 24, 1880; soprano; studied with L. A. Torrens, Chicago, Mr. and Mrs. Toedt, N. Y.; sang widely in concert and oratorio; 1908, début in opera at Covent Garden; returned to concert work.

Riechers (rē′-khĕrs), **Aug.**, Hanover, 1836—Berlin, 1893; maker and repairer of vlns.; writer.

Riedel (rē′-d′l) **(1) Karl**, Kronenberg, Oct. 6, 1827—Leipzig, June 3, 1888; pupil Leipzig Cons.; 1854, founded the noted choral society Riedelverein; pres. Wagnerverein, etc.; pub. colls. **(2) Hn.**, Burg, near Magdeburg, Jan. 2, 1847—Brunswick, Oct. 6, 1913; pupil Vienna Cons.; ct.-cond. Brunswick, composer. **(3) Fürchtegott Ernst Aug.**, Chemnitz, May 22, 1855—Plauen, Feb. 6, 1929; pupil Leipzig Cons.; from 1890, town cantor, Plauen, Saxony, also cond.; c. cantatas, etc.

Riedt (rēt), **Fr. Wm.**, Berlin, 1712—1784; flute-virtuoso; writer and composer.

Rieger (rē′-gĕr), **Wallingford**, b. Albany, Ga., April 29, 1885; composer; grad., Inst. of Mus. Art, N. Y., also studied at Berlin Hochsch.; cond. at Würzburg Op.; at Königsberg and with Blüthner Orch., Berlin; taught at Drake Coll. and Ithaca Cons.; Paderewski Prize, 1922, for piano trio in B minor; Coolidge Prize, 1924, for chamber work, *"La Belle Dame sans Merci"*; c. Rhapsody for Orch. (N. Y. Philh.); *"Study in Sonority"* (Phila. Orch.); *"Frenetic Rhythms"*; (chamber music) Chromatic Quartet; *"Dichotomy"*; canons for woodwinds; Divertissement; suite for flute solo, etc.

Riehl (rēl), **Wm. H. von**, Biebrich, 1823 —Munich, 1897; director, writer and composer.

Riem (rēm), **Fr. Wm.**, Kölleda, Thuringia, 1779—Bremen, 1857; organist, conductor and composer.

Riemann (rē'-män), **Hugo**, Grossmehlra, near Sondershausen, July 18, 1849—Leipzig, July 10, 1919; notable theorist. Son of a farmer who taught him the rudiments of mus., and who had prod. an opera and choral pcs. at Sondershausen, but opposed his son's mus. ambitions; the youth, however, studied theory with Frankenberger, and piano with Barthel and Ratzenberger, at Sondershausen. Studied law, then philosophy and history, at Berlin and Tübingen; after serving in the campaign of 1870–71, entered Leipzig Cons.; 1873, Dr. Phil. Göttingen; wrote dissertation "*Musikalische Logik*"; until 1878, a cond. and teacher at Bielefeld, then lecturer Leipzig Univ.; 1880–81, teacher of mus. at Bromberg; then till 1890, Hamburg Cons., then the Wiesbaden Cons.; 1895, lecturer at Leipzig Univ.; m. in 1876. Notable at times under pseud. "Hugibert Ries" as an essayist, writer of theoretical treatises of much originality, also an important historian and lexicographer; mus.-ed. of Meyer's *Konversationslexikon* and ed. a valuable "*Musik-Lexikon*" (1882; Engl. ed. 1893); c. chambermus., vln.-sonata, etc.

Riemenschneider (rē'-mĕn-shnī-dĕr), (1) **G.**, Stralsund, April 1, 1848—Breslau, Sept. 14, 1913; pupil of Haupt and Kiel; th.-cond. Lübeck (1875) and Danzig; later cond. Breslau concert-orch.; c. operas "*Mondeszauber*" (Danzig, 1887), and "*Die Eisjungfrau*" (symphonic picture), "*Julinacht*," etc. (2) **Albert**, b. Berea, O., Aug. 31, 1878; organist, conductor, teacher; pupil of Reinhold, Fuchs, Widor and Guilmant; dir. Baldwin-Wallace Cons., Berea, and cond. of annual Bach fests. there.

Riepel (rē'-pĕl), **Jos.**, Horschlag, Upper Austria, 1708 — Ratisbon, 1782; chamber-musician, theorist and composer.

Ries (rēs), (1) **Fz.** (der alter), Bonn, 1755—Bremen, 1846; leader, later ct.-mus. dir., Bonn. (2) **Fd.**, Bonn, Nov. 29, 1784—Frankfort-on-Main, Jan. 13, 1838; noted pianist; pupil of Beethoven (of whom he wrote a valuable sketch) and Albrechtsberger; toured, 1813–24, London, m. an English woman; from 1830, l. Frankfort as cond.; c. 8 operas, 6

symphs., etc. (3) **Peter Jos.**, 1790 —London, 1882; bro. of above; Royal Prussian Prof. (4) **Hubert**, Bonn, April 1, 1802—Berlin, Sept. 14, 1886; bro. of above; violinist, teacher and composer of valuable method, studies, etc., for vln. (5) **Fz.**, Berlin, April 7, 1846—Naumburg, June 20, 1932; son and pupil of (4); studied with Massart at Paris Cons. and with Kiel (comp.); concert-violinist till 1875 when he retired, and entered mus.-publishing (Ries & Erler, Berlin), c. orch. and chamber-mus., etc.

Riesenfeld (rēs'-ĕn-fĕld), **Hugo**, b. Vienna, 1883; Los Angeles, 1939; played in orch. of Vienna Op. as violinist; came to U. S. and served as concertm. of orch. at Manhattan Op. House, N. Y.; later as cond. in film theatres; former dir. of Rialto, Rivoli and Criterion Theatres, N. Y.; active in Hollywood as mus. dir. of film productions; c. operettas, orch. works, songs, etc.

Rieter-Biedermann (rē'-tĕr-bē'-dĕr-män), **J. Melchior**, 1811—Winterthur, Switz., 1876; founded pub.-house, 1849; 1862, branch at Leipzig.

Rieti (rē-ā'-tē), **Vittorio**, b. Alexandria, Jan. 28, 1898; composer; grad. Bocconi Univ., Milan; pupil in music of Frugatta and Respighi; c. (ballets) "*Arche de Noè*," "*Barabau*" and "*Le Bal*" (the two latter works prod. by Diaghileff); (opera) "*Orphee*"; also concerto for wind and orch., piano concerto, string quartet and other chamber music.

Rietsch (rētsh), **Heinrich**, Falkenau, Sept. 22, 1860—Prague, Dec. 13, 1927; professor and composer; pupil of Krenn, Mandyczewski, and Fuchs; from 1892 teacher in Vienna; from 1900 prof. at the German Univ., Prague; author, and historian; c. opera, chamber music, etc.

Rietz (rēts), (1) **Jn. Fr. R.**, d. Berlin, 1828; vla.-player, royal chambermus. (2) **Eduard**, Berlin, 1802—1832; son of above, violinist and tenor; founded the Berlin Philh. Soc., 1826; was its cond. till death. (3) **Julius**, Berlin, Dec. 28, 1812—Dresden, Sept. 12, 1877; son of (1); 'cellist and cond.; pupil of Schmidt, Romberg and Ganz; 1834, asst.-cond. to Mendelssohn, Düsseldorf opera; 1835, his successor; 1847, cond. Singakademie, Leipzig, later also cond. Gewandhaus and prof. of comp. at the Cons.; 1860, ct.-cond. at Dresden; later dir. of the Cons.; editor of scores; c. 4 operas, 3 symphs., various overtures, masses, etc.

Riga (rē′-gä), **Frantz (François)**, Liége, 1831—Schaerbeek, near Brussels, 1892; conductor and composer of male choruses, etc.

Righini (rē-gē′-nē), **V.**, Bologna, Jan. 22, 1756—Aug. 19, 1812; tenor, singing-teacher and court-cond. at Mayence, later Berlin; c. 20 operas, etc., incl. vocalises.

Rille. Vide LAURENT DE RILLE.

Rimbault (rĭm′-bōlt), (1) **Stephen Francis**, organist and composer, 1773—1837. (2) **Edw. Fran.**, London, June 13, 1816—Sept. 26, 1876; son and pupil of above; organist and noted lecturer, editor, essayist and writer of numerous valuable historical works based on research.

Ri′mini, Giacomo, b. Verona, Italy; barytone; studied with Mme. Conti-Forono; début at Desenzano, 1910; mem. of Chicago Op. for a number of years after 1914, and sang at Ravinia Op.; has been heard in Eur. theatres, esp. in Italy, also South America; m. Rosa Raisa, soprano.

Rimsky-Korsakov (rĭm′-shkĭ-kôr′-sä-kôf), **Nikolas Andrejevitch**, Tikhvin, Novgorod, May 18 (new style), 1844—near St. Petersburg, June 21, 1908; notable Russian composer; studied at the Naval Inst., Petersburg; also took pf.-lessons; 1861, took up mus. as a profession after study with Balakirev; at 21 prod. his first symph.; 1871, prof. of comp. and instr. at Petersb. Cons., also 1873–84 inspector of Marine Bands; 1874–87, dir. Free Sch. of Mus., and until 1881, cond. there; 1883, asst. cond. (to Balakirev) of the Imp. Orch.; from 1886, cond. Russian Symph. Concerts; 1889, cond. 2 Russian concerts at the Trocadero, Paris. He orchestrated Dargomyzsky's "*Commodore*," Moussorgsky's "*Boris Godounoff*" and "*Khovanstchyna*" and Borodin's "*Prince Igor*"; pub. coll. of Russian songs and a harmony. C. operas "*Pskovitjanka*" ("The Girl from Pskov") (St. Petersburg, Imp. Th. 1873); "*A May Night*" (do. 1880); "*Snegorotchka*" ("*The Snow Princess*") (do. 1882); "*Mozart und Salieri*" (Moscow); opera ballet

"*Mlada*" (Petersburg, 1892); opera "*Christmas Eve*" (1895); opera "*Zarskaja Newjesta*" ("*The Tsar's Bride*") (1901), as well as 3 symphs. incl. "*Antar*" (1881), Sinfonietta; "*Russian*" overture; Servian fantasia, mus. tableau "*Sadko*" (1876); pf.-concerto, etc.; symphonic suite, "*Schêhêrazade*" (Boston Symph., 1897), used for the Russian ballets in Paris, 1911, with immense success; in 1901 he ceased to cond. Russian symph.; 1905 he wrote a letter protesting against the use of armed force in the Cons. to repress students' political expression, and he was dismissed; Glazounoff, Liadov, and others at once resigned, public feeling was aroused, and his opera "*Kotschei*" was prod. at the Théâtre du Passage, 1905, with great acclaim; later he was reinstated and Glazounoff chosen director. His opera "*Kitesch*" was prod. the same year, "*Le Coq d'Or*," a satiric comedy of a mythical kingdom (a thinly veiled criticism of Imp. Russia in his day), which was for a time forbidden prod. by the censor, reached the stage 1910. A master of orchestration, he carried on the Liszt tradition of the tone-poem but added his own brilliant finesse of instrumental colouring. His operas include attractive folksong elements. Previously pub. in Russian, his autobiography, "*My Musical Life*," was issued in English tr., 1923. He wrote a treatise on instrumentation, ed. by Steinberg (2 vols., 1913). Memoirs by Yasrobtsiev, Findeisen, Lapshin, Montagu-Nathan, Newmarch.

Rinaldi (rē-näl′-dē), **Giov.**, Reggiolo, Italy, 1840—Genoa, 1895; pianist.

Rinck (rĭnk), **Jn. Chr. H.**, Elgersburg, Thuringia, Feb. 18, 1770—Darmstadt, Aug. 7, 1846, famous organist, writer and composer; pupil of Kittel, etc.; town organist Giesen, then, 1805, at Darmstadt, where he also taught in the seminary; 1813 ct.-organist there; autobiog. (Breslau, 1833).

Ringel, Federico. Vide F. D'ERLAN-GER.

Rinuccini (rē-noot-chē′-nē), **Ottavio**, Florence, 1562—1621; the librettist of the first opera ever performed, Peri (q. v.) and Caccini's "*Dafne*" (1594), also of Peri's "*Euridice*"

(1600), and Monteverde's *"Arianna a Nasso"* (1608).

Riotte (rĭ-ôt), **Phillip J.**, St. Mendel, Trèves, Aug., 1776—1856; conductor and dram. composer.

Ripa (rē'-pä), **Alberto da** (called **Alberto Mantovano**), b. Mantua—d. 1551; lutenist and composer.

Rischbieter (rĭsh'-bë-tĕr), **Wm. Albert**, Brunswick, 1834—Dresden, Feb. 10, 1910; pupil of Hauptmann, theory; violinist in Leipzig and other cities; from 1862 teacher harm. and cpt., Dresden Cons., pub. treatises, etc.; c. symph., overtures, etc.

Riseley (rĭz'-lĭ), **George**, Bristol, Aug. 28, 1845—April 12, 1932; organist; pupil of Corfe, his successor at Bristol Cathedral; cond. orch. societies; pensioned, 1898, then cond. London; c. *Jubilee Ode*, 1887, etc.

Risler (rēs'-lĕr), **Edouard**, Baden-Baden, Feb. 23, 1873—July 22, 1929; notable pianist; pupil of Diemer and d'Albert, Stavenhagen, etc.; taught at Paris Cons. after 1907; Chev. of the Legion of Honour.

Ristori (rēs-tō'-rē), **Giov. Alberto**, Bologna, 1692—Dresden, Feb. 7, 1753; organist and conductor; c. 2 of the earliest comic operas, also church-music.

Rit'ter, (1) **G. Wenzel**, Mannheim. April 7, 1748—Berlin, June 16, 1808; bassoonist, Berlin ct.-orch.; composer. (2) **Aug. Gf.**, Erfurt, Aug. 25, 1811—Magdeburg, Aug. 26, 1885; organ-virtuoso, editor and composer. (3) **Alex**, Narva (or Reval), Russia, June 27 (new style), 1833—Munich, April 12, 1896; violinist; c. succ. operettas, etc. (4) **Frédéric Louis**, Strassburg, June 22, 1834—Antwerp, July 22, 1891; prof. of mus. and conductor at Loraine; 1856, Cincinnati (U. S. A.), organist Philh. orch. and Cecilia Soc.; 1861 New York, cond. the Arion; 1867 prof. Vassar Col.; wrote *"Music in England,"* and *"Music in America"* (both N. Y., 1883); and other historical works; c. 3 symphs., etc. (5) **(Raymond-Ritter), Fanny**, b. Philadelphia, 1840; wife of above; writer and translator. (6) (rightly **Bennet**) **Théodore**, near Paris, 1841—Paris, 1886; pianist and composer. (7) **Hermann**, Wismar, Sept. 16, 1849—Würzburg, Jan. 22, 1926; violinist; studied Berlin with Joachim, etc.; invented and played a viola alta; for 20 yrs. teacher

at Würzburg. (8) **Josef**, Salzburg, Oct. 3, 1859—June 21, 1911; baritone at Vienna.

Ritter-Götze (gĕt-'tsĕ), **Marie**, Berlin, Nov. 2, 1865—London, 1922; mezzo-sopr.; pupil of Jenny Meyer and Levysohn; début R. Opera, Berlin; later Hamburg for 4 years; sang at Met. Op. and in concert U. S. A., 1890–1902; then Berlin R. Opera.

Rivarde (rē-vär'-dĕ), **Serge Achille**, b N. Y., Oct. 31, 1865—London, March 31, 1940; violinist; at 11 taken to Europe, pupil of Dancla, Paris Cons.; dividing first prize, 1879, with Ondriček; 1885–90, solo violinist Lamoureux orch., from 1899, prof. R. C. M., London.

Rivé-King (rē'-vā-kĭng), **Julie**, b. Cincinnati, 1857—Indianapolis, 1937; noteworthy pianist; toured the world with great succ.; c. pop. pf.-pcs.; taught Bush Cons., Chicago.

Rivier (rē'-vē-ā), **Jean**, b. Villemeuble, France, 1896; won 1st prize counterpoint and fugue, Paris Cons.; c. orch. works, among which an *"Overture for a Don Quichotte"* has been played by several Amer. orchestras.

Rob'erton, Sir Hugh, b. Glasgow; conductor and composer; has won an important place as a choral leader with his Toynbee House Choir and particularly the Glasgow Orpheus Choir, which made a tour of America; a pioneer in the competitive fest. movement in Scotland; knighted by British gov't. for musical work; c. songs and other pieces.

Roberts, John Varley, near Leeds, 1841 —Oxford, 1920; eminent English organist; 1882–1918 succeeded Parratt as org. at Magdalen Coll., Oxford; cond. Univ. Glee and Madrigal Soc.; c. cantatas, organ works, etc.

Robeson, (1) **Lila**, b. Cleveland, O., 1880; contralto; pupil of Burnham, Mrs. Ford, Luckstone and Saenger; sang in concerts after 1905 and in 1912 at Met. Op., New York; later active as a teacher in Cleveland. (2) **Paul**, b. Princeton, N. J., April 9, 1898; Negro bass and actor; grad. of Rutgers Univ. and Columbia; has appeared on dram. stage, incl. *"Othello"* in London, also as song recitalist and in films.

Rob'inson, (1) **Jos.**, Dublin, 1815—1898; famous cond. and composer; his wife, (2) **Fanny Arthur**, 1831—1879, was a pianist and composer.

(3) **Franklin,** b. New York, Jan. 27, 1875; organist, theorist; studied music at Columbia Univ. with MacDowell and Rybner; grad. Coll. of the City of N. Y.; after 1908 taught at Inst. of Mus. Art; devised novel system of teaching harmony through ear-training; author of *"Aural Harmony."*

Robyn (rō'-bĭn), (1) **Alfred G.,** St. Louis, Mo., April 29, 1860—New York, Oct. 18, 1935; son of (2) **Wm. R.** (who organised the first symph. orch. west of Pittsburgh); at 10 **A.** succeeded his father as organist at St. John's Church; at 16 solo-pianist with Emma Abbott's Co.; prod. comic opera *"Jacinta"*; c. pf.-concerto, etc., also pop. songs (incl. *"Answer"*), etc.

Roc'ca, Lodovico, b. Turin, Nov. 29, 1895; composer; studied Milan Cons.; doctorate, Turin Univ., 1920; won hon. diploma from Parma Cons. operatic competition; also prizes offered by Musica e Musici, Milan, and Italian Music League, N. Y.; c. (opera) *"Il Dibuk"* (after Anski drama), which had a striking succ. at Milan and Rome, and was given in N. Y., Chicago and Detroit (in English tr.) by Civic Op. Co. of last-named city, 1936; also considerable music for orch., among which the suite *"Chiaroscuri"* and the poem *"La Cella Azzurra"* have had frequent hearings; and many chamber music works.

Rochlitz (rŏkh'-lĭts), **Jn. Fr.,** Leipzig, Feb. 12, 1769—Dec. 16, 1842; composer, editor and prominent writer of essays, biog. and librettos.

Röckel (rĕk'-ĕl), (1) **Jos. Aug.,** Neumburg-vorm-Wald, Upper Palatine, 1783—Anhalt-Cöthen, 1870; singer, prof. and operatic dir. at Aix; 1829-32, of a German co. at Paris; 1832, London. (2) **Aug.,** Graz, 1814—Budapest, 1876; joint-conductor at Dresden opera (with Wagner); 1848, abandoned mus. for politics. (3) **Edw.,** Trèves, Nov. 20, 1816—Bath, Nov. 2, 1889; pupil of his uncle, J. N. Hummel; toured as pianist; from 1848 lived Bath, Eng.; c. pf.-pcs. (4) **Jos. (Ld.),** London, April 11, 1838—1923; bro. of above; pupil of Eisenhofer, Götze, and of his father and bro. Eduard (pf.); lived in Bristol, as teacher and pianist; c. cantatas, pf.-pcs., pop. songs, etc.

Rock'stro (rightly **Rackstraw**), **Wm. Smyth,** North Cheam, Surrey, Jan. 5, 1823—London, July 2, 1895; notable historian; pupil Leipzig Cons.; pianist and teacher, London; 1891, lecturer R. A. M. and R. C. M.; wrote treatises, biog. and *"General History of Music"* (1886); c. overture, cantata *"The Good Shepherd,"* etc.

Roda (rō'-dä), **Fd. von,** Rudolstadt, 1815—near Kriwitz, 1876; mus.-dir. and composer.

Rode (rŏd), **(Jacques) P. (Jos.),** Bordeaux, Feb. 16, 1774—Château-Bourbon, near Damazon, Nov. 25, 1830; notable violinist; pupil of Fauvel and Viotti; début, Paris, 1790; toured; prof. at the Cons.; 1800, soloist to Napoleon, later to the Czar; c. 13 concertos, famous études, etc.; wrote a method (with Baillot & Kreutzer).

Rode (rō'-dĕ), (1) **Jn. Gf.,** Kirchscheidungen, Feb. 25, 1797—Potsdam, Jan. 8, 1857; horn-virtuoso; c. tone-pictures, etc. (2) **Th.,** Potsdam, 1821—Berlin, 1883; son of above; singing-teacher and writer. (3) **Wilhelm,** b. Hanover, Germany, Feb. 17, 1887; noted barytone and theatre manager; pupil of R. Moest in native city; début in Bremen; sang later in Breslau, Stuttgart, Munich, Vienna and Berlin, also as guest in London; after 1934 he was the manager of the Berlin Deutsches Opernhaus (formerly the Städtische Oper), but also continued his singing career.

Röder (rä'-dĕr), (1) **Jn. Michael,** d. ca. 1740; Berlin org.-builder. (2) **Fructuo'sus,** Simmershausen, March 5, 1747—Naples, 1789; notable organist. (3) **G. V.,** Rammungen, Franconia, ca. 1778-—Altötting, Bavaria, 1848; ct.-cond. and composer. (4) **Carl Gl.,** Stötteritz, near Leipzig, 1812—Gohlis, 1883; 1846, founded the largest mus. and engraving establishment in the world; in 1872, his sons-in-law, C. L. H. Wolf and C. E. M. Rentsch, became partners. (5) **Martin,** Berlin, April 7, 1851—Boston, Mass., June 10, 1895; pupil R. Hochschule; conductor and teacher of singing in various cities, incl. Dublin and Boston; critic and writer under pseud. *"Raro Miedtner"*; wrote essays, librettos, etc.; c. 3 operas, a symph., 2 symph. poems, etc.

Rodio (rō'-dĭ-ō), **Rocco,** b. Calabria, ca. 1530; famous Neapolitan contrapuntist and theorist.

Rodolphe (rō'-dôlf) (or **Rudolph**), **Jean Jos.,** Strassburg, Oct. 14, 1730—Paris, Aug. 18, 1812; horn-virtuoso and violinist; pub. treatises; prod. operas.

Rodzinski (rŏd-zhēn'-skē), **Artur,** b. Spolato, Dalmatia, 1896; conductor; LL. D., Vienna Univ.; studied Acad. of Music there, under Marx, Schreker, Sauer, Lalewicz and Schalk; cond. Lemberg Op., later Warsaw Op. and Philh.; asst. cond. Phila. Orch., cond. Grand Op. Co. of that city and Curtis Inst. Orch.; 1930, Los Angeles Philh.; 1933, Cleveland Orch.; 1936–37, N. Y. Philh. for part of season; as guest in Hollywood Bowl, San Francisco, Detroit and Rochester, also at Salzburg Fest.

Rogel (rō'-hĕl), **José,** Orihuela, Alicante, Dec. 24, 1829—Cartagena, Feb. 25, 1901; conductor and composer of 61 zarzuelas, etc.

Roger (rō-zhā), (1) **Gve. Hip.,** La Chapelle St.-Denis, near Paris, Dec. 17, 1815—Paris, Sept. 12, 1879; noted tenor; created "*Le Prophète*"; 1868, prof. of singing at the Cons. (2) **Victor,** Montpellier, France, July 22, 1853—Paris, Dec. 2, 1903; pupil École Niedermeyer; critic of *La France*; prod. about 20 operettas, etc., incl. "*La Petite Tâche*" (1898); succ. "*Poule Blanche*" (1899); and succ. "*Mlle. Georges*" (1900).

Roger-Ducasse. Vide DUCASSE.

Rogers (rä'-jĕrs), (1) **Benj.,** Windsor, 1614—Oxford, 1698; organist at Dublin; later at Windsor; c. the hymn sung annually at 5 A. M., May 1, on the top of Magdalen tower, Oxford. (2) **John,** d. Aldersgate, ca. 1663; lutenist to Chas. II. (3) Sir **John Leman,** 1780—1847; composer; pres. Madrigal Soc. (4) **Clara Kathleen** (née **Barnett**), Cheltenham, Engl., Jan. 14, 1844—Boston, March 8, 1931; daughter and pupil of John Barnett; pupil of Leipzig Cons.; studied also singing with Götze and Sangiovanni, at Milan; début Turin, 1863 (under name "Clara Doria"); sang in Italy, then in London concerts; 1871, America with Parepa-Rosa Co.; 1872–73, also with Maretzek Co.; lived in Boston as singer and teacher; 1878, m. a Boston lawyer, Henry M. R.; pub.

"*The Philosophy of Singing*" (New York, 1893), c. songs, sonata for pf. and vln., etc. (5) **Roland,** West Bromwich, Staffordshire, Nov. 17, 1847—Bangor, July 30, 1927; at 11, organist at St. Peter's there; 1871–91, organist at Bangor Cath. and cond. of the Penrhyn and Arvonic Choirs, teacher in Wales; 1875, Mus. Doc. Oxford; c. cantatas "*Prayer and Praise*" (with orch.), "*The Garden*" (prize, Llandudno, 1896); and "*Florabel*"; Psalm 130, for soli, chorus and strings; a symph., etc. (6) **James H.,** Fair Haven, Conn., 1857; at 18 studied in Berlin with Löschhorn, Haupt, Éhrlich and Rohde, and at Paris with Firsot, Guilmant and Widor; after 1883 lived in Cleveland, Ohio, as organist, pianist, critic and composer of notable songs; org. Euclid Ave. Temple, and cond. (7) **Francis,** b. Roxbury, Mass., April 14, 1870; barytone; grad. Harvard Univ.; appeared widely as recitalist; taught singing at Yale Univ. for a time, later privately, and at Juilliard Grad. School of Mus.; chairman, Amer. committee, Fontainebleau Cons.; Chevalier of the Legion of Honour. (8) **Bernard,** b. New York, Feb. 4, 1893; composer; studied Inst. of Mus. Art and with Ernest Bloch; Guggenheim Fellowship and Pulitzer Music Award; after 1930 taught comp. at Eastman School of Mus., Rochester, N. Y.; c. (orch.) symphony; "*Adonais*"; prelude to "*Hamlet*"; "*Fairy Tales*" (N. Y. Philh., 1936); (chamber orch.) "*Soliloquy*" for strings; "*Pastorale*"; "*Nocturne*"; (choral work) "*The Raising of Lazarus*"; string quartet, ballet, etc.

Rognone (rōn-yō'-nĕ), (1) **Riccardo,** a Milanese violinist. His son (2) **Fran.,** pub. a vln. method, 1614, etc.

Roguski (rō-goo'-skĭ), **Gustav,** Warsaw, 1839—April 5, 1921; pupil there and of Marx, Kiel, and Berlioz; from 1865 prof. of composition at the Warsaw Cons.; c. symph., 2 masses, chamber music, etc.

Rohde (rō'-dĕ), **Eduard,** Halle-on-Saale, 1828—Berlin, March 25, 1883; writer of pf.-method; singing teacher and composer.

Röhr (rär), **Hugo,** b. Dresden, Feb. 13, 1866—Munich, 1937; conductor; pupil of the Cons.; 1896–1934, cond. at Munich State Opera; also prof. at

Akad.; c. oratorio *"Ekkehard,"* opera *"Vater unser"* (Munich, 1904), etc.

Rokitansky (rō-kĭ-tän'-shkĭ), **Victor,** Freiherr **von,** Vienna, 1836—1896; pub. treatises on singing.

Rol'la, Ales., Pavia, April 22, 1757—Milan, Sept. 15, 1841; violinist and teacher; prof. of vln. and vla.; Paganini was his pupil.

Rolland (rŭl-län), **Romain,** b. Clamecy, Jan. 29, 1866; teacher of history at the École normale supérieure, at Paris; 1900 organised an international congress of music; historian at Paris; author of many historical and critical works, dramatic poems, and the musical romance *"Jean Christophe"* (1905-1908); notable works on Beethoven, Handel, early French music, etc.

Rolle (rôl'-lĕ), **Jn., H.,** Quedlinburg, Dec. 23, 1718—Magdeburg, Dec. 29, 1785; son and successor of the town mus.-dir. of Magdeburg; 1741-46, vla.-player, Berlin ct.-orch.; c. 4 Passions, 20 oratorios, etc.

Röllig (rĕl'-lĭkh), **K. Ld.,** Vienna, 1761—March 4, 1804; harmonica-player, inv. of the "Orphika" and "Xanorphika" (v. D. D.); wrote treatises on them; c. comic opera.

Rôman, Johann Helmich, Stockholm, 1694—near Calmar, 1758, called the father of Swedish music; pupil of Händel in London with a municipal stipend; 1727, court cond. at Stockholm; c. funeral march for King Fredrik (1751), coronation march for King Adolph Fredrik; 2 symphonies, etc.

Romaniello (rō-män-ĭ-ĕl'-lō), (1) **Luigi,** Naples, Oct. 27, 1858—Buenos Aires, Dec., 1916; pianist; pupil of his father, his brother (2) **Vincenzo** (b. Naples, 1858) and at Naples Cons.; graduating with highest honours; dir. of the pf.-dept. there, later member of the Soc. del Quartetto, also pianist Ferni Quartet; instructor in the R. "Educandato di San Marsellino" and critic; Chev. of the Italian Crown; 1896, Buenos Aires; pub. a pf.-method (prize at Naples, 1886); c. 3 operas, symphonic poems *"Corsair"* and *"Manfrèd,"* 2 symphs., etc.

Romanini (rō-mä-nē'-nē), **Romano,** Parma, 1864—1934; pupil of Mandovani (vln.) and Dacci (comp.) at the Cons.; 1st vln. Teatro Regio; then cond. concert and theatre-orch.

at Savigliano; 1890, prof. of vln.; 1897, director "Istituto Venturi," Brescia; c. succ. opera *"Al Campo"* (Brescia, 1895), symph., etc.

Romano, (1) **Alessandro** (q. v.). (2) **Giulio.** Vide CACCINI.

Romberg (rôm'-bĕrkh), (1) **Anton** (a) and (2) **H.,** two brothers, lived in Berlin, 1792. (3) **Anton** (b), Westphalia, 1745—1812 (1742—1814, acc. to Riemann); bassoonist. (4) **Gerhard H.,** b. 1748; clarinettist and mus.-dir. at Münster. (5) **Bd.,** Dincklage, near Münster, Nov. 11, 1767—Hamburg, Aug. 13, 1841; the head of the German sch. of 'cellists; prof.; ct.-cond., 1815-19; c. many operas, incid. mus.; 9 excellent concertos. (6) **Andreas** (Jakob), Vechta, near Münster, 1767—Gotha, 1821; vln.-virtuoso; son of (7) **Gerhard H.,** b. 1748; dir. and clarinettist. (8) **Sigmund,** b. Hungary, 1887; composer of popular light operas; a cousin of Alfred Grünfeld, pianist (q. v.); grad. Bucharest Univ.; pupil of Heuberger in Vienna; has long been res. in N. Y.; his extensive list of stage works includes *"The Blue Paradise," "Maytime," "The Student Prince," "The Desert Song,"* and many other pop. operettas.

Ron'ald, Sir Landon, b. London, June 7, 1873—Aug. 14, 1938; composer; son of Henry Russell, composer, and bro. of the impresario of that name; studied R. Coll. of Music, London, with Parry, Stanford and Parratt; début as pianist; former cond. at Covent Garden and with Augustus Harris Op. Co. on tour; with London Symph., Royal Albert Hall Orch., and at various times with Scottish Orch., Manchester Symph., London and Liverpool Philh. Orchs., also widely as guest in continental cities; prin. Guildhall School of Music, 1910–38; fellow R. Coll. of Music, 1924; c. ballets, orch. and piano music, and songs; served as music critic of various publications; author, *"Variations on a Personal Theme," "Schumann," "Tschaikowsky."*

Ronchetti-Monteviti (rôn-kĕt'-té môn-tä-vē'-tē), **Stefano,** Asti, 1814—Casale Monferrato, 1882; pupil of B. Neri, Milan; 1850, prof. of comp. at the Cons.; 1877, dir.; c. an opera, a motet, etc.

Ronconi (rôn-kō'-nē), (1) **Dom.,** Lendinara, Rovigo, July 11, 1772—

Milan, April 13, 1839; singer and famous vocal-teacher; tenor, 1809, dir. of the ct.-opera, Vienna, 1819–29; singing-master to the princess, Munich; 1829, founded a singing-sch. at Milan; pub. vocal exercises. (2) **Giorgio**, Milan, 1810—1890; son of above; barytone; 1863, teacher at Cordova, Spain; from 1867, New York; composer. (3) **Felice**, Venice, 1811—St. Petersburg, 1875; singing-teacher and writer. (4) **Sebastiano**, b. Venice, 1814; barytone, violinist and teacher, Milan.

Röntgen (rĕnt'-gĕn), (1) **Engelbert**, Deventer, Holland, 1829—Leipzig, 1897; violinist. (2) **Julius**, Leipzig, May 9, 1855—Utrecht, Sept. 13, 1932; pianist; son of above; pupil of Hauptmann and E. F. Richter, Plaidy, Reinecke and Fr. Lachner; at 10 began to c.; at 17 pub. a vln.-sonata; début as pianist, 1878; teacher mus.-sch., Amsterdam; 1886-98, cond. to the Soc. for the Promotion of Mus., also Felix Meritis Soc.; co-founder (1885) of the Cons.; dir. after 1913; c. "*Toskanische Rispetti*," an operetta for voices and pf.; a pf.-concerto, symphony, 'cello concerto, 3 vln. sonatas, 3 'cello sonatas, 2 piano sonatas, piano trio, opera "*Agnete*" (1914), etc.

Root, (1) **G. Ed. Fr.**, Sheffield, Mass., Aug. 30, 1820—Barley's Island, Aug. 6, 1895; teacher of singing and conductor; pupil of Webb, Boston; studied Paris, 1850; c. "*Battle-cry of Freedom*," "*Tramp, Tramp, Tramp*," "*Just before the Battle, Mother*," etc. (2) **Fr. Woodman**, Boston, Mass., June 13, 1846—Chicago, 1916; son and pupil of above; pupil of Blodgett and Mason, New York; organist; 1869-70, studied in Europe; later lecturer, writer and teacher of large vocal classes.

Roo'tham, (1) **Daniel Wilberforce**, Cambridge, Aug. 15, 1837—April, 1922; pupil of Walmesley and Schira; 1865-77, cathedral org.; Bristol; cond. Bristol madrigal society. His son (2) **Cyril Bradley**, Bristol, Oct. 5, 1875—Cambridge, Engl., March 18, 1938; Mus. B. at Cambridge, 1900; from 1901, organist there, St. John's College; pupil also at R. C. M., London; c. overture "*The Spirit of Comedy*," and vocal works with orch. "*Albert Graeme's Song*"; "*Andromeda*" (Bristol Festival, 1908),

"*Coronach*," etc.; after 1912, dir. of Cambridge Univ. Music Soc.

Rooy, van. Vide VAN ROOY.

Ropartz (rō-pärs), **J. Guy**, b. Quingamp, France, June 15, 1864; pupil Dubois, Massenet, and César Franck; from 1894, dir. Nancy Cons., and cond. symph. concerts; from 1919, dir. Strasbourg Cons.; c. symph. on a Breton chorale; incid. music to Loti's "*Pêcheur d'Islande*"; suite "*Dimanche breton*"; *Psalm 136* for organ and orch., chamber music, pf.-pcs., songs, etc.

Rore (rō'-rĕ), **Cipriano de**, Mechlin, 1516—Parma, 1565; eminent composer of Venetian sch.; pupil of Willaert, 1550, and his successor, 1563; ct.-conductor.

Rorich (rō'-rĭkh), **Carl**, b. Nürnberg, Feb. 27, 1869; pupil of R. Sch. of Mus., Würzburg; from 1892, teacher Gr. Ducal Sch. of Mus., Weimar; after 1914 dir. of school of music, Nürnberg; c. an overture "*Märchen*," a suite "*Waldleben*," etc.

Ro'sa, (1) **Salvato're**, Ranella, Naples, 1615—Rome, 1673; famous painter and poet; wrote a satire on mus., etc.; composer. (2) **Carl** (rightly **Carl Rose**), Hamburg, 1842—Paris, 1889; violinist; 1867, m. Parepa-Rosa, and with her organised an English opera-company; toured with great frequency, especially at head of an Engl. opera syndicate.

Rösch (rĕsh), **Friedrich**, Memmingen, Dec. 12, 1862—Berlin, Oct. 29, 1925; author and conductor of male choruses, etc.; pupil of Wohlmuth and Rheinberger; lived in various cities; from 1898 in Berlin.

Rosé (rō'-zā), **Arnold Josef**, b. Jassy, Oct. 24, 1863; pupil of Heissler, Vienna Cons.; 1st vln. Rosé Quartet; since 1881, soloist, Vienna ct.-orch., and 1888, leader Bayreuth Festivals; long prof. at Vienna State Acad. of Mus., and concertm. at the State Opera; 1902, m. a sister of Mahler.

Roseingrave (rōz'-ĭn-grāv), **Thos.**, Dublin—London, 1753 (?); 12 years organist at St. George's, Hanover Square; composer and writer.

Rösel (rä'-zĕl), **Rudolf Arthur**, Münchenbernsdorf, Gera, Aug. 23, 1859—Weimar, April 3, 1934; pupil of Weimar Mus.-Sch., later of Thomson; 1877-79, 1st vln. various cities; from 1888 in the Weimar ct.-orch.; also teacher at Mus.-Sch.; c. fairly succ. "lyric stage-play" "*Halimah*" (Weimar, 1895), symph. poem "*Frühlingsstürme*," a notturno for horn with orch., a notturno for oboe with orch., etc.

Rosellen (rō-zĕl-läṅ), **H.**, Paris, 1811 —1876; pf.-teacher, writer and composer.

Ro'sen, Max, b. Rumania, 1900; violinist; lived in New York as child; studied there and in Europe; début, Dresden, 1915; after 1918 appeared in U. S. with success.

Ro'senfeld, (1) **Leopold,** Copenhagen, July 21, 1850—July 19, 1909; studied in Germany; critic and teacher in Copenhagen; c. vocal works with orch., "*Henrik og Else*," "*Liden Helga*," "*Naar Solen daler*," songs, etc. (2) **Maurice,** b. Vienna, Dec. 31, 1867—Chicago, Feb. 25, 1939; studied Columbia Univ.; piano with Hyllested and Spanuth; grad. Chicago Mus. Coll.; where later taught and became dir.; in 1916 estab. his own school in Chicago; critic for the *Examiner* and after 1917 for the *News*. (3) **Paul,** American writer; author of books and articles on modern music, incl. *Musical Chronicle, Musical Portraits, An Hour with American Music*, etc.

Rosenhain (rō'-zĕn-hīn), **Jacob** (**Jacques**), Mannheim, 1813—Baden-Baden, 1894; pianist and dram. composer.

Rosenmüller (rō'-zĕn-mĭl-lĕr), **Jn.,** 1619 —Wolfenbüttel, 1684; mus.-director and composer.

Rosenthal (rō'-zĕn-täl), (1) **Moriz,** b. Lemberg, Dec. 18, 1862; brilliant pianist; at 8 his ability enlisted the aid of Mikuli; at 10, pupil of R. Joseffy; at 14, gave a concert Vienna; Royal Pianist; 1876–86, pupil of Liszt; from 1887, toured America and Europe; pub. (with L. Schytte) "*Technical Studies for the Highest Degree of Development*." (2) **Hedwig Kanner,** his wife, also an accomplished pianist and teacher in Vienna.

Rosetti (rô-sĕt'-tē), **Fran. Ant. (Fz. Anton Rössler,** rĕs-lĕr), Leitmeritz, Bohemia, 1750—Ludwigslust, 1792; ct.-conductor and composer.

Ross, Hugh, b. Langport, England, Aug. 21, 1898; conductor; studied Oxford Univ., R. Coll. of Music; cond. Winnipeg (Can.) Male Choir after 1921; Winnipeg Symph., 1923–

27; beginning latter year, **Schola Cantorum, N. Y.**

Rossi (rôs'-sē), (1) **Giov. Bat.,** Genoese monk; theorist, ca. 1618. (2) **Abbate Fran.,** b. Bari, Italy, ca. 1645, canon and dram. composer. (3) **Gaetano,** Verona, 1780—1855; librettist. (4) **Luigi Felice,** Brandizzo, Piedmont, 1804—Turin, 1863; essayist and translator. (5) **Lauro,** Macerata, 1810—Cremona, 1885; wrote a harmony and c. operas. (6) **Giov. Gaetano,** Borgo, S. Donino, Parma, 1828—Genoa, 1886; c. 4 operas. (7) **Carlo,** Lemberg, April 4, 1839— Venice, Oct., 1906; pupil of Menzel; from 1851 in Venice; c. symph., etc. (8) **Cesare,** near Mantua, Jan. 20, 1858—Casalmaggiore, July 27, 1930; c. operas "*I fugitivi*" (Trient, 1896), and "*Nadeya*" (Prague, 1903).

Rossini (rôs-sē'-nē), **Gioacchino A.,** Pesaro, Feb. 29, 1792—Ruelle, near Paris, Nov. 13, 1868; eminent Italian opera-composer. His father was inspector of slaughter-houses and also horn-player in strolling troupes in which the mother (a baker's daughter) was *prima donna buffa*. Left in charge of a pork-butcher, R. picked up some knowledge of the harpsichord from a teacher, Prinetti; 1802 studied with Angelo Tesci; this began his tuition; he made rapid progress, and sang in church, and afterwards joined his parents as a singer, horn-player and accompanist in the theatre. At 14 he studied comp. with Padre Mattei, and 'cello with Cavedagni at the Bologna Liceo. At 15 he prod. a cantata "*Il Pianto d'Armonia per la Morte d'Orfeo*," which won a prize. Mattei soon told him that, though he had not enough cpt. to write church-mus., he knew enough to write operas, and he ceased to study. At 17 he prod. a succ. 1-act opera buffa "*La Cambiale di Matrimonio*" (Venice, 1810); next year, a succ. 2-act opera buffa "*L'Equivoco Stravagante*," Bologna. He received various commissions, writing 5 operas during 1812. 1813, his "*Tancredi*" (Fenice Th., Venice) was an immense succ. and "*L'Italiana in Algeri*," an opera buffa (San Benedetto Th.), was also succ. Two failures followed with disheartening effect, but "*Elisabetta*" (its libretto curiously anticipating Scott's "*Kenilworth*") was a succ. (Naples, 1813), and in it he dropped *recitativo secco*. A failure followed and on the first night of the next work the public resentment at his daring to set to mus. the text of one of Paisiello's operas led to its being hissed. This work *"Almaviva"* (Rome, 1816) was better received the second night and gradually est. itself in its subsequent fame under the title *"Il Barbiere di Siviglia"*; 1815–23 he was under contract to write two operas yearly for Barbaja, manager of La Scala at Milan, the Italian opera, Vienna, and Neapolitan theatres. His salary was 12,000 lire (about $2,400). During these 8 years he c. 20 operas, travelling from town to town and working under highest pressure. 1821 he m. Isabella Colbran (d. 1845), who had sung in his operas. The ill-succ. of his most carefully written *"Semiramide"* (Venice, 1823) and an offer from Benelli, a mgr., led him to London where he was lionised and in 5 months earned £7,000. For 18 months he was mgr. of the Th. Italien at Paris, and prod. several operas with artistic but not financial succ. He was, however, "Premier compositeur du roi" and "Inspector-général du chant en France," sinecures with a salary of 20,000 francs ($4,000). He lost these in the Revolution of 1830, but afterwards on going to law received a pension of 6,000 francs. At the Gr. Opéra he prod. with succ. revisions in French of earlier Italian succs. 1829 he gave there his greatly succ. masterpiece *"Guglielmo Tell."* At the age of 37, having prod. under his direction Meyerbeer's first opera and having heard *"Les Huguenots,"* R. foreswore opera and never wrote again anything more dramatic than his famous *"Stabat Mater"* (1832), not performed entire till 1842; *"Petite messe solennelle,"* with orch.; a cantata for the Exposition of 1867; and pf.-pcs. with burlesque names. He retired to Bologna and Florence, returning to Paris in 1855. 1847 he m. Olympe Pelissier. He c. 35 operas, 16 cantatas, canzonets and arias, *"Gorgheggi e solfeggi per soprano per rendere la voce agile,"* *"Chant des Titans"* for 4 basses with orch.; *"Tantum ergo"* for 3 male voices with orch.; *"Quoniam"* for solo bass with orch.; *"O salutaris"* for solo quartet. etc. Biog. by Stendhal

(1823), Azevedo (1865), H. S. Edwards (London, 1869), Zanolini (1875), Struth (Leipzig), Dr. A. Kohut (Leipzig, 1892). Other memoirs by Carpani, d'Ortigue, Bettoni, Blaze de Bury, Escudier, Mirecourt, Montazio, Pougin, Silvestri, Sittard, Thrane, Checchi, Gandolfi, Dauriae, Corradi, Istel, Curzon, and Francis Toye (1934).

Rössler, F. A. Vide ROSETTI, F. A.

Rost (rôst), (1) **Nicolas**, pastor at Kosmenz, Altenburg; composer, 1583 —1614. (2) **Fr. Wm. Ehrenfried**, Bautzen, 1768—Leipzig, 1835; writer.

Roth (rōt), (1) **Ph.**, Tarnowitz, Silesia, 1853—Berlin, 1898; 'cellist. (2) **Bertrand**, b. Degersheim, St. Gallen, Feb. 12, 1855; pianist; pupil of Leipzig Cons. and Liszt; teacher Hoch Cons., Frankfort, co-founder. Raff Cons., 1882; 1885–90, Dresden Cons.; then opened a private mus.-sch. there. (3) **Feri**, b. Zolyon, Hungary, July 18, 1899; violinist; grad. R. Hungarian School of Music, Budapest; played in orch. at Budapest Op. and Berlin Volksop.; in 1922 formed well-known Roth Quartet, and has toured with it in leading Eur. and Amer. cities.

Rothier (rō'-tē-ā), **Léon**, b. Rheims, Dec. 26, 1874; bass; studied Paris Cons., won 1st prizes in 3 years; sang with Paris Op., and after 1910 with Met. Op., N. Y.

Rothmühl (rōt'-mül), **Nikolaus**, Warsaw, March 24, 1857—Berlin, May 24, 1926; tenor; pupil of Gänsbacher; début, Dresden ct.-theatre, then Berlin, etc.; toured widely, incl. America; then at Stuttgart ct.-opera; for some years dir. of opera school at Stern Cons., Berlin.

Roth'well, Walter Henry, London, Sept. 22, 1872—Los Angeles, March 11, 1927; conducted the first English performance of *"Parsifal"* in America; pupil Vienna Royal Acad.; cond. in various cities, and at Amsterdam Royal Opera; 1903, America to conduct English productions of *"Parsifal,"* and *"Madame Butterfly"*; 1908–15, cond. St. Paul, Minn., Orch.; 1916, at N. Y. Stadium concerts; 1917–18, guest cond., Cincinnati and Detroit; after 1919 until his death, of the Los Angeles Philh. Orch.

Rotoli (rō-tō'-lē), **Augusto**, Rome, Jan. 17, 1847—Boston, Nov. 26, 1904; pupil of Lucchesi; founded and

cond. "Società corale de' concerti
sagri," 1876, singing-master to Princess Margherita; 1878, maestro,
Capella reale del Sudario; 1885, invited to Boston, Mass., as teacher in
the N. E. Cons.; Chev. of the Ital.
Crown, etc.   C. mass for the funeral
of Victor Emmanuel, 1878; "*Salmo
elegiaco*," with orch. (1878), etc.

Rot'tenberg (-bĕrkh), Dr. **Ludwig,**
Czernowicz, Oct. 11, 1864—Frankfort-on-Main, May 6, 1932; studied
vln. and piano with Fuchs, and
theory with Mandyczewski; début as
pianist; 1888, director; 1891, cond.
at Brünn, then 1st opera cond. at
Frankfort; in 1912–13, cond. of
Wagner at Covent Garden; c. opera,
vln. sonata, songs.

Rotter (rôt'-tĕr), **L.,** Vienna, 1810—
1895; pianist, conductor, theorist and
composer.

Rottmanner (rôt'-män-nĕr), **Ed.,** Munich, 1809—Speyer, 1843; organist.

Rouget de l'Isle (roo-zhā dŭ-lēl),
Claude Jos., Lons-le-Saulnier, Jura,
May 10, 1760—Choisy-le-Roy, June
27, 1836; composer of the "*Marseillaise*," military engineer, poet,
librettist, violinist and singer; wrote
"*La Marseillaise*," picking out the
air on his vln.; he called it "*Chant
de Guerre*," but it grew popular first
in Marseilles, and was brought to
Paris by Marseillaise volunteers in
1792; R. was imprisoned for refusing
to take an oath against the crown,
but was released, and lived in Paris
in great poverty.

Rousseau (roos-sō), (1) **Jean Jacques,**
Geneva, June 28, 1712—Ermenon-
ville, near Paris, July 3, 1778. The
great writer; mainly self-taught in
mus., but aiming to reform notation
by the substitution of numerals for
letters and note-heads, read before
the Académie, 1742, a "*Dissertation
sur la musique moderne*" (1743); his
opera, "*Les Muses Galantes*," had
one private representation (1745); his
revision of the intermezzo "*La Reine
de Navarre*" (by Voltaire and Rameau) was a failure; but his opera
"*Le Devin du Village*" (Gr. Opéra,
1752) was succ. for 60 years. He
wrote mus. articles for the "*Encyclopédie*," which were roughly handled
by Rameau and others, but revised
and re-pub. as "*Dictionnaire de musique*" (1768). In 1752 he participated in the "Guerre des Bouffons,"

between the partisans of French and
Italian opera, **R.** siding with the
Italianists and declaring that a
French national music was impossible and undesirable; for which
the members of the opera burned
him in effigy. "*Pygmalion*" (1773)
was v. succ. being a novelty—a
melodrama, all the dialogue spoken,
the orch. furnishing interludes and
background. Six new arias for "*Le
Devin du Village*," and a coll. of 100
romances and duets "*Les consolations
des misères de ma vie*" (1781), and
fragments of an opera, "*Daphnis et
Chloé*," were pub. (1780). (2) **Samuel
Alex.,** Neuvemaison, Aisne, June 11,
1853—Paris, Oct. 1, 1904; pupil of
Paris Cons., 1878, won the Prix
Cressent, and 2d Grand Prix de
Rome; prod. 1-act comedy-opera
"*Dianorah*" (Op.-Com., 1879); 1891,
won the Prize of the City of Paris,
with opera "*Merowig*"; 1892, 1st
cond. Th. Lyrique; 1898, prod. fairly
succ. lyric drama "*La Cloche du
Rhin*"; c. also a solemn mass, etc.

Roussel (roos'-sĕl), **Albert,** b. Tour-
coing, April 5, 1869—Royan, France,
Aug. 23, 1937; composer; a naval
student, he made a voyage to China
as an ensign; but resigned in 1894
and took up music, studying harmony with Gigout; 1898 entered
the Schola Cantorum and studied
under d'Indy till 1907; 1902–14, prof.
of counterpoint at the Schola Cantorum.   His comps. include symph.
prelude, "*Résurrection*" (after Tolstoi's novel); symph., sketch, "*Ven-
danges*"; "*Le poème de la Forêt*"
(1904–06); symph. sketches "*Evoca-
tions*" (1910–11), poem for orch.
"*La Menace*" (1907), etc. Inspired
by his visit to the East in 1909–10,
R. prod. a Hindu ballet, "*Padma-
vati*," which had a markedly successful première at the Paris Op., 1923.
Other productions include the orch.
works, "*Le Festin de l'Araignée*" and
"*Pour une Fête de Printemps*"; 4
symphonies; concerto for orch.; concerto for piano and orch.; "*Petite
Suite*"; "*Psaume*," for orch. with
employment of choral voices; the
ballet, "*Bacchus and Ariadne*"; the
opera, "*La Naissance de la Lyre*,"
which treats an allegorical theme; 2
sonatas for piano and vln.; trio for
flute, viola and 'cello; quintet; sextet;
and various piano pieces and smaller

vocal compositions. He visited the U. S. and took part in perfs. of his works at the Chicago Chamber Music Fest. under the patronage of Mrs. F. S. Coolidge in 1930.

Roussier (roos-sĭ-ā), Abbé **P. Jos.;** Marseilles, 1716—Écouis, Normandy, ca. 1790; canon and theorist.

Rovel'li, (1) **Giu.,** Bergamo, 1753—Parma, 1806; 'cellist. (2) **P.,** Bergamo, 1793—1838; nephew of above; violinist and composer.

Rovet'ta, Giov., d. Venice, 1668; pupil of Monteverde, and his successor (1644) at San Marco; c. operas, etc.

Row'botham, John F., b. Edinburgh, April 18, 1854; studied Oxford, Berlin, Paris, Vienna, Dresden; wrote numerous histories of mus., biogs., etc.; d. London, 1925.

Roze (rôz), (1) **Marie,** Paris, 1846—June 21, 1926; eminent operatic soprano; pupil of Paris Cons.; long active as singer and teacher in Paris; from 1912 also in London. Her son (2) **Raymond,** London, 1875–1920; pupil of Brussels Cons.; 1911, cond. London Op. House; cond. His Majesty's Theatre, and c. incid. music for Beerbohm Tree's prods. of Shakespeare's "*Macbeth*," etc., c. text and music of operas "*Joan of Arc*" (in concert from Queen's Hall, 1911); "*Antony and Cleopatra*"; a symph. poem on the same subject (Queen's Hall, 1911); songs, etc.

Rozkošny (rōz'-kōsh-nē), **Josef Richard,** Prague, Sept. 21, 1833—1913; pianist; pupil of Jiranek, Tomaschek and Kittl; toured, then lived in Prague; prod. there 9 Bohemian operas; c. also overtures, 2 masses, etc.

Różycki (roo-zhĕt'-skĭ), **Ludomir von,** b. Warsaw, 1883; pupil of the Cons. and of Humperdinck; from 1908 teacher at the Cons. in Lemberg and cond. at the Opera; then in Warsaw; c. operas "*Boleslas der Kühne*" (Lemberg, 1909); "*Eros and Psyche*" (1917), "*Beatrice Cenci*" (1922), 6 symphonic poems, piano quintet, piano trio, sonatas for vln., for 'cello and piano; many songs, etc.

Ru'benson, **Albert,** Stockholm, Dec. 20, 1826—1901; violinist; pupil of David; 1872 dir. of the Stockholm Cons.; c. symph., incid. music to Björnson's "*Halte Hulda*," etc.

Rubert (roo'-bĕrt), **Johann Martin,** Nuremberg, 1614—Stralsund, 1680; organist and comp.

Rubinel'li, **Giovanni Battista,** Brescia, ca. 1753—1829; Italian opera singer; début at 18, Stuttgart.

Rubini (roo-bē'-nē), **Giov. Bat.,** Romano, Bergamo, April 7, 1795—at his castle, near Romano, March 2, 1854; famous tenor, said to have been the first to use the vibrato and the sob, both since abused; his range was from E—b' (with a falsetto register to f'. (v. PITCH, D. D.); Bellini wrote many operas for him; toured with Liszt, earning by one concert over $10,000; had one of the largest fortunes ever amassed by a singer.

Rubinstein (roo'-bĭn-shtīn), (1) **Anton Gregorovitch,** of Jewish parents, Wechwotynecz, Bessarabia, Nov. (16) 28, 1829—Peterhof, near St. Petersburg, Nov. 20, 1894; one of the greatest of the world's pianists. Early taken to Moscow, where his father est. a pencil factory, he was at first a pupil of his mother; at 7, of Alex. Villoing, who was his only pf.-teacher. At 9 he made a tour with Villoing as far as Paris, where, in 1840, he played before Chopin and Liszt, who advised him to study in Germany. He toured further and returned to Moscow in 1843. His brother, Nikolai (v. below), was also musical, and in 1844 both were taken to Berlin, where Anton studied comp. with Dehn. Returning to Russia after a tour through Hungary, with the flutist Heindl, he lived in Petersburg under the patronage of the Grand Duchess Helen; he prod. 2 Russian operas; 1854–58, with the assistance of Count Wielhorski and the Grand Duchess, he made a wide tour, finding himself now well known as composer and pianist; 1858, ct.-pianist and cond. of ct.-concerts, Petersburg; 1859, dir. Russian Mus. Soc.; 1862, founded the Imp. Cons. at Petersburg, and was its dir. until 1867; 1865, he m. Vera Tchekuanoff. 1867–70, he toured Europe, with greatest imaginable succ.; 1872–73, he gave in America 215 concerts, from which he earned $40,000 (£8,000); but he could never be induced to cross the ocean again, though offered $125,000 (£25,000) for fifty concerts. 1887–91, again dir. Petersburg Cons., then lived in Berlin; 1891, in Dresden. The Czar bestowed on him the Order of Vladimir carrying with it nobility, and the title of Imp. Russian State Councillor; he was an officer of the Legion of Honour, a Knight of the Prussian Ordre pour le mérite, etc. He instituted the *Rubinstein prizes* of 5,000 francs each for pf.-playing and composition open every 5 years to men between 20 and 26 of any nationality.

He wrote his *"Memoirs,"* also *"Die Musik und ihre Meister"* (1892), *"Gedankenkorl"* (1892).

As a pianist R. is second only to Liszt, whom he perhaps excelled in fire and leonine breadth. He was, however, frequently inaccurate in his performance. He chiefly wished to be remembered as a composer but his music has lost its erstwhile popularity in recent years, save for occasional hearings of his piano works. He placed great hope in the creation of what he called "Sacred Opera" (oratorio to be enacted with costume and scenery). In this "new form" he c. *"The Tower of Babel," "Paradise Lost," "Moses," "Christus."* Besides the noteworthy operas *" Nero"* (Hamburg, 1879), *"The Demon"* (Russian, P., 1875), and *"Die Makkabäer"* (German, Berlin, 1875), he c. 11 other operas, a ballet *"La Vigne"* (*Die Rebe*), and 2 cantatas with orch. C. also 6 symphs. (incl. the famous *"Ocean,"* op. 42, in C, in 7 movements); op. 95, in D min. (*"Dramatic"*); op. 107, in G min. (in memory of Gr. Duch. Helen). *"Character-pictures" "Faust," "Ivan IV.,"* and *"Don Quixote"*; 3 concert-overtures, incl. op. 43 (*"Triomphale"*), and op. 116 (*"Anthony and Cleopatra"*); a Suite in 6 movements, op. 119 (his last work); symph. poem *"La Russie"*; 5 pf.-concertos; fantasia eroica with orch.; vln.-concerto; romance and caprice for vln. with orch.; 2 'cello-concertos; vln.-sonatas; vln.-sonata (arr. for vln. by David), etc. FOR PIANO SOLO: suite; 4 sonatas, 6 preludes, 6 études, 5 barca-rolles; *" Kamenoi-Ostrow"* (*"Isle of Kamenoi"* in the Neva, a series of 24 "pictures"); *"Soirées de St. P.,"* *"Miscellanies," "Le Bal,"* 10 pcs. op. 14; *"Album de Peterhof,"* etc. FOR PF. 4 HANDS, sonata, *"Bal Costumé,"* 6 Charakterbilder, fantasia for 2 pfs.; over 100 songs, 18 duets, choruses, etc.

Autobiog. *"Memoirs"* (St. P., 1889; Leipzig, 1893). Biogr. by McArthur (London, 1889). Other studies by Baskin, Vogel, Lissowski, Sveriev, Zabel, Soubies, Cavos-Degtarev, Martinov, Rodenberg, Droucker, Findeisen, La Mara, Bernstein and Arthur Hervey.

(2) **Nikolai,** Moscow, June 2, 1835—(of consumption), Paris, March 23, 1881; bro. of above, who declared N. to be the better pianist of the two; founder Moscow Mus. Soc.; dir. Moscow Cons. from its foundation, 1864; c. pf.-pcs. etc. (3) **Jos.,** Staro-Constantinow, Russia, Feb. 8, 1847—(suicide) Lucerne, Sept. 15, 1884; pianist for rehearsals at Bayreuth; composer. (4) **Jacques,** Russia. 1874—Paris, 1902; son of (1). (5) **Arthur,** b. Lodz, Poland, 1886; pianist; pupil of Breithaupt in Berlin; since his 12th year touring in recitals as a prodigy; has been heard as mature artist with much succ. in Europe, Far East and U. S. (6) **Beryl,** b. Athens, Ga., Oct. 26, 1898; pianist; composer; studied with Alexander Lambert, Vianna da Motta and Busoni; début with Met. Op. orch. at 13; played with leading Amer. orchs. and in London (1925); dean (later, dir.) and head of piano dept., Cleveland Inst. of Music; former cond. of Singers Club in that city; c. opera, orch., piano works. (7) **Ida,** b. Kharkov, Russia, 1893; noted actress and dancer; pupil of the tragedian Lensky; gave series of dance productions in Paris, which incl. creation of D'Annunzio's and Debussy's *"Martyre de St. Sebastien"* (written for her) at Théâtre du Châtelet, 1911; also many other modern ballet scores created for and premièred by her, incl. title rôle in Stravinsky's *"Perséphone,"* which utilises mime-reciter, tenor soloist, chorus and orch.

Rückauf (rĭk'-owf), **Anton,** Schloss Alt-Erloa, Prague, March 13, 1855—Sept. 19, 1903; composer; pupil of Proksch, and teacher at his institute, then pupil of Nottebohm and Navratil, at Vienna; c. opera *"Die Rosenthalerin"* (Dresden, 1897), songs, etc.

Ruckers (rook'-ĕrs), family of clavecin-makers at Antwerp, superior to all others. (1) **Hans** (Senior), d. ca. 1640; father of (2) **Fz.,** b. 1776. (3) **Hans** (Junior), b. 1578. (4) **Andries** (Senior), b. 1579. (5) **Anton,**

b. 1581; the last mfr. was (6) **Andries** (Junior), 1607–67.

Rucsicska. Vide RUZICKA.

Rudersdorff (roo'-dĕrs-dôrf), **Hermine,** Ivanowsky, Ukraine, Dec. 12, 1822 —Boston, Mass., Feb. 26, 1882; noted soprano and teacher.

Rudhyar (rŭd'-yĕr), **Dane,** b. Paris, 1895; composer; has lived in U. S. since 1916; won Los Angeles Orch. prize, 1920, for symph. poem, "*Surge of Fire*"; author of book on Debussy; his orch. works incl. also Three Dance Poems, Sinfonietta, "*Desert Chants,*" "*Ouranos*"; "*Five Stanzas*"; "*To the Real*"; symphony; "*Hero Chants,*" etc.

Rudnick (root'-nĭk), **Wilhelm,** Dammerkow, Pomerania, Dec. 30, 1850— Liegnetz, Aug. 7, 1927; pupil of Kullak's Acad., and of Dienel; org. at Liegnitz; c. opera "*Otto der Schütz*" (1887); oratorio "*Judas Iscariot,*" "*Der Verlorene Sohn,*" etc.

Ru'dolph, (1) **Jn. J. R.,** Arch-duke of Austria, Florence, 1788 — Baden, Vienna, 1831; pianist and composer; pupil and intimate friend of Beethoven. (2) **Jn. J.,** 1730—1812, vln. and horn player.

Rudorff (roo'-dôrf), **Ernst Fr. K.,** Berlin, Jan. 18, 1840—Dec. 31, 1916; pupil of Bargiel (pf.) and Leipzig Cons.; private pupil of Hauptmann and Reinecke; 1865, pf.-teacher, Cologne Cons.; 1867 founded the Bach-verein; 1869 head pf.-teacher Berlin Hochschule; 1880–90 cond. Stern Gesangverein; c. symphs., overtures, etc.

Ruegger (rüg'-gĕr), **Elsa,** b. Lucerne, Dec. 6, 1881; 'cellist; studied with Jacobs and Anna Campowski at the Cons. there, taking 1st prize at 13; toured widely America and Europe; 1908–14, taught Scharwenka Cons., Berlin; later res. in San Francisco, m. Edmund Lichtenstein, violinist.

Rüfer (rü'-fār), (1) **Ph. (Barthélémy),** Liége, June 7, 1844—Berlin, Sept. 15, 1919; son of a German organist. (2) **Philipp R.,** pupil of Liége Cons.; 1869–71, mus.-dir. at Essen; pf.-teacher Stern's Cons., Kullak's Cons., and from 1881 Scharwenka's, Berlin, c. operas "*Merlin*" (Berlin, 1887); succ. "*Ingo*" (Berlin, 1896); symph. in F.; 3 overtures, etc.

Ruffo (roof'-fō), (1) **V.,** b. Verona; maestro of the Cath.; composer (1550–88). (2) **Titta,** b. Pisa, June

9, 1877; eminent barytone; pupil of St. Cecilia Cons., Rome; after two years dismissed and advised to give up singing; then Cassini of Milan taught him gratis; he won his first success at Rio Janeiro and throughout South America, then triumphed in Italy, later in Vienna; 1912 a sensation in Paris and engaged for Chi.-Phil. Opera Co., appearing Philadelphia, Nov. 4, 1912; 1922–9, with Met. Op., N. Y., and widely in U. S. and Europe.

Ruggeri (**Ruggieri**) (rood-jā'-rē), a Cremonian family of vln.-makers, (1) **Fran.,** flourished, 1668—1720. (2) **Giov. Bat.** (1700—1725), and (3) **P.** (1700—1720), probably his sons. (4) **Guido** and (5) **V.,** both of Cremona in 18th cent. **R.** violins resemble Amatis. (6) **Giov. M.,** Venetian composer; prod. operas there 1696—1712.

Ruggi (rood'-jē), **Fran.,** Naples, 1767— 1845; conductor, professor and dram. composer.

Rug'gles, Carl, b. Marion, Mass., 1876; composer; studied Harvard Univ., founded and cond. Winona (Minn.) Symph. for several years; c. orch. and chamber works of highly original harmonic and rhythmic style, incl. "*Portals*" for string orch., "*Men and Angels,*" "*Sun-Treader,*" and "*Men and Mountains,*" also songs with orch.; several of his works perf. at fests. of Internat'l. Soc. for Contemp. Music in Europe.

Rühlmann (rül'-män), (**Ad.**) **Julius,** Dresden, 1816—1877; court-trombonist; professor, writer and composer.

Rum'ford, R. Kennerly, b. London, Sept. 2, 1871; concert barytone; studied in Frankfort, Berlin and Paris; m. Clara Butt, 1900.

Rummel (room'-mĕl), (1) **Chr. (Fz. L. Fr. Alex.**), Brichsenstadt, Bavaria, 1787—Wiesbaden, 1849; clarinettist, and composer. (2) **Josephine,** Manyares, Spain, 1812 — Wiesbaden, 1877; daughter of above; ct.-pianist. (3) **Jos.,** Wiesbaden, 1818—London, 1880; son and pupil of (1); ct.-pianist and composer. (4) **Franziska,** Wiesbaden, 1821—Brussels, 1873; ct.-singer; sister of above; m. Peter Schott, the pub. (5) **Aug.,** Wiesbaden, 1824—London, 1886; pianist. (6) **Fz.,** London, Jan. 11, 1853—Berlin, 1901; pianist; son of

(3); pupil of Brassin, Brussels Cons., winning 1st prize, 1872, 1877–78, toured Holland with Ole Bull; toured America 3 times; teacher Stern's Cons., then Kullak's, Berlin; 1897 "Professor" from the Duke of Anhalt. (7) **Walter Morse**, b. Berlin, July 19, 1882; noted pianist; son of (6); pupil of Fabian, Godowsky, Kaun and Debussy; after 1913 toured in Europe; m. Therese Chaigneau, pianist.

Run'ciman, John F., England, 1866— London, April, 1916; prominent critic. Educated at the science school (now Rutherford College), Newcastle-on-Tyne; organist from childhood; 1887, took position in London; from 1894 musical critic *Saturday Review;* later, until 1898, also acting editor and managing director; also editor of the quarterly *The Chord,* and of the *Musician's Library;* for some years correspondent Boston *Musical Record;* 1901, of New York *Musical Courier;* some of his essays were published as *"Old Scores and New Readings"* (1899); wrote biographical studies of Wagner and of Purcell.

Rung (roongk), **Henrik**, Copenhagen, 1807—1871; conductor and dram. composer.

Runge (roong'-ĕ), **Paul**, Heinrichsfeld, Posen, Jan. 2, 1848—Colmar, July 4, 1911; pupil of Church Music Institute, Berlin, and J. Schneider; from 1873 at Colmar as historian and comp.

Rungenhagen (roong'-ĕn-hä-gĕn), **K. Fr.**, Berlin, 1778—1851; Professor, conductor and dramatic composer.

Rünger (rēng'-ĕr), **Gertrud**; b. Posen, Poland; dramatic soprano (originally contralto); studied in Berlin; sang at Erfurt, Magdeburg, Cologne, then at Vienna State Op. for a number of seasons; in 1935 became member of the Berlin State Op. assuming soprano rôles; guest appearances at Salzburg Fest., Amsterdam, Paris and London; in 1936–37 engaged for Met. Op., New York.

Rupff. Vide LUTHER, M.

Rus'sell, (1) **Wm.**, London, 1777—1813; pianist. (2) **Henry**, Sheerness, 1812—London, Dec. 6, 1900; v. pop. Engl. song-composer. (3) Sir **Henry**, London, 1871—London, Oct. 11, 1937; son of (2); noted English impresario and voice teacher; pupil of

R. C. M., London; 1903, dir. of Covent Garden Op.; 1905 brought his co. to Boston; 1909–14, dir. Boston Op. Co., with which he visited Paris, 1914; bro. of Sir Landon Ronald. (4) **Louis Arthur**, b. Newark, N. J., Feb. 24, 1854—Sept. 5, 1925; pupil of Warren, Bristow, and C. C. Müller, New York; studied, London, 1878–95; organist and choirm., Newark; after 1879, cond. Schubert Vocal Soc.; after 1885, Easton (Pa.) Choral Soc.; 1885, founded the Newark Coll. of Mus., of which he was dir. and teacher; 1893, organised Newark Symph. Orch.; wrote various books; c. cantata with orch., *"A Pastoral Rhapsody,"* etc. (5) **Ella (Countess de Rhigini)**, Cleveland, O., March 30, 1864—Florence, Jan. 16, 1935; soprano; pupil of Cleveland Cons., Mme. de la Grange and Ed. Pluque (acting); début, *"Il Trovatore,"* Prato, Italy, 1882; sang with succ. on Continent; Covent Garden, 1885; later with Carl Rosa Opera Company.

Rust (roost), (1) **Fr. Wm.**, Wörlitz, near Dessau, July 6, 1739—Dessau, Mar. 28, 1796; violinist; bro. and pupil of an amateur violinist in J. S. Bach's orch. at Leipzig; ct.-mus. director; c. stage pieces, etc. (2) **Wm. K.**, 1787—1855; son of above; pupil of Türk; organist and composer. (3) **Wm.**, Dessau, Aug. 15, 1822—Leipzig, May 2, 1892, nephew of above; composer; notable organist and teacher; cond. Berlin Bach-Verein and editor of Bach's text.

Ruta (roo'-tä), **Michele**, Caserta, 1827—Naples, Jan. 24, 1896; theorist and dram. composer.

Rüter (rē'-tĕr), **Hugo**, b. Hamburg, Sept. 7, 1859; pupil of the Cons.; from 1882 singing teacher and cond. at Wandsbeck; 1897, Hamburg; c. symph.; 2 operas, etc.

Ruthardt (root'-härt), (1) **Fr.**, 1800—1862; oboist and composer. (2) **Julius**, Stuttgart, Dec. 13, 1841—Constance, Oct. 13, 1909; son of above; violinist, th.-conductor 1885 at Bremen; c. incid. mus. songs. (3) **Ad.**, Stuttgart, Feb. 9, 1849—Leipzig, Sept. 12, 1934; bro. of above; pupil of the Cons.; 1868–85, teacher in Geneva, then Leipzig Cons.; writer and composer.

Ruzicka (Rucsicska, Rutschitschka,

etc.) (root-shētsh'-kä), **Wenzel**, Jaumentz, Moravia, 1758—Vienna, 1823; bandm. and dram. composer and ct.-organist; Schubert was his pupil.

Ry'an, Thos., Ireland, 1827—New Bedford, Mass., March 25, 1903; at 17 went to the U. S.; studied Boston, 1849; co-founder "Mendelssohn Quintet Club," with which he toured America; clarinet and vla.-virtuoso; c. quintets, quartets, songs, etc.; wrote "*Recollections of an Old Musician*" (New York, 1890).

Ryba (rē'-bä), **Jakob Jan.**, Przestitz, Bohemia, 1765—Roczmittal, 1815; c. 6 comic operas, etc.

Rybakov (rē'-bä-kôf), **Sergei Gavrilovich**, b. 1867; pupil of St. Petersburg Cons.; author studies of music in Russia and Turkestan.

Rybner (rib-ner), (1) **Cornelius**, Copenhagen, Oct. 26, 1855—N. Y., Jan. 21, 1929; pupil Gade, Reinecke; 1892, cond. Carlsruhe Philh. Soc.; 1904–19, he succeeded MacDowell as prof. of music Columbia University, N. Y., c. 3-act dance legend "*Prinz Ador*" (Carlsruhe, 1903), etc.; had given piano recitals, often with his daughter (2) **Dagmar**, b. 1890; also a talented pianist, début Carlsruhe, playing the Schumann concerto under Mottl; toured the U. S.; c. songs.

Ryelandt (rē'-länt), **Joseph**, b. Bruges, April 7, 1870; composer; pupil of Tinel; c. choral works with orch., "*St. Cécile*," and "*Purgatorium*," chamber music, etc.

S

Saar (zär), **Louis Victor Fz.**, Rotterdam, Dec. 10, 1868—St. Louis, Nov. 23, 1937; composer; studied with Rheinberger and Abel, Munich Cons.; then with Brahms; 1891 took the Mendelssohn composition prize for a pf.-suite and songs; 1892–95, opera-accompanist, New York; 1896–98, teacher, comp. and cpt., National Cons., N. Y.; 1898, Coll. of Mus.; critic and composer for piano; principal of the dept. of theory at Cincinnati College of Music from 1906; after 1917 at Chicago Mus. Coll.; prizes for composition; c. string quartet, piano quartet, sonatas for vln., for 'cello and for horn; organ, choral pieces; many songs, etc.

Sabane'iev, Leonid, b. Moscow, Nov. 19, 1881; pianist and writer on music, also composer; after 1920, dir. of State Inst. for Musical Science; c. piano trios and other pieces; author, "*History of Russian Music.*"

Sabata. Vide DE SABATA.

Sabbatini (säb-bä-tē'-nē), (1) **Galeazzo**, b. Pesaro; ct.-maestro and composer (1627–39). (2) **Luigi A.**, Albano Liziale, Rome, 1739—Padua, 1809; maestro, writer and composer.

Sacchi (säk'-kē), **Don Giovenale**, Barfio, Como, 1726—Milan, 1789; writer.

Sacchini (säk-kē'-nē), **A. M. Gasparo**, Pozzuoli, near Naples, June 23, 1734 —Paris, Oct. 8, 1786; eminent Neapolitan opera composer, son of a poor fisher. Discovered and taught by Durante and others; 1756, prod. succ. intermezzo "*Fra Donata*," followed by others in Neapolitan dialect; 1762–66, at Rome in a keen rivalry with Piccinni; 1772–82, London, succ. as composer but not as financier. Fled from creditors to Paris where he had succ. and prod. many works, incl. "*Œdipe à Colone*," his best work. He c. over 60 operas, 6 oratorios, etc.

Sachs (zäkhs), (1) **Hans**, Nürnberg, Nov. 5, 1494—Jan. 19, 1576; a cobbler; chief of the Meistersinger (v. D. D.) and hero of Wagner's opera of that name; he wrote over 4,000 poems, 1,700 tales and 200 dramatic poems; also c. melodies. (2) **Julius**, Waldhof, Meiningen, 1830—Frankfort-on-Main, 1888; pianist. (3) **Melchior Ernst**, Mittelsinn, Lower Franconia, Feb. 28, 1843—Munich, May 18, 1917; pupil Munich Cons. and of Rheinberger; 1868–72, cond. "Liederkranz"; 1871, teacher of harm. Sch. of Mus.; founded and long cond. "Tonkünstlerverein" concerts; c. opera, ballade with orch., etc. (4) **Curt**, b. Berlin, 1881; noted critic and musicologist, Ph. D., Berlin Univ.; an authority on instruments, author of many works on the subject. (5) **Léo**, b. Alsace, 1868; c. operas, chamber music, songs.

Sachse-Hofmeister (zäkhs'-ĕ-hôf'-mī-shtĕr), **Anna**, Gumpoldskirchen, near Vienna, July 26, 1850—Berlin, Nov. 15, 1904; soprano.

Sacrati (sä-krä-tē), **Francesco**, d. Modena, May 20, 1650; court cond. and important early composer of opera.

Saen'ger, (1) **Gustav**, New York, May 31, 1865—Dec. 10, 1035; violinist, conductor, editor; played in orch. at Met. Op., with N. Y. Philh. and Symph.; cond. Empire Theatre after 1893; ed. *The Metronome* and *The Musical Observer;* c. instrumental pieces, songs. (2) **Oscar,** Brooklyn, N. Y., Jan. 5, 1868—Washington, D. C., April 20, 1926; barytone, vocal teacher; pupil of Bouhy; taught Nat'l. Cons., N. Y.; sang with Hinrichs Amer. Op. Co.; teacher of many prominent artists.

Saf'onoff, (1) **W.,** Istchory, Caucasus, Feb. 6 (new style), 1852—Kislovodsk, March 13, 1918; pupil of Leschetizky and Zaremba; then of Brassin, Petersburg Cons., taking gold medal, 1881–85, teacher there; 1885, Moscow; 1889, dir. of the Cons. there, and 1890 conductor; in 1906 he visited London and cond. the Phil. Orch.; 1906–09 he cond. the Philh. Orch., New York City, with great success, then returned to Russia. A famous teacher, among his pupils being many eminent Russian musicians. (2) **Maria,** his daughter, is a pianist.

Ságh (säkh), **Jos.,** b. Pesth, March 13, 1852; Hungarian lexicographer; 1885, founder and editor of mus. paper *Zenelap;* d. Vac, Jan. 25, 1922.

Sagitta'rius. Vide SCHÜTZ.

Sahla (zä'-lä) **Richard,** Graz, Sept. 17, 1855—Stadthagen, April 30, 1931; violinist; pupil of David, Leipzig Cons.; début, Gewandhaus, 1873; 1888, ct.-cond. Bückeburg; founded an oratorio-soc. there; c. a Roumanian Rhapsody, etc.

Saint-Amans (săň-tä-mäň), **L. Jos.,** Marseilles, 1749—Paris, 1820; conductor at Brussels and dram. composer.

Saint-Georges (săň-zhôrzh), (1) ——, Chev. **de,** Guadeloupe, 1745—Paris, 1799 (or 1801); mulatto violinist and composer. (2) **Jules H. Vernoy,** Marquis **de,** Paris, 1801—1875; librettist of many works, especially in collaboration with Halévy.

Saint-Huberty (săň-tü-bĕr-tē), **Antoinette Cécile Clavel** (called **St.-Huberty,** rightly **Clavel),** Toul, ca. 1756—London, 1812, noted soprano, Gr. Opéra, Paris, 1777–89; 1790, m. the Count d'Entraigues; they were assassinated at their country seat, near London, 1812 (probably from political motives).

Saint-Lambert (săň-läň-băr), **Michel**

de, Parisian harpsichord-teacher; wrote methods (1680–1700).

Saint-Lubin (săn-lü-băň), **Léon de,** Turin, 1805—Berlin, 1850; violinist and dram. composer.

Sainton (săn-tôň), (1) **Prosper (Ph. Catherine),** Toulouse, 1813—London, 1890; violinist and composer. (2) **Sainton-Dolby, Charlotte Helen** (née Dolby), London, 1821—1885; contralto-singer.

Saint-Saëns (săn-säň), **Chas. Camille,** Paris, Oct. 9, 1835—Algiers, Dec. 16, 1921; eminent French composer. Began to study the piano before 3; at 5 played a Grétry opera from the score; at 7 entered the Cons., pupil of Stamaty (pf.) Maleden and Halévy (comp.), and Benoist (org.); 1st org.-prize, 1851; at 16, prod. a symph.; 1853, organist Saint-Méry; 1858, the Madeleine; also till 1870 pf.-teacher Niedermeyer Sch.; made frequent tours as pianist and conductor of his works, incl. U. S., 1906 and 1915. He was a writer of unusual gifts. 1894, Commander of the Legion of Honour. C. operas: 1-act *"La Princesse Jaune"* (Op.-Com., 1872); *"Le Timbre d'Argent,"* 4-acts (Th.-Lyr., 1877); the very succ. *"Samson et Dalila"* (Weimar, 1877, often sung as an oratorio); *"Proserpine"* (Op.-Com., 1887); *"Ascanio"* (Opéra, 1890); comic *"Phryné"* (Op.-Com., 1893); *"Parisatis"* (Béziers, 1902); *"Lola"* (1901), *"Les Barbares"* (1901), *"Andromaque"* (1903), *"Hélène"* (Monte Carlo, 1904), *"L'Ancêtre"* (do., 1906), *"Dejanire"* (1911); wrote the last 2 acts of Guiraud's unfinished *"Frédégonde"* (Opéra, 1895). C. ballets, music to *"Antigone"* (Comédie-Française); and Gallet's *"Déjanire"* (Béziers, 1898, with orch. of 250, chorus of 200, and ballet of 60 in open air). C. also a Christmas oratorio; the "Biblical opera" *"Le Déluge";* 2 masses; ode *"La Lyre et la Harpe"* (Birmingham Fest., 1879); cantata *"La feu céléste"* (1900); fantaisie for violin and harp (1907); *"La Muse et le Poète"* for violin and orch., 1909; *"Overture de Fête,"* op. 133, 1909; songs, piano pieces, string quartet, septet, 2 piano trios, 2 vln. sonatas, organ works, *"La jota aragonese"* for orch.; 5 pf.-concertos; 2 vln.-concertos, Introduction and Rondo Capriccioso, *"Havanaise"* both for v!n. and orch.; *"Carneval des Animaux,"* descriptive suite (humorous) for 2 pianos and orch.; 2 'cello-concertos; cantata *"Les Noces de Prométhée"* (1867); Psalm 19, with orch. (London, 1885); 5 symphs., symphonic poems, *"Le rouet d'Omphale," "Phaëton," "Danse macabre," "La jeunesse d' Hercule"*; 2 orch. suites, the first *"Algérienne,"* etc. A highly versatile composer, his works showed refinement, spirit, genial melody and a fine sense of form. He was one of the leading figures in the restoration of French symphonic music. His nature lacked, however, qualities of depth and universality.

A thematic catalogue of his works was pub. by Durand, 1897, and revised, 1907. Memoirs by Loanda, Blondel, Bellaigue, Neitzel, Baumann, Bonnerot, Montargis, Hervey, Rolland, Jullien, Séré, etc.

Sala (sä'-lä), **Nicola,** near Benevento, Italy, ca. 1715—Naples, 1800; maestro, theorist and dram. composer.

Sal'aman, Chas. Kensington, London, March 3, 1811—June 23, 1901; pianist; pupil of Rimbault and Chas. Neate; début 1828, then studied with H. Herz, Paris; 1831, teacher in London; 1840, founded a choral soc.; 1858, founded the Mus. Soc. of London; also the Mus. Assoc., 1874; critic and essayist; c. orch. pcs., etc.

Saldoni (säl-dō'-nē), Don **Baltasar,** Barcelona, 1807 — 1890; organist, singing-teacher, writer and dram. composer.

Sale (säl), **Fran.,** Belgian ct.-tenor and composer, 1589.

Saléza (säl-ā-zä), **Albert,** Bruges, Béarn, 1867—Paris, 1916; notable tenor; pupil Paris Cons.; 1st prize in singing, 2d. in opera; début Op.-Com., 1888; 1889-91, at Nice; from 1892, engaged at the Opéra, Paris; 1898-1901, Met. Op., New York; after 1911 he taught at the Paris Cons.

Salieri (säl-ĭ-ā'-rē), (1) **Ant.,** Legnano, Verona, Aug. 19, 1750—Vienna, May 7 (12 ?), 1825; noted operatic composer and organist; pupil of his brother (2) **Francesco** (violinist) and of Simoni, Pascetti and Pacini; taken to Vienna by Gassman; his successor as ct.-composer and cond. of Italian opera; he prod. many operas there, then one at Paris under Gluck's

name, G. kindly confessing the ruse when the opera was a succ.; 1788, ct.-cond. Vienna; was a rival of Mozart and unjustly accused of poisoning him; c. 40 operas, 12 oratorios, etc.

Salimbeni (säl-ĭm-bä'-nē), **Felice,** Milan, ca. 1712—Laibach, 1751; soprano-musico.

Salinas (sä-lē'-näs), **Fran.,** Burgos, Spain, ca. 1512—1590; professor.

Sal'mond, Felix, b. London, Nov. 19, 1888; 'cellist; studied with Whitehouse, R. Coll. of Music, and Edouard Jacobs, Brussels; début, London, 1909; appeared widely in Europe; after 1922 in N. Y., where gained rep. as fine technician; has played with leading orchs. and in chamber music and recital programmes; head of 'cello dept., Juilliard School of Music, N. Y.

Salò, Gasparo da. Vide GASPARO.

Saloman (zä'-lō-män), **Siegfried,** Tondern, Schleswig, 1816—Stockholm, 1899; violinist, lecturer and dram. composer.

Salomé (säl-ō-mä), **Th. César,** Paris, 1834—St. Germain, 1896; composer and organist.

Salomon (zä'-lō-mōn), (1) **Jn. Peter,** Bonn, Jan., 1745—London, Nov. 25, 1815; vln.-virtuoso; from 1781, London; 1786, organised famous Salomon concerts for which Haydn, whom he brought over, c. special works. (2) **Hector,** Strassburg, May 29, 1838—Paris, 1906; pupil of Jonas and Marmontel (pf.), Bazin (harm.) and Halévy (comp.); in 1870, 2d chorusm., later *chef de chant,* Gr. Opéra; c. operas, etc.

Salter (sôl'-tĕr), (1) **Sumner,** b. Burlington, Iowa, June 24, 1856; studied at Amherst Coll. and music in Boston; 1900-02, taught at Cornell Univ. and Ithaca Cons.; 1905, mus. dir. at Williams College; active as recitalist, organist and mus. dir.; ed. *The Pianist and Organist,* N. Y.; c. church-mus. (2) **Mary Turner,** Peoria, Ill., 1856—Orangeburg, N. Y., 1938; studied singing with Alfred Arthur, Burlington, Ia.; then pupil of Max Schilling, John O'Neill, and Mme. Rudersdorf, Boston; 1877 succeeded Emma Thursby as soprano of Broadway Tabernacle, N. Y.; 1879, soprano Trinity Church, New Haven, teaching also at Wellesley College; 1881, married Sumner Salter, who was her teacher in composition; 1893 retired from church and concert work, devoting her time to teaching and composition of songs.

Salvayre (săl-văr) (**Gervais Bd.**), **Gaston,** Toulouse, June 24, 1847— May 16, 1916; studied at the cath.-maîtrise, then at Toulouse Cons.; later Paris Cons., taking the Grand Prix de Rome, 1872, with cantata "*Calypso*"; 1877, chorusm. at the Opéra-Populaire; 1894 in Servia; later critic of "*Gil Blas*"; Chev. of the Legion of Honour; c. operas "*Le Bravo*" (1877), "*Richard III.*" (Petersburg, 1883), "*Egmont*" (Op.-Com., 1886), "*La Dame de Montsoreau*" (Opéra, 1888), etc.; c. also Biblical symph., "*La Resurrection*," 113th Psalm with orch., etc.

Salzedo (säl-zä'-dō), **Carlos,** b. Arcachon, France, April 6, 1885; harpist, composer; studied Bordeaux and Paris Cons., 1st prize solfege, piano and harp; toured in Europe as harpist, later with Amer. orchs. and in recital; dir. harp dept., Curtis Inst. of Music, Phila.; founded Salzedo Harp Ensemble; c. works for harp and orch., in which he has appeared as performer or cond.

Samara (sä-mä'-rä), **Spiro,** Corfù, 1861 —Athens, 1917; pupil of Enrico Stancampiano in Athens; later of Délibes, Paris Cons.; prod. succ. opera, "*Flora Mirabilis*" (Milan, 1886); "*Medge*" (Rome, 1888); "*Lionella*" (Milan, 1891); "*La Martire*" (Naples, 1894; Paris, 1898); "*La Furia Domata*" (Milan, 1895); "*Histoire d'amour*" (Paris, 1902), etc.

Samar'off (née Hickenlooper), **Olga,** b. San Antonio, Texas, Aug. 8, 1882 (of German-Russian parents); pianist; at 9 pupil of Von Sternberg, later of Marmontel, Widor, and the Paris Cons.; studied again with Ernest Hutcheson and with Jedliczka; début, N. Y., 1905; 1906, London; toured widely; 1911 married Leopold Stokowski; divorced; she retired from concert work following an injury to her wrist sustained in a fall; for 2 seasons she was guest music critic of the New York *Post;* founder and dir. of the "Laymen's Music Courses," and has made many lecture appearances throughout the country to promote music appreciation; faculty mem. of the Juilliard School of Music, N. Y. C., and of

the Phila. Cons. of Music; secretary of the Schubert Memorial, Inc.

Samazeuilh (săm-ä-zŭ'-ē), **Gustave,** b. Bordeaux, June 2, 1877; Parisian critic and composer; pupil of Chausson and d'Indy; c. notable orch., chamber and vocal music; secretary of the Société Nationale de Musique and contributor to numerous publications. Wrote life of Paul Dukas (1913).

Samin'sky, Lazare, b. in the Crimea, 1883; composer; studied at St. Petersburg Cons., also with Rimsky-Korsakoff, Tcherepnine and Liadoff; 1918, dir. of Tiflis People's Cons.; cond. at Duke of York Theatre, London, 1920; after 1921 lived in N. Y.; mem. of board of directors, League of Composers; dir. of music at Temple Emanu-El; has been active as cond. of modern music programmes; c. (ballets) "*Vision of Ariel*," "*Lament of Rachel*," "*Gagliarda of a Merry Plague*," "*Jephtha's Daughter*"; 5 symphonies with descriptive titles; "*Litanies of Women*" for mez.-sopr. and chamber orch.; piano works, song cycles, etc.

Sammar'co, Mario, Palermo, Sicily, 1873—Milan, Jan. 24, 1930; noted barytone; pupil of Cantelli; after 1894 sang in Milan, later in other Eur. cities; 1905-14 at Covent Garden, 1907-10 with much succ. at Manhattan Op. House, N. Y.; and after 1910 for some seasons with the Chicago Opera Company.

Sammartini (säm-mär-tē'-nē), (1) **Pietro,** ct.-mus. at Florence, etc. (1635-44). (2) **Giov. Bat.** Milan, 1701—1775; organist, conductor and composer. (3) **Giu.,** d. London, 1740; oboist; bro. of above.

Sam'mons, Albert, b. London, Feb. 23, 1886; violinist; studied with his father, with Saunders and Weist-Hill; début, Harrowgate, 1906; has appeared widely as soloist, also as concertm. of Beecham Symph. Orch. and for a time as a mem. of the London String Quartet.

Samuel (säm-wĕl), (1) **Ad.,** Liége, 1824 —Ghent, 1898; theorist and dram. composer. (2) **Harold,** London, May 23, 1879—Jan. 15, 1937; pianist; studied R. C. M. with Stanford and Dannreuther; début, London, 1894; had attained internat'l. rank as a Bach performer particularly, but also in other music of classical period; had given Bach cycles of clavier music (played on modern piano but brilliantly suggesting harpsichord), covering a week in both London and N. Y.; toured U. S. after 1925; appearances with leading orchs.; had also lectured and served as examiner for the R. C. M. and R. A. M.

San'born, Pitts, b. Port Huron, Mich., d. N. Y., March 7, 1941; critic; M. A., Harvard, 1902; music ed. N.Y. *Globe*, 1905–25; later with N. Y. *Daily Mail* and continuing on the N.Y. *Telegram* when merged with this paper; also with *World-Telegram* following merger with N. Y. *World;* has written novel in 2 vols., *"Prima Donna,"* also many programme annotations and magazine articles; dir. of Inst. of the Audible Arts.

Sances (sän'-chĕs), **Giovanni Felice,** Rome, 1600—Vienna, Nov. 24, 1679; tenor and court cond. at Vienna; one of the first to write "cantatas"; c. operas, oratorios, etc.

Sanctis, de. Vide DE SANCTIS.

Sandberger (zänt'-bĕrkh-ĕr), **Ad.,** b. Würzburg, Dec. 19, 1864; studied at the R. Sch. of Mus. there, and at Munich, also with Spitta; 1887, Dr. Phil.; mus. libr., Munich Library, and lecturer at the Univ.; 1898 prof. of mus. at Prague Univ.; 1909–29, prof. mus. history, Munich Univ.; ed. Orlando di Lasso's complete works; wrote biog., hist., essays, etc.; c. opera *"Ludwig der Springer"* (Coburg, 1895), overture, etc.

Sanders, C. Vide LEUCKART.

San'derson, (1) **Jas.,** Workington, Durham, 1769—ca. 1841; violinist, teacher and composer. (2) **Lillian,** b. Sheboygan, Wis., Oct. 13, 1867; concert mezzo-soprano; pupil of Stockhausen, Frankfort-on-Main; début Berlin, 1890; toured Europe. (3) **Sibyl,** Sacramento, Cal., 1865—Paris, May 16, 1903; soprano, opera-singer; pupil of de la Grange and Massenet, who wrote his *"Thaïs"* and *"Esclarmonde"* for her; succ. début, Op.-Com., 1889; sang there for several years; 1898 in New York Met. Op., and variously in Europe.

Sandoni. Vide CUZZONI.

Sandt (zänt), **Max van de,** Rotterdam, Oct. 18, 1863—Cologne, July 14, 1934; pianist; pupil of his father and Liszt; toured Europe; 1889, pf.-teacher Stern Cons., Berlin; 1896, Cologne Cons.; 1910, Bonn Conservatory.

Sangiovanni (sän-jō-vän'-nē), **A.,** Bergamo, 1831—Milan, 1892; prof. of singing.

Santini (sän-tē'-nē), Abbate **Fortunato,** Rome, 1778—1862; coll. a notable mus.-library.

Sant'ley, (1) Sir **Chas.,** Liverpool, Feb. 28, 1834—Hove near London, Sept. 22, 1922; noted operatic and concert barytone; pupil Nava, Milan, Garcia, London; début, 1857; won pre-eminence in England at festivals, etc.; operatic début, Covent Garden, 1859; 1875 with Carl Rosa Co.; 1871 and 1891, America; retired 1900; knighted 1907; also a painter; c. a mass with orch.; a berceuse for orch.; songs (pub. under the pseud. **"Ralph Betterton"**), etc. His wife, (2) **Gertrude Kemble** (Charles Kemble's granddaughter) (d. 1882), was a soprano; their daughter (3) **Edith** was a successful soprano, till her marriage in 1884 with the Hon. R. H. Lyttleton.

Santoliquido (sän-tō-lē-kwē'-dō), **Francesco,** b. Naples, Aug. 6, 1883; composer; grad. St. Cecilia Liceo, Rome; for a time res. in Tunis; a delicate and colourful style is revealed in his chamber music and songs; c. (operas) *"La Favola di Helga," "L'Ignota"* and *"Ferhuda"*; (Mimo-drama) *"La Bajadera dalla Maschera Gialla"*; (cantata) *"L'Ultima Visione di Cassandra"*; (overture) *"La Morte di Tintagiles"*; (symph. poem) *"Nelle Oasi Sahariani"*; 2 symphonies; (suites) *"Paesaggi"* and *"Acquerelli,"* piano music and songs; wrote essay on music after Wagner, Debussy and Strauss.

Santucci (sän-toot'-chē), **Marco,** Camajore, 1762—Lucca, 1843; conductor and composer.

Sapell'nikoff, Wassily, b. Odessa, Nov. 2, 1868; pianist; pupil of Fz. Kessler, and then (with a stipend from the city of Odessa) of L. Brassin and Sophie Menter, Petersburg Cons., 1888, début Hamburg; toured; taught Moscow Cons., 1897–99; c. opera and pf.-pieces.

Sap'io, Romualdo, b. Palermo, 1858; conductor, vocal teacher; pupil Naples Cons.; toured U. S. after 1888 as cond. for Patti, Albani, Nordica; beginning 1892 taught at Nat'l. Cons., N. Y.; later privately; m. Clementine de Vere, soprano.

Saran (zä'-rän), **Aug. (Fr.),** Altenplathow, Province of Saxony, Feb. 28, 1836—Bromberg, Feb. 23, 1922; pupil of Fr. Ehrlich and of R. Franz; teacher, army-chaplain (1873); 1885 cond. of a church-choral soc. at Bromberg; writer and composer.

Sarasate (sä-rä-sä′-tĕ), **Pablo (Martin Meliton Sarasate y Navascuez) de,** Pamplona, Spain, March 10, 1844—Biarritz, Sept. 20, 1908; eminent violinist; at 10 played before the Queen, who presented him with a Stradivari, after succ. concerts in Spain he studied with Alard (vln.) and Reber (comp.), Paris Cons., taking 1st vln.-prize 1857, and a *premier accessit*, 1859, in harm.; he made very wide and very succ. tours; 1889, America. For him Lalo c. his 1st vln.-concerto and the "Symph. espagnole"; Bruch, his 2nd concerto and the Scotch Fantasia; A. C. Mackenzie, the "Pibroch" Suite. S. pub. *"Zigeunerweisen"* for vln. and orch.; *"Spanische Tänze"* for vln. and pf., fantasias, etc. He left a large coll. of mementos to his native city, later housed in a special museum. Memoir by Altadill, 1910.

Sarmiento (sär-mĭ-ĕn′-tō), **Salvatore,** Palermo, 1817—Naples, 1869; conductor and dram. composer.

Saro (sä′-rō), **J. H.,** Jessen, Saxony, 1827—Berlin, 1891; bandmaster and writer.

Sarrette (sär-rĕt), **Bd.,** Bordeaux, 1765—Paris, 1858; founder and director till 1814 of the Paris Cons. which he gradually developed from a sch. started by the band of the Paris National Guard.

Sarri (sär′-rē), **Dom.,** Trani, Naples, 1678—after 1741; conductor and dram. composer.

Sarti (sär′-tē), **Giuseppe (called Il Domenichino)** (ēl dō-mĕn-ĭ-kē-nō), Faenza, Dec. 1, 1729—(of gout) Berlin, July 28, 1802; pupil of either Vallotti or Padre Martini; 1748–50 organist Faenza Cath.; 1751 he prod. at Faenza succ. opera *"Pompeo in Armenia,"* followed by *"Il Re Pastore"* (Venice, 1753) and others so succ. that at 24 he was called to Copenhagen as dir. Italian opera and court-cond.; he was summarily dismissed for political reasons; 1775–99, dir. Cons. dell' Ospedaletto, Venice; in competition (with Paisiello and others) he won the position of cond. at Milan Cath.; he prod. from 1776–

84, 15 operas; he also prod. grand cantatas and several masses, etc. Catherine II. invited him to Petersburg. As he passed Vienna, he was received by the Emperor, and met Mozart, complaining, however, of the "barbarisms" in M.'s quartets and finding 19 mortal errors in 36 bars. Lived at Petersburg 18 years, excepting a brief period of disgrace, due to Todi, during which exile he founded a fine sch. at Ukraine. 1793 he was restored to the Empress' favour, and placed at the head of a Cons. He raised the Italian opera to high efficiency, inv. a very accurate machine for counting vibrations and was ennobled in 1795. In a Te Deum (on the taking of Otchakow by Potemkin) the music was reinforced by fireworks and cannon. He set the libretto *"Hega"* by the Empress. He c. 40 operas, masses, some still performed, etc.

Sartorio (sär-tō′-rĭ-ō), **A.,** Venice, ca. 1620—ca. 1681; conductor and dram. composer.

Saslav′sky, Alex., b. Kharkov, Russia, Feb. 9, 1876; violinist; pupil of Gorsky and Gruen; after 1903 concertm. of N. Y. Symph.; 1904–08 of Russian Symph., N. Y.; after 1919 of Los Angeles Philh.; d. San Francisco, Aug. 2, 1924.

Sass (säs) (at first sang under the name **Sax**), **Marie Constance,** Ghent, Jan. 26, 1838—Auteuil near Paris, Nov. 8, 1907; a chansonette-singer in a Paris café, found and taught by Mme. Ugalde; début Th.-Lyrique, 1859, as soprano, 1860–71, at the Opéra, then in Italy; 1864, m. the barytone Castelmary, divorced 1867.

Satie (sä′-tē), **Erik,** Honfleur, France, May 17, 1866—Arcueil, Aug. 5, 1925; composer; early musical training rather irregular, with periods of study at Paris Cons. and Schola Cantorum; research in Gregorian music influenced him; pioneer in forming original style of extreme simplicity, which was innovational in a day of exaggerated romanticism; had marked influence on Debussy, whom he met 1889, and later on a whole generation of modern composers, incl. Group of Six (Honegger, Milhaud, Poulenc, Auric, Durey and Germaine Tailleferre), and even a younger coterie known as the École d'Arcueil (named after village where

S. was assistant postmaster); he was influenced by classic Greek art, but above all was a satirist of pretences, naming many of his works by absurd titles; c. (opera) "*Paul et Virginie*," (symph. drama) "*Socrate*"; (ballets) "*Uspud*" and "*Parade*"; many piano pieces, of which "*Ogives*," "*Gymnopédies*" (several of latter orchestrated by Debussy and widely perf.) antedated and were strikingly like later harmonic style of that composer.

Satter (zät′-tĕr), **Gustav**, Vienna, Feb. 12, 1832—Savannah, Ga., 1879; studied Vienna, Paris; 1854–60 toured the U. S. and Brazil; returned to Paris, where Berlioz warmly praised his compositions; lived in various cities; c. opera "*Olanthe*," overtures "*Lorelei*," "*Julius Cesar*," "*An die Freude*," 2 symphs., a symph. tone-picture "*Washington*," etc.

Sauer (zow′-ĕr), (1) **Wm.**, Friedland, Mecklenburg, 1831—Frankfort, 1916; org.-builder from 1857 at Frankfort-on-Oder. (2) Vide LEIDESDORF. (3) **Émil, von**, b. Hamburg, Oct. 8, 1862; notable pianist; pupil of his mother; of N. Rubinstein at Moscow, 1881, and of Liszt at Weimar; from 1882 toured Europe and 1898–99 U. S. with great succ.; 1901–07, and again after 1915, head of pf.-dept. Vienna Cons.; c. suite moderne, "*Aus lichten Tagen*," 2 piano concertos, concert-études, etc.

Sauret (sō-rā), **Émile**, Dun-le-Roi, Cher, France, May 22, 1852—London, Feb. 12, 1920; notable violinist; pupil of Paris Cons. and of de Bériot, Brussels Cons.; at 8 began succ. European tours; America 1872, and frequently thereafter; 1880–81, t. Kullak's Acad., Berlin; lived in Berlin till 1890, then prof. R. A. M., London; wrote "*Gradus ad Parnassum du violoniste*" (Leipzig, 1894); c. 2 vln.-concertos, etc.

Sauveur (sō-vŭr′), **Jos.**, La Flèche, 1653—Paris, 1716; a deaf-mute, who learned to speak at 7, and became a notable investigator in acoustics (which word in fact he invented); he was the first to calculate absolute vibration-numbers and to explain overtones; pub. many treatises (1700–13).

Sauzay (sō-zĕ′), (**Chas.**) **Eugène**, Paris, July 14, 1809—Jan. 24, 1901; violinist, pupil of Vidal; later of Baillot at

the Cons.; won 1st and 2nd vln.-prize, and prize for fugue; 2nd vln. and afterwards vla. in Baillot's quartet, and m. B.'s daughter (a pianist); 1840 solo violinist to Louis Philippe; later leader of 2nd vlns. Napoleon III.'s orch.; 1860 vln.-prof. at the Cons.; pub. a treatise; c. a string-trio, "*Études harmoniques*," etc.

Savage, Henry W., New Hampshire, 1860—Boston, Nov. 29, 1927; impresario; graduate of Harvard; as a builder and real estate owner in 1895 took over the Castle Square Theatre, Boston, and organised a stock co. which gave light and serious operas for many years in Boston, New York, etc.; produced many new American operettas as well as plays; made the immensely successful productions of "*Parsifal*" and "*Madame Butterfly*" in English by the touring Savage Opera Company.

Savard (să-văr), (1) **M. Gabriel Aug.**, Paris, 1814—1881; prof. of harm. and thorough-bass at the Cons.; pub. treatises. (2) **M. E. A.**, b. Paris, May 15, 1861; pupil of the Cons., taking the Prix de Rome, 1886; from 1902 dir. Lyons Cons.

Savart (să-văr), **F.**, Mézières, 1791—Paris, 1841; acoustician.

Saw′yer, F. J., Brighton, June 19, 1857—April 29, 1908. Bachelor of music, Oxford, 1877; Mus. Doc., 1884, Fellow R. C. of organists; organist for over 30 years; prof. of singing; c. oratorios, cantatas, etc.

Sax (săx), (1) **Chas. Jos.**, Dinant-sur-Meuse, Belgium, 1791—Paris, 1865; studied flute and clarinet, Brussels Cons.; from 1815 managed an instr.-factory at Brussels, making a specialty of brass instrs.; he made many improvements; 1853 he joined his son Ad. in Paris. (2) (**Ant. Jos.**) **Adolphe**, Dinant, Nov. 6, 1814—Paris, Feb. 4, 1894; son of above; eminent maker and inv. of instrs.; he inv. the family of instrs. called the saxophone (v. D. D.); in Paris he continued to make improvements inventing the saxhorns, saxotromba, etc.; 1857 teacher of the saxophone, Paris Cons. and pub. a saxophone method; he had much litigation over the priority of his inventions, but always won. (3) **Alphonse**, bro. and co-worker of above. (4) **Marie**, Vide SASS.

Sayão (sä-yä-nō), **Bidu**, Brazilian soprano; sang Met. Op., from 1936-7.

Sbriglia (sbrēl'-yä), **Giovanni**, b. Naples, 1840; tenor and famous teacher; pupil of De Roxas; début Naples, 1851; sang throughout Italy and toured America with Patti and others; became a very successful teacher in Paris, numbering the De Reszkés, Plançon, Nordica, Sanderson, etc., among his pupils. Mem. French Académie; d. Paris, (?).

Scacchi (skäk'-kē), **Marco**, b. Rome; ct.-conductor 1618-48; writer and composer.

Scalchi (skäl'-kē), **Sofia**, b. Turin, Nov. 29, 1850; alto or mezzo-soprano of unusual range f-b″; pupil of Boccabadati; début Mantua (1866); she sang throughout Europe, often in North and South America with much succ.; 1875 m. Count Luigi Lolli; after 1896 retired from stage and lived at her villa near Turin.

Scalero (skä-lä'-rō), **Rosario**, b. near Turin, Dec. 24, 1870; violinist, composer, teacher; pupil of Turin Liceo and in London and Leipzig; taught St. Cecilia Liceo, Rome (comp.), there in 1913 founded Societa del Quartetto; after 1919 res. in N. Y., as comp. teacher; c. orch., chamber and choral works.

Scaletta (skä-lět'-tä), **Orazio**, Cremona -Padua, 1630; conductor and composer.

Scandel'li, **Ant.**, Brescia, 1517—Dresden, 1580; conductor and composer.

Scaria (skä'-rĭ-ä), **Emil**, Graz, 1838—Blasewitz, 1886; bass; created "Wotan" at Bayreuth, 1876, and "Gurnemanz" ("Parsifal"), 1882.

Scarlatti (skär-lät'-tē), (1) **Alessandro**, Trapani, Sicily, 1659—Naples, 1725; founder of the "Neapolitan Sch."; noted teacher and an important innovator in opera (he prod. over 115); in 1680 he is first heard of as conducting his own opera; he introduced the innovation of the orchestral ritornello, and a partial *recitativo obbligato* (v. D. D.); 1684 court-cond.; 1703, 2nd cond. S. Maria Maggiore, Rome; 1707-09, 1st. cond.; teacher at 3 conservatories, San Onofrio; de' Poveri di Gesù Christi, and the Loreto. (2) **Domenico (Girolamo)**, Naples, Oct. 26, 1685—1757; son and pupil of above; studied also with Gasparini; eminent virtuoso and composer for harpsichord; founded modern pf.-technic; devised many now familiar feats; the first to compose in free style without contrapuntal elaboration and mass; in a competition with Händel he proved himself equal as a harpsichordist, but confessed himself hopelessly defeated as an organist; he was thereafter a good friend, almost an idolater, crossing himself when he mentioned Händel; 1715-19 he was maestro at St. Peter's, 1720 at London; 1720 court-cembalist Lisbon; his gambling left his family destitute; from 1710 he prod. operas, incl. the first setting of "*Amleto*" (1715). (3) **Giuseppe**, Naples, 1712—Vienna, 1777; grandson of (1); dram. composer. (4) **Fran.**, c. a melodrama in MS. at Rome. (5) **Pietro**, c. opera "*Clitarro*," with intermezzi by Hasse.

Schachner (shäkh'-něr), **Rudolf Jos.**, Munich, 1816—Reichenhall, 1896; pianist, teacher and composer.

Schack (Cziak) (shäk or chäk), **Benedikt**, Mirowitz, Bohemia, 1758—Munich, 1826; tenor and dram. composer.

Schad (shät), **Jos.**, b. Steinach, Bavaria, 1812—Bordeaux, 1879; pianist and composer.

Schade (shä'-dě), (1) **(Schadaus) Abraham**, pub. a valuable coll. of 384 motets (1611-16). (2) **Carl**, singing-teacher and writer (1828-31).

Schäffer (shěf'-fěr), (1) **Aug.**, Rheinberg, 1814 — Baden-Baden, 1879; dram. composer. (2) **Julius**, Crevese, Altmark, Sept. 28, 1823—Breslau, Feb. 10, 1902; studied with Dehn, Berlin; 1855 mus. dir. to the Grand Duke at Schwerin; founded and conducted the "Schlosskirchenchor", 1860 mus.-dir. at the Univ. and cond. Singakademie, Breslau; 1871, "R. Mus.-Dir."; 1878 prof.; Dr. Phil. *h. c.* (Breslau), 1872; wrote defence of his friend Franz' accompaniments to Bach and Händel; composer.

Schafhäutl (shäf'-hī-tl), **K. Fz. Emil von**, Ingolstadt, 1803—Munich, 1890; professor and theorist.

Schalk (shäl'k), (1) **Franz**, Vienna, May 27, 1863—Sept. 2, 1931; pupil of Bruckner; notable cond., first at Graz, then 1st cond. at the Prague Opera and Philh. concerts; 1899 1st cond. ct.-opera, Berlin; 1898 at Covent Garden, 1899 gave the complete Wagner Ring cycle in New York; after 1900, first cond. of the Vienna Op., of which after 1918 he was dir. (with Richard Strauss from 1919, and 1924–28 sole dir.); also led Gesellschafts concerts there until 1921, and dir. a class for conductors at the State Akad. until 1909. His bro. (2) **Josef**, Vienna, 1857—1911; prof. of pf., Vienna Cons.; writer.

Scharfe (shär'-fĕ), **Gustav**, Grimma, Saxony, 1835—Dresden, 1892; barytone, teacher and composer.

Scharfenberg (shär'-fen-bĕrkh), **Wm.**, Cassel, Germany, 1819—Quogue, N. Y., 1895; pianist, teacher and editor.

Scharwenka (shär-vĕn'-kä), (1) (**L., Philipp**, Samter, Posen, Feb. 16, 1847—Bad Nauheim, July 16, 1917; pupil of Würst and Kullak's Acad., Berlin, also of H. Dorn; 1870, teacher of theory and comp. at the Acad.; 1880 founded (with his bro. Xaver) the "Scharwenka Cons."; 1891, accompanied his bro. to New York; returned, 1892, as co-dir. of the Cons., later, 1893, merged in the Klindworth Cons.; also a caricaturist and illustrated a satire by Alex. Moszkowski (Berlin, 1881); 1902, R. Professor; c. "Herbstfeier" and "Sakuntala," for soli, chorus and orch., 2 symphs., "Arkadische Suite" and "Serenade" for orch., festival overture, Trio in G, op. 112, etc. (2) (**Fz.**) **Xaver**, Samter, Jan. 6, 1850— Berlin, Dec. 8, 1924; bro. of above; distinguished pianist and composer; pupil of Kullak and Würst, Kullak's Acad.; 1868, teacher there; at 19 gave public concert at the Singakademie, with succ.; for 10 years he gave annually 3 chamber-concerts there (with Sauret and H. Grünfeld); cond. of subscription concerts; 1874, toured Europe and America; 1880, co-founder the "Berlin Scharw. Cons.," dir. till 1891 then founded a Cons. in New York; 1898, Berlin, as dir. Klindworth-Scharwenka Cons.; ct.-pianist to the Emperor of Austria, "Prof." from the King of Prussia; c. succ. opera "Mataswintha" (Weimar, 1896); symph., 3 pf.-concertos, etc.

Schebek (shā'-bĕk), **Edmund**, Petersdorf, Moravia, 1819—Prague, 1895; amateur authority on vln.-construction, etc.

Schebest (shā'-bĕst), **Agnes,** Vienna,

1813—Stuttgart, 1869; mezzo-soprano.

Schechner-Waagen (shĕk'-nĕr-vä'-gĕn), **Nanette**, Munich, 1806—1860; noted soprano; 1832, m. Waagen, a painter.

Scheel (shēl), **Fritz**, Lübeck, Germany, Nov. 7, 1852—Philadelphia, March 13, 1907; conductor; son of a long line of musicians; studied with his father and with David at Leipzig; cond. in Bremerhaven, 1869; Schwerin, 1873; Chemnitz, 1884; Hamburg, 1890; Chicago Exp., 1894; founded and cond. San Francisco Symph., 1895-99; 1899, summer concerts in Woodside Park in Phila. met with succ. and led to founding of Phila. Orch., which he led from 1900 to his death; also Orpheus and Eurydice Clubs after 1905.

Scheibe (shī'-bĕ), (1) **Jn.**, d. Leipzig, 1748; celebrated org.-builder. (2) **Jn. Ad.**, Leipzig, 1708—Copenhagen, 1776; son of above; organist, editor and composer.

Scheibler (shī'-blĕr), **Jn. H.**, Montjoie, near Aix-la-Chapelle, 1777—Crefeld, 1837; acoustician and inventor.

Scheidemann (shī'-dĕ-män), (1) **Heinrich**, Hamburg, ca. 1596—1663; organist; pupil and successor of his father (2) **Hans S.**, organist Katherinenkirche.

Scheidemantel (shī'-dĕ-män-tĕl), **K.**, Weimar, Jan. 21, 1859—June 26, 1923; pupil of Bodo Borchers; sang at the ct.-th., 1878–86; pupil of Stockhausen; 1885, "Kammersänger"; 1886, Dresden ct.-opera; 1886, sang "Amfortas" in "Parsifal" at Bayreuth.

Scheidt (shīt), **Samuel**, Halle-on-Saale, 1587—1654; famous organist and composer; pupil of Sweelinck; organist of Moritzkirche and ct.-conductor; c. notable chorals, etc.

Schein (shīn), **Jn. Hermann**, Grünhain, Saxony, 1586—Leipzig, 1630; soprano; ct.-conductor and composer.

Scheinpflug (shīn'-pflookh), **Paul**, Loschwitz, Dresden, Sept. 10, 1875 —Memel, Lithuania, March 12, 1937; pupil of the Cons.; from 1909 cond. at Königsberg; 1914, led Blüthner Orch., Berlin; 1920, city mus. dir. at Duisburg; c. opera "Das Hofkonzert" (Berlin, 1922), "Frühlings Symph," chamber music, etc.; overture to a comedy of Shakespeare (based on English melody of 16th century), Boston Symph. Orch., 1909; tone-poems for orch., songs, etc.

Schelble (shĕl'-blĕ), **Jn. Nepomuk**, Hüfingen, Black Forest, 1789—Frankfort-on-Main, 1837; notable cond. and singing-teacher; tenor; c. operas, etc.

Schelle (shĕl'-lĕ), (1) **Jn.**, Geising, Saxony, 1648—Leipzig, 1701; cantor Thomaskirche. (2) **K. Ed.**, Biesenthal, near Berlin, 1816—Vienna, 1882; critic, lecturer and writer.

Schel'ling, Ernest Henry, b. Belvidere, N. J., July 26, 1876—N. Y., Dec. 8, 1939; pianist, composer; 1st appeared as child pianist in Phila.; pupil of Mathias at Paris Cons., and of Moszkowski, Pruckner, Leschetizky, Huber, Barth and Paderewski; has appeared widely as recitalist and soloist with orchs. in Europe and U. S.; in recent years has been esp. prominent as composer and conductor; in latter capacity has led young people's concerts of N. Y. Philh. Orch. annually, also appearing with Los Angeles and other orchs. as lecturer-conductor; guest with Phila. Orch. and Boston Symph.; in 1935-36 appointed cond. of Baltimore Symph. Orch.; c. *"Fantastic Suite"* for piano and orch., in which he appeared as soloist with Amsterdam Concertgebouw, 1907, and with Boston, N. Y., and Chicago Symphs.; also Symphony in C Minor; Orchestral Suite; *"Symphonic Legend"*; violin concerto (played by Kreisler, with Boston Symph., 1916); sonata for vln. and piano; *"A Victory Ball,"* vivid orch. depiction of dance on Armistice Day, after poem by Noyes, given its première in 1923 by N. Y. Philh. and subsequently widely played; *"Impressions from an Artist's Life"* (Boston Symph., 1915), in form of variations for piano and orch.; *"Divertimento"* for string quartet and piano (Flonzaley Quartet, 1925); tone poem, *"Morocco,"* for orch., premièred by N. Y. Philh., 1927; various other chamber music and piano works.

Schelper (shĕl'-pĕr), **Otto**, Rostock, April 10, 1840—Leipzig, Jan. 10, 1906; an actor, later barytone in opera, at Bremen; 1872-76, Cologne, then sang leading rôles, Leipzig City Theatre.

Schenck (shĕnk), (1) **Jean (Johann)**, gamba-player and dram. composer, 1688-93, Amsterdam. (2) **Jn.**, Wiener-Neustadt, Lower Austria, 1761—Vienna, 1836; c. operettas. **Peter Petrovich**, b. St. Petersburg, Feb. 23, 1870; pupil of the Cons., and of Saloviev; librarian and critic; c. operas, 3 symph., etc.

Schenker (shĕnk'-ĕr), **H.**, 1868—Vienna, 1935; pianist, theorist.

Scherchen (shĕr'-khĕn), **Hermann**, b. Berlin, June 21, 1891; conductor; viola player; largely self-taught; played in Berlin Philh. Orch.; cond. of symph. concerts at Riga, 1914; interned during war in Russia; founded and led Neue Musikgesellschaft, Berlin, 1918; Grotrian-Steinweg Orch., Leipzig, 1921-22; after latter year, the Museum Concerts in Frankfort, and cond. as guest in England and other countries; noted as an exponent of contemporary music, appearing at international festivals; ed. *Melos*, Berlin music paper, 1920-21; c. string quartet, piano sonata, songs.

Scherer (shä'-rĕr), **Sebastian Anton**, organist at Ulm Minster and composer, 1664.

Schering (shä'-rǐnk), **Arnold**, b. Breslau, April 2, 1877; violinist and historian, pupil of Joachim and Succo; prof. of music history at Leipzig Univ. after 1915; author of many musicological treatises; 1928, prof. mus. science, Berlin Univ.

Scherzer (shĕr'-tsĕr), **Otto**, Ansbach, 1821—Stuttgart, 1886; violinist and organist.

Schetky (shĕt'-kē), **Chp.**, Darmstadt, 1740—Edinburgh, 1773; 'cellist and composer.

Schicht (shǐkht), **Jn. Gf.**, Reichenau, Saxony, 1753—Leipzig, 1823; pupil of an uncle (org. and pf.); pianist, conductor and writer; c. 4 oratorios, chorals, etc.

Schick (shǐk) (née **Hamel**), **Margarete Luise**, Mayence, 1773—Berlin, 1809; soprano; pupil of Steffani and Righini; début, Mayence, 1791; from 1794, Royal Opera, Berlin.

Schiedermayer (shē'-dĕr-mī-ĕr), **Johann Baptist**, June 23, 1779—Linz-on Danube, Jan. 6, 1840; cath.-organist; wrote a textbook on chorals and a vln.-method, c. symphs., sacred mus., org.-pcs., etc.

Schiedmayer (shēt'-mī-ĕr) & **Söhne,** Stuttgart firm of piano-makers, founded in 1806 by **Johann Lorenz S.** (1786—1860).

Schikaneder (shē'-kä-nä-dĕr), **Emanuel Jn.,** Ratisbon, 1748—Vienna, 1812, the librettist of Mozart's *"Zauberflöte"* in which he created "Papageno"; a manager, actor and singer.

Schildt (shīlt), **Melchior,** Hanover (?), 1592—1667; organist.

Schilling (shǐl-ling), **Gv.,** Schwiegershausen, near Hanover, 1803—Nebraska, U. S. A., 1881; wrote textbooks and treatises, etc.

Schil'lings, Max (von), Düren, April 19, 1868—Berlin, July 24, 1933; notable composer; studied with Brambach and von Königslöw; 1892, stage-manager at Bayreuth; 1890 while studying law, at Munich, c. the opera *"Ingwelde"* (prod. by Mottl, Carlsruhe, 1894); played in many other cities; c. also opera *"Der Pfeifertag"* (Schwerin, 1901); 2 symph. fantasias *"Meergruss,"* 1895, and *"Seemorgen"*; incid. music to plays; *"Hexenlied"* for reciter, with piano or orch.; successful opera, *"Mona Lisa"* (Stuttgart, 1915; Met. Op., 1923, and Chicago Op.); and many other works; Royal Prof., 1903; 1908–18, gen. mus. dir., Stuttgart; 1919–25, intendant, Berlin State Op.; and active as guest cond. elsewhere; 1932, pres., Prussian Acad. of Arts; 1933, intendant of Berlin Städtische Op.; he was granted a patent of nobility by the King of Würtemberg; toured the U. S., 1930, as cond. of Wagnerian Op. Co.; m. Barbara Kemp, soprano.

Schimon (shē'-mōn), (1) **Ad.,** Vienna, 1820—Leipzig,1887; singing-teacher, accompanist and dram. composer, etc.; 1872, m. the soprano (2) **Anna Regan,** Bohemia, 1842—Munich, 1902; pupil of Manuel Garcia and Stockhausen; sang in Italy and Germany; court-singer in Russia; 1874, teacher of singing Leipzig Cons.; 1877–86, R. Sch. of Mus., Munich; again at Leipzig Cons. where his wife taught and was also after death of her husband, singing-teacher at Munich.

Schindelmeisser (shǐn'-dĕl-mīs-sĕr), **L.,** Königsberg, 1811—Darmstadt, 1864; ct.-conductor and dram. composer.

Schindler (shǐnt'-lĕr), (1) **Anton,** Meedl,

Moravia, 1795—Bockenheim, near Frankfort, 1864; violinist and conductor; friend and biographer of Beethoven. (2) **Kurt,** Berlin, Feb. 17, 1882—New York, Nov. 16, 1935; conductor, musicologist; studied Berlin and Munich Univ., music with Ansorge, Bussler, Gernsheim and Thuille; cond. Stuttgart Op., 1902; Würzburg, 1903; ass't cond. to Mottl and Zumpe, Munich, and to Strauss at Berlin, 1903–05; same capacity at Met. Op., N. Y., 1905–08; founded MacDowell Chorus, N. Y., 1909, which he developed into one of the city's most important choruses, the Schola Cantorum in 1912; made collections of Russian, Finnish, Spanish folk music.

Schipa (skē'-pä) **Tito,** b. Lecce, 1889; tenor; Chicago Op., from 1919; Met. Op., 1934.

Schirmer (shĕr'-mĕr), (1) **Gustav,** Königsee, Saxony, 1829—Eisenach, Thuringia, 1893; son and grandson of court piano-makers at Sondershausen; 1837 came to New York; founded pub. firm, Beer & Schirmer, 1866 S. obtained the entire business since known as G. Schirmer; 1893 incorporated under management of (2) **Rudolf E.** (New York, 1859—Santa Barbara, Cal., 1919) and (3) **Gustav** (New York, 1864—1907), sons of above. After 1915 the firm pub. the notable *Musical Quarterly.*

Schjelderup (shĕlt'-ĕr-oop), **Gerhard,** Christiansand, Norway, Nov. 17, 1859—Benedikt Beuern, July 29, 1933; composer and 'cellist; pupil of Franchomme, Savard and Massenet; c. operas *" Norwegische Hochzeit"* (Prague, 1900), and *"Frühlings Nacht,"* a symph. and orch. works, *"Eine Sommernacht auf dem Fjord,"* etc.

Schladebach (shlä'-dĕ-bäkh), **Julius,** Dresden, 1810—Kiel, 1872; wrote treatise on the voice.

Schläger (shlä'-gĕr), **Hans,** Filskirchen, Upper Austria, 1820—Salzburg, 1885; conductor and dram. composer.

Schleinitz (shlī'-nǐts), **H. Conrad,** Zschaitz, Saxony, 1802—Leipzig, 1881; dir. Leipzig Cons. (vice Mendelssohn).

Schlesinger (shlä'-zǐng-ĕr), two mus.-pub. firms. (a) at Berlin, founded 1810 by (1) **Ad. Martin,** from 1851 managed by his son (2) **Heinrich**

(d. 1879); 1864 under R. Lienau.
(b) at Paris, founded 1834 by (3)
Moritz Ad., son of (1); under Louis
Brandus in 1846. (4) **Sebastian
Benson**, Hamburg, Sept. 24, 1837—
Paris, 1917; at 13 went to U. S.;
studied at Boston with Otto Dresel;
for 17 years Imp. German Consul at
Boston; then lived in Paris; pub.
many pop. songs and piano-pieces.

Schletterer (shlĕt'-tĕr-ĕr), **Hans
Michel**, Ansbach, 1824—Augsburg,
1893; mus.-dir., writer and composer.

Schlick (shlĭk), (1) **Arnold**, ct.-organist
to the Elector Palatine, and com-
poser, 1511. (2) **Jn. Konrad**, Münster (?), Westphalia, 1759—Gotha,
1825; 'cellist and composer.

Schlimbach (shlĭm'-bäkh), **G. Chr.
Fr.**, b. Ohrdrof, Thuringia, 1760,
organist, writer on org.-building, etc.

Schlögel (shlä'-gĕl), **Xavier**, b. Brillon-
ville, Belgium, 1854—Ciney, 1889;
pupil Liége Cons.; c. mass with orch.,
chamber music, etc.

Schlösser (shlĕs'-sĕr), (1) **Louis**, Darmstadt 1800—1886; ct.-conductor and
dram. composer. (2) (**K. Wm.**)
Ad., Darmstadt, Feb. 1, 1830—near
Dorking, Engl., Nov. 10, 1913; son
and pupil of above; pianist, début
Frankfort, 1847; toured; from 1854,
teacher in London; c. pf.-quartet and
trio, etc.

Schlottmann (shlôt'-män), **Louis**, Berlin, Nov. 12, 1826—June 13, 1905;
concert-pianist, pupil of Taubert
and Dehn; lived in Berlin as teacher;
1875, R. Mus.-Dir.; c. overture to
"*Romeo and Juliet*," "*Trauermarsch*"
for orch., etc.

Schlusnus (shlōōs'-nōōs), **Heinrich**, b.
Braubach, Germany, Aug. 6, 1888;
barytone; pupil of Louis Bachner;
début, Hamburg Op., 1915; Nuremberg Op., 1915–17; after that year
with Berlin State Op., for a season
with Chicago Op., and has appeared
with prominent orchs. in Europe
and U. S.; also a distinguished Lieder
recitalist.

Schmedes (shmä'-dĕs), **Erik**, near
Copenhagen, Aug. 27, 1868—Vienna,
March 23, 1931; originally a pianist;
then studied singing with Rothmühl;
sang as barytone in various theatres;
studied with Iffert and, 1898–1924,
sang tenor rôles at Vienna; 1899
"*Siegfried*" and "*Parsifal*" at Bayreuth; also in N. Y., 1908–09; long
one of most eminent heroic tenors.

Schmelzer (shmĕl'-tsĕr), **Jn. H.;**
b. ca. 1630—d. June 30, 1680,
Vienna; ct.-cond. and composer.

Schmid(t) (shmĭt), (1) **Bd.**, organist at
Strassburg, 1560. He was succeeded
by (2) **Bd. Schmid**, the younger.
(3) **Anton**, Pohl, Bohemia, 1787—
1857; mus. libr. Vienna Library;
writer.

Schmidt (shmĭt), (1) **Jn. Phil. Samuel**,
Königsberg, 1779—Berlin, 1853;
Govt. official, critic, writer and dram.
composer. (2) **Jos.**, Bückeburg, 1795
—1865; violinist, ct.-conductor and
composer. (3) **Hermann**, Berlin,
1810—1845; ballet-conductor and
ct.-composer; c. operetta. (4) **Gustav**, Weimar, 1816—Darmstadt,
1882; ct.-conductor and dram. composer. (5) **Arthur P.**, Altona, Ger.,
April 1, 1846—1921; est. mus.-pub.
business, Boston and Leipzig, 1876.
(6) **Leopold**, Berlin, Aug. 2, 1860—
April 30, 1927; writer on music; Ph.
D.; early in life an operetta cond.;
from 1897 critic of the Berlin *Tageblatt;* author of studies of Mozart
and Haydn, etc.; adapted Offenbach
works for modern perfs. (7) **Franz**,
b. Pressburg, Hungary, Dec. 22,
1874—Vienna, 1940; comp.; pupil of
Hellmesberger; 1892–1910, played
as solo 'cellist in Vienna Ct.-Op.;
from 1910 teacher of advanced piano
perf. at the Akad. der Tonkunst
there, of which he was dir. after 1925;
1927–30, rector of the Hochsch. für
Musik; c. operas, "*Notre Dame*,"
"*Fredegundis*"; 4 symphonies; 2
string quartets; piano concerto;
piano quintet for left hand (written
for Paul Wittgenstein); organ works,
songs, etc.

Schmitt (shmĭt), (1) **Jos.;** 1764—
Frankfort-on-Main, 1818; writer,
violinist and composer. (2) **Nikolaus**, b. Germany; bassoonist and
composer; from 1779, *chef de musique* of the French Guards at Paris.
(3) **Aloys**, Erlenbach, Bavaria, 1788
—Frankfort-on-Main, 1866; eminent
teacher, pianist, writer and dram.
composer. (4) **Jacob** (**Jacques**),
Obernburg, Bavaria, 1803—Hamburg, 1853; bro. and pupil of above;
wrote a method and c. (5) (**G.**)
Aloys, Hanover, Feb. 2, 1827—Dresden, Oct., 1902; pianist and cond.;
son and pupil of (3); pupil Vollweiler
(theory), Heidelberg; toured; then
th.-cond. at Aix-la-Chapelle, etc.,

1857–92, ct.-cond. at Schwerin; from 1893, dir. "Dreyssig'sche Singakademie," Dresden. He c. 3 operas, incl. "*Trilby*" (Frankfort, 1845); incid. music; overtures, etc. He arranged the fragments of Mozart's C minor mass into a complete work; died of an apoplectic stroke while conducting his own "*In Memoriam.*" (6) **Hans,** Koben, Bohemia, Jan. 14, 1835—Vienna, Jan. 14, 1907; pianoteacher and oboist; pf.-pupil of Dachs, Vienna Cons., taking the silver medal; later, teacher there; wrote a vocal method; c. important instructive pcs., etc. (7) **Florent,** b. Blâmont, France, Sept. 28, 1870; studied at Nancy; 1889, entered Paris Cons. winning second Prix de Rome 1897; first 1900, with cantata "*Sémiramis.*" He sent from Rome a symph. poem "*Combat des Raksasas et Délivrance de Sita,*" a symph. étude based on Poe's "*Le Palais hanté*" and the "*46th Psalm,*" which was later played with success, 1906, increasing to furore (1910 and Colonne Concerts, 1912); his piano quintet (1909) has won fame; his "*Tragédie de Salomé*" was danced by Loie Fuller 1907; his symph. poem "*Sélamlik*" (1904), chamber music, piano pieces, and songs have given him a high place in France. He was dir. of the Lyons Cons. after 1921, and is a mem. of the exec. committee of the Société Musicale Independante and the Société Nationale de Musique. He has participated as pianist in many concerts of his works, visiting the U. S. in this capacity under the auspices of Pro Musica. His comps. also include: the ballet "*Le Petit Elfe Ferme-l'œil*" (Op.-Comique, 1924); music for Shakespeare's "*Antony and Cleopatra*" (Paris, 1921); the choral works, "*Chansons à Quatre Voix,*" "*Pendant la Tempête,*" "*Danse des Devadasis,*" and "*Chant de Guerre,*" the last for soprano soloist, male chorus and orch. (Paris, 1928); the orch. works, "*En Été,*" "*Reflêts d'Allemagne,*" and "*Puzazzi,*" suites, orig. for piano; "*Musiques de plein-air,*" "*Rapsodie Viennoise,*" "*Danse d'Abisag,*" (Paris, 1926); "*Fonctionnaire MCMXII, Inaction en Musique,*" an amusing satire (Paris, 1927); "*Salambo*" (do.); "*Rêves*"; "*Légende*";

"*Dionysiaques*"; "*Keroshal*" for tenor and orch.; "*Chant du Soir*", "*Sonata Libre*" and "*Quatre Pièces*" for vln. and piano; "*Deux Pièces*" and "*Chant Élégiaque*" for 'cello and piano; Andante et Scherzo, for harp and string quartet; Lied et Scherzo for double wind quartet; piano works; songs with piano; four-part songs with orch.; a cappella choral songs; choruses with orch.; also orch. versions of piano pieces by Chopin and Schubert. **S.** is the subject of studies published by Séré, Calvocoressi, Ferroud and Coeuroy.

Schmitz, E. Robert, b. Paris, 1889; pianist, teacher; studied at Paris Cons., with Diémer and Chevillard; 1st prize in piano; founded and dir. A. M. M. A. Choir, Paris, 1911, and also estab. his own orch.; first Amer. concert tour, 1919; formed Franco-Amer. Musical Soc., 1920, devoted to perf. of French music in N. Y. and elsewhere; this after 1923 became Pro Musica, Inc., with branches in many cities, presenting eminent composers in concerts of their works.

Schmul'ler, Alexander, Mozyr, Russia, Dec. 5, 1880—Amsterdam, March 29, 1933; noted violinist; pupil of Sevcik, Hrimaly and Auer; took up res. in Berlin, 1908, where he taught at the Stern Cons. until 1914, when he was called to the Amsterdam Cons.; he made many concert tours, incl. some with Max Reger.

Schnabel (shnä'-bĕl), (1) **Jos. Ignaz,** Naumburg, Silesia, 1767—Breslau, 1831; conductor and composer. (2) **Michael,** Naumburg, 1775—Breslau, 1842; bro. of above; founded at Breslau (1814) a piano factory, carried on by his son (3) **K.** (1809—1881) pianist and composer. (4) **Artur,** b. Lipnik, Carinthia, April 17, 1882; notable pianist; pupil of Leschetizky, 1888–97; played in leading Austrian and German cities; lived in Berlin, 1901–33, where he was heard in many sonata recitals with Flesch; 1925–33, prof. at the Hochschule there; attracted a wide following for his Beethoven sonata programs, giving complete cycles of these piano works in London, Berlin and N. Y.; has played as soloist with leading orchs. in Europe and U. S., also prominent as a teacher; c. songs and piano music, also chamber works in ultramodern idiom; m.

388 DICTIONARY OF MUSICIANS

Therese Behr, contralto; ed. Beethoven piano sonatas. (5) **Karl Ulrich,** son of (4), b. 1909, pianist; pupil of Berlin Hochsch., studied with Leonid Kreutzer; after 1925 appeared widely in Eur. cities; first Amer. tour, 1936–7.

Schneegass (shnā'-gäs) **(Snegas'-sius), Cyriak,** Busleben, near Gotha, 1546—1597; theorist and composer.

Schneevoigt (shnā'-foikht), **Georg,** b. Wiborg, Nov. 8, 1872; Finnish conductor and 'cellist; studied with Schröder, Klengel and Jacobs; lived in Helsingfors as teacher in the Cons., 1894–99; cond. Kaim Orch., Munich; 1903–07; Kiev Orch., 1909–10; Riga Orch., 1910–12; Helsingfors Symph., 1912–14; Stockholm Konsertförenigung Orch., 1914–24, besides also leading summer concerts at Scheveningen, Holland; founded Oslo Philh. Orch., 1919; 1927–29, cond. Los Angeles Philh. Orch.; latter year, gen. dir. Riga Op.; after 1932, cond. in Malmö; mem. French Legion of Honour; m. Sigrid Lindblom, pianist.

Schneider (shnī'-dĕr), (1) **Jn.,** Lauter near Coburg, 1702—Leipzig, 1787; famous improviser and organist. (2) **G. Abraham,** Darmstadt, 1770—Berlin, 1839; horn-virtuoso; conductor, composer of masses, etc. (3) **Louis,** Berlin, 1805—Potsdam, 1878; son of (2); writer. (4) **(Jn. G.) Wm.,** Rathenow, Prussia, 1781—Berlin, 1811; pianist, teacher, composer and writer. (5) **Wm.,** Neudorf, Saxony, 1783—Merseburg, 1843; organist and writer. (6) **Jn. Gottlob,** 1753—Gernsdorf, 1840; organist. (7) **(Jn. Chr.) Fr.,** Alt-Waltersdorf, Saxony, Jan. 3, 1786—Dessau, Nov. 23, 1853; son and pupil of (6); at 10 c. a symphony; 1821 ct.-conductor at Dessau; wrote textbooks and c. 15 oratorios, incl. famous *"Das Weltgericht"*; biog. by F. Kempe. (8) **Jn. (Gottlob),** Alt-Gersdorf, Oct. 28, 1789—Dresden, April 13, 1864; bro. of above; eminent organist and teacher. As a boy a soprano of remarkable range (to f'' acc. to Riemann,   ); later, tenor; 1825 ct.-organist, Dresden, also conductor; made tours; c. fugues, etc., for organ. (9) **Jn. Gottlieb,** Alt-Gersdorf, 1797—Hirschberg, 1856; bro. of above; organist. (10) **Theodor,** Dessau, May 14, 1827 —Zittau, June 15, 1909; son and

pupil of (7); pupil of Drechsler ('cello); 1845, 'cellist, Dessau ct.-orch.; 1854 cantor and choir-dir. court and city churches; 1860–96 cantor and mus.-dir. Jakobikirche, Chemnitz; also cond. (11) **(Jn.) Julius,** Berlin, 1805—1885; pianist, organist and mus.-director; and c. operas; son of (12) **Jn. S.,** pf.-mfr. at Berlin. (13) **K.,** Strehlen, 1822—Cologne, 1882; tenor. (14) **K. Ernst,** Aschersleben, 1819—Dresden, 1893; writer.

Schnitzer, Germaine, b. Paris, May 28, 1889; pianist; pupil of Paris Cons., grad. at age of 14; also of Pugno and Sauer; after 1904 toured widely, 1906 in U. S., where following her marriage in 1913 to Dr. Leo Bürger of N. Y., she has made her home.

Schnorr von Karolsfeld (shnôr fōn kä'-rōls-fĕlt), (1) **L.,** Munich, 1836—Dresden, 1865; noted tenor; created Wagner's "Tristan"; c. opera at Munich (1865), his wife, (2) **Malwina** (née **Garrigues**) (d. Carlsruhe, 1904), created "Isolde."

Schnyder von Wartensee (shnē'-dĕr fōn vär'-tĕn-zā), **X.,** Lucerne, 1786—Frankfort-on-Main, 1868; teacher, writer and composer.

Schoberlechner (shō'-bĕr-lĕkh-nĕr), **Fz.,** Vienna, 1797—Berlin, 1843; pianist, conductor and dram. composer.

Schöberlein (shā'-bĕr-līn), **L.,** Kolmberg, Bavaria, 1813—Göttingen, 1881; writer.

Schobert. Vide SCHUBART (3).

Schoeck (shĕk), **Othmar,** b. Brunnen, Sept. 1, 1886; Swiss composer; pupil of Reger; cond. in Zurich and St. Gallen; c. opera, orch., chamber music.

Schoenefeld (shā-'nĕ-fĕlt), **H.,** Milwaukee, Wis., Oct. 4, 1857—Los Angeles, Aug. 4, 1936; son and pupil of a musician; later studied Leipzig Cons.; winning a prize for a chorus with orch. performed at the Gewandhaus; then studied with E. Lassen (comp.), Weimar; toured Germany as a pianist; from 1879, Chicago, as pianist and teacher, also cond. the "Germania Männerchor." After 1904 lived in Los Angeles, where in 1915 he cond. the first Pacific Sängerfest; C. *"The Three Indians,"* ode with orch.; 2 symphs. (*"Rural," "Springtime"*); 2 overtures, *"In the Sunny South"* (based on Ethiopian

themes) and *"The American Flag"*;
vln.-sonata (Henri Marteau prize,
1899), pf.-pcs., etc.

Schöffer (shĕf'-fĕr), **Peter** (the
younger), mus.-printer at Mayence
and Strassburg, 1530–39.

Schœlcher (shĕl-shār) **Victor**, Paris,
1804—1893; writer, statesman and
biographer of Händel.

Scholes (skōls), **Percy A.**, b. Leeds,
England, 1877; writer; grad. Oxford
Univ.; associate R. Coll. of Music;
formerly master of music at Kent
Coll., Canterbury; 1901–03, Kings-
wood Coll., S. Africa; 1904, taught
Leeds Munic. School of Music; and
inspector for London Board of
Education; extension lecturer for
Oxford, London and Manchester
Univs.; founded Home Music Study
Union; after 1915 he visited America
several times as lecturer; later lived
in Switzerland; author, *"Purcell,"*
*"Arthur Bliss," "Crotchets," "Every-
man and His Music," "The Columbia
History of Music"* (compilation of
phonograph records), *"Listener's
Guide to Music," "Listener's History
of Music," "The Puritans and Music,"
"An Introduction to British Music"*;
and with W. Earhart, *"Complete Book
of the Great Musicians."*

Scholtz (shôlts), **Hn.**, Breslau, June 9,
1845—Dresden, July 13, 1918;
pianist; pupil of Brosig, Liszt, von
Bülow and Rheinberger; teacher in
Dresden, 1880 chamber virtuoso;
c. concerto; edited Chopin's text.

Scholz (shôlts), (1) **F.**, Gernstadt,
1787—Moscow, 1830; in latter city
after 1815 as opera cond.; c. ballets,
etc. (2) **Bd. E.**, Mayence, March
30, 1835—Munich, Dec. 26, 1916;
pupil of Ernst Pauer, Mayence,
and of Dehn, Berlin; 1856 teacher
R. Sch. of Mus., Munich; 1859–65,
ct.-conductor Hanover Th.; 1871–78,
cond. Breslau Orch. Soc.; 1883–
1908, dir. of the Hoch Cons., Frankfort (vice Raff); Dr. Phil. *h. c.* (Breslau Univ.), *"Royal Prussian
Professor,"* etc.; pub. essays *"Wohin
treiben wir?"* (Frankfort, 1897); prod.
9 operas incl. succ. *"Ingo"* (Frankfort, 1898). C. *"Das Siegesfest"* and
"Das Lied von der Glocke" for soli,
chorus and orch.; symph. poem
"Malinconia"; symph. overtures
"Iphigenia" and *"Im Freien,"* etc.

Schönberg (shän'-bĕrkh), **Arnold**, b.
Vienna, Sept. 13, 1874; eminent

composer and theoretician; has exer-
cised profound effect on other composers of his period by his path-
breaking system of free harmonic
writing; the "father" of atonality,
and in his later works the exponent
of the theory that any of the tones
of the chromatic scale may be combined with equal effectiveness; the
form of his works is, however, in the
classical tradition. He began quite
early to compose chamber music,
and studied vln. and 'cello; in theory
he evolved his own method, except
for a brief period of study in 1894
with his future brother-in-law,
Alexander Zemlinsky. He made a
piano version of latter's opera,
"Sarema"; an early string quartet
from this period has been lost; some
songs were heard in Vienna about
1900. From the previous year dates
his popular string sextet, *"Verklärte
Nacht,"* in a romantic, somewhat
Tristanesque idiom, which has had
wide currency in its arrangement for
string orch. In 1901, following his
marriage to Mathilde Zemlinsky, S.
took up res. in Berlin; there he produced his symph. poem, *"Pelleas
und Melisande."* In 1903 he returned to Vienna and began his
important labors as a theory teacher;
in the next 4 years he continued his
early post-Wagnerian period with
his 6 orch. songs, his string quartet,
8 songs (op. 6), 2 ballades (op. 12),
his much-played *"Kammersinfonie,"*
and the second string quartet with
voice; also from 1910–11 dates his
"Gurrelieder" for soloists, chorus,
orch. Later his music began to
reveal an abstract, anti-romantic
quality; his 3rd and most important
manner (which has been called
"expressionistic" and said to have
parallels with the painting of such
a figure as Kokoschka) is heralded
by his songs to lyrics of Stefan
George, op. 15. The compositions
of this period include 3 piano operas
(op. 11), the radical *"Five Orchestral
Pieces"* (op. 16), which created a
sensational effect when 1st played
in Europe and U. S.; the monodrama,
"Erwartung," for one woman singer
and orch., which portrays the
anguish in the mind of one waiting
for her lover (one of S's. most
original works, 1st staged at Prague
in 1924); *"Die Glückliche Hand"*

(The Hand of Fate), a form of opera to the composer's own text. It symbolically narrates the struggle of a man to preserve the joy and dignity of life against the malign effects of an evil incubus, the mysterious menace of the world about him, and the snares of a rich dandy who wins away his wife (prod. Vienna Volksop., 1924; also in N. Y. by Phila. Orch. under Stokowski in stage version, 1930). 1911 marked S's. 2nd removal to Berlin, and the production of his highly original "*Pierrot Lunaire*" (op. 21), settings of a cycle of 21 poems by Albert Giraud, which describe the somewhat decadent and haunted longings of a moonstricken Pierrot for his native Bergamo; this work is called a "melodrama" and introduced to the world of music, in its score for a woman reciter-singer and chamber ensemble, S's. famous device of the "*Sprechstimme*," or voice that half speaks, half sings. 1915–17, he worked on an oratorio, "*Jacob's Ladder*," writing both text and music (not completed); and the following year founded in Vienna a Society for Private Perfs. of Music, which introd. the scores of his immediate circle to a small group of those interested; 1920–21, he lectured on comp. in Amsterdam; 1923, after return to Vienna, he issued some piano pieces, a quintet, and Serenade for barytone and chamber orch. Beginning 1923 he was Busoni's successor as teacher of master class in comp. at Berlin Hochschule, for about a decade; then came to America 1933 and taught comp. in Boston and N. Y.; 1935 faculty mem. of Univ. of Cal. at Los Angeles, occupying chair of comp. Apart from his compositions, his influence has been preëminent in the field of theory, which he may be said to have revolutionised with his publication of a "*Harmonienlehre*"; also c. (operas) "*Von Heute auf Morgen*" (1-act attempt at work in more pop. style, not highly successful); "*Moses and Aaron*"; (orch.) theme and variations; suite for strings (in oldtime style); 'cello concerto after an early work by Monn; and a reworking for string quartet and orch. of a Händel concerto grosso; in 1936 the 4th of his string quartets was to have its première in a fest. given at Los Angeles under the patronage of Mrs. F. S. Coolidge. Studies of his music have been published by Wellesz, Erwin Stein and others, besides an essay by Huneker, etc.

Schönberger (shän'-bĕrkh-ĕr), **Benno,** b. Vienna, Sept. 12, 1863; pianist; pupil of Vienna Cons., studied also with Liszt; toured; 1885 teacher, Vienna; later in Sweden (1886), then London; 1894 toured America; c. pf.-sonatas, rhapsodies, etc.

Schorr (shôr), **Friedrich,** b. Nagyvarad, Hungary, Sept. 2, 1888; barytone; studied with Robinson in Vienna; sang at Graz, 1911–16; Prague, 1916–18; Cologne, 1918–23; then Berlin; came to U.S. with Wagnerian Op. Co., 1923; mem. Met. Op. Co. after 1924; has sung widely in Europe and S. America, and at Covent Garden, esp. in Wagnerian rôles.

Schott (shôt), (1) **Bd.,** d. 1817; founded (Mayence, 1773) the mus.-pub. firm of B. Schott, carried on by his sons (2) **Andreas** (1781—1840) and (3) **Jn. Jos.** (1782—1855), under the firm-name of "B. Schott's Söhne"; later managers at Mayence and the London branch were Fz. von Landwehr and Dr. L. Strecker. (4) **Anton,** Schloss Staufeneck, Swabian Alp, June 25, 1846—Stuttgart, Jan. 8, 1913; tenor; 1865–71 an artillery officer in the French campaign; then studied with Frau Schebest-Strauss; 1871, Munich opera; 1872–75 Berlin opera; leading tenor at Schwerin and Hanover, made concert-tours; 1882 in Italy with Neumann's Wagner troupe.

Schradi(e)ck (shrä'-dĕk), **Henry,** Hamburg, April 29, 1846—Brooklyn, N. Y., March 28, 1918; noted violinist; pupil of his father and of Leonard, Brussels Cons., David, Leipzig; 1864–68 teacher Moscow Cons., then leader Philh. Concerts, Hamburg; 1874–82, co-leader, Gewandhaus Orch. and theatre-orch., Leipzig, also teacher for a time at the Cons. 1883–89, prof. of vln., Cincinnati Cons., U. S. A.; returned to Germany as leader of the Hamburg Philh. Soc.; afterward head vln.-prof. Nat. Cons., N. Y., and later Broad St. Cons., Philadelphia; after 1912 also at Amer. Inst. of Applied Mus.,

N. Y.; pub. excellent technical studies for vln.

Schramm (shräm), (1) **Melchior,** German organist and contrapuntist, 1595. (2) **Paul,** b. Vienna, Sept. 22, 1892; pianist and composer; pupil of R. Kaiser and Leschetizky.

Schreck (shrĕk), **Gustav,** Zeulenroda, Sept. 8, 1849—Leipzig, Jan. 22, 1918; pupil of Leipzig Cons.; 1885 teacher of theory and comp., Leipzig Cons.; 1892, mus.-dir. and cantor, and cond. of the "Thomanerchor"; prod. concert-cantatas, oratorio, *"Christus der Auferstandene"* (Gewandhaus, 1892), church-music, etc.

Schreker (shrĕk'-ĕr), **Franz,** Monaco, March 23, 1878—Berlin, March 21, 1934; composer; pupil of Fuchs, Vienna; founded and cond. Philh. Chorus, Vienna, 1911; prof. of comp., Vienna Acad., 1912; dir. Berlin Hochsch., 1920–32; master class, Akad. der Künste there, 1931–32; noted for his original music dramas, usually on somewhat Freudian erotic subjects, with musical system based on new and unusual "clang-tints," and using his own texts; c. (operas) *"Der Ferne Klang"* (Frankfort, 1912); *"Das Spielwerk und die Prinzessin"* (Vienna, 1913); *"Die Gezeichneten"* (1918); *"Der Schatzgräber"* (1920); *"Irrelohe,"* *"Memnon,"* *"Der Schmied von Ghent"*; (pantomime) *"Der Geburtstag der Infantin"* (after Wilde); Sinfonietta, *" Nachtstück"* and prelude to a drama for orch., choral works and songs; his influence as a teacher was considerable; his style excelled in richness of orchestral color and subtlety of detail, but his works for the stage were of such a complicated nature that they have never been produced outside of Germany and Austria. Studies of his music have been written by Kapp and Bekker.

Schrems (shrĕms), **Jos.,** Warmensteinach, Upper Palatinate, 1815—Ratisbon, 1872; conductor, editor and teacher.

Schröder (shrā'-dĕr), (1) **Hermann,** Quedlinburg, July 28, 1843—Berlin, Jan. 31, 1909; violinist, writer and composer; pupil of A. Ritter, Magdeburg; from 1885, teacher R. Inst. for church-mus., Berlin, and at a mus.-sch. of his own. (2) **Karl,** Quedlinburg, Dec. 18, 1848—Bremen, Sept. 22, 1935; bro. of above; 'cellist and composer; pupil of Drechsler, Dessau and Kiel, Berlin; at 14, 1st 'cello ct.-orch. at Sondershausen, and teacher in the Cons.; 1873, 'cello Brunswick ct.-orch.; 1874, solo 'cellist Gewandhaus Orch., and th.-orch., Leipzig, also teacher at the Cons., and made tours; 1881, ct.-cond., Sondershausen; cond. German Opera at Amsterdam; until 1888, Berlin ct.-opera; till 1890, the Hamburg Opera; returned to Sondershausen as ct.-cond. and dir. Cons.; 1911–24, at Stern Cons.; wrote 'cello-method, catechism on conducting and the 'cello. C. succ. opera *"Aspasia"* (Sondershausen, 1892); a succ. 1-act opera *"Der Asket"* (Leipzig, 1893); succ. operetta *"Malajo"* (Bunzlau, 1887); 1871, founded the "Schröder Quartett," with his brothers (1) **Hermann** (3) **Fz.** and (4) **Alwin,** b. Neuhaldensleben June 15, 1855—Detroit, Nov. 10, 1920; pupil of his father and brother Hermann, André (pf.), and De Ahna (vln.), W. Tappert (theory); self-taught as a 'cellist, as which he has won his fame; 1875, 1st 'cello in Liebig's "Concert-Orchester," later under Fliege and Laube (Hamburg); 1880, Leipzig, as asst. of (1), whom he succeeded, 1881, in the Gewandhaus, theatre and Cons.; 1886, Boston, as first 'cellist Symph. Orch.; member of the Kneisel Quartet; 1903 he resigned from the Boston Symph. Orch., and joined the Kneisel Quartet; 1905–7, teacher at New York Institute of Musical Art; 1907, first 'cello teacher at Hoch Cons., Frankfort-on-Main; 1908, returned to Boston as co-founder of Hess-Schroeder Quartet; 1910, first 'cellist of Boston Symph; resigned 1912 for concert tours; later a mem. of the Margulies Trio and Boston String Quartet until 1919.

Schröder-Devrient (shrā'-dĕr-dā'-frĭ-ĕnt) **Wilhelmine,** Hamburg, 1804—Coburg, 1860; eminent soprano; daughter of Fr. Schröder, barytone, and the actress, Antoinette Sophie Bürger; pupil of Mazatti; début, Vienna, 1821; m. the actor Karl D. (divorced 1828, after bearing him 4 children; married twice afterward); she created the rôle of "Adriano

Colonna" in the "*Rienzi*" of Wagner, whose style she deeply affected.

Schröder-Hanfstängl. Vide HANF-STÄNGL.

Schröter (shrā-tĕr), (1) **Leonhardt**, Torgau, ca. 1540—d. in Magdeburg, 1595; eminent contrapuntist. (2) **Chp. Gl.**, Hohenstein, Saxony, 1699 —Nordhausen, 1782; noted organist; claimed in a pamphlet (1763) to have invented, 1717, the pianoforte, but was forestalled by Cristofori; composer. (3) **Corona (Elisabeth Wilhelmine)**, Guben, 1751—Ilmenau, 1802; celebrated soprano; pupil of her father, (4) **Joh. Fr. S.**, chambersinger. (5) **Joh. Samuel**, Warsaw, 1750—London, 1788, son of (4); pianist. (6) **Joh. H.** (b. Warsaw, 1762), son of (4); violinist.

Schubart (shoo'-bärt), (**Chr. Fr.**) **Daniel**, Sontheim, Swabia, 1739—Stuttgart, 1791; poet; organist and composer.

Schubert (shoo'-bĕrt), (1) **Jos.**, Warnsdorf, Bohemia, 1757—Dresden, 1812; violinist and dram. composer. (2) **Jn. Fr.**, Rudolstadt, 1770—Cologne, 1811; violinist, writer and composer, (3) **Fd.**, Lichtenthal, near Vienna, 1794—Vienna, 1859; elder bro. of the great composer (4) and passionately devoted to him; dir. Normal Sch., Vienna; c. church-mus., a requiem for his brother, etc.

(4) **Franz (Peter)**, Lichtenthal, near Vienna, Jan. 31, 1797—of typhus, Vienna, Nov. 19, 1828; one of the most eminent of the world's composers. One of the 14 children of a schoolmaster at Lichtenthal, who taught him the vln.; also studied with Holzer there; at 10, first soprano in the church-choir, and c. songs and little instrumental pcs. 1808, a singer in the Vienna court choir, and also in the "Convict" (the training-sch. for the court singers). He played in the sch.-orchestra, finally as first vln., and studied theory with Ruczicka and Salieri. His earliest extant composition is a 4-hand fantasia of 12 movements written when he was 13. He had a frenzy for writing, and a fellow-pupil, Spaun, generously furnished him with mus.-paper, a luxury beyond the means of Schubert. At 15 he had written much, incl. an overture; at 16 he c. his first symph.; 1813, his voice broke and he left the "Con-

vict," where the unrestrained license allowed him in his compositions accounts for the crudeness of some of his early works and the faults of form that always characterised him, as well as for his immediate and profound individuality; at 17 he c. his first mass. In order to escape military conscription he studied a few months at the Normal Sch. and took the post of elementary teacher in his father's sch. He taught there until 1816, spending his leisure in studying with Salieri, and in comp. particularly of songs, of which he wrote as many as 8 in one day—144 in his 18th year (1815), including "*Der Erlkönig*"; 1814–16, he also c. 2 operettas, 3 Singspiele and 3 incomplete stage-pieces, 4 masses. 1816, he applied, without succ., for the directorship of the new State mus.-sch. at Laybach (salary $100 (£20) a year). From 1817 he lived in Vienna, except two summers (1818 and 1824), spent at Zelész, Hungary, as teacher in Count Esterházy's family. How S. existed is a matter of mystery, except for the help of such friends as Fz. von Schober, who aided him with the utmost generosity. The famous tenor Michael Vogl popularised his songs. By his 21st year (1818) S. had c. six of his symphs. and a great mass of work. His mus. farce "*Die Zwillingsbrüder*" was prod. (Kärnthnerthor Th., 1820, but ran only six nights). 1821, after he had written over 600 compositions, his "*Erlkönig*" was sung at a public concert of the "Musikverein" and elsewhere, with a wide sale that attended most of his subsequent publication of songs and pf.-pcs.; though he was sadly underpaid by his publishers, sometimes receiving only a gulden (20 cents, less than a shilling) for them. In 1822 he declined the post of organist at the court chapel; but could never obtain a salaried position, though many efforts were made. At 31 he gave his first concert of his own works, with good succ. (1828). In 1822, he had finished a grand opera "*Alfonso und Estrella*," the libretto bad, the scoring too difficult for the musicians at Graz, where it was put in rehearsal; it was withdrawn, not to be prod. till 1854 under Liszt and in 1881 when Jn. Fuchs rewrote the libretto and prod. it at Carlsruhe with great succ. In 1825 a work, "*Rosamunde,*" was prod. at the Th. an-der-Wien, with applause for the music, but it was withdrawn after a second performance. Other works of his had not even productions, his stubborn refusal to alter a note preventing the profitable performance of dram. scenes, etc. His health finally broke under the strain of composition all day on a little food and revelry till late at night. He died of typhus and was buried, at his own request, in the "Ostfriedhof" at Währing, near Beethoven.

A complete critical edition of his works is pub. by Breitkopf & Härtel. These incl., besides those mentioned, an opera "*Adrast*" (unfinished), 3-act operettas "*Der Teufels Lustschloss*" and "*Der Spiegelritter*"; SINGSPIELE: "*Der Vierjährige Posten,*" "*Fernando*"; "*Claudine von Villabella*" (unfinished); "*Die Freunde von Salamanca*" and "*Der Minnesänger*"; all written 1814–1816; none performed; 3-act melodrama, "*Die Zauberharfe*" (Aug. 19, 1820); 3-act opera, "*Sakuntala*" (not finished or performed); 1-act operetta, "*Die Verschworenen, oder der häusliche Krieg*" (Vienna, 1861); 3-act opera, "*Fierabras*" (Vienna, 1861); "*Die Burgschaft,*" 3-act opera (c. 1816; prod. by Fz. Lachner, Pesth, 1827); unprod. operas "*Der Graf von Gleichen*" (1827) and "*Die Salzbergwerke*"; 6 masses; "*Deutsche Messe*"; unfinished oratorio "*Lazarus,*" "*Tantum ergo*" (with orch.); 2 "*Stabat Mater,*" etc. CHORAL WORKS WITH ORCH., OR INSTRS.: "*Miriams Siegesgesang*"; prayer, "*Vor der Schlacht*"; hymn, "*Herr unser Gott,*" "*Hymne an den Heiligen Geist,*" "*Morgengesang im Walde,*" "*Nachtgesang im Walde*" and "*Nachthelle,*" "*Schlachtlied,*" "*Glaube, Hoffnung und Liebe,*" several cantatas and part-songs. ORCH. AND CHAMBER-MUS.: 10 symphs., No. 8 the "unfinished" in B min., 7 overtures (Nos. 2 and 5 "in the Italian style"); vln.-concerto; rondo for vln. with orch.; octet; pf.-quintet ("*Forellenquintet,*" with double bass); string-quintet with 2 'celli; 14 string-quartets; 2 pf.-trios; 2 string-trios; rondo brilliant, phantasie in C, sonata, 3 sonatinas, nocturne for 'cello and pf.; introd. and vars. for flute and pf.; 17 pf.-sonatas (incl. op. 78, fantasia), 3 grand sonatas, posthumous; 8 impromptus, 6 moments musicaux; many variations, many waltzes, incl. "*Valses sentimentales,*" "*Homage aux belles Viennoises,*" "*Valses nobles,*" 12 "*Grätzer Wälzer,*" "*Wanderer-Fantasie*"; FOR PF., 4 HANDS: 2 sonatas, "*Divertissement à l'hongroise,*" "*Grand rondo,*" "*Notre amitié,*" rondo in D, "*Lebensstürme,*" fugue, polonaises, variations, waltzes, 4 Ländler; marches, incl. "Trauermarsch" and "héroique."

SONGS WITH PIANO: "*Erlkönig,*" op. 1; "*Gretchen am Spinnrade,*" op. 2; "*Heidenröslein,*" op. 3; "*Der Wanderer*" and "*Der du von dem Himmel bist,*" op. 4; Suleika songs, Mignon's songs, 2 song cycles by Wilhelm Müller, "*Die Schöne Müllerin*" and "*Die Winterreise,*" containing 20 and 24 numbers; 7 songs from "*Fräulein vom See*" (Scott's "*Lady of the Lake*"), 9 songs from "*Ossian*"; 6 songs by Heine in the "*Schwanengesang,*" etc. (more than 600 in all). As part of the celebration of his death centenary in 1928, the Columbia Phonograph Co. offered a prize for internat'l composers to complete the Unfinished Symph. This aroused so much protest from musicians, however, that the contest was changed to one for a work "in the style of" Schubert, and was won by Kurt Atterberg of Sweden.

Biog. by Kreissle von Hellborn (Vienna, 1861, 1865); Reissman, Berlin, 1873); A. Niggli (1880); Barbedette (Paris, 1866); Max Friedländer; other studies by La Mara, Risse, Austin, Frost, H. Ritter, Skalla, Curzon, Zenger, Heuberger, Duncan, Klatte, Bourgault-Ducoudray, Antcliffe, Dahms, Deutsch and Schiebler, Bie, Clutsam, Flower, Kobald and Ewen. His songs are the subject of studies by Capell and Le Massena. His letters and other writings were pub. in English translation (Knopf, 1928).

(5) **Fz. Anton,** 1768—1824; violinist; R. Konzertmeister. (6) **Fz.,** Dresden, 1808—1878; son and pupil of (5); violinist, Konzertmeister R. orch. and composer. (7) **Maschinka,** wife of (6) and daughter of G. A. Schneider, 1815—Dresden, 1882; soprano. (8) **Georgine,** Dresden, 1840 —Potsdam, 1878; daughter and pupil

of (7); pupil also of Jenny Lind and Garcia; sang in many European cities. (9) **Louis,** Dessau, 1828—Dresden, 1884; violinist; singing-teacher and composer.

Schuberth (shoo'-bĕrt), (1) **Gottlob,** Karsdorf, 1778—Hamburg, 1846; oboist and clarinettist. (2) **Julius (Fd. G.),** Magdeburg, 1804—Leipzig, 1875; son of above; founded firm of "J. Schuberth & Co.," Hamburg, 1826; Leipzig branch, 1832; New York, 1850. His brother (3) **Fr. Wm.** (b. 1817), took the Hamburg house, 1853 (under firm-name "Fritz Schuberth"); 1872, at Weimar founded the mus.-library "Liszt-Schuberth Stiftung"; 1891 succeeded by Felix Siegel; New York branch later owned by J. H. F. Meyer. (4) **L.,** Magdeburg, 1806—St. Petersburg, 1850; son and pupil of (1) and von Weber; at 16 dir. Stadt Th. at Magdeburg; conductor Oldenburg, 1845; cond. German opera, St. Petersburg; c. operas, symphs., etc. (5) **K.,** Magdeburg, 1811—Zurich, 1863; bro. of above; noted 'cellist; pupil of Hesse and Dotzauer; toured widely; soloist to the Czar; ct.-cond., dir. at the U.; c. 2 'cello-concertos.

Schubiger (shoo'-bĭkh-ĕr), **Anselm,** Uznach, Canton of St. Gallen, 1815—1888; important writer.

Schuch (shookh), (1) **Ernst von,** Graz, Styria, Nov. 23, 1847—Dresden, May 10, 1914; pupil of E. Stoltz and O. Dessoff; 1872, cond. Pollini's It. Op.; from 1873 ct.-cond. Dresden, then R. Ct.-Councillor and Gen.-Mus.-Dir. (2) **Clementine Proska,** Vienna, Feb. 12, 1853—June 11, 1932; wife of above; 1873-1904, coloratura-sopr., Dresden ct.-theatre.

Schucht (shookht), **Jean F.,** Holzthalleben, Thuringia, 1822—Leipzig, 1894; critic and composer.

Schücker (shĭk'-ĕr), **Edmund,** Vienna, 1860—Bad Kreuznach, 1911; harpist; pupil of Zamara, Vienna Cons.; 1884, teacher Leipzig Cons., and harpist Gewandhaus Orch.; 1890, ct.-harpist to Duke of Saxe-Altenburg; 1891, Chicago Orchestra.

Schulhoff (shool'-hôf), (1) **Julius,** Prague, 1825—Berlin, 1898; notable pianist; pupil of Kisch, Tedesco and Tomaschek; début, Dresden, 1842; lived in Paris as teacher, then Dresden and Berlin; c. pf.-pcs., etc. (2) **Erwin,** b. Prague, June 8, 1894;

composer; studied at Cons. there, also at Leipzig (comp. with Reger), and at Cologne (cond. with Steinbach); won Mendelssohn Prize in piano at Berlin Hochsch.; also in comp.; c. 2 symphonies, with vocal solos; overtures, orch. variations, piano concerto, suite for chamber orch., string quartet, vln. suite, piano variations, and smaller pieces for piano, all in advanced modern style, incl. atonality.

Schultheiss (shoolt'-hīs), **Benedict,** d. 1693; organist and composer, Nürnberg.

Schulthesius (shool-tā'-zĭ-oos), **Jn. Paul,** Fechheim, Saxe-Coburg, 1748—Leghorn, 1816; theorist and composer.

Schultz-Adaiewski (shoolts-ä-da-yĕf'-ski), **Ella von,** St. Petersburg, Feb. 10, 1846—Bonn, July 29, 1926; pupil of Henselt and the St. Petersburg Cons.; pianist; toured and from 1882 lived at Venice; c. opera *"Die Morgenröte der Freiheit"*; *"Sonate grecque"* for clarinet and piano, etc.

Schultze (shoolt'-tsĕ), (1) **Jn.,** organist and composer, Dannenberg, Brunswick, 1612. (2) **Chp.,** cantor, etc., Delitzsch, Saxony (1647 — 1668). (3) **Dr. Wm. H.,** Celle, Hanover, 1827—Syracuse, N. Y., 1888; violinist and professor. (4) **Ad.,** b. Schwerin, Nov. 3, 1853; pianist; pupil of Kullak's Acad., Berlin; teacher there; 1886-90 ct.-cond., Sondershausen and dir. of the Cons.; later in Berlin; c. a pf.-concerto, etc.

Schulz (shoolts), (1). Vide PRÄTORIUS. (2) **Jn. Abraham Peter,** Lüneburg, March 30 (31 ?), 1747—Schwedt, June 10, 1800; important predecessor of Schubert as a song-writer; pupil of Kirnberger, Berlin; teacher there, 1780, ct.-cond. at Rheinsberg; 1787-94, ct.-cond. Copenhagen; and theorist; c. operas, oratorios, etc. (3) **Jn. Ph. Chr.,** Langensalza, Thuringia, 1773—Leipzig, 1827; cond. and composer. (4) **Fd.,** Kossar, 1821—Berlin, 1897; 1856 conductor, mus.-dir., singing-teacher and composer. (5) **August,** Brunswick, June 15, 1837—Feb. 12, 1909; violinist; pupil of Zinkeisen, Leibrock, and Joachim; leader of the Ducal Orch. there; c. pop. male quartets. (6) **Leo,** b. Posen, March, 28, 1865; 'cellist; pupil of Berlin Hochsch.; soloist in Philh. Orch. there; after 1890 with N. Y.

Philh.; taught at Nat'l Cons.; mem. Margulies Trio, 1904-15.

Schulz-Beuthen (shoolts-boi'-tĕn), **H.**, Beuthen, Upper Silesia, June 19, 1838—Dresden, March 12, 1915; pupil of Leipzig Cons., and of Riedel; 1881, pf.-teacher, Dresden Cons.; 1893, in Vienna; after 1895 again at Dresden Cons.; prof., 1911; a Wagner and Liszt disciple; c. 4 operas, 8 symphonies, "*Haydn,*" "*Frühlingsfeier,*" E♭, "*Schön Elizabeth,*" "*Reformation-S.*" (with organ); "*König Lear,*" and a "*Kinder-Sinfonie*"; symph. poem, "*Die Todteninsel*"; 3 overtures, incl. "*Indianischer Kriegstanz*"; cantatas with orch., "*Befreiungsgesang der Verbannten Israels,*" and "*Harald,*" requiem and Psalms 42, 43, and 125 with orch. Psalm 13, *a cappella* male choruses, etc.

Schulz-Schwerin (shoolts-shvä'-rēn), **K.**, Schwerin, Jan. 3, 1845—Mannheim, May 24, 1913; pianist; pupil of Stern Cons., Berlin; ct.-pianist to Grand Duke of Mecklenburg; 1885–1901, teacher at Stern Cons., Berlin; then in Mannheim; c. a symph., overtures "*Torquato Tasso,*" "*Die Braut von Messina,*" and "*Triomphale*"; Sanctus, Benedictus, etc., with orch., etc.

Schulze (shoolts'-ĕ), (1) **Jn. Fr.**, Milbitz, Thuringia, 1793—Paulinzelle, 1858; org.-builder with his sons at Mühlhausen. (2) **Ad.**, Mannhagen, near Mölln, April 13, 1835—Jena, April, 1920; concert-bass; pupil of Carl Voigt, Hamburg, and Garcia, London; head-prof. of singing R. Hochschule, Berlin.

Schumacher (shoo'-mäkh-ĕr), **(Peter) Paul (H.),** Mayence, 1848—1891; conductor, critic, teacher and composer.

Schumann (shoo'-män), (1) **Robert (Alex.),** Zwickau, Saxony, June 8, 1810—insane, Endenich, near Bonn, July 29, 1856; one of the most individual and eminent of composers. Youngest son of a book-seller (of literary taste and author of a biog. gallery to which R. contributed at 14). Pupil of a local organist, Kuntzsch (pf.), who prophesied immortality for him; at 6 he began to compose, at 11, untaught, he c. for chorus and orch. At 17 he set poems of his own to mus. 1820–28, attended Zwickau Gymnasium; then

matriculated at Leipzig Univ. to study law and philosophy. 1829 Heidelberg, where he also studied mus., practising the piano 7 hours a day; played once in public with great succ. 1830, Leipzig, where he lived with Friedrich Wieck, with whom he studied the piano; he also studied comp. with H. Dorn. In trying to acquire independence of the fingers by suspending the fourth finger of the right hand in a sling while practising with the others he crippled this finger and foiled his ambition to be the chief virtuoso of his time. He now made comp. his first ambition. In 1833, his first symph. was performed with little succ., the first movement having been played in public by Wieck's 13-year old daughter, Clara, with whom S. fell in love. The father liked S. as a son, but not as a son-in-law, and put every obstacle in his way, until in 1840, after a year's law-suit, the father was forced to consent and the two lovers, both now distinguished, were united in one of the happiest marriages known in art; she giving his work publicity in her very popular concerts; he devoted to her and dedicating much of his best work to her. 1834 he founded the *Neue Zeitschrift für Musik,* and was its editor till 1844. His essays and criticisms (signed FLORESTAN, EUSEBIUS, MEISTER RARO, 2, 12, 22, ETC., JEANQUIRIT, etc.) are among the noblest works in the history of criticism, particularly in the matter of recognising new genius and heralding it fearlessly and fervently. (Chopin, Berlioz, and Brahms, profited by this quality. Of Wagner he did not altogether approve.) In his writings he constructed an imaginary band of ardent young Davids attacking the Goliath of Philistinism. He called this group the "Davidsbündler." His pen-name "EUSEBIUS," represents the vehement side of his nature, "FLORESTAN," the gentle and poetic side. His paper had some succ., which was not bettered by a removal to Vienna, 1838–39, and a return to Leipzig. 1840, Dr. Phil., Jena. 1840 was mainly devoted to his important song-composition; 1841 to symph. work; 1842 to chamber-mus., incl. his pf.-quintet (op. 44) which gave him European fame.

1843 was choral, *"Das Paradies und Peri"* (from Moore's "Lalla Rookh"), having a great succ.; he also began his choric mus. for *"Faust."* The same year, on the invitation of his warm personal friend Mendelssohn, he became teacher of pf. and comp., and of playing from score at the newly founded Leipzig Cons.; 1844, after going with his wife on a concert-tour to Russia, he removed to Dresden and resigned the editorship of the *Neue Zeitschrift;* lived at Dresden until 1850 teaching and composing such works as the great C-major symph., 1846, and the opera *"Genoveva"* (1848; prod. 1850 without succ.; its exclusion of recitative displeasing the public). 1847 cond. of the "Liedertafel"; 1848 organised the "Chorgesangverein." 1850, Düsseldorf as town mus.-dir. (vice Fd. Hiller). 1853, signs of insanity, first noted in 1833 and more in 1845, compelled him to retire. 1854 he threw himself into the Rhine, whence he was rescued by some boatmen; he was then taken to an asylum at Endenich near Bonn, where he remained in acute melancholia, varied by intervals of complete lucidity, when he composed as before. A complete ed. of his comps. is edited by Clara Schumann and publ. by Breitkopf & Härtel. It includes, besides the works mentioned, mus. to Byron's *"Manfred,"* Goethe's *"Faust,"* cantatas, *"Der Rose Pilgerfahrt,"* with orch.; *"Adventlied,"* for sopr., chorus and orch.; *"Abschiedslied,"* chorus with wood-wind or pf.; requiem for *"Mignon"*; *"Nachtlied,"* for chorus and orch.; ballades *"Der Königssohn,"* *"Des Sängers Fluch"* (op. 139), *"Vom Pagen und der Königstochter,"* *"Das Glück von Edenhall,"* and *"Neujahrslied";* Missa sacra, and requiem mass, with orch.; 4 symphs. (No. 3, op. 97, in Eb the *"Rheinische,"* or *"Cologne,"* symph.); *"Ouvertüre, Scherzo und Finale,"* op. 52; 4 concert overtures *"Die Braut von Messina,"* *"Festouvertüre,"* *"Julius Cæsar"* and *"Hermann und Dorothea";* pf.-concerto; Concert-stück, and concert-allegro, 'cello-concerto; fantasia for vln. with orch., etc.
Much remarkable CHAMBER MUSIC: incl. pf.-quintet in Eb op. 44; 3 pf.-trios, etc.; 6 org.-studies in canon-form, *"Skizzen für den Pedal-flügel";* 6 org.-fugues on B–A–C–H, op. 60. FOR PF.: Op. 1, Variations on A–B–E–G–G (the name of a young woman); op. 2 *"Papillons";* op. 3, *"Studies after Paganini's Caprices";* op. 5, *"Impromptus on theme by Cl. Wieck";* op. 6, *"Davidsbündlertänze";* op. 9, *"Carnaval";* op. 10, *"Studies on Paganini's Caprices";* op. 15, thirteen *"Kinderscenen";* op. 16, *"Kreisleriana";* op. 21, *"Novelletten"* (4 books), 3 sonatas (No. 3 "Concert sans orchestre"), and 3 sonatas for the young; op. 23 *"Nachtstücke";* op. 26 *"Faschingsschwank aus Wien";* op. 68, *"Album für die Jugend,"* a canon on *"An Alexis."* FOR PF. 4 HANDS: Op. 66, *"Bilder aus Osten,"* after Rückert, 12 *"Clavierstücke für kleine und grosse Kinder";* op. 109, *"Ballscenen."* Many choruses *a cappella;* many songs and duets, incl. ten *Spanische Liebeslieder,* with 4-hand accomp., op. 138; Liederkreis (Heine), song-cycle, op. 24, and Liederkreis (12 poems by Eichendorff), op. 39; *"Myrthen,"* op. 25; Lieder und Gesänge, 5 sets; 12 poems (Körner), op. 35; 6 poems (Rückert), in collaboration with his wife, op. 37; *"Frauenliebe und Leben,"* op. 42; *"Dichterliebe,"* op. 48; *"Liederalbum für die Jugend,"* op. 79; 6 songs from Byron's *"Hebrew Melodies,"* op. 95 (with pf. or harp); nine Lieder und Gesänge from *"Wilhelm Meister,"* op. 98a, etc. In 1937 a posth. vln.-concerto in D minor, never perf. but willed by Joachim to the Prussian State Library, was premiered by Yehudi Menuhin.
His writings are pub. in 4 vols., 1854; 4 vols. in English, London, 1875; and his letters ed. by his wife (1885) and (1886) by Jansen.
Biogr. by von Wasielewski (1858), Reissmann (1865), Ambros (1860), L. Mesnard (Paris, 1876), H. Reimann (1887), H. Erler (1887), S. Bagge (1879), Waldersee (1880), and by Ph. Spitta (1882). Other biographical studies by La Mara, Fuller-Maitland, Batka, Abert, Patterson, Schneider and Maréchal, Oldmeadow, Mauclaire, Wolff, Hartog, Steiner, Calvocoressi, Dahms, Von der Pforten, Basche, Bedford, Niecks, Ronald, and Eugenie Schumann, his daughter (in English, 1931).

(2) **Clara (Josephine)**, née **Wieck**, Leipzig, Sept. 13, 1819—Frankfort-on-Main, May 20, 1896; eminent pianist; wife of above (q. v.). She played in public at 9; at 11 at the Gewandhaus; toured from 1832; Vienna (1836) received the title of Imp. Chamber-virtuoso. On Sept. 12, 1840, m. Schumann (q. v.). After he died she went with her children to Berlin; 1863 to Wiesbaden, resuming her public career as a concert-pianist; 1878–92 pf.-teacher Hoch Cons., Frankfort. Besides editing Schumann's works, his early letters and finger-exercises from Czerny, she c. pf.-concerto, preludes and fugues, pf.-trio, Vars. on a theme by Schumann, many songs, incl. 3 in Schumann's op. 37 (Nos. 2, 4, and 11). Biog. by Litzmann, 1902. (3) **Georg (Alfred)**, b. Königstein, Saxony, Oct. 25, 1866; pianist, son and pupil of the city mus.-dir., pupil of his grandfather, a cantor, and of K. A. Fischer, B. Rollfuss, and Fr. Baumfelder, Dresden, then of Leipzig Cons., where he c. 2 symphs., a serenade for orch., a pf.-quintet, a vln.-sonata, etc., taking the Beethoven prize, 1887; lived 2 years in Berlin; 1892–96, cond. at Danzig; 1896–1900, Bremen Philh. Orch. and chorus; after 1900 of Berlin Singakademie, a notable chorus; 1916, hon. Mus. D.; Berlin Univ.; mem. of the Acad. of Arts; after 1913 leader of master class in comp. at the Univ.; c. oratorios, 2 symphonies, and many other works for orch., chamber music, choruses, piano pieces, songs, etc. (4) **Elisabeth**, b. Merseburg, Germany, June 13, 1891; soprano; 1909–15, sang at Hamburg Op.; after 1919 at Vienna State Op., also for a time at Met. Op., and toured U. S. 1921 in programs with Richard Strauss; m. Karl Alwin, conductor.

Schumann-Heink (shoo'-män-hĭnk), **Ernestine** (née **Rössler**), n. Prague, June 15, 1861—Hollywood, Nov. 17, 1936; famous contralto; pupil of Marietta von Leclair, Graz; début Dresden, 1878, in *"Il Trovatore"*; sang there 4 years; 1883 Hamburg City Th.; 1896, sang "Erda," "Waltraute," and the First Norn at Bayreuth; m. Herr Heink, 1883; m. Paul Schumann, 1893; from 1898, in America; 1899–1904 she sang at Berlin Royal Opera as well as at Met. Op., N. Y.; 1904 she starred in a comic opera, *"Love's Lottery"*; 1909 she created "Clytemnestra" in Strauss's *"Elektra"* at Dresden; Paul Schumann, d. 1904; she m. William Rapp, Jr., 1905; divorced him, 1912; she had sung in concert with enormous success in America and in opera abroad; became naturalised American, 1908. In recent years she had been engaged as a radio singer and had played parts in the films, also to some extent active as a teacher.

Schünemann (shü'-nĕ-män), **G.**, b. Berlin, March 13, 1884; musicologist; Ph.D., Leipzig Univ.; taught Berlin Univ.; dir. Prussian State Library, div. of music.

Schuppan (shoop'-pän), **Adolf**, b. Berlin, June 5, 1863; pupil of B. Härtel; c. chamber music.

Schuppanzigh (shoop'-păn-tsĭkh), **Ignaz**, Vienna, 1776—1830; violinist, conductor and teacher.

Schürer (shü'-rĕr), **Jn. G.**, Raudnitz, Bohemia, 1720—Dresden, 1786; dram. composer.

Schuricht (shōō'-rēkht), **Carl**, b. Danzig, July 3, 1880; conductor; studied at Berlin Hochsch.; with Humperdinck and Rudorff; cond. opera and concerts, Zwickau, Dortmund, Frankfort, and after 1912 at Wiesbaden; has made guest appearances in other countries, incl. London and U. S. (guest cond. St. Louis Symph., 1929).

Schurig (shoo'-rĭkh), **(Volkmar) Julius (Wm.)**, Aue, Saxony, 1802—Dresden, 1899; composer and teacher.

Schuster (shoo'-shtĕr), **Jos.**, Dresden, 1748—1812; ct.-conductor; c. pop. operas, symphs., etc.

Schütt (shüt), **Eduard**, Petersburg, Oct. 22, 1856—near Merano, July 28, 1933; pianist; pupil of Petersen and Stein, Petersb. Cons.; studied at Leipzig Cons.; in 1881 succeeded Mottl as cond. Akademischer Wagnerverein, Vienna; c. succ. comic opera *"Signor Formica"* (Vienna, 1892); pf.-concerto, etc., but is best known as the composer of many popular small pf.-pieces.

Schütz (shüts), **(Sagitta'rius) H.**, "The father of German music," Köstritz, Saxony, Oct. 8, 1585—Dresden, Nov. 6, 1672; in 1607 entered Marburg Univ. to study law, but, 1609, was sent to Venice by Landgrave

Moritz of Hesse-Cassel to study with Giov. Gabrieli; 1612 returned to Cassel as ct.-organist; 1615 cond. to the Elector of Saxony at Dresden; he frequently revisited Italy, whence he brought much to modify and enlarge German mus.; also made long visits to Copenhagen as ct.-cond. 1627, on royal invitation for the wedding of Princess Sophie of Saxony, he c. the first German opera, the libretto being a transl. from the *"Dafne"* of Peri (q. v.); this work is lost, as is also the ballet, *"Orpheus und Eurydice,"* 1638, for the wedding of Jn. Georg II. of Saxony. Carl Riedel revived interest in S. by pub. and producing *"Die 7 Worte Christi am Kreuz,"* and a *"Passion."* A complete ed. of S.'s works is pub. by Breitkopf and Härtel in 16 vols.; they include sacred and secular mus. of great historical importance as the predecessor whom Händel and Bach rather developed than discarded; he was born just a hundred years before them and shows great dramatic force and truth in his choral work, combining with the old polyphonic structure a modern fire that makes many of his works still beautiful. Biog. by Ph. Spitta, and Fr. Spitta (1886), also André Pirro (1913).

Schwalm (shvälm), (1) **Robt.,** Erfurt, Dec. 6, 1845—Königsberg, March 6, 1912; pupil of Pflughaupt and Leipzig Cons.; cond. at Königsberg; c. opera, male choruses with orch. oratorio, etc. (2) **Oscar,** Erfurt, Sept. 11, 1856—Berlin, Feb. 11, 1936; pupil of Leipzig Cons.; 1886–88, proprietor of Kahnt's pub.-house in Leipzig; also critic for the *Tage-blatt*, etc.; c. an overture; pf.-pcs., etc.

Schwanenberg (shvän'-ĕn-bĕrkh), **Jn. Gf.,** Wolfenbüttel, 1740—Brunswick, 1804; ct.-conductor and dram. composer.

Schwantzer (shvän'-tsĕr), **Hugo,** Oberglogau, 1829—Berlin, 1886; organist, teacher and composer.

Schwarz (shvärts), (1) **Wm.,** Stuttgart, 1825—Berlin, 1878; singer and teacher. (2) **Max,** Hanover, Dec. 1, 1856—Frankfort-on-Main, July 3, 1923; son of above; pupil of Bendel, Bülow, and Liszt; pianist; 1880–83, teacher Hoch Cons., Frankfort; then co-founder, after Raff's death, of the Raff Cons.; from 1885 its dir.

Schwedler (shvät'-lĕr), **(Otto) Maximilian,** b. Hirschberg, Silesia, March 31, 1853; flutist; pupil of Fr. Meinel, Dresden; in Leipzig municipal and Gewandhaus Orch.; 1895–1918, 1st flute; after 1908 taught at Leipzig Cons.; inv. the "Schwedler flute"; wrote a pamphlet on it and c. transcriptions, etc.

Schweitzer (shvīt'-tsĕr), (1) **Anton,** Coburg, 1735—Gotha, 1787; conductor and composer. (2) **Albert,** b. Colmar, Alsace, 1875; eminent organist and writer of life of Bach; ed. B.'s organ works.

Schwencke (shvĕnk'-ĕ), (1) **Jn. Gl.,** 1744—1823; bassoonist. (2) **Chr. Fr. Gl.,** Wachenhausen, Harz, 1767—Hamburg, 1822; son of above; cantor and mus.-dir. (3) **Jn. Fr.,** Hamburg, 1792—1852; son and pupil of (2); composer. (4) **K.,** Hamburg, 1797—?; pianist; son of (2). (5) **Fr. Gl.,** Hamburg, 1823—1896; virtuoso on the pf. and organ; composer.

Schwindel (shvīnt'-l), **Fr.,** d. Carlsruhe, 1786; violinist; c. operettas, symphonies, etc.

Schytte (shĕt'-tĕ), **L. (Th.),** Aarhus, Jutland, April 28, 1848—Berlin, Nov. 10, 1909; druggist, then studied with Ree, Neupert, Gebauer, Gade, Taubert, and Liszt (comp.); 1887–88 teacher Horák's Institute, Vienna; lived in Vienna as concert-pianist and teacher; c. 2 comic operas; pf.-concerto; pantomimes for 4 hands, sonata, etc.

Scontrino (skôn-trē'-nō), **A.,** Trapani, 1850—Florence, Jan. 7, 1922; pupil of Platania, Palermo; lived in Milan as teacher; after 1897 prof. of cpt. at Florence Cons.; c. 5 operas, incl. succ. 1-act *"Gringoire"* (1890), and *"La Cortigiana"* (Milan, 1896); c. *"Sinfonia marinaresca"* (Naples, 1897).

Scott, (1) **Lady John Douglas** (née Alicia Ann Spottiswoode); Spottiswoode, 1810—March 12, 1900; composer of *"Annie Laurie,"* and other songs. (2) **Cyril,** b. Oxton, England, Sept. 27, 1879; composer; studied Hoch Cons., Frankfort, with Ivan Knorr and Uzielli; has c. many attractive modern-style works (esp. in smaller forms), some of them exotic in coloring, incl. 2 symphonies, 4 overtures, 2 passacaglias on Irish themes; piano concerto, various chamber music works; also (opera) *"The*

Alchemist," piano music and songs; author "*The Philosophy of Modernism*"; visited U. S. as perf. in his music, 1920.

Scot'ti, Antonio, Naples, Jan. 25, 1866 —Feb. 26, 1936; notable barytone; début Malta, 1889; sang in various cities; from 1899 at Covent Garden and Met. Op. House, N. Y., regularly; famous as "Don Giovanni," and in later years as "Falstaff," "Scarpia," in "*Tosca*," and the evil Chinese villain in Franco Leoni's 1-act "thriller," "*L'Oracolo*." One of the most distinguished dram. artists of his period, he was a regular mem. of the Met. Op. Co. until 1933, his 25th anniversary with this co. being marked by special ceremonies in 1924. His last few years were clouded by ill health and poverty, as his fortune had been lost and his farewell perf. was given as a benefit for him; his death occurred obscurely in Naples.

Scotto (skŏt'-tŏ), (1) **Ottaviano,** and his son (2) **Girolamo,** mus.-printers at Venice, 1536–39, and 1539–73, respectively; the latter was also a composer.

Scriabine (skrē-ä'-bĕn), **Alexander Nicolaievitch,** Moscow, Jan. 10, 1872 —April 14, 1915; eminent composer and pianist; pupil of Moscow Cons., studying with Safonoff (piano) and Taneiev (comp.) also with Arensky; after 1892 he lived in Paris, Brussels and Amsterdam, and also toured in various cities of Europe as a pianist; but returned to Moscow and taught in the Cons., 1898–1903; in 1907 he visited the U. S. and in 1914 England, as performer in his works. He devoted the latter part of his life exclusively to composition, living in other countries until 1910, when he again took up res. in Moscow. In his earliest piano works, he was influenced by Chopin, Liszt and Wagner, but he soon developed a markedly personal style, which also shows traces of folk-song inspiration and the nationalist idiom of the Russian Five. The earliest period includes op. 1 to 25, and numbers the 1st 2 symphonies in E (with chorus) and C minor, the piano sonatas, op. 6, 19 and 23; the études of op. 8, and the preludes, op. 11, 15 and 17. In his 2nd period his creative work took on a new, somewhat mysterious

and ecstatic note, and he developed a highly original harmonic system, while his orch. writings were also individual, as exemplified in his "*Divine Poem*" and "*Poème de l'Extase*," the intensely poignant style of which bears a resemblance to Wagner's "*Tristan*" but is extended to new vehemence of expression. The 2nd period includes also the 4th piano sonata, op. 30; the "*Poème Satanique*," the 8 études, op. 42, 5th sonata, op. 53, and many smaller pf. works. His 3rd period saw the development of an entirely original harmony based on a so-called "synthetic chord" composed of 7 tones—C, F sharp, B, E, A, D, G —which S. sometimes called the "mystic chord." His theories at this time turned more and more toward the mystical and semireligious, so that he conceived his music as a sort of rite. The works of the final period include "*Prometheus*" (subtitled "*The Poem of Fire*"), scored for orch., piano, organ, chorus and color-organ, the 5 sonatas, op. 62, 64, 66, 68 and 70; the "*Poème Nocturne*," "*Guirlande*" and "*Vers la Flamme*," and many briefer piano numbers. He sought to combine the arts of tone, light, and even—in the "*Mysterium*" on which he was working at his death—various elements of smell by the use of perfumes. Studies of S. and his music have been written by Sabaneiev, Karatygin, Gunst, de Schloezer, Hull, Swan, etc. His letters were ed. by Sabaneiev and pub. in Moscow, 1923.

Scribe (skrēb), **Eugène,** Paris, 1791— 1861; most prolific of French dramatists, and wrote over 100 librettos, incl. "*Fra Diavolo*," "*Prophète*," "*L'Africaine*."

Scudo (skoo'-dŏ), **Paolo,** Venice, 1806 —insane, Blois, 1864; writer.

Sea'shore, Carl Emil, b. Mörlunda, Sweden, Jan. 28, 1866; psychologist; grad. Gustavus Adolphus Coll., U. S. A.; Ph. D., Yale Univ., where he taught until 1902; after latter year at State Univ. of Iowa (dean, Grad. Coll., 1908), where he has carried on important experimentation in musical psychology, esp. to determine bases of musical talent; has invented instruments such as audiometer, tonoscope, chronograph, etc., to measure tonal vibrations and the like; author *"The Psychology of Musical Talent,"* 1917, and many important monographs.

Sebald (zä'-bält), **Alex.**, Pesth, April 29, 1869—Chicago, June 30, 1934; violinist; pupil of Saphir and C. Thomson; member of Gewandhaus orch., Leipzig, and toured with Gewandhaus Quartet; toured widely from 1903; was concertm. Berlin Royal Orch.; 1906 taught in Chicago; 1907 opened a school in Berlin; wrote a method and c. violin pieces, etc.

Sebastiani (sä-bäs-tĭ-ä'-nē), Jn., b. Weimar, 1622; conductor and composer.

Šebor (shä'-bôr), **K. (Karel)**, Brandeis, Bohemia, July 18 (Aug. 13 ?), 1843—Prague, May 17, 1903; pupil Prague Cons. and of Kittl; 1864–67, cond. Nat. Opera; from 1871 military bandm., Vienna; prod. at Prague 5 Czech operas; c. symphs., overtures, etc.

Sechter (zĕkh'-tĕr), **Simon**, Friedberg, Bohemia, Oct. 11, 1788—Vienna, Sept. 10, 1867; eminent contrapuntist and teacher, ct.-organist, prof. of harm.; wrote valuable treatises; c. burlesque opera *"Ali Hitch-Hasch."*

Seck'endorff, Karl Siegmund, Freiherr von, Erlangen, Nov. 26, 1744—Ansbach, April 26, 1785; c. a monodrama and songs to Goethe's texts.

Seeg(e)r (sä'-gĕr) (or **Segert** or **Zeckert**), **Joseph Norbert**, Rzepin, Bohemia, March 21, 1716—Prague, April 22, 1782; composer; famous organist and teacher; c. toccatas, masses, etc.

Seeling (zä'-lĭng), **Hans (Hanuš)**, Prague, 1828—1862; piano-virtuoso and composer.

Seghers (sŭ-gärs'), **Fran. J. Bap.**, Brussels, 1801 — Margency, near Paris, 1881; violinist and conductor.

Segond (sŭ-gôn), **L. A.**, a physician at Paris; studied singing with Manuel Garcia, and wrote *"Hygiène du chanteur"* (1846), etc.

Segovia (sĕ-gō-vē'-ä), **Andrés**, b. Jaén, Spain, 1894; guitarist; most eminent performer of his period, incl. Bach and other classics, Spanish romantic school of 19th cent. and modern composers of his country; has toured Europe and U. S.

Seguro'la, Andres de, b. Spain; studied law Madrid Univ.; practised a year at Barcelona; then took up singing with success; member of Met. Op.

Co. for a decade, then manager of series of morning musicales in N. Y. with distinguished clientèle; in later years a voice teacher in Los Angeles, also making film appearances.

Seguin (sĕg'-wĭn), (1) **Albert Edw. S.**, London, 1809—New York, 1852; bass. (2) **Elizabeth**, his sister, mother of Parepa Rosa. (3) **Ann Childe**, wife of (1); operatic singer; début, 1828; retired and lived New York, 1880. (4) **Wm. H.**, 1814—1850; bro. of (1); bass.

Seidel (zī'-dĕl), (1) **Fr. L.**, Treuenbrietzen, Brandenburg, 1765—Charlottenburg, 1831; organist and dram. composer. (2) **Jn. Julius**, Breslau, 1810—1856; organist and writer. (3) **Toscha**, b. Odessa, Nov. 17, 1899; violinist; studied Petersburg Cons. with Auer; early attracted attention by precocious gifts as youthful virtuoso; début, Oslo, 1915; toured in leading Eur. cities, later in America with succ. as orch. soloist and recitalist; has transcribed many pieces for vln.; founded string trio, and has been heard in radio programs.

Seidl (zīt'-'l), (1) **Anton**, Pesth, May 7, 1850—New York, March 28, 1898; eminent cond., particularly of Wagnerian mus.; pupil Leipzig Cons.; 1870 chorusm. Vienna opera; 1872–79, assisted Wagner in score of *"Nibelungen Ring";* 1879–83 cond. for Neumann's Wagner-troupe; 1883–85 cond. Bremen opera (m. there the soprano (2) Frl. Krauss); 1885–91 Met. Op., N. Y., also from 1895–97 cond. N. Y. Philh. Orch.; 1886 and 1897 cond. at Bayreuth; 1897 cond. Covent Garden, London. (3) **Arthur**, b. Munich, June 8, 1863; pupil R. Sch. of Mus. at Ratisbon and of Paul, Stade, Spitta, and Bellermann; Dr. Phil., Leipzig, 1887; critic; lectured at Leipzig Cons., 1904–09; writer.

Seifert (zī'-fĕrt), **Uso**, Römhild, Thuringia, Feb. 9, 1852—Dresden, June 4, 1912; pupil of Dresden Cons.; teacher there and organist; wrote pf.-method, pf.-pcs., etc.

Seiffert (zīf'-fĕrt), **Max**, b. Beeskow, Feb. 9, 1868; historian and composer; pupil of Spitta; from 1891 at Berlin as author and 1907 Royal Prof.; 1914, mem. of Prussian Academy of Arts.

Seifriz (zī-frĭts), **Max**, Rottweil, Würtemberg, 1827—Stuttgart, 1885; violinist, ct.-cond. and composer.

Seiss (zīs), **Isidor (Wm.)**, Dresden, Dec. 23, 1840—Cologne, Sept. 25, 1905; pianist; pupil of Leipzig Cons.; 1871 pf.-teacher Cologne Cons.; 1878 Prof.; conductor Musikalische Gesellschaft; c. studies in bravura, etc.

Séjan (sā-zhäṅ), **Nicolas**, Paris, 1745—1819; famous organist; 1772, Notre Dame; 1783, St. Sulpice; 1783, royal chapel; teacher and composer.

Sekles (zĕk'-lĕs), **Bernhard**, Frankfort-on-Main, June 20, 1872—Dec. 15, 1934; pupil of Hoch Cons., 1896 teacher of theory there, and after 1923 its dir.; also serving as theatre cond. at Heidelberg and Mainz from 1893; c. opera, "*Schahrazade*" (1917); ballet, "*Der Zwerg und die Infantin*" after Wilde's story (1913); a burlesque stage work, "*Die Hochzeit des Faun*" (1921); symph. poem, "*Aus den Gärten der Semiramis*"; "*Kleine Suite*" for orch.; "*Die Temperamente*," serenade for 11 instruments; passacaglia and fugue for string quartet; 'cello sonata, men's and women's choruses; a number of songs. Wrote book on music dictation, 1905.

Sel'by, Bertram Luard, Kent, Engl., Feb. 12, 1853—Rochester, England, 1919; organist, Salisbury Cath.; 1900–16, at Rochester Cath.; c. 2 operas; a 1-act operetta ("duologue"), successful "*Weather or No*" (London, 1896), Berlin as "*Das Wetterhäuschen*," 1896; org.-sonatas, etc.

Seligmann (za'-lĭkh-män), **Hippolyte Prosper**, Paris, 1817—Monte Carlo, 1882; 'cellist and composer.

Selle (zĕl'-lĕ), **Thos.**, Zorbig, Saxony, 1599—Hamburg, 1663; cantor and composer.

Sellner (zĕl'-nĕr), **Jos.**, Landau, Bavaria, 1787—Vienna, 1843; oboevirtuoso, teacher, writer and composer.

Sel'mer, Johann, Christiania, Jan. 20, 1844—Venice, July 21, 1910; Norwegian composer; cond. and author; pupil of A. Thomas, Paris, Richter and Paul, Leipzig; 1883–86 cond. Phil. orch., Christiania; c. Norwegian Festival March, "*Scène funèbre*," Finnish Festival Bells, "*In the Mountains*," "*Carnival in Flanders*," etc., for orch., choral works with orch., songs, etc.

Sembach (zĕm'-bakh), **Johannes**, b. Berlin, March 9, 1881; tenor; sang

Vienna, 1903; Dresden, 1907; Met. Op., 1914–17, and after 1920.

Sembrich (zĕm'-brĭkh), **Marcella** (rightly **Praxede Marcelline Kochanska**, Sembrich being her mother's maiden name), Wisniewszyk, Galicia, Feb. 15, 1858—New York, Jan. 11, 1935; eminent colorature soprano; pupil (later the wife) of Wm. Stengel (piano), Lemberg Cons.; studied with Epstein at Vienna, and singing with Victor Rokitansky and with G. B. Lamperti, Jr., at Milan, début, May, 1877, at Athens; studied German opera at Berlin with Lewy; sang for 18 months Dresden ct.-th.; from June, 1880, London, and, 1883–84, toured Europe and America; 1884, studied with Francesco Lamperti, Sr.; 1898–1909 sang at Met. Op. and in concert in America with greatest succ.; 1900, managed her own opera co. in Germany; in later years she was active as a master teacher at Juilliard School of Music, N. Y., and Curtis Inst. of Music, Philadelphia.

Semet (sŭ-mā), **Théophile (Aimé Émile)**, Lille, 1824—Corbeil, near Paris, 1888; drummer and dram. composer.

Senaillé (sŭn-ī-yā), **Jean Baptiste**, Paris, Nov. 23, 1687—Oct. 8, 1730; famous violinist; at court of Louis XV.; c. violin sonatas, etc.

Senesino (sān-ĕ-sē'-nō), **Bernardi Francesco** (called the Sienese), Siena, 1680—ca. 1750; male contralto or mezzo-sopr.; sang in Händel's operas till 1729, where he quarrelled with H. and went over to Bononcini; made a fortune and returned to Siena.

Senff (zĕnf), **Bartholf**, Friedrichshall, near Coburg, 1815—Badenweiler, 1900; founder Leipzig mus.-pub. house (1850), also editor.

Sen(f)fl (zĕnf'l) (or **Senfel**), **L.**, Zurich (?), ca. 1492—Munich, ca. 1555; eminent contrapuntist, ct.-cond. and composer.

Senger-Bettaque (zĕng'-kĕr-bĕt-täk-vĕ), **Katharina**, b. Berlin, Aug. 2, 1862; soprano; a ballet dancer at the Imperial Opera, Berlin, then studied with Dorn, and 1879 appeared on the same stage in soubrette rôles; sang in various cities, 1888 in Bayreuth as "Eva"; 1895 married the actor Alex. Senger; in later years a teacher.

Senkrah (zān'-krä) (rightly **Hark'ness**), **Arma Leorette**, New York, 1864—

suicide, Weimar, Aug. 4, 1900; violinist; pupil of Arno Hilf, Leipzig; Wieniawski, and Massart, Paris Cons.; toured with succ.

Serafin (sä'-rä-fēn), **Tullio**, b. Rottanova di Cavazzere, Dec. 8, 1878; conductor; studied at Milan Cons.; début at Ferrara; later cond. opera at La Scala, at Rome, Florence, Bologna, Venice, Turin (also symph. concerts), in South America; leading cond. of Italian works at Met. Op. House, for a decade after 1924; thereafter general dir. of Rome Royal Op.; m. Elena Rakowska, soprano.

Serafino (sä-rä-fē'-nō), (1) **Santo**, vln.-maker at Venice, 1730–45; his label is "Sanctus Seraphin Utinensis fecit Venetiis, Anno, 17—". (2) **Gregorio**, his nephew, also was a vln.-maker, label "Georgius Seraphin Sancti nepos fecit Venetiis, 17—."

Serassi (sä-räs'-sē), Italian family of org.-builders at Bergamo. The founder (1) **Giuseppe** (*il vecchio*), Gordano, 1694—Crema, 1760. His son (2) **Andrea Luigi**, 1725—1799. (3) **Giuseppe** (*il giovane*), Bergamo, 1750—1817; succeeded by his sons (4) **Carlo** and (5) **Giuseppe**.

Serato (sä-rä'-tō), **Arrigo**, b. Bologna, Feb. 7, 1877; violinist, son and pupil of a violinist and prof. at the cons.; later pupil of Sarti; played with success in Germany and elsewhere; after 1914 taught at Liceo of Santa Cecilia, Rome.

Ser'kin, **Rudolf**, b. Eger, Bohemia, March 28, 1903; pianist; his parents were Russian, but became Austrian citizens; pupil of Richard Robert, also in comp. with Marx and Schönberg; at 12 played concerto in Vienna, after 1920 appeared with succ. in Berlin; esp. known for sonata recitals with Adolf Busch, with whom he made Amer. début at Washington Festival.

Sermisy (sĕr-mē-sē), **Claude de** (called **Claudin**, not Claudin Lejeune), ca. 1490—1562; French ct.-cond., composer.

Serov (or **Sjeroff, Syeroff** (s'yä-rôf)); **Alex. Nikolajevitch**, Petersburg, Jan. 23, 1820—Feb. 1 (new style), 1871; important Russian composer and critic; a lawyer, studied 'cello with Karl Schuberth; 1863 prod. grand opera (text and mus.) "*Judith*," and the Czar granted him a pension; he was a lecturer on mus. at Moscow and

Petersb. Universities and wrote his own librettos; 1865 prod. "*Rogneda*" with succ.; laid aside 2 unfinished operas to finish "*Wrazyiasiela*" but died before it was done. Soloviev finished it and it was prod. with succ.

Serpette (sĕr-pĕt), (**H. Chas. A.**) **Gaston,** Nantes, Nov. 4, 1846—Paris, Nov. 3, 1904; pupil of Thomas, Paris Cons.; 1871, taking 1st Grand prix de Rome, wrote cantata "*Jeanne d'Arc*"; 1874, prod. opera-bouffe "*La Branche Cassée*" (Bouffes-Parisiens), followed by 30 other light works.

Serrão (sĕr-rä'-nō), **Paolo**, Filadelfia, Catanzaro, 1830—Naples, March 17, 1907; pupil of Naples Cons.; political troubles prevented the prod. of his opera "*L'Impostore*" in 1852, and another in 1857, but he prod. "*Pergolesi*" and "*La Duchessa di Guisa*" (1865), and "*Il Figliuol prodigo*" (1868); c. also an oratorio, a requiem, a funeral symph. (for Mercadante), etc.

Serran'o (or **Serrão**), **Emilio**, b. Vitoria, 1850; court pianist at Madrid; prof. at the Cons., and dir. of Royal Opera; c. operas.

Servais (sĕr-vĕ), (1) **Adrien Fran., Hal,** near Brussels, 1807—1866; eminent 'cellist and teacher; pupil of his father and of Platel, début Paris. 1834; 1848, Prof. Brussels Cons. and soloist to the King; toured widely; c. 3 concertos for 'cello, etc. (2) **Jos.,** Hal, 1850—1885; son and pupil of above; 'cellist and prof. Brussels Cons. (3) **Franz** or **François** (**Matthieu**), 1844—Asnières, Jan. 14, 1901; cond. at Brussels; c. opera "*L'Appolonide*" or "*Ion*" (Carlsruhe 1899). Son of Adrien Fr. (q. v.).

Sessions (sĕsh'-ŏns), **Roger,** b. Brooklyn, N. Y., Dec. 28, 1896; composer; studied Yale School of Music with Parker, also with Ernest Bloch; taught theory, Cleveland Inst. of Music, 1921–25; awarded Damrosch Fellowship at Amer. Acad. in Rome, 1928; founded (with Aaron Copland) Copland - Sessions Concerts; dir. school of music, N. Y.; c. 2 symphonies (1st played by Boston Symph. and at Internat'l Soc. for Contemp. Music Fest., Geneva); incidental music to Andreyeff's "*Black Maskers*", suite which has been perf. by many Amer. orchs.; vln. concerto, piano sonata, works for organ, etc.

Setaccioli (sā-tä-chē-ōl'-ē), **Giacomo,** Corneto Tarquinia, Italy, Dec. 8, 1868—Siena, Dec. 5, 1925; composer; studied at Liceo of Santa Cecila, Rome, where his opera, "*La Sorella di Mark*," was given at Costanzi Theatre, 1896; c. (opera) "*Adrienne Lecouvreur*"; theory teacher after 1922 at St. Cecilia Acad., and succeeded Pizzetti as dir. of Cherubini Cons., Florence, 1925.

Ševcik (shĕf'-chĭk), **Otokar,** Horaždiowitz, Bohemia, March 22, 1852—Pisek, Jan. 18, 1934; famous violin teacher; pupil of Prague Cons.; from 1870 concertmaster various cities; 1875 prof. at Kiev; 1892-1906 at Prague Cons.; 1909-19, dir. of master school of vln., Vienna State Cons.; later taught in U. S. and at Pisek; teacher of Kubelik, Kocian, etc.; author of methods; c. Bohemian dances, variations, etc.

Sévérac (sā-vā-răk), **Déodat de,** Saint Felix, July 20, 1873—Roussillon, March 23, 1921; writer and composer; pupil Toulouse Cons., and the Schola cantorum, Paris; c. 2-act lyric drama "*Le Cœur de Moulin*" (Op. Com. Paris, 1909); lyric tragedy "*Héliogabale*" (Arènes de Beziers, 1910); "*Muguetto*" (1911); "*Hélène de Sparte*" (Paris 1912); symph. poems, "*Nymphes au Crépuscule*" and "*Didon et Enée*"; a piano sonata, etc.

Sevitzky (sē-vēt'-skē), **Fabien,** b. Vishni Volotchek, Russia, Sept. 30, 1893; (family name, Koussevitzky, nephew of Serge); conductor; studied Petersburg Cons. with Siloti and Liadoff, grad. with gold medal; played with Moscow Imp. Theatre orch.; coming to America, he founded Chamber String Sinfonietta at Phila.; also for a time cond. of Boston People's Symph.; 1937, appointed cond. of Indianapolis Symph.; m. Maria Koussevitzky, singer.

Seyffardt (zīf'-färt), **Ernst Hn.,** b. Crefeld, 1859; pupil of Cologne Cons. and of Kiel; 1892-1924, conductor Neuer Singverein, Stuttgart; c. dram. scene "*Thusnelda*," "*Trauerfeier beim Tode einer Jungfrau*," symph., sonatas, MS. opera "*The Bells of Plurs*," etc.

Seyfried (zī'-frēt), **Ignaz X.,** Ritter von, Vienna, 1776—1841; conductor, writer and dram. composer.

Sey'mour, John Laurence, b. Los An-

geles, 1893; c. 1-act opera, "*In the Pasha's Garden*," Met. Op., 1935.

Sgambati (sgäm-bä'-tē), **Giovanni,** Rome, May 28, 1843—Dec. 15, 1914; important pianist and conductor; pupil of Aldega, Barbieri and Natalucci, later of Liszt; at 6 played in public, sang in Church and cond. small orchestras; later he toured Italy and Germany; 1877, headteacher Accad. di S. Cecilia, Rome; 1896, founded "Nuova Società Musicale Romana"; admirer and friend of Wagner; c. requiem with orch. (1896), 2 symphs., overtures, pf.-concerto, an octet, 2 pf.-quintets, a string-quartet (op. 17) and piano pcs., etc.

Shakespeare, Wm., Croydon, Engl., June 16, 1849—Golders Green, Nov. 1, 1931; noted voice teacher; at 13 organist; pupil of Molique (comp.); 1866, won King's scholarship R. A. M., and studied there with Bennett; 1871, took Mendelssohn Scholarship for pf.-playing and comp.; studied with Reinecke, Leipzig; 1872, singing at Milan; from 1875, concert and oratorio-singer; 1878, prof. of singing, R. A. M.; in 1880, 1886, cond. of the concerts there; resigned; won high reputation as a singing-teacher; c. overtures, a symph., pf.-concerto, etc.

Sha'porin, Yuri, b. Glukhov, Chernigovski Province, Russia, 1889; composer; pupil of Leningrad Cons., studying with Sokolov, Tcherepnine and M. Steinberg; c. incidental music for plays, piano sonatas, choral and orch. works; (opera) "*The Decembrists*" (text by A. N. Tolstoy), and a symph. in C minor with chorus, portraying events in Russian revolution of 1917 (perf. in London and U. S.).

Sharp, Cecil James, London, Nov. 22, 1859—Hampstead, England, June 23, 1924; writer and collector of folk music; grad. Cambridge Univ.; assoc. to Chief Justice of So. Australia, 1883-89; principal, Hampstead Cons. of Music, London, 1896-1905; after 1911 dir. of Stratford-on-Avon School of Folk-song; author of valuable collections of British folk-songs, dances, etc.; spent several years in Kentucky Mountains, collecting material.

Sharpe, Herbert Francis, Halifax, Yorkshire, March 1, 1861—London, Oct. 14, 1925; Queen's Scholar, Nat. Training Sch., London; gave pf.-concerts; 1884, prof. R. C. M.; 1890, examiner; wrote *"Pianoforte Sch."* (with Stanley Lucas); c. comic opera, etc.

Shat'tuck, Arthur, b. Neenah, Wis., April 19, 1881; pianist; pupil of Leschetizky; début as soloist with Copenhagen Philh., 1901; has made tours of Europe and U. S.

Sha'vitch, Vladimir, b. Russia; conductor; studied with Godowsky, Busoni, Kaun and Juon; cond. Syracuse (N. Y.) Symph. for several years after 1924; appeared at Moscow State Op., 1929; guest cond. of London Symph., and orchs. in Berlin, Paris, Madrid, Moscow, Leningrad, also in Detroit, San Francisco and Los Angeles; res. in London, where he has promoted a mechanical device to reproduce orch. and chorus in opera, synchronised with actual soloists; m. Tina Lerner, pianist.

Shaw, (1) **Mary,** London, 1814—Hadleigh, Suffolk, 1876; noted contralto and teacher. (2) **Bernard,** b. Dublin, July 26, 1856; the eminent playwright, in his early days a music and dram. critic; author, *"The Perfect Wagnerite,"* etc. (3) **Geoffrey,** b. Clapham, Nov. 14, 1879; studied at St. Paul's Cath. Choir School; at Derby School and at Cambridge with Wood and Stanford; c. church and other music. His bro. (4) **Martin,** b. London, March 9, 1876; composer; studied at R. C. M. with Stanford; organist and dir. of League of Arts; c. church music, a ballad opera, *"Mr. Pepys,"* incidental music to plays, chamber and orch. works, etc.; author, *"Principles of Church Music Comp.";* ed. *"Songs of Britain,"* etc.

Shed'lock, John South, Reading, Engl., 1843—London, Jan. 9, 1919; graduate, London Univ., 1864; pupil of E. Lübeck (pf.) and Lalo (comp.), Paris; teacher and concert-pianist, London, 1879; critic for the *Athenæum;* also lectured at the R. A. M.; pub. articles, *"The Pianoforte Sonata, Its Origin and Development"* (London, 1895); editor and translator; c. string-quartet, etc.

Shel'ley, Harry Rowe, b. New Haven, Conn., June 8, 1858; pupil of Stoeckel at Yale, Dudley Buck, Vogrich and Dvořák (New York); organist various churches, also teacher of theory and comp. Metropolitan College, N. Y.; c. *"The Inheritance Divine,"*

sacred cantata, 2 symphs. (the first Eb, performed, N. Y., 1897), vln.-concerto (1891), cantata *"Vexilla Regis"* (N. Y., 1894), and suite *"Baden-Baden,"* etc., for orch.; church-mus., pf. and org.-pcs. and songs, many very pop.

Shep'ard, (1) **Thos. Griffin,** Madison, Conn., April 23, 1848—Brooklyn, N. Y., 1905; pupil of G. W. and J. P. Morgan; organist various churches in New Haven; instructor, Yale Glee Club and cond. Oratorio Soc., also dir. Apollo Club (male voices); teacher and critic; c. comic opera, Christmas cantata, etc. (2) **Frank Hartson,** Bethel, Conn., Sept. 20, 1863—Orange, N. J., 1913; pupil of Thayer, Boston; organist various towns; 1886–90, studied Leipzig; 1888, organist English Chapel there; 1891, est. a sch. at Orange, N. J.; organist there; writer of text-books and treatises.

Shepherd, Arthur, b. Paris, Idaho, Feb. 19, 1880; 1892, pupil at N. E. Cons. Boston, of Dennée and Faelten (piano), Benj. Cutter (harmony); Goetschius and Chadwick (comp.); graduated 1897, and settled in Salt Lake City as teacher; cond. Salt Lake Symph. Orch.; from 1909, teacher of piano, harmony and cpt. at N. E. Cons.; 1902, won Paderewski prize with *"Ouverture Joyeuse";* 1909 won two Nat. Fed. prizes with piano sonata, and song, *"The Lost Child";* c. also barytone solo with chor. and orch., songs and piano pieces; 1920, asst. cond., Cleveland Orch.; prof. of music, Western Reserve Univ. and critic.

Sher'wood, (1) **Wm. Hall,** Lyons, N. Y., Jan. 31, 1854—Chicago, Jan. 7, 1911; noteworthy pianist and teacher of piano; son and pupil of Rev. L. H. Sherwood, founder of Lyons Mus. Acad.; pupil also of Heimberger, Pychowski and Wm. Mason; studied 5 years under Th. Kullak, Weitzmann, Wuerst and Deppe (Berlin), Richter (Leipzig), K. Doppler and Scotson Clark (Stuttgart) and Liszt (Weimar); début with succ., Berlin; returned 1876 to the U. S., and toured with great succ.; teacher N. E. Cons., Boston, later, New York; 1889, Chicago, as head of the pf.-section of the Cons.; 1897, founded "Sherwood Piano Sch."; 1887 he m. his pupil, Estella F. Adams, also pianist; pub. pf.-pcs. (2) **Percy**, b. of English parents, Dresden, May 23, 1866; pupil of Hermann Scholtz (pf.); later of Dresden Cons.; concert-pianist and until 1914, teacher, Dresden Cons.; later active in London; c. pf.-pcs.

Shield, Wm., Whickham, Durham, 1748—London, 1829; violinist, writer and composer.

Shostako'vitch, Dimitri, b. St. Petersburg, Sept. 16, 1906; composer; pupil of Glazounoff and Steinberg at Cons.; precocious musician; while still in his twenties he attracted attention for an opera, "*The Nose*"; this was followed by other stage works and orch. music, incl. several symphs., chamber music, and piano works; his symphs. played in America by Stokowski with the Phila. Orch., were given speedily by other ensembles, as were subsequent works in this form; in substance, his music is synthetic, combining older styles, and marked by a virtuosic, often flippant and ironic touch; a consummate orchestrator and a humorist of pungent variety, S. made an international furore with his opera, "*Katerina Ismailova*" (known also as "*Lady Macbeth of Mzensk*"), which treats a brutal drama of lust, intrigue and murder in a bold, realistic manner; first prod. at Leningrad, it was highly popular in other Russian theatres and was prod. in America by the Cleveland Orch. and Russian singers under Rodzinski both in its own city and N. Y. at the Met. Op. House in 1935; this work, heard in concert form in London also, was later suppressed by the Soviet authorities, together with his ballet, "*Limpid Stream*," on the grounds that the composer was misusing his talents by cultivating a "formalistic" and sensational style of writing; he was encouraged to hew closer to the classic line of Russian music by being commissioned to prepare a new ballet; c. also a piano concerto, a sonata and smaller works for this instrument; some of his symphs. (notably that known as "*May Day*") include programs of revolutionary content.

Shudi. Vide BROADWOOD.

Sibelius (sē-bā'-lē-ōōs), **Jan**, b. Tavastehus, Finland, Dec. 8, 1865; one of the most important and original

composers of his period, influential not so much through any outward modernity of musical speech, as by the power and freedom with which he has used traditional material to gain new expressive results. As a boy he played piano, improvised and wrote simple compositions; at 15 began vln. study with a local bandmaster; played in school orch. and in chamber music groups, but was entered as a student of law at Univ. of Helsingfors, 1885. Later he gave up law and in 1889 went to Berlin for further study, then to Vienna, where he was a pupil of Carl Goldmark, Robert Fuchs and others. He married Aino Järnefelt, and returned to his native country, 1892. His first composition to attract wide attention was his orch. work, "*En Saga*." He taught comp. and vln. at the Helsingfors Music Inst. for a brief period, but after 1900 received a stipend from the Finnish Government to devote himself exclusively to comp. He visited Paris in 1900 and led some of his works at the Exposition there with the Helsingfors Orch. under Kajanus. In the following year he also conducted at Heidelberg Fest. His later career has been one of increasing honours, with esp. esteem from his countrymen, who celebrated his 70th birthday anniversary in 1935 with an official fest. at Helsingfors, when the highest tributes were paid him. His journeys to other countries included a visit to America in 1914, when he led his symph. poem, "*Daughters of the Ocean*," at the Norfolk Fest., and Yale Univ. conferred on him the degree of Mus. D. His music in the larger forms, incl. 8 monumental symphs., was fairly slow in making its way into the repertoires of other countries, but esp. in England and America has in recent years been assigned a place among the most important of the present day. In addition, his works include: (orch.) "*Pohjola's Daughter*"; "*The Swan of Tuonela*"; "*Karelia*"; "*Tapiola*"; "*Frühlingslied*"; "*Lemminkainen's Homecoming*"; "*The Dryads*"; "*Pelleas und Melisande*"; "*Night Ride and Sunrise*"; "*Pan and Echo*" (dance intermezzo); 2 orch. suites, called "*Scènes Histo-*

riques"; *"Suite caracteristique"*; 2 Serenades for vln. and orch.; *"The Bard"*; (symph. poem); and the pop. nationalistic tone poem, *"Finlandia"*; (chamber music) *"Voces Intimae"* for string quartet; vln. pieces; (opera) *"Die Jungfrau im Turme"*; incid. music to Ad. Paul's drama, *"King Christian II."*; to Procope's *"Belshazzar,"* and to the morality play, *"Everyman"*; (chorus) Academic Festival Cantata; *"Gesang der Athener"* and *"Die Gefangene Königin,"* both for chorus and orch.; *"Des Fahrmanns Braut"* for barytone and orch.; *"My Land"* for mixed chorus and orch.; *"Jordens Sang"* (Der Erde Lied) for mixed chorus, female solo choir and orch.; *"Maan Virsi,"* cantata for mixed chorus and orch.; (pantomime) *"Scaramouche"* (Copenhagen, 1922); also many male choruses, songs and piano works.

In his larger compositions, S. has shown an original method of construction, developing his themes out of short units which later coalesce into their final form. His inspirations are drawn very largely from Nature, and though his works are "absolute" music in the highest sense, many of them contain picturesque legendary suggestions from the Finnish epics, such as the *"Kalevala."* It is, however, not true that his personality is essentially a gloomy or mystical one, for there are boisterous humor and rude strength in many of his works. S. is the subject of important biographies and studies by Rosa Newmarch, Cecil Gray, Walter Niemann, etc.

Siboni (sē-bō′-nē), (1) **Giu.**, Forli, 1780 — Copenhagen, 1839; tenor. (2) **Erik (Anton Waldemar)**, Copenhagen, 1828—1892; pianist, organist, teacher and dram. composer. (3) **Johanna Frederika** (née Crull), Rostock, Jan. 30, 1839—(?); pianist; pupil of Moscheles; 1866 m. above.

Sichra (sĭkh′-rä), **Andreas Ossipovich**, Wilna, 1772—St. Petersburg, 1861; guitarist and composer.

Sick (sĭk), **Theodor Bernhard**, Copenhagen, Nov. 7, 1827—1893; artillery officer and composer of chamber music.

Sieber (zē′-bĕr), **Fd.**, Vienna, 1822—Berlin, 1895; famous singing-teacher.

Siegel (zē′-gĕl), (1) **E. F. W.**, d. 1869;

founded, 1846, mus.-pub. firm at Leipzig, later owned by R. Linnemann. (2) **F.** Vide SCHUBERTH, J.

Sieveking (zē′-vĕ-kĭng), **Martinus**, b. Amsterdam, March 24, 1867; notable pianist; pupil of his father, of J. Röntgen, Leipzig Cons., and Coenen (harm.); 1890 played in London; made v. succ. tours; 1895 Boston; 1896—97 American tour; from 1915 dir. of a music school in N. Y.; c. a suite (played by Lamoureux, Paris), etc.

Siface (sē-fä′-chĕ) (rightly **Grossi**), **Giov. Fran.**, robbed and murdered in Northern Italy, ca. 1699; soprano-musico; ca. 1675 member Papal Chapel.

Sighicelli (sē-gĭ-chĕl′-lē), family of violinists. (1) **Filippo**, San Cesario, Modena, 1686—Modena, 1773; violinist. (2) **Giu.**, Modena, 1737—1826; son of above; violinist. (3) **Carlo**, Modena, 1772—1806; son of (2), also attached to court. (4) **A.**, Modena, 1802—1883; son of (3); eminent violinist and conductor. (5) **V.**, Cento, July 30, 1830—Paris, Feb. 15, 1905; son and pupil of (4); pupil of Hellmesberger, Mayseder, and 1849 solo-violinist and 2nd ct.-cond. Modena; from 1855, teacher Paris; c. vln.-fantasias, etc.

Sigismondi (sē-jĭs-môn′-dē), **Giu.**, Naples, 1739—1826; singing-teacher and dram. composer.

Silas (sē′läs), **Eduard**, Amsterdam, Aug. 22, 1827—West Kensington, England, Feb. 8, 1909; pianist; début Amsterdam, 1837; pupil of Neher, Kalkbrenner, etc.; later of Benoist and Halévy, Paris Cons.; winning 1st prize for org. playing, 1849, in competition with Saint-Saëns and Cohen; since 1890 lived in England as organist; 1866 Assemblée général des Catholiques en Belgique awarded him 1st prize (gold medal and 1,000 francs) for a mass; later prof. of harm. Guildhall Sch. and the London Acad. of Mus.; c. oratorio *"Joash"* (Norwich Fest., 1863), Kyrie Eleison with orch., 3 symphs., 3 overtures etc.

Silbermann (zēl′-bĕr-män), (1) **Andreas**, Klein-Bobritzsch, Saxony, 1678 — Strassburg, 1734; org. builder at Strassburg. (2) **Gf.**, Klein-Bobritzsch, 1683 — Dresden, 1753; bro. of above and his apprentice; the first German to manufacture pianofortes, but preceded by Cristo-

fori; inv. *cembal d'amour* (v. D. D.).
(3) **Jn. Andreas**, Strassburg, 1712—
1783; son of (1); org.-builder.
(4) **Jn. Daniel**, 1717—Leipzig, 1766;
son of (1), successor of (2). (5) **Jn.
H.**, Strassburg, 1727—1799; son of
(1); pf.-maker. (6) **Jn. Fr.**, 1762—
1817; son of (5), org.-builder, organist and composer.

Silcher (zĭl'-khĕr), **Fr.**, Schnait,
Württemberg, 1789—Tübingen, 1860;
noted song-composer; pupil of his
father and of Auberlen; teacher at
Stuttgart, 1817; mus.-dir. at Tübingen Univ.; pub. a text-book and
collected and c. chorals, etc.

Siloti (sē'-lō-tē), **Alex.**, b. Charkov,
Russia, Oct. 10, 1863; pianist, pupil
of Zwereff and of N. Rubinstein and
Tchaikovsky, Moscow Cons.; winning a gold medal; début, Moscow,
1880; studied with Liszt 3 years;
1887–90, prof. Moscow Cons.; made
v. succ. tours, 1898–90, America;
1901, appeared as cond. with Philh.
in Moscow; 1904, founded his own
orch. in St. Petersburg for notable
concerts, until 1919; since 1922 he
has lived in N. Y., as faculty mem.,
Juilliard School of Music, and has
made appearances as recitalist and
orch. soloist; c. pf.-pieces.

Silva (zēl'-vä), (1) **Andreas de**, 16th
cent. contrapuntist; c. motets, etc.
(2) **David Poll de**, St. Esprit, near
Bayonne, 1834 — Clermont, Oise,
1875; blind; pupil of his mother who
c. operas, oratorios, etc.; wrote out
his comp. by dictation.

Silver (sĕl-vär), **Chas.**, Paris, April 16,
1868; pupil of Dubois and Massenet
at the Cons.; won Grand prix de
Rome with cantata "*L'Interdit*"; c.
operetta, elegiac poem "*Raïs*"; 4-act
fairy opera "*La Belle au Bois Dormant*" (Paris, 1895), oratorio "*Tobie*"; opera, "*La Megère Apprivoi-
sée*," 1922, etc.

Simandl (zē'-mänt'l), **Fz.**, Blatna, 1840
—Vienna, 1912; 1st double-bass
Vienna court orch.; 1869 teacher at
the Cons.; pub. method for contrabass.

Simão. Vide PORTUGAL.

Simon (sē'-môṅ), (1) **Jean Henri**, Antwerp, 1783—1861; violinist. (2) **Anton Yulievich**, France, 1851—?;
composer; pupil of Paris Cons.; 1871
theatre cond. in Moscow; 1891 prof.
at Phil. Society School; c. 6 operas,
symph. poems, etc.

Simons-Candeille. Vide CANDEILLE.
Simp'son (or **Sympson**), (1) **Chp.**, d.
London, ca. 1677; player on the
viola da gamba; pub. text-books.
(2) **Thos.**, b. England; from ca. 1615,
violinist in Germany; composer.

Sim'rock, (1) **Nicolaus**, Bonn, 1752—
1834; founded there 1790 mus.-pub.
house; 1805 Berlin branch founded
by his son (2) **Peter Jos.**; 1870 in
Berlin under (3), **Fritz**, 1841—
Lausanne, Sept., 1901.

Sin'clair (sink'lĕr), **J.**, near Edinburgh, 1791—Margate, 1857; tenor.

Sinding (zĭnt'-ĭng), **Christian**, b.
Kongsberg, Norway, Jan. 11, 1856;
notable composer; pupil of Reinecke,
Leipzig Cons., later with Royal
Scholarship, studied at Dresden,
Munich, and Berlin; lived in Christiania as organist and teacher; in
1915 he was granted a govt. pension
for life to enable him to give all his
time to comp.; in 1921–22 he accepted a call to the Eastman School,
Rochester, N. Y., as guest teacher of
comp., returning afterward to Norway. In his own country he is
accounted next to Grieg in importance as a nationalistic composer.
His large output includes 3 symphs.;
piano concerto; 3 vln. concertos and
many smaller pieces of this instrument; suite "*Episodes Chevale-
resques*"; "*Rondo Infinito*"; suite in
A minor; "*Legende*" and Romanze
in D, for orch. with vln.; piano
quintet; string quartet; 3 piano trios;
2 serenades for two violins and
piano; vln. suites, variations, etc.;
pf.-sonata, suite, variations, and
many smaller pieces, incl. the pop.
"*Frühlingsräuschen*"; also an opera,
"*Der Heilige Berg*" and more than
200 songs and other vocal works.

Singelée (săṅzh-lä), **J. Bap.**, Brussels,
1812—Ostend, 1875; violinist and
composer.

Singer (zĭng'-ĕr), (1) **Peter**, Häfelgehr
(Lechthal), 1810—Salzburg, 1882;
monk; inv. (1839) the "Pansym-
phonikon" (v. D. D.); composer.
(2) **Edmund**, Totis, Hungary, Oct.
14, 1830—Stuttgart, Jan. 23, 1912;
violinist; pupil of Ellinger, at Pesth,
then of Kohne; toured, then studied
with Jos. Böhm, Vienna, and at Paris
Cons.; 1853–61 leader at Weimar,
then leader at Stuttgart, and prof.
at the Cons. (3) **Otto**, Sora, Saxony,
1833—New York, 1894; pianist,

conductor, teacher and composer.
(4) **Otto,** Jr., Dresden, Sept. 14, 1863
—Leipzig, Jan. 8, 1931; violinist;
studied in Paris, in Berlin under Kiel,
and in Munich under Rheinberger;
1890 teacher in Cologne Cons., and
conductor; from 1892 lived in Leipzig; c. vln.-Concertstück, etc. (5)
Richard, b. Budapest, May 9, 1879;
d. N. Y., Feb. 29, 1940; pianist;
pupil Fiedler, Barth, Leschetizky
and Busoni; esp. known as a Liszt
performer; toured Europe and U.S.A.
Sin'ico, (1) **Francesco,** Trieste, 1810—
1865; conductor and composer. His
son (2) **Giuseppe,** Trieste, Feb. 10,
1836—Dec. 31, 1907, c. operas.
Sinigaglia (sē-nĭ-gäl'-yä), **Leone,** b.
Turin, Aug. 14, 1868; pupil of the
Cons. and of Mandyczewski; c. violin
concerto, rhapsody *"Piemontese,"* for
violin and orch., string quartet, concert étude for quartet, overture *"Le
baruffe chiozzotte,"* etc.
Sir'men (Syrmen), (1) **Luigi,** violinist
and cond. at Bergamo; his wife,
(2) **Maddalena Lombardini de,** b.
Venice, 1735—d. towards end of
cent.; prominent violinist; pupil of
Tartini; later singer and composer.
Sistermanns (zĭst'-ĕr-mäns), **Anton,**
Herzogenbusch, Holland, Aug. 5,
1865—March 18, 1926; bass; pupil
of Stockhausen; 1899, sang "Pogner"
at Bayreuth; 1904–15, taught Scharwenka Cons., Berlin, later lived in
The Hague.
Sitt (zĭt), **Hans,** Prague, Sept. 21, 1850
—Leipzig, March 10, 1922; violinist;
studied Prague Cons.; 1867, leader
theatre-orch., Breslau; 1869, cond.
there, later in Prague, etc.; 1883,
teacher of vln. Leipzig Cons. and
vla.-player Brodsky Quartet; cond.
of various societies; c. 3 vln.-
concertos, a vla.-concerto, a 'cello-
concerto, etc.
Sittard (sĭt-tär), (1) **Josef,** Aix-la-
Chapelle, June 4, 1846—Hamburg,
Nov. 23, 1903; pupil, Stuttgart
Cons., later teacher of singing and
pf. there; lecturer on mus.; 1885,
critic; 1891, prof.; writer and composer. (2) **Alfred,** b. Stuttgart,
Nov. 4, 1878; organist; son and pupil
of (1), also of Armbrust and Koehler,
later of Cologne Cons.; won Mendelssohn Prize 1902; 1903, org. of
Dresden Kreuzkirche; after 1912 of
the new Michaeliskirche in Hamburg
and also cond. of choir there.

Sivori (sē-vō'-rē), **Ernesto Camillo,**
Genoa, 1815—1894; famous violinist
and composer; début at 6; pupil of
Costa and Paganini; toured widely.
Sjögren (shäkh'-rĕn), (Jn. Gv.) **Emil,**
Stockholm, June 16, 1853—March 4,
1918; pupil of the Cons. there; later
of Kiel (cpt.) and Haupt (org. at
Berlin); 1890, organist Johankirke,
Stockholm; c. sonatas, vln. and piano
works, songs, etc.
Skil'ton, Charles Sanford, b. Northampton, Mass., 1868—Lawrence,
Kan., Mar. 12, 1941; studied Berlin
Hochsch. with Bargiel and Boise,
also Dudley Buck in N. Y.; prof.
organ, theory and history of music,
State Univ. of Kansas after 1903;
c. orch. and other music, some of it
based on Indian themes, which has
had repeated hearings.
Skriabine, vide SCRIABINE.
Skroup (or **Skraup**) (shkroop or shkrä'-
oop), (1) **Fz.** (František), Vosic,
Bohemia, 1801—Rotterdam, 1862;
conductor and dram. composer.
(2) **Jan Nepomuk,** Vosic, 1811—
Prague, 1892; bro. of above; conductor, singing-teacher, writer and
dram. composer.
Skuhersky (skoo'-hĕr-shkē), **Fz.** (František) **Sdenko,** Opocno, Bohemia,
1830—Budweis, 1892; organist, conductor, theorist and composer.
Slaughter (slôt'-ĕr), **A. Walter,** London,
1860—March 2, 1908; chorister at St.
Andrew's, Wells St., London; pupil of
A. Cellier and Jacobi; cond. Drury
Lane and St. James's Th.; prod. comic
operas, and a succ. mus.-comedy,*"The
French Maid"* (1897), etc.
Slavik (slä'-vēk), **Jos.,** Jince, Bohemia,
1806—Pesth, 1833; violinist.
Slenczynski (slĕn-chēn'-skē), **Ruth,** b.
Sacramento, Cal., Jan. 15, 1925;
pianist of remarkable precocity; the
daughter of a violinist; had 1st piano
lesson at age of 3 and at 4 gave her
1st concert in Oakland, Cal.; at 5,
played before audience of 3,500 at
San Francisco; she was taken to
Berlin for further study, and a year
later, in 1931, gave a concert at the
Bach Saal there, astonishing an
audience of musical authorities by
the ease with which she played an
extended program of taxing masterpieces; 1932, at 7 made début in
Paris with equally amazing results;
one of her typical recitals incl. a
Bach and Mozart sonata, a Chopin,

group, Beethoven's theme and variations on "*Nel cor piu mi sento*," and 2 Schubert works; following this she returned to the U. S. and gave concerts to triumphal ovations.

Slezak (slĕt'-säk), (1) Leo, b. Schönberg (Moravia), Aug. 18, 1875; opera tenor; studied with Robinson in Brünn; later with Jean de Reszke; début as "Lohengrin," Brünn Op., 1896; sang in Berlin and Breslau; after 1909, member of Vienna Op.; Covent Garden, 1909 ("Otello"); Met. Op., N. Y., 1909–13; also in Munich, Dresden, Wiesbaden, Budapest, Paris, Prague and La Scala, singing heroic rôles. (2) Walter, his son, has sung with succ. in operetta in New York.

Slivinski (slĭ-vēn'-shkĭ), Jos. von, Warsaw, Dec. 15, 1865—March 2, 1930; pianist; pupil of Strobl, Leschetizky and Anton Rubinstein; début, 1890; America, 1893; toured with Leipzig Philh. orch.; lived Paris.

Slonim'sky, Nicholas, b. St. Petersburg, April 15, 1894; conductor, pianist; studied at Cons. there; gave concerts in Eur. cities; cond. Chamber Orch. of Boston and also as guest in programs of modern music abroad; has taught and lectured; c. chamber, piano and vocal music.

Slo'per (Edw. Hugh), Lindsay, London, 1826—1887; pianist, teacher, writer and composer.

Smal'lens, Alexander, b. St. Petersburg; conductor; studied at Inst. of Mus. Art, N. Y., and at Paris Cons.; asst. cond., Boston Op., 1911; later with Century Op. Co., on tours with Pavlowa; at Chicago Op., 1919–22 (premières of De Koven and Prokofieff works); Phila. Civic Op., 1923–30; also as asst. cond. with Phila. Orch., and as leader of operas with that ensemble; cond. opera, Lewisohn Stadium summer seasons and elsewhere.

Smareglia (smä-rāl'-yä), A., Pola, Istria, May 5, 1854—Grado, April 15, 1929; studied Vienna and at the Milan Cons., graduating with a symph. work "*Eleanora*"; prod. 6 operas, incl. "*Preziosa*"; (Milan, 1879), "*Bianca da Cervia*" (Milan, La Scala, 1882), "*Il Vassallo di Szigeth*" (Vienna, 1889, as "*Der Vasall von Szigeth*," New York, 1890), and "*La Falena*" (Venice, 1897; "*Oceana*," 1903; "*Notte di S.*

Silvestro*," 1907; "*L'Abisso*," 1914; 1921, prof. of comp., Trieste Cons.

Smart, (1) Sir G. (Thos.), London, 1776—1867; noted conductor, pupil of Dupuis and Arnold; knighted, 1811; cond. Phil. Soc., 1813–44. (2) Henry, Dublin, 1778—1823; bro. of above; violinist; leader Drury Lane, 1812–21; piano-manufacturer. (3) Henry, London, Oct. 26, 1813—(blind) July 6, 1879, son and pupil of (2); studied with Kearns; organist in London from 1836; c. an opera "*Bertha*" (1855), many cantatas, etc.

Smetana (smä'-tä-nä), Fr. (Bedrich), Leitomischl, Bohemia, 1824—insane, Prague, 1884, noted composer and pianist; pupil of Proksch and Liszt; 1848, organised a sch. at Prague; 1866–74, cond. Nat. Theatre Prague. Partially because of alleged intrigues against him and his growing deafness, he resigned this post in the latter year. The state of his health grew worse and finally his reason gave way. C. a string-quartet, 8 operas, incl. the comic masterpiece "*Prodaná nevešta*" ("*The Bartered Bride*"), 1866; 9 symph. poems, incl. a cycle of 6 "*Má Vlast*" ("*My Country*"), symph. of "*Triumph*," etc.

Smet'erlin, Jan, b. Bielsko, Poland, 1892; pianist; studied at Vienna Piano Master School, and with Godowsky; has appeared with succ. as piano virtuoso in Paris, London, Vienna, Berlin, Warsaw and other cities, and after 1930 in Amer. cities as orch. soloist and in recitals.

Smith, (1) Bd. (Bd. Schmidt) (called "Father Smith"), Germany, ca. 1630 —London, 1708; ct. org.-builder. (2) Robt., Cambridge, 1689—1768; acoustician. (3) J. Christopher (Johann Chr. Schmidt), Ansbach, 1712 —Bath, 1795; dram. composer. (4) John Stafford, Gloucester, Engl., ca. 1750—London, 1836; organist and composer. (5) Edw. Woodley, 1775—1849, lay-vicar at Windsor. (6) Geo. Townshend, Windsor, 1813 —Hereford, 1877; son of above; composer. (7) Montern, bro. of above; singer. (8) Samuel, b. Eton, 1821; bro. of above; organist. (9) John, Cambridge, 1795—1861; composer and prof. (10) Robt. Archibald, Reading, 1780—1829; composer and violinist. (11) Alice Mary (Mrs. Meadows White), London, 1839—1884; composer. (12) Sydney, Dor-

chester, Engl., 1839—London, 1889;
pianist, teacher, writer, etc. (13)
Wilson G., Elyria, Ohio, Aug. 19,
1855—1929; composer; pupil of Otto
Singer, at Cincinnati; at Berlin,
1880–82, of Kiel, the Scharwenkas,
Neumann, Moszkowski and Raif;
after 1882, lived in Cleveland as
teacher of pf., voice and comp.; pub.
numerous graceful pf.-pcs. and songs,
also *"Octave Studies"* and other
valuable technical works. (14) **David
Stanley,** b. Toledo, Ohio, July 6,
1877; pupil of Horatio W. Parker, at
Yale, where he graduated 1900 with
a "Commencement Ode" for barytone (Herbert Witherspoon), chorus
and orch.; studied then with Thuille
and Widor abroad; 1903 Mus. Bac.
Yale; from 1904 teacher; from 1912
dir. of music dept. (vice Parker) at
Yale; 1909, won Paderewski Prize
with *"The Fallen Star,"* for chorus
and orch. Other comps. include
symphs. in F minor and D; symph.
poem, *"Darkness and Dawn"*; overtures in E flat, *"Joyeuse," "Sérieuse"*
and *"Prince Hal"*; *"Commemoration
March"*; Allegro Giocoso; Symph.
Ballad; *"L'Allegro," "Il Pensieroso"*
and *"Four Impressions"*; prelude,
choral and fugue for organ, and orch.;
fantasy for piano and orch.; string
quartets in E minor and A; piano
trio; and (chorus) *"Commencement
Ode," "The Djinns," "Rhapsody of
St. Bernard,"* anthems and songs; he
has cond. the New Haven Symph.
Orch. and Oratorio Soc. since 1912.
Smolen'ski, Stephan V., Kasan, 1848—
St. Petersburg, Aug. 6, 1909; prof. of
history of Russian church music at
Moscow Cons.; 1901 cond. court
chapel at St. Petersburg; author of
important historical works.
Smyth, Dame Ethel, b. London,
April 23, 1858; daughter of artillery
general; pupil of Leipzig Cons. and
of Herzogenberg. Her string quintet
was played there 1884; her violin
sonata 1887; c. orch. serenade
(London, 1890), overture *"Antony
and Cleopatra"* (do.); *"Mass in D"*
(London, 1893 under Barnby), and
operas, *"Fantasio"* (her own libretto,
Weimar 1898, Carlsruhe, 1901);
1-act *"Der Wald"* (her own German
libretto, Dresden, 1901, Covent
Garden, 1902 and 1903, Met. Op.,
N. Y., 1903); 3-act *"Les Naufra-
geurs"* (book by Leforestier), given

at Leipzig, 1906, as *"Strandrecht"*
(Prague, do.); c. also the operas
"The Boatswain's Mate" (1917),
"Fête Galante" (1923), *"Entente
Cordiale,"* 1-act, 1925; string quintet,
sonata for vln. and pf.; pf. sonatas;
choral work, *"The Prison"*; concerto
for vln. and horn with orch., etc.;
author, *"Impressions That Remained"*
(1919), *"Streaks of Life"* (1921); created Dame Commander of Empire,
1920.
Soãres, João. Vide REBELLO.
Sodermann (sā'-dĕr-män), **August
Johan,** Stockholm, 1832 — 1876;
theatre-conductor there; pupil of
Hauptmann and Richter; c. Swedish
operetta, a notable mass with orch.,
etc.
So'dero, Cesare, b. Naples, Aug. 2,
1886; conductor and composer; grad.
Naples Cons., has cond. with Aborn
and Savage Op. Cos., and in leading
operatic radio programs in U. S.;
c. operas and many orch. works.
Soffredini (sŏf-frĕ-dē'-nē), **Alfredo,**
from 1896, ed.-in-chief, Milan *Gaz-
zetta Musicale*; prod. (text and
mus.) 2-act children's opera *"Il Piccolo Haydn"* (Pavia, 1893), etc.
Sokal'ski, Peter Petrovich, Charkov,
Sept. 26, 1832—Odessa, April 11,
1887; author and composer of operas
and piano pieces.
Sok'oloff, Nikolai, b. Kiev, Russia,
May 28, 1886; conductor; came to
America at early age; studied Yale
School of Music, also vln. with
Loeffler; played in Boston Symph.,
cond. newly organised Cleveland
Orch. from 1918 for a decade and a
half; founded and led N. Y. Orch.
for several seasons; has appeared as
guest with London Symph., orchs.
in Chicago, Cincinnati, Phila., San
Francisco and elsewhere; national
dir. of Fed. Mus. Proj.; 1938–9 cond.
Seattle Symph. Orch.
Sokolov (sō'-kō-lôf), **Nicholas,** Petersburg, March 26, 1859—March 27,
1922; pupil at the Cons.; taught
harm. in the Imp. Chapel; c. an elegy
(op. 4), and intermezzo for orch., etc.
Soldat (zōl'-dät), **Marie,** b. Graz,
March 25, 1864; violinist; pupil of
Pleiner and Pott, and of Joachim,
1889; m. Herr Röger (Vienna). In
1887 she founded a women's string
quartet and toured widely.
Soliê (sōl-yā) (rightly **Soulier**), (1) **J.
P.,** Nîmes, 1753—Paris, 1812; bary-

tone; c. comic operas, many pop.
(2) **Chas.**, son of above; conductor;
prod. a comic opera (Nice, 1877).

Soloviev (or **Solowiew**) (sō'-lō-věf),
Nicolai Theopometovitch, Petrosa-
vodsk, Russia, April 27 (May 9),
1846—St. Petersburg, Dec. 14, 1916;
pupil of N. J. Zaremba (theory),
Imp. Cons. at Petersburg; 1874 prof.
there; also critic, editor and Councillor of State; c. comic opera
"*Vakula, The Smith*" (Petersb.,
1875), and grand opera "*Cordelia*"
(Petersb., 1883, in German, Prague,
1890); finished Seroff's opera "*The
Demon's Power*"; c. symph. picture,
"*Russia and the Mongols*" (Moscow,
1882); prize chorus "*Prayer for
Russia*" (Imp. Russ. Mus. Soc.,
1876), cantata "*The Death of Samson,*" etc.

Soltys (sól'-tēs), **Mieczyslaw**, Lemberg,
Feb. 7, 1863—Nov. 12, 1929; pupil of
Krenn and Gigout; director and
teacher Lemberg Cons.; c. operas,
symph., oratorio, etc.

Som'ervell, Sir **Arthur**, Windermere,
1863—London, May 2, 1937; pupil
Berlin Hochschule, Stanford and
Parry, R. C. M.; c. mass, with orch.
(1891), "*A Song of Praise,*" "*The
Forsaken Merman*" (Leeds Fest.,
1895), "*The Power of Sound,*" elegy
for alto with orch., suite for small
orch. "*In Arcady,*" song cycle on
Tennyson's "*Maude,*" etc.; writer.

Somis (sō'-mēs), **Giov. Bat.**, Piedmont,
1676—Turin, 1763; violinist, teacher
and conductor.

Sommer (zôm'-měr), Dr. **Hans** (rightly
Hans Fr. Aug. Zincke) (tsĭnk'-ě),
Brunswick, July 20, 1837—April 28,
1922; pupil of Meves and J. O.
Grimm; graduate, later prof. at
Göttingen Univ.; from 1888 lived in
Weimar; c. succ. opera "*Lorelei*"
(Brunswick, 1891), 1-act "*Bühnen-
spiel,*" "*Saint Foix*" (Munich, 1894),
1-act "*Der Meerman*" (Weimar,
1896), "*Rübezahl*" (1902), etc.

Son'neck, Oscar Geo. Th., Jersey City,
N. J., Oct. 6, 1873—New York,
Oct. 31, 1928; noted editor and
author; at 20 studied at Heidelberg,
Munich and Italy; 1899 returned to
America; music librarian at the Library of Congress, and after 1902
dir. of music division; 1915, ed. of
The Musical Quarterly; wrote valuable works on early history of music
in America.

Sonnleithner (zôn'-līt-něr), (1) **Chp. S.**,
Szegedin, 1734—Vienna, 1786; dean
of jurisprudence, Vienna; composer.
(2) **Jos.**, Vienna, 1765—1835; son of
above; 1827, discovered the famous
9th cent. Antiphonary of St. Gallen
in neume-notation. (3) **Ld. von,**
Vienna, 1797—1873; nephew of
above; devoted friend of Schubert.

Sontag (zôn'-täkh), **Henriette (Gertrude Walpurgis)**, Coblenz, Jan. 3,
1806—of cholera, Mexico, June 17,
1854; famous coloratura-soprano, her
voice taking e''' easily; daughter of
two actors; operatic singer; 1823
created von Weber's "*Euryanthe.*"

Sontheim (zôn'-tīm), **H.**, Jebenhausen,
Feb. 3, 1820—Stuttgart, Aug. 2,
1912; notable tenor; début Carlsruhe, 1839; 1872, pensioned.

Sor (rightly **Sors**) (sôr), **Fdo.**, Barcelona, 1778—Paris, 1839; guitar-
virtuoso and dram. composer.

Sorge (zôr'-gě), **G. Ands.**, Mellenbach,
Schwarzburg, 1703 — Lobenstein,
1778; famous organist and theorist;
ct.-organist and composer.

Soriano, (1) **Fran.** Vide SURIANO.
(2) **Soriano-Fuertes** (sō-rĭ-ä'-nō-foo-
ěr'-tēs), Don **Mariano**, Murcia, 1817
—Madrid, 1880; son and pupil of the
dir. royal chamber-mus. (1841);
prod. several zarzuelas, aiming to
estab. national opera; conductor and
writer of historical works.

Sormann (zôr'-män), **Alfred (Richard
Gotthilf)**, Danzig, May 16, 1861—
Berlin, Sept. 17, 1913; pianist; pupil
of R. Hochschule, Berlin, and of
Liszt; début 1886; 1889, ct.-pianist
to Grand Duke of Mecklenburg-
Strelitz; taught Stern Cons., Berlin;
c. concerto, etc.

Soubies (soo-bĭ-ěs), **Albert**, Paris,
May 10, 1846—March 19, 1918;
mus.-historiographer and critic; a
lawyer, then pupil of Savard and
Bazin (harm. and comp.) at the
Cons.; 1874 he revived the famous
"*Almanach des spectacles*, *Alm.
Duchesne*"; for this the Académie,
1893, awarded him the Prix Voirac;
1876, critic for *Le Soir*, under
name "*B. de Lomagne*"; officer of
public instruction, and Legion of
Honour, also of the Russian order
Stanislas; writer of valuable historical works, etc.

Soubre (soobr), **Etienne Jos.**, Liége,
1813—1871; director and dram.
comp.

Souhaitty (soo-ĕt-tē'), **J. Jac.**, Franciscan monk at Paris, the first to use figures for popular notation, 1665–78.

Soulier (soo-yā). Vide SOLIE.

Sousa (soo'-sä), **John Philip**, Washington, D. C., Nov. 6, 1856—Reading, Pa., March 6, 1932, while on tour; son of a Spanish trombonist in the U. S. Marine Corps band. Pupil of John Esputa and G. F. Benkert (harm. and comp.); at 17 cond. of travelling theatrical troupes; 1877, violinist in Offenbach's orch. in America; dir. "Philadelphia Church-choir Pinafore Co."; 1880–92, bandm. U. S. Marine Corps; resigned and organised the military band bearing his own name, which toured America and Europe with greatest succ.; (1900), Paris, Exposition. Compiled, by Govt. order, "*National Patriotic and Typical Airs of All Countries*"; wrote instruction-books for trumpet and drum, and for vln. C. 7 comic operas incl. v. succ. "*El Capitan,*" succ. (text and music) "*The Bride Elect,*" "*The Charlatan*" and "*Chris and the Wonderful Lamp,*" a symph. poem "*The Chariot Race*" (from "*Ben Hur*"); suites, "*The Last Days of Pompeii,*" "*Three Quotations,*" and "*Sheridan's Ride*"; and many immensely succ. marches popular throughout the world, "*Washington Post,*" "*High School Cadets,*" "*Stars and Stripes Forever,*" "*Imperial Edward,*" etc.

Sow'erby, Leo, b. Grand Rapids, Mich., May 1, 1895; composer; grad. of Amer. Cons., Chicago; won fellowship at Amer. Acad. in Rome, 1921; active as org. and teacher of comp. in Chicago; c. symph. works, piano concerto, Ballad for 2 pianos and orch., choral and piano pieces, songs.

Spaeth, Sigmund, b. Philadelphia, April 10, 1885; critic, author, lecturer; grad. Haverford Coll., Ph. D., Princeton, 1910; critic of N. Y. *Evening Mail*, 1914–18; active as writer of musical essays and books, also in radio programmes; exec. of Community Concerts Corp., N. Y.; author,"*The Common Sense of Music,*" "*Barber Shop Ballads,*" "*Words and Music,*" "*Read 'Em and Weep,*" "*Weep Some More, My Lady,*" "*American Mountain Songs,*" "*The Facts of Life in Popular Song.*"

Spal'ding, (1) Albert, b. Chicago,

Aug. 15, 1888; violinist; studied in New York, Paris and Florence; début in Paris, 1905; first Amer. appearance as soloist with N. Y. Symph.. 1908; took rank as one of foremost performers, both for technical excellence and refined musicianship; has played with leading orchs. in U. S. and Europe, also in many recital tours; c. and arr. works for vln. (2) **Walter Raymond**, b. Northampton, Mass., May 22, 1865; organist and pedagogue; pupil of Guilmant, Widor, Rheinberger and Thuille; org. in various Boston churches; after 1895 associated with Harvard Univ. as theory teacher, (prof. in 1907), also at Radcliffe Coll; author of books on theory.

Spanuth (spän'-oot), **August**, Brinkum, Hanover, March 15, 1857—Berlin, Jan. 9, 1920; pianist and critic; pupil of Hoch Cons., Frankfort-on-Main; 1886–1893 Chicago as pianist and teacher; then in New York as critic; 1906 returned to Berlin as teacher at Stern Cons.; 1907, ed. periodical *Signale für die Musikalische Welt.*

Spataro (spä-tä'-rō) (or **Spat'arus, Spada'ro, Spada'rius**), **Giov.**, Bologna, ca. 1460—1541; conductor and theorist.

Speaight (spāt), **Joseph**, b. London, Oct. 24, 1868; violinist; composer; pupil of his father and of the Guildhall School of Music, where he taught after 1894; c. 2 symphonies, various other orch. works, chamber music incl. string quartet, piano pieces, choruses, songs, etc.

Speaks, Oley, b. Canal Winchester, O., c. of many popular ballads, incl. "*Sylvia*" and "*The Road to Mandalay*"; res. in N. Y.; mem., board of directors, Amer. Soc. of Composers, Authors and Publishers.

Specht (spĕkht), **Richard**, Vienna, Dec. 7, 1870—March 18, 1932; well-known critic and writer on music; author, "*Gustav Mahler,*" "*Richard Strauss und Sein Werk,*" "*Julius Bittner,*" "*Reznicek,*" "*Brahms,*" "*Puccini,*" etc.

Speer, (1) Charlton T., Cheltenham, Nov. 21, 1859—London, 1921; pupil R. A. M. London, winning a scholarship; from 1885 prof. of piano there, also organist at various churches; c. 2 operas, "*The Battle of Lake Regillus,*" for chorus and orch.; symph. poem, "*King Arthur,*" etc. His cousin (2) **William Henry,** b. London, 1863; organist; pupil of Lloyd and the R. C. M.; 1906 Mus. Doc. Cambridge; c. symph., overture, orch., rhapsody, ballad, *"The Jackdaw of Rheims,"* etc.

Speidel (shpī'-dĕl), **Wm.,** Ulm, 1826— Stuttgart, 1899; pianist, conductor, composer.

Spel'man, Timothy Mather, b. Brooklyn, N. Y., Jan. 21, 1891; composer; pupil of Spalding and Hill (Harvard), also of Courvoisier; for some years res. in Florence.

Spen'cer, Eleanor, b. Chicago, Nov. 30, 1890; pianist; pupil of Leschetizky; début with London Philh., 1912; made N. Y. début following year; has appeared as soloist with orchs. in Europe and U. S., also in recitals.

Spen'diarov, Alexander Afanasovitch, Kachov, Province of Taurien, Russia, Nov. 1, 1871—May, 1928, at Erivan, Armenia, where since 1924 he was dir. of the State Cons.; early in life a lawyer, but later studied with Rimsky-Korsakoff; passed most of his life in the Crimea; c. operas, orch. *"Sketches from the Crimea,"* *"The Three Palm Trees,"* songs, piano works incl. *"Erivan Studies,"* etc.

Spengel (shpĕng'-ĕl), **Julius H.,** Hamburg, June 12, 1853—April 17, 1936; pupil of Cologne Cons. and Berlin Hochschule, taught in Hamburg, and studied with Gradener and Armbrust; 1878–1927, cond. Cäcilienverein; singing-teacher and organist; c. symph., 'cello-sonata, etc.

Speyer (Speier) (shpī'-ĕr), **Wilhelm,** Frankfort, 1790—1878; violinist and composer.

Spicker (shpĭk'-ĕr), **Max,** Königsberg, Prussia, Aug. 16, 1858—New York, Oct. 16, 1912; pupil of Louis Köhler, then of Leipzig Cons.; theatre conductor various cities; 1882–88, cond. "Beethoven Männerchor," New York; 1888–95 Dir. Brooklyn Cons.; teacher Nat. Cons., New York; arranged operatic scores for pf.; c. orch. suite, cantata with orch., etc.

Spiering (shpē'-rĭng), **Theodor,** St. Louis, Missouri, 1871 — Munich, Aug. 11, 1925; violinist; pupil of H. Schradieck, Cincinnati; then of Joachim, Berlin; founder and 1st v̶n. "Spiering Quartet," Chicago, taught in his own school there; 1905–06 at Stern Cons., Berlin; 1909, concertm., N. Y., Philh., and

in 1911 cond. as Mahler's substitute; later led Blüthner and Philh. Orchs. in Berlin; toured as cond. with Pavlowa, etc.

Spindler (shpĭnt'-lĕr), **Fritz,** Würzbach, near Lobenstein, Nov. 24, 1817— near Dresden, Dec. 26, 1905; pianist; studied mus. with Fr. Schneider at Dessau; from 1841, lived in Dresden as teacher; c. 3 symphs., pf.-concerto, v. pop. salon-pcs., etc.

Spinelli (spĭ-nĕl'-lĭ), **Nicola,** Turin, 1865—Rome, Oct. 17, 1909; notable opera composer; pupil of Naples Cons.; 1890 took 2nd Sonzogno prize with 1-act opera *"Cobilla,"* Mascagni winning 1st prize; prod. v. succ. 3-act lyric drama *"A Basso Porto"* (1894, New York, 1899).

Spiridio (spē-rē'-dĭ-ō), **Berthold,** monk, organist and composer, Bamberg, 1665–91.

Spirid'ion. Vide XYNDAS.

Spitta (shpĭt'-tä), (**Julius Aug.**) **Philipp,** Wechold, near Hoya, Hanover, Dec. 27, 1841—Berlin, April 13, 1894; teacher and prof. musical history; wrote many essays and a notable life of J. S. Bach (2 vols., 1873–80), etc.

Spof'forth, Reginald, Nottingham, Southwell, 1769—Kensington, 1827; c. glees, etc.

Spohr (shpōr), **Ludwig** (in his autobiography he calls himself **Louis**), Brunswick, April 5, 1784—Cassel, Oct. 22, 1859; eminent violinist and conductor; notable composer and teacher. Son of a physician who removed to Seesen, 1786; pupil of his mother, and at 5 studied with Riemenschneider (vln.) and Dufour; then with Kunisch, Hartung and Maucourt, Brunswick; at 14 he played a concerto of his own at court. He became a member of the Ducal Orch.; 1802 pupil of Fz. Eck, whom he accompanied to St. Petersburg; 1803, returned to the Ducal Orch.; 1804 toured with great succ.; 1805, leader Duke of Gotha's orch.; m. Dorette Scheidler (d. 1834), the harpplayer and toured with her, 1807 and 1809. 1836 he m. the pianist Marianne Pfeiffer (d. 1892); 1812, after brilliant concerts at Vienna, leader at the Th. an der Wien; 1815, toured Italy (playing a concertante of his own with Paganini at Rome); 1817– 19 opera-cond. at Frankfort; prod. here succ. opera *"Faust";* 1820, visited England with his wife, played at Philharm. Concerts, and prod. there two symphs.; introducing into England the habit of conducting with a bâton. Gave concerts at Paris with little succ. From 1822 ct.-cond. at Cassel; 1857, retired for political reasons on a reduced pension. During his period as a cond. he prod. Wagner's *"Fliegende Holländer"* (1842), and *"Tannhäuser"* (1853), but could not overcome the opposition to a production of *"Lohengrin."* He soon recognised Wagner as the greatest living dramatic composer, but did not care for Beethoven or Weber. He is among the first of the second-best composers, his highest attainments being the opera *"Jessonda"* (Cassel, 1823), the oratorio *"Die Letzten Dinge"* (Cassel, 1826; in England as *"The Last Judgment"*); the grand symph. *"Die Weihe der Töne"* (*"The Consecration of Tone,"* 1832) and the classic vln.-concertos. His *"Violin-School"* (1831 in 3 parts), is a standard. He c. 11 operas in all; dram. cantata, *"Das Befreite Deutschland"*; a mass, etc., with orch.; 9 symphs.; No. 4 op. 86 in F (*"Weihe der Töne"*); No. 6 op. 116, G (*"Historical"*; dedicated to the London Philh. Soc.); 7 op. 121, C (*"Irdisches und Göttliches im Menschenleben"*) for 2 orchs.; 8 op. 137, G min. (ded. to the London Philharm.); 9 op. 143, B min. (*"Die Jahreszeiten"*), 18 overtures, and 15 vln.-concertos; No. 8 (op. 47, in A min., *"in modo d'una scena cantante"*) "quartet-concerto" for 2 vlns., vla., and 'cello with orch.; 2 concertantes for 2 vlns. with orch.; grande polonaise for vlns. with orch., 2 clar.-concertos; much chamber-mus. Autobiogr. (Cassel, 1860, 1861, 2 vols.); Biogr. by Malibran (Frankfort, 1860); by H. M. Schletterer (1881).

Spontini (spôn-tē'-nē), Gasparo (Luigi Pacifico), Majolati, Ancone, Nov. 14, 1774—Jan. 24, 1851; noteworthy cond. and dram. composer. Son of poor peasants who intended him for the church, he ran away, and an uncle, at San Vito, provided him with teaching. At 17 entered the Cons. della Pietà de' Turchini at Naples. 1796, commissioned to write an opera for the Teatro Argentina at Rome, its director having heard some

of his church-mus. in Naples, he left the Cons. without permission and prod. succ. opera, *"I Puntigli delle Donne"*; Piccinni secured his reinstatement and gave him valuable advice. He prod. operas with succ. in various cities and in Palermo, where he was cond. to the Neapolitan court which had fled before the French. After having produced 16 light Italian operas, he went to Paris (1803), where three successive failures and a study of Mozart's works led him to change his style. After supporting himself as a singing-teacher he won succ. with his substantial 1-act opera *"Milton"* (Th. Feydeau Nov. 27, 1804); the Empress Josephine, to whom he had dedicated the score, appointed him "chamber-composer." He c. a cantata *"L'eccelsa Gara,"* celebrating the victory of Austerlitz. The Empress's power secured a hearing for his opera *"La Vestale,"* which after three years of delay and polishing, was prod. with greatest succ. 1807; by a unanimous verdict of the judges, Méhul, Gossec and Grétry, Napoleon's prize for the best dram. work of the decade was awarded to it. It was followed with equal succ. by the grand opera *"Fernand Cortez,"* 1809. 1810, dir. It. opera; dismissed for financial irregularity; 1814 Louis XVIII., appointed him ct.-composer. He c. 2 stage-pieces in glorification of the Restoration. The opera *"Olympie"* was prod. 1819 without succ., though when revised and prod. 1826 it prospered. 1820, he became ct.-composer and gen. mus.-dir. at Berlin; he prod. his old operas with succ., and c. the festival play *"Lalla Rukh"* (1821), remodelled as *"Nurmahal"* (1822); *"Alcidor"* (1825) and *"Agnes von Hohenstaufen"* (1829), none of which were widely succ. A period of violent jealousies and quarrels with the Intendant Brühl, and virulent intrigues, culminated after a score of stormy years in his being royally reprimanded, and finally driven out of the theatre by a hostile audience. He retired in 1841 on full pay. He went to Paris, then to Italy. 1844 the Pope gave him the rank and title of "Conte di Sant' Andrea"; he was a knight of the Prussian "Ordre pour le mérite," member of the Berlin Akademie (1839), and Paris

Académie, and D1. Phil., Halle Univ. Biog. by L. de Loménie (1841); Montanari (1851); Raoul-Rochette (1882).

Sporck, Georges, b. Paris, April 9, 1870; pupil of the Cons. and of d'Indy; c. symph. poems, symphonie *"Vivaraise," "Esquisses symphoniques,"* etc.

Spross, Chas. Gilbert, b. Poughkeepsie, N. Y., Jan. 6, 1874; composer, pianist; pupil of X. Scharwenka, Emil G1amm and Carl Lachmund; org. in various cities; accompanist for noted artists; c. choral works, songs, etc.

Squire, (1) **Wm. Henry,** b. Ross, Herefordshire, Aug. 8, 1871; 'cellist; son and pupil of an amateur violinist; début at 7; won scholarship at the R. C. M., and studied with Powell and Parry; second début, 1891; c. 'cello-concerto. (2) **William Barclay,** London, Oct. 18, 1855—Jan. 14, 1927; historian and author, educated at Cambridge, 1879, B. A.; 1902, M. A.; critic, librettist and antiquarian; ed. works of Purcell, Byrd and Palestrina, and with Fuller-Maitland, the *"Fitzwilliam Virginal Book."*

Stabile (stä'-bē-lĕ), **Annibale,** d. Rome, ca. 1595; conductor and composer.

Stade (shtä'-dĕ), (1) **H. Bd.,** Ettischleben, 1816—Arnstadt, 1882; organist and composer. (2) **Fr. Wm.,** Halle, Aug. 25, 1817—Altenburg, March 24, 1902; organist, pupil of Fr. Schneider, Dessau; mus.-dir. and Dr. Phil. *h. c.* Jena Univ.; 1860-1891, ct.-organist and cond. at Altenburg; c. 2 symphs.; Festouvertüre, music to *"Orestes"*; cantatas, with orch.; choral works; vln.-sonata; *"Kindersonate"* (4 hands), etc. (3) **Dr. Fritz (L. Rudolf),** Sondershausen, Jan. 8, 1844—Leipzig, June 12, 1928; pupil of Riedl and Richter, Leipzig, and teacher there; pub. an answer to Hanslick's *"Vom Musikalisch-Schönen,"* etc.

Staden (shtä'-dĕn), (1) **Jn.,** Nürnberg, 1581—1634; organist and composer. (2) **Sigmund Theopil,** 1607-1655, son and successor of above; c. *"Seelewig,"* one of the earliest extant German operas (cf. H. SCHÜTZ' opera *"Dafne"*).

Stadler (shtät'-lĕr), **Maximilian,** Melk, Lower Austria, 1748—Vienna, 1833; composer and writer.

Stadlmayer (shtät'-'l-mī-ĕr), **Jn.,** Frei-

sing, Bavaria, 1560 — Innsbruck, July 12, 1648; conductor, composer.

Stadtfeldt (shtät'-fĕlt), **Alex.,** Wiesbaden, 1826—Brussels, 1853, dram. composer.

Stägemann (shtä'-gĕ-män), (1) **Max,** Freienwalde-on-Oder, May 10, 1843 —Leipzig, Jan. 29, 1905; pupil of Dresden Cons.; barytone and "chamber-singer" at Hanover; 1877, dir. of Königsberg Th.; later, manager Leipzig City Th.; his daughter, (2) **Helene,** d. Dresden, Aug. 24, 1923; noted Liedersinger, m. Botho Sigwart (Count Eulenberg).

Stahlknecht (shtäl-k'nĕkht), two brothers, (1) **Ad.,** Warsaw, 1813—Berlin, 1887; violinist and dram. composer. (2) **Julius,** Posen, 1817—Berlin, 1892; 'cellist royal orchestra.

Stainer (or **Steiner**) (shtī-nĕr), (1) **Jakob,** Absam, Tyrol, 1621—1683; inventor and manufacturer of instrs. (2) **Markus,** his brother, also vln.- and vla.-maker.

Stainer (stā'-nĕr), Sir **John,** London, June 4, 1840—Verona, Mar. 31, 1901; chorister at St. Paul's; studied with Bayley (harm.) and Steggal (cpt.), and later Cooper (org.); 1854-60, organist various places, then Univ. organist at Oxford; (1859) Bac. Mus., and (1865) Mus. Doc.; 1866, Examiner for mus. degrees; 1872-88, organist of St. Paul's, resigning on account of his eyesight; 1876, prof. of org. and harm. Nat. Training Sch. for Mus.; 1881, principal in R. C. M.; 1883, again at Oxford; 1882, Govt. Inspector of Mus. in the Training-Sch.; 1878, Chev. of the Legion of Honour; knighted, 1888; 1889, prof. of mus. at Oxford Univ.; pub. treatises and (with Barret) a *"Dict. of Mus. Terms,"* 1875; c. oratorio *"Gideon,"* cantatas *"The Daughter of Jairus"* (Worc. Fest., 1878), *"St. Mary Magdalene"* (Gloucester, 1883), and *"The Crucifixion"* (London, 1887), services, etc.

Stamaty (stä-mä-tē), **Camille M.,** Rome, 1811—Paris, 1870; pianist and composer.

Stamitz (shtä'-mĭts), (1) **Jn. Wenzel Anton,** Deutsch-Brod., Bohemia, 1717—Mannheim, 1757; notable violinist and composer. (2) **Anton Thaddäus,** Deutsch-Brod., 1721—Altbunzlau, 1768; bro. of above; canon; 'cellist, Mannheim. (3) **K.,**

Mannheim, 1746—Jena, 1801; violinist and viole d'amour-performer, conductor and composer. (4) **Anton,** Mannheim, 1754—Paris, ca. 1820, bro. of above; violinist and composer.

Stan'ford, Sir Chas. Villiers, Dublin, Sept. 30, 1852—London, March 29, 1924; pianist and notable composer; pupil of Sir Robt. Stewart and Arthur O'Leary (comp.), and Ernst Pauer (pf.), London; 1870 won organ scholarship at Queen's Coll., Cambridge; 1873–92, organist of Trinity Coll., Cambridge, also cond. Univ. Mus. Soc. (till 1893); 1875–76, studied comp. with Reinecke at Leipzig, and Kiel, Berlin. M. A., Cantab., 1878; Mus. Doc., Oxford, 1883, Cambridge, 1888; 1883, prof. of comp. and cond., R. C. M.; 1885, cond. Bach Choir; 1887, prof. of Mus. at Cambridge; 1897, cond. Leeds Philh. Soc.; he was knighted, 1901, and made cond. of the Leeds Festival, resigning the Bach Choir, 1904. C. operas, *"The Veiled Prophet of Khorassan"* (Hanover, 1881); *"Savonarola"* (Hamburg, 1884); *"The Canterbury Pilgrims"* (London, Covent Garden, 1884); v. succ. *"Shamus O'Brien"* (London, 1896); *"Much Ado about Nothing"* (Covent Garden, 1901, Leipzig, 1902); incid. mus. to various plays; operas, *"The Critic,"* *"Travelling Companion,"* oratorio, *"The Resurrection"* (1875); *"The Three Holy Children"* (Birmingham, 1885); Psalm 96 (1877); *"Elegiac Ode"* (Norwich, 1884); *"The Revenge"* (Leeds, 1886); *"Jubilee Ode"* (1887), etc. *"The Bard"* (Cardiff, 1895); *"Phaudrig Crochoore"* (Norwich, 1896); requiem, 3 Morning and Evening Services; a Communion Service, etc.; 6 symphs. *"Elegiac,"* in D min. (No. 3); *"Irish,"* (No. 4); *"Thro' Youth to Strife, Thro' Death to Life"*; and No. 5 *"L'allegro ed il penseroso"*; 2 overtures, a pf.-concerto; *"Irish Rhapsody"* (1902); motet with orch., *"The Lord of Might"* (1903); symphony No. 6, *"In Memoriam G. F. Watts,"* 7th symphony (London Phil., Feb., 1912), *"Stabat Mater,"* with orch. (Leeds Fest., 1907); *"Wellington,"* for voices and orch., incid. mus. to *"Attila"* (1907), overture *"Ave atque Vale"* (Haydn Centenary, 1909), etc. **Stan'ley, (1) (Chas.) John,** London,

1713–1786; organist and conductor. (2) **Albert Augustus,** Manville, Rhode Island, May 25, 1851—Ann Arbor, Mich., May 19, 1932; studied in Providence, and at Leipzig; organist, Providence; 1888–1922, prof. of mus., Univ. of Michigan; from 1893, cond. important series of Ann Arbor Fests., by Choral Union of that city; c. *"The City of Freedom,"* ode, with orch. (Boston, 1883); Psalm 21 (Providence, 1892), and Commemoration Ode *"Chorus triumphalis,"* with orch.; symph. *"The Awakening of the Soul"*; symph. poem *"Altis,"* etc.

Starczewski (stär-chĕf′-skĭ), **Felix,** b. Warsaw, 1868; critic and author; pupil of the Music Institute and of Humperdinck, Fleischer, and d'Indy; taught piano at Warsaw Cons.; c. orchestral pieces, etc.

Stark (shtärk), **L.,** Munich, 1831—Stuttgart, 1884; teacher, editor and composer.

Starke (shtärk′-ĕ) **Fr.,** Elsterwerda, 1774—Döbling, near Vienna, 1835; banam., writer and composer.

Stasny (shtäs′-nē), (1) **L.,** Prague, 1823 —Frankfort, 1883; conductor and dram. composer. (2) Vide STIASTNY.

Stassof, Vlad., 1824—1906; Russian critic and writer.

Statkov′ski, Roman von, near Kalisch, Jan. 5, 1860—Warsaw, 1926; pupil of Zelenski, and of St. Petersburg Cons.; teacher of instrumentation and history at Warsaw Cons. His opera *"Philaenis"* took an international prize in London and was prod., Warsaw, 1904; c. also opera *"Maria"* (Warsaw, 1906); fantasie and polonaise for orch., piano pieces, etc.

Staudigl (shtow′-dēkh-'l), (1) **Josef,** Wöllersdorf, Lower Austria, 1807—(insane), Michaelbeuerngrund, near Vienna, 1861; bass and ct.-conductor. (2) **Josef,** Vienna, March 18, 1850—Carlsruhe, 1916; son of above; barytone; pupil of Rokitansky at the Cons.; chamber-singer to the Grand Duke at Carlsruhe and a member of the ct.-opera. His wife (3) **Gisela,** singer; pupil of Marchesi, 1899 Wiesbaden ct.-opera.

Stavenhagen (shtä′-fĕn-hä-gĕn), **Bd.,** Greiz, Reuss, Nov. 24, 1862—Geneva, Dec. 26, 1914; pianist; pupil of Kiel, at the Meisterschule, and of Rudorff, at the Hochschule, Berlin; 1880, won the Mendelssohn prize for pf.; pupil of Liszt, 1885; toured Europe with succ. and the U. S. (1894–95); 1890, ct.-pianist and ct.-conductor at Weimar; Knight of the White Falcon order; from 1898 ct.-cond. at Munich; c. pf.-pcs.

Stcherbatcheff (stchĕr'-bät-chĕf), (1) **Nicolas**, St. Petersburg, Aug. 24, 1853–?; prominent figure in the neo-Russian sch.; c. "*Deux idylles pour orchestre*"; "*Féeries et pantomimes*," "*Mosaïque, album pittoresque*," etc., for pf.; songs "*Au soir tombant*," etc. (2) **Vladimir**, b. Warsaw, Jan. 24, 1889; pupil of St. Petersburg Cons.; composer of 2 symphonies, chamber music, piano pieces, songs.

Stearns, Theodore, Berea, O., 1880– Los Angeles, Nov. 1, 1935; composer, grad. Würzburg Univ.; cond. musical comedies in N. Y.; served as music critic on N. Y. *Morning Telegraph* and Chicago *Herald Examiner;* awarded Guggenheim Fellowship, 1927; c. (operas) "*Snowbird*" (Chicago Op. 1922, Dresden State Op. 1927), "*Atlantis*," both to own librettos; "*Suite Caprese*" and other orch. music and songs; author books and articles on music.

Stefan (stā'-fän), **Paul**, b. Brünn, Nov. 25, 1879; music critic and writer; Ph. D.; after 1888 lived in Vienna; ed. *Musikblätter des Anbruch*, publication of Universal Edition; author of studies of Mahler, Schubert, Schönberg, Oskar Fried, etc.

Stefani (stā'-fä-nē), (1) **Jan**, Prague, 1746–Warsaw, Feb. 24, 1829; Mus. Director; director at Warsaw Cathedral; c. opera "*Die Krakowiter und die Bergvölker*," 1794, and others, also masses and polonaises. His son (2) **Josef**, Warsaw, April 16, 1800 — (?); pupil of Elsner; c. ballets, operettas, also 10 masses, etc.

Stef'fan, **Joseph Anton**, Copidino, Bohemia, March 14, 1726–Vienna, 1800; court piano teacher at Vienna, numbering among his pupils Marie Antoinette and Queen Caroline of Naples; c. piano pieces and songs.

Steffani (stĕf-fä'-nē), Abbate **Agostino**, Castelfranco, Venetia, 1654– Frankfort-on-Main, 1728; eminent composer of daring originality and great power both in instrumentation and general construction; ct.- and chamber-musician and ct.-organist; prod. 20 operas.

Steffens (shtĕf'-fĕns), **Julius**, Stargard,

Pomerania, 1831–Wiesbaden, 1882; 'cellist and composer.

Steg'gall, (1) **Chas.**, London, June 3, 1826–June 7, 1905; pupil of Bennett, R. A. M., 1851; prof. of org. and harm. there; Mus. Bac. and Mus. Doc., Cambridge; from 1864, organist Lincoln's Inn Chapel; wrote method for org.; ed. colls., and c. Psalms 105, and 33 with orch.; services, etc. (2) **Reginald**, b. London, April 17, 1867; son and asst.-organist of above, later his successor; pupil R. A. M.; from 1895, prof. of org. there; c. mass with orch. and organ, "*Festival Evening Service*" with orch., a symph., 3 overtures, etc.

Stegmann (stākh'-män), **K. David**, Dresden, 1751–Bonn, 1826; tenor, cond. and dram. composer.

Stegmayer (shtākh'-mī-ĕr),**Fd.**, Vienna, 1803 — 1863; conductor, singing-teacher and composer.

Stehle (shtā'-lĕ), **Gv. Ed.**, Steinhausen, Würtemberg, Feb. 17, 1839–St. Gallen, June 21, 1915; cond. at St. Gallen Cath.; c. symph. tone-picture "*Saul*," for org.

Steibelt (shtī'-bĕlt), **Daniel**, Berlin, 1765–St. Petersburg, 1823; a most unvirtuous virtuoso. Under patronage of the Crown Prince, a pupil of Kirnberger, early début; 1790, favourite pianist, teacher and composer at Paris; prod. v. succ. opera "*Roméo et Juliette*" (1793). He seems to have suffered from kleptomania and general dishonesty, which with his insolence, snobbery, and his debts, forced him to leave Paris in 1797, for London, where he was equally succ.; the "*Storm Rondo*" (or the finale of his 3rd concerto "*L'Orage, précédé d'un rondeau pastoral*"), rivalling the notorious "*Battle of Prague*," by Koczwara. 1799, he toured Germany, challenging Beethoven at Vienna with disastrous results. He carried Haydn's "*Creation*" back to Paris and prod. it, 1800, with great succ., with himself as cembalist; but had to leave Paris again, remaining in London, until 1805, when he revisited Paris for 3 years; 1808 toured and settled in Petersburg; 1810, Imp. ct.-cond. and cond. of French Opera; here prod. 2 new operas, as well as earlier ones. In spite of his odious personality, his virtuosity was remarkable, and his compositions show much originality in modulation and scoring. He wrote a pop. pf.-method; c. 6 operas, 5 ballets, and much piano-mus., including 50 études, many programme-pcs. of extraordinary vogue.

Stein (shtīn), (1) **Jn.** Andreas, Heidelsheim, Palatinate, 1728—Augsburg, 1792; inv. "German (Viennese) pf.-action"; organist and famous pf.-maker. Succeeded by son (2) **Matthäus Andreas** (Augsburg, 1776—Vienna, 1842), who 1802 set up for himself in Vienna. (3) **Maria Anna** (or **Nanette Streicher**), Augsburg, 1769—Vienna, 1838; daughter of (1); a devoted friend of Beethoven; also a manager of the pf.-factory. Her son (4) **Jn. Bapt.** (b. Vienna, 1795), was her successor. (5) **Fr.**, Augsburg, 1781 — (of consumption) Vienna, 1808; bro. of above; prominent pianist. (6) **Karoline** (née **Haar**), pianist and teacher. (7) **K. Andreas**, Vienna, 1797—1863; son and successor of (2); pupil of Förster, ct.-pf.-maker and composer. (8) **Eduard**, Kleinschirma, Saxony, 1818 —Sondershausen, 1864; ct.-conductor and composer. (9) **Theodor**, Altona, 1819—St. Petersburg, March 9, 1893; pianist; début at 12; 1872, pf.-prof. Petersburg Cons. (10) **Fritz**, b. Heidelberg, Dec. 17, 1879; theologian at first, then studied music; 1902, organist and cond. at Heidelberg; 1906, musical dir. of Jena University, cond. academic concerts; 1914, ct.-cond. in Meiningen (vice Reger); 1928-33, prof. of musical science and munic. mus. dir. in Kiel; after 1933, dir. of State Hochschule, Berlin; ed. thematic catalogue of Reger's works and wrote his biography.

Steinbach (shtīn'-bäkh), (1) **Emil**, Lengenrieden, Baden, Nov. 14, 1849 —Mayence, Dec. 6, 1919; pupil Leipzig Cons.; 1877, cond. Mayence town-orch.; c. orch. and chamber-mus., etc. (2) **Fritz**, Grünsfeld, Baden, June 17, 1855—Munich, Aug. 13, 1916; bro. and pupil of above; also pupil Leipzig Cons.; won Mozart Scholarship; 1880–86, 2nd cond. at Mayence; 1886 ct.-cond. Meiningen; pub. a septet, 'cello-sonata, songs.

Stein'berg, **Maximilian**, b. Vilna, Russia, June 22, 1888; composer and teacher; studied at Petersburg Univ.

and Cons. with Rimsky-Korsakoff and Glazounoff; teacher of comp. at latter school; c. orch. works, oratorio and songs.

Steindel (shtīn'-děl), **Bruno**, b. Zwickau, Saxony, Aug. 29, 1869; 1st 'cello, Berlin Philh.; later in the Chicago Orch.

Steiner. Vide STAINER.

Steingräber (shtīn'-grāp-ĕr), **Theodor**, Neustadt-on-the-Orla, Jan. 25, 1830 —Leipzig, April 5, 1904; founder of Hanover mus.-pub. firm; from 1890 in Leipzig; wrote a pf.-method under the pseud. "**Gustav Damm.**"

Stein'way & Sons, firm of pf.-makers, New York and Hamburg; founded by (1) **H. Engelhard Steinweg** (shtīn'-väkh), Wolfshagen, Harz, 1797—New York, 1871; journeyman org.-builder, Seesen, ca. 1820; he worked at night on his first piano, which combined the good points of Old English and recent German instrs.; it made immediate succ.; after the Revolution of 1848, he emigrated to New York in 1850 with four sons, (2) **Chas.**, Seesen, 1829— 1865. (3) **H.**, Seesen, 1829—New York, 1865. (4) **Wm.**, Seesen, 1836 —New York, 1896; (5) **Albert**, Seesen, 1840—New York, 1877; leaving the business in charge of (6) **Theodor** (Seesen, 1825—Brunswick, 1889). Father and sons worked in different factories till 1853, when they combined as Steinway & Sons. In 1865 Theodor, who had moved to Brunswick, sold the business to the firm Grotrian, Helferich & Schulz, Theodor Steinwegs Nachfolger (i. e. "successors") (v. STEINWEG), and became a partner in the N. Y. firm, now the largest of its kind in the world.

Steinweg, Original form of "Steinway" (q. v. No. 6).

Stelzner (shtělts'-nĕr), **Alfred**, Hamburg, Dec. 29, 1852—Dresden, July 14, 1906 (suicide); inv. the violotta and cellone, etc. (v. D. D.); they were used in the orch. of his fairy opera "*Rübezahl*" (Dresden, 1902).

Stendhal (stän-däl), pen-name of **Marie Henri Beyle** (běl), Grenoble, Jan. 23, 1783—Paris, March 23, 1842; French consul at Civitavecchia, 1831-42, and author of numerous books on music.

Sten'hammar, (1) **Fredrika**, Wisby, 1836—Stockholm, 1880; operatic soprano; born Andrée. (2) **Ulrik,** Stockholm, 1829–1875; composer of oratorio *"Saul,"* etc. His son (3) **Wilhelm,** Stockholm, Feb. 7, 1871– Nov. 20, 1927; pianist; pupil of the Cons., and of H. Barth; from 1898 cond. Phil. Society in Stockholm; from 1900 assistant cond. at the Royal Theatre; 1907–23, cond. of Gothenburg Symph. Orch.; c. symph., *"Prinsessan och Svennen"* for voices and orch., music. dramas *"Tirfing"* (Stockholm, 1898), and *"Das Fest auf Solhaug"* (Stuttgart, 1899), overture *"Excelsior,"* and many songs.

Sterkel (shtĕr′-kĕl), Abbé **Jn. Fz. X.,** Würzburg, 1750–Würzburg, 1817; conductor, organist and composer.

Ster′ling, (1) **Antoinette,** Sterlingville, N. Y., Jan. 23, 1850–Hampstead, Jan. 10, 1904; concert and oratorio contralto, range *e* flat–*f′′* pupil of Mme. Marchesi, Viardot-Garcia and Manuel Garcia; sang for a time in Henry Ward Beecher's Ch., at Brooklyn; from 1873, London; 1875, m. John Mac-Kinlay. (2) **Winthrop S.,** b. Cincinnati, 1859; pupil of Coll. of Mus. and Leipzig Cons., also under R. Hoffman (comp.) and Frau Unger-Haupt (voice), later in London under Turpin, Behnke and Shakespeare; organist West London Tabernacle; from 1887, prof. Cincinnati Coll. of Mus.; 1903, founder and dean of Met. Coll. of Music there.

Stern (shtĕrn), (1) **Julius,** Breslau, 1820 –Berlin, 1883; cond., teacher and composer. (2) **Leo,** Brighton, Engl., 1870–London, Sept. 3, 1904; 'cellist; pupil of Piatti and of Klengel and Davidoff, Leipzig; first tour, 1888 (with Piatti); made succ. tours in France; 1897, America; c. 'cello pieces, etc.

Sternberg (stĕrn′-bĕrkh), **Constantin (Ivanovitch),** Edler **von,** St. Petersburg, July 9, 1852–Philadelphia, March 31, 1924; pianist; pupil of Leipzig Cons., Berlin Akademie, and of Liszt; conductor various churches; from 1877, toured widely; 1880, United States; from 1890, dir. "Sternberg Sch. of Mus.," Philadelphia; c. 2 pf.-trios, *"Danses cosaques"* for vln., 'cello-fantasia, etc.

Ste′venson, (1) Sir **J. Andrew,** Dublin, ca. 1762–1833; Mus. Doc.; c. Irish operas; son of (2) **John** (vio-

linist in the State-Band at Dublin).

Stew′art, (1) Sir **Robt. Prescott,** Dublin, 1825–1894; organist, professor, conductor and composer. (2) **Humphrey John,** London, May 22, 1856– San Diego, Cal., Dec. 28, 1932; eminent organist; after 1886 in San Francisco; 1915, at San Diego Exp. where he remained to give annual series of several hundred recitals on Spreckles outdoor organ in Balboa Park; also active as conductor and composer.

Stiastny (Stastný) (sht′yäst′-nē), (1) **Bd. Wenzel,** Prague, 1760—1835; 'cellist, professor and composer. (2) **Fz. Jn.,** Prague, 1764—Mannheim, ca. 1820; bro. and pupil of above; 'cello-virtuoso and composer.

Stich (stĭkh), **Jan Václav (or Jn. Wenzel)** (Italianised as **"Giovanni Punto"),** Zchuzicz, Bohemia, 1746— Prague, 1803; eminent horn-virtuoso, writer and composer.

Stiedry (shtē′-drē), **Fritz,** b. Vienna, Oct. 11, 1883; conductor; pupil of Mandyczewski; 1907–08, ass't cond. at Dresden Op.; then in various opera theatres; 1916–23, first cond. at Berlin State Op.; 1924–05, dir., Vienna Volksoper; 1929–33 cond. at Municipal Op., Berlin; 1933–08, gen. mus. dir. of Leningrad Philh. Orch.; 1938, cond. New Friends of Music Chamber Orch., New York.

Stierlin (shtēr′-lĭn), **Joh. Gottfr. Adolf.,** b. Adenau, Oct. 14, 1859—Münster, April 26, 1930; bass; pupil of F. Schmidt; 1897 founded a Cons. in Münster.

Still, William Grant, b. Woodville, Miss., 1895; Negro composer; among his works, marked by exotic note and modern use of instrumental color, are: (ballet) *"La Guiablesse,"* perf. in Rochester also by Chicago Op.; works for orch., incl. *"Afro-American" Symphony* (N. Y. Philh.); *"Darker America," "Africa," "From the Black Belt," "Puritan Epic," "Levee Land," "From the Journal of a Wanderer," "Log Cabin Ballads,"* etc.

Stock, Frederick, b. Dülich, Nov. 11, 1872; conductor; son and pupil of a military bandmaster; then studied with Humperdinck, Zöllner, Jensen and Wüllner, at the Cologne Cons.; 1891–95 violinist in the City Orch.; then joined the Symph. Orch. in Chicago; 1899 became assistant cond.

to Theodore Thomas, on whose death in 1905 he was chosen as conductor; c. symphonic poems, symph., variations, chamber music, songs, etc.

Stockhausen (shtôk'-how-zĕn), (1) **Fz.**, 1792—1868; harpist and composer. His wife (2) **Margarethe** (née **Schmuck**), Gebweiler, 1803—Colmar, 1877; pupil of Cartruffo, Paris; concert-soprano; toured with her husband. (3) **Julius**, Paris, July 22, 1826—Frankfort, Sept. 22, 1906; barytone and eminent teacher; son of above; pupil of Paris Cons. and of Manuel Garcia; succ. concert-singer; 1862–67, cond. Philh. Concerts and Singakademie, at Hamburg; 1869–70, chamber-singer at Stuttgart; 1878–79 and 1882–98, teacher of singing, Hoch Cons., Frankfort; then private teacher; pub. a Method. (4) **Fz.**, Gebweiler, Jan. 30, 1839—Strassburg, Jan. 4, 1926; pupil of Alkan and of Leipzig Cons.; 1868–79, cond. at Strassburg; from 1871 to 1907, teacher Strassburg Cons.; 1892, R. Prof.

Stoessel (stĕs'-ĕl), **Albert**, b. St. Louis, Mo., Oct. 11, 1894; composer, conductor, violinist; studied at Berlin Hochsch., début in that city as violinist; cond. N. Y. Oratorio Soc., succeeding Damrosch, 1921; also Worcester, Mass., and (formerly) Westchester, N. Y., Fests.; 1924, dir. music faculty, N. Y. Univ.; 1930, dir. of opera dept. and cond. of Orch. at Juilliard School, N. Y.; mus. dir. at Chautauqua, N. Y.; c. orch. works, incl. "*Suite Antique*," vln. sonata, works for piano, songs and choruses; author, *Technique of the Baton*.

Stojowski (stō-yôf'-shkĭ), **Sigismond**, b. Strelce, Poland, May 2, 1870; pianist; pupil of L. Zelenski at Cracow, and at Paris Cons., winning 1st prizes for pf. and comp.; studied with Paderewski; he has lived in New York since 1905 as piano prof. Musical Art Inst. 1905–11, then till 1917 at Von Ende School; afterwards teaching privately and giving frequent recitals, particularly of his own works. C. symph. (Leipzig, 1898); romance for violin and orch.; chor. with orch. "*Spring*"; Polish Rhapsodie for piano and orch.; violin concerto (1908); 3 piano concertos and many other works for this instrument; variations and fugue for string quartet; 2 vln. sonatas;

'cello sonata; choral work, "*A Prayer for Poland*"; Fantaisie for trombone; orch. suite, songs, etc.; m. Luisa Morales-Machado, pianist.

Stokowski (stō-kôf'-skĭ), **Leopold**, b. London, April 18, 1882; of Polish parentage; graduated at Oxford; studied at Paris Cons., acted as cond. there; 1905–08 mus. dir. St. Bartholomew's, N. Y.; 1908, cond. in London; 1909–12, cond. Cincinnati Symph. Orch; after 1912, cond. Philadelphia Orch., vice Carl Pohlig; 1911, married the pianist Olga Samaroff; divorced; (2) Evangeline Brewster Johnson. One of the most brilliant and individual conductors of his day, distinguished by his Spartan discipline over the orch., his tendency to select unconventional music for his programmes, esp. of modern composers. His musical style excels in great clarity and transparency of musical texture, beauty of tone, and exquisite finish of detail. He has arranged for orch. many remarkable transcriptions of works by Bach. In 1930–31 he was guest cond. of the N. Y. Philh. Orch.; in 1936 he took his own orch. for a transcontinental tour of the U. S. He has been identified also with productions of modern operas and ballets by the Phila. Grand Op. Co., the Phila. Orch. and the League of Composers, New York. In 1936 he announced that he would lead only a score of concerts in the following season, devoting part of his time to research in new mechanical means of reproducing music. Mus. D., Univ. of Pennsylvania, 1917.

Stoltz, (1) **Rosine** (rightly **Victorine Nöb**) (shtôlts or năp), Paris, Feb. 13, 1815—July 31, 1903; pupil of Choron's Sch.; mezzo-soprano; 1837–47, Gr. Opéra, Paris; other stage names **"Mme. Ternaux," "Mlle. Héloise," "Rose Niva";** m. successively a baron and 2 princes; c. songs. (2) **Therese**, Bohemia, 1834—Milan, 1902; soprano; début, La Scala, 1865; created "Aïda" in Italy; intimate friend of Verdi; married after 1875 and retired.

Stoltzer (shtôlts'-ĕr), **Thos.**, Silesia, ca. 1490—Ofen, 1526; ct.-conductor and composer.

Stölz(e)l (shtĕlts'-ĕl), **Gf. H.**, Grünstädtl, Saxony, 1690—Gotha, 1749; ct.-conductor and dram. composer.

Stolzenberg (shtôl'-tsĕn-bĕrkh), **Benno,** Königsberg, Feb. 25, 1829—Berlin, 1908; tenor; pupil of Mantius and H. Dorn; début, Königsberg, 1852; dir. Danzig City Th.; teacher, Berlin; 1885, Cologne Cons.; from 1896, dir. of a vocal sch. at Berlin.

Stöpel (shtā'-pĕl), **Fz. (David Chp.),** Oberheldrungen, Saxony, 1794—Paris, 1836; theorist.

Stör (shtär), **K.,** Stolberg, Harz, 1814 —Weimar, 1889; violinist, cond. and dram. composer.

Sto'race, (1) **Stephen,** London, 1763 —(of gout) 1796, prod. 18 stage-works; son and pupil of (2) **Stefano S.,** an Italian double-bass-player. (3) **Anna Selina** (1766—1817), famous colorature-soprano; daughter and pupil of (2); sang in public at 8; then début, Florence, 1780; created "Susanna" in Mozart's *"Figaro."*

Stracciari (strä-chä'-rē), **Riccardo; b.** Bologna, June 26, 1875; eminent barytone; pupil of Liceo in native city; début in *"La Bohème"* at birthplace, 1900; later sang in succ. in many cities of Italy, Spain, North and South America; after 1926 taught at the Naples Conservatory.

Stradal (strä'-däl), **August,** Teplitz, 1860—Schönlinde, Bohemia, March 13, 1930; pupil of Door, Bruckner and Liszt; pianist and composer.

Stradella (strä-dĕl'-lä), **Alessandro,** probably Naples or Venice, ca. 1645 —Genoa, after 1681 (the date of his last cantata); important Italian composer, of whom little is actually known, though he is the hero of an extraordinarily melodramatic legend of jealous nobility, paid assassins, and love pursued. In a work by Bonnet-Bourdelot (1715), it is said that his name was Stradel and being engaged to write an opera for Venice, he eloped with the mistress of a nobleman who sent paid *bravi* to assassinate him in Rome. These men were overcome by the beauty of an oratorio of his and warned him of his danger. He fled to Turin with the woman who passed for his wife, and after being followed here and there, and recovering from numerous wounds, was finally slain in Genoa. Flotow made an opera of this story, in which there is much that is incredible. S. was also credited with being a singer and poet, and a wonderful harpist. In any case, 148 of his works exist in MS. in the Modena Library, and others elsewhere, incl. 8 oratorios, many cantatas, madrigals, duets, etc. The church-aria *"Pietà, Signore,"* and the arias *"O del mio dolce ardor"* and *"Se i miei sospiri,"* are probably wrongly attributed to him. Monographs by P. Richard, "A. Stradella" (1866), and Calelane.

Stradivari (Stradivarius) (sträd-ĭ-vä'-rē, or vä'-rĭ-oos), (1) **Antonio,** Cremona, 1644 (1650 ?)—Dec. 17 (18 ?), 1737; maker of vlns., vlas., 'cellos, etc., who established a type and proportion never improved; his tone is also supreme among vlns. (with the possible exception of those of Jos. Guarneri); he probably worked for Niccolò Amati, 1667–79; 1680, he purchased the house in which his workshop thereafter was situated; 1700–25, is his best period, but he worked to 1736; his label reads "Antonius Stradivarius Cremonensis. Fecit Anno . . . (A † S)." Of his eleven children, 2 sons, (2) **Fran.** (1671—1745) and (3) **Omobono** (1679 —1742), were his assistants. Monographs, by Lombardini (1872), Fétis (1856); Wasielewski and Riechers.

Straeten, van der. Vide VANDER-STRAETEN.

Strakosch (shträ'-kôsh), (1) **Moritz,** Lemberg, Galicia, 1825—Paris, Oct. 9, 1887; pianist and impresario; c. operas; teacher of Adelina, and husband of Carlotta, Patti. (2) **Max,** d. New York, 1892; bro. of above and equally famous as impresario.

Stran'sky, Josef, Humpolec, Bohemia, Sept. 9, 1872—New York, March 6, 1936; of German parents; studied medicine at first; and then music while at the universities of Vienna, Leipzig and Prague; début as cond. at Prague Opera, succeeding Muck, later succeeded Mahler at Hamburg; cond. Blüthner orch., Berlin; 1911, succeeded Mahler as cond. N. Y. Philh. Orch., of which he was the successful sole leader until 1923; 1923–24, cond. State Symph. Orch., N. Y., then resigning to become a dealer in paintings.

Straube (strow'-bĕ), **C., b.** Berlin, Jan. 6, 1873; noted organist; pupil of Riemann, Rüfer, and A. Becker; 1902 organist Thomaskirche (vice C. Piatti); from 1903 he also cond.

the Bach Verein there; 1907 organ teacher at Leipzig Cons.; after 1918, Cantor of the Thomaskirche; 1919, merged the B.-Verein with the Gewandhaus Choir; led notable Bach Festivals.

Straus (shtrows), **Oskar,** b. Vienna, April 6, 1870; pupil of Grädener and Max Bruch; cond. theatres in various cities; c. overture *"Der Traum ein Leben,"* chamber music and many operas, some of them extremely successful, especially *"Ein Walzertraum"* (Vienna, 1906; London and America as *"The Waltz Dream"*); *"Der tapfere Soldat"* (Vienna, 1908), (*"Chocolate Soldier"*), etc.

Strauss (shtrows), (1) **Jos.,** Brünn, 1793—Carlsruhe, Dec. 1 (2 ?), 1866; violinist, mus.-director, ct.-conductor; c. operas. (2) **Jn.** (Sr.), Vienna, March 14, 1804—(of scarlet fever) Sept. 25, 1849, "The Father of the Waltz"; son of proprietor of a beer and dance-hall; conductor and composer of 152 waltzes all more or less famous. (3) **Jn.** (Jr.), Vienna, Oct. 25, 1825—June 3, 1899; "The Waltz-King"; son of above, who opposed the mus. tastes of the three sons, for whom the mother secured secret instruction. In 1844 conductor of court-balls and very succ. orch. concerts. He had c. a waltz at 6, and his later comps. eclipsed the success of those of his father, after whose death he united the two orchestras. 1862, he m. the singer Henriette Treffz (d. 1878), and later the singer Angelica Dittrich; c. 400 pcs. of dance-music; his waltzes *"The beautiful blue Danube,"* *"Künstlerleben,"* *"Wiener Blut,"* *"The 1001 Nights,"* *"Wine, Women and Song,"* etc., are dance-rhapsodies whose verve and colour have deserved and won the highest praise of severe musicians. His light operas rival his waltzes in charm and succ. and incl. the v. succ. *"Die Fledermaus"* ('74). (4) **Jos.,** Vienna, Aug. 22, 1827—July 22, 1870; bro. of above, during whose illness in 1853 he served as cond.; later formed an orch. of his own and learned the vln.; on a tour to Warsaw he was maltreated by Russian officers for whom he had refused to play, and died in the arms of his wife (whom he had m. in 1857); he c. 283 dances. (5) **Eduard,** Vienna, Feb. 14, 1835—

Dec. 28, 1916; bro. and succ. of Johann as cond. of the ct.-balls and orch.; took his orch. to America 1892 and 1900; c. dance-mus. (6) **Ludwig,** Pressburg, March 28, 1836—Cambridge, Engl., 1899; violinist. (7) Victor von, Royal opera conductor, Berlin, 1902. (8) **Richard,** b. Munich, June 11, 1864; composer; in early life a brilliant musical genius; son of (8) **Fz. S.** (chambermus. and horn-player); studied also with W. Meyer. At 4 he c. a polka. He took a regular Gymnasium course 1874–82, and spent two years at the univ. At 17 his first symph. was prod. by Levi; his *"Serenade"* for 13 wind-instrs. had much succ. with the Meiningen orch. under von Bülow, to whom S. became asst., and (1885) successor as ct.-mus. dir. at Meiningen; 1886, 3rd cond. at Munich; 1889, ct.-cond. at Weimar under Lassen; 1894, cond. at the ct.-opera, Munich, also 1894, cond. Berlin Philh., and from 1898, cond. at Berlin Royal Opera. He m. the soprano, Pauline de Ahna, who created "Freihilde" in his opera *"Guntram"* (Weimar, 1894, Munich, '95). His 1-act opera *"Feuersnoth"* ("Fire-Famine"), libretto by Wolzogen, was prod. Dresden, Nov. 21, 1901, with much success. He has also cond. with great succ. in various cities. A Strauss Festival was given in London, 1903, with S. conducting the Amsterdam Orch.; 1904 he was made general musical director of the Berlin Royal Opera. In the same year he cond. in the U. S. C. symph. op. 12; symphonic fantasie *"Aus Italien,"* *"Wanderers Sturmlied"* (Goethe), for 6-part chorus, and full orch.; tone-poems, *"Don Juan,"* op. 20; *"Macbeth,"* op. 23; *"Tod und Verklärung,"* op. 24, the symph. poems *"Also sprach Zarathustra"* (after Nietzsche), *"Ein Heldenleben"* (op. 40), and *"Don Quixote"*; op. 28, Orchester-Rondo *"Till Eulenspiegel's lustige Streiche"*; chamber-mus.; vln.-concerto; 5 *"Stimmungsbilder"* for pf.; concerto for Waldhorn; *"Enoch Arden,"* melodrama for pf. and recitation, and many songs. 16-part *a cappella* chorus *"Der Abend"* (1902), ballad for chorus and orch. *"Taillefer"* (1902); *"Sinfonia Domestica"* (1904); operas *"Salomé"* (1 act after Oscar Wilde, Dresden,

1905, and throughout Europe; prod. at Met. Op., 1907; it was withdrawn after one performance but restored 1934 with succ.); *"Elektra"* (Dresden, 1909, and at Manhattan Op., N. Y., 1910); *"Der Rosenkavalier"* (Dresden, June 26, 1911, and at Met. Op., 1913); *"Ariadne auf Naxos"* (Stuttgart, Oct. 25, 1912, revised 1917); *"Die Frau ohne Schatten"* (1921); *"Intermezzo"* (1924, a work said to be based on a mild marital misunderstanding in his own career); *"Die Aegyptische Helena"* (Dresden, 1928, also at Met. Op. House, without succ.); *"Arabella"* (1933, comedy which uses waltz themes somewhat in manner of *"Rosenkavalier"* but not as strong as that world-conquering work); *"Die Schweigsame Frau"* (1933); the ballets *"Josephslegende"* (1914) and *"Schlagobers"* ("Whipped Cream," allegory of pastry shop, 1923). Also a pf.-concerto for the left hand, *"Parergon zur Sinfonia Domestica und Panathenaeen-zug,"* written for Paul Wittgenstein. His last important orch. work was the rather weak *"Alpensinfonie"* (1915), a literal description in tone of a climb to the mountain summits. His later works have tended to revert to a greater simplicity in scoring, some, like his incidental music to *"Der Bürger als Edelmann,"* have Mozartian influence. His post-war works have displayed a decline in invention, though his scoring wizardry is still in evidence. S. made a notable tour of the U. S. in 1921, when he led a cycle of his works in N. Y. with the Phila. Orch.; cond. in many Eur. cities; 1919–24, dir. with Schalk of the Vienna Op.; 1933–35, he was pres. of the Reich Music Chamber in Germany; in 1938 a 1-act opera, *"Friedenstag,"* was premièred at the Munich State Op.; and *"Daphne,"* at Dresden Op., 1938.

Biographical works by Seidl, Klatte, Hutschenruijter, Brecher, Urban, Bie, Newman, Steinitzer, Finck, Waltershausen, and studies of his comps. by Gilman, Hutcheson, Rose and Pruewer, Schattmann, etc. S. revised and completed Berlioz's treatise on instrumentation.

Stravinsky (strä-vēn'-skē), **Igor,** b. Oranienbaum, Russia, June 17, 1882;

composer; one of most striking technical innovators of his period, a remarkable craftsman and highly influential upon other composers; studied comp. with Rimsky-Korsakoff, in whose memory he wrote a *"Chant Funèbre"* and also his early symph. piece, *"Fireworks,"* for the wedding of the latter's daughter; his first productions were marked by original and highly brilliant impressionistic use of orch. color, exploiting strange timbres and instrumental effects, and drew upon Russian folklore, esp. for his pop. ballets *"L'Oiseau de Feu"* and *"Petrouchka,"* which created much interest when prod. by Diaghileff. With *"Le Sacre du Printemps"* (1913), the strident and bizarre effects that made *"Petrouchka"* a masterpiece of bitter irony were augmented with an unprecedented complexity of rhythm and harsh, grinding dissonances which literally portrayed the earth-beating dances of a prehistoric race in a spring fest.; to this period belongs also his Chinese fairy opera, *"Le Rossignol,"* more delicately dissonantal and based on an Andersen story, which was given by the Met. Op. Co., 1926. After *"Les Noces,"* written as a "symphony" but prod. as a ballet which portrays Russian wedding customs of the past with salty gusto, the style of S. became progressively more reticent and also economical of means. His ironic *"Histoire du Soldat"* with a chamber ensemble and narrator, has been danced and also presented in concert form; his *"Renard,"* a sort of animal fable in chamber style with voice and instruments, is also marked by delightful wit; a short opera, *"Mavra,"* oddly echoes (with intent) Glinka and Italian styles. The tendency to compose in the manner of earlier creators asserts itself increasingly in his later works, which has been construed as symptomatic of his attempt to find new paths, but by others as a confession of lack of inspiration. Beginning with his post-war productions, his music is increasingly neo-classic in style. It takes the form of compositions for small instrumental combinations, for various solo instruments with orch. and in concertante form, which embody his strivings after an ideal of "pure music," in which emotion and overemphasis are sternly restricted. Parallel to this, S. has shown a fondness for antique subjects and Greek myths, treated in heroic manner and in neo-classic garb: such are his "*Oedipus Rex*," a dram. cantata for soloists, male chorus, narrator and orch. (prod. in Paris, N. Y. and elsewhere); his "*Symphonie de Psaumes*" for chorus and orch., settings of 3 Hebrew psalms stressing warlike spirit in austere fashion; "*Apollon Musagète*" for orch.; and "*Perséphone*," a mimetic cantata based on the Greek myth, in which a woman mime-reciter, tenor, chorus and orch. take part (given in concert form by the Boston Symph., under the composer); has also c. (ballets) "*Pulcinella*" (after Pergolesi), "*Baiser de la Fée*" and "*Les Abeilles*"; (orch.) "*Scherzo Fantastique*," a symphony; suites based upon his most pop. ballet scores; "*Le Rossignol*" (symph. poem); "*Symphonie Concertante*" and Octuor for wind instruments; Concertino; a Concerto and a Capriccio for piano and orch.; two-piano concerto; vln. concerto; "*Duo Concertante*" for piano and vln., and many other smaller pieces for piano and other instruments, also songs. S. has visited the U. S. several times as guest cond. of various orchs., incl. N. Y. Philh., Phila., Boston, Chicago and elsewhere. Soon after the war he took up res. in France and has become a citizen of that country. He has toured with Samuel Dushkin, violinist, and with his son, Soulima Stravinsky, pianist, in chamber programmes; has visited leading Eur. cities and S. A. as a guest cond.; Eliot Chair of Poetry, Harvard, 1940. S. has published a book of reminiscences, as well as various "manifestos" and the like, setting forth his artistic ideals. A biography (in French) by André Schaeffner was pub. 1931. A large number of essays on the composer and his work have been issued, by Van Vechten, Wise, Montagu-Nathan, Boris de Schloezer and others. Edwin Evans has written a study of his "*Firebird*" and "*Petrouchka*."

Streabbog. Vide GOBBAERTS.

Streat'feild, Rich. Alex., Carshalton, 1866—London, 1919; writer; 1898–1912, critic of London *Daily Graphic*; author, "*Masters of Italian Music*," "*The Opera*," "*Modern Music and Musicians*," "*Handel*," "*Life Stories of Great Composers*," etc.

Street (shtrāt), G. Ernest, of French parents, Vienna, 1854—1908; pupil of Bizet and Damcke, Paris; critic there; 1898, of *L'Éclair*; c. operettas, 1-act mimodrama "*Fides*" (Op.-Com., 1894), 3-act opera "*Mignonette*," parody of Thomas's "*Mignon*" (1896), ballet, "*Scaramouche*" with Messager, 1891, etc.

Streicher (shtrī'-khĕr), (1) Jn. Andreas, Stuttgart, 1761—Vienna, 1833; piano-maker and professor; 1793 inv. the pf.-action which drops the hammer from above; succeeded 1832 by his son (2) Jn. Bapt., 1794—1871, who was succeeded by his son (3) Emil.

Strelezki (strĕ-lĕt'-shkĭ), Anton (rightly Burnand), Croydon, Engl., Dec. 5, 1859—1907; pupil of Leipzig Cons., and of Frau Schumann; c. popular songs, and pf.-pcs.

Strepponi. Vide VERDI.

Striggio (strĭd'-jō), Ales., b. Mantua, ca. 1535; lutenist, composer and conductor.

Strinasacchi (strē-nä-säk'-kē), Regina, Ostiglia, near Mantua, 1764—Dresden, 1839; violinist.

String'ham, Edwin John, b. Kenosha, Wis., July 11, 1890; composer, educator; grad. Northwestern Univ.; Ped. Doc., Cincinnati Cons., studied with Respighi at St. Cecilia Acad., Rome; hon. Mus. D., Denver Coll, of Music; dean, College of Music, Denver, 1919–29; mem. faculty of music education, Teachers College, Columbia Univ.; also taught Union Seminary, N. Y.; c. orch. works, incl. symphony, suites, overtures, etc., played by several major Amer. orchestras.

Strong, (1) G. Templeton, b. New York, 1856; pupil of Leipzig Cons.; c. symph. "*In den Bergen*"; symph. poem "*Undine*" (op. 14); "*Gestrebt—Gewonnen—Gescheitert*"; f. orch. with vln.-obbligato; choral works with orch.; pf.-pcs., etc. (2) Susan, b. Brooklyn, N. Y., 1875; operatic soprano; studied with Korbay; sang in Italy, England and in U. S. with companies under Mapleson and Damrosch; Met. Op., 1899–1900.

Strozzi (strôd'-zē), (1) **Pietro,** b. Florence, 16th cent.; co-founder of the *stile rappresentativo* (v. PERI); set to music Caccini's "*La Mascarada degli Accecati,*" 1595. (2) Abbate **Gregorio,** apostolic protonotary at Naples; composer, 1683.

Strube (shtroo'-bĕ), **Gustav,** b. Ballenstedt, Harz, March 3, 1867; violinist; pupil of his father; at 10 in Ballenstedt orch.; at 16 pupil of Leipzig Cons.; played in the Gewandhaus Orch., later prof. at Mannheim Cons.; 1889, Boston, Mass., in Symph. Orch.; c. symphony in C minor, in B minor; overtures "*The Maid of Orleans*"; "*Fantastic*"; "*Puck*"; symph. poems "*Longing,*" "*Fantastic Dance*"; concertos, violin, 'cello, etc.; 1909 he became a cond. of the Worcester Festivals; 1913 taught Peabody Cons., Baltimore; after 1916 he cond. Symph. Orch. there.

Stueckgold (shtēk'-gôlt), **Grete,** b. London, July 6, 1895; soprano; of English-German parentage; studied voice in Germany with Jacques Stueckgold; operatic début in Nuremberg; engaged for Berlin Städtische Oper, where she sang with succ., incl. leading rôle in Handel's "*Otto and Theophanes*" under Bruno Walter; mem. Met. Op. Co., N. Y., for several seasons after 1929; also a high-ranking concert artist (esp. Lieder singer) and has appeared in radio programmes; m. Gustav Schuetzendorf, barytone.

Stuntz (shtoonts), **Jos. Hartmann,** Arlesheim, near Basel, 1793—Munich, 1859; dram. composer.

Such (zookh), **Percy,** b. June 27, 1878; 'cellist; studied with Robt. Haasmanns; toured widely.

Sucher (zoo'-khĕr), (1) **Josef,** Döbör, Hungary, Nov. 23, 1844—Berlin, April 4, 1908; eminent cond.; studied singing and the vln., Vienna; pupil of Sechter (comp.); vice-cond. of the acad. Gesangverein; coach for solo singers at the ct.-opera; 1876, cond. Leipzig City Th.; 1877, m. the distinguished Wagnerian soprano, (2) **Rosa Hasselbeck,** Velburg, Upper Palatinate, Feb. 23, 1849—Eschweiler, April 16, 1927; 1878–88 they were engaged by Pollini at Hamburg; later as cond. of the Royal Opera at Berlin (retired 1899), and prima donna (retired 1898). Frau S. was daughter of a musician and sang small rôles at Munich and elsewhere at first, later prominent in Wagner opera which she sang at Bayreuth and in America.

Suk (sook), **Josef,** Křečovic, Bohemia, Jan. 4, 1874—Beneschau, May 29, 1935; composer and violinist; pupil and son-in-law of Dvořák at Prague Cons., 1896, 2nd vln. "Bohemian String-Quartet"; c. a dramatic overture "*Winter's Tale,*" suite for orch. op. 16 "*Ein Märchen,*" 2 symphonies, 2 string quartets, piano quartet and trio, and a choral work, "*Under the Apple Tree,*" etc.

Sul'livan, Sir **Arthur Seymour,** London, May 14, 1842—Nov. 22, 1900; eminent composer of national English comic opera; v. succ. in church-mus. also; at 12 a chorister under Helmore, Chapel Royal; at 13 pub. a song; 1856, the first Mendelssohn Scholar of the R. A. M.; studied also at Leipzig Cons., etc. At 18 cond. his overture "*Lalla Rookh*"; at 20 prod. his mus. to "*The Tempest*" (Crystal Palace); at 22 his notable cantata "*Kenilworth*" (Birmingham festival); cond. of the London Philharm. (1885–87); and from 1880, the Leeds Festivals. 1876–81, principal, and prof. of comp. at the Nat. Training Sch. for Mus.; Mus. Doc. *h.c.*, Cambridge (1876), and Oxford (1879), Chev. of the Legion of Honour, 1878; grand organist to the Freemasons, 1887; knighted, 1883. C. symphony (played at the Gewandhaus, Leipzig, etc.) overtures "*In Memoriam*" (on his father's death), "*Marmion,*" "*Di ballo,*" and "*Sapphire Necklace*"; oratorios and cantatas, incl. "*The Golden Legend*" (1886); "*A Festival Te Deum*" (1872), Ode "*I Wish to Tune my Quivering Lyre,*" with orch., and succ. incid. mus. to 8 of Shakespeare's plays and others; c. much v. succ. church-mus. of all kinds. His operas include the grand opera, "*Ivanhoe*" (1891), the romantic opera, "*Rose of Persia*" (1900), neither a succ.

His chief contribution to music was his brilliant series of truly English comic operas, with the equally brilliant librettos of W. S. Gilbert. Some of these had a world-wide

succ., and "*Patience*" was a satire
of equal effectiveness. with Molière's
"*Les Précieuses Ridicules.*" Among
16 comic operas were the following
great successes: "*Cox and Box*"
(1867), "*Trial by Jury*" (1875),
"*H. M. S. Pinafore*" (1878), "*The
Pirates of Penzance*" (1880), "*Patience*" (1881), "*Iolanthe*" (1882),
"*The Mikado*" (1885), "*Ruddigore*"
(1887), "*The Yeomen of the Guard*"
(1888), "*The Gondoliers,*" "*Utopia
(Limited)*" (1893); "*Contrabandista*"
(1867, revised 1894 as "*The Chieftain*"), "*The Emerald Isle*" (1901),
finished by Edw. German, libretto
by Basil Hood. Among many works
on S. and his music are those by
Lawrence, Wells, Wyndham, Findon,
Goldberg, Bridgeman, Mackenzie,
Dunhill, Godwin, and a life (with
letters and diaries) by Herbert
Sullivan and Newman Flower (1927).

Sulzer (zool'-tsĕr), (1) **Jn. G.**, Winterthur, 1720—Berlin, 1779; writer and
professor. (2) **Salomon**, of Jewish
parents, Hohenems, Vorarlberg, 1804
—Vienna, 1890; prof. of singing and
composer. (3) **Julius**, Vienna, 1834
—1891; son of above; violinist and
conductor, and c. operas. His sisters
(4) **Marie** and (5) **Henriette**, singers.
Supervia (soo-pĕr-vē'-ä), **Conchita**,
Spain, 1899—London, March 30,
1936; coloratura mezzo-soprano;
début, Buenos Aires, at 14; sang
with Madrid Op., later at La Scala,
Paris, Vienna with succ., acquiring
rep. for great flexibility of voice and
wide range; also with Chicago Op.,
1932 as "Carmen" and "Rosina"; at
Covent Garden in "*L'Italiana in
Algeri*" and "*Cenerentola*"; she was
also a popular recitalist, esp. in
Spanish music, and esteemed for
her beauty and charm of personality.
Suppé, Fz. von (fōn-zoop'-pā), Spalato,
Dalmatia, 1819—Vienna, May 21,
1895; very popular operetta composer; pupil of Padua, Cigala, and
Ferrari; at first unpaid cond. at the
Josephstädter Th.; then at Pressburg
and Baden and at Vienna; he c. 2
grand operas, a symph., a Missa Dal-
matica, a requiem, "*L'estremo giudizio,*" overtures (incl. the immensely
pop. "*Dichter und Bauer,*" pub. for
59 combinations). Of his Singspiele,
comediettas, etc., some (like "*Tan-
nenhauser*" and "*Dinorah*") are

parodies, of the others the most succ.
are "*Fatinitza*" (Vienna, 1876), and
"*Boccaccio*" (1879).
Surette (sū-rĕt'), **Thos. Whitney**, b.
Concord, Mass., Sept. 7, 1862—
May 19, 1941; graduated Harvard,
1891; pupil there of Arthur Foote
(pf.), and J. K. Paine; organist, Baltimore; then University Extension
lecturer (Phila., Pa.); after 1921,
taught at Bryn Mawr Coll., Pa.;
wrote treatises, etc.; pub. 2-act
operetta "*Priscilla,*"[2] etc.
Suriano (or **Soriano**) (soo'-[or sō']
rĭ-ä-nō), **Fran.**, Rome, 1549—Jan.,
1620; conductor and notable composer; pupil of Nanini and Palestrina; cond. S. Maria Maggiore, and
1603, at St. Peter's, Rome.
Süssmayer (züs'-mī-ĕr), **Fz. X.**, Steyr,
Upper Austria, 1766—Vienna, 1803;
conductor and dram. composer.
Suter (zoo'-tĕr), **Hermann**, Kaiser-
stuhl, Switzerland, April 28, 1870—
Basel, June 22, 1926; pupil of his
father, an organist, and of the Stuttgart and Leipzig Cons.; from 1892,
organist and cond. in Zürich, from
1902 in Basel as cond.; c. quartets
and choruses.
Sutor (zoo'-tôr), **Wilhelm**, Edelstetten,
1774—Linden, Sept. 7, 1828; court
cond. at Hanover; c. operas, etc.
Su'tro, (1) **Rose Laura** (Baltimore,
1870), pianist, and (2) **Ottilie** (Baltimore, 1872), pianist, sisters noted
for their two-piano concerts; pupils
of Berlin Hochsch.; touring in Europe and after 1914 in U. S.; in
recent years lived in Washington,
D. C., where they organised musicales.
Svecinski (svä-chĕn'-skē), **Louis**,
Osijek, Croatia, 1862—New York,
June 18, 1926; violinist and violist;
pupil of Vienna Cons.; 1885-1903
played in Boston Symph.; 1885-
1917, viola of Kneisel Quartet;
taught at Inst. of Mus. Art, N. Y.,
and later at Curtis Inst., Philadelphia.
Svendsen (svĕnt'-zĕn), (1) **Oluf**,
Christiania, 1832—London, 1888;
flutist. (2) **Johan** (Severin),
Christiania, Sept. 30, 1840—Copenhagen, June 13, 1911; important,
though eclectic composer; son of a
bandm.; at 11 c. vln.-pcs.; at 15
enlisted in the army and was soon
bandm., and played flute, clarinet,
and vln.; with a stipend from

Charles XV., he studied vln.; at 23 he became pupil of David and Hauptmann, Richter, and Reinecke, Leipzig Cons.; toured 1868-69, in Musard's orch.; and at the Odéon, Paris; 1869, Leipzig; 1871, m. an American in New York; 1872-77, and 1880-83, cond. Christiania Mus. Assoc.; 1883-1908, ct.-cond. at Copenhagen; from 1896, cond. Royal Th. there. C. 2 symphonies, overture to Björnson's "*Sigurd Slembe*"; "*Romeo and Juliet*," funeral march for Charles XV., coronation march (for Oscar II.), wedding-cantata, etc., with orch.; op. 16, "*Carnaval des artistes norvégiens*," humorous march; 4 "*Norwegian Rhapsodies*" for orch.; vln. and 'cello concertos, chamber-music and songs, etc.

Swar'thout, (1) **Donald Malcolm**, b. Pawpaw, Ill., Aug. 9, 1884; educator; studied in Chicago, at Leipzig Cons., and piano with Philipp; formerly assoc. dir. of music, Oxford Coll., Ohio, and Millikin Univ.; after 1923, prof. of pf. and dean, School of Fine Arts, Univ. of Kansas, where he served as cond. of Lawrence Choral Union and of annual music fests.; sec'y, Music Teachers Nat'l Assoc.; ed. *University Course of of Music Study*. (2) **Gladys**, b. Deepwater, Mo., Dec. 25, 1904; mezzo-soprano; studied in Kansas City and at Bush Cons., Chicago; début, 1923, as soloist with Minneapolis Symph.; mem. Chicago Civic Op. Co., 1924-25; Ravinia Op. Co., 1927-29; after latter year mem. Met. Op. Co.; also active as concert, radio and film artist; m. Frank Chapman, barytone.

Sweelinck (or **Swelinck**, the best 2 of the 7 spellings) (svä'-lĭnk), (1) **Jan Pieter** (called **Jan Pieterszoon**), Amsterdam, 1562—Oct. 16, 1621; chief of Dutch organists. Son and (1577-81) successor, probably also pupil, of (2) **Pieter** (d. 1573), who had won pre-eminence as the org.-virtuoso and teacher of his own time. (1) was the first to employ the pedal in a real fugal part, and originated the org.-fugue; c. psalms, motets, etc.

Sweet, Reginald, b. Yonkers, N. Y., Oct. 14, 1885; composer; pupil of Noyes, Eisenberger, Koch and Kaun; taught at Chautauqua and in N. Y.; c. (one-act opera) "*Riders to the Sea*," chamber music, etc.

Swert, Jules de. Vide DESWERT.

Swieten (svē'tĕn), **Gf.**, Baron **von**, 1734—Vienna, 1803; eminent patron, but unimportant composer, of music; c. 6 symphs.

Swinnerton, Heap. Vide HEAP.

Sympson. Vide SIMPSON.

Szanto (shän'tō), **Theodore**, Vienna, June 3, 1877—Budapest, Jan. 1, 1934; noted pianist; pupil of Koessler at Budapest Acad.; also of Busoni; lived in Budapest, 1914-21 in Switzerland, then in Paris and Helsingfors; composer.

Szarvady. Vide CLAUSZ-SZARVADY.

Székely (shā'-kĕ-lē), **Imre** (**Emeric**), Matyasfalva, Hungary, May 8, 1823 —Budapest, April 8, 1887; pianist; studied in Budapest; toured 1846; from 1852 teacher Budapest; c. Hungarian fantasias on national airs; pf.-concertos, etc.

Szell (shĕl), **Georg**, b. Budapest, June 7, 1897; conductor, composer; studied with Robert, Mandyczewski and Reger; début with Tonkünstler Orch., Vienna, at 11; asst. cond. R. Opera, Berlin, 1915; cond. Strasbourg, 1917; dir. Düsseldorf Op., 1921; cond. Berlin State Op., 1924-29; dir. Prague Op. after 1929; has appeared with leading orchs. in Europe, incl. London and U. S. (guest cond. St. Louis Symph., 1930-31); c. orch., chamber and piano works.

Szenkar (shĕn'-kär), **Eugen**, b. Budapest, April 9, 1891; conductor; pupil of Budapest Acad.; after 1911 active as opera cond.; 1922 in Frankfort; 1923-24, at Berlin Volksop.; 1924-33, in Cologne; after 1934 cond. of Moscow Philh. Orch.

Szigeti (shē'-gĕ-tē), **Joseph**, b. Budapest, Sept. 2, 1892; violinist; studied with Hubay; performer of high musicianship and purity of style; an outstanding virtuoso; has appeared with important orchs. in Europe and U. S., also as recitalist and chamber music player; particularly noted for his perfs. of Beethoven and Bach; has ed. and transcribed many works for violin.

Szumowska (shoo-môf'-shkä), **Antoinette**, Lublin, Poland, Feb. 22, 1868 —Rumson, N. J., Aug. 18, 1938; pianist; pupil of Strobel, Michalowski and Paderewski; played with great succ. at London, Paris, New

York, Boston, etc.; m. Joseph Adamowski; lived in Boston.

Szymanowska (shē-mä-nôf'-shkä), **Maria** (née **Wolowska**), Poland, 1790—(of cholera), Petersburg, 1832; pianist; pupil of Field at Moscow; ct.-pianist at Petersburg; Goethe was infatuated with her and she with him; c. 24 mazurkas, etc.

Szymanowski (shē-män-ôf'-skē), **Karol,** Timoshovka, Ukraine, 1883—near Lausanne, March 27, 1937; Polish composer, considered the most important creative figure of his nation since Chopin; early composed piano pieces during study with Noskowski, which have marked individuality; about 1914 his style underwent a change to more complex harmony; the transitional period in his work marked by the music drama, (one act) "*Hagith*," comp. 1912 but not prod. in Warsaw until 1922, which shows a somewhat Straussian style; later his works are increasingly marked by atonality and post-impressionism, also by greater subtlety, refinement of effect, and emotional power; c. (operas) "*Hagith*"; "*King Roger*"; (ballet) "*Harnasie*" (with vocal soloist); (masques) "*Scheherazade*"; "*Tantris the Fool*"; "*Don Juan's Serenade*"; (orch.) 3 symphonies; "*Penthesilea*"; Serenata; Sinfonia Concertante; vln. concerto; (chamber music) string quartet, vln. and piano sonata; (choral works) "*Stabat Mater*," "*Demeter*," "*Agave*"; and many piano works incl. "*Masks*" and "*Myths*," songs, etc.

T

Tacchinardi (täk-kǐ-när'-dē), (1) **Nicola,** Florence, 1772—1859; at 17 a violinist; later a tenor of greatest European popularity, even singing "Don Giovanni" (transposed) with succ., though he was hideous and a hunchback. His daughter (2) **Fanny Tacchinardi-Persiani** (v. PERSIANI). His daughter (3) **Elisa** was a pianist.

Tadolini (tä-dō-lē'-nē), (1) **Giov.,** Bologna, 1793—1872; dram. composer; m. (2) **Eugenia Savorini** (b. Forli, 1809), a singer.

Taffanel (tǎf'-fǔ-něl), **Claude Paul,** Bordeaux, Sept. 16, 1844—Paris,

Nov. 22, 1908; flutist, pupil of Dorns (flute) and Reber (comp); 3rd cond. Grand Opéra, Paris; 1892, dir. Paris Cons. concerts—resigned, 1901; 1893, prof. of flute there.

Tag (täkh), **Chr. Gotthilf,** Bayerfeld, Saxony, 1735—Niederzwönitz, 1811; composer.

Tagliafico (täl-yä-fē'-kō), **Jos. Dieudonné,** Toulon, Jan. 1, 1821—Nice, Jan. 27, 1900; operatic singer and stage-manager in London.

Tagliana (täl-yä'-nä), **Emilia,** b. Milan, 1854; pupil of the Cons. there, also of Lamperti; colorature-soprano in various cities; 1873-77, Vienna; pupil of Hans Richter; 1881-82, chamber-singer, Berlin.

Täglichsbeck (täkh'-lǐkhs-běk), **Thos.,** Ansbach, 1799—Baden-Baden, 1867; violinist, conductor and dram. composer.

Taglioni (täl-yō'-nē), **Fdo.,** Naples, Sept. 14, 1810—?; son of the famous ballet-master **Salvatore T.** (1790—1868). 1842-49, cond. at Laziano; till 1852, leader San Carlo Th., Naples; editor and conductor; founded a sch. for choral singing; pub. pamphlets and sacred songs.

Tailleferre (tǐ'-fěr), **Germaine,** b. Pau-St.-Maur near Paris, April 19, 1892; composer, pianist; pupil of Paris Cons.; belonged to "Group of Six"; her works marked by taste and sensitiveness, not radical in manner, but in tradition of Debussy, Fauré, etc.; visited U. S. as guest pianist in her works; c. Ballade for piano and orch.; "*Pastorale*," "*Les Jeux de Plein Air*"; string quartet; (ballet) "*Le Marchand d'Oiseaux*" (Swedish Ballet, Paris, 1923), etc.

Tal'ich, Vaclav, b. Kromentz, Moravia, 1883; conductor; pupil of Prague Cons., of Reger and Nikisch in Leipzig, also studied in Milan; played vln. in Berlin Philh.; later active as cond. in Tiflis, Prague, Laibach, Pilsen, and after 1918 with the Czech Philh. Orch.; toured in other countries; 1936, appointed dir. of Prague National Theatre, succeeding the late Ottakar Ostrcil.

Tal'ley, Marion, b. Nevada, Mo., 1907; coloratura soprano; early studied piano and vln., then voice with a local instructor; sang in a church choir, and gave public concert in Kansas City; her unusual vocal promise led to a subscription by residents of latter city for further study in N. Y. and Italy; made début with Met. Op. Co., as "Gilda," 1926, an occasion attended by sensational public interest; sang other coloratura rôles with this company during the next few seasons; later appeared at Ravinia Op. and as guest with Chicago Op. Co.; also in concerts, radio and musical films.

Tal(l)ys (or **Tallis**), **Thos.**, ca. (1520–29) —London, Nov. 23, 1585; an early English composer whose remarkable contrapuntal ability and harmonic richness place him close to Palestrina. His training is not known; 1540, he ceased to be organist at Waltham Abbey and joined the Chapel Royal; he was co-organist with Byrd and shared his monopoly of mus.-paper and printing; he c. notable church mus. for both Catholic and English services, also a song in 40 parts, etc.

Tamagno (tä-män'-yō), **Fran.**, Turin, 1851—Varese, Aug. 31, 1903; robust tenor; début, Palermo; sang with great succ. at La Scala, Milan, 1880, throughout Europe and in both Americas. 1887, he created Verdi's "Otello."

Tam'berlik, **Enrico**, Rome, 1820— Paris, 1889; famous tenor; pupil of Borgna and Guglielmi; début, Naples, 1841; he had a powerful high c'''.

Tamburini (täm-boo-rē'-nē), **A.**, Faenza, March 28, 1800—Nice, Nov. 9, 1876. Next to Lablache, perhaps the most succ. of male singers; a lyric bass with compass of 2 octaves; the son and pupil of a bandm. A horn-player first, then pupil of Boni and Asioli; début, Centi, 1818.

Tanaka (tä-nä'-kä), **Shohé**, Japanese theorist; pupil of Spitta; inv. the enharmonium with just intonation.

Tanejew (or **Taneiev**) (tä'-nä-yĕf), (1) **Sergei**, b. near Vladimir, Russia, Nov. 13, 1856—Moscow, June 18, 1915; pupil of N. Rubinstein and Tchaikowsky; prof. of theory and comp. Moscow Cons.; after 1878, dir.; prod. 3-act opera "Oresteia" (St. Petersburg, 1895); a cantata "John of Damascus," 1884; four symphonies, No. 1 pub. 1902, a Russian overture, seven string quartets. His uncle (2) **Alexander Sergeivich**, St. Petersburg, Jan. 5, 1850 —Feb. 7, 1918; statesman and high chancellor; was a pupil of Reichel and later of Rimsky-Korsakov and

Petrov; c. 3 symphs.; symph. poem "Alecha Popovich"; operas, 3 string quartets, etc.

Tans'man, **Alexandre**, b. Lodz, Poland, June 12, 1897; composer; studied at Warsaw Univ., also with Gawronski, Vas and others; one of most talented modern composers and has made tours in leading Eur. countries, also in America after 1927, appearing as guest cond. and pianist with important orchs.; c. (opera) "Nuit Kurde"; (orch.) symphony; "Danse de la Sorcière"; Symphonic Overture; Polish Dances; Sinfonietta; 2 piano concertos, chamber music, etc.

Tansur (tän'-sŭr), **Wm.**, Dunchurch in Warwickshire, 1706—St. Neots, 1783; organist, teacher, writer and composer.

Tappert (täp'-pĕrt), **Wm.**, Ober-Thomaswaldau, Silesia, Feb. 19, 1830 —Berlin, Oct. 27, 1907; important theorist; a schoolmaster, then 1856, studied with Dehn theory; Kullak's Acad.; lived in Berlin from 1866 as a writer, editor and composer.

Tarchi (tär'-kē), **Angelo**, Naples, 1760 —Paris, 1814; dramatic composer.

Tarditi (tär-dē'-tē), **Orazio**, d. after 1670; from 1648, maestro Faenza Cath.; composer.

Tartini (tär-tē'-nē), **Giuseppe**, Pirano, Istria, April 8, 1692—Padua, Feb. 26, 1770; eminent violinist, composer and scientist; at first he studied for the priesthood at his father's wish; then law, finally mus.; apparently self-taught as a violinist. A charge of abduction, due to his secret marriage with a niece of Cardinal Cornaro, led him to take refuge in the Franciscan monastery at Assisi, where for two years he practiced the vln. and studied comp. After a reconciliation he returned to Padua. Later he heard the violinist Veracini at Venice, and sending his wife to relations, retired to Ancona for further study. 1714, he discovered the combinational tones (v. D. D., "RESULTANT") and utilised them in perfecting intonation; 1721, solo-violinist and cond. at St. Antonio, Padua; 1723–25, chamber-mus. to Count Kinsky, Prague; 1728, founded a vln.-school at Padua; pub. treatises on harm. and acoustics; he published 18 vln.-concertos, 50 sonatas with bass, etc., incl. the famous, posthumous "Il Trillo del

Diavolo," an effort to reproduce a sonata played to him by the devil in a dream. Biog. Fanzago (Padua, 1770); J. A. Hiller (1784), Fayolle (1810).

Tasca (täs'-kä), **P. Ant.** (Baron), Noto, Sicily, April 1, 1864—May 14, 1934; composer of opera "*A Santa Lucia,*" succ. in Germany, 1902; symph., string quartet, etc.

Taskin (täs-kǎň), (1) **Pascal,** Theux (Liége), 1723—Paris, 1793; celebrated instr.-maker in Paris; introd. the piano-pedal worked by the foot instead of the knee; inv. leather tangents for clavichord, the armandine, etc. (2) **Jos. Pascal,** 1750—1829; nephew of above; keeper of the King's Instruments. (3) **H. Jos.,** Versailles, 1779—Paris, 1852; son of above; organist. (4) **(Emile) Alex.,** Paris, 1853—1897; grandson of (3); barytone.

Tauber (tow'-běr), **Richard** (rightly **Ernst Seiffert**), b. Linz, Austria, May 16, 1892; tenor; studied at Hoch Cons., Frankfort, with Carl Beines; début as "Tamino" in "*Magic Flute,*" Chemnitz, 1913; mem. Dresden Op., 1914–24; after latter year sang principally at Vienna and Berlin State Ops., also in Paris, Salzburg, Munich, etc.; won wide popularity in the light operas of Lehár, in whose "*Land of Smiles*" he later made London début; 1st Amer. appearances in recitals, 1931.

Taubert (tow'-běrt), (1) **(K. Gf.) Wm.,** Berlin, 1811—1891; noted pianist and composer of operas, incid. mus. to Shakespeare, etc.; pupil of Neidthardt, Berger and Klein; ct.-cond. at Berlin. (2) **Otto,** Naumburg-on-Saale, June 26, 1833—Torgau, Aug. 1, 1903; pupil of O. Claudius and "prefect" of the cath.-choir; 1863, prof., cantor and cond. at Torgau; pub. treatises; composer. (3) **Ernst Eduard,** Regenwalde, Pomerania, Sept. 25, 1838—Berlin, July, 14, 1934; studied at the Stern Cons., Berlin; Prof., 1898; pub. chamber-mus., etc.

Taubmann (towp'-män), **Otto,** Hamburg, March 8, 1859—Berlin, July 4, 1929; mus. director; pupil Dresden Cons.; 1886–89 dir. Wiesbaden Cons.; 1891 theatre cond. in St. Petersburg; from 1895 in Berlin as critic; c. mass with orch. (1898), choral drama "*Sängerweihe*" (Elberfeld, 1904), "Psalm 13" with orch., etc.

Taudou (tō-doo), **A.** (Antonin Barthélémy), Perpignan, France, Aug. 24, 1846—Paris, July 6, 1925; violinist; pupil of Paris Cons., winning Grand prix de Rome, 1889; member of the Opéra-orch.; from 1883, prof. of harm. at the Cons.; c. vln.-concerto, etc.

Tausch (towsh), **Fz.,** Heidelberg, 1762—Berlin, 1817; clarinettist and composer.

Tausig (tow'-zǐkh), (1) **Aloys,** 1817—1885; pianist and composer, pupil of Thalberg. (2) **Karl,** Warsaw, Nov. 4, 1841—(of typhoid fever), Leipzig, July 17, 1871; remarkable piano-virtuoso; son and pupil of above; and of Liszt; début, Berlin, 1858; lived Dresden and Vienna as notable cond.; 1865 founded a sch. at Berlin; c. brilliant exercises, transcriptions, etc.

Tauwitz (tow'-vǐts), **Eduard,** Glatz, Silesia, 1812—Prague, 1894; conductor; c. more than 1,000 comps. incl. 3 operas.

Tav'erner, (1) **John,** d. Boston, England; organist and composer at Oxford, 1530. (2) **Rev. J.,** d. Stoke Newington, 1638; organist and composer.

Tayber. Vide TEYBER.

Tay'lor, (1) **Edw.,** Norwich, Engl., 1784—Brentwood, 1863; bass, conductor, critic, lecturer and writer. (2) **Franklin,** Birmingham, Engl., Feb. 5, 1843—London, 1919; pianist and teacher; pupil of C. Flavell (pf.) and T. Redsmore (org.); also of Leipzig Cons.; 1876–82, prof. Nat. Training Sch., and from 1883, at the R. C. M.; Pres. of Acad. for the Higher Development of pf.-playing; writer and translator. (3) **(Joseph) Deems,** b. New York, Dec. 22, 1885; composer, critic, editor; grad. N. Y. U., from which also hon. Mus. D., 1927; mem. editorial staff, Nelson Encyclopedia, 1906–07; Encyclopedia Britannica, 1908; assistant Sunday ed., N. Y. *Tribune,* 1916; served as correspondent for *Tribune* in France, 1916–17; associate ed., *Collier's Weekly,* 1917–19; music critic, N. Y. *World,* 1921–25; ed., *Musical America,* 1927–29; mem. producing board, Amer. Op. Co., advisory board, Encyclopedia Brittanica; member, Nat'l Institute of Arts and Letters, Society for the Publication of American Music, Authors' League of America; c. musical comedy, "*The Echo*," prod. on Broadway, 1910; symph. poem, "*The Siren Song*," awarded National Fed. of Music Clubs prize, 1912; (cantatas) "*The Chambered Nautilus*" and "*The Highwayman*," latter for MacDowell Fest., 1914; suite for orch., "*Through the Looking Glass*"; rhapsody for small orch., "*Portrait of a Lady*"; (pantomime) "*A Kiss in Xanadu*"; symph. poem, "*Jurgen*" commissioned by N. Y. Symph., 1925; suite for jazz orch., "*Circus Day*," 1925, later arranged for symph. orch.; (operas) "*The King's Henchman*" (to libretto by Edna St. Vincent Millay), commissioned by Met. Op. Co., 1927; "*Peter Ibbetson*" (after Du Maurier novel), commissioned by Metropolitan, 1930–31; incid. music to Obey's drama "*Lucrece*" for Katharine Cornell; also choral works and arrangements, songs, piano pieces; has appeared as guest cond. of his works with leading Amer. orchs.; author of magazine articles; consultant in music for Columbia Broadcasting System.

Tchaïkovsky (or **Tschaïkowsky**, etc.) (tshä-ē-kôf'-shkĭ), Peter Iljitch, Wotkinsk, in the Government of Wiätka, May 7, 1840—(of cholera) Petersburg, Nov. 6, 1893; eminent Russian composer. Studied law, and entered the government civil service; did not take up mus. seriously till 22; then entered the newly founded Petersburg Cons., under Zaremba and A. Rubinstein, 1865, winning a prize medal for Schiller's ode "*An die Freude*" (also used in Beethoven's 9th symph.); 1866–77, instructor of harm. there; then lived Petersburg, Italy, Switzerland, as composer. He visited England and appeared at Phil. Concerts, 1888 and '89; visited New York for the dedication of the new Carnegie Music Hall, and cond. his own compositions. 1893, Mus. Doc. *h. c.*, Cambridge. Writer, and translator of harm. text-books. C. 11 Russian operas, incl. "*The Voyevode*" (Moscow, 1869), "*Opritchnnyk*" (Petersb., 1874), "*Vakula, the Smith*" (Petersb., 1876); "*Jevgenjie Onegin*"; 1879, "*Eugene Onegin*," in German (Hamburg, 1892), and posthumous "*Pique Dame*" (Vienna ct.-th., 1902); 3 ballets, "*Le Lac des Cygnes*" (op. 20), "*La Belle au Bois Dormant*"

(1890), and "*Le Casse-Noisette*" (op. 71); a coronation cantata with orch.; 2 masses; 6 symphs., incl. No. 6 in B minor, the famous "*Pathétique*"; 7 symph. poems, "*The Tempest*," "*Francesca da Rimini*," "*Manfred*," "*Romeo and Juliet*" (a fantasy-overture); "*Hamlet*," "*Fatum*," and "*Le Voyevode*" (symph. ballad); 4 orch. suites incl. "*Mozartiana*;" 3 overtures "*1812*" (op. 49), "*Triomphale*" on the Danish natl. hymn; "*L'Orage*"; "Marche slave," coronation march; 3 pf.-concertos; a pf.-fantasia with orch.; vln.-concerto; capriccio for 'cello with orch.; string-sextet "*Souvenir de Florence*," 3 string-quartets, a pf.-trio, pieces for vln. and 'cello; and pf.-pcs., incl. "*Souvenir de Hapsal*," sonata "*The Seasons*," 12 characteristic pcs., "*Kinder Album*"; 6 duets, Russian songs, etc. Also pub. a harmony; his "*Erinnerungen*" and translations of Gevaert, etc. Among many biographical works are those in English by Evans, Lee, Newmarch, Ronald, Bowen and Meck; the one by Mrs. Newmarch containing extracts from T's. critical writings and the diary of his 1888 tour. The composer's bro. Modeste pub. a "*Life and Letters of T.*", 1906.

Tebaldini (tä-bäl-dē'-nē), Giovanni, b. Brescia, Sept. 7, 1864; historian; pupil Milan Cons., and in musical history of Amelli, Haberl and Haller; 1889 cond. at St. Mark's, Venice; 1894 at San Antonio, Padua; from 1897, dir. Parma Cons., after 1902 church cond. at Loreto; 1926, in Naples as prof.; wrote historical works, and c. orch., also church music.

Tedesco (tä'-děs'-kō), Ignaz (Amadeus), Prague, 1817—Odessa, Nov. 13, 1882; brilliant pianist ("the Hannibal of octaves"); composer.

Telemann (tä'-lĕ-män), (1) G. Philipp, Magdeburg, March 14, 1681—Hamburg, June 25, 1767; mainly self-taught; conductor; 1709, ct.-cond.; he overshadowed J. S. Bach in contemporary esteem and was one of the most prolific and facile composers incl. 40 operas, 44 passions, etc.; autobiog., 1731. (2) G. Michael, Plön, Holstein, 1748—Riga, 1831; grandson of above; cantor, theorist and comp.

Tel'ford. Vide FRANCIS BOOTT.

432 DICTIONARY OF MUSICIANS

Tel'lefsen, Thos. Dyke Acland, Trondheim, Norway, 1823—Paris, 1874; pianist and composer.

Telman'yi, Emil, b. Arad, Hungary, June 22, 1892; violinist; pupil of Moritz Unger, Hubay, Koessler and Herzfeld; début in Berlin, 1911, playing Elgar concerto; toured U. S. and Europe; m. daughter of Carl Nielsen, composer; res. in Copenhagen.

Tem'pleton, J., Riccarton, Scotland, 1802—New Hampton, near London, 1886; tenor.

Tenaglia (tä-näl'-yä), **Anton Fran.,** b. Florence; conductor at Rome; c. the first known opera using an aria da capo, "*Clearco,*" 1661.

Ten Brink. Vide BRINK, TEN.

Tenducci (ten-doot'-chē), **Giusto F.,** b. Siena, 1736; famous male operatic soprano.

Ten Kate. Vide KATE, TEN.

Ternina (tär-nē'-nä), **Milka,** b. Begisše, Croatia, Dec. 19, 1863; notable dramatic soprano; studied with Gänsbacher; début Leipzig, 1883; then sang Graz and Bremen; 1890 Munich, named "court-singer"; sang in Bayreuth and in America 1899–1904 (Met. Op. Co.).

Terpan'der, b. Antissa, Lesbos, 7th cent. B. C.; called the "Father of Greek music."

Terrabugio (tär-rä-boo'-jō), **Giuseppe,** Primiero, May 13, 1843—Jan. 9, 1933; writer; pupil of Rheinberger, etc.; from 1883 editor of *Musica Sacra* at Milan, and active in the reform of church music; author of organ methods; c. overtures, 12 masses, and much church music.

Terradellas (Terradeglias) (tär-rä-děl'-läs or däl'-yäs), **Domingo** (Domenico), Barcelona, Spain (baptised, Feb. 13, 1711)—Rome, 1751; dram. composer.

Ter'ry, (1) Sir **Richard Runciman,** Ellington, 1865—London, April 18, 1938; organist; 1890–92 at Elston School, then in Antigua, West Indies, at St. John's Cathedral; 1896–1901 Downside Abbey; 1901–24 at Westminster Cathedral; active in reviving early English Catholic music. (2) **Charles Sanford,** Newport Pagnell, Oct. 24, 1864—Aberdeenshire, Nov. 5, 1936; studied Clare Coll., Cambridge; after 1903 prof. at the Univ. of Aberdeen; honorary Mus. Doc., Edinburgh; founded 1st competition

fest. in Scotland, 1909; a specialist in the music of Bach, of whom he wrote biog. and many other studies; also tr. cantata texts into English.

Terschak (tĕr'-shäk), **Ad.,** Prague, 1832—Breslau, 1901; flutist; pupil of Zierer, Vienna Cons.; toured; c. flute-pcs.

Ter'tis, Lionel, b. West Hartlepool, England, Dec. 29, 1876; viola virtuoso; studied at Leipzig and R. Coll. of Music, London, originally piano, then vln. and viola; he is the most eminent British performer on last instrument and a number of composers have written works for him; has toured United States.

Terziani (tĕr-tsĭ-ä'-nē), **Eugenio,** Rome, 1824—1889; prof., conductor and dram. composer.

Teschner (tĕshĭ-nĕr), **Gv. Wm.,** Magdeburg, 1800—Dresden, 1883; teacher, composer and editor.

Tesi-Tramontini (tä'-zē-trä-mŏn-tē'-nē), **Vittoria,** Florence, Feb. 13, 1700 —Vienna, 1775; famous contralto.

Tessarin (tĕs'-sä-rēn), **Fran.,** Venice, Dec. 3, 1820—Rome, June 30, 1889; pianist and teacher; pupil of A. Fanno and G. B. Ferrari; c. opera "*L' Ultimo Abencerragio*" (Venice, 1858); a cantata, etc.

Tessarini (tĕs-sä-rē'-nē), **Carlo,** b. Rimini, 1690; famous violinist, writer and composer.

Testoré (tĕs-tō'-rä), (1) **Carlo Giu.,** vln.-maker at Milan, ca. 1687—1710, with his sons (2) **Carlo A.** and (3) **Pietro A.**

Tetrazzini (tĕt-rä-tsē'-nē), **Luisa,** b. Florence, 1871—Milan, April 28, 1940; soprano; pupil of Ceccherini, and her sister Eva, wife of Cleofonte Campanini; début 1895 as "Inez" in "*L'Africaine,*" Teatro Pagliano, Florence; later at Rome and elsewhere, touring widely in Russia and South America; a favourite in San Francisco, her fame had not reached eastward till after a season of great success at Covent Garden, 1907, she made a sensation at the Manhattan Opera, N. Y., 1908–10; Chicago Op., 1913–14; she long held a foremost position among the world's sopranos in opera and concert.

Teyber (or **Tayber**) (tī'-bĕr), (1) **Anton,** Vienna, 1754—1822; conductor, cembalist and composer. (2) **Fz.,**

Vienna, 1756—1810; bro. of above; organist and dram. composer.

Teyte (tāt), **Maggie** (rightly **Tate**), b. Wolverhampton, England, April 17, 1890; soprano; studied R. Coll. of Music and with Jean de Reszke; début as "Zerlina," Monte Carlo, 1907; sang with Paris Op.-Comique, Beecham Op. Co., Chicago Op., 1911–14; Boston Op., 1915–17; Covent Garden, 1923, 1930; has also appeared with orchs. and in recital.

Thadewaldt (tä'-dĕ-vält), **Hermann**, Bodenhagen, Pomerania, April 8, 1827—Berlin, Feb. 11, 1909; 1850–55, bandm. at Düsseldorf; 1893–95, cond. at Dieppe; 1857 at Berlin. Founded (1872) Allgemeine Deutscher Musikverband.

Thalberg (täl'-bĕrkh), (1) **Sigismund**, Geneva, Jan. 7, 1812—Naples, April 27, 1871; famous piano-virtuoso and composer. "Being the son of Prince Dietrichstein, who had many wives without being married, **T.** had several brothers of different family names" (Grove). His mother was the Baroness von Wetzlar. Both of the parents took the greatest interest in his education. He was intended for a diplomatic career, but after his succ. as a pianist at 14, gave himself up to mus. He had some tuition from Hummel (pf.) and Sechter (comp.), but chiefly from Mittag, a bassoonist. At 16 three florid compositions appeared; at 18 a pf.-concerto. The same year he toured Germany with much succ.; 1834, ct.-pianist at Vienna; 1835, he conquered Paris, and later the rest of Europe. 1843, he m. Mme. Boucher, daughter of Lablache; 1851, his first opera "Florida," failed in London, and 1855, "Cristina di Svezia" failed in Vienna. He then toured Brazil (1855), and 1856, United States; retiring in 1858 to his villa at Posilippo, near Naples. 1862, Paris and London; 1863, second Brazilian tour; 1864, retired again. He was remarkable for his legato effects and for the singing-tone, Liszt saying "Thalberg is the only artist who can play the violin on the keyboard." He originated the subsequently abused scheme of dividing a central melody between the two thumbs, and enveloping it in arpeggiated ornament. His comps. include many florid transcriptions of opera-tunes,

also a grand concerto, 6 nocturnes, "La Cadence," and "Marche funèbre variée," etc. (2) **Marcian**, b. Odessa, 1877; pianist; pupil of Leipzig Cons.; toured in Europe; after 1913 teacher of advanced students at Cincinnati Conservatory.

Thayer (thā'-ĕr), (1) **Alex. Wheelock**, South Natick, Mass., Oct. 22, 1817—Trieste, July 15, 1897; graduated Harvard, 1843; was librarian there for some years; 1849 went to Europe and began materials for life of Beethoven; 1862, America as journalist; 1854 returned to Germany and frequently afterwards as his means permitted; 1862, U. S. consular agent at Vienna; later, till death, consul at Trieste; besides many articles he wrote a great but uncompleted life of Beethoven; though written in English it was first pub. in a German trans. by H. Deiters, in 5 vols. (Berlin, 1866–1908). The English edition, completed by H. E. Krehbiel, was pub. 1921, under the sponsorship of the Beethoven Ass'n, N. Y. (3 vols.). (2) **(Whitney) Eugene**, Mendon, Mass., 1838—Burlington, Vermont, 1889; organist, editor, lecturer and composer.

Theile (tī'-lĕ), **Jn.**, Naumburg, 1646—1724; conductor and composer.

Theo'deri'cus, Sixtus. Vide DIETRICH.

Thern (tĕrn), (1) **Karl (Karolý)**, Iglo, Upper Hungary, 1817—Vienna, 1886; conductor, professor and dram. composer. His sons and pf.-pupils (also pupils of Moscheles and Reinecke), (2) **Willi** (Ofen, June 22, 1847—Vienna, April 7, 1911) and (3) **Louis** (Pesth, Dec. 18, 1848—Vienna, March 12, 1920) were teachers.

Thibaud (tē'-bō), (1) **Jos.**, b. Bordeaux, Jan. 25, 1875; pianist; pupil of L. Diémer, Paris Cons., taking 1st prize for pf.-playing, 1892; 1895–96, accompanied Marsick to America. (2) **Jacques**, b. Bordeaux, Sept. 27, 1880; violinist; pupil of Marsick at Paris Cons., winning first prize at 16; played at the Café Rouge and was engaged for Colonne's orch., became soloist 1898; has toured widely in Europe and America; one of the leading virtuosi of the vln.; mem. of trio with Casals and Cortot.

Thibaut IV. (tē-bō-kătr), King of Navarre; Troyes, 1201—Pamplona, 1253; composer.

Thibaut (tē'-bowt), **Anton Fr. Justus,** Hameln, 1774—Heidelberg, 1840; professor and writer.

Thiele (tē'-lĕ), **Jno. Fr. Ludwig,** Harzgerode, near Bernburg, 1816—Berlin, 1848; organist and composer.

Thierfelder (tēr'-fĕlt-ĕr), **Albert (Wm.),** Mühlhausen, April 30, 1846—Rostock, Jan. 5, 1924; pupil of Leipzig Univ. and Dr. Phil.; studied with Hauptmann, Richter and Paul; cond. various cities; from 1887 mus.-dir. and prof. Rostock Univ.; writer of important treatises; prod. 5 operas, incl. succ. *"Der Heirathstein"* (text and music) (Rostock, 1898), *"Zlatorog,"* and *"Frau Holde,"* for soli, chorus, and orch., and 2 symphs., etc.

Thieriot (tē'-rĭ-ō), (1) **Paul Emil,** Leipzig, 1780 — Wiesbaden, 1831; violinist. (2) **Fd.,** Hamburg, April 7, 1838—Aug. 4, 1919; pupil of E. Marxsen, and Rheinberger; mus.-dir. at Hamburg, Leipzig, and Glogau; lived in Hamburg; c. symph. fantasy *"Loch Lomond,"* vln.-concerto, etc.

Thill (tēl), **Georges,** b. Paris, 1899; tenor, studied with de Lucia, Pandolfini, Dupré, and at Paris Cons.; début, Paris Op. 1924; sang at Monte Carlo, Brussels, Covent Garden, La Scala, Buenos Aires, and with Met. Op. Co., 1931–32.

Thillon (tē-yôn), **Anna** (née **Hunt**), London, 1819—Torquay, 1903; very succ. soprano; pupil of Bordogni, Tadolini, and Thillon, marrying the last named at 15; début, Paris, 1838; 1844, Auber's *"Crown Diamonds"* was written for her; 1850–54, in America, the first to produce opera in San Francisco; retired 1867 to Torquay.

Thimus (tē'-moos), **Albert,** Freiherr von, Cologne, 1806—1846; writer.

Thoinan, E. Vide ROQUET.

Thoma (tō'-mä), **Rudolf,** Lesewitz, near Steinau-on-Oder, Feb. 22, 1829 —Breslau, Oct. 20, 1908; pupil of R. Inst. for Church-mus., Berlin; 1857, cantor, Hirschberg, then Breslau, 1870, "R. Music Dir."; founder of a singing-soc., dir. of a sch.; c. 2 operas, 2 oratorios, etc.

Thomas (tō-mäs) (**Chas. Louis**), **Ambroise,** Metz, Aug. 5, 1811—Paris, Feb. 12, 1896; pupil of Paris Cons.; winning 1st pf.-prize, 1829; harm., 1830; Grand prix de Rome (1832),

with cantata *"Hermann et Ketty."* After 3 years in Italy, returned to Paris, and up to 1843, prod. nine stage-pcs., at the Opéra and Op.-Com. with fair succ. The failure of the last was retrieved after a silence of 5 years by *"Le Cid"* (1849), *"Le Songe d' Une Nuit d'Été"* (1850, both at the Op.-Com.). 1851 elected to the Académie. The next 6 operas were only moderately succ.; but *"Mignon"* (Op.-Com., 1866) made a world-wide succ. and *"Hamlet"* (Opéra, 1868) a lasting succ. in Paris, where it is still sung. *"Gille et Gillotin"* (1874), *"Françoise de Rimini"* (1882), and the ballet, *"La Tempête"* (Opéra, 1889), were his last dram. works; 1871, dir. of the Cons.; 1845, Chev.; 1858, Officier; 1868, Commander of the Legion of Honour. C. also cantatas; messe solennelle (Nôtre-Dame, 1865); many excellent *"chœurs orphéoniques"* (3-part male choruses), etc.

Thomas (täm'-üs), (1) **J.,** Bridgend, Glamorganshire, March 1, 1826— March 19, 1913; 1861 made "Pencerdd Gwalia," *i.e.,* Chief Bard of Wales; pupil at the R. A. M.; 1851, harpist, R. It. Opera; toured Europe, 1852–62 played at the Gewandhaus, etc. 1862, cond. of the first annual concert of Welsh mus., with a chorus of 400, and 20 harps; 1871, harpist to the Queen; leader in the Eisteddfodau, and harp-prof. R. C. M. C. dram. cantata *"Llewelyn"* (1863); a Welsh scene *"The Bride of Neath Valley"* (1866); patriotic songs, with harp; 2 harp-concertos, etc. (2) **Lewis Wm.,** Bath, April, 1826— London, 1896; concert-bass, editor and critic. (3) **Robert Harold,** Cheltenham, July 8, 1834—London, July 29, 1885; pianist; pupil of Sterndale Bennett, C. Potter, and Blagrove; début 1850; pf.-prof. R. A. M. and Guildhall Sch., London; c. overtures, etc. (4) **Theodor(e),** Esens, East Friesland, Oct. 11, 1835 —Chicago, Jan. 4, 1905; eminent cond., educator and stimulator of mus. taste in America; son and pupil of a violinist, at 6 played in public; at 10 was brought to New York, where he soon entered an orch.; 1851, toured as soloist, later with Jenny Lind, Grisi, etc.; 1855, began the Mason and Thomas Soirées (with DR. WM. MASON); 1864–69 cond.

"Symph. Soirées"; 1869 made concert-tour with an orch. of 54; 1876 made Philadelphia Centennial with ill-succ. leading to disbandment; 1878–80, pres. Cincinnati Coll. of Mus.; 1880, cond. New York, Philh. Orch.; from 1888, dir. Chicago Cons., also cond. Chicago Orch. (5) **Arthur Goring**, Ralton Park, near Eastbourne, Sussex, Nov. 21, 1850— London, March 20, 1892; took up music at 24 and studied with Emile Durand, later with Sullivan and Prout R. A. M., London, winning Lucas Prize, 1879; lived in London, C. 2 operas, v. succ. *"Esmeralda"* (Drury Lane, 1883, · New York, 1900); *"Nadeshda"* (1885); *"The Golden Web"* (score finished by Waddington, Liverpool, 1893); a choral ode, *"The Sun Worshippers"* (Norwich, 1881), v. succ. cantata, *"The Swan and the Skylark"* (Birmingham, 1894, instrumented by C. V. Stanford); psalm with orchestra (1878); 3 vocal scenes, *"Hero and Leander"* (1880), etc. (6) **John Charles**, b. Meyersdale, Pa.; notable barytone; early designed for medical career, but while studying in a Baltimore medical coll., won scholarship at Peabody Cons.; pupil of Blanche S. Blackman and Adelin Fermin; début, 1912, in a stage production; sang in operettas in N. Y. where he made début as recitalist, 1921; op. first appearance in Washington, D. C., in *"Aïda"*; sang for several seasons after 1925 with La Monnaie Op., Brussels; 1929, with Phila. Grand Op.; Chicago Op., 1930–31; mem. Met. Op. after 1933; also with San Francisco and Los Angeles Op. Cos.; has wide following as concert singer and in radio.

Thomé (tō-mā), **Francis** (rightly **François Luc. Jos.**), Port Louis, Mauritius, Oct. 18, 1850—Paris, Nov. 16, 1909; pupil of Marmontel (pf.), and Duprato (theory), Paris Cons.; lived in Paris as teacher and critic; c. *"Roméo et Juliette"*; a mystery, *"L'Enfant Jésus"*; symph. ode *"Hymne à la Nuit"* and many pop. songs and pf.-pcs.

Thomp'son, (1) **Randall**, b. New York, April 12, 1899; composer; grad. Harvard Univ.; studied music there and with Ernest Bloch; 1922, awarded Fellowship at American Acad. in Rome; also Guggenheim Fellowship, 1929–31; for a time asst. prof. of music, Wellesley Coll. and lecturer on music at Harvard; 1931–32, cond. Dessoff Choirs, New York; c. 2 symphonies (the second, in E minor, perf. by Rochester Philh. and N. Y. Philh., 1933–34); *"Piper at the Gates of Dawn"* for orch.; *"Seven Odes of Horace"* for chorus, 3 with orch. accompaniment; *"Americana,"* setting of amusing news notes from provincial papers, quoted from *American Mercury*, for chorus; *"The Peaceable Kingdom,"* oratorio (Boston, 1935–36); also piano sonata and suite; important string quartet; songs, piano pieces, etc. (2) **Oscar**; critic, N. Y. *Post*, 1927–34; N. Y. *Sun*, from 1936, vice Henderson; author; *"Debussy," "How to Listen to Music," "Practical Music Criticism,"* etc.; ed., *Musical America*.

Thomson (täm'-sŭn), (1) **Geo.**, Limekilns, Fife, 1757—Leith, 1851; notable coll. and pub. of Scotch, Welsh and Irish melodies, to which he had special instrumental accompaniments written by Beethoven. Pleyel, etc. (2) **Virgil**, b. Kansas City, Kan., 1896; composer; studied U. S. and Paris; has c. much chamber music of witty and ironic style, attracting particular attention for his opera, *"Four Saints in Three Acts,"* to text by Gertrude Stein, prod. in Hartford, Conn., and N. Y., 1934; also masses for men's and women's voices; *"Saints' Procession"* for male voices and piano; *"Five Phrases from the Song of Solomon"* for soprano and percussion; *"Sonata da Chiesa"*; vln. sonata, *"Oraison Funèbre"* for chamber orch.; *"Three Psalms"* for feminine chorus; smaller works for piano and voice.

Thomson (tôn-sôn), **César**, Liége, March 17, 1857—Lugano, Aug. 21, 1931; notable violinist; from 7 pupil of Liége Cons.; at 11, winning the gold medal; then pupil of Vieuxtemps, Léonard, Wieniawski and Massart; 1873–83, chamber-mus. to Baron von Derwies at Lugano, and a member of Bilse's orch., Berlin; 1883–97, teacher at Liége Cons.; 1898, vln.-prof. Brussels Cons. (vice Ysaye); toured widely; after 1894 United States; 1924 taught at Ithaca, N. Y., Cons.

Thooft (toft), **Willem Frans**, Amsterdam, July 10, 1829—Rotterdam,

Aug. 27, 1900; pupil of Dupont, Hauptmann and Richter; founded the German opera at Rotterdam, 1860; c. choral prize symphony, "*Karl V.*" (1861); 3 other symphs., an opera, etc.

Thor'borg, Kerstin; Swedish contralto; esp. noted as a Wagnerian singer; has appeared with succ. in Vienna, Prague and elsewhere on the Continent; 1936, at Salzburg Fest. and at Covent Garden; engaged for Met. Op. Co., 1936–37.

Thorne (thôrn), **Edw. H.**, Cranborne, Dorset, May 9, 1834 — London, Dec. 26, 1916; pianist and org.; chorister under Elvey; organist various churches; from 1891, at St. Anne's, Soho, London; cond. St. Anne's Choral and Orch'l Soc. C. Psalm 57, with orch.; Magnificat and Nunc dimittis with orch. and organ; an overture; "*Sonata elegia*" for pf.

Thrane (trä-ně), **Waldemar**, Christiania, 1790–1828; violinist; c. overtures, etc.

Thuille (too-ē'-lě), **L. (Wm. Ands. M.)**, Bozen, Tyrol, Nov. 30, 1861— Munich, Feb. 5, 1907; pupil of Jos. Pembaur (pf., cpt.), at Innsbruck; Baermann (pf.) and Rheinberger (comp.) Munich Mus.-Sch.; from 1883, teacher of pf. and theory there; also cond. "*Liederhort*"; 1891, R. Prof. of Mus.; c. succ. opera "*Theuerdank*" (Munich, 1897, Luitpold Prize), opera "*Lobetanz*" (Carlsruhe and Berlin, 1898); "*Romantic*" overture, sextet for piano and wind, sonatas, etc.

Thurner (toor'-něr), **Fr. Eugen**, Montbeliard, 1785—Amsterdam, 1827; oboe-virtuoso; composer.

Thurnmayer. Vide AVENTINUS.

Thurs'by, Emma, Brooklyn, N. Y., Nov. 17, 1857—New York, July 4, 1931; famous concert-soprano; pupil of Meyer (Brooklyn), Errani (New York) and Mme. Rudersdorff (Boston), then of Lamperti and San Giovanni, Milan; concert-début, America, Plymouth Church, Brooklyn, 1875; sang in concert and oratorio, and with Gilmore (1875); frequently toured Europe and America with great succ.; compass c'–e'''

Tib'bett, Lawrence, b. Bakersfield, Cal., Nov. 16, 1896; barytone; studied with Joseph Dupuy, Basil Ruysdael, and Frank La Forge; early acted on dram. stage; recital début, Los Angeles, 1917; sang in opera at Hollywood Bowl, 1923, and same year made début with Met. Op. Co., where in 1925 he leaped into sudden prominence with his dram. perf. as "Ford" in "*Falstaff*"; he is a singing actor of much resource and a finished vocalist; has since sung leading rôles in Italian, French, German and English works, particularly character parts; created "Col. Ibbetson" in Deems Taylor's "*Peter Ibbetson*" and "Brutus Jones" in Louis Gruenberg's "*Emperor Jones*"; has sung widely in concert and with orchs., also as "Don Juan" in Goossens' opera, Covent Garden, 1937, at Vienna, Prague, etc.

Tichatschek (tēkh'-ät-shěk), **Jos. Aloys**, Ober-Weckelsdorf, Bohemia, 1807— Dresden, 1886; tenor; created Wagner's "Rienzi" and "Tannhäuser."

Tieffenbrücker. Vide DUIFFOPRUGGAR.

Tiehsen (tě'-zěn), **Otto**, Danzig, 1817 —Berlin, 1849; c. comic opera.

Tiersch (tērsh), **Otto**, Kalbsrieth, Thuringia, 1838—Berlin, 1892; singing-teacher and theorist.

Tiersot (tǐ-ěr'-sō), **(J. Bapt. Elisée) Julien**, Bourg-en-Bresse, France, July 5, 1857—Aug., 1936; pupil of Franck, Paris Cons.; from 1883, asst. libr. there; pub. essays, incl. "*Histoire de la chanson populaire en France*," Bordun Prize, 1885; c. "*Hellas*" for soli, chorus and orch.; rhapsodies on popular airs, etc.

Tiessin (tě'-sěn), **Heinz**, b. Königsberg, Germany, April 10, 1887; composer; pupil of Stern Cons., and of Wilhelm Klatte; critic of Berlin *Allgemeine Zeitung*, 1912–17; asst. cond. at Berlin Op. and Volksbühne, and dir. of Univ. Orch. there; after 1925 taught comp. at Berlin Hochschule; c. (opera) "*Revolutionsdrama*" (Berlin, 1927); (dance drama) "*Salambo*" (Duisburg, 1929); several symphonies, other orch. works, chamber music, piano pieces, songs.

Tietjens (rightly **Titiens**) (tēt'-yěns), **Therese Johanne Alex.**, of Hungarian parents, Hamburg, July 17, 1831—London, Oct. 3, 1877; famous soprano; teachers unknown; début, Hamburg, 1849; from 1858, chiefly in London in grand and comic opera.

Til'borghs, Jos., Nieuwmoer, Sept. 28, 1830—?; theorist; pupil of Lemmens (org.) and Fétis (comp.), Brussels Cons.; from 1882, prof. of org.,

Ghent Cons.; and of cpt. Antwerp Mus.-Sch.; comp. organ-pieces and motets.

Till'metz, Rudolf, Munich, April 1, 1847—Jan. 25, 1915; flutist; pupil of Bohm; 1864 soloist in court orch.; 1883 teacher in Royal Musichsch., and cond. to Prince Ludwig Fd.; c. flute works.

Tilman (tēl'-män), **Alfred,** Brussels, 1848—1895; composer and pianist.

Tilmant (tēl'-mäṅ), **(1) Théophile Alex.,** Valenciennes, 1799—Asnières, 1878; conductor. His brother **(2) Alex.,** 1808—Paris, 1880; 'cellist.

Timanoff (tē'-män-ôf), **Vera,** b. Ufa, Russia, Feb. 18, 1855; pianist; pupil of L. Nowitzky, A. Rubinstein, Tausig and Liszt; lived in Peters-burg, Prague (1871) and Vienna (1872).

Tim'mermans, Armand, b. Antwerp, 1860; pupil of the Cons., and teacher in Antwerp, c. prize winning choral works.

Tinc'toris, Johannes (called **John Tinctor;** or Giov. Del Tintore; rightly **Jean de Vaerwere** (vär'-wä-rĕ), Poperinghe, ca. 1446 (or 35, some say 1450)—Nivelles, 1511; canon; wrote, 1477, the earliest known dict. of mus. (ca. 1475), etc.; composer.

Tinel (tē-nĕl'), **Edgar,** Sinay, Belgium, March 27, 1854—Brussels, Oct. 28, 1912; pianist and composer; son and pupil of a poor school-teacher and organist; pupil also of Brussels Cons.; 1st pf.-prize, 1873, and pub. op. 1, 4 nocturnes for solo-voice with pf.; 1877, won Grand prix de Rome w. cantata "*Klokke Roeland*" (op. 17); 1881, dir. Inst. for Sacred Mus. at Malines; 1888, prod. very succ. oratorio, "*Franciscus*" (op. 36); 1889, inspector State mus. schs.; 1896, prof. of cpt. and fugue, Brussels Cons.; pub. a treatise on Gregorian chant, and prod. a "*Grand Mass of the Holy Virgin of Lourdes,*" for 5 parts (op. 41), Te Deum, Alleluia, motets and sacred songs, incid. mus., pf.-pcs., etc.

Tiraboschi (tē-rä-bôs'-kē), **Girolamo,** Bergamo, 1731 — Modena, 1784; writer.

Tirindelli (tē-rĭn-dĕl'-lē), **P. Adolfo,** Conegliano, 1858—Rome, Feb. 6, 1937; pupil Milan Cons., then of Boniforti; cond. at Gorizia 3 years, then studied with Grün and Massart; 1887, vln.-prof. Liceo Benedetto

Marcello, Venice; 1893, dir., also cond. "Verdi Orchestra"; made Cavaliere, 1894; played with the Boston Symph. Orch. in 1895; 1896–1922 taught Cincinnati Cons., and led orch. there; afterward in Rome. C. 1-act opera "*L'Atenaide*" (Venice, 1892), etc.

Tischer (tĭsh'-ĕr), **Gerhard,** b. Lübnitz, Nov. 10, 1877; historian, Ph. D., Berlin, 1903; from 1904 teacher of musical history in Cologne; later pub. and editor.

Titelouze (tēt-looz), **Jean,** St. Omer, 1563—Rouen, Oct. 25, 1633; organ-ist; called the "founder of French organ music"; 1585 org. at St. Jean, Rouen, from 1588 at the cathedral there; c. mass, and organ works.

Titov or **Titoff** (tē'-tôf), **(1) Vas-sili,** 17th century church composer. **(2) Alexei Nikolaievich,** 1769—St. Petersburg, Nov. 2, 1827; Russian cavalry general; c. 13 operas. His brother **(3) Sergei N.,** b. 1770; c. operas and ballets. **(4) Nikolai Alexeivich,** St. Petersburg, May 10, 1800—Dec. 22, 1875; son of (2) called the "grandfather of Russian song"; a lieutenant-general, whose songs were the first to obtain foreign vogue; c. also popular dances and marches.

Toch (tôkh), **Ernst,** b. Vienna, Dec. 7, 1887; composer; pupil of Willi Rehberg in Frankfort (piano); 1913–14, taught comp. at Mannheim Hochsch., later privately; in com-position largely self-taught; one of the more original creators in modern musical idiom; visited U. S. as soloist in his piano concerto with Boston Symph., 1933, and estab. residence here as teacher and composer; c. (operas) "*Die Prinzessin auf der Erbse,*" "*Der Fächer*"; incid. music to Euripides' "*Bacchantes*"; "*Die Chinesische Flöte*" for soprano soloist and chamber orch.; several string quartets; 2 piano concertos; "*An mein Vaterland*" for org. and orch.; Five Pieces for chamber orch.; "*Bunte*" Suite for small orch.; Dance Suite for chamber orch.; concerto for 'cello and chamber orch.; "*Phan-tastische Nacht-Musik*" and Fantasy on the Chimes of Westminster for orch.; 2 Divertimenti for string duo; also many piano pieces, songs, etc.

Todi (tō'-dē), **Luiza Rosa** (née de Aguiar), Setubal, Portugal, Jan. 9,

1753—Lisbon, Oct. 1, 1833; famous mezzo-soprano; an actress at 15, then pupil of Perez; sang London, 1712; 1777 v. succ. at Madrid; 1783 provoked a famous rivalry with Mara; 1780 ct.-singer, Berlin.

Todt (tōt), **Joh.** Aug. **Wilhelm,** Düsterort, July 29, 1833—Stettin, Oct. 26, 1900; organist, cantor and composer.

Toeschi (tō-äs'-kē) (in German tä'-shē), (1) **Carlo Giu.** (rightly **Toesca della Castella-Monte**), Romagna, 1724—Munich, 1788, ct.-mus., director and composer. (2) **Jn. Bapt.,** Mannheim, ca. 1745—Munich, May, 1800; son and successor of above; noted violinist; c. 18 symphs., etc.

Tofano (tō-fä'-nō), **Gustavo,** Naples, Dec. 22, 1844—June 30, 1899; pupil at the Bologna Cons. and prof. there; pianist and composer.

Tofft, Alfred, Copenhagen, Jan. 2, 1865 —Jan. 30, 1931; pupil of Nebelong and Bohlmann; c. opera "*Vifandaka*" (Copenhagen, 1898), songs, etc.

Tofte (tōf'-tě), **Lars Waldemar,** Copenhagen, Oct. 21, 1832—June, 1907; court violinist and teacher at the Cons.

Tokat'yan, Armand, b. Alexandria, 1898; tenor Met. Op. from 1922.

Tolbecque (tōl'-běk), four Belgian brothers. (1) **Isidore Jos.,** Hanzinne, 1794—Vichy, 1871; conductor and composer. (2) **Jean. Bapt. Jos.,** 1797—Paris, 1869; violinist and conductor. (3) **Aug. Jos.,** 1801—Paris, 1869; violinist. (4) **Chas. Jos.,** Paris, 1806—1835; violinist and conductor. (5) **Aug.,** Paris, March 30, 1830—Niorte, March 8, 1919; son of (3); 'cellist; pupil of the Cons., and 1849 took 1st prize; 1865–71, teacher Marseilles Cons.; later 'cellist in the Paris Cons. concerts; pub. "*La Gymnastique du Violoncelle*" (op. 14); prod. succ. 1-act comic opera "*Après la Valse*" (Niort, 1895).

Toll'efsen, (1) **Augusta** (née **Schnabel**), b. Boise, Idaho, 1885; pianist; studied with Käthe Widmann, a pupil of Mme. Clara Schumann; and with Godowsky and Gallico; toured in Europe and U. S., with orchs. in N. Y.; mem. of Tollefsen Trio; m. Carl Tollefsen. (2) **Carl,** b. Hull, Yorkshire, England, 1882 (Scandinavian parents); violinist; pupil of Lichtenberg, Kneisel, Schradieck,

Goetschius and Rubin Goldmark; played in N. Y. Symph.; mem. of Schnabel Trio (afterward Tollefsen Trio); active as teacher.

Tol'lius, Jan. b. Amersfort, 1550 (?)— Copenhagen, 1603; church-cond. in Italian cities; 1601 court-cond. at Copenhagen; c. motets, madrigals, etc.

Tolstoi (tŏl'-stō-ē), **Count Theophil Matveievich,** 1809—St. Petersburg, March 4, 1881; critic under penname "Rostislav" and composer; studied singing with Rubini, comp. with Fuchs, Miller, Raimondi and Hebel; 1832 prod. opera "*Birichino di Parigi*," Naples; 1835 at St. Petersburg, its failure led Nicholas I. to forbid the Italian singers to appear in Russian works. He c. also songs.

Tomaschek, Jn. Wenzel (rightly **Jar Václav Tomášek**) (täm'-ä-shěk), Skutsch, Bohemia, April 17, 1774— Prague, April 3, 1850; notable pianist, organist; also c. operas and pf.-pcs.

Tomasini (tō-mä-sē'-nē), **Luigi (Aloysius),** Pesaro, 1741—Esterház, 1808; violinist and director; he had two daughters who sang in opera at Eisenstadt and 2 sons.

Tombelle (tōñ-běl'), **Fd. de la,** Paris, Aug. 3, 1854 — Castelnau-Feyrac, Aug. 13, 1928; pupil of Guilmant and Dubois, Paris Cons.; his quartet and symph. won 1st prize of the "Société des compositeurs;" Officer of Pub. Instruction, Paris; c. orch. suites, etc.

Tomeoni (tō-mä-ō'-nē), (1) **Florido,** Lucca, 1757—Paris, 1820; teacher and theorist. (2) **Pellegrino,** b. Lucca, ca. 1759; bro. of above; teacher and writer in Florence.

Tom'kins, (1) **Rev. Thos.,** Engl. composer, Gloucester, 1600. His son (2) **J.,** d. 1638; organist and composer. (3) **Thos.,** d. 1656; organist at Worcester cath.; composer; son of (1). (4) **Giles,** d. 1668; bro. and succ. of above. (5) **Robt.,** son of (2); 1641 one of the King's musicians.

Tommasi (tôm-mäs'-sē), **Giu. M.,** Cardinal, Alicante, Sicily, 1649—Rome, 1713; writer.

Tommasini (tŏ-mä-sē'-nē), **Vincenzo,** b. Rome, Sept. 17, 1880; composer; grad. Univ. of Rome; studied piano with Mazzarella, vln. with Pinelli, comp. with Falchi; won Rome Nat'l

Prize, 1912; mem. of St. Cecilia Acad.; c. a ballet, *"The Good-Humoured Ladies"* based on Scarlatti sonatas, which was prod. by Diaghileff; also 2 operas, *"Medée"* and *"Uguale Fortuna,"* heard, resp. at Trieste, 1906, and Rome, 1913; (orch.) *"Chiari di Luna," "Il Beato Regno," "Paesaggi Toscani,"* prelude, fanfare and fugue, *"Carnevale di Venezia";* 2 string quartets, sonata for vln. and piano, songs.

Ton'ning, Gerard, b. Stavanger, Norway, 1860—N. Y., 1940; comp. and teacher; pupil of Munich Cons.; 1887, active in Duluth as choral cond.; also led trio; after 1905 in Seattle; c. opera, *"Leif Erikson,"* instrumental works, songs, etc.

Topfer (tĕp'-fĕr), Jn. Gl., Niederrossla, Thuringia, 1791—Weimar, 1870; organist, writer and composer.

Topler (tĕp'-lĕr), Michael, Ullersdorf, Jan. 15, 1804—Brühl, Nov. 12, 1874; teacher and composer of church music.

Torchi (tôr'-kē), Luigi, Mordano, Bologna, Nov. 7, 1858—Sept. 18, 1920; graduate, Bologna Cons., 1876, then studied with Serrao (comp.) at Naples Cons. and at Leipzig Cons. where he c. a symph., an overture, a string quartet; 1885–91, prof. of mus. history, Liceo Rossini, Pesaro; then at Bologna Cons., 1895 also prof. of comp.; began a great 34-vol. coll. of the chief Italian works of the 15–18 centuries, *"L'arte musicale in Italia"* (7 vols. pub.).

Torelli (tō-rĕl'-lē), Giu., Verona, ca. 1660—Ansbach, 1708; violinist and composer; developer of the "concerto grosso."

Tor'rance, Rev. G. Wm., Rathmines, near Dublin, 1835—Kilkenny, Aug. 20, 1907; chorister, Dublin; organist at St. Andrew's, and St. Anne's; studied at Leipzig, 1856; 1866, priest; 1869, Melbourne, Australia; 1895, incumbent at St. John's there; Mus. Doc., *h. c.* Dublin, 1879; he returned to Ireland, 1897, and 1900 became canon at Kilkenny. His madrigal *"Dry be that tear,"* won Molyneux prize and London Madrigal Society medal, 1903; c. succ. oratorios, *"Abraham"* (Dublin, 1855), *"The Captivity"* (1864), and *"The Revelation"* (Melbourne, 1882), services, an opera, etc.

Torri (tôr'-rē), Pietro, ca. 1665—

Munich, 1737; court-conductor and dram. composer.

Tor'rington, Fr. Herbert, Dudley, Engl., Oct. 20, 1837—Toronto, 1917; pianist and conductor; articled pupil of Jas. Fitzgerald; at 16 organist at Bewdley; 1856–68, organist, Great St. James's Church, Montreal, Canada; also solo-violinist, cond. and band-master; his orch. represented Canada at the Boston Peace Jubilee, 1869; then teacher New Engl. Cons.; 1st vln. Handel and Haydn, and other socs.; from 1873, organist Metropolitan Ch., Toronto, Canada, and cond. Toronto Philh. Soc.; 1886, organised the first Toronto mus. festival; 1888, founded Toronto Coll. of Mus.; c. services, etc.

Toscanini (tŏs-kä-nē'-nē), Arturo, b. Parma, Italy, March 25, 1867; most eminent conductor of his period; pupil of the Cons. in his native city, where he won a diploma in 'cello playing and comp. in 1885; he had already participated ably in a concert tour as 'cellist the preceding year, incl. appearances at the Exposition in Turin; in the spring of 1886 he was engaged as 'cellist for the opera season in Rio de Janeiro, and his début as conductor occurred on the second night of the season, when he took over the orch. after the batonist of the occasion had been hissed by the public; he at once proved his mettle; and the perf. was a triumph. In 1887 he conducted in Turin the première of Catalani's *"Edmea."* He led many orchestral concerts there, incl. more than 40 programs during the Exposition of 1898, when he gave the first perfs. in Italy of Verdi's 3 sacred works, *"Stabat Mater," "Te Deum"* and *"Laudi alla Vergine."* He also appeared in Bologna and Genoa. In 1895 he gave the 1st Italian perfs. of Wagner's *"Götterdämmerung"* at the Regio in Turin. He conducted opera and symph. concerts at La Scala under the management of Gatti-Casazza from 1898 to 1908. When that impresario came to the Met. Op. in the latter year, he engaged Toscanini as conductor. T. remained in N. Y. until 1915, giving a long series of brilliant perfs., incl. the premières of works by Puccini, Dukas, Wolf-Ferrari, Montemezzi and Giordano, and conducting *"Göt-*

terdämmerung" and Gluck's *"Armide."* During this period in N. Y., he also led 2 symphonic concerts in 1913. He left the Met. as a result of a reported dissatisfaction with its artistic policy and returned to Italy in 1915, where he was active during the war as a conductor of concerts for welfare work. He toured the U. S. and Canada with an orch. composed of musicians from La Scala, and also led fests. in Turin and Milan in 1920. In the following year he became the mus. dir. at La Scala, a post which he retained until 1929. During this period he led the world premières of Boito's *"Nerone"* in 1924, of Puccini's posthumous opera *"Turandot"* in 1926. Beginning with the season of 1926–27 he was guest conductor of the N. Y. Philh. Orch. He immediately estab. a reputation as perhaps the most brilliant cond. who had ever appeared in N. Y. After 1928 he became permanent cond. of this orch., and later musical director, sharing the podium with several others during each season. In 1930 he took the orch. for a tour of leading Eur. cities. In summer of 1932 he conducted at the Bayreuth Fest., but severed his connection with Bayreuth later as the result of his disapproval of discriminations made by the Nat'l Socialist régime in that country against musicians of Jewish birth. He was one of a number of prominent musicians who addressed a cablegram of protest to the German govt. He led a few concerts (exchanging the Philh. bâton with Stokowski) at head of the Phila. Orch. in 1930–31. In 1933 he began a series of annual appearances at the Salzburg Fest., but resigned 1938; has also conducted brilliant concerts at London, Vienna and Paris. In 1936 he announced his resignation as cond. of the N. Y. Philh. Orch. because of the strain imposed by a regular post. His special virtues as a cond. consist in his fidelity to the composer's score, the extreme perfection of detail and the lyrical tone with which he endows even the most abstruse modern works. He invariably conducts without a score. He agreed to lead 10 concerts by a specially formed orch. for the Nat'l Broadcasting Co., 1937–38.

Tosel'li, Enrico, Florence, March **13,** 1883—Jan. 15, 1926; composer and pianist; pupil of Sgambati and Martucci; début Monte Carlo, 1896; played in London and America, 1901; he eloped with Princess Louise of Saxony, whom he m.; c. pop. operettas, songs and pf.-pieces; his *"Serenade"* esp. well-known.

Tosi (tō'-zē), **Pier Fran.,** Bologna, 1647 —London, 1727; celebrated contralto musico and singing-teacher.

Tosti (tôs'-tē), **Fran. Paolo,** Ortona, Abruzzi, April 7, 1846—Rome, Dec. 6, 1916; pupil of the R. C. di S. Pietro a Majella, Naples; subteacher there till 1869; then ct.-singing-teacher at Rome; 1875 sang with great succ. London, and lived there as a teacher; 1880, singing-master to the Royal family; 1894, prof. R. A. M.; pub. a coll. of *"Canti popolari abruzzesi"* (Milan), and c. pop. songs.

Tottmann (tôt'-män), **Carl Albert,** Zittau, July 31, 1837—near Leipzig, Feb. 26, 1917; studied Dresden, and with Hauptmann, at Leipzig Cons.; violinist in the Gewandhaus Orch.; teacher of theory and history at Leipzig, also lecturer; 1873, Prof., for his valuable compendium of vln.-literature; pub. also essays, etc.; c. a melodrama *"Dornröschen,"* Ave Maria, etc.

Toulmouche (tool-moosh), **Fr.,** Nantes, Aug. 3, 1850—Paris, Feb. 20, 1909; pupil of Victor Massé; 1894, dir. theatre *"Menus-Plaisirs";* prod. many operettas.

Tourjée (toor-zhā), **Eben,** Warwick, Rhode Island, 1834—Boston, 1891; organist, teacher and founder of N. E. Cons.

Tournemire (toorn-mēr), **Charles Arnould,** b. Bordeaux, Jan. 22, 1870; d. Paris, Oct., 1939; successor of César Franck at Ste. Clothilde; pupil of the Paris Cons. (winning first organ prize 1891); then of d'Indy. The City of Paris prize was awarded to his *"Le Sang de la Sirène,"* for voices and orch. 1904, and it has been given in various cities; c. 8 symphonies, lyric tragedy *"Nittetis,"* chamber music, etc.

Tours (toors), **Berthold,** Rotterdam, Dec. 17, 1838—London, March 11, 1897; violinist, composer and editor; pupil Brussels and Leipzig Conservatory.

Tourte (toort), **Fran.**, Paris, 1747—1835; famous maker of vln.-bows; est. the standard since followed.

To'vey, Sir Donald Francis, b. Eton, July 17, 1875—Edinburgh, July 10, 1940; pupil Sophie Weisse (piano), Parratt, Higgs and Parry (comp.); graduated at Oxford, 1898; began to compose at 8; at 19 gave a concert at Windsor with Joachim; from 1900 played in London and on the continent; 1914 succeeded Niecks as prof. at Edinburgh Univ.; 1917 founded Reid Orch. in Edinburgh; 1924, hon. Fellow of R. C. M., London; knighted, 1935; c. 4 pf. trios, pf. quartet, string quartet, pf. sonata and concerto; symphony; 3 vln. sonatas; incid. music to plays, etc.; writer on music.

Traetta (trä-ĕt'-tä) (not **Trajetta**), (1) **Tommaso** (Michele Fran. Saverio), Bitonto, Naples, March 30, 1727—Venice, April 6, 1779; pupil of Durante; 1758, maestro to Duke of Parma; 1765, given a life-pension by the Spanish King; 1768, ct.-composer at Petersburg; he prod. 37 operas, many of them v. succ.; c. also an oratorio, masses, etc. (2) **Filippo**, Venice, 1777—Philadelphia, 1854; son of above; from 1799 in America as an exile; wrote a vocal method; c. opera, oratorios, etc.

Trapp (trŏp), **Max**, b. Berlin, Nov. 1, 1887; composer; studied with Juon, also with Dohnanyi at Berlin Hochsch., c. 4 symphonies, vln. and piano concertos, 2 string quartets, 2 piano quartets, a piano quintet, and other orch. works, piano pieces and songs.

Trasuntino (trä-soon-tē'-nō), **Vito**, harps.-maker and inv., Rome, 1555—1606.

Traubel, **Helen**, b. St. Louis, Mo.; soprano; Met. Op., début 1937.

Trebelli (trä-bĕl'-lē), **Zella** (rightly Guillebert), Paris, 1838—Étretât, Aug. 18, 1892; noted mezzo-soprano; pupil of Wartel; début, Madrid, 1859; 1863, m. Bellini; sang in Europe and (1884) U. S. with great succ.

Tre'harne, **Bryceson**, b. Merthyr Tydvil, Wales, May 30, 1879; composer; pupil of Parry, Stanford and Davies at R. Coll. of Music, also in Paris, Milan, Munich; taught at Adelaide (Australia) Univ., 1901–11; after 1912 in Paris where worked with Gordon Craig; interned in Germany during war; later res. in London and Boston; c. several hundred songs and orch. pieces of popular nature.

Tren'to, **Vittorio**, b. Venice, 1761 (or 1765); d. after 1826; mus.-dir. and dram. composer.

Treu (Italianised **Fedele**) (troi, or fä-dā'-lĕ), **Daniel Gl.**, Stuttgart, 1695—Breslau, 1749; violinist, conductor and dram. composer.

Tréville (trä-vē-yŭ), **Yvonne de** (rightly **Le Gièrce**), b. Galveston, Tex., 1881; of French father and American mother; soprano; pupil of Marchesi; 1901 sang in Spain; 1902, at Paris Opéra Comique; 1911–12, Boston Op. Co.

Trevisan (trä'-vē-săn), **Vittorio**, b. Venice; operatic bass; sang buffo rôles, of which he was a specialist, for a number of seasons with Chicago and Ravinia Op. Cos.; afterward active as teacher in Chicago.

Trial (trǐ-ăl), (1) **Jean Claude**, Avignon, 1732—Paris, 1771; dir. Paris Opéra and dram. composer. (2) **Antoine**, 1736—suicide, 1795; bro. of above; tenor; his wife (3) **Marie Jeanne** (née Milon) was a coloraturesopr. Their son (4) **Armand Emmanuel**, Paris, 1771—1803; dram. composer.

Triébert (trǐ'-ā-bǎr'), (1) **Chas. L.**, Paris, 1810—July, 1867; oboist and professor and manufacturer of instrs. (2) **Frédéric**, 1813—1878; bro. and partner of above, and maker of bassoons. (3) **Frédéric**, son of (2); oboist.

Trit'to, **Giacomo**, Altamura, Naples, 1733—Naples, 1824; professor of cpt. and dram. composer.

Tromboncino (trŏm-bŏn-chē'-nō), **Bartholomaeus**, c. at Verona, 1504–10.

Tromlitz (trŏm'-lǐts), **Jn. G.**, Gera, 1726—Leipzig, 1805; flute-player, maker and teacher.

Trot'ter, **Thomas Henry Yorke**, Nov. 6, 1854—London, March 11, 1934; writer on music and pedagogue; grad. New College, Oxford; 1892, Mus. Doc.; after 1915 prin. of the Incorp. London Acad. of Music; devised influential new method of teaching, based upon ear training and rhythmic exercise; author "*Constructive Harmony*"; "*Ear-Training and Sight-Reading Gradus*"; "*The Making of Musicians*"; "*Music and Mind*."

Trout'beck, Rev. **J.**, Blencowe, Cumberland, 1832—London, 1899; pub. psalters and transl. libretti.

Tschaikowsky. Vide TCHAIKOVSKY.

Tscherep'nine, (1) **Nikolai,** b. St. Petersburg, May 15, 1873; .eminent composer; pupil of Cons. in native city, studying with Van Arck and Rimsky-Korsakoff; after 1907 dir. of class for orch. there, and of the Maryinsky Theatre company; 1908, cond. at Paris Op.-Comique of Rimsky-Korsakoff's *"Snow Maiden"*; 1909–14, cond. of Diaghileff Russian Ballet; 1918–21, dir. of Tiflis Cons.; after 1921 took up residence in Paris; originally much influenced by Rimsky-Korsakoff and Tschaikowsky; his later works have shown modernistic elements, esp. some derived from Debussy and Ravel; there is a strong ingredient of Russian folk-music in his scores; c. (ballets) *"Le Pavillon d' Armide," " Narcisse et Echo," "Le Masque de la Mort Rouge"* (after Poe), *"La Favola della Principessa Ulyba," "Dionysius"* (1921), *"Favola Russa"* (1923), *"Romance of a Mummy"* (1926); (orch.) Sinfonietta; Overture to *"La Princesse Lointaine"* of Rostand; *"Fantasie Dramatique"*; symph. poems, *"Dans la Caverne des Sorcières"* (after Shakespeare's *"Macbeth"*) and *"Das Verzauberte Königsreich"; "Six Impressions"* (after Puschkin's *"The Gold Fish"*); piano concerto, and other pieces for that instrument; *"Poème Lyrique"* for vln. and orch.; string quartet in A minor; *"Songs of Sappho"* for soprano, women's chorus and orch.; also liturgical works, other choruses and songs. (2) **Alexander,** b. St. Petersburg, Jan. 8, 1899; son of Nikolai T.; at 19 completed musical studies in native city and was appointed dir. of Tiflis Op.; after Russian Revolution lived with his family in Paris, where he entered Cons. for further study in piano (Philipp) and comp.; made début with prod. of his first piano concerto at Monte Carlo, 1923; his opera, *"Ol-Ol"* (based on Andreyev's *"The Days of Our Life"*), prod. in Weimar, 1928, also in N. Y. by Russian opera troupe in 1934; made a world tour, incl. the U. S.; appeared as guest cond. of his works with Boston Symph., 1931; and later was resident for some time in China; c. also (opera) *"Hochzeit der Sobeide"*; (ballet) *"Ajanta's Frescoes"*; (orch.) 2 piano concertos, *"Rhapsodie Geor-*

gienne," incid. music to plays, etc.; (chamber music) string quartet, concerto da camera, trio; also Three Pieces for chamber orch.; Suite Divertissement for piano and string quartet, etc.

Tscheschichin (chĕsh-ē'-chēn), **Vsevolod Ievgrafovich,** b. Riga, Feb. 18, 1865; critic and author.

Tschirch (tshērkh), **Fr. Wm.,** Lichtenau, 1818—Gera, 1892; ct.-conductor and dram. composer.

Tschudi. Vide BROADWOOD.

Tua (too'-ä), (1) **Teresina,** b. Turin, April 23, 1866; violinist; pupil of Massart, Paris Cons., took 1st prize 1880; toured Europe, and, 1887, America, with great succ.; 1889, m. Count Franchi-Verney della Valetta (d. 1911); (2) Count **Emilio Quadrio;** 1915–24, taught Milan Cons., then at Liceo of Santa Cecilia, Rome.

Tucher (too'-khĕr), Gl., Freiherr von, Nürnberg, 1798—1877; writer.

Tuck'erman, Samuel Parkman, Boston, Mass., 1819—Newport, 1890; organist, editor and composer.

Tuczek (toots'-sĕk), Fz., Prague, ca. 1755—Pesth, 1820; tenor; conductor and dram. composer.

Tud'way, Thos., England, ca. 1650—London, 1726; organist and professor, Cambridge, 1704–26; Mus. Doc. there, 1705; made a coll. of contemporary services, also c. services, etc.

Tulou (tü-loo), **J. L.,** Paris, Sept., 1786 —Nantes, 1865; chief flutist of his time; at 14 at the Opéra; 1826–56, flute-prof. at the Cons.; composer.

Tuma (too'-mä), Fz., Kostelecz, Bohemia, 1704—Vienna, 1774; gamba-virtuoso and composer.

Tunder (toon'-dĕr), Fz., 1614—Lübeck, 1667; organist Marienkirche, as predecessor of Buxtehude.

Tunsted(e) (tŭn'-stĕd) (or **Dunstede**), **Simon,** b. Norwich, d. Bruisyard, Suffolk, 1369; writer. (Cousemaker.)

Turina (tōō-rē'-nä), **Joaquin,** b. Seville, Dec. 9, 1882; composer, after De Falla perhaps most important contemporary creative figure of Spain; studied piano with Trago and Moszkowski; comp. with Torres and then with d'Indy at Paris Schola Cantorum; returned to Spain with De Falla; has served as music critic, as cond. of Spanish perfs. by Russian Ballet, and as pianist of Quinteto de

Madrid, which he founded; his music is imbued with folk rhythms and is richly colored in impressionistic style; c. (stage works) *"Margot,"* *"La Adúltera Penitente,"* *"Jardin de Oriente"*; (orch.) *"La Procesión del Rocio,"* *"Evangelio de Navidad,"* *"Sinfonia Sevillano,"* *"Danzas Fantasticas"*; (chamber music) piano quintet, string quartet, *"Escena Andaluza"* for viola, piano and quartet; *"Poema de una Sanluquena,"* suite for vln. and piano; also many vocal works; ed. encyclopedia of music (2 vols.), and pub. collected articles and criticisms.

Turini (too-rē'-nē). (1) **Gregorio**, Brescia, ca. 1560—Prague, ca. 1600; singer, cornet-player and composer. (2) **Fran.**, Brescia, ca. 1590—1656; son of above; organist and comp.

Türk (türk), **Daniel Gl.**, Claussnitz, Saxony, Aug. 10, 1750—Halle, Aug. 26, 1813; eminent organist and teacher, theorist and composer.

Turle (tŭrl), **Jas.**, Somerton, Engl., 1802—London, 1882; organist, conductor, editor and composer.

Tur'ner, Wm., 1652—1740; English Mus. Doc. Cambridge; composer.

Turnhout (tĭrn'-hoot), (1) **Gerard de** (rightly **Gheert Jacques**), Turnhout, Belgium, ca. 1520—Madrid, 1580; cond. at Antwerp Cath. and to the Court at Spain, 1572; composer. (2) **Jean**, son of above; ct.-conductor and composer, ca. 1595.

Tur'pin, Edmund Hart, Nottingham, May 4, 1835—London, Oct. 25, 1907; concert-organist; lecturer, editor and writer; pupil of Hullah and Pauer, London; organist various London churches; from 1888 at St. Bride's; in 1889 Mus. Doc.; then c. masses, 2 oratorios, cantatas, symph. *"The Monastery,"* overtures, etc.

Turtshaninoff (toort-shä'-nĭ-nôf), **Peter Ivanovitch**, St. Petersburg, 1779—1856; composer.

Tutkov'ski, Nikolai Apollonovich, b. Lipovetz, Feb. 17, 1857; pianist; pupil of Puchalski; from 1881–90 teacher of history at St. Petersburg Cons.; from 1893 dir. of Cons. in Kiev; c. symph. *"Pensée élégiaque"* and *"Bachanale bohêmienne"* for orch., etc.

Tye (tī), **Christopher**, d. Westminster, 1572; 1554–61, organist Ely cathedral and composer.

Tyn'dall, J., Leighlin Bridge, Ireland, 1820—Haslemere, Engl., 1893; famous scientist and acoustician.

U

Ubaldus. Vide HUCBALD.

Uber (oo'-bĕr), (1) **Chr. Benj.,** Breslau, 1764—1812; dram. composer. (2) **Chr. Fr. Hermann,** Breslau, 1781—Dresden, 1822; son of above; opera-conductor and composer. (3) **Alex.,** Breslau, 1783—Carolath, Silesia, 1824; bro. of (2); 'cellist, conductor and composer.

Überlée (ü'-bĕr-lā), **Adelbert,** Berlin, June 27, 1837 — Charlottenburg, March 15, 1897; organist and royal director; c. opera, oratorio, etc.

Uberti (oo-bĕr'-tē), (**Hubert**) **A.,** Verona, 1697 (?)—Berlin, 1783; brilliant soprano-musico and teacher of Malibran, Grisi, etc.

Uccellini (oo-chĕl-lē'-nē), **Don Marco,** conductor and composer at Florence, 1673.

Ugbaldus, Uchubaldus. Vide HUCBALD.

Ugalde (ü-gắld), **Delphine** (née **Beauce**), Paris, Dec. 3, 1829—July 18, 1910; soprano at Op.-Com., etc.; 1866, also managed the Bouffes-Parisiens; twice m.; c. an opera.

Ugolini (oo-gō-lē'-nē), **V.,** Perugia, ca. 1570—1626; teacher and important composer; pupil of Nanini; 1620–26 maestro at St. Peter's.

Uhl (ool), **Edmund,** Prague, Oct. 25, 1853—Wiesbaden, March, 1929; pupil of Leipzig Cons. winning Helbig pf.-prize, 1878; after that year teacher at the Freudenberg Cons., Wiesbaden; organist at the Synagogue; and critic; c. Romance for vln. with orch., etc.

Uhlig (oo'-lǐkh), **Th.,** Wurzen, Saxony, 1822—Dresden, 1853; violinist, theorist and composer.

Ujj (oo'-yǐ), **Bela von,** b. Vienna, July 2, 1873; Hungarian composer, blind from his 7th year; c. opera *"Der Bauernfeind"* (Baden, near Vienna, 1897); operettas *"Der Herr Professor"* (Vienna, 1903), *"Kaisermanöver"* (do., 1907), and *"Der Müller und sein Kind"* (Graz, 1907).

Ulibisheff (in French **Oulibischeff**) (oo-lē'-bǐ-shĕf), **Alex. D.,** Dresden, 1794—Nishnij Novgorod, 1858; diplomat and writer of biographies.

Ulrich (ool'-rǐkh), **Hugo (Otto),** Oppeln, Silesia, 1827—Berlin, 1872; teacher and dram. composer.

Umbreit (oom'-brīt), **K. Gl.**, Rehstedt, near Gotha, 1763 — 1829; org.-virtuoso and composer.

Umlauf (oom'-lowf), (1) **Ignaz**, Vienna, 1756—Mödling, 1796; music director; asst.-conductor to Salieri. (2) **Michael**, Vienna, 1781—1842; son of above; conductor and dram. composer.

Umlauft (oom'-lowft), **Paul**, Meissen, Oct. 27, 1853—Dresden, June 7, 1934; pupil Leipzig Cons.; with Mozart scholarship 1879–83; c. succ. 1-act opera "*Evanthia*" (Gotha, 1893) (won Duke of Coburg-Gotha's prize); dram. poem "*Agandecca*," with orch. (1892); "*Mittelhochdeutsches Liederspiel*," etc.

Unger (oong'-ĕr), (1) **Jn. Fr.**, Brunswick, 1716—1781; inventor. (2) (in Ital. **Ungher**) **Caroline**, Stuhlweissenburg, Hungary, 1803—at her villa, near Florence, 1877; soprano; 1840, m. Sabatier. (3) **G.**, Leipzig, 1837—1887; tenor.

Up'ton, G. Putnam, Roxburg, Mass., Oct. 25, 1835—Chicago, May 20, 1919; graduate Brown Univ., 1854; 1861–85, on the editorial staff, Chicago *Tribune;* founder (1872) and first pres. Apollo Club; translator and writer of valuable essays, incl. "*Standard Operas*" (1890); "*Standard Oratorios*" (1891); "*Standard Symphs.*" (1892), etc.

Urbach (oor'-bäkh), **Otto**, Eisenach, Feb. 6, 1871—Dresden, Dec. 14, 1927; composer; pupil of Müller-Hartung, Stavenhagen, Scholz, Knorr and Humperdinck; won the Liszt stipend, 1890, and the Mozart stipend 1896, and studied with Draeseke and Klindworth; from 1898 piano teacher at the Dresden Cons.; c. opera "*Der Müller von Sanssouci*" (Frankfort, 1896).

Urban (oor'-bän), (1) **Chr.**, b. Elbing, 1778; mus.-director, theorist and composer. (2) **H.**, Berlin, Aug. 27, 1837—Nov. 24, 1901; pupil of Ries, Laub, Helman, etc.; violinist and theorist; 1881, teacher at Kullak's Acad.; c. symph. "*Frühling*," overtures to "*Fiesco*" (Schiller), "*Scheherazade*," and "*Zu einem Fastnachtsspiel*," etc. (3) **Fr. Julius**, Berlin, Dec. 23, 1838—July 17, 1918; bro. of above; solo boy-soprano in the Domchor; pupil of H. Ries, and

Helmann (vln.), Grell (theory), Elsner and Mantius (singing); singing-teacher, Berlin; wrote vocal methods and songs.

Urbani. Vide VALENTINI.

Urhan (ür-äṅ), **Chrétien**, Montjoie, 1790—Paris, 1845; eccentric and gifted player on stringed instrs., ancient and modern; organist and composer.

Urich (oo'-rĭkh), **Jean**, Trinidad, 1849 –1939; pupil of Gounod; prod. operas "*Der Lootse*," "*Hermann und Dorothea*," and 2-act "*Le Carillon*" (Berlin, 1902).

Urio (oo'-rĭ-ō), **Fran. A.**, b. Milan, 1660; writer and composer.

Urlus (ōōr'-lōōs), **Jacques**, Amsterdam, 1868—Noordwyk, June 6, 1935; noted tenor; pupil of Hol, Noltenius, the Amsterdam Cons., making his début in latter city in 1894; after 1900 at Leipzig Stadttheatre; sang also in many other Eur. cities; at Bayreuth from 1911, and in N. Y., 1913–17; one of leading Wagnerian tenors of his day.

Ursillo (oor-sĭl'-lō), **Fabio** (or simply **Fabio**), 18th cent. archlute virtuoso and composer at Rome.

Urso (oor'-sō), (1) **Camilla**, Nantes, France, 1842—New York, Jan. 20, 1902; vln.-virtuoso (daughter of (2) **Salvator**, organist and flutist); pupil of Massart; she played in America with great succ. at 10; toured the world; m. Fr. Luères.

Urspruch (oor'-sprookh), **Anton**, Frankfort-on-Main, Feb. 17, 1850—Jan. 11, 1907; pupil of Ignaz Lachner and M. Wallenstein, Raff and Liszt; pf.-teacher Hoch Cons.; from 1887 at Raff Cons.; c. opera "*Der Sturm*" (based on Shakespeare's "*Tempest*," Frankfort, 1888), comic opera (text and music) "*Das Unmöglichste von Allem*" (Carlsruhe, 1897), a symph., pf.-concerto, etc.

Ursus. Vide BÄHR.

U(u)tendal (or **Utenthal, Uutendal**) (ü'-tĕn-däl), **Alex.**, d. Innsbruck, May 8, 1581; Flemish conductor and composer.

V

Vaccai (väk-kä'-ē), **Niccolò**, Tolentino, Papal States, 1790—Pesaro, 1848, noted singing-teacher; prof. of comp. Milan Cons.; wrote vocal method; c. an opera, funeral cantata, etc.

Vacqueras (vă-kä'-răs), **Beltrame**, 1481 singer at St. Peter's, Rome; 1483–1507 papal chapel singer; c. motets, etc.

Vaet (vät), **Jacques**, d. Vienna, 1567; Flemish conductor and composer.

Valente (vä-lĕn'-tĕ), **Vincenzo**, Corigliano, near Cosenza, Feb. 21, 1855 —Naples, Sept. 6, 1921; c. operas and songs.

Valentini (vä-lĕn-tē'-nē), (1) **Giov.**, ca. 1615; organist and composer. (2) **Giov.**, Naples, 1779–1788; dram. composer. (3) **P. Fran.**, Rome, ca. 1570—1654; eminent contrapuntist; pupil of Nanini. (4) (Rightly **Valentino Urbani**) (oor-bä'-nĕ), celebrated contralto-musico; later a tenor; London, 1707. (5) **Giu.**, b. Rome(?), 1681; violinist and composer.

Valentino (văl-äṅ-tē'-nō), **Henri Justin Armand Jos.**, Lille, 1785—Versailles, 1856; conductor Paris Opéra, 1820–31, then at Op. Com. till 1837.

Valet'ta, Ippolito. Vide FRANCHI-VERNEY.

Vallas (väy'-äs), **Léon**, b. Roanne, May 17, 1879; writer; author of studies of Debussy and Georges Migot.

Vallin (vä'-yăn), **Ninon**, b. Montalieu-Vercieu, prov. of Dauphiné, France; soprano; studied at Lyons Cons.; début, Paris Op.-Comique in *"Carmen"*; later sang in opera at Buenos Aires, also at Paris Op., La Scala, Rome R. Op., Madrid, Vienna, Budapest, Barcelona, Stockholm and Constantinople; esp. known as a recitalist of modern French music, incl. Debussy; toured U. S. in concerts.

Valotti (väl-lŏt'-tē), **Fran. A.**, Vercelli, June 11, 1697—Padua, Jan. 16, 1780; noted organist, theorist and composer.

Valverde (väl-vär'-dä), (1) **Joaquin**, d. Madrid, March 19, 1910; c. zarzuelas and songs. His son (2) **Quirino**, d. Mexico, Nov., 1918; also a prolific comp. of stage works, incl. some 60 zarzuelas.

Van den Eeden (ā'-dĕn), (1) **Gilles**, d. 1792; first teacher of Beethoven; son or nephew of (2) **Heinrich**; ct.-mus. to the Elector of Cologne.

Van der Straeten (strä'-tĕn), **Edmond**, Oudenaarden, Belgium, 1826—1895; writer of valuable treatises based on research and c. an opera, etc.

Van der Stucken (vän'-dĕr-shtook'-ĕn), **Frank** (**Valentin**), Fredericksburg, Gillespie Co., Texas, Oct. 15, 1858— Hamburg, Aug. 18, 1929; son of Belgian father and German mother; notable composer and conductor; at 8 taken by his parents to Antwerp, studied with Benoît, later with Reinecke, Sänger and Grieg; 1881–82, cond. at Breslau City Th.; 1883, in Rudolstadt with Grieg, and in Weimar with Liszt; prod. opera *"Vlasda"* (Paris, 1883); 1884, called to be mus.-dir. of the "Arion," New York; he was dean of the Cincinnati College of Music 1897–1901; cond. Cincinnati Symph. 1895–1907, when he returned to Germany, retaining the conductorship of the Cincinnati May Festivals; c. symph. prologue *"William Ratcliff"* (Cincinnati, 1899); orch. episode, *"Pagina d'amore,"* with choruses and songs; *"Festival March,"* for orch., *"Pax Triumphans,"* etc.

Van der Veer', **Nevada**, b. Springfield Center, N. Y.; contralto; studied with Beigel, Arthur Fagge, and Marie Roze, Paris; has appeared widely as oratorio soloist and with orchs.; later active as teacher at Cleveland Inst. of Music; m. Reed Miller, tenor.

Van Dier'en, **Bernard**, Holland, Dec. 27, 1884—London, April 24, 1936; composer; of mixed Dutch and French parentage; studied in Rotterdam, Leyden, Berlin and London, first in science, and after 1904 exclusively in music; came to London 1909 as musical corr. for the *Nieuwe Rotterdamsche Courant*, where he remained; developed complex contrapuntal style, partly influenced by early choral schools of the Netherlands; c. symph. for soloists, chorus and orch., after Chinese text; 4 string quartets, several of which were heard at European modern music fests.; *"Diaphonie"* for barytone and chamber orch., after 3 Shakespeare sonnets; (opera buffa) *"The Tailor"* (text by Robert Nicholls); and various other chamber music and vocal works; m. Frida Kindler, pianist.

Van Dres'ser, **Marcia**, Memphis, 1880 —London, 1937; soprano; studied Chicago, Munich and Paris; after 1898 sang in light and grand opera in Europe and, beginning 1914, in United States.

Van Duyze (vän doi'-zĕ), **Florimond,** Ghent, Aug. 4, 1848—May 18, 1910; lawyer and amateur; pupil of Ghent Cons., winning Grand prix de Rome, 1873, with cantata "*Torquato Tasso's Dood*"; prod. 7 operas, Antwerp and Ghent; c. also ode-symphonie "*Die Nacht.*"

Van Dyck (vän dīk), **Ernest (Marie Hubert),** Antwerp, April 2, 1861—Berlaer-les-Lierre (Antwerp), Aug. 31, 1923; noted tenor; studied law, was then a journalist at Paris; studied singing with St. Yves; début Paris, 1887, as "Lohengrin"; 1892 sang "Parsifal" at Bayreuth; 1888 engaged for the Vienna ct.-opera; sang in the chief capitals, London, and 1899–1902, New York; later taught at Antwerp and Brussels conservatories.

Van Gordon, Cyrena, b. Camden, Ohio, Sept. 4, 1896; contralto; name originally Procock; studied Cincinnati Coll. of Music; début, Chicago Op. as "Amneris," 1913; sang many contralto rôles with this co.; for a time with Met. Op. Co.; her repertoire incl. German, Italian and French parts.

Van Hoog'straten, Willem, b. Utrecht, March 18, 1884; conductor; studied Cologne Cons.; début as cond., Hamburg, 1911; he also appeared at Hamburg, Vienna and Salzburg; as cond. N. Y. Philh., 1923–24; of Portland, Ore., Symph., after 1925, regularly at the Lewisohn Stadium concerts in N. Y. following 1921; and as a guest with many Eur. and Amer. ensembles, incl. Bonn Beethoven Fest.; hon. Music D., Univ. of Oregon, 1926; m. Elly Ney, pianist; divorced.

Van Hoose, Ellison, Murfreesboro, Tenn., Aug. 18, 1869—Houston, Tex., March 24, 1936; tenor; studied U. S. and Europe, teachers incl. Jean de Reszke and Cotogni; after 1897, sang with Damrosch-Ellis Op. Co.; at Mayence Op., and 1911–12, Chicago Op. Co.; also in oratorio and concerts; later church mus. dir. in Houston.

Vanneo (vän-nä'-ō), **Stefano,** b. Recanati, Ancona, 1493; monk and writer.

Van Rooy (vän rō'-ĭ), **Anton,** Rotterdam, Jan. 12, 1870—Munich, Nov. 28, 1932; notable barytone; pupil of Stockhausen at Frankfort; sang in oratorio and concerts; later at Bay-

reuth, 1897; then at Berlin ct.-opera; sang with succ. London (1898), 1898–1908 in New York annually; then at Frankfort Opera; his greatest rôle was "Wotan."

Van Vech'ten, Carl, b. Cedar Rapids, Iowa, 1880; writer; Grad. Univ. of Chicago; on staff of N. Y. *Times,* later N. Y. *Press;* ed. program notes of N. Y. Symph., 1910–11; in later years esp. known as a novelist, but also pub. books on music and art criticism; author, "*Music after the Great War*," "*Music and Bad Manners*," "*Interpreters and Interpretations*," "*The Merry-Go-Round*," "*The Music of Spain*," etc.

Van Vliet, Cornelius, b. Rotterdam, Sept. 1, 1886; 'cellist; pupil of Eberle and Mossel; played Concertgebouw Orch. under Mengelberg; 1st 'cellist Leipzig Philh.; Prague Philh.; solo appearances, Munich, Vienna, and Helsingfors, where taught in Cons.; after 1911 in U. S. as recitalist, 'cellist in N. Y. Trio and long first 'cellist of N. Y. Philharmonic.

Van Westerhout (wĕs'-tĕr-howt), **Niccolo** (of Dutch parents), Mola di Bari, 1862—Naples, 1898; dram. composer.

Van Zanten, Cornelie, see **Zanten.**

Varèse (vä-rĕs'), **Edgar,** b. Paris, Dec. 22, 1885; composer; studied at Schola Cantorum with Roussel and d'Indy, at Paris Cons. with Widor; 1907, won Bourse Artistique of City of Paris; 1909, founded Symphonischer Chor., Berlin; after 1916 res. in N. Y., where founded New Symph. Orch., giving modern scores for several years; has c. orch. and chamber works in uniquely dissonant style and with piercing sonorities, incl. "*Hyperprism*," "*Integrales*," "*Ionisation*," "*Equatorial*," etc.

Varney (vär-nē), (1) P. **Jos. Alphonse,** Paris, 1811—1879; conductor and composer of operettas. (2) **Louis,** Paris, 1844—Cauterets, 1908; son and pupil of above; prod. over 30 operettas, comic operas, "revues."

Vasconcellos (väs-kōn-sĕl'-lōs), **Joaquim de,** Oporto, Feb. 10, 1849—?; Portuguese lexicographer and historian.

Vasquez y Gomez (văs'-kĕth ē gō'-mĕth), **Marino,** Granada, Feb. 3, 1831—Madrid, June, 1894; concertmaster at Madrid Royal Theatre; c. zarzuelas, etc.

Vasseur (văs-sŭr), **Léon** (**Félix Aug. Jos.**), Bapaume, Pas-de-Calais, May 28, 1844—Paris, 1917; studied École Niedermeyer; from 1870 organist Versailles Cath.; cond. Folies-Bergères and the Concerts de Paris (1882); prod. over 30 light operas; c. also masses, etc.

Vassilen'ko, Sergei Nikiforovich, b. Moscow, March 31, 1872; writer; pupil of the Cons., winning gold medal, 1901; c. cantata "*The Legend of the Sunken City of Kitesch*" (given as an opera, Moscow, 1903); "*Epic Poem*" for orch., choral works "*Nebuchadnezzar*," and "*Daphnis*," etc.

Vatielli (vä-tĭ-ĕl'-lē), **Francesco,** b. Pesaro, Jan. 1, 1877; pupil of Liceo Rossini; 1905 librarian at Bologna, teacher and writer on history; c. intermezzi, etc.

Vaucorbeil (vō-kôr-bĕ'), **Aug. Emanuel,** Rouen, 1821—Paris, 1884; 1880, dir. the Opéra; c. comic-opera, etc.

Vaughan-Williams, Ralph; see **Williams, Ralph Vaughan.**

Vavrinecz (vä'-vrē-nĕts), **Mauritius,** Czegled, Hungary, July 18, 1858—Budapest, Aug. 5, 1913; studied Pesth Cons., and with R. Volkmann; cath. cond. at Pesth; c. 4-act opera "*Ratcliff*" (Prague, 1895), succ. 1-act opera "*Rosamunda*" (Frankfort-on-Main, 1895), oratorio, 5 masses, a symph., etc.

Vecchi(i) (vĕk'-kē-[ē]), (1) **Orazio,** Modena, 1550—Feb. 19, 1603; noted composer; from 1596 maestro Modena cath.; his "mus.-comedy" "*Amfiparnasso*," in which the chorus joined in all the mus., even the monologues, appeared the same year as PERI's (q. v.) "*Dafne*"; c. also madrigals, etc. (2) **Orfeo,** Milan, 1540—ca. 1604; maestro, and composer.

Vecsey (vĕt'-chĕ-ē), **Franz von,** Budapest, March 23, 1893—Rome, April 4, 1935; violinist; at 8, pupil of Hubay; at 10 accepted by Joachim, and toured Germany, England and America with immense success; toured South America, 1911; reappeared in London, 1912; later toured as mature artist.

Veit (vīt), **Wenzel H. (Václav Jindřich),** Repic, near Leitmeritz, Bohemia, 1806—Leitmeritz, 1864; composer.

Velluti (vĕl-loo'-tē), **Giov.˙Bat.,** Monterone, Ancona, 1781—San Burson, 1861; the last of the great male soprani.

Venatorini. Vide MYSLIWECZEK.

Venosa, Prince of. Vide GESUALDO.

Venth (vĕnt), **Karl,** Cologne, Feb. 10, 1860—San Antonio, Tex., Jan. 29, 1938; pupil of the Cons. and of Wieniawski; 1880 in New York as concertmaster at Met. Op. House; founded 1888 a cons. in Brooklyn; c. Schiller's "*Bells*" for chorus and orch., etc.; after 1908 lived in Texas; dean of woman's coll. and orch. cond., Dallas.

Ven'to, (1) **Ivo de,** b. Spain; ct.-organist at Munich and composer (1561–91). (2) **Mattia,** Naples, 1735—London, 1777; c. operas.

Venturelli (vĕn-too-rĕl'-lē), **V.,** Mantua, 1851—(suicide) 1895; essayist and dram. composer.

Venturini (vĕn-too-rē'-ne), **Francesco,** d. Hanover, April 18, 1745; from 1698 in the Hanoverian court chapel as cond.; c. concertos, etc.

Venzano (vĕn-tsä'-nō), **Luigi,** Genoa, ca. 1814—1878; 'cellist and teacher; c. opera, pop. songs, etc.

Veracini (vä-rä-chē'-nē), (1) **A.,** violinist at Florence (1696). (2) **Fran. Maria,** Florence, ca. 1685—near Pisa, ca. 1750; nephew and pupil of above; notable violinist, the greatest of his time; composer.

Verbrug'ghen, Henri, Brussels, Aug. 1, 1873—Northfield, Minn., Nov. 12, 1934; conductor, violinist; studied at Brussels Cons., 1st prize in vln., also with Hubay and Ysaye; soloist with English orchs. and with Lamoureux; 1902, concertm. and asst. cond.; Scottish Orch., Glasgow; succeeded Coward as cond. of Choral Union in that city; also org. string quartet and served as guest leader in London and Continental cities; was dir. for 8 years of New South Wales State Cons., Sydney, and there founded and led State Orch.; came to N. Y. after war and was guest cond. of Russian Symph., 1918; guest cond. of Minneapolis Symph., 1922; appointed regular cond. and served until 1931, when illness caused him to resign post; he led this orch. on tour, incl. N. Y., with eminent succ. and founded and played 1st vln. in quartet bearing his name; headed music dept. at Carleton Coll., Northfield, for several years before his death.

Verdelot, (vărd-lō) (Italianised, **Verdelot'to),** **Philippe,** d. before 1567; famous Flemish madrigal-composer and singer at San Marco, Venice; between 1530–40 in Florence.

Verdi (vĕr'-dē), **(Fortunio) Giuseppe (Fran.),** Le Roncole, near Busseto, Duchy of Parma, Oct. 9, 1813—Milan, Jan. 27, 1901; eminent Italian opera composer. Son of an innkeeper and grocer; pupil, and at 10 successor of the village organist, Baistrocchi, for three years pupil of Provesi at Busseto; 1831 with the aid of his father's friend, Barezzi, he went to Milan, where he was refused admission to the Cons. by Basili, who thought him lacking in mus. talent. He became a pupil of Lavigna, cembalist, at La Scala; 1833, cond. Philh. Soc., and organist at Busseto; 1836 m. Barezzi's daughter Margherita. 1839, his opera *"Oberto"* was prod. with fair succ. at La Scala, Milan. He was commissioned by Merelli, the manager to write three operas, one every eight months, at 4,000 lire ($800 or £160) apiece, and half the copyright. The first was a comic opera *"Un Giorno di Regno,"* which failed (1840), doubtless in part because his two children and wife had died within three months. V.'s combined distress drove him to rescind his agreement and renounce composition for over a year, when he was persuaded by Merelli to set the opera *"Nabucco"* ("Nebuchadrezzar"), prod. at La Scala, 1842, with great applause, the chief rôle being taken by Giuseppina Strepponi (1815–97), whom he m. in 1844. *"I Lombardi alla prima Crociata"* (La Scala, 1843) was still more succ. and is still played in Italy (in Paris as *"Jérusalem"*). *"Ernani"* (Venice, 1844) was prod. on 15 different stages in 9 months. 8 unsucc. works followed, incl. *"I due Foscari"* (Rome, 1844), *"Macbeth"* (Florence, 1847; revised Paris, 1865), and *"I Masnadieri"* (after Schiller's *"Robbers"* London, H. M. Th., 1847). *"Luisa Miller"* (Naples, 1849) was well received and is still sung in Italy. *"Stiffelio"* (Trieste, 1850); later as *"Guglielmo Welingrode"*; also with another libretto as *"Arnoldo"* (1857), was

three times a failure. *"Rigoletto,"* c. in 40 days (Venice) (also given as *"Viscardello"*), began a three years' period of universal succ., it was followed by the world-wide successes *"Il Trovatore"* (Rome, 1853) and *"La Traviata"* (Venice Th., 1853; also given as *"Violetta"*), a fiasco at first because of a poor cast; *"Les Vêpres Siciliennes"* (Paris Opéra, 1855; in Italian *"I Vespri Siciliani"*; also given as *"Giovanna di Guzman"*) was fairly succ.; *"Simon Boccanegra"* (Venice, 1857; succ. revised, Milan, 1881), *"Un Ballo in Maschera"* (Rome, 1859), *"La Forza del Destino"* (Petersburg, 1862), and *"Don Carlos"* (Paris, Opéra, 1867), made no deep impression, though they served as a schooling and marked a gradual broadening from mere Italian lyricism to a substantial harmony and orchestration. *"Aïda"* (written for the Khedive of Egypt) was prod. Cairo, 1871, at La Scala, Milan, 1872, and has had everywhere a great succ. The Khedive gave him £3,000 for it. His *"Manzoni Requiem"* (1874) made a sensation in Italy; *"Otello"* (Milan, 1887) was a work worthy of its composer, and in his last opera *"Falstaff,"* written at the age of eighty, he showed not only an unimpaired but a progressive and novel style. He also c. 2 symphs., 6 pf.-concertos, *"Inno delle Nazioni,"* for the London Exhibition (1862), songs, etc.

In 1893 he was offered the title "Marchese di Busseto," but was too democratic to accept it. He lived at his villa Sant' Agata, near Busseto. His funeral brought 100,000 witnesses, though his will ordered that it should be simple and quiet. He left the bulk of his fortune to found a home for aged and outworn musicians in Milan, where there is also a Verdi museum.

Following a period in which V.'s operas were unfavourably compared with Wagner's, there has been a marked tendency to rank him as an even superior musical dramatist in some respects. Particularly in Germany, after 1920, a new interest in his works arose, partly as the result of translations and adaptations made by Franz Werfel, who also pub. a novel based on V.'s life.

Biog. by Gino Monaldi (in German,

trans. by L. Holthof, Leipzig, 1898);
Checchi, 1887; Blanche Roosevelt
(London, 1887); Crowest (1897);
Visetti (1905); Bonavia (1930) and
Toye (1931). Other memoirs by
Pougin, Hanslick, Prince Valori,
Parodi, Perinello, Cavaretta, Basso,
Boni, Colonna, Sorge, Voss, Gari-
baldi, Bragagnolo and Bettazzi,
d'Angeli, Bellaigue, Lottici, Righetti,
Mackenzie, Chop, Roncaglia, and
Neisser.

Verdonck', Cornelius, Turnhout, Belgium, 1563—Antwerp, 1625; composer.

Vere-Sapio (vär-sä′-pǐ-ō), **Clementine
(Duchêne) de,** b. Paris; soprano;
daughter of a Belgian nobleman, and
an Englishwoman; pupil of Mme.
Albertini-Baucarde, Florence; début
there at 16, sang at leading theatres,
Europe, later in concert, also in the
United States; 1896, she returned to
opera; 1899, toured U. S. with an
opera troupe of which her husband,
Romualdo Sapio, was mgr.; 1900–
1901 at Metropolitan, N. Y., and
Covent Garden.

Verhey (vĕr′-hī), **Th. H. H.,** Rotterdam, 1848—Jan. 28, 1929; pupil of
the Royal Music Sch., at The Hague
and of Bargiel; teacher at Rotterdam; c. operas, a mass, chamber
music, etc.

Verhulst (vĕr-hoolst′), **Jns.** (Josephus
Herman), The Hague, 1816—1891;
cond.; famous composer; pupil of
Volcke at the Cons. there, later R.
mus.-dir.; cond. many societies, etc.;
intimate friend of Schumann; c.
symphony, 3 overtures, etc.

Vernier (vĕrn-yā), **Jean Aimé,** b. Paris,
1769; harpist and composer.

Véron (vä-rôṅ), **Désiré,** Paris, 1798—
1867; critic, writer and manager of
the Opéra.

Verstovsky (or **Werstowski**), **Alexei
Nikolaievich,** Tambov, Feb. 18
(March 1), 1799—Moscow, Nov. 5
(17), 1862; composer; while studying
civil engineering at the Institute in
St. Petersburg, he was also a pupil
of John Field and Steibelt (piano),
Böhm (violin), Tarquini (voice),
Brandt and Tseiner (theory); c. a
vaudeville at 19, and soon acquired
a vogue; at 25 was inspector of the
Imp. Opera, Moscow; at 29, c. a
succ. opera, *"Pan Tvardovski,"* followed by five others, including
"Askold's Tomb" (1835), which had

enormous success and was revived
in 1897; was accepted as a beginning
of national opera and had undoubted
influence on its development. He c.
also cantatas and 29 popular songs.

Vesque von Püttlingen (vĕsk fōn
pǐt′-lǐng-ĕn), **Jn.,** Opole, Poland,
1803—Vienna, 1883; pianist of Belgian parentage; c. 6 operas; used
pen-name **"J. Hoven."**

Ves′tris, Lucia E., London, 1797—
Fulham, 1856; opera-singer.

Vetter (fĕt-tĕr), **Nikolaus,** Königsee,
1666—Rudolfstadt, 1710; court organist and important choral composer.

Viadana (vē-ä-dä′-nä), **Ludovico (da)**
(rightly **L. Grossi**), Viadana, near
Mantua, 1564 — Gualtieri, 1645;
noted church-composer; maestro at
Mantua cath.; important early figure
in the development of basso continuo
(v. D. D.).

Vian′na da Mot′ta, José, see **Da Motta.**

Vianesi (vē-ä-nä′-zē), **Auguste Chas.
Léonard François,** Leghorn, Nov. 2,
1837—New York, Nov. 11, 1908;
studied in Paris 1859, cond. Drury
Lane, London; then at New York,
Moscow and Petersburg; 12 years
cond. at Covent Garden; also in
other cities; 1887, 1st cond. Gr.
Opéra, Paris; cond. New York,
1891–92.

Viardot-Garcia (vǐ-är′-dō-gär-thē′-ä),
(1) (**Michelle Fde.**) **Pauline,** Paris,
July 18, 1821—May 18, 1910; famous
mezzo-soprano and teacher; daughter
of Manuel Garcia (q.v.), studied pf.
with Vega at Mexico Cath., then
with Neysenberg and Liszt, and
Reicha (harm.); and singing with
her father and mother; concert
début, Brussels, 1837; opera début,
London, 1839, engaged by Viardot,
dir. Th. Italien, Paris, and sang
there until 1841, when she m. him
and made European tours with him.
In 1849 she created "Fides" in *"Le
Prophète,"* Paris, "Sapho" (Gounod's
opera), 1851; 1863, retired to Baden-
Baden; from 1871 lived in Paris as
teacher. Her voice had the remarkable compass of more than 3 octaves
from bass c–f′′′. Wrote a vocal
method and c. 3 operas, 60 songs,
and also 6 pcs. for pf. and vln.
Biogr. by La Mara. (2) **Louise
Héritte Viardot,** Paris, Dec. 14, 1841
—Heidelberg, Jan., 1918; daughter
of above; singing-teacher Hoch

Cons., Frankfort (till 1886); then est. a sch. at Berlin; c. 2 comic operas, a pf.-quartet, etc. (3) Mme. **Chamerot,** and (4) **Marianne V.,** daughters of (1) were concert-singers.

Vicentino (vē-chĕn-tē'-nō), **Nicola,** Vicenza, 1511—Rome, 1572; conductor, theorist and composer; inv. "archiorgano."

Victorio. Vide VITTORIA.

Vidal (vē-dăl, (1) **B., d.** Paris, 1880; guitar-virtuoso, teacher and composer. (2) **Jean Jos.,** Sorèze, 1789 —Paris, 1867; violinist. (3) **Louis A.,** Rouen, July 10, 1820—Paris, Jan. 7, 1891; 'cellist and writer; pupil of Franchomme; pub. important historical works. (4) **Paul Antonin,** Toulouse, June 16, 1863— Paris, April 9, 1931; pupil of Paris Cons., winning first Grand prix de Rome, 1881; from 1894, taught at the Cons.; 1896, cond. at the Opéra; prod. 3-act lyric fantasy "*Éros*" (1892), a ballet "*La Maladetta*" (1893), 2 1-act operettas; lyric drama "*Guernica*" (Op. Com., 1895); "*La Reine Fiammette*" (1898); "*La Burgonde*" (1898); "*Ramses*" (1908); orch. suite, "*Les mystères d'Eleusis,*" etc.

Vierdank (fēr'-dänk), **Jn.,** organist and composer at Stralsund 1641.

Vierling (fēr'-lĭng), (1) **Jn. Gf.,** Metzels, near Meiningen, 1750—Schmalkalden, 1813; organist and composer. (2) **Jacob V.,** 1796—1867, organist. (3) **Georg,** Frankenthal, Palatinate, Sept. 5, 1820—Wiesbaden, May 1, 1901; son and pupil of above, also of Rinck (org.), Marx (comp.); 1847, organist at Frankfort-on-Oder; 1852-53, cond. Liedertafel, Mayence; then lived in Berlin, founder and for years cond. Bach-verein; prof. and R. Mus.-Dir.; c. notable secular oratorios, "*Der Raub der Sabinerinnen*" (op. 50), "*Alarichs Tod*" and "*Konstantin*"; Psalm 137, with orch.; and other choral works; a symph.; 5 overtures, incl. "*Im Frühling*"; capriccio for pf. with orch., etc.

Vierne, Louis Victor Jules, Poitiers, France, Oct. 8, 1870—at organ, Notre Dame, Paris, June 2, 1937; pupil of Paris Cons. under Franck and Widor, the latter making him his asst. as org. at St. Sulpice in 1892, and in his classes at the Cons.,

1894; after 1900 he was org. at Notre Dame; from 1911 instructor in organ master class at the Schola Cantorum; he gave recitals in many Eur. cities; teacher of Nadia Boulanger, Joseph Bonnet and Marcel Dupré; c. 5 symphonies for organ and other works for this instrument; Missa Solemnis for choir and orch.; various other church comps.; orch., chamber music and piano pieces, etc.

Vieuxtemps (v'yŭ-täṅ), (1) **Henri,** Verviers, Belgium, Feb. 20, 1820—Mustapha, Algiers, June 6, 1881; eminent violinist and composer; son and pupil of a piano-tuner and instr.-maker, then pupil of Lecloux, with whom he toured at 8; then pupil of de Bériot (vln.), Sechter (harm.), Reicha (comp.); he toured Europe with great succ., and three times America (1844, 1857 and 1870); 1845, m. Josephine Eder, a Vienna pianist; 1846-52, solo-violinist to the Czar and prof. at the Petersburg Cons.; 1871-73, prof. at the Brussels Cons.; then paralysis of his left side stopped his playing. He c. 6 concertos, several concertinos, an overture on the Belgian national hymn (op. 41), fantaisie-caprice, with orch.; fantaisies on Slavic themes, "*Hommage à Paganini,*" caprice, sonata, vars. on "*Yankee Doodle,*" 2 'cello-concertos, a grand solo duo for vln. and 'cello (with Servais), etc. Biog. by Radoux (1891). (2) **Jules Jos. Ernest,** Brussels, March 18, 1832—Belfast, March 20, 1896; bro. of above; solo-'cellist It. Opera, London; also in Hallé's orch. at Manchester. (3) **Jean Joseph Lucien,** Verviers, July 5, 1828—Brussels, Jan. 1901; pianist and composer; pianist, teacher, and c. of piano pieces, brother of **Henri** and **Jules V.** (q. v.).

Viganò (vē-gä-nō'), **Salvatore,** Naples, 1769—Milan, 1821; ballet-dancer and succ. composer of ballets.

Vigna (vēn'-yä), **Arturo,** Turin, 1863— Milan, Jan. 5, 1927; cond. Met. Op. House, N. Y., 1903-07; pupil Milan Cons.

Vilbac(k) (vēl-băk), (**Alphonse Chas.**) **Renaud de,** Montpellier, 1829— Paris, 1884; pianist and organist; c. comic operas.

Vil'la-Lo'bos, Heitor, b. Rio de Janeiro, March 5, 1890; composer; studied with Franca, Braga and Nyendemberg; début as 'cellist at 12; made tour of Brazil, where has led orchs. as well as in Europe; attracted attention for his comps. in chamber music and other forms, based on Brazilian folk-music, marked by unusual pungency and originality in expression; he is advanced in modern technical devices, and independent in idiom and personality; c. sonatas, trios, quintet, sextet, octet, 4 concertos, many symphonic works, and piano pieces, some of which are based on characteristic African dances, and several suites for children; adaptations of native folksongs, with Portuguese, French and Spanish texts.

Villanis (vēl-lä′-nēs), **Luigi Alberto,** San Mauro, near Turin, June 24, 1863—Pesaro, Sept. 27, 1906; LL.D. Turin Univ., 1887, then pupil of Thermignon, and Cravero (comp.); 1890 prof. of mus. æsthetics and history, Turin Univ.; critic and writer.

Villarosa (vēl-lä-rō′-sä), **Carlantonio de Rosa, Marchese di,** Naples, 1762 —1847; Royal Historiographer, 1823, and writer on music.

Villars (vē-yärs), **Fran. de,** Ile Bourbon, 1825—Paris, 1879; critic and historian.

Villebois (vē′-yŭ-bwä), **Constantin Petrovitch,** 1817—Warsaw, 1882; composer.

Vil′loing, Alex, St. Petersburg, 1808—1878; pf.-teacher; wrote method and c. pf.-pcs.

Villoteau (vē′-yŏ-tō), **Guillaume André,** Bellême, 1759—Paris, 1839; tenor and writer.

Vincent (văn-sän), (1) **Alex. Jos. Hydulphe,** Hesdin, Pas-de-Calais, 1797 —Paris, 1868; pub. treatises claiming that the Greeks used harm., etc. (fĭn′-tsĕnt), (2) **H. Jos.,** Teilheim, near Würzburg, Feb. 23, 1819— Vienna, May 20, 1901; gave up theology and law and became a tenor in theatres at Vienna (1849), Halle and Würzburg; from 1872, singing-teacher and conductor; lived at Czernowitz, Bukowina and later in Vienna; pub. treatises advocating the "Chroma" Theory; c. operas, operettas, and pop. songs.

Vinci (vēn′-chē), (1) **Pietro,** b. Nicosia, Sicily, 1540; maestro and composer. (2) **Leonardo;** Strongoli, Calabria,

1690—Naples, 1730; maestro and dram. composer.

Viñes (vēn′-yĕs), **Ricardo,** b. Lérida, Spain, Feb. 5, 1875; pianist; pupil of Pujol at Barcelona Cons., also of de Bériot, Lavignac and Godard at Paris Cons.; esp. known as interpreter of modern French, Russian and Spanish music, and a pioneer in the playing of Debussy; lived in Paris.

Viola (vē-ō′-lä), (1) **Alfonso della,** ct.-composer at Ferrara, 1541–63 to Ercole II. (2) **Fran.,** pupil of Willaert; maestro at Ferrara, and composer, 1558–73.

Viole (fē′-ō-lĕ), **Rudolf,** Schochwitz, Mansfield, 1825—Berlin, 1867; pianist and composer.

Viotta (fē-ŏt′-tä), **Henri,** Amsterdam, July 16, 1848—Montreux, Feb. 18, 1933; studied Cologne Cons.; also a lawyer, 1883; founder and cond., Amsterdam Wagner Soc., etc.; 1889, ed. *Maandblad voor Muziek;* 1896 —1917, dir. Cons. at The Hague; 1903–17, cond. of Residentie Orkest; publ. a *"Lexicon der Toonkunst."*

Viotti (vē-ŏt′-tē), **Giov. Bat.,** Fontaneto da Pò, Vercelli, Italy, May 23, 1753—London, March 3, 1824; son of a blacksmith; at first self-taught, then, under patronage of Prince della Cisterna, studied with Pugnani at Turin; soon entered the ct.-orchestra; 1780 toured with Pugnani, was invited to become ct.-violinist to Catherine II., but went to Paris, then London, playing with greatest succ.; 1783 an inferior violinist drew a larger audience, and in disgust he retired from concerts and became a teacher and accompanist to Marie Antoinette and cond. to the Prince de Soubise. Failing to be dir. of the Opera, 1787, he joined Léonard, the Queen's hairdresser, and est. It. Opéra, 1789; prospering till the Revolution. He went to London as a violinist and played with great succ. 1795, mgr. It. Opéra and dir. Opera Concerts there; failing he went into the wine-trade. Later returned to Paris, and became dir. of the Opera, 1819–22, then pensioned with 6,000 francs. He pub. 29 vln.-concertos (the first written in the modern sonata-form, and supported with broadened orchestration. C. also 2 Concertantes for 2 vlns., 21 string-quartets, 51 vln.-

duos, 18 sonatas, etc. Biogr. by Fayolle (Paris, 1810); Baillot (1825), and Arthur Pougin (1888).

Virdung (fēr'-doongk), **Sebastian,** priest and organist at Basel, 1511; writer and composer.

Visetti (vē-sĕt'-tē), **Alberto Ant.,** Spalato, Dalmatia, May 13, 1846—London, July 9, 1928; pupil of Mazzucato, Milan Cons., concert-pianist at Nice; then Paris, cond. to the Empress Eugénie; 1871, on the fall of the Empire, vocal teacher in the R. C. M., London; dir. Bath Philh. Soc., 1878–90; pub. a "*History of the Art of Singing*," and translations.

Vitali (vē-tä'-lē), (1) **Filippo,** b. Florence, singer and composer, 1631. (2) **Giov. Bat.,** Cremona, ca. 1644—Modena, Oct. 12, 1692; 2d ct.-cond. and composer of important sonatas, ballets, etc. (3) **Tomaso,** b. Bologna, middle of 17th cent.; leader there, and c. a chaconne.

Vitry (vē-trē), **Philippe De (Philippus di Vitria'co),** b. Vitry, Pas-de-Calais; d. 1361, as Bishop of Meaux; theorist.

Vittadini (vē-tä-dē'-nē), **Franco,** b. Pavia, Italy, April, 1884; composer; pupil of Cons. Verdi, Milan; c. (operas) "*Anima Allegra*" (Costanzi, Rome, 1921, also at Met. Op. House); "*Nazareth*" (based on Selma Lagerlöf story), (Pavia, 1925); "*La Sagredo*"; also masses, motets and organ pieces.

Vittori (vĭt-tō'-rē), **Loreto,** Spoleto, 1604—Rome, 1670; composer.

Vittoria (vĭt-tō'-rĭ-ä), **Tomaso Ludovico da** (rightly **Tomas Luis De Victoria),** Avila(?), Spain, ca. 1540—Madrid, Aug. 27, 1611; went to Rome early; 1573 maestro Collegium Germanicum; 1575, of S. Apollinaris; friend and disciple of Palestrina; 1589–1602 vice ct.-conductor, Madrid; c. notable works incl. a requiem for the Empress Maria, 1605.

Vivaldi (vē-väl'-dē), **Abbate Ant.,** Venice, ca. 1675—1743; celebrated violinist; from 1713 dir. Cons. della Pietà. One of the early masters of Italian music, V. in his remarkable *concerti* developed the form created by Corelli and G. Torelli and thus was one of the precursors of the symphony. Sixteen of his concerti were transcribed by Bach for clavier or otherwise musically extended, and the concerto in D minor by Friedemann Bach for organ is a

transcription of one of his for vln. He c. some 150 vln. concerti; 18 vln. sonatas; 12 trios for vlns. and 'cello; 6 quintets for flute, vln., viola, 'cello and organ-bass; some 40 operas, as well as many cantatas, arias and other vocal works.

Vives (vē'-väs), **Amadeo,** Barcelona, 1871—Madrid, Dec. 2, 1932; composer of many Spanish zarzuelas and other stage works; succeeded Tomas Breton as teacher of comp. at Madrid R. Cons. of Music; also a leading writer on music in Spain.

Vivier (vēv-yā), (1) **Albert Jos.,** Huy, Belgium, Dec. 15, 1816—Brussels, Jan. 3, 1903; pupil of Fétis; c. opera and wrote a harmony. (2) **Eugène Léon,** Ajaccio, 1821—Nice, Feb. 24, 1900; remarkable horn-virtuoso; pupil of Gallay, then joined orch. at Paris Opéra; made many tours, was a favourite of Napoleon III., then retired to Nice; a wit and a composer of excellent songs.

Vix, **Géneviève,** 1887—Paris, 1940; soprano; sang at Madrid, Buenos Aires and (1917–18) with Chicago Opera Company.

Vizentini (vē-zĕn-te'-nē), **Louis Albert,** Paris, Nov. 9, 1841—Oct. 1906; violinist; pupil of the Paris and Brussels Cons.; critic on the *Figaro;* cond. in theatres in various cities; c. operettas, ballets, etc.

Vleeshouwer (flās'-hoo-vĕr), **Albert de,** b. Antwerp, June 8, 1863; pupil of Jan Blockx; prod. 2 operas, "*L'École des Pères*" (1892) and "*Zryni*" (Antwerp, 1895), symphonic poem, "*De wilde Jäger*," etc.

Vock'ner, **Josef,** Ebensee, March 18, 1842—Vienna, Sept. 11, 1906; organ teacher at the Cons.; c. oratorio, organ fugues, etc.

Vogel (fō'-gĕl), (1) **Jn. Chr.,** Nürnberg, 1756—Paris, 1788; dram. composer. (2) **L.,** flutist and composer. Paris, 1792—1798. (3) **Fr. Wm. Fd.,** Havelberg, Prussia, Sept. 9, 1807—Bergen, 1892; pupil of Birnbach, Berlin; toured as organist; from 1852, at Bergen, Norway; pub. a concertino for org. with trombones; symph., overture, 2 operettas, etc. (4) **(Chas. Louis) Ad.,** Lille, 1808—Paris, 1892; violinist and dram. composer. (5) **(Wm.) Moritz,** Sorgau, near Freiburg, Silesia, July 9, 1846—Leipzig, Oct. 30, 1922; pianist; pupil of Leipzig Cons.;

teacher, critic and conductor of choral socs., Leipzig; pub. pf. method, c. rondos, etc. (6) **(Ad.) Bd.**, Plauen, Saxony, 1847—Leipzig, 1898; journalist, writer and composer. (7) **Emil**, Wriezen-on-Oder, Jan. 21, 1859—Berlin, June 18, 1908; Dr. Phil., Berlin, 1887; 1883, sent to Italy by the govt. as Haberl's asst. in studying Palestrina's works; from 1893, lib. Peters Mus. Library, Leipzig; pub. monographs, etc. (8) **Vladimir**, b. Moscow, Feb. 29, 1896; noted modern composer; pupil of Busoni in comp.; in his works strongly influenced by atonal theories of Schönberg; he lived in Berlin 1918–33, after latter year in Strasbourg; a number of his works have been perf. at fests. of the I. S. C. M. c. oratorio, symph., suite, orch. pieces, string quartet, piano works, chorus, etc.

Voggenhuber (fôg′-gĕn-hoo-bĕr), **Vilma von** (Frau **V. Krolop**), Pesth, 1845—Berlin 1888; dram. soprano at Berlin ct.-opera 1868–88.

Vogl (fōkh′-′l), (1) **Jn. Michael**, Steyr, 1768—Vienna, 1840; tenor and conductor (v. FZ. SCHUBERT). (2) **Heinrich**, Au, Munich, Jan. 15, 1845— on the stage, Munich, April 21, 1900; famous tenor; début Munich ct.-opera, 1865; sang there thereafter; eminent in Wagnerian rôles at Bayreuth; prod. an opera *"Der Fremdling"* (Munich, 1899). (3) **Therese** (née **Thoma**), Tutzing, Lake of Starnberg, Nov. 12, 1845—Munich, Sept. 29, 1921; from 1868, wife of above, and like him, eminent in Wagner opera; dram. soprano; pupil of Hauser and Herger, Munich Cons.; 1864, Carlsruhe; 1865–92, Munich, then retired.

Vogler (fōkh′-lĕr), **Georg Jos. ("Abbé Vogler"),** Würzburg, June 15, 1749 —Darmstadt, May 6, 1814; famous organist; theorist and composer; pupil of Padre Martini and Vallotti; took orders at Rome; 1786–99, court-conductor Stockholm; 1807, ct.-cond. at Darmstadt; he was eminent as a teacher of radical methods; toured widely as a concert organist with his "orchestrion"; he wrote many treatises; c. 10 operas, a symphony, etc.

Vogrich (fō′-grĭkh), **Max (Wm. Carl),** Szeben (Hermannstadt), Transylvania, Jan. 24, 1852—New York,

June 10, 1916; pianist, at 7 he played in public, then pupil of Leipzig Cons.; 1870–78, toured Europe, Mexico and South America; then U. S. with Wilhelmj; 1882–86, in Australia, where he m.; after 1886, lived in New York; c. 3 grand operas (text and music) incl. *"Wanda"* (Florence, 1875); c. also an oratorio *"The Captivity"* (1884; Met. Op. 1891); 2 cantatas, Missa Solemnis; 2 symphs., vln.-concerto, etc.

Vogt (fōkht), (1) **Gustave**, Strassburg, 1781—Paris, 1870; oboist, professor and composer. (2) **Jn. (Jean),** Gross-Tinz, near Liegnitz, 1823— Eberswalde, 1888; pianist and composer. (3) **Augustus Stephen,** Washington, Ont., Aug. 14, 1861 —Toronto, Sept. 17, 1926; pianist, teacher; studied Leipzig Cons.; after 1888 taught in Toronto, 1892 at Cons., of which dir. after 1913; founded and led Mendelssohn Choir there, 1894–1917; Mus. D.

Voigt (foikht), (1) **Jn. G. Hermann,** Osterwieck, Saxony, 1769—1811; organist and composer. (2) **K.,** Hamburg, 1808—1879; conductor. (3) **Henriette** (née **Kunze**), 1808— Oct. 15, 1839; distinguished amateur musician at Leipzig; intimate friend of Schumann.

Volbach (fōl′-bäkh), **Fritz,** b. Wipperfürth, Dec. 17, 1861; organ-virtuoso; pupil of Cologne Cons. for a year; studied philosophy; then took up music again at the Royal Inst. for church mus., Berlin; from 1887 teacher there; 1892 cond. at Mainz; 1907 at Tübingen; after 1919 at Münster Univ.; has written biogs. and edited musical texts; c. symph., symph. poems, *"Ostern"* (Easter), for organ and orch. (Sheffield Fest., 1902); *"Es waren zwei Königskinder," "Alt Heidelberg, du Feine,"* a series of vocal works with orch. which he cond. in London, 1904, etc.

Volckmar (fôlk′-mär), **Wm. (Valentin),** Hersfeld, Cassel, 1812—Homberg, near Cassel, 1887; mus.-teacher, organist, writer and composer.

Volkland (fôlk′-länt), **Alfred,** Brunswick, April 10, 1841—Basel, 1905; pupil Leipzig Cons.; ct.-pianist at Sondershausen; from 1867, ct.-cond. there 1869–75, cond. Leipzig Euterpe, also co-founder the Bach-Verein; after 1875, cond. at Basel; 1889, Dr. Phil. *h. c.* (Basel Univ.).

Volkmann (fôlk'-män), **(Fr.) Robt.,**
Lommatzsch, Saxony, April 6, 1815
—Budapest, Oct. 30, 1883; notable
composer; son and pupil of a cantor;
studied with Friebel (vln. and 'cello),
Anacker (comp.) and K. F. Becker,
at Leipzig; 1839–42, taught mus. at
Prague; thereafter lived in Pesth,
excepting 1854–58, Vienna; for years
prof. of harm. and cpt. at the Nat.
Acad. of Mus., Prague; c. 2 symphs.;
3 serenades for strings; 2 overtures,
incl. *"Richard III."*; concerto for
'cello, Concertstück for pf. and
orch.; 2 masses with orch.; Christmas
Carol of the 12th cent.; old German
hymns for double male chorus; 6
duets on old German poems; 2 wed-
ding-songs; alto solo with orch.,
"An die Nacht"; dram.-scene for
soprano with orch., *"Sappho"*; pf.-
pcs. and songs. Biog. by Vogel
(Leipzig, 1875).

Vollerthun (fôl'-ĕr-tōōn), **G.,** b. Fürstenau, Sept. 29, 1876; composer.

Vollhardt (fôl'-härt), **Emil Reinhardt,** Seifersdorf, Saxony, Oct. 16,
1858—Zwickau, Feb. 10, 1926; pupil
of Leipzig Cons.; cantor Marienkirche and cond. at Zwickau; c.
motets and songs.

Vollweiler (fôl'-vī-lĕr), **K.,** Offenbach,
1813—Heidelberg, 1848; piano-
teacher and composer.

Volpe (vôl'-pē), **Arnold,** b. Kovno,
Russia, July 9, 1869—Miami, Fla.,
Feb. 2, 1940; studied at Warsaw
Cons., with Auer in St. Petersburg,
and comp. with Soloviev; came to
America in 1898; 1904, founded
Volpe Symph. Orch. in N. Y.; 1916,
led Stadium Concerts at College of
the City of New York; 1922, dir. of
Kansas City Cons.; has since taught
at Miami, Fla., Univ., and led orch.
concerts there.

Voretzsch (vō'-rĕtsh), **Jns. Felix,**
Altkirchen, July 17, 1835—Halle,
May 10, 1908; pianist and conductor.

Voss, (1) **(Vos'sius) Gerhard Jn.,**
Heidelberg, 1577—Amsterdam, 1649;
writer on mus. (2) **Isaak,** Leyden,
1618—Windsor, Engl., 1689; son of
above; canon and writer. (3) **Chas.,**
Schmarsow, Pomerania, 1815—
Verona, 1882; pianist and composer.

Vredemann (frä'-dĕ-män), (1) **Jakob,**
teacher and composer, Leuwarden,
ca. 1600—1640. (2) **Michael,** teacher
and theorist, Arnheim, 1612.

Vreuls (vrŭls), **Victor,** b. Verviers,

Feb. 4, 1876; pupil Liége Cons.
and of d'Indy, at whose Schola cantorum he became teacher of harmony; 1906–20, dir. of Luxembourg
Cons.; 1903 won the Picard prize
of the Belgian Free Academy; c.
symphonic poems, *"Triptyque"* for
voice and orch., chamber music and
songs.

Vroye (vrwä), **Th. Jos. De,** Villers-la-
Ville, Belgium, 1804—Liége, 1873;
canon and theorist.

Vuillaume (vwē-yōm), **Jean Baptiste,**
Mirecourt, Dept. of Vosges, France,
Oct. 7, 1798—Paris, March 19, 1875;
1821–25, in partnership with Lete;
he was v. succ. and a remarkable
imitator of Stradivari; inv. 1851,
"octobasse" (v. D.D.); 1855, a
larger viola "contre-alto"; in 1867 a
mute, the "pedale sourdine"; also
a machine for manufacturing gut-
strings of unvaried thickness, etc.

Vulpius (fool'-pĭ-oos), **Melchior,** Wa-
sungen, ca. 1560—Weimar, 1616,
cantor and composer.

W

Waack (väk), **Karl,** Lübeck, March 6,
1861—Neuminster, March 7, 1922;
pupil of Grand-ducal School,
Weimar; cond. in Finland and at
Riga; 1890 studied with H. Riemann,
returned to Riga as editor, cond. and
author; after 1915 led pop. concerts of
Musik-Freunde in Lübeck.

Wachtel (väkh'-tĕl), (1) **Theodor,**
Hamburg, 1823—Frankfort-on-Main,
1893; noted tenor; son and successor
of a livery-stable keeper; studied
with Frl. Grandjean. His son (2)
Th. (d. Dessau, 1875) was for a time
a tenor.

Wad'dington, Sidney Peine, b. Lincc'n,
July 23, 1869; composer; pupil
R. C. M., London; later teacher there
and pianist to Covent Garden; c.
"John Gilpin" for chorus and orch.
(1894); *"Ode to Music,"* do.; violin
and 'cello sonatas, etc.

Waelput (väl'-poot), **Hendrik,** Ghent,
1845—1885; cond., professor and
dram. composer.

Waelrant (wäl'-ränt), **Hubert,** Ton-
gerloo, Brabant, ca. 1517—Antwerp,
1595; a mus.-pub. and teacher; introduced "Bocedisation"
c. motets, etc.

Wagenaar (väkh'-ĕ-när), (1) **Johan,**
Utrecht, 1862–1941; organist at

the Cathedral; 1904, dir. of mus. school there; 1919, dir. of Cons. of Music in The Hague; c. *"Fritjofs Meerfahrt"* and *"Saul and David"* for orch., overture *"Cyrano de Bergerac,"* etc. (2) **Bernard,** b. Arnhem, Holland, Aug. 18, 1894; composer; studied Utrecht Music School of the Toonkunst Soc., comp. with Johan Wagenaar; came to America in 1925; has taught comp. at Juilliard School of Music, N. Y.; c. (orch.) 2 symphonies, Divertimento, Sinfonietta (chosen to represent U. S. at Liége Fest. of I. S. C. M. 1930); sonata for vln. and piano (prize of Soc. for Pub. of Amer. Music, 1928); also *"Three Songs from the Chinese"* for voice, flute, harp and piano; his works have been performed by N. Y. Philh., Detroit Symph., and other ensembles.

Wagenseil (vä'-gĕn-zīl), (1) **Jn. Chp.,** Nürnberg, 1633 — Altdorf, 1708; writer. (2) **G. Chp.,** Vienna, 1715—1777; teacher and composer.

Wagner (väkh'-nĕr), (1) **K. Jakob,** Darmstadt, 1772—1822; hornvirtuoso; concert-conductor; c. operas. (2) **Ernst David,** Dramburg, Pomerania, 1806—Berlin, 1883; cantor, organist, mus.-director and composer; pub. essays.

(3) (**Wm.**) **Richard,** Leipzig, May 22, 1813—Venice, Feb. 13, 1883; eminent opera composer; son of a clerk in the city police-court, who died when W. was six months old; the mother m. an actor and playwright, Ludwig Geyer of Dresden. W. attended the Dresden Kreuzschule until 1827; he transl. 12 books of the Odyssey, and at 14 wrote a bombastic and bloody Shakespearean tragedy; 1827, he studied at the Nikolai Gymnasium, Leipzig, where the family lived while his sister Rosalie was engaged at the City Theatre there. Wagner was impelled music-ward by hearing a Beethoven symph. and took up Logir's "Thoroughbass." He then studied theory with the organist Gottlieb Müller and c. a string-quartet, a sonata and an aria. 1830, after matriculation at Leipzig Univ., he studied six months with Th. Weinlig (comp.) and c. a pf.-sonata, and a 4-hand polonaise. He studied Beethoven's symphs. very thoroughly. At 30 he c. a symph. in 4 movements,

prod. at the Gewandhaus, Leipzig, 1833. He wrote the libretto for an opera, *"Die Hochzeit,"* an introduction, septet, and a chorus 1832, but his sister Rosalie thought it immoral and he gave it up; 1833 his brother Albert, stage-manager and singer at the Würzburg Theatre invited him to be chorusm. there. He c. a romantic opera in 3 acts *"Die Feen,"* to his own libretto (after *"La Donna serpente,"* by Gozzi); it was accepted but never performed, by the Leipzig th.-dir. Ringelhardt (given at Munich, 1888). 1834, he became cond. at the Magdeburg Th. Here he c. (text and music) *"Das Liebesverbot* (after Shakespeare's *"Measure for Measure"*), performed by a bankrupt troupe, 1836. Th.-cond. at Königsberg, and m. (1836) an actress Wilhelmine Planer, who d. 1866, after they had separated in 1861.

He c. an overture *"Rule Britannia."* 1837 cond. Riga opera. Moved by Meyerbeer's triumphs at the Gr. Opéra at Paris, W. went there, July, 1839, by sea. The voyage lasted 3½ weeks and was very stormy; the experience suggested to him the opera *"Flying Dutchman."* Meyerbeer gave him letters to musicians and pubs. in Paris; here he suffered poverty and supported himself by songwriting, arranging dances for piano and cornet, preparing the pf.-score of Halévy's *"Reine de Chypre,"* and writing articles. His operas were scornfully rejected and he could get no hearing till the v. succ. *"Rienzi"* was prod., Dresden, 1842, and *"Der Fliegende Holländer,"* Jan. 2, 1843. The novelties in this work provoked a furious opposition that never ceased. 1843–49 he was cond. of Dresden Opera, also cond. Dresden Liedertafel, for which he wrote a biblical scene, *"Das Liebesmahl der Apostel,"* for 3 choirs, a cappella, later with full orch. *"Tannhäuser"* was prod., Dresden, 1845, with succ. in spite of bitter opposition. In 1848 *"Lohengrin"* was finished; but the mgr. of the Opera did not care to risk the work. He now wrote out a little sketch *"Die Nibelungen, Weltgeschichte aus der Sage"*; a prose study on *"Der Niebelungen-Mythus als Entwurf zu einem Drama"* (1848), and a 3-act drama with Prologue, written in alliterative verse, *"Sieg fried's Tod,"* preparations for the great work to follow. A rashly expressed sympathy with the revolutionary cause (1849) made flight necessary; he went to Weimar with Liszt, but had to go on to Paris to escape the order for his arrest. 1849 he proceeded to Zurich, were he wrote a series of remarkable essays: *"Die Kunst und die Revolution"* (1849), *"Das Kunstwerk der Zukunft,"* *"Kunst und Klima,"* *"Das Judenthum in der Musik"* (1850), *"Oper und Drama,"* *"Erinnerungen an Spontini,"* a prose drama *"Wieland der Schmiedt,"* and the 3 poems of the Niebelungen trilogy (privately printed 1853). The music of *"Das Rheingold"* was finished 1854, *"Die Walküre,"* 1856. He cond. orch. concerts with much succ., lectured on the mus. drama, prod. *"Tannhäuser"* (Zurich, 1855); 1855 he cond. 8 concerts of the London Philh. Soc. 1857 he left *"Siegfried"* unfinished and c. *"Tristan und Isolde."* 1860 he gave concerts of his own works, winning many enthusiastic enemies and some valuable friends. The French Emperor ordered *"Tannhäuser"* to be prod. at the Gr. Opéra, March 13, 1861. It provoked such an elaborate and violent opposition (for omitting the ballet) that it was withdrawn after the third performance. W. was now permitted to return to Germany; *"Tristan"* was accepted at the Vienna ct.-opera, but after 57 rehearsals the singers declared it impossible to learn. In 1863, he pub. text of the *"Nibelung Ring"* despairing of ever completing the mus. When his financial state was most desperate, King Ludwig II. of Bavaria (1864) invited him to Munich and summoned von Bülow as cond. to prod. *"Tristan und Isolde"* (June 10, 1865); but opposition was so bitter that W. settled at Triebschen, Lucerne, and completed the scores of *"Die Meistersinger"* (prod. Munich, 1868) and *"Der Ring des Nibelungen,"* *"Siegfried"* (1869) and *"Götterdämmerung"* (1874). Though King Ludwig's scheme for a special Wagner Theatre in Munich was given up, there were by now enough Wagner-lovers and societies throughout the world, to subscribe funds for a theatre at Bayreuth, where the corner-stone was laid in 1872, on his 60th birthday. In August, 1876, complete performances of *"Der Ring des Nibelungen"* were given there under most splendid auspices, but with a deficit of $37,500, paid off by a partially succ. festival in London, 1877, and by the setting aside of the royalties from performances at Munich. He now set to work on the *"Bühnenweihfestspiel"* (Stage - consecrating - festival - play) *"Parsifal,"* finished, and prod. in 1882. The same year ill-health sent him to Venice, where he d. suddenly. His writings (extravagantly praised and condemned) are pub. in various eds. There is an English translation in 8 volumes, by Wm. Ashton Ellis.

1870 he m. Cosima, the divorced wife of von Bülow and natural daughter of Liszt (she d. 1930). After his death she had charge of the Bayreuth Festivals for a number of years, but 1909 yielded the direction to her son, Siegfried. Since his death, 1930, his widow, Winifred has been in charge.

In the half century since W.'s death his music has been universally accepted as the corner-stone of modern operatic repertoires. Concerning his personal character there has been much polemical writing, ranging from actual vilification to the most fervid veneration. Particularly about his autobiography, controversy has centred, with some commentators asserting that his life history was altered somewhat after a few privately printed copies of the original edition were struck off. It was therefore of sensational interest when, in 1929, the so-called "Burrell Collection" of Wagneriana, made by an Englishwoman of that name, who wrote a biog. of his earlier years, was discovered in a strongbox in Great Britain after her death. This collection was bought by Mrs. Mary Louise Curtis Bok and now is housed at the Curtis Inst. of Music, Phila. But the "revelations" it was supposed to contain, as thus far made public, only in minor details altered the impressions contained in his book, *"Mein Leben."*

Besides his operas and the other works mentioned he c. a symph. (1832); 6 overtures, incl. *"Konzertouvertüre ziemlich fugirt,"* *"Polo-*

nia," "Columbus," "Rule Britannia"; "*New Year's Cantata*"; incid. mus. to Gleich's farce "*Der Berggeist*" (Magdeburg, 1836); "*Huldigungs-marsch*" (1864, finished by Raff); "*Siegfried Idyll*" (1870, for his son then a year old), "*Kaisermarsch*" (1870), "*Festival March*" (for the Centennial Exposition, Philadelphia, 1876), "*Gelegenheits-Cantata*" (for unveiling a statue of King Friedrich, August, 1843), "*Gruss an den König*" (1843, pf.), "*An Weber's Grabe*" (Funeral March for wind-instrs. on motives from Weber's "*Eu-ryanthe*," and double quartet for voices, 1844). For Pf.: sonata; polonaise, for four hands; fantaisie, "*Albumsonate, für Frau Mathilde We-sendonck*" (1853); "*Ankunft bei den Schwarzen Schwanen*" (1861); "*Ein Albumblatt für Fürstin Metternich*" (1861), "*Albumblatt für Frau Betty Schott*" (1875). Songs: "*Carna-valslied*" from "*Das Liebesverbot*" (1835–36); "*Dors, mon enfant,*" "*Mignonne,*" "*Attente*" (1839–40), "*Les deux Grenadiers*" (1839); "*Der Tannenbaum*" (1840); "*Kraftlied-chen*" (1871), "*Fünf Gedichte*"; 1, "*Der Engel*"; 2, "*Stehe still*"; 3, "*Im Treibhaus*"; 4, "*Schmerzen*", 5, "*Träume*" (1862).

Biog. by C. F. Glasenapp (1876); F. Hueffer (1881); R. Pohl (1883); W. Tappert (1883); H. v. Wolzogen (1883); Ad. Jullien (1886); H. T. Finck (1893); H. S. Chamberlain (1897); E. Dannreuther, F. Präger (1893); G. Kobbé; Glasenapp and Ellis (1900). There are many trea-tises on his works. His letters have also been published in various forms. Among the vast number of other studies of his life and music are works by Torchi, Lidgey, Henderson, Kienzl, Newman, Mrs. Burrell, Adler, Buerkner, Koch, Schjelderup, Lichtenberger, E. Schmitz, Hadden, Kapp, Pfohl, Batka, Runciman, Huckel, Aldrich, Becker, Blackburn, Buesst, Heintz, Krehbiel, Lavignac, McSpadden, Neumann, Pourtalès, Shaw, Thompson and Wallace. "*Wagner-Lexikons*" have been pub-lished by Tappert and Stein, a "*Wagner-Encyclopedia*" by Glase-napp, while a comprehensive list of more than 10,000 books and essays on his life and music is contained in Oesterlein's "*Katalog einer Wagner-*

Bibliothek." There is also a "*Wagner-Jahrbuch*" and much material has been issued in the "*Bayreuther Blätter,*" ed. by Wolzogen.

(4) **Siegfried,** Triebschen, Lucerne, June 6, 1869—Bayreuth, Aug. 4, 1930; only son of above; attended a polytechnic sch., but took up mus. as pupil of Kniese and Humperdinck; 1893, concert-cond. in Germany, Austria, Italy and England; from 1898 he was teacher in Vienna; 1901 cond. Acad. Singing Society, and Tonkünstler Orch.; 1912, cond. special concert of the London Symph. orch.; from 1896 he cond. at Bay-reuth; later co-director with his mother, and 1909 both artistic and mus. dir.; in 1924 he visited the U. S. as cond. to raise funds for resumption of the fests. (discon-tinued 1914); m. Winifred Klind-worth, who since his death has had charge at Bayreuth; c. operas "*Der Kobold*" (Hamburg, 1904), "*Bruder Lustig*" (do., 1905), "*Das Sternenge-bot*" (do., 1908), "*Banadietrich*" (Elberfeld, 1910) and "*Schwarz-schwanenreich*" (Black-swan Coun-try), "*Sonnenflammen,*" "*Der Heidenkönig,*" "*Der Friedensengel,*" also male and female choruses; a symph. poem "*Sehnsucht*" (Schiller), text and music of mod. succ. comic-romantic opera "*Der Bärenhäuter*" (Munich Ct. Th., 1899), unsucc., "*Herzog Wildfang*" (1901). (5) (Jachmann-Wagner), Johanna, near Hanover, Oct. 13, 1828—Würzburg, Oct. 16, 1894; niece of (1); dram. soprano; created "Elizabeth," 1845; m. a Judge Jachmann.

Waissel (vīs'-sĕl), (Waisse'lius) **Matthias,** b. Bartenstein, Prussia; lutenist and composer at Frankfort, 1573.

Walcker (väl'-kĕr), (1) **Eberhard Fr.,** Cannstadt, 1794—Ludwigsburg, 1872; son of a skilled org.-builder; himself a noted org.-builder; suc-ceeded by his five sons, (2) **H.** (b. Oct. 10, 1828), (3) **Fr.** (b. Sept. 17, 1829), (4) **K.** (b. March 6, 1845), (5) **Paul** (b. May 31, 1846), and (6) **Eberhard** (b. April 8, 1850).

Waldersee (väl'-dĕr-zā), **Paul,** Count **von,** Potsdam, Sept. 3, 1831—Königsberg, June 14, 1906; a Prussian officer from 1848–71, then took up mus.; editor of Beethoven and Mozart works.

Waldteufel (vält'-toi-fĕl), **Emil**, Strassburg, Dec. 9, 1837—Paris, Feb. 16, 1915; pupil Paris Cons.; pianist to Empress Eugénie; c. immensely succ. waltzes.

Wa'ley, Simon, London, 1827—1875, pianist and composer.

Walker (wôk'-ĕr), (1) **Jos. Casper**, Dublin, 1760—St.-Valéry, France, 1810; writer. (2) **Jos. and Sons**, org.-builders, London. (3) **Edyth**, b. Hopewell, N. Y., March 27, 1870; contralto; studied Dresden Cons. with Orgeni; engaged at the Vienna opera for 4 years as 1st alto; also in concert; Met. Op. Co., 1903–06; then in Berlin, Hamburg and, 1912–17, Munich Op.; after 1933 taught at Amer. Cons., Fontainebleau. (4) **Ernest**, b. Bombay, July 15, 1870; composer; Mus. Bac. Oxford, 1893; Mus. Doc. 1898; from 1900, dir. at Balliol College; mainly self-taught as composer of *"Stabat Mater," "Hymn to Dionysus,"* and *"Ode to Nightingale"* for voices and orch.; overture, chamber music, songs, etc.

Wal'lace, (1) **Wm. Vincent**, Waterford, Ireland, June 1, 1814—Château de Bages, Haute Garonne, Oct. 12, 1865; violinist; wandered over the world; c. very pop. pf.-pcs. and c. 6 operas includ. the very succ. *"Maritana"* (London, 1845); and *"Lurline"* (do. 1860). (2) **William**, b. Greenock, July 3, 1860; at first a surgeon; in 1889 took up music and studied at the R. A. M., London, till 1890; c. symph. *"The Creation"* (New Brighton, 1892); choral symph. *"Koheleth"*; 6 symph. poems, *"The Passing of Beatrice"* (Crystal Palace, 1892), *"Amboss oder Hammer"* (do., 1896), *"Sister Helen"* (do. 1899), *"Greeting to the New Century"* (London Phil., 1891), *"Sir William Wallace"* (Queen's Hall, 1905), *"François Villon"* (New Symph., 1909; also by New York Phil., 1910, 1912), overtures, suites, song cycles, 1-act lyric tragedy *"Brassolis,"* etc.; author of poetry and a critical work, *"The Threshold of Music."*

Wallaschek (väl'-lä-shĕk), **Richard**, Brünn, Nov. 16, 1860—Vienna, April 24, 1917; after 1896 docent at Univ. in latter city; pub. 1886, valuable treatise *"Æsthetik der Tonkunst."*

Wallenstein (väl'-lĕn-shtīn), (1) **Martin**, Frankfort-on-Main, 1843—1896; pianist; c. comic opera. (2) **Alfred**, b. Chicago, Oct. 7, 1898; 'cellist and conductor; studied with Julius Klengel; début, Los Angeles, 1912; solo 'cellist in Chicago Symph., afterwards for several seasons with N. Y. Philh., with which he also appeared as soloist; cond. of orch. on the radio, and after 1935, dir. of music for Station WOR, Newark.

Wallerstein (väl'-lĕr-shtīn), **Anton**, Dresden, 1813—Geneva, 1892; violinist and composer.

Wall'is, J., Ashford, Kent, 1616—London, 1693; acoustician.

Walliser (väl'-lĭ-zĕr), **Chp. Thos.**, Strassburg, 1568—1648; mus.-dir., theorist and composer.

Wallnöfer (väl'-nä-fĕr), **Ad.**, b. Vienna, April 26, 1854; pupil of Waldmüller, Krenn and Dessoff (comp.), Rokitansky (singing); barytone at Vienna; 1882, with Neumann's troupe; 1897–98, N. Y.; after 1908 lived in Munich; for a time active as theatre dir. in Stettin and Neustrelitz; c. succ. op. *"Eddystone"* (Prague, 1889), etc.

Walmisley (wämz'-lĭ), (1) **Thos. Forbes**, London, 1783—1866; organist and composer. (2) **Thos. Attwood**, London, 1814—Hastings, 1856; son of above; professor and composer.

Walsh, John, d. London, 1736; mus.-publisher.

Walter (väl'-tĕr), (1) **Ignaz**, Radowitz, Bohemia, 1759 — Ratisbon, 1822; tenor and composer. (2) **Juliane** (née **Roberts**), wife of above; a singer. (3) **Aug.**, Stuttgart, 1821 —Basel, Jan. 22, 1896; mus.-director and composer. (4) **Gustav**, Bilin, Bohemia, Feb. 11, 1834—Vienna, Jan. 31, 1910; tenor; pupil of Prague Cons.; début in Brunn; 1856–87, principal lyric tenor at Vienna ct.-opera. (5) **Bruno**, b. Berlin, Sept. 15, 1876; family name Schlesinger; noted conductor; studied at Stern Cons., Berlin, with Radecke, Ehrlich and Bussler; early held bâton posts in both opera and orchestral music at Cologne, Hamburg, Breslau, Pressburg and Riga; 1900–01, Berlin Ct.-Opera; 1901–12, Vienna Ct.-Opera; 1913–22, gen. mus. dir. at Munich, succeeding Mottl; he made visits to the U. S. as guest cond. of the N. Y. Symph. in the next 2 seasons; 1925–29, mus. dir. of Berlin

Städtische Oper; 1929-33, cond. of
Gewandhaus Orch., Leipzig; also
led annual series with Berlin Philh.
Orch.; appeared much in other
countries, including Covent Garden,
London, at the Salzburg Fest., in
Paris, Vienna and Amsterdam; in
1933 he resigned his Berlin posts following accession to political power of
the Nat'l Socialists; co-dir. Vienna
Op., and Philh. Orch., 1936-38; cond.
part of season with N. Y. Philh.
Orch. in 1933 and 1934; c. orch.
works, chamber music and songs.

Walther von der Vogelweide (väl'-
ter fōn děr fō'-gĕl-vī-dĕ), in the
Tyrol (?), ca. 1160—Würzburg, after
1227; the chief Minnesinger and
lyric poet of mediæval Germany.

Walther (väl'-tĕr), (1) Jn., Thuringia,
1496—Torgau, 1570; singer and
composer; ct.-conductor. (V. MAR-
TIN LUTHER.) (2) Jn. Jakob, b.
Witterda, near Erfurt, 1650; ct.-
musician, publisher and composer.
(3) Jn. Gf., Erfurt, 1684—Weimar,
1748; organist, writer and composer.
(4) Jn. Chp., Weimar, 1715-71;
organist and composer.

Wal'thew, Richard H., b. London,
Nov. 4, 1872; pupil of the Guildhall and with scholarship at R. C. M.
under Parry; 1907 prof. at Queen's
College, and cond. opera class at the
Guildhall; 1909 cond. at Finsbury,
c. "Pied Piper" for chorus and orch;
piano concerto, two operettas, etc.

Wal'ton, William Turner, b. Oldham,
England, March 29, 1902; composer;
pupil at 10 at Christ Church Cath.,
Oxford; later studied music at that
Univ. with Sir Hugh Allen and E. J.
Dent, but mostly self-trained; he
came to the fore while still young
with a piano quartet, a string quartet, and esp. successfully with an
amusing work called "Façade,"
settings of poems by Edith Sitwell,
for reciter and small ensemble, the
speaking voice issuing from a mega-
phone in a backdrop; he also c.
"Portsmouth Point" overture, "Dr.
Syntax," a "pedagogical overture";
"The Passionate Pilgrim" for tenor
and orch.; a viola concerto, and a
symph. which was anticipated with
so much interest that parts were
performed before it was completed
(1935); his cantata, "Belshazzar's
Feast" (1933) first heard at an
English fest., later in London, N. Y.

and elsewhere, has striking qualities
of color and rhythmic variety.

Wälzel (vĕl'-tsĕl), **Camillo**, Magdeburg, 1829—Vienna, 1895; librettist,
(pseud. **F. Zell**).

Wambach (väm'-bäkh), **Émile (X.)**,
Arlon, Luxembourg, Nov. 26, 1854—
Antwerp, May 6, 1924; pupil of
Antwerp Cons.; c. symph. poem,
"Aan de boorden van de Schelde,"
orch. fantasias, Flemish drama
"Nathan's Parabel"; 2 oratorios;
a hymn for chorus and orch., etc.

Wangemann (väng'-ĕ-män), **Otto**,
Loitz-on-the-Peene, Jan. 9, 1848—
Berlin, Feb. 25, 1914; pupil of G.
Flügel, Stettin and Fr. Kiel at Ber-
lin; 1878, organist and singing-teacher
Demmin Gymnasium; wrote org.
treatise.

Wanhal (Van Hal) (vän'-häl), Jn.
Bapt., Neu-Nechanitz, Bohemia,
1739—Vienna, 1813; composer.

Wannenmacher (vän'-nĕn-mäkh-ĕr)
(or **Vannius**), **Johannes**, d. Inter-
laken, ca. 1551; important Swiss
church composer and canon; renounced Catholicism, was tortured,
and banished.

Wanski (vän'-shkĭ), (1) Jn. Nepomuk, b. ca. 1800 (?); son of (2) Jan
(a pop. Polish song-composer); violinist; pupil of Baillot; toured widely,
then lived at Aix; wrote a vln.
method and c. études, etc.

Ward, J., d. before 1641; English
composer.

Ware, Harriet, b. Waupun, Wis., 1877;
graduated at Pillsbury Cons. Owa-
tonna, Minn., 1895; pupil of Wm.
Mason, N. Y. for 2 years, then of
Stojowski (piano and comp.) and
Juliana, Paris, later of Hugo Kaun,
Berlin; c. "The Fay Song"; cantata
"Sir Olaf" (New York Symph. 1910),
piano pieces and many songs.

Warlamoff (vär'-lä-môf), **Alex. Jegoro-
vitch**, Moscow, 1801—1848; singing-
teacher and composer.

"Warlock, Peter", see **Heseltine,
Philip**.

War'ner, H. Waldo, b. Northampton,
England, Jan. 4, 1874; composer,
violinist; studied Guildhall School
of Music, London; laureate, R. A. M.,
1895-96; assoc., Guildhall School
with gold medal, 1899, fellow, 1924;
mem. of London String Quartet
1908-29 as viola player; c. string
quartets, orch. music, 3 piano trios,
piano quintet, and other works, incl.

"The Pixie Ring," popular with quartets; awarded Coolidge and Cobbett chamber music prizes and that of Phila. Mus. Fund Soc.

War'nery, Edmond, b. Elbeuf, 1876; operatic tenor (originally barytone); pupil of Paris Cons.; 1899—1907, sang at Paris Op.-Comique; after 1910 with Chicago Op.

Warn'ke, Heinrich, b. near Heide, Holstein, 1871; 'cellist; studied at Hamburg and Leipzig Cons.; after 1898 played in Kaim Orch., Munich; mem. of trio with Weingartner and Rettich; from 1905 mem. of Boston Symphony Orchestra.

Warnots (văr-nō), (1) **Jean Arnold,** (1801—1861). (2) **Henri,** Brussels, 1832—1893; opera-tenor; son and pupil of above; c. operetta. His daughter and pupil (3) **Elly,** b Liége, 1862; soprano; début, Brussels, 1879; sang there, then at Florence, Paris Op.-Com., etc.

Warot (vă-rō), (1) **Charles,** Dunkirk, Nov. 14, 1804—Brussels, July 29, 1836; violinist and theatre-cond.; pupil of Fridzeri; c. operas, 3 grand masses, etc. His brother (2) **Victor,** Ghent, 1808—Bois Colombes, 1877; cond. and teacher; c. operettas, a mass, etc. (3) **Victor Alex. Jos.,** Verviers, 1834—Paris, 1906; son of (2); opera tenor, later teacher at Paris Cons.

War'ren, (1) **Jos.,** London, 1804— Kent, 1881; organist, pianist, violinist, composer and writer. (2) **G. Wm.,** Albany, N. Y., Aug. 17, 1828— New York, 1902; self-taught organist; from 1870, organist St. Thomas's Ch., New York; prof. Columbia Univ.; c. church-mus. (3) **Samuel Prowse,** Montreal, Canada, Feb. 18, 1841—New York, Oct. 7, 1915; organist; pupil of Haupt, Gv. Schumann (pf.) and Wieprecht (instr.); 1865-67, organist of All Souls' Ch., New York; later at Trinity Ch.; c. church-mus., org.-pcs., etc. (4) **Richard Henry,** Albany, N. Y., Sept. 17, 1859—South Chatham, Mass., Dec. 3, 1933; son and pupil of (2), also studied abroad; from 1886 org. at St. Bartholomew's, N. Y.; founder and cond. of church choral soc., which gave many important works their first hearing; Parker's *" Hora Novissima"* was written for this society. C. anthems, services, a comic opera, songs, etc.

Wartel (văr-těl), (1) **Pierre Fran.,** Versailles, 1806—Paris, 1882; tenor. (2) **Atala Thérèse** (née **Adrien**), Paris, July 2, 1814—Nov. 6, 1865; wife of above; 1831-38, prof. at Paris Cons.; c. pf.-studies, etc. (3) **Emil,** son of above; sang for years Th. Lyrique, then founded a sch.

Wasielewski (vä-zē-lěf'-shki), **Jos. W. von,** Gross-Leesen, Danzig, 1822 —Sondershausen, 1896; violinist, conductor, critic, composer, and important historical writer.

Wassermann (väs'-sĕr-män), **H. Jos.,** Schwarzbach, near Fulda, 1791— Riehen, n. Basel, 1838; violinist and composer.

Wat'son, (1) **Thos.,** Eng. composer, 1590. (2) **Wm. Michael,** Newcastle-on-Tyne, 1840—E. Dulwich, London, 1889; teacher and composer under pen-name **Jules Favre.**

Watts, Wintter, b. Cincinnati, O., March 14, 1886; composer; studied painting and architecture, also singing in Florence, and theory with Goetschius; 1919, won Loeb Prize; c. (orch.) *"Two Etchings"*; incid. music to *"Alice in Wonderland,"* ballads and songs, some of them with orch., and the vocal cycles, *"Vignettes of Italy," "Wings of Night," "Like Music on the Water."*

Webb, (1) **Daniel,** Taunton, 1735— Bath, 1815; writer. (2) **G. Jas.,** Rushmore Lodge, near Salisbury, Engl., 1803—Orange, N. J., 1887; organist and editor.

Webbe (wĕb), (1) **Samuel, Sr.,** Minorca, 1740—London, 1816; ed. colls., etc. (2) **Samuel, Jr.,** London, 1770 —1843; son of above; writer and composer.

Web'ber, Amherst, b. Cannes, Oct. 25, 1867; studied music at Oxford, then at Dresden with Nicodé and at Paris Cons.; pianist to Covent Garden and Met. Op., N. Y.; c. symph. (Warsaw Phil., 1904, Boston Symph., 1905); 1-act opera *"Fiorella"* (London, 1905), songs, etc.

Weber (vā'-bĕr), (1) **Fridolin** (b. Zelli, 1733—d. 1764), and his bro. (2) **Fz. Anton** (Freiburg, 1734— Mannheim, 1812), were violinists in the orch. of the Elector K. Theodor. **Fz.** became cond. of Eutin town orch. His four daughters were (3) **Josepha** (d. 1820), soprano; m. the violinist Hofer, 1789, later **m.**

a bass, Meyer. For her Mozart c. "The Queen of the Night" in the "*Magic Flute.*" (4) **Aloysia**, 1750—Salzburg, 1839. Mozart's first love; she m. an actor, Lange, 1780 and toured as a singer. (5) **Constanze**, Zell, 1763—Salzburg, 1842. Mozart's wife (1782); 1809, m. Nissen. (6) **Sophie**, 1764—Salzburg, 1843; m. the tenor Haibl. (7) **Fr. Aug.**, Heilbronn, 1753—1806; physician and c. (8) **Bd. Anselm**, Mannheim, April 18, 1766—Berlin, March 23, 1821; pianist, conductor and dram. composer. (9) (**Fr.**) **Dionys**, Welchau, Bohemia, Oct. 9, 1766—Prague, Dec. 25, 1842; 1811, founder and 1st dir. Prague Cons., c. operas, etc. (10) **Gf.**, theorist and composer, Freinsheim, near Mannheim, 1779—Kreuznach, Sept. 12, 1839; amateur pianist, flutist and 'cellist, also cond.; wrote essays and valuable treatises; c. 3 masses, a requiem and a Te Deum with orch. and pf.-sonata. (11) **Fridolin** (II.), b. 1761; son of (2), and step-broth. of (12); pupil of Haydn; singer and mus.-director. (12) **K. Maria** (**Fr. Ernst**), Freiherr von, Eutin, Oldenburg, Dec. 18, 1786—(of consumption) London, June 5, 1826; son of the second wife of (2) and cousin, by marriage, of Mozart; the founder of German national opera (Wagner shows his influence deeply), and of the Romantic Sch.; perhaps the most widely influential German composer of the cent. He was important not solely as a path-finder, but also showed a striking artistic individuality; he was also a notable pianist (he could stretch a 12th), and a pioneer in modern pianistic composition. At first a pupil of his step-bro. (11). His mother, Genoveva (d. 1798, of consumption), was a dram. singer, and the family led a wandering life. At 10 he became pf.-pupil of J. P. Heuschkel. As a chorister in the cathedral at Salzburg, 1797, he had gratuitous lessons in comp. from Michael Haydn, to whom he dedicated his first published comps., six fughettas (1798). 1798—1800, at Munich, he studied singing with Valesi, and comp. with Kalcher. At 12 he c. an opera (the MS. lost or burned). He also appeared as concert-pianist. He met Aloys Senefelder, the inv. of lithography, and

engraved his own op. 2, 1800, and made improvements in the process. At 13 he c. and prod. with succ. the opera "*Das Waldmädchen*" (Freiburg, also played at Chemnitz, Prague, Vienna and St. Petersburg). In 1801, he c. a third opera "*Peter Schmoll und seine Nachbarn*" (Augsburg, 1803?); 1803, in Vienna, he became a pupil of Abbé Vogler. 1804, cond. Breslau City Th.; resigned 1806; supported himself by lessons, then mus.-intendant to Duke Eugen of Würtemberg; 1807, private secretary to Duke Ludwig at Stuttgart, and mus.-master to his children. In a turmoil of intrigue and dissipation he forgot his art, until he became involved in a quarrel leading to his banishment in 1810. This sobered him and awoke his better self. Going to Mannheim, he prod. his first symph.; then rejoined Abbé Vogler, at Darmstadt. His opera "*Silvana*" was prod. (Frankfort-on-Main, 1810), and "*Abu Hassan*," a comic Singspiel (Munich, 1811). He made a concert-tour to various cities, 1813, cond. of the Landständisches Th. at Prague, where he reorganised the opera, and won such note that in 1816 the King of Saxony called him to Dresden to reorganise the Royal Opera. At 20 he began "*Der Freischütz*," but gave it up till later (the incid. mus. to Wolff's "*Preciosa*" took 3 weeks). In 1817, he m. the singer Karoline Brandt, a member of his company to whom he had long been engaged. They toured together as pianist and singer. "*Der Freischütz*" was prod. with tremendous succ., Berlin, 1821; its strong nationalism provoking a frenzy of admiration. But "*Euryanthe*" (Vienna, 1823) had much less succ. 1824, he was commissioned to write "*Oberon*," for Covent Garden, London, but consumption delayed its completion; it was prod. (London, 1826) with much succ. He lived only eight weeks longer; his body was taken to the family vault at Dresden. DRAMATIC WORKS: Besides the operas already mentioned are c. "*Rübezahl*" (begun 1804, not completed): "*Die Drei Pintos*" (completed by G. Mahler, written and prod. Leipzig, 1888). Incid. mus. to Schiller's "*Turandot*," Müllner's "*König Yngurd*," Gehe's "*Heinrich IV.*,"

and Houwald's *"Der Leuchtthurm."*
C. also cantatas, incl. *"Der erste Ton"*
(1808); and *"Kampf und Sieg"* (on
the battle of Waterloo), with orch.
(1815); *"Natur und Liebe,"* 1818;
hymn, *"In seiner Ordnung schafft
der Herr,"* with orch.; (1812), 2
masses and 2 offertories, with orch.;
some very pop. songs, four scenas
and arias for soprano with orch.; 2
scenas and arias for tenor, chorus
and orch.; 19 part-songs, some very
pop.; and children's songs; 6 canons
à 3–4; duets (op. 31); 2 symphs.
(both in C); Jubel-Ouvertüre; 2
clarinet-concertos; bassoon-concerto;
adagio and rondo ungarese for bassoon with orch.; variations for many
instrs.; chamber-mus.; 2 pf.-concer-
tos, Concertstück with orch., 10 sonatas, a 4-hand sonata, the famous
waltz *"Aufforderung zum Tanze"*
(*"Invitation to the Dance"*), op. 65;
12 Allemandes; 6 Ecossaises; 18
*"Valses favorites de l'impératrice de
France"*; several sets of Variations,
etc. The so-called *"Weber's Last
Waltz"* (*Thought or Farewell*) was
written by Reissiger; a MS. copy
of it being found in W.'s papers.
Biog. by Barbedette (Paris, 1862,
Leipzig, 1864–68). Jähns (Leipzig,
1873); Carl v. Weber (W.'s grandson) pub. his beautiful letters to his
wife (1886); Th. Hell (1828). An
almost ideal biog. is that of W.'s son
the Baron Max Maria von W. (in 3
vols., 1866–68). Other memoirs by
Benedict, Reissmann, Nohl, Skalla,
Gehrmann, Höcker, Von der Pfordten,
O. Schmidt, etc. Thematic catalogue by Jähns, 1871.
(13) **Edmund von,** Hildesheim, 1766
—Würzburg, 1828; mus.-director
and composer. (14) **Ernst H.,**
Wittenberg, June 24, 1795—Leipzig,
Jan., 1878, with his brother (15)
Wm. Ed. (1804—1891), prof. at
Göttingen; writer on acoustics, etc.
(16) **Fz.,** Cologne, 1805—1876; or-
ganist, conductor and composer. (17)
Eduard W., town-musician, Franken-
berg. (18) **K. H.,** Frankenberg,
Aug. 9, 1834—?; son of above;
pupil of Leipzig Cons., 1866–70;
from 1877, dir. Imp. Russian Mus.
Soc. at Saratov, pub. a pf.-method.
(19) **G. Victor,** Ober-Erlenbach,
Upper Hesse, Feb. 25, 1838—May-
ence, Sept. 24, 1911; pupil of
Schrems, Ratisbon; took orders;

since 1866, cond. at Mayence Cath.,
expert and writer on org.-building;
composer. (20) **Gustav,** München-
buchsee, Switzerland, 1845—Zurich,
1887; organist, conductor and composer. (21) **Miroslaw,** Prague,
Nov. 9, 1854—Munich, Jan. 2, 1906;
violinist; pupil of his father; at 10
played before the Austrian Emperor,
and toured; pupil of Blazek, Prague;
also of the Cons.; Konzertmeister,
royal orch. at Wiesbaden, and 2nd
cond. at the opera (resigned, 1893);
1889, R. Mus.-Dir. C. incid. mus.
to ballet *"Die Rheinnixe"* (Wiesbaden, 1884), 2 string quartets (the
2nd taking prize at Petersburg,
1891), etc.
Webern (vā'-bĕrn), **Anton von,** b.
Vienna, Dec. 3, 1883; composer;
Ph. D., Vienna Univ., studied theory
with Guido Adler and comp. with
Schönberg, whose atonal musical
system he adopted, but with some
individual changes; one of the outstanding members of the Schönberg
circle, W. has in recent years developed a highly reticent musical
style, writing extremely short pieces,
with fragile timbres only employed
and with much economy of design;
these have an exquisite quality, if
rather abstract and aloof; c. (orch.)
Passacaglia, Six Pieces, Five Pieces,
5 symphs.; (chamber music) quartet,
trio, vln. and 'cello works, choruses,
songs, piano pieces, etc.; winner
of Vienna State Prize, 1924.
Wecker (vĕk'-ĕr), **Georg Kaspar,**
Nuremberg, 1632—1695; organist,
teacher and composer.
Weckerlin (vĕk-ĕr-lăṅ), **Jean Bapt.
Th.,** Gebweiller, Alsatia, Nov. 9,
1821—Trottberg, Alsatia, May 10,
1910; entered his father's business of
cotton-dyeing; in 1844, studied singing with Ponchard and comp. with
Halévy at the Paris Cons., prod.
heroic choral symph. *"Roland,"*
1847; gave mus.-lessons; 1853, prod.
succ. 1-act opera, *"L'Organiste dans
l'embarras"* (100 performances, Th.-
Lyrique), followed by several
privately performed operettas, 2
comic operas in Alsatian dialect,
1-act opera *"Après Fontenot"* (Th.-
Lyrique, 1877); 1869, asst.-libr.
Paris Cons.; 1876, libr.; wrote
bibliogr. and other articles and
treatises, and ed. valuable colls.
C. *"Symphonie de la forêt,"* an

oratorio *"Le Jugement Dernier,"* 2 cantatas, incl. *"Paix, Charité, Grandeur"* (Opéra, 1866); the ode-symphonie *"Les Poèmes de la Mer,"* etc.

Weckmann (věk'-män), **Matthias,** Oppershausen, 1621—Hamburg, 1674; organ-virtuoso and comp.

Wedekind (vā'-dě-kǐnt), **Erika,** b. Hanover, Nov. 13, 1869; coloratura soprano; pupil of Orgeni at Dresden Cons.; 1894—1909 at court opera Dresden, then at Berlin Comic Opera.

Weelkes (wēks), **Thos.,** organist Chichester Cathedral; c. notable madrigals, etc.; d. London, Nov. 30, 1623.

Wegeler (vā'-gě-lěr), **Fz. Gerhard,** Bonn, 1765—Koblenz, 1848; physician and biographer of Beethoven.

Wegelius (vā-gā'-lǐ-oos), **Martin,** Helsingfors, Nov. 10, 1846—March 22, 1906; pupil of Bibl, Vienna, and Richter and Paul, Leipzig; 1878, opera cond. and dir. of the Cons. at Helsingfors; pub. text-books; c. overture *"Daniel Hjort"*; a ballade with orch; *"Mignon"* for sopr. with orch., etc.

Wehle (vā'-lě), **K.,** Prague, 1825—Paris, 1883; pianist and composer.

Wehrle (vār'-le), **Hugo,** Donaueschingen, July 19, 1847—Freiburg, March 29, 1919); violinist; pupil of Leipzig Cons. and Paris Cons.; toured and played in Singer's Quartet till nervous trouble lamed his hand; 1898 retired to Freiburg; c. violin pieces.

Weidig (vī'-dǐkh), **Adolf,** Hamburg, Nov. 28, 1867—Hinsdale, Ill., Sept. 24, 1931; pupil of the Cons. and winning Mozart stipend, pupil of Rheinberger; from 1892, teacher in Chicago and co-director of the American Cons.; c. orch. and chamber music.

Weidt (vīt), (1) **K.,** b. Bern, March 7, 1857; 1889 cond. at Klagenfurt; lived in Heidelberg; c. male choruses. (2) **Lucy,** Troppau, 1880—Vienna, 1927; noted opera soprano, 1910-11 at Met. Op., N. Y., also sang at Munich, Milan and in South America.

Weigl (vīkh'-'l), (1) **Jos.,** Eisenstadt, Hungary, 1766—Vienna, 1846; ct.-conductor and dram. composer. (2) **Taddäus,** Vienna, 1774 (?)—1844; bro. of above; c. operettas.

Weill (vīl), (1) **Kurt,** b. Dessau, Germany, March 2, 1900; composer; studied at Berlin Hochsch. for a time; then with Busoni; came into prominence with orch. Fantasy, Passacaglia and Hymn (1923); 1st major succ. with one-act opera, *"Der Protagonist"* (Dresden Op.), has since c. highly versatile and ingenious modern stage works, incl. *"Mahagonny," "Drei-Groschen"* Oper (jazz treatment of Gay's *"Beggar's Opera,"* with new text by Brecht, which had great vogue in Central Europe and was sung in English version in N. Y.); *"Na und?"; "Der Czar lässt sich photographieren"; "Der Jasager"* (school opera, based on Japanese story, prod. by Neighborhood Music School, N. Y.); *"Royal Palace"* (Berlin Op., work using cinema and in jazz style); *"The Seven Cardinal Sins," "Marie Galante," "A Kingdom for a Cow";* (orch.) Divertimento; *"Quodlibet"; "Lindbergh's Flight"* (with solo male voice); also string quartet, and choral works, *"Recordare"* and *"The New Orpheus,"* latter given in stage version at Berlin Op.; visited America and was present at concert of his works by League of Composers, 1935; his music interdicted in Germany since National Socialist rule; commissioned to write score for *"The Eternal Road,"* Jewish morality play, prod. in N. Y. by Max Reinhardt. (2) **Hermann,** b. Germany, May 29, 1878; barytone; pupil of Mottl and Adolf Dippel; début, Freiburg, 1900; sang at Bayreuth, and many Eur. theatres; Met. Op., 1911-17.

Weinberger (vīn'-běrkh-ěr), (1) **K. Fr.,** Wallerstein, 1853—Würzburg, 1908; teacher and cath. cond. at Würzburg. (2) **Karl,** b. Vienna, April 3, 1861; c. 9 succ. operettas, incl. *"Die Ulanen"* (Vienna, 1891), *"Lachende Erben"* (1892), *"Die Blumen-Mary"* (ib., 1897), *"Adam und Eva"* (ib., 1898). (3) **Jaromir,** b. Vinohrady, Bohemia, 1896; composer; pupil of Kricka and Karel Hofmeister; also studied at Leipzig Cons. with Reger; taught at Ithaca Cons., 1923; c. (operas) *"Schwanda the Bagpipe Player"* (Prague, 1927, but later trans. into German and enjoyed enormous vogue for several years in Germany and Austria because of its sprightly Czech folk tunes and modern orch. treatment; also given at Met. Op., 1931); *"The Beloved*

Voice" (Munich Op., 1930); (orch.) *"Overture to a Marionette Play";* *"Scherzo Giocoso," "Don Quichote";* (pantomime) *"Die Entführung der Eveline";* piano sonata, cham. music; op., *"Wallenstein,"* Vienna, 1937.

Weiner (vī'-nĕr), **Leo,** b. Budapest, April 16, 1885; composer; studied with Koessler at the Prague Acad., also in other countries; after 1913, teacher of theory at Buda-Pest Acad.; c. orch. works, string quartets, trio, vln. sonata; quartet in F sharp minor winning Coolidge Prize, 1921; also arr. works of Bach' and others for orchestra.

Weingartner (vīn'-gärt-nĕr), **(Paul) Felix,** b. Zara, Dalmatia, June 2, 1863; notable conductor; pupil of W. A. Remy; later of Leipzig Cons., winning Mozart prize; friend of Liszt at Weimar, where his opera *"Sakuntala"* was prod. 1884; until 1889, theatre cond. at Königsberg, Danzig, Hamburg; 1889, Mannheim; 1891–97, was cond. Berlin ct.-opera, also cond. symph. concerts at the Royal orch.; from 1898 lived in Munich as cond. Kaim concerts as well as the R. Orch. Berlin; in 1908–11, he succeeded Mahler as dir. of the Vienna Royal Op., also leading concerts of the Philh. Orch. in that city; in 1912–14, 1st. cond. at the Hamburg Op.; then ct.-cond. at Darmstadt and dir. of the Cons. there; he continued to make notable guest appearances in various cities, incl. visits to America in 1905–06 and 1912–13; 1919–20 he was dir. of the Vienna Volksoper; 1928–35, dir. of Basel Cons., and cond. of orch. there; in 1935 he was again called to the directorship of the Vienna Op., but resigned in 1936 after differences with the state officials over artistic policy; c. operas *"Sakuntala"* (1884), *"Malawika"* (Munich, 1886), *"Genesius"* (Berlin, 1893), withdrawn by the author because of press attacks and revived with succ. at Mannheim and elsewhere; *"Orestes"* (Berlin, June 15, 1902); c. symph. poems *"König Lear," "Das Gefilde der Seligen,"* a drama *"Golgotha"* (1908), 3 symph., *"Frühlingsmärchenspiel"* (Weimar, 1908), music to *"Faust"* (do., 1908); operas, *"Dame Kobold"* (to his own libretto), 1916; *"Meister Andrea"* (1920); *"Terokayn"* (1920); *"Julian the Apostate."* He orches-

trated Beethoven's Hammerklavier pf.-sonata and ed. an unfinished Schubert symphony (not the famous one); wrote *" Über das Dirigieren," "Die Symphonie nach Beethoven,"* etc.; m. Marie Juillerat, 1891; Baroness Feodora de Dreyfus, 1903; Lucille Marcel, singer, 1912 (she d. 1921); Mme. Kalisch, actress, 1922; and later Carmen Studer, a talented conductor. Resides in England.

Weinlig (or **Weinlich**) (vīn'-lĭkh), (1) **Chr. Ehregott,** Dresden, 1743—1813; organist and composer. (2) **(Chr.) Th.,** Dresden, 1780—Leipzig, 1842; nephew and pupil of above; cantor, theorist and composer.

Weinwurm (vīn'-voorm), **Rudolf,** Schaidldorf-on-the-Thaja, Lower Austria, April 3, 1835—Vienna, May 25, 1911; chorister, ct.-chapel, Vienna; 1858, studied law and founded the Univ. Gesangverein; mus.-dir.; 1880 mus.-dir. of the Univ.; pub. treatises and composer.

Weinzierl (vīn'-tsĕrl), **Max,** Ritter von, Bergstadl, Bohemia, 1841—Mödling, near Vienna, 1898; conductor and dram. composer.

Weis (vīs), **Karel,** b. Prague, Feb. 13, 1862—1936; composer of a succ. 2-act opera *"The Polish Jew"* (Berlin, 1902); comic opera *"The Twins"* (Frankfort, 1903), etc.

Weismann (vīs'-män), **Julius,** b. Freiburg, Dec. 26, 1879; pupil of Royal Musicschool, Munich, then with Herzogenberg and Thuille; from 1905 in Freiburg as composer of choral works, a symph., the operas, *"Traumspiel"* (after Strindberg play), *"Schwanenweiss," "Leonce und Lena,"* etc.

Weiss (vīs), (1) **K.,** Mühlhausen, ca. 1738—London, 1795; composer. (2) **K.,** b. 1777, son and pupil of above; writer and composer. (3) **K.,** bro. of above; prod. the opera *"Twelfth Night"* (Prague, 1892). (4) **Fz.,** Silesia, 1778—Vienna, 1830; violavirtuoso and composer.

Weissheimer (vīs'-hī-mĕr), **Wendelin,** Osthofen, Feb. 26, 1838—Nuremberg, June 16, 1910; mus. director and composer; pupil Leipzig Cons., teacher and theatre-cond. in various cities; c. 2 operas, *"Theodor Körner"* (Munich, 1872), and *"Meister Martin und seine Gesellen"* (Carlsruhe, 1897), bass solo with orch., *"Das Grab in Busento,"* etc.; wrote memoirs.

Weist-Hill, H., London, 1828—1891; violinist; pupil R. A. M.; cond. various concerts with much hospitality to novelties; 1880 principal Guildhall Sch.

Weitzmann (vīts'-män), **K. Fr.,** Berlin, 1808—1880; eminent theorist; c. operas, etc.; wrote valuable treatises,

Welcker von Gontershausen (vĕl'-kĕr fōn gôn'-tĕrs-how-zĕn), **H.,** Gontershausen, Hesse, 1811—Darmstadt, 1873; ct.-pf.-maker and writer.

Wel'don, (1) **J.,** Chichester, Engl., 1676—London, 1736; organist and composer. (2) **Georgina,** Clapham, May 24, 1837—Brighton, Jan. 11, 1914; singer and composer.

Wellesz (vä'-lĕsh), **Egon,** b. Vienna, Oct. 21, 1885; composer, educator; Ph. D., Vienna Univ., 1908, Mus. D., 1909; studied history of music with Guido Adler, comp. with Schönberg, by whose atonal methods he was influenced; prof. of musicology, Vienna Univ., after 1929; vice-pres., Austrian Composers' Soc. and active on juries of I. S. C. M.; c. (operas) *"Die Prinzessin Girnara"* (Frankfort, 1921); *"Alkestis"* (Mannheim, 1924); *"Scherz, List und Rache"* (chamber opera), (Stuttgart, 1928); (ballets) *"Die Nächtlichen"* (Berlin, 1925), *"Persisches"* (1925); *"Opferung des Gefangenen"* (Cologne 1926); *"Achilles auf Skyros"*; string quartets, piano music and songs; has written historical works on music.

Wels (vĕls, **Chas.,** Prague, Aug. 24, 1825—New York, 1906; pupil of Tomaschek; 1847, ct.-pianist; 1849, New York as concert-pianist and teacher; c. concert-overture and suite for orch.; a pf.-concerto, etc.

Welsh (1) **Thomas,** Wells, Somerset, 1780—Brighton, 1848; bass and singing-teacher. (2) **Mary Anne** (née **Wilson**), 1802—1867; wife and pupil of above; v. succ. soprano, earning £10,000 ($50,000) the first year of her short career.

Wendel (vĕn'-dĕl), **Ernst,** b. Breslau, 1876; violinist and director; pupil of Wirth, Joachim, Lucco and Bargiel; 1896 joined Thomas Orch., Chicago; 1898 cond. Königsberg Musikverein; 1909 cond. Bremen Phil.; gen. mus. dir., 1921; 1912–15, cond. also of Berlin Musikfreunde concerts; c. choruses with orch., etc.

Wendling (vĕnt'-lĭng), (1) **Jn. Bapt.,** from 1754–1800 flutist in Mannheim;

band composer. His wife (2) **Dorothea** (née **Spurni**), Stuttgart, 1737—Munich, 1811, was a singer. (3) **K.,** d. 1794; violinist in Mannheim band. His wife (4) **Auguste Elizabethe,** was a singer. (5) **K.,** Frankenthal, Rhine Palatinate, Nov. 14, 1857—Leipzig, 1918; pianist; pupil Leipzig Cons.; performer on Jankó keyboard; teacher of it from 1887 at Leipzig Cons; ct.-pianist to Prince of Waldeck.

Wenzel (vĕn'-tsĕl), (1) **Ernst Fd.,** Walddorf, near Lobau, 1808—Bad Kösen, 1880; pf.-teacher and writer. (2) **Leopold,** Naples, Jan. 23, 1847 —Paris, Aug., 1925; studied Cons. S. Pietro a Majella; at 13 toured as violinist; 1866 joined Métra's orch. at Marseilles; 1871, conductor; later cond. of the Alcazar, Paris; 1883, London; from 1889 cond. at the Empire Th.; prod. operettas, many ballets, etc.

Wenzel von Gamter (or **Szamotulski**) (shä-mō-tool'-skĭ), Gamter, 1525—Cracow, 1572; Polish composer of church music.

Werbecke, Gaspar van. Vide GASPAR.

Werckmeister (vărk'-mī-shtĕr), **Ands.,** Beneckenstein, 1645—Halberstadt, 1706; organist, important theorist and composer.

Wermann (văr'-män), **Fr. Oskar,** Neichen, near Trebsen, Saxony, April 30, 1840—near Dresden, Nov. 22, 1906; pianist and organist; pupil of Leipzig Cons.; 1868, teacher R. Seminary, Dresden; 1876, mus. dir. 3 churches and cantor at the Kreuzschule there; c. *"Reformations-Cantate,"* mass in 8 parts, etc.

Werner (văr'-nĕr), (1) **Gregorius Jos.,** 1695—Eisenstadt, 1766; conductor and composer. (2) **Jn. Gottlob,** Hoyer, Saxony, 1777—Merseburg, 1822; organist, mus.-director, teacher and composer. (3) **H.,** near Erfurt, 1800—Brunswick, 1833; composer. (4) **Josef,** Würzburg, June 25, 1837 —Munich, Nov. 14, 1922; 'cellist; pupil of the Cons. there; teacher Munich School of Music; pub. a method; c. pcs. for 'cello, etc.

Wer'renrath, Reinald, b. Brooklyn, N. Y., Aug. 7, 1883; barytone; grad. N. Y. U., pupil of Frank King Clark, Carl Dufft, Percy Rector Stephens, Arthur Mees and Victor Maurel; début in N. Y. concert, 1907; appeared widely as a concert and oratorio singer; also with Met. Op.

(début as "Silvio," 1919); 1921, London; made many recital tours; assoc. as vocal counsel with leading radio corp.; has acted as choral conductor.

Wert (vārt), **Jacob van**, b. Netherlands, 1536—Mantua, 1596; conductor and composer.

Wesembeck. Vide BURBURE DE W.

Wes'ley, (1) **Chas.**, Bristol, Engl., Dec. 11, 1757—London, May 23, 1834; nephew of the evangelist John W.; teacher, organist and composer. (2) **Samuel**, Bristol, Engl., 1766—London, 1837; bro. and pupil of above; organist and composer. (3) **Samuel Sebastian**, London, Aug. 14, 1800—Gloucester, April 19, 1876; son of above; organist.

Wessel (věs'-sěl), **Chr. R.**, Bremen, 1797 — Eastbourne, 1885; mus.-publisher, London.

Wessely (věs'-sě-lē), (1) **Jn.**, Frauenburg, Bohemia, 1762—Ballenstedt, 1814; violinist; c. comic operas. (2) **(K.) Bd.**, Berlin, 1768—Potsdam, 1826; dram. composer. (3) **Hans**, Vienna, Dec. 23, 1862—Innsbruck, Sept. 29, 1926; violinist; pupil of the Cons.; toured with success; from 1889 prof. R. A. M., London, leader of the W. Quartet.

West, J. Ebenezer, South Hackney, London, Dec. 7, 1863—Feb., 1929; concert-organist and pianist; pupil of Bridge and Prout, R. A. M.; 1891, organist S. Hackney Parish Ch.; c. 2 cantatas; Psalm 130; services, etc.

West'brook, Wm. Jos., London, 1831 —Sydenham, 1894; organist, conductor and composer.

West'lake, Fr., Romsey, Hampshire, 1840—London, 1898; composer.

Westmeyer (věsht'-mī-ěr), **Wm.**, Iburg, near Osnabrück, 1832—Bonn, 1880; c. operas.

Westmore'land, J. Jane, Earl of, London, 1784 — Apthorpe House, 1859; dram. composer.

Westphal (věsht'-fäl), **Rudolf (G. Hn.)**, Oberkirchen, Lippe-Schaumburg, 1826—Stadthagen, 1892; writer.

West'rop, H. J., Lavenham, Suffolk, 1812—1879; pianist, violinist, singer, organist and composer.

Wettergren (vět'-těr-grěn), **Gertrud**, b. Esloev, Sweden; contralto; studied at Stockholm Acad. and R. School of Op.; début at R. Op. there, 1922, as "Cherubino"; sang leading rôles with this co.; esp. noted as "Carmen";

début, Met. Op. Co., N. Y., as "Amneris," 1935.

Wetzel (vět'-tsěl), **Hermann**, b. Kyritz, Pomerania, March 11, 1879; teacher at Riemann Cons. 1905–07; then in Potsdam as teacher and author; c. songs, etc.

Wetzler (věts'-lěr), **Hermann Hans**, b. Frankfort-on-Main, Sept. 8, 1870; pupil of Frau Schumann (pf.), B. Scholz (comp.), Ivan Knorr (cpt.), H. Heerman (vln.), and Humperdinck (orchestration); 1893, New York, as pianist and teacher; asst.-org. Trinity Ch.; from 1902 cond. his own symphony orch.; 1905, dir. Hamburg Op.; 1908 cond. in Russia, then in various German cities; c. opera "*The Basque Venus*," etc.

Weweler (vā'-vě-lěr), **August**, b. Recke, Westphalia, Oct. 20, 1868; composer; pupil Leipzig Cons.; c. fairy opera "*Dornröschen*" (Kassel, 1903), comic opera "*Der grobe Märker*" (Detmold, 1908), etc.

Weymarn (vī'-märn), **Paul Platonovich**, b. St. Petersburg, 1857; son of a lieut.-general and himself an officer; gave up the army for music; wrote biographies, criticisms, 'cello-pieces, etc.

Weyse (vī'-zě), **Chp. Ernst Fr.**, Altona, 1774—Copenhagen, 1842; dram. composer.

Whelp'ley, Benj. Lincoln, b. Eastport, Maine, Oct. 23, 1864; studied with B. J. Lang, etc., at Boston, 1890 in Paris; lived in Boston as teacher and composer.

White, (1) **Robt.**, d. Westminster, Nov. 7 (11 ?), 1574; organist at Ely Cath. (1562–67); noted in his day as organist and composer. Often confused with (2) **Wm.** (c. fantasias and "fancies" for org., etc.) and (3) **Rev. Matthew**, Mus. Doc. 1629; c. anthems and catches. (4) **Alice Mary, Meadows** (née **Smith**), 1839—1884; pupil of Bennett, and Macfarren, London; c. symphs., cantatas, etc. (5) **J.**, W. Springfield, Mass., March 12, 1855—Bad Neuheim, Germany, July 18, 1902; pupil of Dudley Buck; then of Haupt (org. and cpt.), Rheinberger; gave org.-concerts in various German cities; 1887–96, organist, New York; from 1897 lived in Munich; pub. Missa Solemnis; O salutaris; c. an oratorio "*Alpha and Omega*," etc. (6) **Maude Valérie**, b. of English parents, Dieppe,

June 23, 1855—London, Nov. 2, 1937; pupil of O. May and W. S. Rockstro, and of R. A. M., Mendelssohn Scholar, 1879, also studied in Vienna; lived in London; c. mass; pf.-pcs.; *"Pictures from Abroad"* and pop. songs, etc. (7) **Carolina**, b. Dorchester, Mass., Dec. 23, 1883; pupil of Weldon Hunt; concert début, 1905; 1907 studied with Sebastian at Naples; début at San Carlo Theatre, 1908; sang in Italy, and from 1910 with Chicago Op. Co.; 1911 with Boston Op.

White'hill, Clarence, Marengo, Iowa, Nov. 5, 1871—New York, Dec. 18, 1932; notable bass; début in *"Roméo et Juliette,"* Brussels, 1899; sang Paris Op. Com. and Bayreuth; Met. Op., 1900–31, except during 1911–15, when he sang with Chicago Op.

Whitehouse, William Edward, b. London, May 20, 1859—Jan. 12, 1935; 'cellist; pupil of Pettit and R. A. M., winning prize, 1878; and from 1882 teacher there; later prof., member of Ludwig Quartet and London Trio.

White'man, Paul, b. Denver, Colo., 1891; conductor; son of a supervisor of music in Denver public schools; early studied to be viola player; during World War became cond. of a U. S. Navy Orch., and began experiments in original style of syncopated dance music, for which he acquired internat'l reputation; has toured widely in U. S., also one season in Europe as head of his own orch.; encouraged prod. of symphonic jazz comps. by giving concerts of new works of this form in New York.

Whith'orne, Emerson, b. Cleveland, O., Sept. 6, 1884; composer; studied with James H. Rogers, Leschetizky, Schnabel and Robert Fuchs; lived in London, 1907–14, where was critic of Pall Mall *Gazette*, 1913; served as exec. ed., Art Publication Soc., St. Louis, 1915–20; c. (orch.) symphonies, *"Fata Morgana,"* *"New York Days and Nights"* (Salzburg Fest., 1923); *"Ranga," "The City of Ys," "The Aeroplane"*; vln. concerto; *"Saturday's Child"* for mezzosoprano, tenor, and small orch.; string quartets, incl. *"Three Greek Impressions* '; (dance satire) *"Sooner or La r'* (prod. in N. Y.); piano quintet, also music to plays incl. O'Neill's *"Marco Millions"*; *"The Grim Troubadour"* for voice and

string quartet; songs and piano pieces; m. Ethel Leginska, composer; separated.

Whi'ting, (1) **G. Elbridge**, Holliston, Mass., Sept. 14, 1842—Cambridge, Mass., 1923; organist at Worcester when 13; later at Hartford, Conn. (where he founded the Beethoven Soc.); later organist in various Boston churches; studied with G. W. Morgan, New York, and Best, Liverpool; Haupt and Radecke, Berlin; till 1879, teacher at the N. E. Cons., Boston; till 1882, at the Cincinnati Coll. of Mus.; then again at the N. E. Cons.; c. masses with orch. and organ, cantatas, ballade with orch., *"Henry of Navarre,"* pf.-concerto, etc. (2) **Arthur Battelle** (Cambridge, Mass., June 20, 1861—Beverly, Mass., July 21, 1936; nephew of above; pf.-pupil of W. H. Sherwood; début at 19, Boston; studied with Chadwick and J. C. D. Parker; then with Rheinberger, in Munich; lived in Boston, organist of N. E. Cons. until 1897; organised concerts at Harvard, Yale and Princeton; teacher of pf. and comp.; c. fantasy with orch., concert-overture, concert-étude, church-service, concerto, song cycles, etc.

Whitney, Samuel Brenton, Woodstock Vermont, June 4, 1842—Brattleboro, Vt., 1914; organist; pupil of Chas. Wells and J. K. Paine; 1871, organist, Ch. of the Advent, Boston; conductor of church-choir festivals; org.-prof. and lecturer, Boston U. and N. E. Cons.; c. anthems, org.-sonatas, etc.

Whit'taker, William Gillies, b. Newcastle-on-Tyne, England, July 23, 1876; composer and conductor; studied with Frederic Austin and G. F. Huntley; hon. Mus. Doc., Durham Univ., 1921; c. orch., chamber, choral and piano music in modern style; author of books on music.

Whyt'horne (or **Whitehorne**), **Thos.**, b. 1528; Engl. composer.

Wichern (vēkh'-ĕrn), **Karoline**, Horn, near Hamburg, Sept. 13, 1836—March 19, 1906; soprano; led choruses at the houses of correction for 20 years, then for 15 years taught in Manchester, returning 1896 to her previous task; 1900 cond. at Hamburg a concert of her own orchestral works; c. vocal works.

Wichmann (vĭkh'-män), **Hermann,**

Berlin, Oct. 24, 1824—Rome, Aug. 27, 1905; studied at R. Akademie; also with Taubert, Mendelssohn and Spohr; then lived in Berlin; c. symphs., sonatas, etc.

Wichtl (vĭkht'-'l), **G.**, Trostberg, Bavaria, 1805—Bunzlau, Silesia, 1877; violinist, conductor and dram. composer.

Wickenhausser (vĭk'-ĕn-hows'-sĕr), **Richard,** Brünn, 1867—Vienna, 1936; pupil of Leipzig Cons.; 1894 was given a stipend on the advice of Brahms and Hanslick; 1895 leader of a singing society in Brünn; 1902 in Graz; 1907 dir. Vienna Singakademie, c. choral works, also 2 piano sonatas, a violin sonata, etc.

Widmann (vĕt'-män), (1) **Erasmus,** poet-laureate, organist and conductor at Weikersheim; publisher and composer (1607). (2) **Benedikt,** Bräunlingen, March 5, 1820—Frankfort, 1910; rector at Frankfort; theorist and composer. (3) **Jos. Victor,** Nennowitz, Moravia, Feb. 20, 1842 —Berne, 1912; at 3 taken to Switzerland; wrote librettos and biog. of Brahms.

Widor (vē-dôr), **Chas. (M.),** b. Lyons, Feb. 24, 1845—Paris, March 12, 1937; son of an Alsatian of Hungarian descent (organist at Lyons); studied with Lemmens (org.) and Fétis (comp.), Brussels; at 15 organist at St. François, Lyons, and 1869–1935, organist at St. Sulpice, Paris; 1890, teacher at the Paris Cons.; from 1896 prof. of cpt., fugue and comp.; critic (under pen-name "Aulètes") and dir. of the soc. "La Concordia," c. v. succ. ballet "La Korrigane" (Opéra, 1880); music to "Conte d'Avril" (Odéon, 1885); "Les Jacobites" (Odéon, 1885); unsucc. lyric drama "Maître Ambros" (Op.-Com., May 6, 1896); 3 pantomimes; a mass for 2 choirs and 2 orgs.; Psalm 112, with orch. and org.; "La nuit de Walpurgis," for chorus and orch.; 3 symphs.; 10 org. symphs. incl. "Gotique," a concerto for vln., 'cello, and pf., org.-sonatas, etc.; Chevalier, Legion of Honour; 1910, member of Académie, and after 1913 secretary of this body.

Wieck (vēk), (1) **Fr.,** Pretzsch, near Torgau, 1785—Loschwitz, near Dresden, 1873; est. a pf.-factory and library at Leipzig; eminent pf.-teacher; also singing-teacher and composer;

teacher also of his daughter (2) **Clara.** (Vide SCHUMANN.) (3) **Alwin,** Leipzig, 1821—1885; son of (1); pupil of David; violinist at St. Petersburg; later pf.-teacher at Dresden. (4) **Marie,** Leipzig, Jan. 17, 1832—1916; pianist; daughter of (1); played in public at 8; 1858, ct.-pianist to the Prince of Hohenzollern; toured; est. a sch. in Dresden; 1914, Royal Professor.

Wiedemann (vē'-dĕ-män), **Ernst Jn.,** Hohengiersdorf, Silesia, 1797—Potsdam, 1873; organist, teacher and composer.

Wiederkehr (vē'-dĕr-kār), **Jacob Chr. Michael,** Strassburg, 1739—Paris, 1823; 'cellist, bassoonist, tambourinist and composer.

Wiedermann (vē'-dĕr-män), **K. Fr.,** Görisseiffen, Dec. 25, 1856—Berlin, 1918; organist and Royal Dir., in Berlin; c. overture, songs, etc.

Wiegand (vē'-gänt), **Josef Anton H.,** Fränkisch-Crumbach in the Odenwald, 1842—Frankfort, 1899; bass.

Wiehmayer (vē'-mī-ĕr), **Theodor,** b. Marienfeld, Westphalia, Jan. 7, 1870; pianist; pupil Leipzig Cons. and of Krause; début Leipzig, 1890; teacher there; 1902–06 at the Cons.; from 1908 at Stuttgart Cons., 1909 prof.; c. piano pieces and songs.

Wielhorski. Vide WILHORSKI.

Wiemann (vē'-män), **Robert,** b. Frankenhausen, Nov. 4, 1870; pupil Leipzig Cons.; cond. various theatre orchs. and singing societies; from 1899 in Osnabrück; 1910, munic. dir. of music, Stettin; c. orch. works, "Erdenwallen," "Kassandra," etc.; choral works with orch., etc.

Wieniawski (v'yä-nē-äf'-shkĭ), (1) **H.,** Lublin, Poland, July 10, 1835—Moscow, April 12, 1880; eminent violinist and composer; début, at Petersburg, at 13; studied with Clavel and Massart, and Colet (harmony) Paris Cons.; won 1st vln.-prize, 1846; 1860, solo-violinist to Czar, and 1862–67, teacher at the Petersburg Cons.; 1875–77, vln.-prof. Brussels Cons. (vice Vieuxtemps); toured widely, 1872 U. S. with Rubinstein; c. 2 concertos, etc. (2) **Jos.,** Lublin, May 23, 1837—Brussels, Nov. 11, 1912; famous pianist; at 10 pupil of Paris Cons.; at 13 toured with his brother, then studied with Marx at Berlin; 1866, teacher at the Moscow Cons.; est. a pf.-sch. of his own; later teacher in Brussels Cons.; c. 2 overtures, suite romantique for orch., pf.-concerto, etc.

Wieprecht (vē'-prĕkht), **Wm. Fr.**, Aschersleben, 1802—Berlin, 1872; famous trombonist and violinist; inv. the bass tuba (1835).

Wietrowetz (vē'-trō-vĕtz), **Gabriele**, b. Laibach, Carmola, Jan. 13, 1866; violinist; pupil of Joachim, winning Mendelssohn prize at Berlin Hochsch.; début 1885 at Münster; toured and from 1904, teacher at the Berlin Hochsch.; founded quartet.

Wig'man, Mary, b. Hanover, Germany; dancer; studied Berlin, Dresden-Hellerau and Rome; pupil of and asst. to Rudolf von Laban in Munich and elsewhere; after 1919 came forward with her own dance recitals, which exhibited style of notable freedom and force, a feature of which was discarding of all conventional "prettiness" and pirouetting of the classic ballet school; Frl. Wigman, as she has expressed it, danced "man's kinship with the earth and with feet flat on the earth"; although the general tendency was apparent in dance world since Isadora Duncan, the Wigman style developed into an internat'l cult known as the "free dance" and she estab. schools in many German cities, also in other countries incl. U. S. after 1920; has also toured several times in America as soloist and with her girl dance group; one of her tenets is dancing to percussion, with special scores created for her.

Wihan (vē'-hän), **Hans (Hanuš)**, Politz, near Braunau, June 5, 1855—Prague, May 3, 1920; 'cellist; pupil of Prague Cons.; 1873, prof. of 'cello, Mozarteum, Salzburg; 1877-80, chamber-virtuoso to Prince Schwarzsburg-Sondershausen; 1880, 1st solo-'cellist Munich ct.-orch.; 1888, prof. at Prague Cons., a member "Bohemian String Quartet."

Wihtol (vē'-tôl), **Jos.**, b. Wolmar, Livonia, 1863; studied at Mirau; then with Johansen (harm.) and Rimsky-Korsakov (comp. and instrumentation) Petersburg Cons.; 1886, prof. of harm. there; 1918, dir. of Riga Opera; 1919, founded New Cons. there; c. "La fête Ligho," symph. picture, "Dramatic" overture, etc.

Wilbye (wĭl'-bĭ), **J.**; lutenist and teacher, London, 1598; most brilliant composer of madrigals.

Wild (vēlt), **Fz.**, Niederhollabrunn, Lower Austria, 1792—Oberdöbling, near Vienna, 1860; tenor.

Wilder (vēl-dăr), **Jérome Albert Victor van**, Wettern, near Ghent, 1835—Paris, 1892; writer and translator.

Wilhelm (vēl'-hělm), **K.**, Schmalkalden, 1815—1873; "R. Prussian Mus. Dir."; c. "Die Wacht am Rhein," etc.

Wilhelmj (vēl-hěl'-mē), (1) **Aug. (Emil Daniel Fd.)**, Usingen, Nassau, Sept. 21, 1845—London, Jan. 22, 1908; eminent violinist; pupil of Fischer at Wiesbaden; played in public at 8; at 16 recommended to David by Liszt as a young Paganini; he studied 1861-64, with David (vln.), Hauptmann and Richter, Leipzig Cons.; 1862, the Gewandhaus; 1864, studied with Raff at Frankfort; from 1865, toured the world; 1876, leader of Bayreuth orch.; lived for years at Biebrich-on-Rhine, where he est. (with R. Niemann) a "Hochschule" for vln.; 1886, lived at Blasewitz, near Dresden; 1894, head-prof. Guildhall Sch., London; 1895, he m. the pianist Mariella Mausch; c. "Hochzeits-Cantate" with orch., vln.-pcs., etc. His son (2) **Adolf**, b. 1872, violinist; after 1898 vln.-prof. at Belfast Cons.

Wilhem (rightly **Bocquillon**) (vēl-än or bôk-ē-yôn), **Guillaume Louis**, Paris, 1781—1842; dir.-gen. of all Paris schools; founder of the great system of popular singing societies or "Orphéonistes" (v. D. D.); pub. many treatises on his method of "mutual instruction" and a 10-vol. coll. of comps.

Wi(e)lhôrski (vēl-hôr'-shkĭ), (1) **Count Matvéi Júrjevitch**, Volhynia, 1787—Petersburg (?), 1863; 'cellist. His brother (2) **Count Michaíl Júrjevitch**, Volhynia, 1788—Moscow, 1856; composer.

Willaert (wĭl'-lärt) (**Wigliar'dus, Vigliar, Vuigliart**), **Adrian** (called **Adriano**), Flanders, ca. 1480—Venice, 1562; eminent composer and teacher; called the founder of the Venetian Sch.; a very prolific composer; pupil of Mouton and Josquin Desprès; 1516 at Rome, later at Ferrara; then mus. to the King of Bohemia; Dec. 12, 1527, maestro at San Marco, Venice, where he organised a famous sch.; c. 5 masses, many motets, psalms, madrigals, etc.; the first to write for two choirs.

Wil'lan, Healey, b. Balham, England, 1880; composer and organist; studied St. Savior's Choral School, Eastham; org. in leading British churches; after 1913 res. in Toronto as theory teacher at Cons., and later vice-pres. and dir.; c. choral and organ works.

Wille (vĭl'-lĕ), **Georg,** b. Greiz, Sept. 20, 1869; 'cellist; from 1899 court-concertmaster at Royal Chapel in Dresden and teacher in the Cons.; pupil of Leipzig Cons.

Willeke (vĕl'-ä-kĕ), **Willem,** b. The Hague, 1878; 'cellist, conductor; studied Hague and Amsterdam Cons., pupil of Hartog; solo 'cellist Leipzig Philh., 1901–03; afterward at Covent Garden and Vienna Op., mem. Kneisel Quartet, 1907–17; founded in latter year the Elshuco Trio and was its 'cellist; life dir. of Berkshire Music Colony; taught at Inst. of Musical Art, N. Y., where cond. orch.; appeared in U. S. as orch. soloist and in recitals.

Willent-Bordogni (vē-yäṅ-bȯr-dōn-yē), **Jean Bapt. Jos.,** Douai, 1809—Paris, 1852; bassoon-virtuoso, teacher, writer and dram. composer. 1834, m. the daughter of Bordogni.

Williams, (1) **Charles Lee,** Winchester, May 1, 1853—Gloucester, Aug. 29, 1935; organist; pupil of Arnold; 1882–98 org. at Gloucester Cathedral; cond. of festivals; c. cantatas, church music, etc. (2) **Charles Francis Abdy,** Dawlish, July 16, 1855 —Milford, Feb. 27, 1933; took music degrees at both Cambridge and Oxford; later pupil Leipzig Cons.; organist at various posts; authority on Greek music and Plain song; c. church music, choruses for *"Alcestis," "Antigone,"* and *"Agamemnon."* (3) **Ralph Vaughan,** b. Down Ampney, England, Oct. 12, 1872; composer; grad. Trinity Coll., Cambridge; Mus. D., Oxford and Cambridge; studied R. Coll. of Music with Moore, Parry, Stanford, Wood, Parratt, Sharpe, Gray, also with Ravel and Bruch; was early active as an organist, and has been extension lecturer at Oxford; it is, however, as a composer that he has estab. a rank among the outstanding musical figures of the day; as a symphonist he has an especial aptitude, and some of his

music has been influenced by English folk-song in which he has been a leading investigator; esp. popular in other countries are his *"London" Symphony,* a programmatic work depicting sights of that metropolis, but welded cleverly into impressive symph. form; and his *"Pastorale" Symphony,* which is exquisitely compounded of English country traditional tunes treated with the hand of a poet and an expert craftsman; his extremely large output includes also stage works and various forms of chamber music, part-songs, choral arrangements of folk-music; in his later music, **W.** has shown a tendency to depart from descriptive writing into more abstract realms and to court aggressive dissonance; c. (opera) *"Hugh the Drover";* (ballet) *"Old King Cole";* (orch.) *"Three Impressions," "In the Fen Country,"* three *"Norfolk Rhapsodies"; "Bucolic Suite"; "Heroic Elegy"; "Serenade"; "Fantasia on a Theme by Thomas Tallis";* suite for *"The Wasps"* of Aristophanes; Fantasie for piano and orch.; *"Concerto Academico"* for vln. and orch.; *"Studies in English Folk Music"* for vln.; a string quartet, (masque for dancing) *"Job";* Symphony in F (no program or title); 2 piano quintets; (choral works) *"Toward the Unknown Region"; "A Sea Symphony"; "The Garden of Proserpine";* five *"Mystical Songs";* (oratorio) *"Sancta Civitas";* 3 Nocturnes for barytone with orch.; (song cycles) *"The House of Life," "Songs of Travel," "On Wenlock Edge";* arr. Purcell's *"Welcome Songs,"* also many folk-songs, madrigals, etc.; ed. *"The English Hymnal."*

Wil'liamson, John Finley, b. Canton, O., June 23, 1887; conductor, educator; studied with Bispham and Witherspoon, also Otterbein Coll.; hon. Mus. D., Wooster Univ.; served as dean of Ithaca Cons.; founder and dean of Westminster Choir School, now at Princeton Univ.; and cond. Westminster Choir, with which he toured U. S. and Europe; c. and arr. choral works.

Willing (vĭl'-lĭng), (1) **Jn. L.,** Kühndorf, 1755—Nordhausen, 1805; organist and composer. (2) (wĭl'-lĭng) **Chr. Edwin,** London, Feb. 28, 1830— St. Albans, Dec. 1, 1904; organist various London churches, conductor and teacher.

Wil'lis, (1) **H.**, England, April 27, 1821 —London, Feb. 11, 1901; prominent org.-builder and improver. (2) **Richard Storrs**, Boston, Mass., Feb. 10, 1819—Detroit, May 7, 1900; bro. of N. P. Willis the poet; critic and editor in N. Y., later Detroit; composer.

Will'man, (1) **Magdalena**, d. 1801; famous soprano; her brother, (2) **K.**, violinist.

Willmers (vĭl'-mĕrs), **H. Rudolf**, Berlin, 1821—Vienna, 1878; pianist and composer.

Wilm (vĭlm), **Nicolai von**, Riga, March 4, 1834—Wiesbaden, Feb. 20, 1911; pianist; studied Leipzig Cons.; 1857, 2nd cond. Riga City Th.; then Petersburg, 1860; teacher of pf. and theory Imp. Nicolai Inst.; 1875, Dresden; 1878, Wiesbaden; c. pop. string-sextet, 'cello and vln.-sonatas, male-choruses, etc.

Wilms (vĭlms), **Jan Willem**, Witzhelden, Schwarzburg-Sondershausen, 1772—Amsterdam, 1847; teacher and org.-composer.

Wilsing (vĭl'-zĭng), **Daniel Fr. Ed.**, Hörde, near Dortmund, Oct. 21, 1809 —Berlin, May 2, 1893; 1829–34, organist in Wesel, then Berlin; c. oratorio *"Jesus Christus,"* in 2 parts (Bonn, 1889); a De profundis à 16 (gold medal for Art, Berlin); pf.-sonata, etc.

Wil'son, (1) **J.**, Faversham, Kent, 1594 —London, 1673; famous lutenist and composer. (2) **J.**, Edinburgh, 1800 —(of cholera) Quebec, 1849; tenor. (3) **Mortimer**, Chariton, Iowa, Aug. 6, 1876—New York, Jan. 27, 1932; composer; studied in Chicago with Jacobsohn, Gleason and Middleschulte; 1901–07, taught theory, Univ. Sch. of Mus., Lincoln, Nebr.; then a pupil of Sitt and Reger in Leipzig; 1911, taught Atlanta Cons.; and cond. symph. orch. there; 1916–18, at Brenau Coll., Gainesville, Ga.; later consultant at Nat'l Acad. of Mus., N. Y.; author of many orch. and other pieces, incl. musical scores for motion pictures.

Wilt (vĭlt), **Marie** (née **Liebenthaler**), Vienna, Jan. 30, 1833—(suicide) Sept. 24, 1891; famous operatic soprano; début 1865 at Graz; sang throughout Europe, also popular in concerts. In 1866–67 she sang at Covent Garden under the name "Vilda," again in 1874–75.

Wiltberger (vĭlt'-bĕrkh-ĕr), **Heinrich**, Sobernheim, Aug. 17, 1841—Colmar, 1916; son of an organist; 1872–1906 teacher in Alsace; co-founder of the Cecilia society and composer of church music, and favourite Alsatian composer of male-choruses.

Winderstein (vĭn'-dĕr-shtīn), **Hans** (Wm. Gv.), Lüneburg, Oct. 29, 1856 —Hanau, June 23, 1925); violinist; pupil of Leipzig Cons.; also playing in Gewandhaus Orch.; 1880–84, leader in Baron von Derwies' orch. at Nice; till 1887, vln.-teacher at Winterthur (Switzerland) Cons., then cond. at Nürnberg; 1893–96, dir. Philh. Orch., at Munich, and at the Kaim Concerts; 1896, organised and conducted the "Winderstein Orch."; 1898, cond. Leipzig Singakademie; c. Trauermarsch, Valse-Caprice and Ständchen for orch.; orch. suite, etc.

Winding (vĭn'-dĭng), **Aug. (Henrik)**, Taaro (Laaland), Denmark, March 24, 1835—Copenhagen, June 16, 1899; pianist; pupil of Reinecke, Ree, Dreyschock and Gade; dir. and prof. Copenhagen Cons.; c. vln.-concerto, sonatas, etc.

Wing'ham, **Thos.**, London, 1846— 1893; organist and composer.

Winkel (vĭnk'-ĕl), **Dietrich Nikolaus**, Amsterdam, ca. 1780—1826; a mechanician; inv. the "componium" and "metronome," which later Mälzel (q. v.) appropriated.

Winkelmann (vĭnk'-ĕl-män), **Hermann**, Brunswick, March 8, 1849—Mauer (Vienna), Jan. 18, 1912; tenor; pupil of Koch at Hanover; début Sondershausen; 1875; sang at Altenburg, Darmstadt and Hamburg; then at ct.-opera, Vienna, 1882; created "Parsifal" at Bayreuth.

Winkler (vĭnk'-lĕr), **Alex. Adolfovich**, Charkov, March 3, 1865—Leningrad, 1935; pianist; studied at Charkov and at Vienna under Leschetizky and Navrátil; teacher at Charkov; from 1896 at St. Petersburg Cons.; c. prize-winning string quartet, op. 7, piano pieces, etc.

Win'ner, **Septimus**, Philadelphia, 1826 —Nov. 23, 1902; writer of pop. songs and methods; said to have written 200 technical books on instruments and to have c. and arranged over 2,000 pcs. for vln. and piano; also wrote for *Graham's Mag.*, when

Poe was editor. His songs include *"Listen to the Mocking Bird,"* and *"Give us Back our old Commander"*; founder of Musical Fund Soc.

Winogradsky (vē-nō-grät'-shkĭ), **Alex.**, Kiev, Russia, Aug. 3 (new style), 1856—1912; noted cond.; pupil of Soloviev, Petersb. Cons.; 1884–86, dir. Imp. Sch. of Mus. at Saratov; 1888, of Imp. Soc. of Mus. at Kiev; in Paris, 1894, he cond. Russian programmes at the concerts "d'Harcourt" and "Colonne," 1896.

Winter (vĭn'-tĕr), **Peter von**, Mannheim, 1754—Munich, 1825; studied with Abbé Vogler, but mainly self-taught; violinist and ct.-conductor; composer of v. succ. operas, 38 in all; c. 9 symphs. incl. *"Die Schlacht"* and much church-mus.

Winter-Hjelm (vĭn'-tĕr-hyĕlm), **Otto**, Christiania, Oct. 8, 1837—Oslo, May 3, 1931; organist; pupil Leipzig Cons. and of Kullak and Wüerst; dir. Phil. concerts; c. 2 symph., 50 Psalms, 46 Norwegian *"Fjeld melodier"* or mountain songs, etc.

Winterberger (vĭn'-tĕr-bĕrkh-ĕr), **Alex.**, Weimar, Aug. 14, 1834—Leipzig, Sept. 23, 1914; pianist; pupil of Leipzig Cons. and of Liszt. 1861, pf.-prof. at Petersburg Cons.; 1872, lived in Leipzig; c. pf.-pcs. and songs.

Winterfeld (vĭn'-tĕr-fĕlt), **K. G. Aug. Vivigens von**, Berlin, 1784—1852; libr. and writer of valuable historical works.

Wippern (vĭp'-pĕrn), **Louise (Harriers-Wippern)**, Hildesheim (or Bückeburg), 1835(?)—Görbersdorf, Silesia, 1878; operatic singer.

Wirth (vērt), **Emanuel**, Luditz, Bohemia, Oct. 18, 1842—Berlin, Jan. 5, 1923; violinist; pupil of Prague Cons., 1864–77; teacher at Rotterdam Cons., and orch.-leader; then vla.-player in the Joachim Quartet, Berlin, and vln.-prof. at the Hochschule; Royal Prof.

Wirtz (vērts), **Charles Louis**, The Hague, Sept. 1, 1841—Breda, 1935; pupil of the Cons.; later piano teacher there; c. church music.

Wise, Michael, England, 1648 ?—in a street brawl, Salisbury, 1687; tenor and notable early composer of anthems, etc.

Wis'ke, Mortimer, Troy, N. Y., Jan. 12, 1853—Lewiston, Me., July 9, 1934; long active as cond. and fest. dir. in New York, New Jersey and elsewhere; from 1872 organist and dir. Brooklyn; c. church and organ music.

Wit (vēt), **Paul de**, Maastricht, Jan. 4, 1852—Leipzig, Dec. 10, 1925; 'cellist and viola da gambist; coll. of ancient instrs.

Witek (vē'-tĕk), **Anton**, Saaz, Bohemia, 1872—Winchester, Mass., Aug. 19, 1933; noted violinist; pupil of Bennewitz; at Prague Cons.; 1894 concertm. Berlin Philh.; toured in solo recitals and with Vita Gerhardt (whom he later m.); in 1903 with her and Joseph Malkin formed Trio; 1905, played concertos by Beethoven, Paganini and Brahms in one concert; after 1910, concertm. of Boston Symph.; 1918 resigned this post and gave himself to solo work and teaching; in 1926, after the death of his first wife, he m. Alma Rosengron, a former pupil.

With'erspoon, Herbert, Buffalo, N. Y., July 21, 1873—New York, May 10, 1935; notable basso cantante; graduated Yale Univ.; pupil of J. W. Hall, N. Y., and Dubulle, Paris; sang in opera, Castle Square Co., N. Y., and with Boston Symph. and other orchs. throughout U. S.; v. succ. début in recital, N. Y., 1902; coached with Lamperti in Berlin; in 1908 he joined the Met. Op., N. Y., and sang there until 1916 with increasing success, making especially deep impression in the rôles of "Gurnemanz," "King Mark," etc. Gave recitals in London with great success, 1910, and continued his concert and oratorio appearances; he was active in later years as a voice teacher and choral cond. in N. Y. and Chicago; 1925–29, pres. of Chicago Musical Coll.; vice-pres. and artistic dir. of Chicago Civic Op. Co., 1931; dir. Cincinnati Cons., 1932–33; 1935 appointed general manager of Met. Op. Co., N. Y., to succeed Giulio Gatti-Casazza, and had begun intensive work on the repertoire for the following season when he was stricken fatally with a heart attack in his offices at the opera house; he m. (1) Greta Hughes, singer; divorced; (2) Florence Hinkle, soprano (d. 1933); (3) Mrs. Blanche Skeath.

Witkowski (vĭt-kôf'-skĭ), **Georges Martin** (rightly **Martin**), b. Mostagneux, Algiers, Jan. 6, 1867; French composer; son of a Polish woman and a French military officer; himself trained in the officers' school at St. Cyr; but early showed talent for composition; after producing a 1-act opera and various symph. works, he entered the Paris Schola Cantorum, where he studied under D'Indy; in 1902, when he left the army, he founded in Lyons a mixed chorus and in 1905 the Soc. des Grands Concerts; his earlier style was based on the classical, but in later works he has shown modern tendencies; c. 2 symphs., piano quintet, string quartet, sonata for vln. and piano; choral work, "*Poème de la maison*"; and "*Mon Lac*" for piano and orch., prod. in Paris, 1921.

Witt (vĭt), (1) **Fr.**, Halten-Bergstetten, 1770 — Würzburg, 1837; violinist, conductor and dram. composer. (2) **Theodor de,** Wesel, 1823—(of consumption) Rome, 1855; organist and composer. (3) **Fz.,** Walderbach, Bavaria, 1834—Schatzhofen, 1888; editor and writer.

Witte (vĭt'-tĕ), (1) **Chr. Gl. Fr.,** d. 1873; org.-builder. (2) **G. H.,** Utrecht, Nov. 16, 1843—Essen, 1929; son of above; pupil of R. Mus. Sch. at The Hague, then of Leipzig Cons.; teacher in Leipzig till 1867, then in Alsatia, 1871; cond. at Essen, 1882; R. Mus. Dir.; c. pf.-quartet (prize at Florence), grand Elegy for vln. and orch., etc.

Wittgenstein (vĭt'-gĕn-stīn), **Paul,** b. Vienna, Nov. 5, 1887; pianist; lost one arm in the war, but acquired notable facility in performing works for one hand; among noted composers who wrote works for him were Ravel (concerto for one hand) and Richard Strauss, whose symph. study, "*Panathenaenzug*" (piano and orch.) was given première by W. and Vienna Philh. under Schalk in 1929; toured U. S. with succ., 1935.

Wittich (vĭt'-tĭkh), **Marie,** Giessen, May 27, 1868—Dresden, Sept., 1931; soprano; studied with Frau Otto-Ubridy; sung various cities; 1901 Dresden ct.-opera.

Witting (vĭt'-tĭng), **Karl,** Jülich, Sept. 8, 1823—Dresden, June 28, 1907; tenor singer; pupil of Reichel in Paris; teacher in various cities; c. 'cello sonata, etc.

Wladigeroff (vlăd-ē-gă'-rôf), **Pantscho,** b. Zurich, 1899, of Bulgarian parents; composer; studied with Paul Juon and Georg Schumann; orig. a theatre cond. with Max Reinhardt in Berlin; has c. incid. music to Strindberg's "*Dream Play*," works for orch., piano and violin.

Wohlfahrt (vōl'-färt), **H.,** Kössnitz, near Apolda, 1797—Connewitz, 1883; noted teacher, writer and composer.

Woldemar (vôl-dŭ-măr) (rightly **Michel),** Orléans, 1750—Clermont-Ferrand, 1816; conductor and composer; wrote methods; inv. a mus.-stenography "*Tableau melotachigraphique*," and mus.-correspondence "*Notographie*."

Wolf (vôlf), (1) **Ernst Wm.,** Grossheringen, 1735—Weimar, 1792; ct.-conductor; c. 42 pf.-sonatas. (2) **Fd.,** Vienna, 1796—1866; writer. (3) **L.,** Frankfort-on-Main, 1804—Vienna, 1859; pianist, violinist and composer. (4) **Wm.,** Breslau, April 22, 1838—Berlin, 1913; pupil of Kullak, teacher of mus.-history, Berlin, also writer and composer. (5) **Hugo,** Windischgrätz, Styria, March 13, 1860—Vienna, Feb. 22, 1903; notable composer, esp. famed for his many beautiful songs; began study of vln. and piano with his father at 5; for a time attended the Vienna Cons. but was expelled as "incorrigible." A shy, sensitive figure he was principally self-taught, and held only minor posts, as asst. and chorusmaster at the Salzburg Op., under Muck, 1881–82, and as critic for the Vienna *Salonblatt,* 1884–87. His life was a desperate struggle with poverty and was attended by little recognition; he eked out his income by giving occasional piano and vln. lessons; after 1888 he began writing the series of more than 275 songs which were later to make him immortal. He had ambitions to compose for the stage, and his opera, "*Der Corregidor*," based on a Spanish comedy, Alarcon's "*Three-Cornered Hat*," was prod. in Mannheim, 1896, but despite the praise it received was not given repetitions; he was at work on another opera, "*Manuel Venegas*," when his mind failed. After spending some months in an asylum he was released but had to return in 1898; paralysis set in and he lived for 5 years in a helpless condition. His great genius was discovered only slowly, but today he is generally ranked among the few foremost

Lieder composers, including Schubert, Brahms and Franz. His songs have had a great and growing popularity with recitalists the world over. His comps. include, besides the pop. Spanish and Italian "*Liederbücher*," the "*Lieder aus der Jugendzeit*," his Goethe, Mörike and Eichendorff songs; choral works, most pop. being "*Elfenlied*" and "*Feuerreiter*"; also a partially completed symph., "*Italian Serenade*" for small orch., a vln. concerto and other works. His "*Corregidor*" has been cond. by Bruno Walter at the Munich and Salzburg Fests. and in 1936 an official ceremony was held at the latter event. More than a score of unknown songs, some youthful, were discovered in 1936. His literary productions were ed. by Batka and Werner and pub. in 1911. Memoirs have been issued by Decsey, Haberlandt, P. Mueller, E. Schmitz, Newman, Morold, Schur and others. There are W.-Vereins in various Eur. cities.

Wolf-Ferrari (vôlf-fä-rä'-rē), **Ermanno,** b. Venice, Jan. 12, 1876; noted composer; son of a German father and Italian mother; studied at the Munich Acad. with Rheinberger; 1902–07, dir. Liceo Benedetto Marcello, Venice; after latter year lived in Neubiberg, Bavaria, for the most part devoting himself to comp.; c. (operas) "*La Sulamita*" (1889); "*Aschenbrödel*" (Venice, 1900); "*Le Donne Curiose*" (Munich, 1903; also sung at Met. Op. House, 1912); "*I Quattri Rusteghi*" (Munich, 1906); "*L'Amore Medico*" (after Molière), (Dresden, 1913); the 3 previous works as well as "*Il Segreto di Susanna*" (1-act, called an "Intermezzo," Munich, 1909), being comic in theme and musically reviving a somewhat Mozartean type of sparkling melody; totally different is "*The Jewels of the Madonna*" (Berlin R. Op., 1911, Chicago, 1912), a melodrama which provides the composer's single attempt to imitate the works of the *veristic* school; later productions include: "*Liebesband der Marchesa*" (Dresden, 1925); "*Das Himmelskleid*" (Munich, 1927); "*Sly*" (La Scala, Milan, 1927); "*La Vedova Scaltra*" (1931) and "*Il Campiello*" (Rome, 1936). He also c. the choral work, "*La Vita Nuova*," and opuses for orch.

and piano, and for various chamber combinations; a symphony da camera, vln. sonata, piano quartet, etc.

Wolff (vôlf), (1). Vide WOLF (4). (2) **Edouard,** Warsaw, 1816—Paris. 1880; pianist and composer. (3) **Auguste Désiré Bd.,** Paris, 1821—1887; pianist, pf.-teacher and maker; head of firm "Pleyel-Wolff." (4) **Hermann,** Cologne, 1845—Berlin, 1902; pupil of Fz. Kroll and Würst; editor, concert-agent and mgr. at Berlin; c. pf.-pcs. and songs. (5) **Erich,** Vienna, Dec. 3, 1874—New York, March 20, 1913; notable song composer; pupil of Door, Robert Fuchs and J. N. Fuchs at the Cons. of the Musikfreunde in his native city; he lived there until 1906 and later in Berlin; made many tours as an accompanist for Lieder singers, incl. visits to the U. S.; his death occurred on one of these tours; c. ballet, "*Zlatorog*," prod. in Prague, 1913; a vln. concerto and a number of Lieder which have won marked popularity since his death; he wrote a study of Schumann's songs in their original and later published forms.

Wölf(f)l (vělf'-'l) (**Woelfel, Woelfle**), **Jos.,** Salzburg, 1772—London, 1812; composer; his enormous hands and great contrapuntal skill made him a pf.-virtuoso whose rivalry with Beethoven divided Vienna into factions; but the rivals had mutual respect and W. dedicated his op. 6 to B.; c. light operas (1795–98).

Wolfram (vôl'-främ), (1) **Jn. Chr.,** d. 1828; organist and writer at Goldbach, near Gotha. (2) **Jos. Maria,** Dobrzan, Bohemia, 1789—Teplitz, 1839; conductor and dram. composer.

Wolfrum (vôl'-froom), **Philipp,** Schwarzenbach-am-Wald, Bavaria, Dec. 17, 1854—Samaden, May 8, 1919; pupil Munich Sch. of Mus.; mus.-dir. Heidelberg Univ.; Dr. Phil. h. c. (Leipzig, 1891); c. "*Grosses Halleluja*," and other choruses, pf.-pcs., etc.

Wolkenstein (vôl'-kěn-shtīn), **Oswald von,** Tyrol, ca. 1377—Aug. 2, 1445; a knight, ambassador, and wanderer, "the last of the Minnesinger," c. poems and melodies.

Wollanck (vôl'-länk), **Fr.,** Berlin, 1782—1831; amateur composer of an opera.

Wolle (vôl'-lě), **John Frederick,** Bethlehem, Pa., April 4, 1863—Jan. 12,

DICTIONARY OF MUSICIANS

1933; founder of a choir with which from 1900 he gave important productions of the works of Bach; in 1901 at a three-day festival the Christmas oratorio, *"Passion According to St. Matthew,"* and Mass in B minor were given entire; 1904, a nine-day festival of Bach's works was given; 1905 prof. University of California and cond. symph. concerts at the Open Air Greek Theatre at Berkeley, Cal.; later again active in Bethlehem until his death.

Wollenhaupt (vôl′-lĕn-howpt), **H. Ad.,** Schkeuditz, near Leipzig, 1827—New York, 1865; pianist, teacher and composer; from 1845 in New York.

Wollick (vôl′-lĭk) (Volli′cius, Bolli′-cius), **Nicolas,** b. Bar-le-Duc; teacher and writer at Metz, 1501–12.

Wol′stenholme, William, Blackburn, Feb. 24, 1865—Hampstead, July 23, 1931; organist, blind from birth; pupil of Dr. Done, Mus. B. Oxford, 1887, from 1888 organist in London; toured the U. S. 1908; c. organ music of all kinds, piano sonata, choral ballad, *"Sir Humphrey Gilbert,"* etc.

Wolzogen (und Neuhaus) (vôl′-tsō-gĕn oont noi-hows), (1) **K. Aug. Alfred, Freiherr von,** Frankfort, 1823—San Remo, 1883; writer. (2) **Hans (Paul), Freiherr von,** Potsdam, 1848—Bayreuth, June 2, 1938; son of above; lived as writer at Potsdam till 1877. Wagner made him editor of the *Baireuther Blätter.* Author of many books on Wagner's music.

Wood, (1) Mrs. **Mary Ann.** Vide PATON. (2) Sir **Henry J.,** b. London, March 3, 1870; prominent cond.; pupil of his father; at 10 an organist; 1883–85, gave org.-recitals; studied at R. A. M. with Prout and others; then cond. societies; 1891–92, Carl Rosa Op. Co.; 1894, Marie Roze Co.; after 1895, Queens Hall Prom. Concerts, London; visited U. S. as cond. of Boston Symph., at Hollywood Bowl, etc. C. oratorio *"Dorothea,"* operettas, masses, songs, etc.; wrote treatise on singing; cond. of the Sheffield Festivals in 1902 and of the Norwich Festivals in 1908. (3) **Charles,** Armagh, June 15, 1866—Cambridge, England, July 11, 1926; pupil of T. O. Marks, and at R. C. M., London, winning the Morley scholarship, later teacher there, and cond. Cambridge U. Musical Society; Mus. Doc. Cambridge, 1894; LL. D.

Leeds, 1904; c. *"Ode to the West Wind,"* voices and orch., incid. music to Greek plays; *"Dirge for Two Veterans"* (Leeds Fest., 1901), *"Ballad of Dundee"* (do., 1904); symphonic variations on *"Patrick Sarsfield"* (London, 1907), songs, etc.

Wood′forde-Fin′den, Amy, b. Valparaiso, Chile, of British parents; d. London, March 13, 1919; her father British Consul in Valparaiso; composer; studied with Adolph Schlosser, Winter and Amy Horrocks; c. many songs, among which the cycle of *"Indian Love Lyrics"* to verses of Laurence Hope, have had world-wide popularity; m. Col. Woodforde-Finden, officer in Indian Army (retired).

Wood′man, Raymond Huntington, b. Brooklyn, N. Y., Jan. 18, 1861; pf.-pupil of his father, of Dudley Buck, and César Franck; 1875–79, asst.-organist to his father, at Flushing, L. I.; 1894–97, mus.-editor *N. Y. Evangelist;* 1880, organist First Presb. Ch., Brooklyn; 1889, head of org.-dept. Metr. Coll. of Mus., N. Y., etc.; c. pf.- and org.-pcs.

Wool′dridge, H. Ellis, Winchester, March 28, 1845—London, 1917; writer; historian; at first a painter and 1895 Slade Prof. of Fine Arts at Oxford; wrote extensively on mediæval music.

Wooll′ett, Henry, Havre, 1864—1936; noted teacher, composer; dir. of music school in native city.

Wormser (vôrm-zăr), **André (Alphonse Toussaint),** Paris, Nov. 1, 1851—Nov. 4, 1926; pupil of Marmontel (pf.) and Bazin, Paris Cons., taking 1st pf.-prize, 1872; Grand prix de Rome, 1875; lived in Paris; c. the opéras-comique *"Adèle de Ponthieu"* (Aix-les-Bains, 1877), *"Rivoli"* (Paris, 1896); v. succ. pantomime *"L'Enfant Prodigue"* (Paris, 1890, London, 1891, New York, 1893); pantomime *"L'Idéal"* (London, 1896); ballet, *"L'Étoile"* (Paris, 1897), etc.

Worobkiewicz (vôr-ôp-k′-yā′-vĭch), **Isidor,** Czernowitz, 1836—Sept. 18, 1903; priest in the Greek church, and pupil on stipend at Vienna Cons.; later teacher of church music at Czernowitz and author; c. Roumanian sngs., etc.

Wot′quenne, Alfred, b. Lobbes, Hennegau, Jan. 25, 1867; pupil Brussels Cons.; from 1894 librarian.

Wouters (voo'-tărs), (Fran.) Adolphe, Brussels, May 28, 1849—April 16, 1924; pupil, and 1871–1920, pf.-prof. at the Cons. there; 1886, organist Nôtre-Dame de Finistère, and cond. at Saint-Nicolas; c. 3 masses solennelles (under pseud. "Don Adolfo"), a grand Te Deum, overture, etc.

Woyrsch (voirsh), Felix von, b. Troppau, Austrian Silesia, Oct. 8, 1860; studied with A. Chevallier, Hamburg, but mainly self-taught; after 1895, organist and conductor at Altona; c. 4 comic operas incl. succ. "*Wikingerfahrt*" (Nürnberg, 1896), 4 choral works with orch.; symph.; symph. prologue to "*Divina Commedia*," etc.

Wranitzky (frä-nēt'-shkĭ), (1) Paul, Neureisch, Moravia, 1756—Vienna, 1808; violinist, conductor and dram. composer. (2) Anton, Neureisch, 1761—Vienna, 1819; violinist; bro. and pupil of above; conductor and composer.

Wüerst (vü'-ĕrst), Richard (Fd.), Berlin, 1824—1881; teacher, critic and dram. composer.

Wüllner (vĭl'-nĕr), (1) Fz., Münster, Jan. 28, 1832—Cologne, Sept. 8, 1902; noted conductor; studied Münster, later at Berlin, Brussels, Cologne, Bremen, Hanover and Leipzig, and gave concerts as pianist; 1854, pf.-teacher Munich Cons.; 1858, town mus.-dir. at Aix-la-Chapelle; 1861, "R. Mus.-Dir." 1864, 1882, 1886 and 1890 he conducted the Lower Rhine Mus. Fest.; cond. the ct.-chapel, Munich; 1867, dir. choral classes in the Sch. of Mus.; in 1869, cond. ct.-opera and the Acad. Concerts (vice von Bülow), giving Wagner's "*Rheingold*" and "*Walküre*" their first hearing. 1870, 1st ct.-cond., R. Prof. 1875; in 1877, ct.-cond. at Dresden, and artistic dir. of the Cons.; 1883–84, cond. Berlin Philh.; 1884, dir. Cologne Cons.; was Dr. Phil. Leipzig U.; c. cantata "*Heinrich der Finkler*," with orch. (1st prize, Aix-la-Chapelle "Liedertafel" 1864); new arrangement (with added recitatives) of von Weber's "*Oberon*"; Psalm 125, with orch.; Miserere and Stabat Mater, for double chorus, masses, chamber-mus., etc. (2) Ludwig, Münster, Aug. 19, 1858—Berlin, March 22, 1938; son of above; Dr. phil., then studied Cologne Cons.; 1888, dir. a church choir;

became an actor in spite of a vocal impediment, then a tenor singer in concert, also in opera (as "Tannhäuser," etc.). Eminent as a Lieder singer and reciter; toured widely, incl. United States.

Wunderlich (voon'-dĕr-lĭkh), Jn. G., Bayreuth, 1755—Paris, 1819; flutevirtuoso and prof. Paris Cons.; also composer.

Würfel (vür'-fĕl), Wm., Planian, Bohemia, 1791—Vienna, 1852; pianist, prof., conductor and dram. composer.

Wurm (voorm), (1) Mary J. A., b. Southampton, 1860—Munich, 1938; pianist; pupil of Pruckner and Stark, Anna Mehlig, Mary Krebs, Jos. Wieniawski, Raff and Frau Schumann; 1884, won the Mendelssohn Scholarship; studied with Stanford, Sullivan, Bridge and Reinecke; played with succ. Leipzig, Berlin, etc.; c. an overture; a pf.-concerto; sonatas, etc. Her sisters (2) Alice and (3) Mathilde, also pianists, the latter known as Verne (d. London, June 4, 1936), a notable recitalist and teacher.

Wylde (wĭld), H., Bushy, Hertfordshire, 1822—London, 1890; pianist, organist and teacher.

Wyszkowski. Vide HOFMANN, C.

X

Xylander (rightly Holtzmann) (ksē'-länt-ĕr or hôlts'-män), Wm., Augsburg, 1532—Heidelberg, 1576, writer.

Xyndas (ksēn'-däs), Spiridion, Corfú, 1812—(in poverty) Athens, 1896; Greek composer of succ. balladoperas.

Y

Yon, Pietro, b. Settimo Vittone, Italy, 1886; organist, composer; studied with Fumagalli, at Turin Cons. and at Acad. of St. Cecila, Rome, winning honours; after 1907 res. in N. Y., where is mus. dir. and org. at St. Patrick's Cathedral; known as organ recitalist; hon. org. of Bas. of St. Peter's, Rome; c. many masses, an oratorio "*The Triumph of St. Patrick*"; and many choral and organ works, and songs.

Yonge (yŭng). Vide YOUNG.

Yost (yôst), Michel, Paris, 1754—1786; celebrated clarinettist and composer.

Young, (1) (or Yonge), Nicholas, b. Lewis, Sussex; d. 1619; pub. "*Musica*

Transalpina," colls. of Italian madrigals, 1597. (2) **J. Matthew Wilson,** Durham, Engl., 1822—W. Norwood, 1897; organist and composer.

Yradier (ē-rädh'-ĭ-är), **Sebastian,** Sauciego, Spain, Jan. 20, 1809—Vitoria, Dec. 6, 1865; Spanish song-composer.

Yriarte (ē-rĭ-är'-tĕ), **Don Tomas de,** Teneriffe, ca. 1750—Santa Maria, near Cadiz, 1791; writer.

Ysaye (ē-sī'-yŭ), (1) **Eugène,** Liége, July 16, 1858—Brussels, May 13, 1931; prominent violinist, son and pupil of a cond. and violinist, then pupil of Liége Cons., and of Wieniawski and Vieuxtemps; later with govt.-stipend studied in Paris; till 1881, leader in Bilse's orch., Berlin, made v. succ. tours throughout Europe and N. America; from 1886, head prof. of vln. Brussels Cons., and leader "Ysaye Quartet"; 1893, Chev. of the Legion of Honour; 1918-22, cond. Cincinnati Symph. and biennial fest.; later again in Belgium; c. opera, *"Peter the Miner"* (1930); suffered amputation of one leg in 1929 and never fully recovered health; c. vln.-concertos; variations on a theme by Paganini; Poème élégiaque for vln. with orch. (or pf.), etc. (2) **Théopile,** Verviers, 1865—Nice, 1918; bro. of (1); composer, pianist; pupil of Liége Cons. and of Franck; dir. of Brussels Acad. of Music.

Yussupoff (yoos'-soo-pôf), Prince **Nicolai,** Petersburg, 1827—Baden-Baden, 1891; violinist; pupil of Vieuxtemps; writer of treatises, and c. a programme-symph. *"Gonzalvo de Cordova,"* with vln. obbligato; *"Concerto symphonique,"* for vln., etc.

Yzac (ē'-zäk). Vide ISAAC.

Z

Zabalza y Olaso (thä-bǎl'-thä ē ŏ-lä'-sō), Don **Damaso,** Irurita, Navarre, 1833—Madrid, 1894; pianist and teacher; prof. Madrid Cons.; c. studies.

Zabel (tsä'-bĕl), **Albert,** Berlin, 1835—St. Petersburg, 1910; harpist; pupil Berlin Royal Inst. for church mus.; soloist Berlin Opera; from 1851 at Royal Ballet orch. St. Petersburg; from 1862 prof. at the Cons.; c. harp concertos, etc.

Zacconi (tsäk-kō'-nē), **Ludovico,** b. Pesaro, 1555—1627; monk and important theorist.

Zach (tsäkh), **Johann,** (1) Czelakowicz, 1699—Bruchsal, 1773; director at Mayence and composer of church music. (2) **Max Wilh.,** Lemberg, 1864—St. Louis, 1921; violinist and conductor; pupil of Vienna Cons.; played in Boston Symph., and 1887-97 cond. summer concerts there; 1900, mem. Adamowski Quartet; after 1907, cond. of St. Louis Symphony.

Zachau (tsäkh'-ow), (1) **Peter,** town-musician, Lübeck, composer for viola da gamba, 1693. (2) **Fr. Wm.,** Leipzig, 1663—Halle, 1712; Händel's teacher; organist and composer.

Zahn (tsän), **Johannes,** Espenbach, Franconia, Aug. 1, 1817—Neudettelsau, Feb. 17, 1895; historian of church music, and compiler of hymn books, etc.

Zajczek (zä'-ĭ-tsĕk), **Julius,** Vienna, 1877—1929; composer of opera *"Helmbrecht"* (Graz, 1906).

Zajič (zä'-yēch), **Florian,** Unhoscht, Bohemia, May 4, 1853—Berlin, May 17, 1926; violinist; son of poor parents; on a stipend studied at Prague Cons.; member theatre-orch., Augsburg; 1881, leader at Mannheim and Strassburg; 1889, at Hamburg; 1891, teacher Stern Cons., Berlin; later at Klindworth-Scharwenka Cons.; toured widely and was made chamber-virtuoso 1885 and given Russian order of Stanislas.

Zamara (tsä-mä'-rä), (1) **Antonio,** Milan, June 13, 1829—Hietzing, near Vienna, Nov. 11, 1901; harp-virtuoso, pupil of Sechters; teacher at Vienna Cons.; c. for harp, flute, etc. (2) **Alfred Maria,** b. Vienna, April 28, 1863; c. operettas.

Zamminer (tsäm'-mē-nĕr), **Fr.,** Darmstadt, 1818 (?)—Giessen, 1856; acoustician.

Zanardini (tsä-när-dē'-nē), **Angelo,** Venice, 1820—Milan, 1893; c. opera, also writer and translator of libretti.

Zandonai (tsän-dō-nä'-ē), **Riccardo,** b. Sacco (Trentino) May 28, 1883; pupil of Gianferrai at Trento; from 1899 at Rossini Cons., Pesaro, in 1902 winning comp. prize with symph. poem for voices and orch.; c. also *"Serenata Mediævale"* for cello, 2 harps, and strings; *"Ave Maria"* for female voices, harp, and strings; *"O Padre Nostro"* (from Dante's Purgatorio), for chorus, orch., and organ; operas, *"Grillo del Focolare"*

(Cricket on the Hearth) (Turin, 1908), and with great success elsewhere, and the highly succ. *"Conchita"* (based on Pierre Louy's *"Femme et le Pantin"* (Milan, 1911, Covent Garden, 1912, etc.); *"Melænis"* (Milan, 1912); *"Francesca da Rimini,"* to a libretto drawn by Tito Ricordi from the tragedy of D'Annunzio (adjudged his masterpiece), (Teatro Regio, Turin, 1914; Met. Op., 1916); *"La Via della Finestra,"* on a comic theme from a play by Scribe, book by Adami (Pesaro, 1919); *"Giulietta e Romeo,"* a new version of the original Italian story on this subject, book by Rossato (Rome, Teatro Costanzi, 1921); *"I Cavalieri di Ekebù,"* after Selma Lagerlöf's novel, *"Gösta Berling,"* book by Rossato (La Scala, Milan, 1925); *"Giuliano,"* a mystic legend based on Flaubert's story, with book by Rossato (Naples, 1928); *"La Farsa Amorosa,"* based on the Spanish comedy, *"Three-Cornered Hat,"* (Rome and Milan, 1935–36); also symph. works, *"Concerto Romantico"* for vln. and orch.; Requiem Mass, and various other vocal compositions.

Zandt, van (fän-tsänt), **Marie,** New York, Oct. 8, 1861—Cannes, Dec. 31, 1919; (daughter of (2) Jeanie van Z., singer formerly in Royal and Carl Rosa Companies); pupil of Lamperti, Milan; début, Turin, 1879; sang in London, then from 1880 at Op.-Com., Paris, with great succ.; 1884, temporary loss of voice due to prostration brought on her such violent criticism that she took a leave of absence and sang with succ. at St. Petersburg, etc.; on her return, 1885, she met the same opposition and sang thereafter in England, etc.; compass *a-f'''*.

Zanella (tsä-něl'-lä), **Amilcare,** b. Monticelli d'Ongina, Sept. 26, 1873; pupil of Parma Cons. and from 1903 director, after years as operatic cond. in South America, etc.; c. a symph. fantasie and fugue for piano and orch., operas, etc.

Zanettini. Vide GIANETTINI.

Zang (tsäng), **Jn. H.,** Zella St. Blasii 1733—Mainstockheim, 1811; cantor; pianist.

Zange (tsäng'-ĕ) (Zang'ius), **Nicolaus,** d. Berlin, before 1620; conductor and composer.

Zani de Ferranti (dsä'-nē dä fĕr-rän-tē), **Marco Aurelio,** Bologna, 1800—Pisa, 1878; guitar-virtuoso.

Zanobi. Vide GAGLIANO.

Zan'ten, Cornelie Van, b. Dordrecht, Aug. 2, 1855; operatic soprano, pupil of Geul, Schneider, and Fr. Lamperti; début in Turin, sang throughout Europe, and with the "National Opera" in America; then sang at Amsterdam and taught in the Cons.; from 1903 teacher in Berlin.

Zarate (thä-rä'-tĕ), **Eleodoro Ortiz de,** b. Valparaiso, Dec. 29, 1865; pupil of Collegio di San Luis there; 1885 won 1st govt. prize, and studied Milan Cons. with Saladino; won prize 1886, for opera *"Giovanna la Pazza"*; studied in Italy; 1895, prod. the first Chilean opera, the succ. *"La Fioraia de Lugano"* (Santiago, Chile, Nov. 10).

Zaremba (tsä-räm'-bä), **Nicolai Ivanovitch de,** 1821—Petersburg, 1879; teacher.

Zarembski (tsä-rěmp'-shkĭ), **Jules de,** Shitomir, Russian Poland, 1854—1885; pianist, pf.-prof. and composer.

Zarlino (dsär-lē'-nō), **Gioseffo** (called **Zarlinus Clodiensis**), Chioggia, March 22, 1517—Venice, Feb. 14, 1590; eminent theorist, conductor and composer; a Franciscan monk; pupil of Willaert at Venice; from 1565 cond. at San Marco, also chaplain at San Severo; his comps. are almost all lost; he was commissioned by the Republic to write mus. in celebration of Lepanto, a mass for the plague of 1577 and in welcome of Henri III., 1574, on which occasion he also c. a dram. work *"Orfeo"*; his theoretical ability is shown by the great work *"Instituzioni harmoniche"* (1558).

Zarzycki (zär-zěk'-ē), **Alex,** Lemberg, Austrian Poland, 1834—Warsaw, 1895; pianist, conductor and dram. composer.

Zaytz (dsä'-ēts), **Giovanni von,** Fiume, Jan. 21, 1832—Agram, Dec. 17, 1914; pupil of Lauro Rossi, Milan Cons.; 1870 theatre-conductor and singing-teacher at the Cons. at Agram; c. the first Croatian opera *"Nicola Subic Zrinjski"* (1876), also 20 German Singspiele, masses, etc.

Zeckwer (tsěk'-vär),(1) **Richard,** Stendal, Prussia, April 30, 1850—Philadelphia, Dec. 30, 1922; pianist; pupil Leipzig Cons.; from 1870 organist at

Philadelphia; 1870 teacher Phila. Mus. Acad.; 1876 director, composer. (2) **Camille**, son of (1) b. Phila., 1875 —Aug. 7, 1924; pianist, composer.

Zelenka (zĕ-lĕn'-kä), **Jan Dismas**, Lannowicz, Bohemia, 1679—Dresden, 1745; conductor and composer.

Želenski (zhĕ-lĕn-shkĭ), **Ladislas**, on the family estate Gradkowice, Galicia, July 6, 1837—Cracow, Jan. 23, 1921; pupil of Mirecki at Cracow, Krejči at Prague, and Damcke at Paris; prof. of comp., later dir., Warsaw Cons.; c. a symph., 2 cantatas, etc. for orch.; succ. opera *"Goplana"* (Cracow, 1896), etc.

Zell, F. Vide WÄLZEL.

Zel'ler (tsĕ'-lĕr), **Dr. Karl**, St. Peterin-der-Au, Lower Austria, July 19, 1842—Baden, near Vienna, Aug. 17, 1898; c. operettas.

Zellner (tsĕl'-nĕr), (1) **Ld. Alex.**, Agram, 1823—Vienna, 1894; son and pupil of an organist; editor, professor, writer and composer. (2) **Julius**, Vienna, 1832—Mürzzuschlag, Styria, 1900; c. 2 symphs., etc.

Zelter (tsĕl'-tĕr), **Karl Fr.**, Berlin, Dec. 11, 1758—May 15, 1832; son of a mason; studied with Kirnberger and Fasch, to whom he was assistant and 1800 successor as cond. of the Singakademie; 1809 he founded the "Liedertafel" from which grew the great "Deutscher Sängerbund" of 50,000 members, for which he c. famous male choruses; 1819, founder and dir. R. Inst. for church-mus.; friend of Goethe, whose songs he set; c. also oratorios, etc.

Zemlin'sky, Alexander von, b. Vienna, Oct. 4, 1872; composer, conductor; studied Vienna Cons.; cond. at various theatres, then at the Op. in that city; also at Mannheim, Prague, Berlin and elsewhere; c. (operas) *"Sarema,"* *"Es War Einmal,"* *"Kleider Machen Leute,"* *"Kreidekreis"*; orch. and choral works, chamber music, piano pieces and songs; he is the brother-in-law and teacher of Schönberg.

Zenatello (tsĕn-ä-tĕl'-lō), **Giovanni**, b. Verona, Feb. 22, 1879; popular operatic tenor, appearing at Covent Garden 1905, and from 1907 in America; 1907–09 at Manhattan Op., N. Y.; 1909–14, Boston Op. Co.; later active as voice teacher in N. Y. and Europe; m. Maria Gay, contralto.

Zenger (tsĕng'-ĕr), **Max**, Munich, Feb. 2, 1837—Nov. 16, 1911; pupil of Stark, and Leipzig Cons.; 1860, cond. at Ratisbon; 1869 mus.-dir. Munich ct.-opera; 1878–85, Munich Oratorio Soc., etc.; Dr. Phil. *h. c.*, 1897; c. 4 operas; succ. oratorio *"Kain"* (after Byron, Munich, 1867), cantatas with orch., "tragic" symph., chamber music, songs, etc.

Zenta. Vide AUGUSTA HOLMES.

Zeretelev. Vide LAWROWSKAJA.

Zerr (tsĕr), **Anna**, Baden-Baden, 1822 —on her estate, near Oberkirch, 1881; singer.

Zerrahn (tsĕr-rän), **K.**, Malchow, Mecklenburg, July 28, 1826—Milton, Mass., Dec. 29, 1909; distinguished conductor; studied with Fr. Weber and at Hanover and Berlin; 1848, America, as a member of Germania Orch.; 1854–95, cond. Handel and Haydn Soc., Boston; also cond. Harvard Symph. Concerts, and prof. of harm., instr. and singing, N. E. Cons

Zeugheer (tsoikh'-hār), **Jakob** (known as J. Z. Hermann), Zurich, 1805— Liverpool, 1865; violinist and conductor.

Zeuner (tsoi'-nĕr), **K. Traugott**, Dresden, 1775—Paris, 1841; pianist, teacher and composer.

Ziani (dsē-ä'-nē), (1) **P. Andrea**, Venice, ca. 1630—Vienna, 1711; organist and dram. composer. (2) **Marco A.**, Venice, 1653—Vienna, 1715; nephew of above; ct. conductor and dram. composer.

Zichy (tsē'-shē), **Count Géza**, Sztára, Hungary, July 22, 1849—Budapest, Jan. 14, 1924; noted left-handed piano-virtuoso, having at 17 lost his right arm; pupil of Mayrberger, Volkmann and Liszt; holding high legal positions; also made tours for charity. 1890–94, Intendant Nat. Th. and Opera, Pesth. C. succ. operas, *"Aldr"* (Pesth, 1896); *"Meister Roland"* (Pesth, 1899, Magdeburg, 1902), cantata, etc.; pf.-pcs., for the left-hand and studies (with preface by Liszt), etc.

Zieg'ler, Edw., b. Baltimore, March 25, 1870; critic, opera executive; studied music with F. X. Arens; critic, N. Y. *World*, 1903–08; mus. and dram. critic, *Herald*, 1908–17; *American*, 1920; after 1917 exec. of Met. Op. Co., asst. gen. manager, after 1920.

Ziehn (tsēn), **Bernhard**, Erfurt, Jan.

20, 1845—Chicago, Sept. 8, 1912;
theorist; came to Chicago 1868;
teacher and organist; author of important works: "*Harmonie und
Modulationslehre*" (Berlin, 1888),
"Five and Six Part Harmonies"
(Milwaukee, 1911), etc.

Ziehrer (tsē'-rĕr), **Carl Michael,** Vienna,
May 2, 1843—Nov. 14, 1922; mili-
tary bandmaster; toured; c. 600
dances and an operetta "*Ein tolles
Mädel*" (Nuremberg, 1908).

Zilcher (tsĭlkh'-ĕr), **Hermann,** b.
Frankfort-on-Main, Aug. 18, 1881;
pupil of the Hoch Cons.; c. concerto
for 2 violins with orch., violin concerto, etc.; 1901, won Mozart Prize
for comp.; 1905, taught Hoch Cons.,
Frankfort; 1908, Munich Akad. der
Tonkunst; after 1920, dir. of State
Cons., Würzburg, and cond. of orch.
concerts there; c. operas, choral,
orch., chamber music, etc.

Zimbalist (tsĭm'-bä-lĭst), **Efrem,** b.
Rostov, Russia, May 7, 1889; notable
violinist; pupil of his father, a conductor; 1901–07 at St. Petersburg
Cons. under Auer, winning gold
medal and scholarship; toured Europe and 1911 America, where he has
made his home for a number of years;
c. Slavic dances, etc., for violin.
M. Alma Gluck, soprano.

Zimmermann (tsĭm'-mĕr-män), (1) **Anton,** Pressburg, 1741—1781; conductor, composer and organist. (2)
Pierre Jos. Guillaume, Paris, March
19, 1785—Oct. 29, 1853; famous
pf.-teacher; pupil, later, 1816–48,
prof., at Paris Cons., c. comic opera
and many pf.-pcs. (3) **Agnes,** Cologne, July 5, 1845—London, Nov.
14, 1925; pianist; at 9 pupil of
London R. A. M., winning King's
Scholarship twice, and also silver
medal; début, Crystal Palace, 1863;
toured with great succ.; ed. scores
and c. a pf.-trio, etc.

Zingarelli (tsĭn-gä-rĕl'-lē), **Nicola A.,**
Naples, April 4, 1752—Torre del
Greco, near Naples, May 5, 1837;
violinist, teacher and eminent composer; the succ. of his grand operas
throughout Europe was almost
equalled by his noble and devout
sacred mus.; pupil of Fenarolo and
Speranza; his first opera was prod.
at 16, and followed by another at
21, but he had no succ. till "*Al-
sinda,*" written in 7 days (La Scala,
Milan, 1785); he followed this with

many others, incl. his best, "*Giulietta
e Romeo*" (ibid., 1796); 1792, cond.
at Milan Cath.; 1794, at Loreto;
1804 at St. Peter's, Rome, 1811, imprisoned for refusal to conduct a service in honour of the King of Rome,
the son of Napoleon, who took him
to Paris, released him, and paid him
well for a mass; 1813, dir. Naples
Cons.; 1816, cond. at the cath.; he
was a notable teacher; c. 34 operas,
masses of all kinds in a series
"*Annuale di Loreto*" for every day
in the year, 80 magnificats, etc.

Zingel (tsĭng'-ĕl), **Rudolf Ewald,** b.
Liegnitz, Sept. 5, 1876; pupil Berlin
Royal Hochsch.; from 1899 dir.
Singakad. at Frankfort-on-Oder;
from 1907 at Greifswald; c. operas
"*Margot*" (Frankfort-on-Main, 1902),
"*Liebeszauber*" (Stralsund, 1908),
"*Persepolis*" (Rostock, 1909).

Zinkeisen (tsĭnk'-ī-zĕn), **Konrad L.**
Dietrich, Hanover, 1779—Brunswick, 1838; violinist, conductor and
composer.

Zipoli (dsē'-pō-lē), **Dom.,** organist,
Jesuit Church, Rome; pub. important clavier-sonatas, treatises, etc.
(1726).

Zoeller (tsĕl'-lĕr), **Carl,** Berlin, 1840—
London, 1889; writer and notable
composer.

Zoilo (dsō'-ē-lō), **Annibale,** conductor
at Laterano, Rome, 1561–70, 1571,
singer, Papal Chapel; c. madrigals,
etc.

Zöllner (tsĕl'-nĕr), (1) **K. H.,** Oels
Silesia, 1792 — Wandsbeck, near
Hamburg, 1836; org.-virtuoso, writer
and dram. composer. (2) **K. Fr.,**
Mittelhausen, Thuringia, March 17,
1800—Leipzig, Sept. 25, 1860; famous composer of male choruses;
pupil of Schicht, Thomasschule,
Leipzig; vocal-teacher there, founded
a Liedertafel "Zöllner-verein," other
socs. of similar nature, organised
1859 to form a "Z.-band." (3) **H.,**
b. Leipzig, July 4, 1854; son of
above; pupil Leipzig Cons.; 1878,
mus.-dir. Dorpat Univ.; 1885, Cologne Cons. and conductor various
vocal socs.; 1889, toured Italy with
a male chorus; from 1890, cond.
New York "Deutscher Liederkranz";
1898, mus.-dir. Leipzig University
and cond. "Paulinerchor"; critic of
Tageblatt there; 1907 taught Stern
Cons., Berlin; 1908, cond. Antwerp
Op., after 1912 in Freiburg; c. **10**

operas, 11 choral works with orch.,
cantata *"Die neue Welt"* (won international prize, Cleveland, Ohio,
1892), a symph., oratorio, male
choruses, etc.

Zopff (tsôpf), **Hermann**, Glogau, 1826
—Leipzig, 1883; editor, writer and
dram. composer.

Zschiesche (tshē'-shĕ), **Aug.**, Berlin,
1800—1876; dram. bass.

Zschocher (tshôkh'-ĕr), **Jn.**, Leipzig,
1821—1897; pianist.

Zumpe (tsoom'-pĕ), **Hermann**, Tauben-
heim, Upper Lusatia, April 9, 1850—
Munich, Sept. 4, 1903; grad. Seminary at Bautzen; taught a year at
Weigsdorf; from 1871 at Leipzig;
also studied with Tottmann; 1873-
76, at Bayreuth, as copyist and asst.
to Wagner; thereafter th. cond.
various cities; 1891, ct.-cond. at
Stuttgart; 1895, ct.-cond. Munich;
later at Schwerin; 1901, Meiningen;
c. 2 operas; v. succ. operettas
"Farinelli" (Vienna, 1886), *"Karin"*
(Hamburg, 1888), and *"Polnische
Wirtschaft"* (Berlin, 1891); overture
"Wallenstein's Tod," etc.

Zumsteeg (tsoom'-shtäkh), (1) **Jn.**
Rudolf, Sachsenflur, Odenwald, 1760
—Stuttgart, 1802; 'cellist and ct.-
conductor; c. operas and important
"durch-komponirten" ballads, before
Löwe (q.v.). His daughter (2)
Emilie, Stuttgart, 1797—1857, was
a pop. song-composer.

Zur Mühlen (tsoor-mü'-lĕn), **Raimund
von**, on his father's estate, Livonia,
Nov. 10, 1854—Steyning, Sussex,
Dec. 9, 1931; concert-tenor; studied
at Hochschule, Berlin, with Stockhausen at Frankfort, and Bussine at
Paris; later active as an important
voice teacher.

Zur Nieden (tsoor nē'-dĕn), **Albrecht**,
Emmerich-on-Rhine, 1819 — Duis-
burg, 1872; mus.-director, conductor
and composer.

Zuschneid (tsoo-shnīt'), **Karl**, Oberglogau, Silesia, May 29, 1854—
Weimar, Aug. 18, 1926; pupil Stuttgart Cons.; director of societies in
various towns; from 1907 dir. Mannheim Hochschule; c. male choruses
with orch., etc.

Zvonař (tsvō'-närzh), **Jos. Ld.**, Kublov,
near Prague, 1824—Prague, 1865;
teacher, theorist and dram. composer.

Zweers (tsvārs), **Bernard**, Amsterdam,
May 18, 1854—Dec. 9, 1924; com-
poser of 4 symphs., sonatas, etc.;
studied with Jadassohn.

Zweig (tsvīg), **Fritz**, b. Olmütz, Sept. 8,
1893; conductor; pupil of Schönberg
in Vienna; after 1912, opera conductor at Mannheim; 1921-3, in
Barmen-Elberfeld; 1923-5, at the
Berlin Grosse Volksoper; 1925, Municipal Op., Berlin; 1927-33, at Berlin
State Op.; from 1934 in Prague.

Zwintscher (tsvĭnt'-shĕr), **Bruno**, Zie-
genhain, Saxony, May 15, 1838—
near Dresden, March 4, 1905; pianist;
pupil of Julius Otto, then of Leipzig
Cons.; 1875-98, teacher there; writer.

Zwyssig (tsvēs'-sĭkh), **P. Alberich**,
(rightly **Joseph**), Bauen, Nov. 17,
1808—Mehrerau, Nov. 17, 1854;
lived at Cistercian abbey Mehrerau;
entered the Cistercian order 1826; c.
"Swiss Psalm," etc.